WOMEN and CRIME

SECOND EDITION

SAGE Text/Reader Series in Criminology and Criminal Justice

Craig Hemmens, Series Editor

1. *Introduction to Criminology: A Text/Reader 3rd Edition* by Anthony Walsh/Craig Hemmens
2. *Corrections: A Text/Reader 2nd Edition* by Mary Stohr/Anthony Walsh/Craig Hemmens
3. *Courts: A Text/Reader 2nd Edition* by Cassia Spohn/Craig Hemmens
4. *Policing: A Text/Reader* by Carol Archbold
5. *Community-Based Corrections: A Text/Reader* by Shannon Barton-Bellessa/Robert Hanser
6. *Race and Crime: A Text/Reader* by Helen Greene/Shaun Gabbidon
7. *Criminological Theory: A Text/Reader 2nd Edition* by Stephen Tibbetts/Craig Hemmens
8. *Victimology: A Text/Reader* by Leah Daigle
9. *Women and Crime: A Text/Reader 2nd Edition* by Stacy Mallicoat
10. *White Collar Crime: A Text/Reader* by Brian Payne
11. *Juvenile Justice: A Text/Reader* by Richard Lawrence/Craig Hemmens
12. *Organization and Management in the Criminal Justice System: A Text/Reader* by Matthew Giblin

Other Titles of Related Interest

Introduction to Criminal Justice by Kenneth Peak
Introduction to Criminology by Pamela Schram/Steven Tibbetts
Introduction to Criminology 8th Edition by Frank Hagan
Criminology: The Essentials 2nd Edition by Anthony Walsh
Criminological Theory 6th Edition by J. Robert Lilly/Frank Cullen/Richard Ball
Criminological Theory: The Essentials 2nd Edition by Stephen Tibbetts
Criminals in the Making 2nd Edition by John Wright, Steven Tibbetts/Leah Daigle
Crime and Everyday Life 4th Edition by Marcus Felson/Rachel Boba
Criminal and Behavioral Profiling by Curt and Anne Bartol
Criminal Justice Ethics 3rd Edition by Cyndi Banks
Introduction to Policing 2nd Edition by Steven Cox/William McCamey/Gene Scaramella
Introduction to Corrections by Robert Hanser
Corrections: The Essentials by Mary Stohr/Anthony Walsh
Community Corrections 2nd Edition by Robert Hanser
Correctional Theory by Frank Cullen/Cheryl Lero Jonson
Violence 2nd Edition by Alex Alvarez and Ronet Bachman
Juvenile Delinquency by Kristin Bates/ Richelle Swan
Race and Crime 3rd Edition by Shaun Gabbidon, Helen Greene
Women and Crime: The Essentials by Stacy Mallicoat and Connie Ireland
Juvenile Justice 8th Edition by Steven Cox, Jennifer Allen/Robert Hanser/John Conrad
Victimology: The Essentials by Leah Daigle
Victims of Crime 4th Edition by Robert Davis/Arthur Lorigio/Susan Herman
Responding to Domestic Violence 4th Edition by Eve Buzawa/Carl Buzawa/Evan Stark
White Collar Crime: The Essentials by Brian Payne
Deviance and Social Control by Michelle Inderbitzen/Kristin Bates/Randy Gainey
Drugs and Drug Policy 2nd Edition by Clay Mosher/Scott Akins
Criminal Justice Policy by Stacy Mallicoat/Christine Gardner
Understanding Terrorism 4th Edition by Gus Martin
Terrorism: The Essentials by Gus Martin
Gangs in America's Communities by James Howell
Criminal Courts, 2nd Edition by Craig Hemmens, David Brody/Cassia Spohn
Criminal Procedure 2nd Edition by Matthew Lippman
Contemporary Criminal Law 3rd Edition by Matthew Lippman
Crime Analysis With Crime Mapping 3rd Edition by Rachel Boba Santos
The Practice of Research in Criminology and Criminal Justice 5th Edition by Ronet Bachman/Russell Schutt
Fundamentals of Research in Criminology and Criminal Justice 3rd Edition by Ronet Bachman/Russell Schutt
Statistics for Criminal Justice by Jacinta Gau
The Mismeasure of Crime 2nd Edition by Clay Mosher/Terence Miethe/Timothy Hart

WOMEN and CRIME

SECOND EDITION

A Text/Reader

Stacy L. Mallicoat

California State University, Fullerton

Los Angeles | London | New Delhi
Singapore | Washington DC

SAGE

Los Angeles | London | New Delhi
Singapore | Washington DC

FOR INFORMATION:

SAGE Publications, Inc.
2455 Teller Road
Thousand Oaks, California 91320
E-mail: order@sagepub.com

SAGE Publications Ltd.
1 Oliver's Yard
55 City Road
London, EC1Y 1SP
United Kingdom

SAGE Publications India Pvt. Ltd.
B 1/I 1 Mohan Cooperative Industrial Area
Mathura Road, New Delhi 110 044
India

SAGE Publications Asia-Pacific Pte. Ltd.
3 Church Street
#10-04 Samsung Hub
Singapore 048763

Acquisitions Editor: Jerry Westby
Associate Editor: Jessica Miller
Editorial Assistant: Laura Kirkhuff
Production Editor: Jane Haenel
Copy Editor: Patricia Sutton
Typesetter: C&M Digitals (P) Ltd.
Proofreader: Ellen Howard
Indexer: Karen Wiley
Cover Designer: Janet Kiesel
Marketing Manager: Terra Schultz

Printed in the United States of America

Library of Congress Cataloging-in-Publication Data

Women and crime : a text/reader / [edited by] Stacy L. Mallicoat, California State University, Fullerton. — 2nd edition.

p. cm. — (SAGE text/reader series in criminology and criminal justice)
Includes bibliographical references and index.

ISBN 978-1-4833-5665-5 (pbk. : alk. paper)

1. Feminist criminology. 2. Women—Crimes against. 3. Female offenders. 4.—Sex discrimination in criminal justice administration. I. Mallicoat, Stacy L.

HV6030.W66 2015
364.082—dc23   2014019010

This book is printed on acid-free paper.

SUSTAINABLE FORESTRY INITIATIVE
Certified Chain of Custody
Promoting Sustainable Forestry
www.sfiprogram.org
SFI-01268
SFI label applies to text stock

15 16 17 18 10 9 8 7 6 5 4 3 2

Brief Contents

Detailed Contents

Foreword

You hold in your hands a book that we think is a different approach to this subject matter and to student learning. It is billed a "text/reader." What that means is that we have blended the two most commonly used types of books, the textbook and the reader, in a way that will appeal to both students and faculty.

Our experience as teachers and scholars has been that textbooks for the core classes in criminal justice (or any other social science discipline) leave many students and professors cold. The textbooks are huge and crammed with photographs, charts, highlighted material, and all sorts of pedagogical devices intended to increase student interest. Too often, however, these books end up creating a sort of sensory overload for students and suffer from their focus on "bells and whistles," such as fancy graphics, at the expense of coverage of the most significant and current research on the subject matter. And, in the end, isn't that what matters most? We study crime and justice to better understand why crime happens and how society processes it, and it is research—not pretty pictures—that inform this process. Our students deserve more than a nicely packaged recitation of boring facts; they need to understand what the research says, and this research needs to be presented in a fashion that does not scare them off.

Readers, on the other hand, are typically composed of recent and classic research articles on the subject matter. They generally suffer, however, from an absence of meaningful explanatory material. Articles are simply lined up and presented to the students with little or no context or explanation. Students, particularly undergraduate students, are often confused and overwhelmed by the jargon and detailed statistical analyses presented in the articles. It is unrealistic to expect students to fully grasp criminal justice research if this research is not placed in context and presented in a manner suited to their knowledge level.

This text/reader represents our attempt to take the best of both textbook and reader approaches. The book includes a combination of previously published articles on women and crime and of textual material introducing the articles and providing structure and context. The text/reader is intended to serve either as a supplement to a core undergraduate textbook or as a stand-alone text.

The book is divided into a number of sections. The sections of the book track the typical content and structure of a textbook on the subject. Each section of the book has an introductory chapter that introduces, explains, and provides context for the readings that follow. The readings are a selection of the best recent research from academic journals, as well as some classic readings where appropriate. The articles are edited as necessary to make them accessible to students. This variety of research and perspectives will provide the student with a grasp of the development of research, as well as an understanding of the current status of research in the subject area. The approach gives the student the opportunity to learn the basics (in the introductory portion of each section) and to read some of the most interesting research on the subject.

There is also a preface and an introductory chapter. The preface explains the organization and content of the book, and the introductory chapter provides a framework for the material that follows and introduces relevant themes, issues, and concepts to assist the student in understanding the articles.

Each section concludes with a summary of the material covered, as well as a set of discussion questions. Discussion questions also appear at the end of each reading. These summaries and discussion questions should facilitate student thought and class discussion of the material.

Ancillary materials, such as PowerPoint slides, a testbank, and lecture outlines, are available to help assist the instructor in moving from a standard textbook to this hybrid approach.

We acknowledge that this approach may be viewed by some as more challenging than the traditional textbook. To that we say "Yes! It is!" But we believe that, if we raise the bar, our students will rise to the challenge. Research shows that students and faculty often find textbooks boring to read. It is our belief that many criminal justice instructors welcome the opportunity to teach without having to rely on a "standard" textbook that covers only the most basic information and that lacks both depth of coverage and an attention to current research. This book provides an alternative for instructors who want more than a basic textbook aimed at the lowest common denominator and filled with flashy but often useless features that merely drive up its cost. This book is intended for instructors who want their students to be exposed to more than the ordinary, basic coverage of criminal justice.

We also believe students will find this approach more interesting. They are given the opportunity to read current, cutting-edge research on the subject while also being provided with background and context for this research. In addition to including the most topical and relevant research, we have included a short entry, "How to Read a Research Article." The purpose of this entry, placed toward the beginning of the book, is to provide students with an overview of the components of a research article. It helps walk them through the process of reading a research article, lessening their trepidation and increasing their ability to comprehend the material presented therein. Many students will be unfamiliar with reading and deciphering research articles; we hope this feature will help them do so.

In addition, we provide a student study site on the Internet with supplemental research articles, study questions, practice quizzes, and other pedagogical material to assist the student in learning the material. We chose to put these pedagogical tools on a companion study site rather than in the text to allow instructors to focus on the material, while still offering students the opportunity to learn more.

To date, there have been twelve books published in the text/reader series. Many of them have gone into (or are in the process of going into) multiple editions. The feedback we have received from early adopters has been overwhelmingly positive. Instructors have successfully used these books in community colleges and universities at both the undergraduate and graduate levels. Faculty tell us they find the books more interesting to use and teach from, and that students appreciate the different approach.

We hope that this unconventional approach will be more interesting to students and faculty alike and thus make learning and teaching more fun. Criminal justice is a fascinating subject, and the topic deserves to be presented in an interesting manner. We hope you will agree.

Craig Hemmens, JD, PhD, Series Editor

Department of Criminal Justice and Criminology
Washington State University

Preface

The purpose of this book is to introduce readers to the issues that face women as they navigate the criminal justice system. Regardless of the participation, women have unique experiences that have significant effects on their perspectives of the criminal justice system. In order to effectively understand the criminal justice system, the voices of women must be heard. This book seeks to inform readers on the realities of women's lives as they interact with the criminal justice system. These topics are presented in this book through summary essays highlighting the key terms and research findings and incorporating cutting-edge research from scholars whose works have been published in top journals in criminal justice, criminology, and related fields.

Organization and Contents of the Book

This book is divided into thirteen sections, with each section dealing with a different subject related to women and crime. Each section begins with an introduction to the issues raised within each topic and summarizes some of the basic themes related to the subject area. Each introductory essay concludes with a discussion of the policy implications related to each topic. This discussion is followed by selected readings that focus on research being conducted on critical issues within each topical area. These readings represent some of the best research in the field and are designed to expose students to the discussions facing women's issues within contemporary criminal justice. These thirteen sections include

- Women and Crime: Introduction
- Theories of Victimization
- Women and Victimization: Rape and Sexual Assault
- Women and Victimization: Intimate Partner Abuse and Stalking
- International Issues in the Victimization of Women
- Theories on Female Offending
- Girls and Juvenile Delinquency
- Female Offenders and Their Crimes
- Processing and Sentencing of Female Offenders
- The Incarceration of Women
- The Supervision of Women: Community Corrections, Rehabilitation, and Reentry
- Women Professionals and the Criminal Justice System: Police, Corrections, and Offender Services
- Women Professionals and the Criminal Justice System: Courts and Victim Services

The first section provides an introduction and foundation for the book. In setting the context for the book, this section begins with a review of the influence of feminism on the study of crime. The section looks at the different types of data sources that are used to assess female offending and victimization. The section concludes with a discussion on feminist methodology and how it can contribute to the discussions of women and crime. The first article in this section, by Meda Chesney-Lind, looks at the role of patriarchy in developing a feminist criminology in light of traditional and contemporary theories of crime. The second article, by Jody Miller, focuses on issues of gender in qualitative research.

The second section begins with a review of the victim experience in the criminal justice system. This section highlights the experience of help seeking by victims and the practice of victim blaming. The section then turns to a discussion of victimization and focuses on how fear about victimization is a gendered experience. The section then turns to the discussion of victimization and how theories seek to understand the victim experience and place it within the larger context of the criminal justice system and society in general. The section includes two readings on victimization. The first article in this section, by Bonnie S. Fisher and David May, investigates the effects of gender on the fear of victimization by college students. The second article, by Chiara Sabina, Carlos A. Cuevas, and Jennifer L. Schally, looks at how ethnicity can impact the help-seeking experience.

The third section focuses on the victimization of women by crimes of rape and sexual assault. From historical issues to contemporary standards in the definition of sexual victimization, this section highlights the various forms of sexual assault and the role of the criminal justice system in the reporting and prosecution of these crimes, and the role of victims in the criminal justice system. The readings in this section highlight some of the critical research on issues related to rape and sexual assault. Beginning with a discussion of sexual assault resources on college campuses, Rebecca M. Hayes-Smith and Lora M. Levett investigate whether information about these resources altered students' beliefs in rape myths. The second reading, by Clare Gunby, Anna Carline, and Caryl Beynon, investigates how alcohol consumption alters perceptions of rape and sexual assault claims.

The fourth section presents the discussion of victimization of women in cases of intimate partner abuse and stalking. A review of the legal and social research on intimate partner violence addresses a multitude of issues for victims, including the barriers to leaving a battering relationship. The articles in this section address some of the contemporary issues facing victims of intimate partner violence. The section concludes with a discussion of stalking. The readings for this section begin with an essay by Martin D. Schwartz and Walter S. DeKeseredy on the role of patriarchy in the culture of battering and how a male-dominated society can stop violence against women. The second article, by Katie M. Edwards, Christina M. Dardis, and Christine A. Gidycz, investigates the disclosure practices of victims of dating violence.

The fifth section focuses on international issues for women and includes discussions on crimes such as human trafficking, honor killings, witch burnings, genital mutilation, and femicide. In the first article in this section, Frances P. Bernat and Heather C. Winkeller present an issue that has engaged communities around the world: human trafficking. While human trafficking is a global issue, much of the intervention efforts are facilitated at the local level. This article discusses how local agencies can prepare to deal with victims of these crimes. The second article, by Sujay Patel and Amin Muhammad Gadit, explains honor killings of women in Pakistan.

The sixth section focuses on the theoretical explanations of female offending. The section begins with a review of the classical and modern theories of female criminality. While the classical theories often described women in sexist and stereotypical ways, modern theories of crime often ignored women completely. Recent research has reviewed many of these theories to assess whether they might help to explain female offending. The section concludes with a discussion of gender-neutral theories and feminist criminology. This section includes two articles that involve testing criminological theory on female populations. The first article is by April Bernard who uses a case study to assess which theories of crime might best explain this offender's criminal behavior. The second article, by Felipe Estrada and Anders Nilsson, uses data from the Stockholm Birth Cohort to assess gender differences in offending from a life-course perspective.

Section VII focuses on girls and the juvenile justice system. Beginning with a discussion on the patterns of female delinquency, this section investigates the historical and contemporary standards for young women in society and how the changing definitions of delinquency have disproportionately and negatively impacted young girls. The readings for this section begin with an article by Barry C. Feld and looks to the question of whether girls are becoming more violent, or whether the system is changing how it deals with young girls who "act out." The section concludes with an article by Juliette Noel Graziano and Eric F. Wagner and investigates the role of trauma within the LGBTQ girls in the juvenile justice system.

Section VIII deals with women and their crimes. While female crimes of violence are highly sensationalized by the media, these crimes are rare occurrences. Instead, the majority of female offending is made up of crimes that are non-violent in nature or are considered victimless crimes, such as property-based offenses, drug abuse, and sexually based offenses. The readings for this section include an article by Judith A. Ryder and Regina E. Brisgone that focuses on the experiences of women and girls living and growing up during the era of crack cocaine and an article by Jennifer E. Cobbina and Sharon S. Oselin that looks at how the age of entry impacts the experience of women involved in street prostitution.

The ninth section details the historical and contemporary patterns in the processing and sentencing of female offenders. This section highlights research on how factors such as patriarchy, chivalry, and paternalism within the criminal justice system impact women. Two articles in this section investigate the effects of gender on the processing of offenders: Tina L. Freiburger and Carly M. Hilinski investigate how race, gender, and age impact decision making in cases of pretrial detention; and Jill K. Doerner and Stephen Demuth look at whether women in the federal courts benefit from chivalrous sentencing practices.

The tenth section examines the incarceration of women. Here, the text and readings focus on the patterns and practices of the incarceration of women. Ranging from historical examples of incarceration to modern-day policies, this section looks to how the treatment of women in prison varies from that of their male counterparts and how incarcerated women have unique needs based on their differential pathways to prison. The readings in this section begin with a discussion by Katarzyna Celinska and Jane A. Siegel on how women cope with being separated from their children during their incarceration and conclude with research by Holly M. Harner and Suzanne Riley on the mental health effects of the incarceration experience.

Section XI looks at the experience of women in the community corrections setting. The section begins with a discussion on gender-specific programming and how correctional agents and programs need to address these unique issues for women. The section then looks at the role of risk assessment instruments and how they need to reflect gender differences between male and female offenders. The section concludes with a discussion on the reentry challenges of women exiting from prison. The first article, by Tara D. Opsal, focuses on how women handle the stigmatized identity of being on parole. The second article, by Carolyn Leitzell, Natalie Madrazo, and Reverend Carmen Warner-Robbins, looks at how one particular program helps women in transition from prison, particularly in terms of the physical and mental health needs.

Section XII focuses on women who work within criminal justice occupations within traditionally male-dominated environments: policing and corrections. The readings for this section bring attention to the women who work within the domain of the criminal justice system and how gender impacts their occupational context. Following a discussion of the history of women in these occupations, this section looks at how gender impacts the performance of women in these jobs and the personal toll it has on their lives. The first article by Kimberly A. Lonsway, Rebecca Paynich, and Jennifer N. Hall looks at the issues of sexual harassment in policing. The section concludes with research by Cassandra Matthews, Elizabeth Monk-Turner, and Melvina Sumter on promotional opportunities for women in corrections.

Section XIII concludes this text with a discussion of women in the legal and victim services fields. The section looks at both women who work as attorneys as well as women in the judiciary. While women are a minority in this realm of the criminal justice system, women are generally overrepresented within victim services agencies. Here, gender also plays a significant role both in terms of the individual's work experiences as well as in the structural organization of the agency. The readings for this section include an article by Madhavi McCall on whether gender impacts judicial voting practices and conclude with research by Sarah E. Ullman and Stephanie M. Townsend on the barriers that rape crisis workers experience in working with victims.

As you can see, this book provides an in-depth look at the issues facing women in the criminal justice system. From victimization to incarceration to employment, this book takes a unique approach in its presentation by combining a review of the literature on each of these issues followed by some of the key research studies that have been published in academic journals. Each section of this book presents a critical component of the criminal justice system and the role of women in it. As you will soon learn, gender is a pervasive theme that runs deeply throughout our system, and how we respond to it has a dramatic effect on the lives of women in society.

Ancillaries

Instructor Teaching Site

A password-protected site, available at www.sagepub.com/mallicoat2e, features resources that have been designed to help instructors plan and teach their courses. These resources include an extensive test bank, chapter-specific PowerPoint presentations, lecture notes, sample syllabi, video and web resources, and links to SAGE journal articles with accompanying questions.

Student Study Site

An open-access study site is available at www.sagepub.com/mallicoat2e. This site includes mobile-friendly eFlash-cards and web quizzes as well as web resources, video resources, and links to SAGE journal articles.

Acknowledgments

I have to give tremendous thanks to Jerry Westby, publisher of the Criminology and Criminal Justice Division at SAGE Publications. I continue to be indebted to you for your faith and encouragement in me as an author and for allowing me the amazing opportunity to share my passion for all things crime and justice. I also have to give thanks to Craig Hemmens, series editor for the Text/Reader series, for his support. Special thanks as well to the staff at SAGE Publications who have also helped to breathe life into this book.

Throughout my career, I have been blessed with amazing colleagues and mentors—Jill Rosenbaum, Denise Paquette Boots, Hank Fradella, Allison Cotton, Hillary Potter, Joanne Belknap, Anthony Peguero, Christie Gardiner, and my colleagues in the Division of Politics, Administration and Justice at California State University, Fullerton. Thanks to all of you who make me laugh every day even when I might want to kick, scream, and cry. Finally, thank you to my amazing network of friends from the Division on Women and Crime and the Division on People of Color and Crime. I am honored to get to work in an environment that is caring and supportive of my adventures in research and scholarship.

Finally, I am deeply indebted to my husband, Jeff, my son, Keegan, and our families for their love, support, and care and their endless encouragement for my adventures in academia and beyond.

SAGE Publications gratefully acknowledges the contributions of the following reviewers for this second edition:

Kathleen A. Cameron, Pittsburgh State University

Dorinda L. Dowis, Columbus State University

Katherine J. Ely, Lock Haven University

Allison J. Foley, Georgia Regents University

Bob Lilly, Northern Kentucky University

Johnnie Dumas Myers, Savannah State University

Sue Uttley-Evans, University of Central Lancashire

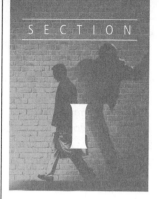

Women and Crime

Introduction

Section Highlights

- Introduction to women as victims, offenders, and workers in the criminal justice system
- The emergence of feminism in criminology
- Data sources that estimate female offending and victimization rates
- The contributions of feminist methodologies in understanding issues about women and crime

S ince the creation of the American criminal justice system, the experiences of women either have been reduced to a cursory glance or have been completely absent. **Gendered justice**, or rather injustice, has prevailed in every aspect of the system. The unique experiences of women have historically been ignored at every turn— for victims, for offenders, and even for women who have worked within its walls. Indeed, the criminal justice system is a gendered experience.

Yet the participation of women in the system is growing in every realm. Women make up a majority of the victims for certain types of crimes, particularly when men are the primary offender. These gendered experiences of victimization appear in crimes such as rape, sexual assault, intimate partner abuse, and stalking, to name a few. While women suffer in disproportionate ways in these cases, their cries for help have traditionally been ignored by a system that many in society perceive is designed to help victims. Women's needs as offenders are also ignored as they face a variety of unique circumstances and experiences that are absent from the male offending population. Traditional approaches in criminological theory and practice have been criticized by feminist scholars for their failure to understand the lives and experiences of women (Belknap, 2007). Likewise, the employment of women in the criminal justice system has been limited, as women were traditionally shut out of many of these male-dominated occupations. As women began to enter these occupations, they were faced with a hyper-masculine culture that challenged the introduction of women at every turn. While the participation of women in these traditionally male-dominated fields has grown significantly in modern-day times, women continue to struggle for equality in a world where the effects of the "glass ceiling" continue to pervade a system that presents itself as one interested in the notion of justice (Martin, 1991).

In setting the context for the book, this section begins with a review of the influence of feminism on the study of crime. Following an introduction of how gender impacts victimization, offending, and employment experiences in the criminal justice system, the section presents a review of the different data sources and statistics within these topics. The section concludes with a discussion on the research methods used to investigate issues of female victimization, offending, and work in criminal justice-related fields.

▨ The Influence of Feminism on Studies of Women and Crime

As a student, you may wonder what **feminism** has to do with the topic of women and crime. Feminism plays a key role in understanding how the criminal justice system responds to women and women's issues. In doing so, it is first important that we identify what is meant by the term *woman*. Is "woman" a category of *sex* or *gender*? Sometimes, these two words are used interchangeably. However, *sex* and *gender* are two different terms. *Sex* refers to the biological or physiological characteristics of what makes someone male or female. Therefore, we might use the term *sex* to talk about the segregation of men and women in jails or prison. In comparison, the term *gender* refers to the identification of masculine and feminine traits, which are socially constructed terms. For example, in early theories of criminology, female offenders were often characterized as *masculine*, and many of these scholars believed that female offenders were more like men than women. While sex and gender are two separate terms, the notions of sex and gender are interrelated within the study of women and crime. Throughout this book, you will see examples of how sex and gender both play an important role in the lives of women in the criminal justice system.

The study of women and crime has seen incredible advances throughout the 20th and 21st century. Many of these changes are a result of the social and political efforts of feminism. The 1960s and 1970s shed light on several significant issues that impacted many different groups in society, including women. The momentum of social change as represented by the civil rights and women's movements had significant impacts for society, and the criminal justice system was no stranger in these discussions. Here, the second wave of feminism expanded beyond the focus of the original activists (who were concerned exclusively about women's suffrage and the right to vote) to topics such as sexuality, legal inequalities, and reproductive rights. It was during this time frame that criminology scholars began to think differently about women and offending. Prior to this time, women were largely forgotten in research about crime and criminal behavior. When they were mentioned, they were relegated to a brief footnote or discussed in stereotypical and sexist ways. Given that there were few female criminologists (as well as proportionally few female offenders compared to the number of male offenders), it is not surprising that women were omitted in this early research about criminal behavior.

Some of the first feminist criminologists gained attention during the 1960s and 1970s. The majority of these scholars were focused primarily on looking at issues of equality and difference between men and women in terms of offending and responses by the criminal justice system. Unfortunately, these liberal feminists focused only on gender and did not include discussions that reflected a multicultural identity. Such a focus resulted in a narrow view of the women that were involved in crime and how the system responded to their offending. As Burgess-Proctor (2006) notes,

> By asserting that women universally suffer the effects of patriarchy, the dominance approach rests on the dubious assumption that all women, by virtue of their shared gender, have a common "experience" in the first place. . . . It assumes that all women are oppressed by all men in exactly the same ways or that there is one unified experience of dominance experienced by women. (p. 34)

While second wave feminism focused on the works by these White liberal feminists, third wave feminism addresses the multiple, diverse perspectives of women, such as race, ethnicity, nationality, and sexuality. With these new perspectives in hand, feminist criminologists began to talk in earnest about the nature of the female offender and began to ask questions about the lives of women involved in the criminal justice system. Who is she? Why does she engage in crime? And, perhaps most importantly, how is she different from the male offender and how should the criminal justice system respond to her?

As feminist criminologists began to encourage the criminal justice system to think differently about female offenders, feminism also encouraged new conversations about female victimization. The efforts of second- and third-wave feminism brought increased attention to women who were victims of crime. How do women experience victimization? How does the system respond to women who have been victims of a crime? How have criminal justice systems and policies responded to the victimization of women?

Feminism also brought a greater participation in the workforce in general, and the field of criminal justice was no exception. Scholars were faced with questions regarding how gender impacts the way in which women work within the police department, correctional agencies, and

▲ Photo 1.1   The icon of Lady Justice represents many of the ideal goals of the justice system, including fairness, justice, and equality.

the legal system? What issues do women face within the context of these occupations? How has the participation of women in these fields affected the experiences of women who are victims and offenders?

Today, scholars in criminology, criminal justice, and related fields explore these issues in depth in an attempt to shed light on the population of women in the criminal justice system. While significant gains have been made in the field of feminist criminology, the field continues to grow, particularly as scholars investigate issues of gender and crime within a diverse and intersecting world of race, ethnicity, class, sexuality, and other identities (Burgess-Proctor, 2006).

CASE STUDY

Spotlight on Women and the Academy

Like many other fields, the academy has historically been a male-dominated profession. Yet the number of women faculty has grown significantly over the past four decades. This is also true in the academic study of crime and the criminal justice system. While the number of men in senior faculty positions outnumbers women, the presence of women entering the academy is growing. In 2007, 57% of doctoral students were female. This marks a significant trend for a field (practitioners and the academy) that has been historically dominated by men (Frost & Clear, 2007).

(Continued)

(Continued)

As a national organization, the roots of the American Society of Criminology date back to 1941. The founding members of the organization were all male (ASC, n.d.). It was not until 1975 that the annual conference showcased a panel on women and crime. Even with the growing interest in female crime and victimization, not to mention an increase in the number of female scholars, the majority of the association members questioned whether gender was a valuable variable to study. In response to these challenges, a small group of female scholars combined their efforts to lobby for more panels on the study of women and crime. In 1984, the Division on Women and Crime was instituted as an official branch of the American Society of Criminology. Today, the Division is the largest division of the ASC, with 384 members in 2012.

As a result of the work of these early female criminologists, the number of panels and papers presented annually on issues related to gender and crime research has grown substantially and includes discussions related to offending, victimization, and employment issues within the criminal justice system. Between 1999 and 2008, there were 3,050 (16.13%) presentations on themes related to the study of women and crime. The top five topic areas of these presentations include (1) domestic violence/intimate partner violence, (2) gender-specific programming and policies, (3) gender differences in criminal behavior, (4) victimization of women, and (5) international perspectives on women and crime (Kim & Merlo, 2012).

While much of the work of feminist criminology involves female scholars, there are also men who investigate issues of gender and crime. At the same time, there are female scholars whose work does not look at issues of gender. Over the past decade, there has been a body of work that has looked at the productivity of criminologists, and in particular how female scholars compare to male scholars. While men publish more than women, the **gender gap** on publishing is reduced when we take into account the length of time in the academy, as the men generally report a longer career history (Snell, Sorenson, Rodriguez, & Kuanliang, 2009). Men are also more likely to be the lead author of articles published in the top-tier journals in the field (Tewksbury, DeMichele, & Miller, 2005). However, the number of publications with women is growing at a rapid pace. Indeed the rise of female scholars led some researchers to note that the future of the "most productive and influential scholars will have a more markedly feminine quality" (Rice, Terry, Miller, & Ackerman, 2007, p. 379).

Women are also becoming more active in the leadership roles within these academic organizations. What was once a "boys club" now reflects an increase in the participation of women on the executive boards as well as officer positions within the organization. In 2013, Joanne Belknap and Karen Heimer will serve as president and vice president of the American Society of Criminology. Their election to these positions by the general membership illustrates just how far women in criminology have traveled, as this will be the first time in the 74-year history of the organization where the top positions of the association were both held by women (and only the seventh time that the presidential role has been filled by a woman). The trend of a female president of the ASC continues in 2015 with the election of Candace Kruttschnitt. The recent election of Ruth Peterson as president for 2016 represents the first time that an African American female will serve in this lead position of the ASC.

As the Division on Women and Crime of the American Society of Criminology celebrates its 30-year anniversary in 2014, it is evident that feminist scholars have made a significant impact on the study of crime over the past 40 years.

✉ Women and Crime

How does the criminal justice system respond to issues of gender? While there have been significant gains and improvements in the treatment of women as victims, offenders, and workers within the criminal justice system and related fields, there is still work to be done in each of these areas.

Women as Victims of Violence

The experience of victimization is something that many women are intimately familiar with. While men are more likely to be a victim of a crime, women compose the majority of victims of certain forms of violent crime. In addition, women are most likely to be victimized by someone they know. In many cases when they do seek help from the criminal justice system, charges are not always filed or are often reduced through plea bargains, resulting in offenders receiving limited (if any) sanctions for their criminal behavior. Due to the sensitive nature of these offenses, victims can find their own lives put on trial to be criticized by the criminal justice system and society as a whole. Based on these circumstances, it is no surprise that many women have had little faith in the criminal justice system. You'll learn more about the experience of victimization in Section II.

Women who experience victimization have a number of needs, particularly in cases of violent and personal victimization experiences. While these cases can involve significant physical damage, it is often the emotional violence that can be equally, if not more, traumatic for victims to deal with. While significant gains have been made by the criminal justice system, the high needs of many victims, coupled with an increased demand for services, means that the availability of resources by agencies such as domestic violence shelters and rape crisis centers are often limited. You'll learn more about the experience of women in crimes such as rape, sexual assault, intimate partner violence, and stalking in Sections III and IV, while Section V highlights issues of victimization of women around the globe.

Women Who Offend

How do female offenders compare to male offenders? When scholars look at the similarities and differences between the patterns of male and female offending, they are investigating the *gender* gap. What does this research tell us? We know that men are the majority of offenders represented for most of the crime categories, minus a few exceptions. Gender gap research tells us that the gender gap, or difference between male and female offending, is larger in cases of serious or violent crimes, while the gap is narrower for crimes such as property and drug related offenses (Steffensmeier & Allan, 1996).

While men are more likely to engage in criminal acts, women offenders dominate certain categories of criminal behavior. One example of this phenomenon is the crime of prostitution. Often called a victimless crime, prostitution is an offense where the majority of arrests involve women. Status offenses are another category where girls are overrepresented. Status offenses are acts that are considered criminal only because of the offender's age. For example, the consumption of alcohol is considered illegal only if you are under a designated age (generally 21 in the United States). Section VIII highlights different offense types and how gender is viewed within these offenses. A review of these behaviors and offenders indicates that most female offenders share a common foundation—one of economic need, addiction, and abuse.

Gender also impacts the way that the criminal justice system responds to offenders of crime. Much of this attention comes from social expectations about how women "should" behave. When women engage in crime (particularly violent crimes), this also violates the socially proscribed gender roles for female behavior. As a result, women in these cases may be punished not only for violating the law but also for violating the socially proscribed gender roles. In

Section IX, you'll learn more about how women can be treated differently by the criminal justice system as a result of their gender. As more women have come to the attention of criminal justice officials, and as policies and practices for handling these cases have shifted, more women are being sent to prison rather than being supervised in the community. This means that there is a greater demand on reentry programming and services for women. These collateral consequences in the incarceration of women are far reaching, as the identity as an *ex-offender* can threaten a woman's chances for success long after she has served her sentence.

The Intersection of Victimization and Offending

One of the greatest contributions of feminist criminology is the acknowledgment of the relationship between victimization and offending. Research has consistently illustrated that a history of victimization of women is a common factor for many women offenders. Indeed, a review of the literature finds that an overwhelming majority of women in prison have experienced some form of abuse—physical, psychological, or sexual—and in many cases, are victims of long-term multiple acts of violence. Moreover, not only is there a strong relationship that leads from victimization to offending, but the relationship between these two variables continues also as a vicious cycle. For example, a young girl who is sexually abused by a family member runs away from home. Rather than return to her abusive environment, she ends up selling her body as a way to provide food, clothing, and shelter as she has few skills to legitimately support herself. As a result of her interactions with potentially dangerous clients and pimps, she continues to endure physical and sexual violence and may turn to substances such as alcohol and drugs to numb the pain of the abuse. When confronted by the criminal justice system, she receives little if any assistance to address the multiple issues that she faces as a result of her life experiences. In addition, her *criminal* identity now makes it increasingly difficult to find valid employment, receive housing and food benefits, or have access to educational opportunities that could improve her situation. Ultimately, she ends up in a world where finding a healthy and sustainable life on her own is a difficult goal to attain. You will learn more about these challenges in Sections X and XI and how the criminal justice system punishes women for these crimes.

Women and Work in the Criminal Justice System

While much of the study of women and crime focuses on issues of victimization and offending, it is important to consider how issues of sex and gender impact the work environment, particularly for those who work within the justice system. Here, the experiences of women as police and correctional officers, victim advocates, probation and parole case managers, and lawyers and judges provide valuable insight on how sex and gender differences affect women. Just as the social movements of the 1960s and 1970s increased the attention on female offenders and victims of crime, the access to opportunities for work within the walls of criminal justice expanded for women. Prior to this era of social change, few women were granted access to work within these occupations. Even when women were present, their duties were significantly limited compared to those of their male counterparts, and their opportunities for advancement were essentially nonexistent. In addition, these primarily male workforces resented the presence of women in "their" world. Gender also has a significant effect for fields that are connected to criminal justice. One example of this is found within the field of victim services, which has typically been viewed as women's work.

Women continue to face a number of sex- and gender-based challenges directly related to their status as women, such as on-the-job sexual harassment, work-family balance, maternity, and motherhood. In addition, research reflects on how women manage the roles, duties, and responsibilities of their positions within a historically masculine environment. The experience of womanhood can impact the work environment, both personally and culturally. You'll learn more about these issues in Sections XII and XIII of this book.

⬚ Data Sources on Women as Victims and Offenders

In order to develop an understanding of how often women engage in offending behaviors or the frequency of victimizations of women, it is important to look at how information about crime is gathered. While there is no one dataset that tells us everything that we want to know about crime, we can learn something from each source as they each represent different points of view. Datasets vary based on the type of information collected (quantitative and/or qualitative), who manages the dataset (such as government agencies, professional scholar, community organization) and the purpose for the data collection. Finally, each dataset represents a picture of crime for a specific population, region, and time frame, or stage, of the criminal justice system.

The **Uniform Crime Reports (UCR)** represents one of the largest datasets on crime in the United States. The Federal Bureau of Investigations (FBI) is charged with collecting and publishing the arrest data from over 17,000 police agencies in the United States. These statistics are published annually and present the rates and volume of crime by offense type, based on arrests made by police. The dataset includes a number of demographic variables to evaluate these crime statistics, including age, gender, race/ethnicity, location (state), and region (metropolitan, suburban, or rural).[1]

UCR data give us a general understanding of the extent of crime in the United States and are often viewed as the most accurate assessment of crime. In addition, the UCR data allow us to compare how crime changes over time, as it allows for the comparison of arrest data for a variety of crimes over a specific time frame (e.g., 1990–2000) or from one year to the next. Generally speaking, it is data from the UCR findings that are typically reported to the greater society through news media outlets and that form the basis for headline stories that proclaim the rising and falling rates of crime.

A review of arrest data from the UCR indicates that the overall levels of crime for women increased 2.9% between 2003 and 2012. For the same time period, the number of arrests for men declined 12.7%. Such results might lead us to question why the number of women involved in crime increased while the percentage of men fell. In order to understand this issue, we need to take a deeper look. Table 1.1 illus-

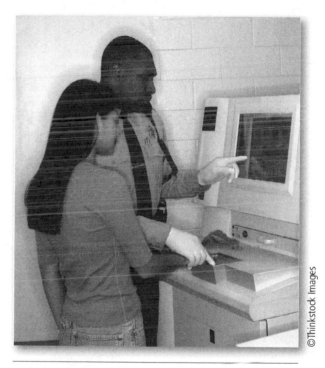

▲ Photo 1.2   Most official crime statistics are based on arrest data. Here, a woman has her fingerprints entered into a database as part of her arrest process.

trates the UCR data on arrest trends for men and women for 2003 and 2012. In 2003, the UCR shows that women made up 23.2% of all arrests (8,985,000 total number of arrests, with women accounting for 2,080,990 arrests). In contrast, 2012 UCR data indicate that 8,169,312 arrests were made, and women accounted for 26.2% of these arrests (2,140,934) (Crime in the United States 2012 [CIUS], 2012. Note that while the number of arrests involving women

---

[1]Up-to-date statistical reports on crime data from the Uniform Crime Reports can be accessed at http://www.fbi.gov/ucr/ucr.htm

Table 1.1 10-Year UCR Arrest Trends

	Men			Women		
	2003	2012	% Change	2003	2012	% Change
All arrests	6,904,010	6,028,378	−12.7	2,080,990	2,140,934	+2.9
Violent crime	326,975	278,167	−14.9	71,077	69,074	−2.8
Homicide	7,353	6,303	−14.3	905	830	−8.3
Forcible rape	16,578	11,782	−28.9	210	109	−48.1
Robbery	63,555	59,033	−7.1	7,512	9,032	+20.2
Aggravated assault	239,489	201,049	−16.1	62,450	59,103	−5.4
Property crime	745,246	694,051	−6.9	334,418	417,033	+24.7
Burglary	170,581	161,450	−5.4	28,275	32,432	+14.7
Larceny-theft	486,870	488,888	+0.4	288,894	374,332	+29.6
Motor vehicle theft	78,642	37,237	−52.6	15.531	8,833	−43.1
Arson	9,153	6,476	−29.2	1,718	1,436	−16.4

SOURCE: Crime in the United States 2012 (CIUS), 2012.

NOTE: 9,529 agencies reporting

increased by approximately 60,000, the total number of arrests decreased by almost 800,000. This change inflates the proportion of women engaged in crime between these two time periods.

When assessing trends in crime data, it is important to consider the time period of evaluation, as this can alter your results. While the 10-year arrest trends demonstrate an increase for women and a decrease for men, the data for 2012 actually represent a decrease from the overall crime rates for both men and women compared to 2011. Table 1.2 demonstrates the arrest trends for these 2 years. The proportion of crime involving men fell 2.4%, while the proportion for women decreased 0.7%. While this gives us a picture of overall crime trends, we see the picture differently when we look at the trends for specific crime categories. Here, a deeper look at the data shows that violent crime fell 2.2% for men and 0.1% for women between 2011 and 2012, while property crime declined 0.1% for men and increased by only 1.0% for women.

While the UCR data can illustrate important trends in crime, the reporting of UCR data as the true extent of crime is flawed for the majority of the crime categories (with the exception of homicide), even though these data represent arrest statistics from approximately 95% of the population. Here, it is important to take several issues into consideration. First, the UCR data represent statistics on only those crimes that are reported to the police. As a result, the data are dependent on both what police know about criminal activity and how they use their discretion in these cases. If the police are not a witness to a crime or are not called to deal with an offender, they cannot make an arrest. Arrests are the key variable for UCR data. This means that unreported crimes are not recognized in these statistics. Sadly, many of the victimization experiences of women, such as intimate partner abuse and sexual assault, are significantly underreported and therefore do not appear within the UCR data.

Table 1.2 1-Year UCR Arrest Trends

	Men			Women		
	2011	**2012**	**% Change**	**2011**	**2012**	**% Change**
All arrests	6,784,643	6,619,871	−2.4	2,394,448	2,376,547	−0.7
Violent crime	311,164	304,438	−2.2	75,435	75,335	−0.1
Homicide	6,827	6,822	−0.1	932	892	−4.3
Forcible rape	13,641	12,900	−5.4	154	128	−16.9
Robbery	66,172	63,239	−4.4	9,192	9,546	+3.9
Aggravated assault	224,524	221,477	−1.4	65,157	64,769	−0.6
Property crime	768,202	767,677	−0.1	459,132	463,609	+1.0
Burglary	185,517	178,258	−3.9	35,001	35,620	+1.8
Larceny-theft	537,318	543,384	+1.1	414,059	417,168	+0.8
Motor vehicle theft	38,233	38,894	+1.7	8,557	9,254	+8.1
Arson	7,134	7,141	+0.1	1,515	1,567	+3.4

SOURCE: Crime in the United States 2012 (CIUS), 2012.

NOTE: 11,407 agencies reporting

Second, the UCR collects data only on certain types of crime (versus all forms of crime). The classification of crime is organized into two different types of crime. Part 1 offenses and Part 2 offenses. Part 1 offenses, known as *index crimes*, include eight different offenses: aggravated assault, forcible rape, murder, robbery, arson, burglary, larceny-theft, and motor vehicle theft. However, these categories may have limited definitions that fail to capture the true extent of arrests made for these crimes. Consider the category of forcible rape. Historically, the UCR defined forcible rape as "the carnal knowledge of a female forcibly and against her will" (CIUS, 2012, para. 1). While the UCR also collects data on attempted rape by force or threat of force within this category, the definition failed to capture the magnitude of sexual assaults, which may not involve female victims or may involve other sexual acts beyond vaginal penetration. In January 2012, the FBI announced a revised definition for the crime of rape to include "the penetration, no matter how slight, of the vagina or anus with any body part or object, or oral penetration by a sex organ of another person, without the consent of the victim" (FBI, 2012a, para. 1). This new definition went into effect in January 2013. Not only does the new law allow for both males and females to be identified as victims or offenders, but it also allows the UCR to include cases where the victim either was unable or unwilling to consent to sexual activity (for example, in cases involving intoxication). In addition, the new definition removes the requirement of force. As a result of these changes, the category of rape will now capture a greater diversity of sexual assaults. This new definition is more in line with the variety of laws related to rape and sexual assault that exist for each state. With this change in how these sexually based offenses are counted, it is expected that we will see an increase in the UCR for the crime of rape in the following years. This does not mean that the crime of rape has increased dramatically in practice, only that we have changed the way we collect the data for these cases. Over time, these changes will help present a more accurate picture of the prevalence of rape and sexual assault in society.

Third, the reporting of the crimes to the UCR is incomplete, as only the most serious crime is reported in cases where multiple crimes are committed during a single criminal event. These findings skew the understanding of the prevalence of crime, as several different offenses may occur within the context of a single crime incident. For example, a crime involving physical battery, rape, and murder is reported to the UCR by the most serious crime, murder. As a result, the understanding of the prevalence of physical battery and rape is incomplete.

Fourth, the reporting of these data is organized annually, which can alter our understanding of crime as police agencies respond to cases. For example, a homicide that is committed in one calendar year may not be solved with an arrest and conviction until the following calendar year. This might initially be read as an "unsolved crime" in the first year, but as an arrest in the subsequent year.

Finally, the participation by agencies in reporting to the UCR has fluctuated over time. While there are no federal laws requiring agencies to report their crime data, many states today have laws that direct law enforcement agencies to comply with UCR data collection. However, this means that the analyzers of crime trends over time need to take into consideration the number of agencies involved in the reporting of crime data. Failure to do so could result in a flawed analysis of crime patterns over time.

These flaws of UCR data can have significant implications for members of society about the understanding of crime data. Most of us get our information about crime from news headlines or other media reports about crime. These 30-second clips about crime rates do little to explain the intricate nature of UCR data definitions and collection practices. Indeed, when the UCR was first assigned to the FBI, early scholars commented, "In light of the somewhat questionable source of the data, the Department of Justice might do more harm than good by issuing the Reports" (Robison, 1966, p. 1033).

In an effort to develop a better understanding of the extent of offending, the **National Incident-Based Reporting System (NIBRS)** was implemented in 1988. Rather than compile monthly summary reports on crime data in their jurisdictions, agencies now forward data to the FBI for every crime incident. The NIBRS catalog involves data on 22 offenses categories and includes 46 specific crimes known as Group A offenses. Data on 11 lesser offenses (Group B offenses) are also collected. In addition to an increased diversity in the types of crimes that data are collected on, the NIBRS abolished the hierarchy rule that was part of the UCR. This means that cases that involve more than one specific offense will now count all of the different offenses that are reported and not just the most serious event. In addition, NIBRS data are collected on both completed as well as attempted crimes.

Overall, NIBRS allows for a more comprehensive understanding of crime in the United States compared to the UCR. However, the transition of agencies to the NIBRS has been slow, as only 32 states have been certified by the FBI as of June 2012. The data obtained from these states represent 27% of the reported crime and 43% of all police agencies in the United States. Eight additional states are currently testing NIBRS in their jurisdictions, and seven more states or territories are in the process of developing plans for NIBRS (Justice Research and Statistics Association [JRSA], n.d.). While the NIBRS is an improvement over the UCR, this system still carries over a fatal flaw from the UCR in that both are limited to reported crimes. In spite of this, it is hoped that the improvements in official crime data collection will allow an increased understanding of the extent of female offending patterns.

In contrast to the limitations of the UCR and NIBRS datasets, the **National Crime Victimization Survey (NCVS)** represents the largest victimization study conducted in the United States. National-level victimization data were first collected in 1971 to 1972 as part of the Quarterly Household Survey conducted by the Census Bureau. In 1972, these efforts evolved into the National Crime Survey (NCS), which was designed to supplement the data from UCR and provide data on crime from the victims' perspective. The NCS was transferred to the Bureau of Justice Statistics in 1979, where the bureau began to evaluate the survey instrument and the data collection process. Following an extensive redesign process, the NCS was renamed the National Crime Victimization Survey in 1991.

The greatest achievement of the NCVS lies in its attempt to fill the gap between reported and unreported crime, often described as the **dark figure of crime**. The NCVS gathers additional data about crimes committed and gives criminologists a greater understanding of the types of crimes committed and characteristics of the victims. In 2011, the NCVS interviewed 143,120 individuals aged 12 and older in 79,800 households. Based on these survey findings, the Bureau of Justice Statistics make generalizations to the population regarding the prevalence of victimization in the United States (Truman & Planty, 2012).

In addition to reporting the numbers of criminal victimizations, the NCVS presents data on the rates of crime. You may ask yourself, "What is a crime rate?" A crime rate compares the number of occurrences of a particular crime to the size of the total population. The NCVS presents its findings in relation to how many instances of the crime per 1,000 people. Crime rates make it easy to understand trends in criminal activity and victimization over time, regardless of changes to the population.

According to the National Crime Victimization Survey, the rate of violent victimization of women in 2002 was 30.7 per 1,000 people. By 2011, the crime rate had fallen to 19.8. This change amounts to a 36% decrease. Serious violent victimization also saw a significant decrease from 9.5 (2002) to 6.7 (2011).[2] Table 1.3 highlights the rates of crime for 2011 for violent and serious violent victimization. While NCVS data highlight these decreases, these patterns are not necessarily reflected in the UCR/NIBRS data, as many victims do not report these crimes to the police. With only 49% of victims reporting violent crime and 37% of victims reporting property crime, the NCVS provides valuable insight about the dark figure of crime that is missing in official crime statistics. This dark figure of crime varies by offense. For example, while 67% of cases of aggravated assault were reported, victims reported only 43% of simple assault cases. Similar patterns are observed in cases involving property crimes. While 83% of cases of motor vehicle theft were reported, other thefts were only reported 30% of the time (Truman & Planty, 2012).

Just as the UCR/NIBRS is not the only data source on offending, the NCVS is not the only national-level data source on victimization. A number of different studies investigate victims of crime and how the justice system responds to their victimization. One example of this type of survey is the National Violence Against Women Survey

Table 1.3   NCVS Crime Rates by Sex: 2002, 2010, and 2011

	Violent Crime					Serious Violent Crime*				
	Rates			Percent Change		Rates			Percent Change	
	2002	2010	2011	2002–2011	2010–2011	2002	2010	2011	2002–2011	2010–2011
Total	32.1	19.3	22.5	−30%	+17%	10.1	6.6	7.2	−28%	+9%
Sex:										
Male	33.5	20.1	25.4	−24%	+27%	10.4	6.4	7.7	−26%	+20%
Female	30.7	18.5	19.8	−36%	+7%	9.5	6.8	6.7	−30%	−2%

SOURCE: Truman & Planty (2012).

*Includes rape or sexual assault, robbery, and aggravated assault

---

[2]Includes rape, sexual assault, robbery, and aggravated assault.

(NVAWS). The NVAWS consisted of a random sample of 8,000 women over the age of 18. The NVAWS was first administered between November 1995 and May 1996 and represented one of the first comprehensive data assessments of violence against women for the crimes of intimate partner abuse, stalking, and sexual assault. Another example is the **National Intimate Partner and Sexual Violence Survey (NISVS)**, which is conducted by the Centers for Disease Control and the National Center for Injury Prevention and Control. In 2010, the NISVS included data from 16,507 interviews. The NISVS reports victimization from a variety of crimes, including sexual assault, intimate partner abuse, and stalking. These findings are then used to create estimates about the extent of crime throughout the United States. Figure 1.1 highlights the lifetime prevalence of rape by race and ethnicity based on data from the NISVS. These results demonstrate that 1 in 5 White (18.8%) and Black (22%) women and 1 in 7 (14.6%) Hispanic women in the United States have been raped at some point in their lifetime. By breaking up these data based on race and ethnicity, we can highlight how the issue of rape is even more dramatic within the American Indian/Alaska Native population, where 1 in 4 (26.9%) women experience rape in their lifetime. Unfortunately, we do not know much about how race and ethnicity impact rates of male rape from these data, only to say that less than 1 in 50 (2%) White men are impacted by the crime of rape in their lifetime (Black et al., 2011). Figure 1.2 presents the findings from this study for the crime of sexual assault. Here, we can see that not only are these crimes much more prevalent in general but also that we are able to see differences for both men and women by race/ethnicity. Studies such as these provide valuable data in understanding the experiences of victims (both men and women) that may not be reflected by the NCVS or UCR data.

While the UCR, NIBRS, and NCVS are examples of official data sources in the United States, there are several examples of international crime surveys that can shed light on the nature of crime and victimization in other countries. The Australian Bureau of Statistics (ABS) collects data on arrested individuals throughout Australia. Unlike the UCR, which collects data on a calendar year basis, the ABS data cycle runs from July 1 to June 30. In its 2012 to 2013 cycle, there were 391,117 individuals aged 10 and older processed by the police for eight different offenses (homicide, assault, sexual assault, robbery, kidnapping, unlawful entry with intent, motor vehicle theft, and other theft; Australian Bureau of Statistics, 2014). Another example of an official source of crime statistics is the annual report produced by the Bundeskriminalamt (Federal Criminal Police Office of Germany). The Bundeskriminalamt (BKA) statistics include data for all crimes handled by the police. In 2012, of the 5,997,040 crimes reported to the police, 3,259,822 were considered "cleared" or solved. Violent crime represents only 3.25% of crime in Germany. The largest crime category is theft and represents 39.68% of all criminal offenses. Men are much more likely to be considered a suspect by the police in these criminal activities—out of 2,094,118 suspects, only 25.4% are women. Men are also more likely to be victims of these crimes as 59.88% of victims are male (BKA, 2013). Australia's and Germany's crime statistical agencies are just two examples of official international data sources on criminal offending at the country level. Due to the differences in laws and reporting practices, it is difficult to compare such statistics at a global level. However, there have been attempts to collect basic information on recorded crime across several jurisdictions. The United Nations Survey of Crime Trends and Operations of Criminal Justice Systems (UN-CTS) compiles crime data from a variety of different sources, including the World Health Organization, Eurostat, and national police organizations from individual countries (to name a few). Their data indicate that there were 378,776 global victims of homicide reported to the police in 2012, or a crime rate of 10 per 100,000 (United Nations Office on Drugs and Crime, 2013).

Similar to the NCVS, the Crime Survey for England and Wales (CSEW) is administered to a random sample of households and is designed to develop estimates about the rate of crime and victimization in England and Wales. The Crime Survey for England and Wales first began as part of the British Crime Survey in 1984 and included data from Scotland and Northern Ireland. Today, these jurisdictions carry out their own victimization survey though the design and intent of these data collections are similar. In 2012 and 2013, approximately 50,000 households participated in the CSEW. Like the NCVS, the CSEW attempts to shed light on the dark figure of crime by capturing victimizations that may not be reported to the police. In 2013, the Crime Survey for England and Wales estimated that there were approximately 7.5 million incidents of victimization. Not only were these findings 15% lower than the previous year's

Figure 1.1 National Intimate Partner and Sexual Violence Survey: Lifetime Prevalence of Rape of Men and Women by Race/Ethnicity

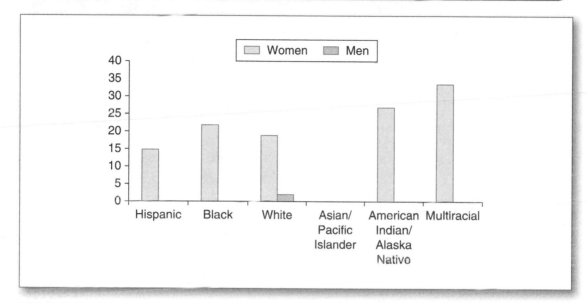

SOURCE: Black et al. (2011).

Figure 1.2 National Intimate Partner and Sexual Violence Survey: Lifetime Prevalence of Sexual Assault of Men and Women by Race/Ethnicity

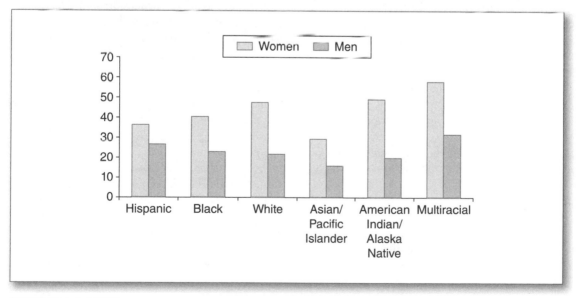

data, they represent as well the lowest level of victimizations since data were first collected in 1981. However, only half of these crimes (3.7 million) were reported to the police (Office for National Statistics, 2014).

Finally, there are data sources that are collected as part of criminological research. These data typically focus on a particular crime within a particular region. These data can be either quantitative or qualitative (or both) and represent either a snapshot in time or follow a group of individuals over a range of time (longitudinal studies). While the findings of these studies are often not generalizable to the masses, they provide valuable insight about victimization and offending. Throughout this text, you'll be exposed to a number of these studies, both within the chapters as well as the highlighted readings.

In summary, official crime statistics offer only one perspective on the extent of crime in society. While the UCR and NCVS data and other international data sources provide a wealth of statistics about crime, their results are limited. Through the use of these official data programs, combined with self-report studies and victimization surveys, scholars can investigate issues of gender and crime in a variety of different ways. While each source of data has its strengths and weaknesses in terms of the types of data that are collected and the methods that are utilized, together, they provide a wealth of information that is invaluable in understanding the complex nature of gender and crime.

The Contributions of Feminist Methodology to Research on Women and Crime

One of the criticisms of traditional mainstream criminology (and a central theme of feminist criminology) is that traditional perspectives on crime fail to recognize the intricate details of what it means to be a woman in society. The feminist movement has had a significant effect on how we understand women and their relationships with crime. As a result, the methods by which we conduct research on gender have also evolved. While many scholars who do research on gender engage in quantitative methods of research and analysis, this is not the only approach, particularly when dealing with sensitive issues. Here, the influence of feminism can alter the ways in which we conduct research, evaluate data, and make conclusions based on the findings yielded from the research experience. By incorporating a feminist perspective to the research environment, scholars are able to present a deeper understanding of the realities of women's lives by placing women and women's issues at the center of the research process.

The concept of giving women a voice, particularly in situations where they have been historically silenced, is a strong influence on **feminist research methods**. Many of the research studies in this book draw on feminist research methods. From the conceptualization of the research question to a discussion of which methods of data collection will be utilized and how the data will be analyzed, feminist methods engage in practices that are contrary to the traditional research paradigms. While the scientific method focuses on objectivity and the collection of data is detached from the human condition, the use of feminist methods requires a paradigm shift from what is traditionally known as research. While many of the researchers who first engaged in research through a feminist lens were women, feminist methodology does not dictate that the gender of the research participant or researcher be a woman. Rather, the philosophy of this method refers to the types of data a researcher is seeking and the process by which data are obtained (Westervelt & Cook, 2007). Feminist methods are largely qualitative in nature and allow for emotions and values to be present as part of the research process. While some feminist methodologists have criticized the process by which data are often quantified, as it does not allow for the intricate nature and quality of women's lives to be easily documented, others argue that quantitative data have a role to play within a feminist context. Regardless of the approach, the influence of feminism allows for researchers to collect data from a subject that is theoretically important for their research versus data that are easily categorized (Hessy-Biber, 2004; Reinharz, 1992).

There is no single method of research that is identified as the *feminist method*. Rather, the concept of feminist methodology refers to *the process by which data are gathered* and *the relationship between the researcher and the subject*. This process involves five basic principles: (1) acknowledging the influence of gender in society as a whole (and inclusive of the research process), (2) challenging the traditional relationship between the researcher and the subject and its link to scientific research and the validity of findings, (3) engaging in consciousness raising about the realities of women's lives as part of the methodological process, (4) empowering women within a patriarchal society through their participation in research, and (5) an awareness by the researcher of the ethical costs of the research process and a need to protect their subjects (Cook & Fonow, 1986).

For many researchers who study women in the criminal justice system, the use of feminist methodologies is particularly beneficial. Not only does it allow for researchers to explore in depth the issues that women face as victims and offenders, but it also provides the opportunity for the researchers to delve into their topics in a way that traditional methods fail to explore, such as the context of women's lives and their experiences in offending and victimization. For example, a simple survey question might inquire about whether an incarcerated woman has ever been victimized. We know that scholarship on incarcerated women has consistently documented the relationship between early life victimizations and participation in crime in their adolescent and adult lives. Yet traditional methods may underestimate the extent and nature of the victimization as the women may not understand the question or identify their experiences in this way. Feminist methodologies allow not only for the exploration of these issues at a deeper level, but also they allow for scholars to develop an understanding of the multifaceted effects of these experiences.

While many feminist researchers largely employ qualitative tactics, it is important to note that the use of feminist methods does not exclude the use of quantitative methods. In fact, quantitative methods can yield valuable data on the experiences of women (Westmarland, 2001). For example, survey data can yield information on the presence of gender discrimination, such as the sexual harassment among women in policing. In addition, the use of quantitative data and statistics is often useful for legislators when developing policies. Reinharz (1992) provides the example of the use of statistics in the development of sexual harassment policies whereby quantitative data "encouraged the establishment of sexual harassment committees in universities and . . . eventually provided legal redress for individuals" (p. 80). Indeed, researchers who study issues of women and crime can benefit from the lessons of feminist methodologies in their use of both quantitative and qualitative methods.

While feminist methods can provide valuable resources for the study of women and crime, feminist methods are not limited to issues of gender. Rather, feminist methodologies employ tools that are applicable across criminological topics.

By recognizing from the outset the class, racial, and gendered structures of oppression that may be at work in women's lives, this method gives voice to the larger structural processes that shape the experiences that often go unseen and unheard by others. Thus, this method provides a framework for building trust with those participants who may be unsure about the research process and creates opportunities for understanding individuals and groups who may very well be inaccessible when approached in any other way (Westervelt & Cook, 2007, p. 35).

⬙ Conclusion

The feminist movement has had a significant effect on the experience of women in the criminal justice system—from victims to offenders to workers. Today, the efforts of the pioneers of feminist criminology have led to an increased understanding of what leads a woman to engage in crime and the effects of her life experiences on her offending patterns, as well as the challenges in her return to the community. In addition, the victim experience has changed for many women in that their voices are beginning to be heard by a system that either blamed them for their victimization or ignored them entirely in years past. The feminist movement has also shed light on what it means to be a woman working within the criminal justice system and the challenges that she faces every day as a woman in this field. While women have experienced significant progress over the last century, there are still many challenges that they continue to face as offenders, victims, and workers within the world of criminal justice.

⊠ Summary

- The terms *sex* and *gender* are often used interchangeably, but they have different implications for research on women and crime.
- Women are significantly more likely to be victimized by someone they know and are overrepresented in crimes such as sexual assault and intimate partner violence.
- Feminist criminologists have identified a significant link between victimization and offending.
- Many criminal justice occupations are male dominated and reflect gendered assumptions about women and work within these realms.
- Data from the Uniform Crime Reports (UCR) and National Incident-Based Reporting System (NIBRS) often fail to identify much of female victimization, as crimes of rape, sexual assault, and intimate partner abuse go largely underreported.
- Victimization studies, such as the National Crime Victimization Survey (NCVS), help illuminate the dark figure of crime by collecting data on crimes that are not reported to police.
- Self-report studies, such as the National Intimate Partner and Sexual Violence Survey (NISVS), provide estimates of the prevalence of rape, sexual assault, intimate partner abuse, and stalking in the United States.
- Feminist research methods give women a voice in the research process and influence how data on gender are collected.

KEY TERMS

Dark figure of crime	Gendered justice	National Intimate Partner and Sexual Violence Survey (NISVS)
Feminism	National Crime Victimization Survey (NCVS)	National Violence Against Women Survey (NVAWS)
Feminist criminology	National Incident-Based Reporting System (NIBRS)	Uniform Crime Reports (UCR)
Feminist research methods		
Gender gap		

DISCUSSION QUESTIONS

1. What impact has feminism had in the study of women and crime?

2. Discuss how the Uniform Crime Reports (UCR) and the National Incident-Based Reporting System (NIBRS) represent the measure of female offending and victimization in society.

3. How do datasets, such as the National Crime Victimization Survey (NCVS), the National Violence Against Women Survey (NVAWS), and National Intimate Partner and Sexual Violence Survey (NISVS), investigate issues of violence against women?

4. How do feminist research methods inform studies on women and crime?

WEB RESOURCES

Centers for Disease Control: http://www.cdc.gov

Crime in the United States 2010: http://www.fbi.gov/about-us/cjis/ucr/crime-in-the-u.s/2010/crime-in-the-u.s.-2010/index-page

National Crime Victimization Survey: http://www.icpsr.umich.edu/icpsrweb/NACJD/NCVS/

National Incident-Based Reporting System: http://www.icpsr.umich.edu/icpsrweb/NACJD/NIBRS/

Uniform Crime Reports: http://www.fbi.gov/about-us/cjis/ucr/ucr

United Nations Survey of Crime Trends and Operations of Criminal Justice Systems: https://www.unodc.org/unodc/en/data-and-analysis/statistics/data.html

Visit **www.sagepub.com/mallicoat2e** to access additional study tools including eFlashcards, web quizzes, web resources, video resources, and SAGE journal articles.

How to Read a Research Article

As a student of criminology and criminal justice, you may have learned about the types of research that scholars engage in. In many cases, researchers publish the findings of their studies as articles in academic journals. In this section, you will learn how to read these types of articles and how to understand what researchers are saying about issues related to criminology and criminal justice.

There are several different types of articles that are published in academic journals. As a student of criminology and criminal justice, you may at some point be given an assignment as part of your class that asks you to combine the findings of several articles. This is an example of a literature review. In some cases, a journal may publish a literature review, which is designed to provide a consolidated review of the research on a particular issue related to crime and justice. Articles can also be theoretical in nature. In these cases, the author is using the literature to advance a new idea or perspective. You will find several examples of these types of articles throughout this text.

In addition to theoretical articles or articles that review the existing literature in the field, journal articles publish pieces that contain original research. These articles are very different from a theoretical article or a review of the literature. These types of article focus on examining a hypothesis (or set of hypotheses) through an examination of information (or data) the researcher has collected. Generally speaking, a research article that is published in an academic journal includes five basic elements: (1) an introduction, (2) a review of the literature related to the current study, (3) the methods used by the researcher to conduct the study, (4) the findings or results of the research, and (5) a discussion of the results and/or conclusion.

Research in the social sciences generally comes in two basic forms: quantitative research and qualitative research. Quantitative research often involves surveys of groups of people or an examination of some previously collected data, and the results are reported using numbers and statistics. Qualitative research can involve interviews, focus groups, and case studies and relies on words and quotes to tell a story. In this book, you will find examples of both of these types of research studies.

In the introduction section of the article, the author will typically describe the nature of the study and present a hypothesis. A hypothesis frames the intent of the research study. In many cases, the author will state the hypothesis directly. For example, a research study in criminology or criminal justice might pose the following hypothesis: As the number of arrests increases, the length of the prison sentence will increase. Here, the author is investigating whether a relationship exists between a defendant's prior criminal record and sentence length. Similar to a hypothesis is the research question. Whereas a hypothesis follows an "if X happens, then Y will occur" format, research questions provide a path of inquiry for the research study. For example, a research question in criminology might ask, "What are the effects of a criminal record on the likelihood of incarceration?" While the presentation of a hypothesis and the presentation of a research question differ from each other, their intent is the same as each sets out a direction for the research study and may reference the expected results of the study. It is then left up to the researcher(s) and their data findings to determine whether they prove or disprove their hypothesis or if the results of their study provide an answer to their research question.

The next section of the article is the literature review. In this section, the author provides a review of the previous research conducted on this issue and the results of these studies. The purpose of the literature review is to set the stage for the current research and provide the foundation for why the current study is important to the field of criminology and criminal justice. Some articles will separate the literature review into its own section, while others will include this summary within the introductory section. Using the example from our earlier sample hypothesis, a literature review will consider what other scholars have said about the relationship between criminal history and incarceration and how their findings relate to the current research study. It may also point out how the current study differs from the research that has previously been conducted.

In the methods section, the researcher presents the type of data that will be used in the current study. As mentioned earlier, research can be either quantitative or qualitative (and some studies may have both types of data within the same research project). In the methods section, the researcher will discuss who the participants of the study were; how the data were collected (interview, survey, observation, etc.); when, where, and how long the study took place; and how the data were processed. Each of these stages represents a key part of the research experience, and it is important for researchers to carefully document and report on this process.

The results section details the findings of the study. In quantitative studies, the researchers use statistics (often accompanied by tables, charts, or graphs) to explain whether the results of the study support or reject the hypothesis/research question. There are several different types of statistics and analysis that might be used. These can generally be divided into three categories: (1) descriptive, (2) bivariate, and (3) multivariate. Descriptive statistics are generally used to describe the demographics of the sample, such as the average age of the respondents, their racial/ethnic identity, or their sex/gender. Bivariate statistics are used to compare two different variables. In this book, you may find examples where survey responses are compared between males and females. You should note which of these relationships are significant, meaning that the effect is not likely to have occurred by chance but instead reflects an important difference or result in the data. Most research places statistical significance at the .05 level. Finally, multivariate statistics, such as regression analyses, are used to look for differences in one variable while controlling for the effect of other variables. In qualitative studies, the researchers look for themes in the narrative data. Whereas quantitative studies rely on numbers, the qualitative studies in this text use words to describe the stories related to women and crime.

The research article concludes with a discussion and summary of the findings. The findings are often discussed within the context of the hypothesis or research question and relate the findings of this research study to related research in the field. Often, scholars will highlight their findings in light of the methods used in the study or the limitations of the study. The section concludes with recommendations for future research or may discuss the policy implications of the research findings.

Now that you've learned a bit about the different types of articles and the different components of a research article, let us apply these concepts to one of the articles here in your book. Depending on the type of article, some of these concepts may not apply to your analysis. This article appears in the second section of this book.

College Students' Crime-Related Fears on Campus: Are Fear-Provoking Cues Gendered?

1. What type of article is this? Is it a theoretical article, a review of the existing literature, or an article that contains original research?
   - This article contains original research.

2. What is the thesis or main idea from this article?
   - The main idea of this article looks at fears on crime victimization on college campuses and how factors such as the type of offense, cue-specific fear of crime measures, and gender impact these experiences of fear.

3. If this is a research article, what is the hypothesis or research question?

- Are there gender differences in fear-provoking cues of victimization on college campuses? For what crimes do these fear-provoking cues have the greatest impact?

4. How does the previous literature answer these issues?

- Yes. The authors list three different bodies of literature that assess whether crime-related fears are gendered. The first category looks at environmental factors, such as poor lighting and foliage, and whether gender impacts the experience of fear. The second category looks at the issue of loitering and whether this provokes fear of victimization. The third category looks at police presence and whether this increases feelings of fear.

5. What is the sample used in this study? How were the data for this research collected?

- This study involves data from a campus survey that was administered to 24 randomly selected general education courses on a college campus. There were 904 students registered in these classes, and a total of 607 students completed the survey.

6. Is this a quantitative or qualitative study? If it is a quantitative study, what types of statistics are used? If it is a qualitative study, how are the data organized?

- In looking at the results section, you can determine that this is a quantitative study through its use of numbers and statistics.

7. What are the results, and how do(es) the author(s) present the results?

- The authors present the data in three different tables and look at the general demographics of the study as well as gender differences in terms of whether the cue provoked the student to be fearful of victimization while on the campus. The authors find that women are most fearful of poorly lit parking lots, sidewalks, and common areas while men are more likely to experience fear when groups congregate or loiter. The final table looks at whether these fears change based on the particular crime that is feared, such as larceny-theft, simple assault, aggravated assault, or sexual assault. Their findings indicate that only in cases of sexual assault are women more likely to experience fear-provoking cues in cases where there is overgrown shrubbery or the lack of visibility of public safety officials.

8. Do you believe the author(s) provided a persuasive argument? Why or why not?

- While the assessment of whether the authors provided a persuasive argument is ultimately up to the reader, the data in this study do provide an interesting assessment of gender and fear of victimization. Unlike the previous research on this topic, the findings of this study did not support the claim that fear cues are gendered.

9. Who is the intended audience of this article?

- In thinking about the intended audience of the article, it may be useful to ask yourself, "Who will benefit from reading this article?" This article appeared in an academic journal, which is typically read by students, professors, scholars, and justice officials. Here, the information in their article can not only add to the classroom experience for students and professors who study this issue, but also it can ultimately influence groundskeeping on college campuses as well as staffing decisions for campus police officers.

10. What does the article add to your knowledge of the subject?

- The answer to this question will vary for each student, as it asks students to reflect about what they learned from this research and how it relates to their previous experience with the topic. An example from this article might be the understanding that while men and women experience different types of fears about victimization, these results are not necessarily significant in all cases.

11. What are the implications for criminal justice policy that can be derived from this article?

- While this article does not necessarily influence criminal justice policy, the results from this study can have an impact on administrative decisions and practices for a college campus. These results also impact how people feel about crime and victimization-related fears.

Now that you've seen these concepts applied to an article, continue this practice as you go through each reading in your text. Some articles will be easier to understand while others will be more challenging. You can refer back to this example if you need help with additional articles in the book.

READING 1

As you learned in the section, feminist criminology challenged not only the male-dominated views of criminality but also provided a new perspective to understand the offending behaviors of women. Here, Dr. Chesney-Lind argues for the importance of examining the interrelationship of race, gender, and crime in order to effectively address issues of racism and sexism within the political agenda of crime control policies. She provides three examples where feminist criminology has been effective in fighting against the right-wing, tough-on-crime philosophy: the use of the media in creating the image of the "bad" girl, the criminalization of victimization, and the negative effects of "equality" in the institutionalization of female offenders.

Patriarchy, Crime, and Justice

Feminist Criminology in an Era of Backlash

Meda Chesney-Lind

A product of the second wave of the women's movement, feminist criminology has been in existence now for more than three decades. Although any starting point is arbitrary, certainly one could point to the publication of key journal issues and books in the 1970s,[1] and it is clear that a signal event was the founding of the Women and Crime Division of the American Society of Criminology in 1982 (Rafter, 2000, p. 9). Since that time, the field has grown exponentially, which makes it increasingly impossible to do justice to all its dimensions in the space of an article. This article, instead, focuses on the challenges facing our important field as we enter a millennium characterized by a deepening backlash against feminism and other progressive movements and perspectives.

⊠ Feminist Criminology in the 20th Century: Looking Backward, Looking Forward

The feminist criminology of the 20th century clearly challenged the overall masculinist nature of theories of crime, deviance, and social control by calling attention to the repeated omission and misrepresentation of women in criminological theory and research (Belknap, 2001; Cain, 1990; Daly & Chesney-Lind, 1988). Turning back the clock, one can recall that prior to path-breaking feminist works on sexual assault, sexual harassment, and wife abuse, these forms of gender violence were ignored, minimized, and trivialized. Likewise, girls and women in conflict with the law were overlooked or excluded in mainstream works while demonized, masculinized, and sexualized in the marginalized literature that brooded on their venality. Stunning gender discrimination, such as the failure of most law schools to admit women, the routine exclusion of women from juries, and the practice of giving male and female "offenders" different sentences for the same crimes went largely unchallenged (see Rafter, 2000, for a good overview of the history in each of these areas).

The enormity of girls' and women's victimization meant that the silence on the role of violence in women's lives was the first to attract the attention of feminist activists and scholars. Because of this, excellent work exists on the problem of women's victimization—especially in the

SOURCE: Chesney-Lind, M. (2006). Patriarchy, crime, and justice: Feminist criminology in an era of backlash. *Feminist Criminology, 1*(1), 6–26.

AUTHOR'S NOTE: The author thanks Lisa Jean Pasko for early conversations on topics addressed in this article as well as Susan Sharp and three anonymous referees for their very useful suggestions on earlier drafts of this article.

areas of sexual assault, sexual harassment, sexual abuse, and wife battery (see, e.g., Buzawa & Buzawa, 1990; Dziech & Weiner, 1984; Estrich, 1987; D. Martin, 1977; Rush, 1980; Russell, 1986; Schechter, 1982; Scully, 1990).

In retrospect, the naming of the types and dimensions of female victimization had a significant impact on public policy, and it is arguably the most tangible accomplishment of both feminist criminology and grassroots feminists concerned about gender, crime, and justice. The impact on the field of criminology and particularly criminological theory was mixed, however, in part because these offenses did not initially seem to challenge androcentric criminology per se. Instead, the concepts of *domestic violence* and *victimology*, although pivotal in the development of feminist criminology, also supplied mainstream criminologists and some criminal justice practitioners with a new area in which to publish, "new" crimes to study (and opportunities to secure funding), and new men to jail (particularly men of color and other marginalized men). More recently, the field of domestic violence has even been home to a number of scholars who have argued that women are as violent as men (for critical reviews, see DeKeseredy, Sanders, Schwartz, & Alvi, 1997; DeKeseredy & Schwartz, 1998; S. Miller, 2005). In part because of these trends, the focus on girls' and women's victimization has produced a range of challenges for feminist criminology and for feminist activists that have become even more urgent as we move into the new century.

Compared to the wealth of literature on women's victimization, interest in girls and women who are labeled, tried, and jailed as *delinquent* or *criminal* was slower to fully develop[2] in part because scholars of *criminalized* women and girls had to contend early on with the masculinization (or "emancipation") hypothesis of women's crime, which argues in part that "in the same way that women are demanding equal opportunity in the fields of legitimate endeavor, a similar number of determined women are forcing their way into the world of major crimes" (Adler, 1975, p. 3; see also Simon, 1975). Feminist criminologists, as well as mainstream criminologists, debated the nature of that relationship for the next decade and ultimately concluded it was not correct (Chesney-Lind, 1989; Steffensmeier, 1980; Weis, 1976), but this was a costly intellectual detour (and also a harbinger of things to come, as it turned out).

The 1980s and 1990s, however, would see breakthrough research on the lives of criminalized girls and women. Rich documentation of girls' participation in gangs, as an example, challenges earlier gang research that focuses almost exclusively on boys (see Chesney-Lind & Hagedorn, 1999; Moore, 1991). Important work on the role of sexual and physical victimization in girls' and women's pathways into women's crime (see Arnold, 1995; Chesney-Lind & Rodriguez, 1983; Chesney-Lind & Shelden, 1992; Gilfus, 1992) began to appear, along with work that suggests unique ways in which gender and race create unique pathways for girl and women offenders into criminal behavior, particularly in communities ravaged by drugs and overincarceration (Bourgois & Dunlap, 1993; Joe, 1995; Maher & Curtis, 1992; Richie, 1996). Needless to say, the focus on girls' and women's gender also highlights the fact that masculinity and crime need to be both theorized and researched (Bowker, 1998; Messerschmidt, 2000).

Instead of the "add women and stir" (Chesney-Lind, 1988) approach to crime theorizing of the past century (which often introduces gender solely as a *variable* if at all), new important work on the gender/crime nexus *theorizes gender*. This means, for example, drawing extensively on sociological notions of "doing gender" (West & Zimmerman, 1987) and examining the role of "gender regimes" (Williams, 2002) in the production of girls' and women's behavior. Contemporary approaches to gender and crime (see Messerschmidt, 2000; J. Miller, 2001) tend to avoid the problems of reductionism and determinism that characterize early discussions of gender and gender relations, stressing instead the complexity, tentativeness, and variability with which individuals, particularly youth, negotiate (and resist) gender identity (see Kelly, 1993; Thorne, 1993). J. Miller and Mullins (2005), in particular, have argued for the crafting of "theories of the middle range" that recognize that although society and social life are patterned on the basis of gender, it is also the case that the *gender order* (Connell, 2002) is "complex and shifting" (J. Miller & Mullins, 2005, p. 7).

Feminist Criminology and the Backlash

Feminist criminology in the 21st century, particularly in the United States, finds itself in a political and social milieu that is heavily affected by the backlash politics of a sophisticated and energized right wing—a context quite different from the field's early years when the initial intellectual agenda of the field evolved. Political backlash eras have long been a fixture of American public life, from reconstruction after the Civil War to the McCarthy era of the 1950s. Most of these have certain common characteristics, including a repression of dissent, imperialistic adventure, a grim record of racism, and "resistance to extending full rights to women" (Hardisty, 2000, p. 10).

The current backlash era, however, uses crime and criminal justice policies as central rather than facilitating elements of political agenda—a pattern clearly of relevance to feminist criminology. The right-wing intent to use the *crime problem* became evident very early. Consider Barry Goldwater's 1964 unsuccessful presidential campaign where he repeatedly used phrases such as *civil disorder* and *violence in the streets* in a "covertly racist campaign" to attack the civil rights movement (Chambliss, 1999, p. 14). Both Richard Nixon and Ronald Reagan refined the approach as the crime problem became a centerpiece of the Republican Party's efforts to wrest electoral control of southern states away from the Democratic Party. Nixon's emphasis on law and order and Reagan's war on drugs were both built on "white fear of black street crime" (Chambliss, 1999, p. 19). With time, crime would come to be understood as a code word for race in U.S. political life, and it became a staple in the Republican attacks on Democratic rivals. When Reagan's former vice president, George Bush Sr., ran for office, he successfully used the Willie Horton incident (where an African American on a prison furlough raped and murdered a woman) to derail the candidacy of Michael Dukakis in 1988 (Chambliss, 1999).

His son George W. Bush would gain the presidency as a direct result of backlash criminal justice policies, because felony disenfranchisement of largely African American voters in Florida was crucial to his political strategy in that state (Lantigua, 2001). In Bush's second election campaign, however, another feature would be added to the Republican mix: an appeal to moral values. Included in the moral values agenda, designed to appeal to right-wing Christians, is the rolling back of the gains of the women's movement of the past century, including the recriminalization of abortion and the denial of civil rights to gay and lesbian Americans. Bush's nominee to the Supreme Court, John Roberts, has even questioned "whether encouraging homemakers to become lawyers contributes to the public good" (Goldstein, Smith, & Becker, 2005).

The centrality of both crime and gender in the current backlash politics means that feminist criminology is uniquely positioned to challenge right-wing initiatives. To do this effectively, however, the field must put an even greater priority on *theorizing patriarchy and crime*, which means focusing on the ways in which the definition of the crime problem and criminal justice practices support patriarchal practices and worldviews.

To briefly review, patriarchy is a sex-gender system[3] in which men dominate women and what is considered masculine is more highly valued than what is considered feminine. Patriarchy is a system of social stratification, which means that it uses a wide array of social control policies and practices to ratify male power and to keep girls and women subordinate to men (Renzetti & Curran, 1999, p. 3). Often, the systems of control that women experience are explicitly or implicitly focused on controlling female sexuality (such as the sexual double standard; Renzetti & Curran, 1999, p. 3). Not infrequently, patriarchal interests overlap with systems that also reinforce class and race privilege, hence, the unique need for feminist criminology to maintain the focus on intersectionality that characterizes recent research and theorizing on gender and race in particular (see Crenshaw, 1994).

Again, in this era of backlash, the formal system of social control (the law and criminal justice policies) play key roles in eroding the rights of both women and people of color, particularly African Americans but increasingly other ethnic groups as well. Feminist criminology is, again, uniquely positioned to both document and respond to these efforts. To theorize patriarchy effectively means that we have done cutting-edge research on the interface between patriarchal and criminal justice systems of control and that we are strategic about how to get our findings out to the widest audience possible, issues to which this article now turns.

Race, Gender, and Crime

If feminist criminology is to fully understand the interface between patriarchal control mechanisms and criminal justice practices in the United States, we must center our analysis on the race/gender/punishment nexus. Specifically, America's long and sordid history of racism and its equally disturbing enthusiasm for imprisonment must be understood as intertwined, and both of these have had a dramatic effect on African American women in particular (Bush-Baskette, 1998; Horton & Horton, 2005; Johnson, 2003; Mauer, 1999).

More than a century ago, W. E. B. Du Bois saw the linkage between the criminal justice system and race-based systems of social control very clearly. Commenting on the dismal failure of "reconstruction," he concluded,

> Despite compromise, war, and struggle, the Negro is not free. In well-nigh the whole rural South the black farmers are peons, bound by law and custom to an economic slavery from which the only escape is death or the penitentiary. (as quoted in Johnson, 2003, p. 284)

Although the role of race and penal policy has received increased attention in recent years, virtually all of the public discussion of the issues has focused on African American males (see, e.g., Human Rights Watch, 2000). More recently, the significant impact of mass incarceration on African American and Hispanic women has received the attention it deserves. Current data show that African American women account for "almost half (48 percent)" of all the women we incarcerate (Johnson, 2003, p. 34). Mauer and Huling's (1995) earlier research adds an important perspective here; they noted that the imprisonment of African American women grew by more than 828% between 1986 and 1991, whereas that of White women grew by 241% and of Black men by 429% (see also Bush-Baskette, 1998; Gilbert, 2001). Something is going on, and it is not just about race or gender; it is about both—a sinister synergy that clearly needs to be carefully documented and challenged.

Feminist criminologist Paula Johnson (2003), among others, advocated a "Black Feminist analysis of the criminal justice system." An examination of Black women's history from slavery through the Civil War and the postwar period certainly justifies a clear focus on the role that the criminal justice system played in the oppression of African American women and the role of prison in that system (Rafter, 1990). And the focus is certainly still relevant because although women sometimes appear to be the unintended victims of the war on drugs, this "war" is so heavily racialized that the result can hardly be viewed as accidental. African American women have always been seen through the "distorted lens

of otherness," constructed as "subservient, inept, oversexed and undeserving" (Johnson, 2003, pp. 9–10), in short, just the "sort" of women that belong in jail and prison. Hence, any good work on criminalized women must also examine the ways in which misogyny and racism have long been intertwined themes in the control of women of color (as well as other women) in the United States, as the next section demonstrates.

✉ Media Demonization and the Masculinization of Female Offenders

As noted earlier, the second wave of feminism had, by the 1980s, triggered an array of conservative political, policy, and media responses. In her book *Backlash: The Undeclared War Against American Women*, Susan Faludi (1991), a journalist, was quick to see that the media in particular were central, not peripheral, to the process of discrediting and dismissing feminism and feminist gains. She focused specific attention on mainstream journalism's efforts to locate and publicize those "female trends" of the 1980s that would undermine and indict the feminist agenda. Stories about "the failure to get husbands, get pregnant, or properly bond with their children" were suddenly everywhere, as were the very first stories on "bad girls"; Faludi noted that "NBC, for instance, devoted an entire evening news special to the pseudo trend of 'bad girls' yet ignored the real trends of bad boys: the crime rate among boys was climbing twice as fast as for girls" (p. 80).

Faludi's (1991) recognition of the media's fascination with bad girls was prescient. The 1990s would produce a steady stream of media stories about violent and bad girls that continues unabated in the new millennium. Although the focus would shift from the "gansta girl," to the "violent girl," to the "mean girl" (Chesney-Lind & Irwin, 2004), the message is the same: Girls are bad in ways that they never used to be. As an example, the Scelfo (2005) article titled "Bad Girls Go Wild," published in the June 13, 2005, issue of *Newsweek*, describes "the significant rise in violent behavior among girls" as a "burgeoning national crisis" (p. 1).

Media-driven constructions such as these generally rely on commonsense notions that girls are becoming more like boys on both the soccer field and the killing fields.[4] Implicit in what might be called the "masculinization" theory (Chesney-Lind & Eliason, in press; Pollock, 1999) of women's violence is the idea that contemporary theories of violence (and crime more broadly) need not attend to gender but can, again, simply add women and stir. The theory assumes that the same forces that propel men into violence will increasingly produce violence in girls and women once they are freed from the constraints of their gender. The masculinization framework also lays the foundation for simplistic notions of *good* and *bad* femininity, standards that will permit the demonization of some girls and women if they stray from the path of "true" (passive, controlled, and constrained) womanhood.

Ever since the first wave of feminism, there has been no shortage of scholars and political commentators issuing dire warnings that women's demand for equality would result in a dramatic change in the character and frequency of women's crime (Pollak, 1950; Pollock, 1999; Smart, 1976). As noted earlier, in the 1970s, the notion that the women's movement was causing changes in women's crime was the subject of extensive media and scholarly attention (Adler, 1975; Chesney-Lind, 1989; Simon, 1975). Again, although this perspective was definitely refuted by the feminist criminology of the era (see Gora, 1982; Steffensmeier & Steffensmeier, 1980; Weis, 1976), media enthusiasm about the idea that feminism encourages women to become more like men; hence, their "equals" in crime, remains undiminished (see Chesney-Lind & Eliason, in press).

As examples, *Boston Globe Magazine* proclaimed in an article as well as on the issue's cover, over the words *BAD GIRLS* in huge red letters, that "girls are moving into the world of violence that once belonged to boys" (Ford, 1998). And from *San Jose Mercury News* came a story titled "In a New Twist on Equality, Girls' Crimes Resemble Boys'" that features an opening paragraph arguing that

> juvenile crime experts have spotted a disturbing nationwide pattern of teenage girls becoming more sophisticated and independent criminals. In the past, girls would almost always commit crimes with boys or men. But now, more than ever, they're calling the shots. (Guido, 1998, p. 1B)

In virtually all the stories on this topic (including the Scelfo, 2005, article appearing in *Newsweek*),

the issue is framed as follows. A specific and egregious example of female violence is described, usually with considerable, graphic detail about the injury suffered by the victim—a pattern that has been dubbed "forensic journalism" (Websdale & Alvarez, 1997, p. 123). In the *Mercury News* article, for example, the reader hears how a 17-year-old girl, Linna Adams, "lured" the victim into a car where her boyfriend "pointed a .357 magnum revolver at him, and the gun went off. Rodrigues was shot in the cheek, and according to coroner's reports, the bullet exited the back of his head" (Guido, 1998, p. 1B). Websdale and Alvarez (1997) noted that this narrative style, while compelling and even lurid reading, actually gives the reader "more and more information about less and less" and stresses "individualistic explanations that ignore or de-emphasize the importance of wider social structural patterns of disadvantage" (p. 125).

These forensic details are then followed by a quick review of the Federal Bureau of Investigation's arrest statistics showing what appear to be large increases in the number of girls arrested for violent offenses. Finally, there are quotes from "experts," usually police officers, teachers, or other social service workers, but occasionally criminologists, interpreting the narrative in ways consistent with the desired outcome: to stress that girls, particularly African American and Hispanic girls whose pictures often illustrate these stories, are getting more and more like their already demonized male counterparts and, hence, becoming more violent (Chesney-Lind & Irwin, 2005).

There are two problems with this now familiar frame: One, there are considerable reasons to suspect that it is demonstrably wrong (i.e., that girls' violence is not increasing), and two, it has created a "self-fulfilling prophecy" that has had dramatic and racialized effects on girls' arrests, detentions, and referrals to juvenile courts across our country.

Although arrest data consistently show dramatic increases in girls' arrests for *violent* crimes (e.g., arrests of girls for assault climbed an astonishing 40.9%, whereas boys' arrests climbed by only 4.3% in the past decade; Federal Bureau of Investigation, 2004), other datasets, particularly those relying on self-reported delinquency, show no such trend (indeed, they show a decline; Chesney-Lind, 2004; Chesney-Lind & Belknap, 2004; Steffensmeier, Schwartz, Zhong, & Ackerman, 2005). It seems increasingly clear that forces other than changes in girls' behavior have caused shifts in girls' arrests (including such forces as zero-tolerance policies in schools and mandatory arrests for domestic violence; Chesney-Lind & Belknap, 2004). There are also indications that although the hype about bad girls seems to encompass all girls, the effects of enforcement policies aimed at reducing "youth violence" weigh heaviest on girls of color whose families lack the resources to challenge such policies (Chesney-Lind & Irwin, 2005).

Take juvenile detention, a focus of three decades of deinstitutionalization efforts. Between 1989 and 1998, girls' detentions increased by 56% compared to a 20% increase seen in boy's detentions, and the "large increase was tied to the growth in the number of delinquency cases involving females charged with person offenses (157%)" (Harms, 2002, p. 1). At least one study of girls in detention suggests that "nearly half" the girls in detention are African American girls, and Latinas constitute 13%; Caucasian girls, who constitute 65% of the girl population, account for only 35% of those in detention (American Bar Association & National Bar Association, 2001, pp. 20–21).

It is clear that two decades of the media demonization of girls, complete with often racialized images of girls seemingly embracing the violent street culture of their male counterparts (see Chesney-Lind & Irwin, 2004), coupled with increased concerns about youth violence and images of "girls gone wild," have entered the self-fulfilling prophecy stage. It is essential that feminist criminology understand that in a world governed by those who self-consciously manipulate corporate media for their own purposes, newspapers and television may have moved from simply covering the police beat to constructing crime "stories" that serve as a "nonconspiratorial source of dominant ideology" (Websdale & Alvarez, 1997, p. 125). Feminist criminology's agenda must consciously challenge these backlash media narratives, as well as engage in "newsmaking criminology" (Barak, 1988), particularly with regard to constructions of girl and women offenders. The question of how to do this is one that must also engage the field. As a start on such a discussion, consider the advice of Bertold Brecht (1966):

> One must have the courage to write the truth when the truth is everywhere opposed; the keenness to recognize it, and although it is everywhere concealed; the skill to manipulate it as a

weapon; the judgment to select in whose hands it will be effective, and the cunning to spread the truth among such persons. (p. 133)

The advocacy work coupled with excellent research that one sees with reports issued by The Sentencing Project and the Center for Juvenile and Criminal Justice provide models of how this work might be done. It certainly requires that we work more closely with progressive journalists than many academics are used to, but given the success of these agencies in doing just that, feminist criminologists should consider this a priority and use our national and regional meetings, as a start, to develop strategies toward this end.

Criminalizing Victimization

Many feminist criminologists have approached the issue of mandatory arrest in incidents of domestic assault with considerable ambivalence (see Ferraro, 2001). On one hand, as noted earlier, the criminalization of sexual assault and domestic violence was in one sense a huge symbolic victory for feminist activists and criminologists alike. After centuries of ignoring the private victimizations of women, police and courts were called to account by those who founded rape crisis centers and shelters for battered women and those whose path-breaking research laid the foundation for major policy and legal changes in the area of violence against women (see Schecter, 1982).

On the other hand, the insistence that violence against women be handled as a criminal matter threw victim advocates into an uneasy alliance with police and prosecutors—professions that feminists had long distrusted and with good reason (see Buzawa & Buzawa, 1990; Heidensohn, 1995; S. Martin, 1980). The criminal justice approach, however, was bolstered in the mid-1980s by what appeared to be overwhelming evidence that arrest decreased violence against women (Sherman & Berk, 1984). Although subsequent research would find that arrest was far less effective than originally thought (see Ferraro, 2001; Maxwell, Garner, & Fagan, 2002), for the policy world, the dramatic early research results seemed to ratify the wisdom of a law enforcement-centered approach to the problem of domestic violence. Ultimately, the combined effects of the early scientific evidence; political pressure from the attorney general of the United States, the American Bar Association, and others; and the threat of lawsuits against departments that failed to protect women from batterers "produced nearly unanimous agreement that arrest was the best policy for domestic violence" (Ferraro, 2001, p. 146).

As the academic debate about the effectiveness of arrest in domestic violence situations continued unabated, the policy of mandatory arrest became routinized into normal policing, and quite quickly, other unanticipated effects began to emerge. When arrests of adult women for assault increased by 30.8% in the past decade (1994 to 2003), whereas male arrests for this offense fell by about 5.8% (Federal Bureau of Investigation, 2004, p. 275), just about everybody from the research community to the general public began to wonder what was happening. Although some, such as criminologist Kenneth Land, quoted in a story titled "Women Making Gains in Dubious Profession: Crime," attributed the increase to "role change over the past decades" that presumably created more females as "motivated offenders" (Anderson, 2003, p. A1), others were not so sure. Even the Bureau of Justice Statistics looked at a similar trend (increasing numbers of women convicted in state courts for "aggravated assault") and suggested the numbers might be "reflecting increased prosecution of women for domestic violence" (Greenfeld & Snell, 1999, pp. 5–6).

Much like the increases seen in girls' assaults, this trend requires critical review, a process that takes the reader through the looking glass to a place that the feminists who worked hard to force the criminal justice system and the general public to take wife battery seriously could never have imagined. In this world, as in California recently, the female share of domestic violence arrests tripled (from 5% in 1987 to 17% in 1999; S. Miller, 2005, p. 21); and as it turned out, it was not just a California phenomenon.

Despite the power of the stereotypical scenario of the violent husband and the victimized wife, the reality of mandatory arrest practices has always been more complicated. Early on, the problem of "mutual" arrests—the practice of arresting both the man and the woman in a domestic violence incident if it is not clear who is the "primary" aggressor—surfaced as a concern (Buzawa & Buzawa, 1990). Nor has the problem gone away, despite efforts to clarify procedures (Bible, 1998; Brown, 1997); indeed, many jurisdictions report similar figures. In Wichita, Kansas, for example, women were 27% of those

arrested for domestic violence in 2001 (Wichita Police Department, 2002). Prince William County, Maryland, saw the number of women arrested for domestic violence triple in a 3-year period, with women going from 12.9% of those arrested in 1992 to 21% in 1996 (Smith, 1996). In Sacramento, California, even greater increases were observed; there, the number of women arrested for domestic violence rose by 91% between 1991 and 1996, whereas arrests of men fell 7% (Brown, 1997).

A Canadian study (Comack, Chopyk, & Wood, 2000) provides an even closer look at the impact of mandatory arrest on arrests of women for crimes of violence. Examining the gender dynamics in a random sample of 1,002 cases (501 men and 501 women) involving charges filed by the Winnipeg, Manitoba, police services for violent crimes during the period 1991 through 1995, the researchers found that the zero-tolerance policy implemented by the police force in 1993 had a dramatic effect on women's arrest patterns. Although the policy resulted in more arrests of both men and women for domestic violence, the impact on women's arrests was most dramatic. In 1991, domestic violence charges represented 23% of all charges of violence against women; by 1995, 58% of all violent crime charges against women were for partner violence (Comack et al., 2000, p. ii). Most significantly, the researchers found that in 35% of the domestic violence cases involving women, the accused woman had actually called the police for help (only 5% of male cases showed this pattern; Comack et al., 2000, p. 15).

Susan Miller's (2005) study of mandatory arrest practices in the state of Delaware adds an important dimension to this discussion. Based on data from police ride alongs, interviews with criminal justice practitioners, and observations of groups run for women who were arrested as offenders in domestic violence situations, Miller's study comes to some important conclusions about the effects of mandatory arrest on women.

According to beat officers who S. Miller (2005) and her students rode with, in Delaware, they do not have a "pro-arrest policy, we have a pro-paper policy" (p. 100) developed in large part to avoid lawsuits. What initially surfaces as a seemingly minor, and familiar, lament begins to take on far more meaning. It emerges that, at least in Delaware (but one suspects elsewhere), police departments, often in response to threatened or real lawsuits, have developed an "expansive definition" (S. Miller, 2005,

p. 89) of domestic violence, including a wide range of family disturbances. As a consequence, although the officers "did not believe there was an increase in women's use of violence" (p. 105), "her fighting back now gets attention too" (p. 107) because of this sort of broad interpretation of what constitutes domestic violence.

Another significant theme in police comments reflects male batterers' increased skill in deploying the criminal justice system to further intimidate and control their wives. Officers reported that men are now more willing to report violence committed by their wives and more willing to use "cross-filings" in securing protective orders against their wives and girlfriends. Police particularly resent what they regard as "bogus" violations of protective orders that are actually just harassment (S. Miller, 2005, p. 90).

None of the social service providers and criminal justice professionals S. Miller (2005) spoke with felt women had become more aggressively violent; instead, they routinely called the women "victims." They noted that at least in Delaware, as the "legislation aged," the name of the game began to be "get to the phone first" (S. Miller, 2005, p. 127). Social service workers noted that male batterers tended to use their knowledge of the criminal justice system and process as a way to threaten their wives with the loss of the children, particularly if they had managed to get the woman placed on probation for abuse. Workers echoed the police complaints about paperwork, noting it takes 8 hours to do the paperwork if an arrest is made, but then they made a crucial link to the arrest of women, noting that police, weary of being told they were the problem, have channeled at least some of their resentment into making arrests of women who act out violently (regardless of context or injury) because "according to police policy," they have to make an arrest.

Essentially, it appears that many mandatory arrest polices have been interpreted on the ground to make an arrest if any violent "incident" occurs, rather than considering the context within which the incident occurs (Bible, 1998). Like problematic measures of violence that simply count violent events without providing information on the meaning and motivation, this definition of *domestic violence* fails to distinguish between aggressive and instigating violence from self-defensive and retaliatory violence. According to S. Miller (2005) and other critics of this approach, these methods tend to produce results showing "intimate violence is committed by women at an

equal or higher rate than by men" (p. 35). Although these findings ignited a firestorm of media attention about the "problem" of "battered men" in the United States (Ferraro, 2001, p. 137), the larger question of how to define *domestic violence* in the context of patriarchy is vital. Specifically, much feminist research of the sort showcased here is needed on routine police and justice practices concerning girls' and women's "violence." In particularly short supply are studies of girls' arrests, particularly those of girls of color (who are often detained for "assault"), although indirect evidence certainly suggests this is happening (see Chesney-Lind & Irwin, 2005). The evidence to date suggests the distinct possibility that in addition to the well-documented race and class problems, with draconian criminal justice approaches to domestic violence (S. Miller, 1989, Richie, 1996), we have a gender issue: Are these policies criminalizing women's (and girls') attempts to protect themselves?

Women's Imprisonment and the Emergence of Vengeful Equity

When the United States embarked on a policy that might well be described as mass incarceration (Mauer & Chesney-Lind, 2002), few considered the impact that this correctional course change would have on women. Yet the number of women in jail and prison continues to soar (outstripping male increases for most of the past decade), completely untethered from women's crime rate, which has not increased by nearly the same amount (Bloom & Chesney-Lind, 2003). The dimensions of this shift are staggering: For most of the 20th century, the justice system imprisoned about 5,000 to 10,000 women. At the turn of the new century, the United States now has more than 100,000 women doing time in U.S. prisons (Harrison & Beck, 2004, p. 1). Women's incarceration in the United States not only grew during the past century but also increased tenfold; and virtually all of that increase occurred in the final two decades of the century.

The number of women sentenced to jail and prison began to soar at precisely the same time that prison systems in the United States moved into an era that abandoned any pretense of rehabilitation in favor of punishment. As noted earlier, decades of efforts by conservative politicians to fashion a crime policy that would challenge the gains of the civil rights movement as well as other progressive movements in the 1960s and 1970s had, by the 1980s, borne fruit (Chambliss, 1999). Exploiting the public fear of crime, particularly crime committed by "the poor, mostly nonwhite, young, male inner-city dwellers" (Irwin, 2005, p. 8), policy makers adopted all manner of mean-spirited crime policies. The end of the past century saw the war on drugs and a host of other "get tough" sentencing policies, all of which fueled mass imprisonment (see Mauer, 1999). The period also saw the development of what Irwin (2005) has called "warehouse prisons," a correctional regime that focuses on a physical plant designed to control (not reform), rigid enforcement of extensive rules, and easy transfer of unruly prisoners to even more draconian settings.

Although feminist legal scholars can and do debate whether equality under the law is necessarily good for women (see Chesney-Lind & Pollock-Byrne, 1995), a careful look at what has happened to women in U.S. prisons might serve as a disturbing case study of how correctional equity is implemented in practice. Such a critical review is particularly vital in an era where decontextualized notions of gender and race "discrimination" are increasingly and successfully deployed against the achievements of both the civil rights and women's movements (Pincus, 2001/2002).

Vengeful equity could have no better spokesperson than Sheriff Joe Arpaio who, when he defended his controversial chain gang for women in Maricopa County, Arizona, proclaimed himself an "equal opportunity incarcerator" and went on to explain his controversial move by saying,

> If women can fight for their country, and bless them for that, if they can walk a beat, if they can protect the people and arrest violators of the law, then they should have no problem with picking up trash in 120 degrees. (Kim, 1996, p. A1)

Other examples of vengeful equity can be found in the creation of women's boot camps, often modeled on the gender regimes found in military basic training. These regimes, complete with uniforms, shorn hair, humiliation, exhausting physical training, and harsh punishment for even minor misconduct, have been traditionally devised to "make men out of boys." As such, feminist researchers

who have examined them contended, they "have more to do with the rites of manhood" than the needs of the typical woman in prison (Morash & Rucker, 1990).

Although these examples might be seen as extreme, legal readings by correctional administrators and others that define any attention to legitimate gender differences as "illegal" have clearly produced troubling outcomes. It is obviously misguided to treat women as if they were men with reference to cross gender supervision, strip searches, and other correctional regimes, while ignoring the ways in which women's imprisonment has unique features (such as pregnancy and vulnerability to sexual assault). Recently, this approach has been correctly identified by Human Rights Watch (1996) as a major contributing factor to the sexual abuse of women inmates.

Reviewing the situation of women incarcerated in five states (California, Georgia, Michigan, Illinois, and New York) and the District of Columbia, Human Rights Watch (1996) concluded,

> Our findings indicate that being a woman prisoner in U.S. state prisons can be a terrifying experience. If you are sexually abused, you cannot escape from your abuser. Grievance or investigatory procedures where they exist, are often ineffectual, and correctional employees continue to engage in abuse because they believe they will rarely be held accountable, administratively or criminally. Few people outside the prison walls know what is going on or care if they do know. Fewer still do anything to address the problem. (p. 1)

Human Rights Watch also noted that their investigators were "concerned that states' adherence to U.S. antidiscrimination laws, in the absence of strong safeguards against custodial sexual misconduct, has often come at the [cost of] fundamental rights of prisoners" (p. 2).

Institutional subcultures in women's prisons, which encourage correctional officers to "cover" for each other, coupled with inadequate protection accorded women who file complaints, make it unlikely that many women prisoners will formally complain about abuse. In addition, the public stereotype of women in prison as bad makes it difficult for a woman inmate to support her case against a correctional officer in court. Finally, what little progress has been made is now threatened by recent legislation that curtails the ability of prisoners and advocates to commence a legal action concerning prison conditions (Stein, 1996, p. 24).

Finally, it appears that women in prison today are also recipients of some of the worst of the more traditional, separate-spheres approach to women offenders (which tends to emphasize gender difference and the need to focus on "saving" women by policing even minor behaviors, particularly sexual behaviors; Rafter, 1990). Correctional officers often count on the fact that women prisoners will complain, not riot, and as a result, often punish women inmates for offenses that would be ignored in male prisons. McClellan (1994) found this pattern quite clearly in her examined disciplinary practices in Texas prisons. Following up two cohorts of prisoners (one male and one female), she found most men in her sample (63.5%) but only a handful of women (17.1%) had no citation or only one citation for a rule violation. McClellan found that women prisoners not only received numerous citations but also were charged with different infractions from men. Most frequently, women were cited for "violating posted rules," whereas males were cited most often for "refusing to work" (McClellan, 1994, p. 77). Women were more likely than men to receive the most severe sanctions.

Much good, early feminist criminology focuses on the conditions of girls and women in training schools, jails, and prisons (see Burkhart, 1976; Carlen, 1983; Faith, 1993; Freedman, 1981). Unfortunately, that work is now made much harder by a savvy correctional system that is extremely reluctant to admit researchers, unless the focus of the research is clearly the woman prisoner and not the institution. That said, there is much more need for this sort of criminology in the era of mass punishment, and the work that is being done in this vein (see Bloom, 2003; Owen, 1998) points to the need for much of the same. Huge numbers of imprisoned girls and women are targeted by male-based systems of "risk" and "classification" (Hannah-Moffat & Shaw, 2003) and then subjected to male-based interventions, such as "cognitive behaviorism," to address their "criminal" thinking as though they were men (Kendall & Pollack, 2003). Good work has also been done on the overuse of "chemical restraints" with women offenders (Auerhahn & Leonard, 2000; Leonard, 2002). In short, as difficult as it might be to do, in this era of mass imprisonment, feminist criminology needs to find creative ways to continue to engage core issues in girls' and women's carceral control as a central part of our intellectual and activist agenda. As Adrian Howe (1994) put it, "Academics must not let 'theoretical rectitude' deter them from committing themselves as *academics* and *feminists* to campaigns on behalf of women lawbreakers" (p. 214).

Theorizing Patriarchy: Concluding Thoughts

In 1899, Jane Addams was asked to address the American Academy of Political and Social Science. She took the occasion to reflect on the role of the social science of her day:

> As the college changed from teaching theology to teaching secular knowledge the test of its success should have shifted from the power to save men's souls to the power to adjust them in healthful relations to nature and their fellow men. But the college failed to do this, and made the test of its success the mere collecting and dissemination of knowledge, elevating the means unto an end and falling in love with its own achievement. (Addams, 1899, pp. 339–340)

Perhaps Addams's use of the generic *he* to describe the universities of her day was more a simple convention. Recall that when Addams worked in Chicago, criminology as a discipline was taking shape at the University of Chicago, whose researchers often relied heavily on contacts made at Hull House while systematically excluding women from its faculty ranks and distancing themselves from the female-dominated field of social work (see Deegan, 1988).

How do we avoid the pitfalls Addams (1899) observed in the male-dominated criminology of her day? This article argues that although feminist criminology has made a clear contribution to what might be described as the criminological project, it is positioned to play an even more central role in the era of political backlash. Certainly, we, as feminist scholars, shoulder many burdens, but perhaps the most daunting is the one articulated by Liz Kelly (as quoted in Heidensohn, 1995): "Feminist research investigates aspects of women's oppression while seeking at the same time to be a part of the struggle against it" (p. 71).

For feminist criminology to remain true to its progressive origins in very difficult times, we must seek ways to blend activism with our scholarship (and senior scholars, in particular, need to make the academy safe for their junior colleagues to do just that by redefining tenure criteria to make this work a part of scholarship). We must discuss the many tensions and difficulties with this work, again in an era of backlash when the right is actively patrolling faculty behavior (Horowitz & Collier, 1994), and be honest about the many challenges ahead. We must create venues for feminist criminology, including peer-reviewed journals (such as *Critical Criminology*, *Feminist Criminology*, and *Women & Criminal Justice*) while also writing for broader audiences, particularly practitioners and policy makers (see *Women, Girls & Criminal Justice*). We must engage in continued activism on the part of girls and women who are the victims of crimes and whose very experiences are being trivialized by well-funded backlash research (Hoff Sommers, 1994) while also documenting the problems those same girls and women have when they take their cases to court (see Estrich, 1987; Matoesian, 1993). It means close attention and continued vigilance about the situations of women working in various aspects of the criminal justice system, particularly as the right wing cynically appropriates concepts such as discrimination. Finally, and most importantly, it means activism on behalf of criminalized girls and women, the least powerful and most marginalized of all those we study.

Again, given the focus of the backlash, this article argues that feminist criminology is uniquely positioned to do important work to challenge the current political backlash. To do so effectively, however, it is vital that in addition to documenting that gender matters in the lives of criminalized women, we engage in exploration of the interface between systems of oppression based on gender, race, and class. This work will allow us to make sense of current crime-control practices, particularly in an era of mass incarceration, so that we can explain the consequences to a society that might well be ready to hear other perspectives on crime control if given them (consider the success of drug courts and some initiatives that encourage alternatives to incarceration; Mauer, 2002). Researching as well as theorizing both patriarchy and gender is crucial to feminist criminology so that we can craft work, as the right wing does so effectively, that speaks to backlash initiatives in smart, media-savvy ways. To do this well means foregrounding the role of race and class in our work on gender and crime, as the work showcased here makes clear. There is simply no other way to make sense of key trends in both the media construction of women offenders and the criminal justice response that increasingly awaits them, particularly once they arrive in prison.

Finally, we must also do work that will document and challenge the policy and research backlash aimed at the hard-fought and vitally important feminist and civil rights victories of the past century. To do any less would be unthinkable to those who fought so long to get us where we are today, and so it must be for us.

Notes

1. One might cite the appearance of the classic special issue on women and crime of *Issues in Criminology*, edited by Dorie Klein and June Kress (1973); two important books on the topic of women and crime by Rita Simon (1975) and Freda Adler (1975); and the publication of Del Martin's (1977) *Battered Wives* and Carol Smart's (1976) *Women, Crime and Criminology*.

2. Early but important exceptions to this generalization are Klein and Kress (1973); Smart (1976); Crites (1976); Bowker, Chesney-Lind, and Pollock (1978); Chapman (1980); and Jones (1980). There has also been an encouraging outpouring of more recent work on women offenders in the past decade. See Belknap (2001), Chesney-Lind and Pasko (2004), and DeKeseredy (1999) for reviews of this recent work.

3. Sex-gender systems include the following elements: (a) the social construction of gender categories on the basis of biological sex, (b) a sexual division of labor in which specific tasks are allocated on the basis of sex, and (c) the social regulation of sexuality, in which particular forms of sexual expression are positively and negatively sanctioned (Renzetti & Curran, 1999, p. 3).

4. I owe this analogy to Frank Zimring who, in response to a question from a reporter, quipped, "Women's liberation didn't turn girls into boys—violence is still particularly male. There has been much more diversification of gender roles on the soccer field than the killing field" (Ryan, 2003, p. 2).

References

Addams, J. (1899). A function of the social settlement. *Annals of the Academy of Political and Social Science, 13*, 323–345.

Adler, F. (1975). *Sisters in crime*. New York: McGraw-Hill.

American Bar Association and the National Bar Association. (2001, May 1). *Justice by gender: The lack of appropriate prevention, diversion and treatment alternatives for girls in the justice system.* Retrieved from http://www.abanet.org/crimjust/juvjus/justice bygenderweb.pdf

Anderson, C. (2003, October 28). Women making gains in dubious profession: Crime. *Arizona Star*, p. A1.

Arnold, R. (1995). Processes of criminalization. From girlhood to womanhood. In M. B. Zinn & B. T. Dill (Eds.), *Women of color in American society* (pp. 136–146). Philadelphia: Temple University Press.

Auerhahn, K., & Leonard, E. (2000). Docile bodies? Chemical restraints and the female inmate. *The Journal of Criminal Law and Criminology, 90*(2), 599–634.

Barak, G. (1988). Newsmaking criminology: Reflections on the media, intellectuals, and crime. *Justice Quarterly, 5*(4), 565–587.

Belknap, J. (2001). *The invisible woman: Gender, crime and justice* (2nd ed.). Belmont, CA: Wadsworth.

Bible, A. (1998). When battered women are charged with assault. *Double-Time, 6*(1/2), 8–10.

Bloom, B. (Ed.). (2003). *Gendered justice.* Durham, NC: Carolina Academic Press.

Bloom, B., & Chesney-Lind, M. (2003). Women in prison: Vengeful equity. In R. Muraskin (Ed.), *It's a crime: Women and the criminal justice system* (pp. 175–195). Upper Saddle River, NJ: Prentice Hall.

Bourgois, P., & Dunlap, E. (1993). Exorcising sex—For crack. An ethnographic perspective from Harlem. In M. Ratner (Ed.), *The crack pipe as pimp* (pp. 97–132). New York: Lexington Books.

Bowker, L. (Ed.). (1998). *Masculinities and violence.* Thousand Oaks, CA: Sage.

Bowker, L., Chesney-Lind, M., & Pollock, J. (1978). *Women, crime, and the criminal justice system.* Lexington, MA: D. C. Heath.

Brecht, B. (1966). *Galileo* (E. Bentley, Ed., C. Laughton, Trans.). New York: Grove.

Brown, M. (1997, December 7). Arrests of women soar in domestic assault cases. *Sacramento Bee.* Retrieved July 31, 2005, from http://www.sacbee.com/static/archive/news/projects/violence/part12.html

Burkhart, K. W. (1976). *Women in prison.* New York: Popular Library.

Bush-Baskette, S. (1998). The war on drugs as a war against Black women. In S. L. Miller (Ed.), *Crime control and women* (pp. 113–129). Thousand Oaks, CA: Sage.

Buzawa, E., & Buzawa, C. G. (1990). *Domestic violence: The criminal justice response.* Newbury Park, CA: Sage.

Cain, M. (1990). Realist philosophy and standpoint epistemologies or feminist criminology as a successor science. In L. Gelsthorpe & A. Morris (Eds.), *Feminist perspectives in criminology* (pp. 124–140). Buckingham, UK: Open University Press.

Carlen, P. (1983). *Women's imprisonment: A study in social control.* London: Routledge.

Chambliss, W. (1999). *Power, politics and crime.* Boulder, CO: Westview.

Chapman, J. R. (1980). *Economic realities and the female offender.* Lexington, MA: Lexington Books.

Chesney-Lind, M. (1988, July–August). Doing feminist criminology. *The Criminologist, 13,* 16–17.

Chesney-Lind, M. (1989). Girls' crime and woman's place: Toward a feminist model of female delinquency. *Crime & Delinquency, 35*(10), 5–29.

Chesney-Lind, M. (2004, August). Girls and violence: Is the gender gap closing? National Online Resource Center on Violence Against Women. Retrieved from http://www.vawnet.org/DomesticViolence/Research/VAWnetDocs/ARGirlsViolence.php

Chesney-Lind, M., & Belknap, J. (2004). Trends in delinquent girls' aggression and violent behavior: A review of the evidence. In M. Putallaz & P. Bierman (Eds.), *Aggression, antisocial behavior and violence among girls: A development perspective* (pp. 203–222). New York: Guilford.

Chesney-Lind, M., & Eliason, M. (in press). From invisible to incorrigible: The demonization of marginalized women and girls. *Crime, Media, Culture: An International Journal.*

Chesney-Lind, M., & Hagedorn, J. M. (Eds.). (1999). *Female gangs in America: Essays on gender and gangs.* Chicago: Lakeview Press.

Chesney-Lind, M., & Irwin, K. (2004). From badness to meanness: Popular constructions of contemporary girlhood. In A. Harris (Ed.), *All about the girl: Culture, power, and identity* (pp. 45–56). New York: Routledge.

Chesney-Lind, M., & Irwin, K. (2005). Still "the best place to conquer girls": Gender and juvenile justice. In J. Pollock-Byrne & A. Merlo (Eds.), *Women, law, and social control* (pp. 271–291). Boston: Allyn & Bacon.

Chesney-Lind, M., & Pasko, L. (2004). *The female offender.* Thousand Oaks, CA: Sage.

Chesney-Lind, M., & Pollock-Byrne, J. (1995). Women's prisons: Equality with a vengeance. In J. Pollock-Byrne & A. Merlo (Eds.), *Women, law, and social control* (pp. 155–176). Boston: Allyn & Bacon.

Chesney-Lind, M., & Rodriguez, N. (1983). Women under lock and key. *The Prison Journal, 63,* 47–65.

Chesney-Lind, M., & Shelden, R. G. (1992). *Girls, delinquency and juvenile justice.* Belmont, CA: Wadsworth.

Comack, E., Chopyk, V., & Wood, L. (2000). *Mean streets? The social locations, gender dynamics, and patterns of violent crime in Winnipeg.* Ottawa, Ontario: Canadian Centre for Policy Alternatives.

Connell, R. W. (2002). *Gender.* Cambridge, UK: Polity.

Crenshaw, H. (1994). Mapping the margins: Intersectionality, identity politics, and violence against women of color. In M. A. Fineman & R. Mykitiuk (Eds.), *The public nature of private violence* (pp. 93–118). New York: Routledge.

Crites, L. (Ed.). (1976). *The female offender.* Lexington, MA: Lexington Books.

Daly, K., & Chesney-Lind, M. (1988). Feminism and criminology. *Justice Quarterly, 5*(4), 497–538.

Deegan, M. J. (1988). *Jane Addams and the men of the Chicago School, 1892–1918*. New Brunswick, NJ: Transaction Books.

DeKeseredy, W. (1999). *Women, crime, and the Canadian criminal justice system*. Cincinnati, OH: Anderson.

DeKeseredy, W., Sanders, D., Schwartz, M., & Alvi, S. (1997). The meanings and motives for women's use of violence in Canadian college dating relationships. *Sociological Spectrum, 17*, 199–222.

DeKeseredy, W., & Schwartz, M. (1998, February). *Measuring the extent of woman abuse in intimate heterosexual relationships: A critique of the conflict tactics scales*. National Online Resource Center on Violence Against Women. Retrieved from http://www.vawnet.org/DomesticViolence/Research/VAWnetDocs/AR_ctscrit.php

Dziech, B. W., & Weiner, L. (1984). *The lecherous professor*. Boston: Beacon.

Estrich, S. (1987). *Real rape*. Cambridge, MA: Harvard University Press.

Faith, K. (1993). *Unruly women: The politics of confinement & resistance*. Vancouver, British Columbia, Canada: Press Gang.

Faludi, S. (1991). *Backlash: The undeclared war against American women*. New York: Anchor Doubleday.

Federal Bureau of Investigation. (2004). *Crime in the United States, 2003*. Washington, DC: Government Printing Office.

Ferraro, K. (2001). Women battering: More than a family problem. In C. Renzetti & L. Goodstein (Eds.), *Women, crime and criminal justice* (pp. 135–153). Los Angeles: Roxbury.

Ford, R. (1998, May 24). The razor's edge. *Boston Globe Magazine*, pp. 3, 22–28.

Freedman, E. (1981). *Their sisters' keepers: Women and prison reform, 1830–1930*. Ann Arbor: University of Michigan Press.

Gilbert, E. (2001). Women, race, and criminal justice processing. In C. Renzetti & L. Goodstein (Eds.), *Women, crime and criminal justice* (pp. 222–231). Los Angeles: Roxbury.

Gilfus, M. (1992). From victims to survivors to offenders: Women's routes of entry into street crime. *Women & Criminal Justice, 4*(1), 63–89.

Goldstein, A., Smith, J., & Becker, J. (2005, August 19). Roberts resisted women's rights. *Washington Post*, p. A1.

Gora, J. (1982). *The new female criminal: Empirical reality or social myth*. New York: Praeger.

Greenfeld, A., & Snell, T. (1999). *Women offenders: Bureau of Justice Statistics, special report*. Washington, DC: U.S. Department of Justice.

Guido, M. (1998, June 4). In a new twist on equality, girls' crimes resemble boys'. *San Jose Mercury News*, p. 1B–4B.

Hannah-Moffat, K., & Shaw, M. (2003). The meaning of "risk" in women's prisons: A critique. In B. Bloom (Ed.), *Gendered justice* (pp. 25–44). Durham, NC: Carolina Academic Press.

Hardisty, J. V. (2000). *Mobilizing resentment*. Boston: Beacon.

Harms, P. (2002, January). *Detention in delinquency cases, 1989–1998* (OJJDP Fact Sheet No. 1). Washington, DC: U.S. Department of Justice.

Harrison, P. M., & Beck, A. J. (2004). *Prisoners in 2003*. Washington, DC: U.S. Department of Justice, Bureau of Justice Statistics.

Heidensohn, F. (1995). Feminist perspectives and their impact on criminology and criminal justice in Britain. In N. H. Rafter & F. Heidensohn (Eds.), *International feminist perspectives in criminology* (pp. 63–85). Buckingham, UK: Open University Press.

Hoff Sommers, C. (1994). *Who stole feminism? How women have betrayed women*. New York: Simon & Schuster.

Horowitz, D., & Collier, P. (1994). *The heterodoxy handbook: How to survive the PC campus*. Lanham, MD: National Book Network.

Horton, J. O., & Horton, L. (2005). *Slavery and the making of America*. Oxford, UK: Oxford University Press.

Howe, A. (1994). *Punish and critique: Towards a feminist analysis of penality*. London: Routledge.

Human Rights Watch. (1996). *All too familiar: Sexual abuse of women in U.S. state prisons*. New York: Human Rights Watch.

Human Rights Watch. (2000, May). Punishment and prejudice: Racial disparities in the war on drugs. *Human Rights Watch Reports, 12*(2). Retrieved from http://www.hrw.org/reports/2000/usa/

Irwin, J. (2005). *The warehouse prison*. Los Angeles: Roxbury.

Joe, K. (1995). Ice is strong enough for a man but made for a woman: A social cultural analysis of methamphetamine use among Asian Pacific Americans. *Crime, Law and Social Change, 22*, 269–289.

Johnson, P. (2003). *Inner lives: Voices of African American women in prison*. New York: New York University Press.

Jones, A. (1980). *Women who kill*. New York: Fawcett Columbine.

Kelly, D. M. (1993). *Last chance high: How girls and boys drop in and out of alternative schools*. New Haven, CT: Yale University Press.

Kendall, K., & Pollack, S. (2003). Cognitive behaviorism in women's prisons. In B. Bloom (Ed.), *Gendered justice* (pp. 69–96). Durham, NC: Carolina Academic Press.

Kim, E.-K. (1996, August 26). Sheriff says he'll have chain gangs for women. *Tuscaloosa News*, p. A1.

Klein, D., & Kress, J. (Eds.). (1973). Women, crime and criminology [Special issue]. *Issues in Criminology, 8*(3).

Lantigua, J. (2001, April 30). How the GOP gamed the system in Florida. *The Nation*, pp. 1–8.

Leonard, E. (2002). *Convicted survivors: The imprisonment of battered women*. New York: New York University Press.

Maher, L., & Curtis, R. (1992). Women on the edge: Crack cocaine and the changing contexts of street-level sex work in New York City. *Crime, Law and Social Change, 18*, 221–258.

Martin, D. (1977). *Battered wives*. New York: Pocket Books.

Martin, S. (1980). *Breaking and entering: Police women on patrol*. Berkeley: University of California Press.

Matoesian, G. (1993). *Reproducing rape domination through talk in the courtroom*. Chicago: University of Chicago Press.

Mauer, M. (1999). *Race to incarcerate*. New York: New Press.

Mauer, M. (2002). State sentencing reforms: Is the "get tough" era coming to a close? *Federal Sentencing Reporter, 15*, 50–52.

Mauer, M., & Chesney-Lind, M. (Eds.). (2002). *Invisible punishment: The collateral consequences of mass imprisonment*. New York: New Press.

Mauer, M., & Huling, T. (1995). *Young Black Americans and the criminal justice system: Five years later.* Washington, DC: The Sentencing Project.

Maxwell, C., Garner, J. H., & Fagan, J. A. (2002). The preventive effects of arrest on intimate partner violence: Research, policy and theory. *Criminology & Public Policy, 2*(1), 51–80.

McClellan, D. S. (1994). Disparity in the discipline of male and female inmates in Texas prisons. *Women & Criminal Justice, 5*(20), 71–97.

Messerschmidt, J. W. (2000). *Nine lives: Adolescent masculinities, the body, and violence.* Boulder, CO: Westview.

Miller, J. (2001). *One of the guys: Girls, gangs, and gender.* New York: Oxford University Press.

Miller, J., & Mullins, C. (2005). *Taking stock: The status of feminist theories in criminology.* Unpublished manuscript.

Miller, S. (1989). Unintended side effects of pro-arrest policies and their race and class implications for battered women: A cautionary note. *Criminal Justice Policy Review, 3,* 299–317.

Miller, S. (2005). *Victims as offenders: Women's use of violence in relationships.* New Brunswick, NJ: Rutgers University Press.

Moore, J. (1991). *Going down to the barrio: Homeboys and homegirls in change.* Philadelphia: Temple University Press.

Morash, M., & Rucker, L. (1990). A critical look at the idea of boot camp as a correctional reform. *Crime & Delinquency, 36*(2), 204–222.

Owen, B. (1998). *"In the mix": Struggle and survival in a women's prison.* Albany: State University of New York Press.

Pincus, F. (2001/2002). The social construction of reverse discrimination: The impact of affirmative action on Whites. *Journal of Inter-Group Relations, 38*(4), 33–44.

Pollak, O. (1950). *The criminality of women.* Philadelphia: University of Pennsylvania Press.

Pollock, J. (1999). *Criminal women.* Cincinnati, OH: Anderson.

Rafter, N. H. (1990). *Partial justice: Women, prisons and social control.* New Brunswick, NJ: Transaction Books.

Rafter, N. H. (Ed.). (2000). *Encyclopedia of women and crime.* Phoenix, AZ: Oryx Press.

Renzetti, C., & Curran, D. J. (1999). *Women, men and society.* Boston: Allyn & Bacon.

Richie, B. (1996). *Compelled to crime: The gender entrapment of battered Black women.* New York: Routledge.

Rush, F. (1980). *The best kept secret: Sexual abuse of children.* New York: McGraw-Hill.

Russell, D. (1986). *The secret trauma.* New York: Basic Books.

Ryan, J. (2003, September 5). Girl gang stirs up false gender issue: Data show no surge in female violence. *San Francisco Chronicle,* p. 2.

Scelfo, J. (2005, June 13). Bad girls go wild. *Newsweek.* Retrieved July 31, 2005, from http://www.msnbcnsn.com/id.8101517/site/newsweek/page/2/

Schecter, S. (1982). *Women and male violence: The visions and struggles of the battered women's movement.* Boston: South End.

Scully, D. (1990). *Understanding sexual violence.* Boston: Unwin Hyman.

Sherman, L. W., & Berk, R. A. (1984). The specific deterrent effects of arrest for domestic assault. *American Sociological Review, 49*(1), 261–272.

Simon, R. (1975). *Women and crime.* Lexington, MA: Lexington Books.

Smart, C. (1976). *Women, crime and criminology: A feminist critique.* London: Routledge Kegan Paul.

Smith, L. (1996, November 18). Increasingly, abuse shows a female side: More women accused of domestic violence. *Washington Post,* p. B1.

Steffensmeier, D. J. (1980). Sex differences in patterns of adult crime, 1965–1977. *Social Forces, 58,* 1080–1108.

Steffensmeier, D. J., Schwartz, J., Zhong, H., & Ackerman, J. (2005). An assessment of recent trends in girls' violence using diverse longitudinal sources. *Criminology, 43,* 355–406.

Steffensmeier, D. J., & Steffensmeier, R. H. (1980). Trends in female delinquency: An examination of arrest, juvenile court, self-report, and field data. *Criminology, 18,* 62–85.

Stein, D. (1996, July). Life in prison: Sexual abuse. *The Progressive,* 23–24.

Thorne, B. (1993). *Gender play.* New Brunswick, NJ: Rutgers University Press.

Websdale, N., & Alvarez, A. (1997). Forensic journalism as patriarchal ideology: The newspaper construction of homicide-suicide. In D. Hale & F. Bailey (Eds.), *Popular culture, crime and justice* (pp. 123–141). Belmont, CA: Wadsworth

Weis, J. G. (1976). "Liberation and crime": The invention of the new female criminal. *Crime and Social Justice, 6,* 17–27.

West, C., & Zimmerman, D. H. (1987). Doing gender. *Gender & Society, 1,* 125–151.

Wichita Police Department. (2002). *Domestic violence statistics: 2001.* Retrieved from http://wichitapolice.com/DV/DV_statistics.htm

Williams, L. S. (2002). Trying on gender, gender regimes, and the process of becoming women. *Gender & Society, 16,* 29–52.

DISCUSSION QUESTIONS

1. How have attempts of "vengeful equity" failed to meet the needs of women offenders?

2. How is the experience of patriarchy influencing the criminal justice system?

3. How has feminist criminology shed light on the race/gender/punishment nexus? Provide examples from the reading to support your answer.

READING 2

In Section I, you learned about how feminist research methods can provide an alternative perspective when researching issues of gender and crime. In this chapter, Dr. Jody Miller discusses how her research on issues of gender and female offending has benefited by placing gender at the center of her research methodology. Through the use of this process, Dr. Miller demonstrates how qualitative research (and in particular, in-depth interviews) can yield a meaningful understanding of how issues of crime and victimization are a gendered experience.

Grounding the Analysis of Gender and Crime

Accomplishing and Interpreting Qualitative Interview Research

Jody Miller

Introduction

As a feminist scholar and sociological criminologist, a primary question guiding my research concerns the impact of gender stratification, gendered practices, and gender ideologies on criminal offending. I seek to challenge and complicate binary assumptions about women and men and in doing so carefully attend to the complex ways in which gender—as one of the most basic organizing structures within and across societies—configures individuals' life experiences in ways that lead them to crime and that influences their motivations for offending, strategies for accomplishing it, and the situations and contexts in which this offending takes place. My method of choice for doing this research is the analysis of qualitative in-depth interview data.

In this chapter, I address the following questions: What makes in-depth interviewing a particularly useful methodological approach for feminist criminology? How is research that utilizes interview data put to use for understanding the relationships between gender, inequality, and crime? Finally, how do those of us who analyze in-depth interviews in our research go about doing

so—what's the actual process by which we turn our data into meaningful theoretical contributions? I draw from three of my research projects—on young women's participation in gangs, women's and men's accomplishment of robbery, and young men's sexual violence against young women—to describe why qualitative interviews are my data of choice, and how I use inductive analytic techniques to produce my research findings.

Feminist Criminology and Qualitative Interview Accounts

Sociologist Christine Williams (2000: 9) describes academic feminism as "a general approach to understanding the status of women in society." Notwithstanding the range of theoretical and methodological approaches brought to bear on the question, she observes that "all feminist social scientists share the goals of understanding the sources of inequality and advocating changes to empower women" (ibid.). Thus, what differentiates *feminist* criminology from other criminological analyses that

SOURCE: Miller, J. (2012). Grounding the analysis of gender and crime: Accomplishing and interpreting qualitative interview research. In D. Gadd, S. Karstedt, & S. F. Messner (Eds.), *The SAGE handbook of criminological research methods* (pp. 49–62). Thousand Oaks, CA: Sage.

consider women and crime is the conceptual understanding of gender that guides our research: a concern with understanding *gender* is as much a starting point in feminist criminological analyses as is the concern with understanding *crime* (Daly, 1998).

Early treatises on feminist methodology, particularly the use of in-depth interview techniques, were situated in women's standpoint theory (Oakley, 1981). These were grounded in feminist goals of "giving voice" to women and their experiences, which had historically been silenced (see DeVault, 1999; Smith, 1987). This remains an important goal of feminist scholars, though with critical understandings of its challenges. Initially, there was a relatively uncritical assumption that when women interviewed women, their shared experiences *as women* would result in identification, rapport, and consequently, the authentic revelation of "women's experiences." These rather romanticized assumptions have since been problematized, however. Most scholars now recognize, for example, that no research can provide authentic access to individuals' experiences or unmediated access to "truth," and this includes the accounts produced in the context of interviews (see Miller and Glassner, 2004; Silverman, 2006). Moreover, feminist scholars now recognize that women do not simply share experiences *as women*. Instead, many facets of difference come into play when we attempt to understand women's and men's lives, including race, ethnicity, cultural identity, nation, class, and age, as well as individual life trajectories and experiences (Presser, 2005; Song and Parker, 1995; Veroff and DiStefano, 2002).

Given this multifaceted understanding of the research process and its goals, many feminist scholars identify unique contributions that qualitative interview approaches can make in theorizing about gender and crime. This results both from how feminist scholars conceptualize gender and from our insistence that examining the meaning and nature of gender relations and inequalities are a critical component of understanding and theorizing about crime and criminality. To begin with, feminist scholarship challenges the premise that gender is simply an individual-level independent variable. Instead, our research starts with the understanding that the social world is systematically shaped by relations of sex and gender, and these operate at all levels of society, including individual, interactional, organizational,

and structural (see Connell, 2002; Risman, 2004). As Daly and Chesney-Lind (1988: 504) sum up, "[G]ender and gender relations order social life and social institutions in fundamental ways."

As a consequence, feminist scholars recognize that gender operates both within the practices and organization of social life, as well as within "the discursive fields by which women [and men] are constructed or construct themselves" (Daly and Maher, 1998: 4). Taken for granted ideologies about gender are profoundly embedded in social life and often include commonsense notions of fundamental difference between women and men, coupled with the perception of maleness as the normative standard. These deeply engrained assumptions are regularly found in academic research and theory; the policies, practices, and operation of organizations and institutions; and in the interpretive frameworks women and men bring to their daily lives. Moreover, it is through the enactment of these gendered meanings that the most persistent, yet often invisible, facets of gender inequality are reproduced.

Perhaps most pronounced is the tendency to reproduce conventional understandings of gender *difference* (see Miller, 2002). Such interpretive frameworks—particularly cultural emphases on a psychologically based "character dichotomy" between women and men (Connell, 2002: 40) often guide the understandings of those we investigate and can also seep into researchers' conceptualizations. Thus, feminist scholars grapple with what Daly and Maher (1998: 1) refer to as an *intellectual double shift*: the dual challenge of examining the impact of gender and gender inequality in "real" life, while simultaneously deconstructing the intertwined ideologies about gender that guide social practices (see Connell, 2002). Indeed, illuminating the relationship between ideological features of gender and gendered practice is a key facet of feminist scholarship.

In addition, feminist conceptualizations of gender often require us to move beyond what broad, global explanations provide. While our starting point is the recognition that social life is patterned by gender, we also recognize—and empirical evidence demonstrates—that this gender order (Connell, 2002) is complex and shifting. For this reason, a key feature of feminist scholarship is the development of what Daly (1998) refers to as "middle range" theorizing—developing theoretical understandings that seek primarily to explain how broader structural forces are realized within particular organizational, situational, and interactional contexts.

So what does the analysis of qualitative in-depth interviews have to offer in our attempts to attend to these complexities and challenges? From my point of view, the strength of such interviews lies in what they are: reflective accounts of social life offered from the points of view of research participants. As such, they provide two intertwined kinds of data: descriptive evidence of the nature of the phenomena under investigation—including the contexts and situations in which it emerges—as well as insights into the cultural frames that people use to make sense of their experiences (Miller and Glassner, 2004). Both are especially useful for feminist theorizing about gender and crime, particularly in the context of the intellectual double shift I noted previously.

In general, qualitative research is oriented toward the creation of contextual understandings of social worlds, emphasizing complexities in the meanings and social processes that operate within them. Interview data, in which people describe and explain their behaviors and experiences, help us identify and understand social processes and patterns at the interactional and situational levels, as well as the meanings people attribute to their experiences and behaviors (see Charmaz, 2006; Spradley, 1979; but compare Silverman, 2006). In criminology, this includes, for example, examining in situ motivations for behaviors such as offending or desistance (Maruna, 2001); social processes associated with crime, criminally involved groups, or the streets (Maher, 1997); situational analyses of crime events (Mullins and Wright, 2003; Wright and Decker, 1997), as well as life history analyses that examine pathways into and out of offending (Giordano, 2010). As such, qualitative in-depth interviews can provide us with ground level understandings of crime and criminal behavior.

In addition, because in-depth interviews are *accounts*, they hold promise for examining the social world from the points of view of research participants and for exploring how meanings are constructed together, including in the interview itself (see Miller, 2010). When analyzed not just as a source of information about the *who, what, when, where*, and *how* of criminal offending but also as a "linguistic device employed whenever an action is subjected to valuative inquiry" (Scott and Lyman, 1968: 46), the narrative accounts within in-depth interviews provide insight into "culturally embedded normative explanations [of

events and behaviors, because they] represent ways in which people organize views of themselves, of others, and of their social worlds" (Orbuch, 1997: 455).

Given feminist scholars' concerns with how language and discourse "reflect and help constitute" gendered meaning systems (Cameron, 1998: 946), the analysis of in-depth interviews thus offers an especially useful tool for feminist scholars in simultaneously examining both social patterns and social meanings associated with gender, inequality, and crime. Recognizing interview accounts as evidence of both the nature of the phenomenon under investigation and the cultural frameworks that individuals use to interpret their experiences means that, in one's analysis, juxtaposing these facets of accounts—even or especially when they appear incongruous—can be useful for developing theoretical insight. Qualitative interview data are thus particularly well suited for addressing the goals of feminist criminologists for understanding how gender and gender inequality shape the experiences of those involved in crime.

Analyzing Qualitative Interview Data

Most qualitative researchers use some version of grounded theory techniques in their data analysis. Charmaz (2006: 2–3) provides the following explanation of what this entails:

> Stated simply, grounded theory methods consist of systematic, yet flexible guidelines for collecting and analyzing qualitative data to construct theories grounded in the data themselves. The guidelines offer a set of general principles and heuristic devices rather than formulaic rules. . . . Thus, data form the foundation of our theory and our analysis of these data generates the concepts we construct.

One of the most important principles of grounded theory analyses is that preliminary data analysis begins at the start of the project. Initial analyses of both what people say and how they say it open up new avenues of inquiry and also generate preliminary hypotheses to be further explored during ongoing data collection and analysis. This is accomplished through close and continuous reading of the data, during which the researcher codes the data and begins documenting preliminary analytic observations and hypotheses, which are then compared with and analyzed in light of additional data collected. Coding, as Charmaz explains, is a process by which "we attach labels to segments of data that depict what each segment is about. Coding distills data, sorts them, and gives us a handle for making comparisons with other segments of data" (ibid., 3).

The particular analysis strategy a qualitative interview researcher uses may vary for any given project. What they share in common, however, is recognition of the importance of beginning initial data coding by using grounded, open coding strategies.

This process helps avoid the application of preconceived concepts, assists in generating new ideas, and keeps the researcher thoroughly grounded in the data (Charmaz, 2006). Initial coding can take a variety of forms, including reading the interview text word by word, line by line, and incident by incident. The more closely we read the data, the more readily we can move beyond taken for granted or preconceived ideas we bring to our research, and the more

likely we are to discover emergent concepts and patterns in the data.

An important part of the process is paying specific attention to interview participants' unique language and speech patterns (Spradley, 1979). Charmaz (2006: 55) refers to these as *in vivo* codes—terms or phrases that provide telling insights into social worlds or processes. In my recent work, *Getting Played* (2008), for example, the insider term *play* and its iterations became central to my analysis, and it was even the basis of the book's title. While analyzing interviews with urban African American youth about interactions between young women and young men and their relation to gendered violence, I was struck by the common and varied ways in which the term *play* entered into youths' accounts. Treating this as an in vivo code, I carefully examined its usage to identify the actions it represented and the implicit meanings *play* attached to them. This led me to an analysis of the variety of ways that play claims are used to minimize the significance of behavioral patterns that are harmful to girls. To illustrate, Reading Box 2.1 provides a partial excerpt of my analysis of play claims associated with sexual harassment

---

Reading Box 2.1 Contested Play Claims: Humor or Disrespected?

[Y]oung men often downplayed the seriousness of sexual harassment by couching it in terms of "play." Antwoin said, "[Y]eah, I grabbed a girl bootie a couple of times . . . we was playing." Such touching, he said, was best understood as "like playing around. Sometimes the boys'll be messing with the girls and they'll just grab they bootie or something." . . . Similarly, asked why he and his friends touched on girls, Curtis said, "I don't know, just to have fun. Just playing."

"Just playing," however, was a characterization young women roundly rejected. Instead, to quote Nicole, girls found boys' sexually harassing behaviors to be "too much playing." . . . Katie complained, "[M]ost of the time boys and girls get into it because boys, they play too much. . . . Like they try to touch you and stuff, or try to talk about you, or put you down in front of they friends to made them feel better. . . . Just talk about you or something like in front of they friends so they can laugh."

Katie's comments tapped into an important feature of boys' play claim: The primary audience for this "play" was other young men. As Anishika argued young men's "humour" was for the benefit of their friends, and at the expense of the young woman:

They just tryin' to be like person and that person. They already know, they know what's right. They know right from wrong. But when it's a lot of 'em, they think that stuff is cute, calling girls B's [bitches] and rats and all that stuff. They think that stuff cute, and some of these girls think that stuff cute. But it's not cute.

(Continued)

(Continued)

In fact, [young men's accounts] are indicative of the role male peers played in facilitating young men's behaviors. Thus, Frank [explained], "some people, when they see [you touch on a girl], they'll laugh or they give you some props. They give you like a little five of something like that. That's what the dudes do." . . . Thus, a number of girls said boys simply used play claims as an excuse for their behavior, and described explicitly rejecting these claims. For example, angry after a young man made sexual comments about her, Destiny said he responded to her anger by saying, "you ain't even gotta get that serious. I was just playin' wit' you." She replied, "I don't care. I don't want you playin' with me like that, stop playin' with me like that." And Nicole explained, "sometimes boys make it like, act like it's funny. But it's not. 'Cause you touchin' a girl and she don't wanna be touched. So don't touch me, period. Don't even think about touchin' me."

Indeed, despite young men's routine use of play claims, their own accounts belied the notion that their behaviors were simply intended as harmless fun. For example, several young men said part of the fun in taunting girls was getting an angry response. . . . Moreover, several young men described treating girls in a a derogatory way specifically to demarcate their (male) space and make it clear to the girl that she wasn't welcome. . . . [O]ne additional factor belies young men's characterizations of their behavior as "just play". Asked when harassing behaviors took place or whether they were directed at particular girls, a number of young men described targeting young women they deemed to be "stuck up," unwilling to show sexual or romantic interest, or otherwise unimpressed with the boy. . . . Curtis said, "[W]e'll see a girl in like a short skirt or short shorts, and we be kind of talking to her, and she don't, she ain't giving nobody no play. So we just get to playing with her, touching on her butt and all that."

SOURCE: From Miller, 2008, pp. 82–87.

In vivo codes can also be phrases that condense and distill significant analytic concepts. During her interview for *Getting Played,* one of the young women described offering the following advice to her sister for avoiding sexual violence: "Protect yourself, respect yourself. 'Cause if you don't, guys won't." Read in passing, it could easily be seen as simple advice. But my line-by-line coding flagged it as a phrase worth further examination. I made note of it in an analytic memo and then paid close attention to how youths talked about protection and respect. Ultimately, my analysis revealed that it succinctly crystallized youths' understandings of the causes of sexual violence and girls' risk-management strategies in the face of limited interpersonal and institutional support (see Miller, 2008: 143–149).

Beyond the importance of open and in vivo coding, qualitative researchers employ a variety of specific coding and analysis strategies, depending on the research question at hand. Charmaz (2006) recommends that grounded theory research should code for *action* within the data, using gerund codes to preserve social processes. Lofland and

Lofland (1984) encourage scholars to identify *topics* for analysis by combining particular units of analysis (e.g., practices, episodes, encounters, or relationships) with their aspects (e.g., cognitive, emotional, or hierarchical). Once identified, the researcher rigorously examines the data for instances that are topically relevant. Spradley (1979) utilizes domain analysis, by using semantic relationships to ask structured questions from the data (e.g., X is a kind of Y; X is a way to do Y). Each of these strategies allow us to approach the data in a systematic way, with the goal of moving from initial coding to systematic theoretical analyses.

Good qualitative research emerges from the thoroughness and rigor of the inductive analysis. In the process, *emergent* hypotheses are identified in the course of analysis as patterns begin to emerge. These hypotheses are then tested, refined, or rejected using the project data. A variety of strategies have been devised to ensure the rigor of the analytic induction process. Most important is the use of constant comparative methods, which are strengthened through the use of tabulations to identify the strength of patterns (see Silverman, 2006: 296–301, for a concise description of these strategies) and to aid in the identification of and analysis of deviant cases. As Charmaz (2006: 54) describes,

> You use *"constant comparative method"* . . . to establish analytic distinctions and thus make comparisons at each level of analytic work. . . . For example, compare interview statements and incidents within the same interview and compare statements and incidents in different interviews.

This allows you to test and refine emergent hypotheses against the data. It is also the case that qualitative researchers tend to reject the position that any research can tap into "pure" objective data, regardless of the methodological approach of the researcher. Thus, consideration of the researcher's place in the research process—from formulating research questions, to data collection, to analysis—is necessary. To illustrate these analytic strategies—focusing specifically on the utility of qualitative interview research for studying gender and crime—I now turn to a more detailed description of several of my research projects.

Up It Up: Studying Gender Stratification and the Accomplishment of Robbery

Early in my career, I was afforded the opportunity to utilize my colleagues' in-depth interview data with armed robbers (Wright and Decker, 1997) to examine the impact of gender on the enactment of robbery (Miller, 1998). My analysis of these data helps illustrate several key features of qualitative analysis techniques. I approached the data with two guiding questions: How do women, as compared to men, account for their motivations to commit robbery? And how do women, as compared to men, describe the process by which they accomplish robbery? The use of comparative samples—in this case, female and male robbers—is a particularly useful approach when doing qualitative research, because it allows for some specification of similarities and variations in social processes and meaning systems across groups or settings.

In this particular investigation, I coded the data with these two specific research questions in mind. First, I looked for evidence in the data for how robbers described their motivations to commit robbery and compared accounts both within and across gender. Next, I coded incident by incident, examining how women and men in the sample described accomplishing the robberies they committed. My identification within the data of both similarities and differences across gender led me to theorize about the impact of gender stratification in offender networks on women's participation in crime. This is an example of the type of middle range theorizing described previously—my research findings pointed me in the direction of stratification as the best fit for explaining the patterns I identified, and it offered an incisive analytic framework for explaining the structures and processes I uncovered.

Specifically, I found congruence across gender in interview participants' accounts of their *motivations* for committing robberies. For both women and men, the incentives to commit robbery were primarily economic—to get money, jewelry, and other status-conferring goods, but [they] also included elements of thrill seeking, attempting to overcome boredom, and revenge. However, women's and men's accounts of *how* they went about committing robberies were strikingly different. And within gender comparisons of incident accounts, [they] were equally illuminating.

Specifically, men's descriptions of their commission of robbery were markedly similar to one another. Their accounts were variations around a single theme: using physical violence and/or a gun placed on or at close proximity to the victim in a confrontational manner. The key, one explained, was to make sure the victim knew "that we ain't playing." Another described confronting his victims by placing the gun at the back of their head, where "they feel it," while saying, "Give it up, motherfucker, don't move or I'll blow your brains out." Explaining the positioning of the gun, he noted, "When you feel that steel against your head . . . [it] carries a lot of weight." Closely examining each man's accounts of strategies for committing robberies, as well as their descriptions of particular incidents, revealed that they accomplished robberies in noticeably uniform ways.

In contrast, women's accounts were notable both for the greater variation in the strategies they described using to accomplish robberies and for their absence of accounts that paralleled those provided by men, except under very specific circumstances: when they committed robberies in partnership with male accomplices. In short, though men described routinely using firearms to commit robberies and placing them on or in close proximity to the back of the victim's head, women's strategies for committing robberies varied according to the gender of their victim, and the presence or absence of co-offenders. They described three predominant ways in which they committed robberies: targeting female victims in physically confrontational robberies that did not involve firearms, targeting male victims by appearing sexually available, and participating with male co-offenders during street robberies of men.

Insights about the role of gender stratification in the commission of robbery emerged particularly prominently when I examined women's accounts of robbing men. These incidents nearly always involved firearms but rarely involved physical contact. Notably, the rationale women provided for this strategy was especially telling. As one explained,

[I]f we waste time touching men there is a possibility that they can get the gun off of us, while we wasting time touching them they could do anything. So we just keep the gun straight on them. No touching, no moving, just straight gun at you.

The circumstances surrounding the enactment of female-on-male robberies were unique as well. The key, in each case, was that the woman pretended to be sexually interested in her male victim. When his guard dropped, this provided a safe opportunity for the robbery to occur.

Moreover, women specifically described playing on the stereotypes men held about women in order to accomplish these robberies—including the assumptions that women would not be armed, would not attempt to rob them, and could be taken advantage of sexually. For example, one woman explained,

[T]hey don't suspect that a girl gonna try to get 'em. You know what I'm saying? So it's kind of easier 'cause they like, she looks innocent, she

ain't gonna do this, but that's how I get 'em. They put they guard down to a woman. . . . Most of the time, when girls get high they think they can take advantage of us so they always, let's go to a hotel or my crib or something.

Another said, "[T]hey easy to get, we know what they after—sex."

This and other evidence of the role that gender ideologies played in the enactment of robberies pointed explicitly to the importance of gendered organizational features of the street environment as an important explanatory factor. Most notable was the incongruity between the similarities in women's and men's motives for committing robbery and the dramatic differences in their strategies for accomplishing robbery. As such, the research highlighted the gender hierarchy present on the streets: while some women were able to carve out a niche for themselves in this setting, they were participating in a male-dominated environment, and their robbery strategies reflected an understanding of this. The differences in the way women, as compared to men, accomplished robberies were not a result of differences in their goals or needs. Instead, they reflected practical choices women made in the context of a gender stratified environment—one in which, on the whole, men were perceived as strong and women as weak. In this particular project, it was not just the availability of in-depth interview data that resulted in the analysis briefly described here but also specifically the *comparative* nature of the data. My ability to juxtapose women's and men's accounts facilitated the identification of commonalities and differences across gender and thus allowed me to build an analytic framework to make sense of them. Moreover, as illustrated in Reading Box 2.2, deviant case analysis further strengthened my analytic framework.

Reading Box 2.2   Deviant Case Analysis: The "Masculine" Woman Robber

Once emergent hypotheses are identified in inductive analysis, it is necessary to actively seek out and account for cases in the data that are counter to the emergent hypotheses. In the robbery project, my emergent hypothesis was that women's enactment of robbery differs from men's based on strategic choices thay make in recognition of gender stratification on the streets, including men's perceptions of women as weak, and thus ineffectual or nonthreatening as robbers.

Closely examining robbery incident accounts, there was one clear outlier: a lone woman who described committing a 'masculine' style robbery by herself and against a male victim. When using analytic induction techniques, it is necessary for researches to revise their emergent hypotheses until such deviant cases can be accounted for by their analysis. In this case, the answer was straightforward, and actually buttressed the original hypothesis. The outlier (or deviant case) perfectly fit my explanatory framework:

Ne Ne explicitly indicates that this robbery was possible because the victim did not know she was a woman. Describing herself physically, she says, "I'm big, you know." In addition, her dress and manner masked her gender. "I had a baseball cap in my car and I seen him . . . . I just turned around the corner, came back down the street, he was out by hisself and I got out of the car, had the cap pulled down over my face and I just went to the back and upped him. Put the gun up to his head." Being large, wearing a ballcap and enacting the robbery in a masculine style (e.g., putting a gun to his head), allowed her to disguise the fact that she was a woman and thus decrease the victim's likelihood of resisting. She says, "He don't know right now to this day if it was a girl or a dude." (Miller, 1998: 60)

While it is rare to have such a seamless answer when analyzing deviant cases, this example illustrates both its utility and import for ensuring rigorous inductive analysis in qualitative research.

One of the Guys: Studying Gender Inequality and Gender Ideologies in Youth Gangs

The next example I draw from is especially useful for illustrating the intellectual double shift described earlier—in which feminist researchers seek to analyze both the reality of experiences and the sometimes incongruent cultural frames used to make sense of them—as well as the importance of constant comparative techniques for enhancing qualitative analysis. When analyzing in-depth interviews in a study of young women's experiences in gangs, I was faced with two sets of discrepancies that required address. First, while most young women I interviewed were adamant that they were *equals* with the boys in their gangs,[1] they simultaneously described systematic gender inequalities within these groups. Second, [whereas] much of the extant literature on young women in gangs led me to expect strong bonds of solidarity among young women, I found the opposite. Many of the young women I spoke with held openly misogynistic attitudes about other girls. Thus, my analysis required me to make sense of both the disconnect between girls' claims that they were "one of the guys" and their experiences of inequality and to account for why my research findings were so disparate from the reports of previous research.

A dominant theme in my interviews with young women was their insistence that their gangs were a space of gender equality, where males and females were treated as equals. As one explained,

"[T]hey give every last one of us respect the way they give the males." Another was visibly frustrated with my line of questions about gender, and repeatedly cut me off in response:

JM: "You said before that the gang was about half girls and half guys? Can you tell me more about that? Like you said you don't think there are any differences in terms of what—"

Interviewee: "There isn't!"

JM: "Ok, can you tell me more—"

Interviewee: "Like what? There isn't, there isn't like, there's nothing—boy, girl, white, black, Mexican, Chinese."

Another explained: "We just like dudes to them. We just like dudes, they treat us like that 'cause we act so much like dudes they can't do nothing. They respect us as females though, but we just so much like dudes that they just don't trip off of it."

Despite this prevailing discursive construction of gender equality, the young women's descriptions of the activities and behaviors of gang members markedly contradicted these statements. Instead, without exception, young women described a distinct gender hierarchy within mixed-gender gangs that included male leadership, a sexual double standard with regard to sexual activity, the sexual exploitation of some young women, perceptions of girls as *weak* and boys as *strong*, and most girls' exclusion from serious gang crime—specifically, those acts that built status and reputation within their groups (Miller, 2001).

It would be easy to simply discount girls' claims of gender equality as wrong or misguided. But, as I noted earlier, making sense of such contradictions provides an important basis for building theoretical insight. My task, then, was to explain the basis on which girls made claims to gender equality and the functions that such claims served. First, I looked carefully at *how* girls made the case that they were treated as equals. Examining their accounts closely, it became apparent that the means by which this was accomplished was not to make broad claims that all women should be treated as equals but to differentiate themselves from *other* girls—and in the process, uphold the masculine status norms of their groups. As one explained,

> A lot of girls get scared. Don't wanna break their nails and stuff like that. So, ain't no need for them to try to be in no gang. And the ones that's in it, most of the girls that's in act like boys. That's why they in, 'cause they like to fight and stuff. They know how to fight and they use guns and stuff.

In addition, because the young women I interviewed also described a range of gender inequalities in their gangs, they also had to account for these descriptions of girls' mistreatment—and do so in ways that were consistent with their central belief in the norm of gender equality. Again, this required me to look at not only *what* they said about girls' mistreatment but also *how* they made sense of it. Closely analyzing their accounts, I discovered that young women drew on two types of frames. First, they individualized acts they recognized as involving the mistreatment of females, describing them as unique or exceptional cases. When this was not possible—for instance, when the mistreatment was

recurring or routine—they sought ways to hold young women accountable for their mistreatment. They did so both by justifying particular acts as deserved because of the behaviors of the young women in question and by characterizing *other* young women as possessing particular negative "female" traits—having "big mouths," being "troublemakers," or being "ho's" or "wrecks."[2]

The other piece of the puzzle that required explanation was *why* young women both insisted on their equality and strongly differentiated themselves from other girls. Answering this question was key to providing an analytic framework that could link the structures of gender inequality in gangs to the processes by which they were reproduced and maintained. I did so by situating their gang participation in the broader contexts of their environments and life experiences, including evidence that gender hierarchies in girls' gangs were not unique, but embedded within a broader social environment in which gender inequalities were entrenched.

Thus, to the extent that there *was* normative space within gangs for gender equality—however narrowly defined—gang participation actually provided individual young women with a means of empowerment and self-definition not available in other contexts. But this required them to accept a "patriarchal bargain" (Kandiyoti, 1988) by which *they* could lay claim to being one of the guys only by supporting and justifying the mistreatment of *other* girls. Identifying with dominant beliefs about women, and rejecting such images for themselves, allowed them to construct a space of gender equality *for themselves* and to draw particular advantages from their gangs that were less available in other social spaces in their lives (see Miller, 2001, chapter 8, for a more detailed account of the analysis).

As noted, the other challenge I faced with this research was that my findings were in contrast to previous research on young women in gangs, which tended to uncover bonds of solidarity among young women (see Joe and Chesney-Lind, 1995; Lauderback, Hansen, & Waldorf, 1992). This also required an explanation. I began by looking closely at what differences might exist between the gangs previous researchers had studied and those represented in my sample, and what I noticed was that the gender composition of many of the gangs from which my sample was drawn were *skewed* groups, in which the preponderance of members were male. In contrast, other studies reported findings on gangs that appeared to be either gender balanced or were all female. This led me to think about the role of group proportion in shaping gender dynamics in gangs. Sociological research on organizations, for example, has long shown that the "*relative* numbers of socially and culturally different people in a group are . . . critical in shaping interactional dynamics" (Kanter, 1977: 965). Why wouldn't this also apply in youth gangs?

To test this hypothesis, I employed a constant comparative method within my own data, whereby, the researcher "always attempt[s] to find another case through which to test out a provisional hypothesis" (Silverman, 2006: 296). I carefully sought instances in my data in which girls strongly articulated their position as one of the guys, as well as instances in which girls were critical of gender inequalities and espoused closer and more supportive relationships with other girls. What I discovered supported my hypothesis—the handful of girls in my study who were in gender-balanced or all female gangs tended not to match the pattern I had previously uncovered. My distinct findings about one of the guys were shaped by the gendered organizational structure of their groups, and this pattern was revealed to me through the use of constant comparative methods in the analytic process.

Running Trains: Gaining Insight Through Attention to the Interview as a Joint Accomplishment

Earlier in the chapter, I noted that qualitative researchers tend to reject the position that research can uncover pure objective data. In the context of in-depth interviewing, an important part of this is recognizing that the interview itself is a particular kind of interaction, in which both participants—the interviewer and the interviewee—are constructing narrative versions of the social world. The accounts produced in the context of interviews are, as noted earlier, "linguistic device[s] employed whenever an action is subjected to valuative inquiry" (Scott and Lyman, 1968: 46). We saw this in gang girls' claims of being one of the guys. It is also the case that our social positioning vis-à-vis those we interview affects the interview exchange. Attention to these interactional dynamics within the interview exchange offers an important site for social inquiry (Grenz, 2005; Miller, 2010; Presser, 2005). This is not about trying to control for interviewer effects per se; instead, "what matters is to understand how and where the stories [we collect] are produced, which sort of stories they are, and how we can put them to honest and intelligent use in theorizing about social life" (Miller and Glassner, 2004: 138).

Earlier, I argued that in-depth interview research utilizing comparative *samples* is particularly useful for theory building. Here, I provide an illustration of how comparative analysis of the data collected by different *interviewers* also provides an important opportunity for theorizing about social life. I draw from one particular set of data from my recent project on violence against young women in urban African American neighborhoods (Miller, 2008)—young men's accounts of *running trains* on girls: a sexual encounter that involved two or more young men engaging in penetrative sexual acts with a single young woman. Specifically, this example shows that paying attention to how interviewers' social positioning matters in the interview context can reveal a great deal about how individuals construct particular sorts of accounts of their offending and about the contexts and meanings of this behavior.

Running trains was an all too common phenomenon in the data, with nearly half of the boys interviewed admitting that they had done so. Though researchers routinely classify such incidents as gang rape, and the young women interviewed described their experiences in this way as well, the young men in the study defined girls' participation in trains as consensual. Thus, it was particularly important in the project to examine how young men understood running trains and especially how they came to perceive these behaviors as consensual. In this case, interviews conducted by two different research assistants—one a White European man (Dennis), the other an African American woman who grew up in the same community as the research participants (Toya)—revealed two sets of findings about boys' constructions of running trains. These offered distinct types of accounts of the behavior, each of which revealed different dimensions of the meaning and enactment of running trains. Reading Box 2.3 provides excerpts from several of Dennis's and Toya's interviews with young men.

Comparing these two sets of accounts suggests a variety of ways in which Dennis's and Toya's social positions of similarity and difference with these African American adolescent boys shaped the ways in which they spoke about their participation in running trains. Moreover, the interviewers themselves took different approaches toward the interview exchanges, which are tied to their interviewing techniques, the kinds of information they were most interested in obtaining, and their own positionality vis-à-vis the interviewees.

An especially striking feature of the accounts provided in young men's interviews with Dennis was the adamancy with which boys claimed that girls were willing, even eager participants. Moreover, their descriptions were particularly graphic, focusing specific attention on the details of their sexual performances. Dennis was responded to by the young men as a naïve White male academic who knows little about street life (see also Miller, 2008: 232–234). His foreignness, as evidenced by his Dutch accent, further heightened the young men's perceptions of him as different. Thus, they appear to tell their stories in ways that simultaneously play on what they do have in common—maleness (and thus a perceived shared understanding of women as sexual objects)—and position themselves as particularly successful in their sexual prowess, an exaggerated feature of hegemonic masculinity in distressed urban neighborhoods in the United States (Anderson, 1999) that marks their difference from Dennis.

Notice that these accounts emphasized their sexual performance. In fact, research on gang rape suggests that group processes play a central role. The enactment of such violence increases solidarity and cohesion among groups of young men, and the victim has symbolic status and is treated as an object (Franklin, 2004; Sanday, 1990). Just as performance played a central role in young men's accounts of these incidents, their accounts were themselves a particular sort of masculine performance in the context of their interview exchange with a young, White male researcher far removed from their world on the streets (see also Presser, 2005).

In contrast, when young men were interviewed about their participation in running trains by Toya—the African American female interviewer—two different features emerged. First, they were much less sexually graphic in their accounts. Second, due in part to Toya's interview style and the specific concerns about consent she brought to the interview exchange, her conversations with young men about running trains challenged their attempts to construct the events as consensual. The interview excerpt with Terence in Box 2.3 reveals, for example, that the young woman in this incident arrived at the house of a boy [who] she knew and may have been interested in; waiting on her arrival were four additional young men whom she did not know or know well. And they had come specifically for the purpose of running a train on her. Because Terence's friend said "she was down for it," he either did not consider or discounted the question of whether the young woman may have felt threatened or had not freely consented. Instead, he took his turn and left.

Reading Box 2.3   Young Men's Accounts of Running Trains

INTERVIEW EXCERPTS WITH DENNIS

Lamont: I mean, one be in front, one be in back. You know sometimes, you know like, say, you getting in her ass and she might be sucking the other dude dick. Then you probably get her, you probably get her to suck your dick while he get her in the ass. Or he probably, either I'll watch, and so she sucking your dick, or while you fuck her in the ass. It, I mean, it's a lot of ways you can do it.

Frank: There's this one girl, she a real, real freak. . . . She wanted me and my friend to run a train on her . . . . [Beforehand], we was at the park, hopping and talking about it and everything. I was like, "man, dawg, I ain't hitting her from the back." Like, "she gonna mess up my dick." . . . He like, "Oh, I got her from the back dude." So we went up there . . . [and] she like, "which one you all hitting me from the back?" [I'm] like, "there he go, right there. I got the front." She's like, "okay." And then he took off her clothes, pulled his pants down. I didn't, just unzipped mine 'cause I was getting head. She got to slurping me. I'm like, my partner back there 'cause we was in the dark so I ain't see nuttin.' He was back, I just heared her [making noises]. I'm like, "damn girl, what's wrong with you?" [More noises] [I'm like], "you hitting her from the back?" He's like, "yeah, I'm hitting it."

INTERVIEW EXCERPT WITH TOYA

Terence: It was some girl that my friend had knew for a minute, and he, I guess he just came to her and asked her, "is you gon' do everybody?" or whatever and she said "yeah." So he went first and then, I think my other partna went, then I went, then it was like two other dudes behind me.... It was at [my friend's] crib.

Toya: Were you all like there for a get together or party or something?

Terence: It was specifically for that for real, 'cause he had already let us know that she was gon' do that, so.

Toya: So it was five boys and just her?

Terence: Yeah.

....

Toya: And so he asked her first, and then he told you all to come over that day?

Terence: We had already came over. 'Cause I guess he knew she was already gon' say yeah or whatever. We was already there when she got there.

Toya: Did you know the girl?

Terence: Naw, I ain't know her, know her like for real know her. But I knew her name or whatever. I had seen her before. That was it though.

....

Toya: So when you all got there, she was in the room already?

Terence: Naw, when we got there, she hadn't even got there yet. And when she came, she went in the room with my friend, the one she had already knew. And then after they was in there for a minute, he came out and let us know that she was 'gon, you know, run a train or whatever. So after that, we just went one by one.

Similar inconsistencies were revealed in Tyrell's—see above account, again precisely because of Toya's particular style of probing and concern with issues of consent:

This girl was just like, I ain't even know her, but like I knew her 'cause I had went to work [where she did] last year.... Then my boy, when he started working there, he already had knew her, 'cause he said he had went to a party with her last year. And he was gonna have sex with her then, but . . . [her] grandmamma came home or something, so they ain't get to do it. So one day he was just like, we was all sitting watching this movie [at work] and it was real dark or whatever. And she had come in there or whatever, and he was just talking to her, and he was like, "Let's all go 'head and run a train on you." She was like, "What?" And she started like, "You better go on." Then, like, [he said], "For real, let's go over to my house." And then, you know what I'm saying, she was like, "Naw."

Tyrell explained that later that day, he and his friend were leaving work and saw the girl "walking over there to the bus stop." His friend invited the girl over to his house, and she agreed to go. Tyrell admitted, "I think she liked him," and this was the reason she came over. However, because they had previously introduced the idea of running a train on her, Tyrell and his friend appear to have decided that her consent to go to his house was consent to have a train run on her. The discussion continued:

Toya: "Do you think she really wanted to do it?"
Tyrell: "I can't really say. 'Cause at first she was like laughing and stuff, like, 'Don't!' But we didn't pressure her. I didn't say nothing to her for the rest of the [work] day. I probably talked to her, but I say nothing about like that. And then she just came with us, so I mean, she had to want to."

Thus, in his account, Tyrell maintained his interpretation that the incident was consensual, offering evidence that the fact that he and his friend did not mention running a train on the girl again during the day they spent at work together meant they had not "pressured" her. He did not appear to consider an alternative interpretation—that their silence on the issue allowed the girl to interpret the earlier comments as innocuous. Instead, he insisted that "she knew" (see also King, 2003; Willan and Pollard, 2003).

> Further, Tyrell's account of the young woman's behavior afterwards—which, again, emerged as a result of Toya's continued questioning, also belied his insistence that she had engaged willingly. He explained that "she missed like a week of work after that." And while he believed the girl liked his friend before the incident, he said, "I know she didn't like him after that. . . . She don't even talk to him at all. Every time they see each other they'll argue." In addition, Tyrell said, "She go to my cousin's school now, and she be talking all stuff like, 'I hate your cousin!' "But I don't care, I mean I don't even care. She shouldn't have did that."

Given this evidence, Toya asked whether he thought she felt bad about it, the conversation continued:

> *Tyrell:* "I can't even say. I don't even know her like that. I really can't say. She do that kinda stuff all the time."
>
> *Toya:* "She does?"
>
> *Tyrell:* "No. I'm just saying. I don't know. If she don't she probably did feel bad, but if she do she probably wouldn't feel bad. . . . But if she didn't really wanna do it, she shouldn't have did it."

Notice how Tyrell slipped easily into noting that "she do that kinda stuff all the time," but when pressed, [he] conceded that he had no basis on which to draw such a conclusion.

In part, accounts like Terence's and Tyrell's emerged because they responded to Toya as a young African American woman who had an understanding of life in their neighborhoods. She was marked by similarities where Dennis was marked by difference, except when it came to gender. Young men thus did not portray running trains as graphic sexual exploits that demonstrated their manhood. And the commonalities Toya shared with them allowed her to probe for factual details without evoking a defensive response that closed down communication within the interview.

These differences could be read as support for the position that social distance between researcher and research participant results in suspicion and lack of trust, which affects the process of disclosure (DeVault, 1999; Taylor, Gilligan, & Sullivan, 1995). My reading is somewhat different. While the role that social similarities and differences played in producing these disparate accounts of the same phenomenon is notable, both sets of interviews revealed important insights about the nature and meanings of running trains. Dennis's interviews demonstrated their function as masculine performance. In fact, young men's acts of *telling* Dennis about the events were themselves masculine performances, constructed in response to *whom* they were doing the telling. In contrast, Toya's interviews revealed important evidence of the processes by which young men construct their interpretations of girls' consent and reveal the various ways in which they do so by discounting the points of view of their female victims (see King, 2003).

This example suggests that it is both necessary and useful to pay close attention to how the interview context shapes accounts. Doing so can reveal multifaceted features of behaviors and their meanings, as they emerge in disparate accounts. Moreover, it reveals the benefits for data analysis that can emerge by utilizing diverse research teams, particularly when using this diversity itself as a means of furthering the analysis (see Miller, 2010).

Conclusion

A primary concern of feminist scholars in criminology is to examine, understand, and ameliorate the gender inequalities that shape crime, victimization, and justice practices. In this chapter, my goals were to describe why the use of in-depth interviews is an especially valuable methodological approach for conducting research on these issues and to explain how research that utilizes interview data puts them to use for understanding the relationships between gender, inequality, and crime.

What I find most useful with interview data is the simultaneous access these provide to both social processes—the *who, what, when, where,* and *how* of crime—and the cultural frames that individuals use to make sense of these activities and their social worlds. This makes interview accounts particularly useful for addressing the intellectual double shift I noted earlier: the dual challenge of examining the impact of gender and gender inequality in real life, while simultaneously deconstructing the intertwined ideologies about gender that guide social practices, including the strong tendency to view gender through an individualistic and binary lens.

Drawing on my own research, I have shown some of the ways in which the analysis of interview data can illuminate the impact of gender stratification, gendered practices, and gender ideologies on criminal offending. Key to the success of doing so is ensuring the rigor of one's inductive analyses. This includes, for example, working to ensure that initial data coding begins early in the process and remains open, and further into the project, utilizing techniques such as constant comparative methods and deviant case analyses to strengthen the internal validity of one's findings. Finally, I have illustrated how attention to the social locations of interview participants—researchers and those researched alike—offer important opportunities to advance our understandings.

As a feminist scholar, the relevance of qualitative interview research for studying gender is specific to my particular theoretical goal of "illuminat[ing] gender as central to our understanding of social life" (Lewis, 2007: 274). Nonetheless, my discussion in this chapter has import for a broader criminological audience. It illustrates the unique contributions that qualitative interview research can provide in theorizing about crime and justice by offering a vital window through which to better understand the life, worlds, and experiences of those we study and the social processes and patterns in which they are embedded.

Notes

1. Thus, again note that the title of the book—*One of the Guys*—made direct use of an in vivo code that became central to my analysis.

2. *Wreck* was a slang term used by young women to refer to girls who were seen as sexually promiscuous.

References

Anderson, E. (1999). *Code of the street*. New York: W.W. Norton.

Cameron, D. (1998). "Gender, language, and discourse: A review essay." *Signs 23*: 945–973.

Charmaz, K. (2006). *Constructing grounded theory: A practical guide through qualitative analysis*. Thousand Oaks, CA: Sage.

Connell, R. W. (2002). *Gender*. Cambridge, UK: Polity Press.

Daly, K. (1998). "Gender, crime and criminology." In M. Tonry (ed.), *The handbook of crime and justice* (pp. 85–108). Oxford, UK: Oxford University Press.

Daly, K., and Chesney-Lind, M. (1988). "Feminism and criminology." *Justice Quarterly 5*(4): 497–538.

Daly, K., and Maher, L. (1998). "Crossroads and intersections: Building from feminist critique." In K. Daly & L. Maher (eds.), *Criminology at the crossroads: Feminist readings in crime and justice* (pp. 1–17). Oxford, UK: Oxford University Press.

DeVault, M. L. (1999). *Liberating method: Feminism and social research*. Philadelphia, PA: Temple University Press.

Franklin, K. (2004). "Enacting masculinity: Antigay violence and group rape as participatory theater." *Sexuality Research & Social Policy 1*(2): 25–40.

Giordano, P. (2010). *Legacies of crime: A follow-up of the children of highly delinquent girls and boys*. Cambridge, UK: Cambridge University Press.

Grenz, S. (2005). "Intersections of sex and power in research on prostitution: A female researcher interviewing male heterosexual clients." *Signs 30*: 2092–2113.

Joe, K. A., and Chesney-Lind, M. (1995). "'Just every mother's angel': An analysis of gender and ethnic variations in youth gang membership." *Gender & Society 9*(4): 408–430.

Kandiyoti, D. (1988). "Bargaining with patriarchy." *Gender & Society 2*(3): 274–290.

Kanter, R. M. (1977). "Some effects of proportions of group life: Skewed sex ratios and responses to token women." *American Journal of Sociology 82*(5): 965–990.

King, N. (2003). "Knowing women: Straight men and sexual certainty." *Gender & Society 17*(6): 861–877.

Lauderback, D., Hansen, J., and Waldorf, D. (1992). "'Sisters are doin' it for themselves': A Black female gang in San Francisco." *The Gang Journal 1*(1): 57–70.

Lewis, L. (2007). "Epistemic authority and the gender lens." *The Sociological Review 55*(2): 273–292.

Lofland, J., and Lofland, L. H. (1984). *Analyzing social settings: A guide to qualitative observation and analysis*. Belmont, CA: Wadsworth.

Maher, L. (1997). *Sexed work: Gender, race and resistance in a Brooklyn drug market*. Oxford, UK: Clarendon Press.

Maruna, S. (2001). *Making good*. Washington, DC: American Psychological Association.

Miller, J. (1998). "Up it up: Gender and the accomplishment of street robbery." *Criminology 36*(1): 37–66.

Miller, J. (2001). *One of the guys: Girls, gangs and gender.* New York: Oxford University Press.

Miller, J. (2002). "The strengths and limits of 'doing gender' for understanding street crime." *Theoretical Criminology 6*(4): 433–460.

Miller, J. (2008). *Getting played: African American girls, urban inequality, and gendered violence.* New York: New York University Press.

Miller, J. (2010). "The impact of gender when studying 'Offenders on offending.'" In W. Bernasco and M. Tonry (eds.), *Offenders on offending: Learning about crime from criminals* (pp. 161–183). London, UK: Willan Press.

Miller, J., and Glassner, B. (2004). "The 'inside' and the 'outside': Finding realities in interviews." In D. Silverman (Ed.), *Qualitative Research* (2nd ed., pp. 125–139). London, UK: Sage.

Mullins, C. W., and Wright, R. (2003). "Gender, social networks, and residential burglary." *Criminology 41*(3): 813–840.

Oakley, A. (1981). "Interviewing women: A contradiction in terms." In H. Roberts (ed.), *Doing feminist research* (pp. 30–61). London, UK: Routledge and Kegan Paul.

Orbuch, T. L. (1997). "People's accounts count: The sociology of accounts." *Annual Review of Sociology 23*(1): 455–478.

Presser, L. (2005). "Negotiating power and narrative in research: Implications for feminist methodology." *Signs 30*: 2067–2090.

Risman, B. J. (2004). "Gender as social structure: Theory wrestling with activism." *Gender & Society 18*(4): 429–450.

Sanday, P. R. (1990). *Fraternity gang rape: Sex, brotherhood, and privilege on campus.* New York: New York University Press.

Scott, M. B., and Lyman, S. M. (1968). "Accounts." *American Sociological Review 33*: 46–62.

Silverman, D. (2006). *Interpreting qualitative data: Methods for analyzing talk, text, and interaction.* Thousand Oaks, CA: Sage.

Smith, D. E. (1987). *The everyday world as problematic: A feminist sociology.* Boston, MA: Northeastern University Press.

Song, M., and Parker, D. (1995). "Commonality, difference and the dynamics of disclosure in in-depth interviewing." *Sociology 29*(2): 241–256.

Spradley, J. (1979). *The ethnographic interview.* New York: Holt.

Taylor, J. M., Gilligan, C., and Sullivan, A. M. (1995). *Between voice and silence: Women and girls, race and relationship.* Cambridge, MA: Harvard University Press.

Veroff, J., and DiStefano, A. (2002). "Researching across difference: A reprise." *American Behavioral Scientist 45*(8): 1297–1307.

Willan, V. J., and Pollard, P. (2003). "Likelihood of acquaintance rape as a function of males' sexual expectations, disappointment, and adherence to rape-conducive attitudes." *Journal of Social and Personal Relationships 20*(5): 637–661.

Williams, C. L. (2000). "Preface." *The Annals of the American Academy of Political and Social Science 571*: 8–13.

Wright, R., and Decker, S. H. (1997). *Armed robbers in action: Stick ups and street culture.* Boston, MA: Northeastern University Press.

DISCUSSION QUESTIONS

1. How can feminist research methods provide insight on the role of gender for victims and offenders?

2. How can different coding strategies reveal important issues for feminist research?

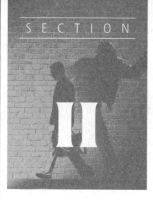

Theories of Victimization

This section is divided into three topics. The section begins with a review of the victim experience in the criminal justice system. This section highlights the experience of help seeking by victims and the practice of victim blaming. The section then turns to a discussion of victimization and focuses on how fear about victimization is a gendered experience. The section concludes with a discussion of victimization and how theories seek to understand the victim experience and place it within the larger context of the criminal justice system and society in general.

Victims and the Criminal Justice System

Why do victims seek out the criminal justice system? Do they desire justice? What does *justice* mean for victims of crime? Is it retribution? Reparation? Something else? Victims play an important role in the criminal justice process—indeed, without a victim, many cases would fail to progress through the system at all. However, many victims who seek out the criminal justice system for support following their victimization are often sadly disappointed in their experiences. In many cases, human victims of crime are reduced to a tool of the justice system or a piece of evidence in a criminal case. As a result, many of these victims express frustration over a system that seems to do little to represent their needs and concerns; victims can even be further traumatized based on their experiences in dealing with the criminal justice system.

As a result of increased pressures to support the needs of victims throughout the criminal justice process, many prosecutors' offices began to establish victim-assistance programs during the mid-1970s to provide support to victims as their cases moved through the criminal justice process. In some jurisdictions, nonprofit agencies for particular crimes, such as domestic violence and rape crisis, also began to provide support for victims during this time (Perona, Bottoms, & Sorenson, 2006; U.S. Department of Justice, 1998). Community agencies such as rape crisis centers developed in response to the perceived need for sexual assault prevention efforts, a desire for increased community awareness, and a wish to ameliorate the pain that the victims of crime often experience (Parsons & Bergin, 2010). In response to a backlash against the rights of criminal defendants as guaranteed by the U.S. Constitution, citizens and legislatures increased their efforts toward establishing rights for victims in the criminal justice process.

In an effort to increase the rights of victims in the criminal justice system, several pieces of federal legislation have passed. These policies increase the voice of victims throughout the process, training for officials who deal with victims and funding programs that provide therapeutic resources for victims. Some of these focus on victims of a specific crime. For example, the Violence Against Women Act provides support for criminal justice researchers studying issues related to intimate partner violence. You'll learn more about this important piece of legislation in Section III. Other examples of federal legislation provide protections for all crime victims, such as the Crime Victim's Rights Act of 2004. While attempts to pass an amendment to the U.S. Constitution on victims' rights have been unsuccessful, each of the 50 states includes references to the rights of victims in criminal cases. Table 2.1 illustrates some of the **core rights of victims** that are included in many state laws and constitutions.

Much of what we know about victims comes from official crime datasets or research studies on samples of victimized populations. A comparison between official crime data (arrest rates) and victimization data indicates that many victims do not report their crime to law enforcement, which affects society's understanding regarding the realities of crime. According to the Bureau of Justice's National Crime Victimization Survey, only about half of all victims surveyed report their victimization to law enforcement (Hart & Rennison, 2003). Victims of serious violent crime are generally more likely to report these crimes compared to property offenses. Robbery was the most likely crime reported (66%), followed by aggravated assault (57%). While women are generally more likely to report crimes to law enforcement than men, cases of personal violence are significantly underreported among female victims (Patterson & Campbell, 2010). For example, the NCVS indicates that only 42% of rapes and sexual assaults are reported, and the Chicago Women's Health Risk Study showed that only 43% of women who experience violent acts from a current or former intimate partner contacted the police (Davies, Block, & Campbell, 2007). Certainly, the relationship between

Table 2.1 Core Rights of Victims

The core rights for victims of crime include

- the right to attend criminal justice proceedings;
- the right to apply for compensation;
- the right to be heard and participate in criminal justice proceedings;
- the right to be informed of proceedings and events in the criminal justice process, of legal rights and remedies, and of available services;
- the right to protection from intimidation and harassment;
- the right to restitution from the offender;
- the right to prompt return of personal property seized as evidence;
- the right to a speedy trial; and
- the right to enforcement of these rights.

SOURCE: From VictimLaw (n.d.).

the victim and offender is a strong predictor in reporting rates, as women who are victimized by someone known to them are less likely to report than women who are victimized by a stranger (Resnick et al., 2000).

There are many reasons why victims might choose not to report their victimization to the police. Some victims feel embarrassed by the crime. Still others may decide not to report a crime to the police out of the belief that nothing could be done. In many cases, people do not report their crime because they believe that the crime was not serious enough to make a big deal over it, while others believe it is a personal matter.

However, a failure to report does not mean that victims do not seek out assistance for issues related to their victimization experience. Several studies on sexual assault and intimate partner violence indicate that victims often seek help from personal resources outside of law enforcement, such as family and friends, and many seek assistance through formal mental health services following a victimization experience (Kaukinen, 2004). While many victims may be reluctant to engage in formal help seeking, research suggests that victims who receive positive support from informal social networks, such as friends and family, are subsequently more likely to seek out formal services, such as law enforcement and therapeutic resources. In these cases, informal networks act as a support system to seek professional help and to make an official crime report (Davies et al., 2007; Starzynski, Ullman, Townsend, Long, & Long, 2007).

▲ Photo 2.1   Much of the victimization that women experience involves offenders known to them. In many cases, their relationship with an offender leads many victims to not report the crime to the police.

©iStock/lofiolo

The literature on barriers to help seeking indicates that fears of retaliation can affect a victim's decision to make a report to the police. This is particularly true for victims of intimate partner violence where research indicates that violence can indeed increase following police intervention in intimate partner violence (Dugan, Nagin, & Rosenfeld, 2003). The presence of children in domestic violence situations also affects reporting rates as many victims may incorrectly believe that they will lose their children as a result of intervention from social service agents.

Victim Blaming

Reporting practices and help-seeking behaviors by victims are also influenced by the potential of **victim blaming**. Victim blaming is the practice whereby the responsibility of the crime is diffused from the offender and blame is shifted to the victim. Researchers on this issue have investigated how victim characteristics can influence this process. For example, if a victim engages in behaviors that place her at increased risk, she might be blamed for contributing to her own victimization. For example, if a woman engaging in street prostitution is robbed by one of her clients, she may be viewed as responsible for placing herself in a dangerous situation.

The presence of victim blaming has been linked to the low reporting rates of crime. Here, victims reach out to law enforcement, community agencies, and family or peer networks in search of support and assistance and are often met with blame and refusals to help. These experiences have a negative effect on the recovery of crime victims.

Consider a high profile case of sexual assault. In situations like these, there can be widespread discussions about victims in the media, including headlines reporting on their mental instability and sexual history. For example, the alleged sexual assault by Kobe Bryant in 2003 at a hotel in Colorado involved significant acts of victim blaming. While most accounts of sexual assault generally use the term *victim*, the media overwhelming used the term *accuser* in this particular case, which underscored the popular belief that either no crime occurred, or it was somehow her fault (Franiuk, Seefelt, Cepress, & Vandello, 2008). In addition to impacting the individual victim in this case, her experience certainly had an effect on other victims of rape and sexual assault. In the year following the Kobe Bryant case, official reports for rape offenses decreased 10%. Rape crisis counselors indicate that the decrease in reporting was directly related to concerns of victim blaming: "I talked to specific survivors (of sexual assault) that said, 'I don't want to report this because I saw what happened in the Kobe Bryant case'" (Lopez, 2007, para. 8).

Victim blaming is not limited to high-profile cases that make news headlines. Victims are often blamed by those closest to them, such as friends and family, who suggest that the victim "should have known better." Victim blaming can even be internalized, leading the victims to blame themselves for their own victimization, and in many cases, shift the responsibility away from the offender.

Secondary Victimization and Victim Blaming

The concept of **secondary victimization** refers to the practice whereby victims of crime feel traumatized as a result of not only their victimization experience but also by the official criminal justice system response to their victimization. For those cases that progress beyond the law enforcement investigative process, few have charges filed by prosecutors, and only rarely is a conviction secured. Indeed, the "ideal" case for the criminal justice system is one that represents stereotypical notions of what rape looks like rather than the realities of this crime. The practice of victim blaming through **rape myth acceptance** is an example of secondary victimization. Given the nature of the criminal justice process, the acceptance of rape myths by jurors can ultimately affect the decision-making process. In an attempt to limit victim blaming in cases of sexual assault, many jurisdictions developed rape shield laws, which are used to limit the types of evidence that can be admitted regarding a victim's background and history (Yeum, 2010). Despite their existence, many of these laws allow for judges to make decisions about when and how these laws will be applied. The experience of secondary victimization indicates that many rape victims would not have reported the crime if they had known what was in store for them (Logan, Evans, Stevenson, & Jordan, 2005).

Why do we blame the victim? The process of victim blaming is linked to a belief in a just world. The concept of a just world posits that society has a need to believe that people deserve whatever comes to them—bad things happen to bad people, and good things happen to good people (Lerner, 1980). Under these assumptions, if a bad thing happens to someone, then that person must be at fault for the victimization because of who he or she is and what he or she does. A just world outlook gives a sense of peace to many individuals. Imagining a world where crime victims must have done something foolish, dangerous, or careless allows members of society to distinguish themselves from this identity of victimhood—"I would never do that, so therefore I must be safe from harm"— and allows individuals to shield themselves from feelings of vulnerability and powerlessness when it comes to potential acts of victimization. There are several negative consequences stemming from this condition: (1) Victim blaming assumes that people are able to change the environment in which they live, (2) victim blaming assumes that only "innocent" victims are true victims, and (3) victim blaming creates a false sense of security about the risks of crime.

Given the nature of victimization patterns in society, few meet the criteria of a culturally ideal victim. This process of victim blaming allows society to diffuse the responsibility of crime between the victim and the offender. For example, the battered woman is asked, "Why do you stay?"; the rape victim is asked, "What were you wearing?"; the assault victim is asked, "Why didn't you fight back?"; the burglary victim is asked, "Why didn't you lock the door?"; and the woman who puts herself in harm's way is asked, "What were you thinking?" Each of these scenarios shifts the blame away from the perpetrator and assigns responsibility to the victim. Victim blaming enables people to make sense of the victimization. In many cases, the process of victim blaming allows people to separate themselves from those who have been victimized—"I would never have put myself in that situation"—and this belief allows people to feel safe in the world.

How does the **just world hypothesis** work, and what are the implications for this application in the criminal justice system? Consider the crime of sexual assault. Under the just world hypothesis, victim blaming occurs in subtle ways in typical cases and may be more obvious in high-profile cases. For example, in the accusations against Kobe Bryant, extensive news reports questioned why the victim entered the hotel room with Mr. Bryant. There was also significant speculation about the victim's sexual activity prior to and following the alleged act with Mr. Bryant. Under the just world hypothesis, the victim begins to assume responsibility for this alleged assault in the eyes of the public. This can impact future reporting trends, as victims may be less likely to report their own victimizations after observing what happened to the victim in the Bryant case. The just world hypothesis may also have an effect on potential offenders as college males who view newspaper articles in support of myths about rape were less likely to view nonconsensual sexual acts as criminal compared to females in general or males who read neutral news accounts of sexual assault (Franiuk et al., 2008).

⊠ Fear of Victimization

The majority of Americans have limited direct experience with the criminal justice system. Most are left with images of crime that are generated by the portrayal of victims and offenders in mass media outlets (Dowler, 2003). These images present a distorted view of the criminal justice system, with a generalized understanding that "if it bleeds, it leads." This leads to the overexaggeration of violent crime in society (Maguire, 1988; Potter & Kappeler, 2006; Surette, 2003). Research indicates that as individuals increase their consumption of local and national television news, their fears about crime increase, regardless of actual crime rates, gender, or a personal history of victimization (Chiricos, Padgett, & Gertz, 2000). In addition to the portrayal of crime within the news, stories of crime, criminals, and criminal justice have been a major staple of television entertainment programming. These images, too, present a distorted view of the reality of crime, as they generally present crime as graphic, random, and violent incidents (Gerbner & Gross, 1980).

Consider the following scenario:

Imagine yourself walking across a parking lot toward your car. It's late and the parking lot is poorly lit. You are alone. Standing near your car is a man who is watching you. Are you afraid?

When this scenario is presented to groups, we find that men and women respond to this situation differently. When asked who is afraid, it is primarily women who raise their hands. Rarely, do men respond to this situation with emotions of fear. This simple illustration demonstrates the **fear of victimization** that women experience in their daily lives. As De Groof (2008) explains, "Fear of crime is, in other words, partly a result of feelings of personal discomfort and uncertainty, which are projected onto the threat of crime and victimization" (p. 281). Indeed, research demonstrates that girls are more likely than boys to indicate fears about victimization in situations that involve things such as poorly lit parking lots and sidewalks, overgrown shrubbery, and groups loitering in public spaces (Fisher & May, 2009).

Gendered socialization is also a powerful tool in explaining why women experience greater levels of fear about victimization. From a young age, girls are often taught about fear, as parents are more likely to demonstrate concern for the safety of their daughters, compared to their sons (De Groof, 2008). This fear results in a relative lack of freedom for girls, in addition to an increase in the parental supervision of girls. These practices, which are designed to protect young women, can significantly affect their confidence levels in regarding the world around them. The worry that parents fear for their daughters continues as they transition from adolescence to adulthood (De Vaus & Wise,

1996). Additionally, this sense of fear can be transferred from the parent to the young female adult as a result of the gendered socialization that she has experienced throughout her life.

Gender also plays a role in feelings of vulnerability, which can translate to fears about victimization. Women are more likely to feel physically vulnerable as a result of their gender and their smaller stature. Age also impacts feelings of physical vulnerability for women (Snedker, 2012). Research indicates that the fear of crime for women is not necessarily related to the actual levels of crime that they personally experience. Overall, women are less likely to be victimized than men, yet they report overall higher levels of fear of crime than their male counterparts (Fattah & Sacco, 1989). These high levels of overall fear of victimization may be perpetuated by a specific fear of crime for women—rape and sexual assault. Indeed, rape is the crime that generates the highest levels of fear for women. These levels of fear are somewhat validated by crime statistics, as women make up the majority of victims for sexually based crimes (Warr, 1984, 1985). However, research indicates that this fear of sexual victimization extends beyond fear of rape to fear of all crimes, not just crimes of a sexual nature. The "shadow of sexual assault" thesis suggests that women experience a greater fear of crime in general, because they believe that any crime could ultimately become a sexually based victimization (Fisher & Sloan, 2003).

For women, fear of victimization is often related to feelings of vulnerability. Research suggests that "a loss of control over the situation and a perceived inadequate capacity to resist the direct and indirect consequences of victimization" can influence women's fears about crime (Cops & Pleysier, 2011, p. 59). Yet even when women engage in measures to keep themselves safe, their fear of sexual assault appears to increase, rather than decrease (Lane, Gover, & Dahod, 2009). This sense of vulnerability is portrayed by "movie of the week" outlets that showcase storylines of women being victimized by a strange man who lurks in dark alleys and behind bushes (Jones-Brown, 2007; Skolnick, 1966). Unfortunately, these popular culture references toward criminal victimization generally (and rape and sexual assault specifically) paint a false picture of the realities of crime and victimization. Most women are victimized not by strangers, as these films would indicate, but instead by people known to them (Black et al., 2011). Indeed, research indicates that many women fail to see *acquaintance rape* as something that could impact them personally (Pryor & Hughes, 2013). While the fear of sexual assault is a common theme in the literature, some scholars indicate that fears about crime can involve acts other than sexual assault. Cook and Fox (2012) found that fear of physical harm is a stronger predictor of fear about crime for women over the fear of sexual assault. Snedker (2012) found similar evidence, as the majority of women in her study expressed fears over being robbed, not raped.

The fear of crime and victimization has several negative consequences. Women who are fearful of crime, particularly violent or sexual crimes, are more likely to isolate themselves from society in general. This fear reflects not only the concern of potential victimization but also a threat regarding the potential loss of control that a victim experiences as a result of being victimized. Fear of crime can also be damaging toward one's feelings of self-worth and self-esteem. Here, potential victims experience feelings of vulnerability and increased anxiety.

The effects of fears of victimization are also reflected in societal actions (Clear & Frost, 2007). For example, public transit agencies may increase security measures, such as the presence of personnel, the use of video cameras in stations, and improving service reliability (Yavuz & Welch, 2010). Fear also impacts policy practices within the criminal justice system. Agents of criminal justice can respond to a community's fear of crime by increasing police patrols, while district attorneys pursue tough-on-crime stances in their prosecution of criminal cases. Politicians respond to community concerns about violent crime by creating and implementing tough-on-crime legislation, such as habitual sentencing laws like "three strikes," and targeting perceived crimes of danger, such as the war on drugs. While the public's concern about crime may be very real, it can also be inflamed by inaccurate data on crime rates or a misunderstanding about the community supervision of offenders and recidivism rates. Unfortunately, "public policy is influenced more by media misinformation and sensationalized high profile cases than by careful or thoughtful analysis" (Frost & Phillips, 2011, p. 88).

⬚ Theories on Victimization

In an effort to understand the victim experience, social science researchers began to investigate the characteristics of crime victims and the response by society to these victims. While criminology focuses predominantly on the study of crime as a social phenomenon and the nature of offenders, the field of victimology places the victim at the center of the discussion. Early perspectives on victimology focused on how victims, either knowingly or unconsciously, can be at fault for their victimization, based on their personal life events and decision-making processes.

One of the early scholars in this field, **Benjamin Mendelsohn** (1956), developed a typology of victimization that distinguished different types of victims based on the relative responsibility of the victims in their own victimization. Embedded in between his typology is the degree to which victims have the power to make decisions that can alter their likelihood of victimization. As a result of his work, the study of victimology began to emerge as its own distinct field of study.

Mendelsohn's theory of victimology is based on six categories of victims. The first category is the innocent victim. This distinction is unique in Mendelsohn's typology, as it is the only classification that does not have any responsibility for the crime attributed to the victim. As the name suggests, an innocent victim is someone who is victimized by a random and unprecipitated crime, such as a school shooting. Unlike the other categories in Mendelsohn's typology, the innocent victim is one with no responsibility in his victimization. In contrast, the other five categories assign a degree of blame or responsibility to the victim. Mendelsohn's second category is the victim with minor guilt. In this case, victimization occurs as a result of one's carelessness or ignorance. The victim with minor guilt is someone who, if she had given better thought or care to her safety, would not have been a victim of a crime. For instance, someone who was in the wrong place at the wrong time or one who places herself in dangerous areas where she is at risk for potential victimization is characterized as a victim with minor guilt. An example of this is a case of a victim who is walking alone down the street in a high-crime area and is robbed. Mendelsohn's third category is a victim who is

Table 2.2 Mendelsohn's Categories of Victims

Category	Definition	Example
Innocent victim	No responsibility for the crime attributed to victim	Institutionalized victims, the mentally ill, children, or those who are attacked while unconscious
Victim with minor guilt	Victim precipitates crime with carelessness/ignorance	Victim lost in the "wrong part of town"
Voluntary victim	Victim and offender equally responsible for crime	Victim pays prostitute for sex; then prostitute robs victim ("rolling Johns")
Victim who is more guilty than the offender	Victim who provokes or induces another to commit crime	Burning bed syndrome: victim is killed by the domestic partner he abused for years
Victim who alone is guilty	Victim who is solely responsible for his or her own victimization	An attacker who is killed in self-defense; suicide bomber killed by detonation of explosives
Imaginary victim	Victim mistakenly believes he or she has been victimized	Mentally ill person who reports imagined victimization as real event

SOURCE: Adapted from Sengstock (1976).

equally as guilty as the offender. This victim is someone who shares the responsibility of the crime with the offender by deliberately placing himself or herself in harm's way. An example of this classification is the individual who seeks out the services of a sex worker, only to contract a sexually transmitted infection as a result of their interaction. The fourth category represents the case whereby the victim is deemed "more guilty" than the offender. This is a "victim" who is provoked by others to engage in criminal activity. An example of this category is one who kills a current or former intimate partner following a history of abuse. The fifth category is a victim who is solely responsible for the harm that comes to him or her. These individuals are considered to be the "most guilty" of victims as they engaged in an act that was likely to lead to injury on their part. Examples of the most guilty victim include a suicide bomber who engages in an act that results in his or her death, or when a would-be attacker is killed by another in an act of self-defense. Mendelsohn's final category is the imaginary victim. This is an individual who, as a result of some mental disease or defect, believes that he or she has been victimized by someone or something, when in reality this person has not been victimized.

While Mendelsohn focused on the influence of guilt and responsibility of victims, **Hans von Hentig's** (1948) typology of victims looked at how personal factors, such as biological, psychological, and social factors, influence risk factors for victimization. The categories in von Hentig's typology of victims include the young, the female, the old, the mentally defective and deranged, immigrants, minorities, dull normals, the depressed, the acquisitive, the wanton, the lonesome or heartbroken, the tormentor, and the blocked, exempted, or fighting.

While the application of von Hentig's theory helped develop an understanding of victims in general, his typology includes only a single category for females. However, experiences of female victimization can fit within each of von Hentig's other categories. For instance, young girls who run away from home are easy targets for pimps who "save" girls from the dangers of the streets and "protect" them from harm. The youth of these girls places them at a higher risk for violence and prostitution activities under the guise of protection. While von Hentig's category of mentally defective was designed to capture the vulnerability of the mentally ill victim, he also referenced the intoxicated individual within this context. Under this category, women who engage in either consensual acts of intoxication, or who are subjected to substances unknown to them, can be at risk for alcohol- or drug-facilitated sexual assault. Likewise, consider von Hentig's category of immigrants and the way in which immigration status can also play a key role for women victims. Many abusers use a woman's illegal immigration status as a threat to ensure compliance. In these cases, women may be forced to endure violence in their lives or are induced into sexual slavery out of fear of deportation. Von Hentig also discusses how race and ethnicity can affect the victim experience, and significant research has demonstrated how these factors affect the criminal justice system at every stage.

CASE STUDY

Spotlight on the Cleveland House of Horrors

On May 6, 2013, three women were rescued from a home in Cleveland, Ohio. Amanda Berry, Georgina "Gina" DeJesus, and Michelle Knight had been held captive by Ariel Castro, a 52-year-old man who had emigrated to the United States as a child from Puerto Rico. Each of the women had accepted a ride from Castro, who then abducted them and forced them into his basement where he kept the girls physically restrained. Michelle Knight was his first victim and was 21 years old when she was taken on August 22, 2002. His next victim, Amanda Berry, disappeared on April 21, 2003, just before her 17th birthday. Finally, Gina DeJesus was abducted on April 2, 2004. She was only 14. All three girls endured significant physical and sexual assaults throughout their captivity. Michelle Knight reported that she suffered several miscarriages, and

Amanda Berry gave birth to a daughter fathered by Castro, born on Christmas Day 2006 (BBC, 2013). After a decade in hell, the women were rescued after garnering the attention of a neighbor, who helped them escape (Steer, 2013).

While the prosecutors originally considered charging Castro with aggravated murder (in the cases of the forced miscarriages of Knight), he ultimately pled guilty to 937 counts of kidnapping, rape, and other crimes such as child endangerment and gross sexual imposition (Krouse, 2013; Mahoney, 2013; Sheeran, 2013). In speaking at his sentencing hearing, Michelle Knight told Castro, "I spent 11 years in hell, where your hell is just beginning" (DeLuca, 2013). However, Castro served very little of his sentence before he hung himself by a bedsheet in his cell. Some might argue that Castro's suicide cheats the

© Aaron Josefczyk/Reuters/Corbis

▲ Photo 2.2   Amanda Berry reads her victim impact statement during the sentencing hearing for Ariel Castro. Castro was convicted on several counts of kidnapping and rape against Berry and her two co-victims.

justice system—"This man couldn't take, for even a month, a small portion of what he had dished out for more than a decade" (Mungin & Alsup, 2013).

While the victims in this case focus on moving on and rebuilding their lives following this tragedy, Ohio is trying to find ways to provide support to Berry, DeJesus, and Knight, as well as other victims of similar tragedies that may occur in the future. In October 2013, a victim's reparations bill (designed with Castro's victims in mind) passed initial review. The bill would target victims who were held in involuntary servitude for at least eight years and provide compensation of $25,000 for each year that they were held in captivity, as well as free tuition, medical care, and living expenses at a state university. The bill is currently being considered by the Ohio State House of Representatives (Connor, 2013). In addition, the local community has demolished the home once owned by Castro where the three women were held after Castro signed over the deed as part of his plea bargain. The local community hopes that the lot will be used to develop a healing garden or some other peaceful space (Lindgren, Stanglin, & Alcindor, 2013).

Routine Activities Theory

While early theories of victimization provided a foundation to understand the victim experience, modern victimization theories expand from these concepts to investigate the role of society on victimization and to address how personal choices affect the victim experience. One of the most influential perspectives in modern victimology is Cohen and Felson's (1979) **routine activities theory**. Routine activities theory suggests that the likelihood of a criminal act (and in turn, the likelihood of victimization) occurs with the convergence of three essential components: (1) someone who is interested in pursuing a criminal action (offender), (2) a potential victim (target) "available" to be victimized, and (3) the absence of someone or something (guardian) that would deter the offender from making contact with the available victim. The name of the theory is derived from a belief that victims and guardians exist within the normal, everyday patterns of life. Cohen and Felson posit that lifestyle changes during the second half of the 20th century created additional opportunities for the victim and offender to come into contact with each other as a result of changes to daily routines and activities. Cohen and Felson's theory was created to discuss the risk of victimization in property crimes. Here, if individuals were at work, or out enjoying events in the community, they were less likely to be at home to guard their property against potential victimization, and burglary was more likely to result.

Routine activities theory has been used to understand a variety of different forms of crime, particularly related to demographic differences in victimization. Research by Navarro and Jasinski (2013) indicates that girls are at a greater risk for cyber-bullying than boys, even though boys engage in similar risky online behaviors. Meanwhile, minority women are more likely to experience risk of victimization when riding public transportation, and neighborhood factors can affect the odds of women's victimization (Like-Haislip & Miofsky, 2011). Finally, while men are more likely to experience increased risks of violent victimization because they go out at night, women have an increased risk of theft based on increased shopping activities (Bunch, Clay-Warner, & Lei, 2012).

Routine activities theory has been criticized by feminist criminologists, who disagree with the theory's original premise that men are more vulnerable to the risks of victimization than women. Indeed, the guardians that Cohen and Felson suggest protect victims from crime may instead be the ones most likely to victimize women, particularly in cases of intimate partner abuse and sexual assault. For example, research by Schwartz, DeKeseredy, Tait, and Alvi (2001) indicates that women who engage in recreational substance use (such as alcohol or drugs) are considered to be a suitable target by men who are motivated to engage in certain offending patterns. Attempts by administrators to increase safety on college campuses by implementing protections, such as escort patrols, lighted paths, and emergency beacons (modern-day guardians), may have little effect on sexual assault rates on campus, given that many of these incidents take place behind closed doors in college dormitories and student apartments. In addition, the concept of self-protective factors (or self-guardians) may not be able to ward off a potential attacker, given that the overwhelming majority of sexual assaults on college campuses are perpetrated by someone known to the victim (Mustaine & Tewksbury, 2002). In addition, perceptions of being a "good" girl can also lead women to believe they are at a reduced risk for victimization. "I'm not running around in tiny little dresses anymore" (Snedker, 2012, p. 86). Another woman expressed a similar sentiment of recognizing potential risks of victimization based on her patterns of behavior: "I'm not going to do anything stupid. If I'm coming home really late drunk and I'm by myself, I might be more of a target" (Snedker, 2012, p. 89). This scenario highlights the perception that a shift in routine activities can reduce the risk of victimization. Unfortunately, this adds to the myth that girls who dress provocatively or consume alcohol somehow deserve to be sexually assaulted, which shifts the blame to the victim and not the perpetrator.

Like routine activities theory, **lifestyle theory** seeks to relate the patterns of one's everyday activities to the potential for victimization. While routine activities theory was initially designed to explain victimization from property crimes, lifestyle theory was developed to explore the risks of victimization from personal crimes. Research by Hindelang, Gottfredson, and Garafalo (1978) suggests that people who engage in risky lifestyle choices place themselves at risk for victimization. Based on one's lifestyle, one may increase the risk for criminal opportunity and victimization through both an increased exposure to criminal activity and an increased exposure to motivated offenders. However, crime is not the only lifestyle that can place people at risk for victimization, as nonviolent deviant behaviors, mental health status, and substance use can place people at potential victimization. Gender also plays a role in how these factors influence victimization risk. For example, males who engage in binge drinking have an increased risk of victimization while females who abuse prescription drugs experience significantly higher odds of victimization (Zaykowski & Gunter, 2013).

Given the similarities between the foundations of lifestyle theory and routine activities theory, many researchers today combine the tenets of these two perspectives to investigate victimization risks in general. These perspectives have been used to explain the risks of sexual assault of women on college campuses. For example, young women in the university setting who engage in risky lifestyle decision-making processes (such as the use of alcohol) and have routine activity patterns (such as living alone or frequenting establishments such as bars and clubs where men are present and alcohol is readily available) are at an increased risk for sexual victimization. In addition, women who are at risk for a single incident remain at risk for recurrent victimizations if their behavior patterns remain the same (Fisher, Daigle, & Cullen, 2010).

Feminist Pathways Perspective

Feminist pathways perspective research draws upon the historical context of women's and girls' lives to relate how events (and traumas) affect their likelihood to engage in crime. Researchers have identified a cycle of violence for female offenders that often begins with their own victimization and results with their involvement in offending behavior. While the pathways perspective is discussed at length in Section VI, the topic deserves a brief introduction as we conclude our discussion on theories of victimization.

The feminist pathways approach may provide some of the best understanding about female offending. Research on women's and girls' pathways to offending provide substantial evidence for the link between victimization and offending, as incarcerated girls are three to four times more likely to have been abused compared to their male counterparts (Belknap & Holsinger, 2006). A review of case files of delinquent girls in California indicates that 92% of delinquent girls in California reported having been subjected to at least one form of abuse, including emotional (88%), physical (81%), or sexual (56%) abuse (Acoca & Dedel, 1998b). Particularly for young female offenders, a history of abuse leads to a propensity to engage in certain types of delinquency, such as running away and school failures. The effects of sexual assault are also related to drug and alcohol addiction and mental health traumas, such as post-traumatic stress disorder and a negative self-identity (Raphael, 2005). In a **cycle of victimization and offending**, young girls often run away from home in an attempt to escape from an abusive situation. In many cases, girls were forced to return home by public agencies, such as the police, courts, and social services—agencies designed to "help" victims of abuse. Unfortunately, in their attempt to escape from an abusive situation, girls often fall into criminal behaviors as a mechanism of survival.

Indeed, there are several ways to think about the victimization of women and girls. As you move through the next three sections in this text, consider how each of these theoretical perspectives impact the victim experience for women and how the criminal justice system responds to these cases. How would you improve the experience of women as victims? What police recommendations would you recommend to agents of criminal justice? Finally, what remedies exist to limit the victimization of women, and what can you as a member of society do to affect change in this realm?

⬦ Summary

- Not all victims report their crimes to the police but may seek out support from other sources.
- Victim-assistance programs have emerged as a key response to the secondary victimization often experienced by victims who come forward to the criminal justice system.
- Victim blaming has been linked to low reporting rates.
- Women experience higher rates of fear of crime compared to males.
- Gendered socialization and vulnerability to specific crime types such as rape may explain the gendered fear of crime.
- Mendelsohn's typology of victimization distinguishes different categories of victims based on the responsibility of the victim and the degree to which victims have the power to make decisions that can alter their likelihood of victimization.
- Von Hentig's typology of victimization focuses on how personal factors, such as biological, social, and psychological characteristics, influence risk factors for victimization.

- The just world hypothesis, which holds that people get what they deserve, is a form of victim blaming.
- Routine activities theory and lifestyle theory have been used to investigate the risk of sexual assault of women.
- The pathways perspective suggests a cycle of criminal justice involvement for women whereby early victimization is sometimes a precursor to later criminal offending.

KEY TERMS

Core rights of victims	Just world hypothesis	Routine activities theory
Cycle of victimization and offending	Lifestyle theory	Secondary victimization
Fear of victimization	Mendelsohn, Benjamin	Victim blaming
Feminist pathways perspective	Rape myth acceptance	von Hentig, Hans

DISCUSSION QUESTIONS

1. How do early theories of victimization distinguish between different types of victims? How might the criminal justice system use these typologies in making decisions about which cases to pursue?

2. What type of help-seeking behaviors do female crime victims engage in? How are these practices related to the reporting of crimes to law enforcement?

3. What effects does the practice of victim blaming have for future potential crime victims and the criminal justice system?

4. In what ways do media outlets support or dispel rape myths and victim blaming? How is this related to help-seeking behavior, official reporting, and revictimization?

5. How is fear of crime a gendered experience? What factors contribute to the differences in male versus female fear of crime? Do official crime statistics support or dispel the basis for these fear differences?

6. How might feminist criminologists critique modern-day victimization theories, such as routine activities theory and lifestyle theory?

7. How have historical theories on female offending failed to understand the nature of female offending?

8. What contributions has feminist criminology made in understanding the relationship between gender and offending?

WEB RESOURCES

Bureau of Justice Statistics: http://bjs.ojp.usdoj.gov

The National Center for Victims of Crime: http://www.ncvc.org

Office of Victims of Crime: http://www.ojp.usdoj.gov/

Feminist Criminology: http://fcx.sagepub.com

Visit **www.sagepub.com/mallicoat2e** to access additional study tools including eFlashcards, web quizzes, web resources, video resources, and SAGE journal articles.

READING 3

In the chapter, you learned that many of the fears of crime are gendered. Women experience different levels of fear about crime than men do. This reading highlights how gender impacts how someone experiences fear about being victimized on a college campus for certain types of crimes but that no differences exist between males and females for other types of crimes. In addition, the authors expose what factors lead to increased levels of fear for both men and women.

—— College Students' Crime-Related Fears on Campus ——

Are Fear-Provoking Cues Gendered?

Bonnie S. Fisher and David May

The notion that gender plays a central role in determining crime-related fear levels is so tightly woven into thinking about fear that it is by and large no longer subject to question. Decades of empirical scrutiny by sociologists, victimologists, psychologists, planners, and geographers have established that there are gender-based differences in fear levels across crime types and in certain types of environments, such as public places (Day, 1994; Fisher & Sloan, 2003; Klodawsky & Lundy, 1994; Lane & Meeker, 2003; May, 2001a; Nasar & Fisher, 1993; Reid & Konrad, 2004).

Despite these widely accepted gendered findings, much of the crime-related research has focused almost exclusively on why women are fearful (Madriz, 1997; Pain, 1997; Starkweather, 2007). A small, but growing, number of researchers have turned their attention to men as victims of fear and why they are fearful (Brownlow, 2005; Day, Stump, & Carreon, 2003). Only recently, a few comparative research pieces have been published that identify and explain which factors, if any, differentiate crime-related fear between women and men (Lane & Meeker, 2003; May,

2001b; May & Dunaway, 2000; May, Vartanian, & Virgo, 2002; Reid & Konrad, 2004; Schafer, Huebner, & Bynum, 2006; Smith & Torstenson, 1997; Wallace & May, 2005).

Despite researchers' efforts and explanations, gaps in understanding the relationship between fear-provoking cues and subsequent fear of crime are evident. The current research takes several important steps in a long overdue effort to close the gaps about what is known about which, if any, fear-provoking cues differ across gender and which ones, if any, influence males' and females' fear of specific types of crime. We employ survey data from a large sample of undergraduate students at a 4-year public university to address three research questions about the possible gendered nature of cues and crime-related fear that have not been previously addressed. First, are fear-provoking cues gendered? Simply stated, do males and females evaluate cues known to provoke fear of crime the same way or differently? Second, which of these cues, if any, predict males' and females' fear of specific types of crimes? That is, are fear-provoking cues offense specific? For example, do

SOURCE: Fisher, B. S., & May, D. (2009). College students' crime-related fears on campus: Are fear-provoking cues gendered? *Journal of Contemporary Criminal Justice*, 25(3), 300–321.

AUTHORS' NOTE: This study was supported by a research grant awarded to Professor David May from the College of Justice and Safety Research Committee at Eastern Kentucky University in 2007. The opinions expressed in this article do not represent those of Eastern Kentucky University; they are the authors' opinions.

certain fear-provoking cues predict fear of theft but not fear of violent crime? Third, do these cues equally predict specific crime-related fear across males and females? Simply put, do fear-provoking cues equally predict the same types of fear for males and females alike? Addressing these questions is among the first attempts to enhance our understanding about whether the relationship between fear-provoking cues and crime-related fears is a gendered one among college students while on campus.

Cognitive Mapping and Fear-Provoking Cues

From an evolutionary perspective, individuals use a cognitive map as an efficient mechanism for managing spatial and temporal information about the physical and social nature of their environment to guide behavioral decisions (Kitchin, 1996). Cognitive maps are important to individuals' safety; they protect people from harm. Environmental psychologists have suggested that these maps give individuals "a selective advantage in a difficult and dangerous world that is necessary for survival" (Kitchin, 1994, p. 2). Sighted individuals scan their immediate environment for cues of danger, physical threat, or harm that would make themselves, others, or their property vulnerable to attack. Merry (1981, pp. 11–12) described this process when she explained,

> [C]ues are structured into spatial, temporal, and personal cognitive maps that define places, times, and categories of persons who are likely to be safe or dangerous. The decision that a situation is (is not) dangerous depends on the intersection of these maps. To understand fear of crime, it is much less useful to ask how afraid an individual feels than it is to explore the content of his or her cognitive maps and the frequency with which he or she encounters situations these maps define as dangerous.

Ultimately, these cognitive maps shape an individual's sense of potential criminal victimization, and it is from these maps that individuals draw inferences about their fear levels. Van der Wurff, Van Staalduinen, and Stringer (1989, p. 145) noted that as individuals venture into a specific place, they immediately heed the "criminalizability" of that space.

Given the gendered focus of this article, the nexus between cognitive maps and crime-related fear gives rise to an issue directed at possible differences between males and females in their perceptions of fear-provoking cues. At the core of this issue are three quite simple, yet unanswered, questions: (a) Do males and females differ with respect to their assessment of fear-provoking cues? (b) Do the same or different fear-provoking cues predict fear of different types of crimes, namely, property and violent ones? (c) Are these fear-provoking cues the same for males and females? The answers to these questions, however, are not so obvious.

Fear-Provoking Cues

There is ample evidence cutting across a variety of academic disciplines that supports a significant association between specific features of the immediate physical environment and crime-related fear (Brownlow, 2005; Fisher & Nasar, 1992; Merry, 1981; Nasar & Fisher, 1993; Warr, 1990, 2000). However, the findings from fear-provoking cues research suggest that there is not one cue that influences fear but rather a constellation of cues that include specific features of the physical environment from the presence of others to the visibility of police officers whose duty is to provide surveillance and protection.

Are the Cues That Predict Crime-Related Fear Gendered?

As we have discussed, cognitive maps are helpful in understanding how sighted individuals assess their fear of crime level. The growing body of research on fear-provoking cues also provides insights into what cues influence individuals' fear of crime. Bringing these bodies of research together raises issues as to whether the cues that predict crime-related fear are gendered. For example, does poor lighting influence fear of crime for both males and females, or does poor lighting influence only females' fear of crime? Does police presence predict males and females being fearful or predict only males being fearful?

It is somewhat surprising that researchers have largely neglected the integration of these bodies of research to examine if the relationship between cues and crime-related fear are similar or different across males and females. In part, the lack of attention may lie in the fact that researchers' focus has primarily highlighted females' experiences of crime-related fear (Madriz, 1997; Pain, 1997; Starkweather, 2007; for exception see Brownlow, 2005; Day et al., 2003; Lane & Meeker, 2003; May, 2001b; May & Dunaway, 2000).

Among the very few published studies to offer some guidance into addressing our gendered-based questions about the fear-provoking cues relationship is Brownlow's (2005) study of fear among young men and women in Philadelphia's Cobb Creek Park. From the focus group discussions with these youth and their rating of slides from the park, he concluded that "clear differences distinguish how the young men and women of the study negotiated their fears in public spaces" (p. 589). He reported that unlike their female counterparts, males do not judge an environment as safe based on the presence or absence of environmental cues. Brownlow found that males judge an environment based on their sense and perceptions of their negotiation of an environment, namely, whether they see themselves as being able to flee a risky or uncertain situation. Males consider their youth, physical strength, and speed to be a key in managing dangerous situations. These results suggest that environmental cues to crime-related fear differ across sexes. His conclusions provide starting points to unpacking the gendered nature, if it exists, of cues predicting students' crime-related fear while on campus.

Lighting and Gender

Previous research has reported that lighting affects sighted individuals' ability to see a potentially dangerous environment. Research has also shown that lighting is a significant correlate and predictor of fear of crime, in part, because poor lighting does not offer adequate illumination to observe environmental cues to danger such as being physically attacked or having property stolen. Poor lighting in certain areas such as parking garages that have a perceptional tendency to be isolated may

have more pronounced effects on predicting fear than poor lighting in more public spaces, such as sidewalks. Regardless of the exact place of the lighting, poor lighting on campus might have different effects on whether males and females are fearful. In line with Brownlow's conclusions, we would expect that poor lighting might influence whether females' are fearful but not whether male counterparts are fearful. Research has shown that most females are physically and sexually vulnerable to attack and are physically challenged to thwart off such an attack. Most males, however, would have physical strength and ability to thwart off such an attack, but in line with Brownlow's work, if they cannot see how to escape when confronted, this situation might make them fearful. So poor lighting might equally influence both sexes' fearfulness.

Foliage and Gender

Researchers have shown that foliage influences individuals' fear of crime because it provides refuge or hiding places for a predator who can surprise attack a victim or even walk from inside or behind the greenery. On one hand, foliage, such as overgrown shrubbery, might have a positive effect on fear for women because of their sexual and physical vulnerability and physical inability to thwart an attack. Overgrown foliage on campus might not influence males' fear because of their physical confidence to thwart attack but could also present an element of confrontation that might heighten their fear. Hence, the effect of foliage on crime-related fear may be the same for males and females.

Youth Loitering and Gender

The presence of others, especially youth, congregating or loitering has been shown to heighten fear of victimization. Researchers attribute the elevated fear in these types of situations to individuals' perceiving a breakdown in social control, suggesting that if confronted by these youth, the infraction would go unchallenged by others. Much research has shown that this cue results in a lack of a sense of social control in that others may not effectively respond to the situation at hand (Skogan, 1990; Warr, 2000). For males, this might be especially so in light of research that shows that for many men, the public places and situations that challenged their gender identity, in particular their masculinity, generated fear (Day et al., 2003). Supportive of Day et al.'s (2003) results are those reported by Brownlow (2005), who reported that males felt less safety and security in situations where they lack the ability to flee a risky or uncertain situation. Groups loitering around campus may well predict males' fear but not females' fear. Another plausible speculation is that both sexes might sense a lack of social control in this situation in that others may not effectively respond to the situation at hand or that they would be unable to escape attack since they are outnumbered. The fear that confrontation would increase risk of being victimized might loom equally for both sexes.

Police Visibility and Gender

The relationship between police visibility and fear of crime for the sexes is less clear. The relationship appears to be contingent on the type of activities the police are engaged in during the time they are visible. As such, it is quite possible that the impact of police visibility on fear of crime will vary by gender as well. Increased visibility of police might reduce fear of crime among women because of their vulnerabilities discussed above yet may have no effect on male fear because they lack those same vulnerabilities.

Drawing from the research examining cognitive mapping, fear-provoking cues, and fear of crime, it is plausible that fear-provoking cues have different effects on whether or not males and females are fearful of being victimized. But it may be equally likely that there are no cues that significantly predict whether males and females are fearful, and hence, there are no fear-provoking cue differences predicting fear across the sexes. Because we are not certain whether cues that predict crime-related fear are gendered or not, we turn to our empirical analyses to explore this overlooked relationship.

⧖ Method

Data Collection

In March 2008, we asked for and received a list of all the general education courses offered during the current spring term on campus at a large public institution in the South. We randomly selected 25 of those courses and e-mailed each professor who was listed as the instructor for the course, requesting permission to administer the survey at one of his or her class meetings.

At the mutually agreed on time, a research team member visited the classroom and read a protocol that (a) described the process through which their course was selected, (b) asked the students for their cooperation, (c) assured them that their responses were voluntary and anonymous, (d) asked for their assistance with the data collection effort, and (e) advised them that if they had already completed the survey, to inform the research team member. The surveys were then distributed to the students, who took approximately 10 minutes to complete them.

Across the 24 participating courses, there were 904 students enrolled on February 17, 2008, the day the sample was randomly selected. None of the classes that we visited had the same number of students in attendance as were enrolled for that course; as such, data from students not attending were not obtained. In addition, a small number of students (approximately 2% of those contacted) were registered for more than one of the 24 classes we visited and thus completed the survey only in the first course we visited. Furthermore, eight students either declined to participate or submitted a blank survey at the end of the data collection period. Finally, one student indicated that [he was] a graduate student; this person was subsequently deleted prior to data analysis to ensure that only undergraduate students had participated in the study. Our final sample consisted of 607 students, resulting in a response rate of 67.1%.

Dependent Variables

The dependent variable is fear of criminal victimization while on campus. We included a number of questions that asked the student about being afraid of being a victim of different types of crime while on campus. Students were asked to indicate their level of agreement on a 4-point Likert-type scale with the following statements:

While on campus at (name of school):

I am afraid of being attacked by someone with a weapon.

I am afraid of having my money or possessions taken from me.

I am afraid of being beaten up.

I am afraid of being sexually assaulted.

For the purpose of this study, the first item will serve as an indicator of fear of aggravated assault, followed by fear of larceny-theft, fear of simple assault, and fear of sexual assault.

In the original instrument, students were asked to indicate the relative strength with which they agreed with the above statements (e.g., *strongly agree, somewhat agree, somewhat disagree, strongly disagree*). With the exception of one variable (fear of larceny-theft, where 7% strongly agreed), less than 5% of the respondents strongly agreed that they were fearful of that situation. As such, we created a dichotomous measure of each of the four types of fear, with those who strongly agreed or agreed that they were *fearful* coded as 1 and those who *strongly disagreed* or *disagreed* coded as 0.

Independent Variables

The survey data allowed us a unique opportunity to examine the relationship between different fear-provoking cues and types of fear of victimization because included in the survey were five cue-specific fear-of-crime measures. Students were asked to indicate their level of agreement on a 4-point Likert-type scale with the following:

Since the beginning of this school year, I have been fearful of crime victimization on campus because of . . .

poorly lit parking lots

poorly lit sidewalks and common areas

overgrown or excess shrubbery

groups congregating or loitering

visibility of public safety officials

In the original question, students were asked to indicate the relative strength with which they agreed with the above statements (e.g., *strongly agree, somewhat agree, somewhat disagree, strongly disagree*). Due to the skewed nature of the distribution of each variable, we created a dichotomous variable from each of the five cue-specific fear-of-crime measures, with those who *strongly agreed* or *agreed* that they were fearful coded as 1 and those who *strongly disagreed* or *disagreed* were coded as 0.

Each of these cue-specific variables measures a different factor that past research has found to be associated with high levels of fear of crime. The two poor-lighting variables measure students' ability to see if a threatening or dangerous situation is in view (e.g., to observe if predator is close). The overgrown or excess shrubbery variable captures the notion of possible hiding places for would-be offenders. Groups congregating or loitering is an indication of some level of social incivility that could create an impression about the concentration of possible motivated offenders. Visibility of public safety officials is a measure of police presence that provides formal guardianship.

Control Variables

Two sets of control variables were used in our analyses. First, due to their association with fear of criminal victimization reported in the past research, we also included measures of age, student's current academic classification (freshman, sophomore, junior, and senior), course load status (full- or part-time student), and residence status (on or off-campus). Summary statistics for the control variables are presented in Reading Table 3.1.

The results presented in Reading Table 3.1 show that over half (55.9%) of the sample were females. Almost two in three were freshmen or sophomores (66.1%), freshmen being the largest academic group across all categories (37.1%). Most were full-time students (96.4%) and were between the ages of 18 and 24 (86.9%), with the mean age of the sample being nearly 21 (20.88) years of age. Approximately half of the respondents lived on campus (52.6%).

Given that the emphasis of this research is on gender differences in fear of criminal victimization, we examined how the distribution on the aforementioned variables varied by sex. These results, presented in Reading Table 3.1, demonstrate that the distribution of student classification ($p = .002$) and residence status ($p = .078$) were significantly different between females and males.

Second, given previous research, the importance of perceived risk of victimization as a significant predictor of fear of crime cannot be overlooked in any analysis. In light

Reading Table 3.1   Sample Characteristics (N = 607)

Characteristic	Total Sample % (n)	Sex Females % (n)	Males % (n)	p Value
Sex				
Female	55.9 (335)			
Male	44.1 (264)			
Current academic classification				
Freshman	37.1 (221)	43.8 (145)	28.8 (76)	.002
Sophomore	29.0 (173)	26.3 (87)	32.6 (86)	
Junior	20.1 (120)	16.3 (54)	24.6 (65)	
Senior	13.8 (82)	13.6 (45)	14.0 (37)	
Type of student				
Traditional[a]	87.1 (520)	88.9 (296)	84.8 (223)	.145
Nontraditional/exchange	12.9 (77)	11.1 (37)	15.2 (40)	
Current course load				
Full time	96.4 (563)	96.0 (313)	96.9 (249)	.145
Part time	3.6 (21)	4.0 (13)	3.1 (8)	
Residence status				
On campus[b]	52.6 (314)	56.0 (187)	48.5 (127)	.078
Off campus	47.4 (283)	44.0 (147)	51.5 (135)	
	M (SD)	*M (SD)*	*M (SD)*	
Age in years	20.88 (4.53)	20.75 (4.90)	21.06 (3.98)	.418
Perceived risk				
Larceny-theft	4.58 (2.76)	4.86 (2.84)	4.22 (2.58)	.005
Aggravated assault	2.52 (1.90)	2.81 (1.98)	2.13 (1.67)	.000
Simple assault	2.86 (2.03)	3.29 (2.12)	2.26 (1.67)	.000
Sexual assault	2.44 (2.10)	3.13 (2.24)	1.55 (1.48)	.000

[a] Traditional students are those who are between the ages of 18 and 24 years old. Nontraditional students are those 25 years and older. Less than 1% (0.5%, n = 3) of the sample are exchange students.

[b] On campus includes on-campus dormitories (50.9%, n = 304) and on-campus apartments and family housing (1.7%, n = 10).

of the consistent positive effect of perceived risk on fear of crime, we included perceived risk as a control variable. Perceived risk of victimization was defined as the chance that a specific type of crime would happen to the student while on campus during the coming year. Students were asked to rate their perceived risk of specific types of crime on a 10-point scale from 1 meaning that *it is not at all likely to happen* to 10 meaning *it is very likely to happen.*

Perceived risk of four specific types of crimes was used as control variables: larceny-theft and aggravated, simple, and sexual assault. Each specific type risk was used as a control variable for the specific type of fear. For example, perceived risk of larceny-theft was used as a control variable only for predicting fear of larceny-theft.

Much of the past research has shown that females, in particular college women, have higher perceived risk of different types of victimization from males (Fisher & Sloan, 2003; see May, 2001a, for review; for exception, see Lane and Meeker, 2003). As shown in Reading Table 3.1, our student sample follows this previously reported college student risk pattern reported by Fisher and Sloan (2003): females reported being more at risk of victimization than males. In other words, females' perceived risk mean for each type of crime was significantly higher than the respective males' mean.

✖ Results

Are Fears of Criminal Victimization-Provoking Cues Gendered?

The first step in examining whether fear-provoking cues are gendered was to explore the proportion of females and males who reported that a specific cue provoked their fear of victimization while on campus. As presented in Reading Table 3.2, at first glance it appears that fear-provoking cues might be gendered. There are statistically significant differences in the proportion of female students who agreed that specific cues provoked fear of crime victimization while on campus when compared to their male counterparts. For example, 65% of females reported that poorly lit parking lots provoked their on-campus fear of victimization compared to 34% of males, a 30 percentage point difference. About a third of females (32%) reported that overgrown or excessive shrubbery provoked their fear, whereas 19% of males reported feeling fear, a 13 percentage point difference.

These results, however, may be a bit misleading since research has consistently shown that females in general are more fearful than males, and our sample also shows this pattern as female students are more fearful than males for each of our four crime-related fears (larceny-theft, aggravated assault, simple assault, and sexual assault).

Another way to examine these fear-provoking cues results is to look at the ordering of the cues between females and males by rank ordering females' and males' proportion from largest proportion agreeing that the cue provoked them to be fearful of victimization while on campus to smallest proportion who agreed. From this lens, the rank ordering can be seen as an indicator of the relative magnitude of the order of fear-provoking cues between females and males from largest to smallest percentage agreeing. As can be seen in Reading Table 3.2, the Spearman's rank order correlation of their ranking is quite strong, but it is not statistically significant ($p = .19$). There appears to be no significant difference between females and males in the rank ordering of the fear-provoking cues, suggesting that these cues do not vary by gender in their ranking and, therefore, might not be gendered.

Are the Cues That Predict Crime-Related Fear Gendered?

The second step of our analyses examined which cues, if any, predict crime-related fear for females and males and which cues, if any, are different across female and male students. Findings from Reading Table 3.3 indicate that different fear-provoking cues are evident for females and males. Across fear of larceny-theft, aggravated assault, simple assault, and sexual assault, the visibility of public safety officials increased females' fearfulness. Overgrown or excessive shrubbery also increased women's fearfulness of larceny-theft and aggravated and sexual assault. Poor lighting on sidewalks and common areas also increased their fear of larceny-theft and aggravated assault. Groups loitering only increased females' fear of simple assault. Poorly lit parking lots did not predict fearfulness of any type of crime for females. For males, only two cues were significant predictors of fearfulness. Overgrown or excessive shrubbery increased their fear of aggravated assault. Groups congregating or loitering increased their fearfulness of larceny-theft.

Turning to possible gendered effects of cues on crime-related fear, the results from the equality of coefficients test indicate that none of the cues had significantly different effects across females and males. None of the fear-provoking cues had a stronger effect for either sex compared to the other, thus, suggesting that fear-provoking cues are not gendered.

Reading Table 3.2   Type of Fear-Provoking Cue by Sex of Respondent

| Type of Cue | Proportion Agreeing Cue Provoked Them to Be Fearful of Victimization While on Campus | | | | |
| | Females | Males | Proportions Test | Rank Order | |
	% (n)	% (n)	z Score (p Value)	Females	Males
Poorly lit parking lots	64.5 (213)	34.0 (88)	7.37 (.000)	1	2
Poorly lit sidewalks and common areas	62.1 (205)	30.4 (79)	7.66 (.000)	2	3
Groups congregating or loitering	53.0 (175)	37.2 (97)	3.84 (.0001)	3	1
Visibility of public safety officials	35.0 (114)	22.7 (58)	3.24 (.0001)	4	4
Overgrown or excessive shrubbery	32.1 (105)	18.9 (49)	3.63 (.0003)	5	5

Spearman's rank order correlation = .70, p = .19.

Discussion

Among the major goals of this exploratory study was to begin to close the gaps about what is known about fear-provoking cues among females and males and to examine if these cues were gendered. To these ends, the results reported are among the first steps to unpacking the relationship among different fear-provoking cues and crime-related offense specific fear among females and males and provide informative findings for future research.

The wide range in proportions (19%–65%) of both females and males who indicated that specific cues provoked them to be fearful of criminal victimization while on campus gives credence to the past research findings that individuals see and distinguish cues in their immediate environment as fear generating. Interestingly, despite the relative difference in these proportions between females and males, there was not a statistically significant relationship between the rank orders of these proportions, suggesting that fear-provoking cues, at least in at the bivariate level, are not gendered. In addition, when considering the multivariate results, there were no significant differences across gender in the impact of the cues on either fear of larceny-theft, aggravated assault, or simple assault. As such, it appears that the fear-provoking cues under study are not gendered as Brownlow's research suggests.

There are a number of plausible explanations why our results suggest that fear-provoking cues are not gendered.

With the exception of the limited number of lighting and foliage studies, most of the fear-provoking cues research has not been done within a university setting. The unique nature of the university setting, especially being relatively safe and secure, may contribute to the lack of associations found in our study. It might be that the unique setting of a campus, relatively open to all yet populated with young studious adults, faculty, and staff on a daily basis, might influence the type of persons who loiter around the grounds. Many college students may find comfort (and therefore be less fearful) in seeing members of the college community congregating on campus.

Another explanation for the lack of "gendered findings" revolves around the fact that the questions used to measure fear-specific cues were not as detailed as they could have been. As discussed earlier, these questions did not incorporate the element of time of day, which may have reduced the impact of the fear-specific cue on the fear of the respondent. For example, it is possible that groups congregating or loitering and visibility of public safety officials at night might have different impact on fear of crime among females (or, conversely, males) from these cues during the day. Future research should carefully word these measures to distinguish between daytime and nighttime cues to further explore this effect.

Despite the fact that female students are more fearful than their male counterparts for each offense-specific

Reading Table 3.3 Fear of Type of Crime Logit Models Results

Independent Variable: Specific Fear-Provoking Cue	Larceny-Theft			Aggravated Assault			Simple Assault			Sexual Assault
	Females	Males	Equality of Coefficient Test z Score	Females	Males	Equality of Coefficient Test z Score	Females	Males	Equality of Coefficient Test z Score	Females
	b (SE)	b (SE)		b (SE)	b (SE)		b (SE)	b (SE)		b (SE)
Poorly lit parking lots	.12 (.37)	.13 (.53)	-.02	.20 (.44)	.71 (1.01)	-.46	.83 (.56)	.47 (.91)	.34	.49 (.42)
Poorly lit sidewalks and common areas	.86 (.36)**	.47 (.56)	.59	1.03 (.41)***	1.28 (1.02)	-.23	-.05 (.48)	1.32 (.93)	-1.31	.58 (.15)
Overgrown or excessive shrubbery	.64 (.33)**	.32 (.44)	.58	.61 (.35)*	1.86 (.70)***	-1.60	.58 (.39)	.55 (.63)	.04	.70 (.35)**
Groups congregating or loitering	.43 (.29)	.99 (.40)***	-1.13	.27 (.37)	.99 (.63)	-.31	.84 (.39)**	.84 (.70)	.00	.42 (.33)
Visibility of public safety officials	.54 (.31)*	.06 (.47)	.85	.59 (.33)**	.51 (.75)	.10	.61 (.37)*	-.15 (.82)	.84	.95 (.34)***
Constant	-3.14 (1.09)***	-1.71 (1.50)		-4.80 (1.21)****	-4.22 (2.90)		-5.0 (1.38)****	-3.73 (2.07)*		-4.33 (1.17)***
Model chi-square (df)	88.62 (10)	51.75 (10)		76.52 (10)	48.29 (10)		38.11 (10)	34.30 (10)		129.67 (10)
Significance	.000	.000		.000	.000		.000	.000		.000

NOTE: The respective perceived risk, age, and current residence status; academic classification; and course load were used as control variables.

*p < .1, **p < .05, ***p < .01, ****p < .001.

fear, the relative safety and security of the university setting may also reduce the impact of gender on these relationships, as neither male or female students were generally fearful on campus. With the exception of fear of larceny-theft, where two in five respondents (40.0%) agreed that they were fearful of victimization on campus, the levels of fear among these respondents were relatively low (18.4% agreed that they were at least somewhat fearful of aggravated assault, and only 12.2% agreed that they were fearful of simple assault). In light of these findings, future research should attempt to replicate and build from our current study in nonuniversity settings, such as residential communities or even computer-generated settings that vary characteristics by known fear-generating cues, to determine if the relative safety and security of the university setting masks any impact that fear-provoking cues might have on fear of criminal victimization. Equally important to future research is examining whether this relationship is gendered. The past fear-provoking research provides ample evidence to suggest that there is quite a strong association between fear-provoking cues and fear of crime, but the question about this relationship conditioned on gender remains ripe for inquiry.

Despite the lack of gender differences in the association between fear-provoking cues and offense-specific fear, the reported results inform the research community about gender differences in fear of crime on a number of dimensions. First, the multivariate results offer some support for the "shadow of powerlessness" that has been used to explain differences in fear of crime among adolescent males (May, 2001b).

As May (2001b) suggests, males who feel that they have less power in a situation are likely to be more fearful of that situation. Both Day et al.'s (2003) and Brownlow's (2005) research are supportive of May's shadow of powerlessness suggestion. Their research jointly suggests that males are fearful in environments in which they experience a loss of control because, for some males, their masculine gender identity (e.g., aggression, physical strength) is challenged. For males, there were only two significant associations between fear-provoking cues and fear of crime found in the current study. For males, fear of crime because of groups congregating or loitering had a statistically significant association with fear of larceny-theft and fear of crime because of overgrown or excessive shrubbery

had a statistically significant association with fear of aggravated assault. In both of these situations, this relationship might be explained by the challenges to their gender identity [that] some males feel in these types of environments.

Males may feel that their odds of resisting larceny-theft are reduced in a group setting where they are surrounded by a number of young adult males and females (the demographic most likely to loiter and congregate on a university campus); as such, the powerlessness they feel to overcome these odds may be responsible for the significant association between fear caused by groups loitering and fear of larceny-theft. These feelings of powerlessness may also explain male fear of aggravated assault in this sample as well. Although males may think that they can evade a person who wants to commit aggravated assault against them in a poorly lit parking lot or sidewalk or when public safety officials are not present, they may think they are less likely to be able to evade an assailant who confronts them in an area with overgrown shrubbery. As such, those males most fearful because of the overgrown shrubbery cue are significantly more fearful of aggravated assault than their male counterparts who are not as fearful because of that cue. This evidence of the impact of the shadow of powerlessness related to gender identify suggests that this line of thinking is a potentially rich area of exploration for the continued research into the possible gendered relationship between fear-provoking cues and offense-specific fear.

A second interesting gender-specific finding concerns the relationship between the visibility of police and crime-related fear for females. Females (but not males) who were most fearful of crime because of the visibility of public safety officials were significantly more likely than their counterparts to be fearful of every crime under consideration. Given that over 90% of both male and female respondents felt that the university public safety officials were either somewhat or very visible, this finding would appear to indicate that the visibility of police increases fear of crime for females but not for males. Nevertheless, analysis of a follow-up question reveals that this may not be the case. For males, one in three (38.1%) respondents agreed that they would "feel safer if public safety officials were more visible than they currently are"; two in three (67.9%) females agreed with that statement. As such, the presence of police may be more relevant for decreasing fear of crime among females than males. Given that this finding has not been uncovered in any study of which we are aware, this provides another particularly rich area of research that could inform the study of fear of crime.

In much the same way that the shadow of powerlessness may partially explain fear of victimization among the males in this sample, there is some evidence to suggest that the shadow of sexual assault (see May, 2001a, for review; Fisher & Sloan, 2003) may partially explain fear of victimization among the female students in this sample as well. Females who were most fearful because of overgrown or excessive shrubbery and visibility of public safety officials (but none of the other specific fear-provoking cues) were significantly more likely to be fearful of sexual assault than their counterparts were. This finding would suggest that certain cues, in this case, overgrown shrubbery and low police visibility, are relevant to increasing women's fear of sexual assault. This result can also be seen through the lens of several studies that have found that women are primarily fearful of being sexually assaulted, especially in public places at night because they are afraid of being attacked by a stranger (see Fisher & Sloan, 2003; Merry, 1981; Pain, 2001; Valentine, 1990). Again, this line of thinking provides another rich area of exploration in the area of gendered fear-provoking cues and fear of crime, in particular fear of sexual assault.

Although we have uncovered a number of interesting findings, this study is not without limitations. First, and most importantly, future researchers should develop measures of fear-provoking cues that incorporate richer descriptions of a specific cue. For example, although our survey question asked students about fear of groups congregating or loitering, the question was not specific about the demographic or nonstudent status composition of the group, the location, the activity of the group who was loitering, or the time of day the group was loitering. Anecdotal evidence suggests that those groups loitering on the campus under study here were mostly male college students loitering outside of one or more dormitories on campus who routinely verbally harass other students (particularly female students). The one measure included in the survey used to collect group loitering information did not allow us to fully examine these relationships which Warr's (2000) work suggests influences fear of crime. In addition, as alluded to above, the measure of visibility of public safety officials could be improved by . . . including even more types of police visibility (e.g., foot patrol, bicycle patrol, face-to-face interaction) to better unpack the police presence and crime-related fear relationship, especially to see if this relationship is gendered. The day–night distinction with respect to fear-provoking cues and fear of crime is also another measurement issue that was not fully addressed in the current research. It could well be that certain fear-provoking cues, for example poor lighting, only influence certain offense-specific fears during the nighttime but not during daylight. We could not address such issues in our work but leave this issue to future researchers to address.

Whether fear-provoking cues are gendered is clearly an issue deserving more scholarly attention. The current study is an important first exploration for informing an agenda for future researchers to examine the possible gendered nature of fear-provoking cues.

Like we have done in the current research, we would encourage future researchers to draw from the variety of disciplines that has examined different aspects of crime-related fear and integrate their theoretical approaches and findings to more fully comprehend which, if any, fear-provoking cues are gendered and their effects on offense-specific fears. Hopefully, in the next decade, a better understanding of the possible gendered relationship between fear-provoking cues and crime-related fear will mature and provide practical means to address fear-provoking cues and thereby reduce crime-related fears among both females and males.

⊠ References

Brownlow, A. (2005). A geography of men's fear. *Geoforum, 36,* 581–592.

Day, K. (1994). Conceptualizing women's fear of sexual assault on campus. *Environment and Behavior, 26,* 742–767.

Day, K., Stump, C., & Carreon, D. (2003). Confrontation and loss of control: Masculinity and men's fear of public spaces. *Journal of Environmental Psychology, 23,* 311–322.

Fisher, B. S., & Nasar, J. L. (1992). Fear of crime in relation to three exterior site features: Prospect, refuge, and escape. *Environment and Behavior, 24,* 35–65.

Fisher, B. S., & Sloan, J. J. (2003). Unraveling the fear of sexual victimization among college women: Is the "shadow of sexual assault" hypothesis supported? *Justice Quarterly, 20,* 633–659.

Kitchin, R. M. (1994). Cognitive maps: What are they and why study them? *Journal of Environmental Psychology, 14,* 1–19.

Kitchin, R. M. (1996). Are there sex differences in geographic knowledge and understanding? *Geographical Journal, 162,* 273–286.

Klodawsky, F., & Lundy, C. (1994). Women's safety in the university environment. *Journal of Architectural and Planning, 11,* 128–331.

Lane, J., & Meeker, J. W. (2003). Women's and men's fear of gang crimes: Sexual and nonsexual assault as perceptually contemporaneous offenses. *Justice Quarterly, 20,* 337–371.

Madriz, E. (1997). *Nothing bad happens to good girls.* Berkeley: University of California Press.

May, D. C. (2001a). *Adolescent fear of crime, perceptions of risk, and defensive behaviors: An alternate explanation of violent delinquency.* Lewiston, NY: Edwin Mellen Press.

May, D. C. (2001b). The effect of fear of sexual victimization on adolescent fear of crime. *Sociological Spectrum, 21,* 141–174.

May, D. C., & Dunaway, R. G. (2000). Predictors of adolescent fear of crime. *Sociological Spectrum, 20,* 149–168.

May, D. C., Vartanian, L. R., & Virgo, K. (2002). The impact of parental attachment and supervision on fear of crime among adolescent males. *Adolescence, 37,* 267–287.

Merry, S. E. (1981). *Urban danger: Life in a neighborhood of strangers.* Philadelphia: Temple University Press.

Nasar, J. L., & Fisher, B. S. (1993). "Hot spots" of fear and crime: A multi-method investigation. *Journal of Environmental Psychology, 13,* 187–206.

Pain, R. (1997). Social geographies of women's fear of crime. *Transactions of the Institute of British Geographies, New Series, 22,* 231–244.

Pain, R. (2001). Gender, race, age and fear in the city. *Urban Studies, 38,* 899–913.

Reid, L. W., & Konrad, M. (2004). The gender gap in fear: Assessing the interactive effects of gender and perceived risk on fear of crime. *Sociological Spectrum, 24,* 399–425.

Schafer, J. A., Huebner, B. M., & Bynum, T. S. (2006). Fear of crime and criminal victimization gender-based contrasts. *Journal of Criminal Justice, 34*(3), 285–301.

Skogan, W. G. (1990). *Disorder and decline: Crime and the spiral of decay in American neighborhoods.* New York: Free Press.

Smith, W. R., & Torstenson, M. (1997). Gender differences in risk perception and neutralizing fear of crime. *British Journal of Criminology, 37,* 608–634.

Starkweather, S. (2007). Gender, perceptions of safety and strategic responses among Ohio university students. *Gender, Place, and Culture, 14,* 355–370.

Valentine, G. (1990). Women's fear and the design of public space. *Built Environment, 16,* 279–287.

Van der Wurff, A., Van Staalduinen, L., & Stringer, P. (1989). Fear of crime in residential environments: Testing a social psychological model. *Journal of Social Psychology, 129,* 141–160.

Wallace, L. H., & May, D. C. (2005). The impact of relationship with parents and commitment to school on adolescent fear of crime at school. *Adolescence, 40,* 458–474.

Warr, M. (1990). Dangerous situations: Social context and fear of victimization. *Social Forces, 68,* 891–907.

Warr, M. (2000). Fear of crime in the United States: Avenues for research and policy. In D. Duffee (Ed.), *Measurement and analysis of crime and justice: Crime justice* (Vol. 4, pp. 451–490). Washington, DC: Department of Justice.

DISCUSSION QUESTIONS

1. How is the fear of victimization similar for men and women? How is it different?

2. Is a fear of crime related to specific offenses? Does this fear vary by gender?

3. How can university administrators use the findings of this study to increase safety on college campuses?

READING 4

As you learned in the section, women utilize a variety of formal and informal resources when looking for help following a victimization experience. This reading targets women within Latino communities to gain a better understanding of help-seeking behaviors within this community. In addition, the authors of this research look at whether victims of particular crimes are more likely to seek help (both formally and informally) and why.

Help-Seeking in a National Sample of Victimized Latino Women

The Influence of Victimization Types

Chiara Sabina, Carlos A. Cuevas, and Jennifer L. Schally

Women who are victimized rely on both formal and informal resources for help and support. Formal avenues include police, the criminal justice system, legal remedies, social services, and mental health professionals whereas informal avenues include talking to friends, relatives, and clergy about the victimization. Help-seeking is a process that includes defining the problem, deciding to seek help, and selecting a source of support (Liang, Goodman, Tummala-Narra, & Weintraub, 2005). Each of these stages is influenced by individual, interpersonal, and sociocultural factors (Carlson, 1997; Dutton, 1996; Liang et al., 2005).

Help-seeking is best characterized as a dynamic process (Cattaneo, Stuewig, Goodman, Kaltman, & Dutton, 2007; Dutton, 1992, 1996; Stork, 2008) that responds to the changing context of victimized women. The process begins with women defining acts as violence and as unacceptable, resulting in a decision to confront the violence (J. Campbell, Rose, Kub, & Nedd, 1998; Petersen, Moracco, Goldstein, & Clark, 2004; Pilowsky, 1993). Feelings of shame, guilt, self-doubt, and fear can work to undermine women's resolution of help-seeking (Petersen et al., 2004). Nonetheless, women confront the violence in their lives generally in a multifaceted way including informal and formal help-seeking along with more private intrapersonal strategies, such as self-talk, and stress release through personal activities (Smith, Murray, & Coker, 2010). Three factors are especially pertinent here with regard to Latino women's help-seeking—victimization characteristics, cultural factors, and the availability of linguistically and culturally appropriate services—and are reviewed in turn.

Evidence shows that the dynamics of victimization can alter help-seeking responses, including victim–offender relationship, severity, and type of victimization. In regard to victim–offender relationship, it appears that having a known perpetrator is more likely to result in informal help-seeking efforts, specifically in cases of violent victimization among women (Kaukinen, 2002) and sexual assault (Ullman & Filipas, 2001). When focusing on victimization type and severity, it appears that increased severity, such as the presence of a weapon or sexual assault in combination with physical violence, is likely to result in increased likelihood of reporting to police or other formal sources (Duterte et al., 2008; Kaukinen, 2002; Rennison, 2007; Ullman & Filipas, 2001). In contrast, sexual violence alone appears to decrease the odds of reporting victimization to police for violent crime victims generally (Kaukinen, 2002) and Hispanic women specifically (Rennison, 2007). These results seem to suggest that help-seeking behaviors may in part be dictated by who the perpetrator is and the interaction of the severity and type of violence.

Cultural traditions and beliefs also play an important role in the help-seeking process. Gender roles, importance of the family unit, acceptability of sharing private concerns, and patriarchal structures vary among racial/ethnic groups and may alter the process of defining a problem, deciding which responses to enact, and the reactions of help sources. Rates of disclosing victimization vary significantly by racial/ethnic group as does chosen confidants (Ingram, 2007; Rew, 1997; Yoshioka, Gilbert, El-Bassel, & Baig-Amin, 2003) and choice of formal help source (Lipsky, Caetano, Field, & Larkin, 2006). Persons more fluent in English, in the United

SOURCE: Sabina, C., Cuevas, C. A., & Schally, J. L. (2012). Help-seeking in a national sample of victimized Latino women: The influence of victimization types. *Journal of Interpersonal Violence, 27*(1), 40–61.

States for longer periods of time, with a stable legal status, and more acculturated are more likely to seek formal services (Dutton, Orloff, & Hass, 2000; Ingram, 2007; Kelly, 2006; Lipsky et al., 2006). Psychological and cultural barriers pertinent to Latino women include a belief in preserving the family, stigmatization of divorce, fear of abuser, and shame (Bauer, Rodriguez, Quiroga, & Flores-Ortiz, 2000; Dutton et al., 2000; Erez & Hartley, 2003; Kelly, 2006; Lewis, West, Bautista, Greenberg, & Done-Perez, 2005; Lira, Koss, & Russo, 1999). These cultural influences likely shape Latino women's responses to victimization and may work to impede help-seeking among this group.

Poor access to services, along with limitations of available services, further influence the help-seeking responses of Latino women. About 10% of unfulfilled requests for domestic violence services are due to services not being available in languages other than English or limited funding for translators (National Network to End Domestic Violence, 2010). Cultural sensitivity of services may also limit help-seeking such as staff's potential lack of understanding of minority women and disregard for religious and cultural practices. Studies have documented Latino women's frustrations with health care (Bauer et al., 2000; Kelly, 2006), counseling (Kasturirangan & Williams, 2003), the legal system (Erez & Hartley, 2003), and police responses to domestic violence calls (Ammar, Orloff, Dutton, & Aguilar Hass, 2005). According to victims themselves, service providers can be better informed and attuned to Latino culture and practices, immigrant women's legal status and associated fear, and the importance of personalism and sensitivity in service provision, and [victims] stressed the importance of service providers directly asking them about their victimization experiences (Rodriguez et al., 2008; Rodriguez, Sheldon, Bauer, & Pérez-Stable, 2001). Provision of services to this community is important given that help-seeking, including tapping formal resources and social support networks, in an effort to deal with intimate partner violence, is related to positive mental health outcomes and physical safety (Coker et al., 2002; Coker, Watkins, Smith, & Brandt, 2003; Horton & Johnson, 1993; Liang et al., 2005; Sullivan & Bybee, 1999).

Studies that compare Latinos with Whites generally show a decreased likelihood of help-seeking among Latinos. For example, data from a national sample revealed that Latino women who experience physical assault from their partners are less likely (48%) than White women (66%) to seek help, either formal or informal (West, Kaufman Kantor, & Jasinski, 1998). Furthermore, data from the National Crime Victimization Survey reveal that Whites are two times more likely to report rape/sexual assault to police than Latinos (Rennison, 2007). Although a large-scale survey revealed no significant difference between Latinos and non-Latinos on the rate of seeking any type of help, the rate for disclosing intimate partner violence (IPV) to a health care worker was significantly lower among Latino men and women (Ingram, 2007). Another study found Latino women significantly less likely to use health care settings, especially emergency rooms in response to IPV (Lipsky et al., 2006). Together, the research points to a general reluctance for Latino victims to seek formal help in response to IPV and sexual assault relative to their non-Latino counterparts. With regard to informal help-seeking, differences between Latinos and Whites are less consistent. A shelter sample revealed no significant difference in sharing [an experience of] abuse with others (Krishnan, Hilbert, VanLeeuwen, & Kolia, 1997), but a national sample showed Latino women underutilized informal sources, such as talking with a friend or relative (West et al., 1998). The largest study available shows differences among Latinos and non-Latinos, with Latinos relying on family members significantly more often than non-Latinos (31.5% and 25.4%, respectively) but a nonsignificant difference in telling friends about IPV victimization (29.7% and 31.4%, respectively; Ingram, 2007). Each of these studies focuses on intimate partner violence, excluding other forms of victimization and other perpetrators.

The current study addresses some of these gaps in the literature. The Sexual Assault Among Latinas (SALAS) Study undertakes investigation of these questions by assessing formal (reporting to police, going to court, getting medical attention, seeking social services) and informal (talking to others about victimization, such as family members, friends, and partners) help-seeking [for] victimization in general and [for] physical, sexual, stalking, childhood, and threatened victimization among a national sample of Latino women. The aims of this study include (a) a national estimate of help-seeking among victimized Latino women, (b) estimates of help-seeking by victimization type, and (c) an examination of the influence of victimization type on help-seeking.

Method

Participants

This research is based on data from the Sexual Assault Among Latinas (SALAS) Study, a bilingual national phone survey, conducted between May and September 2008. The study assessed the experiences of a national sample of 2,000 Latino women living in the United States, the majority of whom (90%) were living in high-density Latino areas (80% or higher) based on the U.S. Census data.

The average age of the participants was 47.76 years of age and most had a high school education or less (63%). The majority of participants (61%) were U.S. citizens (either U.S. born or naturalized). Those who reported victimization and were asked about their help-seeking responses, differed significantly from those who did not report victimization across all demographic variables.

Of the full sample, 37.6% of the women reported at least one lifetime victimization incident based on physical assault, sexual assault, stalking, threatened violence, or kidnapping. [And] 25.6% reported at least one victimization experience during childhood, whereas 26.6% reported at least one victimization experience in adulthood. For the victimized women, 66.9% of them experienced more than one victimization incident. The rate for any physical assault, which includes weapon assault, was 22.2%. The rate for sexual assaults was 17.2%, which included completed sexual assault/rape, attempted sexual assault, and fondling/forced touch. The rate for stalking victimization was 18.4%. The threat victimization rate for the sample was 21.1%.

Procedures

The sample was obtained through a random digit dial method, applied in high-density Latino areas based on Census data. Related phone exchanges were used and random digits added to produce a random sample within high-density Latino neighborhoods. Telephone interviewing has been found to be comparable with in-person interviews in its reliability and validity (Bajos, Spira, Ducot, & Messiah, 1992; Bermack, 1989; Czaja, 1987; Martin, Duncan, Powers, & Sawyer, 1989). Participants were screened for identifying as a Latino woman and being above the age of 18. For full description of procedures, see Cuevas and Sabina (2010).

All instruments used in this study were translated into Spanish, unless an established translated version was already available, in which case that version was used, and participants could use their language of preference (71.4% completed the interview in Spanish). On completing the survey, participants were asked if they felt distressed and were offered a support hotline or callback to follow up with them. If the participant requested a callback or the interviewer felt they should [receive] a follow-up, the case was screened for follow-up. On follow-up calls, it was ensured that the individual was no longer distressed and [was] provided with additional support information if needed (e.g., local social service agencies, etc.). Approximately 1% of the sample required follow-up. After completing the survey, participants were paid US$10 for their participation.

Measures

Demographic information. Participant background information was asked on personal characteristics including age, country of origin, immigration status, preferred language, educational level, employment status, household income, and relationship status. Age (continuous variable), employment (dichotomized as 1 = *working either full-time or part-time* vs. 0 = *nonemployed*), and socioeconomic status were used as control variables in the regression analyses. Socioeconomic status was calculated by converting education and household income variables into z scores, adding those values, and then restandardizing the summed values.

Lifetime trauma and victimization history (LTVH). A shortened version of the LTVH (Widom, Dutton, Czaja, & DuMont, 2005) was used to assess interpersonal victimization. Participants were asked if any of the following ever happened to them: stalking, physical assaults, weapon assaults, physical assaults in childhood, threats, threats with weapons, sexual assault, attempted sexual assault, sexual fondling, kidnapping, or witnessed victimization. The victimization incidents pertinent to these analyses were then consolidated into four categories: physical assaults, sexual assaults, stalking, and threat victimization. Given the interest in help-seeking responses, two additional categories were created which relate to childhood victimization (i.e., sexual fondling and physical assaults in childhood) and victimization with a weapon (i.e., weapon assaults and threats with weapons) to account for possible severity and/or age influence on help-seeking.

Help-Seeking Questionnaire (HSQ). The Help-Seeking Questionnaire was developed specifically for this study but was formed from two large-scale studies that assessed formal and informal help-seeking behaviors (Block, 2000; Gelles & Straus, 1988). This questionnaire asked about the actions taken by respondents after experiencing an identified incident of victimization. Participants who reported victimization chose the anchor incident by identifying the "most severe incident that occurred in the United States and has upset you the most." Questions included information about the various types of resources, both formal and informal, that participants may have contacted for assistance. Formal help-seeking included reporting it to the police; going to court (getting a restraining order and/or filing criminal charges); getting medical care (i.e., doctor, medical center, or hospital); and contacting a social service agency, counselor, or crisis center. Informal help-seeking responses were gathered through a subsequent open-ended question, "Who did you talk to about the incident?" All responses were coded into the categories of parent, sibling, other family, partner, friend, and professionals (e.g., clergy, coworkers, faculty). Given participants responses to these questions, they were categorized as either not seeking any help, employing informal help-seeking only, formal help-seeking only, or both formal and informal help-seeking.

Results

Overall, 32.5% of the sample engaged in formal help-seeking and 68.9% engaged in informal help-seeking. Help-seeking rates in response to the anchor event are presented in Reading Table 4.1. The most common form of formal help-seeking was getting medical attention for victims who self-reported being injured (34.7%) followed by calling the police (16.9%). The police were most often called for victimizations involving weapons (27.7%) and threatened victimization (26.1%). These two victimization types also resulted in relatively high levels of going to court (23.8% and 24.2%, respectively). Informal help-seeking was commonly sought from parents (26.6%) and friends (21.5%)

among those reporting any victimization. Variations by victimization type again show elevated levels of informal help-seeking for victimizations involving weapons.

Including both formal and informal help-seeking, 76.6% of victimized participants engaged in some type of help-seeking behavior in response to the anchor event (see Reading Table 4.2). The highest rate of not seeking help was related to child victimization (38.8%). Women who had been stalked reported the highest rate of informal only help-seeking (57.0%). Women responded with both formal and informal help-seeking in relation to victimization that involved a weapon. Within each victimization type, significant chi-squares show unequal propensity to engage in each of the types of help-seeking.

Regression results for formal help-seeking. Participants who had been stalked or experienced childhood victimizations had significantly decreased odds of using any formal help resources, In addition, participants who had experienced childhood victimization had significantly decreased odds of reporting to the police.

The odds of any informal help-seeking were decreased by age of respondent, increased by socioeconomic status, increased by victimizations involving weapons, and decreased by child victimizations.

Discussion

The trend for Latino women to engage in informal help-seeking more often than formal help-seeking was supported here as in other studies (Cortina, 2004; Dutton et al., 2000; Ingram, 2007) and is in line with a recent review of the literature (McCart, Smith, & Sawyer, 2010). Moreover, about two thirds of the victimized women engaged in at least one type of help-seeking underscoring the distress caused by victimization. This estimate is lower than those garnered from shelter clients who asked about other forms of help seeking (Krishnan et al., 1997; Yoshioka et al., 2003) but higher than an estimate garnered from a larger sample in regard to help-seeking for intimate partner violence victimization (Ingram, 2007). Ingram's study reported an overall rate of help-seeking of 50% among Latinos, including both men and women, who reported IPV. The current study, which assesses a broader range of victimization, by all perpetrators, correspondingly

Reading Table 4.1   Rate of Help-Seeking Responses by Victimization Type

	Any Victimization (n = 714)	Sexual (n = 212)	Physical (n = 223)	Stalking (n = 116)	Threat (n = 157)	Weapon (n = 101)	Child (n = 167)
Any formal	32.5%	20.8%	39.9%	21.6%	44.6%	45.5%	16.2%
Police	16.9	6.6	19.7	18.1	26.1	27.7	4.8
Courts	16.9	10.8	20.2	11.2	24.2	23.8	6.6
Social services	9.9	10.0	9.5	2.6	15.4	10.9	6.1
Medical[a]	34.7	41.0	31.8	33.3	34.3	39.3	22.2
Any informal	68.9	58.3	69.2	76.3	76.8	84.0	55.8
Parent	26.6	18.0	26.7	33.3	32.9	38.0	21.2
Sibling	14.9	10.4	16.7	14.9	18.1	23.0	9.1
Other family	12.7	5.7	16.3	12.3	16.8	23.0	9.7
Partner	7.9	8.1	6.3	11.4	7.1	11.0	6.1
Friend	21.5	18.5	23.5	25.4	18.7	25.0	14.5
Professional	9.4	10.8	5.8	9.4	12.1	9.9	6.0

[a] Medical help-seeking was only asked of the 190 participants that reported an injury.

Reading Table 4.2   Help-Seeking by Victimization Types

	No Help (%)	Informal Only (%)	Formal Only (%)	Both (%)	χ^2
Any victimization	23.3	43.8	7.8	25.0	185.10***
Sexual	35.5	43.6	6.2	14.7	77.51***
Physical	21.3	38.5	9.5	30.8	41.43***
Stalking	21.1	57.0	2.6	19.3	71.75***
Threat	11.6	43.2	11.6	33.5	47.35***
Child	38.8	44.8	5.5	10.9	76.87***
Weapon	11.0	43.0	5.0	41.0	47.04***

*** $p < .001$.

found a high rate of help-seeking with 76.6% of the victimized sample engaging in some sort of help-seeking behavior. Thus, as documented before, women actively respond to victimization and Latino women are no different in this respect. However, a richer understanding of help-seeking responses is offered by the current study.

Help-seeking responses of victimized Latino women vary by victimization type. From the descriptive analyses, it is apparent that threatened victimization and victimization involving a weapon were most likely to result in formal help-seeking. Sexual, stalking, and child victimization were the least likely to result in formal help-seeking. Perhaps the dynamics of these types of victimization are such that victims respond with more internalizing behavior, thus, hindering help-seeking efforts. Women may also aptly label victimization with a weapon as criminal and thus be more willing to seek help. Another possibility is that women may not know that there are formal recourses available if they are stalked. Informal help-seeking followed similar trends with threat and weapon victimization showing relatively elevated rates of informal help seeking and sexual and child victimization showing lower rates. However, stalking was met with a relatively high degree of informal help-seeking. This adds credence to the notion that women are willing to talk about the victimization but may not realize that formal avenues are also possible.

Unfortunately, victimization that occurred in childhood was met with the least amount of help-seeking efforts, both formally or informally. Children are unlikely to have direct access to help-seeking opportunities (e.g., police or mental health services) with parents and/or school officials often serving as the gateway to these resources (Finkelhor, Wolak, & Berliner, 2001). Hence, this may impair their opportunity to get formal help if primary caretakers are either unaware of the victimization, prefer to handle it themselves, or are the perpetrators of the violence. This lack of disclosure can likely serve to reinforce the negative consequences of victimization. Victimization that occurs during childhood may be especially harmful as emotional development is stymied at a critical period. Furthermore, these victimizations most often occurred at the hands of family, relatives, or other known perpetrators (Cuevas, Sabina, & Milloshi, in press), further undermining the sense of trust and understanding children have of the world. These results are more disheartening in light of research findings that indicate social support during childhood from family and friends could mitigate some of the loss associated with childhood sexual victimization (Murthi & Espelage, 2005) including feeling lost and helpless and loss of childhood. That is, both formal avenues that could safeguard the child and informal avenues that may help to buffer the traumatic impact are both less likely to be sought by child victims.

The increased likelihood in response to victimization involving a weapon speaks to the pragmatic and logical response to victimization with lethal potential. This suggests that women respond in ways that meet the severity of the victimization. Evidence shows that victims actively and persistently engage in help-seeking in response to severe victimization (Duterte et al., 2008; Goodman, Dutton, Weinfurt, & Cook, 2003; Leone, Johnson, & Cohan, 2007; Petersen et al., 2004). In situations of severe violence, as marked by a weapon, the primary objective of women is likely to gain immediate safety thus protecting their lives. Other factors which influence women's help-seeking decisions—psychological barriers of fear and shame, for example—become secondary to survival in these situations.

The relatively low prevalence of formal help-seeking may be due in part to availability of services. For example, a related literature lays emphasis on the lack of mental health services available to the Latino community and the general underutilization of mental health services by Latinos in comparison with non-Latino Whites (Cabassa, Zayas, & Hansen, 2006; U.S. Department of Health and Human Services, 2001). A principal culprit for this problem is the lack of services in Spanish, given that approximately 40% of Latinos in the United States report not speaking English "very well" (Ramirez, 2004), which is consistent with our sample who predominantly indicated Spanish as their preferred language. Lack of linguistically sensitive providers is supported by research which has found that the ratio of mental health professionals to population for Latinos was 29 per 100,000 compared with 173 per 100,000 for Whites (U.S. Department of Health and Human Services, 2001). These data demonstrate that the availability of providers for Latinos is less than one fifth of what is available to the English-speaking population. In addition to this evidence, a recent qualitative study by Barrio and colleagues (Barrio et al., 2008) highlights the perception, by both service providers and consumers, that Latinos have neither sufficient available resources nor adequate information on available mental health services. Some of the issues presented in their study include lack of Spanish-speaking providers or interpreters and general barriers to accessing service providers (e.g., few clinics in Latino neighborhoods, transportation difficulties). Although this information presents an overall picture of the underservicing of Latinos in the mental health field, we can assume that this problem holds true among Latino women who are victims of violence.

Yet we would be remiss in not also ensuring that social services and criminal justice responses are not only available but also address the needs of victimized women and girls such that their safety and psychological well-being are enhanced. Indeed, the goal of increasing service utilization is only worthy if those services are associated with positive and long-lasting outcomes for victimized women. Although it is often assumed that services offer positive effects, an important body of work calls attention to the limitations of services for all women (R. Campbell, 2005; Ullman & Filipas, 2001), and for Latino women specifically (Kelly, 2006). Beyond providing services in Spanish, services attentive to Latino cultural dynamics are essential (Kasturirangan & Williams, 2003; Vasquez, 1998).

Practice implications of the current study include the need to increase knowledge and availability of formal help-seeking venues. Other studies have documented Latinos' lack of knowledge about services (Dutton et al., 2000; Ingram, 2007). Building on the strengths that are already apparent within this Latino sample, service providers may make specific efforts to coordinate with medical providers to educate victims about help-seeking options. Medical providers may also include in their protocol screeners that identify victims of intimate partner or family violence and offer local services. Beyond provision of service directly to the victim, the results here point to the promise of providing information to family members who often learn about the victimization. Efforts could be made to inform families about how to respond to disclosure and possible community resources. For example, school personnel who are culturally informed and bilingual could inform parents about signs of abuse, address misconceptions, and also detail the availability of services. Similar approaches could be taken in community centers, churches, and medical centers. The individualized information and services that characterize our current efforts

to combat violence may not be as applicable to the Latino community. The strong family ties that characterize the population could be the gateway to addressing violence in the community.

Although the current study has documented that Latino women respond differently to varying types of victimization, several questions remain unanswered. Responses to victimization are influenced by a number of factors including the length of the relationship, coping resources, and prior experiences with help-seeking (Waldrop & Resick, 2004). Neither the process influencing help-seeking efforts nor intrapersonal efforts to cope with violence (Davis, 2002; Smith et al., 2010) are examined here. Cultural factors, such as acculturation level, immigrant status, and gender role ideology, also likely moderate these relationships and need to be investigated in subsequent studies. Furthermore, some may contend that specific Latino subgroups, such as Mexican Americans and Cuban Americans, should be separated out (Guarnaccia et al., 2007). These factors also need to be modeled to understand the complex processes that characterize help-seeking efforts, although this is beyond the scope of the current study.

Limitations of the SALAS study include the cross-sectional methodology which misses how help-seeking efforts develop and change over time. In addition, the cultural constructs mentioned above should be included in future studies to offer a fuller understanding of help-seeking. As the SALAS focused on help-seeking responses to one type of victimization identified by the participant to be most distressing, we did not capture help-seeking responses to other forms of victimization. As with all retrospective reports, there is a risk for memory deterioration and distortion in recall. It is also important to note that the SALAS did not garner a nationally representative sample of Latino women but rather a national sample of Latino women living in high-density Latino areas, limiting the generalizability. This method, which relies on phone service, may systematically miss those who are transient and/or very poor, who may be at heightened risk for victimization and may rely on formal help sources less often. In addition, the response rate was low, and we are unable to identify the ways in which potential participants differed from those who chose to participate in the study.

Despite these limitations, the current study examines formal and informal help-seeking among a national sample of Latino women and adds to the literature by examining differences in help-seeking by a wide variety of victimization types. We clearly see the need to include contextual variables, such as type of victimization, in our models of help-seeking and coping. Whereas prior research shows Latino women are less likely than White women to seek help in response to victimization, this study shows that Latino women, in response to certain victimization types, disclose abuse to formal supports and quite often trust family and friends with their experiences.

References

Ammar, N. H., Orloff, L. E., Dutton, M. A., & Aguilar Hass, G. (2005). Calls to police and police response: A case study of Latina immigrant women in the USA. *International Journal of Police Science & Management, 7,* 230–244.

Bajos, N., Spira, A., Ducot, B., & Messiah, A. (1992). Analysis of sexual behaviour in France (ACSF): A comparison between two modes of investigation: Telephone survey and face-to-face survey. *AIDS, 6,* 315–323.

Barrio, C., Palinkas, L. A., Yamada, A.-M., Fuentes, D., Criado, V., Garcia, P., & Jeste, D. V. (2008). Unmet needs for mental health services for Latino older adults: Perspectives from consumers, family members, advocates, and service providers. *Community Mental Health Journal, 44,* 57–74.

Bauer, H. M., Rodriguez, M. A., Quiroga, S. S., & Flores-Ortiz, Y. G. (2000). Barriers to health care for abused Latina and Asian immigrant women. *Journal of Health Care for the Poor and Underserved, 11,* 33–44.

Bermack, E. (1989). Effect of telephone and face-to-face communication on rated extent of self-disclosure by female college students. *Psychological Reports, 65,* 259–267.

Block, C. R. (2000). *Chicago Women's Health Risk Study (Part I and II), final report* (NCJ 183128). Washington, DC: United States Department of Justice, National Institute of Justice.

Cabassa, L. J., Zayas, L. H., & Hansen, M. C. (2006). Latino adults' access to mental health care: A review of epidemiological studies. *Administration and Policy in Mental Health and Mental Health Services Research, 33,* 316–330.

Campbell, J. C., Rose, L., Kub, J., & Nedd, D. (1998). Voices of strength and resistance: A contextual and longitudinal analysis of women's responses to battering. *Journal of Interpersonal Violence, 13,* 743–762.

Campbell, R. (2005). What really happened? A validation study of rape survivors' help-seeking experiences with the legal and medical systems. *Violence and Victims, 20,* 55–68.

Carlson, B. E. (1997). A stress and coping approach to intervention with abused women. *Family Relations, 46,* 291–298.

Cattaneo, L. B., Stuewig, J., Goodman, L. A., Kaltman, S., & Dutton, M. A.(2007). Longitudinal help seeking patterns among victims of intimate partner violence: The relationship between legal and extralegal services. *American Journal of Orthopsychiatry, 77,* 467–477.

Coker, A. L., Smith, P. H., Thompson, M. P., McKeown, R. E., Bethea, L., & Davis, K. E. (2002). Social support protects against the negative effects of partner violence on mental health. *Journal of Women's Health & Gender-Based Medicine, 11,* 465–476.

Coker, A. L., Watkins, K. W., Smith, P. H., & Brandt, H. M. (2003). Social support reduces the impact of partner violence on health: Application of structural equation models. *Preventive Medicine, 37,* 259–267.

Cortina, L. M. (2004). Hispanic perspectives on sexual harassment and social support. *Personality and Social Psychology Bulletin, 30,* 570–584.

Cuevas, C. A., & Sabina, C. (2010). *Final report: Sexual Assault Among Latinas (SALAS) study.* (NIJ Document No. 230445). Washington, DC: National Institute of Justice.

Cuevas, C. A., Sabina, C., & Milloshi, R. (in press). Interpersonal victimization among a national sample of Latino women. *Violence Against Women.*

Czaja, S. J. (1987). Human factors in office automation. In G. Salvendy (Ed.), *Handbook of human factors* (pp. 1587–1616). Oxford, UK: John Wiley.

Davis, R. E. (2002). The strongest women: Exploration of the inner resources of abused women. *Qualitative Health Research, 12,* 1248–1263.

Duterte, E. E., Bonomi, A. E., Kernic, M. A., Schiff, M. A., Thompson, R. S., & Rivara, F. P. (2008). Correlates of medical and legal help seeking among women reporting intimate partner violence. *Journal of Women's Health, 17,* 85–95.

Dutton, M. A. (1992). *Empowering and healing the battered woman: A model for assessment and intervention.* New York, NY: Springer.

Dutton, M. A. (1996). Battered women's strategic response to violence: The role of context. In J. L. Edleson & Z. C. Eisikovits (Eds.), *Future interventions with battered women and their families* (pp. 105–124). Thousand Oaks, CA: Sage.

Dutton, M. A., Orloff, L. E., & Hass, G. A. (2000). Characteristics of help-seeking behaviors, resources and service needs of battered immigrant Latinas: Legal and policy implications. *Georgetown Journal on Poverty Law & Policy, 7,* 245–306.

Erez, E., & Hartley, C. C. (2003). Battered immigrant women and the legal system: A therapeutic jurisprudence perspective. *Western Criminology Review, 4,* 155–159.

Finkelhor, D., Wolak, J., & Berliner, L. (2001). Police reporting and professional help seeking for child crime victims: A review. *Child Maltreatment, 6,* 17–30.

Gelles, R., & Straus, M. (1988). *Intimate violence: The causes and consequences of abuse in the American family.* New York, NY: Simon & Schuster.

Goodman, L., Dutton, M. A., Weinfurt, K., & Cook, S. (2003). The intimate partner violence strategies index: Development and application. *Violence Against Women, 9,* 163–186.

Guarnaccia, P. J., Pincay, I. M., Alegria, M., Shrout, P. E., Lewis-Fernandez, R., & Canino, G. J. (2007). Assessing diversity among Latinos: Results from the NLAAS. *Hispanic Journal of Behavioral Sciences, 29,* 510–534.

Horton, A. L., & Johnson, B. L. (1993). Profile and strategies of women who have ended abuse. *Families in Society, 74,* 481–492.

Ingram, E. M. (2007). A comparison of help seeking between Latino and non-Latino victims of intimate partner violence. *Violence Against Women, 13,* 159–171.

Kasturirangan, A., & Williams, E. N. (2003). Counseling Latina battered women: A qualitative study of the Latina perspective. *Journal of Multicultural Counseling and Development, 31,* 162–178.

Kaukinen, C. (2002). The help-seeking decisions of violent crime victims: An examination of the direct and conditional effects of gender and the victim–offender relationship. *Journal of Interpersonal Violence, 17,* 432–456.

Kelly, U. (2006). "What will happen if I tell you?" Battered Latina women's experiences of health care. *CJNR: Canadian Journal of Nursing Research, 38*(4), 78–95.

Krishnan, S. P., Hilbert, J. C., VanLeeuwen, D., & Kolia, R. (1997). Documenting domestic violence among ethnically diverse populations: Results from a preliminary study. *Family & Community Health, 20,* 32–48.

Leone, J. M., Johnson, M. P., & Cohan, C. L. (2007). Victim help seeking: Differences between intimate terrorism and situational couple violence. *Family Relations, 56,* 427–439.

Lewis, M. J., West, B., Bautista, L., Greenberg, A. M., & Done-Perez, I. (2005). Perceptions of service providers and community members on intimate partner violence within a Latino community. *Health Education & Behavior, 32,* 69–83.

Liang, B., Goodman, L., Tummala-Narra, P., & Weintraub, S. (2005). A theoretical framework for understanding help-seeking processes among survivors of intimate partner violence. *American Journal of Community Psychology, 36,* 71–84.

Lipsky, S., Caetano, R., Field, C. A., & Larkin, G. L. (2006). The role of intimate partner violence, race, and ethnicity in help-seeking behaviors. *Ethnicity & Health, 11,* 81–100.

Lira, L. R., Koss, M. P., & Russo, N. F. (1999). Mexican American women's definitions of rape and sexual abuse. *Hispanic Journal of Behavioral Sciences, 21,* 236–265.

Martin, W. S., Duncan, W. J., Powers, T. L., & Sawyer, J. C. (1989). Costs and benefits of selected response inducement techniques in mail survey research. *Journal of Business Research, 19,* 67–79.

McCart, M. R., Smith, D. W., & Sawyer, G. K. (2010). Help seeking among victims of crime: A review of the empirical literature. *Journal of Traumatic Stress, 23,* 198–206.

Murthi, M., & Espelage, D. L. (2005). Childhood sexual abuse, social support, and psychological outcomes: A loss framework. *Child Abuse & Neglect, 29,* 1215–1231.

National Network to End Domestic Violence. (2010). *Domestic violence counts 2009: A 24-hour census of domestic violence shelters and services.* Washington, DC: Author.

Petersen, R., Moracco, K. E., Goldstein, K. M., & Clark, K. A. (2004). Moving beyond disclosure: Women's perspectives on barriers and motivators to seeking assistance for intimate partner violence. *Women & Health, 40,* 63–76.

Pilowsky, J. E. (1993). The courage to leave: An exploration of Spanish-speaking women victims of spousal abuse. *Canadian Journal of Community Mental Health, 12*(2), 15–29.

Ramirez, R. R. (2004). *We the people: Hispanics in the United States.* Washington, DC: U.S. Census Bureau.

Rennison, C. M. (2007). Reporting to the police by Hispanic victims of violence. *Violence and Victims, 22,* 754–772.

Rew, L. (1997). An exploration of help-seeking behaviors in female Hispanic adolescents. *Family & Community Health, 20,* 1–15.

Rodriguez, M. A., Heilemann, M. V., Fielder, E., Ang, A., Nevarez, F., & Mangione, C. M. (2008). Intimate partner violence, depression, and PTSD among pregnant Latina women. *Annals of Family Medicine, 6,* 44–52.

Rodriguez, M. A., Sheldon, W. R., Bauer, H. M., & Pérez-Stable, E. J. (2001). The factors associated with disclosure of intimate partner abuse to clinicians. *Journal of Family Practice, 50,* 338–344.

Smith, P. H., Murray, C. E., & Coker, A. L. (2010). The coping window: A contextual understanding of the methods women use to cope with battering. *Violence and Victims, 25,* 18–28.

Stork, E. (2008). Understanding high-stakes decision making: Constructing a model of the decision to seek shelter from intimate partner violence. *Journal of Feminist Family Therapy, 20,* 299–327.

Sullivan, C. M., & Bybee, D. I. (1999). Reducing violence using community-based advocacy for women with abusive partners. *Journal of Consulting and Clinical Psychology, 67,* 43–53.

Ullman, S. E., & Filipas, H. H. (2001). Correlates of formal and informal support seeking in sexual assaults victims. *Journal of Interpersonal Violence, 16,* 1028–1047.

U.S. Department of Health and Human Services. (2001). *Mental health: Culture, race, and ethnicity.* Rockville, MD: U.S. Department of Health and Human Services, Substance Abuse and Mental Health Services Administration, Center for Mental Health Services.

Vasquez, M. J. T. (1998). Latinos and violence: Mental health implications and strategies for clinicians. *Cultural Diversity and Mental Health, 4,* 319–334.

Waldrop, A. E., & Resick, P. A. (2004). Coping among adult female victims of domestic violence. *Journal of Family Violence, 19,* 291–302.

West, C. M., Kaufman Kantor, G., & Jasinski, J. L. (1998). Sociodemographic predictors and cultural barriers to help-seeking behavior by Latina and Anglo American battered women. *Violence and Victims, 13,* 361–375.

Widom, C. S., Dutton, M. A., Czaja, S. J., & DuMont, K. A. (2005). Development and validation of a new instrument to assess lifetime trauma and victimization history. *Journal of Traumatic Stress, 18,* 519–531.

Yoshioka, M. R., Gilbert, L., El-Bassel, N., & Baig-Amin, M. (2003). Social support and disclosure of abuse: Comparing South Asian, African American, and Hispanic battered women. *Journal of Family Violence, 18,* 171–180.

DISCUSSION QUESTIONS

1. What are the most common forms of formal and informal help seeking among the women in the study?

2. What sorts of experiences increase the likelihood that women will seek out help following a victimization experience? What sorts of experiences decrease this likelihood?

3. What contributions does this research make to the current literature on this topic?

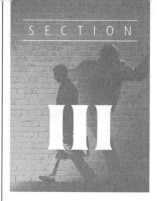

III

Women and Victimization

Rape and Sexual Assault

Historical Perspectives on Rape and Sexual Assault

Rape is one of the oldest crimes in society and has existed in every historical and contemporary society around the world. Laws prohibiting the act of rape, or intercourse under force, threat, or without the consent of the individual, have existed for almost four thousand years. One of the first laws prohibiting the crime of rape can be found in the Code of Hammurabi from Babylon. Ancient Greek, Roman, and Judaic societies also criminalized the act of rape under various circumstances. Some laws distinguished between the rape of a married versus an unmarried woman, and the punishments for these crimes varied based on the status of the victim (Ewoldt, Monson, & Langhinrichsen-Rohling, 2000). Others viewed rape not as a violent sexual offense but as a property crime (Burgess-Jackson, 1999). If the victim was an unmarried woman, the rape tainted her status and value for potential marriage. As a result, many fathers negotiated to have their daughters marry their rapists (Dodderidge, 1632). Even cases of forcible sexual assault (where the victim is compelled to engage in sexually based acts other than intercourse) brought shame to the victim, as the acknowledgment of a rape was an admission of sexual activity. In many cases of forcible sexual assault, women were blamed for tempting offenders into immoral behaviors. During criminal rape trials, a woman's sexual history was often put on display in an attempt to discredit her in front of a jury. By portraying female victims of sexual assault as complicit in the behavior, the responsibility of an offender's actions were mitigated. Such a practice represented a double standard as the courts did not request similar information about a man's sexual history, as it would be considered prejudicial in the eyes of the jury (Odem, 1995).

Until the 20th century, early American statutes on rape limited the definition to a narrow view of sexual assault. Consider the following definition of rape that was included in the Model Penal Code in 1955:

Section 213.1: Rape and Related Offenses

1. Rape. A male who has sexual intercourse with a female not his wife is guilty of rape if

    a. he compels her to submit by force or by threat of imminent death, serious bodily injury, extreme pain or kidnapping, to be inflicted on anyone; or

    b. he has substantially impaired her power to appraise or control her conduct by administering or employing without her knowledge drugs, intoxicants or other means for the purpose of preventing resistance; or

    c. the female is unconscious; or

    d. the female is less than 10 years old.

© Scott Houston/Corbis

▲ **Photo 3.1**　In response to a Toronto police officer's comment that "women should avoid dressing like sluts in order not to be victimized," over 3,000 people gathered at Queen's Park in Toronto on April 3, 2011, to protest the rape myth that women ask to be sexually assaulted based on their appearance. Since then, "Slut Walks" have been organized around the world to raise awareness about the danger of rape myths and their effects on victims.

What is wrong with this definition? First, it reduces the definition of rape to the act of intercourse, and it excludes other acts of sexual assault, such as oral sex, sodomy, or penetration by a foreign object. Second, it limits the victim-offender relationship to a male perpetrator and a female victim. While women make up the majority of victims, such a definition excludes cases of **same-sex sexual assault**, such as a female sexually assaulting a female or a male-on-male assault, or cases where the victim is a male (and the offender is female). Third, this definition requires that force, or the threat of force, must be used in order for an act to qualify as rape, and it focuses on violence and brutality as proof of the crime. Fourth, this definition creates a marital status exemption such that men could not be prosecuted for raping their wives. Finally, the definition fails to acknowledge attempted rapes as a crime and the traumatic effects of these "near misses" of victimization. However, we do see some positive influences from the Model Penal Code that has influenced present-day laws on rape and sexual assault. First, the Model Penal Code acknowledges that the absence of consent for sexual intercourse (including in cases involving intoxication or unconsciousness) constitutes rape. Second, the definition (while limited) acknowledges that sexual acts involving children are a crime.

While contemporary definitions of rape vary from state to state, many present-day laws include similar provisions. Today, most laws broadly define sexual victimization as sexual behaviors that are unwanted and harmful to the victim. Most emphasize the use of force or coercion that is displayed by the offender, rather than focusing on the response or conduct of the victim. This is not to say that the actions of the victim (such as her attire or behaviors) are not chastised by defense counsel or members of the jury, but the law itself does not require victims to demonstrate physical levels of resistance.

Another development in contemporary rape laws involves the abolishment of the marital-rape exemption clause, as every state now has laws on the books that identify rape within the context of marriage as a criminal act. In an effort to resolve some of the limitations with the word *rape*, the term *sexual assault* is often used to identify forms of sexual victimization that are not included under the traditionally narrow definition of rape. These laws have expanded the definitions of sexual assault beyond penile-vaginal penetration and include sodomy, forced oral copulation, and unwanted fondling and touching of a sexual nature. Cases of child sexual assault are treated differently in many jurisdictions, and age of consent laws have led to the development of statutory rape laws. Finally, sex offender registration laws, such as Megan's Law and Jessica's Law, require the community receive notification of sexual offenders and the placing of residential, community, and supervision restrictions on offenders.

▧ Defining Sexual Victimization

What behaviors are included within the definitions of rape and sexual assault? The answer to this question depends on the source. Historically, the Uniform Crime Reports considered only cases of forcible rape. Such a definition excluded the majority of cases of rape and sexual assault. In addition, this practice by the UCR did not account for cases of attempted rape/sexual assault. Although the Federal Bureau of Investigation (2012a, c) changed their data collection practice in 2012 to include both completed and attempted cases of rape and sexual assault, the National Crime Victimization Survey (NCVS) defines rape as the "forced sexual intercourse . . . (including) vaginal, oral, or anal penetration by offender(s)."[1] The NCVS collects data not only on penile penetration but also includes cases of penetration with a foreign object. At the same time, states vary significantly on their own definitions of these crimes. Some states limit rape to penile-vaginal penetration and use sexual assault as a catch-all category of other crimes, while other states use multiple statutes to distinguish between different forms of sexual assault. While some of these statutes are very specific, others combine multiple forms of assault under a single penal code definition.

The limited clarity on the legal definitions of rape and sexual assault, coupled with the personification of these crimes in popular culture and the media can have a significant effect on victims. In many cases, people who experience acts that are consistent with a legal definition of rape or sexual assault may not label their experience as such. As a result, they do not see themselves as such and therefore do not report these crimes to the police, nor do they seek out therapeutic resources. In many of these cases, women who experience these acts do not define themselves as victims because their experience differs from their personal definitions of what rape and sexual assault look like. For example, the crime of sexual assault is perpetuated throughout fiction novels and made for television movies as a stranger who attacks a victim in his home or on a dark sidewalk at night. Despite the high degree to which such events are manifested within popular culture, real life cases of this nature are relatively rare. Indeed, findings from the NCVS data demonstrate that cases of **stranger rape** with female victims account for only 22% of all sexual assaults (Planty, Langton, Krebs, Berzofsky, & Smiley-McDonald, 2013). Such findings highlight that the majority of rapes and sexual assault are perpetuated by people that are known to the victim.

The lack of an understanding of a definition of rape and sexual assault affects offenders, as well. Many people who admit to engaging in behaviors that meet the legal criteria for rape or sexual assault generally do not define their own actions as criminal. One of the most frequently cited studies on rape and sexual assault surveyed 2,971 college

[1]See definitions at http://www.bjs.gov/index.cfm?ty=tda.

men regarding self-reported conduct that met the legal definitions of rape, attempted rape, sexual coercion, and unwanted sexual contact. Based on these reports, the results indicated that 1,525 acts of sexual assault had occurred, including 187 acts of rape. Of those whose acts met the legal definition of rape, 84% of the "perpetrators" believed that their acts did not constitute rape (Warshaw, 1994).

Prevalence of Rape and Sexual Assault

Despite the acknowledgment that rape and sexual assault are two of the most underreported types of crimes, the known data indicate that these crimes pervade our society. According to the Rape, Abuse and Incest National Network (RAINN), a rape, attempted rape, or sexual assault occurs approximately once every 2 minutes. This figure represents roughly 213,000 victims of these crimes that are documented by the U.S. Department of Justice's National Crime Victimization Survey annually (2011 survey).[2] While the U.S. Department of Justice (2003) found that 40% of victims report their crime to the police, other research has placed this number significantly lower, at 16% for adult women (Kilpatrick, Resnick, Ruggiero, Conoscenti, & McCauley, 2007) and only 2% for college women (Fisher, Daigle, Cullen, & Turner, 2003). Given the stigmatizing nature of this crime, it is not surprising that rape, attempted rape, and sexual assault are some of the most underreported crimes, making it difficult to determine the extent of this problem. While researchers attempt to estimate the prevalence of sexual assault, they are faced with their own set of challenges, including differences in defining sexual assault, the emphasis on different sample populations (adolescents, college-aged adults, adults, etc.), or different forms of data (arrest data vs. self-report surveys). Regardless of these issues and the data it yields, it appears that sexual assault affects most individuals in some way (either personally, or through someone they know) at some point in their lifetime.

Prevalence studies report a wide range of data on the pervasiveness of rape and sexual assault in the United States. A national study on rape published in 2007 indicated that 18% of women in America have experienced rape at some point in their lifetime, with an additional 3% of women experiencing an attempted rape. A comparison of these findings to the Violence Against Women survey in 1996 indicates that little change has occurred in the prevalence of this crime over time (15% of all women). Indeed, these results demonstrate an increase in the number of rape cases, which is contrary to the belief that rape has declined significantly in recent times. Rates of sexual assault appear to be higher on college campuses, where it is estimated that between 20% and 25% of women will experience a completed or attempted rape at some point during their collegiate career (Fisher, Cullen, & Turner, 2000). The collegiate experience contains many variables that may increase the risk for sexual assault—campus environments that facilitate a "party" atmosphere, easy access to alcohol and drugs, increases in freedom, and limited supervision by older adults (Sampson, 2003). In this environment, the majority of sexual assaults against university women occurred between the evening and early morning hours during or after a party. Alcohol was involved in most of these cases where the victims knew their attackers. Victims are also more likely to be younger and less knowledgeable about the dangers of sexual assault and its relationship to the school/party experience. In addition, the more that students engage in substance use, the greater the risk for victimization as they are more likely to cross paths with a motivated offender (Hines, Armstrong, Reed, & Cameron, 2012). Findings from studies such as these have led researchers, rape-crisis organizations, and policy makers to posit that one in four American women will be victimized by rape or sexual assault (or an attempt) within their lifetime.

Rape Myths

Rape myths are defined as "attitudes and beliefs that are generally false but are widely and persistently held, and that serve to deny and justify male sexual aggression against women" (Lonsway & Fitzgerald, 1994, p. 134). Table 3.1 highlights some of the most commonly perpetuated myths about rape.

---

[2]The National Crime Victimization Survey does not include victims under the age of 12.

The acceptance of rape myths by society is a contributing factor in the practice of victim blaming. First, the presence of rape myths allows society to shift the blame of rape from the offender to the victim. By doing so, we can avoid confronting the realities of rape and sexual assault in society. This denial serves as a vicious cycle: As we fail to acknowledge the severity of rape and sexual assault, which leads to victims not reporting their crime to authorities, this results in greater acceptance that the crime is not taken seriously by society as a whole. Second, the presence of rape myths lends support to the notion of a just world hypothesis, which suggests that only good things happen to good people and bad things happen to those who deserve it. Rape myths, such as "she asked for it," serve to perpetuate the notion of the just world in action (Lonsway & Fitzgerald, 1994).

Offenders often use rape myths to excuse or justify their actions. Excuses occur when offenders admit that their behavior was wrong but blame their actions on external circumstances outside of their control. In these instances, offenders deny responsibility for their actions. Statements such as "I was drunk" or "I don't know what came over me" are examples of excuses. In comparison, justifications occur when offenders admit responsibility for their actions but argue that their behavior was acceptable under the circumstances. Examples of justifications include "She asked for it" or "Nothing really happened." Miscommunication appears to play a significant role for men, as well, who ask, "When does no mean no, or when does no mean yes?" By suggesting that men "misunderstand" their victim's refusal for sexual activity, the responsibility of rape is transferred from the offender back to the victim.

Some victims accept these excuses or justifications for their assault that minimize or deny the responsibility of their offender. In cases where the male offender "got carried away," female victims often accept the actions of the offender as a natural consequence of male sexuality. In these cases, victims feel that they deserve their victimization as a result of their own actions. Many victims argue that "they should have known better" or that "they didn't try hard enough to stop it." In these cases, victims believe that they put themselves at risk as a result of their own decision-making process.

The prevalence and acceptance of rape myths in society does a significant disservice for both victims and society in general in terms of understanding the realities of rape. These myths permit us to believe that stranger rape is "real" rape, whereas **acquaintance rape,** by persons known to the victim, is interpreted as less serious, less significant, and less harmful because the offender is known to the victim. Rape myths perpetuate the belief that women should be more fearful of the **symbolic assailant**—the stranger who lurks in the alley or hides in the bushes and surprises the victim. Rape myths suggest that in order for a woman to be raped, she needs to

Table 3.1 Rape Myths

- A woman who gets raped usually deserves it, especially if she has agreed to go to a man's house or park with him.
- If a woman agrees to allow a man to pay for dinner, then it means she owes him sex.
- Acquaintance rape is committed by men who are easy to identify as rapists.
- Only women can be raped or sexually assaulted by men.
- Women who do not fight back have not been raped.
- Once a man reaches a certain point of arousal, sex is inevitable, and he cannot help forcing himself upon a woman.
- Most women lie about acquaintance rape because they have regrets after consensual sex.
- Women who say "No" really mean "Yes."
- Certain behaviors such as drinking or dressing in a sexually appealing way make rape a woman's responsibility.
- If she had sex with me before, she has consented to have sex with me again.
- A man cannot rape his wife.
- Only *bad* women get raped.
- Women secretly enjoy being raped.

©iStock/jsp

▲ **Photo 3.2**   The Code of Hammurabi is one of the oldest legal artifacts in the world and dates back to 1772 BC. It includes punishments for 282 different crimes, including rape. Today it is housed at the Louvre Museum in Paris, France.

fight back against her attacker and leave the scene with bruises and injuries related to her efforts to thwart the assault. Rape myths also suggest that real rape victims always report their attackers and have evidence collected and that an offender is identified who is then arrested, prosecuted, and sentenced to the fullest extent under the law. Alas, this rarely occurs within our criminal justice system. Instead, the majority of cases involve victims that know their offender, and victims that do not report these cases to the police. Even when such cases are reported, the prosecution of an offender can be a difficult task. Here, the consequence of pervasive rape myths in society serves to limit the public's understanding about the realities of rape which in turn can limit the victim's opportunity for justice.

Acquaintance Versus Stranger Assault

As illustrated above, cases of stranger rape are not the most common type of sexual assault. Young women are socialized to be wary of walking alone at night, to be afraid that a scary man will jump out of the bushes and attack them. Unfortunately, many prevention efforts that advise women on what they can do to keep themselves safe from sexual assault often focus on these situations of stranger danger. While these tools are certainly valuable in enhancing women's safety, they fail to acknowledge the reality of sexual assault. Acquaintance rape accounts for 90% of all rapes of college women (Sampson, 2003). Additionally, 60% of all rape and sexual assault incidents occur either at the victim's home or at the home of a friend, neighbor, or relative (Greenfeld, 1997). Cases of acquaintance rape and sexual assault tend to entail lower levels of physical force by the offender and involve less resistance by the victim compared to cases of stranger rape (Littleton, Breitkopf, & Berenson, 2008). Alas, each of these realities are missing from the stereotypical scripts about rape and sexual assault.

It is difficult to assess how many sexual assault victims disclose their victimization to police. Research conducted by Millar, Stermac, and Addison (2002) documented that 61% of acquaintance rapes are not reported to the police. In comparison, Rickert, Wiemann, and Vaughan (2005) found that only one of 86 study participants made a report to law enforcement authorities, and an additional four victims sought services from a mental health professional. While these findings demonstrate a dramatic range of reporting rates, it is safe to conclude that acquaintance rape is significantly underreported. Society tends to discount the validity of acquaintance rape, suggesting that it is a lessor criminal act compared to stranger rape (i.e., real rape). Yet research demonstrates that victims of acquaintance rape suffer significant mental health trauma as a result of their victimization. This trauma is often exacerbated by the fact that many victims of acquaintance rape tend to blame themselves for their own victimization. In many cases, these victims are less likely to seek assistance from rape crisis or counseling services.

CASE STUDY

Spotlight on the Steubenville High School Rape Case

Steubenville, Ohio, is a small town located along the Ohio River. According to the 2012 census, the town had only 18,429 residents, 79% of who are White (U.S. Census, 2013). Sporting events at the local high school are popular community events and Steubenville High School stands as one of the best football programs among high schools in the country and has won three state championships.

In August 2012, Steubenville was thrust into the national spotlight after a 16-year-old girl was sexually assaulted by several of her peers. What made this case particularly noteworthy is that her assault was videotaped and her assailants posted the video on social media sites, such as YouTube and Twitter. In the photos and videos, two Steubenville High football team members Trent Mays and Ma'lik Richmond (both 16 at the time of the offense) are shown carrying the victim by her hands and feet as she was so intoxicated that she was unable to walk. Video also documents the accused penetrating the victim's vagina with their fingers and flashing her breasts to the camera (Abad-Santos, 2013). While under many state laws this would be considered sexual assault, Ohio's state law includes digital penetration under its definition of rape (Oppel, 2013).

Many blamed the victim (who was so intoxicated that she did not know she had been violated until she saw the photos and videos online) and called her a "train whore." Even one of the football coaches joined in on the blaming, stating, "What else are you going to tell your parents when you come home drunk like that and after a night like that? She had to make up something. Now people are trying to blow up our football program because of it" (Abad-Santos, 2013). During the trial, the defense counsel introduced testimony that tried to paint the victim as culpable in her own attack by calling two former friends who testified that the victim not only had a history of drinking in excess but also told contradictory stories about the events of the evening (Welsh-Huggins, 2013a).

The judge found that the victim was so intoxicated that she lacked the cognitive ability to consent to sexual activity (Oppel, 2013). Both Mays and Richmond were found guilty in juvenile court and sentenced to one year in the state juvenile correctional facility. Mays received an additional one-year sentence for the crime of distributing nude images of a minor (Ng, 2013). In her report of the verdict, CNN reporter Poppy Harlow critiqued the court's decision, stating that it had been "incredibly difficult [to watch] as these two young men—who had such promising futures, star football players, very good students—literally watched as they believed their life fell apart" (Harlow, 2013). On January 7, 2014, Richmond was released from custody after serving nine months of his sentence. Even though he was sentenced in the juvenile court, he is required to register as a sex offender for the next 20 years (Fox News, 2014). Mays remains incarcerated.

In addition to charging the assailants, officials have questioned whether bystanders and others involved in the event should be charged with a crime. What about those who were not in attendance but shared photos and videos of the assault? What is their responsibility? These are people whose social media commentary included statements such as "the song of the night is 'Rape Me' by Nirvana" and "some people just deserve to be peed on" (Dissell, 2012). While none of these individuals have been charged with any crimes, the case does not end with Mays and Richmond as several school personnel have been indicted by a grand jury on charges related to the rape case. William Rhinaman (who served as the school's information technology director) and

(Continued)

(Continued)

© JASON COHN/Reuters/Corbis

▲ **Photo 3.3**   Trent Mays and Ma'lik Richmond appear in juvenile court in Steubenville, Ohio. Mays and Richmond were adjudicated delinquent of rape in a case that highlighted the use of social media and victimization.

Superindendent Michael McVey have been indicted on charges including tampering with evidence, obstruction of justice, obstructing official business, and perjury. Matthew Belardine, a volunteer football coach, was charged with allowing underage drinking and contributing to the delinquency of a child. In addition, two teenaged girls received 6 months probation for threating the victim with bodily harm on Facebook and Twitter (*Huffington Post*, 2013; Welsh-Huggins, 2013b).

The Steubenville case highlights the role that rape culture continues to play in our society. In many ways, this case mirrors that of Cheryl Araujo who was raped in a bar in New Bedford, Massachusetts, in 1983, a case that inspired the 1988 film *The Accused* starring Jodie Foster. In Araujo's case (and portrayed in the film), several of the bar patrons encouraged and cheered on the offenders (Murtha, 2013). Thirty years later, kids at the party did nothing to protect the victim in the Steubenville case and further victimized her with their taunts and comments on social media. These forms of violence contribute to a culture of rape whereby offender actions are minimized and blame for these events is focused on the victim.

✉ Drug-Facilitated Sexual Assault

A **drug-facilitated rape** is defined as an unwanted sexual act following the deliberate intoxication of a victim. In comparison, an **incapacitated rape** is an unwanted sexual act that occurs after a victim voluntarily consumes drugs or alcohol. In both cases, the victim is too intoxicated by drugs and/or alcohol to be aware of her behavior, and she is therefore unable to consent. Kilpatrick et al. (2007) found that 5% of women experience drug-facilitated or incapacitated rape.

Recent research has discussed a rise in incapacitated rapes through the involuntary drugging of victims. The terms *date rape drug* and *drug-facilitated sexual assault* have been used to identify how the involuntary consumption of substances have been used in sexual assault cases. Table 3.2 provides a description of the different types of substances that are commonly used in cases of drug-facilitated sexual assault. In many cases, these substances are generally colorless, odorless, and/or tasteless when dissolved in a drink and result in a rapid intoxication that renders a potential rape victim unconscious and unable to recall events that occurred while she was intoxicated. One research study identified that less than 2% of sexual assault incidents were directly attributed to the deliberate covert drugging of the victim (Scott-Ham & Burton, 2005). However, these findings document reported cases of sexual assault, and it is reasonable to conclude that many cases of drug-facilitated sexual assault go unreported, as victims may be reluctant to report a crime for which they have little recollection.

Table 3.2 Substances Commonly Used in Drug-Facilitated Sexual Assaults

- GHB (Gamma-Hydroxybutyric acid)
  - GHB comes in a few forms—a liquid that contains no odor or color, a white powder, and a pill. GHB has not been approved by the FDA since 1990, so it is considered illegal to possess or sell. GHB can take effect in as little as 15 minutes and can last for 3 to 4 hours. GHB is considered a Schedule 1 drug under the Controlled Substances Act. GHB leaves the body within 10 to 12 hours, making it very difficult to detect.
- Ketamine
  - Ketamine is an anesthetic that is generally used to sedate animals in a veterinarian's office. Ketamine can be particularly dangerous when used in combination with other drugs and alcohol. It is very fast acting and can cause individuals to feel as if they are disassociated from their body and be unaware of their circumstances. It can cause memory loss, affecting the ability of a victim to recall details of the assault.
- Rohypnol (Flunitrazepam)
  - Rohypnol is a dissolvable pill of various sizes and colors (round, white, oval, green-gray). Rohypnol is not approved for medical use in the United States, and much of the supply comes from Mexico. However, the manufacturer of this drug recently changed the chemistry of the pill such that if it is inserted into a clear liquid, it will change the color of the drink to a bright blue color, allowing for potential victims to increase the chance that they could identify whether their drink has been altered. Rohypnol effects can be noticeable within 30 minutes of being ingested; the individual appears overly intoxicated, and the drug affects their balance, stability, and speech patterns. Like many other substances, Rohypnol leaves the body in a rapid fashion, generally between 36 and 72 hours of ingestion.
- Alcohol
  - Alcohol is one of the most common "date rape" drugs. Here, victims drink to excess, placing themselves at risk for sexual assault. Not only do victims willingly consume alcohol, it is (generally, based on the age of the individual) legal and easily obtained. The consumption of alcohol impairs judgment, lowers inhibition, and affects a victim's ability to recognize potentially dangerous situations.

With the exception of alcohol, the majority of the substances that are used in cases of drug-facilitated sexual assault (such as GHB, or gamma-hydroxybutyrate, ketamine, and Rohypnol) are labeled as controlled substances, and the possession of these drugs is considered a federal offense under the Controlled Substances Act of 1970. In addition, the Drug-Induced Rape Prevention and Punishment Act of 1996 provides penalties for up to 20 years for the involuntary drugging of an individual in cases of violence (National Drug Intelligence Center, n.d.). Many states have enacted laws that provide specific sanctions in cases of drug-facilitated sexual assault. For example, Colorado Penal Code § 18–3–402(4d) distinguishes cases of drug-facilitated sexual assault as one where "the actor has substantially impaired the victim's power to appraise or control the victim's conduct by employing, without the victim's consent, any drug, intoxicant, or other means for the purpose of causing submissions." Here, state law provides an assessment of a victim's ability to consent to sexual relations and holds that the level of intoxication, combined with the resulting mental impairment of the individual, must affect the victim's ability to exercise reasonable judgment. In addition, Colorado's law provides for an elevated punishment of these cases. While sexual assault is generally considered a class 4 felony (punishable by 2–6 years in prison), drug facilitated sexual assault is considered a class 3 felony and calls for a punishment range of 4–12 years. The mandatory parole in these cases also increases from 3 to 5 years.

While there has been increased attention to sexual assault due to involuntary intoxication, this is not the primary form of drug-facilitated sexual assault. Rather, cases where the victim is sexually assaulted following her voluntary intoxication of alcohol make up the majority of drug-facilitated sexual assaults. In a sample of rape cases of college-aged women, alcohol was involved in 79% of cases of nonforcible rape (Kilpatrick et al., 2007). The use of drugs and alcohol places women at a greater risk for sexual assault. Not only may women be less aware of the risk for sexual assault and labeled as a target for potential offenders due to a reduction of their inhibitions, but they may also be unable to resist their attackers due to their incapacitated state. Additionally, while voluntarily intoxicated individuals are legally incapable of giving consent for sexual activity (Beynon, McVeigh, McVeigh, Leavey, & Bellis, 2008), these victims are often held as the most responsible of all sexual assault victims, since they chose to use intoxicating substances recreationally. As a result, the actions of perpetrators in these cases are most likely to be excused or diminished (Girard & Senn, 2008).

CASE STUDY

Spotlight on the Invisible War: Rape in the Military

As a prestigious military academy, the Air Force Academy in Colorado Springs, CO, receives high rankings for their training of pilots (as well as their football team). However, 2003 brought a new level of attention to the Academy, as allegations of sexual abuse among the ranks were made public. Not only did victims suggest that rape and sexual assault occurred within the student body on a regular basis, victims suggested that military officials knew of the abuse but did little to stop the systematic assault of female cadets by their male counterparts. Women who came forward with allegations were often punished by their superiors, leading many victims to remain silent about the abuse they endured. While six cadets came forward as part of the allegations, a survey of female graduates in 2003 suggest that the issue of rape, sexual assault, and sexual harassment is much more prevalent that these few cases. Over 88% of the female graduates participated in the survey, and 12% of women acknowledged that they experienced completed or attempted rape at some point during their college career. An additional 70% of women referenced cases of sexual harassment, including pressure to engage in sexual behaviors (Schemo, 2003). Since news of the 2003 scandal broke, more victims have come forward. Alas, punishment of the offenders is exceedingly rare. Over the past ten years, only two offenders have been court martialed for their abuse of female cadets. Only one case yielded a conviction, and the offender was sentenced to seven months in jail (CBS News, 2009).

There have also been cases of sexual abuse by military officers against prisoners of war. In 2004, allegations of sexual and other forms of abuse came to light involving members of the U.S. Army and prisoners held at the Abu Ghraib prison in Baghdad, Iraq. The allegations involved significant acts of torture of the prisoners, including being sodomized by a baton, forced oral copulation on another male inmate, forced masturbation, and being doused with chemicals. Several photographs of the abuse were released in conjunction with an article in *The New Yorker* magazine (Hersh, 2004), though officials suggest that there are thousands of photographs depicting acts of abuse. In many of these photographs, military personnel are shown posing with the prisoners, smiling and giving the "two thumbs up" signal. Drawing from the Taguba Report, an internal military document not intended for public release, Hersh detailed the acts of abuse and commented how "the 372nd's abuse of prisoners seemed almost routine—a fact of Army life that the soldiers felt no need to hide" (Hersh 2004, para. 12). In an interview on *60 Minutes* with Dan Rather, Former Marine Lt. Col. Bill Cowan said, "We went into Iraq to stop things like this from happening, and indeed, here they are happening under our tutelage" (Leung, February 11, 2009). Over the next two years, eleven military personnel were convicted and dishonorably discharged from the Army for their involvement in the abuse. Two of the officials depicted in the photographs were Specialist Charles Granier and Specialist Lynndie England. Much was made of their participation in the acts, as many of the photos released in *The New Yorker* article included Granier and England perpetuating acts of abuse. At the time of her court-martial, England was pregnant with her then-fiancee Granier's child. England's involvement in the acts was particularly condemned by the media as a result of her gender—how could a woman engage in such horrible actions? During her trial, she claimed that she followed the directions of Granier, her lover and superior officer—"I did everything he wanted me to do. I didn't want to lose him" (England, March 17, 2008). For their involvement in the Abu Ghraib scandal, Granier was sentenced to 10 years (he served 6½ years) and England received 6 years (she served 3½). Despite these punishments, several high-ranking officials continue to suggest that the acts of Abu Ghraib are acceptable techniques of interrogation.

Unfortunately, cases of rape and sexual assault are not limited to the academy or to times of war. In an effort

▲ Photo 3.4   Ariana Klay was gang raped in 2009 by a fellow marine and his civilian friend. When she reported the rape to her commanding officer, he replied, "It's your fault for wearing running shorts and makeup." One of her perpetrators was given immunity in the case while the other was convicted of adultery and indecent language and was sentenced to only 45 days in military jail. Klay and others have fought for changes in the way sexual assault cases are handled in the military.

to bring attention to the issue of rape in the military, filmmakers Kirby Dick and Amy Ziering presented their film *The Invisible War* at the Sundance Movie Festival in 2012. Drawing from real stories from military personnel, the film portrays the victimization of these soldiers and the response, or lack thereof, by military officials. Their story paints a grim picture about sexual violence in the military as they suggest that 20% of all active duty women are sexually victimized. Other scholars have indicated that 34% of active duty women (and 6% of men) suffer harassment of a sexual nature (Lipari, Cook, Rock, & Matos, 2008). Even official Department of Defense data indicate that the number of sexual assault cases is growing, as 3,230 reports were made in 2009, which amounts to an 11% increase over prior year data (U.S. Department of Defense, 2010). Table 3.3 highlights some of the findings from this study. Data from the 2005 Service Academy Sexual Harassment and Assault Survey indicate that 85% of females and 42% of men experienced some form of sexual victimization over the past year. While the most common form of victimization involved sexual harassment, female cadets were significantly more likely to indicate that they had experienced forms of unwanted sexual touching, sexual coercion, or rape. In addition, women were almost four times more likely to experience multiple acts of victimization compared to men (Snyder, Fisher, Scherer, & Daigle, 2012). Given the historical treatment in sexual victimization cases, it is perhaps not surprising that victims in this study had negative perceptions of the leadership in the military academies and their efforts to respond to these issues. These findings have significant implications given that graduates from these academies move on to become leaders within our military branches.

(Continued)

(Continued)

Table 3.3   Sexual Victimization at Military Academies

Type of Victimization	All Victims (%)	Males (%)	Females (%)
Unwanted sexual attention	22.65	10.79	41.24
Sexual harassment	55.73	38.40	82.89
Unwanted sexual contact	15.85	8.96	26.65
Sexual coercion	7.99	4.39	13.64
Rape	3.45	2.41	5.07
Total victimization	58.90	41.85	85.57
Multiple victimizations	25.00	12.23	45.04

SOURCE: Snyder, Fisher, Scherer, & Daigle (2012).

Since [the documentary's] release, the Invisible No More Campaign has generated new conversations about how to combat this issue. Following his review of the film, Secretary of Defense Leon Panetta ordered that all sexual assault investigations be altered to provide multiple avenues for victims to report cases of assault. Previous military policy dictated that the assault be reported to the victim's immediate supervisor. Panetta also directed each branch to develop a Special Victims Unit to respond to allegations of sexual assault.[3]

Changes have also occurred at the Air Force Academy. In response to the sexual assault scandal of 2003, the Air Force Academy established the Sexual Assault Prevention and Response (SARP) team in June 2005. SARP provides a 24/7 hotline for victims and has two victim advocates available to provide services to victims. In addition, SARP delivers approximately 11 hours of training over the cadet's four-year educational experience on rape and sexual assault prevention. Beginning on Day 2 of basic training, the cadets learn about the various different behaviors that constitute rape and sexual assault. As a result, SARP has seen increased reporting rates of these incidents, with approximately 25% of victims reporting their victimization (T. Beasley, personal telephone conversation, September 11, 2012). What is unclear is if these interventions are decreasing behaviors or simply increasing reporting practices. In 2011, 31 victims filed restricted reports with SARP and an additional 21 victims filed unrestricted reports. While a restricted report allows victims to receive counseling and other services from the sexual assault response team, these reports remain confidential and no charges are filed. In an unrestricted case, the Air Force Office of Special Investigations is able to assess whether criminal charges will be filed against the perpetrator (Branum, 2013). However, it appears that many victims do not report these cases when alcohol is involved, as the victim is at risk for being reprimanded for underage drinking (Blackwell, 2012). There does appear to be an increased trend in following through on these cases, as there were five cases

---

[3]See http://www.notinvisible.org/the_movie for information about the film *The Invisible War*.

brought against cadets at the Air Force Academy in 2012 with an additional two cases with pending charges for 2013 (*Air Force Times*, 2012).

Despite recent changes, rape in the military continues to be a problem. In 2012, Air Force Staff Sergeant Luis Walker was convicted on twenty-eight counts of rape, sexual assault, and aggravated sexual misconduct against ten victims. His conviction is a positive step toward fighting for justice for victims of sexual assault in the military. Walker received 20 years in prison for his crimes (Peterson, 2012). These violations occurred at the Lackland Air Force base in San Antonio, Texas, where all Air Force recruits are sent for basic training. While approximately 20% of all recruits are female, the majority of boot camp instructors are male (Associated Press, 2012). Unfortunately, Walker is only one of several boot-camp instructors involved in the scandal at Lackland. The recent arrest of Lieutenant Colonel Jeffrey Krusinski demonstrates that the fight against sexual assault in the military is far from over. In 2013, Krusinski served as the branch chief for the sexual assault prevention and response team. Yet in May of that year, he was accused of sexually assaulting a woman. The victim in this case alleges that Krusinski grabbed her sexually in a parking lot. Cases such as these demonstrate that there is still significant work to be done to change the culture of sexual assault that pervades the military (Ross, 2013).

In an effort to create systemic changes on how sexual assault cases are handled by the military, members of the U.S. Senate have made attempts to change the Uniform Military Code of Justice. Senators Kirsten Gillibrand (D-NY) and Claire McCaskill (D-MO) who are both members of the Senate Armed Services Committee have tackled this issue head on and have challenged military officials to increase their understanding about rape in the military. According to Gillibrand, "Not every single commander necessarily wants women in the force. Not every single commander believes what a sexual assault is. Not every single commander can distinguish between a slap on the ass and a rape because they merge all of these crimes together" (*NY Daily News*, 2013, para. 11). In December 2013, Congress passed the Military Justice Improvement Act, which makes a number of significant reforms for how cases of sexual assault are handled within the military ranks. These include an end to the statute of limitations for rape and sexual assault cases, makes retaliation against victims a crime, and bars military commanders from overturning convictions on sexually based crimes. It also mandates a dishonorable discharge for those convicted of such crimes. While these reforms are significant, Gillibrand was unable to garner support for what some have argued would have been the most controversial policy change: eliminating the involvement of military commanders in these cases and assigning them to independent military prosecutors (O'Keefe, 2013).

▧ Spousal Rape

Earlier in this section, you learned about how early laws on rape included a marital exception clause, which argues that women automatically consent to sex with their husbands as part of their marriage. Even once the legal rights of women began to increase, the relationship between a man and wife was viewed as a private manner, and not one for public scrutiny. This belief system permitted the criminal justice system to maintain a "hands-off" policy when it came to spousal rape. As existing rape laws began to change throughout the 1970s and 1980s, increased attention was brought to the marital rape exception. In 1978, only five states defined marital rape as a crime. By 1993, all 50 states had either eliminated laws that permitted marital rape or had expressly included laws that prohibited this practice. Despite these trends in the United States, marital rape is still legal in many other countries around the world (Fus, 2006).

The majority of cases of marital rape involve cases of emotional coercion, rather than physical force. Examples of emotional coercion include inferences that it is a *wife's duty* to engage in sex with her husband (referred to as social coercion) or the use of power by a husband to exert sexual favors from his wife (referred to as interpersonal coercion). A third form of emotional coercion involves cases where a wife engages in sex for fear of unknown threats or damages that may occur if she refuses. Many of these occurrences are related to cases of domestic violence, where the possibility of violence exists. Cases of marital rape by the use of physical force are referred to as battering rape. In cases of battering rape, the sexual assault is an extension of the physical and emotional violence that occurs within the context of the relationship (Martin, Taft, & Resick, 2007). The physical effects of marital rape are generally greater compared to cases of stranger and acquaintance rape.

Contrary to popular belief, marital rape is as prevalent as other forms of rape, but this victimization is generally hidden from public view. Results from randomized studies showed that 7% to 14% of women experienced completed or attempted rape within the context of marriage, cohabitating, or intimate relationship (Bennice & Resick, 2003). Community samples tend to yield significantly higher rates of marital rape—however, they tend to draw from shelters or therapeutic settings, which offer skewed results. These studies find that 10% to 34% of women studied experienced rape within the context of marriage (Martin et al., 2007).

Despite the criminalization of spousal rape, the cultural acceptance of marital rape still fails to identify these women as victims. By leaving these victims with the belief that their experiences are not considered real rape, these women are less likely to seek assistance for their victimization. Thus, marital rape remains a significant issue in the United States and around the world.

CASE STUDY

Spotlight on Statutory Rape

Statutory rape refers to sexual activity that is unlawful because it is prohibited by legal statute. Unlike other forms of violent sexual assault, statutory rape generally involves individuals who are legally unable to consent to sexual activity due to their age.

Statutory rape laws were initially introduced to protect adolescents from adults, particularly in cases where there was a dramatic age difference. Consider the case of Amy Fisher, a 16-year-old female from New Jersey. She had been engaging in a sexual affair with Joey Buttafuoco, a married man twenty years her senior. The case made headlines in 1991 when Fisher shot Buttafuoco's wife in the head. She survived, and Fisher served seven years in prison for the crime. (Amy Elizabeth Fisher, 2014). Meanwhile, Buttafuoco was sentenced to only 6 months, the maximum sentence under New Jersey law for statutory rape (Marks, 1993). In contrast, the case of Mary Kay Letourneau involved a female offender with a male victim. Mary Kay was a 34-year-old married school teacher in Washington State. She met Vili Fualaau when he was in the second grade. They began a romantic relationship when Vili was just 13. When she began [became] pregnant with Vili's child, Mary Kay's husband reported her to the school authorities and the Department of Social Services. Despite Vili's (and his mother's) assertion that he was not a victim and that they were in love, Mary Kay was arrested for statutory rape. While out on community release, May Kay violated a no-contact order and continued to engage in sexual relations with Vili and became pregnant with their 2nd child. Following a 7½ year sentence, Mary Kay was released from prison in August 2004, and she and Vili were married in May 2005 (Mary Katherine Schmitz, 2014).

Statutory rape laws have also been used against adolescents and their peers. Some would consider these to be victimless crimes as individuals in these cases often do not define themselves as a victim. Rather, they see themselves as willing participants in sexual activity. It is purely the legal distinction of who can, and who cannot consent, that makes these acts a crime. There are two different types of statutory rape laws. The first category includes states where the age of consent is considered a minimum age and sex with anyone under that age is considered a crime. For example, the age of sexual consent in California is 18 and anyone that engages in intercourse that is under the age of 18 is in violation of the state's statutory rape law. So two seventeen year olds that engage in intercourse would be considered to be breaking the law. In the second category are states that define an age range between the individuals. In these cases, it would be considered a crime if one of the individuals was of a minimum age and the other individual was older by a specified number of years under the statute. For example, in Missouri, someone who is at least 21 years old who has sexual intercourse with someone younger than 17 is considered second degree statutory rape. (§ 566.034 (1)). In comparison, Tennessee state law considers statutory rape a criminal act if (1) it involves sexual penetration; (2) the victim is at least 13, but younger than 18; and (3) the offender is at least four years older than the victim. In addition, Tennessee requires that offenders under the age of 18 be tried as a juvenile (§ 39-13-506).

Several states have increased their prosecution of statutory rape cases in an effort to reduce teen pregnancy and the demand on welfare. During the 1990s, legislators targeted welfare reform as a major cause of action. In passing The Personal Responsibility and Work Opportunity Reconciliation Act (PRWORA), legislators noted a significant increase in the number of unwed teen mothers between 1976 and 1991 and indicated that these young single mothers were more likely to apply for welfare benefits. In responding to this issue, legislators noted that "an effective strategy to combat teenage pregnancy must address the issue of male responsibility, including statutory rape culpability" (H.R. 3734-7). Encouraged by this directive, states began to increase their prosecutions of statutory rape cases. One of the most significant examples of this practice comes from California, where then-Governor Pete Wilson allocated additional funding to form a vertical prosecution unit specifically for statutory rape cases. Vertical prosecution units (where prosecutors stay with a case from the beginning and specialize in a particular offense category) generally yield a higher conviction rate as victims are more likely to participate in the process (Donovan, 1996). However, California is not the only state involved in increasing the prosecutions of these crimes. In an effort to assist prosecutors, Mississippi recently passed a law that requires the collection of DNA from babies born to mothers under the age of 16 in case the evidence is needed in statutory rape criminal cases (Diep, 2013).

The increased prosecution of statutory rape cases leads to collateral consequences for offenders. In many states, the conviction of statutory rape requires that offenders must register as a sex offender, which can significantly limit their academic standing as well as their ability to secure employment. Unfortunately, the minimum age of consent laws and state registry requirements fail to distinguish between "two immature high school kids hooking up at a party [and] a pedophile molesting the toddler next door" (Downey, 2007, B1). One suggestion is for states to adopt age-gap provisions to their statutory rape laws. Meanwhile, other states have adopted Romeo and Juliet laws, which maintain the age-gap provision, but do not include the sexual registry requirement. In Florida, if a victim is at least 14 years old and consented to sexual activity with someone who is no more than four years older, the offender can petition to have the registration requirement removed (The Florida Senate, 2011). However, these Romeo and Juliet clauses are not without problems in their own right, as many states do not provide exceptions for cases of same-sex statutory rape. Here, it is important that LGBT youth are protected in the same ways under the law, and states should work to close these gaps (Higdon, 2008). Provisions such as this can help to ensure that the focus of statutory rape prosecution returns to situations of coercion of a victim by an offender, and not on youthful offenders engaging in consensual sexual activity.

⬚ Same-Sex Sexual Violence

Much of the existing research on rape and sexual violence involves a male offender and a female victim. Many of the theories to explain rape involve the use of violence by men to exert power and control over women. This explanation is rooted in a heterosexist ideology. Indeed, our laws, which in many states identify the crime of rape as the unlawful penetration of a penis into a vagina, do not allow for us to legally identify these same-sex cases as rape (though most have additional statutes of sexual assault that would be inclusive of same-sex acts of sexual violation).

Much of the discussion about same-sex rape is limited to male-on-male sexual assault, and many of these studies are conducted within an incarcerated setting. Research on woman-to-woman sexual violence is limited. One study that compared levels of violence experienced by lesbian and heterosexual women found that women involved in same-sex relationships experienced significantly higher levels of nonsexual physical violence (51%) compared to heterosexual women (33%; Bernhard, 2000).

Women (and men) who report same-sex sexual violence are often confronted with a system where agents of the criminal justice system may reflect homophobic views (Wang, 2011). Such perspectives can potentially silence victims and prevent them from seeking legal remedies and social services. Indeed, advocacy services have been slow in responding to the unique and multiple needs of this population (Turrell & Cornell-Swanson, 2005). Some community service providers express a fear that offering services to the lesbian, gay, bisexual, and transgender (LGBT) population could potentially restrict their donations from government or socially conservative individuals and organizations. These conflicts limit the opportunities to identify same-sex sexual assault as a social problem (Girshick, 2002).

⬚ Racial Differences in Sexual Assault

Research suggests that women of color have different experiences of sexual assault, compared to Caucasian women. These differences can be seen in prevalence rates, reporting behaviors, disclosure practices, help-seeking behaviors, and responses by the justice system. For example, research indicates that 18% of White women, compared to 19% of Black women, 34% of American Indian/Alaska Native women, and 24% of women who identify as mixed race report a rape or sexual assault during the course of their lifetime (Tjaden & Thoennes, 2006). Two important issues are raised with these statistics: (1) We already know that rape generally is underreported, so it is possible to assume that the true numbers of rape and sexual assault within different races and ethnicities may be significantly higher than these data indicate; and (2) given the unequal distribution of these statistics by race and ethnicity, compared to their representation in the general population, it is reasonable to conclude that women of color are victimized at a disproportionate rate compared to their White sisters. Despite these issues, the experience of rape and sexual assault within minority communities is significantly understudied in the scholarly research. Here, we ask the question: How do race and ethnicity affect the experience of rape and sexual assault and the response to these crimes by the criminal justice system?

While much of the literature on racial differences in rape and sexual assault focuses on the African American female experience, statistics by Tjaden and Thoennes (2006) highlight the extreme rates of rape within the American Indian and Alaska Native population (AIAN). These data are particularly troubling given that the AIAN population is a small minority in the population, making up only 1.5% of the U.S. population (U.S. Bureau of the Census, 2000). Research using the National Crime Victimization data indicates that compared to other racial and ethnic groups, AIAN women are most likely to experience rape within an intimate partner relationship, versus stranger or acquaintance relationships. Within this context, they were more likely to have a weapon used against them and to be physically assaulted as part of the attack. Alcohol and drugs also play a stronger role in the attacks of AIAN women, with more than two thirds of offenders under the influence of intoxicants, compared to only one third of offenders in cases involving White or Black victims. While AIAN victims are more likely to report these crimes to the police, the majority of these reports come from people on behalf of the victim (family, officials, others) rather than the victim herself (Bachman, Zaykowski, Lanier, Poteyva, & Kallmyer, 2010).

Research by Boykins et al. (2010) investigates the different experiences of sexual assault among Black and White women who sought emergency care following their attack. While no racial and ethnic differences were found between victims in terms of the location of the assault (home, car, outdoors) or whether the offender was known to the victim, Black women were significantly more likely to have a weapon used against them during the attack compared to White women (42% vs. 16.7%). The intoxication of the victim (and offender) also varied by race, as White women were more likely to be under the influence of alcohol (47.2% of White women reported being under the influence, compared to 23.8% of Black women), as were their perpetrators (47.2% of offenders against White women were under the influence, compared to 23.8% of offenders against Black women). In contrast, the use of illicit drugs prior to the assault was more common among Black victims compared to White victims (28.7% vs. 12.5%). However, there were no racial or ethnic differences in the reporting of the assault to police or of the offering or acceptance of counseling resources. Despite the importance of these findings, it is important to keep in mind that few victims seek out emergency services following their assault, which may skew the interpretation of these results.

Not only are women of color less likely to disclose sexual assault, but there are also a number of factors that vary by race and ethnicity that can affect the disclosure and recovery process. Research by Washington (2001) showed that less than half of the women interviewed had disclosed their victimization—when they did disclose, they did so to friends or family members within 24 hours of the assault. However, most of these women experienced incidents of victim blaming as a result of their disclosure. As a result of historical personal and cultural experiences with law enforcement, the majority of these women did not seek out the police to make an official report of their attack. In addition, many of the Black women talked about not reporting as a cultural expectation of keeping their business to themselves. They also mentioned not wanting to perpetuate additional racist views against members of the African American community, particularly if their assailant was also Black.

We have this element in our community that it's the White man or the White race that causes most, if not all, of the problems we have in our communities. If we begin to point out the Black male for specific problems, we tend to get heat . . . and even from some women because we as women have been socialized as well. And it's "Don't bring the Black man down. . . . He's already going to jail, dying, rumored to be an endangered species; so why should we as Black women bring our wrath against him?" (Washington, 2001, p. 1269)

Cultural expectations also limited the help seeking for some African American victims. These women assumed the identity of the "strong Black woman," which in turn restricted many women from seeking out therapeutic resources because "only crazy people went to therapy" (Long & Ullman, 2013, p. 310). Rather than share their victimization, which could make them appear weak, victims would not disclose their assaults, even to close friends or family members. Alas, the lack of support often led to psychological challenges for many survivors. For these women, finding someone that they could trust and talk to about their victimization proved to be a healing experience (Long & Ullman, 2013).

Likewise, cultural expectations also can inhibit the official reporting practices of women within the Asian American and Pacific Islander population (AAPI). Like the African American community, there is a high level of distrust of public officials (often due to negative experiences either in the United States or in the cases of immigrant and refugee individuals, in their home country) as well as a cultural expectation to keep personal issues in the private sphere. Research has highlighted that many AAPI women fail to understand the definitions of rape and sexual assault, which limits the likelihood that such incidents will be reported (Bryant-Davis, Chung, & Tillman, 2009). Concerns over immigration status and language barriers also limit victim reporting. These same factors also affect the use of therapeutic resources as AAPIs have the lowest utilization of mental health services of any racial or ethnic minority group (Abe-Kim et al., 2007).

Within the Hispanic community, Latina women have the highest rates of attempted sexual assault of all ethnic groups. Stereotypes of Latina women as passionate and sexual women can lead to victim blaming by the victim herself and therefore limits the likelihood that they will report (or that their reports will be taken seriously). Given these challenges, it is important for agencies in Hispanic/Latino communities to reach out to the population and dismantle some of the stereotypes and attitudes that can inhibit reporting and help-seeking behaviors (Bryant-Davis et al., 2009). Indeed, research indicates that Hispanic/Latina women are more likely to seek out informal resources (68.9%) versus make a report to the police (32.5%). Their utilization of informal resources included seeking medical attention (34.7%) and disclosing their victimization to a parent (26.6%). However, the rates of disclosure (both formally and informally) were significantly reduced if the victim had a history of childhood victimization (Sabina, Cuevas, & Schally, 2012).

Culture shapes the manner in which people represent themselves, make sense of their lives, and relate to others in the social world. Indeed, the experience of trauma is no different, and we find that women of color are less likely to engage in help-seeking behaviors from traditional models of assistance. While many women of color believe that agencies such as rape-crisis centers can provide valuable resources to victims of sexual assault, they may be hesitant to call upon these organizations for fear that these organizations would be unable to understand their experiences as women of color. In addition, many victims may be unaware that such services are available, particularly given the potential language barriers (Sabina et al., 2012). Instead, victims may turn to sympathetic leaders and women within their own communities. In order to increase the accessibility of these services to women of color, victims and scholars argue that services need to be culturally sensitive and address the unique considerations that women of various racial and ethnic identities face as victims of sexual assault (Tillman, Bryant-Davis, Smith, & Marks, 2010).

The Role of Victims in Sexual Assault Cases

Many women do not identify themselves as victims. According to a national survey of college women, 48.8% of women who were victimized did not consider the incident to be rape. In many cases, victims may not understand the legal definition of rape. Others may be embarrassed and not want others to know. Finally, some women may not want to identify their attacker as a rapist (Fisher et al., 2000).

Several factors increase the likelihood that a victim will report the crime to the police, including injury, concern over contracting HIV, and if they identified the crime as rape. Victims are less likely to report the crime if the offender is a friend or if they were intoxicated (Kilpatrick et al., 2007). For college-aged women, less than 5% of completed and attempted rapes were reported to the police. While women do not report these crimes to law enforcement or school officials, they do not necessarily stay silent, as over two thirds of victims confided in a friend about their attack. The decision by victims to not report their assault to the police stems from a belief that the incident was not harmful or important enough to report. For these women, it may be that they did not believe that they had been victims of a crime or did not want family members or others to know about the attack. Others had little faith in the criminal justice system, as they were concerned that the criminal justice system would not see the event as a serious incident or that there would be insufficient proof that a crime had occurred (Fisher et al., 2000).

Victims who do report their crimes often do so to prevent the crime from happening to others (Kilpatrick et al., 2007). Documented key findings from the National Violence Against Women Survey show that only 43% of reported rapes resulted in an arrest of the offender. Of those reported, only 37% of these cases were prosecuted. Fewer than half (46.2%) of those prosecuted were convicted, and 76% of those convicted were sentenced to jail or prison. Taking unreported rapes into consideration, this means that only 2.2% of all rapists are incarcerated. Of those who reported their rape, less than half of victims indicated that they were satisfied with the way their case was handled by the authorities (Tjaden & Thoennes, 2006).

In other cases, victims decide to report their assaults in an effort to increase community awareness and attention by the criminal justice system on crimes of sexual violence. These victims acknowledge that the small number of successes within the legal system in these types of cases may mean that traditional avenues of justice may not be available to them. In some cases, victims talk of wanting to protect future victims from their assailant, even if nothing came of their report personally. Here, the need to raise awareness in their community trumped their own needs for closure. In the words of one victim,

> I looked back and thought; well I'm not going to let one situation put me off from doing the right thing and going through. I know it would be a harrowing experience sitting there telling them what happened over and over again, but at the end of the day you know people need to be accountable for what they've done. And I thought I've, whether it goes to court or whether it doesn't I've done everything in my power you know to prevent something. (Taylor & Norma, 2012, p. 34)

Many victims make these reports knowing that people and officials may not respond favorably or that family members may reject them, particularly in cases where the offender is a close relative or family friend. These are significant hardships that influence many victims to not disclose their victimization to both officials as well as personal social networks. Despite these challenges, some victims believed that reporting the crime helped in their survival as it validated their victimization experience (Taylor & Norma, 2012).

Victims of rape and sexual assault have both immediate and long-term physical and emotional health needs. Over half of the victims of sexual assault experience symptoms of post-traumatic stress disorder (PTSD) at some point during their lifetime. Symptoms of PTSD can appear months or even years following the assault. The levels of emotional trauma that victims experience lead to significant mental health effects, such as depression, low self-esteem, anxiety, and fear for personal safety. Women with a history of sexual assault are more likely to have seriously considered attempting suicide and are more likely to engage in behaviors that put them at risk, including risky sexual behaviors with multiple partners, extreme weight loss measures, and substance abuse involving alcohol and illegal drugs (Gidycz, Orchowski, King, & Rich, 2008; Kaukinen & DeMaris, 2009). Women who are victimized by strangers may experience anxiety and fear about their surroundings, particularly if the assault occurred in a public setting. For women who were assaulted by a family member, acquaintance, or date, they may experience issues with trusting people.

Given the limits of the criminal justice system, how can we meet the needs of victims in rape and sexual assault cases? The current rape crisis movement developed in response to the perceived need for prevention, community awareness, and amelioration of victims' pain. However, even the best community services are limited and lack adequate resources to effectively combat all needs for victims of sexual assault. While attempts to help survivors of sexual assault involve friends, family members, community agencies, and criminal justice personnel, efforts in help seeking may actually enhance the trauma that victims experience due to lack of support, judgment, and blame by support networks. Additionally, victims may experience further trauma by being forced to relive their trauma as part of the official processing of the assault as a crime (Kaukinen & DeMaris, 2009). Due to these negative experiences in disclosure, many victims choose to keep their assault a secret.

Ultimately, cases of rape and sexual assault can be very difficult to prove in a court of law. Convictions are rare, and many cases are plea-bargained to a lesser charge, many of which carry little to no jail time. Alas, the acceptance of rape myths by police, prosecutors, judges, and juries limits the punishment of offenders in cases of sexual assault. Figure 3.1 highlights how each stage of the criminal justice system reduces the likelihood that offenders will be arrested, charged, and punished for these cases. The effects of these practices can further discourage victims from reporting these crimes, believing that little can be done by criminal justice officials.

Figure 3.1   Punishment and Rape

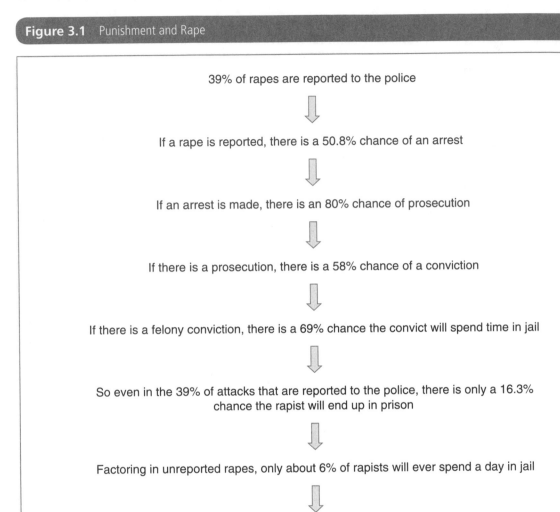

39% of rapes are reported to the police

⬇

If a rape is reported, there is a 50.8% chance of an arrest

⬇

If an arrest is made, there is an 80% chance of prosecution

⬇

If there is a prosecution, there is a 58% chance of a conviction

⬇

If there is a felony conviction, there is a 69% chance the convict will spend time in jail

⬇

So even in the 39% of attacks that are reported to the police, there is only a 16.3% chance the rapist will end up in prison

⬇

Factoring in unreported rapes, only about 6% of rapists will ever spend a day in jail

⬇

15 of 16 walk free

✉ Conclusion

Research on rape and sexual assault indicates a number of areas where the criminal justice system and other social institutions can improve prevention and intervention efforts. Given that adolescents and young adults have higher rates of acquaintance rape and sexual assault, much of these prevention efforts have been targeted toward college campuses. While college campuses have increased their educational activities aimed toward preventing rape on campuses in recent times, these efforts may still be inadequate given the number of assaults that occur on campuses around the nation each year. However, the age of victimization appears to be decreasing, indicating a need for education efforts focused on high school students.

Victims indicate that an increase in public education about acquaintance rape and increased services for counseling would encourage more victims to report their crimes (Kilpatrick et al., 2007). Programs focusing on rape and sexual assault prevention should provide accurate definitions of sexual assault behaviors, the use of realistic examples, discussions about alcohol use and sexual assault, and an understanding of what it means to consent to sexual activity. By tailoring education efforts toward combating myths about rape, these efforts can help reduce the levels of shame that victims may experience as a result of their victimization and encourage them to seek help following a sexual assault. Services need to be made available and known to students, both in terms of services and outreach on campus and information available online.

⊠ Summary

- Rape is one of the most underreported crimes of victimization.
- The risk of rape and sexual assault appears to be higher on college campuses.
- The acceptance of rape myths by society contributes to the practice of victim blaming.
- Many victims of rape and sexual assault fail to identify their experiences as a criminal act.
- Excuses and justifications allow perpetrators of rape and sexual assault to deny or minimize levels of blame and injury toward their victims.
- The majority of rapes and sexual assaults involve individuals who are known to the victim prior to the assault.
- The term *date rape drugs* has been used to identify a group of drugs, such as GHB, Rohypnol, and ketamine, that have been used to facilitate a sexual assault.
- Victims of rape and sexual assault are at risk for long-term physical and emotional health concerns.

KEY TERMS

Acquaintance rape

Drug-facilitated rape

Incapacitated rape

Rape

Same-sex sexual assault

Sexual assault

Spousal rape

Statutory rape

Stranger rape

Symbolic assailant

DISCUSSION QUESTIONS

1. How has the definition of rape evolved over time?

2. Why do many victims of rape and sexual assault choose not to report their crimes to the police?

3. What impact do rape myths play in victim blaming and the denial of offender culpability?

4. Why do many victims of rape and sexual assault fail to identify themselves as victims of a crime?

5. Why are acquaintance rape cases not viewed as "real" rape?

6. What tactics do perpetrators use to coerce sex from their victims?

7. In what ways can prevention efforts be used to educate women and men about the realities of rape and sexual assault?

8. What are the short- and long-term effects of sexual assault? How might early sexual assault yield a pathway to later victimization or offending?

WEB RESOURCES

Bureau of Justice Statistics: http://bjs.ojp.usdoj.gov

Rape, Incest and Abuse National Network: http://www.rainn.org

RAINN—State resources for sexual assault: http://www.rainn.org/get-help/local-counseling-centers/state-sexual-assault-resources

National Clearinghouse on Marital and Date Rape: http://ncmdr.org/

The National Center for Victims of Crime: http://www.ncvc.org

NCVC Rape Shield Laws: http://www.ncvc.org/ncvc/main.aspx?dbID=DB_FAQ:RapeShieldLaws927

Office of Victims of Crime: http://www.ojp.usdoj.gov

Visit **www.sagepub.com/mallicoat2e** to access additional study tools including eFlashcards, web quizzes, web resources, video resources, and SAGE journal articles.

READING 5

Rape myths are a powerful tool that can alter how victims, offenders, and peers of these two populations understand crimes of rape and sexual assault. In this research study, Dr. Hayes-Smith and Dr. Levett look at whether the sharing of information about available sexual resources on college campuses is impacted by student's beliefs in these myths about rape.

Student Perceptions of Sexual Assault Resources and Prevalence of Rape Myth Attitudes

Rebecca M. Hayes Smith and Lora M. Levett

Ground-breaking legislation such as the Student Right-to-Know and Campus Security Act of 1990 (n.d.) requires colleges to publicly report statistics on crime and to educate students on campus about policies designed to prevent crime and secure the campus environment. Later amendments to this Act require the creation of specific policies designed to prevent and respond to sexual assault on campus (Jeanne Clery Disclosure of Campus Security Policy and Campus Crime Statistics Act, 1998, 2011). Now referred to as the Clery Act,[1] it provides guidelines on what information is supposed to be made widely available to students. According to the Act, college administrators should adequately educate students about crime and provide resources for students when crime occurs. Given the prevalence of sexual assault on college campuses, educating students about it and providing resources for victims of sexual assault is especially important. Recent studies, however, demonstrate that resources directed at victims/survivors of sexual assault on campus range in their content and availability to students (Hayes-Smith & Hayes-Smith, 2009; Karjane, Fisher, & Cullen, 2002). However, even in those cases in which adequate resources were available on campus, it was still not clear whether those resources or programming efforts actually reach or affect the student population.

It is no longer a contested issue among researchers and scholars that sexual assault on college campuses is a widespread phenomenon (Bocringer, 1999). One needs only to conduct a search using a library search engine or even Google® to find numerous studies focused on sexual assault issues at universities (e.g., Fisher, Cullen, & Turner, 2000; Karjanc et al., 2002; Koss, Gidycz, & Wisniewski, 1987; Perkins, 1997). A groundbreaking study by Koss (Koss et al., 1987) measured the prevalence of sexual assault beyond official statistics. Even though the Koss study was met with a backlash regarding the prevalence of sexual assault (see Roiphe, 1993), this study is still commonly used to demonstrate that sexual assault is more widely spread on campus than official statistics may suggest. Research has moved beyond simply studying the prevalence of sexual assault on campus and has expanded to things such as the close association between sexual assault and alcohol (Abbey, 2002; Mohler-Kuo, Dowdall, Koss, & Wechsler, 2003; Ullman, Karabatsos, & Koss, 1999) or how common it is for a sexual assault victim to

SOURCE: Hayes-Smith, R. M., & Levett, L. M. (2010). Student perceptions of sexual assault resources and prevalence of rape myth attitudes. *Feminist Criminology, 5*(4), 335–354.

know the offender (Greenfield, 1997), how often women self-blame (Warshaw, 1988), and, important to this study, what colleges [or] universities are doing to remedy the problem (Karjane et al., 2002).

✄ Availability and Adequacy of Sexual Assault Resources on Campus

With researchers and scholars acknowledging the high prevalence of sexual assault occurring among college women and with legislation like the Clery Act, university administrators have taken steps to create programs to educate and assist their student bodies. Recent studies examining the availability and adequacy of resources on college campuses, however, have shown that there appears to be no uniformity across schools on response to sexual assault and resource availability (Hayes-Smith & Hayes-Smith, 2009; Karjane et al., 2002). In one study, researchers found that most of the schools complied with the federal requirement to report crime but were not necessarily consistent with current laws stating how to keep these records (Karjane et al., 2002). Even basic resources such as information about how to file criminal charges were not uniform across schools. Less than half of the institutions reported providing new students with sexual assault educational materials.

Given that students may seek information on the Internet, a subsequent study examined the resources available to students online and found that some schools fared better at providing online resources than other schools (Hayes-Smith & Hayes-Smith, 2009). This content analysis of universities in the Midwest showed that a few schools provided large amounts of information, much of which was victim centered, such as using the term *survivor* and stating, "it is not your fault." Most schools, however, barely provided the basic information online such as sexual assault policies and crime statistics (Hayes-Smith & Hayes-Smith, 2009).

Both of these studies called for better and more information on sexual assault policies and resources for students on campus (Hayes-Smith & Hayes-Smith, 2009; Karjane et al., 2002). Suggestions included developing models for sexual assault education beyond current federal mandates and included recommendations drawn from sexual assault research designed to reduce belief in rape myths. Thus, part

of the goal of disseminating sexual assault resources on campus is to dispel belief in rape myths.

✄ Sexual Assault Programming and Deprogramming

Researchers have noted the difficulty involved with creating programs that attempt to prevent and react to the problem of sexual assault (see Yeater & O'Donohue, 1999). Programs created to either respond to or prevent sexual violence are likely to take into account the correlation between rape myth acceptance and sexual aggression in men (Bohner et al., 1998; Hamilton & Yee, 1990; Lanier, 2001) and rape myth acceptance and victim blaming behaviors in women (Cowan, 2000). Thus, these programs should attempt to dispel rape myths.

Both males and females have shown evidence of adhering to rape myths although men are more likely to endorse rape myths compared to women (Lonsway & Fitzgerald, 1994). For example, in a study conducted by Amnesty International (2005), men were more likely than women to attribute blame to a woman for her own sexual assault if her wardrobe was revealing. This is troubling for a few reasons. First, acceptance of rape myths in men has been associated with their self-reported likelihood [that] they would commit a sexual assault (although rape myths only partially explain the motivation behind men's violence against women; Bohner et al., 1998). One study showed a positive correlation between men's attitudes about rape myths and their inclination toward sexual assault in both written sexual assault scenarios in which men responded to a realistic date rape scenario and in individual items asking about sexual aggression (Bohner et al., 1998). Furthermore, making rape myth attitudes accessible (by measuring them prior to measuring rape proclivity) increased the likelihood that the men would report higher rape proclivity in a subsequent survey. In a related exploratory study testing the validity of a rape myth scale, Burgess (2007) also found that men's acceptance of rape myths was correlated with self-reported sexual aggression. A longitudinal study further supported this and did not find support for the notion of rationalization whereby men who rape will begin to adhere to rape myths as a justification mechanism (Lanier, 2001). This same study also found that reducing adherence to rape myths in males would likely be effective in lowering sexually aggressive behavior (Lanier, 2001). These studies show that men who believe in rape myths may be more likely than men who do not to engage in sexually coercive or aggressive behavior, and programs should address this issue. Alternatively, it is also possible that rape myths may function as a justification for violent behavior although more research is needed to address this possibility.

Programs should attempt to reach both men and women (Yeater & O'Donohue, 1999). Women who are disproportionately likely to be victims of sexual assault and who show evidence of adhering to rape myths make it difficult to reverse the cycle of violence against college-aged women (Cowan, 2000). Specifically, women who believe in rape myths may be contributing to [both] blaming the victim in crimes of sexual assault and the continual de-emphasizing of sexual assault compared to other crimes in our society, [which are] termed "internalized oppression" (i.e., one's own group attributing blame to the victim; Cowan, 2000). Women who report feelings of hostility toward women or hold negative stereotypes about women are more likely than those who do not to victim blame in incidences of sexual assault and to trivialize the occurrence of violence toward women (Cowan, 2000). Ultimately, when a woman believes in rape myths or has negative attitudes toward women, this may exacerbate the problem of sexual assault, thus, increasing victim and self-blame. Thus, programs designed to educate women can attenuate this problem.

False beliefs about sexual assault may result in victims blaming themselves or not believing that a sexual assault actually occurred. Women who endorse rape myths are less likely to define sexual assault behavior as such, despite the fact that the behavior in question meets the legal definition (Fisher et al., 2000; Norris & Cubbins, 1992). In addition, if a victim's claims that a sexual assault occurred are rejected by others because others believe that the victim is at fault, it can reconfirm self-blaming feelings, increasing the likelihood of victims not reporting victimization or seeking help (Schwartz & Leggett, 1999; Warshaw, 1988). The use of alcohol has also been linked with the victim self-blame phenomenon, in which victims will blame themselves and in turn not report the sexual assault because they believe it is their fault due to their use of alcohol (Schwartz & Leggett, 1999). Koss et al. (1987)

found that 74% of perpetrators and 55% of sexual assault victims had been drinking alcohol right before the incident. At least half of sexual assaults include alcohol consumption by both or either parties involved in the assault (see Abbey, 2002 for a complete review). Many women report that the reason they believe the sexual assault is their fault is because they consumed an alcoholic beverage and were too intoxicated to consent. Belief in these types of rape myths can keep women from reporting or seeking out necessary resources to help them recover (Schwartz & Leggett, 1999; Warshaw, 1988).

Another example of a rape myth that likely perpetuates victim-blaming behavior is that rape is committed primarily by strangers. This myth is particularly problematic given that evidence continues to show that the majority of sexual assault is committed by someone the victim knows (Greenfield, 1997). On a college campus, this myth is especially harmful given that students may not exercise appropriate caution around acquaintances in risky situations (such as spending time alone with a friend at a party) yet are cautious when walking alone at night.

Collectively, these studies illustrate the importance of having programs that attempt to educate about *and react* to the occurrence of sexual assault. However, even if we create advocacy programs to assist survivors of sexual assault and educate the general population about sexual assault, we may not be successful in accomplishing those goals if the programs are not reaching the intended audiences. This study attempts to examine whether sexual assault resources are reaching the students and, if resources are reaching students, whether students' attitudes about sexual assault change.

Presumably, students receive educational information about sexual assault and therefore the students should hold more accurate beliefs about sexual assault. That is, past advocates of these types of resources and programs have noted that these programs should educate students through dispelling inaccurate beliefs about sexual assault and ultimately produce attitudinal change consistent with the education proffered; indeed, this is part of the goal in having sexual assault resources available to students (Heppner, Humphrey, Hillenbrand-Gunn, & DeBord, 1995). Thus, in our study, we attempted to measure whether attitudes about sexual assault were changed as a result of receiving sexual assault resources. Theories of attitude change, such as the elaboration likelihood model of persuasion (ELM; Petty & Cacioppo, 1986), demonstrate how attitudes about sexual assault may be changed as a result of exposure to these resources (e.g., Gidycz et al., 2001; Heppner et al., 1995). Specifically, the ELM states that attitude change takes place through two processes: central and/or peripheral processing. If one processes a message centrally (such as a sexual assault education program), change is likely to take place if the target of change is motivated to listen to the message, has the ability to understand the message, and thinks thoughtfully about the content of the message. Processing a message centrally is more likely to result in a stable, long-term attitude change compared to processing a message peripherally (i.e., relying on heuristics like the message sender's expertise or attractiveness in being persuaded; Petty & Cacioppo, 1986). Thus, exposure to sexual assault resources should presumably produce stable attitude change about attitudes toward sexual assault (e.g., rape myths) if students are centrally engaged in learning about those resources. So in our study, . . . exposure to [higher level] resources should be associated with [attitude change toward] lower [quality] beliefs in rape myths if those resources are being properly received (although in this study, the exact causal nature of the relationship cannot be assessed). However, it is possible that beliefs about sexual assault (and rape myths) may be resistant to attitude change due to the continued presence of patriarchy throughout society and the backlash hypothesis (DeKeseredy, 1999).

The backlash hypothesis is concisely defined as a simultaneous surge of criticism onto women as advances are being made in women's favor (Faludi, 1991). For example, DeKeseredy (1999) showed that when research attempts to highlight the prevalence of violence against women, critics immediately emerge and criticize the research methodology, usually by attacking the lack of the male victims. He calls this the "but women do it too" argument, which belittles the importance of raising awareness about violence that is directed mainly toward women (DeKeseredy, 1999). This type of backlash, where the focus is taken off of women, can make it particularly difficult for sexual assault programs to reach female students, whereby they may think sexual assault is not going to happen to them. If an individual does not believe that a topic (e.g., sexual assault) is relevant to him or her or is important, he or she is not as likely to pay attention to the messages

about the topic, making the job of spreading information difficult (Kahlor & Morrison, 2007).

Study Overview

The present study examined whether students were receiving information regarding sexual assault resources at a university that provided several resources. We examined whether students knew of the available resources, believed they would use the information, and considered the information informative. We also asked students how they would recommend the information be disseminated to students. In addition, we explored whether knowledge about the availability of sexual assault resources was associated with lower belief in rape myths. Last, we examined gender differences in knowledge of sexual assault resources and acceptance of rape myths.

Method

Participants

Participants were 224 criminology undergraduate students from a large southeastern university. Students were 61% female and 38% male (2% did not report their sex). The majority of the students were White (60%), followed by Hispanic/Latino (20%), Black (10%), Asian (6%), and other (4%). The average age was 21 ($SD = 2$) ranging from 18 to 46. The largest percentage of students were 3rd years (37%) followed by 4th years (28%), 2nd years (23%), 1st years (8%), and a few 5th years (3%).

Measures

Knowledge of sexual assault resources. Students' knowledge of resources was first measured by asking if they had received information on sexual assault resources when they began their education at the university. If they answered "yes," they were asked the following "yes" or "no" questions: (a) Did it include information about the number of sexual assault incidents? and (b) Do you know where to get information about sexual assault on campus?

To measure more general knowledge of sexual assault resources on campus, students responded to several statements. In responding to each statement, students indicated their agreement on a 7-point Likert-type scale ranging from 1 (*strongly disagree*) to 7 (*strongly agree*). The scale assessing general knowledge of sexual assault resources on campus averaged the items indicated in Reading Table 5.1 ($\alpha = .77$, scale ranging from 1.00 to 6.25). Three additional items were not included in the final scale because they did not factor in with the above scale, but mean responses to these items are reported in the results section. These items are also included in Reading Table 5.1.

Students also were asked nine questions measuring their awareness of each of the nine resources available at the university or in the community. Students indicated with a "yes" or "no" response whether they had knowledge of each of the following campus resources: (a) sexual assault victim advocates, (b) an office of victim services, (c) sexual assault counselors, (d) a "safe place" for victims

of sexual assault, (e) a "Take Back the Night" rally, (f) a sexual assault crisis hotline, (g) a women's resource center, (h) a policy on sexual assault, and (i) a facility to get a forensic medical exam. The total number of "yes" responses were summed to create a scale; students' scores on this scale ranged from 0.00 to 9.00.

Students also were asked a question regarding where they would seek information on sexual assault issues. They responded to the following question: "Which one of the following places would you be most likely to seek information on sexual assault issues?" Students chose one of 6 choices (i.e., phonebook, crisis hotline, police, Internet, the university's web site, and other).

Quality of resources. Those students who responded that they received information about sexual assault from the

Reading Table 5.1 Students' Mean Responses to Knowledge of Sexual Assault Resources Available on Campus

	Mean Response (*SD*)	Median (item range)	% Disagree	% Agree	% Neutral
Scaled Items					
I am familiar with the procedures of reporting incidents of sexual assault at [the university]	3.30 (1.51)	3.00 (1–6)	59.2%	29%	12%
I am knowledgeable about the role of Judicial Affairs in sexual assault cases at [the university]	3.10 (1.49)	3.00 (1–7)	66%	21%	13%
I am familiar with the services offered by an Office of Victims Services	3.02 (1.46)	3.00 (1–7)	68%	19%	14%
I know where to go to receive help if I or someone I know were sexually assaulted at [the university]	4.17 (1.61)	5.00 (1–7)	36%	7%	57%
Individual Items					
If you report a sexual assault at [the university], you *do not* have to file a police report with the police	3.65 (1.55)	4.00 (1–7)	33%	20%	47%
I know what happens at a "Take Back the Night" rally	2.53 (1.62)	2.00 (1–7)	73%	13%	14%
I know the number (or where to get it) to the Sexual Assault Crisis Hotline	3.60 (1.90)	4.00 (1–7)	49%	41%	10%

NOTE: Students responded on a scale ranging from 1 (*strongly disagree*) to 7 (*strongly agree*).

university rated the quality of the information they received. Again, students responded to statements on 7-point Likert-type scales ranging from 1 (*strongly disagree*) to 7 (*strongly agree*). Higher ratings indicate a more positive evaluation of the resources. All items are included in Reading Table 5.2.

Distribution of sexual assault resources. Participants also responded to an open-ended question asking where and how they would like to see information about sexual assault disseminated on campus. This question was coded for common themes using two independent coders. Overall agreement rates were high ($\kappa = .85$, $p < .01$). One hundred ninety eight students answered the open-ended question, and several students gave more than one suggestion.

Rape Myth Scale. The Rape Myth Scale was developed by Burt (1980; see also Burt, 2004) to examine acceptance of rape myths. The scale included 11 statements, and participants indicated agreement with those statements on 7-point Likert-type scales ranging from 1 (*strongly disagree*) to 7 (*strongly agree*). For example, one item reads, "A woman who goes to the home or apartment of a man on their first date implies that she is willing to have sex." The entire Rape Myth Scale was used in the survey (available in Burt, 2004). We also created three additional items to add to the scale because of the relationship between sexual assault and alcohol use and sexual assault and drugs (Mohler-Kuo et al., 2003; Ullman et al., 1999): (a) If the victim of sexual assault was drinking alcohol at the time of the incident, it is partially his or her fault that the sexual assault occurred. (b) If the victim of sexual assault willingly took drugs at the time of the incident, it is partially his or her fault that the sexual assault occurred. (c) Even if a victim of sexual assault was drunk at the time of the incident, the sexual assault is not his or her fault. When conducting factor and reliability analyses on the new scale, two items from the original Rape Myth Scale did not factor on the construct and reduced the reliability of the overall scale ("any female can get raped" and "one reason women falsely report rape is that they frequently have a need to call attention to themselves"). These two items were dropped because they did not factor. Given that we added items to Burt's Rape Myth Scale, we conducted an exploratory factor analysis with varimax rotation to examine the factor structure. Burt (1980) originally proposed a single factor structure; however, this factor structure has been debated in the field (see Lonsway & Fitzgerald, 1994). Some have shown that the items in the scale rotate onto 3 (Hall, Howard, & Boezio, 1986) or 4 (Briere, Malamuth, & Check, 1985) factors. Others, however, report that the scale

Reading Table 5.2   Students' Mean Responses to Quality of Resources Available on Campus

Scaled Items	Mean Response (*SD*)	Median (item range)	% Disagree	% Agree	% Neutral
The sexual assault resources given to students at [the university] is not informative enough	4.02 (1.25)	4.00 (1–7)	18.6%	23.1%	58.2%
I do not know enough about the sexual assault resources at [the university] to use them in a sexual assault situation	4.70 (1.52)	5.00 (1–7)	21.5%	63.3%	15.2%
The sexual assault information was very straightforward and easy to understand	4.40 (1.01)	4.00 (1–7)	9.8%	32%	58.3%
I would probably use the sexual assault information given to me by [the university] if I encountered a sexual assault situation	5.37 (1.25)	6.00 (1–7)	15.8%	80.2%	12.2%

NOTE: Students responded on a scale ranging from 1 (*strongly disagree*) to 7 (*strongly agree*).

retained its original single factor structure (Krahe, 1988; Margolin, Miller, & Moran, 1989). In our factor analysis, a single factor emerged. Items included in the scale had factor loadings between .52 and .78. Items with smaller factor loadings were eliminated from the scale. The three new items were included in the final scale and scores were added according to Burt (2004 α = .86; range: −36.00 to 13.00). Students were also randomly assigned to complete the Rape Myth Scale before or after the measures inquiring about sexual assault resources to test for social desirability of responses to rape myth items.

◪ Results

Student Knowledge of Sexual Assault Resources

When students were asked if they had received sexual assault resources, only roughly half of the students (54%) reported receiving information, 13% reported they had not received any information, and 33% reported not remembering if they had received information. Of the students who reported receiving information, 30% reported that the information included reports of the number of sexual assault incidents, and 39% reported they knew where to get information about sexual assault at the university. A series of chi-square tests revealed male and female students did not differ in their responses to these items, $p > .05$.

For the scale and items measuring knowledge of resources, the means of responses to most items were below the scale average, indicating that overall, many respondents were not aware of many of the resources. For the overall scale, students averaged 3.39 ($SD = 1.17$). This indicates that the overall average of students' knowledge of resources was below the median response. To provide the best picture of the data, we included descriptions of participants' responses in Reading Table 5.1. We also divided participants' responses into categories indicating proportions of students who agreed, disagreed, and were neutral in response to the items on the scales provided. Male and female students did not significantly differ in their knowledge of resources for either the scale or the individual items.

As expected, students who had indicated receiving resource information significantly differed from those students who indicated not receiving resources on the

knowledge of resource scale. Students who remembered receiving information about sexual assault resources were more likely to report more knowledge of resources compared to those students who did not report or did not remember receiving information.

Next, we examined knowledge of specific resources on campus. Students knew an average of 4.00 resources out of the 9 which were available. 58% of students knew between 0 and 4 of the resources, and 42% knew about 5 or more of the available resources. All resources were readily available on campus. The students' knowledge of specific resources scale did not significantly differ by gender. Again, students who had indicated receiving resource information significantly differed on how many specific resources they knew about. Students who reported receiving information on entering the university knew about more resources compared with students who reported they had not received resources or those who did not remember receiving resources.

To determine where students would seek out information on sexual assault, a percentage was calculated for all responses indicating the proportion of students who would seek information from each of the sources. Overall, 41% of the students reported they would refer to the police, 34% reported they would use the Internet, and 11% reported they would go to the university's web site.

We asked students who answered that they had received information on sexual assault if the information was helpful and useful. Again, to provide the best picture of the data, we included descriptions of participants' responses in Reading Table 5.2. After examining the item distributions, it appears that students would use the university's sexual assault resources but still do not know enough about them to indicate whether or not they are informative and/or helpful. Students' responses to these items did not significantly differ by gender.

Students suggested the following mechanisms for distributing sexual assault information: a full school course (21%) or incorporating the information into current classes (11%), informative publications on campus (18%), disseminating information during new student orientation (18%), using the Internet (either through the university's portal or through a separate web site; 14%), organizing a campus event (20%), using an online course similar to the university's currently required alcohol awareness course (10%), using resources outside the university, including media outlets, such as commercials and billboards (2%), and using the school newspaper (1%).

Student Belief in Rape Myths

The Rape Myth Scale was coded so that negative scores mean an overall lowered acceptance of rape myths. The items were summed to create the scale not including the two items that did not factor in as discussed above. Overall acceptance of rape myths was low indicating that overall, students were low in their belief of rape myths.

A one-way ANOVA testing for gender differences in beliefs in rape myths showed an effect of gender on beliefs in rape myths. Women were less likely than men to accept rape myths. The relationship between gender and students' acceptance of rape myths remained significant even when students' knowledge of resources (as measured by a *yes, no,* or *I don't remember* question) was entered into the model in a two-way ANOVA. Both the effects of knowledge of resources and the interaction between gender and knowledge of resources were not significant. That is, knowledge of resources was not related to a lower belief in rape myths.

◤   Discussion

Although some students at this university reported receiving information about sexual assault resources, the majority of our sample did not. Arguably, this group of university students has had more exposure than the average student to the issue of sexual assault because they are criminology students. Only half of the students, however, reported that they had received information about sexual assault resources at the university (despite the fact that all students should have received the information). Two possibilities may explain why so many students reported not receiving information: the university may not be uniformly distributing the information, or students may not be paying attention or actively engaged when they receive the information.

With students reporting low knowledge of the resources available on campus (including general knowledge and knowledge of specific available resources) and women in the sample not significantly differing from men in their knowledge of sexual assault resources, this reveals a problematic picture. Many (if not most) resources available at this campus are directed toward women because

this university has a reactive response as opposed to a preventative response to the problem of sexual assault. Therefore, the resources intended to assist women in case of sexual assault may not be serving women to the best possible capacity. However, students who reported receiving resource information did report more knowledge of sexual assault resources than those who reported that they did not receive such information. The university may need to consider a new dissemination strategy to ensure that the students have knowledge of all the resources available to them and are actively engaged in learning from those resources.

Our main suggestion is that a new approach should be taken by using the Internet as a primary source of dissemination.

In our study, 24% of students indicated that disseminating the information about sexual assault and sexual assault resources through the Internet (either through a required online course or a web site) may be the best way to reach the student body. Even though with this sample many responded they would go to the police for resources—which could be due to the fact they are criminology students—some students also reported that they would turn to the Internet for information in a sexual assault situation, indicating support for the idea that the university should provide sound information for students online (Hayes-Smith & Hayes-Smith, 2009). Places like Facebook® and Twitter®, popular college networking sites, may be an ideal place to disseminate resource information. These sites allow its users to subscribe as a fan to pages and have ways to contact users of an entire network (which each university is a network) notifying them of upcoming events. Given the popularity of these sites, it might make sense for universities to use them in disseminating information about available services at the university, including sexual assault resources.

Indeed, theoretically, creating interactive, long-term Internet-based programs makes sense. That is, research on sexual assault prevention programs has demonstrated that participating in a long-term program designed to teach students about sexual assault issues (e.g., consent) produced the most stable change in students' attitudes (Anderson & Whiston, 2005; Borges, Banyard, & Moynihan, 2008). The interactive nature of the using the Internet may make students more actively engaged and motivated to process the information meaningfully, which according to the ELM is likely to result in central processing of the information (Heppner et al., 1995; Petty & Cacioppo, 1986). This type of processing is likely to result in attitude change that is stable over time and resistant to counterpersuasion arguments (Heppner et al., 1995).

The suggestion of using Internet networking sites is more complicated than it appears; when using these sites, there is more to it than simply creating a profile. As Hayes-Smith & Hayes-Smith (2009) found in their study, simply having a web site with information does not mean it is quality or easily accessible. To use networking sites, there would likely need to be a process in which some marketing strategies might prove helpful to gain proper visibility. For example, on the network site Facebook®, creating a profile that is not public requires users to request inclusion, and because it is not public, it only appears on specific searches versus general keyword searches. The private profile increases security but decreases visibility. Security is an important issue to consider with programs geared toward survivors of sexual assault but may be of less concern when considering the prevention programs, where visibility is more likely to be helpful than harmful. Of course, these are only speculations, and future research should address the effectiveness of networking sites regarding resource dissemination and awareness.

Another interesting student suggestion for disseminating sexual assault resources and educating students about sexual assault was the call for a required online course. This suggestion is particularly pertinent to the university in this study as they already have one required online course to educate students about alcohol. This course is required for all incoming students and may have prompted the students to come up with the idea of an online course for educating students about sexual assault issues and resources. The online course could be given to all freshman-level students prior to their being allowed to register for classes, and they would have to acquire a specific grade. It would be feasible for the university to add sexual assault information to the alcohol course given the established relationship between alcohol and sexual assault (Koss et al., 1987; Mohler-Kuo et al., 2003). Past research suggests that if such programming is to be successful in changing students' attitudes about sexual assault, it would need to engage students and send a meaningful, relevant message likely to invoke stable attitude change (Anderson & Whiston, 2005).

The alternative explanation regarding resource dissemination is that students receive information about sexual assault resources, but they may not be reading or paying attention to these resources. As Kahlor and Morrison (2007) propose, it is possible that students receive information but do not find it relevant. In this study, the majority of students who reported receiving resources seemed unable to evaluate the helpfulness or quality of the resources; this supports the notion that they are not paying attention. In addition, simply knowing that resources on campus exist to help victims of sexual assault may not be enough; universities may need to make more concerted efforts to educate the student population about sexual assault. A more involved program would need to be created to raise visibility *and* awareness. Indeed, research has shown that making the information more personally relevant to students increases the likelihood they will pay attention to the message and therefore change relevant attitudes and behaviors (Grube, Mayton, & Ball-Rokeach, 1994).

Regardless of dissemination, knowledge of resources was not correlated with a reduced acceptance of rape myths by men *or* women, and so maybe universities should implement more sexual assault prevention programs. It is possible that attitudes about sexual assault are engrained in our culture, that the current programming and resources are not successful in reducing acceptance of rape myths because the programming does not successfully combat the backlash that continues to occur against the programs (DeKeseredy, 1999). Proactive programming may be more successful in producing attitude change. Sexual assault prevention programs are more proactive and attempt to educate both men and women about the culture that surrounds the incidence of sexual assault, whereas the programs that are reactive are only geared toward women (the survivors) and are helpful after the fact but not prior to. Scholars have long since suggested the importance of focusing sexual assault programs on men (Karjane et al., 2002; Schwartz & Dekeseredy, 1997). It has been argued that men, especially those who are in college, tend to facilitate a culture surrounding male peer support that is conducive to sexual assault (Sanday, 2007; Schwartz & Dekeseredy, 1997). The fraternity culture oftentimes facilitates the male peer support and encourages the objectification of women (Sanday, 2007).

Research evaluating sexual assault prevention programming is generally supportive of the prevention technique in dispelling commonly held rape myths (Breitenbecher, 2000; Foubert, 2000; Lanier, 2001). There are programs that educate men about how to stop violence against women, such as the national program Men Can Stop Rape (www.mencanstoprape.org) or Men Against Violence (see Choate, 2003 for a description). These programs generally focus on the notion that men are the ones with the most power to stop the violence because they are the typical perpetrator in these types of crimes. Thus, these programs attempt to create a new culture by encouraging men to assert that they will not tolerate violence against women (Schwartz & Dekeseredy, 1997). Fraternity members who were subjected to the Men against Violence training reported positive experiences with the program and expressed that prior to the program they were unaware of many of the issues surrounding sexual assault, such as alcohol and consent (Choate, 2003). Research has shown that men and women may communicate consent in different ways (Hickman & Muehlenhard, 1999), so such programs may help attenuate this gender gap and educate men about sexual assault issues (and therefore, may be successful in preventing sexual assault). These programs compliment programs educating women about the availability of sexual assault resources.

Conclusion

Overall, this study shows that even if sexual assault resources are available at a university, it does not mean students are receiving, using, or learning from them. Our nonprobability sampling method makes it impossible to generalize these findings to the whole university. However, this sample provided a conservative test of whether students were receiving resources; that is, this study was conducted with a sample of students currently enrolled in criminology, law, and society classes (in which they may receive information about those resources). Arguably, this sample should have had higher knowledge of sexual assault resources compared to [those of] the average student. Future research may benefit from using a random sample. However, even with this conservative sample, we demonstrated that merely providing resources about sexual assault may not be able to accomplish purposes intended. That is, if students do not know about the resources available to them, how will they use them in a time of need?

Note

1. The Jeanne Clery Disclosure of Campus Security Policy and Campus Crime Statistics Act (20 USC § 1092) requires all public and private institutions of higher education that receive federal aid to disclose campus crime reports and campus security policies. Schools are required to publish a crime report and policies regarding crime, for example, sexual assault. The manner in which the schools are to disclose this information is not explicitly specified in the report.

References

Abbey, A. (2002). Alcohol-related sexual assault: A common problem among college students [Supplement 14]. *Journal of Studies on Alcohol,* 118–128.

Amnesty International. (2005). *Sexual assault research summary report.* London, UK: ICM.

Anderson, L. A., & Whiston, S. C. (2005). Sexual assault education programs: A meta-analytic examination of their effectiveness. *Psychology of Women Quarterly, 29,* 374–388.

Boeringer, S. B. (1999). Association of rape-supportive attitudes with fraternal and athletic participation. *Violence Against Women, 5,* 81–90.

Bohner, G., Reinhard, M. A., Rutz, S., Sturm, S. Kerschbaum, B., & Effler, D. (1998). Rape myths as neutralizing cognitions: Evidence for a causal impact of anti-victim attitudes on men's self reported likelihood of raping. *European Journal of Social Psychology, 28,* 257–268.

Borges, A. M., Banyard, V. L., & Moynihan, M. M. (2008). Clarifying consent: Primary prevention of sexual assault on campus. *Journal of Prevention and Intervention in the Community, 36,* 75–88.

Breitenbecher, K. H. (2000). Sexual assault on college campuses: Is an ounce of prevention enough? *Applied & Preventive Psychology, 9,* 23–52.

Briere, J., Malamuth, N. M., & Check, J. V. P. (1985). Sexuality and rape supportive beliefs. *International Journal of Women's Studies, 8,* 398–403.

Burgess, G. H. (2007). Assessment of rape-supportive attitudes and beliefs in college men: Development, reliability, and validity of the rape attitudes and beliefs scale. *Journal of Interpersonal Violence, 22,* 973–993.

Burt, M. R. (1980). Cultural myths and support for rape. *Journal of Personality and Social Psychology, 38,* 217–230.

Burt, M. R. (2004). Acceptance of rape myths. In L. Wrightsman, A. L. Batson, & V. A. Edkins (Eds.), *Measures of legal attitudes* (pp. 115–117). Belmont, CA: Thomson-Wadsworth.

Choate, L. (2003). Sexual assault prevention programs for college men: An exploratory evaluation of the Men Against Violence Model. *Journal of College Counseling, 6,* 166–176.

Cowan, G. (2000). Women's hostility toward women and rape and sexual harassment myths. *Violence Against Women, 6,* 238–246.

DeKeseredy, W. S. (1999). Tactics of the antifeminist backlash against Canadian national women abuse surveys. *Violence Against Women, 5,* 1258–1276.

Faludi, S. (1991). *Backlash: The undeclared war against American women.* New York: Crown.

Fisher, B., Cullen, F., & Turner, M. (2000). *The sexual victimization of college women: Findings from two national-level studies.* Washington, DC: National Institute of Justice and Bureau of Justice Statistics.

Foubert, J. D. (2000). The longitudinal effects of a rape-prevention program on fraternity men's attitudes, behavioral intent, and behavior. *Journal of American College Health, 48,* 158–163.

Gidycz, C. A., Lynn, S. T., Rich, C. L., Marioni, N. L., Loh, C., Blackwell, L. M., . . . Pashdag, J. (2001). The evaluation of a sexual assault risk reduction program: A multisite investigation. *Journal of Consulting and Clinical Psychology, 69*(6), 1073–1078.

Greenfeld, L. A. (1997, February). *Sex offenses and offenders: An analysis of data on rape and sexual assault* (Report No. NCJ-163392). Washington, DC: U.S. Department of Justice.

Grube, J. W., Mayton, D. M., & Ball Rokeach, S. J. (1994). Inducing change in values, attitudes, and behaviors: Belief systems theory and the method of value self confrontation. *Journal of Social Issues, 50,* 153–173.

Hall, E. R., Howard, J. A., & Boezio, S. L. (1986). Tolerance of rape: A sexist or antisocial attitude. *Psychology of Women Quarterly, 10,* 101–118.

Hamilton, M., & Yee, J (1990). Rape knowledge and propensity to rape. *Journal of Research in Personality, 24,* 111–122.

Hayes-Smith, R. M., & Hayes-Smith, J. M. (2009). A website content analysis of women's resources and sexual assault literature on college campuses. *Critical Criminology, 17,* 109–123.

Heppner, M. J., Humphrey, C. F., Hillenbrand-Gunn, T. L., & DeBord, K. A. (1995). The differential effects of rape prevention programming on attitudes, behavior, and knowledge. *Journal of Counseling Psychology, 42,* 508–518.

Hickman, S. E., & Muehlenhard, C. L. (1999). "By the semi-mystical appearance of a condom": How young women and men communicate sexual consent in heterosexual situations. *Journal of Sex Research, 36,* 258–272.

Jeanne Clery Disclosure of Campus Security Policy and Campus Crime Statistics Act, 20 U.S.C § 1092(f), (1998 & 2011). The 2011 ed. retrieved from http://www.gpo.gov/fdsys/pkg/USCODE-2011-title20/html/USCODE-2011-title20-chap28-subchapIV-partF-sec1092.htm

Kahlor, L., & Morrison, D. (2007). Television viewing and rape myth acceptance among college women. *Sex Roles, 56,* 729–739.

Karjane, H. M., Fisher, B. S., & Cullen, F. T. (2002). *Campus sexual assault: How America's institutions of higher education respond* (Final Report, NIJ Grant #1999-WA-VX-0008). Newton, MA: Education Development Center.

Koss, M. P., Gidycz, C. A., & Wisniewski, W. (1987). The scope of rape: Incidence and prevalence of sexual aggression and victimization in a national sample of higher education students. *Journal of Consulting and Clinical Psychology, 55,* 162–170.

Krahe, B. (1988). Victim and observer characteristics as determinants of responsibility attributions to victims of rape. *Journal of Applied Social Psychology, 18,* 50–58.

Lanier, C. A. (2001). Rape-accepting attitudes: Precursors to or consequences of forced sex. *Violence Against Women, 7,* 876–885.

Lonsway, K. A., & Fitzgerald, L. F. (1994). Rape myths: In review. *Psychology of Women Quarterly, 18,* 133–164.

Margolin, L., Miller, M., & Moran, P. B. (1989). When a kiss is not just a kiss: Relating violations of consent in kissing to rape myth acceptance. *Sex Roles, 20,* 231–243.

Mohler-Kuo, M., Dowdall, G. W., Koss, M., & Wechsler, H. (2003). Correlates of rape while intoxicated in a national sample of college women. *Journal of Studies on Alcohol, 64,* 37–45.

Norris, J., & Cubbins, L. A. (1992). Dating, drinking and rape: Effects of victim's and assailants alcohol consumption on judgments of their behavior and traits. *Psychology of Women Quarterly, 16,* 179–191.

Perkins, C. A (1997, September). *Age patterns of victims of serious violent crime* (Report No. NCJ-162031). Washington, DC: U.S. Department of Justice.

Petty, R. E., & Cacioppo, J. T. (1986). *Communication and persuasion: Central and peripheral routes to attitude change.* New York: Springer-Verlag.

Roiphe, K. (1993). *The morning after: Sex, fear and feminism.* Toronto, Ontario, Canada: Little Brown.

Sanday, P. R. (2007). *Fraternity gang rape: Sex, brotherhood, and privilege on campus.* New York: New York University Press.

Schwartz, M. D., & DeKeseredy, W. S. (1997). *Sexual assault on the college campus: The role of male peer support.* Thousand Oaks, CA: Sage.

Schwartz, M. D., & Leggett, M. S. (1999). Bad dates or emotional trauma? The aftermath of campus sexual assault. *Violence Against Women, 5,* 251–271.

Student Right-to-Know and Campus Security Act (1990). (n.d.). Retrieved from http://nces.ed.gov/ipeds/glossary/index.asp?id=625

Ullman, S., Karabatsos, G., & Koss, M. (1999). Alcohol and sexual assault in a national sample of college women. *Journal of Interpersonal Violence, 14,* 603–625.

Warshaw, R. (1988). *I never called it rape: The Ms. Report on recognizing, fighting, and surviving date and acquaintance rape.* New York: Harper & Row.

Yeater, E. A., & O'Donohue, W. (1999). Sexual assault prevention programs: Current issues, future directions, and the potential efficacy of interventions with women. *Clinical Psychology Review, 19,* 739–771.

DISCUSSION QUESTIONS

1. How much knowledge do students have about sexual assault resources on their college campus?

2. What can universities do to reduce students' acceptance of rape myths?

3. How might university administrators use the findings of this study to make changes to their programs on campus?

READING 6

In the section, you learned about how alcohol is the most common drug that contributes to rapes and sexual assaults. Drug-facilitated rape victims are often viewed as blameless; however, the discussion changes when someone voluntarily becomes intoxicated and is ultimately sexually violated. This study by Clare Gunby, Anna Carline, and Caryl Beynon includes focus group research with students enrolled at a British university and uses a hypothetical vignette of a potential offender and victim of rape following their consumption of alcohol.

Regretting It After?

Focus Group Perspectives on Alcohol Consumption, Nonconsensual Sex and False Allegations of Rape

Clare Gunby, Anna Carline, and Caryl Beynon

Introduction

It is well documented that young people, including students, are high consumers of alcohol (Kypri, Cronin, and Wright, 2005; YouGov, 2010) and that they frequently use alcohol to facilitate sexual encounters, including increasing their confidence to approach members of the opposite sex (Bellis et al., 2008; Sumnall, Beynon, Conchie, Riley, and Cole, 2007). Research also indicates that this association between alcohol and sexual outcomes serves to influence judgments around the consensual nature of alcohol-involved

intercourse[1] (George and Stoner, 2000). Indeed, recent social network responses to the conviction of the Welsh footballer Ched Evans for the rape of an extremely intoxicated woman, including the public "tweeting" of the victim's name, highlight the profound impact that alcohol consumption can have on third parties assessments of the legitimacy of alcohol-involved rapes (Bancroft, 2012).

Drawing upon the findings of an empirical research project with university students, this article provides a timely examination of young peoples' attitudes and understandings around alcohol consumption, nonconsensual

SOURCE: Gunby, C., Carline, A., & Beynon, C. (2012). Regretting it after? Focus group perspectives on alcohol consumption, nonconsensual sex and false allegations of rape. *Social & Legal Studies, 22*(1), 87–106.

sex, and the role of alcohol in the false allegation process. More specifically, the project examined how, and to what extent, perspectives around false rape allegations and voluntary intoxication intertwine. It also examined more broadly how alcohol-involved intercourse is perceived by students and, by implication, possible attitudinal difficulties that may arise in achieving convictions in alcohol-involved rape cases. To this end, four focus groups were conducted based on a real case in which sex took place between two very drunk acquaintances and consent was contested.

The analysis that follows provides critical insights into how complainant and defendant credibility and responsibility are constructed and explores what is deemed to constitute consent. This is an area where further research is required in order to develop understanding around attitudes that may impinge on the treatment of rape complainants who have been drinking (Stern Review, 2010) and to gain clarity on how the association between alcohol and sex may influence judgments around the consensual nature of intercourse and, by default, link to ideas and understandings around false rape allegations. The article also offers preliminary insights into perspectives that may be drawn upon by jurors in their deliberations of alcohol-involved rape cases.

The article is presented over four sections. To commence, an outline of the law of rape and the key issues and research which relate to this $A = \pi r^2$ are presented. Second, the study methodology is detailed followed by a critical analysis of the research findings. The final section of the article provides conclusions and suggestions for further research.

⬚ The Law of Rape and Research Context

In England and Wales, rape law was reformed in 2003 amongst concerns regarding the low reporting and conviction rate for the offence (Home Office, 2002). Rape is now governed by Section 1 of the *Sexual Offences Act 2003* and involves the nonconsensual penile penetration of a person's mouth, vagina, or anus. As with the previous law, the absence of consent is pivotal: the prosecution must prove beyond a reasonable doubt that the complainant did not consent, and the jury must be satisfied that the accused did not hold a reasonable belief in consent. In making this latter assessment, the jury is to take into account "all the circumstances, including any steps [the defendant] has taken to ascertain whether [the complainant] consents" (Section 1(2)).

For the first time, the 2003 Act implemented a statutory definition of consent. Section 74 states, "a person consents if he agrees by choice, and has the freedom and capacity to make that choice." Further significant reforms were implemented by virtue of Sections 75 and 76, which contain a range of evidential and conclusive presumptions regarding the absence of consent. Under these provisions, if the prosecution proves the existence of certain factors, it will be presumed that the complainant did not consent and/or that the defendant did not hold a reasonable belief in consent. Whilst the presumptions in Section 75 are evidential and can therefore be rebutted by the defendant, under Section 76, lack of consent and/or belief in consent is conclusively presumed. Consequently, the circumstances which fall into this latter section are more narrowly construed, relating to cases involving certain types of deception. In contrast, the presumptions in Section 75 are wider and considered to represent situations in which most people would agree that consent was unlikely to be present (Home Office, 2002: p. 16). They include the use, or threats, of violence along with cases of involuntary intoxication/drink spiking. For the purposes of the present analysis, cases that involve *voluntary* intoxication would only fall within Section 75 if the complainant was so drunk that she became unconscious (Section 75 (2)(d)).

In 2006, a government consultation asked whether Section 75 should be amended to include situations involving extreme voluntary intoxication (Office for Criminal Justice Reform, 2006). One third of respondents argued that presumption Section 75(2)(d) should be changed to include situations in which the complainant was "too affected by alcohol or drugs to give free agreement." Certain respondents referred to situations in which men may "seek to take advantage of the fact that women are drunk [voluntarily] and therefore have less capacity to resist pressure or coercion" (Office for Criminal Justice Reform, 2007: p. 6). These proposals, however, were abandoned due to the fear of "mischievous accusations" (Office for Criminal Justice Reform, 2006: p. 12), arguments that presuppose some linkage between intoxication and the potential for false rape allegations.

Voluntary intoxication short of the point of unconsciousness therefore falls under the general Section 74 definition of consent, where specific consideration is to be given to whether or not the complainant retained the capacity to consent. The complexities of capacity and intoxication are well documented in the case of *R v Bree* (2007). Whilst initially convicted for rape following sex with a complainant who was voluntarily and exceptionally intoxicated, his conviction was quashed on appeal due to the trial judge's inadequate jury directions (see Cowan, 2008; Elvin, 2008; Gunby, Carline, and Beynon, 2010 for a critical analysis of Bree, 2007). The Court of Appeal held that the jury should have received assistance with the meaning of the term *capacity* when a complainant is affected by her own voluntarily induced intoxication and noted that "capacity to consent may evaporate well before a complainant becomes unconscious" (Bree, 2007: p. 167 [case]). However, little further guidance was provided as it was considered to be a "fact-specific" issue and not appropriate to create a "grid system" which would enable the point of incapability to be linked to "some prescribed level of alcohol consumption" (Bree, 2007: p. 167).

⊠ Rape Myths, False Allegations and Intoxication

Despite the reforms to the law of rape in 2003, continued concerns regarding the criminal justice system's handling of rape cases, along with the frequently reported 6% conviction rate and high levels of case attrition (Kelly, Lovett, and Regan, 2005), prompted a review into how rape complaints were handled by public authorities in England and Wales. The review noted that *rape myths* continue to impact upon the criminal justice process (Sanders, 2012; Stern Review, 2010) including myths which presuppose many rape allegations are false (Ellison & Munro, 2010a; Kelly, 2010; Kelly et al., 2005). Such perspectives have historically influenced legal practice, including, for example, the extensive cross-examination of the complainant's sexual history and corroboration warnings (see Temkin, 2002). Whilst many of these provisions have been abandoned, or restrictions around their use applied, beliefs around the frequency of false rape reports continue to influence legal and political thinking and to problematise women's accounts of rape

(Kelly, 2010). Recent suggestions to provide anonymity for those accused of rape, for example, were premised partially on arguments that false allegations impact frequently in rape cases (Almandras, 2010).

Adherence to such perspectives, and their complex relationship to the police recorded no-crime code, has been documented amongst police officers (Kelly, 2010; Kelly et al., 2005) as well as amongst members of wider society. Burton, Kelly, Kitzinger, and Regan (1998) found that from a sample of 2,039 young people, 74% agreed that females often or sometimes "cry rape" when really they just have second thoughts. The London-based Opinion Matters (2010) survey identified one in five participants aged 18–50 years agreed that most claims of rape are probably not true, with men being more likely to endorse this perspective. More recent findings have documented that 47.7% of male students aged 18–24 years, compared to 33.6% of female, agreed with the statement that a significant proportion of rapes reported to the police were false allegations (Gunby, Carline, Bellis, and Beynon, 2012). Whilst gender is not a definitive predictor of adherence to false rape allegation beliefs, studies that have found gender distinctions may partially be explained through reference to differences in sexual expectations amongst young men and women (see Beres, 2007; Gunby et al., 2012; Humphreys, 2007).

Ideas around the elevated nature of false rape allegations remain despite evidence that levels of false rape reporting are no different to (Rumney, 2006), or potentially lower than (Kelly, 2010), the levels of false complaints found across other crimes. Estimates suggest that between 2% and 8% of rape allegations are possibly false (see Kelly et al., 2005; Lonsway, Archambault, and Lisak, 2009). Whilst further research is undoubtedly needed (Stern Review, 2010), ideas around the elevated frequency of false rape allegations appear to have a limited evidence base.

Running parallel are studies which highlight that third parties often hold a woman who was drinking prior to being raped partially accountable and are hesitant to convict the accused (Finch and Munro, 2005, 2007; Gunby et al., 2012). If parties are depicted as equally intoxicated prior to nonconsensual sex, there is an increased reluctance to hold a defendant criminally liable for rape, even when the complainant's degree of intoxication has rendered her incapable of giving consent (Finch and Munro,

2005). However, when a defendant is depicted as sober, or less intoxicated than the victim, participants are more likely to hold the defendant criminally liable (Finch and Munro, 2005). When evaluating whether a complainant is able to consent, participants have been found to focus on a victim's level of consciousness at the time, with a number believing that as long as she maintained consciousness, she retained the capacity to reason (Finch and Munro, 2005), attitudes which contrast with the legal position (Bree, 2007 [case]).

It is possible to hypothesize that hesitance around believing an intoxicated female's account of rape relates to assumptions around the accusation being false and the consequence of a sober retraction of consent (Cowan, 2008). If rape victims believe such assumptions are made, they may feed further into the culture of reluctance to report rape and seek support. Evidence illustrates that such fears are not unfounded with skeptical attitudes around alcohol-involved rape and false allegations impacting on the way cases are dealt with by police, prosecutors, judges, and juries (Stern Review, 2010).

✉ Methodology

Design, Recruitment and Materials

Four single sex focus groups were carried out with a total of 21 students (12 female and 9 male). Single sex groups were used in recognition that men and women often talk differently about rape (Beres, 2007; Gunby et al., 2012; Schneider, Mori, Lambert, and Wong, 2009) and to minimise participants feeling inhibited to discuss perspectives due to having opposite sex individuals present. Participants were full-time undergraduate or postgraduate students studying on psychology (seven participants), criminology (three participants), medicine (two participants), and teacher training (nine participants) courses at an East Midlands university in England. A student sample was selected due to the 18- to 24-year demographic being increasingly at risk of experiencing nonconsensual sex (Abbey, Zawacki, Buck, Clinton, and McAuslan., 2004; Walby and Allen, 2004). In light of students and young people using alcohol to facilitate sexual encounters, and the normalisation of heavy drinking amongst this group (Bellis et al., 2008; Kypri et al., 2005), students were considered an appropriate sample choice to enable informed

debates to be generated which may be specifically pertinent to this demographic. The study vignette (see below description) was based around the behavior of two students, which further made the sample an appropriate choice in terms of asking participants to reflect on experiences they may be able to relate to.

Participants were recruited through nonprobability sampling techniques. Existing contacts at the given university were asked to disseminate information about the study to a subset of individuals. Six individuals volunteered to participate through this process and were asked to invite their peers to take part in the study. It is recognised that a nonrandom sampling approach, and the decision to include individuals within focus groups who were familiar with each other, may impact on the nature of discussions. However, Doherty and Anderson (2004) emphasise the potential for socially desirable responding (the tendency to give positive descriptions) when adopting discussion-based methods that examine controversial rape perspectives.

Ellison and Munro (2010a: p. 799) also acknowledge that individuals may be "well versed" in "socially appropriate" attitudes in relation to rape. Howarth (2002) argues that to enable controversial, sensitive, and distressing topics to be discussed openly and with confidence, group participants should be known to each other at some level. Due to the emotive nature of the research topic, desire to foster uninhibited conversation and potential for socially desirable responding—especially in the presence of unknown individuals—it was rationalised that the recruitment strategy suggested by Howarth (2002) was appropriate. A focus group method was chosen to encourage debate between participants and to allow for the emergence of rich data. This approach also significantly reduces the directive influence of the interviewer (Morgan, 1997) and better corresponds to the process of jury deliberation, thus, highlighting the complex and potentially contradictory ways in which attitudes inform deliberations.

Discussions were based around a vignette that modelled the facts reported in the Bree (2007) case. As discussed, this is recognised to epitomise the problems associated with having sex when parties are extremely drunk, thus, enhancing the study's ecological validity (Doherty and Anderson, 2004). The vignette described Benjamin and Michelle who were briefly acquainted, spending a night out, initially with another couple and then later alone. They were witnessed leaving a bar in the early hours of the morning and walking to Michelle's flat where she vomits due to the alcohol consumed. Sex takes place which Michelle reports to a friend, and later to the police, as being nonconsensual. Michelle argues that her recollection was "very patchy" (Bree, 2007: p. 161) despite recognition that she had not consented at the time. Benjamin maintains throughout his statement to the police that sex was consensual.

Whilst the authors were not aware of other studies that have used this case as a specific vignette, it was selected due to the fact that it has been the catalyst for much debate in the United Kingdom (see Cowan, 2008; Elvin, 2008; Wallerstein, 2009). Study findings are therefore argued to be applicable to, and enhance, the wider international work which has examined the role of alcohol consumption on third parties' attitudes towards sex and its consensual nature (for example, Norris and Cubbins, 1992; Wall and Schuller, 2000).

A focus group guide was used to direct conversation and addressed the following topics:

- Whether participants personally felt that Benjamin should be found guilty of rape and why
- If not guilty of rape, then of some other crime
- The factors that impacted on whether participants personally believed Michelle had been raped
- Whether participants' personal perspectives would have differed if only Michelle had been drinking

Initially, focus group participants were blind to the outcome of the Bree (2007) case. Towards the end of each focus group, participants were told that Bree (2007) was found "not guilty," in order to encourage further reflections on why Benjamin may have been acquitted. In light of the fact that most focus group participants had themselves decided that Benjamin should be acquitted, telling them that this had been the outcome resulted in no further information being elicited. Once focus groups had finished, all participants were informed of the decisions of both the jury and the Court of Appeal in the case.

All participants were provided with written copies of the legal definition of rape, sexual assault, and the Section 74 consent definition to ensure they were aware of these definitions prior to commencing the focus group.

Analysis and Discussion

The following analysis focuses on three primary topics: "not quite rape," "false allegations of rape," and "voluntary intoxication and intercourse." Within each higher order theme, further subthemes were identified and examined in order to draw out key perspectives relating to intoxicated sexual intercourse and false allegations of rape.

Not Quite Rape

Participants were reluctant to label the vignette sex as rape and the subthemes that were developed to compose this topic included "physical injury evidence," which denoted the lack of injury within the case vignette. The subtheme "stereotype of rapist and rape" was also developed to capture arguments around the behaviour of Benjamin failing to conform to that of a stereotypical sex attacker.

Physical Injury Evidence. The majority of participants did not perceive the sex depicted in the vignette to be representative of rape and almost all participants argued that they would have personally acquitted Benjamin. Key to this decision was their inability to be sure beyond reasonable doubt that rape had occurred, with certain misconceptions influencing judgements. It was argued that rape is "difficult to prove" (Focus Group 1, Female 4; (FGl, F4)) and that there were no signs of "physical evidence" (FGl, Fl) indicating rape had taken place. Consistent with past research (Ellison and Munro, 2009, 2010a), multiple participants expected evidence of physical injury: "this is like such an unspeakable, horrible thing to happen to you, and I've no idea what it could possibly feel like. But I'd expect to see some scratches or bruises on her, or something" (FG2, M3).

Several participants focused on this lack of physical evidence and argued that had severe bruising, cuts, or broken bones been present, this would be indicative of rape and convince them of such. Corroborative evidence is typically absent in rape cases and a lack of physical injury undoubtedly makes an allegation harder to prove and the criminal burden of proof more difficult to reach. It was clear that for certain participants, such evidential concerns influenced their arguments regarding the need for physical injury. However, for a smaller subset it was evident that rape was viewed as synonymous with violence. For this latter group, there is perhaps a dissonance between the legal stance and lay expectation. That is, the law does not require evidence of injury in order for consent to be deemed absent (see *R v Heard*, 2007; *R v Olugboja*, 1981). Legally, the harms that arise from rape are viewed in relation to the sex that takes place without consent; the presence of injury simply acts to exacerbate the seriousness of the crime. Perspectives that assume rape involves injury may feed into ideas around false allegations of rape, where it may come to be assumed that if there is no evidence of violence, the allegation is potentially false.

Stereotype of Rapist and Rape. Participants emphasised that the defendant "offered to spend the night in her bed. So, obviously, he does not mean it in a conscious term to be rape" (FG1, F2) and had not "pinned her down and shagged her" (FG1, F4). Certain actions perpetrated by Benjamin prior to the sex, such as bringing Michelle a glass of water and helping to clean her up after having been sick, were perceived to demonstrate he was "obviously quite respectful of her" (FG3, F5). Participants were consequently reluctant to define the sex as involving activity that should be criminalised: ". . . there's a certain lack of morality on his part. He's . . . I think, taking advantage of someone is vastly different to um . . . it's vastly different to committing a sort of offence . . ." (FG4, M1). Instead, it was argued that Benjamin had acted morally wrong, been "foolish" (FG4, M2), made "an error of judgement" (FG4, M1), and although a possible "scumbag" (FG2, M4) for taking advantage, had not necessarily "done anything wrong in the eyes of the law" (FG2, M4). Participants did not consequently feel that his behaviour was sufficient to warrant a prison sentence, and further reasons for this perspective focused on the normalisation of the sex depicted: "it must happen too often to send people to prison for doing that" (FG1, F4). Such normalisation suggests that the sex portrayed has to some extent come to be unquestionably accepted as reflective of the reality of heavy drinking situations, unsurprising in light of the noted research which demonstrates alcohol is used by young people to facilitate their sexual encounters (Bellis et al., 2008; Sumnall et al., 2007).

Whilst reluctant to describe the vignette sex as a crime, participants acknowledged it was "obviously an unpleasant experience" (FG1, F4) but more in line with a "really bad one-night stand" (FG1, F1). Sex was conceptualised to have been the result of mixed messages, poor

communication, and a reduction in inhibitions. Whilst these arguments lend weight to research that suggests when parties are equally intoxicated, participants look for a "mid-point" between rape and consensual sex to describe that intercourse (Finch and Munro, 2005), the current study suggests that this mid-point behaviour is far more aligned with consensual sex (Gunby et al., 2012). The implications that stem from these arguments are that if participants are reluctant to conceptualise the situation depicted in the vignette as one that could involve the commission of a crime initially, they start from an assumption that will doubt the veracity of the complainant's rape allegation. If the scenario is not what constitutes rape for them, then how can her complaint be conceptualised as true?

False Allegations of Rape

The topic of false allegations was spontaneously raised by participants in all four focus groups without direction from the investigator, arguably demonstrating the pervasive nature of the issue. The subthemes that emerged from this topic included participants' perceptions around the "motivations" that drive a false allegation, "their frequency," and the "ramifications of a false allegation."

Motivations for a False Allegation of Rape. Participants in three of the groups raised for debate whether Michelle "regretted it afterwards . . ." (FG2, M3) or questioned whether "she has consented in a way, but she doesn't like the fact that she's done it" (FG3, F4), thus, providing the backdrop for a false allegation to be made:

> . . . being used is a very schoolyard term to have used . . . it kind of shows that her initial reaction was that she'd been used; she hadn't been raped. And then later on, perhaps when she'd thought about it . . . I don't know, perhaps she altered events in her head, to say it's rape. (FG3, F3)

The possibility of a rape allegation being the consequence of events being "altered" to fit with a rape experience is an issue individuals are entitled to consider when assessing the legitimacy of a case. However, the fact Michelle did not initially label her experience as rape is used by several participants to question the validity of her account. This perhaps highlights a limited understanding around the factors that impact on the labelling process (see Bondurant, 2001; Kahn, Jackson, Kully, Badger, and Halvorsen, 2003). Such findings sit within a wider framework that indicates third parties often expect rape complainants to adhere to stereotypical victim scripts which include the display of emotion, immediately reporting to the police (Ellison and Munro, 2009; Temkin and Krahe, 2008), and as currently suggested, to categorically identify and label that experience as rape.

Whilst a subset of participants argued that the vignette was unlikely to be a false report, protests were sometimes qualified: "I don't see what she would get out of crying rape. I mean, unless she's got a boyfriend or something" (FG2, M5). The existence of a relationship appeared to increase the potential for a false allegation, based on the premise that such extreme actions would enable the complainant to "cover-up" (FG4, M2) her indiscretion. False reports were also viewed as a method for seeking revenge, motivations identified in related literature (Ellison and Munro, 2010a; Kelly et al., 2005; Lonsway et al., 2009):

> But also, I look at it um if she's used the term been used, she could also be using this court case as a way to get back at him. If she feels, herself, that she's been used, she could be thinking oh this is my way to get back at him, to show him that I didn't want it to happen; that I feel used, so I'll get my revenge, I'll do payback more than anything, rather than feeling like she's been raped afterwards. (FG3, F2)

Frequency of False Allegations of Rape. After the issue of false rape allegations had been raised by participants, they were asked whether they felt such reports were commonplace. Almost all participants argued they were likely to be infrequent due to there being "no real reward" (FG3, F5) and that women would not want to go through the intrusive physical examination that would stem from making a claim. Whilst this perspective perhaps sits at odds with the frequency with which participants suggested the vignette could be an example of a false report, such a contradiction resonates with existent findings. Ellison and Munro (2010a) for example, identified that when individually questioned on abstract rape perspectives, participants' attitudes did not always mirror those which become apparent via the group process of deliberating a

concrete case example. The social process of discussion, in conjunction with addressing issues of reasonable doubt and belief, resulted in a more complex interplay of factors being considered, which potentially triggered additional logics (including in the current instance, the possibility of an allegation being false). Whilst this may be one explanation for the dissonance in perspectives identified via direct questioning and the more subtle deliberative process, it is also possible that participants were aware that directly agreeing that false reports were frequent could have been perceived unduly unsympathetic (Doherty and Anderson, 2004), with such suggestions consequently remaining unendorsed.

Whilst directly arguing that false rape allegations were likely to be infrequent, participants nevertheless stated that "it's easy to say rape, which I do think happens" (FG1, F1). It may be the perceived ease with which a false allegation can be made which linked to assumptions around the vignette being an example of a false report. As noted, this philosophy has resonated within criminal law and impacted on rape legislation (Rumney, 2006). Whilst Matthew Hale's (1736: p. 634) famed argument that rape is an accusation easily made, yet hard to be defended, no longer resonates as profusely within legal thinking, Ellison and Munro (2010a) argue that the sentiment is still propelled via media reports (Gavey and Gow, 2001; Kitzinger, 2009; Lilith Project, 2008). Lonsway et al. (2009) similarly argue that media accounts of false allegations, often made against popular cultural figures, contribute towards the overestimation of false allegations in everyday life and can serve to enhance assumptions around false allegations being commonplace, despite participants acknowledging to "not knowing anything about it really" (FG2, M3).

The Ramifications of False Allegations. Multiple participants across the groups argued that false reports can "ruin people's lives" (FGl, Fl) and the "rumours will carry on" (FGl, F6), even if the accusation is identified as false. In this sense, the wrongs of a false rape allegation were seen to relate to the impact of having the term *rapist* attributed to an individual. The repeated arguments that focused on men being wrongly and knowingly accused of rape, disproportionately outweighed the conversation held in relation to the harms of the rape offence to the complainant and wider society. Gavey (2005) has noted that an overriding focus around the "wrongness" of false rape allegations, above and beyond the harms of rape itself, is an established feature of Western society and an example of the way in which the traumas of rape are marginalised.

Concern for the defendant was also expressed in relation to rape accusations and decisions to convict generally. Reflecting Ellison and Munro's (2010b) findings, a participant argued, "I don't think his entire life and career should be marred by a conviction, based on this" (FG3, F2), a comment that demonstrates awareness around the ramifications of being found guilty of rape. The majority of participants argued that in such ambiguous circumstances, and with such long-term implications, the defendant should be given the "benefit of the doubt" (FG1, F5). Whilst such verdicts may relate to the problems of being sure beyond reasonable doubt when deciding on guilt, it was clear that for certain participants, in evaluating whether rape had occurred, the focus hinged on the harms of having the rape label attributed to the defendant.

Related to this issue, certain participants argued that the ramifications of being accused of rape made it irresponsible to take a complaint to the police unless the victim was *sure* rape has occurred: "so, if you're not sure, then I think it's quite irresponsible to make that claim" (FG2, M2). Although this perspective was challenged, for a small number of participants, there was the expectation that when memory of events was hampered by alcohol, at a minimum, the complainant should seek legal advice on how to proceed rather than "cry rape" (FG2, M3) at the onset.

This argument again fails to recognise the impact of sexual offences where the associated trauma may inhibit the ability to take immediate coherent action. It perhaps also demonstrates a naivety over the workings of the criminal justice system and a complainant's ability to access such legal advice, outside of the official police reporting route. The comment rightfully suggests that certain individuals may be confused about the sex they have experienced and may benefit from contact with someone suitably trained who could advise, and help categorise, what had been encountered without placing pressure to officially report the incident. It is possible that for certain individuals, the reporting process is a fact-finding endeavour. If at the police reporting stage it is established that rape has not occurred, this may feed into notions of false allegations of rape, with

the genuinely confused complainant being perceived to have made a hasty decision to report, which they subsequently retract, and which may come to be conceptualised as a retraction based upon a sober re-evaluation of the facts.

Voluntary Intoxication and Intercourse

Participants offered more general perspectives on alcohol-involved intercourse, with these conversations implicating potential difficulties in achieving convictions in alcohol-involved rape cases, whilst also elaborating further on the extent to which such views intertwine with wider ideas around false allegations. The subthemes developed included the "impact of alcohol on inhibitions," Michelle's "capacity to consent," and the "dual impact of alcohol on defendant and complainant behaviour."

Impact of Alcohol on Inhibitions. A large proportion of participants argued that alcohol reduces inhibitions and increases the potential for engaging in behaviours that may later be regretted: "alcohol lowers your inhibitions and fuels you to do things that perhaps you shouldn't" (FG3, F6). It was argued that if sex takes place during a period of extreme drunkenness, rape may be the "first reaction when they wake up" (FG1, F3). It was rationalised that whilst sex may have been consensually engaged in at the time, it may be regretted the following day and re-labelled as nonconsensual:

> . . . has she not to some extent woken up and just regretted it, and kind of come to and suddenly thought oh God, what are people gonna think of me, what am I thinking of myself? So, it's kind of an afterthought as well. (FG1, F2)

It was clear that when participants talked about a complainant modifying the sex that took place to align it with a rape act, this was not always deemed a conscious or vindictive process but one that may also be more subtle:

> When you're drunk, you sometimes . . . you know, you're not sure what happened or what was a dream. And when you've spoken to Naomi, when you've still been drunk, that might all mesh into what you remember as well. (FG2, M3)

False allegations were thus constructed as both the product of an overt decision to make a complaint for the purpose of covering up regretted sex as well as potentially being the product of more subtle processes which involved events being "altered" during the course of trying to account for, and rationalise, regretted intercourse. It was clear that it was this impact of alcohol on inhibitions and behaviour specifically, which related to participants' assumptions that false reports were more likely when drinking—either through an intentional decision to make a false claim or via the impact of alcohol on cognition, recollection, and the restructuring of events the next morning. Indeed, this explanation was offered significantly more frequently than motivations that focused on making a false claim for the purpose of revenge or to protect an existent relationship. Whilst certain participants argued that having drank alcohol prior to a rape is likely to decrease a complainant's likelihood of reporting the assault, due to fears around being perceived non-credible, the majority of participants argued that people are more likely to use alcohol "as their excuse" (FGl, F5) for engaging in uninhibited behaviours. These findings support larger scale quantitative data which indicate that 81.1% of students ($N = 869$) aged 18 to 24 years agreed that being drunk when having sex increases the likelihood of a false rape allegation being made (Gunby et al., 2012).

Capacity. Section 74 of the Sexual Offences Act 2003 makes clear that an individual must retain the capacity to consent in order for that consent to be valid. Participants emphasized the difficulties of evaluating the vignette case facts and being able to accurately gauge Michelle's level of alcohol intoxication and, by default, degree of capability. Whilst a subset of participants focused on the complainant having been sick, and felt that this should have been a sufficient indicator to prevent the defendant from having sex with her, it was not deemed sufficient in isolation to convince participants that she lacked the capacity to consent entirely: "you can have a few drinks and be sick, and not even really be that drunk" (FG3, F3). Certain participants also drew upon Michelle's ability to effectively verbalise and walk without staggering to determine her capacity: "if you can walk, you know, quite well, you'd think that someone was okay" (FG3, F3).

Whilst the law acknowledges that an individual may lose the capacity to consent before the point of unconsciousness,

the study suggests that for certain participants, such extreme states of intoxication may only be deemed suitable markers (Finch and Munro, 2006). These comments are perhaps unsurprising in light of arguments around the capacity construct being unhelpful in illuminating the nuanced stages of intoxication. Under such circumstances, it is argued that lack of capacity will typically be judged through reference to an extreme point (Cowan, 2008; Elvin, 2008). Despite these comments, there was a consensus that alcohol impacts differently on people, making it difficult to establish the point at which an individual loses the capacity to consent:

> Alcohol affects different people differently, and there are different times alcohol will affect the same individual. You can have three beers and be absolutely fine on one night. You could have a beer and a cocktail another night and be blasted. (FG1, Fl)

Participants thus expressed their sympathy for the defendant at this point, arguing it would have been impossible "to judge it really" (FG4, M2) and that in the absence of "a breath test" (FG2, M5), it was unreasonable to assume he should be able to appreciate whether the complainant retained the capacity to consent.

The Dual Impact of Alcohol on Defendant and Complainant Behaviour: Constructing Female Responsibility. When participants were asked who they personally felt should take responsibility for ensuring consent was clearly established in a sexual situation, all participants argued that responsibility should be shared, or, it was a man's moral duty to ensure his partner was fully consenting. However, if both parties were equally intoxicated, men were deemed able to forfeit such duties: "I think in a normal sexual situation, it would be shared. But when you're both drunk, I think it's just whoever's the most sober should make the decision" (FG3, F4).

The majority of participants argued that if through alcohol the complainant was left too intoxicated to retain the capacity to consent to intercourse, alcohol may have similarly impacted on the defendant's ability to identify whether his partner had the capacity, thus, "making you more likely to think that they'd [the partner] given reasonable consent" (FG2, M2). Whilst intoxication is not a factor that can be taken into account when determining whether the defendant held a reasonable belief in consent (*DPP v Majewski*, 1977; *R v Heard*, 2007), it was clear participants did not recognise this or, if they did, still sympathised with the drunken defendant: "but if he's drunk to a certain extent that he does reasonably believe that B consents, then he hasn't done anything wrong, in the eyes of the law" (FG2, M6). It is realistic to assume that for certain individuals, extreme intoxication will incorrectly be viewed as a reasonable excuse for believing consent had been given.

When participants were asked whether they personally felt that Benjamin would have been found guilty of rape if only the complainant had been drinking, there was consensus across the groups that there would have been an increased likelihood. If sober, the defendant was perceived to be in a position where he could appreciate the complainant's degree of capacity and had "enough coherence to have the responsibility to make the judgement call" (FG1, F6): "If you're sober and you know that someone is drunk, then you know full well that your moral responsibility is not to take advantage of them ... I dunno if it's a law thing ... you just wouldn't, would you?" (FG2, M6). This argument implies that the law is not the motivator that drives appropriate sexual encounters, but rather, a sense of morality influences behaviour. Moral responsibility, however, still appeared to be something that could be forfeited when parties were equivalently intoxicated, but not when there was a disparity in that intoxication. These findings support the research that has identified that third parties perceive it unfair to hold a defendant criminally liable for rape if each individual is equally intoxicated (Finch and Munro, 2005; Gunby et al., 2012) yet are more inclined to label sex as rape when a complainant is drinking independently (Norris and Cubbins, 1992), or the defendant is less intoxicated (Finch and Munro, 2005). Whilst Finch and Munro (2005) argue that a less drunk or sober defendant is perceived to be in a position whereby he is able to ensure the complainant has the capacity to consent, the current study indicates that an intoxicated defendant is perceived to be in a disadvantageous position whereby he is unable to clearly gauge the complainant's level of intoxication and therefore her capacity. Being in such a position was seen to reduce the defendant's responsibility for ensuring consent was present.

A subset of participants focused on the complainant's lack of verbalised "no" in rationalising why they were insufficiently convinced that rape had taken place: "... at no point has she said ... or she can't recall saying no to sex" (FG4, M1). The dissonance between the law, which does not require consent to be verbally expressed (*R v Heard*, 2007), and lay assumption is again apparent. Female participants specifically emphasised that sexual intentions must be effectively communicated:

> She needs to say no beforehand. There's no point in saying I didn't want to do it afterwards ... that's just gonna confuse everyone. So, like yeah, it's up to the woman to say before it happens, yes or no in an obvious and clear way. (FG3, F3)

The implications of this argument are multiple. It feeds into ideas around the retraction of consent which underpin previous arguments around false allegations being made upon re-evaluation of the sex that occurred, as well as suggesting that if a verbalised "no" is not given, this could be deemed indicative of the allegation being false. It also implies that in the absence of clear articulation, the defendant will be left without sufficient ability to negotiate, or read, the sexual situation. As previously noted, under Section 1(2) of the Sexual Offences Act 2003, juries are required to take into account any steps taken by the defendant to ascertain consent, which could include asking a partner whether they are happy for the sexual interaction to progress. Despite being provided with the legal definition of rape, and participants therefore being aware of this responsibility on defendants, a minority (of women) still deemed the female to be the party who should take control over clarifying sexual expectations. Whilst research suggests that men are more likely to endorse attitudes which feed into beliefs relating to false allegations (Gunby et al., 2012; Opinion Matters, 2010), women have been found to more frequently assume that other women should take some degree of responsibility for nonconsensual sex (Finch and Munro, 2007; Opinion Matters, 2010). This includes taking responsibility for avoiding miscommunication and for effectively communicating nonconsent through overt verbal responses (Ellison and Munro, 2010a).

Whilst emphasising the need for sexual intentions to be clear, it was paradoxically noted that it could be a "passion killer" for the man to ask whether he could have sex with his partner. In this sense, consent was still viewed as more natural and appropriate if controlled by the woman. The articulation of such arguments reflect the traditional sexual scripts that suggest men are responsible for the initiation of sexual encounters and the active pursuit of sexual outcomes, care of their higher sex drive. Women by contrast are seen to set sexual parameters and provide "control" over the time and place of sex (Frith, 2009). It is interesting to note that women still drew upon these scripts of supposedly "normal" male and female sexuality to ground their arguments and which perhaps provided a basis for explaining why women's ability to verbally resist male sexual advances received such scrutiny.

Female participants also highlighted the importance of personal responsibility when drinking and recognising the ramifications of extreme drunkenness: "... I think people do have responsibilities to look after themselves. And I think that the amount that she drank, and the fact that she went out with another couple, will really go against her in that sense" (FG3, F4). The disproportionate focus on women (as opposed to men) taking personal responsibility when drinking may relate to women being at enhanced risk of experiencing sexual offences initially (Kershaw, Nicholas, and Walker, 2008), hence, their perceived role in attempting to reduce that vulnerability. Women are often subject to awareness raising campaign literature that warns them against the dangers of extreme drinking, leaving friends unattended on evenings out, and accepting drinks from strangers (Neame, 2003), also potentially sensitising women to such arguments. Whilst it is acknowledged that campaign literature is increasingly incorporating messages that are directed at men, in attempts to reduce the prevalence of rape, such messages will take time to infiltrate into public consciousness and to temper those which have long focused on the modification of female behaviour (Neame, 2003).

Whilst all individuals should perhaps work towards recognising potential vulnerabilities when drinking, and to equally recognise such vulnerabilities in others, it is noteworthy that there was no comparable discussion around men needing to consider how much alcohol they consumed on a night out, or the possible impacts of their intoxication on their ability to read consent-relevant cues. The overriding focus on the steps that women should take to avoid sexual offences resonates with findings that indicate when rape occurs, the spotlight resides firmly on the female's actions prior to the assault (Finch and Munro, 2005, 2007; Kelly et al., 2005; Temkin and Krahe, 2008).

⚒ Conclusion

A key aim of the research project was to investigate how perspectives towards false allegations and alcohol intoxication intertwine. By investigating such attitudes, it is possible to reflect on the perceived role of alcohol within the false reporting process, provide insights into the way lay individuals apportion responsibility, and illuminate stereotypes that may exist. Accordingly, the study falls within the recommendations of the Stern Review (2010) to provide additional research that can enhance understandings of false rape allegations, thus, enabling unfounded stereotypes to be challenged.

The study highlighted considerable consensus across participants' perspectives regarding alcohol-involved rape. When members of a drinking dyad are presented as equally intoxicated, there was a reduced willingness to label the depiction of nonconsensual sex as rape. Whilst alcohol intoxication is not a defense to a sexual offence, it was evident that participants viewed comparable degrees of drunkenness as a factor that was sufficient to reasonably mitigate the defendant's responsibility for ascertaining consent. When nonconsensual sex took place between equally intoxicated individuals, that intercourse was collectively constructed to be the unpleasant, but somewhat understandable, outcome of extreme intoxication, raising clear concerns around the potential for alcohol-involved nonconsensual intercourse to be re-categorised at trial as simply being constitutive of "bad sex."

The impact of alcohol on cognition and inhibitions was deemed central in encouraging individuals to partake in behaviours they would not if sober. The potential for sex to occur, care of a disinhibited state, and later be reformulated as nonconsensual (either intentionally or via more subtle processes) to account for that behaviour underpinned the assumption that false rape reports are more likely when drinking. Throughout the discussions, it was evident that the focus remained on Michelle's actions prior to the intercourse, including her failures for having not explicitly verbalised nonconsent and for placing herself in a vulnerable position. No equivalent arguments were made in relation to the steps Benjamin could have taken to ensure consent was present and how his extreme alcohol consumption may have increased his potential for misperceiving Michelle's sexual intentions. To this end, additional awareness raising is paramount to help articulate the legal stance on rape, [to articulate] the rape victim experience, to emphasise that intoxication is not a defense to a charge of rape, and to raise awareness around men also being instrumental in preventing nonconsensual experiences. Awareness raising should also focus specifically on attitudes held in relation to false allegations of rape and dissemination of the facts that can dispel such myths. It is acknowledged that further research is needed to help categorically clarify rates of false rape reporting and the factors associated with these allegations. Only then will the extent of the situation, and the contextual factors surrounding false reports, be fully understood.

Note

1. Alcohol-involved intercourse is defined here as sex that takes place between parties when one or both have been drinking voluntarily and are extremely intoxicated.

Cases

Bree, 2 Crim. App. R. 13 [2007].

DPP v Majewski, AC 443 [1977].

R v Heard, EWCA Crim 2056 [2007].

R v Olugboja, 73 Cr. App. R. 344 [1981].

References

Abbey, A., Zawacki, T., Buck, P. O., Clinton, A. M., and McAuslan, P. (2004). Sexual assault and alcohol consumption: What do we know about their relationship and what types of research are still needed? *Aggression and Violent Behavior* 9(3): 271–303.

Almandras, S. (2010). *Anonymity in rape cases.* London, England: House of Commons Library, Home Affairs.

Bancroft, A. (2012). Twitter reaction to Ched Evans case shows rape culture is alive and kicking. Available at: http://www.guardian.co.uk/commentisfree/2012/apr/23/ched-evansrape-culture-twitter (accessed 6 June 2012).

Bellis, M. A., Hughes, K., Calafat, A., Juan, M., Ramon, A., Rodriguez, J. A., . . . Phillips-Howard, P. (2008). Sexual uses of alcohol and drugs and the associated health risks: A cross sectional study of young people in nine European cities. *BMC Public Health* 8: 155–165.

Beres, M. A. (2007). Spontaneous sexual consent: An analysis of sexual consent literature. *Feminism and Psychology* 17(1): 93–108.

Bondurant, B. (2001). University women's acknowledgement of rape: Individual, situational, and social factors. *Violence Against Women* 7(3): 294–314.

Burton, S., Kelly, L., Kitzinger, J., and Regan, L. (1998). *Young people's attitudes towards violence, sex and relationships: A survey and focus group study.* Edinburgh, Scotland: Zero Tolerance Charitable Trust.

Cowan, S. (2008). The trouble with drink: Intoxication, (in)capacity, and the evaporation of consent to sex. *Akron Law Review* 41(4): 899–922.

Doherty, K., and Anderson, I. (2004). Making sense of male rape: Constructions of gender, sexuality and experience of rape victims. *Journal of Community and Applied Social Psychology* 14(2): 85–103.

Ellison, L., and Munro, V. (2009). Reacting to rape: Exploring mock jurors' assessments of complainant credibility. *British Journal of Criminology* 49(2): 202–219.

Ellison, L., and Munro, V. (2010a). A stranger in the bushes, or an elephant in the room? Critical reflections upon received rape myth wisdom in the context of a mock jury study. *New Criminal Law Review* 13(4): 781–801.

Ellison, L., and Munro, V. (2010b). Getting to (not) guilty: Examining juror's deliberative processes in, and beyond, the context of a mock rape trial. *Legal Studies* 30(1): 74–97.

Elvin, J. (2008). Intoxication, capacity to consent and the Sexual Offences Act 2003. *Kings Law Journal* 19(1): 151–157.

Finch, E., and Munro, V. (2005). Juror stereotypes and blame attribution in rape cases involving intoxicants: Findings of a pilot study. *British Journal of Criminology* 45(1): 25–38.

Finch, E., and Munro, V. (2006). Breaking boundaries? Sexual consent in the jury room. *Legal Studies* 26(3): 303–320.

Finch, E., and Munro, V. (2007). The demon drink and the demonized woman: Socio-sexual stereotypes and responsibility attributions in rape trials involving intoxicants. *Social and Legal Studies* 16(4): 591–614.

Frith, H. (2009). Sexual scripts, sexual refusals and rape. In M. Horvath and J. Brown (Eds.), *Rape: Challenging contemporary thinking* (pp. 99–122). Devon, England: Willan.

Gavey, N. (2005). *Just sex? The cultural scaffolding of rape.* Sussex, England: Routledge.

Gavey, N., and Gow, V. (2001). "Cry wolf," cried the wolf: Constructing the issue of false rape allegations in New Zealand media texts. *Feminism and Psychology* 11(3): 341–360.

George, W. H., & Stoner, S. A. (2000). Understanding acute alcohol effects on sexual behaviour. *Annual Review of Sex Research* 11: 92–124.

Gunby, C., Carline, A., Bellis, M. A., and Beynon, C. (2012). Gender differences in alcohol-related non-consensual sex: Cross-sectional analysis of a student population. *BMC Public Health* 12(216): 1–12.

Gunby, C., Carline, A., and Beynon, C. (2010). Alcohol-related rape cases: Barristers' perspectives on the Sexual Offences Act 2003 and its impact on practice. *Journal of Criminal Law* 74: 579–600.

Hale, M. (1736). *History of the pleas of the Crown.* London, England: Professional Books.

Home Office. (2002). *Protecting the public: Strengthening protection against sex offenders and reforming the law on sexual offences.* London, England: Home Office.

Howarth, C. (2002). Identity in whose eyes? The role of representations in identity construction. *Journal for the Theory of Behaviour* 32(2): 145–162.

Humphreys, T. (2007). Perceptions of sexual consent: The impact of relationship history and gender. *Journal of Sex Research* 44(4): 307–315.

Kahn, A., Jackson, J., Kully, C., Badger, K., and Halvorsen, J. (2003). Calling it rape: Differences in experiences of women who do or do not label their sexual assault as rape. *Psychology of Women Quarterly* 27(3): 233–242.

Kelly, L. (2010). The (in)credible words of women: False allegations in European rape research. *Violence Against Women* 16(12): 1345–1355.

Kelly, L., Lovett, J., and Regan, L. (2005). *A gap or a chasm? Attrition in reported rape cases. HORS 293.* London, England: Home Office.

Kershaw, C., Nicholas, S., and Walker, A. (2008). *Crime in England and Wales 2007/08: Findings from the British Crime Survey and police recorded crime.* London, England: Home Office.

Kitzinger, J. (2009). Rape in the media. In M. Horvath and J. Brown (Eds.), *Rape: Challenging contemporary thinking* (pp. 74–98). Devon, England: Willan.

Kypri, K., Cronin, M., and Wright, C. S. (2005). Do university students drink more hazardously than their non-student peers? *Addiction* 100(5): 1672–1677.

Lilith Project. (2008). *Just representation? Press reporting and the reality of rape.* London, England: Matrix Chambers.

Lonsway, K., Archambault, J., and Lisak, D. (2009). False reports: Moving beyond the issue to successfully investigate and prosecute non-stranger sexual assaults. *The Voice* 3(1): 1–11.

Morgan, D. (1997). *Focus groups as qualitative research, qualitative research methods series.* Thousand Oaks, CA: Sage.

Neame, A. (2003). *Beyond drink spiking: Drug and alcohol facilitated sexual assault: Briefing number 2.* Melbourne, Australia: Australian Centre for the Study of Sexual Assault.

Norris, J., and Cubbins, L. (1992). Dating, drinking, and rape: Effects of victim's and assailant's alcohol consumption on judgments of their behaviour and traits. *Psychology of Women Quarterly* 16(2): 179–191.

Office for Criminal Justice Reform. (2006). *Convicting rapists and protecting victims—Justice for victims of crime: A consultation paper.* London, England: Home Office.

Office for Criminal Justice Reform. (2007). *Convicting rapists and protecting victims—Justice for victims of rape: Responses to consultation.* London, England: Home Office.

Opinion Matters. (2010). Wake up to rape research summary report. Available at: http://www.thehavens.co.uk/docs/Havens_Wake_Up_To_Rape_Report_Summary.pdf (accessed 10 June 2011).

Rumney, P. (2006). False allegations of rape. *Cambridge Law Journal* 65(1): 128–158.

Sanders, A. (2012). Speech on the prosecution of rape and serious sexual offences by Alison Saunders, Chief Crown Prosecutor for London. Available at: http://www.cps.gov.uk/news/articles/speech_on_the_prosecution_of_rape_and_serious_sexual_offences_by_alison_saunders_chief_crown_prosecutor_for_london/ (accessed 11 February 2012).

Schneider, L., Mori, L., Lambert, P., and Wong, A. (2009). The role of gender and ethnicity in perceptions of rape and its after effects. *Sex Roles* 60(5–6): 410–421.

Stern Review. (2010). *A report by Baroness Vivien Stern CBE of an independent review into how rape complaints are handled by public authorities in England and Wales.* London, England: Home Office.

Sumnall, H. R., Beynon, C. M., Conchie, S. M., Riley, S. C. E., and Cole, J. C. (2007). An investigation of the subjective experiences of sex after alcohol or drug intoxication. *Journal of Psychopharmacology* 21(5): 525–537.

Temkin, J. (2002). *Rape and the legal process.* Oxford, England: Oxford University Press.

Temkin, J., and Krahe, B. (2008). *Sexual assault and the justice gap: A question of attitude.* Oxford, England: Hart.

Walby, S., and Allen, J. (2004). *Domestic violence, sexual assault and stalking: Findings from the British Crime Survey. Home Office Research Study 276.* London, England: Home Office.

Wall, A., and Schuller, R. (2000). Sexual assault and defendant/victim intoxication: Jurors perceptions of guilt. *Journal of Applied Social Psychology* 30(2): 253–274.

Wallerstein, S. (2009). A drunken consent is still consent: Or is it? A critical analysis of the law on a drunken consent to sex following Bree. *Journal of Criminal Law* 73: 318–344.

YouGov. (2010). Drunk and disorderly. Available at: http://today.yougov.co.u/life/drunk-and-disorderly (accessed 2 May 2011).

DISCUSSION QUESTIONS

1. Did the students think that Benjamin should be found guilty of rape? Are there differences between male and female students in this assessment?

2. What role did voluntary intoxication play in evaluating the victim/offender status of Benjamin and Michelle?

3. How are false allegations of rape viewed in light of the intoxicated state of Benjamin and Michelle?

Women and Victimization
Intimate Partner Abuse and Stalking

Much of history has documented the presence of violence within relationships. Throughout history, women were considered the property of men. Wife beating was a legal and accepted form of discipline of women by their husbands. During ancient Roman times, men were allowed to beat their wives with "a rod or switch as long as its circumference is no greater than the girth of the base of the man's right thumb" (Stevenson & Love, 1999, table 1, 753 B.C.). The "rule of thumb" continued as a guiding principle of legalized wife beating throughout early European history and appeared in English common-law practices, which influenced the legal structures of the early settlers in America. While small movements against wife beating appear in the United States throughout the 18th and 19th century, it was not until 1871 that Alabama and Massachusetts became the first states to take away the legal right of men to beat their wives. However, significant resistance still existed in many states on the grounds that the government should not interfere in the family environment. In 1882, wife beating became a crime in the state of Maryland. While defining wife beating as a crime meant that the act would receive criminal consequences, the enforcement of the act as a crime was limited, and husbands rarely received any significant penalties for their actions.

The rise of the feminist movement in the late 1960s and early 1970s gave a foundation for the **battered women's movement**. Shelters and counseling programs began to appear throughout the United States during the 1970s; however, these efforts were small in scale, and the need for assistance significantly outweighed the availability of services. While police officers across the nation began to receive training about domestic violence calls for service, most departments had a nonarrest policy toward cases of domestic violence, as many officers saw their role as a peacemaker or interventionist, rather than as an agent of criminal justice. In these cases, homicide rates continued to increase due to the murders of women at the hands of their intimate partners, and more officers were dying in the line of duty responding to domestic violence calls.

The grassroots battered women's movement of the 1970s led to systemic changes in how the police and courts handled cases of domestic violence. Many of these changes occurred in respond to research findings by the **Minneapolis Domestic Violence Experiment** (MDVE). The MDVE illustrated that when an arrest was made in a misdemeanor domestic violence incident, recidivism rates were significantly lower compared to cases in which police simply "counseled" the aggressor (Sherman & Berk, 1984). Many departments ushered in new policies based on these findings. However, replication studies did not produce similar experiences and instead indicated that arresting the offender led to increases in violence.

Throughout the 1980s, state and nonprofit task forces assembled to discuss the issues of intimate partner abuse. By 1989, the United States had over 1,200 programs for battered women and provided shelter housing to over 300,000 women and children each year (Dobash & Dobash, 1992; Stevenson & Love, 1999). In 1994, Congress passed the **Violence Against Women Act** (VAWA) as part of the Federal Crime Victims Act. The VAWA provided funding for battered women's shelters and outreach education, as well as funding for domestic violence training for police and court personnel. It also provided the opportunity for victims to sue for civil damages as a result of violent acts perpetrated against them. In 1995, the Office on Violence Against Women (OVW) was created within the U.S. Department of Justice and today is charged with administering grant programs aimed at research and community programming toward eradicating intimate domestic and intimate partner abuse in our communities (Office on Violence Against Women [OVW], n.d.). Table 4.1 highlights the allocation of resources and the provision of services through the different reauthorizations of the Violence Against Women Act.

Defining and Identifying Intimate Partner Abuse

A number of different terms have been used to identify acts of violence against women. Many of these descriptions fall short in capturing the multifaceted nature of these abusive acts. The term *wife battering* fails to identify cases of violence outside of marriage, such as violent relationships between cohabiting individuals, dating violence, or even victims who were previously married to their batterer. Excluding these individuals from the official definition of *battered* often denies these victims any legal protections or services. The most common term used in recent history is *domestic violence.* However, this term combines the crime of woman battering with other contexts of abuse found within a home environment, such as the abuse of children or grandparents. Today, many scholars and community activists prefer the term **intimate partner abuse** (IPA) as it captures any form of abuse between individuals who currently have, or have previously had, an intimate relationship (Belknap, 2007). However, the use of these terms can vary significantly between different research studies, which can make it difficult to understand the extent of these victimizations. For example, the Centers for Disease Control defines intimate partner abuse as "physical, sexual or psychological harm by a current or former partner or spouse" (Centers for Disease Control [CDC], n.d., para. 1). Meanwhile, the National Violence Against Women survey extended the definition of intimate partner abuse to include cases of rape/sexual assault, physical assault, and stalking behaviors. Other agencies such as the Bureau of Justice Statistics (2006) include additional crimes within the discussion of IPA, such as homicides and robberies involving intimate partners (Catalano, 2012).

According to the National Crime Victimization Survey, an estimated 1.3 million women are physically victimized each year by a current or former intimate partner. In the majority of cases, men are the aggressor and women are

Table 4.1 The Violence Against Women Act

1994	**Violent Crime Control and Law Enforcement Act of 1994** **Title IV—Violence Against Women** • Allocated $1.6 billion in grant funds (1994–2000) for investigation and prosecution of violent crimes against women, community services for victims, and the creation of domestic violence helplines • Created new laws that target violators of civil restraining orders and that make interstate domestic violence a federal crime • Allows offenders to use civil justice in cases that prosecutors decline to prosecute • Established the Office on Violence Against Women within the Department of Justice
2000	**Victims of Trafficking and Violence Protection Act of 2000** **Division B—Violence Against Women Act** • Allocated $3.33 billion in grant funds (2001–2005) • Enhanced federal laws for domestic violence and stalking • Added protections for immigrant victims • Added new programs for elderly and disabled victims • Included victims of dating violence into VAWA protections and services
2005	**Violence Against Women Act and Department of Justice Reauthorization Act of 2005** • Allocated $3.935 billion in grant funds (2007–2011) • Created repeat offender penalties • Added protections for trafficked victims • Provides housing resources for victims • Enhanced resources for American Indian and Alaska Native populations • Provides increased training for health care providers to recognize signs of domestic violence • Enhanced protections for illegal immigrant victims
2013	**Violence Against Women Act Reauthorization of 2013** • Allocated 3.378 billion in grant funds (2013–2018) • Continues funding for grants for research and services • Maintains and expands housing protections • Expands options for tribal courts to address domestic violence • Requires reporting procedures for dating violence on college campuses • Prohibits discrimination for LGBT victims in accessing services • Maintains and increases protections for immigrant victims

SOURCES: Seghetti, L. M & Bjelopera, J. P. (2012). The Violence Against Women Act: Overview, legislation and federal funding. Congressional Research Service. Retrieved from http://www.fas.org/sgp/crs/misc/R42499.pdf. National Coalition Against Domestic Violence (2006); Comparison of VAWA 1994, VAWA 2000 and VAWA 2005 Reauthorization Bill. Retrieved from http://www.ncadv.org/files/VAWA_94_00_05.pdf; Office on Violence Against Women. (n.d.). VAWA 2013 summary: Changes to OVW-administered grant programs. Retrieved from http://www.ncdsv.org/images/OVW_VAWA+2013+summary+changes+to+OVW-administered+Grant+Programs.pdf

the victim (85%)[1] (CDC, 2003). Alas, most crimes of intimate partner abuse are considered a misdemeanor offense, even for repeat offenders. In these cases, prosecutors charge offenders with the crime of simple assault (77.9% of cases), which carries with it a penalty of no more than one year in jail (Klein, 2004; Smith & Farole, 2009).

---

[1]Given that the majority of data find men as the perpetrator and women as the victim, this text generally uses the term *he* to refer to the abuser and the term *she* as the victim. The use of these terms is not meant to ignore male victims of violence or abuse within same-sex relationships but only to characterize the majority of cases of intimate partner abuse.

©Thinkstock/BananaStock

▲ **Photo 4.1** Intimate partner violence is composed of a variety of different behaviors used by an offender to have power and control over their victim. These include physical, sexual, emotional, and psychological abuse. Abuse also impacts the children who observe acts of violence.

Much of the abuse within an intimate relationship occurs behind closed doors and is not visible to the community. This makes it difficult for researchers to measure the extent of these acts or for community agencies to provide outreach and services for victims. Many are reluctant to report cases of abuse to anyone (police, friends, or family members) due to the high levels of shame that they feel as a result of the abuse. Others believe that the police will be unable to help. This belief is not unfounded. Research indicates that in some cases, the police scolded victims for not following through on previous court cases. Other victims were either blamed for causing the violence or were told to fix the relationship with the offender (Fleury-Steiner, Bybee, Sullivan, Belknap, & Melton, 2006).

Most people think of physical battering/abuse as the major component of intimate partner abuse. However, abuse between intimates runs much deeper than physical violence. Perhaps one of the most common (and some would argue the most damaging in terms of long-term abuse and healing) is emotional battering/abuse. Those who batter their partner emotionally may call them derogatory names, prevent them from working or attending school, or limit access to family members and friends. An abuser may control the finances and limit access and information regarding money, which in turn makes the victim dependent on the perpetrator. Emotional abuse is a way in which perpetrators seek to control their victims, whether it be in telling them what to wear, where to go, or what to do. They may act jealous or possessive of their partner. In many cases, emotional abuse turns violent toward the victim, child(ren), or pet(s). Following acts of physical or sexual violence, the emotional abuse continues when a batterer blames the victim for the violent behavior by suggesting that "she made him do it" or by telling the victim that "you deserve it." Research indicates that emotional abuse is more common with younger males and females and women are more likely to experience social isolation and property damage within the context of emotional abuse compared to men (Karakurt & Silver, 2013).

Emotional abuse is particularly damaging because it robs the victim of her self-esteem and self-confidence. In many cases, victims fail to identify that they are victims of intimate partner abuse if they do not experience physical violence. Yet the scars left by emotional abuse are significant and long lasting. Unfortunately, few laws characterize the acts of emotional abuse as a criminal offense.

For a small number of women, physical violence in an intimate relationship escalates to murder. For these women, death was the culmination of a relationship that had been violent over time, and in many cases, the violence occurred on a frequent basis. The presence of a weapon significantly increases the risk of homicide, as women who are threatened or assaulted with a gun or other weapon are 20 times more likely to be killed (Campbell et al., 2003). Three fourths of intimate partner homicide victims had tried to leave their abusers, refuting the common question of "why doesn't she leave?" While many of these women had previously sought help and protection from their batterers' abuse, their efforts failed (Block, 2003).

CASE STUDY

Spotlight on Nigella Lawson

By all perceptions, Nigella Lawson lived a charmed life. Her father, Nigel, was the former Chancellor of the Exchequer (a high-ranking British political official), and her mother came from British food royalty. Nigella began her career as a food and restaurant critic and has authored several cookbooks. Her syndicated cooking shows, such as *Nigella Bites* and *Nigella Kitchen,* have made her popular with cooking enthusiasts.

However, it was her relationship with then-husband Charles Saatchi that attracted the attention of legal analysts and paparazzi alike. On June 9, 2013, Nigella and her husband were dining in a London restaurant when Saatchi placed his hands around Lawson's throat. Captured by photographers, the incident made headline news. While Saatchi suggested that the gesture was a "playful tiff" between the couple, others identified her as a victim of intimate partner abuse (Freeman, 2013). Following an investigation by the police, Saatchi was cautioned for assault (Topping & Quinn, 2013). Under U.K law, a caution is a formal warning that stays on police records and could be used against the offender should there be a similar event in the future (Jefferies, 2013). Following the incident, Lawson and her children moved out of the family home. After ten years of marriage, the couple began divorce proceedings in July 2013. In an interesting twist, news media outlets noted that while Lawson filed the court documents, it was Saatchi that claimed that the divorce was initiated after Lawson did not defend him

▲ Photo 4.2 Nigella Lawson leaves court after a divorce hearing. Lawson was highlighted as a victim of intimate partner violence after photos surfaced of her husband Charles Saatchi grabbing Lawson by the throat as they dined at a restaurant in London.

after the restaurant choking incident (Smith-Spark & Nyberg, 2013). While Saatchi threatened to sue Lawson for half a million pounds (approximately $825,000) for defamation, he later dropped the claim (Turvill, 2013).

The Cycle of Violence

The greatest tool of perpetrators of intimate partner abuse is their ability to have power and control over their victim. To explain how violence and abuse occurs in an intimate relationship, Lenore Walker (1979) conceptualized the **cycle of violence.** The cycle of violence is made up of three distinct time frames (see Figure 4.1). The first is referred to as tension building, where a batterer increases control over a victim. As anger begins to build for the perpetrator, the victim tries to keep her partner calm. She also minimizes any problems in the relationship. During this time, the victim may feel as though she is walking on eggshells because the tension between her and her partner is high. It is during the second time frame, referred to as the abusive incident, where the major incident of battering occurs. During this period, the batterer is highly abusive, and engages in an act of violence toward the victim. Following the abusive incident, the perpetrator moves to stage three, which is often described as the honeymoon period. During this stage, the offender is apologetic to the victim for causing harm. He often is loving and attentive and promises to change his behavior. In this stage, the perpetrator is viewed as sincere and in many cases is forgiven by the victim. Unfortunately, the honeymoon phase does not last forever, and in many cases of intimate partner abuse, the cycle begins again, tensions increase and additional acts of violence occur. Over time, the honeymoon stage may disappear entirely.

Victims of Intimate Partner Abuse

Intimate partner abuse can impact victims of any sex, age, race, ethnicity, religion, nationality, and sexual orientation. Offenders who perpetuate these acts of violence are spouses, intimates (boyfriend/girlfriend, cohabitating partners), and ex-intimates. This section highlights some of the different relationship types and populations where IPA occurs. The section also includes a discussion on the challenges that victims face within intimate partner abuse.

Dating Violence

While initial laws on intimate partner abuse recognized only physical violence between married couples, recent laws have been changed to reflect the variety of relationship types where intimate partner abuse can occur. One such

Figure 4.1   The Cycle of Violence

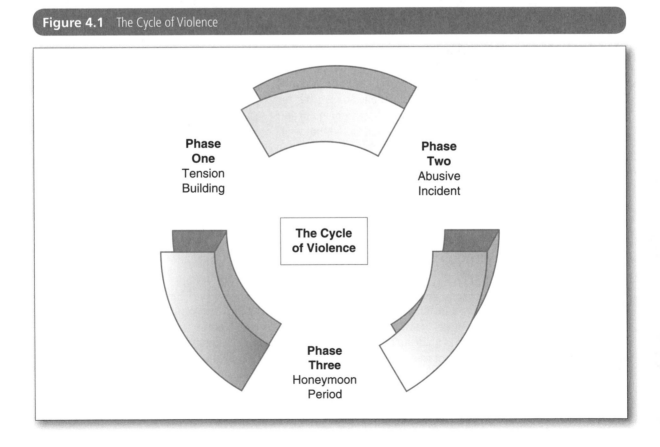

example is **dating violence**. Even though two people are unmarried and may or may not be living together, such relationships are not immune from violence. Prevalence rates of dating violence on college campuses indicate that 32% of students report a history of dating violence in a previous relationship, and 21% of students indicate that they currently experience violence in their dating relationship (Sellers & Bromley, 1996). Teens, in particular, are at high risk for dating violence as a result of their inexperience in relationships and their heightened views of "romantic love," combined with a desire to be independent from their parents (Alabama Coalition Against Domestic Violence [ACADV], n.d.). Given the severity of this issue, it is concerning that few parents believe that dating violence is a significant issue for their children (Women's Health, 2004). Research estimates that one third of youth experience dating violence during adolescence. The early onset of violence and abuse in a relationship continues for victims into adulthood, as adolescent victims often find themselves in a pattern of abusive relationships as adults (Silverman, Raj, Mucci, & Hathaway, 2001).

Children of Intimate Partner Abuse

Children are significantly affected by violence within the home environment, even if they are not the direct victims of the abuse. Research indicates that 68% to 87% of incidents involving intimate partner abuse occur while children are present (Raphael, 2000). One battered woman spoke of the effects this victimization has on children: "Our kids have problems dealing with us. When we argue and fight in front of them, when they see our husbands humiliating, beating, and cursing us, they will get affected. They will learn everything they see" (Sullivan, Senturia, Negash, Shiu-Thornton, & Giday, 2005, p. 928).

Children who reside in a home where violence is present tend to suffer from a variety of negative mental health outcomes, such as feelings of low self-worth, depression, and anxiety. Affected children often suffer in academic settings and have higher rates of aggressive behavior (Goddard & Bedi, 2010). Additionally, many children exposed to violence at a young age continue the cycle of violence into adulthood, as they often find themselves in violent relationships of their own. Research indicates that 30% of young boys who are exposed to acts of intimate partner abuse will engage in violence against an intimate partner later in life. In an effort to respond to families in need, many agencies that advocate for victims of intimate partner violence are connecting with child welfare agencies to provide a continuum of care for children and their families. However, it is important for agencies to make sure that they do not overemphasize this risk factor and label these children as potential offenders and victims, as it could lead to a self-fulfilling prophecy (Boyd, 2001).

Same-Sex Intimate Partner Abuse

While the majority of intimate partner abuse involves a female victim and a male offender, data indicate that battering also occurs in same-sex relationships. The National Crime Victimization survey found that 3% of females who experienced IPA were victimized by another woman, while 16% of male victims were abused by their male counterpart (Catalano, 2007). However, these statistics may not necessarily reflect the reality of this issue. Is same-sex IPA a rare phenomenon (as these data may suggest), or is this issue more common yet hidden within this community? Like heterosexual victims of intimate partner abuse, many same-sex victims are reluctant to report their abuse. The decision to report same-sex IPA involves the same challenges as a heterosexual battering relationship. But these challenges are enhanced for LGBT victims as it exposes their sexual orientation to police, community organizations, peers, and family members (Irwin, 2008).

Research indicates that female victims of **same-sex intimate partner abuse** face many of the same risk factors for violence as heterosexual battering relationships. Figure 4.2 presents the power and control wheel for the LGBT community. While heterosexual IPA relationships face many of these same factors such as economic abuse, emotional abuse, and coercion, this figure adds factors such as heterosexism, external homophobia, and internalized homophobia

Figure 4.2   Lesbian/Gay Power and Control Wheel

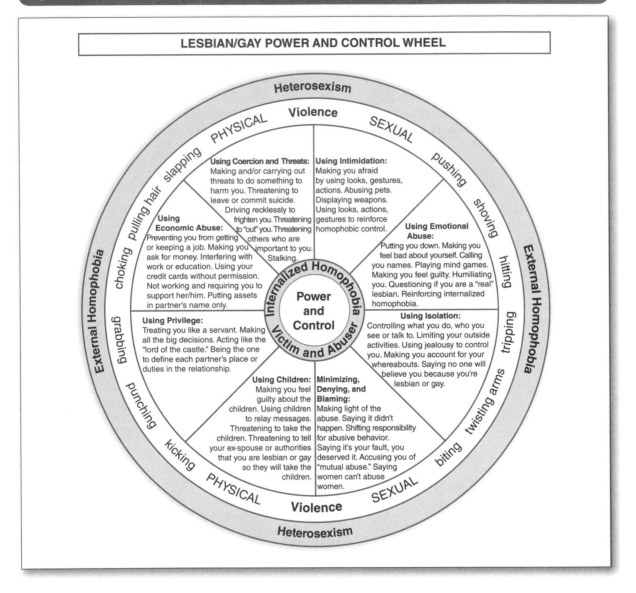

as (further) influences on LGBT IPA relationships. For some victims, these additional factors can complicate their efforts to find support within the LGBT community. As one victim notes, "I think that people are very afraid to add to (the stigma of being queer) by saying . . . not only are we queer, but we also have violence in our relationships and in our community" (Bornstein, Fawcett, Sullivan, Senturia, & Shiu-Thornton, 2006, p. 169). In addition, the connection that an IPA victim has to the LGBT community (or lack thereof) can also play a role in disclosure practices. For example, women who experienced abuse within the context of their first lesbian relationship tended to express fear about discrimination. Since many of these victims lacked a connection to the LGBT community, some wondered whether the abuse was a normal component of a lesbian relationship. This fear of being "outed" also led some victims to stay in the relationship for a longer period of time (Irwin, 2008). In comparison, women who had strong networks or attachments with the LGBT community were more likely to seek out help when their relationships turned violent (Hardesty, Oswald, Khaw, & Fonseca, 2011).

Gender-role stereotyping has a significant effect on the perceptions of female same-sex intimate partner violence (FSSIPV). Research by Hassouneh and Glass (2008) identified four themes where gender-role stereotypes affect women's experience of violence within a same-sex battering relationship. Each of these themes has a significant impact on the denial of harm and victimization. The first theme, "girls don't hit other girls," illustrated that many of the women involved in same-sex battering relationships saw their abuse as an indicator of relationship problems where they were to blame, rather than a relationship where abuse occurred. The second theme, "the myth of lesbian utopia," suggested that the absence of patriarchy meant that there is no oppression or violence within a lesbian relationship. The third theme, labeled "cat fight," discussed how many women thought that violence within their relationship was less significant than the levels of violence that occur in a male-female domestic violence situation. The fourth theme, of "playing the feminine victim," made it difficult for outsiders to identify cases of intimate partner abuse, particularly when agents of law enforcement were involved. Playing the victim allowed offenders to avoid arrest, as law enforcement would rely on traditional gender-role stereotypes to identify who was the victim and who was the perpetrator.

Given that victims of FSSIPV are in the minority, few programs and services exist to meet the unique needs of this population. In addition, resources that are often available to heterosexual victims of IPA are expressly denied for the LGBT population. Three states have explicitly denied LGBT victims from seeking out a protective order in cases involving IPA (Montana, Louisiana, and South Carolina). Only one state (Hawaii) specifically includes language that allows LGBT individuals to seek out a **restraining order** against a current or former intimate. The remaining laws at the state level are silent on the issue as they neither permit nor exclude victims from seeking a restraining order. In these cases, the interpretation of the law is left up to the judiciary (American Bar Association Commission on Domestic Violence, 2008). Even service providers may view same-sex IPA incidents as less serious than cases of heterosexual IPA. This assumption can impact the level and type of services provided by an agency (Brown & Groscup, 2009). Effective programming needs to address the use of gender-role stereotypes when developing education and intervention efforts for the community. Agencies also need to develop "queer-specific" services to meet the needs for the LGBT community (Bornstein et al., 2006).

Effects of Race and Ethnicity on Intimate Partner Abuse

Issues of race and ethnicity add an additional lens through which one can view issues of intimate partner violence. While much of the early research on intimate partner violence focused exclusively on the relationships of gender inequality as a cause of abuse, the inclusion of race and ethnicity (and socioeconomic status) adds additional issues for consideration. For women of color, issues of gender inequality become secondary in the discussion of what it means to be a battered woman. Here, scholars acknowledge the role of cultural differences and structural inequality in understanding the experiences of IPV in ethnically diverse communities (Sokoloff, 2004). When investigating issues of violence among women of color, it is important that scholars not limit their discussions to race and ethnicity. Rather, research needs to reflect on the collision of a number of different factors, as "age, employment status, residence, poverty, social embeddedness, and isolation combine to explain higher rates of abuse within black communities—not race or culture per se" (Sokoloff, 2004, p. 141).

As a population, Black women are at an increased risk to be victimized in cases of intimate partner violence. Scholars are quick to point out that it is not race that affects whether one is more likely to be abused by a partner. Rather, economic and social marginalization can place women of color at an increased risk for victimization (West, 2004). Research by Potter (2007b) highlights how interracial abuse among Black women and men is related to feelings of being "devalued" by social stereotypes about "the Black man." Since men of color experience high levels of discrimination by society, many victims justify the violent acts that are perpetuated by their intimate partner. This can also impact the decision to seek assistance from the criminal justice system as some women of color may not want to further criminalize the men in their communities, as they are already disproportionately represented within the correctional system (Nash, 2006).

Women who experience IPV may be faced with a multitude of physical and psychological issues, and race and ethnicity can affect whether a victim will seek out support and resources from social service agencies, such as thera-peutic and shelter resources. Here, research indicates that Black women were significantly more likely to use emer-gency hospital services, police assistance, and housing assistance, compared to White and Hispanic/Latina women. For example, 65.4% of Black IPV females indicated that they had used housing assistance during the past year, compared to only 26.9% of White IPA women and 7.7% of Hispanic/Latina IPA women (Lipsky, Caetano, Field, & Larkin, 2006). Women of color also express a need for culturally relevant support in their communities. For example, traditional therapeutic communities may be ineffective for some victims of violence: "Black folks don't 'do' group. We 'do' church. . . . I will not sit there and [tell] all these White women my business. [Blacks] don't talk about our stuff [in public]—and especially to White folks" (Nash, 2006, p. 1437).

Unique Issues for Immigrant Victims of Intimate Partner Abuse

While intimate partner abuse is an issue for any community, the effects are particularly significant for immigrant communities. Research indicates that men in these communities often batter their partner as a way to regain con-trol and power in their lives, particularly when their immigrant status has deprived them of this social standing. Battering becomes a way in which these men regain their sense of masculinity. For many, the education and training they may have received in their home countries does not easily transfer upon their arrival to the United States. As Bui and Morash (2008) note, "Vietnamese immigrant men have lost power after immigrating to the U.S. Many felt bad because they lack[ed] language and occupational skills and could not support their families" (p. 202).

Faced with their husband's inability to find a job to support the family, many immigrant women are faced with the need to work, which many immigrant men find to be in opposition to traditional cultural roles and a threat to their status within the family. This strain against traditional roles leads to violence. Many men blame the American culture for the gender clash occurring in their relationships. However, many women accept the violence as part of the relationship, as such behavior is considered normative for their culture. For example, violence is accepted behavior in Vietnamese traditional cultures, wherein men are seen as aggressive warriors and women are seen as passive and meek. Research on intimate partner violence within this community reveals high levels of verbal (75%), physical (63%), and sexual abuse (46%), with 37% experiencing both physical and sexual abuse (Bui & Morash, 2008).

For Ethiopian-immigrant women, the violent behavior of men is also accepted within the community, making it difficult for women to develop an understanding that battering is a crime and that they should seek out services. Help seeking is seen as a complaint by women, and in such cases, members of the community turn to support the perpetrator, not the victim (Sullivan et al., 2005). Intimate partner abuse is also discussed as a normal part of rela-tionships for Russian-immigrant women. One woman stated that domestic violence "is part of the destiny, and you have to tolerate it" (Crandall, Senturia, Sullivan, & Shiu-Thornton, 2005, p. 945). These cultural expectations may inhibit women from seeking out assistance, as it would bring shame upon the victim and her family, both immediate and extended. Strict gender-role expectations may lead women to believe that they do not have the right to disobey their partner, which legitimizes the abuse.

Many perpetrators use the fear of deportation to prevent victims from leaving an abusive relationship. Many Latina immigrant women are likely to remain in a battering relationship for a longer period of time due to fear sur-rounding their undocumented immigration status. In these cases, Latina immigrants are less likely to seek out help for intimate partner abuse compared to Latina nonimmigrants (Ingram, 2007). While the 2005 reauthorization of the

Violence Against Women Act increased the protection of immigrant women who are victims of a crime (including domestic violence), it is unclear how many immigrant women are aware of these protections.

Perpetrators often build upon a negative experience of law enforcement from their home country in an effort to create a sense of distrust of the U.S. legal system. For many Vietnamese women, a call to the police for help was a last resort and often done not to facilitate an arrest but rather to improve the relationship between the perpetrator and the victim by stopping the violence. Most victims did not want to have their partner arrested or prosecuted for domestic violence, but rather, they wanted to send a message that the abuse was wrong. Unfortunately, many were reluctant to seek police intervention as they fear the civil implications that a criminal record would bring, particularly in jurisdictions with mandatory arrest policies (Bui, 2007).

Language barriers may also affect victims' ability to seek help, as they may not be able to communicate with law enforcement and court personnel, particularly when resources for translators may be significantly limited (National Coalition Against Domestic Violence, n.d.). Lack of language skills, combined with a lack of understanding of the American legal system, also can prevent an immigrant/refugee woman from leaving her violent relationship. Not only may a victim not know what services are available, she may not understand how to navigate social systems, such as welfare and housing, and educational opportunities that are necessary in order to achieve economic independence from her batterer (Sullivan et al., 2005). In an effort to expand access to the courts in domestic violence cases, California amended its domestic violence laws in 2001 to ensure that legal documents in domestic violence cases would be made available in multiple languages. Today, paperwork to request a restraining order and other related documents is available in five different languages: English, Chinese, Spanish, Vietnamese, and Korean.[2]

CASE STUDY

Spotlight on Intimate Partner Abuse in India

Intimate partner abuse is a worldwide problem. Alas, issues such as patriarchy, power, and control know no geographical boundaries. In many countries, it is these values about women that exacerbate the abuse of women. Consider the case of India. Like many regions of the world, the marital relationship is considered private, and there are few laws against the abuse of women. Indeed, it is the cultural values that reign supreme and essentially promote the power differential between men and women. It is some of these cultural indicators, such as the dowry and arranged marriages, that can encourage violence. For many families, the arranged marriage is an opportunity for the bride's family to increase their social status within the community as they "marry up" their daughters.

The inability to provide an adequate dowry then serves as a trigger for the abuse. For these women, the abuse begins almost as soon as the marriage begins (44% indicate that it began within a month of the marriage), and it is a regular occurrence. 79% of the women reported abuse within their marriage on a daily basis and another 15.6% once every two days. In many cases, the violence comes not only from her husband but also her in-laws. Women are not only physically beaten (100%) but were also threatened by knives and other weapons (47.8%). Psychological violence was also a common tactic as they were prohibited from contacting their families, friends, and even their own children (82.2%; Panchanadeswaran & Koverola, 2005).

(Continued)

---

[2]Each state has different policies on the availability of legal documents in languages other than English. Forms for the State of California are located at http:www.courtinfo.ca.gov.

(Continued)

Given the cultural context for these abusive relationships, women seek help from a variety of sources. For those women that do leave these abusive relationships, community legal aid and counseling shelters were the most helpful in exiting an abusive situation. The police were essentially useless in dealing with these incidents. Meanwhile, families were only moderately helpful as they were caught up within maintaining their image in the community:

> My parents and sister were very supportive and provided shelter from [*sic*] my daughter and me whenever we went. But after 3–4 days, my parents would always ask me to go back and try to reconcile with my husband. They were worried that if I stayed longer, he would not take me back ...and the family honor will be affected and I would be a stigma to the family and no one would marry my younger sister. (Panchanadeswaran & Koverola, 2005, p. 750)

Barriers to Leaving an Abusive Relationship

When hearing of cases of domestic violence, many members of the public ask, "Why doesn't she just leave?" Leaving a relationship where intimate partner abuse is present is a difficult and complex process. There are many issues that a victim must face. One of the greatest barriers in leaving a battering relationship is the financial limitations that victims face. Women who lack economic self-sufficiency are less likely to report intimate partner abuse and less likely to leave the relationship. The support from extended family and friends can play a critical role in a victim's ability to successfully depart from an abusive partner. However, these same individuals can increase the potential for victim blaming and a withdrawal of support and empathy if the victim returns to the relationship (Moe, 2007).

Inherent in the question of "why doesn't she just leave?" is the question of "why does she stay?" This question places the responsibility on the victim for staying with a violent partner rather than focusing on why her partner chooses to be violent. The reality is that many women do leave their batterers. The average battered woman leaves seven to eight times before she is successful in leaving for good (ACADV, n.d.). Violence does not always end when women report their crimes or leave their abuser. For some women, the levels of violence increase; women who were separated from their batterers reported higher rates of violence, compared to women who were married or divorced from their batterer (Catalano, 2007). These acts of violence can involve not only the initial victim but also can spread out, placing children, friends, and extended family members of the woman at risk. Concerns regarding these potential increases in violence may influence these women to remain in the relationship out of concern for their loved ones.

For some women, their children become the deciding factor in leaving intimate partner abuse. Some mothers believe that it is their responsibility to keep the family together, despite the violence they endure. While many women are more likely to tolerate the abuse when it occurs only to them, they are less likely to continue the relationship once their children are negatively affected. In these cases, the decision to leave is based on either a child's request for safety from the violent parent or the mother's conclusion that her child's physical and emotional needs overruled any question of remaining in the relationship (Moe, 2009).

In their search for support, some women may turn toward religious institutions for assistance in leaving a relationship characterized by intimate partner abuse. For many women, their faith gives them strength to leave (Wang, Horne, Levitt, & Klesges, 2009). Unfortunately, for some of these women, their spirituality may hinder their abilities to leave. Cultural scripts of some religious doctrines may encourage women to try to resolve the struggles of their relationship, as divorce and separation are not viewed as acceptable under the eyes of the church. Here, congregations encourage women to forgive the violence that their partners display (Potter, 2007a). Additionally, clergy may be ill equipped to deal with the issue of intimate partner abuse within their congregations, due to a lack of understanding of the realities of the problem and limited training on service and support needs (Shannon-Lewy & Dull, 2005).

Many women struggle with their decision to leave an abusive relationship. Some women may still love their partner, despite the violence that exists within the relationship. Others may hope that their partner will change and believe the promises made by their loved one for a different life. In some multicultural communities, there is a greater pressure outside of the family unit to return to one's batterer. Members of these communities

▲ **Photo 4.3**   A domestic violence victim wears an alarm necklace that silently signals police in event of danger. Domestic violence agencies distribute the devices, called the A.W.A.R.E. alarm, which stands for Abused Women's Active Response Emergency.

often place significant pressures on victims to reunite with their batterer (Sullivan et al., 2005). For many women, they fear what their lives will be like without their partner. These fears may include how they will support themselves (and their children), the possibility that future relationships will have similar results, and even fear of loneliness. A key to successfully leaving an abusive relationship is the victim's belief that she will be better off without her batterer and have the confidence to make a new life free from violence.

Victim Experiences With Police and Corrections

As the criminal justice system becomes more involved in cases of intimate partner abuse, scholars have begun to ask questions about the victim experience with the criminal justice system. The findings of these studies vary. While some suggest that victims are satisfied by their experience with the police and courts in these cases, others highlight areas for significant improvement within the justice process.

The first step in asking for assistance often involves the police. The victim can either request the presence of the police, or the police may be summoned on behalf of a victim, usually by a neighbor or other family member. A call to the police often represents the first step by a victim to seek protection from intimate partner abuse. Research on this topic provides feedback on how victims feel about these interactions with the police. Women who felt that the officer listened to their concerns and provided information and referrals for help (such as shelters and other protective options) were the most satisfied with their experience with the police (Johnson, 2007). Gender of the responding officer also has an impact on victim satisfaction levels, as victims indicated that female officers were more receptive to their concerns overall and were not just focused on facilitating an arrest (Stalens & Finn, 2000). These positive experiences can encourage victims to seek out police assistance in the future should they need it (Johnson, 2007). In contrast, women who do not feel that the justice system effectively responded to their concerns may be less likely to seek out help in the future. If an offender is let off with a "slap on the hand," victims may experience increased risks of violence in the future (Moe, 2007). Here, the criminal justice system did not serve as an effective deterrent for these offenders. This is also true in cases where the intimate partner abuse is limited to verbal abuse. Some women did not feel that the police took the issue of verbal violence seriously. At the same time, victims often minimized the severity of the verbal violence in order to avoid the police from making an arrest (Stewart, Langan & Hannem, 2013).

Drawing from criticisms regarding the **discretionary arrest** policies of many police departments, mandatory arrest or pro-arrest policies began to surface in police departments across the nation during the 1980s and 1990s. **Mandatory arrest** policies refer to the legal duty of a police officer to make an arrest if the officer has reason to believe that domestic violence has occurred. The laws vary from state to state, but most state laws recognize both current and previous spouses or cohabitants as protected categories under the law, though not all states cover dating or prior dating relationships. Currently, 22 states have some form of mandatory arrest policy in place. In addition, the laws vary when a mandatory arrest can be made. For example, laws in Alaska and Missouri require that a report be made within 12 hours of the assault, whereas Mississippi and Nevada extend the time frame to 24 hours. Washington State and South Dakota represent some of the most narrowly defined time frames and require that the police make an arrest within 4 hours of the assault. Washington State law is also unique in that it limits cases to individuals who are 16 or older (Hirschel, 2008).

The movement toward mandatory arrest clarified roles of officers when dealing with domestic violence calls for service. It also removed the responsibility of arrest from the victim's decision and onto the shoulders of police personnel. For many women, they believed that a mandatory arrest policy would make officers understand that domestic violence is a serious issue and that it would legitimize their victimization. At the same time, the threat of arrest would serve as a deterrent for the offender. Here, women believed that an arrest would decrease levels of violence and send a message to the offender that battering is a crime and he would be punished. However, they acknowledged that the decrease in violence was only a temporary measure and that there existed a possibility of increased violence after an offender returned to the family home following an arrest or court proceedings (Barata & Schneider, 2004; Moe, 2007). Victims can feel disempowered by the mandatory arrest process, as it takes away their decision-making abilities. While mandatory arrest policies removed the victim's responsibility for instituting formal charges against an offender, there were some unintentional consequences. In many cases, a victim's call to the police for help resulted in her own arrest, leaving many victims feeling betrayed by the system that they sought help from (Burgess-Proctor, 2012). Other victims may be less likely to call for intervention knowing that their batterer (or themselves) would be arrested (Gormley, 2007; Miller & Peterson, 2007).

Dual arrests are more likely to occur when state laws or policies do not include a primary aggressor designation. As a result, officers are required to make a determination about who the "real" offender is. Even with a primary aggressor designation, officers may lack the training or experience to make a professional judgment about who to arrest, resulting in both parties being arrested. These dual-arrest practices result in women being arrested for domestic violence with their partner. As a result, many women victims find themselves labeled as offenders of IPA by police and the courts for engaging in acts of self-defense (Miller, 2005). Dual-arrest policies also have negative consequences for the LGBT community. Research by Hirschel et al. (2007) found that in cases of intimate partner violence, same-sex couples were more likely to be involved in dual-arrest situations (female-to-female = 26.1% and male-to-male = 27.3%) compared to heterosexual couples (3.8%).

The increase in arrests has long-reaching implications for women, including the refusal of help by shelter services and challenges in child custody battles as a result of their "criminal" history (Miller & Meloy, 2006). In addition, gender differences in battering also impact programming options for women who engage in acts of IPA. Here, scholars have noted that traditional batterer intervention programming (which is designed primarily for male offenders) may not be appropriate for women. Instead, therapeutic options should focus on the rationale and factors behind women who engage in IPA (Kernsmith, 2005).

In response to many mandatory arrest policies, many jurisdictions have instituted **no-drop policies**. Rather than force a victim to participate against her will, these jurisdictions developed evidence-based practices that would allow the prosecutor to present a case based on the evidence collected at the scene of the crime, regardless of any testimony by the victim (Gormley, 2007). Such policies were developed in response to a victim's lack of participation in the prosecution of her batterer. These policies may actually work against victims. When victims feel that their voice is not being heard by the criminal justice system, they may be less likely to report incidents of intimate partner abuse. While no-drop policies were designed to prevent victims from dismissing charges against their batterer, they instead led to disempowering victims.

When victims feel that the criminal justice system does not meet their needs in a case of intimate partner violence, they are less likely to seek assistance for subsequent victimizations. In many cases, victims felt that the event was not serious enough to report or expressed concerns that they would not be believed by the police. In addition, several victims were concerned about how contacting the police could lead to potential negative consequences for themselves or their families. Here, victims expressed concerns over the possibility of mandatory arrests or dual arrests (and the effects on children in the home), custody battles, and fear of how the offender would respond. Finally, even after multiple victimizations, some victims still express love and compassion for their abuser (Gover, Welton-Mitchell, Belknap, & Deprince, 2013).

CASE STUDY

Spotlight on Intimate Partner Abuse and Shelters

As the grassroots efforts of the battered women's movement began to increase the availability of resources and attention on intimate partner violence during the 1960s and 1970s, shelters began to emerge as a valuable resource for women exiting a violent relationship. Shelter care provides women with support, empowerment, and a safe space to consider options for their future (Bennett, Riger, Schewe, Howard, & Wasco, 2004).

While the types of services vary by agency, victims generally utilize four different resources in their quest to exit an IPA relationship: (1) legal assistance, (2) counseling services, (3) wraparound services, and (4) life-skills assistance. Most shelter residents rely on legal assistance to help file legal protective orders against their abuser. Almost all of the shelter residents receive individualized counseling (95.8%) and a majority of residents participate in group therapy sessions (71.9%). Wraparound services are also popular with survivors of IPA and involve collaborative case management with other community agencies, such as mental health and substance abuse treatment providers. Life-skills resources are the least utilized of all services; just 14.2% received help with finding a job, 11.2% received educational guidance, and 13.9% sought help with economic assistance. In addition to using these services while residing at the shelter, many continued to call on these organizations for assistance to help support their transition. While shelters represent a key resource for many women who leave an IPV relationship, the demand for these resources significantly outweighs their availability. Indeed, many victims can be denied shelter, either due to a lack of general availability or the lack of specific resources to support victims with children (Moe, 2007). This can affect their utilization of services and resources (Grossman & Lundy, 2011).

While the demand for shelter housing is high, the availability of bed space for women and their children . . . often fails to meet the need of this population. When women leave an abusive relationship without somewhere to go, their risk of homelessness increases (Baker, Holditch, Niolon, & Oliphant, 2009). However, many agencies are limited in what they can provide due to budgetary constraints. As a result, shelters need to develop creative strategies in order to deliver these services and resources to populations in need. These

(Continued)

(Continued)

resources are needed not only during a shelter residency but can continue throughout their transition. Here, the use of wraparound services and networking with other community agencies is crucial. While shelters may not be able to provide support for the ongoing, long-term needs of those exiting an abusive relationship, they can provide referrals to related community agencies (Grossman, Lundy, George, & Crabtree-Nelson, 2010). Options such as these allow communities to continue to serve the victims of IPA in light the struggles of a tense economic climate.

Shelters can also represent a valuable alternative to the criminal justice system. While many victims are dissatisfied with their experience with the police and the court process, they are more likely to find positive connections with shelter and related support services. While these organizations typically provided women with financial support and skills training, participants indicated that their greatest satisfaction derived from the support and encouragement that they received from the other women in the group. Given these positive outcomes, it seems that the criminal justice system could learn from the success of shelters (Burgess-Proctor, 2012).

Over time, many victims and advocates have expressed concern that the traditional criminal justice system may not be an effective tool to address the issues posed by intimate partner abuse. In response to these concerns, many jurisdictions have developed specialized courts that deal exclusively with cases of domestic violence. The professionals in these specialized courts (prosecutor, judges, etc.) often have specific training on issues such as the cycle of violence and the role of power and control within an intimate partner relationship. Research demonstrates that the use of specialized court practices can impact the level of satisfaction that victims experience as a result of their interactions with these environments. In their evaluation of a domestic violence court program in South Carolina, researchers Gover, Brank, and MacDonald (2007) found that a collaborative courtroom environment between the prosecutor, victim advocate, and judge had a significant effect on victim satisfaction levels. Unlike traditional criminal justice options that generally focus on punitive measures, this program emphasized the therapeutic options designed to treat the offender. As a result, the majority of victims and defendants believed that the outcome of their case was fair, positive, and respectful.

> Even after cases were decided, members of the court team would approach the victims and make sure that they understood the verdict and also understood what was required by both the victim and defendant. If the victim needed any assistance with shelter or legal assistance, the team members were there to help obtain it. (Gover et al., 2007, pp. 621–622)

Programming Concerns for Victims of Intimate Partner Abuse

Not only are programs needed to address the needs of victims, but it is also important to consider the value of battering prevention programs for men. Over the past three decades, batterer intervention programming has become one of the most popular options when sentencing offenders in cases of intimate partner abuse. Given the high correlation between substance use and intimate partner abuse, most programs also include substance abuse treatment as a part of their curriculum. The majority of these programs offer group therapy, which is popular not only for its cost effectiveness but also because scholars suggest that the group environment can serve as an opportunity for program participants to support and mentor one another. One criticism of battering intervention programs is that they generally assume that all batterers are alike. This approach does not offer the opportunity for programs to tailor their curriculum to address the differences among men who abuse (Rosenbaum, 2009). In addition, victims of domestic violence voice their dissatisfaction with many of these types of programs, arguing that they are ineffective in dealing with the issues that the men face in their lives (Gillum, 2008).

Intimate partner abuse attacks every community, age, religion, race, class, and sexual identity. Programs that provide services for victims of battering must acknowledge the need for programming that is culturally diverse and reflect the unique issues within different racial and ethnic communities. The need for culturally relevant programming also extends to shelter programs for victims of domestic violence. In one program, participants noted the absence of women of color (particularly Black women) within the shelter administration and staff, even though the majority of the clientele was Black. Feeling culturally connected to program practitioners (as women of color and IPV survivors themselves) helped survivors understand what they were going through. As one woman notes, "Black womens understand other Black womens. Ain't no way a White woman understands what a Black women going through. . . . Because . . . we're different, we are totally different" (Gillum, 2009, p. 67). In addition, programs to be based within the targeted community to ensure participation from the community residents—if programs are difficult to access geographically, women are less likely to seek out services as a result of time, money (loss of work hours and cost of child care), and transportation limitations. Programs also need to be proactive and engage in prevention efforts with young women and men in the community (Bent-Goodley, 2004).

Culturally diverse programs are not enough to combat issues of violence between intimate partners. Rather, intervention efforts need to attack the systems that create social inequalities—racism, sexism, classism, and so on. In addition, the legal system and program providers need to understand how these issues are interrelated and not dominated by a single demographic factor (Sokoloff, 2004). Regardless of their individual effects on a single person, many of these interventions have the potential to fail at the macro level, as long as the social culture of accepting male violence against women remains (Schwartz & DeKeseredy, 2008).

▧ Stalking and Intimate Partner Violence

According to the National Crime Victimization Survey, stalking is defined as "a course of conduct directed at a specific person that would cause a reasonable person to feel fear" (Baum, Catalano, Rand, & Rose, 2009, p. 1) Estimates by the Supplemental Victimization Survey (SVS) indicate that more than 5.9 million adults[3] experience behaviors defined as stalking[4] or harassment.[5] Table 4.2 illustrates the types and prevalence of stalking behaviors. In most cases, the acts that constitute stalking, such as sending letters or gifts, making phone calls, and showing up to visit, are not inherently criminal. These acts appear harmless to the ordinary citizen but can inspire significant fear and terror in victims of stalking.

Much of what the general public understands about stalking comes from Hollywood, where celebrities have long experienced acts of stalking. Consider the actions of John Hinckley Jr. who became infatuated with Jodi Foster when she first appeared as a child prostitute in the film *Taxi Driver*. Hinckley's obsession with Foster continued while she was a student at Yale, but he failed to gain her attention after numerous letters and phone calls. In 1981, Hinckley attempted to assassinate President Ronald Reagan in an effort to impress Foster. He was found not guilty by reason of insanity for his crimes and was committed to St. Elizabeth's Hospital for treatment. Another example of celebrity

---

[3]The Supplemental Victimization Survey (SVS) includes only data on respondents aged 18 and older who participated in the National Crime Victimization Survey (NCVS) during January–June 2006. The data assess victimization incidents that occurred during the 12 months prior to the interview.

[4]According to these data, 3.4 million people are victims of stalking each year.

[5]Harassment is defined by the SVS as acts that are indicative of stalking behaviors but do not incite feelings of fear in the victim.

Table 4.2 Prevalence of Stalking

Experienced at least one unwanted contact per week	46.0%
Victims were stalked for 5 years or more	11.0%
Experienced forms of cyberstalking	26.1%
Received unwanted phone calls or messages	66.2%
Received unwanted letters and e-mail	30.6%
Had rumors spread about them	35.7%
Were followed or spied on	34.3%
Experienced fear of bodily harm	30.4%
Believed that the behavior would never stop	29.1%

stalking is Madonna's stalker Robert Dewey Hoskins. He was convicted in 1996 for making threats against the star—he told the star that he wanted to "slice her throat from ear to ear" ("After Court Order," 1996, para. 6) and attempted to break into her house on two separate occasions. During one event, he successfully scaled the security wall of her home and was shot by one of her bodyguards. Other Hollywood victims of stalking include David Letterman, Sandra Bullock, Tyra Banks, and Lindsay Lohan, to name a few. Indeed, it seems that a number of Hollywood personalities have been stalked by an obsessed fan at some point during their careers. While noteworthy events of Hollywood stalkers brought significant attention to the crime of stalking, the attention was done in ways that reduced the social understanding of this crime to one that was limited to celebrities and the Hollywood circuit. Many of these cases involved perpetrators who suffered from mental disease or defect. This narrow definition had significant effects on the legitimization of this crime for ordinary victims of stalking.

Outside of the Hollywood context, a victim's relationship with her future stalker began in a very ordinary sense. Victims described these men as attentive, charming, and charismatic. But these endearing qualities soon disappeared, and their interactions became controlling, threatening, and violent. Many women blamed themselves for not recognizing the true colors of their stalker earlier. This pattern of self-blaming affected their ability to trust their own judgment and led these women to be hesitant about their decision-making abilities in future relationships as a result of their victimization.

Like many crimes, victims of stalking often do not report their victimization to police. According to SVS data, more than half of the individuals who were victims of stalking did not report their victimization. For many victims, their decision to not report these crimes stemmed from a fear of intensifying or escalating the stalking behaviors. Others dealt with their victimization in their own way, believing that their experience was a private and personal matter. Additionally, many believed that stalking was not a serious enough offense (or did not believe that a crime had occurred) to warrant intervention from the criminal justice system. Finally, some victims felt that nothing could be done to stop the behavior by their stalkers. For those individuals who did report their crimes, SVS data indicate that charges were filed in only 21% of these cases, further solidifying a belief for many victims that the criminal justice system was unable to effectively punish their stalkers in a court of law.

Victims engage in several different strategies in an effort to cope with their stalking victimization. Some victims attempted to solve the trauma through self-reflection and sought out therapeutic resources. Women also made significant changes to their behavior patterns. They might avoid community events out of a fear that their stalker would show up at the same function. Other women moved out of the area yet still expressed fear that their stalker would find them. Some victims tried to renegotiate the definitions of their relationship with their offender through bargaining, deception, or deterrence. Finally, some victims moved against their attackers by issuing warnings or pursuing a legal case against them (Cox & Speziale, 2009; Spitzberg & Cupach, 2003).

Victims and Offenders of Stalking

▲ **Photo 4.4** Many victims of stalking experience the constant fear of being followed and observed as they attempt to manage their daily lives. In this situation, the psychological terror that victims experience can be just as violent as any physical confrontation.

Who are the victims of stalking? They are men and women, young and old, of every race, ethnicity, and socioeconomic status. Data indicate that there are certain groups that make up the majority of victims of stalking. A meta-analysis of 22 studies on stalking found that female victims made up 74.59% of stalking victims, while 82.15% of the perpetrators were male. In the majority of cases, the perpetrator was someone known to the victim, with 30.3% of all cases occurring as a result of a current or former intimate relationship. Only 9.7% of stalking cases involved someone who was a stranger to the victim (Spitzberg & Cupach, 2003).

While stalking is a crime in its own right, it is also a common experience for victims of intimate partner abuse. The degree to which victims are stalked is directly related to the levels of physical, emotional, and sexual abuse that they experienced with their intimate partner—the greater the abuse in the relationship, the higher the levels of stalking can be. Several factors appear to influence whether a victim of domestic violence will be stalked. Women who are no longer in a relationship with their abuser are more likely to experience stalking compared to women currently involved in an IPA relationship. Additionally, domestic violence abusers who are more controlling and physically violent toward their victims are more likely to stalk them. Finally, abusers who use drugs and alcohol are more likely to stalk their partners. For those women who had moved on to new relationships, almost three fourths of them indicated that their new partner was harassed, threatened, or injured by their stalker (Melton, 2007).

Economics also impact the stalking experience for victims. Many victims find that they do not have the economic resources or abilities to move out of their communities to escape their stalker. Many of these women received governmental subsidies for housing—moving would mean to give up this assistance. This lack of mobility made it easier for their perpetrators to continue to stalk and harass their victims. In addition, the close-knit nature of many of these communities led to cases where a batterer's friends and family members were able to help the offender harass and intimidate their victim. Unfortunately, these cases of third-party stalking are not always recognized by the criminal justice system, or are not connected to the behaviors of the individual. As a result, many victims believe that an escape from the violence is impossible (Tamborra, 2012).

The experience of stalking has a significant effect on a woman's mental health. Women who experience significant levels of stalking over time are more likely to be at risk for depression and post-traumatic stress disorder. These rates of depression and post-traumatic stress disorder are significantly higher for women who blame themselves for the behaviors of their perpetrator (Kraaij, Arensman, Garnefski, & Kremers, 2007). Victims indicate feelings of powerlessness, depression, sleep disturbances, and high levels of anxiety (Pathe & Mullen, 1997). They are also likely to develop a chronic disease or other injury in response to the high levels of stress that victims of stalking experience (Davis, Coker, & Sanderson, 2002). It is clear that mental health services need to acknowledge how the experience of stalking affects the mental health status of victims and determine how to better provide services to this community.

Cyberstalking

The use of technology has changed the way in which many victims experience stalking. The use of devices such as e-mail, cell phones, and global-positioning systems (GPS) by offenders to track and monitor the lives of victims has had a significant effect on the experience of stalking. The term cyberstalking was created to address the use of technology as a tool in stalking. Of the 3.2 million identified victims of stalking identified by the SVS, one out of four individuals reported experiencing acts that are consistent with the definition of cyberstalking. Table 4.3 highlights examples of stalking aided by technology.

Like traditional methods of stalking, cyberstalking involves incidents that create fear in the lives of its victims. Just because cyberstalking does not involve physical contact does not mean that it is less damaging or harmful than physical stalking. Indeed, some might argue that the anonymity under which cyberstalkers can operate creates significant opportunities for offenders to control, dominate, and manipulate their victims, even from a distance, as there are no geographical limits for stalking within the domain of cyberspace. Indeed, someone can be stalked from just about anywhere in the world. For many victims of "traditional" stalking, cyberstalking presents a new avenue through which victims can be harassed, threatened, and intimidated.

While cyberstalking is a relatively new phenomenon, research indicates that the prevalence of these behaviors is expanding at an astronomical rate. Youth and young adults appear to be particularly at risk for these forms of victimization, given their connections to the electronic world through the use of the Internet, blogs, text messaging, and social networking sites, such as Facebook. Research by Lee (1998) indicated that behaviors that can be identified as cyberstalking are rationalized among college-age students as a form of modern-day courtship and were not considered by the majority of the students to be of any particular significance, particularly in cases where the offender is known to the victim. Research by Alexy, Burgess, Baker, and Smoyak (2005) also utilized a sample of college students

Table 4.3   Behaviors of Cyberstalking and Technology-Aided Stalking

- Monitoring e-mail communications
- Sending harassing, disruptive, or threatening e-mails or cell phone text messages
- Using computer viruses to disrupt e-mail and Internet communications
- Fraudulent use of victim's identity online
- Use of Internet services to gather and disseminate personal information with the intent of harassing the victim
- Use of global positioning devices to track movements of victim
- Use of caller identification services to locate whereabouts of victim
- Use of listening devices to intercept telephone conversations
- Use of spyware and keystroke logging hardware to monitor computer usage
- Use of hidden cameras to observe movement and activities of the victim
- Search of online databases and information brokers to obtain personal information about the victim

and found that only 29.9% of students labeled a simulated encounter as cyberstalking, even though 69% indicated that they felt threatened by the behavior. In addition, participation in activities such as sexting can increase the likelihood that one will be victimized online. Research indicates that 38% of study participants had either sent or received sexually explicit texts or photos. Participation in these activities increases the likelihood of cybervictimization (Reyns, Burek, Henson, & Fisher, 2013). Given the limited understanding of these crimes by victims (and the larger society), it is important that advocates and justice professionals have an understanding about the realities of these crimes in order to provide adequate support for victims.

Laws on Stalking

For the majority of the 21st century, stalking was not considered to be a crime. The first law criminalizing the act of stalking was created in 1990 by the state of California following the murder of actress Rebecca Schaeffer in 1989 by an obsessed fan. Schaeffer had risen to fame as an actress in the popular television show *My Sister Sam*. Robert Bardo had become obsessed with "Patti," the character played by Schaeffer on the show, and made several attempts to contact her on the set. He sent Schaeffer several letters and had built a shrine to her in his bedroom. Undeterred, he traveled cross-country, and he paid a private investigator $250 to obtain her home address. Upon making contact with Schaeffer at her residence, he shot her in the chest, killing her. Bardo was convicted of murder and sentenced to life in prison. Since the death of Rebecca Schaeffer and the creation of the first antistalking law in California, all 50 states, the District of Columbia, and the federal government have created criminal laws against stalking. In addition, the majority of state laws on stalking include details on stalking via electronic methods.

In order to prosecute someone for stalking, many state laws require victims to indicate that they experienced *fear* as a result of the offender's actions. Research indicates that women are more likely to experience fear as a result of being stalked compared to men (Davis et al., 2002). Using data from the National Violence Against Women Survey, Dietz and Martin (2007) found that nearly three fourths of women who were identified as victims of stalking behaviors indicated that they experienced fear as a result of the pursuit by their stalker. The levels of fear depended on the identity of the stalker (women indicated higher levels of fear when they were stalked by a current or former intimate or acquaintance) and how they stalked their victims (physical and communication stalking experiences generated higher levels of fear). Fear levels are also predicted by the severity and frequency of the contact (Reyns & Englebrecht, 2012). But what about women who experienced behaviors consistent with the definition of stalking but who did not feel fearful as a result of these interactions? Are these women not victims of stalking? In many states, they would not be considered victims, and the behaviors perpetrated against them would not be considered a crime.

The challenge with stalking is that many do not perceive stalking to be a significant event. Much of the research in this area is based on hypothetical scenarios, investigating what victims might do in these sorts of situations. From this research, we learn that the perceptions about stalking vary based on the gender of the victim and the offender and the type of relationship as well as the gender of the study participant. In addition, men are more likely to view stalking as a minor event and to engage in victim blaming toward stalking victims (Lambert, Smith, & Geistman, 2013). Victim blaming can be predicated by the type of relationship between the victim and the offender. Victims are the least blameworthy if the offender is a stranger but are considered culpable if the stalking results from a casual sexual relationship, such as a one-night stand. This can in turn impact perceptions of victim reporting—"When the victim reports this to the police, she will have to tell them everything, including how she had sex with him on the first night. This makes her look bad and she might be blamed from leading him on" (Cass & Mallicoat, 2014). If people do not perceive that victims will report these crimes to the police in hypothetical scenarios, we can assume that it is unlikely that they will reach out to the police should they face a similar victimization in their own lives.

Conclusion

Many victims of intimate partner violence and stalking did not report their victimization because they did not believe that what was happening to them was a criminal act, particularly in cases where there was no experience of physical violence. One victim noted that in assessing whether a relationship is healthy, women should look at themselves and any changes in their personal behaviors rather than obsessing on the actions of their stalker. "Think about how you were before this happened and how happy you were, and I think once ladies reminisce on that, I think that's where strength comes from" (Cox & Speziale, 2009, p. 12). Others advised that women should not stay silent on the issues of intimate partner abuse and stalking in order to protect their own safety, whether that meant filing a police report and obtaining a restraining order or letting friends, family, and coworkers know of their victimization. Here, victims acknowledge an increased need for community awareness about the nature of these victimizations and the resources available to them.

Summary

- Intimate partner abuse is difficult to identify, as much of the abuse occurs behind closed doors and victims are reluctant to report cases of abuse.
- The Violence Against Women Act of 1994 provided funding for battered women shelters, outreach education, and training on domestic violence for police and court personnel.
- Children who are exposed to violence in the home are at risk for negative mental health outcomes and may continue the cycle of violence as adults.
- Gender-role stereotypes and homophobic views have a significant effect on identifying victims of same-sex IPA and giving them the assistance they need.
- Immigrant victims of domestic violence face a variety of unique issues such as cultural norms regarding violence, gender-role expectations, and a fear of deportation that affect their experience with battering.
- Walker's cycle of violence (1979) helps explain how perpetrators maintain control within a battering relationship.
- Women are confronted with a variety of barriers in their attempts to leave a relationship where intimate partner abuse is present.
- For many women, mandatory arrest policies have resulted in only a temporary decrease in the violence in their lives, with the potential of increased violence in the future.
- Stalking is defined as a "course of conduct directed at a specific person that would cause a reasonable person to feel fear."
- Cyberstalking involves the use of technology to track and monitor the lives of victims of stalking.
- Many victims do not report their experiences of being stalked to law enforcement, as they fear that a report will escalate the behavior, or they do not believe that stalking is a serious matter or that anything can be done to stop the stalking behavior.
- Stalking is often related to incidents of intimate partner abuse.

KEY TERMS		
Battered women's movement	Harassment	No-drop policies
Cyberstalking	Intimate partner abuse	Restraining order
Cycle of violence	Mandatory arrest	Same-sex intimate partner abuse
Dating violence	Minneapolis Domestic Violence Experiment	Stalking
Discretionary arrest		Violence Against Women Act

DISCUSSION QUESTIONS

1. How have mandatory arrest and no-drop policies improved the lives of women involved in cases of intimate partner abuse? How have these policies negatively affected victims?

2. What unique issues do immigrant victims of intimate partner abuse face?

3. Describe the different forms of violence that can occur within an intimate partner abusive relationship.

4. Explain how the cycle of violence attempts to explain incidents of intimate partner battering.

5. What barriers exist for women in their attempts to leave a battering relationship?

6. How has the use of technology changed the way in which victims experience stalking? What challenges do these changes present for law enforcement and the criminal justice system in pursuing cases of cyberstalking?

7. How do victims cope with the experience of being stalked?

WEB RESOURCES

Bureau of Justice Statistics: http://bjs.ojp.usdoj.gov

National Coalition Against Domestic Violence: http://www.ncadv.org/

Office of Victims of Crime: http://www.ojp.usdoj.gov/

Office on Violence Against Women: http://www.ovw.usdoj.gov/

Stalking Resource Center: http://www.ncvc.org/src/Main.aspx

Stalking Victims Sanctuary: http://www.stalkingvictims.com

The National Center for Victims of Crime: http://www.ncvc.org

The National Domestic Violence Hotline: http://www.ndvh.org/

Visit **www.sagepub.com/mallicoat2e** to access additional study tools including eFlashcards, web quizzes, web resources, video resources, and SAGE journal articles.

READING 7

In this reading, Martin Schwartz and Walter S. DeKeseredy discuss the need for a shift in the way in which we think and respond to acts of violence against women. They argue that while efforts at the individual level may provide assistance to victims, these efforts do little to solve the problems of violence at the societal level. Indeed, they suggest that men can be the strongest tools in fighting a culture that is accepting of violence against women.

Interpersonal Violence Against Women

The Role of Men

Martin D. Schwartz and Walter S. DeKeseredy

Many years ago, there was a story told so often it became a cliché. Because we have not heard it for a while, it might be useful to drag it out again in a new context. In any of the story's variants, a group of people were being tested for mental health, common sense, or intelligence. They were told that it was essential to keep as much water off the floor as possible to prevent damage. They were issued mops, and a faucet was turned on. The winners in this exercise were not the ones who devoted their lives to mopping as long and hard as they possibly could, but the ones who went over and turned off the faucet.

In many ways, this can be applied to the problem of interpersonal violence against women. The authors here have cumulatively put in more than 20 years' work in the shelter house movement and have only the greatest respect for those who are devoted to the sometimes dangerous and always difficult cause of protecting and sheltering battered women from their intimate partners. Unfortunately, such aid sometimes does not solve the problem. It may ameliorate various pieces of the damage caused by violent men, although it may also make things worse, possibly even leading to a male backlash that results in the death of the women (Dugan, Nagin, & Rosenfeld, 2003). Shelters have been called "Band-Aids" to the problem, but sometimes they might not even be that.

Generally, the first call of social scientists is for funds to study the problem more. At least on the level of discovering how much interpersonal violence against women exists, we have and have had for many years ample evidence that a phenomenal amount of such violence is committed in North America every day (not to mention the rest of the world). It is not that we do not have enough data, although the issue is sometimes purposely confused by men's rights groups claiming that minor or self-protection violence by women must be counted as equal to extreme or injury-causing violence by men. The problem is that our policies do not reflect the extraordinary amount of information already in our possession.

To speak directly to the issue of programming, there are several major problems with programming over interpersonal violence against women. In a short article, we will center our comments on three issues, although they will not be given equal attention.

SOURCE: Schwartz, M. D., & DeKeseredy, W. S. (2008). Interpersonal violence against women: The role of men. *Journal of Contemporary Criminal Justice,* *24*(2), 178–185.

Programming—Attention and Money

The first problem is one of attention and money. In a badly divided country where politics and media-induced moral panics too often overrule logic, money tends to flow to the issues *du jour,* rather than the most important problems. Barry Glassner (1999) asks whether we as a people are afraid of the wrong things. The American media and the populace following behind are afraid of whatever is being newly hyped: terrorist attacks, road rage attackers, methamphetamine, rape drugs, school shootings, and other events that are statistically relatively rare. Meanwhile, statistically more likely events are ignored: homelessness, the lack of proper medical care, particularly among pregnant women (leading to a truly embarrassingly large infant mortality rate) and children, malnourishment of children, [and] the most extraordinarily low literacy rate in the Western World. A large percentage of our population is highly organized to protest against abortion, for example, but once the child is born, there seems to be much less interest in helping to keep the child alive, or later to educate the child. And, of course, various studies have provided statistics that show that as many as one in four college women are the victims of some sort of sexual assault and more than 10% of all women are physically abused.

In the United States today, in addition to War in Iraq, the popular place to spend money is on the prevention of terrorist attacks, even in places where it boggles the mind to imagine a terrorist attack ever occurring, and fighting wars against either more minor outbreaks of drug use, or relatively harmless drugs. There is very little call to spend more money, for example, on preventing stalking, a crime that absolutely terrorizes many women and even men. National Institute of Justice-sponsored studies, for example, estimate that more than 13% of college women were stalked in one school year, most often by what they characterize as an intimate partner (Office on Violence Against Women, 2007). Looking at all Americans, the Centers for Disease Control and Prevention (CDC) found that a smaller but still amazingly large number of women have been stalked in their lives (1 in 12 to 1 in 14), and a smaller but still significant number of men (1 in 50) (Basile, Swahn, Chen, & Saltzman, 2006). Not to misrepresent the situation, there has been an enormous reaction to these statistics, resulting in most states passing laws on stalking and the federal government beefing up similar laws. Stalking incidents are now counted so that reports can be written. There does not, however, seem to have been much imaginative interest in developing programs beyond increasing penalties for people we don't often convict, and keeping track of reports. Programs to actually stop stalking are not very popular.

The same CDC basic study also looked at forced sex and found that in a national study that victimization rates have remained constant since the 1990s and that most victims (female or male) were 17 or younger at the time of the first forced sex (Basile, Chen, Black, & Saltzman, 2007). In other words, we have been fairly ineffective not only in preventing *physical* abuse of women and children but also in preventing *sexual* abuse of intimate partners and their children.

One of the most popular pieces of U.S. legislation is the Violence Against Women Act, but most American programs dealing with the results of such violence operate on shoestring budgets. Worse, for a long and complicated set of reasons, those who try to provide services for victimized women find that to maintain funded facilities they must conform to governmental requirements. To get money from county mental health budgets, their clients often must have diagnoses and prognoses. Services must be aimed at the individual problems of the client. Child Protection Services often are required in the first instance to try to maintain the family, even if one member is a batterer or child sexual abuser. Services, money, and programs do not deal with broader social forces in America. Miller and Iovanni (2007) make it clear: "These concessions have shifted the discourse and action away from challenging the root causes of battering—including issues related to power and privilege—and away from prevention efforts" (p. 294).

Most important of all, in a climate where most violence against women consists of men harming women, it is not the women who will stop violence by changing. Rather, men will need to change if there is to be a reduction in the amount of violence against women in North American society. The main place this has been recognized is with the development of batterer intervention programs for men. Although a variety of programs have been tried, and the political popularity of "doing something" has made them the darlings of judges, for the most part, they have not been very successful (Jackson, Feder, Davis, Maxwell, & Taylor, 2003; Saunders & Hamill, 2003). One or two hours now and then of counseling, perhaps an emphasis on anger management, and the lack of a system that motivates men to attend and enforces their attendance, all have created a flawed system in most of the country. Most recently, attention has been centered on sophisticated programs of coordinated community response plans among courts, probation, shelters, and other community agencies. The main thrust of these programs has been to sweep offenders off the street and lock them up to prevent them from repeating their offenses. These programs have been subject to the most detailed evaluation of any batterer intervention programs, but unfortunately what seems to be the finding is that any changes that come from judicial oversight demonstration projects have come in incapacitation, not in changes in attitudes or deterrence (Harrett, Schaffer, DeStefano, & Castro, 2006). In other words, once the men are let go, they pose the same danger that they posed before.

What all of these programs have in common are two things. First, they deal with men one at a time. To incapacitate all of the spousal assaulters in North America would require a hard-to-imagine further dramatic expansion of our already extraordinarily overloaded penal system. Yet the problem only gets worse. If men leave batterer treatment programs or batterer incapacitation jail cells and return immediately to their patriarchal families, patriarchal places of work, and patriarchal places of leisure, it is hard to imagine that there will ever be any change in their attitudes, and eventually in their behavior. And, of course, this is exactly what we have been finding.

Few programs have dealt with the problems that started this article: turning off the faucet. If we live in a patriarchal society that encourages male violence against women, we must deal with that society, not only with men one by one. To take an example, a tremendous amount of outrage was unleashed on Atlanta Falcons quarterback Michael Vick in 2007 when he was alleged to have taken part in the killing of two dogs. It was not only a campaign by the radical People for the Ethical Treatment of Animals but [also] a broad national sense of outrage. People do not like to see dogs harmed. Imagine a Hollywood movie that featured the torture and death of a dog. It will not happen. A few hundred men can be killed in a movie, often very graphically, and rape scenes are no problem at all. In real life, a full-time scorekeeper would be required just to keep track of the number of college and professional athletes in the United States and Canada who have been accused or convicted of beating or raping women, let alone assaulting and/or killing men. It would be quite understandable if Michael Vick were sitting in prison wondering why murderers, rapists, and vicious assaulters of women were playing sports without penalty today. The outrage and economic pressure (e.g., losing lucrative endorsements) just is not there in America for people who harm women. Just dogs.

As we shall see later, the first step thus in programming for the end of interpersonal violence is to actually program for it.

Violence Against Women as a Cause of Crime

Today, there has slowly been a growing recognition that being a witness to woman abuse as a child is dangerous to healthy development. We have known for quite some time that many adult criminals grew up in homes marked by domestic terrorism, where they were forced to witness and sometimes experience woman abuse on a regular basis. We know that although they were still children, these witnesses to violence against women act out in serious problematic ways and suffer from important stress and strain that can lead to drug and alcohol use as time goes on (Emery, 2006).

What has not been commonly recognized has been the relationship between the two. If we have a large number of adult criminals with this background, then we can make the direct connection that growing up in a home marked by extensive violence against women can be seen as a cause of some unknown but certainly large amount of the juvenile and adult delinquency in America. This has been mostly studied in terms of whether there is an intergenerational effect, where children grow up to beat their wives. What has not been studied is the extent to which children who live in terroristic households grow up to join gangs, commit armed robberies, use and sell illegal drugs, commit burglaries, and generally become what society calls street criminals (Schwartz, 1989).

Thus, one important area for study in the future is the extent to which ending interpersonal violence against women can be seen as a strategy for reducing adolescent and adult criminal behavior in later years.

Male Peer Support

Some years ago, we proposed a male peer support model of woman abuse, which has been tested many times on both college and community populations, including a national representative sample (Schwartz & DeKeseredy, 1997; Sinclair, 2002). This complex model starts with the proposition that the ultimate cause of woman abuse is societal patriarchy and provides a corollary that more patriarchal men are more likely to be batterers. What is different about this model is that it suggests that the focus of our attention should not be on women's behavior but on men's behavior. Unfortunately, and this is very difficult to say, services for women are good to ameliorate many kinds of pain. Counseling and therapy can be very important for dealing with the individual suffering of woman and can help them look at their lives to see if they wish to make changes. Shelters can provide short-term protection, and under some circumstances longer term protection, if they can separate the woman some physical distance from the abuser. However, shelters may not solve the problem. Shelter house directors are fond of saying that under the best of circumstances—if this particular woman is put into a permanent protective environment—batterers will just go on to their next victim; it is hard to see how this can solve any problem except for one particular woman one particular time.

Solving Problems

The most obvious beginning in most introduction to sociology books is the distinction made by C. Wright Mills, the difference between private and public troubles. Private troubles are terrible. One may have cancer or gangrene, be unable to find housing or a sufficient amount of food to eat, or any of a host of other problems. For most of us, sleeping under a bridge in the winter while in pain would be a terrible thing, but it is a private problem; it is *our* problem. To be a sociologist is to look at public problems. If it is not one person who is homeless, but a large percentage of the population, then there is a confluence of social forces here that causes a broad amount of pain. The same applies to interpersonal violence against women. Centering attention on counseling, batterer intervention, protection orders, shelter houses, and the like will not end the problem of male violence, although it may ameliorate the private troubles of some smaller group of women.

There is an emerging number of men who believe that if men are the problem here, then men have to be part of the solution. Jackson Katz (2006) in particular has written on this subject, decrying the fact that so few institutions that affect young males (e.g., schools) actively program to

try to reduce misogynist and violent attitudes. Meanwhile, these same institutions may through sports, games, role models, films, and other devices work hard to reinforce the notion that men have an entitlement to be in charge and to force their way if women resist. Katz has found that there are many men willing to listen, if not actively participate in bystander intervention, having been silenced all their lives for fear of not being manly. He developed his extremely popular MVP program with athletes, the Marines, and others, not because these men are the most difficult or dangerous, but because they make effective leaders: If football linemen can speak out against violence against women, others may feel similarly enabled. Others (e.g., Banyard, Moynihan, & Plante, 2007) have found that bystander education can be effective and long lasting.

What these programs point out is something that we have long known in dealing in crime, which is that informal social control is more effective than formal social control. For more than a decade, men have been recommending a variety of informal social controls. Ron Thorne-Finch (1992), for example, has suggested a variety of one-on-one confrontations that men can make to convince their colleagues not to engage in abuse or sexist jokes. Rus Ervin Funk (1992) argued that men could reduce violence against women by engaging in extensive efforts at what he calls "educational activism." DeKeseredy and Schwartz (1996) argued that men can work in community and local political forums to develop political and informational campaigns. None of these ideas are likely to have an immediate dramatic impact, but all might begin to have a smaller impact, chipping away at the problem.

Rather, what is needed is a major national effort to end interpersonal violence against women. The Michael Vick example may be a good one. There are many similar ones of course, such as when filmmakers portrayed the death of an animal, and did not make it clear enough that it was not a real animal. Why do people get so upset by the death of animals but not women? In Pittsburgh, a sports radio personality pointed out that Michael Vick would never have gotten into as much trouble if he had limited himself to raping women. He got into trouble, and was removed from the air, but the fact remains that he was right. Why do most athletes accused of battering or rape end up with the charges dismissed and the woman complainant vilified (Benedict, 1997)?

Many of the activists cited here recommend individual level patterns of confrontation and struggle to let people know that such behavior and the attitudes that facilitate it are not acceptable (Banyard et al., 2007; DeKeseredy & Schwartz, 1996; Katz, 2006). However, this is not enough. Although there are education programs across the country in this area, there must be significantly more. What is needed is a national level discussion of programming sufficient to change people's overall attitudes, to where, who knows, maybe raping a woman will come to be seen as bad as killing a pit bull.

Conclusion

The main argument in this essay has been that interpersonal violence against women will not be ended by ameliorative efforts aimed at women. These may be necessary, important, and useful for the women involved, but they will not stop the flow of violence. It is just as unlikely that individual programs such as batterer intervention programs will have much effect, especially if they remain short interventions that have little effect on men's overall environment. Rather, what is needed is major intervention aimed directly at the patriarchal attitudes that facilitate interpersonal violence against women in the United States and that allow men who commit such crimes to get away with them.

References

Banyard, V. L., Moynihan, M. M., & Plante, E. G. (2007). Sexual violence prevention through bystander education: An experimental evaluation. *Journal of Community Psychology, 35,* 463–481.

Basile, K. C., Chen, J., Black, M. C., & Saltzman, L. E. (2007). Prevalence and characteristics of sexual violence victimization among U.S. adults, 2001–2003. *Violence and Victims, 22,* 437–448.

Basile, K. C., Swahn, M. H., Chen, J., & Saltzman, L. E. (2006). Stalking in the United States: Recent national prevalence estimates. *American Journal of Preventive Medicine, 31,* 172–175.

Benedict, J. (1997). *Public heroes, private felons: Athletes and crimes against women.* Boston: Northeastern University Press.

DeKeseredy, W. S., & Schwartz, M. D. (1996). *Contemporary criminology.* Belmont, CA: Wadsworth.

Dugan, L., Nagin, D. S., & Rosenfeld, R. (2003, November). Do domestic violence services save lives? *National Institute of Justice Journal, 250,* 20–25.

Emery, C. R. (2006). *Consequences of childhood exposure to intimate partner violence.* Washington, DC: National Institute of Justice.

Funk, R. E. (1992). Stopping *rape: A challenge for men.* Philadelphia: New Society.

Glassner, B. (1999). *The culture of fear: Why Americans are afraid of the wrong things.* New York: Basic Books.

Harrett, A., Schaffer, M., DeStefano, C., & Castro, J. (2006). *The evaluation of Milwaukee's judicial oversight demonstration.* Washington, DC: Urban Institute.

Jackson, S., Feder, L., Davis, R. C., Maxwell, C., & Taylor, B. G. (2003). *Do batterer intervention programs work?* Washington, DC: National Institute of Justice.

Katz, J. (2006). *The macho paradox: Why some men hurt women and how all men can help.* Naperville, IL: Sourcebooks.

Miller, S., & Iovanni, L. (2007). Domestic violence policy in the United States. In L. L. O'Toole, J. R. Schiffman, & M. L. Kiter Edwards (Eds.), *Gender violence: Interdisciplinary perspectives* (pp. 287–296). New York: New York University Press.

Office on Violence Against Women. (2007). *Report to Congress on stalking and domestic violence, 2005–2006.* Available from the U.S. Department of Justice web site, http://www.usdoj.gov

Saunders, D. G., & Hamill, R. M. (2003). *Violence against women: Synthesis of research on offender interventions.* Washington, DC: National Institute of Justice.

Schwartz, M. D. (1989). Family violence as a cause of crime: Rethinking our priorities. *Criminal Justice Policy Review, 3,* 115–132.

Schwartz, M. D., & DeKeseredy, W. S. (1997). *Sexual assault on the college campus: The role of male peer support.* Thousand Oaks, CA: Sage.

Sinclair, R. L. (2002). *Male peer support and male-to-female dating abuse committed by socially displaced male youth: An exploratory study.* Unpublished doctoral dissertation, Carleton University, Ottawa, Ontario, Canada.

Thorne-Finch, R. (1992). *Ending the silence: The origins and treatment of male violence against women.* Toronto, Ontario, Canada: University of Toronto Press.

DISCUSSION QUESTIONS

1. How is intimate partner violence a "male" issue?

2. How does a patriarchal society perpetuate violence against women?

3. What type of programming and interventions are necessary to stop violence against women?

READING 8

In this section, you learned about how intimate partner abuse can also occur in dating relationships. This article by Katie M. Edwards, Christina M. Dardis, and Christine A. Gidycz uses both quantitative and qualitative data to look at the issue of dating violence. In particular, this study highlights some of the reasons why women may or may not choose to disclose these victimizations and how these experiences could be used to inform intervention efforts for college campuses and local communities.

Women's Disclosure of Dating Violence

A Mixed Methodological Study

Katie M. Edwards, Christina M. Dardis, and Christine A. Gidycz

The majority of women will be the victim of dating violence during their lifetime (Edwards, Desai, Gidycz, and Van Wynsberghe, 2009). A burgeoning body of research documents the deleterious consequences of dating violence to victims and society (Lewis and Fremouw, 2001). Less research, however, has focused on women's disclosure of dating violence, especially research utilizing mixed methodologies and samples of non-treatment seeking college women in abusive dating relationships. Using a feminist lens, the purpose of the current study was to explore this gap in the literature. In particular, the present study represents a follow-up to Mahlstedt and Keeny's (1993) mixed methodological study about U.S. college women's disclosure of dating violence.

Mahlstedt and Keeny (1993) found that 92% of abused women disclosed the abuse to at least one source and that these women were much more likely to disclose abuse to informal support services than formal support services. Specifically, they found that although only 9% of abused women disclosed dating violence to police, 80% disclosed dating violence to a friend. Other common informal support sources to whom women disclosed were

relatives, including mothers (43%), sisters (47%), brothers (33%), and fathers (15%). These rates of disclosure are similar to rates of sexual assault disclosure found in more recent studies with college (Orchowski and Gidycz, forthcoming) and community (Ullman, 1996, 2010) samples.

Mahlstedt and Keeny (1993) also documented that women endorse barriers to disclosure such as embarrassment about the abuse, believing that the abuse is a private matter, fear for their own safety, or concerns about social reactions. Orchowski and Gidycz (forthcoming) found that women who endorse lower levels of self-blame were more likely to disclose sexual violence than individuals who endorse higher levels of self-blame. The data from these studies are consistent with Ahrens (2006) and Ullman's (2010) assertions that violence against women serves to reinforce women's powerlessness in a patriarchal society and that silence (or nondisclosure) symbolizes this powerlessness.

In addition to assessing rates of disclosure and reasons for nondisclosure, Mahlstedt and Keeny (1993) assessed social reactions to abused women's disclosure. These researchers found that the most commonly

SOURCE: Edwards, K. M., Dardis, C. M., & Gidycz, C. A. (2012). Women's disclosure of dating violence: A mixed methodological study. *Feminism & Psychology, 22*(4), 507–517.

reported responses to disclosure were that confidents "listened," "gave helpful advice," and were "angry with the assailant." The least frequent responses were "trivialized it," "saw me as a failure," and "made decisions for me." Responses that women reported as the most helpful included "understanding," "advice-giving," "listening," and "interrupting victim blame." Mahlstedt and Keeny reported that excessive advice giving (e.g., to leave the abuser) was often interpreted by women as an insinuation of victim blame, and [these] were considered by women to be the most unhelpful responses. These results underscore the differences in social reactions that women receive to their disclosure of dating violence within the context of a patriarchal culture.

Although the Mahlstedt and Keeney (1993) study contributes to our knowledge of disclosure of dating violence, there remains a dearth of research assessing reasons for nondisclosure and the responses from confidants that college-aged women who disclose dating violence perceive as the most and least helpful. Also, there have been considerable efforts in our society (e.g., media awareness campaigns, dating violence prevention, and intervention programming) to raise awareness about dating violence over the past years (Gidycz et al., 2011), which may have contributed to changes in disclosure processes (Ullman, personal communication, January 6, 2011). In order to build upon the results of earlier research, we attempted to answer the following questions utilizing quantitative data: To whom do women disclose dating violence? What are the correlates of women's disclosure of dating violence? Utilizing qualitative data, we attempted to answer the following questions: For women who disclosed, who was the most helpful and why? Who was the least helpful and why? For women who did not disclose, what were their reasons for doing so? Of note, we agree with other researchers (e.g., Ahrens, 2006; Ullman, 2010) that social reactions to interpersonal violence emanate from broader social norms and attitudes related to violence against women and gendered power relations. Although we did not directly assess these social norms and attitudes in our study, we assert that these invariably affect social reactions to disclosure and survivors' perceptions of helpfulness and unhelpfulness of specific responses. We thus use a critical feminist lens when interpreting and discussing our results.

Method

Participants

Participants included 44 women who reported at least one incident of sexual, physical, or psychological abuse in their current heterosexual relationship, as measured by the Conflict Tactics Scale-Revised (CTS2; Straus, Hamby, Boney-McCoy, & Sugarman, 1996) and obtained from a larger screening sample ($N = 107$). The 44 women were predominantly young (mean age = 19.30, $SD = 1.36$) and white (82%).

Results

To Whom Do Women Disclose Dating Violence?

Approximately 75% ($n = 33$) of the sample disclosed dating violence to at least one source. As demonstrated in Reading Table 8.1, the most common disclosure sources were informal supports, specifically friends.

Reading Table 8.1   Rates of Disclosure

Source	Percentage Who Disclosed to Source
Female friend	73%
Male friend	25%
Sister	25%
Brother	2%
Mother	23%
Father	7%
Counselor	5%
Medical doctor	0%
Law enforcement	0%
Priest/minister	0%

NOTE: Percentages exceed 100% because many participants disclosed to multiple sources.

What Are the Correlates of Women's Disclosure of Dating Violence?

Three *t*-tests and a chi-square test were conducted to determine the correlates of women's disclosure of dating violence. Results from the *t*-tests (see Reading Table 8.2) suggested that, compared to nondisclosers, disclosers reported higher levels of stress associated with the experience and higher levels of partner blame. Results from the chi-square test (see Reading Table 8.3) suggested that disclosers were more likely to think about ending the relationship than nondisclosers.

Reading Table 8.2 Means (and standard deviations) for Variables of Interest

	Disclosers	Nondisclosers
Partner blame	3.15 (1.03)	2.45 (1.36)
Self-blame	1.67 (1.19)	1.36 (1.43)
Stress of situation	2.85 (1.03)	1.91 (1.58)

Reading Table 8.3 Rates of Disclosure as a Function of Thoughts About Ending the Relationship

	Thought About Ending Relationship	
	Yes	No
Disclosers	58%	42%
Nondisclosers	18%	82%

For Women Who Disclosed, Who Was the Most Helpful and Why?

Content analyses showed that 56% of disclosers perceived their friends as the most helpful, with the remainder stating family members were most helpful. The most common reasons that disclosers stated people were helpful were

that confidants offered good advice (36%), provided the opportunity to vent/talk about it (28%), and provided comfort and other emotional support (20%). Additional helpful responses were that confidants related to the experience (16%), provided rationalization for the partners' behavior (12%), and provided a neutral perspective (8%). See Reading Table 8.4 for quotes depicting the reasons disclosers stated individuals were helpful.

For Women Who Disclosed, Who Was the Least Helpful and Why?

Content analyses showed that 49% of disclosers felt that friends were the least helpful, with the remainder stating their partner (20%), family member (19%), or counselor (13%) were the least helpful. Reasons that disclosers stated people were unhelpful were because others told them to break up with their partner (33%), provided "bad advice" (27%), did not understand (27%), and joked about the experience (20%). See Reading Table 8.5 for quotes depicting the reasons disclosers stated people were least helpful.

For Women Who Did Not Disclose, What Were Their Reasons?

The most common reason for nondisclosure was that the incident was "no big deal" (80%). Additional reasons included concerns that no one would understand (10%) and concerns about anticipated confidants' reactions (20%). See Reading Table 8.6 for quotes depicting the reasons participants did not disclose.

⬰ Discussion

The purpose of this study was to assess college women's disclosure of dating violence utilizing a mixed methodological design. Similar to Mahlstedt and Keeny's (1993) study, many women were able to break their silence and disclose dating violence. Almost all women who disclosed did so to an informal support, most commonly female friends. Additionally, quantitative results demonstrated that there was a relationship between several factors—stress associated with abuse, partner blame, and thoughts about ending the relationship—and the disclosure of dating violence. However, given the retrospective nature of

Reading Table 8.4 Quotes Depicting Most Helpful Responses

Category	Example Quotes
Offered advice	"My friends told me they never see me and talked about [how] they hated him and my mom hated him so I knew he was no good."
	"My sister because I tell her everything and she gives me good advice."
	"[Friends] gave me a lot of guidance."
	"My friends told me not to talk to him for a couple of days so we can both cool down."
	"My sister and parents always give good advice."
Vent/talk about it	"Just talking it out to some of my girlfriends calmed me down."
	"My best friend just let me talk about it."
	"I talked to my roommate about it."
Emotional support	"They comforted me."
	"Friends [were] very supportive."
	"[My best friend] was very comforting."
Related	"I thought my best friend was helpful because she had it happen to her."
	"My friends were the most helpful because they have been there."
Rationalized behavior	"His friends were the most helpful because they informed me that this was how he always acted when he drank."
	"Male friends. They explained that he needed to cool off."
Neutral perspective	"[My friends] didn't justify the action, but allowed me a different perspective."
	"My best friend because she knows me so well and knows my boyfriend pretty well so she could give me an informed and helpful opinion."

this study, the temporal sequencing of these variables is unclear . . . [for] the temporal sequencing of these variables (i.e., if a certain thought or emotion led to disclosure, or if the act of disclosing and the responses of others led to a certain thought or emotion).

Qualitative content analyses suggested that women's minimization of the abuse was the most commonly mentioned reason for nondisclosure. In fact, 80% of nondisclosers chose not to discuss the experience with anyone because it was "no big deal." This finding may be reflective of larger social ideologies that legitimize and normalize violence against women, often leading victims to internalize these norms and beliefs (Baly, 2010; Wood,

2001). Additional reported reasons for nondisclosure included fear that no one would understand, feelings of embarrassment, or believing that the experience was a private matter, all of which are consistent with Mahlstedt and Keeny's (1993) research and consistent with patriarchal social structures that influence micro-level disclosure processes. For those women who disclosed dating violence to others, responses from confidants varied in their perceived helpfulness. Perhaps due to the fact that 98% of women in this sample who disclosed did so to friends, friends were perceived as both the most helpful (56%) and least helpful confidants (49%). Indeed, consistent with Mahlstedt and Keeny, women often disclosed to

Reading Table 8.5   Quotes Depicting Least Helpful Responses

Category	Example Quotes
Encouraged relationship dissolution	"Female friends just said 'so dump him.'" "They aren't a fan of my boyfriend so they automatically wanted me to leave him." "My brother. He wants us to break up." "My mom wanted me to end the relationship." "[My friends] didn't understand why I wouldn't just leave him."
"Bad advice"	"Some friends said not to do anything which was worthless." "They couldn't give an informed opinion." "Telling me to call his mom." "My father because he didn't think it was appropriate to be dating at the age of 15–16."
Did not understand	"My counselor didn't know how to respond." "[My mom] didn't understand." "[My friends] didn't understand why I would be so upset." "They don't understand our relationship."
Joked	"Male friends because they jokingly asked why I wouldn't [give into sexual pressure]." "Male friends just laugh it off."

Reading Table 8.6   Quotes Depicting Reasons for Nondisclosure

Category	Example Quotes
"No big deal"	"It was not a big deal to me! Stuff happens; you get into fights, not a big deal." "It wasn't that big of a deal." "It was not a big deal—my boyfriend [and I] talked about it afterward." "The incident was no big deal. I just wanted to have sex but he wanted me to perform oral." "It was nothing out of the ordinary for two teenagers. I forgave him b/c he was sorry and we moved on, I did not need to discuss it with others—it was miniscule." "I felt like it was a normal dating thing and that it was unnecessary to tell anyone. Afterwards, I felt like he really didn't mean it to come out that way so I just forgot about it."
Would not understand	"I didn't feel anyone would understand the situation since they weren't there."
Concern about reactions	"Because I was embarrassed and it was my business I didn't want anyone else to know." "I think it's not a good thing to talk to the people who really care about me. I don't want to let them worry about me, especially my family."

multiple friends, some of whom were helpful and some of whom were unhelpful.

Interestingly, we found that whereas some individuals reported a particular response (such as telling one to leave) was helpful, others found the same response unhelpful. This finding is consistent with the transtheoretical model of change (Prochaska and DiClemente, 1984) and other research with abused women (e.g., Enander, 2011), such that for women who are in contemplation or preparation stages of leaving, advice such as being told to leave may be perceived as helpful (and consonant with one's own beliefs), whereas for precontemplative individuals, being told to leave would be dissonant with one's own beliefs about her relationship. This finding may also be related to patriarchal cultural factors and social discourses that maintain some women in abusive relationships and affect how women understand their role in relationships and their subjectivity as women. This notion is related to feminist research suggesting that some women internalize oppressive social norms regarding gender ideologies and hold more accepting attitudes of violence against women (Baly, 2010; Wood, 2001), which undoubtedly affects the extent to which women find certain social responses to their disclosures of dating violence helpful or unhelpful.

Several limitations of the current study and suggestions for future research are noted. First, the sample size was small and the participant demographics of our sample were homogenous (i.e., white, heterosexual women). This limited our ability to assess differences in perceived helpfulness and unhelpfulness among the varying types of supports (e.g., informal vs. formal supports) and different abuse types (e.g., physical, sexual, and psychological). Additionally, the retrospective nature of this study did not allow us to assess the temporal sequencing of the correlates of dating violence or how disclosure of dating violence relates to women's long-term adjustment and relationship stability—questions that could be followed up using longitudinal mixed methodologies with larger, more diverse samples. Additionally, it is unclear from the qualitative data what constituted participants' perceptions of "good" and "bad" advice, as well why some participants viewed responses as helpful and others viewed the same responses as unhelpful. Accordingly, future research could attempt to understand participants' perceptions of various types of advice using more rigorous and in-depth qualitative methodologies (e.g., interviews) and assess readiness to change, empowerment, and cultural variables as possible explanations for variability in what women view as helpful and unhelpful.

Despite these limitations, the findings from the current study offer implications for dating violence programming and social awareness efforts. Given the large percentage of women who minimized the abuse, there is a need for psychoeducation and public awareness campaigns to educate people about dating violence. Further, these data underscore the importance of educating others—especially college students since they are the most likely source of their friends' disclosures—on how to respond to the disclosure of dating violence. Although dating violence prevention programs often provide suggestions on how to help a friend in an abusive relationship (Black and Weisz, 2008; Foshee et al., 1998; Senn, 2011), findings from the current study underscore the complexity in what women deem as helpful and unhelpful responses to their disclosures of dating violence. Indeed, some of the responses that women reported as helpful (e.g., minimize the abuse) are responses that program developers and facilitators discourage and consider harmful. Clearly, this is a critical area for more mixed methodological and participatory action research that must include dialogue between researchers, clinicians, program developers, survivors of dating violence, and their formal and informal supports. Furthermore, programming efforts alone will not lead to widespread change in reactions to disclosure because these interpersonal reactions are situated in larger patriarchal social and institutional contexts that legitimize violence against women, and these too must be addressed.

References

Ahrens, C. E. (2006). Being silenced: The impact of negative social reactions on the disclosure of rape. *American Journal of Community Psychology 38*: 263–274.

Baly, A. R. (2010). Leaving abusive relationships: Constructions of self and situation by abused women. *Journal of Interpersonal Violence 25*: 2297–2315.

Black, B. M. and Weisz, A. M. (2008). Effective interventions with dating violence and domestic violence. In: Franklin, C., Harris, M. B., and Allen-Meares, P. (eds.), *The School Practitioner's Concise Companion to Preventing Violence and Conflict.* New York: Oxford University Press, 127–139.

Edwards, K. M., Desai, A. D., Gidycz, C. A., and Van Wynsberghe, A. (2009). College women's aggression in relationships: The role of childhood and adolescent victimization. *Psychology of Women Quarterly 33*: 255–265.

Enander, V. (2011). Leaving Jekyll and Hyde: Emotion work in the context of intimate partner violence. *Feminism and Psychology 21*: 29–48.

Foshee, V. A., Bauman, K. E., Arriaga, X. B., Helms, R. W., Koch, G. G., and Linder, G. F. (1998). An evaluation of Safe Dates, an adolescent dating violence prevention program. *American Journal of Public Health 8*: 45–50.

Gidycz, C. A., Orchowski, L. M., and Edwards, K. M. (2011). Sexual violence: Primary prevention. In: White, J., Koss, M., and Kazdin, A. (eds.). *Violence Against Women and Children Vol. 2: Navigating Solutions.* Washington, DC: American Psychological Association, 159–179.

Lewis, S. F. and Fremouw, W. (2001). Dating violence: A critical review of the literature. *Clinical Psychology Review 21:* 105–127.

Mahlstedt, D. and Keeny, L. (1993). Female survivors of dating violence and their social networks. *Feminism and Psychology 3:* 319–333.

Orchowski, L. M. and Gidycz, C. A. (forthcoming). Psychological consequences associated with positive and negative responses to disclosure of sexual assault among college women: A prospective study. *Violence Against Women.*

Prochaska, J. and DiClemente, C. (1984). *The transtheoretical approach: Crossing traditional boundaries of therapy.* Homewood, IL: Dow Jones-Irwin.

Senn, C. Y. (2011). An imperfect feminist journey: Reflections on the process to develop an effective sexual assault resistance programme for university women. *Feminism and Psychology 21:* 121–137.

Straus, M. A., Hamby, S. L., Boney-McCoy, S., and Sugarman, D. B. (1996). The revised Conflict Tactics Scales (CTS2): Development and preliminary psychometric data. *Journal of Family Issues 17:* 283–316.

Ullman, S. E. (1996). Social reactions, coping strategies, and self-blame attributions in adjustment to sexual assault. *Psychology of Women Quarterly 20:* 505–526.

Ullman, S. E. (2010). *Talking about sexual assault: Society's response to survivors.* Washington, DC: American Psychological Association.

Wood, J. T. (2001). The normalization of violence in heterosexual romantic relationships: Women's narratives of love and violence. *Journal of Social and Personal Relationships 18:* 239–261.

DISCUSSION QUESTIONS

1. What do the quantitative results of this study tell us about dating violence and the disclosure practices of women?

2. What do the qualitative results of this study tell us about dating violence and the disclosure practices of women?

3. What did victims find were the most helpful resources in their disclosure? The least helpful?

V

International Issues in the Victimization of Women

Within a global environment, millions of women personally experience violence or live within the context of violence. These acts are not random but represent ongoing cultural representations of savagery and brutality that can last for decades. You've already learned about the issues of intimate partner abuse and rape/sexual assault in Sections III and IV. However, these are not the only acts of violence that women around the world endure. Some of the most common forms of violence against women include human trafficking, femicide, genital mutilation, and murder in the name of honor. Each of these crimes are related to the status of women within their communities, and suggestions for change are rooted within a shift of gendered normative values and the treatment of women in these societies. Within this section, you will learn about the nature of these crime, the implications for women in these regions, and how criminal justice policies address these issues within an international context.

As you read through the experiences of the women and their victimizations, it is important to consider how the cultural context of their lives affects their victimization experience. The effects of culture are significant, as it can alter not only how these crimes are viewed by agents of social control (police, legal systems) but also how the community interprets these experiences. These definitions play a significant role in determining how these crimes are reported (or if reports are made), as well as any response that may arise from these offenses. It can be dangerous to apply a White, middle-class lens or an "Americanized identity" to these issues—what we might do as individuals may not necessarily reflect the social norms and values of other cultures.

⊠ Human Trafficking

Rathana was born to a very poor family in Cambodia. When Rathana was 11 years old, her mother sold her to a woman in a neighboring province who sold ice in a small shop. Rathana worked for this woman and her husband for several months. She was beaten almost every day, and the shop owner never gave her much to eat. One day, a man came to the shop and bought Rathana from the ice seller. He then took her to a faraway province. When they arrived at his home, he showed Rathana a pornographic movie and then forced her to act out the movie by raping her. The man kept Rathana for more than 8 months, raping her sometimes two or three times a day. One day, the man got sick and went to a hospital. He brought Rathana with him and raped her in the hospital bathroom. Another patient reported what was happening to the police. Rathana was rescued from this man and sent to live in a shelter for trafficking survivors.

Salima was recruited in Kenya to work as a maid in Saudi Arabia. She was promised enough money to support herself and her two children. But when she arrived in Jeddah, she was forced to work 22 hours a day, cleaning 16 rooms daily for several months. She was never let out of the house and was given food only when her employers had leftovers. When there were no leftovers, Salima turned to dog food for sustenance. She suffered verbal and sexual abuse from her employers and their children. One day while Salima was hanging clothes on the line, her employer pushed her out the window, telling her, "You are better off dead." Salina plunged into a swimming pool three floors down and was rescued by police. After a week in the hospital, she returned to Kenya with broken legs and hands.

Katya, a student athlete in an Eastern European capital city, dreamed of learning English and visiting the United States. Her opportunity came in the form of a student visa program, through which international students can work temporarily in the United States. But when she got to America, rather than being taken to a job at a beach resort, the people who met her put her on a bus to Detroit, Michigan. They took her passport away and forced her and her friends to dance in strip clubs for the traffickers' profit. They controlled the girls' movement and travel, kept keys to the girls' apartment, and listened in on phone calls the girls made to their parents. After a year of enslavement, Katya and her friend were able to reach federal authorities with the help of a patron of the strip club in whom they had confided. Due to their bravery, six other victims were identified and rescued. Katya now has immigration status under the U.S. trafficking law. (U.S. Department of State, 2011)

Each of these scenarios represents a common story for many victims of human trafficking. These examples reflect a life experience where women victims of trafficking have been manipulated, abused, and exploited. These are but a few examples of the crimes that make up the category of human trafficking.

Human trafficking is the second largest criminal activity and the fastest growing criminal enterprise in the world. Estimates by the United Nations (2008) suggest that approximately 2.5 million people from 127 countries are victims of trafficking. Due to the nature of these crimes, it is difficult to determine a precise number of human trafficking victims worldwide. According to data provided by the U.S. State Department, between 600,000 and 820,000 men, women, and children are trafficked across international borders every year. These numbers do not include the thousands, and potentially millions, of individuals who are trafficked within the boundaries of their homelands (U.S. Department of State, 2013).

Trafficking can involve cases within the borders of one's country as well as transport across international boundaries. Thailand is a well-known location for the sexual trafficking of women and girls who migrate from other Southeast Asian countries, such as Cambodia, Laos, Myanmar (Burma), and Vietnam, as well as other Asian countries, such as China and Hong Kong. Others find their way to Thailand from the United Kingdom, South Africa, Czech Republic, Australia, and the United States (Rafferty, 2007). However, examples of trafficking are not limited to countries from the Southeast Asian region. The trafficking of women and children is an international phenomenon and can be found in many regions around the world, even in the United States.

There are several ways in which victims are trafficked. While it is sex-based crimes that garner the greatest attention, there are other examples of trafficking, such as forced labor and debt bondage. Forced labor typically involves immigrants and migrant workers that are in need of employment. Due to their illegal status, they are often taken advantage of, threatened, and in some cases, physically abused. Estimates indicate that forced labor generates more than $30 billion dollars annually (International Labour Organization, 2005). In contrast to forced labor, debt bondage requires victim to pay off a debt through labor. Debt may be inherited as a result of the actions of other family members or may be acquired in response for employment, transportation, and housing or board (U.S Department of Health & Human Services, 2011). In some cases, the costs of these debts are so high that it is impossible for the victim to ever depart the situation. While men, women, and children are all at risk for being victimized, women are disproportionately presented in these cases (U.S. Department of State, 2012).

It is sex trafficking that receives the greatest amount of attention within the discussion of human trafficking. Between January 2007 and September 2008, there were 1,229 documented incidents[1] of human trafficking in the United States. An astounding 83% of these cases were defined as alleged incidents of sex trafficking (such as forced prostitution and other sex crimes), of which 32% of these cases involved child sex trafficking and 62% involved adults (Kyckelhahn, Beck, & Cohen, 2009). According to the U.S. Trafficking Victims Protection Act (TVPA), which was passed by Congress in 2000, sex trafficking occurs when

> a commercial act is induced by force, fraud or coercion, or in which the person induced to perform such an act has not attained 18 years of age; or the recruitment, harboring, transportation provision, or obtaining a person for labor or services through the use of force, fraud or coercion [is] for the purpose of subjection to involuntary servitude, peonage, debt bondage, or slavery. (U.S. Department of State, 2011, p. 8)

Trafficked victims may find themselves working in a variety of settings, including brothels, strip clubs, and sex clubs. They also appear in pornographic films, live Internet sex chats, and on the streets where they solicit money in exchange for sexual services. Traffickers use several methods to manipulate women and girls into the sex trade and prey on their poor economic standing and desires for improving their financial status. These enticements include offers of employment, marriage, and travel. Each of these opportunities is a shield to trap women into sexual slavery. In some cases, women may be kidnapped or abducted, although these tactics are rare compared to the majority of cases, which involve lies, deceit, and trickery to collect its victims (Simkhada, 2008). In some cases, young children are recruited by "family friends" or community members or may even be intentionally sold into servitude by their own parents. According to Rafferty (2007):

> Traffickers use a number of coercive methods and psychological manipulations to maintain control over their victims and deprive them of their free will, to render them subservient and dependent by destroying their sense of self and connection to others, and to make their escape virtually impossible by destroying their physical and psychological defenses. The emotional and physical trauma, as well as the degradation associated with being subjected to humiliation and violence, treatment as a commodity, and unrelenting abuse and fear, presents a grave risk to the physical, psychological and social-emotional development of trafficking victims. (p. 410)

---

[1]The Human Trafficking Reporting System (HTRS) is part of the Department of Justice and tracks incidents of suspected human trafficking for which an investigation, arrest, prosecution, or incarceration occurred as a result of a charge related to human trafficking.

Victims are dependent on their traffickers for food, shelter, clothing, and safety. They may be trafficked to a region where they do not speak the language, which limits opportunities to seek assistance. They may be concerned for the safety of their family members, as many traffickers use threats against loved ones to ensure cooperation (Rafferty, 2007). Girls who are imprisoned in a brothel are often beaten and threatened in order to obtain compliance. They are reminded of their "debts" that they are forced to work off through the sale of their bodies. Most girls have little contact with the world outside the brothel and are unable to see or communicate with the family members that are left behind.

While some girls are able to escape the brothel life on their own, most require the intervention of police or social workers. Girls receive services from "rehabilitation centers," which provide health and social welfare assistance to victims of trafficking. The intent of these agencies is to return girls to their homes; however, many of these girls indicate they experience significant challenges upon return to their communities. Many of these girls are not looked upon as victims but rather as damaged goods when they return home. As such, they are shunned and stigmatized not only by society at large but also by their family members (Simkhada, 2008). As a result, many victims keep their trafficking experiences a secret, which can complicate outreach and recovery efforts. Particularly in cases where women leave home for a job, they may be chastised for not sending money back to the family or feel anguish over having left their children. Even when victims did disclose their experiences to family members, they were not believed. In some cases, the husbands accused their wives of marital infidelity and do not understand that the women were victimized. In others, the stigma of trafficking and the fear of others knowing of their experience led many victims to stay silent about their victimization (Brunovskis & Surtees, 2012).

Despite being aware of trafficking as a social issue, many jurisdictions have failed to effectively address the problem in their communities. Much of the intervention efforts against trafficking involve nongovernmental organizations (NGOs), national and international antitrafficking agencies, and local grassroots organizations. While several countries have adopted legislation that criminalizes the sale and exploitation of human beings, many have yet to enact antitrafficking laws. In some cases, countries may have laws on the books but have limited resources or priorities for enforcing such laws. Still other countries punish the victims of these crimes, often charging them with crimes such as prostitution when they seek out assistance from the police. While grassroots and antitrafficking organizations have developed policies and practices designed to punish traffickers and provide assistance to the victims, few of these recommendations have been implemented effectively or on a worldwide scale.

Responses to Human Trafficking

There are a number of items of national legislation and international policies that outline efforts to address human trafficking worldwide. While there is no uniform standard across jurisdictions, these generally include three basic themes involving the prosecution of traffickers, protection of victims, and prevention of human trafficking.

In the United States, legislation known as the **Trafficking Victims Protection Act of 2000** (TVPA)[2] is designed to punish traffickers, protect victims, and facilitate prevention efforts in the community to fight against human trafficking. Enacted by Congress in 2000, the law provides that traffickers can be sent to prison for up to 20 years for each victim. In 2008, the Department of Justice obtained 77 convictions in 40 cases of human trafficking, with an average sentence of 112 months (9.3 years). Over two thirds of these cases involved acts of sex trafficking. At the state level, 42 states currently have antitrafficking legislation in their jurisdictions and are active in identifying offenders and victims of these crimes (U.S. Department of State, 2008).

While the TVPA includes protection and assistance for victims, these provisions are limited. For example, victims of trafficking are eligible for a T-visa, which provides a temporary visa. However, there are only 5,000 T-visas available

---

[2]Reauthorized by Congress in December 2008.

(regardless of the numbers of demand for these visas), and issuance of this type of visa is limited to "severe forms of trafficking (such as) involving force, fraud or coercion or any trafficking involving a minor" (Haynes, 2004, p. 241). In addition, applications for permanent residency are conditional on a victim's participation as a potential witness in a trafficking prosecution. In the 2 years following the implementation of the T-visa program, only 23 visas had been granted, a far cry from the demand given that over 50,000 people are trafficked into the United States alone each year (Oxman-Martinez & Hanley, 2003).

In an effort to track antitrafficking campaigns on a global level, the U.S. Department of State assesses the efficacy of policies and practices. Each country is organized into one of three tiers, and the United States uses these rankings in making funding decisions for countries in need. Countries need to demonstrate that they are working to prosecute the offenders of trafficking and protect the victims. "If governments fail to meet this minimum standard, or do not make strides to do so, they will be classified as a Tier 3 country. Under those circumstances, the United States will only provide humanitarian and trade-related assistance" (Wooditch, 2011, pp. 475–476). Table 5.1 illustrates data on the global enforcement of trafficking under the Trafficking Victims Protection Reauthorization Act of 2003. While well intentioned, the *Trafficking in Persons (TIP) Report* has been criticized, as there have been few policy recommendations that have been implemented as a result of its findings. Research indicates that over the past decade, antitrafficking efforts have remained stable despite the introduction of the tier ranking system. While countries may have made efforts in combating human trafficking, it may not be enough to impact their tier ranking. In addition, the tier system has not always led to decision making in terms of the grant allocation process as it was initially intended to do (Wooditch, 2011).

In 2000, the United Nations proposed the *Protocol to Prevent, Suppress and Punish Trafficking in Persons, especially Women and Children*. While the intent of this multinational legal agreement was to join together international entities to identify and respond to victims and offenders of human trafficking, efforts have been slow to action. For example, the protocol applies to only those countries that have agreed to comply. While 147 countries have joined, several have raised concerns or objections to the process by which conflicts would be resolved (for example, via a third-party arbitration). So while many applaud the United Nations for attempting to tackle the issue of human trafficking, these efforts have been largely unsuccessful.

Similar to the TVPA in the United States, and as suggested by Cho, Dreher, and Neumayer (2011), the European Union policies on trafficking prioritizes the prosecution of offenders over the needs of victims, and visas are granted only for the purposes of pursuing charges against the traffickers. In addition, there is no encouragement or pressure by the EU for states to develop programs to address the needs of trafficked victims (Haynes, 2004). While the push to *jail the offender* of these crimes appears positive, the reality is that few prosecutions have succeeded in achieving

Table 5.1   Global Law Enforcement on Trafficking

Year	Prosecutions	Convictions	Victims Identified
2008	5,212	2,983	30,961
2009	5,606	4,166	49,105
2010	6,017	3,619	33,113
2011	7,206	4,239	41,210
2012	7,705	4,746	46,570

SOURCE: U.S. Department of State (2013).

this task. Even in cases where prosecutions are "successful" and traffickers are held accountable for their crimes, their convictions result in short sentences and small fines, the effect of which does little to deter individuals from participating in these offenses in the future.

In contrast to the prosecution-oriented approach, several international organizations have developed models to fight trafficking that focus on the needs of the victim. These approaches focus on the security and safety of the victims, allow them to regain control over their lives, and empower them to make positive choices for their future while receiving housing and employment assistance. While this approach provides valuable resources for victims, it does little to control and stop the practice of trafficking from continuing.

Promising Solutions to End Human Trafficking

Given the limitations of the **jail the offender and protect the victim models**, research by Haynes (2004) provides several policy recommendations that would combine the best aspects of these two approaches. These recommendations include the following:

1. *Protect, do not prosecute the victim:* As indicated earlier, many victims find themselves charged with prostitution and other crimes in their attempts to seek help. Not only does this process punish the victim, but it serves also to inhibit additional victims from coming forward out of fear that they too might be subjected to criminal punishments. Antitrafficking legislation needs to ensure that victims will not be prosecuted for the actions in which they engaged as a part of their trafficked status. In addition, victims need to be provided with shelter and care to meet their immediate needs following an escape from their trafficker.

2. *Develop community awareness and educational public service campaigns:* Many victims of trafficking do not know where to turn for help. An effective media campaign could provide victims with information on how to recognize if they are in an exploitative situation, avenues for assistance such as shelters and safety options, and long-term planning support, such as information on immigration. Media campaigns can also help educate the general public on the ways in which traffickers entice their victims and provide information on reporting potential victims to local agencies. Recent examples of prevention efforts in fighting trafficking have included raising public awareness through billboard campaigns, the development of a national hotline to report possible human trafficking cases, and public service announcements in several languages, including English, Spanish, Russian, Korean, and Arabic, to name a few (U.S. Department of State, 2009). These efforts help increase public knowledge about the realities of human trafficking within the community.

3. *Address the social and economic reasons for vulnerability to trafficking:* The road to trafficking begins with poverty. Economic instability creates vulnerability for women as they migrate from their communities in search of a better life. For many, the migration from their homes to the city places them at risk for traffickers, who seek out these women and promise them employment opportunities only to hold them against their will for the purposes of forced labor and slavery. Certainly, the road to eradicating poverty around the world is an insurmountable task, but an increased understanding of how and why women leave could inform educational campaigns, which could relay information about the risks and dangers of trafficking and provide viable options for legitimate employment and immigration.

4. *Prosecute traffickers and those who aid and abet traffickers:* Unfortunately, in many of these jurisdictions, law enforcement and legal agents are subjected to bribery and corruption, which limits the assistance that victims of trafficking may receive. "Police are known to tip off club workers suspected of harboring trafficked women in order to give owners time to hide women or supply false working papers (and) are also known to accept bribes, supply false papers or to turn a blind eye to the presence of undocumented foreigners" (Haynes, 2004, p. 257). In order to effectively address this issue, police and courts need to eliminate corruption from their ranks. In addition, agents

of justice need to pursue cases in earnest and address the flaws that exist within the system in order to effectively identify, pursue, and punish the offenders of these crimes.

5. *Create immigration solutions for trafficked persons:* An effective immigration policy for victims of trafficking serves two purposes: Not only does it provide victims with legal residency rights and protections, but it also helps pursue criminal prosecutions against traffickers, especially since the few effective prosecutions have relied heavily on victim cooperation and testimony. At its most fundamental position, victims who are unable to obtain even temporary visas will be unable to legally remain in the country and assist the courts in bringing perpetrators to justice. In addition, victims who are offered immigration visas contingent upon their participation in a prosecution run the risk of jeopardizing potential convictions, as defense attorneys may argue that the promise of residency could encourage an "alleged" victim to perjure his or her testimony. Finally, the limited opportunities to obtain permanent visa status amount to winning the immigration lottery in many cases, as these opportunities are few and far between and often involve complex applications and long waiting periods.

6. *Implement the laws:* At the end of the day, policy recommendations and legislation does little good if such laws are not vigorously pursued and enforced against individuals and groups participating in the trafficking of humans. In addition, such convictions need to carry stern and significant financial and incarceration punishments if they hope to be an effective tool in solving the problem of trafficking.

While efforts to prioritize the implementation of antitrafficking laws may slow the progress of eliminating these crimes against humanity, the best efforts toward prevention focus on eliminating the need for people to migrate in search of opportunities to improve their economic condition. An ecological perspective suggests that the cause of trafficking lies within issues such as poverty, economic inequality, dysfunction within the family, gender inequality, discrimination, and the demand for victims for prostitution and cheap labor. At its heart, human trafficking "is a crime that deprives people of their human rights and freedoms, increases global health risks, fuels growing networks of organized crime and can sustain levels of poverty and impede development in certain areas" (U.S. Department of State, 2009, p. 5). Until these large-scale systemic issues are addressed, the presence of trafficking will endure within our global society.

The Women of Juarez

A field of crosses stand today in the deserts of Ciudad Juarez, Mexico, where hundreds of bodies of women have been found. Local and international organizations estimate that thousands of other women have gone missing and have yet to be found.

The Mexican city of Ciudad Juarez sits across the Rio Grande from El Paso, Texas. A fast-growing industrial area, the region is known as a major manufacturing center for many American companies. With more than three hundred assembly plants (known as maquiladoras) in the region, Ciudad Juarez is a booming area for production. Since the 1994 passing of NAFTA (North American Free Trade Agreement), U.S. Corporations, such as Ford, General Electric, and DuPont (to name a few), have established manufacturing centers in a region where labor costs are cheap and taxes are low, which result in high profits for companies. With four separate border access points, the region is a major center for exporting goods and transportation between Central Northern Mexico and the United States (Chamberlain, 2007). Awarded the "City of the Future" designation by *fDi* magazine and the Financial Times Group in 2008, Ciudad Juarez represents a region of opportunity and development. "It appears to be a win-win situation for the United States. Americans enjoy relatively inexpensive consumer good[s], and American-owned corporations enjoy the free aspect of the free trade zone: it is free of unions, minimum wages and largely free of enforceable regulations" (Spencer, 2004/2005, p. 505).

However, this City of the Future is also filled with extreme poverty. Drawn to the region with the promise of a better life, Mexican citizens arrive from rural towns only to discover a new form of economic disparity in border towns, such as Juarez. While filled with factories, the city receives few benefits to stimulate its economy. The maquiladoras generated over $10 billion of profit for U.S. companies in 2000, yet the city of Juarez received less than $1.5 million in taxes to provide a sustainable community structure for residents. Shantytowns surround the maquiladoras, as there are few options for housing for the workers. There is no money to build schools or provide services to the residents of the city (Spencer, 2004/2005). The high profit margins for companies come at a price for the **maquiladoras'** workforce, where women make up more than 80% of the workforce and where cases of poor working conditions, low wages ($60 a week for their labor), and traumatic work environments have been documented (Althaus, 2010).

Mexican border towns are also known for their high levels of violence and narcotics trafficking. Today, Ciudad Juarez is considered one of the most dangerous cities in the world due to violent feuds between the drug cartels and police. Juarez is also dangerous for one particular population: young women. Since 1993, estimates suggest that over 400 women have been murdered in and around the city. While some of these girls are students who disappeared as they traveled to and from school, the majority of **femicides** in this region involve young women between the ages of 11 and 24 who traveled from their villages to Ciudad Juarez looking for work in the maquiladoras. Their bodies are discovered days, weeks, and months following their disappearance and are typically abandoned in vacant lots in Juarez and the surrounding areas; some women are never found. Many of these cases involve significant acts of sexual torture, including rape and the slashing of the breasts and genitals of the female victims (Newton, 2003). The women who are killed and tortured in this fashion become members of a club known as *las muertas de Juarez*, or the Dead Women of Juarez.

In describing the murders of these women, several commentaries have pointed toward a clash between the traditional roles for women, a **machista** (chauvinistic) culture, and the rise of women's independence as an explanation for the violence. One author suggests that "these crimes are more murderous than murder, if such a thing is possible—they are crimes of such intense hatred that they seek to destroy the personhood of the women, negating their humanity and erasing their existence" (Revolutionary Worker, 2002, para. 11). According to a 2003 report by the Inter-American Commission on Human Rights (IACHR), the crimes against women in Ciudad Juarez have received international attention due to the extreme levels of violence in the murders and the belief that these killings may have been the result of a serial killer. However, their research indicates that these cases of femicide are not the result of a single serial killer but are part of a larger social issue related to a pattern of gender-based discrimination where the violence against women is not considered to be a serious issue. Given the relationship with gender in these cases, any official response to address these crimes must consider the larger social context of crimes against women and the accessibility of justice for women in these cases.

In attempting to solve these crimes, police have jailed dozens of suspects for the murders throughout the years. Some of these presumed offenders were railroaded by a system desperate to quash an inquisition into police practices. Many of these alleged perpetrators had their confessions coerced from them. Some argue that the authorities have shown little concern for these crimes and its victims, sending a message that these women are unworthy victims. Indeed, victim-blaming tactics have often been used to explain the murders, suggesting that these women wore revealing clothing, frequented bars and dance clubs, and were prostitutes. The National Human Rights Commission has found that the "judicial, state and municipal authorities were guilty of negligence and dereliction of duty" (Agosin, 2006, p. 16).

The quest for justice by journalists, social activists, and the families of these young women has been a challenging road, as many of them have been threatened with violence if they continue their investigations. Others have been silenced due to the inaction by authorities. Given the poor treatment of victims' family members by the authorities, recent improvements have been made in the areas of legal, psychological, and social services. However, there is concern that there are limited funds allocated to meet the demands for these services (Inter-American Commission on

Human Rights, 2003). The Mexican government has also created a victims services fund designed to provide monetary compensation to the families of the women and girls who have been murdered in Juarez. However, the program is poorly organized, and few families have been able to access the funds (Calderon Gamboa, 2007).

While the creation of a special prosecutor's office in 1998 did little to end the killings in Juarez, improvements have been made in recent times regarding the organization of evidence, the tracking of case details, and the streamlining of investigations and assignment of personnel. While Mexican authorities claim they have resolved the majority of the murders, their definition of "resolved" is based on a presumption of motive and the identification of a perpetrator and does not require that an offender be charged, tried, or convicted of the crime. Understandably, many families are dissatisfied by this definition of *resolved*. As of 2003, only three convictions have been handed down, and the community has little faith in the validity of these convictions (Simmons, 2006). Many human rights and activist groups have blamed the Mexican government for the inadequate investigation of these crimes and the lack of accountability by police agents. Indeed, Mexico's failure to act in these cases constitutes a violation of international laws, such as the American Convention of Human Rights and the Inter-American Convention on the Prevention, Punishment and Eradication of Violence Against Women (Calderon Gamboa, 2007).

While it is unclear whether the victims' families will ever receive closure in the deaths of their loved ones, human rights organizations have called for a systematic reform of conditions to ensure the future safety of women in Juarez. Their suggestions are presented within a framework designed to mend the cultural systems that historically have minimized the traumas of female victimizations. A key component of reform includes addressing the root causes of these murders by eliminating the machista culture that is prevalent in these communities. Suggestions include increasing employment opportunities for males in the maquiladoras' labor force, gender-sensitivity training for the workplace, and the creation of safe public spaces for women to gather in and travel to, from, and within the city of Juarez (Calderon Gamboa, 2007).

CASE STUDY

Spotlight on Witch Burnings in Papua New Guinea

Between 1692 and 1693, 200 people were accused and 19 were executed in Salem, Massachusetts, for practicing witchcraft. The paranoia of this region stemmed from a similar craze between the 12th and 15th century in Europe where people believed that the devil could empower individuals to bring harm on his behalf. While the people of Salem ultimately admitted that these trials were conducted in error and provided compensation to the families of the wrongfully convicted, these witch trials mark a unique point of history for colonial America (Blumberg, 2007).

While the Salem witch trials are a part of history, the beliefs of witchcraft remain alive in a number of global regions. One area that has recently been drawing attention is Papua New Guinea, which is located in the South Pacific north of Australia. As a country of over 800 different cultures and language, one of the unifying factors between them is a belief in black magic (Mintz, 2013).

Consider the following case: Kepari Leniata was burned alive in February 2013 after she was accused of being a witch. She was tortured, bound, and soaked with gasoline and set afire among the community trash (Pollak, 2013). She was blamed for engaging in sorcery and causing the death of a young boy in the village. Rather than accept that the child may have died from illness or natural causes, it is not uncommon for villagers to look to the supernatural to explain death (Bennett-Smith, 2013). "Black magic is often suspected when misfortune strikes, especially after the unexplained death of a young man, because it is said that they have a long life ahead of time and it has been cut short" (Alpert, 2013, para. 4). Leniata's death is not the only case of witch burning in recent times as two women narrowly escaped a similar fate, and in June 2013, a local schoolteacher was beheaded for being a witch (Chasmar, 2013). The punishment for sorcery is generally a public display in an effort to deter others from using magic (OXFAM, 2010). Women are most often the victims of accusations of sorcery, and it is often men who make such accusations. While the most egregious punishment for sorcery is death, people who have been accused of these crimes can also lose their land, homes, and be banished from the community (OXFAM, n.d.). The legal system in Papua New Guinea provides little help in preventing acts of witch burning and other tortures of those accused of sorcery. While there are laws that prohibit sorcery, they do little to deter the practice. The 1971 Sorcery Act punishes those who engage in sorcery with a two-year incarceration sentence, a rather insignificant punishment. In addition, people who commit murder can use sorcery as a mitigating factor. Here, murder is justified in the eyes of the offender as an act of greater good of the community. The United Nations has called for an end to witch burning, as "these reports raise grave concern that accusations of sorcery are used to justify arbitrary and inhumane acts of violence" ("UN: 'Sorcery' murders," 2013, para. 8). The Papua New Guinea government recently overturned the Sorcery Act and has called for the expansion of the death penalty for offenders of these crimes. Despite this strong stance by governmental officials, it is unknown what effect, if any, this change will have on the practice of witch burning (UN News Centre, 2013).

✉ Female Genital Mutilation

Female **genital mutilation** (FGM; also known as female cutting or circumcision) includes a number of practices whereby young girls are subjected to the vandalism or removal of their genitalia. The purpose of this process is to both protect the purity of girls' virginity while at the same time eliminating the potential for sexual pleasure. These procedures are far from safe as the tools are rarely sanitized and anesthesia is not used. In addition, the people performing these procedures do not have any sort of medical training. Yirga, Kassa, Gebremichael, and Aro (2012) list the four types of female genital mutilation:

[T]ype 1, partial or total removal of the clitoris and/or the prepuce (clitoridectomy); type 2, partial or total removal of the clitoris and labia minora, with or without excision of the labia majora (excision); type 3, narrowing of the vaginal orifice with creation of a covering seal by cutting and appositioning the labia minora and/or the labia majora, with or without excision of the clitoris (infibulation); and type 4, all other harmful procedures to the female genitalia for nonmedical purposes, e.g., pricking, piercing, incising, scraping, and cauterization. (p. 46)

While there has been significant outrage at an international level, genital mutilation remains a significant issue. Estimates indicate that 100–140 million women across Africa are genitally mutilated every year. This means that the majority of women in these countries have endured this experience. For example, 94% of women in Sierra Leone and 79% in Gambia have been circumcised. Many women who undergo this process experience significant infection and are at risk for sterilization, complications during pregnancy, and sexual and menstrual difficulties. In addition to these physical challenges, victims experience high levels of psychological trauma (Foundation for Women's Health Research and Development, 2012).

Genital mutilation is a cultural normative practice, and it is viewed as an expression of womanhood. Females who have not undergone a circumcision process are often viewed as lower status and less desirable, which impacts their value in marriage. In addition, the failure to be circumcised carries significant examples of urban legend and fear: "A girl that is not circumcised cannot have children because the clitoris is still there. When the baby's head touches the clitoris at birth, the baby will die" (Anuforo, Oyedele, & Pacquiao 2004, p. 108). Other myths suggest that uncircumcised women are unclean, that circumcision aids in childbirth, and the vagina is more visually appealing without it (Akintunde, 2010). It is also believed that circumcision helps maintain sexual purity and prevents promiscuity. For many of these tribal communities, they express hope that the practice of female circumcision will continue and resent the belief by Westerners that the practice is abusive. However, migration and modernization may help encourage these communities to abandon the practice. For example, women who immigrate to the United States are more likely to believe that female cutting practices should end. However, change is not just an American ideal, as some research indicates that women's attitudes about FGM are changing, which could lead to shifts in the practice. Here, experiences such as education and employment influence such changes. For example, women who attend college or who are employed outside of the home are significantly less likely to circumcise their daughters. (Boyle, McMorris, & Gomez, 2002). For those that believe that the practice should continue, they suggest some practical changes that would allow the cultural values of FGM to remain. Here, some suggest that the procedure be performed in a medical environment with trained practitioners who could respond to any complications that might arise (Anuforo et al., 2004).

While social change may be possible within the communities that practice female genital mutilation, few laws have been passed to outlaw the practice. However, several groups have engaged in advocacy work within these communities. The World Health Organization conducts extensive research and public awareness campaigns in hopes of educating African women about the detrimental effects of genital mutilation (World Health Organization, 2012). However, these practices are not limited to the African countries and other regions of the world where the practice is commonly accepted. For example, the United Kingdom has been a major source for immigrants and refugees from these regions. Even though people are physically removed from their countries of origin, their cultures and practices follow with them. As a result, nations such as Great Britain need to engage in outreach with these communities that reside within their borders (Learner, 2012).

⬚ Honor-Based Violence

The category of **honor-based violence** (HBV) includes practices such as honor killings, bride burnings, customary killings, and dowry deaths. Each of these crimes involves the murder of a woman by a male family member, usually a father, brother, or male cousin. These women are killed in response to a belief that the women have offended a family's honor and have brought shame to the family unit. The notion of honor is one of the most important cultural values for members of these communities. "Honor is the reason for our living now . . . without honor life has no meaning. . . . It is okay if you don't have money, but you must have dignity" (Kardam, 2005, p. 16).

At the heart of the practice of honor-based violence is a double standard rooted in patriarchy, which dictates that women should be modest, meek, pure, and innocent. Women are expected to follow the rules of their fathers and, later, their husbands. In some cases, honor killings have been carried out in cases of adultery, or even perceived infidelity. Consider the recent case of a 15-year-old girl who died after an acid attack in her home in Kashmir, Pakistan. Her crime was that she was talking to a boy outside of her family home. Unfortunately, this case, nor the response by her family members, is not uncommon. Upon their arrest, her parents justified their actions as their daughter had brought shame to their family's honor (Burke, 2012). Hina Jilani, a lawyer and human rights activist, suggests that, in some cultures, the "right to life of women . . . is conditional on their obeying social norms and traditions" (Amnesty International, 1999, para. 2). Women are viewed as a piece of property that holds value. Her value is based on her purity, which can be tainted by acts that many Western cultures would consider to be normal, everyday occurrences, such as requesting a love song on the radio or strolling through the park (Arin, 2001). For many women, their crime is that they wanted to become "Westernized" or participate in modern-day activities, such as wearing jeans, listening to music, and developing friendships. For other women, their shame is rooted in a sexual double standard where a woman is expected to maintain her purity for her husband. To taint the purity of a woman is to taint her honor and, thereby, the honor of her family. The concept of honor controls every part of a woman's identity. As Kardam (2005) explains, "When honor is constructed through a woman's body, it entails her daily life activities, education, work, marriage, the importance of virginity (and) faithfulness" (p. 61).

Women who are accused of bringing negative attention and dishonor are rarely afforded the opportunity to defend their actions (Mayell, 2002). Even women who have been victimized through rape and sexual assault are at risk of death via an honor killing, as their victimization is considered shameful for the family. In many cases, the simple perception of impropriety is enough to warrant an honor killing. Amnesty International (1999) explains the central role of *perception* in honor in Pakistan:

> The distinction between a woman being guilty and a woman being alleged to be guilty of illicit sex is irrelevant. What impacts the man's honour is the public perception, the belief of her infidelity. It is this which blackens honour and for which she is killed. To talk of "alleged kari" or "alleged siahkari" makes no sense in this system nor does your demand that a woman should be heard. It is not the truth that honour is about, but public perception of honour. (p. 12)

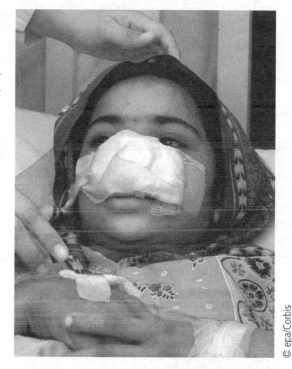

© epa/Corbis

▲ **Photo 5.1** A young woman is treated for injuries that she received in an attempted honor crime in rural Pakistan. While she was lucky to survive the attack, hundreds of women die each year in these honor attacks, which are generally committed by their male relatives (husband, father, brother, etc.) for bringing shame on the family.

The practice of honor and customary killings are typically carried out with a high degree of violence. Women are subjected to acts of torture, and their deaths are often slow and violent. They may be shot, stabbed, strangled, electrocuted, set on fire, or run over by a vehicle. In fact, doing so is expected in certain cases, as "a man's ability to protect his honour is judged by his family and neighbors. He must publicly demonstrate his power to safeguard his honour by killing those who damaged it and thereby restore it" (Amnesty International, 1999, p. 12). One would assume that the women in these countries would silently shame these acts of violence. Contrary to this belief, however, research indicates that the women in the family support these acts of violence against their daughters and sisters as part of the shared community understanding about honor (Mayell, 2002).

While the United Nations (2000, 2010) estimates more than 5,000 honor killings each year around the world, researchers and activists indicate that the true numbers of these crimes are significantly greater. Estimates indicate that tens of thousands of women are killed each year in the practice of honor-based violence. Yet many of these crimes go unreported, making it difficult to develop an understanding of the true extent of the issue. According to research by Chesler (2010), the majority (95%) of the victims of honor killings are young women (mean age = 23). In 42% of cases, there were multiple perpetrators involved in the killing, a characteristic that distinguishes these types of crimes from the types of single-perpetrator femicide that are most commonly reported in Western countries. Over half of these women were tortured to death and were killed by methods such as stoning, burning, beheading, strangulation, or stabbing/bludgeoning. Nearly half (42%) of these cases involved acts of infidelity or alleged "sexual impropriety," while the remaining 58% of women were murdered for being "too Western" and defying the expectations that are set through cultural and religious normative values. Yet men are never criticized for their acceptance of Western culture. Women in such cultures "are expected to bear the burden of upholding these ancient and allegedly religious customs of gender apartheid" (Chesler, 2010, pp. 3–11).

While much of the practice of honor killings occurs outside of the United States (and other Westernized jurisdictions), we do see occasional incidents of honor killings in these regions. These cases are exclusively linked to an immigrant culture or community where honor killings are a more accepted practice. Despite laws that prohibit murder, the perpetrators in these crimes generally maintain that their actions were culturally justified. Perhaps one of the most recent cases of honor violence within the Western world involves the January 2012 conviction of the Shafia family in Ontario, Canada. Mohammad Shafia, his wife Tooba Yahya, and their son Hamen were found guilty of first-degree murder in the deaths of their children/sisters Zainab (age 19), Sahar (age 17), and Geeti (age 13) as well as Rona, Mohammad's first wife from his polygamous marriage. The four women were found in a submerged car staged to look like an accident. Prosecutors argued that the daughters were killed for dishonoring the family. While the Sharia family members all maintained their innocence and have publically stated their intent to appeal their conviction, evidence in the case included wiretapped conversations which included Mohammad stating, "There can be no betrayal, no treachery, no violation more than this . . . even if they hoist me up onto the gallows . . . nothing is more dear to me than my honor" ("Canada Honor Killing Trial," 2012, para. 25).

Even if justice officials do become involved in these cases, perpetrators are rarely identified and even more rarely punished to any extent. When human rights organizations and activists identify these incidents as honor-based violence, family members of the victim are quick to dismiss the deaths of their sisters and daughters as "accidents." In Turkish communities, if a woman has fractured the honor of her family, the male members of her family meet to decide her fate. In the case of "customary killings," the task of carrying out the murder is often given to the youngest male member of the family. Typically, these boys are under the age of criminal responsibility, which further reduces the likelihood that any punishments will be handed down in the name of the victim (Arin, 2001).

One example of honor-based violence is the practice of **karo-kari** murder in Pakistan. Karo-kari is a form of premeditated killing and is part of the cultural traditions of the community. The terms *karo* and *kari* literally translate to "black male" and "black female" and are used in reference to someone who is an adulterer or adulteress. In the majority of karo-kari cases, women are killed for engaging in acts of immoral behavior. These acts can include alleged marital infidelity, refusal to submit to an arranged marriage, or requesting a divorce from a husband (even in cases where abuse is present). While a 2010 U.S. State Department report referenced over 40 victims of karo-Kari in the Kandahan province alone, official data estimate that there are over 1,000 such deaths across the country (U.S. Department of State, 2011). Unofficial statistics place this number as significantly higher, given that many of these crimes occur within the family and may not be reported to the authorities. The practice of karo-kari in Pakistan is unique compared to honor killings in many other countries, as men can also be victims under karo-kari traditions. Generally speaking, cultural norms require the killing of both the man and woman involved in the infidelity in order to restore honor. This distinction is unique to karo-kari, whereas most other forms of customary killings involve only the woman. However, in some cases, the karo (man) is able to negotiate with the tribal counsel for the community to pay money or offer other forms of settlement (property of another woman) to compensate the "victim" (Amnesty International, 1999). Alas, this alternative is rarely available for women.

Honor-based violence is a violation of many international treaties and acts. The laws in many countries contain provisions that permit acts of honor-based violence, including Syria, Morocco, Jordan, and Haiti. The practice of honor killings was condoned under the Taliban, and data indicate that since the fall of the Taliban regime, there has been an increase in reporting acts of violence against women (Esfandiari, 2006). Even in cases where there is no legal legitimization of the practice, cultural traditions and tribal justice sanction these crimes of violence and often shield offenders from punishment, and offenders continue the practice without impunity (Patel & Gadit, 2008). Some countries may offer lesser penalties to men who murder female relatives. Other countries have laws on the books that identify customary killings as a criminal act, yet they offer opportunities for the offender to escape punishment. One such example is Pakistan. Although the Pakistani Parliament passed legislation in 2004 that punished honor killings with a 7-year sentence and would allow for the death penalty for the worst cases, many activists question whether such a punishment will ever be carried out. In addition, the law contains a provision where the offender could "negotiate" a pardon with the victim's family members. Given that many of the offenders are indeed members of the victim's family, many believe that the retention of this provision will enable the offenders of these crimes to escape punishment altogether (Felix, 2005).

There are few options for escape for women in these countries where honor-based violence prevails. International support for women at risk of becoming a victim of an honor killing is limited. There are few shelters for women seeking to escape their families. Not only does any attempt to contact the police or other agents send a woman back to the arms of her family where she is at greatest risk, but her actions in seeking help also create shame and dishonor for the family by exposing their private life to public and community scrutiny. The only customary option for these women is to escape to the tribal leader of the community (sadar), who can provide shelter while they negotiate a safe return of the woman to her home or to another community far from her family. However, this option is limited, as it still requires women to abide by traditional community standards and is not an option for women who are interested in asserting their rights or improving their status as women outside of their cultural norms (Amnesty International, 1999).

In their quest to improve the lives of women who may be victims of the practice of honor killings, Amnesty International (1999) outlines three general areas for reform:

1. *Legal Measures.* The current legal system in many of these countries does little to protect victims from potential violence under the normative structures that condone the practice of honor killings. Women have few, if any, legal rights that protect them from these harms. Legal reforms must address the status of women and provide them with opportunities for equal protection under the law. In cases where women survive an attempted honor killing, they need access to remedies that address the damages they experience. In addition, the perpetrators of these crimes are rarely subjected to punishment for their actions. Indeed, the first step toward reform includes recognizing that violence against women is a crime, and such abuses need to be enforced by the legal communities. International law also needs to recognize these crimes and enforce sanctions against governments that fail to act against these offenders. However, it is unclear how effective these legal measures will be for individual communities. In their discussions of what can be done to stop the practice of honor killings, Turkish activists did not feel that increasing the punishments for honor-based violence would serve as an effective deterrent, particularly in regions where the practice is more common and accepted within the community, as "punishments would not change the social necessity to kill and that to spend long years in jail can be seen as less important than lifelong loss of honor" (Kardam, 2005, p. 51).

2. *Preventive Measures.* Education and public awareness is the first step toward reducing honor-based violence toward women. These practices are rooted in culture and history. Attempts to change these deeply held attitudes will require time and resources aimed at opening communication on these beliefs. This is no easy task given the normative cultural values that perpetuate these crimes. One of the first tasks may be to adopt sensitivity-training programming for judicial and legal personnel so that they may be able to respond to these acts of violence in an impartial manner. In addition, it is important to develop a sense of the extent of the problem in order to provide effective remedies. Here, an enhanced understanding of data on these crimes will help shed light on the pervasiveness of honor-based violence as a first step toward addressing this problem.

3. *Protective Measures.* Given the limited options for women seeking to escape honor-based violence, additional resources for victim services need to be made available. These include shelters, resources for women fleeing violence,

legal aid to represent victims of crime, provisions for the protection of children, and training to increase the economic self-sustainability for women. In addition, the agencies that offer refuge for these women need to be protected from instances of backlash and harassment.

While these suggestions offer opportunities for change, many agents working in the regions most affected by honor-based killings indicate feelings of hopelessness that such changes are even possible. Certainly, the road toward reform is a long one, as it is rooted in cultural traditions that present significant challenges for change. "When an honor killing . . . starts to disturb everybody . . . and when nobody wants to carry this shame anymore, then finding solutions will become easier" (Kardam, 2005, p. 66). Indeed, the first step in reform involves creating the belief that success is possible.

CASE STUDY

Spotlight on Malala Yousafzai

Pakistan has one of the largest populations of children that do not attend school, two thirds of whom are girls. Spending on education represents only 2.3% of the gross national product (GNP) and over 49 million adults are illiterate (Torre, 2013). Girls were prohibited from attending school under Taliban rule and over 170 schools were destroyed between 2007 and 2009 (Brumfield & Simpson, 2013).

Malala Yousafzai was born on July 12, 1997, in Pakistan. As a young girl, Malala became interested in politics and education and became an outspoken advocate for girls' education in her country. At 11 years old, she gave her first speech titled "How dare the Taliban take away my basic right to education" and at 12 she began blogging for the BBC about life under Taliban rule (Kuriakose, 2013). Her public profile began to rise through her speeches and writings and her efforts were applauded by several international organizations. In 2012, she began to develop a foundation to help young girls receive an education. However, she was considered a threat to the Taliban, and on October 9, 2012, she was shot while riding on a bus home from school (Walsh, 2012). The Taliban argued that she was targeted not for promoting education but for using propaganda against the Taliban. "Taliban are not opposed to girls education, but they could not support anti-Islamic agendas and Westernized education systems" (Brumfield & Simpson, 2013, para. 11). For this crime, they have stated that she will continue to remain a target. While a *fatwa* was issued against the Taliban gunman, he remains at large.

▲ Photo 5.2   Malala Yousafzai was shot by the Taliban when she was only 15 years old for speaking out about girls' rights to education. She is a worldwide advocate on the issue and has been nominated for the Nobel Peace Prize.

© Walter McBride/Corbis

Yousafzai was seriously wounded in the attack as the gunman's bullet fired through her head, neck, and shoulder. She was transported to the United Kingdom for treatment where she went through several surgeries, one of which replaced a piece of her skull with a titanium plate. Amazingly, she did not suffer any neurological damage (Brumfield & Simpson, 2013). Since then, she has resided in Birmingham, England, as it is too dangerous for her to return to Pakistan. However, the violence has not silenced Malala. She continues to speak out about the importance of education for girls and created the Malala fund to raise support for educational projects for girls worldwide. She has received a number of international awards and was nominated for the Nobel Peace Prize. Six months after the shooting, Malala returned to school in the United Kingdom, a day she described as the most important day of her life (Quinn, 2013). One year following her attack, Malala released her biography *I am Malala* (Farid, 2014).

Conclusion

While this chapter covers some of the victimizations that women face around the world, it is by no means an exhaustive discussion. Many of these crimes occur due to the status of women in society and gender-role expectations of women. Alas, the needs for victims in these cases are high, and the nature of these crimes can challenge the accessibility and delivery of services. Ultimately, reform for these victims is linked to changing the gendered cultures of our global society.

Summary

- Human trafficking involves the exploitation of individuals for the purposes of forced labor or involuntary servitude, debt bondage, and sexual exploitation. The majority of these cases involve sexual exploitation and abuse, and human trafficking disproportionately affects women.
- Traffickers prey on women from poor communities and appeal to their interests in improving their economic standing as a method of enticing them into exploitative and manipulative work environments.
- International efforts to combat human trafficking have focused on "3Ps": prosecution (of traffickers), protection (of victims), and prevention (of trafficking cases), but there has been little international progress to reduce the prevalence of human trafficking worldwide.
- Recommendations for best practices against trafficking involve improved victim services, increased public awareness about trafficking, and implementation and enforcement of stricter laws against the practice.
- The pattern of femicides in Ciudad Juarez, Mexico, involves the violent rape and torture of hundreds of women and girls who travel from their homes in search of work in the factories where they endure poor working conditions and are paid little for their labor.
- There have been few convictions for these crimes, and most of the cases are unresolved. Victim blaming is a common practice, and many families and victim-rights groups have protested over the lack of attention paid to these incidents.
- Honor-based violence involves the murder of women for violating gendered cultural norms. Most incidents of honor-based violence are committed by a male family member, such as a father, husband, brother, or cousin.
- Offenders of honor-based violence are rarely punished, as the killings are an accepted practice within the communities.
- Efforts toward reducing or eliminating honor-based violence include legal reform, education and public awareness, and additional resources for victim services.
- Female genital mutilation is a cultural practice throughout much of Africa. Much of the Western world views these practices as acts of violence toward women.

KEY TERMS

Femicides

Genital mutilation

Honor-based violence

Human trafficking

Jail the offender and protect
   the victim models

Karo-kari

Machista

Maquiladoras

Trafficking Victims
   Protection Act of 2000

T-visa

DISCUSSION QUESTIONS

1. How is the pattern of femicides in Ciudad Juarez linked to larger social issues, such as patriarchy, masculine identity, and the entry of women into the workforce?

2. What steps have local and national agencies in Mexico taken to solve the cases of the "las muertas de Juarez"? How have these efforts failed the families of the victims?

3. How is the concept of shame created in cultures where honor-based violence is prevalent?

4. To what extent are offenders in honor-based violence cases punished? What measures need to be implemented to protect women from these crimes?

5. How do women enter and exit the experience of sexual trafficking?

6. Compare and contrast the jail the offender and the protect the victim models of trafficking enforcement. What are the best practices that can be implemented from these two models to address the needs of trafficking victims?

7. What suggestions have been made to work within the communities that support genital mutilation?

WEB RESOURCES

Desert Flower Foundation: http://www.desertflowerfoundation.org/en/

Forward UK: http://www.forwarduk.org.uk/key-issues

HumanTrafficking.org: http://www.humantrafficking.org

Not for Sale: http://www.notforsalecampaign.org/about/slavery/

Polaris Project: http://www.polarisproject.org/

Stop Honour Killings: http://www.stophonourkillings.com/

The Juarez Project: http://www.thejuarezproject.com/

Trafficking in Persons Report: http://www.state.gov/g/tip/rls/tiprpt/2011/index.htm

Women of Juarez: http://womenofjuarez.egenerica.com/

Visit **www.sagepub.com/mallicoat2e** to access additional study tools including eFlashcards, web quizzes, web resources, video resources, and SAGE journal articles.

While human trafficking is a global issue, much of the intervention efforts are facilitated at the local level. This article discusses how local agencies can prepare to deal with victims of these crimes. The article also highlights how interventions by criminal justice agencies can engage in secondary victimization in their treatment of these victims.

Human Sex Trafficking

The Global Becomes Local

Frances P. Bernat and Heather C. Winkeller

Human trafficking is modern-day slavery. The number of trafficking victims is estimated to be 27 million worldwide, with between 1 and 2 million trafficked internationally each year (Clawson, Small, Go, and Myles 2003; Free the Slaves 2009; United Nations Population Fund 2009). The problem of human trafficking is being addressed by international and national tribunals, social service agencies, media outlets, and various governmental agencies. The problem has become a focus for global and national action and has resulted in changes to federal and international laws and legal processes. Human sex trafficking is a problem that is being played out on the global stage and that is beginning to get international responses from the highest levels of government.

To combat sex trafficking, the global response needs to be concurrently addressed at the local level. Enacting human trafficking laws is not enough if they fail to adequately define human trafficking and fail to provide resources for prosecuting trafficking cases (Chapkis 2003; Corrigan 2001; Medige 2007; Payne 2006; Tiefenbrun 2002). In addition, the legal system may not help or protect victims who suffer from multiple traumas associated with their enslavement. Too often, trafficking victims are processed as illegal immigrants or prostitution offenders. It is time for the global response to be tailored to local situations so that the local communities that are impacted by trafficking can respond effectively to this immense human rights crisis.

Sex Trafficking and Victim Vulnerabilities

A common factor in the movement of victims across borders is that people are transported from poor nations to more affluent nations, and from underdeveloped nations to developed nations (Cameron and Newman 2008; Clawson et al., 2003; Guinn and Steglich 2003). Governmental corruption and poverty in poor nations can exacerbate the problem and contribute to its perpetuation (Andrews 2004; Kapstein 2006). However, domestic human trafficking also exists. The Polaris Project (2009) found that U.S. citizens and residents are trafficked from state to state and within states. Many of these victims are youth under the age of 18 who enter into prostitution living on the street and who need money to support themselves; traffickers are able to recruit and exploit this vulnerable population. It is estimated that there are 2 million domestic victims within the United States.

Children who are sexually trafficked are quite prone to contracting illnesses because of their immature physical

SOURCE: Bernat, F. P., & Winkeller, H. C. (2010). Human sex trafficking: The global becomes local. *Women & Criminal Justice, 20,* 186–192.

systems (Andrews 2004). Once in a trafficking location, victims are entrapped and find it difficult to leave their enslavement. Gordon and Crehan (1999) explored the complicated issues of sexual violence for victims who are traumatized by violence, who are exposed to HIV, and who experience stigmatization and shame. They asserted that the sexual violence associated with trafficking shows a breakdown in law and order and reflects gendered hegemony. Women's and children's bodies are valued only as commodities in sex trafficking trades.

⬚ Cultural Conditions and Human Bondage

Persons who wish to end human slavery face a very basic problem. Trafficking victims, despite their numbers, can be hard to identify, hard to locate, hard to convince to leave their situation, and hard to provide services for in order to help them escape from bondage. Once freed, many victims return to their previous conditions of bondage. These victims find it hard to work with criminal justice actors, and they might deny that the abuse is occurring out of shame or fear of prosecution. Cultural differences among domestic and internationally trafficked victims also point to problems in the "one-size-fits-all" model for responding to human trafficking. It is essential for victims to join forces in their communities to redefine the nature of gender roles in the family while they seek assistance for their multiple levels of trauma. It is important to differentiate the lies from the truth when a victim is identified. Some traffickers pretend that victims are their family members (spouses or children) in order to thwart authorities; these deceptive practices enable traffickers to dominate further victims who are isolated, poor, and in need of human contact and support. Trafficking victims may come to accept their situation and also learn to accept the abuse and domination as normal.

Like domestic violence victims, victims of human trafficking are threatened with serious injury or death if they attempt to leave. With such abuse, the victims of trafficking also exhibit a lack of self-esteem and are ashamed of their lifestyle. In addition, they are likely to believe that their families will not accept them back or not understand what they experienced. Victims may also feel that they must continue to work in order to send money home or pay off their own debts to the trafficker (Brunovskis and Surtees 2007; Hart 2009). Anti-immigrant sentiment increases the likelihood of learned helplessness, the inability to see avenues of escape, and helps to explain why foreign victims stay with abusers. If social service providers are reluctant to acknowledge that non-immigrant women with ample economic resources find it difficult to leave an abusive home, then they are even less likely to understand the plight of immigrant women whose English language skills, income, and resources are often extremely limited. These victims are likely to be treated as liars or criminal offenders and then dismissed or arrested by persons whose job it is to help (see Moossy 2009). If the victims are housed in shelters, other inhabitants may not wish to associate with former prostitutes, so the trafficking victims may be isolated or shunned.

⬚ Response on the Local Level: Studying Arizona

The ability of anti-trafficking networks and governments to unmask the hidden nature of human trafficking requires attention to the individual and local community. In this sense, the global becomes the local, and the local becomes the global. Bernat (1995) argued that inequalities of race, culture, education, and economic status exist and affect women in differential ways. Distinguishing the characteristics of crime and victimization requires paying special attention to how women, children, and men may be more severely traumatized when their ability to support themselves is negatively associated with their cultural norms and social values and the impact of human trafficking.

Arizona is a major transit state for human trafficking, and human trafficking is connected to other crimes (Goddard 2008). Because of its large and porous southern border, Arizona is on the front lines in U.S. anti-trafficking efforts. The state is a site for human trafficking, and these offenses seem tied to other illegal activities (Goddard 2008), such as illegal immigration, drug trafficking, kidnapping, and homicide. In this regard, Arizona was recently ranked number one in the number of kidnappings (Associated Press 2009; Roberts 2009), and federal prosecutions for illegal immigration, human trafficking, and drug offenses have been increasing (Gaouette 2008). Federal, state, and local law enforcement officials believe such kidnappings are related to Mexican cartels and "coyotes" who engage in human smuggling rings and refuse to release smuggled immigrants unless they pay thousands of dollars for their release (Goddard 2008; Will 2009).

Trafficking victims may come to the attention of the police when "drop houses" are located and victims who are being held for ransom are discovered (Roberts 2009). Phoenix Police Chief Harris has said that he can deploy up to 60 officers to handle one kidnapping case because he oversees a large department, but he would prefer to solve the problem rather than respond to its symptoms (Will 2009). In Phoenix, human trafficking is investigated by the Vice Enforcement Unit, which was reassigned to the Drug Enforcement Bureau in 2005 (City of Phoenix Police Department 2009). Small police agencies do not have the monetary or human resources to devote to the problem, and small departments might not even consider human trafficking to be a problem.

Arizona has adopted a multifaceted approach to countering human trafficking. The state created a border smuggling task force within the Attorney General's office to specifically target some of the tools that traffickers rely on to facilitate their criminal activities (Napolitano 2005; "Testimony of Janet Napolitano" 2007). During the 2005 legislative session, Arizona lawmakers succeeded in passing an anti-trafficking statute that made human trafficking and human smuggling felony offenses within the state (National Conference of State Legislatures 2007). In this regard, the criminal law specifically proscribes sex trafficking as a Class 2 felony with enhanced punishments if the victim is under the age of 15 (Arizona Revised Statutes §13–1307).

The Arizona Attorney General's office also created a Border Trafficking Team tasked with prosecuting those engaged in human smuggling and fraudulent identity cases and with working in conjunction with financial institutions to actively disrupt traffickers' financial networks. As a result of these efforts, by 2006, more than 100 smugglers had been arrested and millions of dollars in assets seized (Goddard 2006). Although the number of smugglers prosecuted for their crimes appears relatively small, Arizona has experienced greater success than other regions, such as southwest Florida, which has seen only nine prosecutions for human trafficking in recent years (CNN 2008). Recent data collected by the U.S. Department of Justice (2009) show that 99 percent of sex trafficking victims are female and more than 70 percent are young (under the age of 25). In addition, most trafficking offenders are male, but about 20 percent of sex trafficking suspects [or]offenders are female. Arizona has also entered into a binational agreement with Mexico to combat human trafficking and other forms of illicit activity in the Southwest (Goddard 2008).

In 2010, a shelter for young women [who were] sexually trafficked is to open in Arizona. StreetLight is a local charitable organization that aims to provide shelter and services to young teens seeking assistance to end their trafficking victimization (StreetLight 2010). Because bringing services to victims of trafficking is in its "infancy," more research needs to be done to document the extent of victimization and the degree to which "rescue and restore initiatives" work (Di Nicola and Cauduro 2007; Gozdziak and Bump 2008). Shelters need to be sensitive to the multiple levels of trauma [that] sex trafficking victims experience and need to understand that treatment efforts may require longer shelter services than may usually be provided for victims of domestic violence.

Local service providers can be a bridge between the victim and the legal system, the victim and the community, and the victim and the victim's family. Restoring a victim to his or her home community or family may be a noble goal, but it might not be feasible if the victim is a person from another nation without proper documentation, is poor and uneducated, or has medical and mental health needs. Because of the large number of victims, it is important to begin to identify and assist victims without preconceived goals of quick integration. Despite the increased attention and new legislation, human trafficking remains a significant social issue for which only a small fraction of victims are identified and few traffickers are successfully prosecuted.

Conclusion

Changing laws are not enough to help sex trafficking victims. Legal and social service workers need to understand how and why trafficking victims find it difficult to break free from their enslavement and why many victims will not cooperate with people who sincerely want to help them. The gendered nature of human trafficking (how women and men are trafficked, and the complexities of child trafficking) needs to be understood to enable anti-trafficking groups and individuals to construct social and political responses that are effective. Individual-level trauma is a major impediment to restoring sex trafficking victims to their families and communities. Efforts aimed at the multiple impacts of victimization and the reasons for human sex trafficking must come about to end trafficking in this lifetime. [Those involved in] such efforts must understand the individual involved, the reasons for his or her entry into commercial sexual work, and the impact of sexual victimization on his or her ability to get and use the assistance offered. Legal changes can only be effective when the cultural dimensions of trafficking are understood and addressed.

⊠ References

Andrews, Sara K. 2004. "U.S. Domestic Prosecution of the American International Sex Tourist." *Journal of Criminal Law & Criminology* 94:415–454.

Arizona Revised Statutes. §13–1307.

Associated Press. 2009, May 8. "Phoenix Police Fear Wave of Kidnappings Could Grow." [Online]. Available: http://www.azcentral.com/news/articles/2009/05/08/20090508drugwar-kidnapping0508-ON.html. Accessed 3–10–10.

Bernat, Frances P. 1995. "Opening the Dialogue: Women's Culture and the Criminal Justice System." *Women & Criminal Justice* 7:1–7.

Brunovskis, Anette and Rebecca Surtees. 2007. *Leaving the Past Behind? When Victims of Trafficking Decline Assistance.* (Fafo Report No. 2007: 40). Oslo, Norway: Fafo.

Cameron, Sally and Edward Newman. 2008. "Structural Factors in Human Trafficking." Pp. 21–57 in *Trafficking in Humans: Social, Cultural and Political Dimensions,* edited by S. Cameron and E. Newman. New York: United Nations University Press.

Chapkis, Wendy. 2003. "Trafficking, Migration, and the Law: Protecting Innocents, Punishing Immigrants." *Gender & Society* 17:923–937.

City of Phoenix Police Department. 2009. *Drug Enforcement Bureau.* [Online]. Available: www.phoenix.gov/Police/deb1.html. Accessed 3–27–09.

Clawson, Heather J., Kevonne M. Small, Ellen S. Go, and Bradley W. Myles. 2003, October. *Needs Assessment for Service Providers and Trafficking Victims* (Document No. 202469). Washington, DC: U.S. Department of Justice.

CNN. 2008, April 28. *Modern Slavery.* [Video Webcast]. Available: http://www.cnn.com/video/#/video/us/2008/04/28/human.trafficking.cnn. Accessed 11–30–09.

Corrigan, Katrin. 2001. "Putting the Brakes on the Global Trafficking of Women for the Sex Trade: An Analysis of Existing Regulatory Schemes to Stop the Flow of Traffic." *Fordham International Law Journal* 25:151–214.

Di Nicola, Andrea and Andrea Cauduro. 2007. "Review of Official Statistics on Trafficking in Human Beings for Sexual Exploitation and Their Validity in the 25 EU Member States From Official Statistics to Estimates of the Phenomenon." Pp. 73–94 in *Measuring Human Trafficking: Complexities and Pitfalls,* edited by E. U. Savona and S. Stefanizzi. New York: Springer.

Free the Slaves. 2009. *Top 10 Facts About Modern Slavery.* [Online]. Available: http://www.freetheslaves.net. Accessed 9=23=09.

Gaouette, Nicole. 2008, June 18. "Federal Prosecution of Illegal Immigrants Soars." *Los Angeles Times.* [Online]. Available: http://articles.latimes.com/2008/jun/18/nation/na-immig18. Accessed 10–10–08.

Goddard, Terry. 2006, March 23. *Message From the Attorney General: Acting to Stop Human Smugglers.* [Online]. Available: http://www.azgov.gov/messages/HumanSmuggling0306.html. Accessed 11–26–09.

Goddard, Terry. 2008. *Arizona Attorney General Terry Goddard: 2008 Annual Report.* [Online]. Available: http://www.azag.gov/AnnualReports/2008AnnualReport.pdf. Accessed 1–14–10.

Gordon, Peter and Kate Crehan. 1999. *Dying of Sadness: Gender, Sexual Violence and the HIV Epidemic.* [Online]. Available: http://www.undp.org/hiv/publications/gender/violencee.htm. Accessed 10–6–09.

Gozdziak, Elzbieta and Micah N. Bump. 2008. *Data and Research on Human Trafficking: Bibliography of Research-Based Literature.* Washington, DC: Georgetown University, Institute for the Study of International Migration.

Guinn, David E. and Elissa Steglich, eds. 2003. *In Modern Bondage: Sex Trafficking in the Americas.* Ardsley, NY: Transnational Publishers.

Hart, Joyce. 2009. *Human Trafficking.* New York: Rosen Publishing Group.

Kapstein, Ethan B. 2006. "The New Global Slave Trade." *Foreign Affairs* 85:103–115.

Medige, Patricia. 2007. "The Labyrinth: Pursuing a Human Trafficking Case in Middle America." *Journal of Gender, Race & Justice* 10:269–284.

Moossy, Robert. 2009. "Sex Trafficking: Identifying Cases and Victims." *NIJ Journal.* [Online]. Available: http://www.ojp.usdoj.gov/nij/journals/262/sex-trafficking.htm. Accessed 10–13–09.

Napolitano, Janet. 2005, November 2. *Message of the Week.* [Online]. Available: http://www.votesmart.org/speech_detail.php?sc_id=195322&keyword=&phrase=&contain=. Accessed 10–1–09.

National Conference of State Legislatures. 2007. *2005 Victims' Rights Enactments.* [Online]. Available: http://ecom.ncsl.org/programs/cj/victimenacts05.htm. Accessed 11–28–09.

Payne, Michael C. 2006. "The Half-Fought Battle: A Call for Comprehensive State Anti-Human Trafficking Legislation and a Discussion of How States Should Construct Such Legislation." *Kansas Journal of Law & Public Policy* 16:48–66.

Polaris Project. 2009. *Domestic Trafficking Within the U.S.* [Online]. Available: http://www.polarisproject.org/content/view/60/81/. Accessed 9–23–09.

Roberts, Laurie. 2009, March 18. "Kidnapping: Valley's Dirty Secret." *Arizona Republic,* B1, B5.

StreetLight. 2010. *Safe House*. [Online]. Available: http://www.street lightphx.com//safe_house. Accessed 1–14–10.

"Testimony of Janet Napolitano, Governor of Arizona." 2007, January 9. Pp. 259–266 in *Ensuring Full Implementation of the 9–11 Commission's Recommendations: Hearing Before the Committee on Homeland Security and Governmental Affairs, United States Senate, One Hundred Tenth Congress, First Session*. [Online]. Available: http://www.gpo.gov/fdsys/pkg/CHRG-110shrg865/pdf/CHRG-110shrg865.pdf. Accessed 11–24–09.

Tiefenbrun, Susan. 2002. "The Saga of Susannah. A U.S. Remedy for Sex Trafficking in Women: The Victims of Trafficking and Violence Protection Act of 2000." *Utah Law Review* 1:107–175.

United Nations Population Fund. 2009. *Gender Equality: Trafficking in Human Misery*. [Online]. Available: http://www.unfpa.org/gender/violence1.htm. Accessed 10–4–09.

U.S. Department of Justice. 2009, January 15. *More Than 1,200 Alleged Incidents of Human Trafficking Reported in the U.S.* [Online]. Available: http://bjs.ojp.usdoj.gov/index.cfm?ty=pb-detail&iid=364. Accessed 1–14–10.

Will, George. 2009, March 22. "Kidnapping Phoenix's Reputation." *Arizona Republic*, B11–B12.

DISCUSSION QUESTIONS

1. How can local service providers serve the needs of women who have been trafficked in the United States?

2. What are the duties and responsibilities of local criminal justice agencies (police and prosecutors) in dealing with cases of sex trafficking?

3. What sort of challenges do victims of sex trafficking face in their attempts to leave?

READING 10

This reading expands on what you learned in the section introduction on honor killings. Karo-kari is a particular form of honor killing that occurs in the rural and tribal areas of Sindh, Pakistan. This reading explains the practices of karo-kari and how issues of culture place women at risk for victimization.

Karo-Kari

A Form of Honour Killing in Pakistan

Sujay Patel and Amin Muhammad Gadit

Introduction

While generally categorized as unlawful, homicide has been justified under particular circumstances by some social and cultural groups. This includes the cultural sanctioning of premeditated killings of women perceived to have brought dishonor to their families, often by engaging in illicit relations with men. This violence exhibits strong gender bias in that, in such settings, men who engage in similar behavior are typically subject to less severe punishments.

SOURCE: Patel, S., & Gadit, A. M. (2008). Karo-kari: A form of honour killing in Pakistan. *Transcultural Psychiatry, 45*(4), 683–694.

There is evidence of legal or cultural sanction for such practices in a number of ancient societies, including Babylon—where the predominant view was that a woman's virginity belonged to her family (Goldstein, 2002), ancient South- and Meso-American civilizations, and the Roman Empire. Incan laws permitted husbands to starve their wives to death as punishment for committing adultery, and Aztec legal codes meted out death by stoning or strangulation for female adultery (Gardner, 1986). In Ancient Rome, the senior male within a household retained the right to kill a related woman who engaged in premarital or extra-marital relations (Goldstein, 2002).

Over the past decade, human rights groups have increasingly exposed various forms of gender-biased "honor killing." A number of countries have legislative positions that allow for partial or complete criminal defense against criminal charges on the basis of honor killing, including those of Argentina, Bangladesh, Ecuador, Guatemala, Turkey, Jordan, Syria, Egypt, Lebanon, Iran, Israel, Peru, Venezuela, and the Palestinian National Authority (UNCHR, 2002). Honor killings have continued to occur in countries where they have been explicitly outlawed, such as Albania, Brazil, India, Iraq, Uganda, and Morocco, as well as in immigrant communities in Europe and North America (UNCHR, 2002).

In Pakistan, honor killings were recently criminalized, but continue to occur frequently in many communities, particularly in four tribal regions of the country: Punjab, NWFP (North West Frontier Province), Baluchistan, and Sindh. The respective names given to the practice of honor killings in these regions are *kala-kali* (Punjab), *tor-tora* (NWFP), *siyahkari* (Baluchistan) and *karo-kari* (Sindh) (Malik, Saleem, & Hamdani, 2001). Although similar, each of these regional practices has a unique set of characteristics that sets them apart from one another. This review paper will focus on karo-kari, the most common type of honor killing in Pakistan.

Karo-kari is a compound word, which means "black male" and "black female," respectively, metaphoric terms for those who commit illicit premarital or extra-marital relations. A female is labeled a *kari* because of the perceived dishonor that she had brought to her family through her illicit relationship with a man (other than her husband) who is subsequently labeled a *karo*. Once labeled a *kari,* male family members have the self-authorized justification to kill her and the co-accused *karo* in order to restore family honor. Because men more commonly have access to economic resources, allowing them to either flee or buy a pardon from the dishonored family, they are less often killed in such crimes of honor.

Given the paucity of information on this topic and the apparent spread of such violent acts, research in this area is crucial. By examining the motives underlying karo-kari and its epidemiological trends, we hope to gain insight into the relative roles of socio-cultural attitudes and psychopathology in shaping such homicidal practices.

Origin of Karo-Kari

The practice of karo-kari dates to the pre-Islamic period when Arab settlers occupied a region adjacent to Sindh, which was known as Baluchistan (Malik et al., 2001). These early settlers had strongly patriarchal traditions, with such practices as the live burial of unwanted newborn daughters. It is likely that karo-kari originated in, or was facilitated by, the subordination of women underlying these cultural practices. Such gender norms have become deeply entrenched in the social psyche of Sindh, leading to the preservation of karo-kari in the feudal social structure of local tribal communities. Although karo-kari, as a practice and term, is specific to Sindh, the general concept of honor has been independently described in many parts of the world.

Motives for Karo-Kari

The most commonly cited warrant for a karo-kari act is a woman's premarital or extra-marital relations with any man who is not her husband. This may include any form of relationship, regardless of whether it is coerced—as in the case of sexual assault—or consensual—as in the case of women who choose romantic partners without their family's approval. Perceptions of what constitutes dishonor to the family have broadened, with some honor killings linked to situations such as pregnancy out of wedlock, sexual misconduct, and marriage against family approval (Kulwicki, 2002).

In recent years, the label of karo-kari has been used to mask killings that likely occurred for reasons other than restoring family honor, in what have been called "fake honor killings" (Amnesty International, 1999a). An example is the use of karo-kari as a camouflage for men who murder other men in personal disputes. The tradition has been manipulated by tribes to settle rivalries and vendettas; in Pakistan, this was the case in the well-publicized story of Mukhtar Mai (Husain, 2006).

Women who demand divorces from their husbands may elicit a karo-kari attack under a false pretext. By categorizing these homicides as acts of karo-kari, men obtain the customary endorsement for their actions and avoid retribution. Another type of factitious honor killing occurs in the poorer communities of Sindh, especially when a woman is felt to have become a financial burden on the household. These communities sometimes use karo-kari as a convenient way of acquiring wealth or land by declaring a woman of their household a kari. This allows the family to obtain the victim's share of inheritance, as well as appropriate compensation from the co-accused karo of their choice. Other financially motivated killings represented as karo-kari are often connected to marriages arranged within a family to retain property, or attempts to prevent a widow or divorced mother from remarrying in order to avoid the transfer of wealth to another family.

Epidemiology of Karo-Kari

The United Nations Population Fund estimates that at least 5,000 women worldwide are victims of honor killings each year (UNCHR, 2002). Many of these homicides occur in Pakistan. This figure is probably an under-estimate since many cases of honor killing go unreported, especially in patriarchal societies that sanction this practice. Additionally, in countries where the practice of honor killing is outlawed but supported by portions of the population, communities attempt to cover up such acts to avoid legal authorities from disrupting a sacred cultural practice.

Although several agencies in Pakistan have attempted to quantify the national incidence rate of honor killings and karo-kari acts, these numbers are also likely to underestimate the actual incidence levels. The inaccuracy of these reported rates is reflected in the wide discrepancies between figures provided by various agencies. For instance, while the Human Rights Commission of Pakistan reports 1,464 honor killings occurred in Pakistan between 1998 and 2002 (HRCP, 2004), the Pakistan government reports

4,101 registered honor killings between 1998 and 2003 (HRCP, 2004). The Madadgaar helpline database gives a figure of 3,339 honor killings between 2000 and 2004 (Awan, 2004), and finally, a police report indicated that a total of 4,383 honor killings were reported in Pakistan between 2001 and 2004, with 2,228 of these occurring in Sindh (*The Daily Jang*, 2006).

It is unclear what proportion of these honor killings were of the karo-kari type. However, during the few years that Human Rights Commission of Pakistan has enumerated separate statistics for karo-kari, such deaths have accounted for the majority of honor killings in Pakistan. These data indicate that the total number of karo-kari deaths since 2004 is 416 (see Reading Table 10.1).

Profile of Karo-Kari Victims, Perpetrators, and Accomplices

Victims of karo-kari are most often married adult females (HRCP, 2006). Nevertheless, those who are single or male may also be affected, and at any age. The same combination of economic vulnerability, limited social support and lack of knowledge regarding their legal rights, which prevent[s] women from changing their subordinate status in society, put[s] them at a higher risk for experiencing violence. Thus, women who are unemployed, illiterate, and live in impoverished conditions have a higher risk than others of becoming a karo-kari victim (Niaz, 2001).

The psychological burden placed on females in a patriarchal society is evident in the high prevalence of mental illness among women in Pakistan. Hence, it is possible that many victims of honor killings may have suffered from mental illness. Moreover, it is inevitable that as soon as a woman is labeled a kari she will endure significant psychological distress, which may even lead her to commit suicide prior to the inevitable homicide.

Almost all perpetrators of karo-kari are male family members, most commonly husbands, followed by brothers (Reading Table 10.1). When possible, families choose males under the age of eighteen to carry out the murder, most likely because juvenile offenders serve the shortest prison terms. However, karo-kari may also be linked to the intense competition for honor, status, and marriage

Reading Table 10.1 Characteristics of Homicides, Honor Killings, and Karo-Kari Deaths in Pakistan Between 2004 and mid-2006

	Year			
	2004	**2005**	**2006 (to June)**	**Total**
Homicides				
Total homicides	624	229	172	1025
Honour killings	302	152	114	568
Karo-kari deaths	277	113	26	416
Perpetrators of karo-kari				
Father	7	5	1	13
Brother	44	13	4	61
Husband	112	52	13	177
In-law	19	4	1	24
Relative	27	9	2	38
Son	5	4	0	9
Non-family	2	0	2	4
Action against perpetrator				
Accused of karo-kari	365	195	66	626
Arrested	68	36	6	110

SOURCE: Adapted from the Human Rights Commission of Pakistan.

ability among young men (Cohen, 1998). Other factors which may lead certain men to commit honor killings include socioeconomic disadvantage and the pressure to fulfill the gender norms of their culture. Specifically, men who find themselves unable to meet their gender role expectations, may resort to violence against women in order to assert their masculinity or as an outlet for frustration (Krishnan 2005).

In countries where honor killings are illegal, some lawyers have employed the "honor defense" as an exculpatory strategy for perpetrators. Underlying this defense

are the ideas that women are considered the property of men and that the protection of honor is a type of self-defense. Other perpetrators have attempted to use the "temporary insanity" or "crime of passion" defense, arguing that their homicidal acts were not premeditated but caused by extreme provocation which led to psychological distress and subsequent loss of self-control and impaired judgment (*Yale Law Journal*, 1934; [Canadian Legal] Can LII, 2006).

To date, no studies have examined the presence of a psychopathological process leading perpetrators to commit karo-kari. However, many of the case reports of karo-kari reviewed indicated the presence of certain psychopathic traits in perpetrators, including a reckless disregard for the safety of women, a failure to conform to lawful behaviors, and a lack of remorse. The fact that some have used the honor killing tradition to conceal other motives for their homicidal actions lends weight to the argument for an underlying psychopathic process. The majority of karo-kari killings are quite violent, most commonly committed using firearms. Other methods include stabbing, strangulation, hanging, electrocution, or poisoning (HRCP, 2006). Finally, the fact that most perpetrators attempt to cover up their actions suggests that they have preserved insight into the criminal nature of karo-kari, although they believe that restoring family honor is more important.

The patriarchal cultural values prevailing in Pakistan have often led victims' relatives and community members, as well as legal and government authorities to act as explicit or implicit accomplices in karo-kari deaths. Because they view karo-kari as a culturally acceptable and even heroic act, many family and community members help to cover up such homicides by maintaining silence during investigations. Others keep silent because they fear retribution. Tribal courts have [been] known to impose death sentences on those who report honor killings to the police (*The Daily Times*, Pakistan, 2006).

Legal and government authorities often contribute to covering up karo-kari deaths simply by avoiding any involvement in such cases. Even when they do become involved, gender discrimination continues to create support for the perpetrator. Corruption among government authorities can result in a further disadvantage for females, who are less likely to have access to monetary resources or social capital. The small percentage of accused perpetrators who are arrested (Reading Table 10.1) illustrates the lack of legal intervention in cases of karo-kari.

⋈ Socio-Cultural Influences and Karo-Kari

Some individuals and communities in Pakistan have maintained traditional patriarchal interpretations of Islam, which valorize female chastity and male superiority. The power dynamics of patriarchy tend to reduce women to their reproductive potential, in the process denying them agency as human beings.

In some communities, women are considered to have monetary value and are the property of their male relatives. It is thought that the preservation of a woman's chastity and fidelity, through segregation and control, is the responsibility of the men to whom she belongs. By engaging in an illicit affair, a woman comes into conflict with the socio-cultural framework of meanings prevalent in much of Pakistan, and [it] is seen as having seriously violated the honor of her family. Some believe that in such cases, it is a man's duty to restore his family's honor by killing those who damaged it. Both notion of honor and the concept of women as property are deeply woven into the socio-cultural fabric of Pakistan, leading many individuals, including women, to support the practice of honor killing and others such as legal authorities to look the other way. Such widely held values have also given perpetrators an excellent legal defense when they commit such acts.

Some national legal codes explicitly allow for "honor killing." For example, in Jordan, part of article 340 of the penal code states that "he who discovers his wife or one of his female relatives committing adultery and kills, wounds, or injures one of them, is exempted from penalty." Despite efforts to rewrite the law, the article was retained by parliament. Similar provisions appear in the penal codes of Syria (article 548), Morocco (article 418), and Haiti (article 269). On the other hand, persons found guilty of honor killings in Turkey are sentenced to life in prison (UNCHR, 2002).

In Sindh (Pakistan), many tribal communities employ an informal legal system based on feudal principles, such as forced domestic labor and custodial violence. Despite being unrecognized by Pakistan's formal legal system, such tribal courts adjudicate the majority of karo-kari cases which obtain any legal hearing. Such courts generally sanction honor killings, and they are preferred by individuals in tribal communities because they provide inexpensive and expeditious access to justice.

Pakistan's formal justice system includes laws which seem to endorse the gender-biased rulings of tribal courts. For instance, the 1979 "Hudood Ordinance" criminalized extra-marital sex by females. The law also made it difficult for a woman to prove an allegation of rape by requiring that at least four adult male Muslim witnesses of good character attest to the act of sexual penetration.

Furthermore, a male suspect had the opportunity to testify against the woman in court. A failure to prove the act of rape placed the woman at risk of prosecution for adultery, the punishment for which was death by stoning. Not only did this law play a role in giving legal sanction to women's subordinate social status, it gave implicit legal and cultural justification for the practice of karo-kari. Fundamentalist social forces in Pakistan strongly opposed any change in the law as they falsely believed it to be in accordance with the teachings of Islam.

In December 2004, under international and domestic pressure, the Pakistani government enacted a law that made the practice of karo-kari punishable by death, in the same manner as other homicides. On the other hand, in March 2005, the Pakistani government allied with opposition conservative Islamic parties to reject a bill, which would have strengthened the law against the practice of karo-kari. Finally, in November 2006, the "Hudood Ordinance" was abolished and replaced by the new "Women's Protection Bill" (Government of Pakistan, 2006). Despite these new laws, socio-cultural patterns and feudal attitudes remain largely unchanged: many Pakistanis feel that karo-kari homicides are justifiable and therefore deserve legal pardon. As a result, perpetrators are rarely brought to justice. The few cases that go to court are usually plagued by gender discrimination resulting in lenient sentences or pardons for men. Also, because karo-kari is a crime of retaliation, judges have the option at their own discretion to allow victims' families to accept a simple apology, money, land, or another female from the perpetrator as compensation for the crime. These factors make it almost inevitable that perpetrators will escape a severe punishment for such homicides.

Mental Health and Karo-Kari

While cultural assumptions about family relationships, the meaning of honor, and appropriate gender roles clearly shape the accepting view many members of tribal communities take toward karo-kari, many other individuals with similar backgrounds do not take part in or endorse such acts. Thus, it is important to also consider the role of psychopathy in the perpetrators of karo-kari.

With respect to the victims, there is global consensus among researchers on the fact that that oppression and violence not only violate women's basic rights but also threaten their health and the very state of their being. Patriarchal values, which greatly contribute to the persistence of karo-kari, often result in domestic disharmony and have an adverse psychological impact on many women in Pakistan (Niaz, 2004). The frequency and unexpectedness of karo-kari killings also contribute to the experience of uncertainty and fear among Pakistani women which, along with a lack of autonomy and equal opportunities, has the potential to erode their self-esteem and thereby increase their risk for developing a variety of psychiatric disorders, such as depression and anxiety.

Studies suggest that domestic strife is a primary cause of psychiatric illness in Pakistani women. A five-year study at the University Psychiatry Department in Karachi showed that out of 212 patients receiving psychotherapy, 65% were women who presented primarily due to conflicts with their spouse and in-laws (Zaman, in press). Interestingly, 50% of these women had no psychiatric diagnosis and were labeled "distressed women" while 28% suffered from depression or anxiety. Additionally, a four-year study of psychiatric outpatients at a private clinic in Karachi found that 66% of the patients were females, of whom 60% had a mood disorder, 70% were victims of violence, and 80% struggled with domestic conflicts (Niaz, 1994).

Some women who are labeled "kari" commit "honor suicides" because of the shame they experience from committing a dishonourable act or because they fear being brutally attacked (Amnesty International, 1999b). Other karo-kari deaths categorized as suicides include cases in which a woman is forced to kill herself or is secretly poisoned. Such cases may partly account for the high rates of suicides among married Pakistani women reported in studies (Niaz, 1997).

In rural Sindh, there are rare instances when a woman manages to escape a karo-kari death. Although these women encounter a lack of social support, they do have the option to seek refuge in the home of a tribal holy man, known as a "wadero." The wadero will protect the woman for the rest of her lifetime as long as she obliges with his conditions, which may include acting as his unpaid servant.

She may also be exposed to significant emotional and physical abuse by the wadero. As a result, even such "safe havens" may have a profoundly negative psychological impact on women who escape from karo-kari.

An additional psychological burden is endured by children who witness domestic conflicts and karo-kari acts. These children face an increased risk for behavioral problems, substance abuse, anxiety, and depression.

Conclusion

Mental health clinicians can play a number of important roles in dealing with psychiatric issues associated with karo-kari. At the clinical level, it is important to take careful histories from women presenting to clinics in areas where "honor killing" is common. Mental health practitioners can report concerns about a patient's safety to law enforcement agencies. While it may not be safe for medical professionals to publicly denounce karo-kari practices in these areas, they can become part of campaigns to raise awareness and educate the public on such issues. Unfortunately, concerns for personal security have generally kept many mental health professionals from becoming involved in such efforts.

Additional research on the relationship between culture and psychopathology in karo-kari will allow clinicians to identify persons at risk and to help potential victims and their families. Many studies have shown that the incidence rate of mental disorders among homicide offenders can be as high as 90% (Fazel & Grann, 2004). Better understanding of the socio-cultural context that leads to karo-kari, would allow clinicians to intervene early when patients at risk for a homicide present with domestic disharmony. In the event of a killing, clinicians can also play a role in managing the psychological sequelae of karo-kari on the victims' families, as well as other community members. Finally, clinicians must consider the possible role of psychopathy, along with socio-cultural influences, as factors that may predispose perpetrators to commit karo-kari acts.

References

Amnesty International. (1999a). *Pakistan: Honour killings of girls and women* (September). Report No.: ASA 33/18/99.

Amnesty International. (1999b). *Pakistan: Violence against women in the name of honour.* AI Index: ASA 33/17/99.

Awan, Z. (2004). *Violence against women and impediments in access to justice.* World Bank.

Canadian Legal Information Institute. Review of Judicial Processes. Available at: http://www.canlii.org/on/cas/onca/2006/20060nca1 0275.html. Accessed: 10 November 2007.

Cohen, D. (1998). Culture, social organization, and patterns of violence. *Journal of Personality and Social Psychology, 75*, 408–419.

Fazel, S., & Grann, M. (2004). Psychiatric morbidity among homicide offenders: A Swedish population study. *American Journal of Psychiatry, 161*, 2129–2131.

Gardner, J. (1986). *Women in Roman law and society.* Bloomington: Indiana University Press.

Goldstein, M. (2002). The biological roots of heat-of-passion crimes and honour killings. *Politics and the Life Sciences, 21*, 28–37.

Government of Pakistan. (2006). Protection of Women (Criminal Amendment) Act, 2006. Available at: www.pakistani.org/pakistan/legislation/2006/wp6.html. Accessed: 18 July 2008.

Human Rights Commission of Pakistan (HRCP). (2004). Honour Killings. Available at: http://www.hrcp-web.org/Women.cfm. Accessed: 6 December 2007.

Husain, M. (2006). "Take my riches, give me justice": A contextual analysis of Pakistan's honour crimes legislation. *Harvard Journal of Law & Gender, 29*, 221–246.

Krishnan, S. (2005). Do structural inequalities contribute to marital violence? Ethnographic evidence from rural South India. *Violence against Women, 11*, 759–775.

Kulwicki, A. D. (2002). The practice of honour crimes: A glimpse of domestic violence in the Arab world. *Issues in Mental Health Nursing, 23*, 77–87.

Malik, N., Saleem, I., & Hamdani, I. (2001). *Karo Kari, TorTora, Siyahkari, Kala Kali: There is no honour in killing.* National Seminar Report, findings from the Shirkat Gah "Women, Law and Status Programme" involving broad based and systematic research into honour crimes in Punjab, North Western Frontier Province and Sindh; November 25; Lahore, Pakistan. WLUML.

Niaz, U. (1994). Human rights abuse in family. *Journal of Pakistan Association of Women's Studies, 3*, 33–41.

Niaz, U. (1997). Contemporary issues of Pakistani women: A psychosocial perspective. *Journal of Pakistan Association of Women's Studies, 6*, 29–50.

Niaz, U. (2001). Overview of women's mental health in Pakistan. *Pakistan Journal of Medical Science, 17*, 203–209.

Niaz, U. (2004). Women's mental health in Pakistan. *World Psychiatry, 3:* 60–62.

The Daily Jang, Pakistan. (2006). "Honour Killings." Available at: http://www.jang.com.pk/thenews/nov2005-daily/27-11-2005/metro/k1.htm. Accessed: 2 February 2007.

The Daily Times, Pakistan. (2006). "Honour Killings." Available at: http://www.dailytimes.com.pk/default.asp?page=

2006%5C04%5C29%5Cstory_29–4–2006_pg7_1. Accessed: 5 May 2007.

The Yale Law Journal Company, Inc. (1934). Recognition of the honour defence under the insanity plea. *Yale Law Journal, 43,* 809–814.

United Nations Commission on Human Rights. (2002). *Working towards the elimination of crimes against women committed in the name of honour.* 57th session of the United Nations Commission on Human Rights, United Nations, Report No.: 0246790.

United Nations Commission on Human Rights. (2002). 58th session "Cultural practices in the family that are violent towards women" E/CN. 4/2002/83.

Zaman, R. (in press). Karachi University Psychology Department: Five-year survey (1992–1996).

DISCUSSION QUESTIONS

1. How is the tradition of karo-kari different from other forms of honor killing?

2. What role does patriarchy play in the continuing practice of karo-kari?

3. How can mental health practitioners help in communities where the practice of karo-kari is common?

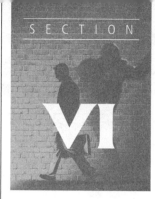

Theories on Female Offending

- Critiques of traditional explanations of crime
- Feminist criminology
- The intersections of criminal victimization and offending

This section is devoted to the theoretical explanations of female offending. The section begins with a review of the failures of mainstream criminology to provide adequate explanations for women who offend. This section first examines how traditional theories of crime failed to understand how female offenders differed from male offenders. While these original authors did little to acknowledge gender, scholars have since looked to whether modern-day applications of these perspectives can help explain female offending. The section then turns to a discussion on how feminist scholars have sought out new theories to represent the female offender and her social world. The section concludes with a discussion on feminist criminology and how the offending patterns of women are often intertwined with their experiences of victimization.

Theoretical Perspectives on Female Criminality

Theories on criminal behavior try to explain why offenders engage in crime. These theories of crime may focus on causes of crime from either macro or micro explanations for criminal behavior. Macro theories of crime explore the large-scale social explanations for crime, such as poverty and community disorganization. In contrast, micro theories of crime focus on individual differences between law-abiding and law-violating behaviors. Since the late 19th century,

Figure 6.1   Timeline on Theories of Female Offending

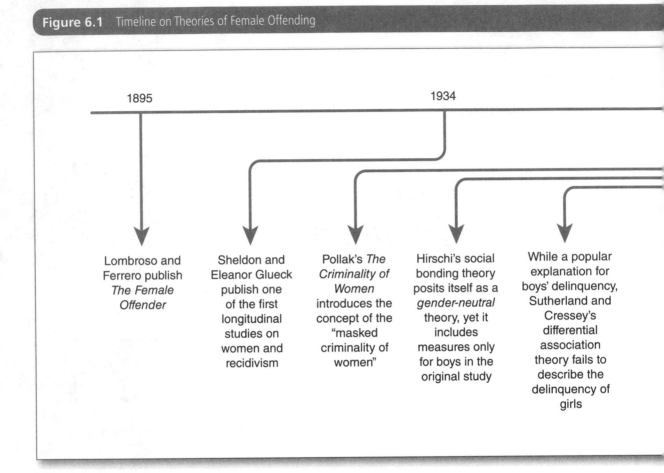

researchers have investigated the relationship between gender, crime, and punishment from macro as well as micro perspectives. As Belknap reflects, "Female lawbreakers historically (and to some degree today) have been viewed as abnormal and as worse than male lawbreakers—not only for breaking the law but also for stepping outside of prescribed gender roles of femininity and passivity" (2007, p. 34). Theories on the nature of female criminality have ranged from describing these offenders as aggressive and violent to women who are passive, helpless, and in need of protection. Consequently, theories on the etiology of female offending have reflected both of these perspectives. While theories on female crime have grown significantly from the early perspectives, it is important to debate the tenets of these historical viewpoints, as they provide a foundation for a greater understanding of female offending (see Figure 6.1).

Historical Theories on Female Criminality

Cesare Lombroso and William Ferrero represent the first criminologists to attempt to investigate the nature of the female offender. Expanding on his earlier work, *The Criminal Man*, Lombroso joined with Ferrero in 1895 to publish *The Female Offender*. Lombroso's basic idea was that criminals are biological throwbacks to a primitive breed of man and can be recognized by various "atavistic" degenerative physical characteristics. To test this theory for female offenders, Lombroso and Ferrero went to women's prisons, where they measured body parts and noted physical

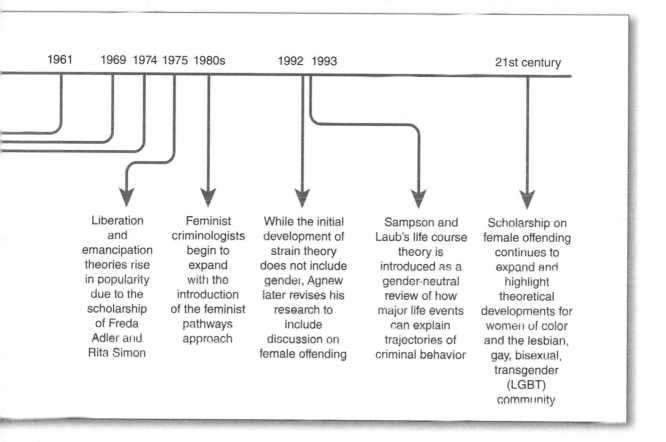

1961   1969 1974 1975 1980s   1992 1993   21st century

Liberation and emancipation theories rise in popularity due to the scholarship of Freda Adler and Rita Simon

Feminist criminologists begin to expand with the introduction of the feminist pathways approach

While the initial development of strain theory does not include gender, Agnew later revises his research to include discussion on female offending

Sampson and Laub's life course theory is introduced as a gender-neutral review of how major life events can explain trajectories of criminal behavior

Scholarship on female offending continues to expand and highlight theoretical developments for women of color and the lesbian, gay, bisexual, transgender (LGBT) community

differences of the incarcerated women. They attributed a number of unique features to the female criminal, including occipital irregularities, narrow foreheads, prominent cheekbones, and a "virile" type of face. Although they found that female offenders had fewer degenerative characteristics compared to male offenders, they explained these differences by suggesting that women, in general, are biologically more primitive and less evolved than men. They also suggested that the "evil tendencies" of female offenders "are more numerous and more varied than men's" (Lombroso & Ferrero, 1895, p. 151). Female criminals were believed to be more like men than women, both in terms of their mental and physical qualities, suggesting that female offenders were more likely to experience suppressed "maternal instincts" and "ladylike" qualities. They were convinced that women who engaged in crime would be less sensitive to pain, less compassionate, generally jealous, and full of revenge—in short, criminal women possessed all of the worst characteristics of the female gender while embodying the criminal tendencies of the male.

The methods and findings of Lombroso and Ferrero have been harshly criticized, mostly due to their small sample size and the lack of heterogeneity of their sample demographics. They also failed to control for additional environmental and structural variables that might explain criminal behavior regardless of gender. Finally, their key assumptions about women had no scientific basis. Their claim that the female offender was more ruthless and less merciful had more to do with the fact that she had violated sex-role and gender-role expectations than the nature of her actual offending behaviors.

The works of Sheldon and Eleanor Glueck represent some of the earliest longitudinal studies on crime and delinquency. In 1934, the Gluecks followed up their study of 500 incarcerated men with a similar study on the female offender, titled *Five Hundred Delinquent Women*. These researchers sought only to distinguish female offenders from male offenders, but this work was also one of the first studies on recidivism among this population. Although *Five Hundred Delinquent Women* was not as well known as their other works, it was similar in philosophy and methodology to their other publications. Most notably, the Gluecks looked at a variety of different factors to explain criminality, which was a dramatically different approach compared to other studies during this time period. For example, they were among some of the first researchers to investigate the role of the family on delinquency. In addition, the Gluecks drew from a multidisciplinary perspective, and they were influenced by a variety of disciplines such as biology, sociology, psychology, and anthropology.

More than a half century passed between the publication of Lombroso and Ferrero's *The Female Offender* and the publication of *The Criminality of Women* by **Otto Pollak** (1961). Pollak believed that criminal data sources failed to reflect the true extent of female crime. His assertion was that since the majority of the crimes in which women engage are petty in nature, many victims do not report these crimes, particularly when the victim is a male. Additionally, he suggested that many police officers exercise discretion when confronted with female crime and may issue only informal warnings in these cases. His data also indicated that women were more likely to be acquitted, compared to their male counterparts. Altogether, he concluded that the crimes of women are underreported, and when reported, these women benefit from preferential treatment by the systems of criminal justice. His discussion of the **masked criminality of women** suggested that women gain power by deceiving men through sexual playacting, faked sexual responses, and menstruation. This power allowed female criminality to go undetected by society. Likewise, Pollak believed that the traditional female roles of homemaker, caretaker, and domestic worker gave women an avenue to engage in crimes against vulnerable populations, such as children and the elderly.

While each of these works represented a new frontier in criminological theory, much of the assumptions about gender were significantly flawed. These early theories of female criminality placed a heavy reliance on stereotypes about the female offender as manipulative, cunning, and masculine—all identities that limited the analysis of female criminality to a narrow perception of the world.

Traditional Theories of Crime and Gender

A number of criminological theories rose to fame during the mid- and late 20th century. The majority of these explanations focused exclusively on male criminality, with little consideration for women's lives. Many of these theorists excluded women from their research on the grounds that they represented such a small proportion of the offending population. Instead, some theorists simply made gross gendered stereotypes about women and girls.

Travis Hirschi's social bond theory (1969) is one example of an alleged gender-neutral theory of crime that failed to consider the lives of girls and women. While most theories up to this point focused on why offenders engage in crime, Hirschi's work was unique in that looked for explanations as to why people might desist from criminal behavior. His theory focused on four criteria, or *bonds,* that prevent people from acting on potential criminological impulses or desires. He identified these bonds as (1) **attachment**, (2) **commitment**, (3) **involvement**, and (4) **belief**. *Attachment* refers to the bond that people have with family, friends, and social institutions (such as government, education, and religion) that may serve as an informal control against criminality. Hirschi posited that people refrain from criminal behavior as a result of these attachments as they do not want to disappoint people in their lives. For example, youth who have positive attachments to parents or peers may limit their delinquent behavior because they do not want to disappoint these important relationships. The second concept, *commitment,* refers to the investment that an individual has to the normative values of society. In many ways, the concept of commitment embodies the spirit of rational choice perspectives. For example, if one is committed to obtaining a college degree, then a violation of the law might limit one's ability to achieve that goal. As a result, one might decide not to engage in the illegal behavior out of fear of jeopardizing one's future. *Involvement* refers to the level at which one might participate in conventional activities such as studying or playing sports. The idea behind involvement is that youth who are more involved in these sorts of activities are less likely to engage in delinquent activities. Finally, *belief* refers to a general acceptance of the rules of society— "the less a person believes he should obey the rules, the more likely he is to violate them" (Hirschi, 1969, p. 26).

For Hirschi, families serve as one of the strongest inhibitors of delinquency. Research shows that the attachment to the family unit varies by gender, as girls are more emotionally attached to their parents. It is this bond that serves to protect girls from delinquency (Heimer, 1996). Likewise, research by Huebner and Betts (2002) showed that a strong attachment bond to parents and other adults serves as a protective factor for girls. However, this attachment to the family may also be related to the increased focus of parents on their daughters. As a result, when girls engage in delinquent behavior, they can experience higher levels of shaming by their parents (Svensson, 2004).

▲ **Photo 6.1** Throughout the 20th century, the number of arrests involving females has increased dramatically. Feminist criminologists highlight that many of the traditional theories of crime fail to address the unique needs of offending women. In addition, much of these data reflect changes in policies regarding societal perspectives of female offending versus a direct increase in the rates of offending by women.

While much has been said about the influence of social bond theory on delinquency, the majority of this scholarship has been restricted to the American criminal justice system. Research by Ozbay and Ozcan (2008) investigate whether **social bond theory** can be used to explain the context of male and female delinquency among Turkish youth. Like findings on American youth, their results indicate that social bonds have a stronger effect on the lives of female students. Within Turkish cultures, the family is an important institution, and girls are highly attached to the family unit. Much of this has to do with differential socialization between the sexes. In contrast, the attachment to school and teachers is a stronger influence in preventing delinquency for boys. While studies on American students indicate that an attachment to school can serve as a protective factor against delinquency for both boys and girls (Lowe, May, & Elrod, 2008), girls who are less attached to school are more likely to engage in nonviolent acts of delinquency (Daigle, Cullen, & Wright, 2007). Educational bonds can also help explain why girls are less likely to engage in alcohol and marijuana use compared to boys (Whaley, Hayes-Smith & Hayes-Smith, 2010).

While Hirschi's social bond theory is considered a macro-level perspective on criminal behavior, his general theory of crime (with Michael Gottfredson) is considered more of a micro-level theory. Gottfredson and Hirschi focus on self-control as the single explanative factor for delinquent and criminal behavior. According to the general theory of crime, those individuals with high levels of social control will remain law abiding, while those with low social control will be more likely to engage in deviant and criminal activities. But the question remains: What influences an individual's self-control, and for the purposes of this discussion, what role does gender play in this process? Gottfredson and Hirschi posit that the development of self-control is rooted in the family. The more involved parents are in their children's lives, the more likely they are to be aware of challenges to the development of their children's self-control. This awareness then leads to action, and parents are more likely to correct these issues at a young age. As a result,

Gottfredson and Hirschi's general theory of crime suggests that early intervention efforts are the only effective tool to deter individuals from crime. From their perspective, variables such as gender, race, and class are irrelevant, as everything comes down to self-control (Gottfredson & Hirschi, 1990).

Since the development of Gottfredson and Hirschi's general theory of crime, many researchers have looked at the role of gender in this process using constructs such as impulsivity, risk taking, and aggression as indicators of self-control. However, these findings demonstrate that the general theory of crime can explain the delinquency of boys but fails in its explanation for girls. For example, research by DeLisi et al. (2010) on delinquent youth housed in the California Youth Authority facility indicate that while self-control measures are effective in predicting behavioral violations for incarcerated males, the misconduct in girls is more likely to be explained by other variables such as age (younger girls are more likely to act out) and the presence of a psychiatric disorder. Meanwhile, research by Shekarkhar and Gibson (2011) noted that while low self-control did predict offending behaviors for Latino boys and girls in terms of violent offenses, it did not predict the behaviors of girls who engage in property offenses (which generally comprise much of female offending patterns). Even in those studies where self-control might explain the offending characteristics for girls, these effects are often eliminated when other variables such as opportunity or social learning theory are introduced (Burton, Cullen, Evans, Alarid, & Dunaway, 1998; LaGrange & Silverman, 1999).

Edwin Sutherland's (Sutherland, & Cressey 1974) **differential association theory** focuses on the influence of how relationships lead to crime, in particular, the influence of peer relationships on delinquent behavior. Differential association theory is influenced by social learning theory, which suggests that criminality is a learned behavior. Differential association theory posits that these learned behaviors are a result of peer associations. As youth spend time with people, these people then influence their knowledge, practices, and judgments on delinquent behavior. The more that people are exposed to these delinquent attitudes and behaviors, the more they are able to influence this person. Like many social theories of the 20th century, discussions of gender were absent in differential association theory.

Recent research has provided mixed results in the application of differential association theory for female offenders. In addition, race and ethnicity also impact the effects of the peer relationship for girls' delinquency. Silverman and Caldwell (2008) find that peer attitudes have the greatest effect on youth behavior for Hispanic girls. Here, the *strength of the peer relationship* plays a key factor—if the peer group deems that delinquency is an acceptable behavior, the rates of violent delinquent behavior increase. In contrast, *time* plays the biggest role for White girls. As the proportion of time that is spent with the peer group increases, the greater the influence these peers have on violent delinquent behavior (Silverman & Caldwell, 2008). However, not all research demonstrates support for the applications of differential association theory to girls. Research by Daigle et al. (2007) and Lowe, May, and Elrod (2008) indicates that influences from delinquent peers does lead to an increase in delinquency for boys but that negative peer influence does not have an effect for girls. Here, it may be that while peer associations can impact delinquency, the effect is stronger for the delinquency of boys than girls (Piquero, Gover, MacDonald, & Piquero, 2005).

Another theory that has frequently been used to explain offending behaviors is *strain theory*. While several theorists have made contributions to the understanding of how an individual's aspirations collide with the goals of society, the works of Robert Agnew represent perhaps the most modern of these applications in terms of criminal behavior. While traditional theories of strain by scholars such as Merton (1938) and Cohen (1955) focused on the structural limitations of success, Agnew's (1992) general strain theory looks into individualized psychological sources as correlates of criminal behavior. Agnew highlights three potential sources of strain: (1) failure in achieving positive goals, (2) the loss of positive influences, and (3) the arrival of negative influences.

Agnew has continued to develop his general strain theory to consider how strain might impact the delinquency and at-risk behaviors for girls as well as boys. Research by Broidy and Agnew (1997) argues that general strain theory can be used to explain gender differences in crime. However, it is important to keep some key distinctions in mind when using a gendered approach to general strain theory. First, males and females have different sources of strain. For example, girls are more likely to experience strain as a result of violence in the home (physical, emotional, and sexual), which in turn leads to delinquent acts, such as running away and substance abuse. Second, boys and girls respond to strain differently. Here, Broidy and Agnew highlight that while strain can manifest as anger for both boys and girls, they exhibit this anger in different ways. For example, girls are more likely to internalize their feelings of anger, which can lead to issues of self-destructive behaviors and depression. In contrast, boys tend to exhibit anger in physical and emotional outbursts (Broidy & Agnew, 1997).

In addition to the work by Broidy & Agnew, other scholars have looked at how gender can impact how youth experience strain. While boys experience higher levels of traditional strain than girls (defined here as aspirations for higher educational success), girls are more likely to have negative life events and report higher levels of conflict

© Bettmann/Corbis

▲ **Photo 6.2**   Susan Atkins, Patricia Krenwinkel, and Leslie Van Houten walk to their hearing in the murder case of Sharon Tate in 1970. The three women, known as the Manson Women, were sentenced to death, but their sentences were commuted to life in prison. While each of the women has faced numerous parole hearings, Krenwinkel and Van Houten remain incarcerated in California Institute for Women, Chino. Atkins died of cancer in 2009.

with their parents. Yet it is these negative life events and higher levels of conflict that increase the involvement in delinquency. Some research indicates that educational success becomes the vehicle for bringing out these issues (Daigle et al., 2007) while others identify specific experiences with strain (such as a history of physical abuse or living with someone who uses drugs and alcohol) as an indirect cause of daily substance abuse (Sharp, Peck, & Hartsfield, 2012). Meanwhile, research by Garcia and Lane (2012) identifies that a major source of strain among female delinquents is relationship strain. Strain within the family (such as with parents) can manifest in behaviors such as running away, substance abuse, or poor relationships choices. These poor relationship choices can also be their own source of strain, particularly when girls become involved with system-involved or older males. Peer relationships can also perpetuate strain, particularly in the cases of *frenemies*. Unlike other theories which discuss how deviant peers might encourage delinquency, Garcia and Lane find that girls may engage in delinquent acts (such as fights) out of anger toward other female peers or status offenses (such as truancy) in an effort to avoid being bullied.

While these classical theories of crime generally offered little evidence or explanation about female criminal activity at their inception, later research has investigated if and how these traditional theories of crime can understand the role of gender in offending. To date, these conclusions are mixed—while some provide evidence that these theories can make contributions to understanding female crime, others are more suited to explain male criminality, as they were originally conceived.

Modern Theories of Female Offending Behaviors

The emergence of works by **Freda Adler** and **Rita Simon** in the 1970s marked a significant shift in the study of female criminality. The works of Adler and Simon were inspired by the emancipation of women that was occurring during the 1960s and 1970s in the United States and the effects of the second wave of the feminist movement. Both authors highlighted how the liberation of women would lead to an increased participation of women in criminal activities. While Adler (1975) suggested that women's rates of violent crime would increase, Simon (1975) hypothesized that women would commit a greater proportion of property crimes as a result of their liberation from traditional gender roles and restrictions. While both authors broke new ground in the discussion of female crime, their research has also been heavily criticized. Analysis on crime statistics between 1960 and 1975 indicates that while female crime rates for violent crimes skyrocketed during this time period, so did the rates of male violent crime. In addition, one must consider the reference point of these statistics. True, more women engaged in crime. However, given the low number of female offenders in general, small increases in the number of crimes can create a large percentage increase, which can be misinterpreted and overexaggerated. For example, if women are involved in 100 burglaries in one year and this number increases to 150 burglaries in the next year, this reflects a 50% increase from one year to the next. If, however, men participated in 1,000 burglaries in one year and in 1,250 during the next, this is only a 25% increase, even though the actual numerical increase is greater for men than women.

Another criticism of Adler and Simon's works focuses on their overreliance on the effects of the women's liberation movement. While it is true that the emancipation of women created increased opportunities and freedoms to engage in crime, this does not necessarily mean that women were more compelled to engage in crime. Changing policies in policing and the processing of female offenders may reflect an increase of women in the system as a result of changes in the response by the criminal justice system to crimes involving women.

In addition to Adler and Simon's focus on the emancipation of women as an explanation for increasing crime rates, theories shifted from a focus on individual pathology to one that referenced social processes and the greater social environment. One of the few theories during this time frame that incorporated gender as a major theme was **power control theory** which assesses how patriarchy can influence gender-role socialization and, in turn, how this process impacts rates of delinquency. Developed by **John Hagan** (1989), power control theory starts with the premise that women and girls are socialized in different ways from men and boys. For example, under a patriarchal family structure, boys will be encouraged to be more aggressive, ambitious, and outgoing and benefit from increased freedom compared to girls. Power control theory suggests that these differences in power lead girls to have lower rates of crime due to reduced opportunities. In contrast, families that are structured in a more egalitarian or balanced manner will socialize their children in a similar fashion regardless of their sex. This in turn leads to fewer gender differences in delinquency. For example, women in South Korea that were raised within a more patriarchial family structure were likely to be law-abiding (regardless if they were high or low risk takers) while families with less patriarchial families were more likely to engage in criminal behaviors (Kim, Gerber, Henderson, & Kim, 2012).

One of the major weaknesses of Hagan's theory is that it focuses on the two-parent family structure—under a patriarchal structure one could assume that the father or male figurehead exerts the primary source of control in the family. As the number of children residing in divorced, separated, and non-cohabitating homes continues to increase, it is important to consider how power control theory might apply in these settings. Research by Bates, Bader, and Mencken (2003) finds that single fathers tend to exert similar levels of parental control over their children compared to two-parent patriarchal families, while single mothers exert lower levels of parental control over children. In families with higher levels of parental control, girls are more likely to refrain from deviant behaviors as they view them as risky. Yet the single parent may be less likely to exert parental control over his child due to reduced opportunities to supervise the youth. As a result, this family structure may present an indirect, though important, effect on youth delinquency.

Another modern theory that has been used to investigate the causes of female offending is **Robert Sampson** and **John Laub's** (1993) **life course theory**. Life course theory suggests that the events of one's life (from birth to death) can provide insight as to why one might engage in crime and highlights the importance of adolescence as a crucial time in the development of youthful (and ultimately adult) offending behaviors. Here, ties to conventional adult activities such as family and work can serve as a protective factor in adulthood, even if the individual has engaged in delinquent acts during adolescence. While not specifically a feminist theory of crime, life course theory does allow for a gender-neutral review of how the different developmental milestones in one's life can explain criminal behavior.

Recent applications of life course theory have included discussions of gender in their analyses. Research by Thompson and Petrovic (2009) investigated how variables such as marriage, education, employment, and children can have gendered effects on an individual's illegal substance use. Their research indicates that these social bonds impact men and women differently. While Sampson and Laub suggested that marriage serves to inhibit criminal behavior in men, Thompson and Petrovic (2009) did not find a similar effect for women in terms of illicit drug use. Their findings indicate that marriage alone is not enough to reduce illicit drug use for women. Instead, it is the strength of the marriage that has an effect in reducing substance abuse for women. Adding to the discussion on life course theory and women, research by Estrada and Nilsson (2012) demonstrates that female offenders are more likely to come from childhoods that are traumatized by poverty. In addition, women who engage in chronic offending into adulthood are less likely to have consistent employment histories and be involved in healthy romantic relationships. Indeed, these instabilities may in fact lead women toward lifestyles that can encourage criminal behavior.

While life course theory can have value for understanding offending behaviors of girls and women, scholars suggest that life course theory needs to expand its understanding of what is considered a "significant life event." In particular, Belknap and Holsinger (2006) point to the effects of early childhood abuse traumas, mental health concerns, and sexual identity as a significant life event that can be used to understanding criminality.

These modern theories made significant improvements in understanding the relationship between gender and crime. Unlike traditional theorists, these modern theories placed gender as a significant focus in their theoretical development. However, critiques of these theories demonstrate that there is increased need for greater discussions about women and crime, particularly given the relationship between the context of their lives and their offending behaviors.

Feminist Criminology

The emergence of feminist criminology builds upon the themes of gender roles and socialization to explain patterns of female offending. Here, scholars begin with a discussion on the backgrounds of female offenders in an effort to assess who she is, where she comes from, and why she engages in crime. Feminist criminology reflects several key themes in its development. Frances Heidensohn (1985, p. 61) suggested that "feminist criminology began with the awareness that women were invisible in conventional studies in the discipline. . . . Feminist criminology began as a reaction . . . against an old established male chauvinism in the academic discipline." While some criminologists suggested that traditional theories of crime could account for explanations in female offending, others argued that in order to accurately theorize about the criminal actions of women, a new approach to the study of crime needed to be developed.

> Theoretical criminology was constructed by men, about men. It is simply not up to the analytical task of explaining female patterns of crime. . . . Thus, something quite different will be needed to explain women and crime. . . . Existing theories are frequently so inconsistent with female realities that specific explanations of female patterns of crime will probably have to precede the development of an all-inclusive theory. (Leonard, 1982, pp. xi–xii)

How can feminist thought influence the field of criminology? Daly and Chesney-Lind (1988) point out that feminist discussions about crime are not limited to "women's issues." They argue that it is important that any discussion of women's lives and criminality incorporates conversations on masculinity and patriarchy. Given the historical distortions and the casual assumptions that have been made about women's lives in relationship to their criminal behaviors, incorporating feminist perspectives can provide a richer understanding about not only the nature of female offending but also the role of how experiences with victimization of women shape this process. In addition, feminist perspectives highlight that feminist criminology is not a single identity but an opportunity to consider multiple influences when understanding issues of gender and crime.

The use of feminist theory, methodologies, and activism in discussions of criminology has led to a variety of new understandings about gender and crime. Perhaps one of the most influential perspectives to date on female offending is the feminist pathways approach. Feminist pathways research seeks to show how life events (and traumas) affect the likelihood to engage in crime. While the pathways approach has many similarities with other theories such as life course or cycle of violence perspectives, these theories do not explain women's criminality from a feminist perspective. In comparison, the feminist pathways approach begins with a feminist foundation (Belknap, 2007). Within the feminist pathways approach, researchers have identified a cycle of violence for female offenders that begins with their own victimization and results with their involvement in offending behavior. Belknap and Holsinger (1998) posit that one of the most significant contributions of feminist criminology is understanding the role of victimization in the histories of incarcerated women, as female offenders report substantially high occurrences of physical, emotional, and sexual abuse throughout their lifetimes. "While such an explanation does not fit all female offenders (and also fits some male offenders), the recognition of these risks appears to be essential for understanding the etiology of offending for many girls and women. Yet this link between victimization and offending has largely been invisible or deemed inconsequential by the powers that be in criminology theory building and by those responsible for responding to women's and girls' victimizations and offenses" (Belknap & Holsinger, 1998, p. 32).

Another example of research incorporating a feminist pathways perspective is Wesely's (2006) research on homeless women and exotic dancers. The levels of childhood abuse and victimization that the women in her study experienced were "located within a nexus of powerlessness, gender-specific sexualization and exploitation, economic vulnerability and destitution, and social alienation and exclusion" (Wesely, p. 309). These women grew up to believe that violence was an ordinary and normal experience, which in turn influenced their decision-making practices throughout their lives. For example, these women learned that sexuality is a tool to manipulate and gain control over others. As a result, many of the women chose to engage in sex work at a young age in an effort to escape the physical and sexual abuse they experienced by their parents and family members. Unfortunately, the decision to live and work on the streets placed them at risk for further violence. These "lived experiences contributed to a downward spiral in which the women were preoccupied with daily survival, beaten down, depressed, and unsuccessful at making choices or having opportunities that improved their life conditions" (Wesely, pp. 314–315).

A third approach by Brennan, Breitenbach, Dieterich, Salisbury, and von Voorhis (2012) on feminist pathways identifies multiple pathways to crime. While abuse still plays a theme in some of these pathways, their work identifies eight different pathways within four unique themes. The first theme describes women who have lower experiences with victimization and abuse but whose major criminality revolves around their addiction. The first pathway in this theme contains women who are younger and are the parents of minor children, while the second pathway involves women who are older and do not have children. The second theme highlights the classic role of victimization and abuse within offending. Many of these women also experience emotional and physical abuse by a significant other. The first pathway within this theme involves younger single mothers who may suffer from depression. Many of their offenses involve drugs and dual arrests from intimate partner violence. The second pathway involves women who engage in higher rates of crime and who have greater issues with drugs and mental health. They are older and not involved in parenting. The third and fourth themes have a common foundation in that these women have been highly marginalized throughout their lives. They typically lived in high-crime areas with high rates of poverty.

They suffered in school and often lack adequate vocational skills to provide sustenance for their lives. Within these similarities, there are also differences. The first theme involves lower rates of victimization and fewer mental health issues. Many of these women were involved in acts of drug trafficking. Within this theme, the first pathway highlights women who tend to be younger and single parents, while the second pathway describes cases where the women have higher rates of crime and noncompliance with the criminal justice system and are less dependent on a significant other. Like in other pathways, these women tend to be older and nonparenting. The final theme involves women who are antisocial and aggressive. They have limited abilities to develop a stable environment for their lives and are often homeless. These women are distinguished primarily by their mental health status. In contrast, the second pathway within this theme involves women who are considered actively psychotic and are at risk for suicide. These women have a significant history with violence and aggression.

Indeed, the feminist pathways approach may provide some of the best information on how women find themselves stuck in a cycle that begins with victimization and leads to offending. Research on women's and girls' pathways to offending provides substantial evidence for the link between victimization and offending, as incarcerated girls are three to four times more likely to be abused than their male counterparts. A review of case files of delinquent girls in California indicates that 92% of delinquent girls in California reported having been subjected to at least one form of abuse (emotional = 88%; physical = 81%; sexual = 56%; Acoca & Dedel, 1997).

For female offenders, research overwhelmingly indicates that a history of abuse leads to a propensity to engage in certain types of delinquency. However, the majority of research points to women committing such offenses as running away and school failure, rather than acts of violence. The effects of sexual assault are also related to drug and alcohol addiction and mental health traumas, such as post-traumatic stress disorder and a negative self-identity (Raphael, 2004). In a cycle of victimization and offending, young girls often ran away from home in an attempt to escape from an abusive situation. In many cases, girls were forced to return home by public agencies, such as the police, courts, and social services—agencies designed to help victims of abuse. Girls who refused to remain in these abusive situations were often incarcerated and labeled as "out of parental control."

A review of case files of girls who had been committed to the California Youth Authority facilities during the 1960s showed that most girls were incarcerated for status offenses (a legal charge during that time frame). Many of these girls were committed to the Youth Authority for running away from home, where significant levels of alcoholism, mental illness, sexual abuse, violence, and other acts of crime were present. Unfortunately, in their attempt to escape from an abusive situation, girls often fell into criminal behaviors as a mechanism of survival. Running away from home placed girls at risk for crimes of survival, such as prostitution, where the level of violence they experienced was significant and included behaviors such as robbery, assault, and rape. These early offenses led these girls to spend significant portions of their adolescence behind bars. As adults, these same girls who had committed no crimes in the traditional sense later were convicted for a wide variety of criminal offenses, including serious felonies (Rosenbaum, 1989). Gilfus's (1992) work characterizes the pathway to delinquency as one of "blurred boundaries," as the categories of victim and offender are not separate and distinct. Rather, girls move between the categories throughout their lives, as their victimization does not stop once they become offenders. In addition to the victimization they experienced as a result of their survival strategies, many continued to be victimized by the system through its failure to provide adequate services for girls and women (Gaarder & Belknap, 2002).

Feminist criminologists have also worked at identifying how issues such as race, class, and sexuality impact criminality (and the system's response to these offending behaviors). From this inquiry, we learn that women of color experience multiple marginalized identities, which in turn impacts their trajectories of offending. Research by Potter (2006) suggests that combining Black feminist theory and critical race feminist theory with feminist criminology allows for an enhanced understanding of how Black women experience crime. This perspective of a *Black feminist criminology* identifies four themes that alter the experiences for Black women in the criminal justice system. First, many Black women experience structural oppression in society. Second, the Black community and culture features unique characteristics as a result of their racialized experiences. Third, Black families differ in their intimate and familial relations. Finally, this perspective looks at the Black woman as an individual, unique in her own right (Potter, 2006). Together, these unique dimensions lead to a different experience for Black women within the criminal justice system that needs to be recognized within theoretical conversations on women and crime.

Developments in feminist research have addressed the significant relationship between victimization and offending. A history of abuse is not only highly correlated with the propensity to engage in criminal behaviors, but also it often dictates the types of behaviors in which young girls engage. Often, these behaviors are methods of surviving their abuse, yet the criminal nature of these behaviors brings these girls to the attention of the criminal justice system. The success of a feminist perspective is dependent on a theoretical structure that not only has to answer questions about crime and delinquency but also has to address issues such as sex-role expectations and patriarchal structures within society (Chesney-Lind, 2006). The inclusion of feminist criminology has important policy implications for the justice system in the 21st century. As Belknap and Holsinger (2006, pp. 48–49) note,

> The ramifications of the traditionally male-centered approaches to understanding delinquency not only involve ignorance about what causes girls' delinquency but also threaten the appropriateness of systemic intervention with and treatment responses for girls.

As feminist criminology continues to provide both an understanding of the causes of female offending and explanations for the changes in the gender-gap of offending, it will also face its share of challenges. Both Chesney-Lind (2006) and Burgess-Proctor (2006) have suggested that the future of feminist criminology centers on expanding the discussions on the intersections between gender, race, and class. For example, recent research has posited that increases in the number of women that are incarcerated as a result of the war on drugs represents not only a war on women in general (Bloom, Owen, & Covington, 2004) but also has had specific and detrimental effects for women of color (Bush-Baskette, 1998, 1999). Feminist scholars also need to continue to pursue opportunities to link their research and activism, particularly given some of the recent trends in crime control policies that have both intentional and unintentional consequences for the lives of women, their families, and their communities.

Summary

- Early biological studies of female criminality were based on gross assumptions of femininity and had limited scientific validity.
- Historical theories of crime saw women as doubly deviant—not only did women break the law, but they also violated traditional gender-role assumptions.
- Applications of social bond theory illustrate that family bonds can reduce female delinquency, while educational bonds have a stronger effect for boys.
- Recent tests of differential association theory indicate that peer associations may have a stronger effect on male delinquency than female delinquency.
- Research on general strain theory illustrates that not only do girls experience different types of strain from boys, but they also respond to experiences of strain differently.
- Life course theory examines how adverse life events impact criminality over time and can provide insight on both female and male offending patterns.
- Theories of female criminality during the 1960s and 1970s focused on the effects of the emancipation of women, gendered assumptions about female offending, and the differential socialization of girls and boys.
- The feminist pathways approach has identified a cycle for women and girls that begins with their own victimization and leads to their offending.

KEY TERMS

Adler, Freda

Attachment

Belief

Commitment

Differential association theory

Hagan, John

Hirschi, Travis

Involvement

Laub, John

Life course theory

Lombroso, Cesare, and
    William Ferrero

Masked criminality of women

Pollak, Otto

Power control theory

Sampson, Robert

Simon, Rita

Social bond theory

Sutherland, Edwin

DISCUSSION QUESTIONS

1. How have historical theories on female offending failed to understand the nature of female offending?

2. What has recent research on gender and traditional theories of crime illustrated about the nature of female offending?

3. What contributions has feminist criminology made in understanding the relationship between gender and offending?

WEB RESOURCES

Bureau of Justice Statistics: http://bjs.ojp.usdoj.gov

Feminist Criminology: http://fcx.sagepub.com

Visit **www.sagepub.com/mallicoat2e** to access additional study tools including eFlashcards, web quizzes, web resources, video resources, and SAGE journal articles.

READING 11

Throughout this section, you learned about how traditional and modern theories of crime failed to include women in their research. This article involves a case study of a young woman convicted of a drug offense. Dr. Bernard looks at the experiences of this woman's offending behaviors as an illustration of feminist criminology in action.

The Intersectional Alternative

Explaining Female Criminality

April Bernard

Introduction

Female criminality has been explained from a variety of feminist perspectives; marginalization from conventional institutions, disrupted family and personal relationships, and institutionalized racism, sexism, and economic disadvantage have all been explored as explanations for the involvement of women in crime (Broidy & Agnew, 1997; Chesney-Lind, 1986, 1997; Daly & Chesney-Lind, 1988; Owen, 1998; Ritchie, 2004). Marginalized women involved in crimes tend to be young, poor, non-white, high school dropouts, unmarried mothers, un-/under-employed and educated, with a history of drug problems, family violence, and sexual abuse. The vulnerabilities that color the lives of marginalized women can be difficult to measure due to the overlapping influence, or intersectionality, of multiple forms of subjugation, such as ingrained racism, sexism, economic disadvantage, abuse, exploitation, and the historical undervaluation of women in society (Collins, 2000; Kelly, 1994).

The need for grounding theorizing about women's criminality in an understanding of intersecting identities that emerge from crosscutting systems of oppression has been emphasized in Black and multiracial feminist and criminology analyses (Baca Zinn & Thornton Dill, 1996; Barak, 1998; Beale, 1995; Belknap, 2001; Britton, 2004; Brown, 2010; Burgess-Proctor, 2006; Collins, 2000; Daly & Stephens, 1995; Gordon, 1987; King, 1988; Potter, 2006; Ritchie, 1996; Wing, 2003). Collins describes this intersectionality as functioning within matrices of domination that represent amalgamations of micro- through macro-level power structures and interrelated systems of oppression. The historically and socially specific ways in which these power structures are constructed and systems of oppression are blended create different kinds of social realities, identities, and experiences. This analysis uses an intersectional approach to provide an explanation of women's criminality in that it seeks to be grounded in an intimate understanding of the multiplicative, overlapping, and cumulative effects of the simultaneous intersections of oppressions that affect women's decisions to engage in crime.

This article begins by challenging aspects of malestream theorizing on crime that fail to capture the multiple forces that serve to construct gender realities (Carlen, 1985; Dekeseredy & Perry, 2006; Maidment, 2006). The significance of the intersectional approach is discussed as a viable alternative paradigm that recognizes the influence of multiple constraining factors on women's criminality. The concept of *doing identity* is then introduced to

SOURCE: Bernard, A. (2013). The intersectional alternative: Explaining female criminality. *Feminist Criminology, 8*(1), 3–19.

describe the unique attempts of individuals, particularly marginalized women, to navigate through power structures and multiple systems of oppression that shape their life experiences. A case study consisting of an exploration of factors contributing to one woman's decision to engage in criminal activity as a means of doing identity is presented. The importance of this intersectional model for feminist criminology is underscored through a discussion of implications and recommendations for theoretical praxis, policy, and programmatic provisions.

⊠ Alternative Theorizing: Strained or Constrained Realities

The primary tenet underlying this alternative approach is that counter to malestream perspectives on crime, women's criminality may be best understood as an adverse response to a lack of legitimate means for women to demonstrate an authentic and efficacious identity that is unfettered by the constraining effects of intersecting systems of oppression. Although my critique seeks to offer an alternative to the malestreaming of mainstream criminal justice research in general, the intention is not to diminish the significance of any of these contributions.

This work should be understood as an attempt to encourage the extension of malestream theorizing on crime by acknowledging the potential of the intersectional approach to encompass the complexities of the realities that are faced by marginalized women. In this vein, an analysis of Merton's strain theory using an alternative intersectional perspective is provided as one, but not the only, example of the limitations of malestream theorizing in general on women's criminality. This application of an intersectional perspective on Merton's strain theory is one demonstration of the need for more in-depth analyses of the underlying causes and complexities that influence women's decisions to engage in crime that hopefully will encourage further intersectional analyses of this and other theories in the future.

According to Merton (1968), deviance is an adaptive response to a lack of legitimate means to achieve shared cultural goals. A commitment to the cultural goals and institutionalized means for success results in conformity, yet when access to the institutionalized means for success is strained or limited (typically due to differences in class), innovative attempts to achieve and retain shared cultural goals are forwarded. Deviance and crime increase in society when the option to conform is not accepted, and this innovation results in illegitimate means to achieve success.

Merton viewed the rejection of cultural goals and/or institutional means as an innovative or adaptive response that occurs within an anomic context in which incongruence between shared cultural goals and institutional means for success exists. Strain, frustration, and stress result where goals exceed means. The alternative intersectional paradigm suggests that women's criminality may be more an expression of constrained rather than strained realities. This alternative approach de-emphasizes individual frustrations and pathologies and instead stresses the ways in which power structures and systems of oppression work to circumscribe the life experiences of persons socially located at the intersections of multiple vulnerabilities.

The proposed alternative framework also suggests that although there may exist agreement on the general nature of the cultural goals that are shared among the population in a society (such as obtaining an education, a job, a house, and a car in Westernized capitalist societies) as described by Merton, the specifics of each individual's desired goals and opportunities may differ in regard to quality and quantity. The intersections that shape unique experiences of privilege/oppression in turn foster the development of multiple realities in which one person's specific goals and opportunities to obtain a particular type of house, number of cars, or quality of education may be very distinct in comparison to another's. Having an understanding of an individual's specific desired goals and opportunities is therefore suggested as taking precedence over having knowledge of shared cultural goals and institutionalized means for success in explaining decisions to engage in criminal activity.

This alternative framework also reconstructs Merton's concept of a class differential and suggests that the disparities that influence access to opportunities and life outcomes represent the cumulative impact of the intersections of multiple inequalities/privileges including (but not limited to) race, class, and gender on the life experiences of individuals. The differential advantage some have over others is less a reflection of their individual merit and propensity toward conformity than of differences in power. The social, economic, and political place and space individuals hold within society relative to the legitimate means, resources, and opportunities for achieving some measure of success may be more or less constrained depending on the ways in which they affect and are affected by existing power structures and systems of oppression. Embedded within the concept of a matrix of domination is the recognition that to achieve the ideals of social justice and equality would require the reduction of the differential advantage of some over others through the restructuring of the domains of power (law, bureaucracy, culture, and relationships/interactions) and the dismantling and eradication of their interconnections that function to maintain (and are maintained by) ideologies and systems of oppression that foster multiple and overlapping inequalities, including, but not limited to, race, class, and gender.

What affects an individual's access to legitimate means for success is not just about social capital, social networks, or other class indicators, but encompasses the micro- through macro-level social, sexual, national, economic, political, and other socially inherited and ascribed histories, norms, and social spaces an individual represents and encounters (Collins, 2000; Harding, 2004). This intersectional approach claims that *social location*, or the combination of micro- through macro-level social identities and social roles and relationships, is a primary contributing factor to decisions about criminality. The decision to engage in crime is influenced by the unique combination of factors that represent a particular social location regardless of an individual or group's relationship to income-generating resources and assets or differences in class as postulated by Merton. Social location can be described as the cumulative impact of intersections of oppression/privilege and represents the intercorrelation of multiple factors and conditions that are unique to each individual that influence his or her experiences, opportunities, and choices.

The significance of Merton's concept of institutionalized means is minimized in this alternative framework due to its ambiguity and the pejorative implications for developing policies that respond to the variety of social and economic conditions affecting marginalized populations. From this alternative perspective, the belief in the existence of omnipresent functional, normal, stable, fixed, and solid social structures, institutions, communities, families, opportunities, or *institutional means* (to which individuals

can choose to conform, accept, or reject) requires rethinking to acknowledge the particular matrix of domination and systems of oppression and the fluidity of associated factors that characterize an individual's social and economic condition. The fluidity of relationships, norms, cultures, and institutions in global and modern societies has been identified as a key contributor to the growing sense of social isolation, decay, risk, and insecurity that depict the challenges of late modernity (Bauman, 2000; Beck, 1992). Instead of institutionalized means, emphasis in the proposed paradigm is placed on the acknowledgment of existing social contradictions (the limitations of capitalist ideology and the erosion of the American Dream), risk (the potential for victimization, exploitation, subjugation), and uncertainty (various forms of insecurity) within contemporary society that function to further disadvantage members of vulnerable populations.

This alternative theoretical framework challenges the assumption that the social contradictions, risk, and uncertainty that are evident in late modernity can be effectively managed through equal opportunity and antidiscrimination legislation, social control, and punitive reforms. The assumption that the impact of these factors on the ability of all individuals to cope with the challenge of navigating through the complexity of their vulnerabilities and inequalities toward achieving success can be mitigated through obedience to the law and conformity to dominant social norms is also challenged. This alternative framework acknowledges the relativity of deviance and rejects paradigms built upon the premise that deviance and conformity are dichotomous states rather than overlapping spheres of potential responses that can be differentially interpreted depending on the circumstances or context (Curra, 2000). What is deemed deviant in one community (fighting among youth, for example) may be viewed as good common sense in another.

Not all marginalized women resort to crime, and some affluent women seek illegitimate means to achieve their goals. Conformity in an intersectional context can be defined as individuals actively engaged in the process of constantly assessing and reassessing their goals and resigning themselves to accept those that can be achieved given their social location in relation to opportunities (means) amid multiple inequalities, risks, and uncertainty that exist in society. For marginalized women, if the consequences of conformity may require an acceptance of a life that is less than their goals prescribe, then crime may become an innovative response. What may distinguish the affluent female criminal from another of less wealth is that though both choose an illegitimate response to their circumstances, their opportunities and agency to commit crimes differ in regard to quality and consequences (Reiman, 2003).

When combined, the concepts of individual (rather than shared) goals for success, social location (as opposed to a class differential), and societal contradictions, insecurity, and risk (instead of institutionalized means) result in a differential means for "doing" identity (navigating through multiple inequalities to achieve a particular or individual-specific measure of success), which leads to an adaptive response that is more or less legitimate depending on the context. Doing identity can be described as a process of producing unique biographical solutions to systemic contradictions (Beck, 1992). This concept of doing identity is based on the work conducted by Carlen (1988) and Messerschmidt (1993) and their perspectives on crime for marginalized populations as an adaptive response to societal circumstances.

Pat Carlen (1988) addresses the issues of conformity, identity, and criminality among underclass women. Based on her study of 39 convicted women between the ages of 15 and 46, Carlen suggests that the cultural goals for success that govern the lives of women are influenced by two social compromises or deals related to gender and class. The *class deal* stipulates that women's conformity is motivated by the opportunity for them to earn their own wages and ultimately achieve financial success, or the "good life," as defined by the society, through their work in the public domain.

The *gender deal* is motivated by the promise of a happy and fulfilling family life that is to result from the woman's labor for and love of a man who is the primary breadwinner. The gender deal breaks down when women are unable to obtain or maintain successful relationships with a male breadwinner, are abused, and/or socially isolated, and the class deal is compromised when women are unable to achieve financial success through work. Carlen's thesis is that women resort to crime when the class and/or gender deals break down.

Although Carlen's thesis is convincing, the question remains whether class and gender are the only socially relevant aspects of women's existence upon which deals can be made and whether there are other aspects of women's

identities or social locations that significantly factor into their responses to adversity and potential criminality. The following analysis will also seek to reveal additional factors as well as consider Carlen's description of the class and gender deals as significant factors that influence women's adaptive responses to risk and contradictions in society.

Messerschmidt (1993) provides a gendered approach to the development of criminological theory to describe the relationship between masculinity and crime. Messerschmidt suggests that to understand male behavior, including crime, one must begin by acknowledging the historical and social structural conditions that construct hegemonic masculine ideologies and social actions. He argues, "Hegemonic masculinity emphasizes practices toward authority, control, competitive individualism, independence, aggressiveness, and the capacity for violence" (p. 82). Crime, he observes, may be one way of "doing gender," or demonstrating one's masculinity, when legitimate means of demonstrating one's identity are stifled.

Messerschmidt's thesis is that crime as a means of doing gender becomes a form of social action or a practical response to structured opportunities and constraints in society that are related to class, race, and gender relationships. Although Messerschmidt's analysis does not involve women and emphasizes the construct of masculinity, I argue that it is not simply "doing masculinity" or "doing femininity" or "doing race" that is the issue, but rather doing identity. How one navigates through multiple oppressions to achieve his or her desired goals and ultimately find space and place for self in contemporary capitalist society is a complex process of which an individual's sex, age, gender, sexual identity, race, nationality, class, level of education, and a host of other factors are significant components.

This alternative paradigm suggests that the issue of crime and women (and perhaps men) with multiple vulnerabilities can be explained based on an understanding of the process of doing identity or the process of becoming somebody (self-defined) while navigating through multiple social contradictions and inequalities. Becoming some-body requires individuals to draw upon complex and advanced decision-making capabilities that can be employed at life's perpetual crossroads to assess the vulnerabilities of their social location amid the solid and liquid aspects of their reality. Here at the crossroads, individuals are challenged with the task of identifying among the plethora of ends the ones that are reasonable and feasible given their social location, circumstances, and context (Bauman, 2000). Establishing priorities in a world that appears to be full of possibilities adds complexity to the challenge, and the uncertainty of life's comparative objectives is all the more perplexing to persons facing multiple vulnerabilities in the process of doing identity.

Method

The primary aim of the methodology was to utilize a feminist and interpretive approach to the data collection, interpretation, and analysis of the life stories and reflections of incarcerated women who have committed drug-related crimes (Denzin, 1989; Lynch, 1996; Oakley, 1981). Rather than seeking results that can be generalized to broader populations, the purpose of the methodology is to ground the findings in the standpoint of the women interviewed, and ultimately, to demystify and humanize their lived experiences and perspectives while providing a range of practical explanations of the choices and behavior of women involved in drug-related crimes. This preliminary analysis focuses on the life story of one young Afro-Caribbean woman who was incarcerated in 2010 due to a drug-related crime. This analysis begins with this single case of one woman as an intentional means of avoiding conundrums inherent in (a) positivists' research that tends to quantify experiences rather than validating nuances, difference, and the production of knowledge based on a single case, and (b) androcentric approaches that reinforce the "malestream" nature of criminology that often omit or misrepresent the experiences of women due to an emphasis on male crime (Belknap, 2001). The intention of this article is not to ignore men or avoid the rigors of scientific study involving multiple cases (both will be considered in future analysis) but simply to begin with the experiences of women and, in this case, one woman as the unit of analysis. The single case that was selected for this analysis is of a Jamaican female in her early 20s serving 2 years for attempting to transport marijuana from Jamaica to St. Maarten with the hope of earning US$900. For the purpose of telling her story, the pseudonym Angelique will be used when referring to the respondent.

The use of a single case as the unit of analysis also provides an opportunity to explore the unique ways in which the conceptual categories that make up the theoretical framework fit the particular case and allows the researcher to assess whether the constructs need further refinement before being applied to a broader set of cases. This process is purposefully iterative in nature and intends to reveal and refine conceptual categories that can be used to further feminist theorizing on the topic of women (and perhaps men) and crime.

In writing this analysis, a difficult methodological consideration I had to make was whether or not to point to a specific theory as an example of malestream criminological theorizing. I was initially uncomfortable with using Merton's strain theory directly as a means to demonstrate the significance of the intersectional approach for examining women's criminality, and I tried to avoid doing so by looking at *strain theories* in general, but the distractions were apparent. I then considered focusing on a single aspect of one strain theory, but that did not allow me to demonstrate the potential breadth and depth of the intersectional analytical approach. To more accurately describe Angelique's circumstances as *constrained* rather than *strained,* I felt strongly that I wanted to compare and contrast the intersectional approach with an existing theoretical framework as a means to develop salient alternative concepts in relation to the findings. With this as my motivation, I felt compelled to maintain a focus on Merton's strain theory, not as a critique of the significance of the theory, but as a means to encourage continued articulation and solidification of the intersectional approach as something distinct from, yet useful within, existing theoretical traditions. The following analysis briefly describes one woman's process of navigating through multiple oppressions within a high-risk context and incorporates the concepts of (a) individual goals for success; (b) social location; (c) social contradictions, risk, and uncertainty; and (d) adaptive responses that include legitimate (legally sanctioned by dominant culture) versus illegitimate (illegal, yet sanctioned by subculture) means to achieve desired success. Together these concepts will be used to describe a unique attempt at doing identity.

Findings: There Is No Safe Place

A safe space, prison is not, but a correction facility may be the only environment where the extent to which inequality, deprivation, and the randomness of uncertainty that affect the lives of marginalized women is to some degree leveled, controlled, or restricted. In prison, there exists no class or gender deal that requires work or marriage to be successful, social location within the dominant social structure has limited significance, and the cultural goals for success are redefined to fit a new (although typically temporary) reality. Angelique's story will be discussed without a particular beginning or ending, using the concepts from the theoretical framework as a guide to explaining her journey toward crime.

Goals

Angelique states that she had her aspirations set on achieving her dream of the good life, which for her meant "becoming somebody" and consisted of obtaining an education, a job, a house, and a future for her children:

> I wanted to better my life I wanted to give my sons a future, a good life, an education—something I never get.
>
> I wanted to own a business—be a hair dresser and own a house. I had the dream. I went to cosmetology school and got a certificate. If my sister no die we would finish school together, save our money together and open a [beauty] parlor and buy a house together.

Angelique shared the socially sanctioned belief that all are entitled to seek an array of possibilities toward achieving the good life. She believed in the class deal that if she could only find a job and work hard that she could obtain financial prosperity. Her specific goals for success included becoming a hairdresser and working in collaboration with her sister to combine the resources necessary to start a business and buy a house. Although her goals seemed reasonable and feasible, Angelique's dream of owning a salon and a home was formally disrupted when her sister died. In time, her commitment to finding legitimate means to achieve her dream of becoming somebody began to wane. She describes how she began to lose faith in her ability achieve her goals:

> When I started college my sister died [her sister was killed by a distant relative]. From that time my life went down. We went to the same school, we were very close. After she died I lived carefree.

Social Location

Unfortunately, Angelique's unique combination of social factors and conditions that influenced her reality included a history of sexual and physical abuse, family disruption, and marginalization from social, educational, and economic resources and support. Her environment was imbued with images that included men who distributed guns to young boys, young girls that danced at strip clubs, and adults and children struggling to survive by selling chicken on the roadside while others were selling drugs. She states, "In my area, people do what they can to survive." For Angelique, these were the only examples and opportunities that were available, and it was within this limited and restricted reality that Angelique sought to achieve success.

Angelique's reality contradicted with her dream of becoming somebody. As a victim of ongoing abuse by her mother and her mother's boyfriend, Angelique found it difficult to reconcile to the fate she seemed to have inherited. Her attempts to try to find a solution to her circumstances were met with disdain; repeatedly, she was silenced or ignored:

> I lived with mother, my mother's boyfriend and six siblings in one bedroom house. My mother beat me all the while. I had to wash for she, her man, and my brothers and sisters. One time after she gave me lunch money, I put it down and her boyfriend took my lunch money and gone. So I asked someone in my yard (a neighbor) for lunch money and my mom chopped me with a knife.
>
> The worst of the abuse was at night. I slept on the ground and my mom, she boyfriend and my brother and sister slept in the bed. Him (the boyfriend) come down and abuse me every night. Me tell her and she never believe me. She love him more than me. He come on the ground and force my foot open every night. The first time I was 9 and this continued until I was 12. I continued to tell my mother what happened. One time she threw hot porridge on me to burn me and I ran. Then I start to runaway.

Compiled upon [in addition to] her experience of being repeatedly silenced at home was her feeling of being socially excluded at school. Angelique describes the first time she contemplated suicide:

> I felt like I was not human. Me don't feel like me loved. I tried to commit suicide when I was 10. My mom abuse me, he abuse me. I felt left out at school. My friends had a good life, and me no have none. She was at work and I tried to do it, then I say why kill myself. I said I will reach my goal and show my mother I can be somebody.

Angelique was not a good student academically and often got into fights at school. She stated she often felt angry at school due to her inability to discuss the victimization she experienced at home. She responded to her feelings of being excluded in school by dropping out and seeking the type of wage-paying employment that was available to young undereducated women in her neighborhood:

> I dropped out of school at age 16 and started to dance at a strip club. I made $600 JA [Jamaican dollars] a night plus tips, and I danced every day. I was able to pay some of my school fees and got in contact with my father and he helped pay my fees for me to start college [to become a hair dresser]. I danced naked freelance to make money. I had to take care of my children.

Angelique's early introduction into adulthood was void of legitimate opportunities to demonstrate the identity she sought to achieve. The abuse she suffered, the death of her sister, and the social exclusion she faced at school were a harsh introduction into the reality of the combined effects of multiple oppressions that shaped her social location and their unique impact on her ability to achieve her goals.

Contradiction and Risk

As a young adult, the only guides through the maze of uncertainty available to Angelique were the local examples of success that she befriended and others to whom she was related. All of them were engaged in socially deviant behavior. Angelique's first child was born when she was 15, and she describes the child's father as worthless because, as she states, "him no want work, I don't want that life so I move out." Angelique's observation of the father of her first child suggests that she initially sought to conform to the gender deal, by seeking a male primary breadwinner to assist her in achieving her desired reality, yet he was unable to fulfill her expectations and hope of achieving her ideal of the good life; therefore, the relationship ended.

A subsequent boyfriend was a drug dealer. This boyfriend offered Angelique an alternative means to achieve the good life and an opportunity to achieve her dreams. Life with this boyfriend meant that Angelique would have to relinquish her desire to conform to the promises of the class deal through her notion of legitimate institutionalized means and adapt to an environment in which the rules that sanctioned behavior deviated from those of the dominant society. Angelique's new reality included the indulgence in drugs, and although this boyfriend could function as the primary breadwinner, his methods for achieving wealth required her to engage in crime:

> My friends set me up with a youth who was a bad man. They had money and things. They would drink, do drugs and gamble for fun. They would rob too. If they want me to carry a gun I say I would do it, for him. With my friends I felt happy, stress free. When I smoke, things just gone. They were kind of like a family. I prefer to be with them than my own. I always felt burdened when I came home [to my mother], but I never felt like that with them. I would rob, but mainly with my boyfriend.

For Angelique, her new family allowed her the freedom to combine the class and gender deals, albeit through illegitimate means, and to adopt an acceptable (if not desired) reality (identity). Unfortunately, this new reality did not free Angelique from risk, as the abuse she suffered from her mother was replaced by exploitation.

> [When I went to England to live with my boyfriend] I had to send money two times a week to my mother because she was taking care of my children. My mother cravin' [is greedy]. She wanted to carry it [drugs] up [from Jamaica

to England]. I told her she was not ready, but she neva stop. She wanted to come to England. So we gave her ganja [marijuana] in a tin and some coke [cocaine]. She get catch [arrested] in Jamaica. I flew down and my boyfriend too. She was in jail and we had to put $100,000 [Jamaican dollars to post bond].

Adaptive Response

Disruption in Angelique's life continued as her boyfriend was also arrested after returning to England. With her primary source of income gone, Angelique adapted to this change by relying on her own income-earning abilities to obtain the means to maintain her mother's now abandoned children as well as her own. With the bulk of her experience, networks, and opportunities concentrated around her boyfriend's illegal endeavors, Angelique inherited his business and began to engage in the transportation of drugs:

> My boyfriend got 17 years. He got caught with drugs and guns in the house. I had to start to carry drugs to small islands in a suitcase. The drugs were built into the suitcase. I traveled every week carrying ganja from Jamaica [to England] and coke [from England] back to Jamaica, Grenada, St. Maarten and Panama. With 3–4 pounds of weed I could make $800 US and with 1 kilo of coke, $900 US for myself. My boss would send money to immigration to clear my way and collect the money, but I don't know his name.

Upon reflection, Angelique says she realizes that she could have made better choices. She stated that she could have obviously continued to go to school to be a hairdresser and potential salon owner after her sister died, as an example, yet with an understanding of her social location and history of risks and contradictions, she may have had little faith that her conformity to the class deal would have resulted in the trappings of the good life she imagined. In Angelique's quest to become somebody, the lack of available legitimate examples, means, and opportunities to help augment her ability to navigate through the complexities of multiple subjugations, uncertainties,

risks, and contradictions she encountered was compensated by adaptive responses characterized by increasing levels of deviance.

As an ex-offender, upon her release, Angelique may find her options for access to education and the formal labor market further restricted. When pressed to specify the choices she plans to make in the future upon her release from prison, as if acknowledging the high degree of uncertainty she will face given the addition of the label of *ex-offender* to the other vulnerabilities that characterize her social location, Angelique spoke with ambiguity and then with resolve:

> I want to get a job and go to [cosmetology] school in England, but me don't know what me may do [when I get out of prison], I don't know my situation. I may go back into it [carrying drugs].

For Angelique, the American Dream has been replaced by a reality that reflects her limitations and the constraints, circumscription, and contradictions within society. For Angelique and other vulnerable men and women, the process of doing identity is wrought with constraints and barriers that place their reach just short of their aspirations. Angelique attempts to define herself, achieve her dreams, and possibly benefit from the class and gender deals ascribed for women in society, yet her attempts are met with a dearth of feasible and legitimate options that are compensated by illicit ones. A life of crime, for Angelique, becomes the practical solution to social and economic conditions that are ripe with uncertainty and contradictions.

Angelique's profile of vulnerabilities and inequalities fits those of other women who may turn to crime as a solution to life's limitations. She is young, poor, non-white, a high school dropout, an unmarried mother, and unemployed and has a history of family violence, sexual abuse, and some drug use. Throughout her life, the impact of the combination of these factors remained virtually ignored by all but one social institution (the prison) and the "family of friends" that she adopted as a refuge and escape from her own. Her new family provided her with an example of how to obtain the tokens and semblance of the good life that could be acquired through illegal means. Due to the random and incremental accumulation of loss and lack in addition to the deprived conditions she inherited, in time

Angelique became removed from her vision of being somebody and achieving her goals through legitimate means and decided to join her new family in search of some remnant of a dream. Eventually, she ends up in prison, with little hope of finding alternative means to navigate through the inequalities and social contradictions that face her upon release.

One of the unanticipated findings this analysis revealed is the extent to which motherhood factors into women's decisions to commit crime or continue to pursue their dreams through legitimate means while confronting adversity. Angelique described how her children were the source of her motivation for achieving her goals and her sole inspiration in difficult times; here, she states how her children give her the will to live despite continued abuse and challenges:

> I tried to commit suicide again. A girl told me what to buy, and I tried to kill myself. I drink some, but not enough, and then I vomit, vomit, vomit. I got weak, and pale and my mother took me to the hospital. During the drive to the hospital my mother told me I was wicked. I spent weeks in the hospital. In the hospital I was thinking about my son. He so bad loves me, and I said I would never do that again. When I came out, I got involved with a youth [a young boy] and got pregnant again. My children give me the strength to move, they make me want to live.

For Angelique, like many mothers, her children function as a tremendous source of encouragement in the midst of uncertainty. Despite the option to forfeit parental responsibilities due to strained social and economic conditions, many mothers continue to try to care for their children. Perhaps this phenomenon of commitment despite uncertainty can be described as another deal that can be added to Carlen's class and gender deals. The mother deal can be found at the intersection between the class and gender deals where the belief that the good life (as defined in noneconomic and more affective terms) results from a mother's dedication to her children. Crime results when illegitimate options for mothers to meet the needs of their children as well as their own are more readily available than those that are legitimate. Tapping into this bond between some mothers and their children as a way to guide and nurture their progress toward the achievement of their goals through legitimate means may lead to innovative policy and programmatic responses to female criminality.

Conclusion: Policy Implications

Although Adler (1975) contends that women's liberation resulted in increasing levels of women's willful criminality, her thesis fails to explain the higher likelihood of young, poor, non-white, high school dropouts, unmarried mothers, un-/under-employed or educated, with a history of drug problems, family violence, and sexual abuse, to be represented among incarcerated women. If a correlation between women's liberation and an increase in women's criminality exists, perhaps this is due to the increased vulnerability of marginalized women to being criminalized as a result of punitive polices that blame them for the same conditions that constrain their progress.

The State through its promotion of policy, norms, and ideology contributes to the illusion that the financial prosperity of the affluent is somehow justified due to their hard work, integrity, and good choices. The consequence of upholding this belief is that it supports the claim that a life of less for others is often attributed to their own individual pathologies, deficiencies, and lack of conformity; and therefore, should the less affluent become deviant, they should be removed from society and punished. To effectively remove the constraints that limit access to *legitimate* options for the vulnerable to achieve an equitable reality would mean breaking the illusion of justified position or class in society and creating a new ideology, norms, institutions (safe places), and social policies that have the notions of interdependency and collective responsibility at the core. Rather than advocating the need for a revolution to combat crime, Left Realists would recommend, and I agree, that the focus of policy and interventions must be on creating communities of care that rebuild neighborhoods and encourage social responsibility and community cohesion as strategies to mitigate against the relative depravation that affects the life outcomes of vulnerable individuals. Left Realist criminologists are critical of conservative policies that seek to build more prisons and lengthen sentences to deal with crime and are supportive of realistic solutions that fit within the existing social framework (Young, 1997). The increasing incarceration rate for women due to drug-related crimes suggests a need to revisit short-sighted legislative policies and to develop opportunities to prevent women's criminality through intervention at the micro (individual and family) and mezzo (groups and community) levels of society. One example of an innovative intervention that seeks to reduce social isolation and capitalizes on the potential bond between mothers and their children is the creation of women-centered kinship networks consisting of a community of fictive and biological mothers, aunts, grandmothers, and nonparents, some of whom may be education and social service providers who can function as sources of support, examples, guidance, and communal child care for young mothers who may be at risk of dropping out of school, engaging in crime, or other forms of deviance (Collins, 2000; Mullins, 1997; White, 1985).

Nonresponsive policies and programs have resulted from a lack of understanding of the complex influence of multiple forms of oppression on women's lives and have rendered many marginalized women virtually invisible (Belknap, 2001). Addressing the problem of women and crime requires society to be willing to confront its failures, including its core ideologies, institutions, norms, and policies that justify a war on marginalized women (and men) under the guise of a war on drugs (Chesney-Lind, 1991). The challenge is for theorizing on female criminality to complicate malestream perspectives on women's criminality by including more empirical studies that seek to deconstruct one-dimensional and essentialist understandings of women's lives while intentionally exploring the interconnected, constraining, and multiple, yet unique, manifestations of power and oppression. The praxis of feminist criminology serves as a reminder that alternative theorizing, policy, and programmatic provisions in support of innovative interventions designed to nurture the development of each member of society are needed. An intersectional approach to feminist criminology functions to confront the collective culpability of all members of society in perpetuating oppressive ideologies and structures that favor the progress of the elite over those who, like Angelique, have limited means to escape the margins.

⊠ References

Adler, F. (1975). *Sisters in crime.* New York, NY: McGraw-Hill.

Baca Zinn, M., & Thornton Dill, B. (1996). Theorizing difference from multiracial feminism. *Feminist Studies, 22*(2), 321–331.

Barak, G. (1998). *Integrating criminologies.* Boston, MA: Allyn & Bacon.

Bauman, Z. (2000). *Liquid modernity.* Cambridge, UK: Polity.

Beale, F. (1995). Double jeopardy: To be Black and female. In B. Guy-Sheftall (Ed.), *Words of fire: An anthology of African-American feminist thought* (pp. 146–155). New York, NY: New Press. (Original work published 1970)

Beck, U. (1992). *Risk society: Towards a new modernity.* New Delhi, India: Sage.

Belknap, J. (2001). *The invisible woman: Gender, crime and justice.* Belmont, CA: Wadsworth.

Britton, D. M. (2004). Feminism in criminology: Engendering the outlaw. In P. J. Schram & B. Koons-Witt (Eds.), *Gendered (in)justice: Theory and practice in feminist criminology* (pp. 49–67). Long Grove, IL: Waveland.

Broidy, L., & Agnew, R. (1997). Gender and crime: A general strain theory perspective. *Journal of Research in Crime and Delinquency, 34*(3), 275–306.

Brown, G. (2010). *The intersectionality of race, gender, and reentry: Challenges for African American women* (Issue Brief, 1–18). Washington, DC: American Constitution Society for Law and Policy.

Burgess-Proctor, A. (2006). Intersections of race, class, gender, and crime: Future directions for feminist criminology. *Feminist Criminology, 1*(1), 24–47.

Carlen, P. (1985). *Criminal woman.* Cambridge, UK: Polity.

Carlen, P. (1988). *Women, crime and poverty.* London, UK: Open University Press.

Chesney-Lind, M. (1986). Women and crime: The female offender. *Signs, 12*(1), 78–96.

Chesney-Lind, M. (1991). Patriarchy, prisons and jails: A critical look at trends in women's incarceration. *The Prison Journal, 51*(11), 51–67.

Chesney-Lind, M. (1997). *The female offender: Girls, women and crime.* Thousand Oaks, CA: Sage.

Collins, P. H. (2000). *Black feminist thought: Knowledge, consciousness, and the politics of empowerment* (2nd ed.). New York, NY: Routledge.

Curra, J. (2000). *The relativity of deviance.* Thousand Oaks, CA: Sage.

Daly, K., & Chesney-Lind, M. (1988). Feminism and criminology. *Justice Quarterly, 5*(4), 497–535.

Daly, K., & Stephens, D. J. (1995). The "dark figure" of criminology: Towards a Black and multi-ethnic feminist agenda for theory and research. In N. Hahn Rafter & F. Heidensohn (Eds.), *International feminist perspectives in criminology: Engendering a discipline* (pp. 189–215). Philadelphia, PA: Open University Press.

Dekeseredy, W., & Perry, B. (2006). *Advancing critical criminology: Theory and application.* Lanham, MD: Lexington Books.

Denzin, N. K. (1989). *Interpretive interactionism.* Thousand Oaks, CA: Sage.

Gordon, V. V. (1987). *Black women, feminism and Black liberation: Which way?* Chicago, IL: Third World Press.

Harding, S. (Ed.). (2004). *The feminist standpoint theory reader.* London, UK: Routledge.

Kelly, M. (1994). *Critique and power: Recasting the Foucault/Habermas debate.* Boston: MIT Press.

King, D. K. (1988). Multiple jeopardy, multiple consciousness: The context of Black feminist ideology. *Signs: Journal of Women in Culture and Society, 14*(1), 42–72.

Lynch, M. J. (1996). Class, race, gender and criminology: Structured choices and the life course. In D. Milovanovic & M. D. Schwartz (Eds.), *Race, gender, and class in criminology: The intersections* (pp. 3–28). New York, NY: Garland.

Maidment, M. (2006). Transgressing boundaries: Feminist perspectives in criminology. In W. DeKeseredy & B. Perry (Eds.), *Advancing critical criminology: Theory and application* (pp. 43–62). Lanham, MD: Lexington Books.

Merton, R. (1968). *Social theory and social structure* (enlarged edition). New York, NY: Free Press.

Messerschmidt, J. (1993). *Masculinities and crime: Critique and reconceptualization of theory.* Lantham, MD: Rowman and Littlefield.

Mullins, L. (1997). *On our own terms: Race, class and gender in the lives of African American women.* New York, NY: Routledge.

Oakley, A. (1981). Interviewing women: A contradiction in terms. In H. Roberts (Ed.), *Doing feminist research* (pp. 30–62). London, UK: Routledge & Kegan Paul.

Owen, B. (1998). *"In the mix": Struggle and survival in a women's prison.* Albany, NY: SUNY Press.

Potter, H. (2006). An argument for Black feminist criminology: Understanding African American women's experiences with intimate partner abuse using an integrated approach. *Feminist Criminology, 1*(2), 106–124.

Reiman, J. (2003). *The rich get richer and the poor get prison: Ideology, class, and criminal justice* (7th ed.). Boston, MA: Allyn & Bacon.

Ritchie, B. E. (1996). *Compelled to crime: The gender entrapment of battered Black women.* New York, NY: Routledge.

Ritchie, B. E. (2004). Feminist ethnographies of women in prison. *Feminist Studies, 30*(2), 438–450.

White, D. (1985). *Ar'n't I a woman? Female slaves in the Plantation South.* New York, NY: Norton.

Wing, A. K. (Ed.). (2003). *Critical race feminism: A reader* (2nd ed.). New York: New York University Press.

Young, J. (1997). Left Realist criminology: Radical in its analysis, realist in its policy. In M. Maguire (Ed.), *The Oxford handbook of criminology* (pp. 473–498). Oxford, UK: Oxford University Press.

DISCUSSION QUESTIONS

1. How does feminist criminology explain the criminality of Angelique?

2. How does this approach differ from other theoretical standpoints? What might other theories of crime have to offer to this analysis?

3. What value do case studies provide when conducting research? What are the limitations to this method of analysis?

READING 12

This article uses data from the Stockholm Birth Cohort (a longitudinal study) to follow individuals throughout their lives. These data contain information on various life events, including criminal behavior. In this study, Drs. Estrada and Nilsson investigate whether there are different pathways to crime for males and females and what the effects of these pathways have in their lives.

Does It Cost More to Be a Female Offender?

A Life-Course Study of Childhood Circumstances, Crime, Drug Abuse, and Living Conditions

Felipe Estrada and Anders Nilsson

◤ Introduction

A long time has now passed since Heidensohn (1968) presented her now classic critique of criminology's failure to illuminate the phenomenon of female offending. Since then, the research field has evolved considerably, but there are still areas where our knowledge remains limited. One such area involves longitudinal studies of female offenders and similarities and differences in the life courses of males and females, respectively. This gap in the knowledge has proved a difficult one to fill, in part because many longitudinal studies have only included males (see, for example, Farrington, Tfofi, & Coid, 2009; Laub & Sampson, 2003; Piquero, Farrington, Nagin, & Moffitt, 2010; Pulkkinen, Lyyra, & Kokko, 2009; Soothill, Christoffersen, Hussain, & Francis, 2010) and in part because those studies that do include females are rarely of a size that permits analysis of the criminal careers of women (see, for example, the conclusions presented in Bergman & Andershed 2009, p. 175; Giordano, Cernkovich, & Rudolph, 2002, p. 1012; Lay, Ihle, Esser, & Schmidt, 2005, p. 47). In addition, on the basis of a review of prospective longitudinal studies which include females, Block, Blokland, van der Werff, van Os, and Nieuwbeerta (2010, p. 75) conclude that very few of these follow women further than young adulthood. A further limitation is that few studies have broadened their analyses to include other gendered adult outcomes than involvement in crime. Thus, although it is well established that many more males than females commit various types of crime, there is much less information available on the extent to which the life courses of males and females who have been involved in crime are similar or distinctive.

In this study, we compare different groups of males and females defined on the basis of their registered crime at different ages. What similarities and differences can we see in their social background, criminality, drug abuse, and living conditions in late midlife? We employ a new and unique longitudinal data set, the Stockholm Birth Cohort Study (SBC), which allows us to follow a cohort of boys and girls born in Stockholm in 1953 until they reach the age of 48 years.

Should We Expect Gender Differences in the Causes and Costs of Crime?

Boys and girls share most of the risk factors associated with juvenile delinquency (e.g., Wong, Slotboom, & Bijleveld, 2010). However, we know less of the existence, or nonexistence, of gender differences in the long-term consequences of criminal involvement. Tanner, Davies, and O'Grady (1999) use the National Longitudinal Survey of Youth to study the long-term impact of self-reported teen delinquency. They show that delinquency has a negative effect on life chances, since it reduces the likelihood of educational and occupational achievements in young adulthood (at ages 25–30). For males, juvenile delinquency predicted both a low academic status and a higher

SOURCE: Estrada, F., & Nilsson, A. (2012). Does it cost more to be a female offender? A life-course study of childhood circumstances, crime, drug abuse, and living conditions. *Feminist Criminology, 7*(3), 196–219.

NOTE: The authors disclosed receipt of the financial support for the research, authorship, and/or publication of this article from Riksbankens Jubileumsfond (RJ P2008–0846:1).

risk for unemployment. For females, however, it was only their educational attainment that was negatively influenced by delinquency. Tanner et al. (1999, p. 269) argue that one possible explanation is that this finding reflects the differing role played by employment among males and females, respectively.

On the basis of the Dunedin longitudinal study (an analysis of 1,000 males and females), Moffitt, Caspi, Rutter, and Silva (2001, p. 46) confirm that both the males and the females who presented conduct disorders in youth had worse living conditions in young adulthood. Males' problems were more often related to the labor market, drug use, and crime, whereas females had worse outcomes in relative terms with regard to relationship problems and physical and mental ill health. Moffitt et al. (2001) conclude that "the extant literature contains very few actual empirical demonstrations of sex differences in the aetiological factors involved with becoming antisocial, in the correlates of antisocial behaviour, or in its long-term consequences" (p. 5). More recently, Odgers et al. (2008) have presented a study of the Dunedin cohort where they follow the men and women up to age 32. According to Odgers et al. (2008, p. 706), their study is the first to highlight differences in adulthood between different female offender groups. One important finding is that persistent offenders experience poor outcomes across multiple domains at age 32 and that persistent female offenders experience the most severe consequences in adulthood. Their findings support similarities across gender with respect to developmental trajectories of antisocial behavior and their associated childhood origins and adult consequences.

The link between crime and gendered negative outcomes in later life is more clear in studies that have employed measures indicating involvement in more serious crime (registered rather than self-reported) or that have focused on samples of more serious offenders, such as institutionalized individuals (e.g., Simpson, Yahner, & Dugan, 2008). Results reported by Bergman and Andershed (2009) indicate[1] that females who were officially *registered* for crime during adolescence were at higher risk for a wide range of problems as adults compared with male offenders (see also Molero Samuelsson, 2011). Studies from the Ohio Life-Course Study (OLS)[2] also show that the females had more negative life outcomes than the corresponding group of males (e.g.,

Giordano et al., 2002, p. 1012). What offenders of both sexes did have in common, however, was low educational achievement, problematic family backgrounds, and poverty (Giordano et al., 2002, p. 1052). In another study from the Ohio project, Lanctot, Cernkovich, and Giordano (2007) conclude that "gender differences were observed in every life domain . . . these results also indicate that previously institutionalized females face the most adverse conditions during young adulthood" (p. 148).

Why should it cost more to be a female offender? Even if delinquent boys and girls share the same risk factors, the considerably lower rate of female offenders indicates that the selection processes into crime may differ for men and women. There is therefore reason to expect it to "take more" to become a female offender. Studies from both sides of the Atlantic have shown that female offenders who end up being dealt with by the justice system have often grown up in very difficult home conditions (e.g., Katz, 2000; Mullings, Pollock, & Crouch, 2002; Nilsson, 2003; Simpson et al., 2008). These do not primarily involve resource deficiencies measured in terms of variables focused on socioeconomic status (SES) or coming from a "broken home" but instead more serious social problems, involving, for example, families characterised by long-term poverty, alcoholism, drug addiction, mental illness, child neglect, and physical and sexual abuse (for reviews of gendered pathways, see Belknap & Holsinger, 2006; Holsinger, 2000; Mullings et al., 2002). Furthermore, it is also reasonable to expect that women will experience more negative consequences as a result of involvement in crime than male offenders. Female offenders are more stigmatized than men as they break not only the law but also the norms and expectations associated with their femininity (Heidensohn, 1968; Kyvsgaard, 1989, p. 58; Steffensmeier & Allan, 1996, p. 476). Gorman-Smith and Loeber (2005) conclude that in consequence, the powerful social sanctions directed against the delinquent behavior of girls mean "that it may take a particularly deviant family to impact risk among girls" (p. 25).

The Importance of Drug Abuse

In previous studies, we have shown that drug abuse is a factor with close links to involvement in crime (Nilsson & Estrada, 2009; see also, for example, Mullings et al., 2002;

Torstensson, 1987) and which also has consequences for future opportunities and life careers (see, for example, Krohn, Lizotte, & Perez, 1997; Laub & Sampson, 2003; Nilsson, 2003; Sarnecki & Sollenhag, 1985; Schroeder, Giordano, & Cernkovich, 2007). This is not [the] least of the case in societies where the prosecution of the possession and use of illicit drugs is a priority in the work of the police and where the explicit goal is that of making it difficult to be a drug abuser (Lenke & Olsson, 2002). Drug abusers risk not only convictions associated with the handling of drugs (possession or sale) but also [those] for a range of minor offences intended to finance their drug use (Mullings et al., 2002). It is also well known that drug use is a key element in the so-called "Street Woman scenario"[3] (Daly, 1992) which in the literature is seen as a central pathway of female lawbreaking (e.g., Simpson et al., 2008).

In their analysis of involvement in crime over the life cycle on the basis of Dutch cohort data, Blokland, Nagin, and Nieuwbeerta (2005, p. 936) note that the offending of the most criminal group involved a wide range of offence types, of which the majority were less serious property offences. The persistent group also tended to perform poorly in both professional and personal life-course domains (Blokland et al., 2005, p. 936). One limitation of the study is that it does not illuminate the question of whether, and in what ways, the results are specific for male offenders or are also applicable to females. In their discussion of the results, Blokland et al. (2005, p. 945) argue that one possible explanation for the crime pattern exhibited by the persistent group is that the group is largely composed of drug addicts who commit offences to finance their drug abuse. Blokland et al. found it difficult to examine this question further in their own study, however, as they lacked reliable data on drug abuse among the members of the cohort. It is noteworthy that in Tanner et al.'s (1999, p. 266) study, drug use was not such an important factor in predicting negative outcomes in young adulthood for either males or females. However, the study in question is based on self-report data and does not separate the more serious use of illegal drugs from alcohol use. The fact that, in the present study, we will look more closely at the significance of drug abuse for the risk for social exclusion in midlife for different offender groups of both sexes has therefore potential to be a significant contribution to the literature.

Objectives and Research Questions

By comparing the lives of delinquent boys and girls, we aim to increase our understanding of gender-specific and gender-neutral long-term consequences of criminal involvement. The fact that we study both sexes, thus, expanding the research field to describe not only the reality of men but also that of women, is clearly one of the strengths of this study. To our knowledge, this is one of the first studies that is able to analyze the significance of involvement in crime, childhood circumstances, and drug abuse for living conditions up to late midlife, while at the same time including comparisons of males and females. Our main research question centers on how life turned out in late midlife for boys and girls with different levels of involvement in crime. Does it take more, in terms of childhood risk factors, and cost more, in terms of long-term negative consequences, to be a female offender?

Our outcome measures in late midlife focus on labor market attachment, income, and family situation. In the following section, we present the SBC and describe the way variables have been operationalized. The results section begins with a presentation of the crime, drug abuse, and social situation of the males and females, respectively, during childhood and adolescence. We then move on to describe living conditions in late midlife. The presentation of findings concludes with multivariate analysis of the associations between gender and the social exclusion of different groups of offenders in midlife, which include controls for both differences in drug abuse and in other conditions during childhood and adolescence.

Data—The SBC

The SBC is a longitudinal database created by combining two data sets (for a more detailed description, see Stenberg et al., 2007; Stenberg & Vågerö, 2006). The first of these is the Metropolitan Study, which comprises all individuals born in 1953 and living in Stockholm 10 years later (Jansson, 1995). The Metropolitan data set includes a large amount of register-based and survey data relating to both the parents and the individuals themselves. For almost the entire length of the Metropolitan project (1963–1986), data were collected from a range of different registers. The data set includes information on, among other things, income, social welfare recipiency, social group, educational achievement, hospital treatment, interventions from Child Welfare Committees, and involvement in crime (for criminological studies that have used this data set, see, for example, Fry, 1985; Kratzer & Hodgkins, 1999; Torstensson, 1987, 1990; Wikström, 1987, 1990). The other data set, to which the Metropolitan study has been linked, is the Health, Illness, Income and Employment database (the HSIA 1980–2001). This database is composed of register data on all individuals living in Sweden in either 1980 or 1990. The data set we have been able to use for the current study includes information on, among other things, income, welfare benefit recipiency, and family type.[4] Since both databases had been anonymized, a probability matching procedure has been employed. It was possible in this way to match a total of 96% of the observations in the Metropolitan study—14,294 individuals.[5] The combination of the two data sets means that it is possible to follow the original cohort of individuals born in 1953 until year 2001 when they were 48 years of age.

Criminality and Drug Abuse

The information on the cohort members' criminality is drawn from the official police register of criminal records. The register contains information on offences that have either resulted in a conviction or, in cases involving younger offenders, been reported to the Child Welfare Committee. For each year from 1966 up to the first 6 months of 1984, that is, the year when the cohort members were 31 years of age, the data set contains information on the number and type of offences committed. These offences have been divided into seven categories: Violence, Theft, Fraud, Vandalism, Motoring offences, Drug offences, and Other offences (Wikström, 1987, 1990). We proceed on the basis of a categorization that distinguishes four different groups on the basis of their criminal activity at different ages (other longitudinal studies have employed similar classifications; see, for example, Bergman & Andershed, 2009; Eggleston & Laub, 2002; Farrington et al., 2006, 2009; Lay et al., 2005):

1. *No crime:* those individuals who have never been registered for crime

2. *Desisters:* those who desist from crime prior to the age of 20

3. *Late onset offenders:* individuals who are registered for crime for the first time after the age of 19

4. *Persisters:* those who persist in crime, that is, individuals who were registered for crime both during their youth and as adults

The question of typologies and classifications of offenders has been the subject of some considerable debate, a discussion that has focused on both theoretical and methodological issues (Skardhamar, 2010). We make no claims that our classification distinguishes homogeneous categories with distinctive careers. By means of our division of the study participants, we distinguish between those who desisted from crime before the transition from youth to adult life and those who were registered for crime as adults. Failure in the transition to adult life, a phase where occupational careers and family formation are initiated, has been shown to have a long-term negative impact on future attainment (Bäckman & Nilsson, 2011). As will be seen below, we are also able on the basis of this rather simple division of the study participants to differentiate between individuals with very different levels of involvement in crime. The SBC includes three different pieces of data relating to the prevalence of drug abuse, which capture the situation both in adolescence and early adulthood (for a further description, see appendix). Together, these official sources provide us with a picture of the cohort members' registered drug abuse from age 13 (1966) to age 30 (1983).

Measures of the Cohort Members' Situation During Childhood and Adolescence

Our measures on circumstances during childhood and adolescence are taken from different registers (see appendix) and capture SES, poverty, and social problems in the family of origin. These are measures that we know to be correlated with the cohort members' registered criminality (Nilsson & Estrada, 2009) and also with social exclusion in midlife (Bäckman & Nilsson, 2011). In our final models, we also include controls for cognitive ability (results from mental tests conducted when the cohort members were 13 years old) and school performance, which is measured by school grades in year 9 of compulsory school (age 16).

Measures on the Cohort Members' Situation in Late Midlife

Our outcome measures in late midlife relate to labor market attachment, income, social exclusion, family status, and mortality. These are all constructed from population based register data (see appendix). Family formation and marital status are measured at two time points: 1991 and 2001. A common child (or marriage) is a prerequisite to be counted as a cohabiting couple. To study formal labor market attachment, we have divided the cohort into different groups on the basis of their employment status and income in 2001. As a first step, the cohort members were divided into groups on the basis of annual earnings recalculated into what are referred to as *price base amounts* (PBAs).[6] The category *In Employment* is composed of those earning at least 3.5 PBA. This threshold was set to correspond to the lowest amount on which individuals can support themselves for a year.[7] The group *Unstable Labor Market Attachment* includes those earning between 1 and 3.5 PBA. The category *No Labor Market Attachment* is composed of those with a very low income (below 1 PBA) or no income at all. We also created categories that distinguish those on disability pensions and students. With regard to income, we divided the cohort into three groups—those with the lowest 20% of incomes, the highest 20%, and the remainder.

Our measure of social exclusion distinguishes the proportion, who, at age 48, were either outside the labor market (those with either no labor market attachment, or on disability pensions) or were in receipt of social welfare benefit. Being unemployed is to be denied both a certain type of social relationships and access to a social institution, the labor market, of which most people of working age are members. Similarly, financial poverty denies people full access to a social activity that is taken for granted by most members of modern societies, that is, consumption. Labor market exclusion and poverty do not fully account for the multidimensionality associated with social exclusion, but it nonetheless captures two of the most important dimensions of this construct. According to Burchardt (2000) exclusion from production activities and financial poverty appear as the most central indicators of social exclusion.

Results

Crime Among Females and Males

As expected, we find substantial differences in criminal participation (Reading Table 12.1). Seven percent of the female cohort members had been registered for offending up to the age of 31 as compared with 33% of the males. These proportions are similar to those reported in other studies (Bergman & Andershed, 2009; Eggleston & Laub, 2002; Moffitt et al., 2001, p. 214). There are approximately nine males for each female among the persisters. The overrepresentation of males is much less marked among the desisters and the late onset offenders (approximately four males for each female).[8] A larger proportion of the female offenders were registered for their first offence subsequent to the teenage years (44% as compared with 31%) which is in line with the results of other studies, which have shown that females have a later age of onset for crime (Block et al., 2010, Eggleston & Laub, 2002; Simpson et al., 2008; Stattin, Magnusson, & Reichel, 1989).

Almost half of the men that were registered for crime as teenagers were also registered as adults. Among females registered for crime as youths, desistance was more common; two thirds did not appear again in the criminal register as adults, which is in line with the results reported by Moffitt et al. (2001), for example. The three groups defined on the basis of their criminality as youths and as adults, respectively, differ substantially from one another with regard to the *frequency* of their registered offending. As expected, a small group of offenders account for a large proportion of the registered offences. Altogether, the group of males who continued to commit offences after their teenage years account for more than 75% of the male cohort members' registered offences, while at the same time constituting 11% of the males in the cohort. Among the females, these individuals compose 1% of the female cohort members but account for 54% of the females' adult registered offending. Looking at those cohort members who committed offences as both teenagers and adults, the level of offending among the males is significantly higher than that found among the females during the teenage

Reading Table 12.1 Proportion (Percentage) in Crime Register and Mean Number of Crimes by Age, Gender, and Categories of Offenders

	Desisters		Late Onset		Persisters	
	Male	Female	Male	Female	Male	Female
Percentage (N)	11.8 (859)	2.6 (181)	10.6 (777)	3.1 (216)	11.0 (803)	1.3 (89)
Mean offences as young	3.4	2.2a	—	—	11.7	3.6[a]
Proportion of youth offences females (NO = 720)	—	55	—	—	—	45
Proportion of youth offences males (NO = 12,336)	24	—	—	—	76	—
Mean offences as adult	—	—	3.3	4.7[a]	12.4	13.0
Proportion of adult offences females (NO = 2,173)	—	—	—	46	—	54
Proportion of adult offences males (NO = 12,534)	—	—	20	—	80	—

Note: Females ($N = 6,989$), males ($N = 7,305$). NO = number of offences.

[a] Female offender group differs from corresponding male offender group ($p < .05$).

period. During the adult period, however, the females in the group have on average been registered for just as many offences as the males (although the number of males in the group is substantially larger).

The cohort's offending, which has been described in previous studies, is dominated by theft, motoring, and fraud offences (Kratzer & Hodgkins, 1999; Wikström, 1987, 1990; see also tables in Nilsson & Estrada, 2009). The clearest difference between the sexes in the *crime mix* (type of crime over the life span) is that the males are registered for motoring offences to a much greater extent, whereas fraud offences account for a larger proportion of the females' criminality. Crimes of violence constitute only a small proportion of the offences committed, irrespective of crime grouping. The individuals who continue to commit offences as adults do not distinguish themselves by being specialized in any particular type of offending. What differentiates the groups is thus first and foremost not the types of crime engaged in but rather the frequency of offending, and this is the case for both males and females.

This pattern corresponds well with the findings of other studies (Block et al., 2010; Blokland et al., 2005, p. 945; Stattin et al., 1989).

Drug Abuse

A large proportion of those who continue to commit offences subsequent to their teenage years are drug abusers (Reading Table 12.2). This is particularly the case among the females; almost two thirds of the female persisters have been classified as drug abusers in the register data. The other two female offender groups also consist of significantly higher proportions of drug abusers by comparison with the corresponding groups of males. It is also noteworthy that most of the drug abusers are already known to the authorities as such when they are teenagers. Among the males and females who are first registered for crime as adults, however, the majority do not appear in the data as known drug abusers until after the age of 18. Another factor which shows that drug abuse and criminality follow a

Reading Table 12.2   Proportion (Percentage) Registered for Drug Abuse Between Ages 13 and 30, by Gender, Categories of Offenders, and Source of Information (*N*)

	No Crime	Desisters	Late Onset	Persisters	Total
Females	(6,503)	(181)	(216)	(89)	(6,989)
Drug abuse total 13–30	0.8	19.9[a,b]	19.4[a,b]	60.7[a,b]	2.6
Drug abuse 13–30 according to Social register (13–18 years)	0.6	18.2[a,b]	10.2[a,b]	43.8[a,b]	1.9
Hospital register (13–30 years)	0.2	4.4[a,b]	11.6[a,b]	31.5[a,b]	1.1
Needle-mark study (15–30 years)	0.1	5.0[a,b]	9.7[a,b]	42.7[a,b]	1.0
Drug abuse 13–18 years	0.6	18.2[a,b]	11.6[a,b]	47.2[a,b]	2.0
Drug abuse 19–30 years	0.2	5.0[a,b]	13.4[a,b]	43.8[a,b]	1.3
Males	(4,866)	(859)	(777)	(803)	(7,305)
Drug abuse total 13–30	0.6	4.3[a]	4.1[a]	29.5[a]	4.6
Drug abuse 13–30 according to Social register (13–18 years)	0.4	3.3[a]	1.4[a]	19.8[a]	3.0
Hospital register (13–30 years)	0.2	0.8[a]	2.1[a]	11.3[a]	1.7
Needle-mark study (15–30 years)	0.0	0.8[a]	2.6[a]	18.7	2.4
Drug abuse 13–18 years	0.4	3.7[a]	1.4[a]	22.2[a]	3.3
Drug abuse 19–30 years	0.2	0.9[a]	3.3[a]	20.4[a]	2.8

[a] Offender group differs from nonoffenders (*p* < .05).

[b] Female offender group differs from corresponding male offender group (*p* < .05).

similar developmental pattern is found in the fact that the proportion of desisters with registered drug abuse declines substantially after the teenage years. There are clear differences as regard the registers in which the different offender groups are found and this, at least in part, can be seen as a reflection of the seriousness of the addiction problem. Both the hospital and needle-mark registers describe more serious drug problems than those found in the files from the Child Welfare Committees.

As we know that drug abuse is correlated with both criminality and adult social bonds, we can expect these findings to have importance for the welfare situation in midlife among male and female offenders. Before we study how their lives turned out, however, we will describe how life started for the girls and boys in the Stockholm cohort.

Conditions During Childhood and Adolescence

It is clear that the cohort members who have been registered for crime are more scarcely resourced. Among the persisters, around one third had grown up in a family categorized as recurrently or chronically poor. The group who persisted in crime is in this regard different from the other two offender groups. There is a tendency in each of the three groups that had been registered for crime for the females to have experienced more poverty during childhood than the males (Reading Table 12.3).

The SBC database also allows for an examination of the significance of childhood conditions which indicate more serious social problems. In the same way as in the case of financial difficulties, it is clear that the females who have been registered for crime tend to have experienced social problems in their childhood environments more often than the corresponding group of males. It seems as though the females who commit offences repeatedly constitute a more highly selected (poorly resourced) group than the corresponding group of males. It is important to note that it is only when we look at indicators of more direct and accumulated resource deficiencies that it becomes apparent that it takes more to become a female offender.

Family, Work, and Social Exclusion at Age 48

The final year to which we are able to follow the cohort in this study is 2001, the year in which the cohort members

Reading Table 12.3   Childhood Conditions, Proportion (Percentage) by Gender and Categories of Offenders (N)

	No Crime	Desisters	Late Onset	Persisters	Total
Females	(6,503)	(181)	(216)	(89)	(6,989)
Social class					
Upper and upper-middle class	17.5	13.9	17.6	9.1[a]	17.3
Lower-middle class	44.4	36.1[a]	32.4[a,b]	34.1[a]	43.7
Skilled blue-collar	22.5	25.6	26.4	25.0	22.7
Unskilled blue-collar	15.5	24.4[a]	23.6[a]	31.8[a]	16.2
Poverty					
Nonpoor	81.6	64.1[a]	67.1[a,b]	42.7[a,b]	80.2
Transient poor	8.9	13.3[a]	11.1	19.1[a]	9.2
Recurrent poor	5.4	11.6[a]	12.5[a,b]	21.3[a]	6.0
Chronic poor	4.1	11.0[a,b]	9.3[a]	16.9[a]	4.6
Social problems family of origin					
Alcohol abuse parents	5.4	14.9[a,b]	13.9[a,b]	24.7[a]	6.2
Mental health problems parents	5.6	12.7[a]	11.1[a]	25.8[a]	6.2
Father registered for crime	5.2	11.0[a]	8.8[a]	23.6[a,b]	5.7
At least one social problem	12.8	27.6[a,b]	23.6[a,b]	53.9[a,b]	14.1

	No Crime	Desisters	Late Onset	Persisters	Total
Males	(4,866)	(859)	(777)	(803)	(7,305)
Social class					
Upper and upper-middle class	19.9	11.5[a]	14.6[a]	7.5[a]	17.0
Lower-middle class	44.8	40.9[a]	42.3	34.8[a]	43.0
Skilled blue-collar	21.1	24.7[a]	23.8	30.8[a]	22.9
Unskilled blue-collar	14.3	22.9[a]	19.3[a]	27.0[a]	17.2
Poverty					
Nonpoor	84.0	69.5[a]	76.1[a]	55.0[a]	78.3
Transient poor	8.9	13.6[a]	11.2[a]	18.1[a]	10.7
Recurrent poor	4.4	10.1[a]	6.3[a]	14.1[a]	6.3
Chronic poor	2.8	6.8[a]	6.4[a]	12.8[a]	4.7
Social problems family of origin					
Alcohol abuse parents	4.0	9.2[a]	7.2[a]	18.7[a]	6.5
Mental health problems parents	4.0	10.2[a]	7.3[a]	14.8[a]	6.8
Father registered for crime	3.6	7.5[a]	6.3[a]	10.3[a]	5.1
At least one social problem	9.8	20.8[a]	15.1[a]	32.9[a]	14.2

[a] Offender group differs from nonoffenders ($p < .05$).

[b] Female offender group differs from corresponding male offender group ($p < .05$).

celebrated their 48th birthdays. However, of the entire cohort, approximately 2% had died prior to the age of 48 (Reading Table 12.4). The mortality rate is approximately seven times as high (at 13%) among the male and female persisters by comparison with those who have not been registered for crime.[9] It is worth noting that the mortality rate is not higher among the females in the persistent crime group than it is among the males. Among the desisters and the late onset group, the mortality rates are considerably lower than among the persisters.

At age 48, most of the men and women were living with others either as married couples or cohabitees (with children in common). They were also in employment, with middle to high incomes, and very few were welfare benefit recipients (Reading Table 12.4). The living conditions of the offenders were significantly worse, however, with a large proportion living by themselves and on low incomes or no income at all. This pattern is more marked among the female cohort members. A majority of the females who had been registered for crime were registered as single at age 48, and this is particularly true among the female persisters, where only a small proportion (20%) were living with a partner. When the focus is directed at labor market attachment, we can see that among the women with no registered involvement in crime, 80% had established themselves on the labor market, which represents more or

Reading Table 12.4   Family Type, Employment Status, Income, and Mortality at 48 Years of Age (2001) by Gender and Categories of Offenders (N)

	No Crime	Desisters	Late Onset	Persisters	Total
Females					
Mortality					
Deceased by age 48	1.7	5.0[a]	4.6[a]	13.5[a]	2.0
Family type	(6208)	(166)	(203)	(76)	(6,653)
Single with children	19.0	24.1[b]	28.1[a,b]	30.3[a,b]	19.5
Single without children	21.0	27.1	35.0[a,b]	48.7[a]	21.9
Married or cohabiting with children	48.3	33.7[a,b]	32.5[a,b]	17.1[a,b]	47.1
Married or cohabiting without children	11.7	15.1[b]	4.4[a]	3.9[a]	11.5
Labor market attachment					
In employment (core labor force)	80.3	68.7[a,b]	59.6[a,b]	36.8[a,b]	78.9
Studying	1.5	1.8[b]	1.5	2.6	1.5
Unstable labor market attachment	8.3	12.7[a,b]	10.3	5.3	8.4
No labor market attachment	5.2	5.4	11.3[a]	19.7[a]	5.5
Disability pension	4.7	11.4[a,b]	17.2[a]	35.5[a,b]	5.6
Income and welfare benefit					
Welfare benefit recipient	1.4	6.6[a,b]	10.3[a,b]	34.2[a,b]	2.2
Income					
Low income (<20%)	19.7	31.3[a,b]	40.4[a,b]	63.2[a,b]	21.1
Middle income	69.5	60.8[a]	53.7[a]	35.5[a]	68.4
High income (>20%)	10.8	7.8[b]	5.9[a,b]	1.3[a,b]	10.5
Social exclusion	10.6	18.1[a,b]	32.0[a,b]	61.8[a,b]	12.0
Males					
Mortality					
Deceased by age 48	2.1	3.3[a]	4.8[a]	12.7[a]	3.7
Family type	(4,647)	(815)	(719)	(684)	(6,865)
Single parent	7.0	9.1[a]	7.1	10.3[a]	7.6

	No Crime	Desisters	Late Onset	Persisters	Total
Single without children	28.2	34.8[a]	42.8[a]	52.5[a]	32.9
Married or cohabiting with children	56.9	46.7[a]	42.6[a]	30.9[a]	51.6
Married or cohabiting without children	8.0	9.3	7.5	6.3[a]	7.9
Labor market attachment					
In employment (core labor force)	86.4	81.8[a]	71.3[a]	53.9[a]	81.1
Studying	0.5	0.4	0.6	1.2[a]	0.5
Unstable labor market attachment	4.9	7.0[a]	8.5[a]	9.2[a]	6.0
No labor market attachment	4.5	6.0	11.0[a]	18.1[a]	6.7
Disability pension	3.7	4.8	8.6[a]	17.5[a]	5.7
Income and welfare benefit					
Welfare benefit recipient	0.9	2.3[a]	3.9[a]	13.6[a]	2.6
Income					
Low income (<20%)	13.6	18.2[a]	28.7[a]	46.2[a]	18.9
Middle income	50.5	61.0[a]	55.1[a]	46.4[a]	51.8
High income (>20%)	36.0	20.9[a]	16.3[a]	7.4[a]	29.3
Social exclusion	8.5	11.8[a]	20.6[a]	39.0[a]	13.2

[a] Offender group differs from nonoffenders ($p < .05$).

[b] Female offender group differs from corresponding male offender group ($p < .05$).

less the same level as that found among the men. Among the female desisters, the level of labor market attachment was also relatively high. However, for the female persisters, it was as common to be on a disability pension as it was to be in employment. Among the males too, the degree of labor market attachment was markedly worse among the persisters, and, at age 48, only half of them were counted among the core labor force. In late midlife, 2% to 3% of the male and female cohort members were welfare benefit recipients. Among male and female persisters, this proportion is many times greater. The same pattern is found in relation to disability pensions. There is a clear tendency among both males and females for those who had been registered for crime for the first time as adults to have living

conditions that were better than those of the persisters but worse than those of the desisters.

In Reading Table 12.4, we also present our summary measure of social exclusion (either outside the labor market or in receipt of social welfare benefit). Of the women registered for crime both during and subsequent to their teenage years, almost two thirds meet this definition of social exclusion, compared with just below 40% of the males in the same group. The corresponding proportions are much lower among those who desisted from crime during their teenage years, who are therefore more reminiscent of those with no registered involvement in crime. Those who belong to the late onset group were living in social exclusion to a greater extent at age 48, and the situation of the women was particularly unfavorable. In summary, it is worth noting that for every welfare outcome where there are clear differences between the males and females who have been registered for crime, these differences are to the disadvantage of the females. Why is this? We already know that a larger proportion of the females with registered involvement in crime were drug abusers, and it would therefore seem reasonable to examine this issue in more detail.

Crime, Drug Abuse, and Social Exclusion

It is clear that drug abuse affects the risk of social exclusion for both sexes, even after controlling for involvement in crime (Reading Table 12.5). Note, for example, that drug abusers with no official criminal record are more socially excluded than desisters with no known drug abuse. After controlling for drug abuse, the higher risk of social exclusion among females only remains for the small group of persistent offenders who are not drug users. This indicates that drug abuse has particular importance for both patterns of criminality and other life-course outcomes among females.

The differences in childhood circumstances that have been described in the article would alone be sufficient to expect to find worse outcomes in late midlife among the females registered for involvement in crime (see, for example, Bäckman & Nilsson, 2011). In addition, we have noted more extensive levels of drug abuse among females with a criminal record. Reading Tables 12.6 and 12.7 present the results from logistic regression analyses which examine how the risk for social exclusion is linked to involvement in crime and gender, given controls for both differences in drug abuse and in other circumstances during childhood and adolescence. The focus is thus directed at the interaction between sex and the different offender categories. The dependant variable is the summary measure of social exclusion. The tables show odds ratios using males with no registered involvement in crime as the reference category. To facilitate comparisons with the other groups, the tables also present confidence intervals for these odds ratios. Reading Table 12.6 shows that the groups who have been registered for crime as adults present a clear excess risk for social exclusion, even when

Reading Table 12.5   Social Exclusion (2001) and Drug Use (1966–1983)

	No Crime	Desisters	Late Onset	Persisters	Total
Females	(6,208)	(166)	(203)	(76)	(6,653)
Social exclusion and drug use					
Exclusion among nonusers	10.5	14.0[a,b]	26.2[a,b]	53.1[a,b]	11.2
Exclusion among drug users	25.0	36.7[a]	60.0[a]	68.2[a]	47.1
Males	(4,647)	(815)	(719)	(684)	(6,865)
Social exclusion and drug use					
Exclusion among nonusers	8.4	11.0[a]	19.1[a]	30.1[a]	11.5
Exclusion among drug users	25.9	30.3[a]	62.5[a]	64.8[a]	56.2

NOTE: Proportion (percentage) who at age 48 were either in receipt of social welfare benefits or who had no attachment to the labor market and proportion registered for drug abuse between ages 13 and 30, by gender, categories of offenders, and drug use (*N*). All differences in social exclusion between non–drug users and users are significant ($p < .05$) except among female persistent offenders.

[a] Group differs from nonoffenders ($p < .05$).

[b] Female offender group differs from corresponding male offender group ($p < .05$).

Reading Table 12.6   The Risk for Social Exclusion at Age 48

	No Crime	Desisters	Late Onset	Persisters
Male	1	1.22 (0.94–1.59)	2.55[a] (2.03–3.21)	4.94[a] (3.88–5.99)
Female	1.28[a] (1.11–1.48)	1.93[a] (1.23–3.03)	4.33[a] (3.12–6.25)	12.20[a,b] (6.72–19.08)

NOTE: Interaction effects of sex and offender category. Results from logistic regression models. Odds ratios (95% confidence interval). Controls included for poverty family of origin, parents alcohol abuse, parents mental health problems, father registered for crime, social class, IQ, and grades in year 9 of compulsory school, N = 12,051.

[a] Group differs from male nonoffenders (p < .05).

[b] Female offender group differs from corresponding male offender group (p < .05).

Reading Table 12.7   The Risk for Social Exclusion at Age 48 (Control for Drug Abuse Included)

	No Crime	Desisters	Late Onset	Persisters
Male	1	1.15 (0.88–1.51)	2.47[a] (1.96–3.11)	3.67[a] (2.91–4.62)
Female	1.28[a] (1.11–1.48)	1.45 (0.91–2.32)	3.56[a] (2.48–5.10)	6.29[a] (3.60–10.99)

NOTE: Interaction effects of sex and offender category. Results from logistic regression models. Odds ratios (95% confidence interval). Controls included for poverty family of origin, parents alcohol abuse, parents mental health problems, father registered for crime, social class, IQ, grades in year 9 of compulsory school, and drug abuse, N = 12,051.

[a] Group differs from male nonoffenders (p < .05).

controls are included for a range of circumstances experienced during childhood and adolescence, whereas the desisters do not differ significantly from the no-crime group. The table also shows that the only group of female offenders that differs from the corresponding group of males is the persisters. In Reading Table 12.7, we have also included a control for drug abuse. As expected, the level of excess risk then declines for both the late onset group and the persisters. The female persisters remain the group at most risk of social exclusion, but the difference in relation to the male persisters is no longer significant.

✉ Concluding Discussion

Our main research question has centered on how life turned out for men and women with different forms of criminal involvement. Does it take more, in terms of

childhood risk factors, and cost more, in terms of long-term negative consequences, to be a female offender? A finding common to both males and females is that those individuals who committed offences come from markedly worse childhood conditions. When we look at more direct indicators of social disadvantage during childhood (families marked by long-term poverty and social problems) rather than more indirect indicators (SES), we also see that the backgrounds of the female offenders are characterized by more serious problems than those of their male counterparts. In this sense, it "takes more" to become a female offender.

By contrast with what has been suggested by Tanner et al. (1999), our results indicate that the situation for female offenders is particularly problematic and that drug use is of significance to this difference. Our results are therefore more in line with the conclusions drawn on the basis of the research conducted by the Ohio Longitudinal Study (e.g.,

Giordano, 2010; Giordano et al., 2002; Lanctot et al., 2007; Schroeder et al., 2007). When we look at the cohort members' family situation and labor market attachment in late midlife, the differences between those who desisted from crime in their teenage years and those with no registered offending is quite small. For those who were registered for crime as adults, however, the situation is more problematic, and this is particularly so for the females. The literature has indicated that the stigma of being registered for crime is greater for females than for males, which, for example, can make it more difficult for female offenders to find conventional males to live with (e.g., De Li & MacKenzie, 2003; Steffensmeier & Allan, 1996). Our study confirms that female offenders appear to be worse off in this regard, at least in late midlife. Moreover, as adults, the majority of the female persisters can be described as socially excluded; a large proportion is not in employment and are experiencing difficulties supporting themselves. Even though these things are also true of many of the men who persisted in offending into adulthood, it is important to note that in middle age, the majority of these men have some level of labor market attachment. Furthermore, a large proportion of these men are involved in stable family relationships. This is not the case for the corresponding group of females. Among the desisters and the late onset group, there is also a tendency for the situation as adults to be worse among the females. Thus, it appears that involvement in crime exacts a higher cost for female offenders.

However, the fact that the situation of the female offenders is worse than that of the males is *essentially* associated with their more problematic backgrounds and their more extensive levels of drug abuse. When controls are included for differences in childhood conditions and drug abuse, female offenders do not differ from the corresponding male offender categories, which is to say that if we compare female offenders with male offenders presenting similar backgrounds and experiences of drug abuse, we see more similarities than differences between the two groups. In short, the same factors seem to produce the same long-term outcome for males and females. This is an important result because it suggests that it is the selection process that is most significant rather than the possibility that the negative consequences of involvement in crime are more pronounced for female offenders. To conclude, the existence of gendered pathways (Simpson et al., 2008; Steffensmeier & Allan, 1996) becomes apparent when we look at indicators

of more direct and accumulated resource deficiencies and drug abuse. This fact also underscores the argument of, among others, Farnworth, Thornberry, Krohn, and Lizotte (1994) that it is not sufficient to use broader categories such as SES as indicators of problematic living conditions. Moreover, even if both male and female drug users share the fate of social exclusion in midlife, we think that it is noteworthy that so many of the female offenders are registered as drug users. This is a finding in line with research that sees drug use as an important feature of both the causes and the outcome of persistent female criminality (Daly, 1992; Simpson et al., 2008) and at the same time a result life-course criminology has not paid enough attention to.

Limitations

The individuals we have studied were born in Sweden in 1953 and thus lived as youths during the 1960s and 1970s. What can we learn today from their experiences? When generalizing on the basis of our findings, it is important to be aware of the fact that there are differences over time and between countries as regard the conditions that affect the prevalence of, for example, risk and protective factors, the social measures employed by a given society and also crime policy. However, we would argue that the specificity of the context of the Stockholm cohort is not a problem. To identify general processes that are not tied to a specific time or place, there is good reason to study the longer term consequences of childhood conditions, crime, and drug abuse for individuals from a society that differs from those which dominate this field of research (see also Bersani, Laub, & Nieuwbeerta, 2009; Savolainen, 2009).

By utilizing a longitudinal data set (the SBC), we have been able, primarily on the basis of various forms of register data, to follow a large number of males and females from childhood into adult life. This has made it possible to analyze questions that have previously been difficult to examine. Our study is limited, however, by problems which are already widely acknowledged. Our conclusions about gendered pathways and consequences relate only to those offences that are detected and registered by the criminal justice system. As has been noted by Steffensmeier and Allan (1996) sex differences are smaller in studies based on self-report data, but these data also tend often to describe less serious forms of involvement in crime by comparison with the criminality that becomes the object of justice system interventions. Although we have been able to use indicators relating to a range of different childhood and living conditions, there remain important areas that we have not been able to examine, including, for example, the significance of childhood trauma and sexual abuse as precursors to offending and vulnerability to abuse from men. These have been identified as important factors in relation to the understanding of gendered pathways and consequences (Belknap & Holsinger, 2006; Cernkovich, Lanctot, & Giordano, 2008; Daly, 1992; Simpson et al., 2008).

Questions that we are interested in examining in future studies focus on the within group variation among those registered for involvement in crime: What differentiates the males and females for whom things turned out well from those for whom things went badly? What are the roles played by childhood conditions, events occurring later in life, and society's responses to their criminality, and in what way does the significance of different live [or life] events vary between males and females?

Appendix

Variables (order of appearance)	Source (for construction of variable)	Variable Description	Further Information[a]	Cohort Age
Categories of offenders	National crime register 1966–1984	See article text	Codebook IV	13–31
Drug abuse	Drug abuse in the social register 1966–1971. Drug-related diagnosis in the in-patient discharge register 1966–1983. The injection mark study. data on intravenous drug abuse in the Stockholm police arrest population 1968–1983	0 = no indications in register; 1 = at least one indication in one of the sources	Codebook II, IV,V	13–30
Social class (mostly fathers occupation)	Population register 1963	1 = upper-middle class; 2 = lower-middle class; 3 = skilled workers; 4 = unskilled workers	Codebook II	10
Poverty	Social register. Receipt of means tested social assistance benefit during 1953–1959 and/or 1960–1965 and/or 1966–1972	1 = no indications in register; 2 = received one period; 3 = received two periods; 4 = received all three periods	Codebook II	0–19
Parents' alcohol problems	Incidents of drunkenness of parent according to the social register 1953–1972	0 = no incidents; 1 = one or more incidents	Codebook II	0–19
Parents' psychological problems	Mother or father showing symptoms of mental illness according to the Social Register 1953–1972	0 = no symptoms; 1 = show symptoms on one or more occasions	Codebook II	0–19
Father's criminality	National crime register 1953–1972	0 = no convictions; 1 = one or more convictions	Codebook IV	0–19
Mortality	The causes of death register 1981–2001	0 = no indication in register; 1 = dead	Codebook VI	27–48

(Continued)

(Continued)

Variables (order of appearance)	Source (for construction of variable)	Variable Description	Further Information[a]	Cohort Age
Family type	Longitudinal Database on Education, Income and Occupation (LOUISE)	1 = *single parent;* 2 = *single without children;* 3 = *married or cohabiting with children;* 4 = *married or cohabiting without children*	Codebook VI	48
Employment	LOUISE	See article text	Codebook VI	48
Welfare benefit	LOUISE	0 = *no indications in register;* 1 = *at least one indication*	Codebook VI	48
Income	LOUISE	1 = *low income;* 2 = *middle income;* 3 = *high income*	Codebook VI	48
Social exclusion	LOUISE	0 = *not socially excluded;* 1 = *either outside the labor market or in receipt of social welfare benefit*	Codebook VI	48
Educational achievement (age 16)	Records from the school boards of Stockholm City and Stockholm County 1969 (1966)	Grade score average from the ninth grade (ranging 1–5). Where data are missing, grade scores from the sixth grade have been used	Codebook II	16
Cognitive ability/IQ	The School Study 1966	Continuous variable based on results from cognitive tests	Codebook I	13

[a] Codebooks available at www.stockholmbirthcohort.su.se

Notes

1. Bergman and Andershed (2009) use data from the IDA longitudinal research program, which follows a cohort of children from a midsize Swedish city, to illuminate questions about differences between male and female offenders. However, as they themselves conclude, "The number of females in some of the offender groups is so small that the results / . . . / must be interpreted with great caution. Hence, although both genders were studied, the reporting was focused on the results for men" (p. 175).

2. OLS is a panel study of adolescents originally surveyed in 1982 when they resided in juvenile correctional institutions. The sample includes 127 female offenders and 127 male offenders. A first follow-up was conducted in 1995 and a second in 2003 (Giordano, 2010).

3. According to the Street Woman scenario, childhood trauma and sexual victimization push young women to run away from home. "Life on the street leads to drug use and addiction, which in turn leads to more frequent lawbreaking to support a drug habit" (Daly, 1992, p. 13; see also Hagan & McCarthy, 1997).

4. For this study, we have had restricted access to the HSIA data (especially regarding the health/illness variables).

5. The matching procedure involved identifying unique combinations of the variables included in both data sets for the individual study subjects. Probability matching is inferior to matching based on personal identification numbers. However, in this case, there are few unmatched individuals (4.4%), and the differences between matched and unmatched (excluded) are small (for a detailed description of the matching procedure, see Stenberg et al., 2007).

6. Annual earnings consist of income from work and work-related social insurance programs, such as sickness benefits and parental insurance, but do not include pensions and unemployment insurance.

7. The size of the price base amount is tied to the consumer price index. In 2007, the price base amount was specified at approximately 4,000 Euros/US$5,500.

8. Comparisons of the outcomes for the four groups (prevalence) have been conducted in part using the chi-square test and with the F test (ANOVA) when the focus is directed at differences in mean values. Females have been compared with the corresponding male offender groups, that is, in Reading Table 12.1, the mean of 3.6 offences as youths among female persisters is significantly lower than the mean of 11.7 offences noted in the corresponding group of males.

9. The differences in mortality rates are underestimated somewhat as we can only study the SBC cohort, that is, those who could be matched with more recent data (and who were thus alive in 1980).

◌ **References**

Bäckman, O., & Nilsson, A. (2011). Pathways to social exclusion. *European Sociological Review, 27,* 107–123.

Belknap, J., & Holsinger, K. (2006). The gendered nature of risk factors for delinquency. *Feminist Criminology, 1,* 48–71.

Bergman, L., & Andershed, A.-K. (2009). Predictors and outcomes of persistent or age-limited registered criminal behaviour: A 30-year longitudinal study of a Swedish urban population. *Aggressive Behaviour, 35,* 164–178.

Bersani, B., Laub, J., & Nieuwbeerta, P. (2009). Marriage and desistance from crime in the Netherlands: Do gender and sociohistorical context matter? *Journal of Quantitative Criminology, 25,* 3–24.

Block, C., Blokland, A., van der Werff, C., van Os, R., & Nieuwbeerta, P. (2010). Long-term patterns of offending in women. *Feminist Criminology, 5,* 73–107.

Blokland, A., Nagin, D., & Nieuwbeerta, P. (2005). Life span offending trajectories of a Dutch conviction cohort. *Criminology, 43,* 919–954.

Burchardt, T. (2000). Social exclusion: Concepts and evidence. In D. Gordon & P. Townsend (Eds.), *Breadline Europe: The measurement of poverty* (pp. 385–405). Bristol, UK: Policy Press.

Cernkovich, S., Lanctot, N., & Giordano, P. (2008). Predicting adolescent and adult antisocial behaviour among adjudicated delinquent females. *Crime and Delinquency, 54,* 3–33.

Daly, K. (1992). Women's pathways to felony court: Feminist theories of lawbreaking and problems of representation. *Review of Law and Women's Studies, 2,* 11–52.

De Li, S., & MacKenzie, D. (2003). The gendered effects of adult social bonds on the criminal activities of probationers. *Criminal Justice Review, 28,* 278–298.

Eggleston, E., & Laub, J. (2002). The onset of adult offending: A neglected dimension of the criminal career. *Journal of Criminal Justice, 30,* 603–622.

Farnworth, M., Thornberry, T., Krohn, M., & Lizotte, A. (1994). Measurement in the study of class and delinquency: Integrating theory and research. *Journal of Research in Crime and Delinquency, 31,* 32–61.

Farrington, D., Coid, J., Harnett, L., Jolliffe, D., Soteriou, N., Turner, R., & West, D. (2006). *Criminal careers up to age 50 and life success up to age 48: New findings from the Cambridge Study in Delinquent Development* (2nd ed.). London, UK: Home Office Research Studies.

Farrington, D., Tfofi, M., & Coid, J. (2009). Development of adolescence-limited, late-onset, and persistent offenders from age 8 to age 48. *Aggressive Behaviour, 35,* 150–163.

Fry, L. (1985). Drug abuse and crime in a Swedish birth cohort. *British Journal of Criminology, 25,* 46–59.

Giordano, P. (2010). *Legacies of crime: A follow-up of the children of highly delinquent girls and boys.* New York, NY: Cambridge University Press.

Giordano, P., Cernkovich, S., & Rudolph, J. (2002). Gender, crime and desistance: Toward a theory of cognitive transformation. *American Journal of Sociology, 107,* 990–1064.

Gorman-Smith, D., & Loeber, R. (2005). Are developmental pathways in disruptive behaviors the same for girls and boys? *Journal of Child and Family Studies, 14,* 15–27.

Hagan, J., & McCarthy, B. (1997). *Mean streets.* Cambridge, UK: Cambridge University Press.

Heidensohn, F. (1968). The deviance of women: A critique and an enquiry. *British Journal of Sociology, 19,* 160–175.

Holsinger, K. (2000). Feminist perspectives on female offending. *Women & Criminal Justice, 12,* 23–51.

Jansson, C.-G. (1995). *On project metropolitan and the longitudinal perspective* (Project Metropolitan, Research Report No. 40). Stockholm, Sweden: Department of Sociology, Stockholm University.

Katz, R. (2000). Explaining girls' and women's crime and desistance in the context of their victimization experiences. *Violence Against Women, 6,* 633–660.

Kratzer, L., & Hodgkins, S. (1999). A typology of offenders: A test of Moffitt's theory among males and females from childhood to age 30. *Criminal Behaviour and Mental Health, 9,* 57–73.

Krohn, M., Lizotte, A., & Perez, C. (1997). The interrelationship between substance use and precocious transitions to adult statuses. *Journal of Health and Social Behaviour, 38,* 87–103.

Kyvsgaard, B. (1989). *Og faengslet tar de sidste* [And prison take the last] (Criminality, Punishment and Living Conditions). Copenhagen, Denmark: Jurist-og okonomforbundets forlag. (in Danish)

Lanctot, N., Cernkovich, S., & Giordano, P. (2007). Delinquent behaviour, official delinquency and gender: Consequences for adulthood functioning and well-being. *Criminology, 45,* 131–157.

Laub, J., & Sampson, R. (2003). *Shared beginnings, divergent lives: Delinquent boys to age 70.* Cambridge, MA: Harvard University Press.

Lay, B., Ihle, W., Esser, G., & Schmidt, M. (2005). Juvenile-episodic, continued or adult-onset delinquency? Risk conditions analysed in a cohort of children followed up to the age of 25 years. *European Journal of Criminology, 2,* 36–66.

Lenke, L., & Olsson, B. (2002). Swedish drug policy in the twenty-first century: A policy model going astray. *Annals of the American Academy of Political and Social Science, 582,* 64–79.

Moffitt, T., Caspi, A., Rutter, M., & Silva, P. (2001). *Sex differences in antisocial behaviour: Conduct disorder, delinquency and violence in the Dunedin Longitudinal Study.* Cambridge, UK: Cambridge University Press.

Molero Samuelsson, Y. (2011). *Antisocial behaviour over the life course among females and males treated for substance misuse.* Solna, Sweden: Karolinska Institutet.

Mullings, J., Pollock, J., & Crouch, B. (2002). Drugs and criminality: Results from the Texas women inmates study. *Women & Criminal Justice, 13,* 69–96.

Nilsson, A. (2003). Living conditions, social exclusion and recidivism among prison inmates. *Journal of Scandinavian Studies in Criminology and Crime Prevention, 4,* 57–83.

Nilsson, A., & Estrada, F. (2009). *Criminality and life chances: A longitudinal study of crime, childhood circumstances and living conditions to age 48* (Report 2009:3). Stockholm, Sweden: Department of Criminology, Stockholm University.

Odgers, C., Moffitt, T., Broadbent, J., Dickson, N., Hancox, R., Harrington, H., . . . Caspi, A. (2008). Female and male antisocial trajectories: From childhood origins to adult outcomes. *Development and Psychopathology, 20,* 673–716.

Piquero, A., Farrington, D., Nagin, D., & Moffitt, T. (2010). Trajectories of offending and their relations to life failure in late middle age: Findings from the Cambridge Study in Delinquent Development. *Journal of Research in Crime and Delinquency, 47,* 151–173.

Pulkkinen, L., Lyyra, A. L., & Kokko, K. (2009). Life success of males on non-offender, adolescence-limited, persistent, and adult-onset antisocial pathways: Follow up from age 8 to 42. *Aggressive Behaviour, 35,* 117–135.

Sarnecki, J., & Sollenhag, S. (1985). *Predicting social maladjustment: Stockholm boys grown up* (Report No. 17). Washington, DC: National Council for Crime Prevention.

Savolainen, J. (2009). Work, family and criminal desistance. *British Journal of Criminology, 49,* 285–304.

Schroeder, R., Giordano, P., & Cernkovich, S. (2007). Drug use and desistance processes. *Criminology, 45,* 191–222.

Simpson, S., Yahner, J., & Dugan, L. (2008). Understanding women's pathways to jail: Analysing the lives of incarcerated women. *Australian and New Zealand Journal of Criminology, 41,* 84–108.

Skardhamar, T. (2010). Distinguishing facts and artefacts in group-based modelling. *Criminology, 48,* 295–320.

Soothill, K., Christoffersen, M., Hussain, M., & Francis, B. (2010). Exploring paradigms of crime reduction: An empirical longitudinal study. *British Journal of Criminology, 50,* 222–238.

Stattin, H., Magnusson, D., & Reichel, H. (1989). Criminal activity at different ages: A study based on a Swedish longitudinal research population. *British Journal of Criminology, 29,* 368–385.

Steffensmeier, D., & Allan, E. (1996). Gender and crime: Toward a gendered theory of female offending. *Annual Review of Sociology, 22,* 459–487.

Stenberg, S-Å., & Vågerö, D. (2006). Cohort profile: The Stockholm birth cohort of 1953. *International Journal of Epidemiology, 35,* 546–548.

Stenberg, S-Å., Vågerö, D., Österman, R., Arvidsson, E., von Otter, C., & Jansson, C.-G. (2007). Stockholm Birth Cohort Study 1953–2003: A new tool for life course studies. *Scandinavian Journal of Public Health, 35,* 104–110.

Tanner, J., Davies, S., & O'Grady B. (1999). Whatever happened to yesterday's rebels? Longitudinal effects of youth delinquency on education and employment. *Social Problems, 46,* 250–274.

Torstensson, M. (1987). *Drug-abusers in a metropolitan cohort* (Project Metropolitan Research Report No. 25). Stockholm, Sweden: Department of Sociology, University of Stockholm.

Torstensson, M. (1990). Female delinquents in a birth cohort: Test of some aspects of control theory. *Journal of Quantitative Criminology, 6,* 101–115.

Wikström, P.-O. (1987). *Patterns of crime in a birth cohort: Age, sex and social class differences* (Project Metropolitan Research Report No. 24). Stockholm, Sweden: Department of Sociology, University of Stockholm.

Wikström, P.-O. (1990). Age and crime in a Stockholm cohort. *Journal of Quantitative Criminology, 6,* 61–84.

Wong, T., Slotboom, A.-M., & Bijleveld, C. (2010). Risk factors for delinquency in adolescent and young adult females: A European review. *European Journal of Criminology, 7,* 266–284.

DISCUSSION QUESTIONS

1. How do childhood conditions impact criminal behavior for the persisters in this study? Which factors have the strongest effect for men? For women?

2. By the age of 48, which factors are strongest for the persisters? For the desisters? How do these effects vary by gender?

3. Does crime have a higher cost for women compared to men?

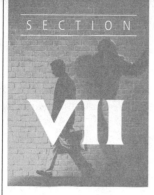

VII

Girls and Juvenile Delinquency

- The rise of the juvenile court
- The "double standard" for girls in the juvenile justice system
- The new *violent* girl
- Contemporary risk factors associated with girls and delinquency
- Gender-specific needs of young female offenders

While the majority of this book focuses on the needs of women and girls generally, this section highlights some of the specific issues facing girls within the juvenile justice system. Beginning with a discussion on the rise of the juvenile courts, this section highlights the historical and contemporary standards for young women in society and how the changing definitions of delinquency have disproportionately and negatively affected young girls. These practices have manifested into today's standards of addressing cases of female delinquents. This section concludes with a discussion of reforms designed to respond to the unique needs of girls within the juvenile justice system.

The Rise of the Juvenile Court and the Sexual Double Standard

The understanding of adolescence within the justice system is a relatively new phenomenon. Originally, the development of the term *juvenile delinquent* reflected the idea that youth were "malleable" and could be shaped into law-abiding citizens (Bernard, 1992). A key factor in this process was the doctrine of *parens patriae. Parens patriae* began in the English Chancery Courts during the 15th century and evolved into the practice whereby the state could assume custody of children for cases where the child had no parents or the parents were deemed unfit care providers. As time passed, parens patriae became the government's justification for regulating adolescents and their behaviors under the mantra in the best interests of the child (Sutton, 1988).

Prior to the development of the juvenile court, the majority of cases of youth offending were handled on an informal basis. However, the dramatic population growth, combined with the rise of industrialization, made it increasingly difficult for families and communities to control wayward youth. The doctrine of parens patriae led to the development of a separate system within the justice system designed to oversee the rehabilitation of youth who were deemed out of control.

Developed in 1825, the New York House of Refuge was one of the first reformatories for juvenile delinquents and was designed to keep youth offenders separate from the adult population. Unlike adults, youths were not sentenced to terms proportionate to their offenses in these early juvenile institutions. Instead, juveniles were committed to institutions for long periods of time, often until their 21st birthday. The doctrine of parens patriae was often used to discriminate against children of the poor, as these youth had not necessarily committed a criminal offense. Rather, youth were more likely to be described as "coming from an unfit home" or displaying "incorrigible behaviors" (Bernard, 1992). The practices at the House of Refuge during the 19th century were based less on controlling criminal behaviors and more on preventing future pauperism, which the reformers believed led to delinquency and crime (Sutton, 1988). Rather than address the conditions facing poor parents and children, reformers chose to respond to what they viewed as the "peculiar weaknesses of the children's moral natures" and "weak and criminal parents" (Bernard, 1992, p. 76).

The Progressive Era of the late 19th and early 20th century in the United States led to the child-saving movement, which comprised middle- and upper-class White citizens who "regarded their cause as a matter of conscience and morality (and) viewed themselves as altruists and humanitarians dedicated to rescuing those who were less fortunately placed in the social order" (Platt, 1969, p. 3). The efforts of the child-savers movement led to the creation of the first juvenile court in Chicago in 1899. The jurisdiction of the juvenile court presided over three youth populations: (1) children who committed adult criminal offenses, (2) children who committed status offenses, and (3) children who were abused or neglected by their parents (Chesney-Lind & Shelden, 2004).

Parens patriae significantly affected the treatment of girls who were identified as delinquent. During the late 19th and early 20th centuries, moral reformers embarked on an **age-of-consent campaign**, which was designed to protect young women from *vicious men* who preyed on the innocence of girls. Prior to the age-of-consent campaign, the legal age of sexual consent in 1885 ranged between 10 and 12 for most states. As a result of the efforts by moral reformers, all states raised the age of consent to 16 or 18 by 1920. While their attempt to guard the chastity of young women from exploitation was rooted in a desire to protect girls, these practices also denied young women an avenue for healthy sexual expression and identity. The laws that resulted from this movement were often used to punish young women's displays of sexuality by placing them in detention centers or reformatories for moral violations with the intent to incarcerate them throughout their adolescence. These actions held women to a high standard of sexual purity, while the sexual nature of men was dismissed by society as normal and pardonable behavior. In addition, the reformers developed their policies based on a White, middle-class ideal of purity and modesty—anyone who did not conform to these ideals was viewed as out of control and in need of intervention by the juvenile court (Chesney-Lind & Shelden, 2004). This exclusive focus by moral reformers on the sexual exploitation of White, working-class women led to the racist implication that only the virtues of White women needed to be saved. While reformers in the Black community were equally interested in the moral education of young women and men, they were unsupportive of the campaign to impose criminal sanctions on offenders for sexual crimes, as they were concerned that such laws would unfairly target men of color (Odem, 1995).

Age-of-consent campaigners viewed the delinquent acts of young women as inherently more dangerous than the acts of their male counterparts. Due to the emphasis on sexual purity as the pathway toward healthy adulthood and stability for the future, the juvenile reformatory became a place to shift the focus away from their sexual desire and train young girls for marriage. Unfortunately, this increased focus on the use of the reformatory for moral offenses allowed for the practice of net widening to occur, and more offenders were placed under the supervision of the juvenile courts. Net widening refers to the practice whereby programs such as diversion were developed to inhibit the introduction of youth into the juvenile justice system. However, these practices often expanded the reach to offenses and populations that previously were outside the reach of the juvenile justice system. The effects of this practice actually increased the number of offenders under the general reach of the system, whether informally or formally.

Beyond the age-of-consent campaign, the control of girls' sexuality extended to all girls involved in the juvenile court, regardless of offense. A review of juvenile court cases between 1929 and 1964 found that girls who were arrested for status offenses were forced to have gynecological exams to determine whether or not they had engaged in sexual intercourse and if they had contracted any sexually transmitted diseases. Not only were these girls more likely to be sent to juvenile detention than their male counterparts, but they also spent three times as long in detention for their "crimes" (Chesney-Lind, 1973). Indeed, throughout the early 20th century, the focus on female sexuality and sexually transmitted infections (STI) reached epic proportions, and any woman who was suspected to be infected with a STI was arrested, examined, and quarantined (Odem, 1995).

In addition to being placed in detention centers for engaging in consensual sex, young women were often blamed for "tempting defendants into immoral behavior" (Odem, 1995, p. 68) in cases where they were victims of forcible sexual assault. Other historical accounts confirm how sexual victimization cases were often treated by the juvenile court in the same manner as consensual sex cases—in both situations the girl was labeled as delinquent for having sex (Shelden, 1981). These girls were doubly victimized, first by the assault and second by the system. During these court hearings, a woman's sexual history was put on display in an attempt to discredit her in front of a jury, yet the courts did not request similar information about a man's sexual history as it would "unfairly prejudice the jury against him" (Odem, 1995, p. 70). These historical accounts emphasized that any nonmarital sexual experience, even forcible rape, typically resulted in girls being treated as offenders.

The trend of using sexuality as a form of delinquent behavior for female offenders continued throughout the 20th and into the 21st century. The court system has become a mechanism through which control of female sexuality is enforced. Males enjoy a sense of sexual freedom that is denied to girls. In regard to male sexuality, the only concern generally raised by the court is centered on abusive and predatory behaviors toward others, particularly younger children. Here, probation officer narratives indicate that court officials think about sexuality in different ways for male and female juvenile offenders. For boys, no reference is made regarding noncriminalized sexual behaviors. Yet for girls, the risk of victimization becomes a way to deny female sexual agency. Here, probation officers would comment in official court reports about violations of moral rules regarding sexuality and displays of sexual behavior. In many cases, these officers expressed concern for the levels of sexual activity in which the girls were engaging. In many cases, such professional concerns are used as grounds for identifying these girls as "out of control" and therefore in need of services by the juvenile court (Mallicoat, 2007).

⊠ The Nature and Extent of Female Delinquency

Girls are the fastest growing population within the juvenile justice system. Not only have the number of arrests involving girls increased, but the volume of cases in the juvenile court involving girls has also expanded at a dramatic rate. Despite the increased attention on females by the agents of the juvenile justice system and the public in general, it is important to remember that girls continue to represent a small proportion of all delinquency cases, as boys' offending continues to dominate the juvenile justice system.

As discussed in Section I, the Uniform Crime Reports (UCR) reflects the arrest data from across the nation. This resource also includes information on juvenile offenders. Given that law enforcement officials represent the most common method through which juvenile offenders enter the system, arrest data provide a first look at the official processing of juvenile cases. Here, we can assess the number of crimes reported to law enforcement involving youth offenders, the most serious charge within these arrests, and the disposition by police in these cases. You have also learned that the UCR data is not without its flaws. Given that juveniles are often involved in acts that are not serious and nonviolent in nature, these practices of crime reporting and how the data are compiled can have a significant effect on the understanding of **juvenile delinquency** by society. Despite these flaws, the UCR remains the best resource for investigating arrest rates for crime (Snyder & Sickmund, 2006).

UCR data on juvenile offenders indicate that in 1980, girls represented 20% of juvenile arrests. By 2003, girls' participation in crimes increased to 27%. Today, juvenile girls make up 29% of the arrests of individuals under the age of 18. Data from 1980 to 2003 show the female proportion of violent crime index offenses increased from 10% to 18%, while property offenses increased from 19% to 32%. These shifts in girls' arrests have certainly increased the attention of parents, juvenile court officials, and scholars (Knoll & Sickmund, 2010; Snyder & Sickmund, 2006). However, it appears that the majority of this increase occurred during the late 1980s to early 1990s when the rise of "tough on crime" philosophies spilled over into the juvenile arena. Figure 7.1 illustrates data on the juvenile arrests

Figure 7.1 Uniform Crime Report Data on Juvenile Arrests, Decreases by Sex Over 10-Year Period (2003–2012)

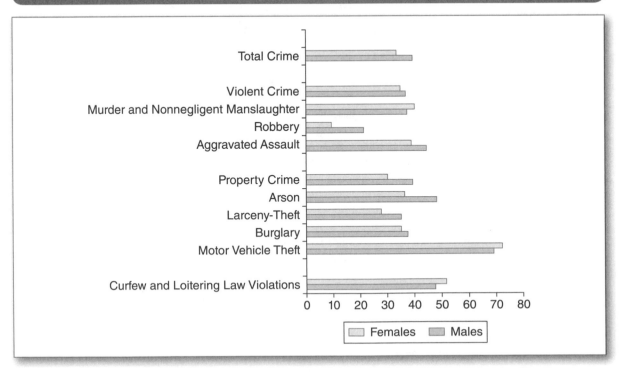

SOURCE: Crime in the United States 2010 (2010).

and the percentages of males and females involved in crimes for 2003 and 2012. Even though the percentage of female arrests within the juvenile population has increased over the past decade, the actual number of arrests has fallen in every crime category.

Despite the fact that females continue to represent a smaller proportion of the offending population compared to males and that the overall number of arrests has decreased significantly, the hype of the female delinquent continues to dominate discussions about juvenile delinquency. The increased attention on female delinquency by law enforcement has, in turn, affected the handling of these cases by the juvenile courts. In 2007, the U.S. juvenile courts were dealing with an estimated 1.7 million cases each year. Since the early 1990s, girls have represented a growing proportion of cases in the juvenile courts. In 1991, girls made up 19% of delinquency cases, 26% in 2002, 27% in 2007, and 28% in 2009. By 2009, female caseloads had increased for all categories compared to 1985 data (Table 7.1). This is particularly noteworthy given that the percentage of arrests has decreased significantly in recent years (Knoll & Sickmund, 2010, 2012; Snyder & Sickmund, 2006). Research by Steffensmeier, Schwartz, Zhong, and Ackerman (2005) showed the increase in arrests and **formal processing** of juvenile cases has disproportionately impacted girls through the practice of up charging by prosecutors and a decrease in tolerance for girls who "act out." Meanwhile, boys benefit from a greater acceptance of these "unacceptable" behaviors (Carr, Hudson, Hanks, & Hunt, 2008).

Table 7.1 Changes in Caseload for Juvenile Offenders by Gender, 1985–2009

Most Serious Offense	Females	Males
Total Delinquency	86%	17%
Person	199%	74%
Property	28%	−30%
Drugs	123%	116%
Public Order	158%	94%

SOURCE: Knoll & Sickmund (2012).

Given the increase in the number of female cases that are handled by the juvenile court, it is no surprise that punishments have also increased for girls. While boys are more likely to be detained for their cases (22% of cases, compared to 17% of girls' cases), girls who are denied release generally spend significantly greater amounts of time in detention compared to boys (Belknap, Dunn, & Holsinger, 1997; Snyder & Sickmund, 2006). Girls of color are disproportionately affected by the shift to formal processing of delinquency cases, as Black and Hispanic girls are more likely to receive detention, whereas White girls are more likely to be referred to a residential treatment facility (Miller, 1994). In addition, girls are subjected to longer periods of supervision, a practice that appears to increase the delinquency in girls due to excessive and aggressive monitoring techniques (Carr et al., 2008). Finally, the number of residential placements or sentences to formal probation terms has also increased for girls.

CASE STUDY

Spotlight on the Sexual Abuse of Girls in Confinement

While the historical discussions on facilities for delinquent girls and offending women have indicated that females experienced high levels of physical and sexual abuse by both guards and other inmates, it is assumed that such experiences are ancient history and are not relevant to modern-day discussions about girls in custody. Unfortunately, these abuses still continue at many juvenile institutions.

The Survey of Youth in Residential Placement was administered to over 7,000 youth in custody during Spring 2003. The results from this survey indicate that 4% of youth in custody experienced sexual victimization. Half of these youth identified staff members as the offenders in these cases (Sedlak, McPherson & Basena, 2013). Fast-forward to several years later, and it appears that the abuse of youth in custody has increased. The National Survey of Youth in Custody surveyed 9,198 adjudicated youth housed in juvenile facilities across the United States between June 2008 and April 2009 (Beck, Harrison, & Guerino, 2010). Like previous studies, the NSYC finds that the majority of these assaults are perpetuated by staff (10.3%). 41.7% of these involved use of force by the staff member and the remaining 58.3% were "consensual" (even though state law would disagree with this definition of consensual given the context of the relationship). Juvenile males were more likely to be victims of staff sexual abuse, and their offenders were typically female staff members. In comparison, juvenile females were more likely to experience acts of abuse from other inmates (9.1% of girls compared to 2.0% of boys). LGBT youth experienced some of the highest levels of victimization (12.1%). In particular, transgendered girls are at extreme risk for victimization (Just Detention International [JDI], 2009). In many cases, staff members not only fail to protect transgendered youth in custody but often join in on the abuse (Fellner, 2010). While surveys such as these yield valuable information about the nature of abuse within juvenile facilities, the data are collected anonymously. This makes it difficult for facility and state officials to follow up on these cases of abuse. In addition, few of these assaults are ever reported to officials. In many cases, victims fear that reporting these crimes will increase the likelihood for future victimization (Human Rights Watch, 2006). While these research findings demonstrate that sexual assault within juvenile confinement facilities is a significant issue, failure to report these cases on even anonymous surveys such as the[se] may skew the findings, and the actual extent of this problem may be even higher.

While the National Prison Rape Elimination Commissions have made a number of recommendations to reduce the extent of abuse within confinement facilities, many of these reforms are costly and out of reach. Public officials have also argued that conducting annual reviews of abuse within juvenile facilities would be too costly. However, allowing such abuse to continue is also an expensive burden, as the emotional experience of victimization impacts youth long after they have departed the facility. In addition, the failure to respond to systemic abuse within the prisons places facilities at risk for lawsuits by youth and their families. In 2007, Alabama paid $12.7 million settlement in response to a class action lawsuit by 48 girls that served time at a state youth correctional facility. The core of their complaint centered on allegations of significant abuse involving over 15 staff members.[1] While international standards prohibit the supervision of female offenders by male staff (a policy that could reduce the cases of abuse of female youth by male guards), many facilities continue to allow cross gender supervision, continuing to place these girls at potential risk (Human Rights Watch, 2006).

---

[1]For a state-by-state review of systematic maltreatment within juvenile facilities, go to http://www.aecf.org/OurWork/JuvenileJustice/~/media/Pubs/Topics/Juvenile%20Justice/Detention%20Reform/NoPlaceForKids/SystemicorRecurringMaltreatmentin JuvenileCorrectionsFacilities.pdf

⊠ The "Violent" Girl

Over the past two decades, media reports have alluded to the rise of the violent juvenile offender. This portrayal of "bad girls" by the media has been linked to data that reflected a significant increase in the number of arrests for crimes of violence involving girls. Based on these findings, researchers ask, Are girls really becoming more violent? Or is there something else to blame for these increases? Have parents, schools, and police changed the way in which they respond to incidents of girls who are deemed to be out of control?

While official crime rates appear to demonstrate that the rate of violent offenses by juvenile girls is increasing, these data reflect only increases in the number of arrests, which is a reflection of the response by the police. Meanwhile, self-report studies do not support this claim and indicate that the levels of violence have actually decreased for both boys and girls. For example, results from the Youth Risk Behavior Survey indicate that between 1991 and 2001, acts of violence by girls decreased 30.5% while boys' violence decreased by 14.1% (Centers for Disease Control, 1992–2002).

A review of recent trends in female juvenile cases indicates an overrepresentation of incidents of family-based violence (Brown,

▲ Photo 7.1   Recent years have seen an increase in the reporting of cases involving "violent girls." Are girls really becoming more violent or have parents, schools, and police changed the way in which they respond to incidents of girls who are deemed to be out of control?

Chesney-Lind, & Stein, 2007). The rise in these cases reflects a shift in the way in which families and officials respond to these cases. Consider that adolescence often corresponds with a new discovery for freedom, which often collides with parents' desire to maintain some control and authority over their children. In some cases, parents may turn to the police and the juvenile court for help. Juvenile authorities may talk to or threaten the youth or use fear as a tool to gain compliance from the youth (Davis, 2007). Once upon a time, the police treated these interventions as a social service, rather than a criminal matter. But this practice is shifting, and cases of domestic dispute and minor assault against family members are now handled as formal acts of delinquency by the police and court system (Brown et al., 2007; Feld, 2009).

Many parents seek out the police because they do not know what else to do and believe that once their kids are involved in the juvenile justice system, they will have greater opportunities for resources such as individual and family therapy (Sharpe, 2009). Once the formal processing of these cases places these girls under the supervision of probation, any subsequent power struggles between the parent and child may then become the grounds for a technical violation of probation. As a result, the court becomes a new and powerful method for enforcing parental authority. Parents in turn can hold a high level of power in the eyes of the court when it comes to the disposition of their child's case. Indeed, it is not uncommon during juvenile court proceedings for a judge to consult with a parent in judicial decisions. If a parent agrees that a child can come home (under the order of obeying house rules), the court may be more likely to return the youth home. If, however, a parent does not want physical custody of the child, a judge may decide to institutionalize the youth (Davis, 2007).

Family-based cases are not the only type of offense that has increased in recent years. Juvenile courts have also seen a marked increase in the number of cases of school-based violence. Once upon a time, outbursts and minor assaults were handled within the school's administration using punishments such as detention and suspension. As a result of zero-tolerance policies, these cases are now dealt with by local police agencies. Given that girls are more likely to engage in acts of violence against family members or peers (whereas boys are more likely to commit acts of violence against distant acquaintances or strangers), such policies may unfairly target girls (Feld, 2009).

Girls that engage in violence often have a history of violence in their own lives. This is an important characteristic to consider as many girls who act out may simply be reacting to the social and personal conditions of their lives. Research by Tasca, Zatz, and Rodriguez (2012) indicates that girls who engage in violence come from home environments that are significantly impoverished. In some cases, there is a history of parental drug abuse. Many of the girls experience sexual abuse and are exposed to violent acts, such as intimate partner abuse, within the home environment. For these girls, home is not a safe place but is one where violence reigns.

Technical Violations: The New Status Offense

Like the historical and contemporary control of female sexuality, status offenses are another realm where doctrines such as parens patriae allow for the juvenile court to intervene in the lives of adolescents. **Status offenses** are acts that are illegal only if committed by juveniles. Examples of status offenses include the underage consumption of alcohol, running away from home, truancy, and curfew violations. While the juvenile court was founded with the idea of dealing with both delinquency and status offenses, today's courts have attempted to differentiate between the two offense categories due to constitutional challenges on status offenses (Bernard, 1992). One of the elements of the **Juvenile Justice and Delinquency Prevention (JJDP) Act of 1974** called for the decriminalization of status offenders in any state that received federal funds. Prior to its enactment, young women were much more likely to be incarcerated for status offenses compared to their male counterparts (Chesney-Lind & Shelden, 2004). While the institutionalization of sexually wayward girls officially ended with the JJDP act of 1974, funds were not made available to provide resources to address the needs of girls. "Status offenders are not a unique or discrete category of juveniles, and they share many of the same characteristics and behavioral versatility as other delinquent offenders" (Feld, 2009, p. 245). Given that status offense charges were frequently used as the basis to incarcerate girls, many assumed that the presence of girls in the juvenile justice system would decrease following the decriminalization of status offenses. However, this decline did not last long. While youth can no longer be incarcerated specifically for status offenses, we still see cases where youth appear before the juvenile court for these cases. Data from an urban county in Arizona indicate that race and gender have an effect on whether youth will be adjudicated for status offenses, such as curfew violations, running away from home, using alcohol and/or tobacco, and truancy. While White girls were the least likely to be adjudicated delinquent for a status offense, Native American boys were the most likely to be adjudicated, followed by girls of color (African American and Hispanic; Freiberger & Burke, 2011).

In addition, researchers contend that the practice of institutionalizing girls who are deemed out of control continues today (Acoca & Dedel, 1998a; Chesney-Lind & Shelden, 2004). The modern-day practice of institutionalizing girls for status offenses is known as **bootstrapping**. The process of bootstrapping involves cases where a girl is currently on probation or parole for a criminal offense and then is prosecuted formally for a probation violation as a result of committing a status offense, such as running away from home or truancy (Owen & Bloom, 1998). While provisions of the **Reauthorization of the Juvenile Justice and Delinquency Prevention (JJDP) Act (1992)** attempted to make the practice of bootstrapping more difficult for courts, evidence indicates that the practice continues in an inequitable fashion against girls. Research by Feld (2009) suggests that acts that were once treated as status offenses are now processed as minor acts of delinquency due to the expansion of the discretionary powers available to schools, police, and juvenile justice officials. The replacement of status offenses by probation violations has allowed justice officials to recommit girls to these residential facilities. While a commitment to a state institution or detention center for these types of status offenses is prohibited by the original authorization of the JJDP Act in 1974, it appears that the juvenile justice system has found a new method to "incarcerate" young girls deemed out of control by the courts (Carr et al., 2008).

Risk Factors for Female Delinquency

Earlier chapters of this text have highlighted the historical failures of criminology to address the unique causes of women and girls' offending. The theoretical inattention to these issues has significantly affected the identification and delivery of services for women and girls. It is a failure for policy makers and practitioners to assume that, just because girls typically engage in nonviolent or nonserious acts of crime and delinquency, their needs are insignificant (Chesney-Lind & Shelden, 2004). Indeed, a historical review of the juvenile justice system finds that programs and facilities are ill equipped to deal with the needs of girls. While boys and girls can exhibit many of the same risk factors for delinquency, such as family dysfunction, school failures, peer relationships, and substance abuse, the effects of these risk factors may resonate stronger for girls than they do for boys (Moffitt, Caspi, Rutter, & Silva, 2001). In addition, research indicates that girls possess significantly higher risk factors toward delinquency than boys. It is interesting to note that while White girls tend to exhibit significantly higher levels of risk for certain categories (such as substance abuse), youth of color, particularly African American youth, are significantly overrepresented in the juvenile court (Gavazzi, Yarcheck, & Lim, 2005). Given these failures of the juvenile courts, it is important to understand the risk factors for female delinquency in an effort to develop recommendations for best practices for adolescent delinquent and at-risk girls. For juvenile girls, the most significant risk factors for delinquency include a poor family relationship, a history of abuse, poor school performance, negative peer relationships, and issues with substance abuse. In addition, these risk factors are significantly interrelated.

Family

The influence of the family unit is one of the most commonly cited references in the study of delinquency. The family represents the primary mechanism for the internalization and socialization of social norms and values (Hirschi, 1969), and social control theorists have illustrated that a positive attachment to the family acts as a key tool in the prevention of delinquency. Yet research indicates that girls may have stronger attachments to the family compared to boys, which can serve as a protective factor against delinquency. However, families can serve as a protective factor only when they exist in a positive, prosocial environment. Research indicates that girls benefit from positive communication, structure, and support in the family environment (Bloom, Owen, Deschenes, & Rosenbaum, 2002b). Just as the family unit can protect girls from delinquency, it can also lead girls into delinquency at a young age. Youth may turn to delinquency to enhance their self-esteem or to overcome feelings of rejection by their families (Matsueda, 1992). Research has indicated that delinquent girls have lower bonds with their family compared to nondelinquent girls (Bourduin & Ronis, (2012). In addition, these negative family issues constitute a greater problem for girls than boys (Shepherd, Luebbers, & Dolan, 2013). Family fragmentation due to divorce, family criminality, and foster care placements, in addition to family violence and negative family attachment, has been identified as family risk factors for female delinquents. Families with high levels of conflict and poor communication skills, combined with parents who struggle with their own personal issues, place girls at risk for delinquency (Bloom et al., 2002b). In addition, once a girl becomes immersed in the juvenile justice system, her delinquency can serve to increase the detachment between her and her family (Girls Incorporated, 1996). Indeed, incarcerated girls are less likely to receive support from their parents compared to boys. This has significant implications in two ways. First, girls are more likely to experience depression, and the lack of family support can contribute to their mental health status. Second, many intervention programs within the juvenile court rely on parental involvement. Measures of success in these programs could be compromised if girls feel less supported by their parents (Johnson et al., 2011).

Abuse

Sexual, physical, and emotional abuse has long been documented as significant risk factors for female offenders. The impact of abuse is intensified when it occurs within the family. Such abuse can be detrimental to the positive development of the adolescent female and can result in behaviors such as running away, trust issues, emotional maladjustment, and future sexual risk behaviors. This is not meant to suggest that violence and victimization are not present in the lives of male delinquents, only that it is more common for girls. Research by Belknap and Holsinger (2006) shows that 58.9% of girls (versus 18.5% of boys) indicated they had been sexually abused by either a family member or other individual in their life. While sexual abuse is the most studied form of abuse for girls, other forms of maltreatment can have a significant effect on the development of girls. Girls experience higher rates of physical abuse than their male counterparts (62.9% of girls compared to 42.8% of boys). Research suggests that girls who are abused may have lower (strength) bonds to protective factors, such as parents and school, that could serve to inhibit their involvement in delinquency (Bourduin & Ronis, 2012).

Experiences of childhood abuse are often the tip of the iceberg for the issues that affect preteen and adolescent females. In many cases, acts such as running away from home reflect an attempt to escape from a violent or abusive home environment. Unfortunately, in their attempt to escape from an abusive situation, girls often fall into criminal behaviors as a mechanism of survival. Widom (1989) found that childhood victimization increases the risk that a youth will run away from home and that childhood victimization and running away increase the likelihood of engaging in delinquent behaviors. A history of sexual abuse also affects the future risk for victimization, as girls who are sexually abused during their childhood are significantly more likely to find themselves in a domestically violent relationship in the future (McCartan & Gunnison, 2010).

Peers

The presence of delinquent peers presents the greatest risk for youth to engage in their own acts of delinquency. While much of the research suggests that girls are more likely to associate with other girls (and girls are less likely to be delinquent than boys), research by Miller, Loeber, and Hipwell (2009) indicates that girls generally have at least one friend involved in delinquent behaviors. While girls in this study indicated that they associated with peers of both genders, it is not the gender of the peers that can predict delinquency. Rather, it is the number of delinquent peers that determines whether a youth engages in problem behaviors. Here, the effects of peer pressure and the desire for acceptance often lead youth into delinquency, particularly if the majority of the group is involved in law-violating behaviors.

Several factors can affect one's association with delinquent peers. First, scholars indicate the shift toward unsupervised *free time* among youth as a potential gateway to delinquency, as youth who are involved in after-school structured activities are less likely to engage in delinquency (Mahoney, Cairns, & Farmer, 2003). However, girls tend to spend less time with their delinquent peers compared to boys and experience less peer pressure as a result (Weerman & Hoeve, 2012). Research indicates that negative peer relationships have a stronger effect for African American girls than boys, while boys' delinquency is more likely to be limited by parental monitoring (O'Donnell, Richards, Pearce, & Romero, 2012). Given the slashing of school-based and community programs due to budgetary funds, there are fewer opportunities to provide a safe and positive outlet for youth in the hours between the end of the school day for youth and the end of the work day for parents. Second, age can also affect the delinquent peer relationship. For girls, peer associations with older adolescents of the opposite sex have an impact on their likelihood to engage in delinquent acts if the older male is involved in crime-related behaviors (Stattin & Magnusson, 1990). Finally, negative family attachment also affects the presence of delinquent peers, as girls whose parents are less involved in their daily lives and activities are more likely to engage in problem behaviors (such as substance abuse) with delinquent peers (Svensson, 2003).

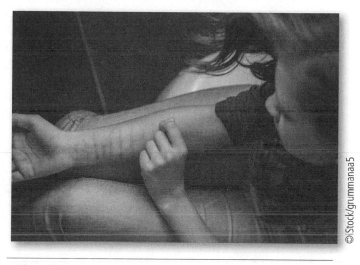

▲ **Photo 7.2**   Many girls with experiences of childhood sexual abuse engage in a variety of self-injurious behaviors, including addiction and cutting.

School

School failures have also been identified as an indicator of concern for youth at risk. Truancy can be an indication of school failures, such as suspension, expulsion, or being held back. In research by Acoca and Dedel (1998a), 85% of incarcerated girls in their study compared their experience in school to a war zone, where issues such as racism, sexual harassment, peer violence, and disinterested school personnel increased the likelihood of dropping out. For girls, success at school is tied to feelings of self-worth—the more students feel attached to the school environment and the learning process and develop a connection to their teachers, the less likely they are to be at risk for delinquency (Crosnoe, Erickson, & Dornbusch, 2002). Additionally, the slashing of prosocial extracurricular activities has also negatively affected girls. Here, activities that involve creativity, build relationships, and enhance personal safety help to build resiliency in young women and guard against delinquent behaviors (Acoca & Dedel, 1998a). Finally, the involvement of a parent in the daughter's school progress can help build resiliency for girls (Bloom et al., 2002b).

Substance Abuse

Several risks have been identified for adolescent females' involvement in alcohol and drug use: early experimentation and use, parental use of drugs and alcohol, histories of victimization, poor school and family attachments, numerous social opportunities for use, poor self-concept, difficulties in coping with life events, and involvement with other problem behaviors (Bloom et al., 2002b). Substance abuse affects female delinquency in two ways. First, girls who experience substance abuse in their families may turn to behaviors such as running away to escape the violence that occurs in the home as a result of parental drug and alcohol use. Second, girls themselves may engage in substance abuse as a mechanism of self-medication to escape from abuse histories (Chesney-Lind & Shelden 2004). In addition, research indicates that the use of substances can be a gendered experience. While boys tend to limit their drug use to marijuana, girls experiment with and abuse a variety of substances, including methamphetamines, cocaine, acid, crack, and huffing chemicals. Not only did their poly-drug use indicate significant addiction issues, but their substance abuse also altered their decision-making abilities, influenced their criminal behaviors, and placed them at risk for danger (Mallicoat, 2007). While substance abuse increases the risk for delinquency for girls, the absence of substance abuse serves as a protective factor against delinquency (McKnight & Loper, 2002).

Mental Health

Youth in custody experience high rates of trauma throughout the course of their lives. Girls experience higher rates of emotional trauma than boys. (See Hennesssey, Ford, Mahoney, Ko, & Siegfried, 2004, for a review of the literature.) For many youth, these traumas place them at risk for post-traumatic stress disorder (Shufelt & Cocozza, 2006) and suicidal ideation. Girls are also more likely to engage in self-injurious behaviors (Shepherd, Luebbers, & Dolan, 2013). This is particularly important for girls under custody as 45% of girls in detention indicated that they had attempted suicide at some point in their lives (Belknap & Holsinger, 2006). Girls are also more likely to suffer from anxiety-related disorders, which typically stem from early childhood experiences with abuse and victimization. In many instances, these anxiety-related disorders are co-occurring with substance abuse and addiction, which can create unique challenges for programming and treatment (Shufelt & Cocozza, 2006). It is important for the juvenile justice system to note and respond to these issues. Unfortunately, many detention facilities are ill equipped to deal with the mental health needs of youth in custody, and these girls end up falling through the cracks. A failure by the system to effectively recognize the mental health needs of delinquent girls not only places these youth at risk for future harm but also places them at risk for increased involvement with the system (Hennesssey et al., 2004).

Meeting the Unique Needs of Delinquent Girls

While girls may make up a minority of offenders in the juvenile justice system, their needs should not be absent from juvenile justice policies. As indicated earlier, girls have a number of different and interrelated issues that historically have been ignored by the system. The 1992 Reauthorization of the Juvenile Justice and Delinquency Prevention Act acknowledged the need to provide gender-specific services to address the unique needs of female offenders. Over the past two decades, research has highlighted the factors that may affect a young woman's road to delinquency, and the reauthorization of the JJDP mandates that states incorporate this understanding into the assessment tools and programming options for girls.

What should **gender-specific programming** for girls look like? Programs must be able to address the wide variety of needs of the delinquent girl—given that many of the risk factors for delinquency involve a web of interrelated issues, programs need to be able to address this tangled web of needs rather than attempt to deal with issues on an individual and isolated basis. Research identifies that a history of victimization is the most significant issue facing at-risk and delinquent girls. According to Belknap & Holsinger (2006), 55.8% of girls believe that their experiences with abuse throughout their childhood had an effect on their offending behaviors. The prevalent nature of a victimization history in adolescent females raises this issue to one of central importance in gender-specific programming. Not only do programs need to provide counseling services for both boys and girls that focus on the trauma in their lives, but placement services for youth need to be expanded as well. Given that many girls run away from home to escape an abusive environment, punishment in detention is not an appropriate place for girls. Because early childhood victimization often leads to risky sexual behaviors with the conclusion of teenage pregnancy and parenthood, education should be offered to these girls as a preventive measure for pregnancy and sexually transmitted diseases.

CASE STUDY

Spotlight on Arts Programming and At-Risk Youth

Once upon a time, schools offered arts programming as part of a child's education. Courses in the visual arts and music were as much a part of the curriculum as math and science. However, budget cuts and an emphasis on standardized testing has led to the minimization or cancelation of arts-related programming. The loss of the arts has had a significant effect on the academic successes of our youth population. Research from the National Education Longitudinal Study of 1988 tells us that children who have a rich experience with the arts demonstrate greater achievements in science and writing and a higher GPA compared to those with a lower engagement in the arts. In addition, these youth were more likely to attend college (71% compared to 48%) and receive an associate's (24% compared to 10%) or bachelor's degree (18% compared to 6%). In addition, the effect of art-related education is stronger for those kids with a lower socioeconomic status background. (Catterall, Dumais, & Hampden-Thompson, 2012).

Arts education programming has been shown to have a positive impact on the lives of at-risk youth. In their evaluation of three arts education programs, the YouthARTS development project has identified that participation in these programs not only provided youth with a positive outlet to express their emotions and to develop their communication skills, but these experiences have also had an impact on recidivism rates for juvenile participants. Not only did the youth in the program receive fewer juvenile court referrals, but their offenses were [also] less serious for those that did engage in delinquency (Americans for the Arts, 2000). Arts-related programming has also had a significant impact on youth in custody. Youth that participated in a visual arts program while in juvenile detention demonstrated significantly lower rates of misbehavior (63%), which increased the time that staff could use for positive interactions, versus disciplinary actions (Ezell & Levy, 2003).

But what about girls? Few of the arts education programs in practice utilize gender responsive practices. The Share Art Program in Flint, Michigan, began as a co-ed program with youth incarcerated at the Genesee Valley Regional Center. The program focuses on visual art and spoken-word poetry as ways that the youth can express themselves and make sense of their lives, which are often very chaotic. As a short-term detention facility, youth serve an average of 21 days, which gives program providers a limited time with most of the youth. In an effort to meet the unique needs of the girls in the facility, the Share Art Program adapted their program design to reflect gender responsive practices. The female-only environment provided the opportunity for the girls to have a safe space to share their emotions through their art, and as they developed their writing, the girls began to feel more confident about their abilities. Through their poetry, the girls began to explore their histories, life experiences, and their visions for the future. Many of the girls commented that the program not only increased their self-confidence but also provided them with a skill set to work through their emotions and decision-making processes. In addition, the girls learned how to work with others and build a support network. Finally, the staff of the program also served as important role models for the girls. By creating a space where the girls could focus on the risk and resiliency factors in their lives, the program was able to effectively serve the needs for this female population and provided a valuable resource for the community (Rosenbaum & Spivack, 2013).

Similar to the needs of high-risk pregnancies, juvenile justice facilities are often ill equipped to deal with the physical and mental health needs of incarcerated females (Tille & Rose, 2007). The emotional needs of developing teenagers, combined with the increase in the prevalence of mental health disorders of incarcerated females, makes this an important component for gender-specific programming for female populations. Physical and mental health complaints by youth need to be interpreted by staff and facilities as a need, not as a complaining or manipulating behavior. Additionally, such interventions must be established on an ongoing basis for continual care, versus limited to an episodic basis (Acoca & Dedel, 1998a).

When designing programs for youth, it is important to consider the variety of different backgrounds and cultures that delinquent girls come from, as this impacts not only their pathways to offending but also affects how they will respond to interventions. Research has indicated that race and ethnicity impact the pathways of girls to the juvenile justice system. While White females experience higher levels of physical and sexual abuse and substance abuse compared to African American girls, the abuse of girls of color remains high. Seventy percent of Black girls indicate a history of physical abuse, and 46% have been sexually abused in their lifetime (compared to 90% of White girls who are physically abused and 62% who are sexually abused; Holsinger & Holsinger, 2005). Other research shows that factors such as lack of parental monitoring, antisocial attitudes, school commitment, and peer pressure can be used to explain delinquency among girls in the Hmong community (Ciong & Huang, 2011).

These factors can alter the way in which girls respond to these experiences. White girls are more likely to engage in self-injurious behaviors compared to girls of color. Here, it appears that White girls are more likely to respond to the abuse experience through internally harming behaviors, whereas girls of color are more likely to engage in outward displays of violence (Holsinger & Holsinger, 2005). The greatest long-term successes come from programs that provide support, not just for the individual girl but for her extended family as well. Unfortunately, many family members resist being involved in programming, as they fail to accept responsibility for the role that they may have played in the development of their daughter's delinquency (Bloom, Owen, Deschenes, & Rosenbaum, 2002a). This lack of involvement raises significant concerns for the family environment of these girls. Although more than one half of girls reported that they do not get along with their parents (51%) and the view that their relationship with their parents contributed to their delinquency (59%), 66% of the girls stated that they would return to live with their parents following their release from custody. This is particularly concerning given that 58% of the girls surveyed reported experiencing some form of violence in the home. It is impossible to develop programs for incarcerated females without reevaluating policies that contribute to the destruction of the family. Gender-specific programming for adolescent females needs to focus on rebuilding the family unit and developing positive role modeling. Here, programs such as family counseling and family substance abuse treatment models can positively affect troubled families.

CASE STUDY

Spotlight on Girls' Voices

As you learned in earlier sections of this text, listening to the stories of women and girls is one of the key strengths of feminist research methods. From this type of research, we learn that girls have a lot to share about their lives [and] their experiences with the juvenile justice and criminal justice systems and have ideas about what they need to improve their lives. Research tells us that girls benefit from a structured environment and that tools such as effective discipline, expectations for behavior, and guidance can provide valuable support for girls (Garcia & Lane 2010). Many of the girls in these research studies discuss the power that a positive role model has for their lives. Strong female staff within the juvenile justice system (and related ancillary organizations) can serve as mentors for girls and provide valuable mentorship support and guidance for girls (Bright, Ward, & Negi 2011). As one female who had spent time in a juvenile facility indicated about the power of a positive mentor, "we depend on that support and that bond with somebody that we can talk to and trust and confide in" (Bright, Ward, & Negi, p. 2011, p. 38). While girls echo the need for therapeutic resources to address drug addiction and victimization histories, they also believe that developing independent life skills and reentry programming is essential in preventing recidivism as a girl transitions into adulthood (Garcia & Lane, 2010). Beyond discussions about the types of programming and the role of mentors in their lives, this research provides a vivid picture of the environments that these girls come from—and ultimately will return to.

The economic marginality that surrounds the lives of girls impacts their future outlooks for success. For many of the girls, what they see within their own families and communities is all they know. To hope and aspire for a better life simply seems like a dream that is out of reach. As a result, many young girls submit themselves to a life filled with violence:

> I came from the ghetto. And people didn't go to college. They barely made it out of high school, if they made it out of high school. So it's not normal for us to think, you know it's just not something that crosses our minds. (Garcia and Lane, 2010, p. 237)

Regardless of the successes that girls may experience within the juvenile justice system, the reality is that these girls will most likely return to the chaotic environments of their families and communities. While some girls fight to maintain the positive changes in their lives by working toward goals for their future, others reference that these will be an uphill battle based on the environments in which they reside:

> It was just harsh, hard. You had to be a rough kid. . . . It was a place that should have been condemned a long time ago. Every day people getting shot. You stand on the sidewalk, you know, somebody running by with a gun, kids getting ran over, people sneaking in people's windows, raping people. (Bright, Ward, & Negi, 2011, p. 40)

For other girls, returning to the juvenile system represents perhaps the safest place for them. Given the economic marginality, violence, and chaos that encompasses their lives, it is no surprise that a structured orderly environment that provides food, clothing, and shelter is viewed as a favorable option, even if it means being incarcerated.

> Here I am back on the streets and if I do this again and get into trouble then I'm just gonna go back to a place where they are gonna feed me and I don't have to worry about somebody beatin' me there/I don't have to worry about somebody molestin' me there, you know? (Garcia and Lane, 2010, p. 235)

Although traditional research on female offenders has focused on the risk factors that lead to negative behaviors, recent research has shifted to include resiliency or protective factors to fight against the risks of delinquent behavior. These factors include intelligence; brilliance; courage; creativity; tenacity; compassion; humor; insightfulness; social competence; problem-solving abilities; autonomy; potential with leadership; engagement in family, community, and religious activities; and a sense of purpose and belief in the future. While these resiliency factors typically develop within the context of the family, the support for such a curriculum needs to come from somewhere else, since many delinquent girls often come from families in crisis (Acoca & Dedel, 1998a).

While the intent to provide gender-specific services indicated a potential to address the unique needs of girls, not all scholars are convinced that girls will be able to receive the treatment and programs that are so desperately needed. While many states embarked on data-heavy assessments reflecting the needs of girls, few of these adventures have translated into effective programmatic changes (Chesney-Lind & Shelden, 2004). Funding remains the most significant barrier in providing effective services for girls. Even when gender-specific programming options exist, the need for these services can outweigh the available options. The limited number of placements, combined with long waiting lists for such services, often makes treatment options unavailable for most girls (Bloom et al., 2002a). However, several individual and community factors also affect program delivery, including lack of information or difficulties in accessing services, resistance toward programming by girls and their families, and distrust of service providers. In addition, racial, economic, and cultural issues can affect whether communities will seek out assistance and the degree to which these services will reflect culturally relevant issues (Bloom et al., 2002b). In order to develop effective and available programming, the system needs to place the allocation of resources as a priority in identifying and addressing the needs of girls in the juvenile justice system.

Summary

- Arrest data and self-report data present contradictory images on the nature and prevalence of female violence.
- While arrests for violent offenses involving girls have increased, self-report data among girls indicate a decrease in the levels of violence.
- Police and the courts have altered the way in which they respond to cases of female delinquency, particularly in cases of family or school violence.
- Many incidents of family violence stem from symbolic struggles for adolescent freedom between girls and their parents.
- For juvenile girls, the most significant risk factors for delinquency include a poor family relationship, a history of abuse, poor school performance, negative peer relationships, and issues with substance abuse.
- Issues of emotional and mental health are a high area of need for delinquent girls.
- Effective gender-specific programming needs to provide long-term programming for girls and their social support network that addresses the causes of delinquency in girls' lives.
- Programming that includes resiliency or protective factors plays a significant role in gender-specific programming.
- Programs face significant barriers in implementing services for girls.

KEY TERMS

Age-of-consent campaign

Bootstrapping

Formal processing

Gender-specific programming

Juvenile delinquency

Juvenile Justice and Delinquency Prevention (JJDP) Act of 1974

Net widening

Parens patriae

Reauthorization of the Juvenile Justice and Delinquency Prevention (JJDP) Act (1992)

Resiliency

Risk factors for female delinquency

Status offenses

DISCUSSION QUESTIONS

1. How did the age-of-consent campaign punish girls and deny healthy expressions of sexuality? What effects of this movement remain today?

2. How have girls continued to be punished for status offenses, despite the enactment of the JJDP Act of 1974?

3. What risk factors for delinquency exist for girls?

4. How has the treatment of girls by the juvenile justice system altered society's understanding of violence among girls?

5. What should gender-specific programming look like? What challenges do states face in implementing these programs?

WEB RESOURCES

Girls Study Group: http://girlsstudygroup.rti.org/

National Center for Juvenile Justice: http://www.ncjj.org

Office of Juvenile Justice and Delinquency Prevention: http://www.ojjdp.gov

Visit **www.sagepub.com/mallicoat2e** to access additional study tools including eFlashcards, web quizzes, web resources, video resources, and SAGE journal articles.

As you've learned, girls were often institutionalized during the early history of juvenile delinquency for being incorrigible or out of control. With the deinstitutionalization of status offenders, policy makers and practitioners have found new ways to relabel female status offenders. There has been a significant amount of hype in the media about the violent girl. This reading explores how the changing definitions of violence and delinquency have resulted in the increases in identifying cases of "crime" for female offenders.

Violent Girls or Relabeled Status Offenders?

An Alternative Interpretation of the Data

Barry C. Feld

Over the past decade, policy makers and juvenile justice officials have expressed alarm over a perceived increase in girls' violence. Official statistics report that police arrests of female juveniles for violent offenses, such as simple and aggravated assault, either have increased more or decreased less than those of their male counterparts and thereby augured a gender convergence in youth violence (Federal Bureau of Investigation, 2006; Steffensmeier, Schwartz, Zhong, & Ackerman, 2005). Reflecting the official statistics, popular media amplify public perceptions of an increase in "girl-on-girl" violence, "bad girls gone wild," "feral and savage" girls, and girl-gang violence (Kluger, 2006 Sanders, 2005; Scelfo, 2004; Williams, 2004). One possible explanation for the perceived narrowing of the gender gap in violence is that gender-specific social structural or cultural changes actually have changed girls' behaviors in ways that differ from boys.

On the other hand, the supposed increase in girls' violence may be an artifact of decreased public tolerance for violence, changes in parental attitudes or law enforcement policies, or heightened surveillance of several types of behaviors such as domestic violence and simple assaults, which disproportionately affect girls (Garland, 2001; Kempf-Leonard & Johansson, 2007; Steffensmeier et al., 2005). Steffensmeier et al. (2005) compared boys' and girls' official arrest rates with other data sources that do not depend on criminal justice system information (e.g., longitudinal self-report and victimization data) and concluded that "the rise in girls' violence . . . is more a social construction than an empirical reality" (p. 397). They attributed the changes in female arrests for violent crimes to three gender-specific policy changes: a greater propensity to charge less serious forms of conduct as assaults, which disproportionately affects girls; a criminalizing of violence between intimates, such as domestic disputes; and a diminished social and family tolerance of female juveniles' "acting out" behaviors.

Their data and analyses support a social constructionist argument that the recent rise in girls' arrests for

SOURCE: Feld, B. C. (2009). Violent girls or relabeled status offenders? An alternative interpretation of the data. *Crime and Delinquency, 55*(2), 241–265.

NOTE: This project was supported by Grant 2004-JF-FX-K001 from the Office of Juvenile Justice and Delinquency Prevention, Office of Justice Programs, U.S. Department of Justice. Points of view and opinions in this document are those of the author and do not necessarily represent the official position or policies of the Department of Justice.

violence is an artifact of changes in law enforcement policies and the emerging "culture of control" rather than a reflection of real changes in girls' behavior (Garland, 2001; Steffensmeier et al., 2005). Although cultural and police policy changes likely contribute to a greater tendency to arrest girls for minor violence, the social construction of girls' violence also may reflect policy changes that occurred within the juvenile justice system itself, especially the deinstitutionalization of status offenders (DSO). After federal mandates in the mid-1970s to deinstitutionalize status offenders, analysts described juvenile justice system strategies to "bootstrap" and/or "relabel" female status offenders as delinquents to retain access to secure facilities in which to confine "incorrigible" girls (Bishop & Frazier, 1992; Feld, 1999).

In this article, I focus on patterns of arrests and confinement of boys and girls for simple and aggravated assaults over the past quarter century. The analysis bolsters Steffensmeier et al.'s (2005) contention that much of the seeming increase in girls' violence is an artifact of changes in law enforcement activities. However, I attribute some of the increase in girls' arrests for violence to federal and state policies to remove status offenders from delinquency institutions. Initially, laws that prohibited confining status offenders with delinquent youth disproportionately benefited girls, whom states most often confined under that jurisdiction. But they provided an impetus to relabel status offenders as delinquents to continue to place them in secure institutions. Within the past two decades, deinstitutionalization polices have coincided with the generic *crackdown* on youth violence in general and heightened concerns about domestic violence in particular, further facilitating the relabeling of status offenders by lowering the threshold of what behavior constitutes an assault, especially in the context of domestic conflict.

I first examine the historical differences in juvenile justice system responses to male and female delinquents and status offender. The next section focuses on the 1974 federal Juvenile Justice and Delinquency Prevention (JJDP) Act, which mandated DSO. In the following section, I analyze arrest data on boys and girls for certain violent crimes—simple and aggravated assault—to highlight differences in the seriousness of the crimes for which police arrest them. The analyses suggest that some girls' arrests for simple assault may be a relabeling of incorrigible girls as delinquents. I then focus on the offender–victim

relationship of boys' and girls' assaults, which differentially affects the likelihood of girls' arrests for family conflicts in domestic disputes. Then, I examine differences between patterns of incarceration for boys and girls sentenced for simple and aggravated assault. A discussion of the findings and conclusions follows.

Historical Differences in Juvenile Justice System Responses to Boys and Girls and DSO

The progressive reformers who created juvenile courts combined two visions, one interventionist and the other divisionary (Zimring, 2002). They envisioned a specialized court to separate children from adult offenders—diversion—and to treat them rather than to punish them for their crimes—intervention (Platt, 1977; Rothman, 1980; Ryerson, 1978; Tanenhaus, 2004). The juvenile court's delinquency jurisdiction initially encompassed only youths charged with criminal misconduct. However, reformers quickly added status offenses—noncriminal misbehaviors, such as "incorrigibility," running away, "immorality," and "indecent and lascivious conduct" (Feld, 2004)—to the definition of delinquency. Historically, juvenile courts responded to boys primarily for criminal misconduct and to girls mainly for noncriminal status offenses (Schlossman, 1977; Sutton, 1988). The status jurisdiction reflected progressives' cultural construction of childhood dependency as well as their sexual sensibilities (Kempf-Leonard & Johansson, 2007; Schlossman & Wallach, 1978). From the juvenile courts' inception, controlling adolescent female sexuality was a central focus of judicial attention and intervention (Sutton, 1988; Tanenhaus, 2004). Historians consistently report that judges detained and incarcerated girls primarily for minor and status offenses and at higher rates than they did boys (Platt, 1977; Schlossman, 1977; Tanenhaus, 2004).

Although juvenile courts' status jurisdiction potentially encompassed nearly all juvenile misbehavior, by the early 1970s, critics argued that juvenile courts incarcerated noncriminal offenders with delinquents in secure detention facilities and institutions, stigmatized them with delinquency labels, discriminated against girls, and provided few beneficial services (Feld, 1999; Schwartz, Steketee, & Schneider, 1990). Judicial intervention at parents' behest to control their children also exacerbated intrafamily conflicts and enabled some caretakers to avoid their responsibilities (Sussman, 1977). In the early 1970s, states charged about three quarters of the girls whom juvenile courts handled as status offenders rather than as criminal delinquents (National Council on Crime and Delinquency, 1975; Schwartz et al., 1990).

The 1974 federal JJDP Act (42 U.S.C. § 223[a][12]) prohibited states from confining status offenders with delinquents in secure detention facilities and institutions and withheld formula grant money from states that failed to develop plans to remove them (Schwartz, 1989). The increased procedural formality and administrative costs of adjudicating delinquent offenders after *In re Gault* (1967) and the JJDP Act's deinstitutionalization goals provided impetus to divert status offenders to services and programs in the community. A 1980 amendment to the JJDP Act, adopted at the behest of the National Council of Juvenile and Family Court Judges, allowed states to continue to receive federal funds and to confine status offenders if juvenile court judges committed them to institutions for violating "valid court orders" (Schwartz, 1989). This exception allowed judges to bootstrap status offenders, disproportionately girls, into delinquents and to incarcerate them for contempt of court for violating court-ordered conditions of probation (Bishop & Frazier, 1992; Hoyt & Scherer, 1998). The 1992 reauthorization of the JJDP Act required states to analyze and provide "gender-specific services" to prevent and treat female delinquency, but most states used the funds to collect data about girls in the juvenile systems rather than to develop new programs (e.g. Bloom, Owen, Deschenes, & Rosenbaum, 2002; Community Research Associates, 1998; Kempf-Leonard & Sample, 2000; MacDonald & Chesney-Lind, 2001).

As a result of the 1974 DSO initiatives, the number of status offenders in secure detention facilities and institutions declined dramatically by the early 1980s. Because states disproportionately confined girls for noncriminal misconduct, they were the primary beneficiaries (Chesney-Lind, 1988; Handler & Zatz, 1982; Krisberg, Schwartz, Lisky, & Austin, 1986; Maxson & Klein, 1997). An early evaluation of the JJDP Act's DSO mandate by the National Academy of Sciences reported a substantial reduction in the detention and confinement of status offenders (Handler & Zatz, 1982). By 1988, the number of status offenders held in secure facilities had declined by 95% from those detained prior to adoption of the JJDP Act (U.S. General Accounting Office, 1991).

Although the JJDP Act prohibited states from incarcerating status offenders, it did not require states to appropriate adequate funds or to develop community-based programs to meet girls' needs. Even as policy makers and lawmakers struggled to find other options to respond to these *troublesome* youths, early analysts warned that states could evade deinstitutionalization requirements by relabeling status offenders as delinquents, for example, by charging them with simple assault rather than incorrigibility (Handler & Zatz, 1982).

Three decades after passage of the JJDP Act, states' failure adequately to fund or inability to offer appropriate community services provides a continuing impetus to use the juvenile delinquency system to circumvent DSO (Hoyt & Scherer, 1998; Maxson & Klein, 1997). *Status offenders* are not a unique or discrete category of juveniles, and they share many of the same characteristics and behavioral versatility as other delinquent offenders. As a result, the juvenile justice system simply could charge a female status offender with a minor crime, adjudicate her as a delinquent, and thereby evade deinstitutionalization strictures (Costello & Worthington, 1981; Federle & Chesney-Lind, 1992; Kempf-Leonard & Sample, 2000).

Macrostructural economic and racial demographic changes during the 1970s and 1980s led to the emergence of an urban Black underclass and increased the punitiveness of juvenile justice policies, and these changes indirectly affected girls' susceptibility to arrest for violence. In the late 1980s and early 1990s, the epidemic of crack cocaine spurred increases in gun violence and Black male homicide, and states adopted punitive laws to *get tough* and crack down on youth crime (Blumstein, 1996; Feld, 1999; Zimring, 1998).

States changed their laws to transfer more juveniles to criminal courts for prosecution as adults, and these amendments reflect a broader cultural and jurisprudential shift from rehabilitative to retributive and managerial penal policies (Feld, 2003; Garland, 2001; Tonry, 2004). Most of the punitive legislative agenda affected boys, particularly urban Black boys, charged with serious, violent crimes (Feld, 1999). Even though girls were not originally the intended subjects of the changes, the shift in juvenile justice responses to youth violence adversely affected girls, whom states could charge with assault (Chesney-Lind & Belknap, 2004; Poulin, 1996). Because the crackdown on youth violence and the rise in girls' arrests for assault coincided with DSO, focusing on the juvenile system's responses to girls provides an indicator of its changing mission and adaptive strategy.

⊠ Arrests of Boys and Girls for Violence: Simple and Aggravated Assaults

Police arrest and juvenile courts handle fewer girls than their proportional makeup of the juvenile population. As Reading Table 13.1 reports, in 2003, police arrested an estimated 2.2 million juveniles. Girls constituted fewer than one third (29%) of all juveniles arrested and fewer than one fifth (18%) of those arrested for Violent Crime Index offenses. Girls constituted about one quarter (24%) of all the juveniles arrested for aggravated assaults and about one third (32%) of juvenile arrests for simple assault. Girls' arrests for simple assault constitute the largest proportion of their arrests for any violent crime. Arrests for Violent Crime Index offenses—murder, forcible rape, robbery, and aggravated assault—account for a very small proportion (4.2%) of all juvenile arrests, and aggravated assaults constitute two thirds (66.6%) of the Violent Crime Index offenses (Snyder & Sickmund, 2006). Significantly, however, police arrested about 85% of all girls arrested for Violent Crime Index offenses for aggravated assault (Federal Bureau of Investigation, 2006). By contrast, police arrested fewer than two thirds (62%) of boys for aggravated assaults and a much larger proportion for the most serious Violent Crime Index crimes of murder, rape, and robbery.

Changes in gender patterns of juveniles' arrests may reflect real differences in rates of offending by boys and girls over time, or they may be justice system artifacts reflecting differences in the ways police and courts choose to respond to boys and girls (Girls Inc., 1996). Although girls constitute a smaller portion of juvenile arrestees than boys, the two groups' arrest patterns have diverged somewhat over the past decade. This divergence distinguishes more recent female delinquency from earlier decades, when male and female offending followed roughly similar patterns and when modest female increases were concentrated primarily in minor property crimes rather than violent crime (Steffensmeier, 1993).

As Reading Table 13.2 indicates, arrests of female juveniles for various violent offenses have either increased more or decreased less than those of their male counterparts. From 1996 to 2005, the total number of juveniles arrested dropped by about 25%, primarily because arrests of boys decreased by 28.8%, whereas those of girls decreased only less than half as much (14.3%). Arrests of boys for Violent Crime Index offenses decreased substantially more than those of female offenders. Over the past decade, arrests of boys for Violent Crime Index offenses declined by 27.9%, whereas those of girls decreased by only 10.2%. Aggravated assaults constitute two thirds of all

Reading Table 13.1 Juvenile and Female Arrest Estimates for Violence, 2003

Crime	Total Juvenile Arrest Estimates for All Offenses	Percentage Female Share of Arrests
Total	2,220,300	29
Violent Crime Index[a]	92,300	18
Aggravated assault	61,490	24
Simple assault	241,900	32

SOURCE: Snyder and Sickmund (2006).

[a] Violent Crime Index includes murder, forcible rape, robbery, and aggravated assault.

Reading Table 13.2   Percentage Changes in Male and Female Juvenile Arrests, 1996 to 2005

Crime	Girls	Boys
Total crime	−14.3	−28.8
Violent Crime Index	−10.2	−27.9
Aggravated assault	−5.4	−23.4
Simple assault	24.0	−4.1

SOURCE: Federal Bureau of Investigation (2006).

juvenile arrests for offenses included in the Violent Crime Index. Boys' arrests for aggravated assaults decreased by nearly one quarter (23.4%), whereas girls' arrests declined much more modestly (5.4%). By contrast, girls' arrests for simple assaults increased by one quarter (24%), whereas boys' arrests declined somewhat (4.1%). Thus, the major changes in arrest patterns for juvenile violence over the past decades are the sharp decrease in boys' arrests for aggravated assaults and the parallel increase in girls' arrests for less serious assaults.

Although the percentages reported in Reading Table 13.2 reflect changes in the numbers of arrests, Reading Figure 13.1 shows changes in the arrest rates per 100,000 male and female juveniles aged 10 to 17 years for Violent Crime Index offenses between 1980 and 2005. Overall, police arrested male juveniles at much higher rates than they did female juveniles. Consistent with Reading Table 13.2, arrest rates for both groups peaked in the mid-1990s, and then, the male rates exhibited a much sharper decline than the female rates. Indeed, the male juvenile arrest rate for Violent Crime Index offenses in 2005 was nearly one quarter (23.3%) lower than in 1980. By contrast, girls' arrest rate for Violent Crime Index offenses rose from 70.4 to 106.9 per 100,000 over the same period, a 51.8% increase. In 1980, Violent Crime Index arrest rates for male juveniles were about 8 times higher than those of female juveniles, whereas by 2005, they were only 4 times higher. Thus, the juvenile *crime drop* of the past decade reflects primarily a decline in boys' arrests.

Reading Figure 13.1   Male and Female Juvenile Arrest Rates, 1980 to 2005, Violent Crime Index Offenses

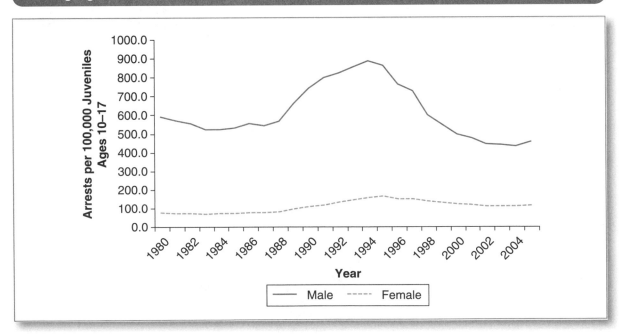

SOURCE: National Center for Juvenile Justice (2008).

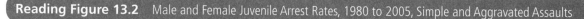

Reading Figure 13.2   Male and Female Juvenile Arrest Rates, 1980 to 2005, Simple and Aggravated Assaults

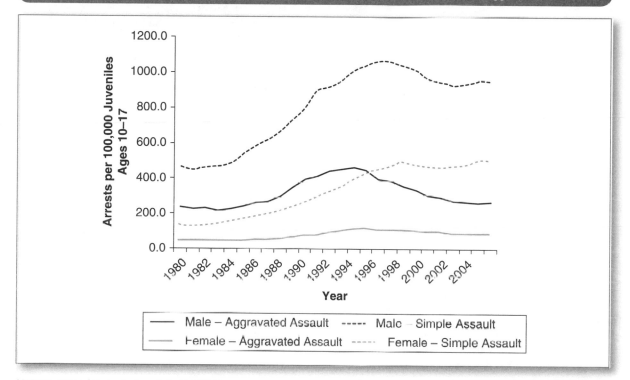

SOURCE: National Center for Juvenile Justice (2008).

Arrests for aggravated assault constituted the largest component of the Violent Crime Index, and arrests for simple assault constituted the largest component of non–Violent Crime Index arrests. Over the past quarter century, clear changes have occurred between boys' and girls' patterns of arrests for these offenses. As Reading Figure 13.2 indicates, boys' and girls' arrests for aggravated assault diverged conspicuously. The female arrest rate in 2005 was nearly double (97%) the arrest rate in 1980 (88.8 vs. 45 arrests for girls per 100,000). Although police arrested male juveniles for aggravated assault about 3 times more frequently than they did female juveniles, the boys' proportional increase (11.8%) was much more modest than that exhibited by the girls over the same period (267.8 vs. 239.4 arrests for boys per 100,000).

Police arrest juveniles for simple assaults much more frequently than they do for aggravated assaults. Again, changes in the arrests rates of female juveniles for simple assaults over the past quarter century greatly outstripped those of their male counterparts. The rate at which police arrested girls for simple assault in 2005 was nearly quadruple (3.9) the rate at which they arrested them in 1980 (499.8 vs. 129.7 female arrests per 100,000). Although the male arrest rate for simple assaults started from a higher base than the female rate, it only doubled (2.1) over the same period (948.9 vs. 462.7 arrests per 100,000).

To gauge the relative seriousness of most juveniles' arrests for violence, Reading Figure 13.3 depicts the ratios of arrest rates for simple assaults and aggravated assaults for boys and for girls. In 1980, police arrested girls for simple assaults about 3 times (2.9) as often as they did for aggravated assaults. They arrested boys for simple assaults about twice (1.9) as often as they arrested them for aggravated assaults. Thus, police arrested girls more frequently than they did boys for less serious types of violence. In part, boys more often use weapons and inflict physical injuries on their victims than do girls, thereby, aggravating many of their assaults. By 2005, police arrested girls more

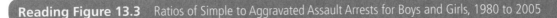

Reading Figure 13.3   Ratios of Simple to Aggravated Assault Arrests for Boys and Girls, 1980 to 2005

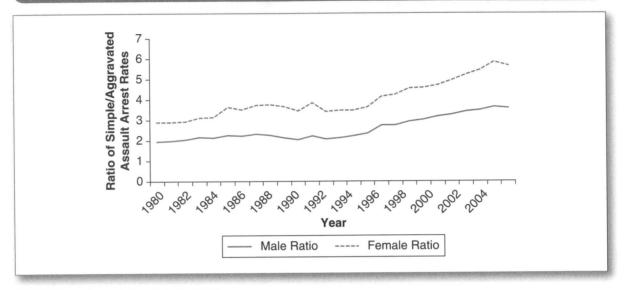

SOURCE: National Center for Juvenile Justice (2008).

than 5 times (5.6) as often for simple assaults as they did for aggravated assaults. By contrast, the ratio of boys' arrests for simple to aggravated assaults only trebled (3.5). Thus, police are arresting even more girls for the least serious forms of violence than they did previously, and that ratio increased more so than for boys. These changes in ratios of arrest rates reflect the two different patterns reported in Reading Table 13.2. The nearly one quarter (23.4%) decline in boys' arrests for aggravated assaults over the past decade increased their ratio of simple to aggravated assaults. By contrast, the nearly one quarter (24%) increase in girls' arrests for simple assaults over the same period substantially increased their ratio of simple to aggravated assaults. Thus, by all the measures—arrests, arrest rates, and ratios of simple to aggravated assaults— the increase in girls' arrests for simple assaults and boys' decrease in arrests for aggravated assaults constitute the most significant change in youth violence over the decades.

Despite these dramatic and gender-linked changes, it remains unclear whether the increase in girls' arrests signifies a real change in girls' underlying violent behavior or reflects police reclassification of assault offenses with a gender-specific component (Steffensmeier et al., 2005). Unlike crimes such as murder and robbery, which have relatively

well-defined elements and clearer indicators, police exercise considerably more discretion when they characterize behavior as an assault at all and whether they classify it as a simple or an aggravated assault, and these meanings have changed over time (Blumstein, 2000). An increase in proactive policing of disorder and minor crimes; a lower threshold to arrest or charge those types of offenses, especially among youth; and more aggressive policing in private settings may create the appearance of a juvenile "crime wave" when none actually exists. Zimring (1998) emphasized the role of police discretion and policy changes in the increase in arrests of youths for assaults. He argued that

since 1980, there is significant circumstantial evidence from many sources that changing police thresholds for when assault should be recorded and when the report should be for aggravated assault are the reason for most of the growth in arrest rates. . . . Any reduction in the threshold between simple and aggravated assault and any shift in the minimum standard for recording an offense would have the kind of statistical impact on assault arrests that has occurred since the late 1980s. (pp. 39–40, 46)

Analysts of the changing characteristics of assaults over the past decades have compared ratios of aggravated assaults to homicides (e.g., Zimring, 1998) or of assaults to robberies (e.g., Snyder & Sickmund, 2006; Zimring & Hawkins, 1997) to demonstrate the malleable and changing definitions of assaults. Because arrests for aggravated assaults increased without any corresponding rise in arrests for homicides or for robberies, they have attributed the escalation in assault arrests to changes in law enforcement policies, such as changing offense seriousness thresholds or responses to domestic violence, rather than to real increases in assaults per se. Similarly, Steffensmeier et al. (2005) compared official arrest statistics for boys and girls from the Federal Bureau of Investigation's Uniform Crime Reports with victims' responses to the National Crime Victimization Survey and juveniles' self-reports in Monitoring the Future and the National Youth Risk Behavior Survey to assess whether the victim and self-report indicators mirrored the increase in girls' arrests for violence over the same period. These indicators revealed no systematic changes in girls' rates or prevalence of offending compared with that of boys, despite the dramatic increase in girls' official arrests for violence over the same period.

Steffensmeier et al. concluded that

recent changes in law enforcement practices and the juvenile justice system have apparently escalated the arrest proneness of adolescent females. The rise in girls' arrests for violent crime and the narrowing of the gender gap have less to do with underlying behavior and more to do, first, with net-widening changes in law and policing toward prosecuting less serious forms of violence, especially those occurring in private settings and where there is less culpability, and, second, with less biased or more efficient responses to girls' physical or verbal aggression on the part of law enforcement, parents, teachers, and social workers. (2005, pp. 387–390)

The demarcation between status offenses and delinquency is as imprecise, malleable, and manipulable as the definition of assaults. "Because many status offenders are not simply runaways or truants but also engage in delinquent activities, it is possible for many such youths to be 'relabeled' delinquents rather than remain classified as status offenders" (Castallano, 1986, p. 496). The ambiguous difference between incorrigible or *unruly* behavior (status offenses) and the heterogeneous and elastic nature of violent behavior, particularly in the context of domestic discord, likely contributes to girls' increased arrests for simple assault. Steffensmeier et al. (2005) argued that

female arrest gains for violence are largely a by-product of net-widening enforcement policies, like broader definitions of youth violence and greater surveillance of girls that have escalated the arrest-proneness of adolescent girls today relative to girls in prior decades and relative to boys. (p. 357)

The near doubling (1.9) in the ratio of simple to aggravated assaults for girls (2.9 vs. 5.6; Reading Figure 13.3) indicates that most girls' arrests are increasingly for violent offenses at the lowest end of the seriousness scale. School *zero-tolerance* policies and police *quality of life, broken windows*, and mandatory domestic violence arrest strategies cumulatively lower the threshold for reporting behavior as an assault or for aggravating it and lead to the arrests of more girls for behaviors previously addressed outside of the purview of police or courts (Chesney-Lind, Morash, & Irwin, 2007). Steffensmeier et al.'s analyses demonstrated that such policies can create an artificial appearance of a girls' violent crime wave when the underlying behavior remains much more stable. Indeed, such policies "tend to blur distinctions between delinquency and antisocial behavior more generally, lump together differing forms of physical aggression and verbal intimidation as manifesting interpersonal violence, and elevate interpersonal violence (defined broadly) as a high-profile social problem (particularly among youth)" (2005, p. 363).

✉ Victims of Boys' and Girls' Violence: Gender-Specific Domestic Disputes

Changing public attitudes and police practices toward domestic assaults have contributed to a growth in reports and arrests for simple assaults that victims and officers previously ignored (Blumstein, 2000; Miller, 2005).

Mandatory arrest policies for domestic violence may have increased girls' risk for arrest by reducing social tolerance for girls' delinquency (Chesney-Lind, 2002; Miller, 2005). The heightened sensitivity to domestic violence combined with the prohibitions on incarcerating status offenders may encourage police to arrest girls more frequently for assault. Charging girls with simple assault rather than with a status offense, such as incorrigibility or unruly conduct, enables families, police, and juvenile courts to relabel the same behaviors as delinquency and thereby evade the prohibitions of the JJDP Act (Chesney-Lind & Belknap, 2004; Girls Inc., 1996; Mahoney & Fenster, 1982; Schneider, 1984).

> Family problems, even some that in past years may have been classified as status offenses (e.g., incorrigibility), can now result in an assault arrest. This logic also explains why violent crime arrests over the past decade have increased proportionately more for juvenile females than males. (Snyder, 2000, p. 4)

Parents' expectations for their sons' and daughters' behavior and obedience to parental authority differ (Chesney-Lind, 1988), and these differing cultural expectations affect how the justice system responds to girls' behavior when they act out within the home (Krause & McShane, 1994; Sussman, 1977). Girls who deviate from traditional gender norms, such as passivity or femininity, may be at greater risk for arrest or domestic violence (Miller, 2005). Girls fight with family members or siblings more frequently than do boys, whereas boys fight more often with acquaintances or strangers (Bloom et al., 2002; Hoyt & Scherer, 1998). Some studies report that girls are 3 times as likely to assault family members as are boys (Franke, Huynh-Hohnbaum, & Chung, 2002). Parents who in the past could have charged their daughters with being unruly or incorrigible now may request that police arrest them for *domestic violence* arising out of the same family scuffle (Russ, 2004). A study in California found that the female share of domestic violence arrests increased from 6% in 1988 to 17% in 1998 (Bureau of Criminal Information and Analysis, 1999).

> Some experts have found that this growth [in girls' assault arrests] is due in part not to a

significant increase in violent behavior but to the re-labeling of girls' family conflicts as violent offenses, the changes in police practices regarding domestic violence and aggressive behavior, [and] the gender bias in the processing of misdemeanor cases. (American Bar Association & National Bar Association, 2001, p. 3)

Policies of mandatory arrest for domestic violence, initially adopted to restrain abusive men from attacking their partners (Miller, 2005), provide parents with another tool with which to control their unruly daughters. Regardless of who initiates a *violent* domestic incident, it is more practical and efficient for police to identify the youth as the offender when a parent is the caretaker for other children in the home (Gaarder, Rodriguez, & Zatz, 2004). As one probation officer observed,

> [I]f you arrest the parents, then you have to shelter the kids. . . . So if the police just make the kids go away and the number of kids being referred to the juvenile court for assaulting their parents or for disorderly conduct or punching walls or doors . . . the numbers have just been increasingly tremendously because of that political change. (Gaarder et al., 2004, p. 565)

Analyses of girls' assault cases referred to juvenile court report that about half were "family centered" and involved conduct that parents and courts previously addressed as incorrigibility cases (Chesney-Lind & Pasko, 2004).

Many cases of girls charged with assault involved nonserious altercations with parents, who often may have been the initial aggressors (Acoca, 1999; Acoca & Dedel, 1998a). Probation officers describe most girls' assault cases as fights with parents at home or between girls at school or elsewhere over boys (Artz, 1998; Bond-Maupin, Maupin, & Leisenring, 2002; Gaarder et al., 2004). School officials' adoption of zero-tolerance policies toward youth violence increases the number of youths referred for school yard tussles that they previously handled internally (Steffensmeier et al., 2005).

Girls typically perpetrate violence at home or at school and against family members or acquaintances, whereas boys are more likely to commit violent acts against acquaintances or strangers (Steffensmeier et al.,

2005). Two pieces of evidence provide indicators of differences between boys and girls in offender–victim relationships and support the inference that more girls' violence arises in the context of domestic conflicts. Obviously, homicide is not an instance of the relabeling of status offenses, but the offender–victim relationship in homicides provides one indicator of gender-specific differences in violent offending. Reading Table 13.3 reports the victim–offender relationships for boys and girls who committed homicides between 1993 and 2002. In more than one third (36%) of cases in which girls killed, their victims were family members, contrasted with only 7% of boys' homicides. By contrast, boys murdered strangers more than twice as frequently as did girls (38% vs. 18%). Thus, the most lethal forms of violence committed by girls were far more likely than for boys to occur in a domestic context.

Reading Table 13.3 Victims of Murders Committed by Juveniles, 1993 to 2002

Victim–Offender Relationship	Boys	Girls
Family	7	36
Acquaintance	55	46
Stranger	38	18

SOURCE: Snyder and Sickmund (2006, p. 69).

Reading Figure 13.4 examines the offender–victim relationships of youths involved in aggravated and simple assaults and provides another instance of gender-specific differences in violent offending in domestic disputes. The Federal Bureau of Investigation's National Incident-Based Reporting System is an incident-based crime reporting program that collects, among other data, information about offenders, victims, and their relationships (Snyder & Sickmund, 2006). More than one quarter of girls (28%), compared with fewer than one fifth (16%) of boys, committed aggravated assaults against family members. By contrast, boys assaulted acquaintances more frequently than did girls, and they assaulted strangers twice as often as girls. A similar pattern occurred for boys and girls involved in simple assaults. Girls' assaults occurred more frequently

within the family than did boys' assaults, whereas boys more often assaulted acquaintances or strangers. Some of the increase in girls' arrests for simple assaults can be attributed to their greater likelihood than boys to "victimize" family members, the decrease in public and police tolerance for all forms of domestic violence, and the ease with which police may reclassify incorrigible behavior as assault.

> The rise in girls' arrests for violent crime and the narrowing gender gap have less to do with underlying behavior and more to do, first, with net-widening changes in law and policing toward prosecuting less serious forms of violence, especially those occurring in private settings and where there is less culpability, and, second, with less biased or more efficient responses to girls' physical or verbal aggression on the part of law enforcement, parents, teachers, and social workers. (Steffensmeier et al., 2005, p. 387)

Several studies provide evidence of the juvenile justice system's relabeling status offenders as delinquents to incarcerate them. A comparison of juvenile court petitions filed against girls before and after Pennsylvania repealed its status jurisdiction in the mid-1970s found that the proportion of girls charged with assaults more than doubled (from 14% to 29%) following the change (Curran, 1984). In response to the JJDP Act's DSO mandate, the proportion of girls confined in training schools for status offenses declined from 71% in 1971 to 11% in 1987, while there was a commensurate increase in the proportion of girls confined for minor delinquencies during the same period (Schwartz et al., 1990). Moreover, states appear to confine girls for less serious offenses than they do boys. In 1987, juvenile courts confined over half (56%) of girls for misdemeanor offenses, compared with only 43% of boys (Schwartz et al., 1990).

⊠ Offense Characteristics of Delinquent Boys and Girls in Confinement

Juvenile court judges possess a wide range of options to sentence delinquents: dismissal, continuance without a finding, restitution or fine, probation with or without conditions,

Reading Figure 13.4 Male and Female Offender–Victim Relationships

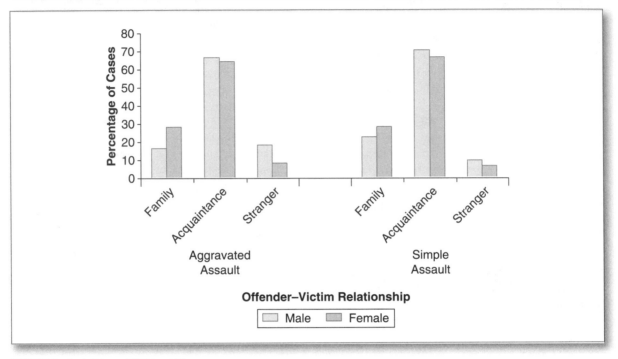

SOURCE: Snyder & Sickmund (2006, p. 145).

out-of-home placement in a public or private facility or group home, confinement in a county institution or state training school, or placement in another secure public or private setting. Because male juveniles commit most of the serious crimes, evaluations of juvenile court sentencing practices typically focus on boys and examine racial rather than gender disparities (e.g., Feld, 1999; McCord, Widom, & Crowell, 2001).

Some sentencing research on gender bias focuses on *chivalrous* or lenient treatment of delinquent girls to explain why girls receive less severe sanctions than do similarly charged boys (Hoyt & Scherer 1998). Other analysts invoke *protectionist* or *paternalistic* explanations to account for why juvenile courts intervene more actively in the lives of sexually active females and status offenders than they do boys charged with minor offenses (e.g., Chesney-Lind, 1977, 1988; Johnson & Scheuble, 1991; Schlossman, 1977; Schlossman & Wallach 1978). Earlier research consistently reported a gender double

standard in the sentencing of girls and boys. Juvenile courts incarcerated proportionally more girls than boys charged with status offenses and sentenced boys charged with delinquency more severely than they did girls (e.g., Bishop & Frazier, 1992). More recent studies have reported fewer gender differences in sentencing status offenders once analysts control for present offense and prior record (e.g., Corley, Cernkovich, & Giordano, 1989; Hoyt & Scherer, 1998; Teilman & Landry, 1981; U.S. General Accounting Office, 1995). However, others contend that the definitions of the offenses for which the research control (e.g., status offenses) already reflect gender bias (Alder, 1984). Johnson and Scheuble (1991) summarized the inconsistent research findings on sentencing girls and reported that

the traditional sex role model has more application to less serious types of violations, such as status offenses, for which females are given a more severe penalty than males for violating role expectation. It also has application for the sentencing of repeat offenders. Such behavior by girls is more strongly in violation of gender role expectations than it is for boys and should result in more punitive disposition for the girls. For the more serious violations of the law, the chivalry model may have the most relevance. Girls are more likely to receive leniency and protection from the consequences of the more serious crimes. (p. 680)

Bishop and Frazier (1992) analyzed juvenile courts' use of contempt power to sanction male and female status offenders who violated valid court orders and reported differential treatment and bootstrapping of girls that covertly perpetuated gender bias.

The next analyses look at characteristics of youths in juvenile residential facilities. Police arrest and juvenile courts file petitions, detain, adjudicate, and place boys in institutions at higher rates and for more serious offenses than they do girls. However, the juvenile justice system processes girls for aggravated and simple assaults at higher rates than it does girls charged with other types of offenses, such as property, drugs, and public order crimes (Feld, in press; Snyder & Sickmund, 2006). Rather than examining the cumulative process by which judges place youths in correctional facilities, the Census of Juveniles in Residential Placement provides a 1-day count of youths in residential placements on a biennial basis.

Reading Table 13.4 adapts the Census of Juveniles in Residential Placement data and reports on juveniles in residential placement (detention and confinement) in 1997, 1999, 2001, and 2003. In 2003, girls constituted about 14% of all delinquents in confinement and 13% of those confined for violent crimes, and both proportions have increased over the four biennia. Nearly three quarters (about 72%) of all girls confined in secure facilities for crimes against individuals were incarcerated for either simple or aggravated assault. In 2003, girls constituted about one seventh (13%) of all delinquents confined for aggravated assault and one fourth (25%) of those confined for simple assault. Confinement for simple assault represents the largest proportion for any offense for which states confine girls, and it has increased steadily over the census years.

To highlight the differences between the offenses for which states confine male and female juveniles, in 2003, girls constituted only about one in seven (14%) of all delinquents in confinement. However, states incarcerated one quarter (25%) of all delinquent girls for either simple or aggravated assaults. By contrast, states confined boys for a more heterogeneous mix of offenses, of which simple and aggravated assaults accounted for only about one seventh (15%).

When changes in confinement for assault are examined, it is found that in each succeeding biennial census, the proportion of girls confined for aggravated and simple assaults increased. Even though boys constituted 92% of all delinquents confined for Violent Crime Index offenses (Sickmund, Sladky, & Kang, 2005), the proportion of girls confined for aggravated assaults, as a percentage of all delinquents confined for aggravated assaults, increased from 12% to 16%. In all four biennia, states confined a majority of all boys for aggravated assaults (62%, 60%, 54%, and 51%) rather than simple assaults. By contrast, the majority of girls whom states confined for assaults were incarcerated for simple assaults rather than aggravated assaults (45%, 45%, 40%, and 38%). Although violent girls may violate gender norms and thereby appear more serious (Schaffner, 1998), by contrast with the boys, larger proportions of girls are confined for less violent and injurious crimes than their male counterparts. The incarceration of larger numbers and proportions of girls for simple assaults suggests a process of relabeling other status like conduct, such as incorrigibility, to obtain access to secure placement facilities.

Conclusion and Policy Implications

Juvenile courts adapt to changes in their organizational environment, and institutional maintenance may explain juvenile courts' continued endurance at least as well as their professed ability to achieve their rehabilitative goals (Schwartz, Weiner, & Enosh, 1998; Sutton, 1988). The breadth and mutability of the juvenile court's mission enable it to redefine the boundaries of social control it administers (Sutton, 1988) and allow court personnel to maintain operational stability in the face of the delinquent male crime drop, with an offsetting increase in female

Reading Table 13.4   Confinement of Boys and Girls for Simple and Aggravated Assaults, 1997 to 2003

Variable	1997	1999	2001	2003
Total delinquents confined	98,222	102,958	99,297	91,831
Female proportion of all delinquents in confinement	11%	12%	13%	14%
Number of girls confined for all person offenses	3612	4365	4443	4401
Proportion of delinquent offenders confined for all person offenses who are female	10%	12%	13%	13%
Number of girls confined for simple and aggravated assault	2,535	3,147	3,211	3,198
% of total delinquents confined for aggravated assault who are female	12	14	15	16
% of total delinquents confined for simple assault who are female	22	23	24	25
% of girls confined for simple and aggravated assaults as a proportion of all girls' delinquency confinements	23	25	25	25
% of boys confined for simple and aggravated assaults as a proportion of all boys' delinquency confinements	16	16	15	16
Girls' % aggravated assaults to all assaults	45	45	40	38
Boys' % aggravated assaults to all assaults	62	60	54	51

SOURCE: Adapted from Sickmund, Sladky, & Kang (2005).

cases (Federle, 2000). DSO coincided with the emergence of a culture of control, greater emphases on proactive policing, and aggressively addressing minor disorder and law violations (Garland, 2001). "The trend has been to lower the threshold of law enforcement, in effect to arrest or charge up and be less tolerant of low-level crime and misdemeanors, and to be more inclined to respond to them with maximum penalties" (Steffensmeier et al., 2005, p. 363).

The broad discretion available to parents, police, prosecutors, and juvenile court personnel allows them to charge many status offenders as minor delinquents and to "bring status offenders under the jurisdiction of the court at a rate almost as great as had existed prior to the [decriminalization] reform" (Schneider, 1984, p. 367). Courtroom observers report that following DSO, prosecutors charged many girls with criminal offenses for behavior

that they previously charged as status offenses (Mahoney & Fenster, 1982). After Washington State temporarily decriminalized status offenders, some police and courts *redefined* them as minor criminal offenders so that juvenile courts could retain jurisdiction and authority over them (Castallano, 1986; Schneider, 1984). Analyses of the changing handling of girls' simple and aggravated assaults strongly suggest that the perceived growth in girls' "violence" may reflect a "criminalization of intra-familial conflicts and aggressive behavior," rather than an actual change in girls' behavior (American Bar Association & National Bar Association, 2001, p. 14).

After three decades of DSO, the juvenile justice system remains committed to protecting and controlling girls, but without responding to their real needs. When Congress passed the JJDP Act in 1974, neither the federal nor state governments made substantial or systematic efforts to provide girls with adequate programs or services in the community (Chesney-Lind & Sheldon, 2005; Maxson & Klein, 1997). Although the 1992 reauthorization of the JJDP Act included provision for gender-specific services, the implementation of that mandate has languished. The failure to provide alternatives to institutional confinement for troublesome girls creates substantial pressures within the juvenile justice system to circumvent DSO restrictions by the simple expedient of relabeling them as delinquents by charging them with assault.

References

Acoca, L. (1999). Investing in girls: A 21st century strategy. *Juvenile Justice, 6*, 3–13.

Acoca, L., & Dedel, K. (1998). *No place to hide: Understanding and meeting the needs of girls in the California juvenile justice system.* San Francisco, CA: National Council on Crime and Delinquency.

Alder, C. (1984). Gender bias in juvenile diversion. *Crime & Delinquency, 30,* 400–414.

American Bar Association & National Bar Association. (2001). *Justice by gender: The lack of appropriate prevention, diversion and treatment alternatives for girls in the justice system.* Washington, DC: American Bar Association.

Artz, S. (1998). *Sex, power, and the violent school girl.* Toronto, Canada: Trifolium.

Bishop, D. M., & Frazier, C. (1992). Gender bias in juvenile justice processing: Implications of the JJDP Act. *Journal of Criminal Law and Criminology, 82,* 1162–1186.

Bloom, B., Owen, B., Deschenes, E. P., & Rosenbaum, J. (2002). Improving juvenile justice for females: A statewide assessment in California. *Crime & Delinquency, 4,* 526–552.

Blumstein, A. (1996). Youth violence, guns, and the illicit-drug industry. *Journal of Criminal Law and Criminology, 86,* 10–36.

Blumstein, A. (2000). Disaggregating the violence trends. In A. Blumstein & J. Wallman (Eds.), *The crime drop in America* (pp. 13–44). New York: Cambridge University Press.

Bond-Maupin, L., Maupin, J. R., & Leisenring, A. (2002). Girls' delinquency and the justice implications of intake workers' perspectives. *Women & Criminal Justice, 13,* 51–77.

Bureau of Criminal Information and Analysis. (1999). Report on arrests for domestic violence in California, 1998. *Criminal Justice Statistics Center Report Series, 1*(2), 5–6.

Castallano, T. C. (1986). The justice model in the juvenile justice system: Washington State's experience. *Law and Policy, 8,* 479–506.

Chesney-Lind, M. 1977. Paternalism and the female status offender. *Crime & Delinquency, 23,* 121–130.

Chesney-Lind, M. (1988). Girls and status offenses: Is juvenile justice still sexist? *Criminal Justice Abstracts, 20,* 144–165.

Chesney-Lind, M. (2002). Criminalizing victimization: The unintended consequences of proarrest policies for girls and women. *Criminology & Public Policy, 1,* 81–90.

Chesney-Lind, M., & Belknap, M. (2004). Trends in delinquent girls' aggression and violent behavior: A review of the evidence. In M. Puytallaz & P. Bierman (Eds.), *Aggression, antisocial behavior and violence among girls: A developmental perspective* (pp. 203–222). New York: Guilford.

Chesney-Lind, M., Morash, M., & Irwin, K. (2007). Policing girlhood? Relational aggression and violence prevention. *Youth Violence and Juvenile Justice, 5,* 328–345.

Chesney-Lind, M., & Pasko, L. (2004). *The female offender: Girls, women, and crime* (2nd ed.). Thousand Oaks, CA: Sage.

Community Research Associates. (1998). *Juvenile female offenders: A status of the states report.* Washington, DC: Office of Juvenile Justice and Delinquency Prevention.

Corley, C. J., Cernkovich, S., & Giordano, P. (1989). Sex and the likelihood of sanction. *Journal of Criminal Law and Criminology, 80,* 540–556.

Costello, J. C., & Worthington, N. L. (1981). Incarcerating status offenders: Attempts to circumvent the Juvenile Justice and Delinquency Prevention Act. *Harvard Civil Rights—Civil Liberties Law Review, 16,* 41–81.

Curran, D. J. (1984). The myth of the "new" female delinquent. *Crime & Delinquency, 30,* 386–399.

Federal Bureau of Investigation. (2006). *Uniform crime reports: Crime in the United States 2005.* Washington, DC: U.S. Department of Justice.

Federle, K. H. (2000). The institutionalization of female delinquency. *Buffalo Law Review, 48,* 881–908.

Federle, K. H., & Chesney-Lind, M. (1992). Special issues in juvenile justice: Gender, race, and ethnicity. In I. Schwartz (Ed.), *Juvenile justice and public policy: Toward a national agenda* (pp. 165–195). New York: Lexington.

Feld, B. C. (1999). *Bad kids: Race and the transformation of the juvenile court.* New York: Oxford University Press.

Feld, B. C. (2003). Race, politics, and juvenile justice: The Warren court and the conservative "backlash." *Minnesota Law Review, 87,* 1447–1577.

Feld, B. C. (2004). *Cases and materials on juvenile justice administration* (2nd ed.). St. Paul, MN: West.

Franke, T. M., Huynh-Hohnbaum, A.-L.T., & Chung, Y. (2002). Adolescent violence: With whom they fight and where. *Journal of Ethnic & Cultural Diversity in Social Work, 11*(3–4), 133–158.

Gaarder, E., Rodriguez, N., & Zatz, M. S. (2004). Criers, liars, and manipulators: Probation officers' views of girls. *Justice Quarterly, 21,* 547–578.

Garland, D. (2001). *The culture of control: Crime and social order in contemporary society.* Chicago: University of Chicago Press.

Girls Inc. (1996). *Prevention and parity: Girls in juvenile justice.* Indianapolis, IN: Author.

Handler, J. F., & Zatz, J. (Eds.). (1982). *Neither angels nor thieves: Studies in deinstitutionalization of status offenders.* Washington, DC: National Academy Press.

Hoyt, S., & Scherer, D. G. (1998). Female juvenile delinquency: Misunderstood by the juvenile justice system, neglected by social science. *Law and Human Behavior, 22,* 81–107.

In re Gault, 387 U.S. 1 (1967).

Johnson, D. R., & Scheuble, L. K. (1991). Gender bias in the disposition of juvenile court referrals: The effects of time and location. *Criminology, 29,* 677–699.

Kempf-Leonard, K., & Johansson, P. (2007). Gender and runaways: Risk factors, delinquency, and juvenile justice experiences. *Youth Violence and Juvenile Justice, 5,* 308–327.

Kempf-Leonard, K., & Sample, L. L. (2000). Disparity based on sex: Is gender-specific treatment warranted? *Justice Quarterly, 17,* 89–128.

Kluger, J. (2006). Taming wild girls. *Time, 167*(18), 54–55.

Krause, W., & McShane, M. D. (1994). A deinstitutionalization retrospective: Relabeling the status offender. *Journal of Crime and Justice, 17,* 45–67.

Krisberg, B., Schwartz, I., Lisky, P., & Austin, J. (1986). The watershed of juvenile justice reform. *Crime & Delinquency, 32,* 5–38.

MacDonald, J. M., & Chesney-Lind, M. (2001). Gender bias and juvenile justice revisited: A multiyear analysis. *Crime & Delinquency, 47,* 173–195.

Mahoney, A. R., & Fenster, C. (1982). Female delinquents in a suburban court. In N. H. Rafter & E. A. Stanko (Eds.), *Judge, lawyer, victim, thief: Women, gender roles and criminal justice* (pp. 221–236). Boston: Northeastern University Press.

Maxson, C. L., & Klein, M. W. (1997). *Responding to troubled youth.* New York: Oxford University Press.

McCord, J., Widom, C. S., & Crowell, N. A. (2001). *Juvenile crime, juvenile justice.* Washington, DC: National Academy Press.

Miller, S. L. (2005). *Victims as offenders: The paradox of women's violence in relationships.* New Brunswick, NJ: Rutgers University Press.

National Center for Juvenile Justice. (2008, October 24). Juvenile arrest rates by offense, sex, and race. Retrieved from http://ojjdp .ncjrs.org/ojstatbb/crime/excel/jar_2007.xls

National Council on Crime and Delinquency. (1975). Jurisdiction over status offenders should be removed from the juvenile court: A policy statement. *Crime & Delinquency, 21,* 97–99.

Platt, A. M. (1977). *The child-savers: The invention of delinquency.* Chicago: University of Chicago Press.

Poulin, A. B. (1996). Female delinquents: Defining their place in the justice system. *Wisconsin Law Review, 1996,* 541–575.

Rothman, D. (1980). *Conscience and convenience: The asylum and its alternative in progressive America.* Boston: Little, Brown.

Russ, H. 2004. The war on catfights. *City Limits, February,* 19–22.

Ryerson, E. (1978). *The best-laid plans: America's juvenile court experiment.* New York: Hill & Wang.

Sanders, J. (2005, June 23). How to defuse "girl on girl" violence. *Christian Science Monitor.* Retrieved from http://www.csmonitor .com/2005/0623/p09s01-coop.html

Scelfo, J. (2004). Bad girls go wild: A rise in girl-on-girl violence is making headlines nationwide and prompting scientists to ask why. *Newsweek.* Retrieved from http://www.newsweek.com/ id/50082

Schaffner, L. (1998). Female juvenile delinquency: Sexual solutions, gender bias, and juvenile justice. *Hastings Women's Law Journal, 9,* 1–25.

Schlossman, S. L. (1977). *Love and the American delinquent: The theory and practice of "progressive" juvenile justice 1825–1920.* Chicago: University of Chicago Press.

Schlossman, S. L., & Wallach, S. (1978). The crime of precocious sexuality: Female juvenile delinquency in the progressive era. *Harvard Educational Review, 48,* 655–694.

Schneider, A. L. (1984). Divesting status offenses from juvenile court jurisdiction. *Crime & Delinquency, 30,* 347–370.

Schwartz, I. M. (1989). *(In)justice for juveniles: Rethinking the best interests of the child.* Lexington, MA: Lexington Books.

Schwartz, I. M., Steketee, M. W., & Schneider, V. W. (1990). Federal juvenile justice policy and the incarceration of girls. *Crime & Delinquency, 36,* 511–520.

Schwartz, I. M., Weiner, N. A., & Enosh, G. (1998). Nine lives and then some: Why the juvenile court does not roll over and die. *Wake Forest Law Review, 33,* 533–552.

Sickmund, M., Sladky, T. J., & Kang, W. (2005). *Census of Juveniles in Residential Placement databook.* Retrieved from http://www .ojjdp.ncjrs.org/ojstatbb/cjrp/

Snyder, H. (2000). *Challenging the myths.* Washington, DC: U.S. Department of Justice, Office of Juvenile Justice and Delinquency Prevention.

Snyder, H. N., & Sickmund, M. (2006). *Juvenile offenders and victims: 2006 national report.* Washington, DC: U.S. Department of Justice, Office of Justice Programs, Office of Juvenile Justice and Delinquency Prevention.

Steffensmeier, D. (1993). National trends in female arrests, 1960–1990: Assessment and recommendations for research. *Journal of Quantitative Criminology, 9,* 411–441.

Steffensmeier, D., Schwartz, J., Zhong, S. H., & Ackerman, J. (2005). An assessment of recent trends in girls' violence using diverse longitudinal sources: Is the gender gap closing? *Criminology, 43,* 355–405.

Sussman, A. (1977). Sex-based discrimination and PINS jurisdiction. In L. E. Teitelbaum & R. Gough (Eds.), *Beyond control: Status offenders in the juvenile court* (pp. 179–199). Cambridge, MA: Ballinger.

Sutton, J. (1988). *Stubborn children: Controlling delinquency in the United Sates, 1640–1981.* Berkeley: University of California Press.

Tanenhaus, D. S. (2004). *Juvenile justice in the making.* New York: Oxford University Press.

Teilman, K. S., & Landry, P. H., Jr. (1981). Gender bias in juvenile justice. *Journal of Research in Crime and Delinquency, 18*, 47–80.

Tonry, M. (2004). *Thinking about crime: Sense and sensibility in American penal culture.* New York: Oxford University Press.

U.S. General Accounting Office. (1991). *Noncriminal juveniles: Detentions have been reduced but better monitoring is needed.* Washington, DC: Author.

U.S. General Accounting Office. (1995). *Minimal gender bias occurred in processing non-criminal juveniles.* Washington, DC: Author.

Williams, C. (2004, December 28). Where sugar and spice meet bricks and bats. *The Washington Post,* p. B01.

Zimring, F. E. (1998). *American youth violence.* New York: Oxford University Press.

Zimring, F. E. (2002). The common thread: Diversion in juvenile justice. *California Law Review, 88,* 2477–2495.

Zimring, F. E., & Hawkins, G. (1997). *Crime is not the problem: Lethal violence in America.* New York: Oxford University Press.

DISCUSSION QUESTIONS

1. What role do family conflicts play in the rise of girls' rates of delinquency?

2. How have status offenses "reemerged" in the juvenile court and impacted the processing of youth offenders?

3. What recommendations would you make for the juvenile justice system in dealing with girls?

READING 14

In this chapter, you learned about how many of the girls involved in the juvenile justice system experience high rates of trauma and victimization in their childhoods. This article reviews both the existing literature as well as the current trends and practices within justice-related agencies. The article concludes with recommendations on how to improve services and treatment for LGBTQ girls in the juvenile justice system.

Trauma Among Lesbians and Bisexual Girls in the Juvenile Justice System

Juliette Noel Graziano and Eric F. Wagner

A large research literature has found that experiencing trauma related to sexual or physical abuse is linked to a host of negative psychological, behavioral, and health-related outcomes among adolescents and adults (Breslau, Davis, Andreski, & Peterson, 1991; Briere & Runtz, 1993; Dembo, Williams, & Schmeidler, 1993; Giaconia et al., 2000; Mullen, Martin, Anderson, Romans, & Herbison, 1996; Neumann, Houskamp, Pollock, & Briere, 1996; Ritter, Stewart, Bernet, Coe, & Brown, 2002; Widom, 1995). While there seems to be a particularly strong relationship between trauma, operationalized as either posttraumatic stress disorder (PTSD) or subsyndromal symptoms of traumatic stress, and delinquency, especially among girls, this topic has only recently received

SOURCE: Graziano, J. N., & Wagner, E. F. (2011). Trauma among lesbians and bisexual girls in the juvenile justice system. *Traumatology, 17*(2), 45–55.

attention (Simkins & Katz, 2002; Smith, Leve, & Chamberlain, 2006; Widom, 1995). Criminological theories have historically focused on men rather than on women, and little attention has been devoted to gender-specific variables that may predict and explain female offending. To this end, feminist researchers argue that there are important gender differences regarding pathways into the justice system, including a particularly strong linkage between girls' experiences of trauma related to physical or sexual abuse and subsequent offending behavior (Bloom, Owen, & Covington, 2005). Since characteristic female responses to such types of trauma (e.g., running away from home, acting out, aggression, etc.) are often viewed as symptoms of conduct disorder or problematic antisocial behavior, and thus are criminalized, traumatized girls become entangled in the justice system without adequate attention to gender-specific needs such as trauma-focused treatment (Chesney-Lind & Shelden, 2004; Simkins & Katz, 2004).

Sexual abuse, physical abuse, traumatic stress, and PTSD are much more likely to be reported by youth with juvenile justice system involvement than by youth without justice system involvement (Acoca & Dedel, 1998; Cauffman, Feldman, Waterman, & Steiner, 1998). While the prevalence of traumatic stress and PTSD among juvenile justice populations (primarily male) has been estimated to be at least 8 times greater than found in adolescent community samples (Wolpaw & Ford, 2004), research shows that the prevalence of trauma-related stress and diagnoses among female juvenile justice populations is *more than 200 times* the national average (Smith et al., 2006). Moreover, histories of physical and sexual abuse are significantly more prevalent among juvenile offender girls than among juvenile offender boys (McCabe, Lansing, Garland, & Hough, 2002). Since trauma-related stress, PTSD, physical abuse, and sexual abuse are especially associated with delinquency for girls, research concerning risk factors for abuse (and subsequent trauma) and delinquency among girls is a priority.

An adolescent subpopulation at particularly high risk for experiencing trauma are lesbian, gay, bisexual, transgender, queer, and/or questioning (LGBTQ) youth. While it is well documented that LGBTQ youth experience significantly higher rates of trauma and sexual orientation violence than do their heterosexual counterparts (Rivers & D'Augelli, 2001; Saewyc et al., 2006; Savin-Williams,

1994), the interconnectedness of trauma, delinquency, and sexual-minority status among teenage girls has not been well studied. There has been a general increase in research concerning the health and well-being of LGBTQ youth; however, there remains a dearth of research specifically focused on PTSD rates. D'Augelli, Grossman, and Starks (2006) did include a measure of PTSD in their study of LGBTQ adolescents and found that 9% of the lesbians, gay, and bisexual youth met criteria for a PTSD diagnosis. Three times the number of girls reported PTSD compared to boys, and PTSD was also significantly associated with gender atypical behavior and physical sexual orientation violence. This is in line with previous studies that show in community samples girls are 2 times more likely than boys to develop PTSD after being exposed to trauma (Breslau et al., 1998). Juvenile offender girls as a group report high rates of trauma, and LGBTQ youth may be at particular risk for experiencing sexual orientation violence, gender atypicality trauma, family rejection, stigmatization, and peer victimization (Berlan, Corliss, Field, Goodman, & Austin, 2010; Birkett, Espelage, & Koenig, 2009; Davis, Saltzburg, & Locke, 2009; Kosciw, Greytak, & Diaz, 2009). Since sexual-minority youth are at an elevated risk for trauma and girls are more prone to meet criteria for PTSD than are boys, the link between trauma and delinquency among lesbians and bisexual girls warrants investigation.

Delinquency during adolescence can have serious long-term negative consequences for physical and mental health and places girls at risk of future arrests, reduced educational and employment opportunities, domestic violence, and dysfunctional parenting (Bardone et al., 1998; Bushway & Reuter, 2002; Clingempeel, Britt, & Henggeler, 2008; Dembo et al., 2000; Giordano, Milhollin, Cernkovich, Pugh, & Rudolph, 1999; Piquero, Daigle, Gibson, Leeper, & Tibbetts, 2007; Serbin, Peters, McAffer, & Schwartzman, 1991; Sweeten, 2006). Given (a) the lack of research focused on sexual-minority women in the justice system and (b) the pronounced trauma-related treatment need among juvenile offending girls, this review will focus on recent trauma research involving juvenile justice system–involved lesbians and bisexual girls. The goals of our review are to identify strengths and weaknesses of current approaches to female juvenile offenders and provide guidance for how services for juvenile offending girls may be improved.

✕ Background

Definitions of Trauma and PTSD

Current definitions of what constitutes trauma and the necessary and sufficient criteria for a diagnosis of PTSD differ regarding the initial stressor needed for a PTSD diagnosis, symptom onset, and duration among those diagnosed with PTSD and the functional impact of PTSD. According to the *Diagnostic and Statistical Manual of Mental Disorders Fourth Edition* (*DSM-IV*; American Psychiatric Association [APA], 1994), a stressor signifies a traumatic event when the person has "experienced, witnessed, or was confronted with an event or events that involved actual or threatened death or serious injury, or a threat to the physical integrity of self or others" (p. 427). In addition, the response of the person includes "intense fear, helplessness, or horror" (p. 428). The *DSM-IV* notes that the response in children may differ and "be expressed instead by disorganized or agitated behavior" (p. 428). In addition, the person must exhibit a variety of symptoms, for a specified duration, with compromised functioning. According to the World Health Organization's (WHO) International Classification of Diseases (ICD-10), PTSD is a response to a stressful event or situation "of an exceptionally threatening or catastrophic nature, which is likely to cause pervasive distress in almost anyone" (WHO, 2007, Section F43.1). Predisposing factors, typical symptoms, and the onset time frame are outlined, and the diagnosis requires evidence of symptom arousal within 6 months of the event.

Abram et al. (2004) argued that the definition of trauma by the *DSM-IV* is somewhat ambiguous, and there are scant reliability and validity studies of PTSD measures based on the *DSM-IV* criteria. They argue that there remains a lack of consistent measures of trauma, and the most utilized instruments measure different types of trauma. For example, violent victimization, sexual victimization, and/or family victimization may be measured differently or not at all, depending on the specific assessment instrument. This state of affairs ultimately reduces reliability and validity and muddies the waters regarding what is the most appropriate way to conceptualize trauma and its impact. PTSD clinical researchers argue in favor of a "consensually understood and empirically validated framework to define and measure traumatic events" (p. 408). That said, such a framework would include narrowing the focus and specifically naming the different types of trauma being investigated for research endeavors that explore trauma and its impact. While important advances have been made regarding the diagnosis of trauma and its impact, notable discrepancies remain (Peters, Slade, & Andrews, 1999), which could have serious implications for populations that have suffered from trauma, such as not meeting criteria for receiving services.

Types of Trauma

Trauma is a risk factor for delinquency and a host of other emotional, physical, and health-risk problems (Chesney-Lind 1989; Gover, 2004; Jaffee, Caspi, Moffitt, & Taylor, 2004; Perez, 2000; Robertson, Baird-Thomas, St. Lawrence, & Pack, 2005; Simkins & Katz, 2002; Smith et al., 2006; Zierler et al., 1991). There are numerous forms of trauma, which include interpersonal violence (sexual abuse, physical abuse, and domestic violence) and/or the witnessing of interpersonal violence. In addition, neglect, the loss of a loved one, serious accidents, terrorism, natural disasters, and wars and other forms of political violence are often traumatic for the individual experiencing them.

Natural disasters, political violence, the loss of a loved one, and serious accidents can be extremely traumatic. However, there is no reason to believe lesbian and bisexual girls are disproportionately affected by such trauma. In contrast, the association between child abuse and victimization and delinquency has been well established, and, in fact, as Steiner, Garcia, and Matthews (1997) found among violent youth in California who met criteria for PTSD, "none of them reported the recent natural disasters in California, which some of them lived through and most of them heard about and saw on television (Loma Prieta earthquakes, Oakland firestorm, Rodney King riots)" as traumatic events (p. 361). Instead, they reported interpersonal violence in the family, including abuse, injury, and murder. Since interpersonal violence seems to be the type of trauma most strongly and directly linked to juvenile offending, this review will focus on the trauma that ensues after interpersonal violence (i.e., physical abuse, sexual abuse, and sexual orientation violence). Moreover, in addition to reporting higher rates of sexual abuse and physical punishment, girls also report experiencing violence, in comparison to boys who more frequently report witnessing violence (Abram et al., 2004; Ford, Chapman, Hawke, & Albert, 2007; Hennessey, Ford, Mahoney, Ko, & Siegfried, 2004).

Trauma and PTSD Among Lesbians and Bisexual Girls Involved in the Justice System

Prevalence of Trauma and PTSD

We conducted an exhaustive literature search and found not a single publication that addresses the prevalence of trauma and PTSD among girls who are both (a) juvenile justice system-involved and (b) lesbian or bisexual. While the empirical literature has documented higher rates of trauma and PTSD among juvenile justice system–involved girls (compared to girls not involved in the juvenile justice system) as well as higher rates of trauma and PTSD among lesbian or bisexual girls (compared to heterosexual girls), the combination has not been examined. Since girls who are both juvenile offenders and lesbian or bisexual exhibit two risk factors known to be positively associated with trauma and PTSD, it may be that the combination of these two risk factors compound risk additively or multiplicatively. However, the absence of empirical research on this topic leaves unknown the issue of how juvenile offending and lesbianism or bisexuality may interact in regard to risk for trauma and PTSD.

While at this time it is unknown how many lesbians and bisexual girls are involved in the juvenile justice system, a handful of studies have included a measure of sexual orientation and can provide some insight. For example, Belknap and Holsinger (2006) studied 444 female and male incarcerated youth and found that sexual identity was an important variable in offending behavior. Twenty-two percent of incarcerated youth self-identified as bisexual, and 5% self-identified as lesbian/gay. Girls, however, were 6 times as likely to identify as bisexual than boys and 3 times as likely to identify as homosexual compared to boys. The authors acknowledge they could not discern "whether boys are less likely to report gay or bisexual identities or if it is an identity that places girls, but not boys, at increased risk of marginalization and delinquency"

(p. 55). In a study that included more than 2,000 youth in detention facilities conducted by Ceres Policy Institute found that 13% of the youth in their sample were LGBTQ, where 11% of the boys and 23% of the girls were "not straight" (Irvine, 2009). In a study that focused on girls only, Schaffner (1999) interviewed and reviewed files of more than 100 justice system–involved young women and reported that between one fifth and one third of the sample were bisexual or lesbian. The consensus among researchers and clinicians working in juvenile offending is that minority sexual orientation is especially overrepresented among female delinquents. This lack of specific information regarding the prevalence of lesbians and bisexual girls severely limits our understanding of their specific risk factors and needs.

Research has documented the prevalence of and specific issues related to abuse, trauma, and PTSD among justice system–involved girls as well as community samples of lesbians and bisexual girls. In addition, qualitative research has started to focus on the experiences of LGBTQ in the juvenile justice system, and collectively, these sources can provide insight regarding the trauma-related treatment needs of lesbians and bisexual girls in the justice system.

Trauma Among Justice System–Involved Girls

Prevalence of Abuse, Trauma, and PTSD

Estimates of the prevalence of abuse, trauma, and PTSD vary depending on the types of abuse or trauma under review; instruments used to detect abuse, trauma, or PTSD; and the segment of the justice population investigated (Teplin, Abran, McClelland, Dulcan, & Mericle, 2002), though in general, offending youth typically report much higher rates of physical and sexual abuse, trauma, and PTSD than do youth not involved in the juvenile justice system (Abram et al., 2004). Having been abused places youth at increased risk for violent behavior and arrests, and among juvenile justice system populations is associated with an earlier age of first offense and a greater number of total offenses (Smith et al., 2006; Widom & Maxfield, 2001).

These associations appear to be particularly strong among justice system–involved girls. Belknap and Holsinger (2006), Brosky and Lally (2004), and Dembo, Williams, Wothke, Schmeidler, and Brown (1992) all documented significantly higher rates of sexual and physical abuse among delinquent girls than among delinquent boys, which range from 28% to 60% of girls reporting sexual abuse and 38% to 75% reporting physical abuse. Cauffman et al. (1998), Ford et al. (2007), and Mueser and Taub (2008) all documented significantly higher rates of PTSD among justice system–involved girls than among justice system–involved boys, with more than 40% of girls reporting PTSD. According to Cauffman, these rates are 50% higher than the rate typically reported by male juvenile delinquents. Studies focused exclusively on juvenile offending girls have confirmed that they are especially likely to report physical abuse, sexual abuse, and trauma related to abuse experiences (Acoca & Dedel, 1998; Simkins & Katz, 2002). Moreover, abuse appears to be a stronger predictor of offending behavior for women than for men, with female abused youth 7 times more likely to be arrested than their nonabused, same-sex counterparts (Makarios, 2007).

It should be noted that epidemiological research has found differences between childhood sexual and physical abuse in the areas of age, race/ethnicity, gender, and relationship between perpetrator and victim, which has important clinical implications (Jason, Williams, Burton, & Rochat, 1982). Likewise, type of abuse may be linked to different behaviors and outcomes. For example, in studies that compared sexual and physical abuse, somatic complaints and anxiety disorders were more prevalent among sexually abused children (Green, Russo, Navratil, & Loeber, 1999), and research consistently documents that sexual abuse may be more related to high-risk sexual behaviors (Buzi et al., 2003; Fergusson, Horwood, & Lynsky, 1997; Robertson, Baird-Thomas, & Stein, 2008). Sexually abused girls in the justice system, in particular, report poorer mental health, such as more suicide attempts and more negative feelings about life, than their female counterparts that do not report sexual abuse (Goodkind, Ng, & Sarri, 2006).

Any type of abuse though, particularly sexual and physical abuse, places youth at risk for both internalizing and externalizing behaviors such as violent and nonviolent delinquency and aggression (Gore-Felton, Koopman, McGarvey, Hernandez, & Canterbury, 2001; Herrera & McClosky, 2003). Moreover, experiencing both forms of abuse have been shown to have even worse outcomes and problem behaviors, and this co-occurrence is more common in clinical versus community samples (Chandy, Blum, & Resnick, 1996; Green et al., 1999). However, it is important to note that while experiencing abuse does increase the risk for a variety of adolescent problem behaviors, most sexually and/or physically abused children do not engage in delinquent behavior as teens.

While the majority of studies examining gender differences in trauma exposure and PTSD have found higher rates among juvenile offending girls than among juvenile offending boys, not all studies have supported gender differences in trauma exposure among teenage offenders. For example, Abram et al. (2004) examined the prevalence estimates of exposure to trauma and 12-month rates of PTSD among youth involved in the justice system and found significantly more number of boys had experienced at least one traumatic event than girls had (93% of boys compared to 84% for girls). Interestingly, while girls reported fewer traumatic experiences, they were just as likely as boys to meet PTSD diagnoses. Wasserman, McReynolds, Ko, Katz, and Carpenter (2005) and McCabe et al. (2002) also found no significant gender differences among justice system–involved youth in rates of PTSD, though those researchers suggest possible methodological issues such as low statistical power, sample selection limitations, and the reliability of measures and diagnostic criteria may have been responsible for their nonsignificant findings.

Trauma Among Lesbians and Bisexual Girls

As previously stated, there have been no empirical studies focusing on trauma among justice system–involved lesbians and bisexual girls, though numerous studies have shown that both sexual and physical victimization is especially prevalent among community samples of lesbians and bisexual girls compared to their heterosexual peers. (Austin et al., 2008; Balsam, Rothblum, & Beauchaine, 2005). For example, Saewyc et al. (2006) in a multisample study found that lesbians and bisexual girls reported the highest rates of sexual abuse and physical abuse by family members. Austin et al. conducted a study of women's past abuse victimization experiences and found lesbians reported higher rates of physical and sexual abuse than heterosexual women. Compared to heterosexual women, bisexual women were more likely to report physical abuse beginning in adolescence. Lesbians were also more likely to report physical abuse in adolescence compared to heterosexual women. Balsma et al. conducted a study, which compared LGB adults with their adult siblings. LGB siblings reported higher rates of childhood sexual abuse, psychological [abuse], and physical abuse by parents or caretakers, as well as partner victimization and sexual assault. Saewyc et al. also found high rates of sexual abuse reported by gay and bisexual boys, which were close to the rates of bisexual girls and lesbians. In conclusion, a growing body of literature supports that lesbians and bisexual girls experience higher rates of sexual and physical abuse than even heterosexual female counterparts.

Lesbians and bisexual girls may also be at increased risk for other potentially harmful behaviors and traumatic experiences. Like bisexual and gay boys, lesbians and bisexual girls may experience high rates of parental rejection and violence. For example, D'Augelli (1998) found that it was more common for lesbians to be threatened with physical violence and actually attacked, most often by their mothers, when they disclosed their sexual orientation to parents. Other studies document strained family relationships and parental rejection (Salzburg, 1996; Savin-Williams & Ream, 2003; Williams, Connolly, Pepler, & Craig, 2005), school violence (Bontempo & D'Augelli, 2002; Hansen, 2007; Kosciw, Diaz, & Greytak, 2008), substance use (Garofalo, Wolf, Kessel, Palfrey, & Durant, 1998; Marshal et al., 2008; Marshal, Friedman, Stall, & Thompson, 2009), suicide risk (Kitts, 2005; Remafedi, French, Story, Resnick, & Blum, 1998; Russell & Joyner, 2001; Silenzio, Peña, Duberstein, Cerel, & Knox, 2007), and high-risk sexual behaviors (Garofalo et al., 1998; Saewyc et al., 2006; Wright & Perry, 2006).

LGBTQ Youth in the Justice System

Unique Considerations Related to Families and Schools

The developmental period of adolescence is marked by a number of additional challenges for LGBTQ youth, which affect their overall well-being. In particular, unique issues related to family and school problems have a significant effect on LGBTQ youth. While family dysfunction and poor academic performance are established risk factors for all youth, particularly girls (Acoca & Dedel, 2000; Henggeler, Edwards, & Borduin, 1987), an extensive study by Majd, Marksamer, & Reyes (2009) outlines how family rejection and school harassment lead to negative outcomes for LGBTQ youth. In their survey of more than 400 justice and legal professions, 90% identified a lack of parental support as a serious problem for LGBTQ youth. Specifically, family rejection often underlies many of the offenses with which LGBTQ are charged, including ungovernability or incorrigibility, runaway, homelessness, survival crimes (i.e., shoplifting and prostitution), substance use, and domestic disputes (Equity Project, 2007, 2008; Feinstein, Greenblatt, Hass, Kohn, & Rana, 2001; Ray, 2006). Irvine in Majd et al. [*Hidden Injustice* (2009)] found LGBTQ youth in detention were twice as likely to have been removed from the home due to someone hurting them and more than twice as likely to be detained for running away from home or placement when compared to their heterosexual peers. The findings speak directly to some of the unique challenges faced by LGBTQ youth.

School harassment, which is associated with multiple negative academic outcomes, also plagues LGBTQ youth (Harris Interactive & GLSEN, 2005; Henning-Stout, James, & McIntosh, 2000; Murdock & Bolch, 2005; Rivers, 2000). GLSEN's 2007 School Climate Survey results revealed that 86% of LGBTQ youth had been verbally harassed, 44% had been physically harassed, and 61% felt unsafe in school due to their sexual orientation (Kosciw, Diaz, & Greytak, 2008). Such types of trauma are directly associated with poor academic performance and truancy (Kosciw et al., 2008). Judges typically interpret such bad behavior at school as the result of antisocial tendencies, best managed by punishment, rather than of PTSD, best managed by treatment.

Current Practices and Policy

Current Trends

Historically, girls have typically entered the justice system because of status offenses. Odem and Schlossman (1991) found that in 1920, 93% of the girls brought into the system were charged with status offenses, of whom 65% were charged with immoral sexual activity. In 1950, there was an increase in the number of Black girls entering the system. By the 1980s, girls were entering the justice system for more serious crimes as opposed to primarily status offenses. Schaffner (2006) argued, "The data reflect a shift away from a criminalization of girls' sexual misconduct toward a focus on girls' violent crimes" (p. 39). Stahl (2008) reported that in 2004, girls composed only 44% of the total petitioned status offenses.

According to the *Juvenile Offenders and Victims: 2006 National Report,* since 1994, there has been a general decline in juvenile violence, though the proportion of girls' violent crimes has increased, particularly for assault (Snyder & Sickmund, 2006). For example, the Violent Crime Index rose 103% for girls between 1981 and 1997, compared to 27% for boys during the same time frame (Acoca, 1999). The trend has continued where the juvenile arrest rate for simple assault increased 19% for girls as opposed to 4% decrease for boys between the years 1997 and 2006 (Snyder, 2005, 2008). Regarding aggravated assault, there was a 24% decrease for boys compared to a 10% decrease for girls during the same period (Snyder, 2005, 2008).

Chesney-Lind and Eliason (2006) argued that recent trends in societal perceptions and media portrayals of the potential for violence among lesbians may have serious negative consequences for sexual-minority and ethnic/racial-minority women. Majd, Marksamer, and Reyes (2009) found that many of the juvenile justice professionals they interviewed lamented that LGBTQ youth are viewed as mentally ill and sexual predators. One respondent remarked, "The whole case was about sensationalizing lesbians . . . [The prosecution] played it like she was a deranged lunatic lesbian" (p. 52). The second trend may result in more harsh treatment by the justice system for women who are perceived as lesbians. According to the authors, these trends affect all girls and women since they serve as a warning of the consequences of countering dominant gender ideals.

In general, gender transgressions in any form challenge traditional views regarding "acceptable" female behaviors. Lesbian and bisexual delinquent girls often enter justice systems that are ill prepared to address their sexuality in affirming ways that often further traumatizes them due to homophobic environments and practices. The ways in which sexism and heterosexism interact may place lesbians and bisexual girls at high risk for justice system

involvement as well as for receiving treatment inappropriate and inadequate for meeting their clinical needs.

Current Practices

Given the preceding, there is a need to examine both the factors that place lesbians and bisexual girls at risk of justice system involvement as well as their unique experiences once they have entered the justice system. The lack of research on LGBTQ youth in the justice system is remarkable since sexual-minority status appears to be a risk factor for juvenile justice system involvement, and LGBTQ youth appear to have particularly negative experiences in the juvenile justice system (Urban Justice Center, 2001).

Majd et al. (2009) documented how at every stage of contact and processing, competent treatment of and services for LGBTQ youth are lacking. They outline practices that serve as barriers to fair treatment when LGBTQ have contact with police and court officials as well as unjust practices within the system. For example, they found that LGBTQ youth have remained a hidden population, where approximately 20% of the juvenile justice professionals interviewed stated that they had not worked with LGBTQ youth in the past 2 years, though they may in fact be an overrepresented group. A combination of different factors contribute to the invisibility of sexual-minority youth. Juvenile justice professionals may lack awareness regarding sexual orientation, and/or youth may choose not to disclose information about their sexual orientation. One interviewee estimated that 75% of the lesbian and bisexual court-ordered girls with whom she works typically do not feel comfortable sharing sexual orientation information initially due to safety concerns.

Misconceptions on the part of professionals serving justice system–involved youth persist, such as the belief that youth are too young to know whether they are LGBTQ, sexual orientation can be changed through treatment, and/or LGBTQ identity is pathological. These misconceptions regarding sexual orientation among key decision makers, juvenile justice professionals, and services providers in turn influence LGBTQ youth contact with system officials. Majd et al. (2009) documented how LGBTQ youth are targeted and abused by police, lack appropriate sentencing options, are overcharged with sex offenses, and undergo inappropriate treatment such as sex offender treatment and reparative therapy. For example, several interviewees indicated that it is more common for LGBTQ youth to be prosecuted for consensual sex that is age appropriate. In addition, interviewees recounted cases where youth were ordered to receive counseling to address or change their sexual orientation. The sum effect is that LGBTQ sexual identity is targeted, criminalized, and ultimately punished. To illustrate, a case was cited where a judge ordered a young lesbian to be placed in a private hospital for 2 weeks because of her sexual orientation.

Once LGBTQ youth enter the justice system, they are often met with a lack of programs and services. Few placements [facility officials] are willing to accept LGBTQ youth, either because they are not competent to do so or cite safety concerns as a major issue (Majd et al., 2009). In general, competent individual mental health and family counselors are scarce (Majd et al., 2009). LGBTQ youth report a host of problems such as abuse inside institutions from peers and staff and discriminatory policies and practices.

LGBTQ youth safety inside juvenile justice programs is a major concern. Unfortunately, there have been high rates of physical, sexual, and emotional abuse of LGBTQ youth reported while in custody (Krisberg, 2009; Majd et al., 2009). Sexual-minority youth are targeted by both peers and staff, and in one study, 80% of survey participants stated that safety was a serious problem for sexual-minority youth, and more than 50% of detention staff reported that they know of situations where LGBTQ youth were mistreated because of their sexual orientation (Majd et al., 2009). More specifically, LGBTQ "often experience rejection, harassment, and discrimination at the hands of their peers, as well as their caretakers and professionals charged with their care" (Estrada & Marksamer, 2006, pp. 171–194), a fact well recognized by juvenile justice officials: "I wonder . . . about how their life is now and how much this traumatized them. . . . It would be hard anyway (to be locked up). But (to be) locked up and verbally abused and told this was a bad sick thing—" (Curtain, 2002, p. 291).

In addition to threats to safety, LGBT youth report services and policies unresponsive to their treatment needs and staff unprepared for treating LGBT youth (Urban Justice Center, 2001). Other discriminatory practices include isolating or segregating youth, utilizing overly harshly discipline, and harassment. While many delinquent youth may feel that they are not receiving the treatment and services they need, the justice system and other out-of-home systems "routinely subject LGBTQ youth to differential treatment, deny them appropriate services and fail to protect them from violence and harassment" (Estrada & Marksamer, 2006, pp. 171–194).

Examples of just how bad it can get inside the system include "the presence of male security personnel, being strapped to beds, forced medication, seclusion, precautions which force disrobing, forced physical exams, and invasive body searches," all of which are almost certainly revictimizing for girls who have suffered from abuse (Ford et al., 2007). Even more common practices that employ physical confrontation, isolation, and restraint may retraumatize girls who suffer from PTSD (Hennessey et al., 2004). In general, the environment is marked by staff insensitivity and loss of privacy, which can increase negative feelings for LGBTQ girls and lead to self-harm (Hennessey et al., 2004). Simply spoken, the conditions faced by LGBTQ juvenile offender girls are uniquely grim and greatly reduce the effectiveness of current treatment and rehabilitation efforts.

Recommendations

Given the preceding, our first recommendation is that much more research should be conducted with juvenile offending LGBTQ youth, focusing on their unique experiences and treatment needs, particularly in regard to trauma. Many juvenile justice agencies do not collect information about sexual orientation, which limits our understanding of how many delinquent youth identify as LGBTQ. Needs assessments should at least include general information about intimate relationships and the role they play in the youth's life. To this end, the National Council on Crime and Delinquency (NCCD) has developed an assessment for girls, called JAIS (Juvenile Assessment and Intervention System), which captures information about sexual orientation in the context of relationships. Juvenile offending girls are not asked directly about their sexual orientation, but instead whether they have a significant/special partner, which gives them the choice to disclose whether they have same-gender relationships. JAIS' inclusion of lesbian and bisexual orientations as possible realities in the lives of offending girls marks the importance of being attentive to sexual identity. Needs assessments should also include general information about trauma experienced prior to and during juvenile justice system involvement, with particular attention to sexual orientation violence. Finally, research is sorely needed that examines girls' risk factors for and trajectories of juvenile offending and how these may differ as a function of sexual orientation; such research would help elucidate the unique prevention and intervention needs of LGBTQ youth.

Our second recommendation is more and better training and education regarding LGBTQ issues among delinquent youth should be provided to juvenile justice professionals. The Model Standards Project's (MSP) work for LGBTQ youth in the juvenile justice system has been cited as a possible resource (Estrada & Marksamer, 2006; Schaffner, 2006). MSP is a national project aimed at establishing a model and disseminating information regarding professional standards for working with LGBTQ youth. The overarching goal of the MSP is to "develop a practice tool to highlight the needs of LGBT youth in out-of-home care and improve services and outcomes" (Wilber, Reyes, & Marksamer, 2006, p. 135). MSP makes several recommendations for how to improve treatment services for LGBTQ youth, including (a) creating an inclusive organization culture, (b) recruiting and supporting competent caregivers and staff, (c) promoting healthy adolescent development, (d) respecting privacy and confidentiality, (e) providing appropriate placements, and (f) providing sensitive support services. Adults working with juvenile offending youth need to understand that while minority sexual orientation does not directly lead to criminality, the negative experiences associated with minority sexual status complicate and exacerbate juvenile offending trajectories.

Our final recommendation is more and better training and education regarding trauma among delinquent youth, and how this may vary by sexual orientation, should be provided to juvenile justice professionals. In the past decade, juvenile justice systems have placed more emphasis on trauma and its impact on the juvenile offending population. Ford et al. (2007) reviewed recent advances in trauma-related treatment that include (a) trauma screening and assessment, and (b) treatment and rehabilitation of traumatic stress disorders. They emphasize the need for screening and assessments since behaviors that occur in response to trauma resemble delinquent behaviors. Several instruments have been developed to measure trauma and symptoms resulting from traumatic events.

Though interventions that target trauma, some of which were designed and evaluated specifically with women, have been implemented, in general, there remains a lack of trauma-informed care for youth involved in the justice system.

Covington and Bloom (2003) argued that services need to be trauma-informed in order to be effective for women. They propose that trauma-informed treatment (a) take the trauma into account; (b) avoid triggering trauma reactions and/or traumatizing the individual; (c) adjust the behavior of counselors, other staff, and the organization to support the individual's coping capacity; and (d) allow survivors to manage their trauma symptoms successfully so that they are able to access, retain, and benefit from the services (Harris & Fallot, 2001). These recommendations are particularly relevant for sexual-minority youth since their specific traumatic experiences should be considered and retraumatizing triggers be avoided. The limited literature in this area suggests that the behavior of staff is an issue in serious need of adjustment in order to be supportive to all youth regardless of sexual orientation. Finally, sexual-minority youth should have access to trauma-related treatment in order to be able to manage their symptoms.

Conclusion

Lesbians and bisexual girls are overrepresented among, and at elevated risk for becoming, juvenile offenders. Lesbians and bisexual girls are at particularly pronounced risk for experiencing trauma, and trauma appears to increase the risk for juvenile justice system involvement. The justice system is ill equipped to deal with sexual-minority girls and underequipped for addressing issues related to trauma. Moreover, it appears they often inflict further trauma through policies and procedures completely at odds with the needs of LGBTQ juvenile offender girls. Specialized efforts are needed to ensure the protection, safety, and appropriate treatment of all youth, including sexual-minority girls involved in the justice system. Recommended actions include (a) more research with juvenile offending LGBTQ youth focusing on their unique experiences and treatment needs, particularly in regard to trauma; (b) more and better training and education regarding LGBTQ issues among delinquent youth for juvenile justice professionals; and (c) more and better training and education regarding trauma among delinquent youth and how this may vary by sexual orientation, for juvenile justice professionals.

References

Abram, K. M., Teplin, L. A., Charles, D. R., Longworth, S., McClelland, G., & Dulcan, M. (2004). Posttraumatic stress disorder and trauma in youth in juvenile detention. *Archives of General Psychiatry, 61,* 403–410.

Acoca, L. (1999). Investing in girls: A 21st century challenge. *Juvenile Justice, 6*(1), 3–13.

Acoca, L., & Dedel, K. (1998). *No place to hide: Understanding and meeting the needs of girls in the California juvenile justice system.* Oakland, CA: National Council on Crime and Delinquency.

Acoca, L., & Dedel, K. (2000). *Educate or incarcerate: Girls in the Florida and Duval County juvenile justice systems.* Oakland, CA: National Council on Crime and Delinquency.

American Psychiatric Association. (1994). *Diagnostic and statistical manual of mental disorders* (4th ed.). Washington, DC: Author.

Austin, S., Jun, H., Jackson, B., Spiegelman, D., Rich-Edwards, J., Corliss, H., & Wright, R. J. (2008). Disparities in child abuse victimization in lesbian, bisexual, and heterosexual women in the Nurses' Health Study II. *Journal of Women's Health, 17,* 597–606.

Balsam, K. F., Rothblum, E., & Beauchaine, T. P. (2005). Victimization over the lifespan: Comparison of lesbian, gay, bisexual and heterosexual siblings. *Journal of Consulting and Clinical Psychology, 73,* 477–487.

Bardone, A. M., Moffitt, T. E., Caspi, A., Dickson, N., Stanton, W. R., & Silva, P. A. (1998). Adult physical health outcomes of adolescent girls with conduct disorder, depression, and anxiety. *Journal of the American Academy of Child & Adolescent Psychiatry, 37,* 594–601.

Belknap, J., & Holsinger, K. (2006). The gendered nature of risk factors for delinquency. *Feminist Criminology, 1,* 48–71.

Berlan, E. D., Corliss, H. L., Field, A. E., Goodman, E., & Austin, S. B. (2010). Sexual orientation and bullying among adolescents in the growing up today study. *Journal of Adolescent Health, 46,* 366–371.

Birkett, M., Espelage, D. L., & Koenig, B. (2009). LGB and questioning students in schools: The moderating effects of homophobic bullying and school climate on negative outcomes. *Journal of Youth Adolescence, 38,* 989–1000.

Bloom, B., Owen, B., & Covington, S. (2005). *Gender-responsive strategies for women offenders: A summary of research, practice, and guiding principles for women offenders* (NIC Accession No. 020418). Washington, DC: National Institute of Corrections.

Bontempo, D., & D'Augelli, A. (2002). Effects of at-school victimization and sexual orientation on lesbian, gay, or bisexual youths' health risk behaviors. *Journal of Adolescent Health, 30,* 364–374.

Breslau, N., Davis, G. C., Andreski, P., & Peterson, E. (1991). Traumatic events and posttraumatic stress disorder in an urban population of young adults. *Archives of General Psychiatry, 48,* 216–222.

Breslau, N.,Kessler, R. C.,Chilcoat, H. D., Schultz, L. R., Davis, G. C., & Andreski, P. (1998). Trauma and posttraumatic stress disorder in the community: The 1996 Detroit Area Survey of Trauma. *Archives of General Psychiatry, 55,* 626–632.

Briere, J., & Runtz, M. (1993). Child sexual abuse: Long-term sequelae and implications for psychological assessment. *Journal of Interpersonal Violence, 8,* 312–330.

Brosky, B. A., & Lally, S. J. (2004). Prevalence of trauma, PTSD, and dissociation in court-referred adolescents. *Journal of Interpersonal Violence, 19,* 801–814.

Bushway, S., & Reuter, P. (2002). Labor markets and crime risk factors. In L. Sherman, D. Farrington, B. Welsh, & D. MacKenzie (Eds.), *Evidence-based crime prevention* (pp. 198–240). New York: Rutledge.

Buzi, R. S., Tortolero, S. R., Roberts, R. E., Ross, M. W., Addy, R. C., & Markham, C. M. (2003). The impact of a history of sexual abuse on high-risk sexual behaviors among females attending alternative schools. *Adolescence, 38,* 595–605.

Cauffman, E., Feldman, S. S., Waterman, J., & Steiner, H. (1998). Posttraumatic stress disorder among female juvenile offenders. *Journal of the American Academy of Child & Adolescent Psychiatry, 37,* 1209–1216.

Chandy, J. M., Blum, R. W., & Resnick, M. D. (1996). Gender-specific outcomes for sexually abused adolescents. *Child Abuse & Neglect, 20,* 1219–1231.

Chesney-Lind, M. (1989). Girls' crime and woman's place: Toward a feminist model of female delinquency. *Crime & Delinquency, 35,* 5–29.

Chesney-Lind, M., & Eliason, M. (2006). From invisible to incorrigible: The demonization of marginalized women and girls. *Crime, Media, Culture, 2,* 29–47.

Chesney-Lind, M., & Shelden, R. G. (2004). *Girls, delinquency, and juvenile justice.* Belmont, CA: Wadsworth.

Clingempeel, W. G., Britt, S. C., & Henggeler, S. W. (2008). Beyond treatment effects: Comorbid psychopathologies and long-term outcomes among substance-abusing delinquents. *American Journal of Orthopsychiatry, 78*(1), 29–36.

Covington, S., & Bloom, B. (2003). Gendered justice: Women in the criminal justice system. In B. Bloom (Ed.), *Gendered justice: Addressing female offenders.* Durham, NC: Carolina Academic Press.

Curtain, M. (2002). Lesbian and bisexual girls in the juvenile justice system. *Child and Adolescent Social Work Journal, 19,* 285–301.

D'Augelli, A. R. (1998). Developmental implications of victimization of lesbian, gay, and bisexual youths. In G. M. Herek (Ed.), *Psychological perspectives on lesbian and gay issues. Vol. 4: Stigma and sexual orientation: Understanding prejudice against lesbians gay men, and bisexuals* (pp. 187–210). Thousand Oaks, CA: Sage.

D'Augelli, A. R., Grossman, A. H., & Starks, M. T. (2006). Childhood gender atypicality, victimization, and PTSD among lesbian, gay, and bisexual youth. *Journal of Interpersonal Violence, 21,* 1462–1482.

Davis, T., Saltzburg, S., & Locke, C. R. (2009). Supporting the emotional and psychological well being of sexual minority youth: Youth ideas for action. *Children and Youth Services Review, 31,* 1030–1041.

Dembo, R., Williams, L., & Schmeidler, J. (1993). Gender differences in mental health service needs among youths entering a juvenile detention center. *Journal of Prison and Jail Health, 12,* 73–10.

Dembo, R., Williams, L., Wothke, W., Schmeidler, J., & Brown, C. H. (1992). The role of family factors, physical abuse and sexual victimization experiences in high risk youths' alcohol/other drug use and delinquency. *Violence & Victims, 7,* 245–266.

Dembo, R., Wothke, W., Shemwell, M., Pacheco, K., Seeberger, W., Rollie, M., . . . Schmeidler, J., (2000). A structural model of the influence of family problems and child abuse factors on serious delinquency among youths processed at a juvenile assessment center. *Journal of Child and Adolescent Substance Abuse, 10,* 17–31.

Estrada, R., & Marksamer, J. (2006). The legal rights of LGBT youth in state custody: What child welfare and juvenile justice professionals need to know. *Child Welfare, 85*(2), 171–194.

Feinstein, R., Greenblatt, A., Hass, L., Kohn, S., & Rana, J. (2001). *Justice for all? A report on lesbian, gay, bisexual and transgendered youth in the New York juvenile justice system.* New York: Urban Justice Center.

Fergusson, D. M., Horwood, J., & Lynsky, M. T. (1997). Childhood sexual abuse, adolescent sexual behaviors and sexual revictimization. *Child Abuse & Neglect, 21,* 789–803.

Ford, J. D., Chapman, J. F., Hawke, J., & Albert, D. (2007). *Trauma among youth in the juvenile justice system: Critical issues and new directions.* Washington, DC: National Center for Mental Health and Juvenile Justice Research Brief, Department of Health and Human Services.

Garofalo, R., Wolf, R., Kessel, S., Palfrey, J., & Durant, R. H. (1998). The association between health-risk behaviors and sexual orientation among a school-based sample of adolescents. *Pediatrics, 101,* 895–902.

Giaconia, R. M., Reinherz, H. Z., Hauf, A. C., Paradis, A. D., Wasserman, M. S., & Langhammer, D. M. (2000). Comorbidity of substance use and post-traumatic stress disorders in a community sample of adolescents. *American Journal of Orthopsychiatry, 70,* 253–262.

Giordano, P. C., Millhollin, Y. J., Cernkovich, S. A., Pugh, M. D., & Rudolph, J. L. (1999). Delinquency, identity, and women's involvement in relationship violence. *Criminology, 37,* 17–39.

Goodkind, S., Ng, I., & Sarri, R. C. (2006). The impact of sexual abuse in the lives of young women involved or at risk of involvement with the juvenile justice system. *Violence Against Women, 12,* 456–477.

Gore-Felton, C., Koopman, C., McGarvey, E., Hernandez, N., & Canterbury, R. J. (2001). Relationships of sexual, physical, and emotional abuse to emotional and behavioral problems among incarcerated adolescents. *Journal of Child Sexual Abuse, 10,* 73–88.

Gover, A. R. (2004). Childhood sexual abuse, gender, and depression among incarcerated youth. *International Journal of Offender Therapy and Comparative Criminology, 48,* 683–696.

Green, S. M., Russo, M. F., Navratil, J. L., & Loeber, R. (1999). Sexual and physical abuse among adolescent girls with disruptive behavior problems. *Journal of Child and Family Studies, 8,* 151–168.

Hansen, A. L. (2007). School-based support for GLBT students: A review of three levels of research. *Psychology in the Schools, 44*(8), 839–848.

Harris, M., & Fallot, R. D. (Eds.). (2001). *Using trauma theory to design service systems. New directions for mental health services series.* San Francisco: Jossey-Bass.

Harris Interactive, & GLSEN. (2005). *From teasing to torment: School climate in America. A survey of students and teachers.* New York: GLSEN.

Hennessey, M., Ford, J., Mahoney, K., Ko, S., & Siegfried, C. (2004). *Trauma among girls in the juvenile justice system.* Los Angeles, CA: National Child Traumatic Stress Network.

Henning-Stout, M., James, S., & McIntosh, S. (2000). Reducing harassment of lesbian, gay, bisexual, transgender and questioning youth in schools. *School Psychology Review, 29,* 180–191.

Henggeler, S. W., Edwards, J., & Borduin, C. M. (1987). The family relations of female juvenile delinquents. *Journal of Abnormal Child Psychology, 15,* 199–210.

Herrera, V. P., & McCloskey, L. A. (2003). Sexual abuse, family violence and female delinquency: Findings from a longitudinal study. *Violence and Victims, 18*(3), 311–334.

Irvine, A. (2009, April 20). The inappropriate use of secure detention for lesbian, gay, bisexual, transgender, and queer youth, presented at the Columbia University Gender on the Frontiers Symposium. In K. Majd, J. Marksamer, & C. Reyes (2009). *Hidden injustice: Lesbian, gay, bisexual, and transgender youth in juvenile courts.* San Francisco: The Equity Project.

Jaffee, S. R., Caspi, A., Moffitt, T. E., & Taylor, A. (2004). Physical maltreatment victim to antisocial child: Evidence of an environmentally mediated process. *Journal of Abnormal Psychology, 113,* 44–55.

Jason, J., Williams, S. L., Burton, A., & Rochat, R. (1982). Epidemiologic differences between sexual and physical child abuse. *The Journal of the American Medical Association, 247,* 3344–3348.

Kitts, R. L. (2005). Gay adolescents and suicide: Understanding the association. *Adolescence, 40,* 621–628.

Kosciw, J. G., Diaz, E. M., & Greytak, E. A. (2008). *2007 National School Climate Survey: The experiences of lesbian, gay, bisexual and transgender youth in our nation's schools.* New York: GLSEN.

Kosciw, J. G., Greytak, E. A., & Diaz, E. M. (2009). Who, what, where, when and why: Demographic and ecological factors contributing to hostile school climate for lesbian, gay, bisexual and transgender youth. *Journal of Youth and Adolescence, 38,* 976–988.

Krisberg, B. (2009). *Special report: Breaking the cycle of abuse in juvenile facilities.* Oakland, CA: National Council on Crime and Delinquency.

Majd, K., Marksamer, J., & Reyes, C. (2009). *Hidden injustice: Lesbian, gay, bisexual, and transgender youth in juvenile courts.* San Francisco: The Equity Project.

Makarios, M. D. (2007). Race, abuse, and female criminal violence. *Feminist Criminology, 2,* 100–116.

Marshal, M. P., Friedman, M. S., Stall, R., King, K. M., Miles, J., Gold, M. A., . . . Morse, J. Q. (2008). Sexual orientation and adolescent substance use: A meta-analysis and methodological review. *Addiction, 103,* 546–556.

Marshal, M. P., Friedman, M. S., Stall, R., & Thompson, A. (2009). Individual trajectories of substance use in lesbian, gay, and bisexual youth and heterosexual youth. *Addiction, 104,* 974–981.

McCabe, K. M., Lansing, A. E., Garland, A., & Hough, R. (2002). Gender differences in psychopathology: Functional impairment, and familial risk factors among adjudicated delinquents. *Journal of the American Academy of Child and Adolescent Psychiatry, 41,* 860–868.

Mueser, K. T., & Taub, J. (2008). Trauma and PTSD among adolescents with severe emotional disorders involved in multiple service systems. *Psychiatric Services, 59,* 627–634.

Mullen, P. E., Martin, J. L., Anderson, J. C., Romans, S. E., & Herbison, G. P. (1996). The long-term impact of the physical, emotional, and sexual term impact of the physical, emotional, and sexual abuse of children: A community study. *Child Abuse & Neglect, 20,* 7–22.

Murdock, T. B., & Bolch, M. B. (2005). Risk and protective factors for poor school adjustment in lesbian, gay, and bisexual (LGB) high school youth: Variable and person-centered analyses. *Psychology in the Schools, 42,* 159–172.

Neumann, D. A., Houskamp, B. M., Pollock, V. E., & Briere, J. (1996). The long-term sequelae of childhood sexual abuse in women: A meta-analytic review. *Child Maltreatment, 1,* 6–16.

Odem, M., & Schlossman, S. (1991). Guardians of virtue: The juvenile court and female delinquency in the early 20th century Los Angeles. *Crime & Delinquency, 37,* 186–203.

Perez, D. M. (2000). The relationship between physical abuse, sexual victimization, and adolescent illicit drug use. *Journal of Drug Issues, 30,* 641–662.

Peters, L., Slade, T., & Andrews, G. (1999). A comparison of ICD10 and *DSM-IV* criteria for posttraumatic stress disorder. *Journal of Traumatic Stress, 12,* 335–343.

Piquero, A. R., Daigle, L. E., Gibson, C., Leeper, N., & Tibbetts, S. G. (2007). Are life-course-persistent offenders at risk for adverse health outcomes? *Journal of Research in Crime & Delinquency, 44,* 185–207.

Ray, N. (2006). *Lesbian, gay, bisexual and transgender youth: An epidemic of homelessness.* New York: National Gay and Lesbian Task Force Policy Institute and the National Coalition for the Homeless.

Remafedi, G., French, S., Story, M., Resnick, M., & Blum, R. (1998). The relationship between suicide risk and sexual orientation: Results of a population-based study. *American Journal of Public Health, 88,* 57–60.

Ritter, J., Stewart, M., Bernet, C., Coe, M., & Brown, S. A. (2002). Effects of childhood exposure to familial alcoholism and family violence on adolescent substance use, conduct problems, and self-esteem. *Journal of Trauma Stress, 15,* 113–22.

Rivers, I. (2000). Social exclusion, absenteeism, and sexual minority youth. *Support for Learning, 15,* 13–18.

Rivers, I., & D'Augelli, A. R. (2001). The victimization of lesbian, gay, and bisexual youths: Implications for intervention. In A. R. D'Augelli & C. J. Patterson (Eds.), *Lesbian, gay, and bisexual identities and youths: Psychological perspectives* (pp. 199–223). New York: Oxford University Press.

Robertson, A. A., Baird-Thomas, C., St. Lawrence, J. S., & Pack, R. (2005). Predictors of infection with chlamydia or gonorrhea in incarcerated adolescents. *Sexually Transmitted Diseases, 32,* 115–122.

Robertson, A. A., Baird-Thomas, C., & Stein, J. A. (2008). Child victimization and parental monitoring as mediators of youth problem behaviors. *Criminal Justice and Behavior, 35,* 755–771.

Russell, S. T., & Joyner, K. (2001). Adolescent sexual orientation and suicide risk: Evidence from a national study. *American Journal of Public Health, 91,* 1276–1281.

Saewyc, E. M., Skay, C. L., Pettingell, S. L., Reis, E. A., Bearinger, L., Resnick, M., . . . Combs, L. (2006). Hazards of stigma: The sexual and physical abuse of gay, lesbian, and bisexual adolescents in the United States and Canada. *Child Welfare, 85,* 195–213.

Salzburg, S. (1996). Family therapy and the disclosure of adolescent homosexuality. *Journal of Family Psychotherapy, 7,* 1–18.

Savin-Williams, R. C. (1994). Verbal and physical abuse as stressors in the lives of lesbian, gay male, and bisexual youths: Associations with school problems, running away, substance abuse, prostitution, prostitution, and suicide. *Journal of Consulting and Clinical Psychology, 62,* 261–269.

Savin-Williams, R. C., & Ream, G. L. (2003). Sex variations in the disclosure to parents of same-sex attractions. *Journal of Family Psychology, 17,* 429–438.

Schaffner, L. (1999). Violence and female delinquency: Gender transgressions and gender invisibility. *Berkeley Women's Law Journal, 14,* 40–65.

Schaffner, L. (2006). *Girls in trouble with the law.* New Brunswick, NJ: Rutgers University Press.

Serbin, L., Peters, P. L., McAffer, V. J., & Schwartzman, A. E. (1991). Childhood aggression and withdrawal as predictors of adolescent pregnancy, early parenthood, and environmental risk for the next generation. *Canadian Journal of Behavioral Science, 23,* 318–331.

Silenzio, V., Peña, J., Duberstein, P., Cerel, J., & Knox, K. (2007). Sexual orientation and risk factors for suicidal ideation and suicide attempts among adolescents and young adults. *American Journal of Public Health, 97,* 2017–2019.

Simkins, S., & Katz, S. (2002). Criminalizing abused girls. *Violence Against Women, 8,* 1474–1499.

Smith, D. K., Leve, L. D., & Chamberlain, P. (2006). Adolescent girls' offending and health-risking sexual behavior: The predictive role of trauma. *Child Treatment, 11,* 346–353.

Snyder, H. (2005). *Juvenile arrests, 2003.* Washington, DC: U.S. Department of Justice.

Snyder, H. (2008). *Juvenile arrests 2005.* Washington, DC: U.S. Department of Justice.

Snyder, H. N., & Sickmund, M. (2006). *Juvenile offenders and victims: 2006 National Report.* Washington, DC: U.S. Department of Justice.

Stahl, A. (2008). *Petitioned status offense cases in juvenile courts, 2004* (OJJDP Fact Sheet, February 2008, #02). Washington, DC: U.S. Department of Justice.

Steiner, H., Garcia, I., & Matthews, Z. (1997). Posttraumatic stress disorder in incarcerated juvenile delinquents. *Journal of the American Academy of Child and Adolescent Psychiatry, 36,* 357–365.

Sweeten, G. (2006). Who will graduate? Disruption of high school education by arrest and court involvement. *Justice Quarterly, 23,* 462–480.

Teplin, L., Abran, K., McClelland, G., Dulcan, M., & Mericle, A. (2002). Psychiatric disorders in youth in juvenile detention. *Archives of General Psychiatry, 59,* 1133–1143.

Urban Justice Center. (2001). *Justice for all? A report on lesbian, gay, bisexual and transgendered youth in the New York juvenile justice system.* New York: Author.

Wasserman, G., McReynolds, L., Ko, S., Katz, L., & Carpenter, J. (2005). Gender differences in psychiatric disorders at juvenile probation intake. *American Journal of Public Health, 95,* 131–137.

Widom, C. S. (1995). *Victims of childhood sexual abuse—Later criminal consequences* (National Institute of Justice: Research in Brief). Washington, DC: U.S. Department of Justice.

Widom, C. S., & Maxfield, M. G. (2001). *An update on the "Cycle of Violence"* (National Institute of Justice: Research in Brief). Washington, DC: U.S. Department of Justice.

Wilber, S., Reyes, C., & Marksamer, J. (2006). The Model Standards Project: Creating inclusive systems for LGBT youth in out-of-home care. *Child Welfare Journal, 85,* 133–149.

Williams, T., Connolly, J., Pepler, D., & Craig, W. (2005). Peer victimization, social support, and psychosocial adjustment of sexual minority adolescents. *Journal of Youth and Adolescence, 34,* 471–482.

Wolpaw, J. W., & Ford, J. D. (2004). *Assessing exposure to psychological trauma and post-traumatic stress in the juvenile justice population.* Los Angeles: National Child and Traumatic Stress Network. Retrieved from http://www.NCTSNet.org

World Health Organization. (2007). *International statistical classification of diseases and related health problems* (10th rev., Chapter 5: Mental and Behavioural Disorders, F00-F99; Neurotic, Stress-Related and Somatoform Disorders, F40-F48). Retrieved from http://apps.who.int/classifications/apps/icd/icd10nline/

Wright, E. R., & Perry, B. L. (2006). Sexual identity distress, social support, and the health of gay, lesbian, and bisexual youth. *Journal of Homosexuality, 51,* 81–109.

Zierler, S., Feingold, L., Laufer, D., Velentgas, P., Kantrowitz-Gordon, I., & Mayer, K. (1991). Adult survivors of childhood sexual abuse and subsequent risk for HIV infection. *American Journal of Public Health, 81,* 572–575.

DISCUSSION QUESTIONS

1. What sort of issues do LGBTQ youth experience related to trauma?

2. How should the juvenile justice system respond to the needs of these youth?

3. How can training of staff improve the treatment of LGBTQ youth in custody?

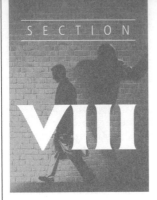

VIII

Female Offenders and Their Crimes

Section Highlights

- Women and drugs
- Property crimes by women offenders
- Prostitution and sex work
- Violent crimes by women
- Women who kill their children

Women engage in every type of criminal activity. Much like their male counterparts, females are involved in a variety of different types of crime. While female crimes of violence are highly sensationalized by the media, these crimes are rare occurrences. Instead, the majority of female offending is made up of crimes that are nonviolent in nature or are considered victimless crimes, such as drug abuse and sexually based offenses.

Males have always engaged in greater numbers of criminal acts. However, women are becoming more involved in crime and the criminal justice system. Research over the past several decades has focused on the narrowing of the gender gap, which refers to the differences in male and female offending for different types of offenses. But what does this really mean? Are women becoming more violent than they were in the past, as media reports have suggested? Is the rise in women's incarceration a result of more women engaging in serious criminal acts? What contributes to these changes? How do we investigate these questions?

In Section I, you learned about the changes in male and female crime participation over a 1-year and 10-year period, using arrest data from the Uniform Crime Reports. Using these same data, we can investigate the gender gap in offending. Table 8.1 compares the percentage of males and females in different offense types. These data illustrate that the proportion of violent crime cases is far greater for males than females. In contrast, the proportion of property

Table 8.1   2012 UCR Arrest Data: Males Versus Females

	Number of Offenders		Percentage of Offense Type Within Gender (%)	
	Males	Females	Males	Females
Violent crime	278,167	69,074	28.6%	14.2%
Homicide	6,303	830	0.6%	0.01%
Forcible rape	11,782	109	1.2%	*
Robbery	59,033	9,032	6.1%	1.9%
Aggravated assault	201,049	59,103	20.7%	12.2%
Property crime	694,051	417,033	71.4%	85.8%
Burglary	161,450	32,432	16.6%	6.7%
Larceny-theft	488,888	374,332	50.3%	77.0%
Motor vehicle theft	37,237	8,833	3.8%	1.8%
Arson	6,476	1,436	0.7%	0.02%

NOTE: Total male arrests for index crimes = 972,218; total female arrests for index crimes = 486,107. Arrests for index crimes make up 16.1% of male arrests and 22.7% of female arrests.

* Less than .01%

crimes is greater for females than males, as property crimes make up 85.8% of all female arrests, compared to 71.4% of male arrests. While these data illustrate that the gender gap may be narrowing in terms of gender proportions of crime, it is important to note that the number of male arrests is twice that of the number of arrests of women for index crimes and it is almost three times greater than the number of arrests for all crimes.

Arrest trends over time also demonstrate an overall decrease in violent crimes for both men and women, but they show an increase in property crimes for women. Table 8.2 demonstrates the 5- and 10-year trends in male and female arrests from 2003 to 2012. For example, between 2003 and 2012, women's arrests in property-related crimes increased 24.9%. It appears that much of this increase occurred between 2003 and 2012, as data indicate that women's participation in this crime increased by only 5.0% between 2008 and 2012. In addition, much of this increase comes from a 29.6% increase in larceny-theft crimes and a 14.7% increase in arrests for burglary. Meanwhile, the number of arrests for men in these cases has continued to decrease at both the 5- and 10-year mark. While these percentages may lead some to believe that women's crime is exploding, it is important to remember that women remain a small proportion of the total number of arrests.

While data from the Uniform Crime Report provide valuable insight into the current state of female offending, research by Steffensmeier and Allan (1996) examines the proportion of male and female arrests for three separate snapshots of time during the 20th century: 1960, 1975, and 1990. Their findings indicate that females make up 15% (or less) of arrestees for most types of major crimes (such as crimes against persons and major property crimes)

Table 8.2   5- and 10-Year Arrest Trends 2003–2012: UCR Arrest Data: Males Versus Females

	Percent Change Within Gender Between 2008 and 2012		Percent Change Within Gender Between 2003 and 2012	
	Males	Females	Males	Females
Violent crime	−13.8	−5.3	−14.9	−2.8
Homicide	−14.7	−9.2	−14.3	−8.3
Forcible rape	−17.0	−36.1	−28.9	−48.1
Robbery	−20.9	−10.2	−7.1	+20.2
Aggravated assault	−11.1	−4.3	−16.1	−5.4
Property crime	−6.4	+5.0	−6.9	+24.7
Burglary	−10.3	+2.4	−5.4	+14.7
Larceny-theft	−2.2	+6.1	+0.4	+29.6
Motor vehicle theft	−29.8	−20.5	−52.6	−43.1
Arson	−20.4	−7.5	−29.2	−16.4

across all time periods. For minor property offenses, the greatest increases are noted between 1960 and 1975 arrest data. Here, the female percentage of arrests increased from 17% in 1960 to 30% in both 1975 and 1990. The only exception where women make up the majority of arrests is for the crime of prostitution (where women make up between two thirds and three fourths of all arrests across all three time periods).

In contrast to Steffensmeir and Allan's research, which relied on UCR data, Rennison (2009) compared offending data from the National Crime Victimization Survey (NCVS) for the 9 years between 1992 and 2001. Her work indicates that there have been negligible differences in the gender gap between male and female offending behaviors during this time frame. By using the data from the NCVS, we see a different view of men's and women's offending behaviors as it includes the dark figure of crime—that is, those crimes that were not reported to the police, as well as the crimes where the police were notified of the crime. These findings note that any differences in the gender gap result not from the increases of female offending but rather from the decreases in male offending rates for particular offenses, which fell at a greater rate than the decrease in female offending rates.

While women participate in many different types of crimes, this section highlights five general categories of crime, all of which involve gendered assumptions about crime and offending. The first category focuses on a topic that is at the heart of the dramatic rise of female participation in the criminal justice system: drug addiction. The second category investigates the role of women in property crime. The third category focuses on prostitution and sex work. While this is a crime that is often identified as a victimless crime, a review of women who engage in sexually based offenses often face high levels of victimization in their lives. The fourth category looks at the role of women within gang organizations. The section concludes with a look at women who engage in acts of murder.

🔀 Women and Drugs

Throughout the majority of the 20th century, women were not identified as the typical addict or drug abuser. In many cases, the use of prescription and illegal substances by women (particularly White women) was normalized, often as a response to the pressures of gender-role expectations. For example, cocaine and opiates were legally sold in pharmacies and were frequently prescribed by doctors for a variety of ailments. Historically speaking, "women's addiction [was] constructed as the product of individual women's inability to cope with changing versions of normative femininity" (Campbell, 2000, p. 30). Examples of this can be found in advertisements depicting women and antianxiety medications in an effort to calm the frenzied housewife who is overwhelmed with her duties as a wife and mother. In the modern era, drug use was once again promoted as desirable (for White women) with the image of the heroin chic fashionista of the 1990s, personified by supermodel Kate Moss.

Without question, the war on drugs has had a significant impact on women with illicit drug addictions. In the last few decades, female incarceration rates grew 108%, but raw numbers grew eightfold (Harrison & Beck, 2006). These increases can be attributed almost exclusively to the female drug offender (or attributed to the rise in other offenses due to her drug use). This disproportionality continues to increase. In 2012, female drug offenders account for 25% of the state prison population whereas in male prisons, these crimes make up only 16% of all offenders (Carson & Golinelli, 2013). This is a significant increase compared to 2008 data, where only 9% of drug offenders were women (Guerino, Harrison & Sabol, 2011).

▲ **Photo 8.1** Research highlights that women and men vary in their drug use, both in terms of their drug of choice as well as their motivations of use. Here, a woman is shown using drugs intravenously.

There is an endless number of pathways to the onset of drug addiction and offending. However, research consistently identifies similar pathways of drug use for women, regardless of race, ethnicity, or drug of choice. Whether the discussion focuses on women addicted to crack cocaine in lower income communities or middle-class women who abuse alcohol or prescription drugs, substance use becomes a method of coping with their lives (Inciardi, Lockwood, & Pottiger, 1993). These primary pathways include exposure to alcohol and drugs at a young age, early childhood victimization and trauma, mental health challenges, and economic challenges (Bloom, Owen & Covington, 2003).

For some women, their experiences with addiction begin at an early age. These girls are often exposed to drug use within their home environment. A family environment can influence the pathway to addiction in terms of an increased availability of these illicit drugs as well as an environment that is accepting of substance use. In some cases, substance abuse becomes a part of the family culture and a way in which children could spend time with their parents and siblings (Carbone-Lopez, Gatewood Owens, & Miller, 2012). On the other hand, lack of parental supervision may also lead to substance use for girls (Bowles, DeHart & Webb, 2012). Early experimentation with substance abuse can also lead to a longer term of addiction (Dennis, Scott, Funk & Foss, 2005).

Another pathway to addition is represented through the issues that result from victimization and trauma, particularly during early childhood. Women who experience violence and abuse during their formative years are more likely to abuse alcohol and other drugs compared to women without a history of abuse. Here, research estimates that 48% to 90% of addicted women have endured physical or sexual victimization during their childhood (SAMHSA, 2009). Left untreated, drugs become a way to escape from the pain of childhood abuse and trauma (Carbone-Lopez et al., 2012). The presence of mental health issues can also serve as a pathway to addiction. Mental illness and substance use go hand in hand as 72% of men and women with severe mental disorders have a co-occurring substance abuse problem (Baillargeon, Binswanger, Penn, Williams, & Murray, 2009). Additionally, research indicates that women have higher rates of mental illness compared to men (James & Glaze, 2006). If effective mental health treatment (including psychotropic medication) is unavailable, many may choose to self-medicate with illicit substances, which can lead to issues with addiction (Harris & Edlund, 2005). Finally, women may engage in substance abuse as part of their romantic relationship with a significant other. In many cases, their experimentation quickly translates into addiction and continues even once the relationship ends (Ryder & Brisgone, 2013).

Addiction limits the abilities for many women to develop a self-sustaining life. In addition to placing them at risk for homelessness, violence, and incarceration in an effort to fund their drug use, addiction has collateral consequences, particularly for her minor children. Indeed, the images of the pregnant addicted mother and crack babies of the 80s and 90s represented the greatest form of evil found in the drug-abusing woman. Many women with addiction issues often fail to recognize that they are pregnant until late in their pregnancy where their substance use and lack of prenatal care can place their child at significant risk for health and developmental issues. However, for some women, the realization that they are expecting may encourage them to seek out treatment and give them a reason to change their lives (Silva, Pires, Guerreiro & Cardoso, 2012). However, relapse issues can threaten this newfound journey toward stability and have lasting effects both for her life as well for her children. Relapse, incarceration, and time in a treatment facility mean that mothers are separated from their children. Even in cases where these mothers were physically present, their addiction meant that they were often emotionally unavailable for their children. Over time, an intergenerational pattern emerges, and these daughters turn to the same addictions that their mothers endure.

Regardless of their pathway to addiction, increases in number of women using drugs and the marginalization of addicts fed the war on drugs. As the behaviors of addicted women shifted toward criminal activity in an effort to support their drug habit, the perception that drug addiction is *dangerous* spread among the general public. Drug use became something to fear by members of society. The shift of addiction from a public health issue to a criminal justice issue fueled the fear about the link of drug use and crime.

The heightened frenzy about the dangerousness of drugs has fueled the war on drugs into an epidemic. The war on drugs and its effects on the criminal justice system have been documented extensively, and the introduction of mandatory minimum sentencing represented a major change in the processing of drug offenders. While these sentencing structures were applied equally to male and female defendants, the role of women's participation in drug offenses often differs substantially from male involvement in drug-related crimes. With the elimination of judicial discretion, judges were unable to assess the role that women played in these offenses (Merolla, 2008). As a result, women now received long sentences of incarceration where they had once been granted probation and other forms of community supervision. The effect of this shift was dramatic. Between 1986 and 1991, the incarceration rates of women for drug-related offenses increased 433%, compared to a 283% increase for males (Bush-Baskette, 2000). Drug-convicted women make up 72% of the incarcerated population at the federal level (Greenfeld & Snell, 2000). Most of these cases involve women as users of illegal substances. Even in the small proportion of cases where women are involved in the sale of drugs, they rarely participate in mid- or high-level management in the illegal drug market, often due to sexism within the drug economy (Maher, 2004b). In addition, the presence of crack shifted the culture of the street economy, particularly for women involved in acts of prostitution. The highly addictive nature of crack led more women to the streets in an effort to find a way to get their next high. At the same time, the flood of women in search of sex work created an economy whereby the value of sexual services significantly decreased.

While recent changes in federal drug sentencing laws have reduced the disparities in sentencing, the damage has already been done. The effects of these laws created a new system of criminal justice where the courts are overloaded with drug possession and distribution cases, and the growth of the prison economy has reached epic proportions. Yet these efforts appear to have done little to stem the use and sale of such controlled substances. Indeed, the overall rates of crimes other than drug-related cases have changed little during the last 40 years. The effects of these policies have produced significant consequences for families and communities, particularly given the increase in the incarceration rates of women. Sections X and XI explore in depth the consequences in the incarceration of women, both for themselves and their families, as well as their communities. It is these consequences that have led some scholars to suggest that the war on drugs has in effect become a war on women (Chesney-Lind, 1997).

🗙 Property Crime

The category of property crime is relatively broad and encompasses a number of different offenses. Generally speaking, property crime refers to the illegal acquisition of money, goods, or valuables, but without the use of force or fear to obtain the property. While the Uniform Crime Report includes arson, burglary, larceny-theft, and motor vehicle theft as Part 1 offenses under the category of property crime, the National Crime Victimization Survey (NCVS) includes only burglary, motor vehicle theft, and theft (larceny) in its definition. As a more inclusive representation of crime, the National Incident Based Reporting System incorporates many more types of property offenses into its definition, such as arson, bribery, burglary, vandalism, embezzlement, blackmail, fraud, larceny-theft, motor vehicle theft, stolen property offenses, and bad checks.

▲ Photo 8.2   The majority of crimes involving women are property offenses and include crimes such as burglary and theft. Here, a woman engages in shoplifting from a store.

According to the Bureau of Justice Statistics, the rate of property crime victimization within U.S. households (property crime per 1,000 households) has steadily declined since 1993. While the 2010 property crime victimization rate was approximately 5% lower compared to 2009, today's rate is roughly one third of the 1993 victimization rate (120 victimizations per 1,000 households in 2010, compared to 320 in 1993) (Truman, 2011). While females are more likely to be involved in property offenses compared to other types of crimes, males still commit the overwhelming majority of these crimes. Men committed 62% of property crimes in 2010, while women were responsible for about 38% of theses offenses.

Earlier in this section, you learned about how women's lives are shaped by addiction. Addiction can also shape women's participation in crimes, particularly for property offenses as women may engage in these crimes to either support their drug habit or commit crime while under the influence. Indeed, drugs are the most common factor among females who engage in property crimes. Research by Johnson (2004) finds that 52% of property offenders engage in crime to get money so that they can buy drugs. In comparison, only 15% of violent offenders stated that their crime was directly related to obtaining drugs for personal use.

Another factor in female property offending is economic survival. Given that only 40% of incarcerated women were employed prior to their arrest, it appears that many women engage in these crimes in order to provide for themselves and their families. However, to suggest that poverty and unemployment leads people to engage in property-based offending is a narrow view of the issue. Certainly, addiction can play a role for some offenders. Here, the decision to engage in crime helps not only to fund their substance abuse, but it also provides support to maintain a household. This is particularly poignant given that many individuals who suffer from addiction are unable to hold down functional employment.

The image of women in property crimes varies dramatically. On one hand, shoplifting is typically described as a "pink-collar" crime. While shoplifting may be an act that some undertake to support other areas of criminality, such as drug use, others use shoplifting as their primary occupation and sell their goods to buying customers. These women view themselves as professionals, and their ability to shoplift is a skill. Much like the drug dealer, the shoplifter develops a list of clients who will purchase their goods from her. Her attire is based on what types of stores she will steal from so that she blends in with the rest of the legitimate shoppers and goes undetected by security personnel (Caputo & King, 2011). Another example involves women and the crime of robbery. Some scholars highlight how women engage in robbery as solo offenders; how women choose to engage in crime is gendered in that they typically do not engage in overt acts of violence and select other women as their victims (Miller, 1998a). Meanwhile, other cases show women who use their femininity to draw in their victims as part of a larger mixed-gender group (Contreras, 2009). In each of these cases, women use their gender in their favor.

CASE STUDY

Spotlight on Women and Bank Robbery

Historically, male offenders have dominated the crime of bank robbery. Even in cases where women have been involved in these crimes, they were either co-conspirators with a male or were reduced to a minor role. Consider the example of Bonnie Elizabeth Parker (1910–1934) who was romantically involved with Clyde Chestnut Barrow (1909–1934). Barrow and his gang committed over a dozen bank robberies during the Great Depression. Urban legend suggested that Bonnie was an equal participant in these crimes. However, evidence suggests that Bonnie never actually killed a single victim.

While the days of Bonnie and Clyde are long gone and men remain the most likely offender of these crimes, times are changing. Women are becoming more involved in these crimes. In the last decade, the number of bank robberies committed by women has shifted. While there were more females involved in bank robberies in 2003, there were more of these offenses in general. According to the Uniform Crime Reports, women made up 524 of the 9,714 offenders involved in these crimes. This means that women made up 5.5% of all bank robbery offenders in 2003. In 2011, they made up 429 of the offenders for these crimes. However, the overall number of offenders in these cases fell by 37% to 6,088 (Federal Bureau of Investigation [FBI], 2003, 2011).

Perhaps one of the most famous cases of bank robbery involved Patricia Hearst. Hearst was the 19-year-old socialite granddaughter of newspaper publishing mogul William Randolph Hearst. In 1974, Patty Hearst was kidnapped by members of the Symbionese Liberation Army, a domestic terrorist group. The SLA manipulated Hearst to join their criminal actions. During her 18 months under SLA captivity, she participated in three bank robberies and several other criminal activities. Despite her defense that she had been brainwashed by her captors, Hearst was sentenced to seven years in prison for her part in the robbery. Her sentence was commuted after two years by then President Jimmy Carter, and she was pardoned by President Clinton (Cable News Network [CNN], 2001).

A recent example of a female bank robber is Lee Grace Dougherty. In August 2011, Lee Grace, with her brother Ryan and stepbrother Dylan, robbed a local bank in Georgia. While all three had previously been involved with the criminal justice system, Lee Grace drew the attention of the media both for her status as a woman as well as online statements that "I like causing mayhem with my siblings." She was sentenced to 35 years in prison for her involvement in the bank robbery and faces additional time, for her subsequent offenses as part of their multi-state crime spree (Coffman, 2012; Gast, 2011; MacIntosh, 2011).

Prostitution

Hollywood images of prostitution depict a lifestyle that is rarely found in the real world. Movies such as *Pretty Woman, Leaving Las Vegas*, and *Taxi Driver* paint a picture of the young, beautiful prostitute who is saved from her life on the streets. In reality, there are few Prince Charming's available to rescue these women. The reality that awaits most of these women is one filled with violence, abuse, and addiction—deep scars that are challenging to overcome.

Prostitution involves the act of selling or trading sex for money. Prostitution can take a variety of forms, including escort services, massage parlors, or work in brothels, bars, and truck stops. However, street-level prostitution is perhaps the most visible form of sex work. According to the Uniform Crime Reports, police agencies arrested 36,931 offenders for the crime of prostitution in 2012. Two thirds of such offenders were female (see FBI, 2011, 2012b). Most of these offenders are workers of the trade and not the traffickers or customers associated with these crimes.

For those women who engage in street-level prostitution, money may not be the only commodity available in exchange for their bodies, as they also trade sex for drugs or other tangibles such as food, clothing, and shelter. In addition, women in this arena experience the high levels of risk for violence and victimization.

The journey into prostitution is not a solitary road. Rather, it involves a variety of individual, contextual, and environmental factors. A history of abuse is one of the most commonly referenced risk factors for prostitution, and research by Dalla (2000) indicates that drug addiction almost always paves the way for work in prostitution. However, poverty also plays a role. In Section V, you learned about the issue of forced prostitution and human trafficking, yet many women choose to enter street prostitution and brothel work out of financial need (Karandikar, Gezinski & Meshelemiah, 2013).

One of the most common pathways for women in prostitution is the experience of early childhood sexual victimization. Although there is no direct link that indicates that the experience of incest is predictive of selling one's body, research indicates that there is a strong correlation between the two (Nokomis Foundation, 2002), and one prostitution recovery program indicates that 87% of their participants experienced abuse throughout their early childhood, often at the hands of a family member. For these women, incest became the way in which they learned about their sexuality as a commodity that could be sold and traded, and some suggest this process of bargaining became a way in which these victims could once again feel powerful about their lives (Mallicoat, 2006). In Section VII, you learned about how young girls who have been abused within the home often run away to escape the ongoing violence and victimization. Once on the streets, they are at risk for even more violence. Many of these girls turn to prostitution to support their basic survival needs, such as food and shelter. While childhood abuse is a common factor among many women in prostitution, girls who enter prostitution as teens experience higher rates of emotional abuse compared to those who enter the lifestyle as adults (Roe-Sepowitz, 2012).

Women in prostitution experience high levels of violence during their careers. On the streets, they witness and experience violence on a daily basis. More than 90% of these women are brutally victimized (Romero-Daza, Weeks, & Singer, 2003). They are robbed, raped, and assaulted by their customers and pimps alike (Raphael & Shapiro, 2004). Many do not report these incidents out of fear that they will be arrested for engaging in prostitution, coupled with a

©iStock/microgen

▲ **Photo 8.3** Street prostitution is one of the most visible and dangerous forms of sex work. Many women who work as street prostitutes risk significant victimization from their johns. Unfortunately, many victims do not report these crimes to the police out of fear of victim blaming by the criminal justice system.

belief that the police will do little to respond to these crimes. Indeed, women often return to the streets immediately following their victimization. This temporary intervention is viewed as a delay in work, rather than an opportunity to search for an exit strategy. One woman characterized her experience as normal—"society and law enforcement consider a prostitute getting raped or beat as something she deserves. It goes along with your lifestyle. There's nothing that you can do" (Dalla, Xia, & Kennedy, 2003, pp. 1380–1381).

Female sex workers also witness significant acts of violence perpetuated against their peers, an experience that often leads to significant mental health issues. Drug use becomes a way to cope with the violence in their daily lives. As the pressure to make money increases in order to sustain their substance abuse addiction or to provide a roof over their head at night, women may place themselves in increasingly risky situations with their customers (Norton-Hawk, 2004). In an effort to protect against potential harms, women rely on their intuition to avoid potentially violent situations. Many girls indicate that they will not leave a designated area with a client and generally refuse to get into a car with a client. Others carry a weapon, such as a knife. Despite the risks, some women reference the thrill and power they experience when they are able to survive a violent incident (Dalla, Xia, & Kennedy, 2003). Many women are surprised when they reflect on the levels of violence that they experienced on the streets. Some may disassociate themselves from the realities of this journey and believe that the experience was not as traumatic as they originally believed. However, the battle scars from their time on the streets provide the evidence for the trauma they endured, both physically and mentally.

The role of substance abuse is central to the discussion of risk for prostituting women. About 70% of women in prostitution have issues with drug addiction. Some women begin their substance use prior to their entry in prostitution to cope with the pain associated with past or current sexual violence in their lives. They then resort to prostitution to fund their drug habits (Raphael, 2004). For others, entry into substance abuse comes later in an effort to self-medicate against the fear, stress, and low self-esteem resulting from the selling of sex (Nixon, Tutty, Downe, Gorkoff, & Ursel, 2002). As their time on the streets increases, so does their substance abuse. Indeed, the relationship between drug use and prostitution may be a self-perpetuating circle in which they feed off one another. A sample of women in jail for prostitution had significantly higher rates of drug use compared to women arrested for non-prostitution-related offenses (Yacoubian, Urbach, Larsen, Johnson, & Peters, 2000).

In recent years, media accounts have focused significant attention on the use of crack cocaine by street prostitutes. Research has linked the presence of crack to an increased number of individuals working on the street, which in turn decreases the price that women receive for their services. Addiction to drugs like crack has created an economy where money is no longer traded for sex. Rather, sexual acts become a commodity to be exchanged for drugs. The levels of violence associated with the practice of selling sex increases in this drug-fueled economy (Maher, 1996).

While drug addiction presents a significant health concern for women in prostitution, additional issues exist for women in terms of long-term physical health. Women engaged in sex work are at risk for issues related to HIV, hepatitis, and other chronic health concerns, including dental, vision, neurological, respiratory, and gynecological problems (Farley & Barkin, 1998). Finally, the death rate of women in prostitution is an astonishing 40 times higher than the death rate of the overall population (Nokomis Foundation, 2002).

Mental health concerns are also a significant issue for women engaged in the sex trade. Cases of **post-traumatic stress disorder (PTSD)** are directly related to the levels of violence that women experience on the streets, and an estimated two thirds of prostituted women experience symptoms of PTSD (Schoot & Goswami, 2001). Prostitutes suffering from PTSD may be unable to accurately assess the levels of threat and violence that surround their lives, which in turn places them at increased risk for ongoing physical and sexual victimization (Valera, Sawyer, & Schiraldi, 2000).

The Legalization Debate

The question of whether prostitution should be considered a criminal activity is one of considerable debate. In Nevada, legal prostitution is limited to counties with a population under 400,000, excluding high-traffic areas, such as Reno and Las Vegas, from offering legalized brothels.[1] The laws within Nevada focus almost exclusively on the minimization of risk and reduction of violence for women in prostitution. Since 1986, Nevada has required that prostitutes who work in brothels must submit to weekly exams to assess for any sexually transmitted infections or the presence of HIV. Brothels also implement a variety of regulations to ensure the safety and security of the facility and the women who work there, such as audio monitoring and call buttons in the rooms. Most brothels limit services outside of the brothel environment to control any potentially negative behaviors of clients. Research indicates that women who work in brothel settings feel safe and rarely experienced acts of violence while working as a prostitute. Indeed, it is these safety mechanisms that led women to believe that brothel sex work is by far the safest environment in which to engage in prostitution, compared to the violence and danger that street prostitutes regularly experience (Brents & Hausbeck, 2005).

In the Netherlands, the legalization of brothels in 2000 created a new way to govern the sex trade. While the act of prostitution has been legalized since the early 20th century, it was the brothel environment (popularized by the red light district and "window" shopping in the city of Amsterdam and other cities) that was illegal. At the time of brothel legalization, the practice of prostitution in the Netherlands was not an uncommon phenomenon, and estimates suggest that over 6,000 women per day were working in prostitution-related activities (Wagennar, 2006). The effects of the legislation lifted the formal prohibition of the brothel, even though many municipalities tolerated their presence, and agents of social control, such as law enforcement and the courts, largely refrained from prosecuting cases. By creating a system whereby brothels had to be licensed, authorities were able to gain control over the industry by mandating public health and safety screenings for sex workers. As part of the decriminalization of prostitution, the state created the opportunity for brothel owners to have a legal site of business. Labor laws regarding the working conditions for prostitutes were put into effect. In addition, it created a tax base in which revenue could be generated (Pakes, 2005). The goals of decriminalization allowed for the Dutch government to improve the lives of women in prostitution by creating safe working conditions, creating a system of monitoring of the sex trade, and regulating illegal activities that might be associated with the selling of sexuality, such as streets crimes associated with prostitution, the exploitation of juveniles, or the trafficking of women into the sex industry (Wagenaar, 2006).

By creating a sustainable economy of prostitution, some critics suggest not only that the needs of the customer are met but also that these regions create an economic strategy for women, particularly women within challenged economic situations. However, creating a system of legislation is no guarantee that laws will be followed; even with the legalization of prostitution in New South Wales, Australia, the majority of brothels fail to register their businesses

---

[1] However, evidence exists that street prostitution and escort services are still prevalent within these regions.

and pay little attention to the regulatory rules for operation. In addition, illegal sexual practices have continued to flourish—the Netherlands is identified as a leading destination for pedophiles and child pornographers, many of which operate under the belief that the promotion of legalized prostitution has created opportunities for illegal prostitution in these regions, as well (Raymond, 2004).

Other legislation focuses on the criminalization of the demand for sexual services. In addressing the issue of prostitution in Sweden, legislatures have focused on making the purchasing of sex from women a criminal act. The belief here is that by criminalizing the male demand for sex, it may significantly decrease the supply of women who engage in these acts. By criminalizing the "johns," Sweden has taken a stand against a practice that they feel constitutes an act of violence against women (Raymond, 2004). In the passing of these laws, the parliament indicated, "[I]t is not reasonable to punish the person who sells a sexual service. In the majority of cases . . . this person is a weaker partner who is exploited" (Ministry of Labour, Sweden, 1998, p. 4).

In the United States, even in an environment where both the purchaser and seller of sex can be subjected to criminal prosecution, the data indicate that women are significantly more likely to face sanctions for selling sex, compared to men who seek to purchase it (Farley & Kelly, 2000). Although the focus on demand is an important characteristic in the selling of sex, it is not the only variable. Indeed, larger issues such as economics, globalization, poverty, and inequality all contribute to a system where women fall victim to the practices of sexual exploitation.

Farley and Kelly (2000) suggest that even with the legalization of the brothel environment, prostitution remains a significant way in which women are brutalized and harmed. The social stigma of women who engage in the selling of sex does not decrease simply because the act of prostitution becomes legal. Indeed, the restriction of brothels to specific regions only further isolates women from mainstream society and magnifies the stigma they may experience (Farley, 2004). In cases of victimization, women employed in sex work continue to experience significant levels of victim blaming when they are victimized, even if prostitution is decriminalized. The system of public health, which is promoted as a way to keep both the prostitute and her client safe, fails to meet some of the most critical needs of women in this arena, as these efforts toward promoting safety are limited exclusively to physical health, and little to no attention is paid to the mental health needs of women engaged in prostitution (Farley, 2004).

Research indicates that women involved in street prostitution often want to leave the lifestyle, but they express concern over how their multiple needs (including housing, employment, and drug treatment) may limit their abilities to do so. There are few programs that provide adequate levels of services to address the multiple needs of women during this transition. A review of one prostitution recovery program found that affordable safe housing is the greatest immediate need for women in their transition from the streets (Mallicoat, 2011). Homelessness puts women at risk for relapse: "Without reliable housing, it is challenging to escape the cycle of prostituting" (Yahne, Miller, Irvin-Vitela, & Tonigan, 2002, p. 52).

In addition, women must possess necessary skills and have access to support in order to facilitate this process. Women exiting the streets indicate a variety of therapeutic needs, including life skills, addiction recovery programming, and mental health services designed to address the traumas they experienced. An exit strategy needs to acknowledge the barriers to success and continuing struggles that women will experience as a result of these traumas.

Women and Violence

True crime documentaries and fictionalized television dramas give the perception that the rates of female offending, particularly in cases involving violence, have increased dramatically in recent years. Yet rates of crime for women in these types of cases have actually decreased. This discussion about women and violent crimes investigates three different categories of female offenders. The first topic highlights the role of women in gangs. The second topic looks at general crimes of female violence, including murder. The section concludes with a specific type of female homicide with women who kill their children.

Girls and Gangs

While girls have traditionally made up a small proportion of gang members, there was significant media attention on the rise of gang girls throughout the late 20th century. Surveys conducted by law enforcement agencies in the 1990s estimated that between 8% and 11% of gang members were female (Moore & Terrett, 1998). However, not all law enforcement jurisdictions include girls in their counts of gang members, a practice that can skew data about the number of girls involved in gangs (Curry, Ball, & Fox, 1994). Whereas the National Youth Gang Center suggests that these rates have remained consistent and reflect little change in rates of female gang participation (2009), other data tell a different story. Self-report studies during this same time frame reflect a higher percentage of female gang participation compared to law enforcement data and suggest that 38% of the self-identified gang members between the ages of 13 and 15 were female (Esbensen, Deschenes, & Winfree, 1999). Recent self-report data indicate that girls represent between 31% and 45% of gang members (Esbensen and Carson, 2012).

Who are female gang members? Much of the early literature on girls and gangs looked at female gang members as secondary to issues surrounding male gangs. Classic studies by Campbell (1984) and Moore (1991) illustrated that girls entered the gang lifestyle as a result of a brother or boyfriend's affiliation. Girls in the gang were often distinguished from their male counterparts by their sexuality. This sexualization manifested in several ways: (1) as a girlfriend to a male gang member, (2) as one who engages in sex with male gang members, and (3) as one who uses her sexuality in order to avoid detection by rival gang members and law enforcement (Campbell, 1995). Modern research builds upon this early work, suggesting that female gangs are not only increasing their membership ranks but also expanding their function and role as an independent entity separate from the male gang. Girls in the gang are no longer the sexual toy of the male gang, but have become active participants in crimes of drugs and violence.

The lives of girls in gangs tell a story filled with violence, poverty, racism, disenfranchisement, and limited resources. They come from families who struggle to make ends meet in economically depressed areas. In these communities, opportunities for positive, prosocial activities are significantly limited, and the pressure to join a gang runs rampant. Many of the girls have limited achievements in the classroom, and their educational experience has little to do with books or teachers. Instead, they share stories of disorder, threats, and crime (Molidor, 1996). The majority of their parents never married, and the presence of intimate partner abuse within the home was not uncommon. Many of the girls had a parent or other family members who were involved in the criminal justice system and were either currently incarcerated or had been incarcerated during some part of their lives.

For some girls, membership in a gang is a family affair, with parents, siblings, and extended family members involved in the gang lifestyle. Research by Miller (2000) indicates that 79% of girls who were gang involved had a family member who was a gang member, and 60% of the girls had multiple family members in gangs. For these girls, gang affiliation comes at an early age. During the childhood and preteen years, their gang activities may consist of limited acts of delinquency and drug experimentation. During junior high, girls exhibit several risk factors for delinquency, including risky sexual behavior, school failures, and truancy. By the time these girls become teenagers, they are committed to the gang and criminal activity and participate in a range of delinquent acts, including property crimes, weapons offenses, and violent crimes against persons. The later adolescent years (ages 15–18) represent the most intense years of gang activity (Eghigian & Kirby, 2006).

While the gang is a way of life for some girls, many others find their way to the gang in search of a new family. Many girls involved in gangs have histories of extensive physical and sexual abuse by family members during early childhood. Many of the girls run away from the family residence in an attempt to escape the violence and abuse in their lives. In an attempt to survive on the streets, the gang becomes an attractive option for meeting one's immediate and long-term needs such as shelter, food, and protection. Not only does the gang provide refuge from these abusive home environments, but it provides as well a sense of family that was lacking in their families of origin (Joe & Chesney-Lind, 1995). Research by Miller (2000) indicates that it is not so much a specific risk factor that propels girls into the gang but rather the relationship among several life situation factors, such as a neighborhood exposure to gangs, a family involvement in the lifestyle, and the presence of problems in the family, that illustrates the trajectory of girls into the gang lifestyle.

The literature on female gangs indicates that the lifestyle, structure, and characteristics of female gangs and their members are as diverse as male gangs. Some girls hang out with gangs in search of a social life and peer relationships, but they typically do not consider themselves as members of the gang. The structure of the girl gang ranges from being a mixed-gender gang to functioning as an independent unit. For girls involved in mixed-gender gangs, their role ranged from being an affiliate of the male gang unit to even, in some cases, having a "separate but equal" relationship to their male counterparts (Schalet, Hunt, & Joe-Laidler, 2003).

The initiation process for girls varies from being "jumped" in or **walking the line**, whereby the girls were subjected to assault by their fellow gang members, to being "sexed" in or **pulling a train**, an experience that involved having sex with multiple individuals, often the male gang members. However, not all of these initiation rites came with a high degree of status within the gang, as those girls who were sexed in generally experienced lower levels of respect by fellow gang members (Miller, 2000). Girls who had been "sexed into the gang" were subjected to continued victimization from within the gang. Although not all girls were admitted to the gang in this manner, this image negatively affected all of the girls.

> The fact that there was such an option as "sexing in" served to keep girls disempowered, because they always faced the question of how they got in and of whether they were "true" members. In addition, it contributed to a milieu in which young women's sexuality was seen as exploitable. (Miller, 1998a, p. 444).

Recent media attention has targeted the gang girl and [thus created] the perception that violence by these girls is increasing. Yet data indicate that female gang members participate in criminal acts at rates similar to male gang members (Esbensen & Carson, 2012). Research by Fleisher and Krienert (2004) indicated that among girls who described themselves as active members of a gang, almost all (94%) had engaged in a violent crime during the previous 6 months, and two thirds (67%) had sold drugs during the past 2 months. More than half (55%) had participated in property crimes, such as graffiti or destruction to property, while two thirds (67%) engaged in economic crimes, such as prostitution, burglary, robbery, or theft, in the previous 6 months. Here, violence is more than just engaging in criminal offenses. Indeed, the participation in a delinquent lifestyle that is associated with gang membership places girls at risk for significant victimization. Girls who are "independent" of a male gang hierarchy tend to experience high levels of violence as a result of selling drugs and their interactions on the streets with other girls. These independent girls are aware of the potential risk they face and take a number of precautionary measures to enhance their safety, such as possessing a weapon, staying off the streets at night, and traveling in groups. While the close relationship with the male gang can often serve as a protective factor, it can also place the girls at risk of rape and sexual assault by their "homeboys" (Hunt & Joe-Laidler, 2001). In addition, girls whose gang membership is connected to a male gang unit tend to experience higher levels of violence on the streets compared to girls who operate in independent cliques. These girls are at a higher risk of victimization due to the levels of violence that they are exposed to from assaults and drive-by shootings that involve the male gang members. Indeed, many of these crimes (and potential risks of victimization) would not be present if they were not involved in the gang lifestyle (Miller, 1998b).

The exit from the gang lifestyle for girls can occur in several ways. For most girls, this exit coincides with the end of adolescence. They may withdraw from the lifestyle, often as a result of pregnancy and the need to care for their young children. For others, their exit is facilitated by an entry into legitimate employment or advanced education. Others will be removed from their gangs as a result of incarceration in a juvenile or adult correctional facility. While some may choose to be "jumped out," most will simply diminish their involvement over time rather than be perceived as betraying or deliberately going against their gang peers (Campbell, 1995). The few women who choose to remain in the gang have several pathways from which to choose. They may continue their gang participation as active members and expand their criminal resume. Their relationships with male gang members may continue with their choice of marriage partners, which allows them to continue their affiliation in either a direct or indirect role (Eghigian & Kirby, 2006).

Gender and Violent Crime

Despite public perceptions, females make up a small proportion of violent offenders. While violent crime perpetuated by women does occur, it is rare. As you learned earlier in this chapter, men engage in far more acts of violence than females. For example, women's participation in the crime of homicide accounts for less than half of the arrests of men. And like the rates of male violence, women's participation in these crimes has decreased, with homicide offending rates for females declining from 3.1 offenders per 100,000 in 1980 to 1.6 offenders per 100,000 in 2008 (Cooper & Smith, 2011). Women are more likely to kill someone known to them, compared to a stranger. Research by Kellermann & Mercy (1992) indicates that while 60% of female offenders knew their victims, only 20% of male murders had known victims. Generally speaking, women generally kill their spouses, significant others, or their children (Cooper & Smith, 2011).

CASE STUDY

Spotlight on Women and Self Defense

Much of the fascination about women who kill comes from the perception of these offenders either as cold and calculating murderers or cases where women just "snap." But what about those cases of women who kill in self-defense? How do we make sense of these crimes of violence?

Consider the case of Marissa Alexander. During a confrontation with her husband in August 2010, Marissa fired a bullet into the wall to scare her husband. She testified that she felt threatened and luckily no one was hurt in the incident. Even though Alexander drew upon Florida's Stand Your Ground Law, the jury convicted her of aggravated assault with a deadly weapon, and she was sentenced to twenty years in prison. Her actions triggered a mandatory minimum gun law which increases the sentence in certain felonies if a gun is brandished or fired. Even lawmakers in the state argued that the intent of the law was not to punish cases like Alexander's but was designed to increase sentences for those who brandished or used a firearm during the commission of a crime such as robbery or assault (Stacy, 2012). While the case was overturned on appeal for errors by the trial judge in the instructions to the jury, Alexander's case continues to face significant scrutiny. While out on bond, prosecutors argued that she violated the conditions of her house arrest, even though her requests to leave her residence were approved by her case manager. She remains out on bond until her new trial (Hannan, 2014). The court is currently considering whether Alexander will be allowed to seek a hearing under Florida's Stand Your Ground Law as part of her retrial in this case (Whitaker, 2014).

Another case of self-defense that has drawn recent attention involves Sara Kruzan. In 1995, Kruzan was only 16 years old when she was convicted of first-degree murder and sentenced to life without the possibility

(Continued)

(Continued)

of parole. She had no juvenile record and had been an honor student as a young child. The victim was her pimp, a 31-year-old man named G. G. Howard who had begun grooming Sara when she was only 11 years old and had been sexually trafficking her for the past four years (Sharma, 2013). Even though her age made it possible for the case to be tried in juvenile court (where the maximum sentence would have resulted in her incarceration until age 25), prosecutors transferred her case to criminal court where she was tried as an adult. In January 2011, new legislation was enacted that allowed for the reconsideration of juvenile cases where life sentences were handed down. Following the new law, then-Governor Schwarzenegger granted clemency to Kruzan and commuted her [life without parole] LWOP sentence to 25 years with the possibility of parole. Additional legislation signed into law by Governor Jerry Brown required parole boards to give special considerations in parole decisions involving juvenile offenders who were tried as adults and who had served at least fifteen years of their sentences. After serving nineteen years, Kruzan was paroled in part due to these new policies (St. John, 2013).

In both of these cases, public attention played a significant role in raising awareness about these cases. Sara Kruzan was featured in social action campaigns by Abolish Slavery and Human Rights Watch and drew the attention of lawmakers who were seeking changes in how juvenile cases were handled. Kruzan has become the face for thousands of youth who are serving sentences for crimes they committed as juveniles (De Atley, 2013). In contrast, Alexander's story has drawn significant criticism, and the treatment of her case has been compared to that of George Zimmerman, who during the same time was considering Florida's Stand Your Ground Law as part of his defense in the Trayvon Martin homicide. In expressing her dissatisfaction of the decision to retry Alexander, Florida Congresswoman Corrine Brown made the following remarks: "The Florida criminal justice system has sent two clear messages today. . . . One is that if women who are victims of domestic violence try to protect themselves, the Stand Your Ground Law will not apply to them. . . . The second message is that if you are black, the system will treat you differently" (Dahl, 2012).

Much of the fascination about female violent crime stems from how these crimes are portrayed by popular culture. The cable television show *Snapped* (Oxygen network) focuses on true crime cases of women who kill and their motivations for crime. Movie story lines have included both fictional and "ripped from the headlines" examples of women who stalk, torture, and murder their victims. The 1987 film *Fatal Attraction* tells the story of Alex (portrayed by Glenn Close) who obsesses over her married lover Dan (played by Michael Douglas). Alex engages in all sorts of crimes toward Dan, including pouring acid on his car and killing the family rabbit (Maslin, 1987). The Broadway show (and film adaption) *Chicago* tells the story of Velma Kelly and Roxie Hart who are arrested for the murders of their paramours. The backdrop for this story came from several true crime cases from the 1920s where women were tried and ultimately acquitted for killing their husbands or lovers. These cases were sensationalized in local newspapers, and these women became celebrities throughout their trials (Perry, 2010). Even popular song lyrics draw attention (and justify) the actions of women who damage the side panel, vandalize its interior, and slash the tires of their cheating boyfriend's car (*Before He Cheats*).

Beyond the Hollywood portrayals of violence by women, the public is fascinated by the real world examples of women who kill. Consider the case of Pamela Smart. Twenty-two years old and married after a quick courtship, she and her husband Gregory Smart had been having significant problems in their marriage and they began to spend time apart. Pamela began spending time outside of her job at Winnacunnet High School with several students. She ultimately began an intimate relationship with one of these youth, William "Billy" Flynn. On May 1, 1990, Smart arrived at her home in Derry, New Hampshire, after the workday to find her husband Gregory dead of a bullet wound to the head. The case immediately aroused the suspicions of the local police. While the crime scene appeared to be staged to look like a robbery gone bad, Gregory Smart had been killed execution style. While Pam had an alibi at the time of the murder, police began to suspect that she was involved in her husband's murder. An anonymous call to the police suggested that Pam had orchestrated the killing. Billy Flynn and two of his friends were arrested for murder. Although the police believed they had the individuals who were responsible for carrying out the murder, they conducted audio surveillance on Pam Smart, where she admitted details of planning the murder of her husband with Flynn (Rideout, 2007). Billy Flynn testified against Smart that she convinced him to murder her husband so that they could be together (Dinan, 2005). While Flynn was sentenced to 40 years to life, Pamela Smart received a sentence of life without the possibility of parole.

The trial of Pamela Smart gained national attention, and it was the first to be televised on the cable television channel Court TV (Rideout, 2007). By the time the trial began, there were over 400 various articles written about the case in local and national newspapers. By the end of the trial, this number approached 1,200. These articles portrayed Flynn as "hot for teacher" and Smart as seducing her young student (even though Smart was an administrator for the school district and not a teacher). They also described Smart's cold demeanor during the trial, labeling her as the *Ice Princess* (Lyons, 2006). This real life case became iconized by the movie *To Die For* starring Nicole Kidman and Joaquin Phoenix.

A more contemporary example of the media's fascination with a female murder trial is the case of Casey Anthony, who was tried for the 2008 murder of her 2-year-old daughter Caylee in Orange County, Florida. The police began to suspect Anthony after several discrepancies in her story regarding her daughter's disappearance. Anthony had alleged that Caylee was kidnapped by her nanny (Zenaida Fernandez-Gonzalez), who it was later determined never existed. In addition, Anthony had not reported her daughter missing, which further raised the suspicions of her family and the police. Caylee's decomposed body was found in a wooded area on December 11, 2008 (Casey Anthony, 2014).

Casey Anthony's trial began in June 2011 with significant media attention. In portraying Anthony as responsible for her daughter's death, the state linked [the death to] a search on Casey's computer for chloroform. Remnants of this toxic chemical were found in the trunk of Anthony's car, coupled with the smell of decomposing waste. Anthony was also described as an out of control party animal that did not want to be a mother. However, there was no evidence that directly linked Anthony to the murder of her daughter (Alvarez, 2011). Following her acquittal in July 2011, Anthony's attorneys vilified the press for their role in creating a sensationalized image of Casey to the public that assumed her guilt. However, newspapers were not the only ones to blame for these behaviors. Like Pamela Smart, the trial of Casey Anthony was televised. Twenty years later, however, there are many other sources of information that dominate the public perceptions of crime. These included a live video feed online of the trial, numerous Facebook pages in the names of Casey and her daughter, and even a Twitter account managed by the Ninth Judicial Circuit Court of Florida (Cloud, 2011). This level of intimate accessibility allowed the public to feel as if they were a part of the trial experience and had a personal investment in its outcome. Indeed, the public outcry over Anthony's acquittal was significant. "Because many American murder cases, such as the Casey Anthony trial, are shown on television, they sometimes appear to the public as if they were reality television shows. There is great disappointment, therefore, when the result is a verdict of not guilty" (Dershowitz, 2011, para 8). Not surprisingly, the public's fascination with women who engage in crimes of violence appears to have increased with the times as there are now multiple sources through which one can satisfy their desires for this dramatized portrayal of crime and justice. These themes were once again displayed in the case of Jodi Arias.

CASE STUDY

Spotlight on the *State v. Jodi Arias*

Violence. Murder. Lies. And a woman behind it all. The case of Jodi Arias had everything it needed to be a television movie. Yet this was a real case that was set on fire by the media. Over the course of her four-month trial, every moment of the trial was broadcast on cable television. In addition, there was no shortage of "legal experts" waiting to give their opinion on the events of the day, the evidence presented, or the demeanor of the defendant. Arias was charged and ultimately convicted for the murder of her boyfriend, Travis Alexander. Alexander was found in his shower where he had been stabbed 27 times, his throat had been slit, and he had been shot in the head. This was no simple murder but rather an act of extreme aggression as any one of these wounds would have resulted in his death. Yet the excessive nature of the crime drew the attention of the media. Arias was the perfect candidate for this media frenzy as she had changed her story about the crime several times. At first, she denied any involvement in his murder. Later, she alleged that she and Alexander had been attacked by two masked intruders who murdered Travis, but allowed her to live. During the trial, her story was amended once again to one of self-defense. Jodi asserted that Travis Alexander had frequently abused her throughout their relationship, and she killed him during one of these attacks. However, she claimed that she did not remember the specific events of his death and that she had blocked out these events due to her emotional trauma (Sholchet, 2013). One of the particularly sensationalized parts of the trial involved Arias own testimony, which lasted 18 days. Under Arizona law, members of the jury are allowed to submit questions to the accused should they choose to take the stand in their own defense. "Some of the questions seemed to serve no other purpose but to mock Arias and illustrate the jurors' annoyance with her claims" (Fagel, 2013). While she was convicted of first-degree murder, the same jury was unable to come to a verdict on whether Arias should be given the death penalty.

Mothers Who Kill Their Children

While the crime of filicide is a rare occurrence, it raises significant attention in the media. The case of Andrea Yates is one of the most identifiable cases of filicide in the 21st century. After her husband left for work on June 20, 2001, Yates proceeded to drown each of her five children one at a time in the bathtub of the family home. Her case illustrates several factors that are common to incidents of maternal filicide. Yates had a history of mental health issues, including bipolar disorder, and she had been hospitalized in the past for major depression. She was the primary caretaker for her children and was responsible for homeschooling the older children. She and her husband were devout evangelical Methodists. Yates indicated that she felt inadequate as a mother and wife, believed that her children were spiritually damaged, and stated that she was directed by the voice of Satan to kill her children (Spinelli, 2004).

The case involving the children of Andrea Yates is just one tragic example of a mother engaging in filicide, or the killing of her children. There are several different categories of filicide. Neonaticide refers to an act of homicide during the first 24 hours after birth, compared to cases of infanticide, which includes acts whereby a parent kills his or her child within the first year of life. Here, the age of the child distinguishes these cases from general acts of filicide, which include the homicide of children older than 1 year of age by their parent. While the practice of filicide does not exclude the murder of a child by its father, mothers make up the majority of offenders in cases of infanticide and neonaticide.

What leads a woman to kill her child? There are several different explanations for this behavior. Research by Resnick (1970) distinguishes five different categories of infanticide. The first category represents cases where the infant was killed for **altruistic** reasons. In these incidents, the mother believes that it is in the best interests of the child to be dead and that the mother is doing a good thing by killing the child. Here, the mother believes (whether real or imagined) that the child is suffering in some way and that the child's pain should end. Based on Resnick's (1970) typology, Yates would be identified as a mother who kills her children out of altruistic reasons. A review of Yates's case indicates two themes common to altruistic filicide. The first theme reflects the pressure that exists in society for women to be good mothers. For Yates, this pressure was influenced by her religious fundamentalism, which placed the importance of the spiritual life of her children under her responsibility. The pressure to be a perfect mother was exacerbated by her history of mental illness. The second theme reflected the pressure of bearing the sole responsibility to care for the children. Here, Yates expressed feeling overwhelmed by the demands of their children's personal, academic, and spiritual needs, in addition to the responsibilities of caring for the family home. She also lacked any support from outside of the family, which further contributed to her feelings of being overburdened (West & Lichtenstein, 2006).

The second category in Resnick's typology refers to the killing of a child by an acutely psychotic woman. These cases are closely linked with explanations of postpartum psychosis where the mother suffers from a severe case of mental illness and may be unaware of her action or be unable to appreciate the wrongfulness of her behaviors. Examples of this type of filicide may involve a woman who hears voices that tell her that she needs to harm her child. The third category represents the killing of an unwanted infant. In many cases, these are cases of neonaticide. Research indicates that there are similar characteristics within the cases of mothers who kill their children within their first day of life. These women tend to be unmarried, under the age of 25, and generally to conceal their pregnancy from friends and family. Some women may acknowledge that they are pregnant, but their lack of actions toward preparing for the birth of the child indicate that they may be in denial that they may soon give birth. Others fail to acknowledge that they are pregnant and explain away the symptoms of pregnancy (Miller, 2003). They typically give birth without medical intervention and generally do not receive any form of prenatal care. The majority of these women do not suffer from any form of mental illness, which would help to explain the death of their children. Instead, most of the cases of homicide of the infant are simply a result of an unwanted pregnancy. In these instances, the children are typically killed by strangulation, drowning, or suffocation (Meyer & Oberman, 2001). The fourth category involves the "accidental" death of a child following incidents of significant child abuse and maltreatment. Often, the death of a child occurs after a long period of abuse. The fifth category represents cases where the death of a child is used as an act of ultimate revenge against another. In many cases, these vengeful acts are against the spouse and father of the child (Resnick, 1970).

Mothers who kill their children present a significant challenge to the cultural ideals of femininity and motherhood. Society dictates that mothers should love and care for their children, behave in a loving and nurturing manner, and not cause them harm or place their lives in danger. In many cases, the presence of a psychological disorder makes it easier for society to understand that a mother could hurt her child. Information on postpartum syndromes is used at a variety of different stages of the criminal justice process. Evidence of psychosis may be used to determine whether a defendant is legally competent to participate in the criminal proceedings against her. However, this stage is temporary, as the woman would be placed in a treatment facility until such a time that she is competent to stand trial. Given that postpartum syndromes are generally limited to a short period of time (compared to other forms of psychiatric diagnoses), these court proceedings would be delayed only temporarily.

More often, information about postpartum syndromes is used as evidence to exclude the culpability of the woman during a trial proceeding. In some states, this evidence forms the basis of a verdict of "not guilty by reason of insanity." Here, the courts assess whether the defendant knew that what she was doing at the time of the crime was wrong. "The insanity defense enables female violence to coexist comfortably with traditional notions of femininity. It also promotes empathy toward violent women, whose aberrance becomes a result of external factors rather than conscious choice" (Stangle, 2008, p. 709). In cases where an insanity defense is either not available or is unsuccessful, evidence of postpartum syndromes can be used to argue for the diminished capacity of the offender.

A third option allows for courts to find someone guilty but mentally ill (GBMI). Here, the defendant is found guilty of the crime, but the court may mitigate the criminal sentence to acknowledge the woman's mental health status. For many offenders, this distinction can allow them to serve a portion of their sentence in a treatment hospital or related facility (Proano-Raps & Meyer, 2003). While Andrea Yates was convicted of murder and sentenced to 40 years to life by the state of Texas in 2002, her conviction was later overturned. In her second trial, she was found not guilty by reason of insanity and was committed to a state mental health facility for treatment.

Summary

- Women engage in every category of crime, yet their rates of offending are significantly lower than male offending practices.
- Regardless of race, ethnicity, or class, women have similar pathways to addiction: depression, abuse, and social and economic pressures.
- For many women, entry into addiction is rooted in early trauma: Drugs are used for escape, and prostitution and property crimes are then committed for survival.
- The war on drugs has led to increased incarceration rates for both men and women but has had particularly damaging effects for women.
- Women in prostitution face significant mental and physical health issues as a result of their time on the streets. These issues lead to significant challenges as they try to exit prostitution and make a new life off the streets.
- Women are most likely to commit property-based offenses.
- There are several different reasons why mothers may kill their children, but not all involve issues of mental illness.
- Sexuality can be a component of the gang life for some girls, but it is not necessarily the experience for all girls involved in gangs.
- Although female perpetrated homicide is rare, it is generally sensationalized in the media when it occurs.

KEY TERMS

Altruistic	Neonaticide	Street prostitution
Filicide	Post-traumatic stress disorder (PTSD)	Walking the line
Infanticide	Pulling a train	

DISCUSSION QUESTIONS

1. Why is the media obsessed with the image of the female offender? What implications does this have on understanding the realities of female offending?

2. What does research say about the gender gap in offending?

3. How have drug addiction and the war on drugs become a gendered experience?

4. How are drugs, property crimes, and prostitution connected for many female offenders on the streets?

5. What are the risk factors for prostitution? How do these issues affect a woman's ability to exit the streets?

6. Why are jurisdictions reluctant to legalize or decriminalize prostitution?

7. Why do women engage in property offenses?

8. What role does mental illness play in cases of women who kill their children?

9. How do girls use their gender within the gang context?

10. Discuss the types of violent crimes in which women most typically engage.

WEB RESOURCES

Children of the Night: http://www.childrenofthenight.org

National Gang Center: http://www.nationalgangcenter.gov/

Prostitutes Education Network: http://www.bayswan.org

Prostitution Research and Education: http://www.prostitutionresearch.com

SAMHSA Center for Substance Abuse Treatment: http://www.samhsa.gov/about/csat.aspx

SAMHSA National Center for Trauma-Informed Care: http://www.samhsa.gov/nctic/

The Sentencing Project: http://www.sentencingproject.org

Women and Gender in the Drug War: http://www.drugpolicy.org/communities/women

Visit **www.sagepub.com/mallicoat2e** to access additional study tools including eFlashcards, web quizzes, web resources, video resources, and SAGE journal articles.

Reading 15

In the section, you learned how issues with drug use and addiction can contribute to women's criminality. In this article by Drs. Ryder and Brisgone, you'll hear from two groups: women who experienced addiction during the crack cocaine era and girls who grew up with parents addicted to crack during this time frame.

Cracked Perspectives

Reflections of Women and Girls in the Aftermath of the Crack Cocaine Era

Judith A. Ryder and Regina E. Brisgone

In 1983, a new, cheap version of cocaine was disproportionately introduced into poor African American neighborhoods across the United States, where its use quickly expanded. Within only a few years, crack cocaine was entrenched in inner-city New York where it remained popular throughout the 1990s (Johnson, Dunlap, & Tourigny, 2000).[1] In the early years of that decade, however, both national surveys of arrestees and ethnographic neighborhood studies confirmed a significant transition: Inner-city youths preferred marijuana to crack and other hard drugs (Curtis, 1998; Furst, Johnson, Dunlap, & Curtis, 1999; Hamid, 1992). The transition was hailed with cautious optimism and speculation that because the younger generation was not using crack or heroin, youths may not "suffer the severe health and legal problems associated with those [hard] drugs" (Golub, Johnson, Dunlap, & Sifaneck, 2004, p. 362). The current project augments these findings by analyzing in-depth interviews with two generations of females who lived through this devastating period. We confirm the lack of crack use among female youths but find excessive alcohol and marijuana use. In addition, our analysis reveals disrupted emotional attachments between women and their children and concurrent traumatic experiences among the girls. We explore how this potent combination may have contributed to girls' involvement in serious delinquency.

Research on drug use in the Crack Era and the so-called Marijuana/Blunt Era that followed (Johnson, Golub, & Dunlap, 2000) is based primarily on studies of men and boys and generally uses epidemiological methods that may be insufficient for flagging the vulnerabilities of drug-involved females (Maher, 2002). As a result, little is known about how the Crack Era affected the lives of drug-using women and girls. The current project brings a gendered perspective to the generational drug research by analyzing commonalities and differences in female drug involvement. We extend prior research by exploring the ways in which drug involvement shaped family relationships and contributed to the weakening of emotional bonds between mothers and children during a turbulent

SOURCE: Ryder, J. A., & Brisgone, R. E. (2013). Cracked perspectives: Reflections of women and girls in the aftermath of the crack cocaine era. *Feminist Criminology, 8*(1), 40–62.

NOTE: The authors disclosed receipt of the following financial support for the research, authorship, and/or publication of this article: The original research was partially funded by two separate federal grants, NIDA Grant No. F31 DA006065, and NIDA Grant No. R01 DA08679.

social and economic period. We do not make causal claims, but our work is informed by the psychological construct of attachment (Bowlby, 1988) that allows for a developmental understanding of the effects of the Crack Era on the health and legal problems of a younger generation. Our analysis of the narratives of females born into two distinct drug eras is a pooled case comparison, a method situated in a tradition of cross-study comparative analysis. West and Oldfather (1995) liken pooled case comparison to "the overlaying of one transparency on another" (p. 454) in an effort to understand both groups more fully while maintaining the primacy of each group's voice. Finally, we propose recommendations for improving treatment services to better address the needs of drug-using women and girls.

 ## Women and Children in the Crack Era

We examine female drug use within a broad historical context, using the concept of *drug eras,* a term that reflects the fluctuations of disease epidemics but with an emphasis on the cultural aspects of the phenomenon. The term describes a point in a historical period when a substance is introduced, adopted, and "institutionalized within certain segments of the population" (Johnson, Golub, & Dunlap, 2000, p. 21). The drug era model uses aggregated (mostly male) arrest data to delineate generational cohorts based on date of birth. The model marks a distinct historical break between the drug-use patterns of those born between 1955 and 1969 (Cocaine Crack Era) and those born since 1970 (Marijuana/Blunts Era; Johnson, Golub, & Dunlap, 2000).

When crack cocaine hit the streets of America in the 1980s, inner-city communities were already suffering from the prior decade's economic dislocations and widespread unemployment (Small & Newman, 2001; Wilson, 1996). With manufacturing jobs gone and large numbers of men out of work, the number of female head-of-households dramatically increased, and more women became sole caregivers of dependent children (Sampson, 1987; Wilson, 1987). At the same time, women were drawn to crack cocaine in unprecedented numbers, a trend attributed to the drug's low cost and social perceptions of smoking (as opposed to injecting) as a less intrusive method of drug use and more in keeping with established gender norms (Sterk, 1999).

Despite an increase in the number of female primary breadwinners and the number of women using crack, little research investigates this intersection or the effect of crack-era drug dependency on parent–child relationships or includes children's perspectives. Maher and Hudson (2007) conducted an important metasynthesis of the qualitative literature on women *working* in the illegal drug economy but did not include women's own drug use and identified only two themes pertaining to family relationships and children: the importance of kinship structures (Adler, 1985; Denton, 2001; Waldorf, Reinarman, & Murphy, 1991) and women's ability to structure their drug dealer role around parental responsibilities (Dunlap & Johnson, 1996; Morgan & Joe, 1996; Sterk, 1999). Other research specific to female drug use details how, as women's crack dependency increased, their lives became more transient and chaotic, pressuring the women to seek the aid of social networks (Brisgone, 2008; Wilson & Tolson, 1990). By the 1980s, however, kin networks that traditionally had supported impoverished families were economically and emotionally worn down by long-term unemployment, punitive criminal justice policies, and the ravages of HIV/AIDS (Miller-Cribbs & Farber, 2008). Thus, children of crack-using mothers were often left without supportive adults to care for them, and some were placed in the care and custody of the state, solidifying the disruption in the parent–child relationship.

Hardesty and Black's (1999) study of Latina addicts in recovery is one of only a few to explore drug dependency and parent–child relationships. Women discussed the significant effort they employed to maintain their self-image as "good" mothers in the context of Puerto Rican culture, even as their drug activities became all engrossing. In another study, recovering heroin addicts reflected on the consequences of parental drug use, including parents' inability to "be there" to meet children's material and emotional needs, family violence, and family dissolution (McKeganey, Barnard, & McIntosh, 2002).

Distinct from the few studies that analyze parental perspectives on drug use is an ethnographic study of mother–daughter pairs from two crack-user households in New York City's Central Harlem (Dunlap, Stürzenhofecker, Sanabria, & Johnson, 2004). The paired study exposes disruptions in parent–child emotional bonds and suggests that mothers' crack use contributed to the intergenerational cycle of "child abuse, neglect, and abandonment of parental responsibilities" (Dunlap, Golub, & Johnson, 2006, p. 133). Although children born to the Crack Generation did not use the drug, they continued to face major deficits arising from their childhoods. These analyses stop short, however, of exploring how disruptions in the parent–child relationship, and other traumatic events, may have contributed to children's later involvement in delinquency and violence.

The Role of Disrupted Attachments

A primary purpose of the current project is to explore the dynamics underlying parent–child relationships among drug-using women and girls. In particular, we sought to understand how the disruption of emotional attachments between these dyads might contribute to girls' problem behaviors. Many criminological theories stress the importance of social bonds and relationships and some, such as developmental life-course theories, explicitly examine the complexities and messiness of *lives in social context*. However, such theories are primarily supported by research on boys and men and thus are likely to miss gendered behaviors and situations.[2] Life events such as sexual abuse and assault, which feminist scholarship has demonstrated to be much more extensive in the lives of female offenders than among male offenders, are rarely examined despite the potential to negatively redirect victims' life trajectories. The feminist pathway perspective stresses the importance of social bonds and relationships and specifically connects girls' traumatic experiences, such as sexual abuse, with substance abuse and arrests for violent offending (Daly, 1992; Gaarder & Belknap, 2002; Schaffner, 2007; Siegel & Williams, 2003). Both developmental life course and the feminist pathway perspective help, but are not sufficient, to explain how childhood events and experiences might contribute to a young woman adopting delinquent behaviors herself.

In an effort to understand the processes underlying the health and legal problems of a generation of girls growing up during the Crack Era, we place the narratives of women and girls within a developmental framework and employ the psychological construct of attachment. As conceptualized by John Bowlby and others (1973/1969, 1988; Ainsworth, Blehar, Waters, & Wall, 1978), attachment is considered an innate human need. This counters the use of the term in the criminological literature, particularly control theories, that consider attachment the result of proper socialization (e.g., Gottfredson & Hirschi, 1990). Bowlby's attachment theory proposes that children need more than food and shelter; they require security: "a quality of care . . . sufficiently responsive to the child's needs to alleviate anxiety and engender a feeling of being understood" (Ansbro, 2008, p. 234). Attachment behavior is designed to care for and protect the young by forming an affective bond between children and significant others. Furthermore, the role of the caregiver in nurturing and supporting the child's emotional bonds is critical to healthy development across the life span (Cernkovich & Giordano, 1987; Fonagy, 2004; Sroufe & Fleeson, 1986).

When a primary caregiver abandons, neglects, or abuses a child, attachment bonds are weakened. With attachment needs thus unmet, the child becomes emotionally vulnerable and will exhibit a predictable pattern of protest and despair and—without the intervention of loving and attuned adults—detachment (Ainsworth, 1972; Bowlby, 1973/1969; Margolin & John, 1997). This need for connection influences the course of the child's later development, with much research demonstrating that detachment in childhood is associated with long-term negative outcomes (Hayslett-McCall & Bernard, 2002). The detached child may psychically wall off her needs, even as her yearning for connection continues, or she may still cling to those who have caused the trauma because her terror of being abandoned exceeds her terror of the abuser. She also may seek connection to others through violence, sexual activity, or substance abuse and be comforted by an abusive attachment because it is familiar and similar to the original love object (Robinson, 2011; Ryder, 2007; Shengold, 1999; Smith & Thornberry, 1995). Although such behaviors are maladaptive and potentially destructive, a trauma-saturated child may not see the distinction (Herman, 1997).

Narrative Reflections

The current project encompasses two small groups of drug-using females. We begin with the adult women who were crack and heroin users and (most of them) primary caregivers of children. We add to this the perspective of adolescent girls, a rare dimension even in qualitative studies centered entirely on females (Lopez, Katsulis, & Robillard, 2009, cited in McKeganey et al., 2002). The project evolved from the authors' informal discussions about our separate National Institute on Drug Abuse (NIDA)-funded studies and how, in theory, the adult women could be mothers of the teenaged girls.[3] With some common focus areas and similar methodology, each study includes rich data on drug involvement and the importance of family relationships. Both studies posed questions about family functioning, community characteristics, traumatic events, and illegal activities including drug use and trafficking. The adult cohort also answered questions about prostitution activity and periods in jail and drug treatment. Brisgone interviewed the women between 1998 and 2001 as part of an ethnographic study of heavy drug users involved in prostitution. Interviews were conducted in various settings (e.g., streets, HIV outreach offices, and county jail). In her study, Ryder completed face-to-face, semistructured interviews with girls who had been remanded to custody for a violent offense. Interviews were conducted in 1996 in four state-run, juvenile residential facilities.

The two samples, or "cohorts," are primarily females of color, of low socioeconomic status, and from the New York City metropolitan area. They differ from one another, however, in ways predicted by larger, mostly male, studies of the Crack Era and subsequent Marijuana/Blunts Era. In addition to variation in drug choice, of particular interest is the age differential. Each of our two data sets fit squarely within the generational categories established in earlier, mostly quantitative studies (Johnson, Golub, & Dunlap, 2000). Both adults and juveniles told of extensive drug involvement and strained family relationships and, although their perspectives sometimes overlapped, they just as frequently diverged. The spaces where the two groups differed revealed a poignant yearning for connection. As we continued to discuss our work and findings, we dubbed these differing viewpoints the "what I'd tell my daughter, what my mom should have known" model, and considered the dynamics of an imaginary dialogue between the generations. Findings from the separate projects caused us to think about how the female narratives might enhance existing knowledge about the effects of the Crack Era.

Selected demographics are presented in Reading Table 15.1. Each cohort falls within previously established generational drug eras, based on year of birth (Johnson, Golub, & Dunlap, 2000). The women of the Crack Era were born from 1958 through 1971; at the height of the era in 1989, their median age was 23 years. The postcrack cohort was born from 1980 through 1983, placing them a decade into the so-called Marijuana/Blunts Era. In 1989 when the Crack Era peaked, the girls' median age was only 8 years. More than three fourths of the adult females were Black, and approximately one fifth was Hispanic; three fourths of the girls self-identified as Black or Hispanic. Most of the women had at least one child ($n = 51$); the median number of children per woman was two, with a range of one to nine children. Three of the girls had one child. Forty-six women were arrested on prostitution charges, and nearly a fourth (24%) had also been charged with drug sales. The girls were adjudicated and remanded to custody for assault (79%) or robbery (21%).

In presenting portions of the narratives, we examine these complicated relationships first from one side of the mirror and then from the other. On one side sit adult women who discuss how much, how often, and what drugs they used during their adult years and how they perceived the impact of their actions on family relationships, particularly those with their dependent children. On the other side, adolescent girls look back a short distance to review the years growing up in crack-affected families, linked to histories of traumatic loss and victimization.

Drug Involvement

The adult cohort (Crack Era) is characterized by pervasive drug use in an era of historically high female drug use, a traditional outlook regarding dependence on men, and participation in a street drug network perceived as menacing and ruthless. The women began their drug careers with crack or heroin and were abusing the drugs, on average, 4 years before they began prostituting. The narratives of the juvenile cohort (Marijuana/Blunt Era) indicate excessive use of marijuana and alcohol, typically initiated with family members; participation in drug sales; and involvement with street violence. Drug Involvement describes drug initiation, drug use, and drug-related activities.

Reading Table 15.1 Selected Demographics of the Two Cohorts

	Adult Women (*N* = 58)	Juvenile Girls (*N* = 24)
Period of birth	1958–1971	1980–1983
Median age at height of Crack Era (1989)	23 years	8 years
Age (Range [Median])	26–40 years (32 years)	13–16 years (15 years)
Race/ethnicity		
Black	78%	58%
Hispanic/Latina	19%	17%
Biracial/multiracial	—	17%
White	3%	8%
Any children	88%	12.5%
Used regularly (at least 3–4 times a week)	Cocaine 19%	Marijuana 71%
	Heroin 12%	Alcohol 33%
	Both cocaine and heroin 69%	Both marijuana and alcohol 33%

Women's Drug Initiation

The women generally initiated or progressed into hard drug use with intimate partners in the context of family life. Irraida, a poly-drug user, was a new wife and mother when she started using drugs with her husband.

> He would do everything for me. He took care of me and my drug habit. . . . I was 18 [when] I had met him. . . . I had no idea about drugs. He introduced me to it. . . . That's how I started using. He didn't force me to do it, and he told me what it was like. . . . Most likely I never would've done it if I hadn't met him.

Using drugs with male partners was considered romantic and protective, something all the women desired. Women previously in such relationships looked back longingly and were always on the outlook to re-create them. Shawnice spoke of this yearning: "I didn't ever have to come outside [to prostitute]. He would bring me my dope. I could smoke all the cocaine I could. . . . That's what I want to go back to." Many who started with cocaine before trying heroin did not realize their addiction until it was too late: "I liked the warm feeling [of heroin]. . . . I didn't want to get high every day, but I did. . . . Then the girl told me I had a habit. Habit? Habit? What habit!" Women generally moved swiftly from initiation to drug dependence as their habit came to match that of their older, heavy drug-using male partners.

Girl's Drug Initiation

For most girls, drug use began at home. Nearly 80% said that someone in the household drank alcohol or used drugs, and mothers were most commonly mentioned.[4] Other users in the household included mothers' partners, relatives, and siblings. The girls' median initial age for trying tobacco and alcohol was 10 years old; the median initial age for trying marijuana was 12 years old. None of the girls considered initiation a significant event but rather viewed it as a natural progression. Sixteen-year-old Natalie described how she started using marijuana with relatives:

I was used to people around me smoking and like my family being out in the room, catch a contact, so I just started smoking it. . . . I felt like I was already smoking it because I was already in the room where my aunt and uncle were smoking away.

Joanne began smoking marijuana with her mother and siblings "because I guess, if you watch somebody use it for long enough you are gonna want to try it and see how it is." Raised by her grandfather and father, Michelle recalled drinking small glasses of rum "for a chest cold, it broke the cold up." She was about 7 years old when her father gave her beer but, she noted, "he didn't give it to me for colds, he just gave it to me to drink." Her father also introduced her to marijuana, and she continued to drink and smoke regularly on her own: "I was hooked on it some. . . . I was just high almost every day."

Women's Drug Use

Overall, the women were dependent on cocaine and physically addicted to heroin with its debilitating withdrawals. Cocaine was generally smoked and heroin sniffed, but nearly a third of the women injected at least some of the time. Women used from 2 to 10 packets (bags) of heroin a day; cocaine use ranged from less than one to more than 10 vials daily. Cocaine and poly-drug users followed a pattern of binging and resting.

Poly-drug users relied on heroin to level out their mood after a cocaine binge and used cocaine to sharpen their concentration on the street. Said Boobie, "It's like a . . . roller-coaster all the time." Christina explained further,

With a crack hit, five minutes later you're running and chasing that feeling, that high. If you do a lot of coke, you're going to need the dope because the dope eats the coke. If you do a lot of crack, your heart gets all jiggery and you need a lot of dope so you can calm down.

Baby, a poly-drug user and mother of a teenage daughter, was on the streets for a decade. She described how her drug use eliminated most structure and routine: "People like you, you live around a calendar. Me, I get up, and I

don't know what I'm going to do. I'm not on a clock. . . . I use drugs and then I forget. . . . Time flies when you're in a drug haze." Although women did abstain when forced (i.e., in jail), most relapsed unless they broke from the drug scene entirely.

Girls' Drug Use

In stark contrast to the women's cohort, none of the girls reported ever having tried crack, but two tried cocaine in powder form. Jennifer claimed, "The older people smoke crack, it's not . . . you don't see no younger kids that smoke crack." Furthermore, the girls had contempt for those who did use the drug. As one girl declared, "Crack heads are crazy. They'll do anything." Although all girls renounced crack, four had tried hallucinogens and three had tried PCP [phencyclidine, e.g., angel dust]. None reported trying heroin or injecting any drug. A third of the girls drank alcohol on a regular basis (at least 3 to 4 days a week), and nearly three fourths smoked marijuana regularly during the year prior to incarceration. Often, marijuana was smoked as a blunt, wrapped inside a cigar shell. Indicative of the extent of their use, a third of the girls regularly used *both* marijuana and alcohol. At home, in school, in the streets, regardless of the context, "everybody was doing, every teenager used marijuana and alcohol. That was like normal."

Girls incorporated drug use into most of their activities. For example, alcohol and marijuana were a regular part of holidays and personal celebrations, such as birthdays, as well as upsetting or traumatic experiences, of which there were many. One 14-year-old described her response to the fatal shooting of her boyfriend.

We all got ripped at the funeral. I mean that was the first time I ever really got so drunk I could hardly even walk, I was so high I couldn't even see straight. That was the first time. . . . I was already ripped and stuff, I was gone, I was like in another world.

Elena described how after being initiated into her female gang, members used copious amounts of marijuana and alcohol to commemorate "stepping up" through the ranks: "If you succeed when we did something violent you have to smoke at least 25 blunts so you could move up. We didn't do nothing else. Well, oh yeah, we used to drink." The amounts of alcohol and marijuana reported by individual girls may be exaggerated, as some present themselves in a particular "pose," but overall, the amounts are indicative of heavy usage (Majors & Billson, 1993).

Women's Drug-Related Activities

Progression into hard drug use with men led women to a variety of drug-related criminal activities, including check fraud and drug sales, but particularly prostitution. In general, the women were inexperienced and had little heart for street crime. "I don't like robbin' and stealin'. I'm too chicken," Irraida confessed. The few who did deal drugs found that as users they were poor handlers of both the drugs and money; many reported an arrest and/or jail time for drug sales. Sam, a former dealer on the run, explained, "I had to keep away from people who wanted to hurt me. . . . Being on drugs and being in these places put you in danger, and I'm a very scary person" (a local colloquialism for easily frightened). Women dealers also noted the hierarchical, gender-stratified nature of the market and the low-level, exploitive work opportunities. Tina dealt heroin with a younger man but believed such relationships oppressed women:

> They [men] very rarely let women sell drugs. It's because of male chauvinism. A robber try a woman quicker than a man. It's dominance. I learned this back in college. Main thing: They don't want women to get the power. Dealing is dangerous too. They want you to do 80% of the work.

Desiree believed male dealers took advantage of women who then suffered the consequences: "I think they [male drug managers] think we're going to get it easier if we get caught. They just don't know. If we get caught, just like them, we're going to do that time." Because women sold on the streets, they were more visible to police and more vulnerable to arrest than were men.

The women's initiation to hard drug use fostered a relationship between intimacy and drugs and set a path toward street prostitution. Forty percent of the women began to prostitute when intimate partners were no longer available to provide their drugs because of a romantic breakup, incarceration, death, or the loss of the partner's means of obtaining drugs. Sugartoo, for example, started prostituting at age 32 when her boyfriend, a drug dealer, died during a gang fight in jail: "I'm a good person. I just started doing it [prostitution] since my old man passed. . . . It took me a long time to get used to it. I don't like nothing about this running." Prostitution was a pragmatic response to women's relative inexperience in rough drug-using street scenes, combined with their urgent need for drugs. As Toni stated, "After [my kids'] father took off, I wanted men for only one thing. I'd call up a john. I'd use men for my drug addiction. I'd get out there, take care of business, and get what I needed." Pumpkin was adamant that she would never solicit except for her drug habit: "Of course not! I have an income—I work the [prostitution] stroll just for drugs." Another woman explained, "If I didn't have a habit I'd probably be working at something else. But I got a habit so the stroll is it." All of the women reported street prostitution as their *main hustle* for drugs, and half of them said prostitution was their *exclusive* hustle for drugs.

Although most of the women rejected drug dealing and predatory crimes because of the perceived dangers, prostitution greatly increased their vulnerability to street violence. The women were prey to robbers, rapists, and murderers. They reported multiple victimizations especially when, because they were intoxicated or desperate for drugs, they solicited indiscriminately.

Girls' Drug-Related Activities

The girls' early familiarity with drug use facilitated access to people and opportunities in the illegal drug trade. Drug sales, drug use, and crime quickly became closely intertwined with daily activities. For example, Kathy and her friends "used to get together and go to the movies sometimes but mainly it was selling drugs and robberies." Despite their disdain for crack users, the girls were very much involved in the sale of the popular street drug. More than two thirds had participated in some aspect of drug trafficking beginning at the median age of 12; with the exception of one girl, all were still active in the business during the year prior to custody. Generally, girls partnered with other girls or boyfriends and worked low-level jobs in small organizations under the auspices of male suppliers. Several managed to amass a fairly large amount of cash. The economic benefits were a major enticement and, at least initially, mitigated safety concerns. One girl used her drug proceeds to rent a city ice-skating rink for the evening for all her friends. Royale, who desperately wanted a pair of sneakers she could not afford, told how she increased her purchasing power when she began selling crack:

> . . . my cousin gave me some drugs to sell and he said this will get you it quick. And I did and I liked it because I got money real quick. Instead of buying my sneakers I bought my own stuff [drugs] and doubled my money and got more than one pair of sneakers!

Another girl explained that she began selling drugs as a way of obtaining household money for her alcohol- and drug-using mother.

Transactions were conducted primarily in public locales where, despite the high risk of arrest, many believed police were less likely to stop a girl. Young and generally optimistic, girls indicated that if stopped, "All I gotta do is, like, 'no sorry, but I'm a female, you can't do that.' You know, then, they couldn't search me." The girls did complain that "guys used to try to gype me and stuff," and many admitted that they had been shot at, physically threatened, and sexually assaulted. Thus, despite some success on their own, most girls eventually came to rely on older males for protection precisely because of their gender and age. This arrangement, however, put them at great disadvantage and exposed them to additional emotional, physical, and sexual harm.

Even with male "protectors," the work required girls to negotiate volatile and violent situations. As part of their tutelage, they learned to use force against others. Violence (for themselves and their clients) was the cost of not adhering to established business norms and conventions. In one instance, a girl said she "beat this crack head up so bad because she wouldn't pay us and she was sending people that we never seen before to our house . . ." Another young seller told of a nonpaying female customer who put "my life in jeopardy" when her earnings were short. Her male manager verbally threatened her, then gave her a gun and told her she had "better handle your business." The seller and her cousin shot the customer in the head. Minimizing the killing, the girl claimed, "You couldn't do nothing. She was a crack head anyway."

✉ Family Relationships

The two cohorts each suffered from disruptions in their familial relationships. The women espoused conventional aspirations for family life but in their current circumstances failed to live up to them. Their erratic lifestyle and parenting practices created emotional distance between them and their families, especially their children. They believed traditional kinship networks could sufficiently provide for their children, yet this resource had worn thin. From the perspective of girls passed between and among the tattered network of caregivers, adults generated more harm than the interviewed mothers were able or willing to disclose. The girls tell of traumatic losses and emotional detachment, as well as physical and sexual violence—much of which was associated with maternal substance abuse and the lack of intervening, supportive caregivers. This section on Family Relationships describes family composition and structure and emotional connections.

Women's Family Composition and Structure

Though most women in the study were currently not married and not with their dependent children, more than one third reported that they either had been raised in a two-parent family or had raised their own children as part of a stable couple. They described families of origin with "stable enough" finances and parenting and portrayed their mothers as the glue that kept the family together and the ones who upheld mainstream values in difficult circumstances. Lena, for example, credits her mother with raising her two sons and keeping her from getting worse: "It's mainly because I have a mother who's there for me. Without her, God knows where I'd be." When the women were in their worst drug-using phases, they avoided family out of shame and to avoid conflicts that would prevent them from returning home in better times. Women were well aware of how far they had fallen from their own and their family's expectations and, like Sugartoo, remained concerned with others' perceptions: "I'm from an all-right family. I pray to God I never get caught out there soliciting. I'm afraid to [get caught] because of my family."

Most women had at least one child and maintained a committed relationship with the child's father—at least initially—but few were legally married. Of the 51 mothers,

22% were regular drug users when their first child was born. They relied on their family of origin to help raise the children when drug use and criminality forced them to relinquish parental roles. Circumstances forced the majority of the women to disperse their children among relatives so that many siblings were separated and frequently moved. Three fourths had surrendered custody of their children; nine women had ceded custody of at least one child to state child welfare authorities. The women described a pattern of drifting back and forth from their estranged families, and shifting alliances with men as their troubles waxed and waned. They were intermittently homeless or worse, bouncing from home to drug houses to abandoned warehouses as they pursued drugs and engaged in prostitution.

Girls' Family Composition and Structure

Girls depicted home as a shifting configuration of caregivers and locations. At some time in their lives, 71% of the girls had lived with adults other than a parent, residing in both kin and nonrelative foster care, residential treatment centers, and group homes. Locations changed when mothers went to jail or drug treatment, or families were evicted or forced to leave unsafe conditions. The household composition also changed when a mother's new husband or boyfriend arrived or girls ran away, deciding to stay with fathers, extended family, or friends. Mother–daughter separations could be brief stints or last for months—or even years—when mothers could or would not care for their daughters, and the children often were placed in foster care. Paula's description is typical of the cohort's residential instability.

> I was back and forth because I was in—it depends—I would be in foster care, then I would be in group homes, then I would go AWOL, go to my house, . . . I don't know where my house—me saying my house—that meant I would go to my father's house. . . . Other times I would go to my boyfriend's house or my sister-in-law's house.

Women's Emotional Connections

Most of the women did not have custody of their children and in interviews avoided revealing the details of that loss.

Only two mentioned neglect or child abuse and revealed that the events triggered their drug abuse. Dinah said the state took her children because "their father molested them" and added that she had tried to hide and protect the children from him. Sunshine, a poly-drug user, was defensive: "I was falsely accused of child abuse." She added that the courts took custody of her children and gave them to her ex-husband. "I started drugs when my children were taken from me." Prostitution kept women on the streets all hours of the day and night, further disrupting relationships with their children. The lifestyle upset domestic routines and left little time or emotion for family. Too often, the women say, they promised to quit drugs and resume their parental role—only to fail—repeatedly dashing their children's hopes. Gina expressed her regret over relapsing and disappointing her children.

> I was so ashamed. . . . I have beautiful children who I talk to all the time. . . . How many times are they going to put up with the same bullshit again? My kids know about my drug addiction. I don't want to lose them and I'm tired of losing me.

Lena echoed these sentiments: "I want to do something for their lives. They want a mommy who gets up with them in the morning and goes to bed at night. They're tired of their grandmother taking care of them."

Most women said they tried to visit their children regularly but also realized the need to stay away when they were heavily involved in drugs. They contributed financially when they could, handing over government checks or making family members official recipients of the aid for children, and using their illegal earnings for gifts and special occasions. Desiree, whose three young children stayed with her mother, said,

> I try to see them every week. Now and then I see them more. I'll go with them to the park. On their birthdays I chip in and buy them a cake. If they're going on a school trip, I give them what they need.

Despite their love and attempts to bond with their children, the women recognized their inability to offset previously disrupted attachments and physical absences, and they worried about how their behavior affected the children's life chances. Doreen had been gone for a year when, during a brief visit home, she was devastated to see her teenaged daughter's strong bond with the aunt who raised her.

> Sometimes I feel like I made a mistake over there. Sometimes I know I did something right. I took my daughter over to my sister when she was 12 years old. Now she's 18 years old. . . . She calls me mommy, but she goes over and hugs my sister. It upsets me. She goes right over to her and talks with her like a mother.

Doreen's decision to leave her daughter was an act of love and protection.

> Her schoolwork was suffering. She was staying up worrying about me. That's why I took her to my sister's house. I took her over there because I loved her. I didn't want nothing to happen to her. . . . I don't want her to go through what I have gone through.

Girls' Emotional Connections

The girls described physical and sexual violence in their homes and the numerous losses that strained relationships with their mothers and others entrusted with their well-being (Ryder, 2007). By the median age of only 10, three fourths had been physically abused, and 29% had been sexually abused by a family member; more than half had witnessed family physical abuse, and 13% had witnessed family sexual abuse. Girls told of seeing their mothers regularly attacked and beaten by male partners: "He tried to hit her and then I came out you know, I was screaming on him . . . he tried to hit her, he tried to beat her up." They also talked about the violence their mothers and others inflicted on them. One girl described her mother as "very abusive when she was drunk . . . yelling, throwing things. When she was high, she used to take the hangers and beat me with it."

The physical absence and psychological unavailability of mothers further disrupted girls' emotional attachments. Sometimes, a mother's whereabouts were unknown to her daughter. Paula's parents separated when she was an infant, and shortly thereafter, her mother left her with an aunt.

Paula said, "I don't know where she went, then she came back and got me later,"—when the girl was 3 years old. For the most part, however, girls reported that when their mothers were physically absent, it was because they were on the streets, incarcerated, or residing in a mental health or substance abuse facility. Fourteen-year-old Gina had only sporadic contact with her mother, having lived with relatives or in institutional settings most of her life. The girl explained that her mother "used to have a problem with drugs and alcohol and so she gave me to my grandmother." Another girl, Gayle, said her father died before she was born, and her mother was repeatedly incarcerated for selling drugs. Gayle described theirs as "a close relationship," but mother and daughter visited only intermittently: "If I would see her we would talk. We didn't see each other that often. She'll come see me like every six months."

Even when physically present, many mothers were incapable or unwilling to nurture girls' basic emotional needs. The dynamics of substance abuse were a primary contributor to such psychological unavailability. For example, Elena stated, "My mother's like anti-social. She don't like speaking to nobody. She just keeps her problems in. . . . I don't know, it was just the crack just really getting to her." Royale complained that her drug-using mother provided physical necessities but that an emotional void existed between them: "I ate regularly, lived in a regular house, like my mother would cook us dinner . . . it was OK, we, never, we didn't hardly talk 'cause my mother was on drugs so my brother had to take care of us." Joanne similarly confided that her mother's regular drug use and involvement with other users affected the mother–daughter relationship. Late night parties and constant visitors to the home kept the girl up and the mother estranged: ". . . when I got older it bothered me because it started to take more of the relationship out of all of us."

All the girls indicated that their victimizations and losses were exacerbated by the fact that they felt little parental attachment, and nearly a third said there was no one with whom they felt safe and secure. Most never told any of the people they lived with when something was bothering them. Instead, the girls learned to rely on themselves. Fourteen-year-old Jill acknowledged that despite the fact that her mother was present "to protect me and stuff, [I] . . . never felt safe with her. Maybe because we didn't have a good relationship." The lack of emotionally attuned adults to help girls integrate traumatic experiences into their lives and fulfill their attachment needs is a likely contributor to their subsequent use of drugs and involvement in violent activities.

Discussion

In the early 1990s, crack cocaine use began to decline, even in the hardest hit, low-income, minority neighborhoods of New York City (Hamid, 1992). In a related trend, marijuana use was on the rise among individuals born since 1970. Some researchers believe this shift enhanced youths' prospects and limited health and legal risks because marijuana-blunt use tended to promote "conduct norms of controlled alcohol intake" and the sanctioning of "threatening or violent behavior" (Johnson, Golub, & Dunlap, 2000, p. 187). Based primarily on epidemiological studies of male drug patterns, the optimistic projections do not necessarily apply to behaviors and experiences of females. Our study provides the space to hear the stories of women and girls whose lives were shaped by the crack and marijuana drug eras and so posits a more nuanced, gendered perspective on drug involvement and family relationships. The women speak of a desire to explain the reality of their troubled lives and how, contrary to sensationalistic rhetoric about crack-using mothers, they loved and tried to care for their children (see Humphries, 1999; Logan, 1999; Reeves & Campbell, 1994). The girls, however, describe a host of traumatic experiences and describe their caregivers as emotionally and often physically absent. They wanted adults to understand that their mothers' problems, including those associated with illicit drug use, diminished their own chances to live a healthy and productive life. A mother's attempt to shield her daughter from a drug-centered life, for example, may be experienced by the daughter as abandonment and the disruption, or even severance, of primary attachment bonds. The combined narratives reflect a new perspective on the Crack Era and its aftermath by locating drug-related activities of females within the context of disrupted personal and family relationships.

The Gendered Nature of Drug Use

Growing up in families of the poor and working poor, the women had mainstream aspirations of employment and a family life. This vision dissipated, however, after the women became intimately involved with male partners who helped initiate their long careers with crack and heroin. When legitimate work disappeared, personal relationships ended, and supply sources were lost, the women faced a crisis. In a panic of loss and drug cravings, the women chose prostitution to continue to finance their habits. As their drug use escalated and their economic and social stability deteriorated, the women became increasingly estranged from family life. Despite their inability to demonstrate their love for their children in a consistent and meaningful way, the women spoke repeatedly of wanting to "put things right." They struggled to love and protect their offspring as best they could, which sometimes meant leaving children with relatives or friends and acknowledging that at times it was best to stay away. The experience of losing a child, particularly in cases when children were placed with state authorities, presented an enormous challenge to the women's sense of self as a loving parent. The women served their own needs, but they also recognized that involvement with drugs and prostitution contributed to their diminished, or total abandonment of, parental responsibilities (Dunlap et al., 2004).

The girls' drug use patterns diverged from those of the adult women, as did their perceptions of adult caregivers' behaviors. This group of girls reported heavy, regular use of marijuana and alcohol. Typically, girls' drug use began when they were young children as a normal extension of family life, wherein adults regularly drank alcohol and smoked marijuana and crack cocaine. The girls' drug involvement quickly escalated and expanded into peer networks until heavy usage was fully integrated into routine activities and events. Family life, in addition to providing a setting for drug use, was violent and dangerous, where girls were subjected to multiple and repetitive traumatic events including physical and sexual abuse, loss of caregivers, and frequent relocations. Girls characterized their caregivers as emotionally detached and physically absent. Angered and shamed by their sense of loss and abandonment, girls engaged in physical violence, as well as crack cocaine sales where, under the "protection" of older male dealers, their experiences of victimization within the home were often replicated.

Although others have described the Marijuana Generation—the children of Crack Era parents—as "being reared in severely distressed households" (Johnson, Golub, & Dunlap, 2000, p. 185), little research has investigated any further. In contrast to earlier, more hopeful predictions based on male data, the limited qualitative research on women and girls suggests that escalating drug abuse and imprisonment among adults of the Crack Era may have contributed to the subsequent problems of the next generation of girls (Males, 2010, p. 28). Our analysis of narrative data from two generations of females goes deeper to expose the underlying dynamics and suggests a developmental understanding of the younger generation's problems.

Both cohorts refer to the fragility of family relationships and, to varying degrees and from different perspectives, each reference loss, abandonment, neglect, and violence. Considered within the framework of attachment theory, such experiences weaken the bond between mothers and children. Despite the women's desire to care for their children, crack and heroin use interfered with their ability to do so, creating situations detrimental to strong mother–child bonds and to girls' emotional development. Adults' behaviors left the girls in this study feeling alone and seemingly unloved. Without other adults to support and protect them, girls struggled on their own to cope with the effects of trauma (Margolin & John, 1997). Lacking a sense of attachment or safety, the girls sought connections through the maladaptive means of substance abuse and violence.

 # Implications and Recommendations

Bonds between the drug-using females of the Crack and Marijuana Eras were disrupted, but there is also evidence of a yearning to repair the emotional connection. Any policy designed to intervene in women's recovery from drug dependency must first take into account that many women are also mothers and the head of household. Women's role as caregivers of the young deserves the implementation of empathic strategies that balance treatment services with parenting. Furthermore, if policy makers and practitioners seek to interrupt the intergenerational transmission of drug-related problems, they must acknowledge and address the primacy of early attachment bonds and find ways to support mother–child relationships and strengthen family cohesiveness. Appropriate services for recovering women with children must be delivered in the context of total family needs. Women in

substance abuse treatment want "more of a family-focused lens that treats the connection and bond of the family with ongoing nurturance, consideration, and respect" (Smith, 2006, p. 456). Policies that strengthen family cohesiveness have long-term societal benefits unlike, for example, lengthy prison sentences for drug offenses that attenuate family ties and lower children's life chances.

Drug-using mothers and daughters each have their own set of treatment concerns relative to their age and situation, but both also need structured time together to develop or repair emotional bonds. Treatment programs might arrange for mother–child visits that work toward reconnection and reunification. Joint programming between adult and child services may also be possible, necessitating, perhaps, new protocols that enable agencies to share client information. Without improvements in the flow of information between adult-focused agencies and child welfare services, recovery and reconnection may be compromised (McKeganey et al., 2002). Finally, outreach and support for law-abiding and willing family members' participation in treatment and recovery efforts can be extremely helpful in mending mother–daughter relationships and strengthening family unity across generations.

Despite the decrease in the number of crack users nationally, the effects of crack involvement, particularly for those embedded pockets of the urban poor, have carried over into the new millennium. The associated emotional, social, and economic problems continue to plague a younger generation, and yet few holistic and female-oriented drug treatment programs and policies are available to confront this challenge (Sterk, Elifson, & Theall, 2000). As much as we may want to believe that the era is over, "the Age of Crack persists, characterized by whole urban communities demoralized by poor health, violence, poverty, child neglect, and family decay" (Allen, 2003, p. 205). Programs and policies oriented toward changing individual drug use must be accompanied by a parallel commitment to bring down the structural impediments of concentrated poverty, harsh criminal justice sanctions, and widespread sexism and racism. The need for structural transformation, however, must not excuse delays in the implementation of supportive treatment services for women and girls. Neither the mothers nor the daughters of the Crack Era have fared well, and to ignore their stories is to watch the repetition of destructive patterns in future generations, regardless of the next "drug of choice."

Notes

1. Much of this research is based on Drug Use Forecasting surveys that report the number of arrestees who test positive for drugs. Arrestees volunteer to be tested, and results cannot be generalized. City prevalence rates also vary greatly.

2. As Farrington (2003) states, "Generally, DLC [Developmental Life Course] findings and theories apply to offending by lower class urban males in Western industrialized societies in the past 80 years or so" (p. 223). Two exceptions to the all-male study are Moffitt, Caspi, Rutter, and Silva (2001) and Silverthorn and Frick (1999).

3. "Combining Drug Treatment and Law Enforcement for Drug-Addicted Offenders," NIDA Grant No. F31 DA006065; "Learning About Violence and Drug Use among Adolescents (LAVIDA)," NIDA Grant No. R01 DA08679.

4. Nearly two thirds of the girls lived mostly with their mothers for at least part of their lives.

References

Adler, P. A. (1985). *Wheeling and dealing: An ethnography of an upper-level drug dealing and smuggling community.* New York, NY: Columbia University Press.

Ainsworth, M. (1972). Attachment and dependency. In J. L. Gerwitz (Ed.), *Attachment and dependency* (pp. 97–137). Washington, DC: Winston.

Ainsworth, M., Blehar, M., Waters, E., & Wall, S. (1978). *Patterns of attachment. A psychological study of the strange situation.* Hillsdale, NJ: Erlbaum.

Allen, A. (2003). Against drug use. In A. K. Wing (Ed.), *Critical race feminism: A reader* (2nd ed., pp. 197–208). New York, NY: New York University Press.

Ansbro, M. (2008). Using attachment theory with offenders. *Probation Journal, 55*(3), 231–244.

Bowlby, J. (1973). *Attachment and loss* (Vols. 1–2). New York, NY: Basic Books. (Original work published 1969)

Bowlby, J. (1988). *A secure base.* New York, NY: Basic Books.

Brisgone, R. (2008). *Varieties of behavior across and within persons of drug-using street prostitutes: A qualitative longitudinal study* (Doctoral dissertation). Rutgers, The State University of New Jersey, New Brunswick. Available from ProQuest database. (UMI No. 332692)

Cernkovich, S., & Giordano, P. (1987). Family relationships and delinquency. *Criminology, 25*, 295–321.

Curtis, R. (1998). The improbable transformation of inner-city neighborhoods: Crime, violence, and drugs in the 1990s. *Journal of Criminal Law and Criminology, 88*, 1233–1266.

Daly, K. (1992). Women's pathways to felony court: Feminist theories of lawbreaking and problems of representation. *Southern California Review of Law and Women's Studies, 2*(11), 11–51.

Denton, B. (2001). *Dealing: Women in the drug economy.* Sydney, Australia: University of New South Wales Press.

Dunlap, E., Golub, A., & Johnson, B. (2006). The severely distressed African-American family in the Crack Era: Empowerment is not enough. *Journal of Sociology and Social Welfare, 33*(1), 115–139.

Dunlap, E., & Johnson, B. (1996). Family and human resources in the development of a female crack-seller career: Case study of a hidden population. *Journal of Drug Issues, 26*(1), 175–198.

Dunlap, E., Stürzenhofecker, G., Sanabria, H., & Johnson, B. (2004). Mothers and daughters: The intergenerational reproduction of violence and drug use in home and street life. *Journal of Ethnicity in Substance Abuse, 3*(2), 1–23.

Farrington, D. (2003). Developmental and life-course criminology: Key theoretical and empirical issues. *Criminology, 41*, 221–255.

Fonagy, P. (2004). Psychodynamic therapy with children. In H. Steiner (Ed.), *Handbook of mental health interventions in children and adolescents: An integrated developmental approach* (pp. 621–658). New York, NY: Jossey-Bass.

Furst, T., Johnson, B., Dunlap, E., & Curtis, R. (1999). The stigmatized image of the "crack-head": A sociocultural exploration of a barrier to cocaine smoking among a cohort of youth in New York City. *Deviant Behavior, 20*(2), 153–181.

Gaarder, E., & Belknap, J. (2002). Tenuous borders: Girls transferred to adult court. *Criminology, 40*, 481–517.

Golub, A., Johnson, B., Dunlap, E., & Sifaneck, S. (2004). Projecting and monitoring the life course of the marijuana/blunts generation. *Journal of Drug Issues, 34*, 361–388.

Gottfredson, M., & Hirschi, T. (1990). *A general theory of crime.* Stanford, CA: Stanford University Press.

Hamid, A. (1992). The developmental cycle of a drug epidemic: The cocaine smoking epidemic of 1981–1991. *Journal of Psychoactive Drugs, 24*, 337–348.

Hardesty, M., & Black, T. (1999). Mothering through addiction: A survival strategy among Puerto Rican addicts. *Qualitative Health Research, 9*, 602–619.

Hayslett-McCall, K., & Bernard, T. (2002). Attachment, masculinity, and self-control: A theory of male crime rates. *Theoretical Criminology, 6*(1), 5–33.

Herman, J. (1997). *Trauma and recovery.* New York, NY: Basic Books.

Humphries, D. (1999). *Crack mothers: Pregnancy, drugs, and the media.* Columbus: Ohio State University Press.

Johnson, B., Dunlap, E., & Tourigny, S. (2000). Crack distribution and abuse in New York. In M. Natarajan & M. Hough (Eds.), *Illegal drug markets: From research to prevention policy* (pp. 19–57). Monsey, NY: Criminal Justice Press.

Johnson, B., Golub, A., & Dunlap, E. (2000). The rise and decline of hard drugs, drug markets and violence in New York City. In A. Blumstein & J. Wallman (Eds.), *The crime drop in America* (pp. 164–206). New York, NY: Cambridge University Press.

Logan, E. (1999). The wrong race, committing crime, doing drugs, and maladjusted for mother-hood: The nation's fury over "crack babies." *Social Justice, 26*(1), 115–138.

Lopez, V., Katsulis, Y., & Robillard, A. (2009, April). Drug use with parents as a relational strategy for incarcerated female adolescents. *Family relations, 58,* 135–147.

Maher, L. (2002). Don't leave us this way: Ethnography and injecting drug use in the age of AIDS. *International Journal of Drug Policy, 13,* 311–325.

Maher, L., & Hudson, S. (2007). Women in the drug economy: A metasynthesis of the qualitative literature. *Journal of Drug Issues, 37,* 805–826.

Majors, R., & Billson, J. (1993). *Cool pose: The dilemmas of Black manhood in America.* New York, NY: Lexington Books.

Males, M. (2010). Have girls gone wild? In M. Chesney-Lind & N. Jones (Eds.), *Fighting for girls: New perspectives on gender and violence* (pp. 13–32). Albany, NY: SUNY Press.

Margolin, G., & John, R. (1997). Children's exposure to marital aggression: Direct and mediated effects. In G. K. Kantor & J. Jasinski (Eds.), *Out of the darkness: Contemporary research perspectives on family violence* (pp. 90–104). Thousand Oaks, CA: Sage.

McKeganey, N., Barnard, M., & McIntosh, J. (2002). Paying the price for their parents' addiction: Meeting the needs of the children of drug-using parents. *Drugs: Education, prevention and policy, 9,* 233–246.

Miller-Cribbs, J. E., & Farber, N. B. (2008). Kin networks and poverty among African-Americans: Past and present. *Social Work, 53*(1), 43–51.

Moffitt, T., Caspi, A., Rutter, M., & Silva, P. (2001). *Sex differences in antisocial behavior: Conduct disorder, delinquency and violence in the Dunedin Longitudinal Study.* Cambridge, UK: Cambridge University Press.

Morgan, P., & Joe, K. (1996). Citizens and outlaws: The private lives and public lifestyles of women in the illicit drug economy. *Journal of Drug Issues, 26*(1), 125–142.

Reeves, J., & Campbell, R. (1994). *Cracked coverage: Television news, the anti-cocaine crusade, and the Reagan legacy.* Durham, NC: Duke University Press.

Robinson, R. (2011). "Just leave me alone! I'm so afraid to be alone": Helpful lessons from attachment and object relations theory. In R. Immarigeon (Ed.), *Women and girls in the criminal justice system* (Chap. 25, pp. 1–6). Kingston, NJ: Civic Research Institute.

Ryder, J. (2007). "I wasn't really bonded with my family": Attachment, loss and violence among adolescent female offenders. *Critical Criminology. An International Journal, 15*(1), 19–40.

Sampson, R. J. (1987). Urban Black violence: The effect of male joblessness and family disruption. *American Journal of Sociology, 93,* 348–382.

Schaffner, L. (2007). Violence against girls provokes girls' violence: From private injury to public harm. *Violence Against Women, 13,* 1229–1248.

Shengold, L. (1999). *Soul murder revisited: Thoughts about therapy, hate, love, and memory.* New Haven, CT: Yale University Press.

Siegel, J., & Williams, L. (2003). The relationship between child sexual abuse and female delinquency and crime: A prospective study. *Journal of Research in Crime and Delinquency, 40*(1), 71–94.

Silverthorn, P., & Frick, P. (1999). Developmental pathways to antisocial behavior: The delayed-onset pathway in girls. *Development and Psychopathology, 11*(1), 101–126.

Small, M., & Newman, K. (2001). Urban poverty after *The truly disadvantaged:* The rediscovery of the family, the neighborhood, and culture. *Annual Review of Sociology, 27,* 23–45.

Smith, C., & Thornberry, T. (1995). The relationship between childhood maltreatment and adolescent involvement in delinquency. *Criminology, 33,* 451–477.

Smith, N. (2006). Empowering the "unfit" mother: Increasing empathy, redefining the label. *Affilia, 21,* 448–457.

Sroufe, L., & Fleeson, J. (1986). Attachment and the construction of relationships. In W. Hartup & Z. Rubin (Eds.), *Relationships and development* (pp. 51–72). Mahwah, NJ: Erlbaum.

Sterk, C. (1999). *Fast lives: Women who use cocaine.* Philadelphia, PA: Temple University Press.

Sterk, C., Elifson, K., & Theall, K. (2000). Women and drug treatment experiences: A generational comparison of mothers and daughters. *Journal of Drug Issues, 30,* 839–862.

Waldorf, D., Reinarman, C., & Murphy, S. (1991). *Cocaine changes: The experience of using and quitting.* Philadelphia, PA: Temple University Press.

West, J., & Oldfather, P. (1995). Pooled case comparison: An introduction for cross-case study. *Qualitative Inquiry, 1,* 452–464.

Wilson, M., & Tolson, T. (1990). Familial support in the Black community. *Journal of Clinical Child and Adolescent Psychology, 19,* 347–355.

Wilson, W. (1987). *The truly disadvantaged: The inner city, the underclass, and public policy.* Chicago, IL: University of Chicago Press.

Wilson, W. (1996). *When work disappears: The world of the new urban poor.* New York, NY: Knopf.

DISCUSSION QUESTIONS

1. How did women's drug use influence their criminality? How did this differ from girls' drug use and offending?

2. How did women's drug use impact their family relationships? What effect did drug use have on the lives of girls and their relationships with their families?

3. How should treatment providers respond to the needs of women and girls involved in substance abuse?

Reading 16

As you learned, women often turn to prostitution as a way to support a drug habit or provide economic support for food and shelter. In addition, many find themselves on the street, following an abusive childhood and where they are only placed at additional risk for violence. In this article by Jennifer Cobbina and Sharon Oselin, you'll learn how age is an important trajectory for women and girls in prostitution and how their age of entry is shaped by their childhood and also alters their experience of life on the streets.

It's Not Only for the Money

An Analysis of Adolescent Versus Adult Entry Into Street Prostitution

Jennifer E. Cobbina and Sharon S. Oselin

Given the stigma and labeling associated with working in street prostitution, one may wonder what compels individuals to enter the trade. Numerous scholars have attempted to address this question, and the culmination of this work uncovers a variety of explanations that include financial necessity, childhood abuse, runaway behavior, homelessness, interpersonal networks, drug addiction, psychological characteristics, and antisocial personality disorder (Brock 1998; Brody, Potterat, Muth, and Woodhouse 2005; Chapkis 2000; Whelehan 2001). While there is a substantial body of literature that examines the factors that are associated with prostitution entry, most have not considered age of onset (for exception, see Kramer and Berg 2003), which has been shown to impact the pathways women take into crime[1] (Simpson, Yahner, and Dugan 2008). In fact, there is ample theoretical and empirical evidence that indicates age shapes criminal initiation (Laub and Sampson 2003; Moffitt 1993; Sampson and Laub 1993).

The current research bridges the gap in the literature in two ways. First, drawing from feminist and age of onset literatures, we examine how age of onset shapes pathways into prostitution. Second, we consider how entrance pathways are associated with length of time spent in the sex trade and the effect this has on women. Building on Barton's (2006) findings on strippers, we seek to further explicate the unique challenges that street prostitutes face in their line of work over time. We base our analysis on 40 interviews with female street prostitutes from five U.S. cities to assess motivations for entering prostitution as adolescents or adults, analyze how age of onset is linked to time spent in the trade, and whether the length of time in prostitution exacts a greater toll on women. Our results underscore the importance of including age as an organizing feature of women's pathways into prostitution and the potential associated consequences of working in this trade over time.

Women and Crime

Nearly three decades of feminist research have offered much insight into female offenders and the factors associated with female criminality (Reisig, Holtfreter, and Morash 2006).

SOURCE: Cobbina, J., & Oselin, S. S. (2011). It's not only for the money: An analysis of adolescent versus adult entry into street prostitution. *Sociological Inquiry, 81*(3), 310–332.

Indeed, researchers have documented how gender influences criminal pathways, motivations, and involvement with the criminal justice system (Daly 1992; Kruttschnitt 1996). Empirical evidence indicates that victimization, economic marginalization, and substance abuse disproportionately affect women and play unique roles in shaping women's initiation into crime (Daly 1992; Gaarder and Belknap 2002; Gilfis 1992; Simpson et al. 2008). In her examination of female offenders, Daly (1992, 1994) produced a widely used typology of multiple pathways women take into crime including street women, harmed and harming women, drug-connected women, battered women, and other women. Daly's pathways framework underscores the gendered nature of women's offending patterns.

Scholarly research on pathways into crime has also employed a life-course developmental approach, claiming that age of offending is important for establishing trajectories of criminal activity (Laub and Sampson 2003; Moffitt 1993). In spite of the plethora of research analyzing the initiation to offending among men and adolescents, fewer studies have paid specific attention to first-time adult offenders or considered the age of onset among female adult populations (for exceptions see Eggleston and Laub 2002; Simpson et al. 2008). This is surprising given that research shows adult-onset offending comprises [sic] approximately half of the overall adult offender population, and these rates are even greater among female adult offenders (Eggleston and Laub 2002).

Although studies suggest there are distinct routes and trajectories into crime, there is evidence that pathways to crime are age graded, especially when we consider the blurred boundaries between women's victimization and offending. Many girls who have experienced childhood abuse find that the best available means of escape from violence is to rely on survival strategies—such as running away from home, drug use, and illegal street work—that thereby constitute crimes according to the "justice" system (Gilfis 1992; Owen and Bloom 1995). Other scholars contend criminal activity among battered women is a by-product of their emotional attachment to criminally involved boyfriends or spouses (Mullins and Wright 2003; Richie 1996).

In one of the few studies analyzing age of onset into crime and pathways to jail, Simpson et al. (2008) found that individuals who engaged in crimes as children were more likely to have experienced sexual abuse and were more heavily involved in drug dealing, property crime, and offensive violence later on in life compared with adult-onset offenders. In contrast, women whose onset of criminal activity began as adults were more likely to have experienced violent victimization in adulthood compared with earlier onset offenders. While Simpson and colleagues' study highlights the importance of taking into account the age of onset of criminal behavior for criminal trajectories, additional work is needed to further explore these connections.

Motivations for Entry Into Prostitution

Through their extensive research, scholars have identified a variety of factors that are associated with entry into prostitution. One argument in this line of research stresses the link between abuse and prostitution. Indeed, a number of studies on female prostitution have revealed the patterns of victimization at the hands of men (Earls and David 1990; Miller 1993). However, what remains unclear is the causal path linking child abuse with later prostitution. Two models have been proposed as possible explanations. First, the susceptibility model contends that the combination of psychological characteristics (i.e., alienation and feelings of worthlessness) and tragic events (i.e., sexual assault) makes women more vulnerable to entering prostitution. While some scholars argue that childhood victimization is directly related to subsequent prostitution entry (James and Meyerding 1977; Kramer and Berg 2003), others assert that the causal link is indirectly mediated by runaway behavior (Seng 1989; Simons and Witbeck 1991). Nevertheless, according to the susceptibility model, when certain personality attributes are coupled with personal crisis, females become more susceptible to entering the life of prostitution.

The second model used to explain women's motivation for entering prostitution is the exposure model, which refers to interpersonal contacts with and inducement from others who are involved in the subculture of prostitution (Davis 1971). This model is closely tied to the cultural deviance theoretical perspective, which attributes crime to a set of values that exist in disadvantaged neighborhoods. In particular, Sutherland (1939) proposed a theory of differential association, which argues that people learn to commit crime because of regular contact with antisocial values, attitudes, and criminal behaviors. These definitions that are favorable to crime are learned when one's personal networks are primarily filled with individuals who uphold and perpetuate them. For instance, in their Chicago-based study, Raphael and Shapiro (2002) found that 32.5 percent of street prostitutes had a household member [who] work[ed] in prostitution where they grew up, and 71 percent of their sample reported that they were encouraged by another individual to work as a prostitute to earn money. In short, it appears that the cultural deviance framework may partially explain why some women from disadvantaged backgrounds enter prostitution.

Economic necessity is often connected to entry into prostitution. Women who occupy a lower socioeconomic status (SES) have fewer educational and employment opportunities, making it challenging to avoid poverty (Ehrenreich 2001). As a result, some turn to particular survival strategies, such as working in the underground economy to supplement limited welfare (Edin and Lein 1997). Evidence indicates that when women lack viable alternatives, they are more likely to perceive prostitution as a feasible option for income (Brock 1998; Delacoste and Alexander 1998). In fact, many street prostitutes are runaways who have few resources and engage in a myriad of criminal activities to survive (Weitzer 2009).

Moreover, scholars contend that drug addiction can also pull women into the sex trade. In fact, studies find that substance abuse is often prevalent among street-working prostitutes and note that it can be a primary reason they resort to selling their bodies (Epele 2001; Porter and Bonilla 2009). For certain drug-addicted women, prostitution may serve as the only viable means to finance their habit, especially among those who lack education and job skills (Gossop, Powes, Griffiths, and Strang 1994). Other research suggests that while some women may use drugs recreationally prior to engaging in prostitution, the habit intensifies the longer they work in the trade, as drugs may be used as a coping mechanism (Cusick and Hickman 2005; Davis 2000).

We have just reviewed many studies that analyze female involvement in prostitution and the various motivations that account for their entry into sex work. Yet these works offer little explanation as to why some factors appear to have greater impact on certain women compared with others. Building off previous studies that suggest age may be a defining factor that shapes reasons for engaging in prostitution (Kramer and Berg 2003), we use age of entry as an organizing tool that influences pathways into street prostitution. Following Simpson et al. (2008), we distinguish women who enter prostitution in adolescence (18 and under) from those who start in adulthood (19 and over) and create a typology to determine whether such a framework explains why and how prostitution results from multiple interdependent factors.

Previous studies conclude street prostitutes are likely to experience the highest rates of violence, abuse, arrests, and stigma of all sex workers (Miller and Schwartz 1995; Sanders 2007; Weitzer 2009), which may increase the longer a woman works as a prostitute. Thus, beyond exploring the connection between age and pathways, we examine the implications of particular pathways as they are linked to time in the trade and whether the tenure in prostitution exacts a greater "toll" on women.

Methodology and Data Collection

To assess the interaction between gender, age, and prostitution entry, we rely on 40 interviews drawn from two research projects, each conducted by one of the authors. The first project was based on a comprehensive in-depth examination of street prostitutes affiliated with four nonprofit organizations that specifically aid women in prostitution by providing services, resources, and a range of other amenities to them. These sites were located in different U.S. cities: Los Angeles, Chicago, Minneapolis, and Hartford. While there is much structural variation among these organizations, most claim their goal is to help women in prostitution leave the trade. The author was able to act as an intern and researcher at each of these settings for approximately 3 months per site, where she conducted semistructured interviews with 36 clients. This researcher attempted to interview all prostitutes present at each site; however, overall, fewer than 10 either refused to participate or were unable to because of scheduling conflicts. Of these 36 prostitutes, three were excluded from this current study because they did not provide substantial information about their entrance into prostitution. During these interviews, the women discussed their biographies, including how and why they first entered prostitution, and their experiences in the trade.

Data from the second study come from a broader investigation examining the reentry experiences of incarcerated and formerly incarcerated women in St. Louis, some of whom also worked as street prostitutes. As the original study was comparative in nature, the sample included women who returned to custody 2 to 3 years following their release from prison and a matched sample of females who were not reincarcerated during this period. During these interviews, 11 women discussed working in prostitution, and of these individuals, seven were therefore included in the current study.[2] Women were recruited to participate in the project based on the following criteria: (1) They were released on parole between June 2004 and December 2005, and (2) they were released with at least 2 to 3 years to serve on their parole sentence.[3] To ensure the comparative nature of the sample, approximately equal numbers of women were included in the study if (1) they have [had] no documented new crimes, law violation, or technical violation resulting in reincarceration and (2) they were reincarcerated as a result of a new crime, law violation, or technical violation.

In this study, we focus specifically on age of entry into street prostitution and do not analyze when they first engaged in other criminal behaviors (unrelated to prostitution). Drawing on Barton's (2006) study, which concluded that strippers experience a greater *toll* the longer they work in the trade, we also examine whether female street prostitutes feel this toll and whether it increases the longer they remain on the streets. We were able to gauge this toll because in the first research project (which encompasses 83% of the sample for this study), the researcher asked participants questions that specifically addressed the difficulties and negative effects of working in street prostitution. These questions included, What are the negatives of working in prostitution? What were some of the difficulties of being a prostitute? Did your family and friends know you were working in prostitution? How did they react? Did working as a prostitute affect how you felt about yourself? How did you cope with these difficulties?

Because of the differences between strippers and street prostitutes, we developed an alternative definition of the toll that emerged from our qualitative data. Based upon these accounts, the *toll* is defined as the accumulation of violent encounters, elevated levels of exhaustion associated with the job, heightened stigma and broken relationships with family members, increased drug addiction as a way to cope with the difficulties of the job, and severe punishments from the criminal justice system.

In the current study, we employed qualitative research methods because it provides insight into the perspectives and lived experiences of the research participants. In both projects, the interviews followed a semistructured protocol designed to elicit rich accounts relating to prostitution, with interviewers using follow-up probes to obtain a fuller depiction of the context and circumstances surrounding entrance into prostitution and the outcomes of working in the trade. The interview questions that were useful for this study related to crime, entry into prostitution, age of entry, length of time in the trade, and experiences associated with the work. Interviews were voluntary, and research participants were promised strict confidentiality; therefore, pseudonyms were used. The interviews lasted between one and two hours, were recorded and transcribed verbatim, and were subsequently coded.

In the analysis, we took care to ensure that the concepts developed and illustrations provided typified the most common patterns of women's accounts. Inter-reliability was achieved by having both authors independently code the data sets for themes related to how females constructed their understandings of their entrance into prostitution. We then conferred to identify the most common thematic patterns. We ensured internal validity using inductive analytic techniques, including the search for and explication of deviant cases (Charmaz 2006). Although we are cautious of the generalizability of our findings, the study's findings underscore the importance of age as an organizing feature of women's pathways into prostitution and the potential associated consequences of working in this trade.

✖ Findings

The demographics of the women in our sample were racially and ethnically diverse with 67 percent African American, 23 percent Caucasian, and 10 percent Hispanic.[4] They ranged from 20 to 60 years of age, with a mean age of 36.5 years. In addition, 50 percent of women entered prostitution when they were 18 years or younger, and 50 percent entered prostitution when they were 19 years or older. We analyzed pathways according to age group and discovered they varied by age of entry. At the time of the interviews, the women included in these samples had ceased working in prostitution.[5] The women are separated according to their age of entrance categories—adolescents or adults.

Age and Pathways Into Prostitution

Previous research finds numerous pathways into prostitution, yet the relationship between age and entry remains unclear. Thus, we aim to illuminate this topic here by analyzing prostitutes' accounts of how and when they entered the sex trade. To do so, we identified patterns and compared them across two age categories: adolescents (18 and under) and adults (19 and up).

We find pathways into prostitution differ according to age of entry, as illustrated by our typology (see Reading Table 16.1). Among those who entered prostitution during adolescence, we identified two categories or pathways: Prostitution to Reclaim Control of One's Sexuality and Prostitution as Normal. In comparison, women who entered as adults comprised [sic] the two other categories: Prostitution to Sustain Drug Addiction and Prostitution

for Survival. There were three individuals who comprised [sic] a fifth category of Others because their age category did not coincide with corresponding pathways or they exhibited a combination of two or more pathways.[6] While there is some overlap, we contend that overall, each typology encompasses a distinct set of motivations and pathways into prostitution that varies according to age.

Motivations for Entering Prostitution as Adolescents

Fleeing Abuse and Reclaiming Control. A majority of the women (60%) who entered prostitution as adolescents discussed their entry as an attempt to regain control of their lives and their sexuality. A common experience among the women who had an early onset of prostitution (18 years or younger) was enduring childhood victimization, including sexual molestation, rape, incest, and physical assault. As a result, many girls chose to run away and flee their families. Kali, for example, discussed having entered prostitution at 16 years of age because of molestations: "I left home at an early age because there was some molestation in my family. I did it for money and to rebel from my parents." Similarly, Tisha linked her reason for engaging in prostitution at the age of 11 to early sexual abuse:

Reading Table 16.1   Typology of Entrance Into Prostitution

Type of Entrance	Characteristics	Sample
18 and under		
Fleeing abuse and reclaiming control	Childhood physical / sexual abuse, runaway behavior, perception of prostitution as empowering, some use of pimps	$N = 12$
Normal	Economic motivation, learned from family and friends, viewed prostitution as exciting and glamorous	$N = 8$
19 and up		
Sustain drug addiction	Family history of drug use, drug addicted, association with other prostitutes, morally conflicted about prostitution	$N = 11$
Survival	Means of survival, nearly homeless, holds some allure, not motivated by drugs but drug use escalates over time	$N = 6$
Other	Do not fit into other categories	$N = 3$

[My grandmother] was also engaged in a lot of activities such as selling drugs, doing drugs, renting out the rooms of her house and stuff like that. So staying was basically out of the question because she had so many men in the house and I had been sexually molested and raped a lot of times, so I didn't want to stay there anymore and put up with that.

Other women attributed their initial involvement in prostitution to sexual abuse but did not attempt to runaway. Instead, they began to perceive their sexuality as a way to garner power over men and reap monetary rewards. For instance, Jackie who engaged in prostitution at an early age was sexually victimized repeatedly during childhood. Her first memory of sexual abuse was by two family friends she was staying with from the age of 9 to 14 years of age and then by her great-uncle from the age of 15 on. She explained that her mother "gave" her away to family friends who molested her, which ultimately resulted in her entry in prostitution:

The people that my mama gave me to, one [of] their sons molested me real bad. I would go through the house and he would catch me in the kitchen and do stuff to me. But anyway, I got into prostitution. Grandpa, his daddy, he would always give me little money to feel and touch on me and stuff like that, so that's how I got off into that [prostitution]. I learned then that if I wanted something, I had to give up something.

Additionally, some recalled that engaging in prostitution gave them a sense of empowerment, allowed them to exact revenge, or provided a sense of control over their bodies. Janelle engaged in prostitution as a teenager: "[b]ecause from my childhood, I had been molested. And then as time went on, I was still getting molested, so I got tired. And I said well, if a man going to take it from me, why not sell myself?" And CeeCee rationalized her entry into prostitution in the following manner: "At the time it gave me a sense of control because I had been molested as a child. So it was like at some point it felt like I was getting a revenge for the predators in my life at that time." Consistent with prior research, we found that child abuse and runaway behavior became a pathway into prostitution

for certain individuals (Hwang and Bedford 2003; Kramer and Berg 2003; Tyler, Hoyt, and Whitbeck 2000; West and Williams 2000).

Other scholars posit the mechanism between sexual abuse and prostitution often lies within a third-party actor (Williamson and Cluse-Tolar 2002). While not common among the women in our study, a few established relationships with men who then played a main role in their entry into the trade. For Janise, a teenage runaway, a male figure was key to her entrance:

I used to run away from home a lot because my father used to beat us. So I ran away from home and I met this guy and he told me—I explained to him how my father beated on us, he said "well I'm [not] gonna beat you. Call me daddy." He used to buy me anything I wanted, whatever, no matter how much it was.

Janise later discovered that these gifts came with a price. She explained that "later on in the relationship he said 'now you gotta go do this in order to keep me buying you that' which was prostitution. So I did it." In this case, Janise was enticed as an adolescent to engage in prostitution because she believed these acts pleased her pimp, sustained the acquisition of material goods, and gave her a sense of control over her life.

Similarly, Alissa stated she engaged in prostitution at approximately 14 years of age because her boyfriend introduced her to the idea and encouraged her to do so. After she agreed, he became her pimp and profited off her labor:

He said, "[w]ell if you like me, would you like to make some money?" So I'm like, "well yeah, okay." So he took me over to different men's houses, he said, "[y]ou do whatever they want you to do. . . . They'll give you money and when you get the money you bring it back and give it to me." And that's what I did, not knowing that I was prostituting because again I was young and didn't know.

Most of these adolescent girls claimed performing sex work gave them a sense of control over their sexuality (and their lives). Ironically, certain girls (e.g., Janise and Alissa) engaged in prostitution not only because of encouragement from a male figure in their life, who served as their pimp, but also relinquished much of their autonomy and earnings to him within a short time. While some may enter the trade to obtain control, the coercive nature of street prostitution under a pimp's rule is often far from empowering and often abusive. (Williamson and Baker 2009). In entering street prostitution, many girls worked in environments where the risk of violence was heightened, the very circumstances that initially caused them to flee their abusive homes.

Working in Prostitution Is Normal. An additional category of entrance into prostitution as adolescents consisted of the "normalization" of prostitution. Among early-onset females, 40 percent fell under this category and described prostitution as a normal activity in the neighborhoods where they grew up. As a result, these individuals viewed prostitution as a viable option for income. Lisa described her motivation for entering prostitution at 16 years of age in the following manner: "I use to hear [my sister] say stuff like . . . 'don't get up with a wet ass and no money in your pocket.' So instantly that planted that seed for me. When you lay down with a man you ain't gon' get up with an empty pocket and a wet ass." Evette also was exposed to prostitution through family members, as her father was a pimp and routinely kept company with many prostitutes. She explained how this was a normal facet of her childhood and adolescence:

> I wanted to be with my dad and of course these things were going on in my dad's household because I told you my dad was a dope dealer and pimp, so that's when I became attracted to the lifestyle. The glamour part of it, you know, I saw the dressing up and the makeup and really that was the attraction for me. . . . You know my dad kept a lot of street people around and that's how I met this guy that eventually introduced me to prostitution. I was doing it regularly by sixteen.

Both Lisa and Evette viewed prostitution as "normal" because they were surrounded by prostitution from a young age. It was through this socialization that they learned values, beliefs, and behaviors that corresponded with this lifestyle.

Another common theme, alluded to by Evette, was the perception that working in prostitution was glamorous. As these adolescent girls observed women working in the sex trade, they regarded the work and the accoutrements as sophisticated. Thus, they believed prostitution was a way to achieve status. Tina surmised: "[A]fter my father died we were so poor and in that area that's all you see are prostitutes and pimps. . . . The girls are wearing nice clothes and making money, that's what I wanted too, so that's how it started for me." Likewise, Monique entered prostitution at 10 years of age, "Because of the money, the excitement, my environment. . . . When I grew up in the late 60s, the movies and people were glamorizing pimps and hustlers and stuff. . . . All I seen was the money, the furs, the jewelry and the talk . . . so I started and I got a rush out of that quick money, that fast living." The lure of early entry into prostitution can be partly explained by interpersonal contact with others involved in the prostitution and the perception that it is a viable course of action to acquire money, clothes, and material resources.

Even though certain women in this sample claimed that as adolescents they learned to view prostitution as "normal" behavior to engage in, it is noteworthy that they did not also "learn" to use addictive drugs at this point in their lives. Indeed, many studies suggest that women enter prostitution for the purpose of earning money to sustain their drug habit (Potterat, Rothenberg, Muth, Darrow, and Phillips-Plummer 1998); yet we found that most women who entered prostitution as teenagers did not share these motivations, as few contended with severe drug addictions. Rather, they avowed to having used drugs recreationally as adolescents and limited their use to marijuana or alcohol.

In sum, early-onset prostitutes' entrance into the trade was complex, yet they exhibited particular pathways that spanned across these five samples. Those in the first category consistently focused on childhood abuse when explaining their motivation for entering prostitution. In response to these experiences, many of the girls became runaways and engaged in prostitution to earn money in an attempt to reclaim control over their sexuality. The rest of our adolescent-onset sample fell in the second category of learning about prostitution at an early age from others involved in the sex trade and adopting the perception that sex work is normal. In these accounts, they routinely described sex acts as alluring and exciting. Our data suggest that female adolescent entry into prostitution revolves around two particular pathways, associated with specific events and motivations. We now explore the pathways into prostitution as adults.

Motivations for Entering Prostitution as Adults

Sustaining the Drug Habit. In contrast to early-onset prostitutes who depicted their entry as a way to gain control over their sexuality or who viewed the sex trade as a viable course of action in their community, the women who entered as adults provided alternative explanations. Indeed, 65 percent of women who first engaged in prostitution as adults attributed their entrance to drug addiction. Most of these women came from a family or environment where drug use was prevalent and consequently became drug addicted. Chanelle, for example, explained why she engaged in prostitution:

> Because of my drug addiction. I found out that that would enable me to get money for drugs . . . quicker than waiting on county checks or a boyfriend to bring it to me. I could go out there and be assertive and get it myself. . . . And I was propositioned once or twice but then it occurred to me one day—hey, I could sell my body and get some money. I tried it and it worked.

When posed with the same question, Melanie responded, "I have an addiction to money and drugs." And Vanessa explained, "Once I started [drugs] and got hooked is when I first entered prostitution to support my growing habit." For many women, prostitution served as a practical and accessible way to support their substance addiction.

One striking difference between the women who entered the sex trade during adulthood (rather than adolescence) was that the former held strong moral condemnations of prostitution. They stressed that the drugs affected their willingness to enter the trade by making them lose sight of their morals and values. Belinda recalled, "I used to see other girls out there and . . . I'm like 'how could they do that?' Then I had a strong need for a drug. . . . It [prostitution] wasn't something that I liked to do actually, you know, but the need for the drug was so great that it took priority."

And Noelle explained how she initially struggled with moral beliefs about engaging in prostitution at the age of 22:

> It was for the money to support my substance abuse. When I first started prostituting it had a very big impact on me. I would only work when it was dark out. I didn't want my children or family members to see me. God forbid if someone should see me . . . I was so ashamed. As the progression of my disease picked up sooner or later it was early hours of the morning, then it was afternoon, then it was 24 hours a day. Then it became seven days a week. The progression of my disease took hold. And nothing matters. You use to live and live to use.

Although some had been exposed to prostitution in childhood, the women in this category felt conflicted about prostitution, with most having strong moral opposition to it. However, as their addictions progressed, they violated their previously held beliefs about prostitution, as it became a viable means to earn quick cash for drugs. These findings support previous research that asserts drug addiction can lead women into prostitution and keep them "stuck" in the trade (Cusick and Hickman 2005).

Survival Sex. Among adult-onset prostitutes, 35 percent described their entry into prostitution as a means of survival, in that it served as a necessary way to earn money to eat and pay rent for housing. For example, Elena explained, "I lived in the streets and there was no other way to maintain myself for food, clothes—it was really hard for me." As a result, Elena sold drugs but resorted to prostitution "when the sales weren't coming through." And Shondra explained why she first started turning tricks:

> I was still married to my second husband. We were separated. He left me in Atlanta stranded. He packed up our things, my kids, and left—during a time when I was in a mental hospital. I had a real bad breakdown. And when I got out I told him that I couldn't live with him for a minute, that I needed time to adjust. So I moved in with a girlfriend of mine and during the time I was at her house he packed up everything and moved

back North and left me in Atlanta stranded. It kind of messed me up. I guess he felt that my relatives were here I would be okay but it kind of messed me up. I ended up prostituting my way back to the Midwest because I had no money, nothing to my name.

In contrast to those who cited the previous pathway, the women in this category turned to prostitution to survive. Findings corroborate previous research which argues structural conditions can lead impoverished individuals into prostitution (Miller 1986; Weitzer 2009), as they often view it as a survival mechanism and one of the best available opportunities for making money (Rosen and Venkatesh 2008). This pathway, in particular, is similar to Daly's (1992, 1994) "street woman" classification.

While acknowledging structural factors that make prostitution a practical option for lower-class women, some described their work as glamorous or alluring, even though they entered the work primarily for income. After a period where she "tested" prostitution out by walking the streets with a fellow prostitute, Kristin explained: "It was kind of exciting. . . . And I kind of got a thrill out of the guys whistling at me with my mini-skirt on." And though Loretta engaged in prostitution because she was unemployed, when asked whether there were other secondary reasons, she admitted, "I was in my late twenties and I had just had my second child . . . and honestly, I also thought it was exciting."

While there is some overlap between categories, these findings reveal that age of onset is important to consider because it is linked to particular pathways that lead adolescents and women into prostitution. However, these conclusions also generate further inquiries, such as, Why are pathways into prostitution important? And are they associated with other outcomes? We address these concerns in the following section.

Pathways, Time in the Trade, and the Toll

Beyond showing that age appears to be linked to particular pathways into prostitution, the age of entry also holds other implications for street prostitutes. We believe it is especially noteworthy that those who began working in prostitution as adolescents remained in the trade for longer periods of time compared with individuals who first entered as adults. Specifically, the former group spent approximately 22 years in prostitution compared with the latter group who averaged 8 years on the streets (see Reading Table 16.1). This stark difference suggests those who entered earlier are more likely to work in prostitution for a longer duration of time, which in turn can increase the toll the work takes on these individuals. The toll experienced among street prostitutes consisted of an accumulation of violent encounters, elevated levels of exhaustion, heightened stigma that resulted in broken relationships with family members, intensified drug addictions as a way to cope with the difficulties of the work, and arrests and incarceration. Previous work based on a large data set of street prostitutes concludes that drug use and violence, in particular, can also lead to premature mortality among them (Potterat et al. 2004). Likewise, it is evident throughout these accounts that fear of death is a prominent factor that contributes to the toll women experience owing to their work.

The first indicator of the toll is the number and intensity of violent encounters prostitutes experienced on the streets. Like much of the research on prostitution, we found women who remained in the trade for longer periods of time had been exposed to higher levels of abuse and appeared to feel the effects of victimization to a greater degree. Carrie, for example, who began work as a prostitute at the age of 18, remained in the trade for 17 years and recalled countless violent encounters: "I've been raped, woken up rolled up in a tarp, left for dead, had my lung collapse in a street fight, and more. It's amazing I'm still alive." Likewise, Jenna, who was 14 years old when she first started and worked as a prostitute for 27 years, emphasized the violence and abuse she endured: "I was raped many times and left for dead, having people cut my face up and my eye was permanently damaged. I was almost killed by my last john and I ran for my life." Although prostitutes can experience violence at the hands of johns, pimps, or others at any point in their career, abuse appears especially salient among those who had been on the streets a substantial time and had been subjected to numerous attempts on their lives.

In addition, the level of overall exhaustion is another indicator of the toll experienced by street prostitutes, which was frequently reported by those who remained in prostitution for a considerable number of years. For instance, 28-year-old Amy worked as a prostitute for 15 years and claimed she stopped working on the streets because, "I was tired of prostituting and wanted to try and change my life so I could do something else . . . because I'm getting way too old for it. By the end, I was so tired I just sat on the sidewalk from sheer exhaustion until the cops found me."

Likewise, LaTonya, a 52-year-old woman who worked in prostitution since age 13, stated, "I realized that I wanted to stop this lifestyle because I'm way too old for this shit. . . . I'm a mother of 11 kids and 15 grand-kids . . . at this point in life I shouldn't be doing that." When probed to describe specifically the ways in which she felt tired, LaTonya referenced multiple forms of exhaustion: "I was so tired and ill that I went to the hospi-tal, I barely made it. Around that time I got too depressed, that's another issue I struggled with was depression or whatever." Similar to Barton's (2006) assessment, those who emphasized these feelings underscore the difficulties of the work itself, which manifested itself in terms of both mental and physical exhaustion.

Moreover, another toll of prostitution was the stigma-tization women felt upon being labeled by loved ones, which in turn adversely affected these relationships. A few women in this study spoke of their shame and the stigma they experienced while in prostitution and how that shaped their familial relationships. Shondra was a prosti-tute for 12 years, and she explained how the shame she felt over her actions caused her to sever ties with her family members: "Once my family found out I was in county jail on prostitution charges . . . I didn't see them for years after that because I was embarrassed and ashamed of what they would think about me and my lifestyle."

CeeCee, who entered prostitution at 15 and worked in the trade for 25 years, recalled how her relationships with family members completely deteriorated when her brother saw her on the streets and took physical action: "In fact one of my brothers got so angry with me that he physically assaulted me." Thus, consistent with previous research, the stigma and shame women felt and the lack of support from family and friends became a burden for these individuals that took a toll over time (Chapkis 1997; Sanders 2007).

It is well documented that many prostitutes use drugs as a coping mechanism (Davis 2000; Porter and Bonilla 2009; Young, Boyd, and Hubbell 2000). Similarly, our inter-viewees claimed their addictions intensified the longer they remained in the trade to contend with the difficulties of the work (e.g., stigma, shame, violent encounters). Elaine, who worked as a prostitute for 17 years, admitted she occasion-ally used drugs prior to becoming a prostitute, but the habit grew worse after her entrance. She stated, "When I started working the street [prostituting] it got even worse because I didn't have commitments to make. As I got more money I could just blow it on drugs." Monique, who entered prosti-tution at age 10 and spent a total of 39 years working on the streets, discussed how drugs became the way she coped with shame and stigma associated with her work: "Yes, it bothered me that my family found out what I was doing and what they thought about me, but I just went and got high so I wouldn't have to have to deal with it." The follow-ing account by Noelle, who had worked as a prostitute for 16 years, highlights how drugs and prostitution reinforced one another:

> When I was arrested I was so sick and so sick and tired that they had to arraign me from the door-way. My drug of choice was heroin. I couldn't even walk to stand in front of the judge so they arraigned me from the doorway, that's how sick I was. That's how I got out of it finally.

As Noelle's earlier comments imply, she felt shame and stigma about working as a prostitute, and drugs helped to assuage those feelings. As a result, she had a severe drug addiction at the time of her arrest. The women who had been in prostitution for significant lengths of time often had a serious drug habit that grew worse as they grappled with feelings of shame, worthlessness, and powerlessness.

The final indicator of a toll that woman experienced was extensive histories with the criminal justice system, which led to increasingly stiff punitive sentences. Tisha had a substantial history of arrests and jail time, accumu-lated during her 9 years of prostitution. She was "burned out" and felt the costs of being in prostitution were becom-ing too high as she faced another long stint in prison: "I was on parole and I got busted for prostitution again. I knew I was going back to prison for a long time. At that point, I knew something had to change." Janise, who worked in prostitution for 28 years, also expressed that going to prison was her biggest fear and caused her great anxiety. She espoused, "I had been to the penitentiary twice, one more arrest and I would have gone away for a long, long time. I became so scared of getting in a car with an undercover cop . . . that was a big fear for me. Because when you go to prison, you don't really know if you'll get out alive." Anxiety about stiff punitive sentences became especially taxing for those who had significant prior involvement with the criminal justice system.

Many of the issues that caused a toll fueled each other (e.g., feelings of shame, escalated drug use, and strained familial relationships) and culminated in negative outcomes and feelings that prostitutes claimed they endured because of their participation in prostitution. Specifically, we found the women who entered prostitution as adolescents were more likely to remain in the trade longer, as well as experience and recount negative aspects associated with the job. For some of these individuals, the toll became too great to bear and ultimately served as the impetus to pull them out of the sex trade.

Discussion

Many studies examine factors that pull women into prostitution, including economic and structural conditions (Brock 1998; Chapkis 2000; Whelehan 2001), cultural norms (Raphael and Shapiro 2002; Sharpe 1998), and personal experiences, such as past abuse or drug addiction (Cusick and Hickman 2005; Hwang and Bedford 2003; Rosen and Venkatesh 2008; Simpson et al. 2008). However, these works do not provide a clear explanation as to why certain factors shape some women's entrance into prostitution more than others. The current study extends previous research through a qualitative analysis of female entrance into street prostitution. Our study underscores that pathways into prostitution are age-graded; thus, the relevance of certain explanatory factors varies according to age category.

One pathway that accounts for adolescent entry into prostitution centers on childhood victimization, which includes physical abuse, sexual molestation, and incest. Consistent with other research, we find that many in our sample ran away from home to escape assaults (Gilfis 1992; Hwang and Bedford 2003; Owen and Bloom 1995) and subsequently engaged in prostitution to reclaim control over their sexuality. Ironically, those who were encouraged to work as prostitutes by male figures soon felt disempowered as their work was "managed" by others.

The other pathway of adolescent entry into prostitution was based on socialization and learned perceptions about prostitution. Growing up in disadvantaged community contexts where prostitution was prevalent exposed females to this lifestyle at an early age. Because of close interpersonal networks with family, friends, and neighbors who participated in the sex work, adolescents came to view these activities as acceptable and glamorous and prostitution as a viable option of work. Consistent with differential association theory, we find females who had regular contact with prostitutes or those who encouraged prostitution embraced the lifestyle at an early age.

Although some studies argue that childhood victimization and exposure to others involved in sex work account for women's entrance into the trade (Potterat, Phillips, Rothenberg, and Darrow 1985; Simons and Witbeck 1991), our research reveals different motivations for women who entered prostitution as adults. The first pathway into prostitution among our adult-onset sample was primarily fueled by drug addiction. Interestingly, these individuals claimed they were morally opposed and reluctant to engage in prostitution, yet drug addiction led them to violate their beliefs to obtain money to support their habit.

The last pathway into prostitution among adult-onset prostitutes was economic instability. Extant research claims poverty can "pull" women into prostitution, especially when the trade serves as a survival mechanism and rational means for making money (Rosen and Venkatesh 2008; Weitzer 2009). This is consistent with the feminization of poverty theory, which states that many women resort to committing crimes because of their low SES (Daly 1992, 1994).

In uncovering these four pathways into prostitution based on age category, we are aware that none of these pathways are completely distinct from another. However, we assert that each embodies a prevalent pattern of entry into prostitution associated with a particular age group. Our study builds on Simpson et al.'s (2008) work by identifying "risk factors" that pull women into prostitution that vary by age, many of which have been uncovered in previous research on this topic (Brock 1998; Chapkis 2000; Hwang and Bedford 2003; Potterat et al. 1998; Raphael and Shapiro 2002; Rosen and Venkatesh 2008). Yet our study presents nuanced explanations by analyzing how age of onset (adolescence versus adulthood) is associated with different pathways and risk factors. We assert that age is central to understanding this phenomenon because it appears not only to be connected to pathways into prostitution but also [because] entrance types may predict longer durations in the trade, which heightens the toll experienced by prostitutes.

Our age-graded typology provides an organizing framework that bridges both personal and structural features. Dalla (2000: 352) concludes that while "entry into prostitution results from the cumulation of multiple interdependent personal and contextual factors . . . [e]fforts at teasing apart those variables, and the relative significance of each, have left many questions unanswered and uncertainties remaining." By examining age and its connection to pathways into prostitution, this analysis begins to disentangle these concerns and goes beyond them by discussing implications of tenure in prostitution.

Our findings add not only to scholarly research but also can be used to inform public policy relevant to prostitution. From this perspective, our pathways underscore the need for additional support services for "at-risk" women, as the prevalence of these may affect whether girls and women enter street prostitution. To be effective, prevention and intervention programs must address the unique needs of prostitutes. One way to do so is to focus on treating physical and sexual assault victims and to allocate proper guardians and housing for at-risk adolescent girls. Adult prostitutes are primarily in need of services that help them obtain legal employment, secure housing, and maintain their sobriety.

Despite our contributions, we must note a few limitations of this study. First, these data precluded us from addressing psychological factors, which may impact female entry into prostitution (Potterat et al. 1998). Second, each participant in our sample was interviewed once regarding their pathways into the trade; thus, we were unable to capture changes in attitudes or interpretations of personal experiences linked to entrance. Third, given our small sample size, our findings may not be generalizable to all street prostitutes. And, indeed, not all street prostitutes experience the degree of hardships evident among our sample. Nonetheless, future studies can continue to assess not only pathways into prostitution but also tenure in the trade as it engenders a toll on these workers. In spite of these limitations, our study concludes that age of onset is a critical feature that should be considered in future attempts to understand and theorize entrance into prostitution.

NOTES

1. We recognize that there is scholarly debate about the classification of prostitutes as "criminals." It is not our intention to promote this idea; however, owing to the legal and cultural mandates in the United States, being labeled and treated as criminals was especially salient for the women in this sample. Thus, we include this framework because it is derived from our data and sheds light on the perceptions of the individuals included in this study.

2. Although 11 women admitted to having engaged in prostitution, four were excluded from the study because during the course of the interview, no information was gathered regarding the reasons they entered prostitution.

3. Because the purpose of the original study was to explore how women managed their release from prison, this time frame was selected because it provided an ample follow-up period post-release to identify women successful in not recidivating and a similarly situated reincarcerated comparison group.

4. Race was not found to shape prostitution entry among respondents in the sample.

5. Most women in this study claimed they worked consistently in prostitution for the length of time they specified. However, there were some individuals who left for short durations of time; temporary breaks were often attributed to other events such as being incarcerated, pregnant, in a hospital, or in detox programs. We stress that these calculations represent the estimates of tenure in prostitution and are likely not exact measures but overall demonstrate broad patterns and averages. We connect time in the trade with the toll and rely on rich, qualitative data to support our assessment.

6. Rosaria and Sabrina fit into the first typology; however, they entered prostitution as adults rather than as adolescents. Although Rachael entered prostitution as an adult and admits having experimented with drugs recreationally when she was younger, she did not engage in prostitution to sustain a drug habit or to survive while on the streets.

References

Barton, Bernadette. 2006. *Stripped: Inside the Lives of Exotic Dancers.* New York: New York Press.

Brock, Deborah. 1998. *Making Work, Making Trouble: Prostitution as a Social Problem.* Toronto, ON: University of Toronto Press.

Brody, Stuart, John J. Potterat, Stephen Q. Muth, and Donald E. Woodhouse. 2005. "Psychiatric and Characterological Factors Relevant to Excess Mortality in a Long-Term Cohort of Prostitute Women." *Journal of Sex and Marital Therapy* 31:97–112.

Chapkis, Wendy. 1997. *Live Sex Acts: Women Performing Erotic Labor.* New York: Routledge.

———. 2000. "Power and Control in the Commercial Sex Trade." Pp. 181–201 in *Sex for Sale*, edited by Ronald Weitzer. New York: Routledge.

Charmaz, Kathy. 2006. *Constructing Grounded Theory*. Thousand Oaks, CA: Sage.

Cusick, Linda and Matthew Hickman. 2005. "'Trapping' in Drug Use and Sex Work Careers." *Drugs: Education, Prevention and Policy* 12:369–379.

Dalla, Rochelle. 2000. "Exposing the 'Pretty Woman' Myth: A Qualitative Examination of the Lives of Female Streetwalking Prostitutes." *Journal of Sex Research* 37:344–366.

Daly, Kathleen. 1992. "A Woman's Pathway to Felony Court." *Review of Law and Women's Studies* 2:11–52.

———. 1994. *Gender, Crime, and Punishment*. New Haven, CT: Yale University Press.

Davis, Nanette. 1971. "The Prostitute: Developing a Deviant Identity." Pp. 297–322 in *Studies in the Sociology of Sex*, edited by J. M. Henslin. New York: Appleton-Century-Crofts.

———. 2000. "From Victims to Survivors: Working with Recovering Street Prostitutes." Pp. 139–155 in *Sex for Sale*, edited by Ronald Weitzer. New York: Routledge.

Delacoste, Frederique and Priscilla Alexander. 1998. *Sex Work: Writings by Women in the Prostitution*, San Francisco, CA: Cleis Press.

Earls, Christopher M. and Helene David. 1990. "Early Family and Sexual Experiences of Male and Female Prostitutes." *Canada's Mental Health* 38:7–11.

Edin, Kathryn and Laura Lein. 1997. "Work, Welfare, and Single Mothers' Economic Survival Strategies." *American Sociological Review* 62:253–266.

Eggleston, Elaine P. and John Laub. 2002. "The Onset of Adult Offending: A Neglected Dimension of the Criminal Career." *Journal of Criminal Justice* 30:603–622.

Ehrenreich, Barbara. 2001. *Nickel and Dimed: On (Not) Getting by in America*. New York: Metropolitan Books.

Epele, Maria. 2001. "Excess, Scarcity & Desire among Drug-Using Sex Workers." *Body and Society* 7:161–179.

Gaarder, Emily and Joanne Belknap. 2002. "Tenuous Borders: Girls Transferred to Adult Court." *Criminology* 40:481–517.

Gilfis, Mary E. 1992. "From Victims to Survivors to Offenders: Women's Routes of Entry and Immersion into Street Crime." *Women and Criminal Justice* 4:63–90.

Gossop, Michael, Beverly Powes, Paul Griffiths, and John Strang. 1994. "Sexual Behavior and Its Relationship to Drug-Taking among Prostitutes in South London." *Addiction* 89:961–970.

Hwang, Shu-Ling and Olwen Bedford. 2003. "Precursors and Pathways to Juvenile Prostitution in Taiwan." *Journal of Sex Research* 40:201–210.

James, Jennifer and Jane Meyerding. 1977. "Early Sexual Experience and Prostitution." *American Journal of Psychiatry* 134:1381–185.

Kramer, Lisa A. and Ellen C. Berg. 2003. "A Survival Analysis of Timing of Entry into Prostitution: The Differential Impact of Race, Educational Level, and Childhood/ Adolescent Risk Factors." *Sociological Inquiry* 73:511–528.

Kruttschnitt, Candace. 1996. "Contributions of Quantitative Methods to the Study of Gender and Crime or Bootstrapping Our Way into the Theoretical Thicket." *Journal of Quantitative Criminology* 12:135–161.

Laub, John H. and Robert J. Sampson. 2003. *Shared Beginnings, Divergent Lives: Delinquent Boys to Age 70*. Cambridge, MA: Harvard.

Miller, Eleanor. 1986. *Street Woman*. Philadelphia, PA: Temple University Press.

Miller, Jody. 1993. "Your Life Is on the Line Every Night You're on the Streets: Victimization and the Resistance among Street Prostitutes." *Humanity & Society* 17:422–446.

Miller, Jody and Martin D. Schwartz. 1995. "Rape Myths and Violence against Street Prostitutes." *Deviant Behavior* 16:1–23.

Moffitt, Terrie E. 1993. "The Neuropsychology of Conduct Disorder." *Development and Psychopathology* 5:135–152.

Mullins, Christopher W. and Richard Wright. 2003. "Gender, Social Networks, and Residential Burglary." *Criminology* 41:813–840.

Owen, Barbara and Barbara Bloom. 1995. "Profiling Women Offenders: Findings from National Surveys and a California Sample." *The Prison Journal* 75:165–185.

Porter, Judith and Louis Bonilla. 2009. "Drug Use, HIV, and the Ecology of Street Prostitution." Pp. 163–186 in *Sex for Sale*, edited by Ronald Weitzer. New York: Routledge.

Potterat, John J., Devon D. Brewer, Stephen Q. Muth, Richard B. Rothenberg, Donald E. Woodhouse, John B. Muth, Heather K. Stites, and Stuart Brody. 2004. "Mortality in a Longterm Open Cohort of Prostitute Women." *American Journal of Epidemiology* 159:778–785.

Potterat, John J., Lynanne Phillips, Richard B. Rothenberg, and William W. Darrow. 1985. "On Becoming a Prostitute: An Exploratory Case-Comparison Study." *The Journal of Sex Research* 20:329–336.

Potterat, John J., Richard B. Rothenberg, Stephen Q. Muth, William W. Darrow, and Lynanne Phillips-Plummer. 1998. "Pathways to Prostitution: The Chronology of Sexual and Drug Abuse Milestones." *Journal of Sex Research* 35:333–340.

Raphael, Jody and Deborah Shapiro. 2002. "Sisters Speak Out: The Lives and Needs of Prostituted Women in Chicago." Chicago, IL: Center for Impact Research.

Reisig, Michael D., Kristy Holtfreter, and Merry Morash. 2006. "Assessing Recidivism Risk across Female Pathways to Crime." *Justice Quarterly* 23:384–405.

Richie, Beth. 1996. *Compelled to Crime: The Gender Entrapment of Battered Black Women*. New York: Routledge.

Rosen, Eva and Sudhir Alladi Venkatesh. 2008. "A Perversion of Choice: Sex Work Offers Just Enough in Chicago's Urban Ghetto." *Journal of Contemporary Ethnography* 37:417–441.

Sampson, Robert and John Laub. 1993. *Crime in the Making: Pathways and Turning Points through Life*. Cambridge, MA: Harvard University Press.

Sanders, Teela. 2007. "Becoming an Ex-Sex Worker: Making Transitions Out of a Deviant Career." *Feminist Criminology* 2:74–95.

Seng, Magnus J. 1989. "Child Sexual Abuse and Adolescent Prostitution: A Comparative Analysis." *Adolescence* 24:665–675.

Sharpe, Karen. 1998. *Red Light, Blue Light: Prostitutes, Punters, and the Police.* London: Ashgate.

Simons, Ronald L. and Les B. Witbeck. 1991. "Sexual Abuse as a Precursor to Prostitution and Victimization among Adolescent and Adult Homeless Women." *Journal of Family Issues* 12: 361–379.

Simpson, Sally S., Jennifer L. Yahner, and Laura Dugan. 2008. "Understanding Women's Pathways to Jail: Analysing the Lives of Incarcerated Women." *The Australian and New Zealand Journal of Criminology* 41:84–108.

Sutherland, Edwin H. 1939. *Principles of Criminology.* Philadelphia, PA: Lippincott.

Tyler, Kimberly A., Dan R. Hoyt, and Les B. Whitbeck. 2000. "The Effects of Early Sexual Abuse on Later Sexual Victimization among Female Homeless and Runaway Adolescents." *Journal of Interpersonal Violence* 15:235–240.

Weitzer, Ronald. 2009. "Sociology of Sex Work." *Annual Review of Sociology* 35:213–234.

West, Carolyn and Linda Williams. 2000. "Adult Sexual Revictimization among Black Women Sexually Abused in Childhood: A Prospective Examination of Serious Consequences of Abuse." *Child Maltreatment* 5:49–58.

Whelehan, Patricia. 2001. *An Anthropological Perspective on Prostitution: The World's Oldest Profession.* Lewiston, NY: Edwin Mellen Press.

Williamson, Celia and Lynda M. Baker. 2009. "Women in Street-Based Prostitution: A Typology of Their Work Styles." *Qualitative Social Work* 8:27–44.

Williamson, Celia and T. Cluse-Tolar. 2002. "Pimp-Controlled Prostitution." *Violence Against Women* 8:1074–1092.

Young, Amy M., Carol Boyd, and Amy Hubbell. 2000. "Prostitution, Drug Use, and Coping with Psychological Distress." *Journal of Drug Issues* 3:789–800.

DISCUSSION QUESTIONS

1. How did the life circumstances of women entering prostitution differ for those under the age of 18 and for those over the age of 18?

2. How did time on the streets impact the shame and stigma that women experience?

3. What toll does street prostitution have on women and how does time increase this toll?

Processing and Sentencing of Female Offenders

As you learned in Section I, the gender gap in crime has remained consistent since 1990. For most crime types, the increase in female arrests reflects not an increase in offending rates of women but rather a shift in policies to arrest and process cases within the criminal justice system that historically had been treated on an informal basis (Rennison, 2009; Steffensmeier & Allan, 1996; Steffensmeier, Zhong, Ackerman, Schwartz, & Agha, 2006). This section highlights the different ways in which gender bias occurs in the processing and sentencing of female offenders.

How might we explain the presence of gender bias in the processing of female offenders? Research highlights that women and girls can be treated differently from their male counterparts by agents of social control, such as police, prosecutors, and judges, as a result of their gender. Gender bias can occur in two different ways: (1) Women can receive lenient treatment as a result of their gender, or (2) women may be treated harsher as a result of their gender. These two competing perspectives are known as the **chivalry** hypothesis and the **evil woman hypothesis**. The chivalry hypothesis suggests that women receive preferential treatment by the justice system. As one of the first scholars on this issue, Otto Pollak (1950) noted that agents of the criminal justice system are reluctant to criminalize women, even though their behaviors may be just as criminal as their male counterparts. However, this leniency can be costly, as it reinforces a system whereby women are denied an equal status with men in society (Belknap, 2007). While most research indicates the presence of chivalrous practices toward women, the potential for sex discrimination against women exists when they are treated more harshly than their male counterparts, even when charged with the same offense. Here, the evil woman hypothesis suggests that women are punished not only for violating the law but also for breaking the socialized norms of gender-role expectations (Nagel & Hagan, 1983).

Research throughout the past 40 years is inconclusive about whether or not girls receive chivalrous treatment. While the majority of studies indicate that girls do receive leniency in the criminal justice system, the presence of chivalry is dependent on several factors. This section focuses on five general themes in assessing the effects of chivalry on the processing and treatment of female offenders: (1) the stage of the criminal system, (2) the race and ethnicity of the offender, (3) the effects of the war on drugs for female offenders, (4) the effect of legal and extralegal characteristics, and (5) the effects of sentencing guidelines on judicial decision making. This section concludes with a discussion of some of the international sentencing practices of women.

Stage of the Criminal Justice System

Chivalry can occur at different stages of the criminal justice system. Much of the research on whether women benefit from chivalrous treatment looks only at one stage of the criminal justice process. This single snapshot approach makes it difficult to assess the potential effects of chivalrous treatment for each case, region, or time frame. In addition, it can be difficult to determine how the effects of chivalry at one stage of the criminal justice process may impact subsequent decisions as a case moves throughout the system.

Much of our data about crime begins at the arrest stage, since this is generally the first involvement that an offender will have with the criminal justice system. However, the experience of chivalrous treatment can actually begin prior to an arrest. Police officers exercise discretion as part of their everyday duties. As a result, offenders may experience chivalrous treatment as a result of their gender. For example, police use discretion in determining when to engage in stop and frisk tactics. Brunson and Miller (2006) noted that African American boys receive greater levels of attention by police officers compared to girls of the same race, yet this may also be dictated by offense type. For example, the girls in this study indicated that their involvement with the police was typically related to incidents of truancy, curfew violations, and other low-level offenses. In contrast, the police generally made contact with the boys over higher criminal offenses, such as drug possession or distribution.

> The police will mess with the males quicker than the females. If it's a group of girls standing across the street and it's a group of dudes standing across the street, [the police] fina [getting ready to] shine they lights on the dudes and they ain't fina mess with the girls. (Brunson & Miller, 2006, p. 539)

Contrary to popular belief, women do not always experience chivalrous treatment. In an early study on gender, chivalry, and arrest practices, Visher (1983) found that it was not just gender that affected whether chivalrous treatment was extended but that variables such as age, race, and behavior also had a strong effect on whether police exercised their discretion in favor of the women. For example, older Caucasian women benefited the most from chivalrous treatment by the police. In comparison, younger women and women of color were significantly more likely to be arrested, even in cases involving similar offenses.

In Section VII you learned about how some of the changes in police practices and school policies have altered how the juvenile justice system has responded to cases of delinquency. We have also seen a ripple effect in the arrests of women as a result of the introduction of mandatory arrest policies in intimate partner abuse cases. Policies such as these have altered how police deal with cases of simple assault, and it is girls that are disproportionately impacted by these changes. Here, the message has been that girls who act outside of traditional normative expectations for behavior are treated more harshly by police (Strom, Warner, Tichavsky, & Zahn, 2010).

At the pretrial stage, research indicates that women are more likely to be treated leniently than men. In these cases, the power of discretion is held by the prosecutor, who determines the charges that will be filed against an

© Gene Blevins/LA DailyNews/Corbis

▲ **Photo 9.1** Lindsay Lohan enters the Los Angeles courthouse for a probation violation hearing. Lohan has had several run-ins with the law due to substance abuse yet has spent very little time behind bars, leaving many to suggest that she benefits from chivalrous treatment due to her gender and celebrity status.

offender and whether charge-reduction strategies will be employed in order to secure a guilty plea. Charge-reduction strategies involve a guilty plea by an offender in exchange for a lesser charge and a reduction in sentence. Some research indicates that women are less likely to have charges filed against them or are more likely to receive charge reductions, compared to their male counterparts (Albonetti, 1986; Saulters-Tubbs, 1993). Research by Spohn, Gruhl, and Welch (1987) found that women of all ethnic groups were more likely, compared to men of all ethnic groups, to benefit from a charge reduction. Given the shift toward determinant sentencing structures and the reduction of judicial discretion, the power of the prosecutor in this practice increases. While research by Wooldredge and Griffin (2005) indicated an increase in the practice of charge reductions under state sentencing guidelines in Ohio, their results indicated that women did not benefit from this practice any more or less than male offenders. While seriousness of crime and criminal history remain the best predictors of receiving a charge reduction, research is inconclusive on the issue of the effect of gender on this process.

Of all the stages of the criminal justice system, the likelihood of pretrial release is the least studied; given that this stage has one of the highest potentials for discretion by prosecutors and the judiciary, it is important to assess whether gender plays a role in the decision to detain someone prior to trial. Research by Demuth and Steffensmeier (2004) found that females are less likely to be detained at the pretrial stage than men, controlling for factors such as offense severity and criminal history. Several factors can influence the presence of chivalrous treatment for women at this stage. Offense type affects this process, as female offenders who were charged with property-based offenses were less likely to receive pretrial detention compared to males with similar offenses (Ball & Bostaph, 2009). Generally speaking, females are typically viewed as less dangerous than their male counterparts, making them less likely to be detained during the pretrial process (Leiber, Brubacker, & Fox, 2009). Women are also more likely to have significant ties to the community, such as family and childrearing duties, which make it less likely that they will fail to appear for future court proceedings (Steffensmeier, Kramer, & Streifel, 1993). Offense type also plays a role as women who are charged with drug or property crimes are less likely to be detained prior to trial compared to women who engage in crimes against persons (Freiburger & Hilinski, 2010). This gender bias appears throughout the pretrial process, as women are 30% less likely than men to be detained prior to trial and also receive lower bail amounts than men (and therefore run less risk of being forced to remain in custody due to an inability to make bail). While this preferential treatment exists for women compared to men regardless of race and ethnicity, White women do receive the greatest leniency compared to Hispanic and Black women. Here, research indicates that women of color are less likely to be able to post bond, resulting in their detention at the pretrial stage, compared to White women.

Gender also has a significant impact on how cases are disposed of by the courts. In Florida, a felony conviction carries a number of consequences beyond the criminal justice system. Felons lose many of their civil rights as well as professional certifications required for certain occupations, and the restoration of these rights is not an automatic process following the completion of their sentence and requires a lengthy application process. One way of avoiding this process is to avoid a formal conviction and instead be sentenced by the judge to probation. Under state law, the adjudication of the offender is delayed, and if they successfully complete the terms and conditions of their probation, they are not considered a convicted felon (although the case remains a part of their criminal record). Women are more likely to benefit from these withheld adjudications compared to men. This practice continues even in violent offenses, such as assault, and in some cases, women were more likely to benefit from a withheld adjudication for crimes that are dominated by male offenders, such as drug manufacturing (Ryon, 2013).

The appearance of preferential or chivalrous treatment in the early stages of criminal justice processing also affects how women and girls will be treated in later stages. Females who already receive favorable treatment by prosecutors continue to receive such chivalrous treatment as their case progresses. The majority of research indicates that women are more likely to receive chivalrous treatment at sentencing. At this stage of the criminal justice process, women are less likely to be viewed as dangerous (Freiburger & Hilinski, 2010) and are less likely to recidivate (Daly, 1994). Indeed, women are viewed as better candidates for probation supervision compared to male offenders (Freiburger & Hilinski, 2010). Research on the decision to incarcerate reflects that women are less likely to be sent to jail or prison for their crimes, compared to men (Spohn & Beichner, 2000). Offense type also affects the relationship between gender and sentencing, as women are less likely to receive prison sentences for property and drug cases than their male counterparts. In those cases where women are incarcerated for these crimes, their sentences are significantly shorter compared to the sentence length for male property and drug offenders. Here, the disparity in sentencing can be attributed to the levels of discretion exercised by judges in making sentencing decisions (Rodriguez, Curry, & Lee, 2006). Even in cases where sentencing guidelines are used, such as in the federal system, the odds of a substantial assistance departure are significantly greater for women (Ortiz & Spohn, 2014; Spohn & Belenko, 2013). Even in cases where offenders are already involved in the criminal justice system and have received a new charge, women are more likely to receive a substantial assistance departure to either prevent women from having to serve long terms of incarceration or to divert women already under probation supervision from having to go to prison (Ortiz & Spohn, 2014). Although there is a consistent pattern of the preferential treatment in sentencing, not all crime types in all jurisdictions report this experience. While several studies on drug offenders find that women receive preferential treatment by the courts in terms of the decision to incarcerate and the length of the sentence, research by Koeppel (2012) finds that there are no differences in the sentencing practices between male and female property offenders in rural areas.

Race Effects and the Processing of Female Offenders

Historically, African American women have been punished more harshly than White women. This punishment reflected not only a racial bias but also a pattern consistent with their levels of offending, as women of color engaged in higher levels of crimes than White women. In many cases, the types of offenses committed by women of color had more in common with male offenders. Over time, research indicated that the offending patterns of White women shifted such that women, regardless of race or ethnic status, engaged in similar levels of offending.

Significant bodies of research address concerns over the differential processing of male offenders on the basis of race and ethnicity. Here, research consistently agrees that men of color are overrepresented at every stage of the criminal justice system. Given these findings, what effect does discrimination have for female offenders? Several scholars have suggested that chivalry is selective and is more likely to advantage White females over women of color. Research indicates that the rates of incarceration for White women have increased by 47% between 2000 and 2009—during the same period, incarceration rates for Black women declined 31%. However, women of color still dominate the statistics given their proportion in the population. The rate of incarceration for Black women is 142 per 100,000 (compared to 50 per 100,000 for White women; Mauer, 2013). Given these findings, some researchers have questions on whether discriminatory views about women offenders, and particularly women of color, may negatively influence prosecutorial and judicial decision-making processes (Gilbert, 2001). Even though women of color may be deemed as more "salvageable" than men of color (Spohn & Brennan, 2011), the potential effect of racial bias can be significant considering the significant powers of prosecutors in making charge decisions, offering plea agreements and charge reductions, and making sentence recommendations.

You have already learned that gender can impact the decision to hold someone in custody prior to trial. But how does race play into this process? Whereas interactions between gender and race can give the impression that women of color are treated more harshly by the criminal justice system, research findings indicate that the bias may be one of economics rather than race. Katz and Spohn (1995) found that White women are more likely to be released from custody during the pretrial stages, compared to Black women, as a result of the ability to fulfill demands for bail. When defendants cannot make bail, there may be incentives to accept a plea deal that would limit the time spent in custody. Yet this "freedom" comes at a cost, as the label of an *ex-felon* can affect them and limit their opportunities for the rest of their lives. This relationship between race/ethnicity, **legal factors,** and **extralegal factors** can also impact sentencing outcomes. For example, research by Brennan (2006) demonstrated that misdemeanor cases involving female defendants were more likely to be sentenced to incarceration if the offender had a prior criminal history. Here, race serves as an intermediating effect as the Black women in this study had greater criminal histories compared to White and Hispanic women. In addition, women of color were less likely to have strong positive ties to their community. This is a factor that also increased the likelihood of incarceration in these cases.

Research also finds that skin tone can influence the length of a prison sentence for women of color. Black women who are described as "light skinned" received shorter sentences by 12%, compared to offenders that were described as "darker" skinned (Viglione, Hannon, & DeFina, 2011). Similar findings are also demonstrated in research on men of color, where darker Black males were more likely to receive harsher punishments by the criminal justice system compared to lighter skinned Black males (Gyimah-Brempong & Price, 2006).

However, not all research demonstrates that girls and women of color suffer from harsher treatment by the courts. Some scholars find evidence that girls and women of color have benefited from chivalrous treatment. Here, scholars suggest that the preferential treatment of African American girls by judges is seen as an attempt to remedy the biased decision making of criminal justice actors during earlier stages of the criminal justice process that may have led to harsher attention (lack of pretrial release and bail options, less likely to receive charge reductions, etc.; Leiber et al., 2009). Race can have an effect on the sentencing practices for both adult and juvenile offenders. In one study on sentencing outcomes for juveniles, Guevara, Herz, and Spohn (2008) indicated that race effects did not always mean that girls of color were treated more harshly than White girls. Their results indicate that White females were more likely to receive an out-of-home placement. While many would suggest that an out-of-home placement is a more significant sanction, their research indicates that juvenile court officials may be engaging in "child saving" tactics in an effort to rehabilitate young offenders. In another study involving juvenile court practices, race did not impact the decision to detain youth in detention, as girls of all races and ethnicities were more likely to receive leniency in this decision compared to boys (Maggard, Higgins, & Chappell, 2013).

It is important to note that while research on race, ethnicity, and processing can demonstrate valuable results for women of color in the criminal justice system, these results are significantly limited. Much of the research investigating race and gender effects involves a comparison between White and Black women. It has been only within the last few decades that scholars have extended the discussion to the ethnicity and included data on Hispanic/Latina females. Few studies investigate how race can impact the processing for other racial and ethnic groups, such as Asian American, Native Americans, or Pacific Islanders. In addition, while recent implementations of the U.S. Census have utilized the category of "one race or more" to acknowledge that many women of color identify as bi- or multiracial, few studies on the processing of female offenders included this variable in their research. One explanation for this stems from the different sources of data that are used by scholars, such as official data statistics like the Uniform

Crime Reports. These sources are limited in how they collect data about race and ethnicity. In many cases, these assessments about race come not from how the offender self-identifies, but from the perceptions of police officers on the streets, court officials, and correctional personnel.

The War on Drugs and Its Effects for Women

The heightened frenzy about the *dangerousness* of drugs has fueled the war on drugs into an epidemic. The war on drugs first appeared as an issue of public policy in 1971, when President Richard Nixon called for a national drug policy in response to the rise of drug-related juvenile violence. Over the next decade, controlled substances, such as cocaine, were illegally smuggled into the United States by drug kingpins and cartels throughout Mexico and South America (National Public Radio, n.d.).

Since the 1980s and the passage of the Anti-Drug Abuse Act, the incarceration rates for both men and women have skyrocketed. Figure 9.1 demonstrates how these new laws impacted the arrest rates for women. Using 1972 data as a baseline, the passage of the first drug bill by President Ronald Reagan led the arrest rates for drug cases to skyrocket (Merolla, 2008). Yet the majority of persons imprisoned on these charges are not the dangerous traffickers who bring drugs into neighborhoods and place families and children at risk. Rather, it is the drug user who is at

Figure 9.1   Female Arrests for All Crimes Versus Drug Arrests, 1972–2004

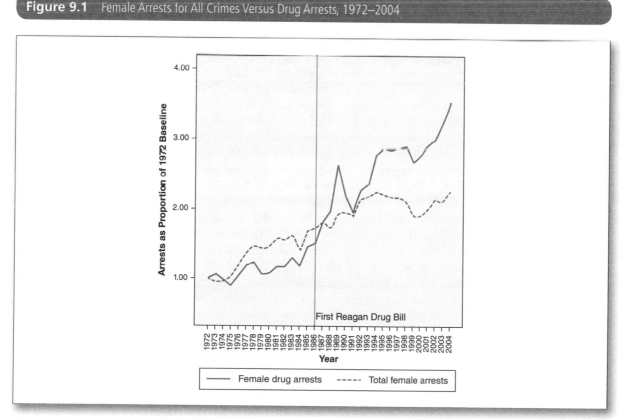

SOURCE: Merolla (2008).

the greatest risk for arrest and imprisonment. In response to the social fears about crack cocaine in the inner city, lawmakers developed tough-on-crime sentencing structures designed to increase the punishments for crack cocaine. Sentencing disparities between powder and crack created a system whereby drug users were treated the same as mid-level dealers. In 1995, the U.S. Sentencing Commission released a report highlighting the racial effects of the crack and powder cocaine sentencing practices and advised Congress to make changes to the mandatory sentencing practices to reduce the discrepancies. Their suggestions fell on deaf ears among congressional members who did nothing to change these laws. For the next 15 years, cases of crack and powder cocaine perpetuated a 100:1 sentencing ratio, whereby offenders in possession of 5 grams of crack were treated the same as dealers in possession of 500 grams of powder cocaine. In 2010, President Obama signed the Fair Sentencing Act, which reduced the disparity between crack and powder cocaine sentences to a ratio of 18:1. Under this revised law, offenders receive a 5-year mandatory minimum sentence for possessing 28 grams of crack (compared to 5 grams under the old law) and a 10-year sentence for possessing more than 280 grams of crack cocaine.

Prior to the war on drugs and mandatory sentencing structures, most nonviolent drug conviction sentences were handled within community correction divisions. Offenders typically received community service, drug treatment, and probation supervision. The introduction of mandatory minimum sentencing represented a major change in the processing of drug offenders. While these sentencing structures are applied equally to male and female defendants, the extent of women's participation often differs substantially from male involvement in drug-related crimes. With the elimination of judicial discretion, judges were unable to assess the role that women played in these offenses. The result was a shift from community supervision to sentences of incarceration, regardless of the extent of women's participation in criminal drug-related activities (Merolla, 2008).

While the focus by the federal government on drugs shifted criminal justice practices during the mid and late-1980s, it was not until the 1990s that state governments began to alter their policies and practices related to drug crimes. In Florida, the legislature introduced the Criminal Punishment Code (CPC) in 1994. This new law called for increases not only for drug crimes but for many other crime categories as well. Here, the influence of the war on drugs reflected a shift toward a more punitive and retributive stance by criminal justice agencies. Not only did these changes have a significant effect for women in general, but these practices were also particularly detrimental for women of color. In particular, these changes increased the number of racial disparities in sentencing, an ironic consequence given that the focus of the mandatory minimum sentencing practices at the federal level were intended to reduce such disparities by race and ethnicity. For example, prior to the implementation of the CPC in Florida, sentences were 27% higher for Black women and 24% greater for Hispanic/Latina women, compared to those sentences given to White women. By 2003, these disparities had increased to 38% longer sentences for women of color, compared to White women.

While much of the attention about the war on drugs has focused on the crack and powder cocaine debate (and the resulting disparities in sentencing between these two substances), these substances no longer reflect the drug of choice trends that currently exist for women. Crack cocaine has been replaced by methamphetamines, to the point where meth has been labeled as the "pink collar crack" (Campbell, 2000). Similar to the changes that occurred to drug laws about crack and powder cocaine in the 1980s and 90s, recent history has seen changes to the laws on methamphetamine production and use that have not only increased likelihood of incarceration but has also increased the sentence length for these crimes as well. As a result, the number of women sentenced for a meth-related drug conviction increased from 10.3% in 1996 to 23.0% in 2006 (Bush-Baskette, 2010). The length of sentences increased 300% as well during this time frame. While the majority of women convicted and sentenced for meth-related offenses were once White (99.5% in 1996), the representation of women of color in these cases is increasing (27% in 2006; Bush-Baskette & Smith, 2012).

The shift to incarceration from community supervision had a detrimental effect on women. Between 1986 and 1991, the incarceration rates of women for drug-related offenses increased 433%, compared to a 283% increase for males (Bush-Baskette, 2000). Drug-convicted women make up 72% of the incarcerated population at the federal level

(Greenfeld & Snell, 2000). Most of these cases involve women as users of illegal substances. Even in the small proportion of cases where women are involved in the sale of drugs, they rarely participate in mid- or high-level management in the illegal drug market, often due to sexism within the drug economy (Maher, 2004a). In addition, the presence of crack in the 1980s and meth in the 90s shifted the culture of the street economy, particularly for women involved in acts of prostitution. The highly addictive nature of these substances led more women to the streets in an effort to find a way to get their next high. At the same time, the flood of women in search of sex work created an economy whereby the value of sexual services significantly decreased.

While recent changes in federal drug sentencing laws have reduced the disparities in sentencing, the damage has already been done. The effects of these laws created a new system of criminal justice where the courts are overloaded with drug possession and distribution cases, and the growth of the prison economy has reached epic proportions. Yet these efforts appear to have done little to stem the use and sale of such controlled substances. Indeed, the overall rates of crimes other than drug-related cases have changed little during the last 40 years. The effects of these policies has produced significant consequences for families and communities, particularly given the increase in the incarceration rates of women. Section X explores in depth the consequences in the incarceration of women, both for herself and her family, as well as her community. It is these consequences that have led some scholars to suggest that the war on drugs has in effect become a war on women (Chesney-Lind, 1997).

⬚ The Effects of Extralegal Factors on Sentencing Women

The assessment of whether women benefit from chivalrous treatment by the criminal justice system is not as simple as comparing the sentences granted to men and women in general. Many factors must be considered, including the severity of the offense, the criminal record of the offender, the levels of injury experienced by the victim, and the culpability, or blameworthiness, of the offender. For example, women generally have a less extensive criminal history than males and are less likely to engage in violent offenses or play a major role in criminal offenses.

In assessing whether women receive chivalrous treatment, it is important to control for these legal and extralegal variables. Research indicates that legal variables do affect the decision-making process for both males and females, albeit in different ways. As you learned earlier in this section, the effects of gender vary with each stage of the criminal justice system. For example, offense type and criminal history influence whether a defendant will be detained during the pretrial stages or receive charge reductions and leniency in sentencing.

Not only do legal factors, such as criminal history and offense severity, appear to affect the pretrial decision process for women, but extralegal factors, such as the type of attorney, affect as well the likelihood of pretrial release for women. Women who were able to hire a private attorney were 2.5 times more likely to make bail, compared to those women who relied on the services of a public defender. Clearly, the ability to hire (and financially afford) a private attorney is linked to the ability to satisfy the financial demands of bail as set by the court. In comparison, women who were represented by a public defender were twice as likely to be detained at the pretrial stage (Ball & Bostaph, 2009). Ties to the community (such as family life) can also serve as an extralegal factor that can mediate sentencing practices. For example, motherhood mitigates the likelihood of a prison sentence, as women with dependent children are less likely to be incarcerated compared to women who do not have children. In these cases, judges appear to consider the social costs of imprisoning mothers and the effects of incarceration on children, particularly in cases of nonviolent or drug offenses (Spohn & Beichner, 2000). Research indicates that variables such as single parenthood and pregnancy have been used by judges to justify a departure from strict sentencing guidelines and offer a reduced sentence (Raeder, 1995). Here, it is not gender specifically that accounts for mitigation but rather concern for the family (as non-"familied" women do not receive similar instances of leniency in sentencing). These departures have been confirmed by the courts in cases such as *U.S. v. Johnson*, 964 F.2d 124 (2d Cir. 1992). Indeed, such departures are not reserved exclusively for women but can also benefit male defendants who are the primary caregiver for minor children (see *U.S. v. Cabell*, 890 F. Supp. 13, 19 [D.D.C. 1995], which granted a departure from the sentencing guidelines for a male offender who was the primary caregiver for the children of his deceased sister).

The Effects of Sentencing Guidelines on Judicial Decision Making

Throughout most of history, judges have had discretion in handing out sentences to offenders. In most cases, judges were free to impose just about any type of sentence, from probation to incarceration. Essentially, the only guidance for decision making came from the judge's own value system and beliefs in justice. This created a process whereby there was no consistency in sentencing, and offenders received dramatically different sentences for the same offenses, whereby the outcome depended on which judge heard their case. While this practice allowed for individualized justice based on the needs of offenders and their potential for rehabilitation, it also left the door open for the potential of bias based on the age, race, ethnicity, and gender of the offender.

During the 1970s, the faith in rehabilitation for corrections began to wane and was replaced with the theory of "just deserts," a retributive philosophy that aimed to increase the punishment of offenders for their crimes against society. In an effort to reform sentencing practices and reduce the levels of discretion within the judiciary, many jurisdictions developed sentencing guidelines to create systems by which offenders would receive similar sentences for similar crimes. At the heart of this campaign was an attempt to regulate sentencing practices and eliminate racial, gender, and class-based discrimination in courts. As part of the Sentencing Reform Act of 1984, the U.S. Sentencing Commission was tasked with crafting sentencing guidelines at the federal level. Since their implementation in November 1987, these guidelines have been criticized for being too rigid and unnecessarily harsh. In many cases, these criticisms reflect a growing concern that judges are now unable to consider the unique circumstances of the crime or characteristics of the offender. Indeed, the only standardized factors that are to be considered under the federal sentencing guidelines are the offense committed, the presence of aggravating or mitigating circumstances, and the criminal history of the offender.

Prior to sentencing reform at the federal level, the majority of female offenders were sentenced to community-based programs, such as probation. Under federal sentencing guidelines, the numbers of incarcerated women are not only expanding, but the length of time that they will spend in custody has increased as well.

Research by Koons-Witt (2006) investigates the effects of gender in sentencing in Minnesota. Minnesota first implemented sentencing guidelines in 1980. Like the federal sentencing guidelines, Minnesota founded their guidelines on a retributive philosophy focused on punishment for the offender. The guidelines were designed to be neutral on race, gender, class, and social factors. However, the courts can consider aggravating and mitigating factors, such as the offender's role in the crime, if they make a decision outside of the sentencing guidelines. Koons-Witt investigated the influence of gender at three distinct points in time: prior to the adoption of sentencing guidelines in Minnesota, following their introduction (early implementation 1981–1984), and in 1994, 14 years after the sentencing guidelines were implemented (late implementation). Her research indicated that female offenders were more likely to be older than their male counterparts and have a greater number of dependent children. In contrast, men were faced with more serious crimes, were more likely to be under community supervision at the time of the current offense, and had more significant criminal histories. Prior to the implementation of sentencing guidelines, gender did not appear to have an effect on sentencing guidelines. This finding contradicted the findings of other research, which illustrated that judges did treat female offenders in a chivalrous fashion. The one exception for Koons-Witt's findings was that sentences were reduced for women who had dependent children. Following the early implementation of sentencing guidelines (1981–1984), several legal outcomes increased the potential for incarceration regardless of gender. These legal factors include prior criminal history and pretrial detention. This pattern was repeated during the late implementation time period (1994). However, the influence of extralegal factors reappeared during this time period, whereby women with dependent children were more likely to receive community correctional sentences compared to women who did not have children. In these cases, Koons-Witt suggests that the courts may be using the presence of dependent children as a mitigating factor in their decision to depart from the sentencing guidelines, producing an indirect effect for the preferential treatment of women.

Not all states deal with directive sentencing in the same way. While Minnesota's sentencing guidelines are similar in design to the federal sentencing guidelines, Pennsylvania's sentencing guidelines are not limited to just a retributive focus but also reference tenets of rehabilitation, deterrence, and incapacitation that allow for additional opportunities for judges to exercise their discretion. Pennsylvania first developed its sentencing guidelines in 1982 but suspended the practice and reinstated the practice with new provisions in 1988. Research by Blackwell, Holleran, and Finn (2008) investigated the effects of gender and sentencing during these three time periods (when the sentencing guidelines were in effect [1986–1987 and 1988–1990] and during the suspension [1987–1988]). Their findings demonstrated that Pennsylvania's sentencing guidelines did not reduce the sentencing disparities by sex. However, it is possible that the higher levels of judicial discretion within Pennsylvania's sentencing guidelines may also contribute to this effect.

Like Minnesota and Pennsylvania, Ohio also utilizes a guided sentencing structure. Felony crimes are organized into five basic categories. Unlike other state sentencing schemes, Ohio's law allows for increased opportunities for judicial discretion as each category has a wide range of options for sentencing (in terms of sentence length). Unlike other states, which demonstrated increases in the number of offenders sent to prison as well as the sentence length, Ohio documented decreases in both of these categories following its implementation of sentencing guidelines. These decreases were observed for both women and men and in the majority of offense categories (with drug cases as the exception). Racial disparities were also reduced for Black female offenders (Griffin & Wooldredge, 2006).

In contrast to the states that have either implemented or later disbanded sentencing guidelines, South Carolina considered the adoption of sentencing guidelines but ultimately failed to implement a practice. Over the two decades when the state debated whether to adopt such a schema, the state's sentencing commissions collected extensive data from the judicial, corrections, and probation/parole departments on all criminal offenses where the minimum punishment was a $500 fine or greater than 90 days in jail. Research by Koons-Witt, Sevigny, Burrow, and Hester (2012) examines these data to determine how factors such as gender, race, age, and offense type affect sentencing outcomes in a region that did not adopt structured guidelines. Their findings indicate that women benefited from chivalrous treatment by the court, as they were less likely to be incarcerated. When women were sent to prison, they received shorter sentences compared to male offenders. However, this benefit is selective, as it is extended only for White women and not for women of color.

Some critics of gender-neutral sentencing argue that directed sentencing structures like the federal sentencing guidelines have affected women in a negative fashion. These sentence structures assume that men and women have an equal position in society and, therefore, the unique needs of women do not need to be considered when making sentencing decisions. Whereas the intent behind the creation of sentencing guidelines and mandatory minimums was to standardize sentencing practices so that offenders with similar legal variables received similar sentences, the effect has been an increased length of incarceration sentences for both men and women. Given the inability of judicial officials to consider extralegal factors in making sentencing decisions, these efforts to equalize sentencing practices have significantly affected women.

◪ International Perspectives on the Processing of Female Offenders

While women in the United States have seen significant progress toward equality over the past century, research on gender and criminal justice processing indicate that women still experience gender bias. Here, women either positively

© POOL/Reuters/Corbis

▲ **Photo 9.2** Amanda Knox reacts after hearing the verdict during her appeal trial in Perugia. An Italian court cleared Knox and her former boyfriend of the 2007 killing of British student Meredith Kercher and ordered they be freed after nearly four years in prison for a crime they always denied committing. Seattle native Knox and Italian student Raffaele Sollecito had appealed against a 2009 verdict where prosecutors asserted that Kercher was murdered during a drug-fueled sexual assault. However, the Italian Supreme Court overturned the appeal, and the case was sent back for a retrial. In 2014, Knox and Sollecito were once again found guilty. Knox and Sollecito remain free during the appeal. If upheld, Knox could face extradition.

benefit from chivalrous treatment or are penalized in part by their gender and receive harsher punishments. Given these experiences throughout the United States, how do women fare in criminal justice systems in other regions of the world, particularly in countries with significant paternalistic views toward women?

China is one example where the paternalistic treatment of women is integrated within the cultural viewpoint. Women are considered as subordinate members of society. As a result, the legal system may treat women with "kid gloves." This need to protect women can potentially lead to reductions in punishment. As women's participation in criminal activity increases, the legal system is faced with how to respond to these cases. In China, there has been a documented increase in the number of women involved in drug possession and trafficking cases. Research by Liang, Lu, and Taylor (2009) indicates that female drug traffickers received significantly lower punishments compared to their male counterparts. In addition, women benefit from chivalrous treatments, even in cases where their offenses and criminal history were similar to male drug traffickers. The most important variable in these cases was the woman's behavior before the court—if the offender was remorseful about her actions and showed respect to the court, she received a more lenient sentence. However, chivalry was extended only to lower level offenders. In cases where the woman was facing a potential death sentence, the desire for equality between men and women overpowered any influence of patriarchy. The offender's demeanor is an important variable for South Taiwanese women as well. If a female defendant demonstrates a submissive and apologetic demeanor toward the judge, she benefits from leniency in her punishment. To a certain extent, the demeanor of the defendant is just as important as the offense type or the criminal history of the offender (Hsu & Wu, 2011).

Women in South Korea also benefit from chivalry in sentencing. Female offenders are less likely to be sent to prison and received significantly shorter sentences compared to male offenders. In addition, offenders who had a prior criminal history and were detained at the pretrial stage received significantly harsher punishments. This practice echoes many of the findings with women in the American justice system. Drug of choice also has a significant impact on sentence outcomes. While cases involving methamphetamines received harsher punishments compared to marijuana cases (a likely response given stricter legal directives), female offenders were more likely to experience chivalrous treatment in terms of the length of sentence that is handed down, as male offenders received a longer sentence of incarceration than women.

However, chivalry may not be extended to all women. Research on sentencing practices in Australia looks at whether indigenous women receive preferential treatment by the courts. The term *indigenous* refers to a minority group that typifies the early inhabitants of a region. For example, we would identify *Native Americans* as an indigenous group in the United States. In Australia, a person who identifies as indigenous is of either aboriginal or Torres

Strait Islander origin. Research by Bond & Jeffries (2012) finds that women of indigenous status do receive preferential treatment by justice officials. In these cases, justice officials appear to consider how unique extralegal variables within these communities (such as the presence of trauma in early childhood and the marginalization of their cultural identity) may have a significant effect on their offending behaviors. These findings suggest that judicial officials weigh the risk that indigenous offenders pose to the community in comparison to the potential consequences that incarcerating indigenous persons for a significant period of time can have for these communities (Bond & Jeffries, 2009, 2012).

Unlike these examples where chivalry can benefit women in certain cases, women in Finland do not benefit from preferential treatment by justice officials. Unlike many of the jurisdictions where chivalry can have an impact, Finland is much more progressive in their policies and practices, and there are greater levels of gender equality between men and women throughout the workplace and home. For example, Finnish family-leave policies are more generous that those in the United States, which has created increased opportunities for mothers to participate in the labor force. Women are also more likely to be active in the political realm in Finland compared to women in the United States. These examples of gender equality have also translated to the criminal justice system, where women and men are considered equal under the law. Gender appears to have no significant effect on sentencing decisions, controlling for legal variables (such as criminal history and crime severity) and social factors (such as employment and family status; Kruttschnitt & Savolainen, 2009).

Conclusion

This chapter reviewed how and when preferential treatment is extended to female offenders. Whether chivalry exists within the criminal justice system is not an easy question to answer, as it is dependent on the stage of the criminal justice system, the intersections of race and ethnicity, legal and extralegal factors, and the implementation of determinate sentencing structures. Even in cases where research suggests that chivalrous treatment serves women through shorter sentences and an increased likelihood to sentence offenders to community-based sanctions over incarceration, not all scholars see this preferential treatment as a positive asset for women. For many, the presence of chivalry is also linked to these gender-role expectations whereby "preferential or punitive treatment is meted out based on the degree to which court actors perceive a female defendant as fitting the stereotype of either a good or bad woman" (Griffin & Wooldredge, 2006, p. 896). Not only does the potential for women to be punished for breaking gender role expectations exist (i.e., the evil woman hypothesis), but there exists as well a double-edged sword in fighting for special treatment models. Gender equality does not necessarily mean "sameness." Rather, this perspective suggests that women possess cultural and biological differences that should be considered in determining the effects of "justice." However, there is a potential danger in treating women differently as a result of these cultural and biological indicators. Given that the law affords reductions in sentencing based on mental capacity and age (juvenile offenders), to extend this treatment toward women can suggest that women "cannot be expected to conform their behavior to the norms of the law . . . thus when women are granted special treatment, they are reduced to the moral status of infants" (Nagel & Johnson, 2004, p. 208).

Summary

- Generally speaking, women are more likely to be released during pretrial stages, receive charge reductions, and receive a jail or probation supervision sentence.
- When women are incarcerated, they typically receive shorter sentences compared to men.
- Research on race and gender is mixed, with some studies indicating that women of color are treated more harshly than Whites, and other researchers finding that women of color are treated in a more lenient fashion.

- Legal factors, such as criminal history and offense type, affect the processing of women.
- Extralegal factors, such as the type of attorney and family status, can affect the likelihood of pretrial release for women.
- Sentencing guidelines have significantly increased the number of women serving time in U.S. prisons.

KEY TERMS

Chivalry	Extralegal factors	Sentencing guidelines
Evil woman hypothesis	Legal factors	

DISCUSSION QUESTIONS

1. Why is it important to study the processing of female offenders at each stage of the criminal justice system, versus just during the final disposition?

2. How do prosecutors and judges use their discretion to give preferential or chivalrous treatment toward women?

3. Which legal and extralegal factors appear to have the greatest impact on the processing of females? Which variables indicate preferential treatment of women in unexpected ways?

4. How do women in foreign countries benefit from chivalrous treatment?

Visit **www.sagepub.com/mallicoat2e** to access additional study tools including eFlashcards, web quizzes, web resources, video resources, and SAGE journal articles.

As you learned in the section introduction, gender can affect the sentencing decisions of females, often resulting in preferential treatment of female offenders. However, the majority of research on the issue of chivalry is conducted at the sentencing stage, after women may have already benefited from chivalrous treatment throughout the justice process. This reading explores whether women receive preferential treatment during the pretrial stage. The authors explore whether gender and race affect the decision to use preventive detention for offenders.

The Impact of Race, Gender, and Age on the Pretrial Decision

Tina L. Freiburger and Carly M. Hilinski

The majority of sentencing literature has examined the final sentencing decision (i.e., the in/out decision) and the sentence length. Few studies have examined earlier decision-making points in the judicial system, such as the pretrial release outcome. Because of this, advancements in final sentencing literature have not extended to pretrial release research. Most notably, the examination of race, gender, and age interactions has not been examined in the pretrial release research. Using the focal concerns perspective, the current research addresses this gap by examining how race, gender, and age affect defendants' odds of pretrial detention.

Instead of focusing solely on race or gender, current sentencing research has carefully examined how courtroom experiences vary across different race and gender combinations. The development of the focal concerns perspective by Steffensmeier et al. (Steffensmeier, 1980; Steffensmeier, Kramer, & Streifel, 1993; Steffensmeier, Ulmer, & Kramer, 1998) has greatly contributed to this line of sentencing research. The focal concerns perspective comprises the three focal concerns of blameworthiness, dangerousness, and practical constraints. Blameworthiness is largely determined by the legal factors of offense severity and prior record. Dangerousness is determined by variables such as offense type (e.g., personal, property, or drug), use of a weapon, and education and employment status of the defendant. Practical constraints consist of factors that influence a defendant's ability to serve a period of incarceration, including organizational factors such as jail space and case flow as well as individual factors such as familial responsibilities (e.g., child care duties and marital status).

According to focal concerns theory, it is through these three focal concerns that judges make their sentencing decisions. However, when judges make sentencing decisions, they must often do so with limited information and with limited time and do not have access to all of the information included in each of the three focal concerns. Thus, the demographic characteristics of an offender are often used to shape the three focal concerns. Certain demographic combinations, specifically age, gender, and race, are especially influential, as judges tend to view younger minority males as more dangerous and more blameworthy, leading to harsher sentences for these individuals (e.g., Spohn & Beichner, 2000; Steffensmeier &

SOURCE: Freiburger, T. L., & Hilinski, C. M. (2010). The impact of race, gender, and age on the pretrial decision. *Criminal Justice Review, 35*(3), 318–334.

Demuth, 2006; Steffensmeier, Kramer et al., 1993; Steffensmeier, Ulmer et al., 1998).

Current research examining these interactions has supported the focal concerns perspective. Specifically, this research has found that both Black and White females are treated more leniently than males (e.g., Freiburger & Hilinski, 2009; Steffensmeier & Demuth, 2006) and that Black males are sentenced more harshly than White males (e.g., Albonetti, 1997; Steffensmeier & Demuth, 2006; Steffensmeier, Ulmer et al., 1998). Research specifically focusing on the treatment of females, however, has been more mixed, with some studies finding that Black females are treated more leniently than White females (e.g., Bickle & Peterson, 1991; Spohn & Beichner, 2000; Steffensmeier & Demuth, 2006) whereas others have found the opposite (Crawford, 2000; Steffensmeier, Ulmer et al., 1998).

Prior sentencing studies also have found that age has varying impacts on the sentences of males and females and Black and White defendants (Steffensmeier, Ulmer et al., 1998). The results here also are mixed, with several studies finding that young Black men are treated most harshly (Spohn & Holleran, 2000; Steffensmeier, Ulmer et al., 1998) and others finding that middle-aged Black men are treated most harshly (Freiburger & Hilinski, 2009; Harrington & Spohn, 2007). Despite the numerous studies examining the impact of race, gender, and age on sentencing decisions, no studies have been conducted that examined the impact of gender, race, and age interactions on early court decisions. The current research fills this gap by examining how these three factors interact to affect the pretrial release decision.

Literature Review

The pretrial release decision is a crucial point in the judicial system. A common finding in the final sentencing research is that the pretrial release status of a defendant is significantly correlated with their [the individual's] likelihood of incarceration; offenders who are detained have a greater chance of receiving a sentence of incarceration (see Freiburger & Hilinski, 2009; Spohn & Beichner, 2000; Steffensmeier & Demuth, 2006). There is also less scrutiny on the pretrial release decision, which allows judges a great deal of discretion. This has led some researchers to argue that it might actually be subject to more bias in judicial

decision making (Hagan, 1974; Steffensmeier, 1980). Pretrial detention can further negatively affect defendants' final sentences by hindering their ability to participate in the preparation of their defense (Foote, 1954). Despite these findings illustrating the importance and significance of the pretrial decision, few studies have been conducted to examine the factors that affect this decision.

Race and Pretrial Release

The majority of research examining the effects of race on pretrial release decisions has found that White defendants receive greater leniency at this stage than Black defendants (Demuth, 2003; Katz & Spohn, 1995). Demuth (2003) and Katz and Spohn (1995) found that Black defendants were less likely to be released than White defendants. Although these studies failed to find a significant relationship between race and bail amount for both White and Black defendants, Demuth found that Black defendants were less likely to make bail. Furthermore, Demuth also found that Black defendants were significantly more likely to be ordered to detention (denied bail). No race difference was found, however, for Black and White defendants' odds of receiving a nonfinancial release (release on recognizance [ROR]) rather than bail.

Other studies examining slightly different outcome measures also have produced evidence to suggest White defendants are granted greater leniency in pretrial release. Patterson and Lynch (1991) found that non-White defendants were less likely than White defendants to receive bail amounts that were lower than the amount recommended by bail guidelines. However, they also found that White and non-White defendants were equally likely to receive bail amounts that were more than the amount recommended by bail guidelines. Albonetti (1989) did not find a direct race effect, though she did find that White defendants were less likely to be detained if they had higher levels of educational attainment and a higher income. White defendants' outcomes, however, were more negatively affected by increases in the severity of the offense.

Gender and Pretrial Release

Few studies have been conducted that examine the effect of gender on pretrial release and outcome. Overall, the studies that have examined this relationship have found that females were treated more leniently than male defendants. Daly (1987b) and Kruttschnitt and Green (1984) found that females were less likely to be detained prior to trial. Additional studies have found that females were more likely to be granted a nonfinancial release (Nagel, 1983) and be assigned lower bail amounts (Kruttschnitt, 1984). Unfortunately, no recent studies were located that focused solely on the effect of gender on pretrial release.

Race-Gender-Age Effects and Pretrial Release

Only one study has examined the interactions of race/ethnicity and gender. Demuth and Steffensmeier (2004) analyzed data from felony defendants in 75 of the most populous counties in state courts for the years 1990, 1992, 1994, and 1996. Their results indicated that race and gender significantly affected whether defendants were released prior to trial. More specifically, females were more likely to be released than males, and White defendants were more likely to be released than Black and Hispanic defendants. Although females experienced leniency at every decision point (they were less likely to be detained due to failure to make bail or ordered to detention, more likely to secure nonfinancial release, and receive lower bail), the findings for race were more mixed across the different decision points. Blacks were more likely to be detained than White defendants, but Black and White defendants were equally likely to be ordered to detention (not granted bail) and be given a nonfinancial release. Demuth and Steffensmeier (2004) also found that there was no difference in the amount of bail assigned to Black and White offenders. It appeared, therefore, that the race effect was due to Black defendants' failure to post bail.

When race and gender interactions were examined, female defendants were less likely to be detained than their male counterparts across all racial and ethnic groups. The gender gap, however, was the smallest for White defendants (followed by Black defendants and Hispanic defendants).

Using categorical gender/race variables, the results further indicated that White women were the least likely to be detained, followed by Black women, Hispanic women, White men, Black men, and Hispanic men.

We were not able to locate any studies that examined the interactions of race, gender, and age on pretrial release; however, prior sentencing studies have examined the interacting effects of these factors on the final sentencing decisions. The findings of these studies are mixed. Steffensmeier, Ulmer et al. (1998) found that young offenders were more likely to be sentenced to incarceration, with young Black males being treated the harshest. In their examination of sentencing decisions in Chicago, Miami, and Kansas City, Spohn and Holleran (2000) found that offenders aged 20–29 received the harshest sentences. When age and race were examined, they found that young and middle-aged Black males were more likely to be incarcerated than middle-aged White defendants. In Kansas City, young Black and White males had higher odds of incarceration than middle-aged White males.

Harrington and Spohn (2007) found that Black males in the middle age (30–39) category were less likely than White males of all age groups to be sentenced to probation versus jail. When the decision to sentence an offender to prison instead of jail was examined, however, the opposite was found. White males of all ages were more likely than middle-aged Black men to receive a prison sentence. Freiburger and Hilinski (2009) found that being young benefited White males but resulted in harsher sentences for Black males. Older Black males were only granted leniency in the decision to incarcerate in jail rather than prison. For Black females, age was not a significant predictor of sentencing. Young White women, however, were treated more leniently in the decision to sentence to probation or jail.

Previous studies that have examined the influence of race and gender on pretrial release decisions have failed to consider factors that are likely to influence release decisions. When judges make pretrial release decisions, they are typically concerned with the level of risk the offender poses to the community and the likelihood that the offender will return to court for future appearances (Goldkamp & Gottfredson, 1979). Although prior record and offense severity are important factors that judges consider in this stage, other factors such as marital status, education, community ties, and employment also are used to assess these concerns (Goldkamp & Gottfredson, 1979; Nagel, 1983; Petee, 1994; Walker, 1993). In addition, the focal concerns perspective notes these factors as influential to the focal concern of dangerousness (Steffensmeier,

Ulmer et al., 1998). The only previous study that examined race and gender interactions (Demuth & Steffenmeiser, 2004) did not assess the impact of these important factors. Additionally, no studies have examined the interactions of race, gender, and age on the pretrial release decision despite the fact that judges are differently influenced by these various combinations. Thus, the current study builds on the previous research by examining the effect of race, gender, and age interactions on pretrial release outcomes while considering other factors (e.g., income, education, and marital status) that have been linked to the pretrial release decision and the focal concerns perspective.

Methods

The current study examined the effects of race, gender, and age on the pretrial detention outcomes of felony offenders in an urban county in Michigan. The data analyzed contain information collected from presentence investigation reports completed for all offenders convicted of a personal, drug, property, or public order offense in the county during 2006. The original data set contained 3,316 offenders. We removed defendants who were Hispanic or of another ethnicity ($N = 73$) from the data set because a meaningful analysis was not possible with such a small number of cases; cases that were missing important information pertaining to offense severity level and prior record level ($N = 608$) also were removed from the data set because it is necessary to include these variables in sentencing research.[1] Thus, the final data set contained 2,635 cases.

Dependent Variable

The dependent variable in the current study was a dichotomized measure of the actual pretrial outcome, with 0 representing "defendants released prior to sentencing" and 1 representing those "detained prior to sentencing." Coding for this variable, and all independent variables, is included in Reading Table 17.1. Although we agree with prior research that argues that the pretrial release is best assessed through the examination of both the judicial decision and the actual outcome (see arguments by Demuth, 2003 and Demuth & Steffensmeier, 2004), the current data only allow for the assessment of the actual

pretrial outcome (whether the defendant was detained or released). This is considered a limitation of the current study; however, the pretrial outcome is the most telling of the decision points. It signifies the actual experience of the defendant by considering the consequences of pretrial detention (e.g., reduced ability to prepare defense and severed social ties due to incarceration). Despite this limitation, the ability to assess race, gender, and age interactions while including other facts relevant to pretrial release contributes substantially to the current literature.

Independent Variables

Several legal variables shown to be relevant in sentencing decisions were included in the analysis. The Michigan Statutory Sentencing Guideline's 6-point offense severity measure was used to control for the seriousness of the crime.[2] The state guideline's 7-point measure of prior record also was used.[3] The analysis also controlled for offense type through four separate dummy variables (property, drug, personal, and public order offense), with personal crimes left out as the reference category. A dummy variable also was included for current criminal justice supervision. Those who were on probation, parole, or incarcerated at the time of the bail decision were considered under criminal justice supervision and were coded as 1.[4]

The main extralegal variables of interest (gender, race, and age) also were included in the analysis. Gender was included and coded as 0 for female and 1 for male and race was coded as 0 for White and 1 for Black. Because age was found to have a curvilinear effect on pretrial detention, it was entered into the models as three categorical variables. Similar to prior research (Freiburger & Hilinski, 2009; Harrington & Spohn, 2007), the three age categories created were 15–29, 30–39, and 40+ years, with 30–39 being left out of the analysis as the reference variable.

Several other variables that measured defendants' stability in the community also were included in the models. These variables also were important in assessing the focal concerns perspective as these factors have been theorized by Steffensmeier and colleagues (Steffensmeier, 1980; Steffensmeier, Kramer et al., 1993; Steffensmeier, Ulmer et al., 1998) to affect judges' perceptions of dangerousness. None of the defendants in the sample had a

Reading Table 17.1 Description of Variables

Independent Variable	Description
Individual characteristics	
Age	Separate dummy variables for ages 15–29, 30–39, and 40+; age 30–39 is the reference category
Race	Black = 1, White = 0
Gender	Male = 1, Female = 0
Marital status	Married = 1, Not married = 0
High school (HS)	HS diploma/GED = 1, No HS diploma/GED = 0
Income over $75/month	Income over $75/month = 1, income less than $75/month = 0
Assets over $1,500	Assets over $1,500 = 1, assets < $1,500 = 0
Case characteristics	
Prior record variable (PRV)	7-category scale (1 = least serious, 7 = most serious[a])
Offense variable (OV)	6-category scale (1 = least serious, 6 = most serious)
Type of conviction charge	Separate dummy variables for property offense, public order offense, personal offense, and drug offense; personal offense is the reference category
CJS supervision	CJS supervision (probation, parole, incarceration) = 1, No CJS supervision = 0
Dependent variable	
Pretrial detention	Detention = 1, Release = 0

NOTE: CJS = Criminal Justice System supervision.

a. None of the cases in the current data set had a prior record score of 7.

college education; therefore, education was entered as a dichotomous variable of high school education or General Education Diploma (GED) coded as 1 or no high school education coded 0. Marital status also was included as a dummy variable; those who were not married were coded as 0 and those who were married were coded as 1. A direct employment measure was not available; however, two income variables were recorded in the presentence investigation (PSI) reports and were included in the analysis. The first assessed whether the defendant had an income of $75 or more a month (0 = no income

above $75 and 1 = income above $75). The second variable indicated whether the defendant had assets of $1,500 or more (0 = no assets totaling $1,500 and 1 = assets totaling $1,500 or more).

Results

The individual and case characteristics of the offenders included in the current research are presented in Reading Table 17.2. The majority of both male and female offenders were 15–29 years of age. Both male and female offenders were more likely to be White, unmarried, and without a high school diploma. Further examination of the descriptive statistics reveals that over half of the females had a monthly income over $75 but less than 40% of the males earned more than $75 per month. Across both males and females, only about 15% had assets that were worth $1,500 or more. Case characteristics reveal that male offenders were charged most often with a personal offense, but female offenders were most often charged with a property offense. Males were also more likely to be under some form of criminal justice supervision at the time of the current offense. Finally, both men and women were more likely to be released prior to trial.

We estimated the effect of race, gender, and age on pretrial release, using logistic regression models. First the effects of race, gender, and age were examined separately. The models were then split by gender and race; z scores also were calculated to determine whether the independent variables had a significantly different effect on the pretrial outcome for male and female and Black and White defendants. The final models contain categorical variables for gender and race and categorical variables for race, gender, and age combinations.

The logistic regression coefficients for pretrial detention are presented in Reading Table 17.3. Four models are presented. The first model presented displays the effects of age, race, and gender without the inclusion of any other independent variables. In this model, gender, race, and both age variables are significant. The variable for gender indicates males have a significantly greater likelihood of being detained than females. Black defendants had a significantly greater likelihood of detention than White defendants. The age variables show that young defendants and older defendants were less likely to be detained than offenders 30–39. Model 2 shows the coefficients after the income variables are controlled. Although the gender and age variables remain significant, race is no longer significant. When the legal variables are added in Model 3, the gender, age, and income variables remain significant. Race, however, is not significant. Therefore, it appears that the initial effect of race was due in part to differences in the financial capabilities of Black and White defendants.

The full model also is presented in Reading Table 17.3 and contains all of the independent variables. As shown in the table, males were significantly more likely to remain

detained than females; however, the coefficient for race was not significant. Young defendants and older defendants were less likely to be detained than defendants in the middle age category. Completing high school or obtaining a GED further resulted in a lower likelihood of being detained. Both income variables also were significant, indicating that defendants with an income over $75 a month and assets exceeding $1,500 were less likely to be detained.

In an attempt to garner a better understanding of the differences in the detention status of male and female defendants, we estimated split models to determine whether the same factors influenced the pretrial status of both groups. The results of this analysis are presented in Reading Table 17.4. Examination of the female model shows that race was significant in the pretrial status for females with Black female defendants having reduced odds of being detained compared to White females. Race did not, however, significantly affect the pretrial release status of males. The z score for race also was significant, indicating that the effect of race was significantly stronger for females than males. The coefficients for age indicate that young males were significantly less likely to be detained than males aged 30–39. Neither the age coefficient for females nor the z score for females was significant. Thus, the impact of age was not significantly different for males and females.

Further examination of the split models indicates that males and females ($b = .716, p < .01$) had an increased odds of detention with each increase in prior record severity. The z score reveals that prior record did not have a significantly greater impact on the pretrial release of males than females; however, it came very close to reaching significance. Severity of offense, conversely, was significant for males but not for females. The z score reveals that the difference was significant for males and females, with offense severity more strongly affecting males' pretrial detention status. Committing a property crime (compared to committing a personal crime) resulted in a decreased likelihood of being detained for females but not for males. The z score was significant, indicating that the differing effect was significant. The coefficient for drug offense was significant for both males and females. The z score also was significant, suggesting that committing a drug offense had a stronger impact for females than for males.

Reading Table 17.2 Descriptive Statistics

	Total (*n* = 2635)		Males (*n* = 2187)		Females (*n* = 448)	
	n	Percentage	*n*	Percentage	*n*	Percentage
Individual characteristics						
Age						
15–29	1,397	53.0	1,184	54.1	213	47.5
30–39	597	22.7	480	21.9	117	26.1
40+	641	24.3	523	23.9	118	26.3
Race						
White	1,421	53.9	1,139	52.1	282	62.9
Black	1,214	46.1	1,048	47.9	166	37.1
Gender						
Male	2,187	83.0	—	—	—	—
Female	448	17.0	—	—	—	—
Marital status						
Married	289	11.0	237	10.8	52	11.6
Not married	2,346	89.0	1,950	89.2	396	88.4
High school (HS)						
HS diploma/GED	1,277	48.5	1,070	48.8	207	46.2
No HS diploma/GED	1,358	51.5	1,117	51.1	241	53.8
Income over $75/month						
Yes	1,081	41.0	835	38.2	246	54.9
No	1,554	59.0	1,352	61.8	202	45.1
Assets over $1500						
Yes	382	14.5	314	14.4	68	15.2
No	2,253	85.5	1,873	85.6	380	84.8

(Continued)

Reading Table 17.2 (Continued)

	Total (n = 2635)		Males (n = 2187)		Females (n = 448)	
	n	Percentage	n	Percentage	n	Percentage
Case characteristics						
Prior record						
1	431	16.4	322	14.7	109	24.3
2	369	14.0	278	12.7	91	20.3
3	571	21.7	469	21.4	102	22.8
4	613	23.3	525	24.0	88	19.6
5	370	14.0	323	14.8	47	10.5
6	281	10.7	270	12.3	11	2.5
Offense severity						
1	1,323	50.2	1,081	49.4	242	54.0
2	812	30.8	672	30.7	140	31.3
3	298	11.3	245	11.2	53	11.8
4	98	3.7	88	4.0	10	2.2
5	70	2.7	69	3.2	1	0.2
6	34	1.3	32	1.5	2	0.4
Conviction charge						
Property offense	805	30.6	580	26.5	225	50.2
Public order offense	190	7.2	140	6.4	50	11.2
Personal offense	963	36.5	871	39.8	92	20.5
Drug offense	677	25.7	596	27.3	81	18.1
CJS supervision						
Supervision	912	34.6	774	64.6	138	30.8
No supervision	1,723	65.4	1,413	35.4	310	69.2
Pretrial detention						
Detained	960	36.4	866	39.6	94	21.0
Not detained	1,675	63.6	1,321	60.4	354	79.0

Reading Table 17.3 Logistic Regression Estimates

Variable	Model 1			Model 2			Model 3			Full Model		
	B	SE	Exp(B)	B	SE	Exp(B)	B	SE	Exp(B)	B	SE	Exp(B)
Offender characteristics												
Age 15–29	−.467**	.102	.627	−.664**	.110	.515	−.341**	.122	.711	−.422**	.125	.656
Age 40+	−.371**	.119	.690	−.254*	.128	.776	−.259*	.139	.772	−.253**	.139	.776
Race (Black = 1)	.253**	.083	1.288	.010	.089	1.010	−.172	.102	.842	−.184	.102	.832
Gender (male = 1)	.909**	.125	2.482	.832**	.132	2.297	.533**	.146	1.705	.565**	.147	1.760
Marital status										−.270	.175	.764
High school										−.287**	.099	.750
Income over $75				−1.292**	.097	.275	−1.087**	.104	.337	−1.072**	.104	.342
Assets over $1,500				−1.255**	.164	.285	−1.056**	.176	.348	−.970**	.179	.379
Case characteristics												
Prior record							.456**	.039	1.578	.461**	.039	1.585
Offense severity							.194**	.048	1.214	.202**	.049	1.224
Property offense							−.542**	.126	.582	−.531**	.126	.588
Public order offense							−.276	.201	.758	−.266	.202	.588
Drug offense							−.530**	.134	.589	−.527**	.135	.590
CJS supervision							.733**	.103	2.082	.745**	.104	2.107
Constant	−1.116***	.138	.328	−.253*	.151	.773	−2.127**	.246	.119	−2.007**	.249	.134
Nagelkerke R^2	.046			.193			.344			.348		
Cox and Snell R^2	.034			.141			.251			.254		

Significance: $*p < .05$; $**p < .01$.

Reading Table 17.4 Female and Male Split Models

Variable	Females			Males			z Score
	B	SE	Exp(B)	B	SE	Exp(B)	
Offender characteristics							
Age 15–29	−.072	.358	.931	−.461**	.135	.631	1.02
Age 40+	−.198	.377	.820	−.243	.151	.784	0.11
Race (Black = 1)	−.979**	.331	.376	−.090	.110	.913	2.55*
Marital status	−.854	.576	.426	−.191	.187	.826	1.09
High school	.137	.302	1.146	−.310**	.106	.733	1.40
Income over $75	−.898**	.296	.407	−1.072**	.112	.342	0.55
Assets over $1500	−.737	.589	.479	−.981**	.190	.375	0.39
Case characteristics							
Prior record	.716**	.139	2.047	.435**	.041	1.545	1.94
Offense severity	−.234	.206	.791	.234**	.051	1.264	2.21*
Property offense	1.531**	.392	.216	−.379	.135	.685	2.78*
Public order offense	−.223	.485	.800	−.553*	.237	.576	0.61
Drug offense	−1.556**	.512	.211	−.452**	.140	.636	2.08*
CJS supervision	.955*	.313	2.598	.723**	.111	2.061	0.70
Constant	−1.811*	.728	.163	−1.465	.241	.231	
Nagelkerke R^2	.423			.308			
Cox and Snell R^2	.272			.229			

*$p < .05$; **$p < .01$.

Discussion

The current study attempted to further the understanding of the effects of race, gender, and age on pretrial release outcomes. Given the logic of the focal concerns perspective (Steffensmeier, 1980; Steffensmeier, Kramer et al., 1993; Steffensmeier, Ulmer et al., 1998), it is not surprising that gender and age directly affect pretrial outcomes as females and young defendants are often viewed as less blameworthy and dangerous. The findings for race, however, were more complex. A strong race effect was found prior to entering the economic variables into the model, with Black defendants less likely to be released pretrial than Whites. Once these variables were included, however, race was no longer significant. In fact, the sign of the coefficient changed, suggesting Whites were actually more likely to be detained. Therefore, it appears that Black defendants are more likely to be detained because they do not have the financial means necessary to secure release. This indicates that Black disadvantage in the court system may not be as simple as racial bias but instead stems from inequality and general disadvantage in society. This is especially noteworthy because prior studies on pretrial releases have not included these variables (e.g., Demuth & Steffensmeier, 2004).

The effect of race was significant, however, when examining the sentences of men and women separately. Consistent with prior research conducted by Demuth and Steffensmeier (2004), the results also indicated that the gender gap was the smallest for White defendants. Unlike Demuth and Steffensmeier, however, White females were not most likely to be released pretrial. Instead, Black females were the least likely to be detained. This finding held across Black females of every age group. The odds of release for White women, however, were not significantly different [from] that of White and Black males. Although Black females were less likely to be detained than White females, the age/race/gender analysis showed that this finding was only applicable to White females aged 30–39. Younger and older White females were not significantly more likely to be detained than their Black female counterparts. When compared to males (both Black and White), however, Black females of all age groups were the least likely to be detained.

Although these findings seem inconsistent with the focal concerns perspective, it is possible that this inconsistency is actually due to the absence of practical constraint factors. Steffensmeier and colleagues (Steffensmeier, 1980; Steffensmeier, Kramer et al., 1993; Steffensmeier, Ulmer et al., 1998) suggest that defendants whose incarceration poses a greater practical constraint (e.g., leaving behind dependent children that will require care, need correctional facilities that are not available) will be granted leniency. It is possible, therefore, that the inclusion of family responsibility variables might account for the increased odds of Black females being released. Daly (1987a) suggests that judges are concerned with the social costs of incarcerating defendants who perform vital familial responsibilities. This is especially pertinent, given that more Black women in the criminal justice system are often single parents to dependent children (U.S. Bureau of the Census [*2000 Census*], 2003). Furthermore, prior research

on the effect of gender on pretrial release has shown that the inclusion of these controls reduces the gender gap (Daly, 1987b; Kruttschnitt & Green, 1984). Unfortunately, the data used for the current study had a great deal of missing data for the measure of dependent children, making it impossible to assess this possibility.

The gender split models also show that judges give less consideration to legal factors for females than for men. This might indicate that judges find males with more serious offenses as posing a greater risk to society. Therefore, it is possible that legal factors play less of a role in shaping the focal concerns associated with early court decisions for women as [*sic*] they do for men. This finding indicates a need for additional studies that closely examine the different factors that affect males' and females' sentencing decisions. It is possible that judges' focal concerns for males and females are influenced by different factors. The inconsistencies across research studies also cause questions of the ability to generalize these findings and signify a need for future research that examines the impact of race, gender, and age on sentencing decisions in other jurisdictions.

Overall, the current study has made an important contribution to the literature examining the factors affecting the pretrial decision. Most notably, it is the only study to date that has examined the effect of race, gender, and age interactions on the pretrial release outcome of defendants while also considering extralegal factors, including income, educational attainment, and marital status. The current study is limited, however, in its examination of only one jurisdiction. Although this is not uncommon in the sentencing literature, it does pose a limitation as findings may vary across location. This study also is limited in its ability to measure the focal concern of practical constraint. It is likely that individual practical constraints (e.g., familial responsibility) as well as organizational constraints (e.g., available jail space) could have an effect on pretrial detention. Additionally, these constraints may have varying effects by race, gender, and age of the defendant.

Future research should assess the impacts of race after controlling for economic factors on a more comprehensive set of dependent variables (e.g., ROR or bail, bail amount, ability to make bail). This is especially important given the finding that the race effect was eliminated once economic variables were included in the analysis. In addition, Demuth (2003) found that Black defendants were less likely to post bail than White defendants. If a more comprehensive dependent variable is assessed, it can be determined whether the Black disadvantage is due to a difference in bail amounts. In other words, are Black defendants receiving higher bail amounts or are Blacks simply more often than Whites in situations where they cannot afford to pay bail? The ability to examine a dependent variable of this nature would greatly contribute to the understanding of the effect of race on the pretrial release.

 Notes

1. Significance tests performed to determine whether any differences existed between the cases excluded from the data set due to missing data and the cases included in the final analysis indicated that there were some significant differences between the two groups (presented below). Two age groups, ages 15–29 and 40+, were significantly different across the two groups; race also was significantly different across the two groups. An examination of the remaining independent variables reveals that cases excluded due to missing information were less likely to have a high school diploma or GED, less likely to have a monthly income of $75 or more, and less likely to have assets of more than $1,500. They were also less likely to be under criminal justice system supervision at the time of their arrest and more likely to be detained prior to trial. Although the missing data pose a limitation to the research, it is not unique to this study; most sentencing literature is limited in the amount of usable data. For instance, Harrington and Spohn (2007) were only able to use 59% of the cases in their original data set, and Freiburger and Hilinski (2009) were only able to use 62.4% of the cases in their original data set. In the current study, nearly 80% of the cases in the original data set were able to be included in the final analysis.

2. Michigan Statutory Sentencing Guidelines assigns an offense variable (OV) to each offense. There are 19 possible offense variables that can be scored, including aggravated use of a weapon, physical or psychological injury to the victim, victim asportation or captivity, and criminal sexual penetration; the sentencing guidelines stipulate which variables will be scored based on the crime group of the current offense (e.g., crimes against a person, crimes against property, and crimes involving a controlled substance). Based on the crime group, each relevant variable is scored and then combined to create a total offense variable that ranges from 1 (least serious) to 6 (most serious; Michigan Judicial Institute, 2007). This offense variable (coded 1–6) was included in each model to control for the severity of the offense.

3. The prior record variable is a composite score based on factors such as prior adult felony and misdemeanor convictions, prior juvenile felony and misdemeanor adjudications, and the offender's relationship with the criminal justice system at the time of the current offense (i.e., whether the offender is a probationer or parolee). For each of the seven prior record variables, a numerical score is assigned. The sum of these seven scores determines the offender's prior record level, which ranges from A (least serious) to F (most serious; Michigan Judicial Institute, 2007). This variable was recoded and included in the models (coded 1–6) to control for prior record.

4. Although it is likely that those who are incarcerated are more likely to be detained pretrial than those on probation or parole, only seven offenders in the sample were actually incarcerated in jail or in prison. Due to the small number, it was impossible to meaningfully assess this difference; therefore, they were combined with those on probation and parole.

 References

Albonetti, C. A. (1989). Bail and judicial discretion in the District of Columbia. *Sociology and Social Research, 74,* 40–47.

Albonetti, C. A. (1997). Sentencing under the federal sentencing guidelines: Effects of defendant characteristics, guilty pleas and departures on sentencing outcomes for drug offenses, 1991–1992. *Law and Society Review, 31,* 789–822.

Bickle, G. S., & Peterson, R. D. (1991). The impact on gender-based family roles on criminal sentencing. *Social Problems, 38,* 372–394.

Crawford, C. (2000). Gender, race, and habitual offender sentencing in Florida. *Criminology, 38,* 263–280.

Daly, K. (1987a). Structure and practice of familial-based justice in a criminal court. *Law & Society Review, 21,* 267–290.

Daly, K. (1987b). Discrimination in the criminal courts: Family, gender, and the problem of equal treatment. *Social Forces, 66,* 152–175.

Demuth, S. (2003). Racial and ethnic differences in pretrial release decisions and outcomes: A comparison of Hispanic, Black, and White felony arrestees. *Criminology, 41,* 873–907.

Demuth, S., & Steffensmeier, D. (2004). The impact of gender and race-ethnicity in the pretrial release process. *Social Problems, 51,* 222–242.

Foote, C. (1954). *Compelling appearance in court: Administration of bail in Philadelphia.* Philadelphia, PA: Temple University Press.

Freiburger, T. L., & Hilinski, C. M. (2009, February 24). An examination of the interactions of race and gender on sentencing decisions using a trichotomous dependent variable. *Crime & Delinquency.* doi:10.1177/ 0011128708330178

Goldkamp, J. S., & Gottfredson, M. R. (1979). Bail decision making and pretrial detention: Surfacing judicial policy. *Law and Human Behavior, 3,* 227–249.

Hagan, J. (1974). Extra-legal attributes and criminal sentencing: An assessment of a sociological viewpoint. *Law and Society Review, 8,* 337–383.

Harrington, M. P., & Spohn, C. (2007). Defining sentence type: Further evidence against use of the total incarceration variable. *Journal of Research in Crime and Delinquency, 44,* 36–63.

Katz, C., & Spohn, C. (1995). The effect of race and gender on bail outcomes: Test of an interactive model. *American Journal of Criminal Justice, 19,* 161–184.

Kruttschnitt, C. (1984). Sex and criminal court dispositions: An unresolved controversy. *Journal of Research in Crime and Delinquency, 12*(3), 213–232.

Kruttschnitt, C., & Green, D. E. (1984). The sex-sanctioning issue: Is it history? *American Sociology Review, 49,* 541–551.

Michigan Judicial Institute. (2007). *Sentencing guidelines manual.* Retrieved from http://courts.michigan.gov/ mji/resources/ sentencing-guide lines/sg.htm–srdanaly

Nagel, I. (1983). The legal/extra-legal controversy: Judicial decision in pretrial release. *Law and Society Review, 17,* 481–515.

Patterson, E., & Lynch, M. (1991). The biases of bail: Race effects on bail decisions. In M. J. Lynch & E. Britt Patterson (Eds.), *Race and criminal justice.* New York, NY: Harrow and Heston.

Petee, T. A. (1994). Recommended for release on recognizance: Factors affecting pretrial release recommendations. *Journal of Social Psychology, 134,* 375–382.

Spohn, C., & Beichner, D. (2000). Is preferential treatment of felony offenders a thing of the past? A multisite study of gender, race, and imprisonment. *Criminal Justice Policy Review, 11,* 149–184.

Spohn, C., & Holleran, D. (2000). The imprisonment penalty paid by young unemployed black and Hispanic male offenders. *Criminology, 38,* 281–306.

Steffensmeier, D. (1980). Assessing the impact of the women's movement on sex-based differences in the handling of adult criminal defendants. *Crime & Delinquency, 26,* 344–358.

Steffensmeier, D., & Demuth, S. (2006). Does gender modify the effects of race ethnicity on criminal sanctions? Sentences for male and female, White, Black, and Hispanic defendants. *Journal of Quantitative Criminology, 22,* 241–261.

Steffensmeier, D., Kramer, J., & Streifel, C. (1993). Gender and imprisonment decisions. *Criminology, 31,* 411–446.

Steffensmeier, D., Ulmer, J., & Kramer, J. (1998). The interaction of race, gender, and age in criminal sentencing: The punishment cost of being young, black, and male. *Criminology, 36,* 763–797.

U.S. Bureau of the Census. (2003). *2000 census of the population.* Washington, DC: U.S. Government Printing Office. Retrieved from http://www.factfinder.census.gov

Walker, S. (1993). *Taming the system: The control of discretion in criminal justice, 1950–1990.* New York, NY: Oxford University Press.

DISCUSSION QUESTIONS

1. What impact does gender have on the decision to release an offender during the pretrial stage?

2. What impact does race have on the decision to release an offender during the pretrial stage?

3. What impact do race and gender have on the decision to release an offender during the pretrial stage?

READING 18

Throughout this text, you have learned about the gender gap between male and female criminality. This section discussed some of the ways in which women are processed through the criminal justice system. This article uses federal data to assess the role that gender plays in sentencing practices and whether legal and extralegal variables impact male and female sentence outcomes.

SOURCE: Doerner, J. K., & Demuth, S. (2012). Gender and sentencing in the federal courts: Are women treated more leniently? *Criminal Justice Policy Review 10*(10), 1–28.

Gender and Sentencing in the Federal Courts

Are Women Treated More Leniently?

Jill K. Doerner and Stephen Demuth

Federal sentencing guidelines are designed to encourage the uniform and proportional treatment of defendants based on legally relevant factors. A main goal of the guidelines is to produce fair and honest outcomes that minimize unwarranted disparities based on defendants' social characteristics. A large body of disparity research has developed over time and, not surprisingly given America's sordid racial history, the overwhelming majority of studies focus on racial and ethnic differences in sentencing outcomes (Demuth, 2002; Demuth & Steffensmeier, 2004; Spohn, 2000; Steffensmeier & Demuth, 2006). What has not been a strong focus of past research is an arguably more common, yet apparently less controversial, form of disparity based on gender.

Like a defendant's race, gender is considered to be an extralegal factor in decision making at the sentencing stage. However, there are at least three factors that might explain both the persistence of gender disparities in sentencing despite guidelines designed to curtail them and a diminished concern for studying and remedying these disparate outcomes. First, unlike claims of racism in the application of laws and sanctions, there is no general presumption that women, the disadvantaged minority group, have historically been subjected to a consistent pattern of discrimination resulting in unwarranted harsher punishments (Nagel & Hagan, 1983). Second, in the context of societal and court concerns about crime and public safety and given the known greater propensity for crime among men, women are viewed as better recidivism risks and more deserving of leniency than men (Spohn, 2002). Third, a major difference in the social lives of men and women is the level of responsibility in caring for family, or more specifically for their dependent children (Bickle & Peterson, 1991; Daly, 1987a, 1987b, 1989). This practical consideration might make the court reluctant to sentence women as harshly as men.

In sum, there is a tension in the guidelines between the goal of a gender-neutral implementation of the law emphasizing uniform treatment based on offense severity and criminal history and the realization that important differences exist between the lives of men and women that might create a need or desire for differential treatment (for a similar argument about race, see Tonry, 1996). In fact, the guidelines recognize this dilemma and provide limited ways for judges and prosecutors to take gender into account. For example, the guidelines allow for some discretion through the use of departures, which enable factors such as family ties and responsibilities to be considered. But, overall, unexplained gender disparities persist despite policy changes designed to minimize them. This suggests that reformers may have had unrealistic expectations about the ability of guidelines to structure outcomes as intended (Spohn, 2000).

For all these reasons, an underdeveloped body of scholarship exists that addresses the topic of gender differences in sentencing. Much of this research is dated, having been published in the 1970s and 1980s using smaller state data sets or single city samples. Another shortcoming of many past studies is a lack of robust controls for legal case characteristics, such as offense seriousness and criminal history. Most importantly, past research tends to examine only whether sex differences exist at the sentencing stage and typically does not explore empirically how gender influences outcomes (for a review, see Chiricos & Crawford, 1995; Daly & Bordt, 1995). Researchers who examine gender and court processing tend to treat gender as a fixed attribute of individuals; however, work by Daly (1986, 1989, 1994) and Kruttschnitt (1984) explores how gender and patterned roles associated with gender can influence court decisions. That male defendants tend to commit more serious offenses and have more extensive criminal records than female defendants helps to explain why men tend to receive harsher sentences than women (Bickle & Peterson, 1991; Daly, 1989, 1994; Daly & Bordt, 1995; Doerner & Demuth, 2010; Spohn, 2000, 2002; Steffensmeier, Kramer, & Streifel, 1993; Steffensmeier, Kramer, & Ulmer,

1995, 1998). But legal factors alone do not appear to fully explain the gender gap, and few studies have attempted to account for the remaining, often sizable, differences in sentence outcomes between men and women.

In the present study, we use data from the United States Sentencing Commission (USSC) to more fully explore the gender gap in federal sentencing and examine the various ways in which gender continues to influence outcomes even within a system of formal rules designed to minimize the impact of extralegal factors. We contribute to the gender and sentencing literature in several important ways. First, we use data that have rich and detailed measures of legal case characteristics. A concern in prior research was that weak or incomplete measures of offense seriousness and criminal history failed to adequately capture the real differences in offending between men and women and made the gender gap in sentencing outcomes look larger than it actually was. With more robust measures, we reduce the likelihood of finding a gender gap that is simply an artifact of model misspecification.

Second, we examine a series of nested regression models to determine not just if a gender gap in incarceration and sentence length outcomes exists, but why. We begin by looking at the gender gap before accounting for differences in legal characteristics between men and women. Next, we control for legal differences to see how much gender differences in sentencing are explained by legal factors. Lastly, and most importantly, we examine the gender gap after adding controls for extralegal characteristics that are associated both with gender and sentencing outcomes: education, marital status, and the number of dependents for which the defendant is responsible. Much prior research tends to add all legal and extralegal variables to the model at the same time, making it difficult to compare the gender gap before and after controlling for legal factors. And central to our earlier criticism of existing gender-sentencing work is that most prior studies examine gender as a fixed attribute and do not attempt to address what aspects of gender influence sentencing. Building upon the research of Daly (1986, 1989, 1994) and Kruttschnitt (1984), we explore several gender-related possibilities.

Third, in addition to examining the main effect of gender, we examine whether legal and extralegal factors have different effects on sentencing outcomes for men and women. Most prior studies focus on the main effect of

gender and do not consider the possibility that sentencing could be a gendered process. Prior research by Daly (1987a, 1987b, 1989) has shown that court personnel assumed gender divisions in the work and family responsibilities of familied defendants, and this resulted in differential outcomes during the sanctioning process. These court officials also viewed caretaking labor, most often provided by women, as more difficult to replace. In addition, Koons-Witt (2002) found that the interaction between gender and number of dependents was a significant predictor of incarceration decisions, with women with dependent children significantly more likely to be sentenced to sanctions within the community. Thus, we explore whether there are differences between men and women with respect to legal and extralegal factors.

Gender and Sentencing Literature

The treatment of women in the courts has not been static in the United States (Farrell, 2004). Historically, female offenders were less likely to be arrested and often sentenced more leniently than similarly situated male offenders. However, such judicial discretion has often been a double-edged sword for women. Rafter (1990) and colleagues (with Stanko, 1982) documented a dual system of punishment for female offenders during the middle of the 19th century. Women deemed "feminine" or "trainable" by the court were most often sent to reformatories, while women viewed as "bad" or "masculine" were subject to incarceration in penal institutions, often alongside male prisoners (Butler, 1997). Gendered sentencing laws at the turn of the 20th century still allowed judges to send women to prison for minor public order offenses (e.g., alcohol-related offenses, DUI, and prostitution) for which men were rarely even arrested (Rafter, 1990; Temin, 1980). Indeed, until the 1970s, state sentencing laws allowed judges to sentence women differently [from] men because female offenders were perceived to be more amenable to rehabilitation and would benefit from longer indeterminate sentences (Pollock-Byrne, 1990).

Currently, a fairly persistent finding in the sentencing literature is that female defendants are treated more leniently than male defendants (Bickle & Peterson, 1991; Daly & Bordt, 1995; Doerner & Demuth, 2010; Griffin &

Wooldredge, 2006; Spohn, 2002; Steffensmeier et al., 1993); however, one study reported no gender differences (Kruttschnitt & Green, 1984). Doerner and Demuth (2010) showed that female defendants were significantly less likely to receive incarceration sentences than male defendants. The odds of incarceration for female defendants were approximately 42% lower than the odds of incarceration for male defendants. Griffin and Wooldredge (2006) found that female defendants in general were less likely than men to be sent to prison both before and after the sentencing reform efforts in Ohio and that the magnitude of this effect did not change significantly over time (.51 to .43 for men, and .38 to .34 for women). Spohn (2002) reported that the odds of receiving a prison sentence were 2.5 times greater for male offenders than for female offenders after controlling for legally relevant factors. Steffensmeier and Motivans (2000) found that female defendants were sentenced less harshly than male defendants—on average they were about 14% less likely to be incarcerated and received prison sentences about 7 months shorter. Similarly, previous research by Steffensmeier et al. (1993) indicated that gender, [and] net of other factors, had a small effect on the likelihood of imprisonment, with female defendants less likely to receive an incarcerative sentence than male defendants. But, they found that gender had a negligible effect on sentence length outcomes.

According to Gruhl, Welch, and Spohn (1984), female defendants were treated more leniently than male defendants, based on a simple breakdown with no controls. Even though they plead[ed] guilty and were convicted at about the same rates as males, females were more likely to have their cases dismissed and were less likely to be incarcerated. When the authors controlled for legal and extralegal factors, significant gender differences remained for dismissal and incarceration, even though the difference between males and females was reduced somewhat.

In terms of gender, women are thought to be less dangerous, less blameworthy, less likely to recidivate, and more likely to be deterred than men (Spohn, 2002). Therefore, the more lenient sentences that are imposed on them might reflect the fact that judges believe them to possess these qualities more than men. According to Belknap (2001), studies consistently show that females generally commit fewer crimes than males but also tend to commit offenses that are less serious and violent in nature. However, [despite] net of case severity, charge severity, type of offense, prior record, and other defendant characteristics, male and female defendants were still treated differently on the basis of their ties to and responsibilities for others. Kruttschnitt (1984) found that controlling for gender-related statuses (i.e., being a wife or mother) mediated the length of probation sentences. In addition, she concluded that women were more likely than men to remain free, both prior to adjudication and after conviction, and that the determinants of these two decisions varied significantly with the offender's gender. Therefore, her analysis provided some insight into why females receive preferential treatment by criminal courtroom personnel.

Familial Responsibility Literature

It has long been observed that female defendants who are married or who have children receive greater leniency from the courts than their male or unmarried and childless female counterparts (Bickle & Peterson, 1991; Daly, 1987a, 1987b, 1989; Eaton, 1987; Farrington & Morris, 1983; Kruttschnitt & Green, 1984; Kruttschnitt & McCarthy, 1985; Simon, 1975). Early explanations of how and why gender-based family roles were important in judicial decision making focused on the impracticality of harsh sanctions for female offenders compared to their male counterparts (Bernstein, Cardascia, & Ross, 1979; Simon, 1975). More specifically, Simon (1975) reported that officials' accounts of gender differentials in sentencing in both New York (1963–1971) and California (1945–1972) emphasized that women have families, both husbands and children, to care for, and sending women to prison would seriously disrupt the family unit.

Kruttschnitt (1982a, 1984), along with her colleagues (with Green, 1984; with McCarthy, 1985) examined gender differentials in sanctioning, specifically pretrial release and sentencing outcomes, using data from Minnesota. In addition to gender, these analyses included either a composite measure of informal social control or one or more sex-based family role factors including family/household composition, number of children, employment status, and sources of support. Overall, the findings from this research indicated that gender-based disparities were affected but not eliminated by including family role factors and that when composite measures of informal control were considered, there was little support for the claim that familial social control was a sex-specific determinant of criminal sanctioning.

In a more recent study of imprisonment decisions in Minnesota, Koons-Witt (2002) found that gender alone did not have a significant influence on sentence outcomes prior to the use of sentencing guidelines, but results indicated a significant interaction between gender and the presence of dependent children. The presence of dependent children for women significantly reduced their likelihood of going to prison. She also found that the interaction between gender and number of dependent children was a significant predictor of the incarceration decisions after sentencing guidelines were enacted. In this instance, women with dependent children were significantly more likely to be sentenced to a community sanction than were women without dependent children.

In her 1989 study, Daly found that a defendant's work-family relations affected the sentencing of both men and women. Furthermore, she reported that what defendants did for families, in terms of providing economic support or care for dependents, mattered to judges. Familied men and women (those with dependent children) were less likely to be detained pretrial, and they were less likely to receive the harsher types of nonjail sentences than childless men and women. In addition, the mitigating effect of being familied was stronger for women than men (Daly, 1987a). Furthermore, having dependents, whether in a marital context or not, was generally the more determining feature of whether defendants receive lenient treatment. For men, being married without dependent children conferred no advantage at the pretrial release or the two sentencing decisions but having dependent children did. Married women, and especially those with dependent children, were accorded greater leniency at the pretrial release decision. In addition, at the sentencing stage, women with dependents received the most lenient sentences.

What appears to matter most for court personnel is whether defendants have day-to-day responsibilities for the welfare of others; such care or economic support can occur with or without a marital tie, and the specific form of care and economic support can vary by gender. In addition, the greater leniency accorded familied women than familied men stems from contemporary gender divisions in work and family life, specifically that women are more

likely to care for others. The mitigating effects of family were found in both the pretrial release and nonjail sentencing decisions. Thus, familied defendants may be accorded leniency even when decisions do not center on a defendant's loss of liberty (Daly, 1987a).

Daly (1987b) found that court officials consistently drew on the categories of work and family in explaining why some defendants deserved leniency. One theme present was that defendants who provide economic support or care for others deserve more lenient treatment than those without such responsibilities. Leniency toward the familied defendants was therefore justified on the grounds that these defendants were more stable and have more to lose by getting into trouble again. Court personnel assume gender divisions in the work and family responsibilities of familied men and women.

These differences, combined with the family profiles of defendants, foster discrepancies in the treatment of familied men and familied women. In addition, officials often justified treating familied defendants more leniently because of the social costs of removing them and jeopardizing the family unit. Sex differentials in outcomes stem from the perceived differential responsibilities of females versus males. Officials viewed it as more costly or impractical to jail women with families than men with families because breadwinning support, usually provided by males, was more readily replaced than caretaking labor (Daly, 1987b).

Overall, research has shown that legal factors play a large role in the sentencing outcomes of male and female defendants, but even after controlling for characteristics like criminal history and offense severity, unexplained differences still persist. As a result, our understanding of why women are sentenced more leniently than men remains limited. In addition, research on familial responsibility indicates that having dependents (more specifically, dependent children) creates leniency at sentencing, especially for women. The present study sets out to explore how legal and extralegal factors play a role in the sentencing of male and female defendants, using data from the United States Sentencing Commission. We pay particular attention to whether characteristics such as education, marital status, and the presence of dependents help to explain the remaining gap in sentencing outcomes, as previous research in this area has discovered, after controlling for legally relevant variables outlined under the federal sentencing guidelines.

⊠ Theoretical Framework and Research Expectations

As previous research has shown, sentencing outcomes continue to be influenced by a host of extralegal factors, even with sentencing guidelines in place (Doerner & Demuth, 2010; Steffensmeier & Demuth, 2000; Steffensmeier et al., 1998; Ulmer, 1995). The focal concerns perspective developed by Steffensmeier (1980) serves as a framework for understanding why extralegal factors, such as gender, race/ethnicity, and age, might influence sentencing decisions, despite the implementation of formal guideline systems. The theory outlines three focal concerns that are important to judges and other criminal justice actors in reaching sentencing decisions: blameworthiness, protection of the community, and practical constraints and consequences. Grounded in research on organizational decision making, inequality and stratification, and criminal stereotyping, Steffensmeier and colleagues (with Kramer & Streifel, 1993; with Kramer & Ulmer, 1998) argue that defendant status characteristics may influence sentencing decisions insofar as stereotypes and behavioral expectations linked to these characteristics relate to the focal concerns of legal agents.

Blameworthiness follows the principle that sentences should depend on the offender's culpability and the degree of injury caused. The primary factors influencing perceptions of blameworthiness are legal factors, such as the seriousness of the offense, the defendant's criminal history or prior victimization at the hands of others, and the defendant's role in the offense (Steffensmeier et al., 1998). Albonetti (1997) suggests that court officials attempt to achieve rational outcomes in the face of incomplete knowledge by relying on stereotypes that differentially link defendant groups to recidivism. Research by Daly (1994) indicates that judges, at least to some extent, share common beliefs portrayed by the media and are influenced by them in their sentencing decisions. In other words, when decisions have to be made quickly, judicial professionals may rely on limited resources to reach an outcome in the time available.

Protection of the community typically focuses on the need to incapacitate the offender or to deter future crime. Albonetti (1991) argues that sentencing is an arena of bounded rationality, in which court actors, particularly judges, confront the goal of protecting the public and preventing recidivism in the context of high uncertainty about offenders' future behavior. Judges' assessments of offenders' future behavior is often based on attributions predicated primarily on the nature of the offense and the offender's criminal history. However, these decisions may also be influenced by extralegal characteristics of the offender, such as gender, race/ethnicity, age, and socioeconomic status (SES). As mentioned previously, criminal justice professionals may give in to stereotypical notions as a means of making decisions more quickly, especially in the face of pressure from the media, victims' families, and members of the community.

Practical constraints and consequences relate to how sentencing decisions impact the functioning of the criminal justice system as well as the circumstances of individual defendants [and] their families and communities. Organizational concerns include maintaining working relationships among courtroom actors, ensuring the stable flow of cases, and being sensitive to local and state correctional crowding and resources (Dixon, 1995; Flemming, Nardulli, & Eisenstein, 1992; Steffensmeier et al., 1993, 1998; Ulmer, 1995; Ulmer & Kramer, 1996). Individual concerns include the offender's ability to do time, health conditions, special needs, the cost to the correctional system, and disruption to children and family (Daly, 1987a; Hogarth, 1971; Steffensmeier, 1980; Steffensmeier et al., 1995).

Expectations

Guided by the focal concerns perspective and the findings of past research on the effect of gender on sentencing outcomes, we develop several hypotheses for the present study to answer two research questions. First, can the gender gap in sentencing be explained by accounting for differences in legal and extralegal factors? Second, do legal and extralegal factors have the same impact for male and female defendants? Drawing on prior research, we expect to find that, on average, female defendants will receive more lenient sentences than male defendants (H1), and that this finding will hold true even after controlling for relevant legal and contextual factors (H2). In addition, we expect that defendants that have more education, more marital stability, and dependents will be afforded greater leniency than defendants that have less education, are single, or have no dependents (H3). Furthermore, we hypothesize that legal and extralegal factors will exert similar effects on sentencing outcomes for both male and female defendants (H4).

Data and Method

In the present study, we use data from three years (2001–2003) of the Monitoring of Federal Criminal Sentences program compiled by the USSC. The data include all cases received by the USSC that had sentencing dates between October 1, 2000, and September 30, 2003, and were assessed as constitutional (total = 194,521 cases). Data from the three years were combined to create one large data set, thus, providing larger case sizes for both male and female defendant groups. These data are especially appropriate as they contain some of the richest and most detailed information available on cases at the sentencing stage. Many of the single-city or state-level data sets used in prior studies have lacked the large number of legal control variables found in the federal guidelines data. Having these variables available enabled a more adequate elimination of alternative explanations for extralegal effects on sentencing outcomes (e.g., Demuth & Steffensmeier, 2004; Spohn & Holleran, 2000). Furthermore, the federal sentencing guidelines provide a more rigid and conservative test of the impact of extralegal factors on sentencing outcomes.

For this analysis, we eliminate several defendant groups from the sample. First, noncitizens are deleted from the analysis. Federal sentencing of noncitizen defendants often differs greatly from sentencing of citizen defendants in many ways and, as a result, makes comparisons of sentencing outcomes between them difficult (Demuth, 2002). For instance, a large proportion of noncitizen cases involve immigration violations. Furthermore, because noncitizens can be deported, the sentencing process for noncitizens is often qualitatively different (the goal being to send the defendant back to his or her country of origin and not to punish) from that of U.S. citizens. Finally, case information provided for noncitizens may be incomplete and this will most likely result in an underestimation of prior criminal history.

Second, defendants under the age of 18 are excluded from the analysis because their cases are substantively and legally different due to their juvenile status. Third, defendants

who receive upward departures are deleted from the analysis as they comprised [*sic*] only 0.8% of departure cases and made comparisons across departure type very difficult. Fourth, using listwise deletion, all cases with missing information for all variables used in the analysis are deleted. Analyses were run predeletion and postdeletion of missing information and the elimination of these cases did not significantly change the overall results. The final analytic sample for the present study is 109,181.

Dependent Variables

The sentencing outcome is the result of a two-stage decision making process: The decision to incarcerate and, once incarceration is selected, the sentence length decision (for discussion, see Spohn, 2002). In the present study, we use logistic regression to model the incarceration decision. The in/out decision variable is coded dichotomously, with 1 indicating a prison sentence and 0 indicating a nonincarceration sentence (e.g., probation, community service). The sentence length decision is modeled using ordinary least squares (OLS) regression and includes only those defendants who receive a prison sentence. Sentence length is a continuous variable representing the logged length of the prison sentence in months. Logging sentence length helps to normalize the distribution, and taking the antilog of the coefficient in the logged sentence length model provides a useful proportional interpretation. Sentence length is capped at 470 months. Any sentence length beyond that duration is considered to be life in prison.[1]

Extralegal Variables

Defendant gender is a dummy variable coded 1 if the defendant is female and 0 if the defendant is male. Race/ethnicity is coded as four dummy variables: White non-Hispanic, Black non-Hispanic, Hispanic of any race, and Other.[2] Defendant age is a continuous variable representing the age of the defendant at the time of sentencing and ranges from 18 to 100. In this case, defendant age has been grouped in logical ranges consistent with Steffensmeier et al. (1998) and is coded as a series of dummy variables (18 to 20, 21 to 29, 30 to 39, 40 to 49, 50 to 59, and 60 and over).

Education level is coded as three dummy variables: less than high school, high school, and more than high school, with those who graduated high school as the reference category. Marital status is coded as six dummy variables: single, married, cohabiting, divorced, widowed, and separated. Those defendants who are single serve as the reference category. Number of dependents[3] is a continuous variable indicating responsibility of support by the defendant of their dependents. For the purposes of this study, number of dependents has been recoded into a dichotomous variable indicating that defendants either have no dependents or have one or more dependents.[4] Many studies have shown that female defendants that are married or have dependents receive greater leniency from the courts than their male or unmarried and childless female counterparts (Bickle & Peterson, 1991; Daly, 1987a, 1987b, 1989; Eaton, 1987; Farrington & Morris, 1983; Kruttschnitt & Green, 1984; Kruttschnitt & McCarthy, 1985; Simon, 1975). Having dependents, whether in a marital context or not, is generally the more determining feature of whether defendants receive lenient treatment. However, while the majority of prior research uses the terms "child or children," the present study uses "dependent" as the data do not specify what type of dependent the defendant is responsible for.

Legal Variables

Under the federal guidelines, federal judges retain discretion for sentencing individuals within the range determined by the offense level and criminal history of the offender. Sentence ranges are determined using a grid that takes these two variables into account, one on each axis. However, it has been argued (see Engen & Gainey, 2000) that a variable representing the presumptive guideline sentence, where criminal history and offense severity are combined into a single measure, is a more appropriate strategy and actually explains more of the variation in sentencing outcomes. This analytic strategy is also used by the USSC (2004). Therefore, we include a variable representing the guideline minimum sentence, in months. We also include a measure of criminal history, which ranges from 1 to 6 and indicates the final criminal history category of the defendant, as assigned by the court. According to Ulmer (2000), measures of offense severity and prior record have important main, curvilinear, and interactive influences on in/out and sentence length that cannot be reduced to the effect of presumptive sentence measures. This suggests that it is statistically and substantively

important to include offense severity and prior record even if one is including a presumptive sentence measure. However, Ulmer also points out that including all three legally prescribed variables results in problematic multicollinearity in the OLS models of sentence length. As a result, an offense severity score variable is not included in the analysis because it is highly collinear with the guideline minimum sentence variable.

Case disposition is a dichotomous variable, which indicates whether the offender's case is settled by plea agreement or trial. It is coded 1 for trial and 0 for guilty plea. We also include a measure of multiple counts. A dummy variable is coded 0 for cases involving a single count and 1 for cases that involve multiple counts. The defendant's offense type (see Appendix for a complete breakdown of categories) is coded as four dummy variables: violent (i.e., murder, manslaughter, sexual abuse), drug (i.e., trafficking, simple possession), white-collar (i.e., fraud, embezzlement, bribery), and other (includes all other offenses in the federal data). Defendants committing other types of offenses serve as the reference group. The variable departure indicates the defendant's departure status. Departure status is dummy-coded into 3 categories: no departure (the reference), downward departure, and substantial assistance departure. Upward departure cases were deleted from the sample as they made up only 0.8% of the sample and deleting them does not significantly change the findings. The federal sentencing statutes include provisions that permit judges to depart either above or below the sentence prescribed by the guidelines. Judges may award these sentencing departures based on a legitimate reason if they feel the defendant does not deserve the sentence stated under the prescribed guidelines. Overall, however, the overwhelming direction of departures is downward.

The narrow range of factors that judges may consider when sentencing either above or below the prescribed guideline range makes the federal sentencing guidelines much more rigid than similar state structured sentencing systems (Farrell, 2004). Consequently, federal courts are prohibited from departing from the guidelines based on the race, gender, religion, or class of an individual defendant. However, the Sentencing Commission has deferred to the courts to interpret how extensively judges may use offender characteristics to justify departures from the guideline range.

Several control variables are also included in the models. Since multiple years of data were used in the present study, a dummy variable for each of the three years was constructed. Prior studies have indicated that judicial circuit, as well as other court contextual variables, may be important influences on sentencing outcomes (Peterson & Hagan, 1984; Steffensmeier & Demuth, 2000). One cause of disparities is that not all states or judicial circuits have implemented guidelines systems. The variable judicial circuit indicates the judicial circuit in which the defendant was sentenced. Judicial circuits are broken down into 11 categories, which were then made into dummy variables.

Results

In the present study, we analyze the data and present the results in several stages. In the first section, we present descriptive statistics for all variables used in the models (Reading Table 18.1). Second, we use logistic and OLS regression (including only those defendants who receive a prison sentence) to examine the independent effects of gender on incarceration and sentence length decisions (Reading Table 18.2) in three separate models. Third, we partition the full model by gender, examining the differential influence of legal and extralegal variables on sentencing outcomes of male and female defendants (Reading Table 18.3). It is important to note that the data set we use in the present study is not a sample. It includes the entire population of defendants sentenced in the federal courts during the period. As such, statistical tests of significance are not particularly meaningful in that there is no sampling error and no need to make inferences (Berk, 2010; Raftery, 1995). In our discussion of results, we focus mostly on the size and direction of coefficients, but nonetheless include indicators of significance ($p < .05$) in the tables.

Descriptive Statistics

Overall, men make up 83% of the sample. In terms of race, we found similar percentages in each racial category for both men and women. The plurality of defendants in the sample is White, approximately 44%, while 34% are Black and 18% are Hispanic. In terms of age, the largest portion of the sample fell in the 21 to 29 age range, followed closely by the 30 to 39 age range.

Looking at sentencing outcomes, a smaller percentage of women are incarcerated than men, with 85% of men receiving a prison sentence while only 62% of females in the sample are incarcerated. The sentence length gap for incarcerated defendants is also quite substantial between male and female defendants; male defendants receive sentence lengths of roughly 70 months, while female defendants are sentenced to approximately 34 months of incarceration. The average sentence length for the total sample falls close to that for male defendants (approximately 65 months).

These large differences in sentencing outcomes may be explained by both legal and extralegal factors. In terms of legal characteristics, male defendants have higher criminal histories, and they also receive higher recommended minimum guideline sentences than do female defendants due to the greater severity of the offenses committed by men. In addition, a higher percentage of male defendants are sentenced on multiple counts. Furthermore, a smaller percentage of female defendants go to trial. However, men and women receive sentencing departures at similar rates. A higher percentage of males commit violent, drug, and other offenses, while a higher percentage of females commit white-collar offenses compared to their male counterparts.

Looking at extralegal factors that might be related to gender, a slightly higher percentage of female defendants have one or more dependents. More specifically, about 62% of female defendants have at least one dependent, compared to 59% for male defendants. Also, male defendants are more likely to be single than female defendants (46% vs. 40%), but female defendants are more likely to be divorced (14% vs. 11%) or separated (8% vs. 5%) than male defendants. Furthermore, a higher percentage of female defendants, roughly 6% more, have more than a high school education compared to their male defendant counterparts.

Independent Effects of Gender

Reading Table 18.2 shows the main effects of gender in three nested models.[5] Model 1 controls only for basic defendant demographics including gender, race, and age. Overall, female defendants have odds of incarceration roughly 74% lower than similarly situated male defendants. Hispanic defendants have the highest odds of incarceration,

Reading Table 18.1 Descriptive Statistics by Gender

Independent variables	Overall		Males		Females	
	N	Percentage	N	Percentage	N	Percentage
Gender						
Male	90,297	82.70	90,297	100	—	—
Female	18,884	17.30	—	—	18,884	100
Race						
White	48,003	43.97	39,568	43.82	8,435	44.67
Black	37,541	34.38	31,408	34.78	6,133	32.48
Hispanic	19,348	17.72	15,988	17.71	3,360	17.79
Other	4,289	3.93	3,333	3.69	956	5.06
Age						
18–20	5,427	4.97	4,516	5.00	911	4.82
21–29	37,777	34.60	31,455	34.84	6,322	33.48
30–39	32,702	29.95	26,950	29.85	5,752	30.46
40–49	20,305	18.60	16,427	18.19	3,878	20.54
50–59	9,537	8.74	8,000	8.86	1,537	8.14
60 & over	3,433	3.14	2,949	3.27	484	2.56
Legal variables						
Multiple counts	23,142	21.20	20,274	22.45	2,868	15.19
Trial	4,536	4.15	4,062	4.50	474	2.51
Prior criminal history (points)	2.40	—	2.57	—	1.60	—
Guideline minimum sentence (months)	58.92	—	65.11	—	29.33	—
Offense type						
Violent	6,092	5.58	5,609	6.21	483	2.56
Drug	48,688	44.59	41,626	46.10	7,062	37.40
White-collar	23,259	21.30	16,371	18.13	6,888	36.48
Other	31,142	28.52	26,691	29.56	4,451	23.57

Independent variables	Overall		Males		Females	
	N	Percentage	N	Percentage	N	Percentage
Departures						
No departure	72,938	66.80	60,816	67.35	12,122	64.19
Downward departure	12,866	11.78	10,289	11.39	2,577	13.65
Substantial assistance departure	23,377	21.41	19,192	21.25	4,185	22.16
Education						
Less than high school	38,587	35.34	32,794	36.32	5,793	30.68
High school	40,484	37.08	33,544	37.15	6,940	36.75
More than high school	30,110	27.58	23,959	26.53	6,151	32.57
Marital status						
Single	48,909	44.80	41,349	45.79	7,560	40.03
Married	30,588	28.02	25,448	28.18	5,140	27.22
Cohabit	10,702	9.80	9,087	10.06	1,615	8.55
Divorced	12,529	11.48	9,817	10.87	2,712	14.36
Widowed	626	0.57	315	0.35	311	1.65
Separated	5,827	5.34	4,281	4.74	1,546	8.19
Number of dependents						
No dependents	44,677	40.92	37,411	41.43	7,266	38.48
One or more dependents	64,504	59.08	52,886	58.57	11,618	61.52
Dependent Variables						
Incarcerated	88,647	81.19	76,979	85.25	11,668	61.79
Sentence length (months)[a]	65.12	—	69.80	—	34.25	—
N	109,181		90,297		18,884	

[a] Sentence length is for those who received an incarceration sentence.

while White defendants have the lowest, and Black defendants fall in the middle. The odds of incarceration follow an upside-down U-shaped pattern with increasing age. Defendants aged 21 to 39 have odds of incarceration roughly 40% to 50% higher than defendants aged 18 to 20. After age 50, the likelihood of receiving an incarceration sentence drops substantially, with defendants aged 60 and over having odds of incarceration roughly half that of the youngest defendants.

For the sentence length decision, female defendants receive sentences that are about 50% (exp[b]) shorter than similarly situated male defendants. Black defendants

Reading Table 18.2 Main Effects Model

Variable	Model 1		Model 2		Model 3	
	In/out	Ln(Length)	In/out	Ln(Length)	In/out	Ln(Length)
Gender						
Male[a]	—	—	—	—	—	—
Female	0.26*	−0.70*	0.61*	−0.25*	0.61*	−0.25*
Race						
White[a]	—	—	—	—	—	—
Black	1.65*	0.40*	0.96	0.04*	0.95	0.03*
Hispanic	1.80*	0.13*	1.40*	−0.03*	1.34*	−0.03*
Age						
18–20[a]	—	—	—	—	—	—
21–29	1.48*	0.26*	1.00	0.05*	1.08	0.06*
30–39	1.42*	0.32*	0.88*	0.04*	0.98	0.05*
40–49	1.05	0.20*	0.84*	0.04*	0.94	0.05*
50–59	0.73*	0.08*	0.74*	0.06*	0.82*	0.07*
60 & over	0.48*	−0.06*	0.54*	0.02	0.59*	0.03
Legal variables						
Multiple counts			1.64*	0.29*	1.65*	0.29*
Trial			1.68*	0.10*	1.71*	0.10*
Prior criminal history			1.66*	0.06*	1.62*	0.06*
Guideline minimum sentence			1.12*	0.01*	1.12*	0.01*
Offense type						
Violent			1.80*	0.39*	1.77*	0.39*
Drug			1.41*	0.26*	1.37*	0.26*
White-collar			1.18*	−0.41*	1.23*	−0.41*
Other[a]			—	—	—	—
Departures						
No Departure[a]			—	—	—	—

Variable	Model 1		Model 2		Model 3	
	In/out	Ln(Length)	In/out	Ln(Length)	In/out	Ln(Length)
Downward departure			0.27*	−0.41*	0.27*	−0.41*
Substantial assistance departure			0.12*	−0.44*	0.12*	−0.44*
Education						
Less than high school					1.35*	0.02*
High school[a]					—	—
More than high school					0.99	−0.01*
Marital status						
Single[a]					—	—
Married					0.92*	−0.01*
Cohabiting					1.07	0.00
Divorced					1.15*	0.01
Widowed					0.67*	0.02
Separated					1.07	0.00
Number of dependents						
No dependents[a]					—	—
One or more dependents					0.92*	0.00
Max-resealed R^2	0.13	—	0.59		0.59	—
Adjusted R^2		0.12	—	0.67		0.63
N	109,181	88,647	109,181	88,647	109,181	88,647

NOTE: Controls for circuit and year are included in all models.

[a] Represents the reference category.

*$p < .05$.

receive the longest sentence lengths, approximately 50% longer than White defendants. Hispanic defendants fall in the middle when it comes to sentence length outcomes. Overall, sentence lengths increase until age 30 to 39 then decrease thereafter, with defendants aged 60 and over receiving sentences similar to those received by defendants aged 18 to 20.

Model 2 builds on the baseline variables by adding legal factors indicating number of counts, trial or guilty plea, prior criminal history, guideline minimum sentence (which accounts for offense severity), offense type, and receipt of departure. As expected, the legal factors are strongly related to whether a defendant receives a prison sentence or probation. Defendants with longer criminal histories are more likely to be sentenced to prison than defendants with shorter criminal records. In addition, defendants that are sentenced for multiple offense counts have odds of incarceration that are 64% higher than defendants sentenced on only a single count. Furthermore, defendants that go to trial are more likely to be sentenced to an incarceration term than defendants that plead guilty (odds ratio = 1.68). Defendants who commit violent offenses have the highest odds of incarceration, roughly 80% higher than defendants in the other offense category. Defendants committing drug and white-collar offenses are also more likely to be incarcerated (41% and 18%, respectively) than the reference group. Finally, defendants receiving a sentencing departure are less likely to receive an incarceration sentence than defendants who do not receive a sentencing departure. Looking at gender, net of legal factors, the odds of incarceration for females are 39% lower than the odds of incarceration for males. This represents a substantial reduction in the gender gap as compared to the findings presented in Model 1 where the odds of incarceration for women are 74% lower for women than men.

Similar findings emerge for sentence length in Model 2. After controlling for legal factors, female defendants receive sentences approximately 23% shorter than those received by male defendants. As with the in/out decision, defendants with longer criminal histories and those who go to trial receive slightly longer sentences. Those defendants with multiple counts receive sentences approximately 34% longer than those sentenced for only a single count. In addition, defendants who commit violent or drug offenses receive significantly longer sentences (48% and 30% longer, respectively) than those defendants in the reference group. However, defendants who commit white-collar offenses, or receive a sentencing departure, are given significantly shorter sentence length outcomes than their respective reference categories. Notably, by including legal variables in the model, the male–female gap in sentence length is reduced from a 50% difference to a 23% difference.

Model 3 represents the full model and includes three groups of variables indicating educational attainment, marital status, and number of dependents. These extralegal variables were added separately because they can be considered gendered in nature. The odds ratio for female defendants remains the same as in Model 2, indicating that female defendants have odds of incarceration approximately 39% lower than male defendants with similar characteristics. Defendants with less than a high school education are more likely to be incarcerated than those with a high school education. Furthermore, defendants that are divorced have higher odds of incarceration than defendants that are single, while married and widowed defendants are less likely to be incarcerated. In addition, defendants that have one or more dependents are significantly less likely to be incarcerated than defendants who have no dependents. In terms of the sentence length decision, female defendants receive the same sentence length outcome as they did in Model 2, even after the addition of educational attainment, marital status, and number of dependents. Overall, there remains a moderately large gender gap that cannot be explained by legal and extralegal factors.

Main Effects Models by Gender

In Reading Table 18.3, we present the results separately for the male and female defendants in the sample. This is done to determine whether legal and extralegal factors differentially influence the sentencing outcomes of male and female defendants.

In terms of race, incarceration outcomes appear to be influenced differently for men and women. Hispanic male and female defendants have the highest odds of incarceration with defendants roughly 44% and 13% more likely to be incarcerated than their respective White counterparts. On the other hand, Black female defendants have the lowest odds of incarceration compared to White females. We use z-tests of difference of means to compare coefficients between models. Z-tests of difference indicate that the having prior criminal history plays a stronger role for female defendants than male defendants. This also holds true for female defendants who commit drug and white-collar offenses. Defendants, male and female, have lower odds of incarceration if they receive a sentencing departure, but the magnitude of the effect appears to be similar for both gender groups who receive substantial assistance departures. In addition, being less educated hurts male defendants more than women. More specifically, male defendants completing less than a high school education are 46% more likely to be incarcerated than those male defendants with a high school education.

Reading Table 18.3 Main Effects Model—Males Versus Females

Variable	Males		Females	
	In/out	Ln(Length)	In/out	Ln(Length)
Race				
White[a]	—	—	—	—
Black	1.02[b]	0.05*[b]	0.81*[b]	−0.04*[b]
Hispanic	1.44*[b]	−0.03*	1.13*[b]	0.00
Age				
18–20[a]	—	—	—	—
21–29	1.19*[b]	0.06*	0.85[b]	0.04
30–39	1.03	0.05*	0.88	0.08*
40–49	1.00	0.03*[b]	0.80*	0.15*[b]
50–59	0.90[b]	0.04*[b]	0.65*[b]	0.23*[b]
60 & over	0.66*[b]	0.01[b]	0.46*[b]	0.18*[b]
Legal variables				
Multiple counts	1.60*	0.29*	1.84*	0.27*
Trial	1.74*	0.09*[b]	1.69*	0.21*[b]
Prior criminal history	1.59*[b]	0.06*[b]	1.70*[b]	0.09*[b]
Guideline minimum sentence	1.12*	0.01*[b]	1.12*	0.01*[b]
Offense type				
Violent	1.78*	0.37*[b]	1.56*	0.65*[b]
Drug	1.27*[b]	0.23*[b]	1.76*[b]	0.42*[b]
White-collar	1.07*[b]	−0.40*[b]	1.75*[b]	−0.24*[b]
Other[a]	—	—	—	—
Departures				
No Departure[a]	—	—	—	—
Downward departure	0.25*[b]	−0.40*[b]	0.31*[b]	−0.47*[b]

(Continued)

Reading Table 18.3 (Continued)

Variable	Males		Females	
	In/out	Ln(Length)	In/out	Ln(Length)
Substantial assistance departure	0.13*	−0.45*	0.12*	−0.44*
Education				
Less than high school	1.46*b	0.01b	1.13*b	0.05*b
High schoola	—	—	—	—
More than high school	1.02	−0.02*b	0.95	0.05*b
Marital status				
Singlea	—	—	—	—
Married	0.90*	−0.01	0.95	−0.03
Cohabiting	1.06	0.00	1.07	0.00
Divorced	1.10*	0.02	1.23*	−0.03
Widowed	0.78	−0.06	0.57*	0.05
Separated	1.06	0.00	1.09	−0.03
Number of dependents				
No dependentsa	—	—	—	—
One or more dependents	0.95	0.01	0.89*	0.02
Max-resealed R^2	0.58	—	0.55	—
Adjusted R^2	—	0.67	—	0.58
N	90,297	76,979	18,884	11,668

NOTE: Controls for circuit and year are included in all models.

a Represents the reference category.

b Coefficients are different between male and female defendants at $p < .05$ level (two-tailed z-test).

*$p < .05$.

In terms of sentence length outcomes, the results for male and female defendants are somewhat different. Black male defendants receive the longest sentence terms, roughly 5% longer than similarly situated White defendants. On the other hand, Black female defendants receive the shortest sentence length outcomes, approximately 4% shorter than their White female counterparts. Defendants, both male and female, who go to trial and those with prior criminal history receive longer sentence lengths overall. Defendants receiving sentencing departures are given significantly shorter sentences than defendants who do not receive a sentencing departure; however, this appears to play a slightly larger role for female defendants who receive downward sentencing departures. Having anything but [or less than] a high school education appears to play a stronger role for females than males, with female defendants receiving sentences 5% longer than female defendants that finish high school.

Overall, when it comes to the incarceration decision, several things were found to weigh differently for male and female defendants. Racial differences were found among defendant groups, with Hispanic males and females most likely to be incarcerated and Black females least likely to be incarcerated. In terms of legal variables, having prior criminal history plays a stronger role for women than men. For the extralegal measures, having less education negatively effects the sentencing outcomes of men. Looking at sentence length outcomes, racial differences were found. Black male defendants receive the longest sentence lengths, while Black female defendants receive the shortest. Educational differences were also found. Having anything but [or less than] a high school education leads to negative effects for female defendants (longer sentences).

Discussion and Conclusions

The current study had several major goals. First, we wanted to perform a rigorous analysis of the possible causes of gender disparities in sentencing outcomes. Gender disparities are quite common and usually discouraged or prohibited by statute yet receive relatively little attention in the literature. Furthermore, many past studies have used older data, small localized samples, or have not had sufficiently robust legal measures with which to provide adequate statistical control. In the current study, we used some of the richest and most detailed data available to examine how differences in the legal and extralegal case characteristics of men and women contribute to the gender gap in sentencing.

Second, beyond explanations based on differences in legal case characteristics, we wanted to gain a better understanding of how gender impacts sentencing outcomes through other extralegal factors related to both gender and sentencing. Past studies typically examine gender as a fixed attribute and do not consider how gendered roles might impact court decisions. In the current

study, we drew on research from the areas of criminology, criminal justice, and family sociology to examine whether differences in marriage, education, and the presence of dependents helped to account for the gender gap. We also looked to see if there were gender differences in the impact of extralegal and legal factors on sentencing outcomes.

Finally and more broadly, the current study set out to address the limitations of the criminal justice system after the implementation of fixed sentencing reforms, like formal guidelines, designed to reduce unwarranted extralegal disparities. Central to the guidelines is the notion that defendant characteristics, such as gender, should not be considered during the sentencing process. However, even with these guidelines in place, gender disparities persist, calling into question the effectiveness of their implementation. In the current study, we examined possible mechanisms by which gender may influence the sentencing process in spite of guidelines.

Consistent with prior sentencing research, we found that legal factors play an important role in determining sentencing outcomes. Overall, regardless of gender, defendants with more extensive criminal histories and those who committed more serious offenses were more likely to receive harsher sentences than defendants with less serious criminal pasts and current convictions. However, the findings of the current research also showed that gender appears to have a significant effect on sentencing outcomes, after accounting for legal and extralegal factors. Female defendants were less likely to receive an incarceration sentence than male defendants and also received shorter sentence length terms.

Several important findings emerged from the analysis in relation to our research questions and hypotheses. As expected in our first hypothesis, female defendants received more lenient sentence outcomes than their similarly situated male counterparts. Second, legal factors accounted for a considerable portion of the gender gap in sentencing. However, even after accounting for these legal factors, a sizable gender gap remained in that male defendants continued to be sentenced more harshly than their female counterparts, as proposed in our second hypothesis. Third, although education level, marital status, and number of dependents appeared to influence sentencing outcomes in some instances, they did not help to minimize the gender gap in sentencing outcomes. Thus, our third hypothesis was supported in the expected direction in that [those] defendants who have more marital stability and dependents received more lenient sentence outcomes, but there were no significant advantages for defendants with more than a high school education. One reason as to why this group of variables may not be helping to narrow the sentencing gap between male and female defendants is that judges on the federal level, compared to the state level, are more insulated from community pressures and political forces and less able to exercise their discretion than their state or local counterparts. Overall, the gender gap in sentencing outcomes cannot be fully explained by accounting for legal and extralegal factors.

Finally, contrary to our expectations in hypothesis four, when each gender group was examined separately we found that some legal and extralegal factors did influence sentencing differently for male and female defendants. In terms of legal variables, prior criminal history played a more important role in receiving an incarceration sentence for female than male defendants. In terms of extralegal variables, having less than a high school education negatively influenced the incarceration decision of male defendants (raising their odds of incarceration). However, when it came to sentence length outcomes, having less than, or more than, a high school education increased sentence lengths for female defendants. Race also influenced male and female defendants differently. For the incarceration decision, Hispanic male and female defendants had the highest odds of being sent to prison, while Black females had the lowest odds of incarceration. For the sentence length decision, Black males received the longest sentence length terms and Black female defendants received the shortest terms. Overall, legal and extralegal factors were found to have differential impacts on male and female defendants.

The results of the current study are consistent with the focal concerns perspective (Steffensmeier, 1980; Steffensmeier et al., 1993, 1998) that argues that legal decision making is organized around concerns of blameworthiness, protection of the community, and practical constraints and consequences. Overall, the primary influences of sentencing decisions are legal factors (e.g., prior criminal history, offense seriousness); however, we also found that extralegal characteristics play an important role in some defendant's outcomes. The findings support the idea that judges attribute meaning to past and present behavior of defendants, as well as stereotypes associated with various gender or racial/ethnic groups. These extralegal sources of

sentencing disparity indicate that these stereotypes may be very influential and that inequalities in the application of the law and subsequent court proceedings may be taking place, despite the existence of sentencing guidelines designed to avoid such unequal treatment.

One limitation of this study was that socioeconomic status (SES) information was not available in the data set (Monitoring of Federal Criminal Sentences) and thus could not be included in the current analysis. It is not unusual for measures of SES to be missing from sentencing research. In prior years of federal data, a variable representing defendant income was available; however, over 50% of defendants listed their incomes as US$0, making it difficult to analyze the true effects of this variable and how it might interact with gender (see Steffensmeier & Demuth, 2000). Future research should explore the extent to which gender disparities are truly a function of gender perceptions versus economic constraints that limit the ability of defendants to resist legal sanctions and acquire appropriate counsel.

Another limitation of the current study is that the variable indicating number of dependents does not differentiate between the types of dependents. In other words, it is unclear as to whether the defendant is claiming responsibility for their dependent children, their spouse or significant other, some other family member, or a combination of all of the above. Much of the prior research cited in the current study specifically explores the effect of children on sentencing outcomes, regardless of the defendant's marital context (Bickle & Peterson, 1991; Daly, 1987a, 1987b; 1989; Eaton, 1987; Farrington & Morris, 1983; Kruttschnitt & Green, 1984; Kruttschnitt & McCarthy, 1985; Simon, 1975). However, in this context, the definition leaves much room for interpretation. This is especially true given the very different worlds of parenting across various racial/ethnic groups, including instances of multiple partner fertility, mixed family households, extended family care, and responsibilities for aged dependents. Therefore, future research would benefit from an analysis broken down by marital status, specifically targeting single defendants, to determine if significant differences are present when children are the only dependent [variable] examined. Furthermore, future research should strengthen our understanding of different family forms, especially across racial/ethnic groups and same-sex partnerships.

In conclusion, the topic of differential treatment at sentencing will continue to be an important topic, given the Supreme Court decisions (*Blakely v. Washington; U.S. v. Booker; U.S. v. Fanfan*) which changed the sentencing guidelines from mandatory to voluntary. While the full implication of these changes are still to come, they will likely result in significant changes in sentencing outcomes and, more specifically, the role that judges and other members of the courtroom work group play in those sentencing decisions.

Appendix

Breakdown of Offense Types by Category

Coding No.	Offense Type	Overall		Males		Females	
	Name	Number	Percentage	Number	Percentage	Number	Percentage
	Violent	*6,092*	*5.58*	*5,609*	*6.21*	*483*	*2.56*
1	Murder	145	0.13	128	0.14	17	0.09
2	Manslaughter	125	0.11	98	0.11	27	0.14
3	Kidnapping/hostage	65	0.06	58	0.06	7	0.04
4	Sexual abuse	585	0.54	566	0.63	19	0.10
5	Assault	1,032	0.95	920	1.02	112	0.59
6	Bank robbery/other robbery	4,140	3.79	3,839	4.25	301	1.59
	Drug	*48,688*	*44.59*	*41,626*	*46.10*	*7,062*	*37.40*
10	Drugs: Trafficking	46,606	42.69	39,992	44.29	6,614	35.02
11	Drugs: Communication facilities	923	0.85	721	0.80	202	1.07
12	Drugs: Simple possession	1,159	1.06	913	1.01	246	1.30
	White-collar	*23,259*	*21.30*	*16,371*	*18.13*	*6,888*	*36.48*
18	Fraud	14,837	13.59	10,535	11.67	4,302	22.78
19	Embezzlement	1,913	1.75	775	0.86	1,138	6.03
20	Forgery/counterfeiting	3,159	2.89	2,353	2.61	806	4.27
21	Bribery	375	0.34	329	0.36	46	0.24
22	Tax offenses	1,333	1.22	1,093	1.21	240	1.27
23	Money laundering	1,642	1.50	1,286	1.42	356	1.89

(Continued)

(Continued)

| Coding No. | Offense Type | Overall | | Males | | Females | |
	Name	Number	Percentage	Number	Percentage	Number	Percentage
	Other Offenses	*31,142*	*28.52*	*26,691*	*29.56*	*4,451*	*23.57*
9	Arson	176	0.16	162	0.18	14	0.07
13	Firearms: Use/ possession	13,339	12.22	12,832	14.21	507	2.68
15	Burglary/breaking & entering	118	0.11	111	0.12	7	0.04
16	Auto theft	370	0.34	352	0.39	18	0.10
17	Larceny	5,125	4.69	3,205	3.55	1,920	10.17
24	Racketeering/ extortion	1,627	1.49	1,492	1.65	135	0.71
25	Gambling/lottery	271	0.25	246	0.27	25	0.13
26	Civil rights offenses	211	0.19	201	0.22	10	0.05
27	Immigration	3,299	3.02	2,597	2.88	702	3.72
28	Pornography/ prostitution	1,714	1.57	1,689	1.87	25	0.13
29	Offenses in prison	741	0.68	638	0.71	103	0.55
30	Administration of justice-related	1,982	1.82	1,324	1.47	658	3.48
31	Environmental, game, fish, and wildlife offenses	312	0.29	297	0.33	15	0.08
32	National defense offenses	16	0.01	12	0.01	4	0.02
33	Antitrust violations	39	0.04	38	0.04	1	0.01
34	Food and drug offenses	171	0.16	151	0.17	20	0.11
35	Traffic violations and other offenses	1,631	1.49	1,344	1.49	287	1.52
	Overall totals	*109,181*		*90,297*		*18,884*	

⊠ Notes

1. Many sentencing studies model the sentence length decision including a correction term for selection bias stemming from the decision to incarcerate (Berk, 1983). This involves controlling for the "hazard" of incarceration (estimated in the in/out model) in the sentence length model. The hazard variable represents for each observation, the instantaneous probability of being excluded from the sample conditional upon being in the pool at risk. However, Stolzenberg and Relles (1997) and

Bushway, Johnson, and Slocum (2007) find that this correction term can often introduce more bias into the sentence length model than it eliminates due to high levels of collinearity between the correction term and other predictors of sentence length. This is especially likely when the predictors of incarceration are very similar to the predictors of sentencing length as in the present study. Also, Stolzenberg and Relles (1997) argue that a correction term is often unnecessary when there is a low level of selection. In the current data, because only 19% of defendants avoid incarceration, it is unlikely that a selection bias will strongly influence the sentence length findings. For these reasons, we do not include a correction term for selection bias in the sentence length model.

2. Defendants in the "Other" racial category have been included in the analysis models but were not included in the regression tables as they are not the focus of this study and only constitute a small percentage of the sample (3.9%).

3. The "number of dependents" variable may not accurately represent a defendant's potential family responsibilities because the Sentencing Commission has not differentiated among types of dependents (e.g., children, spouses, significant others, aged parents, or extended family members, etc.).

4. Initial analyses were conducted using a full range of categories for this variable, but it was found that no differences existed between higher levels of dependents.

5. All models in the analysis control for judicial circuit and year. Model fit for the full in/out model as indicated by the area under the ROC curve (0.931) is very good. For the full sentence length model, an examination of variance inflation factor scores indicates that all variables are well below 10, which is typically considered to be an acceptable cutoff.

References

Albonetti, C. (1991). An integration of theories to explain judicial discretion. *Social Problems, 38,* 247–266.

Albonetti, C. (1997). Sentencing under the federal sentencing guidelines: Effects of defendant characteristics, guilty pleas, and departures on sentence outcomes for drug offenders, 1991–1992. *Law & Society Review, 31,* 789–822.

Belknap, J. (2001). *The invisible woman: Gender, crime, and criminal justice.* Belmont, CA: Wadsworth.

Berk, R. A. (1983). An introduction to sample selection bias in sociological data. *American Sociological Review, 48,* 386–398.

Berk, R. A. (2010). What you can and can't properly do with regression. *Journal of Quantitative Criminology, 26,* 481–487.

Bernstein, I., Cardascia, J., & Ross, C. (1979). Defendant's sex and criminal court decisions. In R. Alvarez & K. G. Lutterman (Eds.), *Discrimination in organizations* (pp. 329–354). San Francisco, CA: Jossey-Bass.

Bickle, G., & Peterson, R. (1991). The impact of gender-based family roles on criminal sentencing. *Social Problems, 38,* 372–394.

Bushway, S., Johnson, B., & Slocum, L. (2007). Is the magic still there? The use of the Heckman two-step correction for selection bias in criminology. *Journal of Quantitative Criminology, 23*(2), 151–178.

Butler, A. (1997). *Gendered justice in the American West: Women prisoners in men's penitentiaries.* Champaign, IL: University of Illinois Press.

Chiricos, T., & Crawford, C. (1995). Race and imprisonment: A contextual assessment of the evidence. In D. F. Hawkins (Ed.), *Ethnicity, race, and crime: Perspectives across time and place* (pp. 281–309). Albany: State University of New York Press.

Daly, K. (1986, November). *Gender in the adjudication process: Are judges really paternalistic toward women?* Revised paper presented at the American Society of Criminology Annual Meeting, San Diego, CA.

Daly, K. (1987a). Discrimination in the criminal courts: Family, gender, and problems of equal treatment. *Social Forces, 66,* 152–175.

Daly, K. (1987b). Structure and practice of familial-based justice in a criminal court. *Law and Society Review, 21,* 267–290.

Daly, K. (1989). Rethinking judicial paternalism: Gender, work-family relations, and sentencing. *Gender and Society, 3*(1), 9–36.

Daly, K. (1994). *Gender, crime, and punishment.* New Haven, CT: Yale University Press.

Daly, K., & Bordt, R. (1995). Sex effects and sentencing: An analysis of the statistical literature. *Justice Quarterly, 12,* 141–175.

Demuth, S. (2002). The effects of citizenship status on sentencing outcomes in drug cases. *Federal Sentencing Reporter, 14,* 271–275.

Demuth, S., & Steffensmeier, D. (2004). Ethnicity effects on sentence outcomes in large urban courts: Comparisons among White, Black, and Hispanic defendants. *Social Science Quarterly, 85,* 994–1011.

Dixon, J. (1995). The organization context of criminal sentencing. *American Journal of Sociology, 100,* 1157–1198.

Doerner, J., & Demuth, S. (2010). The independent and joint effects of race/ethnicity, gender, and age on sentencing outcomes in U.S. federal courts. *Justice Quarterly, 27*(1), 1–27.

Eaton, M. (1987). The question of bail: Magistrate's responses to applications for bail on behalf of men and women. In P. Carlen & A. Worrall (Eds.), *Gender, crime, and justice* (pp. 95–107). Philadelphia, PA: Open University Press.

Engen, R., & Gainey, R. (2000). Modeling the effects of legally relevant and extralegal factors under sentencing guidelines: The rules have changed. *Criminology, 38,* 1207–1229.

Farrell, A. (2004). Measuring judicial and prosecutorial discretion: Sex and race disparities in departures from the federal sentencing guidelines. *Justice Research and Policy, 6*(2), 45–78.

Farrington, D., & Morris, A. (1983). Sex, sentencing, and reconviction. *Journal of British Criminology, 21,* 229–249.

Flemming, R., Nardulli, P., & Eisenstein, J. (1992). *The craft of justice: Work and politics in criminal court communities.* Philadelphia: University of Pennsylvania Press.

Griffin, T., & Wooldredge, J. (2006). Sex-based disparities in felony dispositions before versus after sentencing reform in Ohio. *Criminology, 44*(4), 893–923.

Gruhl, J., Welch, S., & Spohn, C. (1984). Women as criminal defendants: A test for paternalism. *Western Political Quarterly, 37*, 456–467.

Hogarth, J. (1971). *Sentencing as a human process.* Toronto, ON: University of Toronto Press.

Koons-Witt, B. (2002). Decision to incarcerate before and after the introduction of sentencing guidelines. *Criminology, 40*, 297–327.

Kruttschnitt, C. (1982a). Women, crime, and dependency: An application of the theory of law. *Criminology, 19*, 495–513.

Kruttschnitt, C. (1984). Sex and criminal court dispositions: The unresolved controversy. *Journal of Research in Crime and Delinquency, 21*, 23–32.

Kruttschnitt, C., & Green, D. (1984). The sex sanctioning issue: Is it history? *American Sociological Review, 49*, 541–551.

Kruttschnitt, C., & McCarthy, D. (1985). Familial social control and pretrial sanctions: Does sex really matter? *Criminal Law and Criminology, 76*, 151–175.

Nagel, I., & Hagan, J. (1983). Gender and crime: Offense patterns and criminal court sanctions. In M. Tonry & N. Morris (Eds.), *Crime and justice: An annual review of research* (Vol. 4, pp. 91–144). Chicago, IL: University of Chicago Press.

Peterson, R., & Hagan, J. (1984). Changing conceptions of race: Towards an account of anomalous findings of sentencing research. *American Sociological Review, 49*, 56–70.

Pollock-Byrne, J. (1990). *Women, prison, and crime.* Pacific Grove, CA: Brooks/Cole.

Rafter, N. (1990). *Partial justice: Women, prison, and social control.* Piscataway, NJ: Transaction.

Rafter, N., & Stanko, E. (1982). *Judge lawyer victim thief: Women, gender roles, and criminal justice.* Boston, MA: Northeastern University Press.

Raftery, A. (1995). Bayesian model selection in social research. *Sociological Methodology, 25*, 111–163.

Simon, R. (1975). *Women and crime.* Lexington, MA: Lexington Books.

Spohn, C. (2000). Thirty years of sentencing reform: The quest for a racially neutral sentencing process. *Criminal Justice 2000* (Vol. 3, pp. 427–501). Washington, DC: National Institute of Justice.

Spohn, C. (2002). *How do judges decide: The search for fairness and justice in punishment.* Thousand Oaks, CA: Sage.

Spohn, C., & Holleran, D. (2000). The imprisonment penalty paid by young unemployed Black and Hispanic male offenders. *Criminology, 38*, 281–306.

Steffensmeier, D. (1980). Assessing the impact of the women's movement on sex-based differences in the handling of adult criminal defendants. *Crime and Delinquency, 23*, 344–356.

Steffensmeier, D., & Demuth, S. (2000). Ethnicity and sentencing outcomes in U.S. federal courts: Who is punished more harshly? *American Sociological Review, 65*, 705–729.

Steffensmeier, D., & Demuth, S. (2006). Does gender modify the effects of race-ethnicity on criminal sanctioning? Sentences for male and female White, Black, and Hispanic defendants. *Journal of Quantitative Criminology, 22*, 241–261.

Steffensmeier, D., Kramer, J., & Streifel, C. (1993). Gender and imprisonment decisions. *Criminology, 31*, 411–446.

Steffensmeier, D., Kramer, J., & Ulmer, J. (1995). Age differences in sentencing. *Criminal Justice Quarterly, 12*, 701–719.

Steffensmeier, D., Kramer, J., & Ulmer, J. (1998). The interaction of race, gender, and age in criminal sentencing: The punishment cost of being young, Black, and male. *Criminology, 36*, 763–797.

Steffensmeier, D., & Motivans, M. (2000). Older men and older women in the arms of criminal law: Offending patterns and sentencing outcomes. *Journal of Gerontology, 55*, 141–151.

Stolzenberg, R., & Relles, D. (1997). Tools for intuition about sample selection bias and its correction. *American Sociological Review, 62*, 494–507.

Temin, P. (1980). Regulation and the choice of prescription drugs. *American Economic Review, 70*, 301–305.

Tonry, M. (1996). *Sentencing matters.* New York, NY: Oxford University Press.

Ulmer, J. (1995). The organization and consequences of social pasts in criminal courts. *Sociological Quarterly, 36*, 587–605.

Ulmer, J. (2000). The rules have changed—So proceed with caution: A comment on Engen and Gainey's method for modeling sentencing outcomes under guidelines. *Criminology, 38*, 1231–1243.

Ulmer, J., & Kramer, J. (1996). Court communities under sentencing guidelines: Dilemmas of formal rationality and sentencing disparity. *Criminology, 34*, 383–408.

U.S. Sentencing Commission (USSC). (2001, 2002, 2003). *Monitoring of Federal Criminal Sentences* [Computer files]. ICPSR versions. Washington, DC: U.S. Sentencing Commission (Producer), 2001, 2002, 2003. Ann Arbor, MI: Inter-University Consortium for Political and Social Research (distributor).

U.S. Sentencing Commission (USSC). (2004). *Fifteen years of guidelines sentencing: An assessment of how well the federal criminal justice system is achieving the goals of sentencing reform.* Washington, DC: U.S. Sentencing Commission.

DISCUSSION QUESTIONS

1. Do female defendants receive more lenient sentences than male defendants?

2. How does the consideration of legal and contextual factors impact sentencing practices for female defendants? For male defendants?

3. How do extralegal factors impact the sentencing decisions for female defendants? For male defendants?

X

The Incarceration
of Women

- Historical trends in the incarceration of women
- Contemporary issues in the incarceration of women

This section focuses on patterns and practices in the incarceration of women offenders. Ranging from historical examples of incarceration to modern-day policies, this section looks at the treatment and punishment of women in jails and prisons. This section also highlights how children become unintended victims in the incarceration of mothers. This section concludes with a discussion about the lives of women in prison and their survival strategies as they "do time."

Historical Context of Female Prisons

Prior to the development of the all-female institution, women were housed in a separate unit within the male prison. Generally speaking, the conditions for women in these units were horrendous and were characterized by an excessive use of solitary confinement and significant acts of physical and sexual abuse by both the male inmates and the male guards. Women in these facilities received few, if any, services (Freedman, 1981). At Auburn State Prison in New York, women were housed together in an attic space where they were unmonitored and received their meals from male inmates. In many cases, these men would stay longer than necessary to complete their job duties. To no surprise, there were many prison-related pregnancies that resulted from these interactions. The death of a pregnant woman named Rachel Welch in 1825 as a result of a beating by a male guard led to significant changes in the housing of incarcerated women. In 1839, the first facility for women opened its doors. The Mount Pleasant Prison Annex was located on the grounds of Sing Sing, a male penitentiary located in Ossining, New York. While Mount Pleasant had

Figure 10.1   Timeline on the Development of Women's Prisons

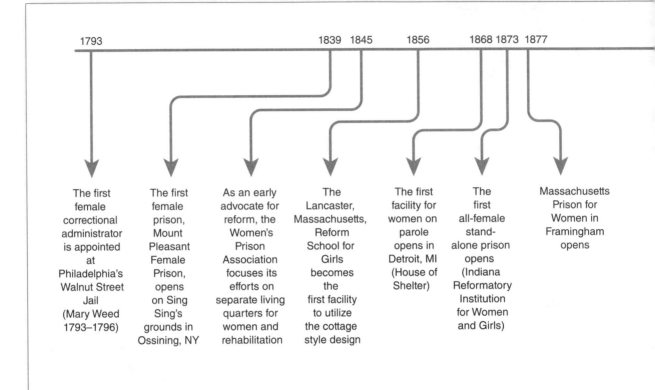

SOURCES: Freedman, E. B. (1984). *Their Sisters' Keepers: Women's Prison Reform in America 1830–1930.* Ann Arbor: University of Michigan Press; Rafter, N. H. (1990). *Partial Justice: Women, Prisons and Social Control.* New Brunswick, CT: Transaction; Watterson, K. (1996). *Women in Prison: Inside the Concrete Womb.* Boston, MA: Northeastern University Press; Women's Prison Association (n.d., "History & Mission"). Retrieved from http://www.wpaonline.org/about/history

a female warden at the facility, the oversight of the prison remained in the control of the administrators of Sing Sing, who were male and had little understanding about the nature of female criminality. Despite the intent by administrators to eliminate the abuse of women within the prison setting, the women incarcerated at Mount Pleasant continued to experience high levels of corporal punishment and abuse at the hands of the male guards.

Conditions of squalor and high levels of abuse and neglect prompted moral reformers in England and the United States to work toward improving the conditions of incarcerated women. A key figure in this crusade in the United Kingdom was **Elizabeth Fry** (1780–1845). Her work with the Newgate Prison in London during the early 19th century served as the inspiration for the American women's prison reform movement. Fry argued that women offenders were capable of being reformed and that it was the responsibility of women in the community to assist those who had fallen victim to a lifestyle of crime. Like Fry, many of the reformers in America throughout the 1820s and 1830s came from upper- and middle-class communities with liberal religious backgrounds (Freedman, 1981). The efforts of these reformers led to significant changes in the incarceration of women, including the development of separate institutions for women. (See timeline in Figure 10.1.)

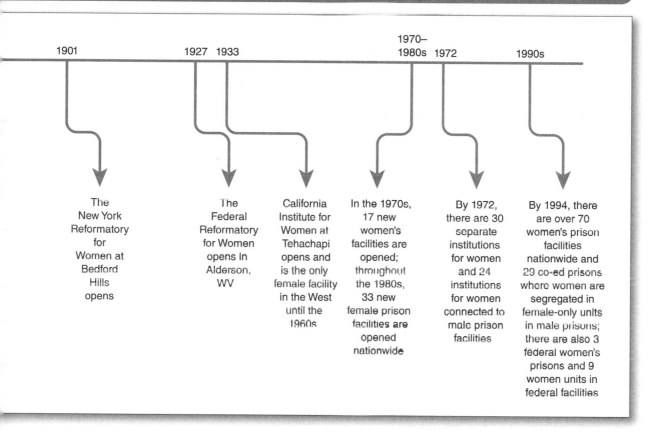

1901	1927	1933	1970–1980s	1972	1990s
The New York Reformatory for Women at Bedford Hills opens	The Federal Reformatory for Women opens in Alderson, WV	California Institute for Women at Tehachapi opens and is the only female facility in the West until the 1960s	In the 1970s, 17 new women's facilities are opened; throughout the 1980s, 33 new female prison facilities are opened nationwide	By 1972, there are 30 separate institutions for women and 24 institutions for women connected to male prison facilities	By 1994, there are over 70 women's prison facilities nationwide and 29 co-ed prisons where women are segregated in female-only units in male prisons; there are also 3 federal women's prisons and 9 women units in federal facilities

The Indiana Women's Prison (IWP) is identified as the first stand-alone female prison in the United States. It was also the first maximum-security prison for women. At the time of its opening in 1873, IWP housed 16 women (Schadee, 2003). By 1940, 23 states had facilities designed to exclusively house female inmates.

A review of facilities across the United States reveals two different models of institutions for women throughout the 20th century: custodial institutions and reformatories. In **custodial institutions**, women were simply warehoused, and little programming or treatment was offered to inmates. Women in custodial institutions were typically convicted on felony and property-related crimes, with a third of women convicted of violent crimes. The custodial institution was more popular with southern states. In cases where a state had both a reformatory and a custodial institution, the distribution of inmates was made along racial lines—custodial institutions were more likely to house women of color who were determined to have little rehabilitative potential, while reformatories housed primarily White women (Freedman, 1981). Black women were also sent to work on state-owned penal plantations under conditions that mimicked the days of slavery in the South. Women of color generally had committed less serious offenses compared to White women, and yet they were incarcerated for longer periods of time. It was rare to see women of color convicted of moral offenses—since Black women were not held to the same standards of what was considered acceptable behavior for a lady, they were not deemed as in need of the rehabilitative tools that characterized the environments found at the reformatory (Rafter, 1985). Prison conditions for women at the custodial institution were characterized by unsanitary living environments with inadequate sewage and bathing systems, work conditions that were dominated by physical labor and corporal punishment, a lack of medical treatment for offenders, and the use of solitary confinement for women with mental health issues (Kurshan, 2000).

Unlike the custodial institution, which was similar in design and philosophy to most male prisons where inmates were simply housed while they did their time, the **reformatory** offered women opportunities for rehabilitation. This was a new concept in incarceration. Women were sent to the reformatory for an indeterminate period of time. In some cases, this meant that women were incarcerated for longer periods of time than their male counterparts, even for the same offenses. The philosophy of the reformatory focused on improving the moral character of women, and these facilities were mostly filled with White, working-class women who were sentenced for a variety of offenses including "lewd and lascivious conduct, fornication, serial premarital pregnancies, adultery [and] venereal disease" (Anderson, 2006, pp. 203–204). Many of these offenses were not serious or violent crimes but rather were public order offenses, and women were punished under the premise that such behaviors were not ladylike.

Reformatories were meant to improve on the conditions that existed in many custodial institutions. For example, the reformatories were staffed with female guards. This was done in response to the historical treatment of women by male guards, which often involved sexual abuse. Reformatories were also the first to provide treatment for female offenders. However, these efforts have been criticized by feminist scholars as this treatment was based on curing women who had violated the socially proscribed norms of womanhood. As a result, the reformatory became a place that embodied an attempt by society to punish the wayward behaviors and autonomy of women and instill in them the appropriate morals and values of society (Kurshan, 2000).

One of the most successful reformatories during this time frame was the Massachusetts Correctional Institution (MCI) in Framington. Opened in 1877, Framington possessed a number of unique characteristics, including an all-female staff, an inmate nursery that allowed incarcerated women to remain with their infants while they served their sentence, and an on-site hospital to address the inmates' health care needs. Several activities were provided to give women opportunities to increase their self-esteem, gain an education, and develop a positive quality of life during their sentence. While MCI Framington is the oldest running prison still in use today, it bears little resemblance to its original mission and design; the modern-day institution bears the scars of the tough-on-crime movement. Today's version of the institution has lost some of the characteristics that made Framington a unique example of the reformatory movement and now mimics the structure and design of the male prisons located throughout the state (Rathbone, 2005).

During the 1960s, the California Institution for Women was also known for its efforts in rehabilitation. Like the early reformatories, women were sentenced to indeterminate terms of incarceration. Any decisions for parole considered not just her offense(s) but also her participation in various rehabilitative efforts during her incarceration. Most of these programs were very gendered and offered little opportunity for sustainable income once she exited prison. "Like the ideal mother, each WCS (women's correctional supervisor) also supervised prisoners' training in homemaking, deportment, dress and grooming, and was expected to participate in the moral regulation of prisoners, particularly as this related to their sexuality" (Gartner and Kruttschnitt, 2004, p. 279).

By the mid-1970s, the focus on sentencing had shifted away from rehabilitation and back to punishment as a punitive and retributive ideal. For example, the passage of California's Uniform Determinate Sentencing Act in 1976 meant that group and individualized counseling was no longer mandatory. Indeed, only a few options for rehabilitation were available and were typically run either by community volunteers or by the inmates themselves:

> Work, educational, vocational and volunteer programs were offered as way for women to empower themselves, boost their self-esteem, and accept personal responsibility for their lives in order to change them.

The prisoner was no longer expected to rely on clinical experts to design her route to rehabilitation but had become a rational actor. (Gartner & Kruttschnitt 2004, pp. 282–283)

Today, most states have at least one facility dedicated to a growing population of female offenders. Unlike male prisons, which allow for different facilities based on the security level of the offender, the smaller incarcerated female population means that women's prisons house offenders of all security levels. In addition, these prison facilities are located in remote areas of the state, far from the cities where most of the women were arrested and where their families reside. The distance between an incarcerated woman and her family plays a significant role in the ways in which she copes with her incarceration and can affect her progress toward rehabilitation and a successful reintegration. In contrast, the sheer number of male facilities increases the probability that these men might reside in a facility closer to their home, which allows for an increased frequency in visitations by family members.

Contemporary Issues for Incarcerated Women

Since the 1980s, the number of women incarcerated in the United States has multiplied at a dramatic rate. As discussed in Section IX, sentencing policies, such as mandatory minimum sentences, and the war on drugs have had a dramatic effect on the numbers of women in prison. These structured sentencing formats, whose intent was to reduce the levels of sentencing disparities, have only led to the increases in the numbers of women in custody. At year-end 2012, there were 108,866 women incarcerated in prisons in the United States (Carson & Golinelli, 2013). Table 10.1 illustrates a profile of women found in the criminal justice system today. Much of the rise in female criminality is the result of minor property crimes, which reflects the economic vulnerability that women experience in society, or cases involving drug-related crimes and the addiction issues facing women.

While Blacks and Hispanics make up only 24% of the U.S. population, 63% of women in state prisons and 67% of women in federal prisons are Black or Hispanic, a practice that indicates that women of color are significantly overrepresented behind bars. Indeed, research indicates that Black women today are being incarcerated at a greater rate than both White females and Black males (Bush-Baskette, 1998). Table 10.2 highlights the rates of incarceration of White, Black, and Hispanic women. Women of color have incarceration rates that are often three times greater than the rates of White women. While White women are typically incarcerated for property offenses, women of color

Table 10.1 Characteristics of Women in Prison	
Race/Ethnicity	
White	33%
African American	48%
Hispanic	15%
Median age	33
High school/GED	56%
Single	47%
Unemployed	62%
Mother of minor children	65%

Table 10.2   Rate of Incarceration of Women by Race/Ethnicity

Race/Ethnicity	Rate of Incarceration Per 100,000
All Women	67
White	47
Black	133
Hispanic	77

SOURCE: Guerino, Harrison, & Sabol (2011).

are more likely to be incarcerated for violent and drug-related offenses (Guerino, Harrison, & Sabol, 2011). Poverty is also an important demographic of incarcerated women, as many women (48%) were unemployed at the time of their arrest, which affects their ability to provide a sustainable environment for themselves and their children. In addition, they tend to come from impoverished areas, which may help explain why women are typically involved in economically driven crimes, such as property, prostitution, and drug-related offenses. Women also struggle with limited education and a lack of vocational training, which places them at risk for criminal behavior. The majority of women in state prisons across the United States have not completed high school and struggle with learning disabilities and literacy challenges. For example, 29% of women in custody in New York have less than a fifth-grade reading ability. Yet many prison facilities provide limited educational and vocational training, leaving women ill prepared to successfully transition to the community following their release. For example, of the 64% of women who enter prison without a high school diploma, only 16% receive their GED, and only 29% participate in any form of vocational training while they are incarcerated (Women's Prison Association [WPA], 2003, 2009a).

The rise in the female prison population means that many facilities are overcrowded, which creates a strain on basic resources within the facility and impacts the delivery of services of women. Overcrowding also can increase stress and anxiety levels leading to increases in negative mental health issues, such as depression, self-harm, and suicidal ideation. As a result, not only may women be unable to receive the treatment that they need, but also staff may be unable to recognize when women are at risk for negative mental health issues. Given the effects that overcrowding can have for female inmates, it is important that prisons be able to provide adequate resources to screen for potential self-harming behaviors and develop necessary therapeutic resources to address these issues (Clements-Nolle, Wolden & Bargmann-Losche, 2009).

CASE STUDY

Spotlight on California Prison Realignment and Its Effect on Female Inmates

In 2011, the U.S. Supreme Court ruled that the current state of overcrowding and the resulting conditions of the state's prisons were a violation of the prisoners' Eighth Amendment protection against cruel and unusual punishment. As a result, the California Department of Corrections was required to substantially reduce the state's prison population. To bring the prison population to 137.5% of the institutional design capacity, the state needed to reduce its prison population by 40,000 prisoners (*Plata v. Brown*, 2011).

Table 10.3   Profile of Women in California's State Prisons

Offense	2010 (n = 9,759)	2012 (n = 5,992)	Percent Change
Violent Crime	40.9%	62.4%	+21.5
• Murder	14.7%	24.6%	+9.9
• Manslaughter	1.3%	2.0	+0.7
• Rape	0.1%	0.2%	+0.1
• Robbery	9.9%	14.5%	+4.6
• Aggravated or Simple Assault	9.6%	13.4%	+3.8
Property Crime	33.3%	22.3%	−10.0
• Burglary	11.2%	10.9%	−0.3
• Larceny-Theft	9.9%	4.8%	−5.1
• Motor Vehicle Theft	3.3%	1.7%	−1.6
• Fraud	6.3%	3.0%	−3.3
Drug Offenses	21.1%	10.9%	−10.2

SOURCE: Carson & Golinelli (2013).

As part of the efforts to reduce the population in the state prison, correctional officials have shifted many of the correctional supervision of lower level offenders, parolees and parole violators, to the local governments. In particular, the state legislature has altered how the state punishes felony crimes. Historically, felons were sent to the state prison and only misdemeanor offenders served their time in local jail facilities. The introduction of Assembly Bill 109 reclassified certain felonies (nonviolent, nonserious, and nonsexual offenses) to permit offenders to serve their time in county jails. Additional legislation allows offenders to receive good time credits based on time served as well as participation in specialized programming (Smude, 2012).

As a result of California's realignment plan, the state prison population has seen dramatic changes in 2011 and 2012, both in terms of its overall size and also in terms of the types of offenders that remain housed in these state prison facilities. While some decreases were noted in 2011,[1] the full effects of realignment are apparent with 2012 data. While there have been noted changes in the prison population for both male and female offenders, women have seen proportionally greater reductions. Table 10.3 highlights how the population of California's female population has shifted as a result of realignment. Not only has the number of women in prison decreased by 39%, but the types of offenders are [also] more likely to be violent offenders. As a result of realignment practices, nonviolent and drug offenders are now no longer housed in state prison facilities. This represents a dramatic change in practices since the growth of women in prison during the late 20th and early 21st centuries.

---

[1]The California Public Safety Realignment program was enacted on October 1, 2011. By end of year 2011, the program had been in effect for only 3 months. 2012 represents the first full year of the program.

©Thinkstock Images

▲ **Photo 10.1** A woman spends time with a family member during a no-contact visit. A no-contact visit means that the inmate cannot touch or hug her family and friends when they come to visit. For many women, the lack of physical contact with their loved ones can contribute to the stress and loneliness of incarceration.

With all the challenges that women face within prison, how do they develop social support networks within the prison walls? Research by Severance (2005) finds that women rely on a variety of experiences to develop these internal support structures. For example, women who are from the same neighborhoods or did time together in jails may bond together. The dormitory style housing environment in prisons can also provide women the opportunity for women to develop these emotional connections. While being in close proximity can help establish relationships, it can also be challenging for some women to build trust within these environments, particularly given the lack of privacy and the high levels of gossip that exist within these correctional settings (Severance, 2005).

The level of attachment and trust can vary as inmates have different types of relationships within the prison walls. Research by Severance (2005) describes four different categories of relationships that are found within women's prisons: acquaintances, friends, family, and girlfriends. Acquaintances are superficial relationships that involve low levels of trust between inmates. Friends are more meaningful than acquaintances as they involve an increased level of trust. Unlike acquaintances, which are typically temporary relationships, friends have the potential to continue once the women have left prison. While family relationships, or **pseudo-families,** can also provide supportive networks, these relationships are not always positive experiences due to the lack of respect that can occur between family members. Finally, girlfriends can provide emotional and romantic support. What makes this type of relationship unique is that the majority of women in prison do not identify as homosexual. These relationships are generally not for sexual purposes, but rather, they are for emotional support and companionship. Intimate relationships can also serve to provide economic benefits, particularly in cases where one partner has more resources (i.e., money for canteen supplies) than the other. Here, sex becomes a commodity that can be exchanged. Unlike the "girlfriends" described by Severance (2005), these relationships are often engaged in by offenders with shorter sentences and are purely sexual (Einat & Chen, 2012).

Physical and Mental Health Needs of Incarcerated Women

Women in custody face a variety of physical and mental health issues. In many cases, the criminal justice system is ill equipped to deal with these issues. Given the high rates of abuse and victimization these women experience throughout their lives, it is not surprising that the incarcerated female population has a high demand for mental health services. Women in prison have significantly higher rates of mental illness compared to women in the general population. Official data indicate that 13% of women in federal facilities and 24% of women in state prisons have been diagnosed with a mental disorder (General Accounting Office, 1999).

The pains of imprisonment, including the separation from family and adapting to the prison environment, can exacerbate mental health conditions. In addition, many offenders with life sentences (45%) often experience suicidal ideation upon receiving this sentence. The experience of prison can also exacerbate mental health conditions, such as depression, particularly given the life experiences of many female inmates. In addition, women with limited support from family on the outside also experience suicidal ideation (Dye & Aday, 2013).

Unfortunately, the standard course of treatment in many facilities involves prescription psychotropic medications. Often these medications are prescribed in excess and often in lieu of counseling or other therapeutic interventions. For example, one study indicates that 21 of the 22 participants were given the prescription Seroquel,[2] which is used to treat bipolar disorder. Yet only one of the women was actually officially diagnosed with bipolar disorder. Although the manufacturer or Seroquel recommends that people who take this medication should be reassessed at regular intervals, few of the women actually received such treatment while in prison. While some drugs were readily available, the same did not hold true for all psychotropic medications. In some cases, women noted that prison doctors would prescribe new drugs to the women rather than continue to offer prescriptions for drugs that had been effective in the past. "Prison doctors just do whatever they want; the opposite of what you were getting before you went in so that they can show you who's boss. It's just a way for them to show you how much control they have" (Kitty, 2012, p. 171). Not only can the failure to comply with a prescribed medication protocol be grounds for a disciplinary action while in prison, but such behaviors can also be used against an offender during a parole hearing.

Some women believe that their mental health status improves during incarceration because they were appropriately medicated, were no longer using illicit substances, and were engaged in therapeutic support programs. However, the majority of women believed that incarceration exacerbated their mental health issues and that a number of variables contributed to this. First, incarceration is a stressful experience and stress can increase feelings of anxiety and insecurity. Second, the majority of resources for mental health were focused on crisis intervention and not therapeutic resources. In particular "lifers" felt that they were often placed at the end of the list and were denied services due to their sentence. Finally, many of the women felt degraded and abused by the staff, which added to their trauma (Harner & Riley, 2013).

Women also face a variety of physical health needs. Women in prison are more likely to be HIV positive compared to women in the community, presenting a unique challenge for the prison health care system. While women in the general U.S. population have an HIV infection rate of 0.3%, the rate of infection for women in state and federal facilities is 3.6%, a tenfold increase. In New York state, this statistic rises to an alarming 18%, a rate 60 times that of the national infection rate. These rates are significantly higher than the rates of HIV-positive incarcerated men. Why is HIV an issue for women in prison? Women who are HIV positive are more likely to have a history of sexual abuse, compared to women who are HIV negative (WPA, 2003). While the rates of HIV-positive women have declined since an all-time high in 1999, the rate of hepatitis C infections has increased dramatically within the incarcerated female population. Estimates indicate that between 20% and 50% of women in jails and prisons are affected by this disease. Hepatitis C is a disease that is transmitted via bodily fluids, such as blood, and can lead to liver damage if not diagnosed or treated. Offending women are at a high risk to contract hepatitis C given their involvement in sex and drug crimes. Few prison facilities routinely test for hepatitis C, and treatment can be expensive due to the high cost of prescriptions (Van Wormer & Bartollas, 2010).

While the physical health needs of women in prison are significant, there are often limited resources for treatment within the prison walls. The medical staff is generally overwhelmed with the high number of inmates that require medical care. In addition, many women expressed concerns about the environment in prison and felt that it put them at risk for increased health issues in a number of ways, such as the physical conditions of the prison and housing that

---

[2]The manufacturer of Seroquel indicates that "Seroquel is an anti-psychotic medication, useful as a mono-drug therapy or as an adjunct to the drugs lithium or divalproex for the treatment of schizophrenia and the acute manic and depressive episodes in bipolar disorder" (Kitty, 2012, p. 168).

© Viviane Moos/CORBIS

▲ **Photo 10.2** The rise of female incarceration has had significant impacts on the lives of their children, who are left to grow up without their mothers. Here, children visit with their mothers at Rikers Island Prison in New York.

combine healthy inmates with inmates with chronic and communicable illnesses. Finally, the women expressed a desire for increased health education on issues such as prevention, diet, and exercise (Morgan, 2013).

Considering the number of women that come to prison on drug-related charges, or whose criminal activity is related to their drug use, the demand for drug treatment in prison is high. Women are more likely to participate in prison-based drug treatment (Belenko & Houser, 2012), and those who participate have lower rates of recidivism over the long term (Grella & Rodriguez, 2011). Many of the drug treatment programs in prison have been based on therapeutic community (TC) models. The TC model is designed to provide individuals with tools to help them live a drug-free lifestyle. However, TC programming may not adequately address some of the gender-specific needs of the female incarcerated population. Research by Messina, Grella, Cartier, and Torres (2010) found that women in the gender-specific drug treatment program were more likely to stay away from drugs for a longer period of time and were more successful on parole compared to those who participated in a TC treatment program. These findings indicate the importance in offering programs designed with the unique needs of women in mind.

While women inmates have a higher need for treatment (both in terms of prevalence as well as severity of conditions) compared to male inmates, the prison system is limited in its resources and abilities to address these issues. For example, most facilities are inadequately staffed or lack the diagnostic tools needed to address women's gynecological issues. Women also have higher rates of chronic illnesses than the male population (Anderson, 2006). However, the demands for these services significantly outweigh their availability, and the lack of accessible services ranks high on the list of inmate complaints regarding quality of life issues in prison (WPA, 2003).

Children of Incarcerated Mothers: The Unintended Victims

Children of **incarcerated mothers** (and fathers) deal with a variety of issues that stem from the loss of a parent, including grief, loss, sadness, detachment, and aggressive or at-risk behaviors for delinquency. Additionally, these children are at high risk for ending up in prison themselves as adults. The location of many prisons makes it difficult for many children to retain physical ties with their mother throughout her incarceration. While more than two thirds of incarcerated mothers have children under the age of 18, only 9% of these women will ever get to be visited by their children while they are incarcerated (Van Wormer & Bartollas, 2010).

A small number of women enter prison already pregnant. Estimates indicate that approximately 6% of women in jail, 4% to 5% of women in state prisons, and 3% of women in federal prison are pregnant when they were arrested for their crimes (Glaze & Maruschak, 2008). While pregnancy is generally a happy time for most expectant mothers, these mothers-to-be face high levels of stress over how their incarceration might affect the lives of their children. One concern centers on the quality of prenatal care that she might experience behind bars. Here, women are concerned about how their physical health before and during their incarceration will impact their unborn child. Most of these women will give birth and return to prison within a few days without their new baby. This separation between mother and child can lead to mental health complications for the mother. In addition, they may be concerned over who will care for their child and fear they will miss out on the physical and emotional connections that mothers traditionally experience with a new baby (Wismont, 2000).

Giving birth while incarcerated can be a traumatizing experience. Consider the following scenario:

> A nurse in the labor room goes to attend to one of her patients who is in active labor and is ready to deliver her baby. The correctional officer removes the women's leg shackles and hand cuffs and immediately replaces them after the baby is born. (Ferszt, 2011, p. 254)

In 2012, 33 states had policies that permitted women to be shackled while they were in labor. Yet even those states that prohibit the practice demonstrate great variability of the law. Some prohibit the use of shackles only during the labor and delivery process. Rhode Island has one of the most comprehensive and liberal laws, in that they prohibit the use of restraints at any time during the second and third trimester, as well as during postpartum (World Law Direct, 2011). These laws state that prisoners needed to be restrained due to safety and security concerns. Several professional organizations, including the American Congress

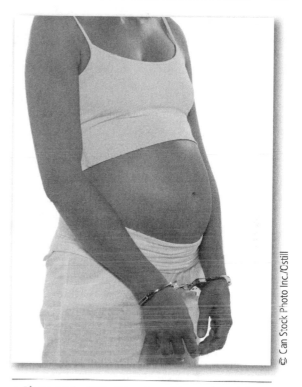

© Can Stock Photo Inc./Cstill

▲ **Photo 10.3** While many states have outlawed the practice of shackling women during childbirth, the use of restraints on pregnant women continues to present a number of health risks for both the mother and the child.

of Obstetricians and Gynecologists and the American Medical Association, have expressed concerns over these policies as they can lead to health risks to both the mother and her baby (Berg, 2011). For example, if a woman is shackled (meaning her legs are either restrained to each other or to the side of the bed), it can be difficult for hospital staff to assist a woman during a normal childbirth experience and can significantly complicate the delivery during an emergency situation. This has potentially disastrous effects for both the women and her baby. "If the fetal heart beat slows, and an immediate Caesarian-section is required, the time lost to fumbling with shackle locks could cause brain damage and even death" (WPA, n.d., "Laws Banning," para. 4).

Over the past several years, a number of states have passed new laws that forbid the practice of shackling female inmates during delivery. For example, Florida recently abolished the use of shackling of any pregnant woman during labor and delivery, the first such law in a southern state (Lopez, 2012). California recently passed a law that prohibits the use of shackles (feet), handcuffs (hands), or belly chains during childbirth ("Shackling Pregnant Inmates", 2012). However, some jurisdictions have been slow to respond to new laws in their jurisdiction. While Illinois in 1999 outlawed shackling inmates during labor, the practice continued up until 2012 at places such as the Cook County Jail in Chicago. Eighty women filed a class action suit alleging that they were unnecessarily shackled during birth and recovery and were awarded 4.1 million dollars in damages in May 2012 (Mastony, 2012).

In an effort to improve both the emotional well-being of the mother and encourage attachment and bonding between a mother and her infant, nine states (New York, California, Illinois, Indiana, Ohio, Nebraska, South

Dakota, Washington, and West Virginia) have integrated prison nurseries into their facilities, which allow for women to remain with their infant children for at least part of their sentence (WPA, 2009b). The oldest prison nursery program is located at Bedford Hills Correctional Facility in New York. Founded in 1901, this program is the largest in the country and allows for 29 mothers to reside with their infant children. Women who participate in these prison nursery programs take classes on infant development and participate in support groups with other mothers. Although most programs limit the time that a child can reside with his or her mother (generally 12–18 months), the Washington Correctional Center for Women is unique in that its prison nursery program allows for children born to incarcerated women to remain with their mothers for up to 3 years (WPA, 2009b). Other states allow for overnight visits with children, either in special family units on the prison grounds or in specialized cells within the facility. At Bedford Hills, older children can participate in programs at the facility with their mothers (Van Wormer & Bartollas, 2010). These programs help families repair and maintain ties between a mother and her child(ren) throughout her incarceration.

Prison nursery programs are not without their critics, as some suggest that prison is an inappropriate place for children. However, separating mothers and their children can also have detrimental effects, as children of incarcerated mothers are more likely to have educational challenges and limited emotional attachments. There is also a cycle of incarceration as children of imprisoned parents have an increased risk toward delinquent and criminal behaviors. Not only do these programs such as the mother-baby nurseries help to end the cycle of incarceration for both the mother and child, but they also assist in the reduction of recidivism once a woman is released from custody (WPA, 2009b). Unfortunately, many prison administrators are unaware of the benefits that a prison nursery can serve. Additional concerns involve the costs of implementing such a program and a belief that prison was an inappropriate place for children (Campbell & Carlson, 2012).

While the concept of the prison nursery and programming for children of incarcerated mothers helps promote the bond between parent and child, what about those states where these types of programs are not available? What happens to these children? The majority of women in the criminal justice system are the primary custodial parents for their young children, and these women must determine who will care for their children while they are incarcerated. Some may have a husband or children's father to turn to for assistance, though many will seek out extended family members, including grandparents. Seventy-nine percent of children who have an incarcerated parent are raised by an extended family member (WPA, 2003). In cases where an extended family member is unable or unavailable to care for a woman's minor child(ren), social services will place them in foster care. When a woman faces a long term of incarceration, the Adoption and Safe Families Act of 1997 terminates the parental rights in cases where children have been in foster care for 15 months (out of the previous 22 months). Given the increases in strict sentencing practices, the effects of this law mean that the majority of incarcerated women will lose their children if a family member is unable to care for them while the mother serves her sentence (Belknap, 2007).

Given that many of these women will regain custody of their children following the completion of their sentence, it is important that they maintain a connection with their children during this time. This can be a challenging prospect. In many cases, prison facilities are far removed from where these children reside. The cost of traveling to visit a parent can be prohibitive, particularly for families that struggle with the day-to-day economics of raising a child. This means that the majority of women in custody do not receive regular physical visits from their children. While 35% of women correspond with their children via the telephone and 49% communicate via letters, this means that half of the children do not have a relationship with their mother during her incarceration. This can have a detrimental impact on the parent–child relationship. In cases where the women will return to an authoritative parental role following their release from prison, it is important for families to maintain a parent–child bond. Here, extended family members play a crucial role in maintaining the connection between incarcerated women and their children (Stringer & Barnes, 2012).

Given that the majority of women in prison are mothers and that many were the primary caregiver of minor children prior to their incarceration, facilities have begun to implement parenting programs designed to help inmates develop effective parenting skills. Not only can these programs help provide a better relationship between a mother and her child(ren), but it can also help to prevent recidivism. As a result of this curriculum, these mothers increased their knowledge about childhood development, altered their attitudes about physical discipline, and developed an understanding about the needs and well-being of their children (Sandifer, 2008).

CASE STUDY

Spotlight on the Girl Scouts Beyond Bars Program

Funded by the National Institute of Justice, the first Girl Scouts Beyond Bars (GSBB) program was offered at the Maryland Correctional Institution for Women in November 1992 (Girl Scouts [GSA], 2008). As part of the program, mothers meet with their daughters twice a month on prison grounds to work on troop projects, such as math and science projects, as well as creative activities that focus on topics such as self-esteem, relationships, and teen development/pregnancy prevention. By 2008, there were over thirty-seven programs nationwide. Research has shown that the Girl Scouts Behind Bars program has been effective in a number of ways. First, the program facilitates regular contact between mothers and their daughter(s), which allows the mothers to have an active role in childrearing. Spending quality time together also strengthens the mother-child bond even though she is incarcerated (Moses, 1995). Research indicates that the majority (85%) of girls who participated in these programs had a closer bond with their mom following their participation in the program (GSA, 2008). Second, the program also benefits the children, as research documents that their behavior at home and educational involvement improve (Block & Potthast, 1998). Additionally, the girls learned a variety of prosocial behaviors, such as respect and leadership, and developed a positive attitude about their personal futures (GSA, 2008).

While there are significant benefits to be gained by participating in the Girl Scouts Behind Bars program, they do require significant emotional and physical investments by its supporters. Similar to traditional Girl Scouts (GS) programs, GSBB programs are run primarily by volunteers. In traditional GS programs, parents serve as the troop leaders. GSBB programs require a commitment by the community and family members to help organize and lead these programs (Block, 1999). Despite these challenges, the Girl Scouts Beyond Bars represents a program with positive effects for both a mother and her daughter.

▨ Summary

- The first prison for women was opened in 1839 in response to the growing concerns of abuse of women in male prison facilities.
- The reformatory prison was designed to rehabilitate women from their immoral ways.
- The custodial institution offered very little in terms of rehabilitative programming for incarcerated women.
- Women of color are overrepresented in women's prisons.
- While in prison, women develop acquaintances, friendships, pseudo-families, and romantic relationships to provide emotional support.
- Women in custody face a variety of unique issues, many of which the prison is ill equipped to deal with.
- Some facilities have prison nursery programs, which allow mothers to remain with their infant children while incarcerated.
- Programs such as Girl Scouts Beyond Bars help to provide the parent–child bond while mothers are incarcerated.

KEY TERMS

Custodial institutions

Fry, Elizabeth

Incarcerated mothers

Pseudo-families

Reformatory

DISCUSSION QUESTIONS

1. If you were to build a women's prison that reflected gender-responsive principles, what key features would you integrate into your facility?

2. Discuss the profile for women who are incarcerated in our prison facilities. In what ways are incarcerated women different from incarcerated men?

3. What challenges do incarcerated women face? How does prison impact the children of these mothers?

WEB RESOURCES

Hour Children: http://www.hourchildren.org

Our Place DC: http://www.ourplacedc.org

The Sentencing Project: http://www.sentencingproject.org

Women's Prison Association: http://www.wpaonline.org

Visit **www.sagepub.com/mallicoat2e** to access additional study tools including eFlashcards, web quizzes, web resources, video resources, and SAGE journal articles.

The majority of women in prison are mothers, and many of them were the primary caregivers for their minor children at the time of their arrest and incarceration. This article by Katarzyna Celinska and Jane A. Siegel includes interviews with 74 women who are awaiting a trial or are incarcerated and discusses the challenges that they face in being separated from their children.

Mothers in Trouble

Coping With Actual or Pending Separation From Children Due to Incarceration

Katarzyna Celinska and Jane A. Siegel

Introduction

Although they constitute only 7.5% of inmates (West & Sabol, 2009), female offenders are the fastest growing population in the America's prisons today. Some attribute this trend to gender-blind sentencing and the "war on drugs," which has been labeled an "unannounced war on women" (Chesney-Lind, 1998; Dolley, 2002).

From 1977 to 2008, the rate of incarceration of women grew by 943%, whereas the incarceration rate for men increased by 520% (Hill & Harrison, 2008; West & Sabol, 2009). Since 2000, women's incarceration rates have increased on average 4.6% annually (West & Sabol, 2009). In 2008, 115,779 women were incarcerated in state and federal prisons, and approximately 5 times more were under correctional supervision in the community (West & Sabol, 2009). The Federal Bureau of Justice Statistics reports that most incarcerated women are mothers and, unlike fathers in prison, were the main caregivers for their children before their imprisonment (Glaze & Maruschak, 2009; Mumola, 2000). In addition, the number of children with a mother in prison more than doubled (131%

increase) since 1991. In 2007, approximately 81% of mothers aged between 25 and 34 in state prison and 75% in federal prisons lived with their minor children prior to incarceration (Glaze & Maruschak, 2009).

Although those statistics indicate a growing social problem, relatively few studies in the fields of criminal justice and corrections focus on women offenders' experiences as mothers (Enos, 2001). This study was intended to fill this gap. It utilizes 74 semistructured interviews conducted with mothers before trial and during incarceration to document coping strategies that they employed to deal with potential or actual separation from their children.

Though there are studies that have examined women's experiences in prison, this study makes several important contributions. First, the sample is relatively large in comparison to other studies in this area: 74 interviews were conducted with women who were either separated or potentially faced pending separation from their children due to incarceration. Second, we analyzed the data using grounded theory to identify coping techniques. In addition, we classified them within a coping framework. Third, unlike other qualitative studies, this study sampled both

SOURCE: Celinska, K., & Siegel, J. A. (2010). Mothers in trouble: Coping with actual or pending separation from children due to incarceration. *The Prison Journal, 90*(4), 447–474.

women who were incarcerated in jail or prison and those who were in the community awaiting trial. This sampling strategy helps to differentiate behavioral patterns among women involved with the criminal justice system at different stages in the criminal justice process.

⬚ Prior Research on Incarcerated Mothers

Research suggests that female prisoners tend to share certain characteristics and many have problems that predate incarceration. They are likely to be poor, single, and disproportionately racial minorities; on average, incarcerated mothers have two children (Covington, 2002; Glaze & Maruschak, 2009; Hairston, 1991; Stanton, 1980). Most incarcerated women experienced multiple traumas in their lives, and many were sexually abused as children and victimized in their adolescence and adulthood (Boudin, 1998; Chesney-Lind, 1998; DeHart, 2008; Greene, Haney, & Hurtado, 2000). Most women in prison are incarcerated for drug-related offenses and were abusing drugs or alcohol before incarceration—arguably as a way of adapting to earlier life-course abuse and violence (Widom, 1989). According to McDaniels-Wilson and Belknap (2008), women's sexual victimization in many cases is a trajectory leading to criminal behavior. Henriques and Manatu-Rupert (2001) suggested that prison is a "safe haven" for some African American women from abuse and from addiction. In that sense, prison may actually mitigate some women's preexisting problems. Compared to men, women are more likely to be incarcerated for property crimes and minor offenses. Lastly, many incarcerated women suffer from mental health problems, such as depression (Bloom & Covington, 2009; Dalley & Michels, 2009; Glaze & Maruschak, 2009; Lindquist & Lindquist, 1997; Mumola, 2000).

Much of the research on women in prison has emphasized the centrality of the maternal role to women's identities and the importance that maintaining a maternal relationship has in adjustment within the institution and postrelease (e.g., Greene et al., 2000). In her study of 25 incarcerated mothers, Enos (2001) found that imprisoned mothers attempt to maintain their relationship with children by presenting themselves as "good mothers" and disassociating from other imprisoned but "unfit" mothers.

Furthermore, research has shown that mothers consider isolation and separation from their children to be the hardest aspects of imprisonment (e.g., Dodge & Pogrebin, 2001; Hairston, 1991). Based on her own experience in prison and observations and interviews conducted with other inmates, Boudin (1998) reported that incarcerated women feel "enormous grief" about time lost with their children. Others have found that women prisoners' primary concern centered on the effects of separation and incarceration on their children's lives and psychological development (Kazura, 2001).

Thus, children continue to play a central role in women's lives even during imprisonment. Mothers in prison often see children as motivation for change and their primary purpose in life (Enos, 2001; Ferraro & Moe, 2003), and they worry about their children's care (Henriques, 1982). Women are concerned about their ability to both sustain their relationships with children during imprisonment and regain or continue it after release from prison (Enos, 2001). While incarcerated, they may idealize their relationships with their children and have high hopes about their family lives following reunification (Hairston, 1991; Stanton, 1980). However, once released, the pains of financial hardship, social stigma, shame, and struggles in addiction recovery often make it difficult for women to reclaim their relationships with their children (Dodge & Pogrebin, 2001; Richie, 2001). According to Arditti and Few (2006), female ex-offenders need assistance in addressing "three threats" to full community reintegration: substance abuse, trauma, and mental disorders. In addition, many researchers report that mothers face not only familial and community barriers to maintaining maternal roles and relationships during and after imprisonment but also criminal justice and child welfare system impediments (e.g., see Beckerman, 1998, for details on the social and personal cost of the Adoption and Safe Families Act of 1997).

The literature on relationships between imprisoned parents and their children tends to focus on the issue of maintaining parent–child contact during incarceration. Many researchers believe that children's visits, phone calls, and mail assist in sustaining a parent–child bond, lessen the deleterious impact of separation, and help parents adjust to the prison environment (Berry & Eigenberg, 2003; Casey-Acevedo & Bakken, 2002). Even correctional officials, who may hold negative stereotypes about incarcerated mothers (Schram, 1999), tend to agree that visitation helps inmates cope with separation from their families (Casey-Acevedo & Bakken, 2002).

Other researchers assert that the benefits from visitation may be contingent upon the type of relationship between child and parent before incarceration, the immediate goals of the visit, and available support for children and parents before, during, and after the visit (Gabel, 1992). Others suggest that, in fact, phone calls are a more effective mode of communication than visits (Owen & Bloom, 1995). Finally, some skeptical researchers argue that prison visitation imposes a very restricted experience of motherhood and, as a result, does little to lessen the pains of imprisonment. Even when mothers are visited by their children, the visits are usually irregular, or of poor quality, due to the same problems that limit some children and their families from visiting mothers in the first place: the distant location of women's prisons, lack of transportation, restrictive and burdensome prison rules, and child-unfriendly visiting areas (Block & Potthast, 1998; Bloom & Steinhart, 1993; Mumola, 2000). For example, Hairston (1998) describes families and children standing in line for hours to be cleared for a short visit in crowded and noisy facilities or visits with jailed mothers who are separated from visitors by a glass barrier. Some correctional facilities impose a no-visitation policy for the first 60 days following a prisoner's arrival in prison (Kazura, 2001). Finally, further challenges to sustaining relationships between imprisoned parents and their families arise when correctional institutions treat family visitation as a behavioral control mechanism, withholding visitation for rule infractions (Dressel, Porterfield, & Barnhill, 1998).

Understandably, given the problems listed previously, some children's caregivers discourage or prohibit visits (Bloom & Steinhart, 1993). Researchers have found that from 40% to 71% of mothers in prison or jail had never been visited by their children (Bloom & Steinhart, 1993; Casey-Acevedo & Bakken, 2002; Hairston, 1991; Mumola, 2000). This low rate of visitation is attributable in part to prisoners' own desires, with many mothers reporting that they prefer not to see family and friends while incarcerated (Casey-Acevedo & Bakken, 2002). Hairston found that 63% of women in her sample claimed that they did not want to be visited by their children. However, they were the same women who had never been visited by any family members in the first place.

Coping With Potential or Actual Separation Due to Imprisonment

Thoits (1995) recommended that research on stress and coping, usually studied within a psychological framework, should be expanded to sociological questions to promote social change. The current study is an attempt to follow this recommendation by analyzing a phenomenon not sufficiently described in the literature, related to the social problem of increasing female incarceration rates and its concomitant impact on family structure.

Clearly, being imprisoned poses many challenges to a woman's ability to sustain her maternal role, given that "they are unable to do mothering on a daily basis" (Berry & Eigenberg, 2003, p. 104). Recognizing that incarcerated women would view separation from their children as one of the most challenging and burdensome aspects of imprisonment, we expected that they would employ diverse approaches to cope with separation and to sustain their maternal identity.

Moreover, based on studies among incarcerated mothers, we expected that a similar pattern would emerge among women anticipating incarceration. Incarceration is not an event that occurs unexpectedly. It takes place after an extended period involving the adjudicatory process and sentencing. The mere act of being arrested raises the specter of possible separation and the need to cope with the prospect of that eventuality.

Coping has been defined as "constantly changing cognitive and behavioral efforts to manage specific external and/or internal demands that are appraised as taxing or exceeding the resources of the person" (Lazarus & Folkman, 1984, pp. 141). In this definition, "coping is a process-oriented" phenomenon and is viewed as a way to manage stressful circumstances and events regardless of what the outcomes are (Lazarus & Folkman, 1984). We presume that pending or actual separation from children due to imprisonment is indeed a "taxing" circumstance that requires coping. Thus, our research attempted to uncover the ways mothers cope with the pressures and strains associated with their roles as mothers.

The concept of coping has its roots in psychoanalytic ego psychology (Lazarus & Folkman, 1984). Accordingly, the literature on coping is concentrated mainly in the field of psychology. Within the fields of criminology and criminal justice, only a limited number of quantitative studies addresses coping by incarcerated females. In one such study of female adjustment to imprisonment, Negy, Woods, and Carlson (1997) found six coping techniques that were positively associated with adjustment and two that were negatively associated. However, this study did not differentiate between mothers and nonmothers. Houck and Loper (2002) surveyed 362 incarcerated mothers to measure parental stress related to imprisonment. They found that mothers exhibited stress associated with self-perceived skills and competence as a parent. Interestingly, the mothers did not report distress related to attachment with their children. Although this study focused on sources of maternal stress during incarceration, it did not address the issue of how mothers managed or coped with stress. Finally, Berry and Eigenberg (2003) examined factors that affected the maternal role strain of incarcerated women. They found minorities, women with shorter sentences, and those who approved of the temporary child care arrangements for their children experienced significantly less role strain than other incarcerated mothers.

We located no qualitative studies that directly examine how mothers cope with possible or actual separation from their children. However, several studies detail the hardships and challenges of separation from children and mothering from prison. For example, Enos (2001) interviewed 25 mothers incarcerated in a state prison, focusing on how imprisoned mothers managed to maintain their roles as mothers. She found that mothers sought to affirm their fitness as mothers by "identity talk"—that is, defending their past and present maternal competence in conversations with others—and by actions like arranging visits with children and being involved in children's current care. Other studies based on interviews with incarcerated mothers (e.g., Datesman & Cales, 1983; Hairston, 1991) tend to focus on the consequences of separation and related programmatic and policy changes.

After identifying different coping styles described by the mothers in this study, we categorized them within Lazarus and Folkman's (1984) binary coping typology of emotion- and problem-focused coping. Emotion-focused coping modifies and decreases stress and trauma via cognitive-emotional means, such as positive reinterpretation and acceptance—both of which are often aided through religion. Mechanic (1962) described emotion-focused coping as a defense used to maintain integrity and to control feelings.

Problem-focused coping, by contrast, involves actively managing the problem that causes the stressful situation. Components of problem-focused coping include defining the problem, planning and choosing solutions, weighing the costs and benefits of action, and the actual behavior engaged in as the coping mechanism.[1] In addition, we also consider whether the coping mechanisms are adaptive or maladaptive (Carver, Scheier, & Weintraub, 1989). Whereas adaptive methods improve the management of stress, maladaptive techniques ultimately pile on more stress and decrease coping capacity. Carver et al. provide examples of maladaptive techniques, such as acting out, withdrawal, or denial.

Methods and Data

The data used in this study come from a larger study examining the impact of parental incarceration on children and included semistructured interviews conducted by the second author between 2002 and 2004. The researcher interviewed 37 incarcerated mothers (20 were in pretrial detention in the county jail of a large northeastern city, and 17 were inmates in a northeastern state prison) and 37 mothers awaiting trial at home. The protocol for this study was reviewed and approved by the Rutgers University Institutional Review Board. The adult participants signed forms for their own participation as well as for their children's participation. The child participants gave assent to participate.

The interviews provided women with an opportunity to share their life stories and discuss their parenting in depth. Ferraro and Moe (2003) suggested that life history narratives are the optimal method to collect data from incarcerated women and other marginalized populations.

Women recruited for the study all had at least one child aged between 8 and 18 years. Those in the pretrial groups (in pretrial detention and at home awaiting trial) were recruited for the purpose of observing mother–child relationships prior to incarceration, whereas the prison sample was recruited in order to better understand the consequences of long-term separation from children. The women in this group were represented by the city's public defender office. Nearly all those interviewed at home were recruited at court when they came in for their arraignment. The public defender provided any female defendant with a brief description of the study and asked her whether she would be willing to speak with the researcher. The women in pretrial detention were recruited in the county jail when a lawyer from the defender's office went to interview them in preparation for case disposition. Finally, flyers describing the study were distributed in the prison by the prison staff. Women interested in participating were then allowed to attend the general meeting with the researcher, after which individual meetings were held.

In our analysis, we let coping categories emerge, using the grounded theory method described by Glaser and Strauss (1967). The grounded theory technique allows for interpretation that aims at generating concepts, hypotheses, and theories from the data. This technique seems to be particularly useful when analyzing narratives and life stories. After identifying the major coping styles, we applied a basic coding scheme described earlier for classifying coping mechanisms as emotion focused, problem focused, and as adaptive or maladaptive.

The sample includes 55 Black (74%), 12 White (26%), and 7 (10%) Latino mothers. Thus, African American women are overrepresented, reflecting the particular racial makeup of the population of defendants and inmates from whom the samples were drawn. The average age of the mother in the sample was 34 years; also, the mother was single and had 3 children from 2 partners; 78% of incarcerated mothers lived with at least one of their children before incarceration; 55 women (81%) admitted to past and/or current drug abuse predominantly of cocaine; 24 mothers (32%) spontaneously reported being abused as children; and 34 mothers (46%) reported having been in a violent intimate relationship. On average, mothers had been arrested 5 times and incarcerated once (including their current incarceration).[2] The women's most common current charges were drug possession and/or sale or assault.

✉ Results

Although mothers' stories and experiences differ in many respects, the central theme that emerged in the interviews was motherhood. Mothers who were incarcerated and mothers who were awaiting trial talked extensively about their experiences as mothers. Incarcerated mothers were aware of their inability to perform most of their maternal duties, whereas mothers awaiting trial were dealing with the possibility of losing their ability to perform them.

As a consequence, mothers were experiencing stress and strain and discussed how they tried to cope with them.

This analysis uncovered seven techniques that incarcerated mothers and mothers who were awaiting trial employed to cope with the problems arising from actual or pending separation from their children: being a good mother, mothering from prison, role redefinition, disassociation from prisoner identity, self-transformation, planning and preparation, and self-blame. In what follows, we discuss each coping strategy in more detail.

Being a Good Mother

"Being a good mother" was an emotion-focused coping strategy that mothers uniformly employed to affirm their fitness as mothers. Mothers in all three groups tended to present themselves as good and capable mothers. However, the arguments and symbols used to construct and convey a self-image as a fit mother differed slightly among the subgroups.

Mothers awaiting trial at home were able to demonstrate their bona fides by focusing on everyday life events and the bond they had with their children, based on these daily and routine activities. For example, one mother of 4 children (age 32) explained, "We eat together, we sleep together, everything. I don't go out and, you know, like a lot of people go out. I don't go out or nothing, it's just me and my children."

Mothers in prison and jail attempted to continue performing their roles as mothers—albeit in a highly circumscribed manner. For many jailed and incarcerated women, establishing their credentials as good mothers also meant having to defend their parenting skills against their criminal and drug-abusing past, the very behavior that had separated them from their children. For example, one mother of 4 children (age 28) who was a heavy drug user before her incarceration discussed how she was able to take good care of her children despite her drug use:

> Drugs were controlling me, but I also had control of my life. I got high in the house, never got high out of the house. The kids stayed clean all the time; I never left them with anyone but my

Reading Table 10.1   Coping Techniques: Definition, Categories, and Prevalence

Coping	Definition	Coping Category	Percentage
Being a good mother	Motherhood as a central identity	Emotion focused, adaptive	100%
Disassociation from prisoner identity	Detachment from prison and other inmates	Emotion focused, adaptive (short-term), and maladaptive (long-term)	31% & 41% (jailed & incarcerated)
Mothering from prison	Maintaining relationship and parental supervision from prison	Problem focused, adaptive	66% & 95% (jailed & incarcerated)
Role redefinition (role reversal)	Children as capable grown-ups: friends and/or confidants.	Emotion focused, adaptive	51% & 49% (before trial)
Self-transformation	Mother resolves to change behavior and lifestyle	Emotion focused and problem focused, adaptive	61% & 88% (incarcerated)
Planning and preparation	Making decisions about future	Problem focused (pretrial sample) and emotion focused (incarcerated mothers), adaptive	54% & 100% (incarcerated)
Self-blame	Guilt and shame for separation from children	Emotion focused, maladaptive	32% & 59% (incarcerated)

NOTE: The first percentage is based on the whole sample (74 cases) and the second percentage is based on the subsample identified in the parenthesis.

mother or my sister. The refrigerator was always filled; my house was clean.

Another mother (age 36, three children) explained,

'Cause you have some mothers who have kids and they get high right there in front of their kids. And a lot of the kids run around the house hungry, being neglected . . . but I didn't do that.

"I was a super mom. They got whatever they wanted," added another incarcerated mother (age 40, two children).

Children sometimes provided further confirmation that a woman was a good mother. For instance, one mother in prison (age 33, two children) incarcerated on a drug conviction said,

That's a good thing to know, that they look at me as a good mom, not a bad mom, because I'm locked up. 'Cause that's what I was thinking, I'm

a bad mom, I'm on drugs, you know. They don't see it like that, and Takann, she just wants to know when I am coming home.

Further evidence of the incarcerated women coping with the need to defend their maternal competence came from statements reflecting concern about their children's current child care, the type of concern that might be expected of a *good* mother. For instance, one 28-year-old mother of two children worried about the health of her children's grandmother, their current caregiver: "And God forbid that something should happen to her—then my kids end up in the system. God forbid! My mom is not capable, you know what I mean? I'm not saying that's what would happen. But it's possible." Another mother (age 24, one child) said that her daughter

[. . .] tells me that I don't love her because if I loved her, I wouldn't be locked up. She tells me that she misses me. Sometimes I can hear in her voice that she's a little depressed. She wants me home. Some things she can't talk to my mother or sister about.

Coping with threats to their maternal identity by reinforcing their maternal role was very important, since many mothers saw their children as the light at the end of the tunnel of their incarceration and had a great deal invested in their self-image as mothers, poignantly expressed by one mother (age 37, four children):

> You see, my kids are my life [Starts crying] Sometimes I think I'm still alive because of them, you know, because I want to go home to them. If it hadn't been for them, I don't think I would have cared. Honestly, I wouldn't care.

Another mother (age 25, one child) said,

> I don't want my daughter to be 18 visiting me in prison. I see a lot of women that have kids and never talk about them. With me, I stay talking about my daughter. I love her to death. She's the best thing that ever happened to me.

There were also similarities in how mothers in the three groups defined and performed their maternal role. Mothers in all three samples, just like any "other mother," expressed concern about their children regularly going to school, doing homework, and staying away from drugs and crime. One incarcerated mother (age 33, two children) explained:

> I know at this age this is when you get introduced to pot. I've been there. And drinks. So, I wonder about that. And I hope and pray that she don't. That's why I'm mad at myself a lot 'cause I'm not there.

Mothers of girls and boys were also concerned about pregnancy at an early age: "When I got locked up, I wrote to her and I told her, 'You know, these boys are looking at you. But if you're out there having sex, please get out there and get some protection'" (age 36, three children).

In general, the mothers viewed their relationships with their children in a positive way. They tended to portray these relationships as unique, special, and emotionally meaningful. One incarcerated mother (age 36, one child) said, "But my son will come to me right now and talk to me about his girl. . . . He tells me everything, like I'm his best friend in the world. That's being a good mother."

Disassociation From Prisoner Identity

Establishing their bona fides as credible mothers was one way to cope with the problem imposed by the incarcerated women's absence from their families. Another emotion-focused technique utilized to cope with threats to their maternal identity was disassociation from the image of a prisoner. Even mothers at home utilized this technique, though it was obviously concentrated mainly among jailed and incarcerated mothers, 41% of whom indicated that they employed it. With striking consistency, incarcerated women distanced themselves from their fellow prisoners. As one mother (age 32, four children) firmly explained when discussing how some women end up in prison multiple times: "You got to be crazy in your head to want to keep going back to a place like that. That's no place for no human being." Another mother (age 35, three children) said,

> I didn't come here to make friends, and there's so much bull crap around here. I'm leaving. I knew the day I walked in that I was leaving sooner or later. When I leave I don't want to take anyone from here with me. I'm not that needy. Like, emotionally, I can handle this on my own. I'm used to it.

Disassociation from prisoner identity was present in several different ways. Some women claimed that though there are people who belong in jail or prison, they do not fit in there. "There is no reason for me to be here. I'm a high school grad. I took some computer classes, some college courses here. . . . I'm too smart to be in jail" (age 24, one child).

Other mothers tended to minimize the behavior that resulted in their incarceration thereby distinguishing themselves from other prisoners. One mother (age 28, two children) said: "I don't understand. Personally, since I've been in here, I've seen women who killed their children leave before me. And it baffles me, I've no understanding. I would never hurt anybody." The same mother added, "All these men that did a hell of a lot more than me [. . .], are still free."

Disassociating themselves from a prisoner's image was both an adaptive and maladaptive coping strategy for the women. Refusing to accept the negative connotations associated with the image of a prisoner helped women hold onto their own identity as somehow different and, therefore, potentially still having the right to be seen as a good mother. On the other hand, distancing themselves as they did to avoid identification with their fellow inmates meant that they were denied any comfort and solidarity other women in similar situations might have provided, which in turn could have helped them adapt to their situation.

Mothering From Prison

In addition to confronting the need to establish and maintain a maternal identity and to distinguish themselves from other prisoners, incarcerated mothers had to find ways to cope with their diminished capacity to provide active mothering. The principle means they utilized to sustain their maternal bond was by maintaining contact with their children and their surrogate caregivers, a problem-focused and adaptive strategy. One mother (age 28, two children) explained:

> Um, when they used to come up and visit me, that was like my bonding session. [. . .] like to be able to speak to them face to face and see them and ask them if everything is okay and look at them in the eye and know.

Another mother (age 35, three children) is serving time in prison for attempted murder. She was a drug and alcohol user in the past. She misses her children and plans to reunify with them after incarceration, making clear that she still tries to be a mother to them while she is locked up: "I write my kids, like each one. They all get individual letters. [. . .] I try to emotionally help them, help support them. I try to put fun and games in there with them, too."

The attempts to maintain their parental authority and remain actively engaged in their children's lives—"mothering from prison"—included decision making about their children's future and staying abreast of their children's whereabouts and their progress in school. Although the visits were often described as a main tool of mothering from prison, 41% of incarcerated mothers and 75% of jailed mothers in the sample received no visits from their children. One of the mothers (age 28, two children) described the disincentives for her children to visit:

> It's crazy. It's really far. It's a hassle. 'Cause the visits out here are nine o'clock in the morning. In the morning traffic, to get here by nine o'clock you have to be here earlier—actually, by eight thirty. You would have to leave so early. . . . My kids would have to be up five o'clock in the morning to come in. It's just a big hassle.

The interviews suggest that phone calls and letters, along with sporadic visits, are the primary channels through which mothering from prison occurs. Arguably, more frequent and better quality visits, phone calls, and letters would aid women in coping. It is also likely that it would help women ease their transition to life in community after release from prison. However, the results of the data also confirm the prior reports and studies about persistent and system-wide barriers to maintain a mother–child relationship in prison via these traditional ways of communication. In their study, Berry and Eigenberg (2003) noted that mothering is not a static characteristic but rather an active and ever-changing attribute. As such, it does not depend exclusively on the number of family visits to prison but rather on myriad factors. For example, the extent to which incarcerated mothers can maintain their authority is tied to the cooperation of the children's caregivers. Women who most effectively mothered from prison were those whose children's guardians included them to the largest extent possible in the children's lives and facilitated communication between the mother and child.

Role Redefinition

Role redefinition and role reversal phenomena have been previously described in the field of psychology and, specifically, in the area of developmental psychopathology. Role reversal, the extreme form of role redefinition, has been defined as a relationship disturbance in which parents rely on children to meet their needs for comfort and intimacy, and children take the roles of parents or peers (Kerig, 2003).

Our analyses revealed a similar type of role redefinition in which mothers redefined their children as friends or even confidants. By attributing exaggerated maturity to their children, these mothers seemed to neutralize the harms they may have caused their children, while minimizing their own guilt and sense of failure, thus making this technique an adaptive strategy, at least in the short term. Although this emotion-focused technique was evident in all three subsamples, it was most prominent among mothers awaiting trial who were living at home.

Mothers living with their children tended to vividly recall circumstances and events in which their children acted in a mature way. One mother (age 46, five children) summarized it as follows: "I learned how to talk up and speak to them. Talk to them like adults now." Similarly, a younger mother of two (age 35) explained her relationship with her daughter: "You know, we're not mother-daughter. We never had a mother-daughter relationship. We were most like sisters. Like, you know, and I don't know if it's a good thing or a bad thing but that's the truth."

The interviews revealed that many children prematurely witnessed or experienced adverse events like violence in the home, their mothers' arrests and incarceration, or their mothers' substance abuse. Often, as a consequence of these experiences, older children had to fulfill some grown-up responsibilities, such as taking care of the younger siblings. In some cases, children actually exhibited some adult-like behavior and assumed the role of protective guardians of their vulnerable and dependent mothers. Such "parentification" (Cox, Paley, & Harter, 2001) or "adult gratification" (Grella & Greenwell, 2006) is aptly illustrated by a short conversation between a drug-using mother and her young daughter, Mariah, that her mother recounted having: "Are you going out to get high today mom?" 'I'd say, "Yeah, why?" "Well, I think that you need some money." 'She'd go in her little piggy bank.' "Well, here's ten dollars to get you started" (age 27, four children). Another mother (age 34, four children) recalled her conversation with her son:

"Either you had too many cigarettes, or you had some bad drugs." And, I was like, "Really?" And, he was like, "Yeah. But, I think it's the drugs though." And ever since that day, I just felt as though even though I didn't want him to know, but I thought it was kind of important that I explain myself to him. But, it really hurt me for him to know that I was doing drugs.

In both examples, mothers seemed to recognize how unhealthy and damaging to their children their relationships were. However, most mothers seemed also to believe that taking the roles of an adult by their children was a sign of maturity and resilience in the face of the harms their mothers' behavior inflicted upon them.

Self-Transformation

Many women explicitly expressed the shame they felt about their situation and about letting their children down when they were imprisoned. One way to cope with such deep disappointment was to focus on self-transformation, an adaptive process that we classified as both emotion and problem focused. Approximately 45 women talked about self-transformation in their narratives. Some women consciously took active steps to improve their lot, which may have actually improved their perceived maternal efficacy. One mother (age 29, six children) explained,

I've been through rehab, detox, programs, all that. This time, I'm gonna leave it in God's hands. I've been clean before. But I want it now more than I ever did. I plan on going to church for help. I want to get a job, and keep my mind occupied.

This quote illustrates the fact that the process of self-transformation often included becoming spiritual or religious, which many saw as a pathway to desistance from drug and alcohol use. Several other mothers mentioned being involved in community and helping others. One mother said,

I had a dream that maybe one day I would be able to help troubled teenagers, so while in their youth they have a chance to do something with themselves before they get too old. That's one of the dreams I have had . . . to help people that have all these different problems. (age 36, one child)

Planning and Preparation

Approximately 40 mothers talked about planning and preparation for the future, an adaptive strategy that was problem focused among those awaiting trial and more emotion focused than problem focused for those in prison. Mothers talked about who would take care of their children in the event they were incarcerated after their cases were heard in court. They generally knew who their children's caregiver would be because in most cases, the same family members were already involved in caring for their children.

Incarcerated mothers talked about getting jobs and finding places to live after release, though these plans were insubstantial and indefinite. Leaving the prison was the main concern: "My priority, first of all, is getting out of here" (age 37, four children). It was followed by concerns of parenting: "Then when I do go home, I'm gonna be like a different person and I got to make him my baby again" (age 24, one child). Another mother (age 24, one child) said,

> Go home, see my mom and my daughter. I want to continue to be positive and live a positive life. I want to do the best I can ... be a better mother and a better daughter. Focus on myself, my mom, my daughter and my sister. Stay away from negativity.

Self-Blame

This emotion-focused technique, which we classified as maladaptive, was present nearly exclusively among incarcerated mothers—a number of whom admitted that their life choices had an adverse impact on their children. Being in prison seemed to have given them a different perspective on their past behavior, leading to the need to cope with feelings of guilt and shame about their past actions. Mothers who utilized self-blame admitted these feelings and expressed responsibility for their past behavior. A mother (age 36, one child) admitted: "The only thing I regret even though my life had been real hard is not being a better mother to my son. I could have been better than I was, but I can't change that." Another mother (age 40, three children) declared, "Like I said, don't nobody really understand how much my children mean to me. Because I could never repay the pain that I put them through. Younger, even though they were younger, they still feel the pain." One woman (age 33, one child) expressed hope that she would be able to "get out of here in enough time to make it up to him [son]. To show him love."

Initially, we tended to view self-blame primarily as a negative and even destructive strategy. However, we realized that self-blame plays an important role in mothers' self-transformation. Self-blame might be self-harmful, especially when no help or assistance is provided to mothers to *counterbalance* it. On the other hand, self-blame, if followed by real opportunities for self-transformation and a change in circumstances might be a step toward positive reinterpretation and adaptive coping.

Conclusions

The questions asked in the interviews allowed women to freely present their life stories and talk about their relationships with children, partners, family members, and friends. We were able to identify seven main coping strategies employed by mothers to deal with separation from their children: being a good mother, mothering from prison, role redefinition, disassociation from prisoner identity, self-transformation, planning and preparation, and self-blame.

In order to categorize coping techniques that emerged from our data, we drew traditional distinctions between emotion-focused and problem-focused and between adaptive and maladaptive coping techniques. We found that mothers used multiple strategies and tended to employ emotion-focused over problem-focused techniques and adaptive over maladaptive techniques.

Lazarus and Folkman (1984) enumerated several so-called coping resources needed to develop and utilize coping strategies effectively: health and energy, positive beliefs, positive solving skills, social skills, social support, and material resources. Although researchers tend to maintain that active, goal-oriented, or problem-focused techniques are more effective in managing stress and trauma (Thoits, 1995), individuals do not have equal access to the resources that would facilitate their ability to employ them. Researchers agree that disadvantaged minority women tend to have very limited access to coping resources (Thoits, 1995) that would enable them to use active or problem-focused strategies. Instead, they are inclined to employ a smaller number of less effective emotion-focused coping techniques.

Most mothers in this study came from disadvantaged, lower social and economic strata. They often struggled with physical and mental problems and suffered from a lack of social support. Thus, though mothers were planning or attempting an active response to stress and separation, most often they were not able to deliver on their efforts. For example, though some mothers attempted to mother their children from prison, their families' economic limitations and prison regulations prevented regular face-to-face visits thereby significantly inhibiting their ability to do so.

As a consequence of the prison context and limited resources both inside and outside the prison, mothers employed mainly emotion-focused coping techniques. Establishing and maintaining a maternal identity emerged in this study as dominant challenges with which women in prison must cope. The present findings confirm prior research about the central role of motherhood among incarcerated mothers (e.g., Enos, 2001). In addition, we found that mothers awaiting trial tended to use the same techniques when faced with potential separation from their children. Being a good mother was linked to the need to disassociate oneself from a prisoner self-image. The finding that more than 40% of mothers who talked about their prison and jail experience tended to disassociate themselves from prison or jail was surprising at first. This rejection might be a counterproductive and maladaptive method of dealing with incarceration and separation. On the other hand, disassociation from prison does appear to be an appropriate way of defending a good-mother image. Mothers isolate themselves in order to protect their core identity as a good mother, which because of the stigma of imprisonment, they see as incompatible with self-identification as a prisoner.

We also found that 51% of mothers in our sample and 49% of mothers who were awaiting trial employed role redefinition as a coping strategy. This technique alleviated pressures resulting from perceived inadequacies and failings as mothers. It seems that mothers who are uncertain about their future (awaiting trial) opt to view their children as mature and probably able to handle a separation from them. Interestingly, this mode of adaptation seems to play a lesser role while mothers are jailed or incarcerated, perhaps because continuing to view their offspring as children helped incarcerated mothers reinforce their sense of motherhood by emphasizing the youthfulness of their children and, thus, their need for a mother. It is also likely that some children of incarcerated mothers actually experience less adversity while their mothers are in prison because they are better taken care of and, thus, can act as children again.

Rather than portraying children as mature individuals, incarcerated mothers tend to feel shame and tend to blame themselves for problems in their relationships with their children more frequently than mothers who still live outside. Thus, not only self-blame but also a commitment to self-transformation were more common among the imprisoned subsample. We suggest that self-blame primarily might be harmful in the short run but that it might lead toward adaptive coping if it is followed by real opportunities for self-transformation.

Some limitations of this research must be noted. The interview questions were not designed specifically to address the issue of coping but rather to focus on all aspects of mothers' lives and their relationships with children. Women who volunteered to participate in this study may have been better able to cope than others, which may explain why maladaptive coping was not as evident. In addition, whereas coping is a process (Lazarus & Folkman, 1984), there were no follow up interviews available that would have permitted investigation of the ongoing utilization of these techniques or their efficacy. Finally, the data on addiction, drug, and alcohol abuse, criminal history, and victimization came from the women themselves and were not compared with any official data.

This study offers also important contributions to the topic of mothers in the criminal justice system. The sampling of women at different stages in the process (before trial, in pretrial detention, and in prison) permits the analysis of coping as a dynamic process. In addition, the sample was uniform across many characteristics of women. Nonetheless, our analysis suggests that the length of incarceration and race might influence the ways mothers cope with separation from their children[3] confirming some results found in quantitative studies. Finally, we also found that traditional coping framework was highly contingent on the context in which women were situated. The division into emotion-focused and problem-focused, and especially adaptive and maladaptive, categories, was not clear-cut. For example, both disassociation from prisoner identity and self-blame could be either adaptive or maladaptive depending on characteristics of a particular mother and her specific life circumstances, including social support. Although we categorized mothering from prison as problem-focused coping, this way of adapting also carries important emotional weight. It appears to be a problem-focused and adaptive coping strategy, but it is plausible to conceive that visits (or rare visits) and phone calls (short and expensive for families) might in fact bring more stress and strain to incarcerated mothers and as such become a maladaptive way of adapting to prison and to separation from family and children.

This study has several important implications for correctional policy and practice. Prisons should consider adopting programs that support emotion-focused coping and model problem-focused coping techniques. For example, being a good mother (emotion-focused) and mothering from prison (problem-focused) [using] coping techniques can be aided by developing and supporting programs that help maintain contact and build relationships between imprisoned parents and their children, such as Girl Scouts Beyond Bars (Block & Potthast, 1998), Parenting From a Distance (Boudin, 1998), or Parents in Prison (Hairston & Lockett, 1987). Parenting classes and legal aid regarding parental rights could help mothers develop problem-focused coping skills.

In addition, certain correctional policy reforms should promote positive coping. Inconvenient and troublesome visiting hours, the distance of women's prisons from the cities, costly phone calls, rigid rules of visitations, and sending packages and letters, all hinder contact between incarcerated mothers and their children. The guiding principle of reforms to address these problems should be that visitation and other parental contact is a right and not a privilege. Removing or loosening restrictions on visitation should help women maintain a good-mother image and may help them accept a prisoner identity.

This study joins prior research in supporting calls for fundamental changes in policies that affect women and mothers in the criminal justice system. Incarcerated mothers differ from incarcerated fathers and differ from women in [the] general population. Women involved in the criminal justice system are more likely to face the *triple threat* of substance abuse; trauma due to sexual abuse; violence in childhood, adolescence, and adulthood; and mental health disorders (Arditti & Few, 2006; Bloom & Covington, 2009; Raj et al., 2008; Staton, Leukefeld, & Webster, 2003). Thus, researchers tend to agree that female prison inmates need a comprehensive gender-specific model of treatment and care (Arditti & Few, 2006; Chesney-Lind, 1998; Covington, 1998; Dalley, 2002;

Hairston, 1991; Staton et al., 2003). Proposed models generally encompass treatment for drug abuse and addiction, trauma recovery, and quality mental and physical health care. Such a model would aid in sustaining and developing important coping techniques, especially self-transformation. It could also reduce role redefinition and self-blame, the techniques that seem to be significant barriers to effective mothering. Finally, focusing on and providing assistance with addressing the triple threats within prison would assist mothers in building the skills necessary for functioning outside of prison and for reuniting successfully with their children.

Of course, successful mother–child reunification can be achieved only if women are not reincarcerated after their release. However, women face formidable challenges upon release. Compounding the challenge of reunification and readjustment to custodial parenting are the struggles to obtain and maintain a job, housing, sobriety, and quality health care (Dalley & Michels, 2009). According to Richie, women who leave the prisons are in need of wraparound and case management services that would focus on gender-specific needs and ensuring continuity of services received in prison, and Dalley (2002) recommends creating a separate counseling unit within probation departments to offer a coordinated, multiagency approach to assist women and their children. Thus, assistance within the community is crucial in women's successful reintegration and reunification with their families and children. It would assist in building problem-focused coping skills while providing vital emotional support. Women could be empowered by being able to find and utilize community resources and care (Richie, 2001).

Finally, the present research highlights the problem of social stigma and its adverse effects on mothering from prison. Negative labeling continues when women are released even though they are not viewed as bad individuals or bad parents by their children, families, and close communities (Hairston, 1998). Female ex-offenders frequently confront community distrust, their own shame and guilt, and social stigma, which often prevent them from finding a job and housing. Support groups, both within prison and in the community, could assist in reducing stigma and promoting positive coping techniques, such as self-transformation, being a good mother, and planning and preparation.

Services and treatment, both inside and outside of the criminal justice system, can assist mothers in effective coping with actual and pending separation from their families and children. A multimodal, continuous, and gender-specific approach can help mothers maintain their maternal identity and provide hope for their and their children's futures.

Notes

1. It is important to note that recent coping research tends to reject the use of simplified dichotomies. Skinner, Edge, Altman, and Sherwood (2003) claimed that the emotion-focused and problem-focused concepts are unclear [and] incomplete and that they overlap. Nonetheless, they also recognize that these concepts can be useful, especially in analyzing topics not examined yet in the coping literature.

2. Incarceration in this case refers to imprisonment either in jail or prison.

3. We found that mothers who lived with at least some of their children (78%) and mothers who did not live with any of their children before incarceration tended to employ similar coping techniques. We divided the sample of incarcerated mothers ($n = 17$) into two subgroups: mothers who were incarcerated for less than 6 months and mothers who were incarcerated for at least 6 months. Women in the first group were more likely to use the following two strategies: being a good mother and mothering from prison. This finding is plausible because separation from families was more recent and these mothers were more likely to be in contact with their children [and] make decisions about their future, and [they] overall believed that they were in fact involved in raising their children. We also found that mothers who were incarcerated for shorter time tended to cope more via self-transformation, disassociation from prisoner identity, and planning techniques. One possible explanation is that women with shorter incarceration had more available social and emotional resources to help them cope in adaptive and active ways. The question remains, however, whether the resources were really available (e.g., partly because these mothers had a stronger and better contact with their families and friends) or whether the women were more hopeful and optimistic about their opportunities and future because of less time spent in prison and their rejection of prison identity. These results appear to confirm Berry and Eigenberg's (2003) finding that women who served shorter sentences and were faced with shorter separation from their children experienced less role strain as mothers. We found two additional trends in the data. First, White mothers tended to employ mothering from prison more frequently than African American mothers. Second, African American mothers were more likely to employ self-blame than their White counterparts. These preliminary findings need to be explored further with a larger sample.

References

Arditti, J. A., & Few, A. L. (2006). Mothers' reentry into family life following incarceration. *Criminal Justice Policy Review, 17,* 103–123.

Beckerman, A. (1998). Charting a course: Meeting the challenge of permanency planning for children with incarcerated mothers. *Child Welfare, 77,* 513–530.

Berry, P. E., & Eigenberg, H. M. (2003). Role strain and incarcerated mothers: Understanding the process of mothering. *Women & Criminal Justice, 15*(1), 101–119.

Block, K. J., & Potthast, M. J. (1998). Girl Scout Beyond Bars: Facilitating parent-child contact in correctional settings. *Child Welfare, 77,* 561–579.

Bloom, B. E., & Covington, S. (2009). Addressing the mental health needs of women offenders. In R. L. Gido & L. P. Dalley (Eds.), *Women's mental health issues across the criminal justice system* (pp. 160–176). Upper Saddle River, NJ: Prentice Hall.

Bloom, B. E., & Steinhart, D. (1993). *Why punish the children? A reappraisal of the children of incarcerated mothers in America.* San Francisco: National Council on Crime and Delinquency.

Boudin, K. (1998). Lessons from a mother's program in prison: A psychological approach supports women and their children. *Women and Therapy, 21,* 103–125.

Carver, C. S., Scheier M. F., & Weintraub, J. K. (1989). Assessing coping strategies: A theoretically based approach. *Journal of Personality and Social Psychology, 56,* 267–283.

Casey-Acevedo, K., & Bakken, T. (2002). Visiting women in prison: Who visits and who cares? *Journal of Offender Rehabilitation, 34*(3), 67–83.

Chesney-Lind, M. (1998). The forgotten offender. *Corrections Today, 60*(7), 66–72.

Covington, S. S. (1998). Women in prison: Approaches in the treatment of our most invisible population. *Women and Therapy, 21,* 141–155.

Covington, S. S. (2002). *A woman's journey home: Challenges for female offenders and their children, 249–273.* Paper presented at The "From Prisons to Home" Conference, sponsored by the National Institutes of Health and U.S. Department of Health and Human Services, Washington, DC.

Cox, M. J., Paley, B., & Harter, K. (2001). Interparental conflict and parent-child relationships. In J. H. Grych & F. D. Fincham (Vol. Ed.), *Interparental Conflict and Child Development.* Cambridge, UK: Cambridge University Press.

Dalley, L. P. (2002). Policy implications relating to inmate mothers and their children: Will the past be prologue? *The Prison Journal, 82,* 234–268.

Dalley, L. P., & Michels, V. (2009). Women destined to failure: Policy implications of the lack of proper mental health and addiction treatment for female offenders. In R. L. Gido & L. P. Dalley (Eds.), *Women's mental health issues across the criminal justice system* (pp. 160–176). Upper Saddle River, NJ: Prentice Hall.

Datesman, S. K., & Cales, G. L. (1983). "I'm still the same mommy": Maintaining the mother/child relationship in prison. *The Prison Journal, 63,* 142–154.

DeHart, D. D. (2008). Pathways to prison. Impact of victimization in the lives of incarcerated women. *Violence Against Women, 14,* 1362–1381.

Dodge, M., & Pogrebin, M. R. (2001). Collateral costs of imprisonment for women: Complications of reintegration. *The Prison Journal, 81,* 42–54.

Dressel, P., Porterfield, J., & Barnhill, S. K. (1998). Mothers behind bars. *Corrections Today, 60*(7), 90–95.

Enos, S. (2001). *Mothering from the inside. Parenting in a women's prison.* New York: State University of New York Press.

Ferraro, K. J., & Moe, A. M. (2003). Mothering, crime, and incarceration. *Journal of Contemporary Ethnography, 23*(1), 9–40.

Gabel, S. (1992). Children of incarcerated and criminal parents: Adjustment, behavior, and prognosis. *Bulletin of American Academy of Psychiatry and Law, 20*(1), 33–45.

Glaser, B., & Strauss, A. (1967). *The discovery of grounded: Strategies for qualitative research.* Hawthorne, NY: Aldine.

Glaze, L. E., & Maruschak, L. M. (2009). *Parents in prison and their minor children.* Washington, DC: Bureau of Justice Statistics, U.S. Department of Justice.

Greene, S., Haney C., & Hurtado, A. (2000). Cycles of pain: Risk factors in the lives of incarcerated mothers and their children. *The Prison Journal, 80,* 3–23.

Grella, C. E., & Greenwell, L. (2006). Correlates of parental status and attitudes toward parenting among substance-abusing women offenders. *The Prison Journal, 86,* 89–113.

Hairston, C. F. (1991). Mothers in jail: Parent-child separation and jail visitation. *Journal of Women and Social Work, 6*(2), 9–27.

Hairston, C. F. (1998). The forgotten parent: Understanding the forces that influence incarcerated fathers' relationships with their children. *Child Welfare, 77,* 617–640.

Hairston, C. F., & Lockett, P. W. (1987). Parents in prison: New directions for social services. *Social Work, 32,* 162–164.

Henriques, Z. W. (1982). *Imprisoned mothers and their children: A descriptive and analytical study.* Washington, DC: University Press of America.

Henriques, Z. W., & Manatu-Rupert, N. (2001). Living on the outside: African American women before, during, and after imprisonment. *The Prison Journal, 61,* 6–19.

Hill, G., & Harrison, P. (2008). *Female prisoners under state or federal jurisdiction.* Washington, DC: U.S. Department of Justice, Office of Justice Programs, Bureau of Justice Statistics.

Houck, K. D. F., & Loper, A. B. (2002). The relationship of parenting stress to adjustment among mothers in prison. *American Journal of Orthopsychiatry, 72,* 548–558.

Kazura, K. (2001). Family programming for incarcerated parents: A needs assessment among inmates. *Journal of Offender Rehabilitation, 32*(4), 67–83.

Kerig, P. K. (2003). In search of protective processes for children exposed to interparental violence. *Journal of Emotional Abuse, 3*(3/4), 149–182.

Lazarus, R. S., & Folkman, S. (1984). *Stress, appraisal and coping.* New York: Springer.

Lindquist, C. H., & Lindquist, C. A. (1997). Gender differences in distress: Mental health consequences of environmental stress among jail inmates. *Behavioral Sciences and the Law, 15,* 503–523.

McDaniels-Wilson, C., & Belknap, J. (2008). The extensive sexual violation and sexual abuse histories of incarcerated women. *Violence Against Women, 14,* 1090–1127.

Mechanic, D. (1962). *Students under stress. A study in the social psychology of adaptation.* New York: Free Press.

Mumola, C. J. (2000). *Incarcerated parents and their children* (A Special Report of Bureau of Justice Statistics). Washington, DC: U.S. Department of Justice.

Negy, C., Woods, D. J., & Carlson, R. (1997). The relationship between female inmates' coping and adjustment in a minimum-security prison. *Criminal Justice and Behavior, 24,* 224–233.

Owen, B., & Bloom, B. (1995). Profiling women prisoners: Findings from national surveys and a Californian sample. *The Prison Journal, 75,* 165–185.

Raj, A., Rose, J., Decker, M. R., Rosengard, C., Hebert, M. R., Stein, M., et al. (2008). Prevalence and patterns of sexual assault across the life span among incarcerated women. *Violence Against Women, 14,* 528–541.

Richie, B. E. (2001). Challenges incarcerated women face as they return to their communities: Findings from life history interviews. *Crime & Delinquency, 47,* 368–389.

Schram, P. J. (1999). An exploratory study: Stereotypes about mothers in prison. *Journal of Criminal Justice, 27,* 411–426.

Skinner, E. A., Edge, K., Altman, J., & Sherwood, H. (2003). Searching for the structure of coping: A review and critique of category systems for classifying ways of coping. *Psychological Bulletin, 129,* 216–269.

Stanton, A. M. (1980). *When mothers go to jail.* Lexington, MA: Lexington Books.

Staton, M., Leukefeld, C., & Webster, J. M. (2003). Substance use, health, and mental health: Problems and service utilization among incarcerated women. *International Journal of Offender Therapy and Comparative Criminology, 47,* 224–239.

Thoits, P. A. (1995). Stress, coping, and social support processes: Where are we? What next? *Journal of Health and Social Behavior, 35,* 53–79.

West, H. C., & Sabol, W. J. (2009). Prison inmates at midyear 2008. *Bureaus of Justice Statistics.* Washington, DC: U.S. Department of Justice.

Widom, C. S. (1989). The cycle of violence. *Science, 244,* 160–166.

DISCUSSION QUESTIONS

1. Identify and define the seven coping strategies that women use to cope with being separated from their children.

2. Discuss the differences between emotion-focused strategies and problem-focused strategies.

3. How did the women who were awaiting a trial differ from those already serving their time in prison?

READING 20

The literature has consistently documented the high mental health needs of women in prison. In addition, we have learned that the prison experience may exacerbate the presence of mental health disorders. This research by Holly Harner and Suzanne Riley looks at the issue of mental health of female inmates from a mixed methods approach: a quantitative survey of inmates and qualitative focus groups involving a smaller subset of the population. Their results provide insights for three groups of inmates: (1) those who believe prison had a negative effect on their mental health status, (2) those who believe prison had a positive effect on their mental health status, and (3) those who believe prison did not have any effect on their mental health status.

The Impact of Incarceration on Women's Mental Health

Responses From Women in a Maximum-Security Prison

Holly M. Harner and Suzanne Riley

Incarcerated women are an extremely vulnerable and often "invisible" (Braithwaite, Treadwell, & Arriola, 2008, p. S173) population in the United States (Kim, 2003). Many women enter correctional institutions with complex mental health issues, including depression, anxiety, posttraumatic stress disorder (PTSD), and addiction (James & Glaze, 2006). Despite the rapid increase in the rate at which women in the United States are being incarcerated, there is often not a commensurate increase in available services and programs to support their complex health needs (Young, 2000). Furthermore, treatment modalities supported by evidence in nonincarcerated populations do not necessarily transfer their efficacy to correctional populations (Covington, 1998). To identify mental health treatment modalities that effectively address incarcerated women's mental health needs, an important first step is to

SOURCE: Harner, H. M., & Riley, S. (2013). The impact of incarceration on women's mental health: Responses from women in a maximum-security prison. *Qualitative Health Research, 23,* 26–42.

better understand the nature and context of incarcerated women's experiences of mental health in prison, as well as their perceptions of how incarceration affects their overall mental health. The purpose of our qualitative investigation, which was guided by the principles outlined in Harris and Fallot's (2001) trauma-informed systems framework, was to better understand women's perceptions of how their mental health was affected by incarceration in a maximum-security prison.

Evolution of the Study

The first author's previous clinical practice as a women's health nurse practitioner in a maximum-security women's prison and her mental-health-related research with women incarcerated in the same prison informed this investigation. The first author's prior investigations (Harner & Burgess, 2011; Harner, Hanlon, & Garfinkel, 2010; Harner, Hentz, & Evangelista, 2011) generated data identifying that many incarcerated women suffer from significant mental health issues—some of which are antecedents to incarceration and some of which are consequences of incarceration. Although the prison population has expanded, with a dramatic rise, especially, in the number of incarcerated women, a similar growth in available prison services, especially mental health services, has not been demonstrated in most institutions. One incarcerated woman commented, "The mental health care in here is busted." Indeed, because of the complex needs of this growing population, correctional mental health professionals often operate out of necessity from a "crisis oriented" model of care. The limitations imposed by this model are felt by incarcerated women, one of whom commented, "They just care if I want to kill myself or someone else" (Harner & Burgess, 2011, p. 473).

Review of the Literature

We examined existing literature related to incarceration and women's mental health. Nurse, Woodcock, and Ormsby (2003) examined, via focus groups, the impact of the prison environment and organization on the mental health of incarcerated men and women and correctional staff in either a medium-security prison (18 men) or a training/rehabilitation unit (13 women) in southern England. The most common factors contributing to poor mental health included (a) isolation and lack of mental stimulation, (b) drug misuse, (c) negative relationships with prison staff, (d) bullying of vulnerable prisoners, and (e) lack of family contact. These themes were often interrelated, because prisoners identified that being locked in cells for long periods of time with little or no mental stimuli adversely affected their mental health. This isolation generally led to drug use to try to cover up the monotony of incarceration. Women commented specifically about the lack of family contact and limited control over external events. One woman noted, "If you've got a relative out there who's ill, you can't do nothing about it, you can't, and that makes you feel ten times worse" (Nurse et al., 2003, p. 2). Prisoners identified a pattern of negative interactions with the prison staff. For example, when an inmate was treated badly by an officer, prisoners would then make the officer's life more difficult, which resulted in increased stress for the officer. Another woman commented, "They respond to us and then we respond to them" (p. 3).

Prison staff who participated in separate focus groups identified experiencing increased stress levels related to perceived lack of management support, a negative work environment, safety issues, and stress-related sickness (Nurse et al., 2003). A *circle of stress* functioned in the following manner: "[L]ow morale and staff shortages increase stress levels, which in turn increase staff sickness rates, reduce staffing levels, further lower the morale of remaining staff and lead to more stress and staff sickness" (p. 3). It is in this circle of stress that the interconnected nature of prisoner mental health and staff mental health becomes evident. Stress-related staff absences lead to staff shortages. Shortages lead to longer inmate lock-up time. Longer lock-up time increases inmate stress and frustration. Finally, inmates release their stress and frustration on prison staff.

Douglas, Plugge, and Fitzpatrick (2009) evaluated "women prisoners' perceptions of the impact of imprisonment on their health" (p. 749). Using both focus groups (6 focus groups; $n = 37$ participants) and individual interviews ($n = 12$), the investigators explored incarcerated women's "perceptions of 'health' and 'healthiness'; health problems of women in prison; personal health status prior to imprisonment; impact of imprisonment on health; experiences of prison healthcare services; and recommendations for service development" (p. 750) in two women's prisons in England. Participants described both short-term and long-term impact on health and well-being. Women reported "shock and fear" on entering prison. Concern and worry for children who were left in the care of others was also commonly identified. Women were fearful about what awaited them in prison (violence, intimidation, isolation), and were deeply disturbed when they witnessed other women's distress (detoxification, seizures, self-injury, and mental health problems). Disempowerment and "inconsistent application of prison rules" (p. 750) were also identified as stressful, frustrating, and anxiety producing. Women reported difficulty coping, which often resulted in depression and, for some, suicidality. As with the women who participated in the Nurse et al. (2003) investigation, women in this study were also affected by the behaviors of others. After witnessing a prison suicide, one participant commented,

> I was mad. I hated the officers, I hated the nurses, I hated—I just went mad, I wouldn't eat. . . . I didn't sleep well. All month, you know, I just kept seeing—and then I started hearing things like, I start hearing that my kids were crying, I started—I was in another world, you know. (Douglas et al., 2009, p. 751)

Women also described that poor hygiene, lack of cleanliness, limited access to physical activities, and nutritionally poor diets also negatively affected health (Douglas et al., 2009). The researchers identified that the aforementioned issues were not problematic for everyone in the study. Women who had a history of "chaotic drug misuse" found "an enforced respite from addiction and associated health neglect" (p. 751). The investigators commented, "For some women, prison offered an opportunity to get the help that they needed. Better nutrition, a stable routine and an opportunity to access healthcare and drug treatment services were important opportunities" (p. 751). Imprisonment also separated victims of domestic violence and sexual exploitation from their abusers. Similar findings were also described by participants in Bradley and Davino's (2002) investigation on perceived levels of safety in prison.

Gaps in the Literature

Research supports that many women enter correctional institutions with complex mental health issues (James & Glaze, 2006). Despite their need, women often have limited access to appropriate resources that might be able to improve their mental health. Findings from two qualitative investigations conducted in England (Douglas et al., 2009; Nurse et al., 2003) suggest that incarcerated women's mental health in prison is closely linked to their experience of incarceration, including their interactions with health and correctional professionals and other inmates. To date, few investigations have specifically examined how women's mental health is affected by incarceration. With this study, we aimed to fill this gap.

Methods

We conducted this investigation in a maximum-security women's prison located in the United States. The prison housed approximately 1,600 women at the time of our investigation. We collected data in two stages via two methods: Stage One: the Prison Health Survey (PHS) and Stage Two: focus groups.

Findings

The first author distributed the PHS to 900 incarcerated women in Stage One. Almost half of the women ($n = 445$) returned a completed survey. The average age of respondents was 38 years (range 20 to 85). Most women were White (68%) and had been convicted for a drug-related crime (27%) or murder (19%; i.e., drug-related crimes and murder accounted for the top 2 offenses committed). Twelve focus groups, consisting of a total of 65 women, were conducted during Stage Two. The average age of respondents was 43 years (range 23 to 46). Most were White (62%), and most were convicted for murder (39%) and drug-related crimes (18%). Analysis of the data from both the PHS and the inmate focus groups revealed three broad categories: worse mental health status, better mental health status, and the same mental health status as a result of incarceration. We reviewed the broad categories as well as the subcategories identified from these data.

Worse Mental Health

Many women described that their mental health worsened while in prison. Several factors led to poor mental health, including fear, stress, being away from loved ones, limited access to mental health services, worry over physical health issues, and poor treatment by health and correctional professionals.

We Fear for Our Lives in Here. Women described experiencing fear for their own personal safety in prison: "You never know who you are put in a cell with. They could just kill you without even thinking about it. There are some crazy women in here." Although violent events between inmates in women's prisons occur less frequently than in men's prisons, a violent incident between two women occurred in the prison just prior to the start of our focus groups. This event was particularly fear inducing for many women and generated much discussion in the focus groups. One woman commented,

> You're put in rooms and you don't know what you're dealing with. Everything gets lost in the sauce—mental-health wise. It's tragic that it [the violent incident] happened, but the fact it doesn't happen more is amazing. It's frightening. Behind closed doors, you fend for yourself. You got to work things out amongst yourself.

Similarly, another woman stated,

> What happened the other night affected everybody. When things like this happen, it puts all the staff on high alert and we suffer. Stuff like this makes the staff stressed and it trickles down to us. They do rounds more and ask us a hundred thousand questions about everything. Women are scared for their lives. Women were even scared to ring the buzzer during the attack because they were scared that the crazy woman would retaliate against them when she got out of the hole [a high security housing unit for women who had broken a prison rule or who needed protective custody]. We fear for our lives in here. I feel safer in an open unit [versus a unit with traditional cells]. If something goes down [happens], there are plenty of people who hear you screaming. It's scary in here. I don't like telling my family horror stories.

The lack of "official" knowledge about the incident, coupled with the rampant (and often inaccurate) *rumor mill* amplified women's fears. One woman described this:

> We all saw the hospital helicopter in the parking lot. We saw it and knew something bad had happened. Girls in the kitchen heard about it from the officers talking about it. They said her throat was slit, [she was] stabbed, brain coming out of her nose. Brains on the walls. Drowned in the toilet. You never know what the real story is, though. There is so much talk in here. Everybody thought she was dead at one time. They need to help us and find out who is upset about it and let us talk about it.

During a later focus group, an inmate who had participated in an earlier focus group entered the day room and announced in a panicked tone to the room, "It happened again. Oh my God, it happened again. Someone just got stabbed in [name] unit." This woman, who had just returned from chapel (where she heard this information from another inmate), was clearly traumatized and fearful. We witnessed her frantic and fearful reaction being transferred to the other women in her housing unit. It was later determined that the event she was describing was actually a planned security training event conducted by the officers.

The Stress Is Tremendous. Women described persistent and high levels of stress in prison. Common sources of stress included their lack of control over their own lives and stress associated with common institutional issues and procedures. One woman wrote, "Before I came in, I was always feeling anxious and stressed. In here, the anxiety is heightened, and with the absolute lack of control over my life, the stress is tremendous." Another participant identified that her mental health was worse and that she was "stressed and worried" about not knowing when her final mandatory program would start, which had implications for when she would be released. For some, stress seemed related to the length of time the women had already been incarcerated, as well as their sentence length. One woman serving a life sentence for murder described being "overwhelmed and stressed" by the amount of time she received (i.e., was sentenced to).

Women, especially those with preexisting mental health issues, experienced stress related to common institutional security procedures, including strip searches, pat downs, and random urine drug screens. One woman, incarcerated for prostitution, recounted,

I've been depressed since I was little. I've been homeless and a prostitute on the streets. I've been down in the dumps and my depression is getting worse. I don't have any help from home. . . . I can't stomach the meds [medications]. I force myself not to isolate. I got bipolar, low self-esteem, severe depression. The racing thoughts keep me awake. I'm so tired, but I can't sleep. I am so stressed. Every single day I'm stressed and scared in here. I got picked for a random drug test in here once, but I couldn't pee [urinate]. I kept trying but it wouldn't come out. They give you a few hours to pee, but I just couldn't go because I was so anxious and stressed. The officers knew I don't do drugs in here but they got to follow their rules. So I got sent to the hole for refusing to pee. Now I'm such a nervous wreck about it. I worry about getting tested again, so I hold my pee each morning until 11:00 a.m. [head] count. After I pee, I drink a lot of water, tea, and coffee so I can always go if they make me. Every day I have to do this, and this stress makes me crazy.

Routine pat downs and full-body strip searches were also stress inducing, especially for women who had suffered past abuse. In fact, several women who described past sexual abuse commented that they avoided seeing visitors, including their children, because they did not want to go through the "stress and humiliation" of full-body strip searches.

Being Away From My Family Is Killing Me. Women expressed how they ached to be with their children and mourned for the time they were losing with family because of their incarceration. Some women described feeling guilty for not being good mothers when they had the chance and longed to make up for past mistakes. Women frequently described separation from their children as one of the most difficult aspects of incarceration. One woman wrote, "My kids think I am dead. My ex [ex-husband] told them I was dead. I don't know where they are." Another woman commented, "It's been hell being taken away from my kid and family."

Being in prison was the first time that many women had ever been away from their children. They often did not know where their children were and, with limited contact, often feared for their health and safety. One 34-year-old woman sentenced for murder wrote, "I stay in constant fear of something happening to them. My oldest daughter has stomach cancer. She is 13. She was in a coma for two weeks." Another woman, incarcerated for 10 to 25 years for theft and larceny, wrote,

The stress related to being away from my family is killing me. My son just turned 18 and I miss him as much as a young child. My husband got killed one month after I got locked up and my kids moved out West. I only see them once a year. I can only call once a week because a 15-minute call costs $10.63 and they take 20% out of each pay for fines and stuff. I don't have the money. If I could call three times a week I would be in a better state of mind. It frustrates me and stresses me out.

Although prison visiting hours were available on a fairly regular basis, many women had family members who lived long distances from the prison, making regular visits difficult, expensive, and often impossible. Women were dependent on friends and family members to bring their children for visitation, which had the potential to be problematic and confrontational. One woman said, "My ex won't let the kids come visit me in here." For security reasons, visitation was also highly regulated by the DOC [Department of Corrections]. A 26-year-old participant angrily described how her then 6-year-old son was no longer allowed to sit on her lap during family visitation:

My son, at age three, was diagnosed with cancer. He is now in remission and this happened during my incarceration. He's six years old now, and six-year-old kids cannot have physical contact with their mothers. These security procedures are designed for men. My son has been visiting for four years and now there is some arbitrary restriction that he can't sit on my lap during our visits because of sex offenders. This made my son so angry because he didn't understand it. I don't understand it. I'm here for drugs. This was the first time I ever saw him angry.

Although many mothers ached for visits from their children, one participant decided that visitation placed too much mental stress on her teenaged children and herself and elected to decline family visits:

> Mentally I had my ups and downs, too. I still have my family support, but I elected not to have my visits. They have a life out there and I don't want me being in here to affect their life. I talk to my family once a week. They coped very hard with not being able to see me. It was hard for them in the beginning. When I was in county [county jail], I would have a visit, and after that I would go downhill after and so would they. I didn't think it was fair for any of us.

Several of the women in our study were pregnant when they entered prison. Universally, these women described that giving birth while incarcerated and then being required to release their newborns to a family member or social service agency immediately after delivery contributed to poor mental health. One woman commented,

> After I delivered, I stayed one night in the infirmary but it was so bad I didn't want to stay. . . . I just had a baby. I was so depressed and upset, and wanted to be around people who actually cared about me, not people who just let me sit there. . . . Having such little time with my son was hard. I refused to let them take him out of my hospital room and got him for the night. The officers who came to pick me up were very nice and tried to give me extra time, saying I wasn't discharged when I really was. But probably because they only wanted to stay out of the prison. I didn't care. I was just thankful to have the extra time with him.

Another woman, who returned to prison for violating parole, described her postpartum experience and her desire to have her newborn return to prison with her following delivery:

> There is no information [in prison] about taking care of yourself after the baby. There is the prenatal and postnatal group, which sucked. It was about nothing. Just people showing off their pictures. The only thing that helped me was using

the phone a lot. My oldest daughter, she's twenty, is watching my daughter. But she is due in June and has her hands full. I think they should let you keep your baby here for the first year. It depends on the crime. But we have dogs in here, and they're okay with that. As long as they were in a separate unit and away from people with crimes against kids.

There's Nothing Here to Help Us. Women identified having few resources available to support their mental health needs. Frequently, women described putting their name "on the list" and waiting to be seen by a mental health professional. Given the vast mental health needs in the institution and the limited resources, placement on the list did not necessarily guarantee a definitive timeline for the receipt of services. Circumstances of the prison mental health system (high need, limited resources) necessitated that services were allocated to the most acute cases. This crisis-oriented system left women believing they had been abandoned by mental health providers and were in competition with their fellow inmates for resources. Access to mental health services was viewed as a zero-sum endeavor by many women. One participant, who described being physically and sexually abused by her father, commented,

> I've had numerous flashbacks and had to deal with issues on my own. I am more emotional now than I ever was, and I have trouble sleeping. Where are the programs for women? Men's prisons have everything and we don't have anything. I wanted to be in the abuse program, but I was told that there were people who were worse off than me; that my abuse wasn't as bad as other people's.

A 28-year-old participant identified that prison mental health was often crisis oriented, focusing primarily on inmates who were homicidal or suicidal:

> This place is set up for the worst-case scenario, but not for the everyday needs of women. By the grace of God, we are surviving. I didn't get the help I needed because I wasn't homicidal or suicidal. It is the squeaky wheel that gets the groups in here. I wrote to mental health and waited for six weeks to talk to someone. They just put you

on the list to see your housing unit's counselor. I don't understand why they would just brush you off. If you're not on meds, they don't care. I tried to speak with the counselor on my unit and [the counselor] said, "Your browns [the color of the prison uniform] are the same color as everyone else's. I have too many files and not enough hours in the day. You have fifteen minutes. What would you like to talk about?" Now how therapeutic is that?

Echoing a common refrain, one woman identified that mental health treatment in prison largely consisted of medication management, with very limited talk therapy:

It's hard to find people to talk to, and if you do, they want to prescribe psych [psychiatric] drugs, which I don't think is the right thing to do all the time. They don't have enough people to help us here. Not enough groups here. The mental health department is overworked. You got the same amount of people when there were only six hundred to seven hundred people here. The population grew but the staff didn't. You try to get help, but they kick you out after fifteen minutes. A lot of things that go wrong in this prison wouldn't happen if things were taken care [of] to start with.

Medication did not always resolve women's mental health symptoms. Women described not getting the "right" psychiatric medication, which resulted in worsening mental health. One participant commented, "I don't get the proper psych meds. When they have prescribed it, it gets crushed and I vomit. Mentally, it helps only a little. But physically, it makes me worse." Another woman wrote, "The doctor took me off my medication and put me on something different all together. So my mental health is worse. The medication he has me on don't work. I'm still depressed, anxiety, etc." Another participant wrote,

I experience anxiety daily but the prison offers no medication for this problem alone. My mental health is worse. I am not a sociable person like I was. I feel lonely, worried, paranoid, stressed and closed-off most of the time.

Women serving life sentences frequently commented that they were "at the bottom of most lists" because (as several women identified), "We aren't going anywhere. We're lifers." One woman said,

The mental health in this jail is horrible. Not enough emphasis is put on the head games we have to play with ourselves to get through every day. It's worse on lifers because we have our guards up for retaliation. It's like all of us are one person. I make it my business to keep my hands to myself, even if I want to bust somebody in the mouth. I deal with it on a regular basis. I'm in my forties but I feel like I am sixty-five. I got to play the old lady so I don't flip out like the young woman I am. . . . It drains you day after day, and it makes people lose their hope. Some people feel like they have to pull their damn hair out to get what they need around here. To get basic responses and treatment. The system needs a new page. A whole damn new manual when it comes to dealing with mental health. Especially when it comes to people dealing with life sentences.

Even access to resources for women serving life sentences did not always result in improved mental health. One woman, who had already served more than 20 years of a her sentence, wrote, "Although there are people I can talk to about my mental health, due to the amount of time I have, sometimes I feel like suicide is my only option."

I'm Worried About My Health. Women's concerns for their physical health contributed to poor mental health. Some women entered prison with complex physical health problems, many of which, by their accounts, were not "taken seriously" by correctional medical professionals. Women described being misdiagnosed, given another inmate's medication (which several women referred to as "being overdosed"), and suffering from chronic, untreated pain, all of which intensified existing mental health issues. Although some women feared they would die in prison, others wished for death rather than continue to agonize in pain. One woman, sentenced to life in prison, suffered a back injury while on a prison work detail. After enduring "three years of pain," she was evaluated by an outside surgeon:

> He said that my disc had exploded. He said he couldn't fix it. I said to him, "Do you think that at the age [of] thirty-eight it's okay that my roommate wipes my ass?" My roommates did everything for me. My personality changed. It was so bad that I didn't even have to stand for count. I was a little devil because of the pain. My personality changed. I gained fifty pounds. I turned into a damn monster. I literally wanted to die because I hurt so bad. It takes a toll on you. I just laid it out for the doctor and he finally said, "I'll see you in the morning for surgery." . . . They think we are all the same and trying to game the system [manipulate the system for personal gain]. In one sense, I worked in the criminal justice system before I came here. I see it from both sides. I can play devil's advocate. But with health, there is no devil's advocate. Point blank. Period. They don't do [treat] us right.

Women also expressed frustration and distrust related to the institutional mandatory copayment ($5 for a visit; $5 for medication) required to see a physical health care provider (copayments were not required for mental health care). Copayments were financially crippling for many women because most had limited sources of income (the highest pay rate in prison for many women was less than 50 cents/hour). Women's frustration and distrust were compounded by both health and correctional professionals making comments such as, "You got it lucky. I wish my copay was only five dollars." One woman commented, "They are five-dollaring us to death in here."

Women acknowledged that medical professionals were overwhelmed by the growing prison population and women's increasing medical needs. One woman commented, "The doctors, a lot of time, their hands are tied. I don't think they have the things they need to do their jobs here. They are overworked and overtired." Women also identified that inmates "trying to game the system or get over on medical [manipulate the prison medical system for personal gain]" and "thinking that they are going to get everything fixed in a two-year bid [sentence]" resulted in medical professionals questioning the veracity of all women's medical complaints:

> They sort of shrug us off and think we are not qualified to make judgments of what we need or are lying about symptoms. But we know our bodies. They just get us in and out as quickly as possible, without actually diagnosing us properly.

Many women in our study had limited knowledge of common health issues. Lack of knowledge and lack of access to health-related resources (health literature or Internet access) left women powerless to understand medical and mental health conditions. This powerlessness contributed to their high levels of stress and worry, and left many feeling vulnerable during medical appointments. Women often did not fully understand their diagnoses or available treatment options (or treatment they had already received). For example, several women described being treated for cancer during their imprisonment, but often did not know what type of cancer they had, or their prognosis. For some women, especially those with histories of mental illness, being diagnosed with even common, non-life-threatening conditions was frightening and necessitated additional explanation by health providers. Without access to basic health literature, women relied on outside family members to investigate symptoms and diagnoses on the Internet and then mail them printed medical information. One former health care provider, then serving a sentence for assault, said,

> We have tons of books banned. . . . It would take an act of God to get a health-related book in this place. They have a PDR [*Physician's Desk Reference*], which, let's face it, isn't the easiest thing to read. It freaks everyone out. . . . Women come to me with questions about the PDR.

Women's limited knowledge and power, coupled with their frustration and lack of confidence in an overburdened prison health system, increased worry about real and perceived medical conditions. This worry and anxiety was compounded by their resentment and anger at being required to pay what to them was an exorbitant sum for medical care in which they had no choice of provider and no input as to treatment. As a result, some women intentionally avoided seeking care for their medical symptoms but then suffered from these symptoms, as well as having their anxiety grow about their etiology. Women's understanding that other inmates similarly avoided seeking medical care resulted in a generalized fear of being unnecessarily exposed to contagious infections, especially methicillin-resistant staph aureus.

It's Like We Aren't Even Human. Although women identified individual health and correctional professionals as "kind," "caring," and "fair," the institutional milieu as a whole was generally characterized as "disrespectful" and at times "degrading." Participants described being treated "like nothing" or "subhuman," and being "put down" and "disrespected" by medical and correctional professionals. One participant wrote, "Most staff treat us as if we are subhuman and assume we're all very stupid, addicted to drugs, or criminal masterminds." Being "yelled at" by correctional officers, especially male officers, resulted in increased anxiety and stress among inmates, particularly those with trauma histories:

> You get yelled at and you are stressed out and don't know what to do. There is nothing you can do. I just get paralyzed. I freeze. I think my mental health is worse because I'm always stressed and very depressed. I know that it's because I'm in prison. But how they treat you doesn't help your mental health, either.

Similarly, another woman wrote, "Officers have no respect in the manner they talk to inmates and/or handle certain situations. Some officers use their authority to go above and beyond what they are actually authorized to do." The power differential was obvious to the women, most of whom were unable to advocate for respectful treatment. One participant described feeling "degraded" while giving birth in prison:

> I had to have an officer stand right in front of me while I was having my baby. Now every time I see her, it makes me uncomfortable. She could have just moved to the side. But she just wanted to watch me deliver. That was so ignorant. Every time I was pushing, I had to look at her face. Tell me, where does "care, custody, and control" [i.e., the principle roles of many

departments of correction] come into that? It was the most degrading experience ever.

Some women were scared to report disrespectful or abusive treatment because they feared receiving disciplinary reports or losing privileges:

> Even when the officers lash out, we can't say anything because then we get it worse from the officer. I have a very abusive boss. He calls us dumb and retarded. I can't say anything, though. I eat that [ignore it] because I want to go home to my kids. But some people can't handle that.

Women who "complained" about inappropriate treatment risked additional punishment. One woman described being removed from an institutional program after she reported inappropriate behavior by an officer:

> They degrade us here as a woman. They cuss at us. We are deprived and denied. The officers can say whatever they want and do whatever they want. We have no voice. It makes me cringe. There is an officer in the kitchen that does inappropriate searches. . . . I am afraid that if I say something I will be reprimanded. All the women try to go to another officer to be searched. Everybody knows about him. You get penalized if you complain. I was kicked out of a program because I said something [about another officer's actions]. They have our life in their hands.

Several inmates who had been incarcerated for longer periods of time commented that, in general, correctional officers' attitudes had changed over the last decade. They attributed these changes to officers needing to manage a larger, younger, more drug-addicted and violent population entering prison. One woman serving a life sentence described how treatment by the officers changed during her 15 years in prison:

> I know from experience that officers can be the liaison to get your sanity back. But not every staff member has the education to deal with us. They don't get the training they used to. They used to tell them, "Their punishment is to be in here. It

is not your job to punish them." But they don't come in with that attitude anymore.

Participants also acknowledged the difficulties health and correctional professionals must face when working with such a "demanding" population. For the most part, women understood that some inmates who were "bad apples" made it more difficult for the rest of them. Women acting simple and stupid and women trying to game the system resulted in harsh and uniform consequences for everyone. One woman serving a life sentence wrote,

The majority of women here have continued/ consistent poor character, poor decision making ability, and low maturity levels. That makes it hard for the ones that are not like that. We are often treated as if we all act that way.

Improved Mental Health

A number of women described that their mental health had improved during their incarceration. In addition to numerous responses on the PHS similar to, "My mental health got better," some women commented that they were "less depressed" and "more positive in thoughts and feelings." They felt "more stable" and that their "mental health was more under control in prison." One woman commented, "I feel good about life." Women described feeling less "hopeless," "being aware of feelings," and "having a real chance at life now." One woman commented that she "didn't think of death so much anymore." The structure available in prison was viewed as positive for some women, including one who expressed, "The structure here has taught me that sanity isn't necessarily boring." Finally, one participant summarized her feelings as, "I've been here seven years. It has been the best seven years. In here, you either get bitter or better. I got better, much better." Women identified several factors that led to improved mental health, including access to the right medication, being "clean" [not taking illegal drugs], having the opportunity to work on their "issues" with mental health providers, being away from violence, becoming closer to God, and allowing time to heal old wounds and adapt to the prison environment.

I'm Getting the Right Medication Now. Women identified that access to psychotropic medication in prison

improved their mental health. Some described currently being on a combination of the "right medications" that were properly treating their symptoms. One 32-year-old woman who suffered from schizoaffective disorder remarked that her medications were adjusted and she felt more "stable." Another participant who suffered from schizophrenia described that medication helped "get the voices under control." In addition to medication actually reducing mental health symptoms, the side effect profile of many of the prescribed psychotropic medications included somnolence or sleepiness. For many women, this was a welcome side effect because improved sleep resulted in a perceived improvement in mental health.

Although access to medication was important, actually taking the medication as prescribed and not self-medicating were equally vital. One participant who had been incarcerated for more than 10 years for murder suffered from bipolar disorder. She identified that her symptoms had lessened because she was then properly taking her medication, writing, "I need to be supervised because I never take medication on my own. I forget to eat, and stay wake for two to three days at a time." Also suffering from bipolar disorder, another woman, incarcerated for theft, commented that her mental health issues had stabilized and, "Again, I realized I had bipolar and needed meds." A combination of access to medication and mental health services also contributed to improved mental health. One woman who was incarcerated for manslaughter wrote, "They've given me more accurate diagnosis now and have gotten me on better medication for me." Similarly, another participant wrote, "My mental health is better only because I see a doctor and take meds."

My Head Is Clearer, and I'm Free From Drugs. Access to drug and alcohol treatment and forced sobriety (being *clean*) also resulted in improved mental health for many women. One 39-year-old woman convicted of robbery wrote, "My mental health has definitely gotten better. I am off drugs and alcohol and working on my negative issues trying to be a better person." Another woman commented, "My mental health is better because I can't get high [take illegal drugs] to deal with life." Some women identified that their minds were "clearer" and less "cloudy" without drugs and alcohol. One 40-year-old participant explained, "The length of time I've been here has given me time to clear my head and body of heroin and, with help from the treatment program, I've actually made some changes." Another woman also commented, "My mind is much clearer off of drugs. And I am able [to] focus on myself, my rehabilitation, and the goals that I am setting for myself." A 20-year-old participant wrote, "I'm beginning to be get stronger and I'm able to think better because I'm clean from drugs and drugs ruined my life." Finally, a 22-year-old woman wrote, "I'm clean and on the right track. I'm thinking more clearly and level-headed and ready to be released into society with a better head on my shoulders."

I'm Working on My Issues. Many women who participated in mental health counseling and supportive programming described improvement in their mental health. Treatment programs available in the study institution addressed issues such as addiction, past victimization, and violence prevention, often via cognitive behavioral approaches. One participant wrote, "I've been lucky enough to finally (after 20+ years of treatment) find a good therapist. I still have tons of issues, but now I can manage them." The ability to work on issues from the past was deemed valuable to inmates. Women learned behavioral skills, such as talking about their issues and relaxation techniques, which helped them cope and adapt to the prison environment.

One 43-year-old woman, convicted of aggravated assault, described how she was able to discontinue her medication because of techniques she learned in group, writing, "I have been off all psych meds about 5 or 6 years. I still have mental issues, but I learned to stop and breathe first and journal and talk about my issues in a mental health group." Similarly, another participant wrote, "I see the psych doctor once a month. The environment is controlled and the structure here forces a person to talk about their problems. The only other option is to be self-destructive." One woman also described, "I've learned to really think things through, choose wisely and keep my circle tight, express how I feel all the time, focus on 'what is' and truly worry about making myself better."

Some women described that they were able to "work through issues" or "talk through tough issues" in groups, including issues related to past victimization and exposure to other traumatic experiences. One sexual assault victim wrote,

Every day is a struggle, coping skills aside, to feel physically and emotionally fit. But I feel better. I

have taken full advantage of the programs and groups available in order to gain a better understanding of my emotional disorders. I have used this prison time for me to learn, change, and love me. Things I didn't really make time for outside this gate. My priority was always others. I'm still learning/changing yet I'm content and have come a long way. Besides groups, I also utilize the mental health unit when I need to reach-out for it.

One 48-year-old woman, convicted of a drug-related crime, had been sexually assaulted by a family member as a child. She commented, "My mental health is better due to the programs I've been in to help with my past abuse issues. They have been great." Another woman, convicted of murder, explained:

I'm a lifer [sentenced to serve the remainder of her life in prison]. I am so ashamed of what I did. I was so damn angry and I stayed angry for years. I finally got into counseling and they saved my life. I needed to come face to face with my issues. Issues I didn't even know that I had. It helped me make it through the tough times. I did the abuse program and it was like I was set free. I deal with a lot of issues all the time. I see psych here. All I have to do is write him a request or call him and he is right on it. But everybody don't have that.

Another participant identified that her mental health had improved because she was in a program in which they were "able to talk about things that caused mental health problems." One such event this woman needed to talk about was witnessing the suicide of a fellow inmate, which occurred in her housing unit. Indeed, several women in this study described needing to "talk to someone" about this specific incident.

Another program viewed positively by participants was the "puppy program," which allowed incarcerated women to train service dogs. Women who trained the puppies and women who lived in the same housing unit as the puppies identified this program as having a positive impact on their mental health. One woman, convicted of murder, described that participating in the puppy program allowed her to "keep her mind off of being in prison." She commented, "My puppy helps me with everything. In some ways it helps me block everything out. I go to work. I see my friends. I sometimes forget that, oh yeah, I am in a maximum-security prison." Another woman, also convicted of murder, offered this description:

> You are so cut off with contact with people, like little stuff like hugs, and it just helps. My puppy is always happy to see me. It's nice having that affection and to cuddle with. I could be having a bad day and I have her and it's not so bad. It gives you something to look forward to every day. The dogs remind me of home. That I'm normal. Not in prison.

One woman, who was not a puppy trainer but lived in the same unit as the puppies, commented,

> At first I didn't want to move in with the puppies. I didn't want all their hair on me and licking me. But once I was in here, I learned that animals, especially the dogs, will make you fall in love with them. I didn't want to fall in love with these damn dogs. But I love them!

I'm Safe Now. Although we did not focus our investigation specifically on trauma, more than 90% of the women who completed our full survey identified that they had experienced a traumatic event in their lives, with almost half meeting the diagnostic criteria for PTSD at Stage One. Several women commented that being in prison got them away from the violence in their personal lives and kept them "safe from the violence on the street." One woman, incarcerated for murder, wrote, "I'm not being abused by my ex-husband anymore. Confinement in prison is so much better than the confinement he had me in." Another woman, also incarcerated for murder, wrote, "My mental health has gotten better because I am no longer in an emotionally abusive relationship. I don't have to worry about being forced to have sex or be verbally abused." Similarly, another participant, convicted of drunk driving, noted that time in prison had allowed her to file for divorce from her abusive husband and to "get help with abuse issues."

I'm Getting Closer to God. Becoming *closer to God* during incarceration resulted in improved mental health for some women. One 40-year-old woman, incarcerated for murder, wrote, "I now have a relationship with God and strive to be a better person." Another participant, who returned to prison after she was found living in a boarded up abandoned building (and thus violating her probation), stated,

> If it had not been for the chapel service here, I would not have made it. There is very little mental health services here in prison. Going to the chapel and finding Jesus saved my life. It has taken a lot of mental strength. I would have cut my throat long before I got to grounds if not for the chapel. I am not saying that for pity, because I am a lot stronger than that. The pastor over there teaches you that you matter. But it is a fight to get to the chapel. The ones who come in new need it the most and get it the least.

Distraught over the death of the nearly three dozen animals in her care (many were taken by Animal Control after she was convicted), one woman wrote,

> My animals in my care were like my children, each with its own personality and endearments. . . . In attending both Protestant and Catholic services and speaking with some of the chaplains, I have reconciled—for the most part—my anger at God for "allowing" so many trials to happen in my life and the death of the animals he placed into my care. I now have a better relationship with God.

Time Helps/Time Heals. Several women attributed their improved mental health to a function of time: time healing old wounds, time helping them to mature as individuals, and time helping them adapt to their new lives behind bars. The process of adaptation was especially evident in women sentenced to longer prison terms:

> I was in a tender mental place when I first came here. In the first evaluation I had when I got here, I had a mental break. There is an adjustment period for long-termers and lifers. Knowing you are doing ten to twenty years is overwhelming. There is a difference between doing a year to two and doing a life sentence. It may not hit you right

away. It may take a year or two for you to realize what this place means. You are numb for the first year. You just exist when you first get here. You just eat and sleep. I had to work. I needed the repetition. There are little things that you struggle with, like going to the bathroom in front of a human being. It is emotionally draining. But you learn to appreciate the small things in life. There is always something beautiful every day in here. You just have to work to find it. You have to find a purpose. You let it out and let it go. As they say, "We're not going anywhere." But it's a struggle inside. I had to work myself to this point.

Several women identified that their mental health had improved over time and that they no longer needed psychotropic medication. One woman who had been incarcerated for more than 15 years for murder described this:

I was deeply depressed when I get here, and I was put on medication for it. I've been off medication since 1995. I did take medicine in 1997 and 1999, but not long. My mind was racing those two times and my thoughts had to be slowed down. No medicine since, and I feel fine.

Another woman, incarcerated for more than 7 years, wrote, "My mental health has gotten better. I was on prescribed medications for depression, anxiety, and sleep upon entering prison. I currently take no medications and haven't for the last 5 years." A 31-year-old participant convicted of murder noted,

My mental health is better because I don't need my meds and I'm staying alert of [or to] everything. Yeah, it's logical that we all get depressed and sad here and there. Especially a person like me with a long bid [prison sentence].

No Change in Mental Health

For some women, mental health issues remained unchanged as a result of incarceration. Many women documented that their mental health was simply "the same." Some identified that they did not suffer from any mental health issues prior to or during incarceration. For other women, their mental health was relatively the same in that they still experienced mental health issues; however, the specific nature of these issues changed as a result of incarceration. For example, one 32-year-old woman wrote, "It was a trade. I was stressed about the unknown on the outside but now I am stressed about my kids on the inside." Similarly, another woman identified, "Since I have been here I was diagnosed with situational depression and grief. On the streets I was diagnosed with depression and anxiety. Not really sure if it's gotten worse; it's about the same."

Discussion

Findings from this investigation add to our understanding of the complex ways in which women's mental health is affected by incarceration. In many instances, our results mirror those of other investigators (Douglas et al., 2009) and suggest that women's mental health can worsen, improve, or remain the same during incarceration. Although presented as isolated themes in this article, it is likely that this is a false trichotomy. Indeed, the impact of imprisonment on mental health is likely more fluid in nature, with women's own physical health, social support, access to resources, maturity level, and life experiences playing significant roles in their immediate perceptions of mental health. Similarly, adaptation to incarceration, especially among women serving long sentences, likely plays a role in women's perceptions of their mental health.

It is important to identify that imprisonment resulted in improved mental health for some women, which has also been described by other investigators (Douglas et al., 2009). For some, access to services prior to incarceration, including mental health care, medication management, and addiction treatment programs, was either limited or inadequate. For others, prison provided a safe place relative to their lives on the street, a phenomenon identified by Bradley and Davino (2002). Indeed, prison did serve as a safety net for women experiencing what one participant described as "the worst-case scenario." However, the fact that women benefited in any way from imprisonment is by itself an alarming commentary on the status of women's health and safety in the United States. These women's accounts expose the larger social issue of the link between disparities in women's health, especially among women experiencing the worst-case scenario (poverty, addiction, serious mental illness, and victimization), and imprisonment.

The women's responses also allow us to evaluate the prison system and the professionals within the system using the principles of the trauma-informed framework (Harris & Fallot, 2001). Women's accounts reflect an institutional milieu that was not fully trauma-informed and reveal the institution's limited understanding of trauma, Harris and Fallot's first principle. Although both health and correctional professionals likely knew that many of the women in their care had experienced victimization, an understanding of trauma did not appear to be fully integrated into institutional procedures. For example, women were clearly distraught by the violent event that occurred just prior to our focus groups. Many described fearing for their own safety. Women identified warning signs prior to the event but, for myriad reasons, felt too helpless and fearful to report their suspicions to officials. Some were even too scared to report the violent event as it was taking place because they feared they could not be protected from later reprisal by the perpetrator. Without an official update from the institution after the event, women were left to reconstruct what had transpired during the chaos, often based on the inaccurate and escalating rumor mill and conversations overheard between correctional officers. These false reconstructions compounded women's sense of powerlessness, helplessness, and fear, themes that might have replicated past traumatic experiences and resulted in retraumatization.

An institution that fully understood trauma might have better anticipated the emotional disruption such a violent event might cause and restored a sense of security and safety for all women. Although women living in the unit in which the violent incident occurred were offered timely crisis mental health treatment, women housed in other units had limited access to similar services. These women, too, bore witness to the violent event, albeit in different ways: They watched the helicopter land within the institution and felt fear. They overheard officers and other staff discuss and respond to the violent event and felt powerless. This fear and powerlessness was still palpable during our focus groups. A broader institutional response during this time of crisis might have benefited the mental health of these women, as well as contributed positively to the institutional mission of safety and security.

Understanding the survivor, Harris and Fallot's (2001) second principle, necessitates that systems and professionals relate to women from a holistic perspective. Women in this study frequently described being labeled and "lumped together" as "addicts," "lifers," "drug seekers," or medical "frequent flyers" by health and correctional professionals. These labels not only described a specific negative characteristic of the woman but, at times, seemed linked to access to care [as well]. For example, women serving life sentences (lifers) reported that they were always "last on the list" to participate in mental health programs because they were "not going anywhere." These labels might have also provided a context for how a woman's health symptoms were perceived within the institution. For example, pain experienced by drug seekers and addicts was often invalidated by health professionals. These labels have the potential to additionally damage women's poor self-images. In fact, these negative labels were often transferred down to, and reinforced by, the women themselves. They were, at times, used to describe other women ("Oh, she's just a junkie") and at other times, used to describe themselves ("I'm just an inmate").

Even the label of *inmate*, although factually accurate, carried not only the negative connotation of someone who had committed a crime but also served to reinforce a gender-neutral stance that equated the circumstances and needs of incarcerated women with their male counterparts. For example, women described being subject to the same policies and procedures used in men's institutions, including routine strip searches before visitation. Women identified the irony of being required to attend a *violence prevention program* when in actuality, most had been victims of violent crimes. And finally, women were angered by policies designed for sexual offenders, most of whom were men, which barred children from sitting on their laps after a certain age.

Data from this investigation provide insight into Harris and Fallot's (2001) third principle, understanding available services. Many women described prison mental health services as primarily crisis oriented and designed for "the worst-case scenarios." Despite this orientation, some women did identify both mental health providers and specific programs that contributed to improved mental health. The most often cited beneficial programs included those that specifically addressed victimization and addiction and those that taught and reinforced positive skill-building techniques (journaling, stopping and thinking, relaxation, deep breathing, and so forth). Although not specifically a mental health program, women who participated in the puppy program, as well as women who simply lived in the same unit as the puppies, expressed that involvement in the program improved their mental health. It is important to note, however, that although these programs were viewed by some women as successful, access was often limited because of inadequate resources. Although women acknowledged that providers were overburdened by the increasing acuity and rapid growth in the inmate population, many remained steadfast in their belief that they deserved and needed care, regardless of institutional circumstances.

Finally, women characterized their relationships with service professionals, including health and correctional professionals, as largely disempowered. Only rarely were these relationships portrayed by women as mutual or collaborative. Women described having limited voice or control in their care and identified that their opinions were largely unappreciated. Their views of their symptoms and their knowledge of their own bodies was rarely considered accurate or valuable by health professionals. Despite being dissatisfied with care, some women did not voice their opinions or question health professionals because they were concerned they would be labeled a *troublemaker* and feared such a label would result in worse care. Unlike nonincarcerated women, women in prison were powerless to seek care elsewhere.

Many women believed they had been ignored and abandoned by the correctional health care system. The copayment system was particularly burdensome for most of the women in our study, and [it] might have reduced women's use of health-related services, a finding that was also identified by Fisher and Hatton (2010). Women expressed lack of confidence and trust in health professionals and were anxious over unfamiliar medical terms and diagnoses they neither understood nor fully believed were accurate. Women yearned to be able to *talk with someone* about their issues and were stymied when they were told their medical symptoms were not severe enough or their abuse not traumatic enough to merit care.

Limitations

Despite remarkably good access to most of the prison population, several key groups of incarcerated women were not allowed to participate in the study. As noted, we did not have access to women in high-security areas, such as the RHU or the MHU. It is possible that these women, by virtue of their classification in the institution, might have different (and likely more negative) responses [from] women housed in the general prison population. It is also possible that women in the general prison population who suffered significant difficulties while incarcerated might have had more incentive to share their negative experiences than women who had more positive experiences, thus, skewing the data negatively. Because the PHS was written in English and the focus groups were conducted in English, non-English speakers might also be underrepresented in our study. It is possible that non-English speakers might have different experiences in prison [from] native English speakers. As with any cross-sectional study, our data provide only snapshots of an overall picture of how women's mental health is affected by incarceration. Data collected at different points in time (Mother's Day, Christmas, a month before release) might result in different findings. Finally, these findings are specific to women incarcerated in one particular institution and might not be generalizable to other women incarcerated in other prisons and jails.

Recommendations

Research

Although our research question was focused broadly on mental health, future investigators might be interested in specific aspects of mental health, such as barriers to care, mental health and stigma, and the process of adaptation to imprisonment. It would also be valuable to better understand the key features of treatment programs and other therapeutic modalities that women in our study felt improved mental health. What are the necessary elements that make a program successful, and how do women (and DOC professionals) measure success? Do certain populations of women (such as women serving life sentences) have different needs [from] women serving shorter sentences?

In light of access to limited resources, investigators should also consider the effectiveness of innovative, alternative modes of delivering mental health treatment, such as using MP3 players (which are allowed in some correctional institutions) to teach inmates relaxation techniques or to provide skill-building exercises. In addition to improving women's mental health, the establishment of evidence-based mental health treatment programs that can be used safely and successfully in women's correctional institutions might have the potential to reduce recidivism, which would be important at individual, community, and societal levels.

Although in this investigation we focused specifically on incarcerated women's perceptions of their mental health, understanding the experiences of correctional, medical, and mental health professionals working in correctional institutions might provide important insight; in many respects, these individuals are also institutionalized. If receptive to beginning a dialogue, these professionals are in a unique position to provide valuable insight into what "works" in prison and, equally important, what does not. It is possible that improvements in inmate well-being might result in a less stressful work environment for institutional professionals. As some women commented, a reduction in staff stress levels might result in a better institutional milieu for women in prison.

Several investigators (Fisher & Hatton, 2010; Hatton & Fisher, 2011; Martin, Murphy, Chan, et al., 2009; Martin, Murphy, Hanson, et al., 2009) have partnered with incarcerated women in the design, conduct, analysis, and dissemination of research addressing the needs of incarcerated women. Collaborating with incarcerated women as coinvestigators is one way researchers can acknowledge incarcerated women's expertise and engage them in developing research that is meaningful to them. Furthermore, this partnering has the possibility of reducing unintentional exploitation and addressing power imbalances in the research process.

Practice

Because most of the women in prison have experienced trauma, it is vital that both correctional systems and the professionals they employ approach the women they serve from a trauma-informed perspective. Harris and Fallot (2001) argued for an administrative commitment to change, including "integrating knowledge about violence and abuse into the service delivery practices of the organization" (p. 5). Knowledge can be integrated in a variety of ways, such as developing specific educational programs for staff, as well as incorporating trauma awareness into an organization's mission statement. Harris and Fallot also urged organizations to adopt a policy of universal screening for trauma among all individuals seeking services. They also argued that organizations should hire individuals who already have a basic understanding of trauma, as well as train and educate all service personnel with introductory information about trauma. Finally, Harris and Fallot identified that organizations should review existing policies and procedures with the goal of identifying anything that might potentially be harmful to or might retraumatize survivors.

The presence of a dedicated trauma treatment program, as well as institutional support of trauma-based research, signifies our study institution's positive movement toward a more trauma-informed model of care. However, women's accounts of their experiences in prison point to the continued need for trauma-based training programs targeting all professionals working in the institution. It is reasonable to believe that correctional officers and health professionals can still maintain custody and control within the institution without degrading the women they serve. Even commonplace actions, such as referring to women by their inmate identification number (often referred to as their *con number*), referring to patients as *inmates* in clinical notes, or describing women as "needy," "drug seeking," or "manipulative" are inconsistent with the trauma-informed perspective of care and should be discouraged.

Prison officials, in conjunction with experts in women's trauma, should also thoroughly examine existing policies and procedures from the perspectives of both gender and trauma. Incarcerated women are not men, and many of the policies that direct common institutional procedures might not be relevant to incarcerated women. Furthermore, these procedures might be unnecessarily traumatogenic. While examining existing policies and procedures that might be harmful to women, it is also important to identify situations that might necessitate the development of new trauma-informed policies. These procedures might be especially relevant in situations that require both security action as well as mental health intervention for victims and bystanders, such as violent events in the institution, medical emergencies, and institutional suicides.

✕ References

Bradley, R. G., & Davino, K. M. (2002). Women's perceptions of the prison environment: When prison is "the safest place I've ever been." *Psychology of Women Quarterly, 26,* 351–359. doi:10.1111/1471–6402.t01–2-00074

Braithwaite, R. L., Treadwell, H. M., & Arriola, K. R. J. (2008). Health disparities and incarcerated women: A population ignored. *American Journal of Public Health, 98*(Suppl. 1), S173-S175. doi:10.2105/AJPH.2005.065375

Covington, S. S. (1998). Women in prison: Approaches in the treatment of our most invisible population. *Women & Therapy, 21,* 141–155. doi:10.1300/J015v21n01_03

Douglas, N., Plugge, E., & Fitzpatrick, R. (2009). The impact of imprisonment on health: What do women prisoners say? *Journal of Epidemiology and Community Health, 63,* 749–754. doi:10.1136/jech.2008.080713

Fisher, A. A., & Hatton, D. C. (2010). A study of women prisoners' use of co-payments for health care: Issues of access. *Women's Health Issues, 20,* 185–192. doi:10.1016/j.whi.2010.01.005

Harner, H. M., & Burgess, A. W. (2011). Using a trauma-informed framework to care for incarcerated women. *Journal of Obstetric, Gynecologic, and Neonatal Nursing, 40,* 469–476. doi:10.1111/j.1552-6909.2011.01259.x

Harner, H. M., Hanlon, A., & Garfinkel, M. (2010). The effect of Iyengar yoga on the mental health of incarcerated women: A feasibility study. *Nursing Research, 59,* 389–399. doi:10.1097/NNR.0b013e3181f2e6ff

Harner, H. M., Hentz, P., & Evangelista, M. C. (2011). Grief interrupted: The experience of loss among incarcerated women. *Qualitative Health Research, 21,* 454–461. doi:10.1177/1049732310373257

Harris, M., & Fallot, R. D. (2001). Envisioning a trauma informed service system: A vital paradigm shift. *New Directions for Mental Health Services, 89,* 3–22. doi:10.1002/yd.23320018903

Hatton, D. C., & Fisher, A. A. (2011). Using participatory methods to examine policy and women prisoners' health. *Policy, Politics, & Nursing Practice, 12,* 119–125. doi:10.1177/1527154411412384

James, D., & Glaze, L. (2006). Mental health problems of prisons and jail inmates, Retrieved from http://bjs.ojp.usdoj.gov/content/pub/pdf/mhppji.pdf

Kim, S. (2003). Incarcerated women in life context. *Women's Studies International Forum, 26*(1), 95–100. doi:10.1016/S0277–5395(02)00358–8

Martin, R. E., Murphy, K., Chan, R., Ramsden, V. R., Granger-Brown, A., Macaulay, A. C., & Hislop, T. G. (2009). Primary health care: Applying the principles within a community-based participatory health research project that began in a Canadian women's prison. *Global Health Promotion, 16*(4), 43–53. doi:10.1177/1757975909348114

Martin, R. E., Murphy, K., Hanson, D., Hemingway, C., Ramsden, V., Buxton, J., & Espinoza-Magana, N. (2009). The development of participatory health research among incarcerated women in a Canadian prison. *International Journal of Prisoner Health, 5,* 95–107. doi:10.1080/17449200902884021

Nurse, J., Woodcock, P., & Ormsby, J. (2003). Influence of environmental factors on mental health within prisons: Focus group study. *British Medical Journal, 327,* 1–5. doi:10.1136/bmj.327.7413.480

Young, D. S. (2000). Women's perceptions of health care in prison. *Health Care for Women International, 21,* 219–234. doi:10.1080/073993300245276

DISCUSSION QUESTIONS

1. Which factors led women to believe that prison had a negative effect on their mental health status?

2. Which factors led women to believe that prison had a positive effect on their mental health status?

3. For those women that believed that prison did not impact their mental health status, what factors made this population different from the others?

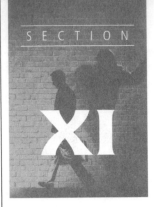

The Supervision of Women
Community Corrections, Rehabilitation, and Reentry

This section focuses on issues related to the supervision of women within the community corrections setting. This section highlights how the differential pathways of female offending affect the unique needs for women and presents a review of the tenets of gender-responsive programming. The section then turns to a discussion on how the needs of women can impact their successes and failures on probation. Within this context, this section also looks at the role of risk assessment tools and how they are used to make decisions about the supervision of women. The section concludes with a discussion on the challenges that female offenders face as they return to their communities following their incarceration.

Gender-Responsive Programming for Women

The needs of women have been significantly neglected by the criminal justice system throughout history. In an effort to remedy the disparities in treatment, several court cases began to challenge the delivery of services for female offenders. Most of these decisions began with the practices in women's prisons; however, their rulings have had implications for women in community correctional settings and programs as well. The case of *Barefield v. Leach* (1974) was particularly important for women as it set the standard through which the courts could measure whether women received a lower standard of treatment compared to men. Since *Barefield*, the courts have ruled that a number of policies that were biased against women were unconstitutional. For example, the case of *Glover v. Johnson* (1979) held that the state must provide the same opportunities for education, rehabilitation, and vocational training for females as provided for male offenders. Cases such as *Cooper v. Morin* (1980) held that the equal protection clause prevents prison administrators from justifying the disparate treatment of women on the grounds that providing such services for women is inconvenient. Ultimately, the courts held that "males and females must be treated equally unless there is a substantial reason which requires a distinction be made" (*Canterino v. Wilson*, 1982).

While these cases began to establish a conversation on the accessibility of programming for women, they generally focused on the issue of parity between male and female prisoners. At the time, women constituted only about 5% of the total number of incarcerated offenders. During the 1970s, prison advocates worked toward providing women with the same opportunities for programming and treatment as men. Their efforts were relatively successful in that many gender-based policies were abolished, and new policies were put into place mandating that men and women be treated similarly (Zaitzow & Thomas, 2003). However, feminist criminologists soon discovered that parity and equality for female offenders does not necessarily mean that women benefit from the same treatment as men (Bloom, Owen, & Covington, 2003, 2004). Indeed, research has documented that programs designed for men fail the needs of women (Belknap, 2007).

These findings led to the emergence of a new philosophy of parity for women—gender-responsive programming. Gender-responsive or gender-specific programming first emerged in response to the dramatic increase in the number of girls that were appearing before the juvenile court. However, few jurisdictions were prepared to address the needs of this new population. As you learned in Section VII, the 1992 reauthorization of the Juvenile Justice and Delinquency Prevention Act mandated that states assess the needs of girls and develop gender-specific options to address the unique needs of female offenders. Following the efforts of the juvenile court, the criminal justice system has engaged in similar conversations regarding the adult female offending population. In an effort to respond to the needs of women and girls, scholars and practitioners were left to determine what it means to be gender responsive in our correctional environments. Research by Bloom et al. (2003, 2004) highlights how six key principles can change the way in which programs and institutions design and manage programs, develop policies, train staff, and supervise offenders. These six principles are (1) gender, (2) environment, (3) relationships, (4) services and supervision, (5) socioeconomic status, and (6) community. Together, these six principles provide guidance for the effective management of female offenders.

The first principle of gender discusses the importance for criminal justice systems and agents to recognize the role that gender plays in the offending of women and the unique treatment needs of women. As you learned earlier in this book, the pathways of women to crime are dramatically different from the pathways of men. Even though they may be incarcerated for similar crimes, their lives related to these offenses are dramatically different. As a result, men and women respond to treatment in different ways and have different issues to face within the context of rehabilitation. To offer the same program to men and women may not adequately address the unique needs for both populations. Given that the majority of programs have been developed about male criminality and are used for male offenders, these programs often fail the unique needs of women.

The second principle of environment focuses on the need for officials to create a place where staff and inmates engage in practices of mutual respect and dignity. Given that many women involved in the criminal justice system come from a background of violence and abuse, it is critical that women feel safe and supported in their journey toward rehabilitation and recovery. Historically, the criminal justice system has emphasized a model of power and control, a model that limits the ability for nurturing, trust, and compassion. Rehabilitative programs for women need to create an environment that is a safe place where women can share the intimate details of their lives (Covington 1999).

The third principle of relationships refers to developing an understanding of why women commit crimes; the context of their lives prior to, during, and following incarceration; and the relationships that women build while they are incarcerated. In addition, the majority of incarcerated women attempt to sustain their relationships with family members outside the prison walls, particularly with their minor children. Given that the majority of incarcerated women present a low safety risk to the community, women should be placed in settings that are minimally restrictive, offer opportunities for programs and services, and are located within reasonable proximity to their families and minor children. The concept of relationships also involves how program providers interact with and relate to their clients. Group participants need to feel supported by their treatment providers, and the providers need to be able to empower women to make positive choices about their lives (Covington, 1999).

The fourth principle identifies the need for gender-responsive programming to address the traumas that women have experienced throughout the context of their lives. As indicated throughout this text, the cycle to offending for women often begins with the experience of victimization. In addition, these victim experiences continue throughout their lives and often inform their criminal actions. Historically, treatment providers for substance abuse issues, trauma, and mental health issues have dealt with offenders on an individualized basis. Gender-responsive approaches highlight the need for program providers and institutions to address these issues as co-occurring disorders. Here, providers need to be cross-trained in these three issues in order to develop and implement effective programming options for women. In addition, community correctional settings need to acknowledge how these issues translate into challenges and barriers to success in the **reentry** process. This awareness can help support women in their return to the community.

The fifth principle focuses on the socioeconomic status of the majority of women in prison. Most women in prison turn to criminal activity as a survival mechanism. Earlier in this volume, you learned that women in the system lack adequate educational and vocational resources to develop a sustainable life for themselves and their families and struggle with poverty, homelessness, and limited public assistance resources, particularly for drug-convicted offenders. In order to enhance the possibilities of success following their incarceration, women need to have access to opportunities to break the cycle of abuse and create positive options for their future. Without these skills and opportunities, many women will fall back into the criminal lifestyle out of economic necessity. Given that many women will reunite with their children following their release, these opportunities will help women make a better life not only for themselves but for their children as well.

The sixth principle of community focuses on the need to develop collaborative relationships among providers in order to assist women in their transition toward independent living. Bloom et al. (2003) call for the need to develop wraparound services for women. **Wraparound services** refer to "a holistic and culturally sensitive plan for each woman that draws on a coordinated range of services within her community" (p. 82). Examples of these services include public and mental health systems, addiction recovery, welfare, emergency shelter organizations, and educational and vocational services. Certainly, wraparound services require a high degree of coordination between agencies and program providers. Given the multiple challenges that women face throughout their reentry process, the development of comprehensive services will help support women toward a successful transition. In addition, by having one case manager to address multiple issues, agencies can be more effective in meeting the needs of and supervising women in the community while reducing the levels of bureaucracy and "red tape" in the delivery of resources.

Table 11.1 illustrates how the principles of gender, environment, relationships, services and supervision, socioeconomic status, and community can be utilized when developing gender-responsive policies and programming. These suggestions can assist institutional administrators and program providers in developing policies and procedures that represent the realities of women's lives and reflect ways that rehabilitation efforts can be most effective for women. Within each of these topical considerations, correctional agencies should be reminded that the majority of female offenders are nonviolent in nature, are more likely to be at risk for personal injury versus harmful toward others, and are in need of services.

Table 11.1   Questions to Ask in Developing a Systemic Approach for Women Offenders

Operational Practices

- Are the specifics of women's behavior and circumstances addressed in written planning, policy, programs, and operational practices? For example, are policies regarding classification, property, programs, and services appropriate to the actual behavior and composition of the female population?
- Does the staff reflect the offender population in terms of gender, race/ethnicity, sexual orientation, language (bilingual), ex-offender, and recovery status? Are female role models and mentors employed to reflect the racial/ethnic and cultural backgrounds of the clients?
- Does staff training prepare workers for the importance of relationships in the lives of women offenders? Does the training provide information on the nature of women's relational context, boundaries and limit setting, communication, and child-related issues? Are staff prepared to relate to women offenders in an empathetic and professional manner?
- Are staff training in appropriate gender communication skills and in recognizing and dealing with the effects of trauma and PTSD?

Services

- Is training on women offenders provided? Is this training available in initial academy or orientation sessions? Is the training provided on an ongoing basis? Is this training mandatory for executive-level staff?
- Does the organization see women's issues as a priority? Are women's issues important enough to warrant an agency-level position to manage women's services?
- Do resource allocation, staffing, training, and budgeting consider the facts of managing women offenders?

Review of Standard Procedures

- Do classifications and other assessments consider gender in classification instruments, assessment tools, and individualized treatment plans? Has the existing classification system been validated on a sample of women? Does the database system allow for separate analysis of female characteristics?
- Is information about women offenders collected, coded, monitored, and analyzed in the agency?
- Are protocols established for reporting and investigating claims of staff misconduct, with protection from retaliation ensured? Are the concepts of privacy and personal safety incorporated in daily operations and architectural design, where applicable?
- How does policy address the issue of cross gender strip searches and pat downs?
- Does the policy include the concept of zero tolerance for inappropriate language, touching, and other inappropriate behavior and staff sexual misconduct?

Children and Families

- How do existing programs support connections between the female offender and her children and family? How are these connections undermined by current practice? In institutional environments, what provisions are made for visiting and for other opportunities for contact with children and family?
- Are there programs and services that enhance female offenders' parenting skills and their ability to support their children following release? In community supervision settings and community treatment programs, are parenting responsibilities acknowledged through education? Through child care?

Community

- Are criminal justice services delivered in a manner that builds community trust, confidence, and partnerships?
- Do classification systems and housing configurations allow community custody placements? Are transitional programs in place that help women build long-term community support networks?
- Are professionals, providers, and community volunteer positions used to facilitate community connections? Are they used to develop partnerships between correctional agencies and community providers?

SOURCE: Bloom, Owen, & Covington (2003).

The Supervision of Women in the Community

Community-based supervision is the most common form of intervention utilized by the criminal justice system. Within community supervision, the most popular option is **probation**. When offenders are sentenced to probation, they are allowed to remain in the community rather than serve out their sentence in jail or prison. In addition, a sentence to probation allows for offenders to access programs and services that focus on rehabilitation. Offenders on probation must follow specific terms and conditions that allow them to remain in the community. These can include a curfew, participation in therapeutic programs such as anger management counseling and drug treatment, or maintaining a job or enrollment in school. Offenders may also be required to pay fines to the court, restitution to the victim, or to complete community service hours. If an offender fails to follow the directives as ordered by the court and her probation officer, she runs the risk of losing her privilege to remain in the community.

In 2011, 4,814,200 adults were supervised in the community through probation services. According to the Bureau of Justice Statistics, 25% of these probationers were female (Table 11.2). This is a slight increase from 2000 where 22% of the probation population were women (Maruschak & Parks, 2012). Probation has traditionally been an option offered for many female offenders as it allowed them to remain in the community. This is particularly important given that many women are often the primary caregivers for young children.

The central tenet of probation is about reducing risk to the community. When offenders are sentenced to serve out their sentence under community supervision, how can we be sure that they will be successful? How can we be sure that they are not a danger to themselves or others? In evaluating the risks and needs of women on probation, many agencies use assessment instruments to gauge the risk that an offender presents to the public. At the same time, these tools can help identify what the needs of the offender are, which can help probation officers provide services and supervision for these offenders. However, these *gender-neutral* assessments may not adequately identify the needs of female offenders (Davidson, 2011). In addition, the needs of women are often misrepresented as risks, which can lead to increased punitive punishments by probation officers.

One of the most common assessment tools used in community corrections is the **Level of Service Inventory-Revised (LSI-R)**. While the LSI-R has been validated within the male offender population, research on the LSI-R for female offenders has been mixed. In some cases, the LSI-R fails to identify the gender-specific needs of women. In others, the LSI-R has led to the overclassification of women. Even when the LSI-R is effective in identifying the

Table 11.2   Characteristics of Women in Community Corrections

	Percentage Under Community Supervision	Percentage in Jail
White	62	36
African American	27	44
Hispanic	10	15
Median age	32	31
High school/GED	60	55
Single	42	48
Unemployed	—	60
Mother of minor children	72	70

risks of recidivism, this tool may not be able to assess the context of these risks. Finally, the LSI-R fails to identify some of the most significant needs of women with their abuse histories, health issues, and motherhood issues (Davidson 2011).

Given some of these limitations of the LSI-R and other assessment tools, scholars have worked to develop gender-responsive tools to provide a better reflection of the needs of female offenders. The first instrument is shorter in length and is designed to supplement existing assessments that are not gender specific, while the second instrument is designed to replace existing measures and be used as a stand-alone tool in evaluating risk and identifying needs for female offenders. The philosophy behind these new tools is to allow for community correctional agencies to record the high needs that many female offenders may have without increasing their risk levels (Salisbury, Van Voorhis, Wright, & Bauman, 2009). These tools allow community correctional agencies to advocate for female-only and smaller caseloads as well as partner with other agencies and providers in the community to develop wraparound services that will help increase the success levels of women on probation (Van Voorhis, Salisbury, Wright, & Bauman, 2008).

▲ **Photo 11.1**   Women walk along a corridor at the Los Angeles County women's jail in Lynwood, California, April 26, 2013. The Second Chance Women's Re-entry Court is one of the first in the United States to focus on women, and it offers a cost-saving alternative to prison for women who plead guilty to nonviolent crimes and volunteer for treatment. Of the 297 women who have been through the court since 2007, 100 have graduated and only 35 have been returned to state prison

The failure by community-based services to develop and implement gender-responsive programs that meet the needs of offenders is connected to recidivism rates. One example of an effective gender-responsive program for female probationers is the *Moving On* program. The curriculum is designed to help women build tools for resiliency in their personal lives and develop ways to generate support and resources within their communities. Here, the focus of the program is to increase women's self-awareness of their challenges and triggers that might lead to recidivism. Assessments of the *Moving On* program have demonstrated its efficacy, as these women had lower rates of recidivism (in terms of new offenses) compared to those women under traditional probation supervision. While the women from the *Moving On* program were more likely to receive a technical violation of probation, these violations occurred in cases where the women failed to complete the program. These findings conclude that the completion of a gender-responsive program can be an effective tool in reducing the recidivism rates of women on probation (Gehring, Van Voorhis, & Bell, 2010).

Once on probation, gender has an effect on how offenders experience probation, as probation officers view male and female offenders differently, which alters their supervision style. Research by Wyse (2013) indicates that probation officers are more likely to focus on the rules of probation with male probationers. Here, the emphasis was placed on whether the men were employed and desisting from criminal behavior. In these cases, the relationship between the offender and the officer was very formal. In contrast, the relationship between the probation officer and female clients was more intimate and emotional in nature. In many cases, this allowed offenders to develop trust with their probation officers, and offenders seek out their help in finding referrals for treatment and support (Hall, Golder, Conley, & Sawning, 2013). Officers frequently encouraged their clients to find ways to increase their self-esteem. Women were also encouraged to build self-reliance and stay away from romantic relationships in general. Indeed, officers spend far greater time policing these relationships for women, while this is rarely mentioned for male offenders (Wyse, 2013).

Women on Parole

The term **parole** invokes a variety of meanings. On one hand, an offender in prison can be up for parole and have her file reviewed by a board of officials to determine whether she should be released back into the community. At the same time, parole also refers to the supervision of offenders following their release from prison. In 2011, of the 853,900 people who were supervised on parole, 11% of the parole population were women (Maruschak & Parks, 2012). Given that women make up such a small proportion of the offenders placed on parole, it has been challenging to provide appropriate gender-responsive programming and services for this population. While parole supervision was once intended to help offenders successfully transition back to the community, the role of parole officers has shifted. Due to the high caseloads that many parole offices face, the opportunities to provide an individualized case to these offenders are limited. Instead, the majority of their time is spent monitoring offenders, waiting to respond if and when an offender violates the conditions of their release. One woman shares the struggles in meeting these demands, expressing fear and the unknown of her new life and her ability to be successful in her reentry process:

> I start my day running to drop my urine [drug testing]. Then I go see my children, show up for my training program, look for a job, go to a meeting [Alcoholics Anonymous], and show up at my part-time job. I have to take the bus everywhere, sometimes eight buses for 4 hours a day. I don't have the proper outer clothes, I don't have the money to buy lunch along the way, and everyone who works with me keeps me waiting so that I am late to my next appointment. If I fail any one of these things I am revoked. I am so tired that I sometimes fall asleep on my way home from work at 2:00 a.m. and that's dangerous given where I live. And then the next day I have to start over again. I don't mind being busy and working hard . . . that's part of my recovery. But this is a situation that is setting me up to fail. I just can't keep up and I don't know where to start. (Ritchie, 2001, p. 381)

Reentry Issues for Incarcerated Women

The needs of incarcerated women returning to their communities are high. While much of the research on reentry issues has focused on whether offenders will reoffend and return to prison (recidivism), recent scholars have shifted the focus on reentry to discussions on how to successfully transition offenders back into their communities. This process can be quite traumatic, and for women, a number of issues emerge in creating a successful reentry experience.

Consider the basic needs of a woman who has just left prison. She needs housing, clothing, and food. She may be eager to reestablish relationships with friends, family members, and her children. In addition, she has obligations as part of her release—appointments with her parole officer and treatment requirements. In addition, the majority of women find themselves returning to the same communities in which they lived prior to their incarceration, where they face the same problems of poverty, addiction, and dysfunction. Finding safe and affordable housing is challenging, and for many women, the only options place them at risk for relapse and recidivism (Hall et al., 2013). For those few women who were able to receive some therapeutic treatment in prison, most acknowledge that these prison-based intervention programs provided few, if any, legitimate coping skills to deal with the realities of the life stressors that awaited them upon their release. Many women also hope to reunite with their children. While a return to motherhood may be a powerful motivation to get their lives back on track, the reality of returning as the authority figure in a family is compromised by a number of factors. These include the separation from her children during incarceration, the loss of her children to other family members or social services, and a lack of confidence to effectively raise her children (Brown & Bloom, 2009). On top of all these struggles, offenders face a new identity upon their release from prison—the *ex-offender* status. This identity can place significant challenges for offenders and threaten their ability to be successful upon release. Consider the number of employment opportunities that require applicants to disclose whether they have ever been arrested for a crime. In many cases, this automatically excludes the applicant from consideration. For women, the inability to find suitable employment has a significant effect, particularly if she is trying to create a stable home environment to regain custody of her children. Many women also reference how their lack of education or training makes it difficult to secure legal and stable employment (Hall et al., 2013). A recent campaign to *ban the box* has many states and companies changing the way they handle ex-convict's applications for employment. In Minnesota, recent legislation makes it illegal for state employers to ask about an offender's criminal history on a job application. As one of the largest retailers, Target has reformed its hiring policies such that questions about any criminal history are not raised until an applicant has been granted an interview (Strachan, 2013).

In addition to the challenges of returning home from prison, many women continue to battle the demons that led them to criminal activity in the first place. As you learned in Section VIII, drug addiction is one of the primary reasons why women are involved in criminal activity and ultimately sent to prison. Given the limited availability of treatment options both behind bars and within the community, issues of addiction can lead to recidivism, particularly for women of color (Huebner, DeJong & Cobbina, 2010). Drug addiction has a multiplying effect in the lives of women—not only can addiction threaten a woman's status on parole, but it impacts as well their ability to maintain stable employment, secure housing, and reunify with their children.

Without community-based resources, many women will return to the addictions and lifestyles in which they engaged prior to their incarceration. In addition, women have limited access to physical and mental health care, often due to a lack of community resources, an inability to pay, or lack of knowledge about where to go to obtain assistance. Given the status of mental and physical health needs of incarcerated women, the management (or lack thereof) of chronic health problems can impede a woman's successful reentry process (Ritchie, 2001). Unfortunately, mental health services within the community overemphasize the use of prescription psychotropic medications. Coupled with the limited availability of therapeutic interventions, these health interventions resemble more of a Band-Aid rather than a comprehensive stable approach for women (Kitty, 2012). This lack of therapeutic support has a significant impact particularly for women with children as both the women and their children could benefit from these resources (Snyder, 2009).

Reentry can also be challenging depending on the offense that brought women to prison in the first place. You've learned in this section about the challenges of reentry for women who continue to struggle with addiction. But what about women who are convicted of one of the most stigmatizing crimes: sexual offenses? What issues do they face? Like other offenders, women convicted of a sexually based offense express concerns about finding housing and a job. In particular, they acknowledged that their offenses come with special terms and conditions of their release such as community notification and residency restrictions. In particular, women were concerned about how this might affect their relationships with their children—would they be allowed to see them participate in activities such as sports if they were held at their children's school or at a local park? Another concern was the stigma that comes with the all-encompassing label of sex offender, regardless of the nature of their specific offense. Indeed, this label can complicate what is already a difficult transition to the community (Tewksbury, Connor, Cheeseman & Rivera, 2012).

While women may turn to public assistance to help support their reentry transition, many come to find that these resources are either unavailable or are significantly limited. The **Welfare Reform Act of 1996** imposed not only time limits on the aid that women can receive, but it has also significantly affected the road to success by denying services and resources for women with a criminal record, particularly in cases of women convicted on a felony drug-related charge (Hirsch, 2001). Section 115 of the welfare reform act calls for a lifetime ban on benefits such as Temporary Assistance for Needy Families (TANF) and food stamps to offenders convicted in the state or federal courts for a felony drug offense. In addition, women convicted of a drug offense are barred from living in public housing developments and, in some areas, a criminal record can limit the availability of Section 8 housing options[1] (Jacobs, 2000). Drug charges are the only offense type subjected to this ban—even convicted murderers can apply for and receive governmental benefits following their release (Sentencing Project, 2006). Indeed, the limits of this ban jeopardize the very efforts toward sustainable and safe housing, education, and drug treatment that are needed in order for women to successfully transition from prison. Table 11.3 presents state-level data on the implementation of the ban on welfare benefits for felony drug convictions.

---

[1]Section 8 housing provides governmental subsidies for housing in nonpublic housing developments. Here, private landlords are paid the difference between the amount of rent that a tenant can afford, based on his or her available income, and the fair market value of the residence.

Table 11.3 State Implementation of Lifetime Welfare Ban (2011)

State	Denies Benefits Entirely	Denies to Drug Manufacturers and Traffickers Only (not possession)	Benefits Dependent on Drug Treatment	Benefits Dependent on Court Compliance	Restores Benefits After Time	Opted Out of Welfare Ban
Alabama						
Alaska	X					
Arizona				X		
Arkansas	X	X				
California			X			
Colorado				X		
Connecticut				X		
Delaware	X					
District of Colombia						
Florida		X				
Georgia	X					
Hawaii			X			
Idaho				X		
Illinois	X					
Indiana				X		
Iowa			X			
Kansas						X
Kentucky			X			
Louisiana					X	
Maine						X
Maryland			X			
Massachusetts				X		
Michigan						X
Minnesota						
Mississippi	X					
Missouri						

State	Denies Benefits Entirely	Denies to Drug Manufacturers and Traffickers Only (not possession)	Benefits Dependent on Drug Treatment	Benefits Dependent on Court Compliance	Restores Benefits After Time	Opted Out of Welfare Ban
Montana				X		
Nebraska	X					
Nevada			X			
New Hampshire						X
New Jersey						X
New Mexico						X
New York						X
North Carolina						
North Dakota		X			X	
Ohio						X
Oklahoma						X
Oregon			X			
Pennsylvania						X
Rhode Island						X
South Carolina	X					
South Dakota	X					
Tennessee			X			
Texas	X					
Utah			X			
Vermont						X
Virginia						
Washington				X		
West Virginia	X					
Wisconsin						
Wyoming						X
U.S. total	11	3	9	8	2	13

SOURCE: Legal Action Center (2011).

How many women are affected by the lifetime bans on assistance? Research by the Sentencing Project indicates that, as of 2006, more than 92,000 women are currently affected by the lifetime welfare ban. They also estimate that the denial of benefits places more than 135,000 children at risk for future contact with the criminal justice system due to economic struggles. The ban also disproportionately affects women of color, with approximately 35,000 African American women and 10,000 Latina women dealing with a loss of benefits. Since its enactment in 1996, 39 states have rescinded the lifetime ban on resources, either in its entirety or in part. However, 11 states have retained this ban on assistance, placing family reunification efforts between women and their children in jeopardy (Sentencing Project, 2006; Legal Action Center, 2011).

Even women without a drug conviction still face significant issues in obtaining public assistance. Federal welfare law prohibits states from providing assistance under programs such as TANF (Temporary Assistance for Needy Families), SSI (Supplementary Security Income), housing assistance, or food stamps in cases where a woman has violated a condition of her probation or parole. In many cases, this violation can be as simple as failing to report for a meeting with a probation officer when she has a sick child. In addition, TANF carries a 5-year life-time limit for assistance. This lifetime limit applies to all women, not just those under the criminal justice system. In addition, the delay to receive these services ranges from 45 days to several months, a delay that significantly affects the ability of women to put a roof over their children's heads, clothes on their bodies, and food in their bellies (Jacobs, 2000). Ultimately, these reforms are a reflection of budgetary decisions that often result in the slashing of social service and government aid programs, while the budgets for criminal justice agendas, such as incarceration, remain supported by state and governmental officials. These limits affect not only the women who are in the greatest need of services but their children as well, who will suffer physically, mentally, and emotionally from these economic struggles (Danner, 2003).

Despite the social stigma that comes with receiving welfare benefits, women in one study indicated that the receipt of welfare benefits represented progress toward a successful recovery and independence from reliance on friends, family, or a significant other for assistance. A failure to receive benefits could send them into a downward spiral toward homelessness, abusive relationships, and relapse.

> We still need welfare until we are strong enough to get on our feet. Trying to stay clean, trying to be responsible parents and take care of our families. We need welfare right now. If we lose it, we might be back out there selling drugs. We're trying to change our lives. Trying to stop doing wrong things. Some of us need help. Welfare helps us stay in touch with society. Trying to do what's right for us. (Hirsch, 2001, p. 278)

Throughout the reentry process, women also struggle with gaining access to addiction-based services. Without these referrals by probation and parole, most women are denied access to treatment due to the limited availability of services or an inability to pay for such resources on their own. Here, women are actually at risk for recidivism, as their needs continue to be unmet. In addition, many of these programs fail to work within the context of their lives. For example, the majority of inpatient drug treatment programs do not provide the option for women to reside and care for their children. These programs promote sobriety first and rarely create the opportunity for family reunification until women have successfully transitioned from treatment, have obtained a job, and can provide a sustainable environment for themselves. For many women, the desire to reunite with their children is their primary focus, and the inability for women to maintain connection with their children can threaten their path toward sobriety (Jacobs, 2000).

Clearly, women who make the transition from prison or jail back to their communities must achieve stability in their lives. With multiple demands on them (compliance with the terms and conditions of their release; dealing with long-term issues such as addiction, mental health, and physical health concerns; and the need for food, clothing, and shelter), this transition is anything but easy. Here, the influence of a positive mentor can provide significant support for women as they navigate this journey.

> While it is true a woman in reentry has many tangible needs (housing, employment, family reunification, formal education), attention to intangible needs (empowerment, a sense of belonging, someone to talk to) can promote personal growth through positive reinforcement of progress, encouragement and support in the face of defeat and temptation, and a place to feel like a regular person. (Women's Prison Association [WPA], 2008, p. 3)

Several key pieces of legislation have focused on the need for support and mentorship throughout the reentry process and have provided federal funding to support these networks. For example, the Ready4Work initiative (2003), the Prisoner Reentry Initiative (2005), and the Second Chance Act (2007) all acknowledged the challenges that ex-offenders face when they exit the prison environment. These initiatives help support community organizations that provide comprehensive services for ex-offenders, including case management, mentoring, and other transitional services (WPA, 2008). Given the struggles that women face as part of their journey back from incarceration, it is clear that these initiatives can provide valuable resources to assist with the reentry process.

✄ Recidivism and Female Offenders

Whether it is probation, prison, or parole, the goal of the corrections is to reduce and prevent recidivism. But does it? Recidivism can be a difficult thing for scholars to measure. What "counts" as recidivism? Is it being arrested or convicted for a new criminal offense? Is it a technical violation of probation or parole? What is the time limit that we use to determine recidivism? One year following release? Five? Ten?

Research by Mears, Cochran, and Bales (2012) indicates that prison can produce a criminogenic effect for women. This means that prison can actually encourage offenders to engage in crime, rather than prevent it, at least in terms of particular offenses. While time in prison is more likely to increase property and drug crimes for male offenders, incarceration for women increases their recidivism for property offenses. In addition, prison produces the strongest effect for recidivism, compared to probation. Similar results were indicated by McCoy and Miller (2013), who found that women were more likely to recidivate in prostitution cases. Younger women were also more likely to recidivate. However, protective factors did serve to inhibit recidivism for women. While romantic and familial relationships increased recidivism risk for male offenders, these relationships (when positive in nature) served to protect women from recidivism (Cobbina, Huebner & Berg, 2012). These results indicate that the *most punitive* punishment may be the least effective in terms of rehabilitation and that reentry efforts need to consider these factors when providing support.

Building Resiliency for Women

With so much attention on the negative focus of women's lives and their relationships, there has been little discussion within the research about how women involved in the criminal justice system build strength and resiliency in their lives. In Section VII, you learned about how factors such as a positive mentor and support networks are important factors for delinquent girls, and the same holds true for incarcerated women. Research by Wright, DeHart, Koons-Witt, and Crittenden (2013) indicates that there are several relationships that can serve as buffers against criminal behavior, including positive family relationships, prosocial peer relationships, supportive significant others, and motherhood. In some cases, family members helped them escape from dangerous situations like an intimate partner. "Normal" friends may inspire women to want normalcy in their lives. While much has been written about the power of a negative romantic relationship, a healthy relationship can also provide support throughout incarceration and provide a sense of stability upon release. Finally, the presence of children may encourage women to turn away from a life of crime and focus on their roles as mothers. While these relationships presented positive opportunities, these women also had negative associations to battle, and it was these bad contexts and relationships that would overpower the positive opportunities in their lives. In the words of one woman,

> It all goes back to trying to please people that you care about. . . . It keeps you focused. If you care about your family and love them, you aren't going to put yourself in a position to have yourself taken away from them. (Wright et al., p. 81)

Summary

- Probation allows for women to receive correctional supervision while remaining in the community.
- Upon release, many women return to the communities in which they lived prior to their incarceration, where they face issues of addiction and dysfunction in their lives.
- Gender-responsive programming is designed to address the unique needs of female offenders.
- Probation allows for women to receive correctional supervision while remaining in the community.
- Upon release, many women return to the communities in which they lived prior to their incarceration, where they face issues of addiction and dysfunction in their lives.

KEY TERMS

Barefield v. Leach

Canterino v. Wilson

Cooper v. Morin

Gender-responsive programming

Glover v. Johnson

Level of Service Inventory-Revised (LSI-R)

Parole

Probation

Reentry

Welfare Reform Act of 1996

Wraparound services

DISCUSSION QUESTIONS

1. If you were to design a program that reflected gender-responsive principles, what key features would you integrate into your curriculum?

2. What challenges do women face during their reentry process? How does the Welfare Reform Bill limit access to resources for some women following their incarceration?

3. How do traditional risk assessment instruments fail female offenders? What are the implications of these findings?

WEB RESOURCES

Hour Children: http://www.hourchildren.org

Our Place DC: http://www.ourplacedc.org

The Sentencing Project: http://www.sentencingproject.org

Women's Prison Association: http://www.wpaonline.org

Visit **www.sagepub.com/mallicoat2e** to access additional study tools including eFlashcards, web quizzes, web resources, video resources, and SAGE journal articles.

READING 21

Women who leave prison are faced with a number of challenges. This article focuses on three of these challenges: (1) dealing with addiction, (2) reconnecting with their children, and (3) overcoming their identity as an ex-offender. Each of these challenges serves as a stigma that the women must manage and overcome in order to successfully transition from prison back into the community.

Women Disrupting a Marginalized Identity

Subverting the Parolee Identity Through Narrative

Tara D. Opsal

Introduction

Knowing the challenges women face post-incarceration, I was cautiously optimistic about Liz's circumstances after our first interview. After being released from prison as a parolee to a community unfamiliar to her, Liz had found subsidized and stable housing through an organization that offers support to individuals post-incarceration. And she had found full-time work that not only allowed her to meet her basic needs but also seemed to sustain her in more meaningful ways. Liz explained:

> I don't get paid all that much. . . . Building from scratch is a little difficult, to try to get out on your own like that. But, it'll happen. Like, I—the harder I work, the more I feel like I'm working towards that in a positive way, you know?

There was, however, an unusual aspect to Liz's work that made it tenuous. A day laborer agency had placed her at an apartment complex as a temporary employee doing grounds work and building maintenance. Impressed by her work ethic, the boss there requested

Liz on a long-term basis. She explained to me that even though she outworked all the other employees (who were men), the corporation that owned the complex was unlikely to hire her on a more permanent basis because they had a policy against hiring felons. "Hiring" Liz via the day laborer agency largely dissolved the company of any potential legal liability that could arise from hiring her directly. Liz was aware of how being a felon limited her work opportunities and set her back. Despite these experiences, she explained adamantly that she did not let people's preconceived notions limit her: "I've learned not to let people's opinions affect me."

Three months later at our second interview, Liz's employment circumstances had dramatically changed. Because of her reliability and continued hard work, her boss "decided that they were gonna go to the corporate office and ask them to overlook my felony" in order to hire her on a permanent basis. She explained what happened next:

> Soon as corporate found out I had a felony, there was a person on the property who said, "Get her off the property right this minute." They didn't even know me. They didn't even know how

SOURCE: Opsal, T. D. (2011). Women disrupting a marginalized identity: Subverting the parolee identity through narrative. *Journal of Contemporary Ethnography, 40*(2), 135–167.

much I had done for them. My boss, I thought he was gonna cry . . . they have my back. They wanted me. But, corporate said, "A felony."

Though Liz understood herself in a very different way, her employer ultimately defined her as a felon. Situations like this provide clear evidence that felons are stigmatized (Goffman 1963). U.S. culture clearly demonstrates the social meaning it attaches to this stigmatized identity. Our cultural stories position felons at or near the bottom rung of our social order; Americans view and discuss them primarily in ways that point to their deficits and the problems those deficits cause (Snow and Anderson 1987). These cultural stories also frame offenders as irredeemable criminals (Maruna 2001). Hence, felons, as social deviants, are regarded as fundamentally different from the rest of "us" and, whether they have served their time on the inside or not, remain both culpable and suspect.

Despite a diverse and developed body of research that illustrates the strategies and identity work of individuals with stigmatized identities (Froyum 2007; Riessman 2000; Sandstrom 1990; Snow and Anderson 1987), growing interest in understanding the effects of living with a criminal record for formerly incarcerated individuals (Dodge and Pogrebin 2001; Pager 2003; Rose and Clear 2003; Schnittker and John 2007), as well as the experiences of women post-incarceration (Brown and Bloom 2009; Leverentz 2006; O'Brien 2001; Richie 2001), we still know little about the identity work (Snow and Anderson 1987) of the formerly incarcerated. The focus of this article is on understanding how individuals negotiate a negative social identity (Shinnar 2008) premised on their culpability.

I begin by briefly reviewing the literature on stigma to establish how I conceptualize it for this article. Then, I review the literature on what existing research establishes about the stigmatizing effects of a criminal record and elucidate the interactional and structural processes that institutionalize the stigma of a felony record within U.S. law and policy. Further, I explain how parole—an institution under whose supervision each of the women in this study live—shapes the reentry process. Using this structural and cultural reality as the backdrop, I examine the identity work of women who are simultaneously living as felons and parolees. In the findings, I explain how they resist the stigma associated with a criminal record through narrative work and draw on hegemonic cultural characters

and story lines that assist them in repairing their damaged identities. I illuminate the experiences of women during the reentry process by weaving their own words throughout the analysis.

Contesting Stigma With Identity Talk

In his classic work on stigma, Erving Goffman (1963, 2–3) explains that when people consider an attribute of an individual [as] "bad, or dangerous, or weak," they reduce them [the individual] "from a whole and usual person to a tainted, discounted one." Goffman also posits that individuals who inhabit a stigmatized identity adhere to the same beliefs about their own identities and characteristics; they see and understand themselves as holding a stigmatized identity or attribute. Flowing from Goffman's work, a substantial body of research documents how those with a variety of stigmatizing characteristics—epilepsy, HIV, homelessness, for example—manage whether, how, and when they convey information about their "spoiled identities" (Goffman 1963; Miall 1986; Schnieder and Conrad 1980; Snow and Anderson 1993). However, other scholars argue that individuals do not passively accept the stigmatized identities others bestow upon them. Childless women in India (Riessman 2000), white middle-class singles (Zajicek and Koski 2003), Middle Eastern Americans post-9/11 (Marvasti 2006), and Gulf War veterans (Shriver and Waskul 2006) often refuse to see themselves as "someone with a chronic stigma, or a permanent and enduring negative identity" (Marvasti 2006, 526).

Although these scholars challenge Goffman's framing of stigma management, they do recognize that because stigma is a social construct, attributes of individuals only become stigmatized in comparison to what collectives define as normal and good within the current structural and cultural boundaries of a particular society. This latter notion is consistent with Goffman's (1963) work and flows from the symbolic interactionist tradition. Hence, stigma is not a fixed or immutable trait. Rather, we create it via interaction and therefore can also contest or resist it in the same manner (Goffman 1963).

One way researchers examine how individuals contest or resist a stigmatized identity is by examining their narrative identity work (Riessman 2000; Rosenfeld 1999;

Sandstrom 1990; Snow and Anderson 1987). Schwalbe and Mason-Schrock (1996, 115) explain that identity work can be understood as "anything people do, individually or collectively, to give meaning to themselves or others." Narrative, or verbal identity talk (Snow and Anderson 1987), provides individuals with the opportunity to create vivid versions of their personal identities by challenging existing identities or constructing new ones. Indeed, narratives about the self are powerful in the way they allow individuals to communicate about their lives and, thus, have a purpose that extends "beyond merely conveying information" (Irvine 1999, 44). The selves we constitute through narrative often incorporate past experiences (as we choose to narrate them), present happenings, and future desires about who and how we want to be (Maruna 2001; Polkinghorne 1988; Strauss 1959). Hence, narratives provide individuals with the opportunity to construct personal identities that are consistent with their own self-concept (Snow and Anderson 1987).

Narrative is a particularly powerful tool for marginalized individuals, like the women in this study, who might otherwise lack the political, financial, or social capital needed to do other forms of identity work. In this article, I examine the narrative strategies [that] women returning to their communities as parolees utilize to contest and resist their connection to a stigmatized identity.

Specifically, I describe how they draw on conventional scripts and story lines to repair their identity and create a socially valued prosocial self. Next, I describe the context out of which these narratives develop by addressing the social meaning attached to the felon identity and summarizing the growing body of research that examines the material costs of this meaning for individuals previously incarcerated.

⊠ The Stigma of a Criminal Record

Researchers have established that individuals reintegrating into their communities after spending time in prison experience a host of difficulties (O'Brien 2001; Richie 2001; Travis 2005). After walking out of the prison gates, they struggle to meet their basic needs like finding housing and employment and reuniting with their families. They must restart their lives, often in similar or worse structural circumstances than

prior to their incarceration. Furthermore, they do so—as illustrated at the outset of this article—while contending with the stigma of a criminal record.

Criminal behavior is widespread among the general population, suggesting the line between *offenders* and *non-offenders* is blurry at best. Yet most social groups in the United States consider a criminal record deeply discrediting. As Maruna (2001) describes, culturally circulating narratives about criminal deviants assume an essential, and therefore inescapable, immorality. *Criminal* is not just a reflection of one's past misdeeds but is also a prediction of future behavior because "the idea that people can become essentially good seems to contradict a fundamental belief of contemporary society" (Maruna 2001, 5), individuals branded *criminal* by the state struggle to escape the label. As others have pointed out, this process creates two distinct categories of people: us (the non-offenders) and them (the offenders; Maruna 2001; Rockell 2009; Simon 2000).

Individuals unencumbered by the stigma of a criminal record draw from these circulating cultural stories to understand who former felons are. The women in this study were well aware that many viewed them as part of an underclass because of their time spent in prison. April explained that people who have never been in prison probably believe that "felons are trash." Similarly, Dee explained, "A lot of people don't want felons around. That's a mark against you." Ashley also explained that because she is a felon people see her as a "menace to society." To support this notion, she provided this example:

> [I was on the bus the other day with a friend,] we were coming home from church, and we were talking about prison and the fact that I'm a convicted felon and I'm on parole. She [my friend] said, "When are you gonna see your parole officer again?" This older couple was sitting behind us, and they got up and moved. And I was just like—I'm not a bad person!

The women in this study were generally well aware of the diminished status they held in relation to other non-offenders. However, Ashley's account illustrates how interaction is at the center of how she comes to understand her membership to a stigmatized group as well the meaning behind her membership to this group (Goffman 1963).

Former felons may "pass" (Goffman 1963) in their interactions with others under certain circumstances, for example, in their search for employment (Harding 2003). However, existing law and policy that marginalizes the rights of former felons in favor of "protecting" the law-abiding public comes with a host of emotional and material consequences for individuals with felony records. For the women in this study, like Liz, whose story was presented at the beginning, the material costs included being denied work and housing because of the meaning imbued [in and projected] onto them as a criminal.

Researchers are just beginning to understand the social, economic, and political costs of possessing the label *felon*. Arguably, the most compelling evidence of the "mark of a criminal record" post-release comes from Devah Pager's (2003) work, which illustrates that employers are significantly less likely to hire ex-offenders than their non-offending counterparts. Other research demonstrates the effects of stigma on the previously incarcerated when they perceive that neighbors or other community members view them as flawed. As they become aware of their diminished status in relation to others, some begin to isolate themselves (Rose and Clear 2003) while others report increased psychological stress (Braman 2004; Dodge and Pogrebin 2001) in addition to other health problems (Schnittker and John 2007). Further, women who are felons—like those in the current study—may have a unique experience with stigma because they can be understood as "doubly deviant" (Lloyd 1995, Owen 1998). Hence, community members, employers, and landlords may view them as individuals who have violated gender expectations as well as the criminal law.

The stigma of a criminal record is so diffusive that it has reciprocal effects on the children, partners, and communities where ex-offenders disproportionately reside (Braman 2004; Myers, Smarsh, Amlund-Hagen, and Kennon 1999). Braman's (2004, 174) ethnographic research illustrates this former phenomenon well; the partners of those who were incarcerated "recounted many specific instances in which they felt that they were looked down on by another person because of their family member's incarceration."

This emerging body of research provides important evidence of the consequences that arise from the stigma associated with an offender identity. However, this stigma does not just flow from our cultural stories about the essential immorality of those involved in the criminal

processing system and the resulting interaction between *non*-offenders and offenders; instead, U.S. policy and law institutionalizes a form of second-class citizenry of former prisoners. The government revokes many basic citizenship rights and privileges from individuals who have spent time in prison. Travis (2005, 63) calls this phenomenon "invisible punishments" and explains [that] many convicted felons are deemed ineligible for education loans, public assistance, driving privileges, and public housing. Travis also points out that some felons will have to register with the police for the rest of their lives, be deported, or have their parental rights terminated. This final component is particularly important for incarcerated women given that they are significantly more likely to have custody of their children prior to their incarceration (Mumola 2000). Finally, many felons are not allowed to vote, serve on juries, or be elected to public office. These latter civil penalties truly deny felons access to full citizenship (Uggen, Manza, and Thompson 2006) and reproduce the premise of cultural stories that separate *us* from *them*.

The Parolee Identity

People and social policy, then, stigmatize felons. The participants in this study acknowledged being casted as *other* and experiencing tangible consequences as a result. These women, however, were also forced to contend with an additional stigmatized identity connected to their past misdeeds—that is, the identity of parolee. Some states release individuals from prison unconditionally; however, many individuals leave prison and reenter their communities under the continued supervision of the state. To date, little research has focused on the experiences of parolees; this lack of research is problematic given that returning to the community as parolees significantly alters the reentry process (Petersilia 2003; Travis 2005). On top of meeting their basic needs, these individuals are also required to meet a variety of technical conditions deemed necessary by the state parole board. Typical conditions include submitting to regular drug or alcohol testing, meeting regularly with their parole officer, attending mandated counseling sessions, holding down employment, not associating with other individuals with felony records, and abstaining from committing new crimes. Utilizing methods of surveillance, the parole officer is responsible for making sure the parolee consistently meets these conditions; if the parolee fails to meet a condition, the parole officer is able to use his or her discretion to revoke the individual's parole with the ultimate consequence of being returned to prison (Steen and Opsal 2007).

Although historically the institution of parole was centered on the goals of rehabilitation and reintegration, more recent research indicates that parole has supplanted these former goals with ones centered on surveillance and monitoring an increasingly larger population of parolees (Opsal 2009; Simon 1993). In practice, parole officers are relying more heavily on new surveillance technologies, like electronic monitoring and, especially, drug testing, to monitor their caseload (Petersilia 2003). These new technologies allow parole officers to identify technical violations more efficiently and, as a result, enable parole officers to file for the revocation of an individual's parole more quickly. For individuals on parole, this shift necessarily means their actions have become increasingly subjected to surveillance and that their freedom is more vulnerable.

In this study, I found that because parole is centered on surveillance, *being* a parolee, although inextricably connected to the stigmatized felon identity, has unique consequences for individuals. Most poignantly, the criminal processing system deems parolees to be potentially risky subjects who must be carefully observed lest they reoffend. Hence, this identity exists solely to be regulated and surveyed by the state's gaze. Participants in this study were persistently aware that they lived under a system of surveillance that bounded their behavior. Zaria explained:

> These people have control over my life right now. They know that. Little do they know—no they know it, and I know it, that they have complete control over my life right now, they do. I can't go anywhere, I can't talk to anybody, I can't do nothin.' I have to do everything they tell me to do.

Their connection to the institution of parole not only reminded the women that they held a stigmatized identity but also that they were a part of the criminal processing system, not actually free. Any potential misstep could be the one that sent them back to prison.

Method

Data Collection and Analysis

The analysis I present in this article derives from data gathered through a series of interviews with forty-three women who were newly released from prison onto parole in the Denver-metro area. I conducted up to three semi-structured interviews over a period of one year with each woman and focused on understanding the challenges they faced as they [were] released from prison and returned to their communities as parolees. The interviews lasted, on average, ninety minutes and took place in public locations of the participant's choosing or in their homes. I digitally recorded each interview and then transcribed them verbatim.

Initially I recruited participants by working directly with prison officials from a local women's prison. Officials welcomed me into the prison each week and spoke directly with women who were about to [be] released to the Denver-metro area about the study. As the study was underway, I used additional recruitment methods including advertising at community organizations that offered resources to the recently released and snowball sampling that occurred both on the inside and outside.

I interviewed each participant up to three times over a period of one year. The first interview occurred as soon as possible after their release from prison.[1] In the initial interview, we focused on topics that included the women's perceptions regarding level of preparedness in leaving prison, moment-of-release, sources of support, challenges, and finally, experiences being a part of the parole system. Although participation in illegal activity was not a focus of this study, I did obtain a federal Certificate of Confidentiality in order to provide the participants, and myself, with an extra layer of protection.

I attempted to conduct the second interview as close as possible to three months after the initial interview. The manifest purpose of this interview was to track change among the participants in the study; hence, I repeated questions asked at the first interview. Retaining contact with newly released prisoners proved to be a formidable task. Women struggled to secure stable housing, so their contact information often changed once or several times relatively quickly after our first interview. Therefore, although I attempted to maintain regular contact with the women between interviews, I often had to rely on alternative contacts to track each woman down. Additionally, several participants quickly violated the conditions of their parole agreement and were sent back to jail and could not be contacted for an interview.[2] Even after these obstacles to follow-up, I conducted second interviews with thirty women.[3]

The final interview occurred one year after the initial contact or one year after they had been released on parole. This last interview occurred with a much smaller subset ($n = 9$) of the original sample. I utilized them primarily to develop and fine-tune themes that emerged as central during data analysis. Hence, I only asked participants to continue their participation if concepts they brought to light in earlier interviews became central themes, they remained in the community and were not in prison or jail at the time of data collection, and finally, they expressed interest in continuing their participation in the study. Some feminist researchers view collaboration during the research process as one way to break down the hierarchy that exists between researcher and participant (Acker, Barry, and Esseveld 1991; Cancian 1992; Stack 1996). This third interview was as close to collaboration as I felt I could get in this research design as it gave me the opportunity to tell women what I saw as central in the data and gave them the opportunity to provide me with feedback.

Although the manifest function of using multiple interviews was to track change over time, in the end the follow-up interviews served more important latent functions. Specifically, as Reinharz (1992, 37) explains, conducting multiple interviews strengthens the data because they are "likely to be more accurate than single interviews because of the opportunity to ask additional questions and to get corrective feedback on previously obtained information." Additionally, initial interviews allowed me to establish rapport with participants; at follow-up interviews, they were clearly more willing to share personal stories and emotions with me. Therefore, although subsequent interviews allowed me to collect critical information on basic changes in participants' lives, they also provided me with thicker and richer data than I was able to collect at the first interview.

As I mentioned previously, study attrition was a factor. This raises the question of possible differences between those women who remained in the study and those who did not. Two major reasons were potentially important

theoretically. First, criminal justice officials returned some women to prison, making subsequent contact with them impossible. Second, I was unable to recontact several women because their contact information changed rapidly between first and subsequent interviews. Neither of these reasons, I argue, provides evidence of differences between those women who remained in the study and those who did not. Although women who returned to prison may have been more likely to reoffend or violate the conditions of their parole agreement, they may also have had parole officers who were more likely to rely on revocation. Indeed, a number of women who remained in the study were violating the conditions of their parole agreement, but their parole officers did not return them to prison. Second, the women I was unable to recontact tended to be women who did not have family in the area of their release and were unable to secure stable housing. Again, however, a number of women who were without familial resources or stable housing also remained in the study. Hence, although there may be differences between the women who remained in the study and those who did not, I argue these are not systematic differences that skew the analysis.

Respondent Characteristics

Reading Table 21.1 summarizes some of the demographic characteristics of the women in this sample and, when possible, compares these characteristics to the population of female offenders released onto parole during the study recruitment period. As evidenced in this table, the sample was racially and ethnically diverse. However, in comparing the racial composition of the sample to the racial makeup of *all* women released onto parole in Colorado during the study recruitment period, blacks are overrepresented in the sample. A racial composition similar to this should be anticipated because the sample for the current study was limited to the Denver metropolitan area, and offenders who are black are more likely to [be] released to this area than members of other racial or ethnic categories (Rosten 2007). The age of the participants ranged from twenty-three to fifty-four years with a mean and median of thirty-seven years of age.

Consistent with other research on female offenders, a significant number of the participants were in prison because of drug-related offenses; even those women who officially went to prison for offenses unrelated to drugs

Reading Table 21.1   Demographic Characteristics of the Sample

Characteristics	Participants (n = 43)	All women released to parole in Colorado during sample recruitment (N = 832)
Department of Corrections data		
Age (years)	37	36
Race (percent)		
White	44	54
Black	35	17
Hispanic	16	25
Native American	2.3	3
Asian	2.3	0.4
Most common serious offense	Drug (34.9)	Drug (36.5)
Convicted of on most recent	Theft (14)	Theft (16.7)
Incarceration (percent)	Forgery (9.3)	Attempted escape (6)
Total months in prison	22	—
First incarceration (percent)	81	—
Self-report data		
Percent with children	72	
Percent with children younger than 18	68	
Percent released to		
Family member's home	33	
Reentry facility	33	
Homeless	26	
Other	8	

often reported that the offense occurred because of their drug use. Almost all of the women (n = 39) reported a drug or alcohol dependency history. The role of drug use was important because of the increasing use of drug testing as a form of parole supervision. Drug testing has become a nearly universal parole condition that allows officers virtually round-the-clock supervision of parolees (Simon 1993).[4] Parole officers required each woman in this sample to take regular random drug tests, including women who were not incarcerated for a drug offense.

Of the women, thirty-one reported they were mothers, while twenty-one reported being mothers of children younger than the age of eighteen. Minor children experienced a variety of custody arrangements upon the imprisonment of their mothers. Some children were permanently taken away from their mothers and placed with the state's foster care system. Often, the women asked extended family to temporarily care for their children. Additionally, occasionally the biological fathers of the children—although never in relationships with the mothers—were the primary caretakers of the children. Upon release from prison, no woman had immediate custody of [her] children.

✉ Becoming "Us": Recrafting Personal Identity by Resisting Stigma

Goffman (1963) noted that individuals with stigmatized identities use information management strategies to pass, or "cover." The women in this study reported responding in both of these ways, particularly in their search for employment. Although these kinds of strategies enabled the women to mitigate or at least manage potential harm that might have come to them by virtue of the stigma attached to their identity, the work they did through their narratives went beyond deciding to whom and how to explain their connection with the criminal processing system. The stories they told about inhabiting an identity that was stigmatized centered on separating the suspect meanings attached to being a felon from how they viewed their own selves. In other words, through their narratives, the women worked to detach the meanings associated with being a felon—*untrustworthy, trash, dysfunctional, a menace, negative*—from their self-conception.

The women I interviewed actively resisted the stigma associated with being incarcerated by refusing to internalize its meaning; Riessman (2000), in her research on childless women in India, calls this type of resistance strategy "resistant thinking." The major way these women resisted this label was by complicating the premise that the stigma of a criminal record relies on: that bad people who do bad things end up in prison. Elana illustrates this point. She explained, prior to her experience with prison, that she used to think, "People who were incarcerated, they must be horrible people." However, now,

My mind has changed. . . . I'm actually glad I had the experience [of going to prison] because now I'm not so prejudiced against people like that. I'm glad I had that. It brought me down a little bit. There is nobody better than anybody in this world, and that taught me there isn't.

Other women, similarly, point out that the situations that end with somebody in prison are not, as Ronda states, "black and white." Drawing from her own experiences with being incarcerated, she explained:

They [society] don't see that a person who's doing good, something can happen and their life can change. It happens. *It can happen to anybody* [italics added]. They can go through a really hard time in their life and decide to do something really stupid, and that one step and now you're in front of a judge and you're gonna get in trouble for it.

Likewise, Nicole stated:

Things happen very quick. Sometimes you can't control what happens and end up getting blamed for it. *It could happen to anybody* [italics added]. You could get in a car wreck and they could say it's your fault, and next thing you know, you're doin' time.

Here, Ronda and Nicole (and several other women) use virtually the same language as they describe how they got caught up in the criminal justice system: being incarcerated can "happen to anybody." Many times, as women shared their stories of becoming incarcerated, they described how in the process of living their lives, suddenly, and before they knew what had happened, they were behind bars. Through this kind of story, the women are able to reinterpret what it means to have a criminal record. Specifically, as these stories indicate, good people (i.e., not criminals) often end up in prison after experiencing something that could happen to anybody at anytime. These stories allowed women to alleviate part of the social distance that existed between them and those who did not have to deal with the stigma of a criminal record.

Another type of resistant thinking some women employed paralleled the strategy just explained but uses different reasoning. Specifically, some women resisted stigma by refusing to acknowledge that there were any significant differences between themselves and individuals who had never been a part of the criminal justice system. Vie described this when she stated that it does not "bother" her when people know that she has a criminal record. To explain this, she stated, "I look at it like this: if you don't have a record, I guarantee you're doin' somethin' you ain't got no business doin' and you haven't got caught for it. So you just be a little smarter than others." Similarly, Tamara stated:

> Most people have done a lot of dirt, they just didn't get caught, you know? You just got away with it. You can thank God that you did that. But when the shoe is on the other foot, they can look down at the other person, and they do. . . . Some of them are very judgmental, and if not for the mercy of God they could have been sitting where I'm sitting. Some people don't remember that.

Here Tamara and Vie reject the stigma associated with the felon label by reinterpreting the connection between criminality and being incarcerated. In their stories, they render the label of felon meaningless by arguing that most people participate in the actions that felons are incarcerated for. Further, Tamara refused not only to view herself as stigmatized because of her criminal history, but she also imposed her "own version of stigma on the dominant society" by calling out those who perpetuate the stigma while participating in the same kinds of activities she did (Kusow 2004, 79). In some ways, this latter resistance strategy parallels the technique of neutralization that Sykes and Matza (1957) described as "condemnation of the condemners." This neutralization technique, like the others Sykes and Matza identified, allows individuals to rationalize their own criminal behavior so that they can align themselves with conventional society and moderate potential damage to their self-image. In light of the current study, this particular technique also serves a different kind of function; that is, it enables women to craft self-stories that resist the stigma associated with being a felon rather than simply abdicating responsibility for their actions.

By resisting the stigma associated with a criminal record, the women in this study simultaneously refashion their identity in a way that aligns them with conventional society and actors. As they challenge the cultural meanings attached to this stigmatized identity, they claim common ground with those individuals unmarked by a felony record. Through this particular identity work, then, they are able to craft themselves as an *us* rather than a *them* or *other*.

Building a Post–Drug-Using Self[5]

Parolees are legally mandated to inhabit a stigmatized social identity that exists solely to make sure they do not pose continued risk to the larger community of "non"-criminals. The criminal processing system understands parolee's potential future behavior in the context of their past criminal behavior, and because of this, deems it necessary to monitor their present behavior. The women in this study reported clearly understanding that the purpose of parole was to watch over them—as opposed to assist them in reintegrating into their communities—explaining that parole existed in order to "catch people," "keep up with what ya doin'," or "keep an eye on them." Indeed, the institution of parole subjected the women in this study, and individuals on parole more generally, to explicit daily regulation and surveillance. This regulation and surveillance by the state caused most of the women in this study to be ever aware of their connection and obligations to this identity.

Parole required the women to adhere to a variety of technical conditions; however, the primary way this institution monitored their behavior was via random drug testing.[6] Theoretically, this mode of surveillance is effective for monitoring the *risky* behavior of this group of women because, as established earlier, most of the women were in prison on charges related directly, or indirectly, to their illegal drug use. Yet many women employed a narrative that positioned themselves in direct opposition to this drug-using self (McIntosh and McKeganey 2000). All of the women who had previously used drugs or alcohol explained that after their time away from the streets, drugs, and old acquaintances, they realized that they deeply desired to change their relationship with illegal drugs by "being done with all that illegal stuff." Not only did they state their desire to change, but they also posited themselves as individuals who were already changed and fundamentally different from their past selves. By identifying not just as clean but as different, the women were able to frame their present selves as individuals who no longer made the kinds of choices they did when they were in their addictions. Nisha's story illustrates this process well.

Nisha had a criminal justice record related to her off and on drug use that began for her as a teenager. She spent over two years in prison, was released, and was quickly revoked because she started "meeting the wrong people, getting in with the dope dealers." Nisha, however, looks at her second stint in prison that resulted from this revocation as the time where she changed herself. She explained, "Going back the second time, I decided I wanted to do this sober. I wanted a better life. I wanted to be free from misery." And because of that, she believed:

I'm a new person coming out. . . . I have no desire to go back to Benford where I used to live at, or go looking for these certain people [who I used drugs with]. I could have called everybody that I remember their number, and I just chose not to.

She described this process of leaving behind her drug use and the life that came with it for her as a "rebirth into a new life." This rebirth for Nisha meant that she would no longer be the person she was formerly. As she remarked,

I know I'm better than being beat up. I know I'm better than drinking and doing drugs, and being out there and prostituting off of Jackson Street. I'm better than that. I'm not that person any more.

Nisha used this new and improved refashioned self centered on difference and change to support her belief that she would be able to complete parole successfully this time. To be able to finish parole without going back, she explained, you *really* have to be a different person:

If you want change, you'll do change. But if you don't want change, you can't change. You can only temporarily change. Before, I thought I wanted change, and then I chose to go back on the path I used to lead, because it was easier for me, but I knew, and I chose not to change, so therefore my parole officer sent me back. So I got another chance, and I'm gonna do it this time, because I want change. I want to go home and

be with my kids, I want to live a drug-free life. I want to be able to be an abiding citizen and do what I need to do and not always be in trouble and be bad-ass. That's not me.

In this final passage, Nisha clearly separates her "new" self from her old drug-using and criminal self. Giordano, Cernkovich, and Rudolph (2002) call this process Nisha described as configuring a "replacement self." These authors explain that as individuals work to transition out of deviant behavior, they construct a replacement self who is fundamentally incompatible with their old self who participated in criminal behavior. This is what Nisha does as she identifies her old patterns of behavior [and] supplants them with her new self while explaining, "I'm not that person anymore."

As the women construct these replacement selves they also demonize their past drug-using behavior by identifying why these former selves needed to be replaced (Denzin 1987). They explained [that] while they used drugs or alcohol, they, for example, sacrificed relationships with family, experienced violence, or were consumed with getting their next hit. Most of the women who talked about their drug or alcohol addictions told extremely painful stories about how they believed these behaviors were detrimental to their lives in some way. For example, Tamara explained that being on drugs and out on the streets using was "dangerous." She stated:

It's dangerous, yes, it is, and glory be to God that I made it through, because some people don't. Man, when I think about how many chances I took with my life and didn't care, didn't care, really, really didn't care. That's pretty much how at the bottom I was. It was kind of like I didn't care whether I lived or died today, pretty much.

In the last section, I illustrated how by resisting the stigma associated with a criminal record, the women were able to refashion their identity in a positive light by connecting to conventionality; I describe a similar process in this section. By distancing themselves from their drug-using behavior and their past drug-addicted selves, the women decenter the necessity of being labeled a parolee because it was their past drug-addicted selves who acquired that label. In other words, it was their former selves who the criminal justice system deemed necessary to be monitored; thus, it is only these former selves that justify the requisition of the parolee identity. Not only does this particular narrative function to problematize this (en)forced identity, but by fashioning themselves as changed, they also connect to a valued social identity: one that is drug free and no longer participates in criminal behavior. Hence, this narrative assisted them in subverting the need for others to identify them as parolees and also enabled them to present and see themselves in a different light, and quite literally, as different people.

Negotiating "Slip-Ups"

Time played an important variable in the women's identity work just described because occasionally some who identified strongly with this narrative at an initial interview "slipped up" and in subsequent interviews reported using drugs or alcohol. These actions were almost always characterized as big mistakes and weighed quite heavily on the minds of the women, who expressed a great deal of guilt and remorse. After being drug free for several months, LouLou attended a family party where there was coke. She stated, "I don't know what got into me or what, but I did it. I just tasted it." About this lapse in her post-drug self, LouLou explained:

> I really felt little, like, I just—I—[long pause] don't know. Like, I just let everybody down, that's how I felt. Like stupid, you know? And I know it was stupid, but you know, I just, I'm trying to live with it.

When they relapsed, many women expressed significant concern that their parole officer would find out and they would be returned to prison for violating a parole condition. However, the few women that used and remained on the outside typically emphasized how by using, they sacrificed relationships with other people who were important to them. LouLou, for example, had restarted a relationship with her teenaged daughter before using and was scared she and her other children would find out about her lapse: "I just don't want to lose my kids, and I'm scared of that." In the next section, I will discuss how children served as a source of motivation for staying clean on the outside for many of these women who were also mothers.

Clearly, physically embodying a drug-free and changed identity is different from narrating that identity—especially for this group of women. Many of them had long, serious, and often untreated drug addictions; at the same time, many [were] released to the same social and structural conditions they experienced prior to incarceration. This typically meant they also [were] released to the same conditions that were present in their lives when they used drugs or alcohol. Hence, some women had to account for slip-ups after presenting themselves as drug free and changed. As they negotiated these lapses in their post-drug selves, they almost always continued to identify with their original claims regarding being different people who would still be drug free. As Zaria explained about her lapse:

> That was the first I ever, ever used and came home, ever in my whole entire life. Back in the day, I'd use and use and use and use and days and days . . . and I didn't do that. So I know that it really wasn't what I wanted to do. It wasn't because I knew I had to be home. I just went home. And that's somethin' I would have never done back then.

Reclaiming Motherhood: Connecting to a Culturally Coveted Social Identity

Because motherhood is a readily available and widely accepted identity, being a mom allows many women access to a culturally valued identity. For marginalized women—like those in the current study—becoming a mother may provide a conduit to a meaningful and positive identity in a social context where they have "little access to the academic degrees, high-status marriages, and rewarding professions that provide many middle and upper-class women with gratifying social identities" (Edin and Kefalas 2005, 171). Hence, the final way that the women in this study narratively repaired their damaged identity was by identifying strongly as mothers.

To identify as mothers, however, the women in this study had to engage a strong cultural narrative that challenges their connection to this identity because it is a particular kind of motherhood that is most valued in U.S.

culture. Current standards indicate that mothers must be wholly committed to rearing their children and dedicated to meeting [their] child's needs always at the sacrifice of their own (Hays 1996). This hegemonic version of motherhood is based on an idealized version of white, middle/upper-class mothering practices (Glen 1994). Most "real-life" mothering practices do not coincide with this model of mothering. However, with certainty, the women in this study and many of the experiences they have shared with their children fall outside of these constructed boundaries. For example, the state often rescinded the mothers' custody of their children because of drug addictions, family members or foster parents cared for their children because they were in prison, or they never really had a role in their children's lives because of their addiction histories or getting caught up in the system. Indeed, the media and the public have demonized the mothering practices of many of these women because of their incarceration history and (especially) because of their illegal drug use (Humphries 1999).

Some of the women expressed feeling remorse over the way they believed their drug history had negatively impacted their children or explained that they felt regret being behind bars while their children were on the outside (Brown and Bloom 2009). They were aware, for example, that their actions before becoming incarcerated had exposed their children to the "wrong kinds" of people and left some children temporarily homeless. Some mothers also spoke of feeling guilty for having to leave their children behind when they spent time in jail or prison knowing that few custody arrangements provided their children healthy environments where they received the kinds of caretaking they needed. These aspects of their narratives reveal many of the mothers were aware of how their mothering practices compared to our cultural stories of what qualifies as good mothering. However, although many of the mothers spoke briefly about their mothering practices they identified as harmful and how this resulted in feelings of guilt and remorse, when I attempted to probe these stories further, the path of their narratives, without exception, changed. Specifically, women entirely resisted continuing to talk about stories that might qualify them as bad mothers and challenge their connection to this identity. Instead, they either discontinued their narrative about their identity as a mother or, more commonly, they reconstructed these experiences so they could be understood as

"acceptable mothering practices" (Baker and Carson 1999, 361). By engaging this kind of narrative, they were able to legitimate their connection to the motherhood identity.

The following remarks from Dee, who used illegal substances off and on while she raised two children into adulthood, illustrate this process. She explained, "I took care of my kids all the time. I was a good mother." She pointed to the fact that her daughter was now a registered nurse and her son was a "good father" as evidence of her own quality parenting practices. More so, she expressed that she taught them "you gotta get into this world, you gotta take care, you gotta grow up and do your own thing. You've gotta be responsible for yourself, regardless of me because I'm your mother." Later, she stated that although as her children grew up and "didn't like" that she was using drugs, she explained, "they learned some things about bein' strong because of it. I told them, 'I gotta do me. I love you guys, but you guys gotta do you too.' They grew up that way. So I pushed them to do good."

In another case, Ashley, a mother who had to leave her son with extended family in another state after being extradited back to Colorado for a warrant, explained that she realized when she went back for a weeklong visit that the time apart was a valuable experience for him. She explained:

> In a funny way, this is kind of a good thing for me and Deon, or at least this is how I was trying to look at it. Of course, with me losing my daughter [to the state], I latched onto my son immediately. He wasn't allowed to go out of my sight. He was attached to my hip because I kept him there, for fear of losing him. . . . So with me coming out here [to serve time in prison and on parole] and being gone as long as I have, and I learned this when I went back to Boston, he's so much more independent. . . . And it took me a while to be like, "He is OK." When he falls down, he comes and tells Mommy. It's taught me to let go a little bit and let him grow up, let him fall, let him be a boy and know that he's gonna be OK.

In short, these moms' narratives point to how their children developed strength, autonomy, and responsibility as a result of their mothering practices—clearly valued traits in their eyes. Reconstructing the boundaries of good mothering allowed these women a more valid connection to the socially coveted role of mother because it gave them an opportunity to recast their past and present mother self on their own terms (see also Baker and Carson 1999). And, through this lens, the women presented their mothering practices as acceptable and their children as benefiting from their experiences. Whether or not the women were, in some objective sense, good mothers or whether or not reestablishing relationships with their children would be the best thing for their kids is beyond the scope of this current inquiry (Moe and Ferraro 2006). What is of interest, however, is that the women in this study strategically avoided constructing a narrative that focused on how their childrearing broke with ideal mothering; instead, by narrating a different story, many women connected with the mother identity and, in turn, presented and defined themselves as someone other than criminal, felon, or parolee.

Motherhood as a Source of Motivation

Although the women explained that their mothering practices benefited their children, they also explained how being mothers benefited them. The women in this study often reported that the prospect of reuniting with children and having a presence in their lives served as a motivating factor to do well on parole or stay away from drugs. Nisha, a mother of two children, illustrates this when she explains:

> I know that the sooner I get this [parole] done with the sooner I can go home to my kids, and that's my main and most important focus right now, getting my life straight so I can go be a mother to my kids.

Additionally, Freesia found out she was pregnant several months after she [was] released from prison and saw the future possibility of being a mother as a reason to stay off of the streets. She explained that being pregnant "makes me want to be more responsible." Further, she stated that she was done with drugs and drinking because she was not going to "jeopardize this little kid." In describing this, Freesia was not talking about the possible physical impacts of these substances on the fetus. Instead, she explained that to be a mother, she was not willing to give birth or raise a child from behind bars and that by drinking or doing drugs she was risking having her parole revoked. Therefore, she stated, to get by she was going to focus on "bein' a parent."

A body of research suggests that strong connections to children have important implications for women involved in the criminal justice system who are also mothers. Consistent with findings presented here, this body of research indicates that childbirth provides a strong incentive for women to desist from crime or the use of illegal drugs (Edin and Kefalas 2005; Enos 2001). Scholars also explain that motherhood provides women with an opportunity to develop a prosocial shift in their self-concept (Giordano, Cernkovich, and Rudolph 2002) and that it is a primary turning point for women to exit delinquency and drug use (Kreager, Matsueda, and Erosheva 2010).

Challenges to This Identity Work

Although this body of research indicates that it may benefit formerly incarcerated women to connect with their children, regaining custody post-prison can be an arduous process. For example, many individuals returning to their communities from prison struggle to meet their own basic needs; bringing a child into this financially volatile equation is simply not an option for many caregivers. Indeed, although many women in the current study narratively worked to connect with their mother identity, and deeply desired to *be* mothers on the outside and directly reconnect with their children in a permanent way, this was a reality no woman realized during the study period.

A few women had full custody of their children prior to going to prison and, when sentenced, handed custody over to various family members. Hence, upon release, they knew where their children were, they could have some form of contact with them, and they knew that regaining custody of their children was largely a matter of negotiating this process with their parole officer. Negotiating this process, however, was not easy or straightforward. Ronda's children, for example, were in the custody of her parents who lived several states away. Ronda had hoped that she would be paroled to California, where her parents resided; doing this, she explained, would make the custody transition smoother and would also provide her with built-in emotional and financial support. She noted, however, that upon release, her parole officer was not interested in transferring her parole to California, "She's like, 'No, you have to get established here, you're not going back to California.'"

Similarly, Linda took custody of her son after her mother decided she could not watch him any longer because he was acting aggressively toward her. Linda explained that when her parole officer found out, he said, "You can either send your son back to your mom, he can go into a foster home, or you're goin' back to prison."

Unlike Ronda and Linda, most women in this study did not have custody of their children prior to incarceration. Often, custody had been rescinded by the state due to drug addiction, time spent in prison, or at some point the state had determined them to be negligent parents. As these women worked to understand what their relationship could look like with their children, they worked through greater levels of ambiguity surrounding their relationship with their children. Indeed, although some of these women looked forward to the day when they would connect with their children, most simply hoped they would be able to see, speak with, or live with their children again.

Lola, a mother of three, strongly identified as a mother despite not having had contact with her two youngest children for over four years or with her thirteen-year-old daughter for even longer. Despite this passing of time, and not knowing where her second ex-husband and two youngest children lived, she emphatically explained at our first interview together, "I want to start a relationship with my kids as soon as possible. I've wasted too much time." Lola said that her first husband took her oldest daughter away from her "because I was drinking pretty heavily" and [that] she lost her two youngest kids to social services. Expanding on this, she explained that after she and her second husband started using crack, she was incarcerated in jail for drug-related charges at the same time she was supposed to be in court for her custody hearing. Because of this, she lost custody of her children. After spending over two years in prison, she was trying to figure out how to negotiate the court system and paperwork in order to restore her custody rights. About this process, she stated,

> I don't know, it's confusing, and it's hard. It's complicated and it hurts. But I'm not gonna let that alter what I'm doing. . . . It's like everyone is offering you help as far as the [criminal justice] system, but they don't take it further than that for a mother, a mom.

Here, Lola acknowledges that individuals and groups offered her assistance based on her identity as a parolee. However, she noted that she is also a mother and that the available help out there did not extend to this role with which she identified. Similar to the historical critique of prison programming, this story points to the idea that the resources available to parolees are likely based on a male model and do not consider the role of gender. Because men who spend time in prison do not typically have custody of their children, the institution of parole has traditionally not focused on meeting the needs of parolees who are also parents. This is likely why Lola does not feel recognized or supported in her role as mother.

Several mothers, like Lola, encountered obstacles that—between first and subsequent interviews—prevented them from establishing any kind of relationship or even contact with their children. At our second interview, Lola explained that she had had no contact with any of her children nor had she made any progress toward understanding how to regain custody of them. It was clear at this subsequent interview that because Lola was unable to integrate more fully into this identity, she was less interested in talking about her children, less optimistic about her future as a mother, and less committed to framing herself with this identity. For Lola, and other mothers who were unable to physically realize any part of their mother narrative, as time passed on the outside, there was a decreased commitment to this identity. All mothers in this study experienced financial, legal, emotional, or parole-initiated obstacles in connecting with their children. However, many of the women who continued to rely strongly on their mother identity, despite experiencing these obstacles, had some sort of regular contact with their children or were supported in their narrative work by other family members. For example, although both Ashley and Ronda remained separated from their children by thousands of miles, they talked on the phone regularly. Further, their relationships with their children were supported by the extended family who retained custody of their kids while they were incarcerated. Hence, women who—over time—remained unsupported or unacknowledged as mothers were significantly less likely to remain committed to the identity.

I was unable to systematically gather data on all of the women in the original sample longitudinally because of sample attrition. In turn, I cannot speak with certainty about the consequences of a decreased commitment to using motherhood to do identity work. However, the women who continued to strongly identify as mothers on the outside were significantly more likely to remain optimistic about their desisting selves as well as their reentry process more generally. Women who became less likely to narrate themselves as mothers were not only less optimistic about reconnecting with their children, but they were also more likely to develop a sense of generalized hopelessness about being on the outside. In fact, several of these women—including Lola—became reengaged with illegal activity, in particular, use of illegal drugs.

As illustrated throughout this section, many women strongly connected to their mother identity via narrative. The central focus of this narrative work navigated cultural stories that brand them as inadequate mothers. However, by reconstructing the characteristics of what qualifies as good mothering, they were able to preserve their connection to this social identity. This process allowed them not only to negotiate the stigma attached to them as mothers, but—similar to the other narrative strategies described in this article—[it] also connected them to a normative culturally valued identity that assisted them in repairing their damaged identity. But time served as an important intersecting variable in women's use of this narrative. Although some women found that motherhood continued to exist alongside a hopeful perspective about their present and future circumstances, those who were unsupported in their identity work found that the promise of this narrative strategy waned over time.

Conclusions

U.S. cultural stories as well as policy and law stigmatize felons (Braman 2004; Manza and Uggen 2006; Pager 2003; Uggen, Manza, and Thompson 2006). These avenues perpetuate the idea that felons are untrustworthy, morally reprehensible, and inherently different from the rest of us who retain our moral worth simply by not being one of them. At the beginning of this article, I introduced the reader to Liz who lost her job strictly because she was understood by her employer solely through this lens that positions her identity as a maligned social object. As her story shows, serious emotional and material consequences result when individuals with felony records interact with those who are not implicated by the criminal processing system (Pager 2003; Tewksbury 2005; Western 2002). For

Liz, the consequence was the loss of her job. Despite understanding that others viewed them as a part of a stigmatized group, however, the women in this study did not understand or present themselves in the same way.

In this article, I focused on the narrative strategies a group of formerly incarcerated women used as they returned to their communities as parolees living under the continued supervision and surveillance of the state. This verbal identity work provided them with an opportunity to challenge the public identity imposed on them and enabled them to recast their past, present, and future selves. In this, I illustrated that the women relied on prosocial cultural values, stories, and characters to refashion their identities. Specifically, they challenged the cultural meanings associated with the felon identity, disassociated from their past drug- and alcohol-using selves, and identified as mothers. Identity is not a meaning in and of itself; instead, it is a sign that "evokes meaning" (Schwalbe and Mason-Schrock 1996). Hence, by infusing conventionality into their identity work, they simultaneously challenge the public's presumption of their inherent badness and position themselves as one of us. Although the women rely on hegemonic ideas of what kind of person is valued, these narrative formulas also provided them with the opportunity to regain a sense of control and agency over their personal identities (Sandstrom 1998).

For this group of women, negotiating their stigmatized identity did not just mean refashioning an identity in the present, but it also meant engaging with their past selves. For instance, as they created new post–drug-using selves by narrating stories of self-transformation (Giordano, Cernkovich, and Rudolph 2002; Maruna 2001), women drew on their past experiences as drug users as evidence of the need for their new selves. Additionally, some women reconstructed the boundaries of good mothering to redefine their past mother selves. These claims about their past selves provided them an opportunity to narrate a more credible connection to prosocial conventional story lines and characters in the present and future. This reinforces what is at the center of their claims, which is the refutation that there is an immutable difference between offenders and non-offenders.

Without these types of claims that redeem their past selves (Maruna 2001; Sandstrom 1998), the women are left with an inconsistent life narrative (Gubrium and Holstein 1998; McAdams 1993). Although this is not an article about desistance, redeeming one's past self has emerged as a topic of research among criminologists who examine why and how individuals participating in criminal behavior desist. For instance, Maruna (2001) explains that redeeming the past self is critical for individuals transitioning out of the "offender" identity because it allows individuals to reconstruct their pasts so they are not at odds with how they understand their current desisting selves. Maruna posits that an essential step in fashioning the "ex-offender" narrative is creating and sustaining a coherent prosocial identity. Maruna's conclusions developed out of interviews he conducted with a largely male sample, and he did not theorize the role of parenthood. However, the narratives presented in this article suggest that motherhood may be an important way women exercise agency over their past experiences to create a consistent life narrative and, using Maruna's logic, may also be a conventional identity that lends itself to create an opportunity for desistance, particularly for women (Edin and Kefalas 2005; Kreager, Matsueda, and Erosheva 2010).

Finally, as I posited at the outset of this article, rooted within the symbolic interaction tradition, stigma is a constructed reality that develops out of and finds meaning through interaction and social context. Because of this, the interview process itself is squarely implicated in the self-making claims of these women because it was at this site where they narratively contested and created identity Hence, it is compelling to think analytically about how this space, as a social context, mediated interaction and the production of prosocial identities. McCorkel's (1998) notion of "critical space" is useful for this endeavor. McCorkel examined how incarcerated women resist organizational identities in a *total* institution as a way to defend their "true" selves. In concert, these women constructed a critical space, which was a literal space unmediated by the surveillance of correctional officers where women rejected the institution's claims about their identities and developed and defended their own definitions of self. McCorkel suggests that even outside the confines of total institutions, people find ways to construct critical spaces where they can distance themselves from identities that contradict or threaten their own self-concepts.

Many social situations forced the women in the current study to confront their connection to the felon identity, and their interactions with others held them accountable to those meanings that come with it. Further,

as they reintegrated back into their communities, many of the participants remained hyperaware of their connection to the parolee identity; as objects of the state's gaze, they negotiated their social landscape wary that any misstep could be the one that would send them back behind prison walls (Opsal 2009). Hence, the participants strategically used the social context available to them, an interview in a space of their own choosing where they were explicitly asked to speak about themselves largely on their own terms, to do just that. They used the interview space and process to resist the social claims that cast them as other and constructed prosocial identities that were more consistent with how they understood themselves.

Ultimately, by describing how a group of formerly incarcerated women create and sustain identities in the face of a stigmatizing cultural narrative, this article contributes to the existing research on identity work. It continues and extends the growing tradition of symbolic interactionist scholars who push and widen Goffman's (1963) original conception of stigma because it examines how these women contest and resist stigma rather than framing it as something they manage. Further, by focusing on a group of formerly incarcerated women and by drawing solely on their own words about their experiences, [the basis for] this article provides important insight into the lives of women post-incarceration. In the end, this article demonstrates how, by weaving connections to conventional story lines and characters, this group of women use their own experiences to repudiate the cultural story that casts them as irredeemable offenders of our moral code.

Notes

1. The final sample included eighteen women who were interviewed within 14 days of release, thirteen women who were interviewed within 15 and 31 days of release, and thirteen women who were interviewed within 32 days and 365 days of release.

2. Although I attempted to gain permission to interview women in the custody of local jails, county correction officials denied my access.

3. Of the thirteen women who did not participate in a second interview, seven had already been revoked back to DOC; two had absconded and I was unable to reach them; and I was unable to contact four respondents either because they did not return repeated efforts to contact them or because I could not locate current contact information.

4. This shift in surveillance techniques becomes particularly important when considering the case of female offenders on parole given that incarcerated women are more likely than men to use illegal drugs (Greenfield and Snell 1999; Langan and Pelissier 2001; Peters, Strozier, Murrin, and Kearns 1997). Once on the outside, women may be more likely to turn to illegal drug use, fail mandatory drug tests, and be returned to prison because a drug test turns up positive.

5. The idea for this subtitle comes from Sandstrom (1998, 364).

6. Other common parole conditions the women in this study had to abide by included regular meetings with their parole officer, driving restrictions, no contact with other felons, attending group classes for a variety of issues ranging from drug addiction to anger management, and being employed.

References

Acker, Joan, Kate Barry, and Johanna Esseveld. 1991. Objectivity and truth: Problems in doing feminist research. In *Beyond methodology: Feminist scholarship as lived research,* ed. M. M. Fonow and J. A. Cook, 133–53. Bloomington, IN: Indiana University Press.

Baker, Phyllis L., and Amy Carson. 1999. I take care of my kids: Mothering practices of substance-abusing women. *Gender & Society* 13:347–63.

Braman, Donald. 2004. *Doing time on the outside: Incarceration and family life in urban America.* Ann Arbor: University of Michigan Press.

Brown, Marilyn, and Barbara Bloom. 2009. Reentry and renegotiating motherhood: Maternal identity and success on parole. *Crime and Delinquency* 55:313–36.

Cancian, Francesca M. 1992. Feminist science: Methodologies that challenge inequality. *Gender and Society* 6:623–42.

Denzin, Norman. 1987. *The recovering alcoholic.* Newbury Park, CA: Sage.

Dodge, Mary, and Mark R. Pogrebin. 2001. Collateral costs of imprisonment for women: Complications of reintegration. *The Prison Journal* 81:42–54.

Edin, Kathryn, and Maria Kefalas. 2005. *Promises I can keep: Why poor women put motherhood before marriage.* Berkeley: University of California Press.

Enos, Sandra. 2001. *Mothering from the inside: Parenting in a women's prison.* Albany: State University of New York Press.

Froyum, Carissa. 2007. "At least I'm not gay": Heterosexual identity making among poor black teens. *Journal of Contemporary Ethnography* 10:603–22.

Giordano, P., S. Cernkovich, and J. Rudolph. 2002. Gender, crime, and desistance: Toward a theory of cognitive transformation. *The American Journal of Sociology* 107:990–1064.

Goffman, Erving. 1963. *Stigma: Notes on the management of spoiled identity.* Englewood Cliffs, NJ: Prentice Hall.

Gubrium, James, and James Holstein. 1998. Narrative practice and coherence of personal stories. *The Sociological Quarterly* 39:163–87.

Harding, David J. 2003. Jean Valjean's dilemma: The management of ex-convict identity in the search for employment. *Deviant Behavior* 24:571–95.

Hays, Sharon. 1996. *The cultural contradictions of motherhood.* New Haven, CT: Yale University Press.

Humphries, Drew. 1999. *Crack mothers: Pregnancy, drugs, and the media.* Columbus: Ohio State University Press.

Irvine, Leslie. 1999. *Codependent forevermore.* Chicago: University of Chicago Press.

Kreager, Derek, Ross Matsueda, and Elena Erosheva. 2010. Motherhood and criminal desistance in disadvantaged neighborhoods. *Criminology* 48:221–57.

Kusow, Abdi. 2004. Contesting stigma: On Goffman's assumptions of normative order. *Symbolic Interaction* 27:179–97.

Langan, Neal, and Bernadette Pelissier. 2001. Gender differences among prisoners in drug treatment. *Journal of Substance Abuse* 13:291–301.

Leverentz, Andrea M. 2006. The love of a good man? Romantic relationships as a source of support or hindrance for female ex-offenders. *Journal of Research in Crime and Delinquency* 43:459–88.

Lloyd, Ann. 1995. *Doubly deviant, doubly damned: Society's treatment of violent women.* London: Penguin.

Manza, Jeff, and Christopher Uggen. 2006. *Locked out: Felon disenfranchisement and American democracy.* New York: Oxford University Press.

Maruna, Shadd. 2001. *Making good: How ex-convicts reform and rebuild their lives.* Washington, DC: American Psychological Association.

Marvasti, Amir. 2006. Being Middle Eastern American: Identity negotiation in the context of the war on terror. *Symbolic Interaction* 28:525–47.

McAdams, Dan. 1993. *The stories we live by: Personal myths and the making of the self.* New York: William Morrow.

McCorkel, Jill. 1998. Going to the crackhouse: Critical space as a form of resistance in total institutions and everyday life. *Symbolic Interaction* 21:227–52.

McIntosh, James, and Neil McKeganey. 2000. Addicts' narratives of recovery from drug use: Constructing a non-addict identity. *Social Science and Medicine* 50:1501–510.

Miall, Charlene E. 1986. The stigma of involuntary childlessness. *Social Problems* 33:268–82.

Moe, Angela M., and Kathleen J. Ferraro. 2006. Criminalized mothers: The value and devaluation of parenthood from behind bars. *Women and Therapy* 29:135–64.

Mumola, Christopher. 2000. *Incarcerated parents and their children.* Washington, DC: Bureau of Justice Statistics.

Myers, Barbara, Tina Smarsh, Kristine Amlund-Hagen, and Suzanne Kennon. 1999. Children of incarcerated mothers. *Journal of Child and Family Studies* 8:11–25.

O'Brien, P. 2001. *Making it in the "free world."* Albany: State University of New York Press.

Opsal, Tara. 2009. Women on parole: Understanding the impact of surveillance. *Women and Criminal Justice* 19:306–28.

Owen, Barbara. 1998. *"In the mix": Struggle and survival in a women's prison.* Albany: State University of New York Press.

Pager, Devah. 2003. The mark of a criminal record. *American Journal of Sociology* 108:937–75.

Peters, R., A. Strozier, M. Murrin, and W. Kearns. 1997. Treatment of substance abusing jail inmates: Examination of gender differences. *Journal of Substance Abuse Treatment* 14:339–49.

Petersilia, Joan. 2003. *When prisoners come home: Parole and prisoner reentry.* Oxford, UK: Oxford University Press.

Polkinghorne, Donald E. 1988. *Narrative knowing and the human sciences.* Albany: State University of New York Press.

Reinharz, Shulamit. 1992. *Feminist methods in social research.* Oxford, UK: Oxford University Press.

Richie, Beth. 2001. Challenges incarcerated women face as they return to their communities: Findings from life history interviews. *Crime and Delinquency* 47:368–89.

Riessman, Catherine Kohler. 2000. Stigma and everyday resistance practices: Child-less women in South India. *Gender & Society* 14:111–35.

Rockell, Barbara. 2009. Theoretical and cultural dimensions of the warehouse philosophy of punishment. *Journal of Criminal Justice and Popular Culture* 16:40–62.

Rose, Dina, and Todd Clear. 2003. *Incarceration, reentry, and social capital: Social networks in the balance.* Washington, DC: Urban Institute Press.

Rosenfeld, Dana. 1999. Identity work among lesbian and gay elderly. *Journal of Aging Studies* 13:121–44.

Rosten, Kristi. 2007. *Statistical reports, fiscal year 2007.* Denver, CO: office of Planning and Analysis, Colorado Department of Corrections.

Sandstrom, Kent. 1990. Confronting deadly disease: The drama of identity construction among gay men with AIDS. *Journal of Contemporary Ethnography* 19:271–94.

Sandstrom, Kent. 1998. Preserving a vital and valued self in the face of AIDS. *Sociological Inquiry* 68:354–71.

Schneider, Joseph, and Conrad, Peter. 1980. "In the closet with illness: Epilepsy, stigma potential and information control." *Social Problems* 28(1):32–44.

Schnittker, Jason, and Andrea John. 2007. Enduring stigma: The long-term effects of incarceration. *Journal of Health and Social Behavior* 48:115–30.

Schwalbe, Michael, and Douglas Mason-Schrock. 1996. Identity work as group process. *Advances in Group Processes* 13:113–47.

Shinnar, Rachel. 2008. Coping with negative social identity: The case of Mexican Immigrants. *The Journal of Social Psychology* 148:553–75.

Shriver, Thomas E., and Dennis D. Waskul. 2006. Managing the uncertainties of Gulf War illness: The challenges of living with contested illness. *Symbolic Interaction* 29:465–86.

Simon, Jonathan. 1993. *Poor discipline: Parole and the social control of the underclass, 1890–1990.* Chicago: University of Chicago Press.

Simon, Jonathan. 2000. Fear and loathing in late modernity: Reflections on the cultural sources of mass imprisonment in the United States. In *Mass imprisonment: Social causes and consequences,* ed. D. Garland. London: Sage.

Snow, David, and Leon Anderson. 1987. Identity work among the homeless: The verbal construction and avowal of personal identities. *The American Journal of Sociology* 92:1336–371.

Snow, David, and Leon Anderson. 1993. *Down on their luck: A study of homeless street people.* Berkeley: University of California Press.

Stack, Carol. 1996. Writing ethnography: Feminist critical practice. In *Feminist dilemmas in fieldwork,* ed. D. L. Wolf, 96–106. Boulder, CO: Westview Press.

Steen, Sara, and Tara Opsal. 2007. "Punishment on the installment plan": Individual level predictors of parole revocation in four states. *The Prison Journal* 87:344–66.

Strauss, Anselm. 1959. *Mirrors and masks: The search for identity.* Glencoe, IL: Free Press.

Sykes, Gresham, and David Matza. 1957. Techniques of neutralization: A theory of delinquency. *American Sociological Review* 22:664–70.

Tewksbury, Richard. 2005. Collateral consequences of sex offender registration. *Journal of Contemporary Criminal Justice* 21:67–81.

Travis, Jeremy. 2005. *But they all come back: Facing the challenges of prisoner reentry.* Washington, DC: The Urban Institute.

Uggen, Chris, Jeff Manza, and Melissa Thompson. 2006. Citizenship, democracy, and the civic reintegration of criminal offenders. *AAPSS* 605:281–310.

Western, Bruce. 2002. The impact of incarceration on wage mobility and inequality. *American Sociological Review* 67:526–46.

Zajicek, Anna, and Patricia Koski. 2003. Strategies of resistance to stigmatization among white middle-class singles. *Sociological Spectrum* 23:377–403.

DISCUSSION QUESTIONS

1. Discuss the strategies that women use to manage the stigma that comes with the status of an ex-offender.

2. What challenges do women face in dealing with their addictions and sobriety?

3. How does motherhood serve as a source of motivation for women on parole?

READING 22

As you learned in the section, women may have significant persistent and traumatic health needs that require assistance when they leave prison. Welcome Home Ministries is one program that helps to provide resources to help meet these needs. This chapter discusses strategies for meeting nine different areas of health.

Meeting the Health Needs of Post-Incarcerated Women

How Welcome Home Ministries Helps Bridge the Gap and Implications for Public Health Professionals

Carolyn Leitzell, Natalie Madrazo, and Carmen Warner-Robbins

Imagine a young woman sitting in her cell at Las Colinas Women's Detention Facility. This is not her first time in jail: Last time, she was picked up for prostitution and for using a cocktail of illicit drugs. This time, she was arrested for her addiction to and involvement in selling illicit substances on the streets. Her three children, each fathered by a different man, are staying with her gang-affiliated brother this time while she is in jail. She hopes they will be safe there. As the woman looks down at her drab inmate uniform, she wonders how she wound up back in jail so quickly. After her release last time, she completed a drug rehab program, and it was successful—for a while. However, after she went back to her familiar home with her abusive boyfriend, she again became entangled in the web of gang affiliations in which her whole family was entrenched. It did not take long before her resolution to remain sober waned, and she resumed using drugs. They made her feel good and helped numb the pain and unhappiness. As she had stopped prostituting herself, she needed a source of income to feed her addiction and support her family—so she began working with the prominent drug dealers in her neighborhood. She feels worthless, caught in a vicious cycle, and the way out seems nowhere to [be found]. She knows she needs help, but her situation seems hopeless.

The prison population of the United States today is almost four times as large as it was 25 years ago, and this significant minority of the U.S. population tends to have high rates of viral infections, mental illnesses, and chronic diseases (Wilper et al., 2009). Current research has indicated that these health needs are not met during incarceration and, consequently, [may not be met in] postincarceration for both men and women (Wilper et al., 2009). This health disparity, among other barriers, makes reentry into society much more difficult after release from prison—especially for women, who have special health needs when compared with men. This article will introduce and explain Welcome Home Ministries, a nonprofit

SOURCE: Leitzell, C., Madrazo, N., & Warner-Robbins, Rev. C. (2011). Meeting the health needs of post-incarcerated women: How Welcome Home Ministries helps bridge the gap and implications for public health professionals. *Home Health Care Management and Practice, 23*(3), 168–175.

organization that serves postincarcerated women during their reentry process. It will also describe the health outcome objectives that three Point Loma Nazarene University nursing students created for Welcome Home to measure [its] success with [its] clients as well as discuss the health needs of postincarcerated women and how these needs can be met. Finally, the implications for public and community health nurses in caring for postincarcerated women will be discussed.

⊠ Welcome Home Ministries

Welcome Home Ministries is a peer-driven, faith-based organization located in Oceanside, California, that Reverend Carmen Warner-Robbins founded in 1996 when she discovered the complicated diversity of the needs of incarcerated women both during their incarceration and after their release (Miller, 2009). She had a vision and felt spiritually guided to create an organization that would foster relationships with women in jails and prisons and help connect them with the resources and support that they would need upon release for successful reintegration into society. Reverend Warner-Robbins collaborated with the incarcerated women she frequently visited to uncover the various barriers to success that these women face on release and to figure out how to best meet their needs and improve their outcomes. They identified five main areas of service that would be most beneficial for their success in reintegration: obtaining shelter, securing legal employment and income, rebuilding their relationships and reestablishing interpersonal connections, forming community membership, and discovering intrapersonal consciousness and self-confidence (Miller, 2009).

Over the past 12 years, Welcome Home has supplied resources and support to former and current inmates of Vista Detention Facility, Las Colinas Women's Detention Facility, and California State Prisons. With the exception of the founder herself, all of the women employed by Welcome Home Ministries are peers: They have been incarcerated themselves and have recovered from their past of criminal activity, alcohol abuse, and drug addiction. [Because] of the peer mentors' similar life experiences to the women offenders', the incarcerated women feel comfortable relating to them and are instilled with hope as they

see women similar to themselves now successfully working, gaining an education, rebuilding relationships, and living free from their past addictions. The peers, as encouraging role models, share their personal experiences with the women and can empathetically listen to the struggles of the women. They also attend the court trials of the women, assist with navigation through the legal system, and help the women plan for their futures beyond the confines of the institutional walls—thus majorly impacting their lives (Parsons & Warner-Robbins, 2002).

Three senior nursing students became connected with Welcome Home Ministries through their Community Health clinical internship during their last semester of nursing school at Point Loma Nazarene University in San Diego, California. They had the privilege of accompanying one of the peer mentors and employees of Welcome Home Ministries into the Vista Detention Facility every Tuesday afternoon to meet with two groups of women, hear their stories, watch them interact with the peer mentor, and provide health teaching on various topics. As the students wanted their health teachings to meet the education needs of the women, they asked the women throughout the semester about which areas of health and wellness they would like to know more. The women requested further education on women's health issues, parenting, positive coping strategies, anger management, stress management, dealing with anxiety, and learning to take better care of themselves. Throughout the semester, the students provided education and facilitated discussion on the following topics: child and infant safety in the home, recognizing normal growth and development in children, endometriosis, polycystic ovary syndrome, fibroid tumors, reflexology for headaches, stress reduction techniques, and promoting healthy self-care. Not only were the women extremely receptive to the health teachings, but [they] also asked great questions and shared their experiences on particular topics with their fellow inmates. Their questions and comments acted as springboards from which the students were able to better understand their situations and particular needs (see Reading Table 22.1).

From the students' time with the women at Vista Detention Facility and Welcome Home Ministries, they learned that the women, when they are released, have a myriad of health needs and often lack the education and resources to meet them. Women who enter the prison

Reading Table 22.1   Myth Versus Fact

Women who are incarcerated neither need nor deserve to be treated for health issues.	Actually, there are many [incarcerated] women facing real and potentially life-threatening diseases or health related issues. The women are entitled to and need health care just like everyone else.
Women in prison are not the same as "us." There must be something wrong with them for them to be doing these bad things.	Women in jail and/or prison have the same attributes and aspirations as those out in the community. These women want to go to school, help others, have a successful career, and build loving families.
Incarcerated women are completely ignorant about health and education.	In fact, there are some who are actually highly educated nurses and professionals. These people are knowledgeable about health and are eager to learn more. Women in jail love learning.
Everyone in jail or prison deserves to be there.	Unfortunately, there have been many cases where life serves people unfortunate circumstances (like being born into a gang affiliation). Although the women have committed deeds that render incarceration, they deserve a second chance.
Women in the jail/prison system are dangerous because these women want to hurt others.	These women are human, not monsters. A total of 85% of the women in jail are just like other women: They are funny, easy to talk to, smart, and talented. Most of the women are not dangerous and care deeply about others.
Women in jail choose to be the way they are and where they are.	While decisions and choices facilitate human lives, more than 70% of women who land themselves in jail are suffering from a mental illness that has been left untreated. These women deserve treatment and need help recovering and living with their illness.

system are often victims of physical and emotional abuse, economic disadvantage, substance and drug abuse, and mental illness. They cannot afford the vital health and social services they need before, during, or after incarceration. In addition, they find that in prison, they are medicated inappropriately and are not given the proper attention they need to address the risk factors that influenced their entrance into the justice system (Lukis, 2006). Although Welcome Home Ministries refers the women to various health clinics and helps them apply for affordable health services, many of the women are afraid to obtain the health care they need. A newly released woman visiting the Welcome Home headquarters voiced her concerns about feeling judged and belittled by medical personnel because of her past, her lack of knowledge about health-related issues, and her inability to pay for the cost of services. She and many women like herself have been victims of rape, molestation, abuse, and other kinds of traumatic experiences which make the idea of physical assessments and Pap

smears appear terrifying. A study exploring the factors that affect women's transitions from jails and prisons to the community showed that "more than half (56%) of the women expressed in the course of the interviews that they had experienced abuse/neglect as a child and/or as an adult victim of domestic violence" (Parsons & Warner-Robbins, 2002, p. 15). Another common reason why the women are hesitant to seek health screening and treatment is they do not want to know about frightening conditions potentially affecting their health. Due to their past history of sexual promiscuity, intravenous drug use, alcohol abuse, and years of unhealthy habits, conditions like HIV/AIDS, hepatitis, liver cirrhosis, sexually transmitted diseases, hypertension, cervical cancer, and tuberculosis are a common reality for the former inmates. Realizing this, the ex-inmates often postpone health screenings, because if they are unaware, they can pretend they are not affected. However, the sooner the women's health needs are determined, the better their chances of obtaining the most optimal level of health possible.

Developing Outcome Objectives

As one of their projects in their community health clinical rotation with Welcome Home Ministries, the nursing students were given a task to expand on a section of the Welcome Home intake assessment tool for women who use the organization's services. They developed a list of outcome objectives to help measure the success of the women participating in Welcome Home's services for the following areas of health: mental illness, pap and breast exams, eye exams, hepatitis, tuberculosis, HIV/AIDS, blood pressure, dental hygiene, and medication management. Each of these health areas is a potential area of significant health risk to the former inmates if not addressed soon after release from incarceration: "Attention to women's physical [and psychological] health is . . . essential given the connections between poor health, injury, and substance abuse" (Arditti & Few, 2008, p. 317).

Mental Illness

Mental ailments, such as trauma-related symptoms and bipolar disorders, have been found to be prevalent among formerly incarcerated women (Drapalski, Youman, Stuewig, & Tangney, 2009). An estimated 73% of women in state prisons suffer from some sort of mental illness (Arditti & Few, 2008). Many incarcerated women with mental health problems tend to also meet the criteria for substance dependence and abuse. This comorbidity has been associated with negative family and economic relationships, continued victimization, and increased relapse into the criminal justice system. Effective screening of women inmates' psychological distress on release and subsequent mental health referrals is vital to the long-term success of the women (Arditti & Few, 2008). The goal is that a psychiatrist will evaluate the inmate with mental illness—such as depression, schizophrenia, personality disorder, or posttraumatic stress disorder—within 1 week of release. The woman will receive appropriate education regarding her disorder and will be referred to at least two organizations (such as support groups and counseling) at which she can receive care. Further education regarding the woman's medication regimen and treatment plan will be given to the woman

as well. The woman will verbalize understanding of her treatment plan and the importance of adhering to it. For evaluation and further assessment, the woman will follow up with Welcome Home Ministries within 1 week, and also at the 2-, 4-, 8-, and 12-month marks.

Papanicolau and Breast Exams

Female inmates have an abnormally higher risk for contracting cervical cancer than the general women's population—nearly twice as high. Breast exams and Papanicolau (Pap) smears are important because they allow for early detection of breast and cervical cancer. In a study looking at cancer screening among female jail inmates, only 41% of incarcerated women more than 40 years old had had a mammogram within the past 2 years. In addition, 40% of this same study's participants reported abnormal Pap smear results in the past—which is significant considering only 7% of the general population have abnormal Pap smear results (Nijhawan, Salloway, Nunn, Poshkus, & Clarke, 2010). It is imperative that these women should be educated on the importance of early cancer detection because the earlier cancer is detected, the greater the chances are of eradicating it completely from the body. After the women are educated, they will demonstrate proper breast self-examination techniques and receive further instruction if a knowledge deficit exists. The women will also verbalize understanding of the importance of yearly Pap smears and describe two signs of cervical cancer. The women will also receive proper referrals for breast exams, mammograms, and Pap smears as well as information on clinics that offer free or affordable services. For evaluation and further assessment, the women will follow up with Welcome Home Ministries within 1 week and then at the 2-, 4-, 8-, and 12-month marks.

Hepatitis

Hepatitis is a common liver disease in women with a history of intravenous drug use and heavy alcohol consumption: Consequently, [it is found in] a large proportion of former women inmates. One study showed that 70% of female inmates report being previously tested for hepatitis C: A total of 37% of these women report positive test results, 50% reported negative test results, and 13%

reported being unaware of their test results (Nijhawan et al., 2010, p. 19). The Point Loma Nazarene nursing students found that many of the women they came into contact with at Welcome Home Ministries did have hepatitis B or C because of their previous habits of excessive alcohol intake or intravenous drug use. Not many of these women—those still incarcerated and those recovering from their former lifestyles—had sufficient understanding of hepatitis as a disease process, how it affected their own bodies, and how to treat or prevent worsening of their condition.

At Welcome Home Ministries, the released women will be educated on the differences between hepatitis A, B, and C and symptoms that occur as a result of liver damage and inflammation. After this teaching, they will identify three ways to prevent hepatitis C. They will agree to cease alcohol consumption, if they have not already done so, to prevent further liver damage. A physician will regularly monitor their disease process. For evaluation and further assessment, the client will follow up with Welcome Home Ministries within 1 week and then at the 2-, 4-, 8-, and 12-month marks.

Tuberculosis

Tuberculosis is disproportionately common in poor and marginalized populations, such as homeless people, inner city residents, injection drug users, and those in institutionalized facilities like jails and prisons (Lewis, Heitkemper, Dirkson, O'Brien, & Bucher, 2007). A study by MacNeil, Lobato, and Moore (2005) showed that the rate of tuberculosis infection among jail and prison inmates is significantly higher than [among] the rest of the population: Federal and state prison case rates were 29.4 and 24.2 per 100,000 inmates, whereas the rate of the general population was 6.7 per 100,000 people. As tuberculosis is a highly contagious infectious disease that is transmitted through airborne droplets, it is important that all those who are at risk for exposure to tuberculosis—like incarcerated women—are tested for tuberculosis. Testing for tuberculosis can be done through a simple Mantoux tuberculin skin test in which a purified protein derivative (PPD) is injected intradermally into the woman's forearm and read 48 to 72 hours later. All women postincarceration should be tested for tuberculosis within 1 week of release. After education on tuberculosis, the women will identify two risk factors for contracting the

disease as well as verbalize four signs and symptoms of tuberculosis. Women who test positive for tuberculosis will obtain a chest X-ray to determine if their disease is latent or active. Women will also be educated on and adhere to their required medication regimen and be receptive of doctor therapy as evidenced by community health nurse visit reports and follow-up visits. For evaluation and further assessment, the women will follow up with Welcome Home Ministries within 1 week, and at the 2-, 4-, 8-, and 12-month marks.

Human Immunodeficiency Virus

Substance abuse, which is common among incarcerated women, often leads women to engage in risky behaviors such as the acquisition and sales of drugs, theft, and prostitution (Sheu et al., 2002). All of these behaviors increase the chances of the women acquiring the HIV through either intravenous drug usage or sexual promiscuity, as the HIV is transmittable through blood and body fluids. The common overlap of injection drug use and high-risk sexual activity leads to a higher prevalence of HIV among incarcerated women than in nonincarcerated women. HIV in correctional facilities disproportionately affects women: In one study, 2.4% of female inmates were found to be HIV positive in state prisons (Nijhawan et al., 2010). Dwayne R. Haught, MSN, RN, manager of the HIV medication program in Austin, Texas, says that 99% of HIV-infected inmates are eligible for antiretroviral therapy through the AIDS Drug Assistance Program (ADAP). The issue lies in connecting them with the medication and resources in a timely manner after release from incarceration (AIDS Alert, 2009). Ideally, within 1 week of release, postincarcerated women will be tested for HIV if they have not already been tested during confinement. One goal for the women who test HIV positive would include education on HIV, AIDS, and treatment, such as antiretroviral therapy, that helps slow the progression of this incurable condition. After the teaching, the women will describe how HIV is transmitted from person to person. HIV-positive women will be directed to resources so they can receive antiretroviral therapy. The women will actively participate in a plan of care according to physician orders through taking their medications, attending doctor appointments, and adherence to antiretroviral therapy. For evaluation and further assessment, the women will follow up with Welcome

Home Ministries within 1 week, and [at] the 2-, 4-, 8-, and 12-month marks.

Hypertension

Hypertension in formerly incarcerated women is highly prevalent because of their tendency to use stimulant drugs like cocaine, lower socioeconomic status, and stressful and unhealthy lifestyles. Genetics and increased rates of obesity are also risk factors for hypertension. High blood pressure, if not managed properly, can lead to complications such as coronary artery disease, peripheral vascular disease, and cerebrovascular disease (Lewis et al., 2007). The women will be evaluated for baseline blood pressure within the first couple days of discharge. After receiving education, they will verbalize understanding of high blood pressure, contributing factors, and the complications that can ensue. The women with high blood pressure will adhere to their treatment plan, medication regimen, and attend all follow-up appointments. They will begin to incorporate healthier lifestyle practices, such as exercising regularly, cutting down on dietary sodium and saturated fat, losing weight if necessary, and reducing stress in their lives. For further evaluation and assessment, the women will follow up with Welcome Home Ministries within 1 week, and [at] the 2-, 4-, 8-, and 12-month marks.

Dental Hygiene

Dental hygiene is a major area of health deficiency for the incarcerated population. Studies have shown that men and women inmates have significantly more untreated dental caries and missing teeth than the general population (Boyer, Neilsen-Thomson, & Hill, 2002). Dental hygiene is an important aspect of health, and untreated oral diseases like gingivitis can actually contribute to heart disease. The newly released women will be educated on the resources available to them so they can receive affordable dental care every 6 months. They will verbalize two benefits of maintaining proper oral hygiene and describe what proper oral hygiene looks like. In addition, all women will receive a toothbrush, toothpaste, and floss on a visit to Welcome Home Ministry. For evaluation and further assessment, the women will follow up with Welcome Home Ministries within 1 week, and at the 2-, 4-, 8-, and 12-month marks.

Eye Health

The women who come to Welcome Home seeking help often do not have the adequate visual aids they need to correct their vision impairments. They have not had the resources or money to have eye examinations or pay for glasses or contacts. Many people find it difficult to fully function in society and provide adequate self-care if they have trouble reading or feel disoriented because their vision is blurry (Lewis et al., 2007). The women also need to be screened for other eye conditions, such as cataracts, glaucoma, and retinal degeneration.

Welcome Home will help the newly released women to obtain the visual care that they need and to use appropriate visual aids according to the severity of their vision loss. The women will be given contact information and resources to free clinics to receive appropriate eye care. For evaluation and further assessment, the client will follow up with Welcome Home Ministries within 1 week, and [at] the 2-, 4-, 8-, and 12-month marks.

Medications

Many former women inmates come from disadvantaged neighborhoods or from families where meeting basic health needs are not a priority and largely ignored (Lee, Connolly, & Dietz, 2005). During incarceration, these women do not often receive the attention they require for their health issues, and obtaining medication in jail or prison can be difficult. This is a problem for inmates with chronic conditions—especially in those with mental illnesses. If inmates do not continue their psychotropic drugs, their symptoms cannot be properly managed. Research has shown that unmanaged mental illness increases the risks of former inmates to fall back into crime, be rearrested, and sent back to jail (Lee et al., 2005). Women released from prison may need medication for a variety of psychiatric disorders, hypertension, infections, or pain, among other things. However, many of these women face barriers to obtaining and adhering to the medication regimen they need, such as lack of education, lack of resources, and reluctance to being associated with the double stigma of their criminal past and their sometimes embarrassing health conditions (Lee et al., 2005). Welcome Home recognizes this and acts as an advocate for these women to help them obtain the treatments they need and manage them appropriately. The newly released women will be educated on their list of current medications. They will understand the reason they are taking them, potential side effects, possible drug interactions, and how to take them properly. The women will also verbalize when she needs to report substantial adverse effects to primary care physicians and when to seek medical care if the condition worsens or the side effects become serious. The women will comply with the education and medication therapy and will follow up with Welcome Home Ministries within 1 week, and also after the 2-, 4-, 8-, and 12-month marks for further evaluation and assessment.

⬚ Implications for Community and Public Health Nurses

Nursing professionals will come into contact with postincarcerated women in the health care setting whether aware or unaware—especially in the public health arena. As many of these women lack money and resources to obtain appropriate health care, they need to be directed to clinics that provide free or discounted services, and they also need information on programs like [Women, Infants, and Children] WIC, [State Children's Health Insurance Program] SCHIP, and medical [programs] for which many of them qualify. Public health nurses need to be aware that this marginalized population of women is hesitant about seeking health care because the women are fearful of the unknown health conditions they could have and also fearful of judgment and poor treatment from health care professionals—which is unfortunately more common than might be expected. One woman at Welcome Home Ministries remembers, "I would walk into the clinic and the instant they saw my tattoos and scars I felt judged and belittled by the way they looked and talked to me. I could tell they didn't trust me and I felt stupid asking questions I felt I was supposed to know the answers to." Women like this have special health care needs that must be addressed. These women need to be treated with dignity, respect, and compassion—just as every woman seeking out health care should be treated.

What happens if these women's health needs are not met and the health care community does not welcome them? What consequences ensue when postincarcerated women are pushed away from the health care system by judgmental and cold attitudes portrayed by health care professionals? Women who have just been released from jail or prison are in an extremely sensitive and critical period that heavily influences whether they will move toward recovery and integration into society or slip back into their destructive patterns of the past. Obtaining the health resources that they need is important for holistic recovery and also vital for helping the women learn to function in society. Supporting research has shown that "community willingness to address the challenges of prisoner reentry and available resources—or the lack thereof—constitute one set of environmental influences on prisoners returning home" (Visher & Travis, 2003, pp. 91–92). Therefore, if the women feel rejected by the health community, they may also begin to feel rejected by the rest of society as well. As their self-doubt increases, their resolve to battle through their unfamiliar new path wanes, and they may start slipping back into old familiar habits and social circles. Nurses in the public health setting need to realize the power they have to positively influence the lives of postincarcerated women in their most critical time of need. A little extra warmth and kindness could make all the difference in encouraging a woman's successful journey on a new path; conversely, a frustrated and judgmental tone could be the trigger that nudges her back into the vicious, harmful cycle from which she was newly released.

⬚ Conclusion

In conclusion, the numerous health disparities and barriers that recently released incarcerated women face make reentry into society increasingly more difficult. This article introduced Welcome Home Ministries, a nonprofit organization that serves postincarcerated women during their reentry process and also described the health outcome objectives that three Point Loma Nazarene University nursing students created for Welcome Home to objectively measure the organization's success with [its] clients. The major health needs of postincarcerated women and how to meet these needs were also explored as well as how this impacts the practice of public and community health nurses.

References

AIDS Alert. (2009). Most HIV-infected inmates are eligible for ART: Connecting with medication right away [is the] problem. *AIDS Alert, 24*(7), 75–76. Retrieved from CINAHL Plus with Full Text database.

Arditti, J., & Few, A. (2008). Maternal distress and women's reentry into family and community life. *Family Process, 47,* 303–321. doi:10.1111/j.1545–5300.2008.00255.x

Boyer, E., Nielsen-Thompson, N., & Hill, T. (2002). A comparison of dental caries and tooth loss for Iowa prisoners with other prison populations and dentate U.S. adults. *Journal of Dental Hygiene, 76*(2), 141. Retrieved from Nursing/Academic Edition database.

Drapalski, A., Youman, K., Stuewig, J., & Tangney, J. (2009). Gender differences in jail inmates' symptoms of mental illness, treatment history and treatment seeking. *Criminal Behaviour and Mental Health, 19,* 193–206. doi:10.1002/cbm.733

Lee, C., Connolly, P., & Dietz, E. (2005). Forensic nurses' views regarding medications for inmates. *Journal of Psychosocial Nursing & Mental Health Services, 43*(6), 32. Retrieved from CINAHL Plus with Full Text database.

Lewis, S., Heitkemper, M., Dirksen, S., O'Brien, P., & Bucher, L. (2007). *Medical-surgical nursing: Assessment and management of clinical problems* (7th ed.). St. Louis, MO: Mosby Elsevier.

Lukis, V. (2006). Health effects of an ex-offender's successful reentry into society. *American Journal of Public Health, 96,* 588–589. doi:10.2105/AJPH.2005.083592

MacNeil, J., Lobato, M., & Moore, M. (2005). An unanswered health disparity: Tuberculosis among correctional inmates, 1993 through 2003. *American Journal of Public Health, 95,* 1800–1805. Retrieved from CINAHL Plus with Full Text database.

Miller, D. (2009). Faith-based organization welcomes women back into community: Changing lives, restoring families, and building community. *Family and Community Health, 32,* 298–306.

Nijhawan, A., Salloway, R., Nunn, A., Poshkus, M., & Clarke, J. (2010). Preventive healthcare for underserved women: Results of a prison survey. *Journal of Women's Health, 19*(1), 17–22. doi:10.1089/jwh.2009.1469

Parsons, M., & Warner-Robbins, C. (2002). Factors that support women's successful transition to the community following jail/prison. *Health Care for Women International, 23*(1), 6–18. doi:10.1080/073993302753428393

Sheu, M., Hogan, J., Allsworth, J., Stein, M., Vlahov, D., Schoenbaum, E., . . . Flanigan, T. (2002). Continuity of medical care and risk of incarceration in HIV positive and high-risk HIV-negative women (15409996). *Journal of Women's Health, 11,* 743. Retrieved from Academic Search Premier database.

Visher, C., & Travis, J. (2003). Transitions from prison to community: Understanding individual pathways. *Annual Review of Sociology, 29*(1), 89–113. Retrieved from Academic Search Premier database.

Wilper, A. P., Woolhandler, S., Boyd, W., Lasser, K. E., McCormick, D., Bor, D. H., & Himmelstein, D. U. (2009). The health and health care of US prisoners: A nationwide survey. *American Journal of Public Health, 99,* 666–672.

DISCUSSION QUESTIONS

1. Identify and define the nine health areas for which Welcome Home Ministries provides care.

2. Which of the areas have the most immediate needs upon release? Why?

3. Which of the areas present as long-term health care needs? Why?

Women Professionals and the Criminal Justice System

Police, Corrections, and Offender Services

Throughout history, criminal justice occupations have been dominated by men. Whether the job was that of a police officer or working within the field of corrections, the common perception was that the duties of apprehending and managing dangerous felons was outside the perceptions of what women could—or should—do. Women first began to appear in criminal justice occupations within police organizations in the early 20th century. However, their early presence within the academy was significantly limited, as many believed that policing was a *man's job* and therefore unsuitable as an occupation for women. The duties in these occupations focused on traditional masculine traits, such as aggression, physical skill, and being tough—traits that many argued were lacking for women, making them inherently less capable of doing the job (Appier, 1998).

Society generally assumes that work in the criminal justice system is dominated by events that are dangerous, exciting, and violent. These themes are echoed and reinforced in examples of popular culture, such as television, film, and news outlets, by stories of dangerous offenders and crimes that destroy peaceful communities (Lersch & Bazley,

2012). Certainly criminal justice officials in fields such as policing, corrections, and probation and parole can and do face dangerous situations during their careers. However these extreme examples misrepresent the reality of criminal justice work, which often involves long delays, extensive paperwork, and spending time talking with residents of the community. Unlike the adrenaline rush that is depicted in the media, criminal justice personnel spend significant portions of their time dealing with situations that require empathy, compassion, and nurturing—traits that are stereotypically classified as *feminine* characteristics. For example, the typical duties of a police officer are not limited to the pursuit and capturing of the "bad guys" and more often include responding to victims of a crime and dealing with the welfare of community members. Given the various skills and traits required in criminal justice professions, has the number of women increased in these fields? How does gender contribute to these professions? Are there other differences in how women are hired, do their jobs, and establish careers in criminal justice? This section follows these issues through the fields of policing, corrections, and offender services.

Women in Police

An examination of the history of policing indicates that the work of moral reformers was instrumental in the emergence of policewomen. During the late 19th century, women's advocacy groups were heavily involved in social issues.

Examples of their efforts include the creation of a separate court for juvenile offenders as well as crime prevention outreach related to the protection of young women from immoral sexual influences. However, women were not a formal part of the justice system and served as informal advocates and, when employed, as paid social workers.

With the start of the 20th century, women entered the police force as bona fide, sworn officers. However, there is some debate as to who was the first female police officer. One report indicates that the first female police officer may have been **Marie Owens**. She was a Chicago factory inspector who transferred to the police department in 1891 and served 32 years with the city (Mastony, 2010). Other scholars point to **Lola Baldwin**, who was reportedly hired in 1908 by the Portland, Oregon, police department as a supervisor to

▲ **Photo 12.1** Edyth Totten and the Women Police Reserve, New York City, 1918.

a group of social workers (Corsianos, 2009). However, it is unclear whether Baldwin served as a sworn officer (Los Angeles Almanac, 2012). But it is **Alice Stebbins Wells**, who was hired by the Los Angeles Police Department (LAPD) in 1910, who is most often cited as the first sworn female police officer in the United States. At the time of her hiring, her job duties revolved around working with female offenders and juvenile cases. Her philosophy as a female police officer reinforced the ideal of feminine traits of policing when she stated, "I don't want to make arrests. I want to keep people from needing to be arrested, especially young people" (Appier, 1998, p. 9). As a result of the national and international attention of her hiring, she traveled the country promoting the benefits of hiring women in municipal policing agencies. As an officer with the LAPD, Wells advocated for the protection of children and women, particularly when it came to sexual education. As part of her duties, she inspected dance halls, movie theaters, and locations for public recreation throughout the city. When she came into contact with girls of questionable moral status, she would lecture them on the dangers of premarital sex and advocate for the importance of purity.

Following in the footsteps of Alice Stebbins Wells, many women sought out positions as police officers. The hiring of women by police agencies throughout the early 20th century did not mean that these women were assigned the same duties as male police officers. Rather, these policewomen were essentially social workers armed with a badge. Their duties focused on preventing crime, rather than responding to criminal activity. While hundreds of women joined the ranks of local law enforcement agencies between 1910 and 1920, they were a minority within most departments. Female officers were generally limited to working with juvenile and female offenders, and the male officers resented their presence in the department. In an effort to distinguish the work of policewomen, many cities created separate branches within their organization. These women's bureaus were tasked with servicing the needs of women and girls in the community. Many of these bureaus were housed outside of the walls of the city police department in an attempt to create a more welcoming environment for citizens in need. Some scholars suggest that by making women's bureaus look more like a home, rather than a bureaucratic institution, women and children would be more comfortable and therefore more likely to seek out the services and advice of policewomen.

The mid-20th century saw significant growth in the numbers of women in policing. In 1922, there were approximately 500 policewomen in the United States—by 1960, more than 5,600 women were employed as officers (Schulz, 1995). Throughout this time, the majority of these policewomen remained limited in their duties, due in large part to a traditional policing (i.e., male) model. Policewomen were not permitted to engage in the same duties as policemen, out of fear that it was too dangerous and that women would not be able to adequately serve in these positions. Most importantly, the "all boys club" that existed in most departments simply did not want or welcome women intruding on their territory.

Despite these issues, women occasionally found themselves receiving expanded duties, particularly during times of war. With the decrease in manpower during World War I and II, many women found themselves placed in positions normally reserved for male officers, such as traffic control. In an effort to maintain adequate staffing levels during this period, the number of women hired within police agencies increased. However, the end of these wars saw the return of men to their policing posts and the displacement of women back to their gendered roles and **gendered assignments** within their respective departments (Snow, 2010).

As in many other fields during the 1960s, the civil rights and women's movements had a tremendous effect on the presence of women in policing. Legal challenges paved the way toward gendered equality in policing by opening doors to allow women to serve in more active police capacities, such as patrol. In 1964, **Liz Coffal** and **Betty Blankenship** of the Indianapolis Police Department became the first women in the United States to serve as patrol officers, an assignment that was previously restricted to male officers throughout the country. As policewomen, Coffal and Blankenship were resented by their male colleagues, who believed that the work of a police officer was too dangerous for women. Coffal and Blankenship received little training for their new positions and often had to learn things on their own. They found that dispatch often gave them the mundane and undesirable tasks, such as hospital transports. It soon became clear to Blankenship and Coffal that the likelihood of being requested for any sort of pursuit or arrest cases was slim. In an effort to gain increased experience in their position, they began to respond to calls at their own discretion. Armed with their police radio, they learned to interpret radio codes and began to respond to cases in their vicinity. They successfully navigated calls that most male officers believed they could not handle. As a result of their positive performances in often tense situations, Coffal and Blankenship began to gain some respect from their male colleagues. However, they knew that any accolades could be short lived—one mistake and they ran the risk of being removed from their patrol status, and the traditional philosophy of "police work isn't for women" would be justified. While they eventually returned to some of the "traditional feminine roles" for women in policing, their experiences in patrol set the stage for significant changes for future policewomen (Snow, 2010).

In addition to the differences in their duties, policewomen were historically subjected to different qualification standards for their positions. At the 1922 annual conference of the International Association of the Chiefs of Police, members suggested that policewomen should have completed college or nursing school (Snow, 2010). This standard is particularly ironic, given that male officers were not required to have even a high school diploma in most jurisdictions until the 1950s and 1960s. As a result, the career path of policewomen attracted women of higher educational and intellectual standing.

Not only were policewomen limited by their roles and duties within the department, they faced significant barriers as well in terms of the benefits and conditions of their employment. Like in many other fields, policewomen were paid less for their work compared to policemen, even though these women often had higher levels of education than their male colleagues. In addition, the advancement and promotional opportunities for women were significantly limited, as most departments did not allow women to participate in the exam process that would grant them access for promotional opportunities. Generally speaking, the highest position that a policewoman could hold during this time was the commander of the women's bureau. Still, many agencies disagreed with that level of leadership, suggesting that women did not have the necessary skills or abilities to supervise officers or run a division. In some jurisdictions, women were forced to quit their positions when they got married, as many felt that women did not have enough time to care for a home, care for their husband, and fulfill their job duties. As one male officer explained it, "when they marry they have to resign. You see, we might want them for some job or other when they have to be home cooking their husband's dinner. That would not be much use to us, would it?" (Snow, 2010, p. 23).

In 1967, the President's Commission on Law Enforcement and the Administration of Justice advocated for expanding the numbers of policewomen and diversifying their duties beyond the traditional female roles to which they were typically assigned. In 1967, the commission wrote, "The value should not be considered as limited to staff functions or police work with juveniles; women should also serve regularly in patrol, vice and investigative functions" (p. 125). Despite these assertions, few departments followed these recommendations, arguing that as members of a uniformed police patrol, officers required significant levels of upper-body strength in order to detain resistant offenders. In addition, many agency administrators argued that the job was simply too dangerous for women.

Until the 1970s, women represented only 1% of all sworn officers in the United States (Appier, 1998). However, new legislation and legal challenges in the 1960s and 1970s led to further changes involving the presence and role of policewomen. While the **Civil Rights Bill** of 1964 was generally focused on eliminating racial discrimination, the word *sex* was added to the bill during the eleventh hour by House members, who hoped that this inclusion would raise objections among legislators and prohibit its passing. To the dismay of these dissenters, the bill was signed into law. In 1969, President Richard Nixon signed legislation that prohibited the use of sex as a requirement for hiring— meaning that jobs could not be restricted to men only (or women only). In addition, the Law Enforcement Assistance Administration (LEAA) mandated that agencies with federal funding (and police departments fell under this category) were prohibited from engaging in discriminatory hiring practices based on sex. While sex was now a protected category in terms of employment discrimination, the bill did little on its face to increase the presence of women in sworn policing roles. While the act prohibited discriminatory hiring practices, it had little effect on the types of assignments that were given to women once they joined the police force.

The passage of the Civil Rights Bill began a trend within departments to introduce women into ranks that were previously reserved exclusively for men. While several departments took the initiative to place women into patrol positions, many men in these departments issued strong objections against the practice. Thus, women in these positions often found themselves ostracized, with little support from their colleagues. Eight years later, in 1972, the Civil Rights Act was amended to extend employment protections to state and municipal government agencies, which opened the door to allow women to apply to all law enforcement jurisdictions as sworn officers without restrictions. While these changes increased the number of positions available to women (and to minorities), they also shifted the roles of policing away from the social service orientation that had been historically characteristic for women in policing. Their jobs now included the duties of crime fighting and the maintenance of order and public safety, just like their male counterparts (Schulz, 1995).

Over the past four decades, there have been significant increases in the number of women employed as sworn law enforcement officers. In 1922, there were approximately 500 policewomen in the United States—by 1960, more than 5,600 women were employed as officers, approximately 1.1% of all sworn officers (Schulz, 1995; Rabe-Hemp, 2008). By 1986, approximately 8.8% of municipal officers were female (Rabe-Hemp, 2008), a proportion that almost doubles by 2008 (15.2%). Women are more likely to be employed in larger jurisdictions (22%) and federal agencies (24%) compared to smaller jurisdictions (defined as departments with fewer than 500 officers) where women make up 8% of all sworn personnel (Langton, 2010). Unfortunately, these few women that serve in rural communities are relegated to lower positions within the agency and experience higher degrees of discrimination compared to women in larger metropolitan departments (Rabe-Hemp, 2008).

© Thinkstock/Darrin Klimek

▲ **Photo 12.2** Legal changes have increased opportunities in policing for both women and people of color. Today, police officers reflect a greater diversity among the force than in the past. However, women continue to struggle in this male-dominated field.

Why is the representation of women so low in the field of policing? While legal challenges have mandated equal access to employment and promotional opportunities for women in policing, research indicates that the overemphasis on the physical fitness skills component of the hiring process excludes a number of qualified women from employment (Lonsway, Carrington, et al., 2002). Physical fitness tests typical of law enforcement positions have been criticized as a tool to exclude women from policing, despite evidence that it is not the physical abilities of officers that are most desirable. Rather, it is their communication skills that are the best asset for the job. The number of push-ups that a woman can complete compared to a man says little about how well each will complete their duties. Yet standards such as these are used as evidence to suggest that women are inferior to their male colleagues. Women who are able to achieve the male standard of physical fitness are viewed more favorably by male colleagues, compared to women who satisfy only the basic requirements for their gender (Schulze, 2012).

While some agencies have embraced the inclusion of women on the force, women as sworn police officers still experience discrimination and isolation within some agencies. Some male officers still refuse to accept female officers, while others are indifferent to the presence of women on the force. Research indicates that younger male officers and male officers of color are more likely to accept women among the ranks compared to older and/or White officers (Renzetti, Goodstein, & Miller, 2006).

Despite the continued increase of women in policing, the majority of these women serve within the general ranks as the upper management positions within agencies are still dominated by men. While court rulings in the 1970s opened the possibilities for promotion for policewomen, few women have successfully navigated their way to the top position of police chief. In 2009, there were 212 women serving in the top-ranking position in their departments nationwide (O'Connor, 2012). Most of these women serve in small communities or lead agencies with a specific focus, such as university police divisions or transit authorities (Schulz, 2003). Within metropolitan agencies (more than 100 sworn officers), only 7.3% of the top-level positions and 9.6% of supervisory positions are held by women. Additionally, women of color make up only 4.8% of sworn officers, and minority women are even less likely to appear in upper-level management positions, with only 1.6% of top-level positions and 3.1% of supervisory roles filled by a woman of color. The situation is even bleaker for small and rural agencies, where only 3.4% of the top-level positions are staffed by women (Lonsway, Carrington, et al., 2002).

Given the historical context of women in policing, it is not surprising that attributes such as compassion, fear, or anything else that is considered *feminine* are historically maligned, particularly by male officers. Given this masculine subculture that exists in policing, how does this affect women who are employed within the agency? What does it mean to be a woman in law enforcement?

Although women in policing have made significant advances over the past century, research is mixed on whether the contemporary situation is improving for women in law enforcement. While legal challenges have required equal access to employment and promotion within law enforcement, research indicates that many women continue to be *passed over* for positions that were ultimately filled by a male officer. In many cases, women felt that they continually had to prove themselves to their male colleagues, regardless of the number of years that they spent within an organization. This experience was particularly prevalent when women moved to a new position (Rabe-Hemp, 2012).

In many jurisdictions, female officers acknowledge that sexual harassment by their male peers and superior officers is part of the landscape of policing. For example, one female officer was often told by a male superior, "Why don't you go home and be a normal woman barefoot and in the kitchen," and another was "slapped. . . across my ass after he told me that he likes women on their knees in front of him" (Lonsway, Paynich, & Hall, 2013, p. 191, 193). Research indicates that women in higher ranking positions are less willing to tolerate sexual harassment and discrimination. While some younger officers dealt with sexual harassment by avoiding and ignoring the behaviors, others confronted their colleagues in an effort to end such behaviors early in their tenure (Haarr & Morash, 2013). Still, many others ignored the behavior as they feared retaliation or believed that nothing would be done (Lonsway et al., 2013).

Despite reports of discrimination and harassment within their agencies, they acknowledge that the culture of policing has become more accepting to women throughout their careers. However, these ideals of peace were not easily won and required daily support and maintenance by the women. Female officers reduce the stress of sexual harassment by developing strong social bonds with other officers within their departments (Harrison, 2012). While such an approach may not reduce or eliminate the presence of harassment, it can help mediate its effects. Research by Rabe-Hemp (2008) identifies three additional ways in which policewomen gain acceptance within the masculine culture of policing: (1) experiences in violent confrontations requiring the use of force, (2) achieving a high rank within the department structure, and (3) distinguishing themselves as different from their male counterparts in terms of their skills and experience. Female police officers acknowledge that acceptance in the male-dominated police culture often comes with significant costs to their personal life and ideals. In many cases, policewomen talk about putting up with disrespect and harassment in order to achieve their goals. For others, they renegotiate their original goals and settle for "second best."

While the historical acceptance of women in policing was less than enthusiastic, there have been a few trends in policing which have emphasized characteristics that are traditionally feminine. One such example is the emergence of community policing philosophies in the 1990s, which provided a shift in police culture that increased the number of women working in the field. The values of community policing emphasize relationships, care, and communication between officers and citizens. It allows officers to develop rapport with members of their community and respond to their concerns. Effective community policing strategies have led to improved relationships and respect of officers by residents. Research indicates that policewomen have been particularly successful within models of community policing due to their enhanced problem-solving skills through communication (Lersch & Bazley, 2012). These traditionally female skills serve as an asset to departments that include community-oriented and problem-oriented policing characteristics as part of their mission as well as in dealing with certain offenders such as juveniles and women who have been victimized (Rabe-Hemp, 2009). Even though they may bring a different set of skills to the job, many female officers believe that they do the job just as well as their male counterparts, albeit in different ways. Many female officers argued that their feminine traits served them well on the job. As one officer notes:

I think they [female officers] are very similar to male officers. They do their job. They just handle it differently. They handle calls differently. Where maybe a male might use strength, I think a female might use strength up here [pointing to her head], you know and strength here [pointing to her mouth]. (Morash & Haarr, 2012, p. 13)

Rather than feel that these female traits made them less competent, some research indicates that female officers believed that their male counterparts appreciated the value of feminine qualities in police work (Morash & Haarr, 2012). For example, women officers may have better relationships with members of their community, have fewer citizen complaints compared to their male counterparts, and are less likely to "jump" to physical interventions (Lonsway, Wood, et al., 2002, Harrington & Lonsway, 2004; Rape-Hemp, 2009). Feminine traits, such as care and compassion, were also viewed as an asset particularly when dealing with victims, although some female officers resisted the label that they possessed these traits because of their gender (Morash & Haarr, 2012). In addition to the communication and problem-solving skills that many female officers use in their daily experiences, women officers are typically not involved in cases of police brutality and corruption. Research indicates that male officers are more than 8.5 times more likely than female officers to be accused of excessive force (Lonsway, Wood, et al., 2002).

Perhaps the most masculine of all policing environments is the SWAT (Special Weapons and Tactics) team. Few women serve in these environments, and their participation within these ranks is a fairly new phenomenon. As one of the most physically demanding assignments in policing, some have suggested that few women possess the abilities to work within such an intense setting (Snow, 2010). Indeed, there are significant barriers (both perceived and real) that limit the number of women to seek out and accept these types of positions. First, many female officers view SWAT as the pinnacle of hyper-masculinity in policing that would exclude women within its ranks. Second, the nature of SWAT includes physical challenges and abilities that may discourage many women from applying. Here, many of the women acknowledged that they believed they would be accepted by the *team* if they were strong enough. Finally, both male and female officers see that women would be challenged by the male SWAT officers and need to prove that they had the skills necessary to do the job, not unlike the early experiences of women in policing:

I would see it as a constant, day-to-day battle. Any woman in that type of unit would be forced to "do more and do it better" in order to prove herself to the men in the group. This is how women were first initiated into police work, and that type of probative acceptance continues and may even be more pronounced in units such as SWAT. (Dodge, Valcore, & Klinger, 2010, p. 229)

Despite the significant increases that women have made in the realm of policing, female officers are still viewed differently from their male counterparts. For example, female officers often prefer male officers as backup compared to another female. This may not reflect a distrust of their fellow female officers but rather serve as a way to distance themselves from a feminine identity and reinforce their validity in a male-dominated arena (Carlan, Nored, & Downey, 2011). At the same time, many women still struggle to separate themselves from the stereotypes of days gone by in many ways, in that they are well suited to dealing with cases involving women, children, and victims in general. These perceptions influence not only beliefs about the abilities of female officers but also ultimately have an impact on the types of work assignments that they receive (Kurtz, Linnemann, & Williams, 2012).

⬚ Women in Corrections

Correctional officers are a central component of the criminal justice system. Responsible for the security of the correctional institution and the safety of the inmates housed within its walls, correctional officers are involved with every aspect of the inmate life. Indeed, correctional officers play an important part in the lives of the inmates as a result of their constant interaction. Contrary to other work assignments within the criminal justice field, the position of the correctional officer is integrated into every aspect of the daily life of prisoners. Duties of the correctional officer range from enforcing the rules and regulations of the facility to responding to inmate needs, to diffusing inmate conflicts, and to supervising the daily movement and activities of the inmate (Britton, 2003).

Historically, the workforce of corrections has been largely male and White, regardless of the race or gender of the offender. As discussed earlier, the treatment of female offenders by male guards during the early days of the prison led to significant acts of neglect and abuse of female inmates. These acts of abuse resulted in the hiring of female matrons to supervise the incarcerated female population. However, these early positions differed significantly from the duties of male officers assigned to supervise male inmates, and opportunities for female staff to work outside the population of female-only inmates were rare. For those women who were successful in gaining employment in a male institution, their job duties were significantly limited. In particular, prison policies did not allow female correctional officers to work in direct supervision roles with male offenders. Similar to the realm of policing, the culture within correctional occupations reflected a masculine identity, and administrators believed it was too dangerous to assign a woman to supervise male inmates. In male facilities, female guards were restricted to positions that had little to no inmate contact, such as administrative positions, entry and control booths, and general surveillance (Britton, 2003).

Despite the increased access to employment opportunities for women through the 1970s, many female guards resented these gendered restrictions on their job duties and filed suit with the courts, alleging that the restriction of duties because they were women constituted sex discrimination. While many cases alleged that the restriction of female guards from male units was done to maintain issues of privacy for the offenders, the courts rejected the majority of these arguments. In *Griffin v. Michigan Department of Corrections* (654 F. Supp. 690, 1982), the court held that inmates do not possess any rights to be protected against being viewed in stages of undress or naked by a correctional officer, regardless of gender. In addition, the court held that the positive aspects of offender rehabilitation outweighed any potential risks of assault for female correctional officers; therefore, they should not be barred from working with a male incarcerated population. Other cases such as *Grummett v. Rushen* (779 F.2d 491, 1985) have concluded that the pat-down search of a male inmate (including their groin area) does not violate the Fourth Amendment protection against unreasonable search and seizure. However, the courts have held that the inverse gender relationship can be considered offensive. In *Jordan v. Gardner* (986 F.2d 1137, 1992), the court found that pat-down policies designed to control the introduction of contraband into a facility could be viewed as unconstitutional if conducted by male staff members against female inmates. Here, the court held that a cross sex search could amount to a deliberate indifference with the potential for psychological pain (under the Eighth Amendment) given the high likelihood of a female offender's history of physical and sexual abuse.

As a result of equal employment opportunity legislation, the doors of prison employment have been opened for women to serve as correctional officers. Today, women are increasingly involved in all areas of supervision of both male and female offenders, and all ranks and positions today. Many women choose corrections as a career out of interest in the rehabilitation services, as well as a perception that such a career provides job security (Hurst & Hurst, 1997). According to the 2007 Directory of Adult and Juvenile Correctional Departments, Institutions and Agencies and Probation and Parole Authorities, women made up 37% of correctional officers in state adult facilities and 51% of juvenile correctional officers (American Correctional Association, 2007). Within these facilities, both men and women are assigned to same-sex as well as cross sex supervision positions. In addition, more women are working as correctional officers in exclusively male facilities, where they constitute 24.5% of the correctional personnel in these institutions (DiMarino, 2009).

Despite significant backlash and criticism against women in corrections, research indicates that the integration of women into the correctional field has significant benefits for prison culture. First, female correctional officers are less likely than male officers to be victimized by inmates. This finding contradicts traditional concerns that women would be at risk for harm if they were responsible for the direct supervision of male offenders (Tewksbury & Collins, 2006). However, women are more likely to fear victimization by inmates (Gordon, Proulx, & Grant, 2013). Second, women

© Thinkstock Images

▲ **Photo 12.3**   In the early history of prisons, women were hired to work only with female inmates. In response to equal opportunity policies and lawsuits by women in correctional fields, women today are now assigned to all types of supervision duties within the prison. Here, a female correctional officer engages in a "pat-down" search of an inmate to look for weapons or other contraband items.

officers are more likely than male officers to use communication skills, rather than physical acts of force, to obtain compliance from inmates. Finally, female officers indicate a greater level of satisfaction from their work, compared to male officers (Tewksbury & Collins, 2006).

How does gender affect the perceptions of work in a correctional setting? Like other criminal justice occupations, how do female correctional officers "do" gender in the context of their job duties? Many female correctional officers are hyperaware of their status as women and how gender affects interactions with both fellow staff and inmates. In some cases, female officers utilize skills and techniques that many scholars identify as feminine traits—communication and care for the inmates, mutual respect between inmates and staff, and so on. Female staff members often become very aware of their physical status as a woman, particularly when working with male offenders, and respond by dressing down, wearing baggier clothing (in facilities where officers are not required to dress in uniform), and donning understated hairstyles and makeup to limit physical displays of gender in the workplace.

Women working in the correctional field are more likely to emphasize the "social worker" aspects of the job, compared to their male counterparts (Stohr, Mays, Lovrich, & Gallegos, 1996). Here, women use their gender to their advantage—by drawing upon their communication skills, they are able to diffuse potentially dangerous situations before violence ensues. However, it is important to find balance between the feminine traits and masculine traits—too much communication between staff and inmates can be viewed negatively, out of fear that staff will grow too close to an inmate and risk being taken advantage of (Britton, 2003). At the same time, some female correctional officers perceive that they are not promoted because they are viewed as less capable than their male counterparts (Matthews, Monk-Turner, & Sumter, 2010). Research indicates that gender can affect how officers approach their position, regardless of the inmate's sex. For women involved in the supervision of male inmates, their philosophies often differ significantly from that of male officers. For example, Britton (2003) found that whereas male officers functioned within a paramilitary role and were ready to use force if necessary, women saw their role as mentors and mothers, and they focused on the rehabilitation of the inmates.

Given the increase of the prison population and the opportunities for employment, it is important for facilities to recognize the strengths and weaknesses for women who work in this field and their relationships with the incarcerated population.

However, women still struggle in this masculine, male-dominated environment. Research indicates that female correctional officers are frequent targets of sexual harassment (Chapman, 2009). The **good ol' boy network** remains quite pervasive in many facilities. Many women in leadership positions face significant challenges navigating this culture. For example, as one female officer puts it, "Men will perceive being assertive as a good quality in a guy, [but for women] they will still say, 'oh she's such a bitch.' So you need to couch what you're saying a little differently so as not to offend these poor guys over here" (Greer, 2008, p. 5). However, the perpetration of sexual harassment is not limited to other staff members. Female officers indicate that they experience persistent occurrences of sexual harassment by inmates. However, studies suggest these experiences do not affect female officers' job satisfaction—indeed many accept that incidents of sexual harassment come with the territory of being a woman working in a male-dominated arena (Chapman, 2009).

Given these challenges, are women happy working in the correctional field? Research tells us that women do tend to like their job in corrections more than their male counterparts. This is particularly interesting given that corrections is a male-dominated field, and many women have had to battle for their presence in the correctional setting (Lambert, Paoline, Hogan, & Baker, 2007). There are a number of interacting variables that determine things like job stress and job satisfaction. For example, female correctional officers report higher levels of job stress than male officers. But what factors influence this stress? Cheeseman and Downey (2012) indicate that women who have low levels of job satisfaction will report higher levels of job-related stress. Even in cases where men and women experience on the job stress, the source of this stress varies by gender. While both men and women relate an increased stress level to lower levels of trust in their supervisor, men are more concerned with their abilities of their supervisor to effectively assess their job performance. In comparison, women are more likely to believe that their supervisor's place unreasonable expectations on them and treat them poorly in the context of the work environment. These gender differences of stress also impact levels of job satisfaction (Lambert, Hogan, Altheimer, & Wareham, 2010). While much of the literature on women in corrections focuses on career trajectories and on the job challenges, some scholars also look at how the inmate population can have gendered implications on the work environment. Inmates often have conflicting perceptions about women working in the correctional field. Studies indicate that upon their first interactions, male inmates draw on stereotypical assumptions regarding female officers. Yet women in these positions possess the unique opportunity to offer a positive image of women (Cheeseman & Worley, 2006). In addition, many line officers express distain when they are assigned to work with female offenders. They suggest that girls are much more difficult to work with than the boys and state that the female inmates are more dramatic, manipulative, needy, emotional, and time consuming. Research by Pollock (1986) provides details on why male and female correctional officers believe that working with women is less desirable than supervising men. While both male and female staff members believe that women inmates are more demanding, defiant, and complaining, male officers also express concerns about being accused of inappropriate behaviors against female inmates. Female officers express that they would prefer to work with male inmates because they feel that they are more likely to be respected and appreciated by the male inmates than female inmates. Belief systems such as these have a significant impact on perceptions of working with female offenders and translate into a belief that working with women is an undesirable assignment (Rasche, 2012). Research indicates that among both male and female correctional officers (and regardless of rank), there appears to be a **male inmate preference**, despite the increased risks for violence associated with this population.

⊠ Community Corrections: Female Probation and Parole Officers

While there has been a fair amount of research on women in policing and corrections, the same cannot be said for women who work as parole and probation officers. While probation and parole agents are sworn officials like police officers, their work focuses only on convicted offender populations, whereas police officers deal with the general population as well. Given the high demand on probation services as a tool of the correctional system, it is fair to say that probation officers deal with the largest criminal justice population.

The origins of probation date back to the Middle Ages and English criminal law. In the United States, John Augustus became the first volunteer probation officer in 1841. In 1925, the federal government passed the National Probation Act and established the U.S. Federal Probation Service. By 1951, probation departments were established in every state. One of the earliest female probation officers was Catherine F. Brattan, who has been referenced as the first woman probation officer in California in 1910 (Sawyers, 1922). In contrast, parole was first implemented in the United States by Zebulon Brockway in 1876 and was implemented nationwide by 1942 (Peterselia, 2000) Indeed, like some of the early women in policing, many of these early women in probation and parole were charged with supervising juvenile offenders and, later, female offenders. In 1970, most states limited the caseloads of female parole officers to female offenders. Following the passage of the Civil Rights Act, states began to allow for cross sex supervision (Schoonmaker & Brooks, 1975). In 2012, there were 90,300 probation officers and correctional treatment specialists in the United States (Bureau of Labor Statistics [BLS], 2014). However, it is unclear how many of these positions are held by women.

As you learned earlier in this section, there has been a significant body of work investigating the cultural environment of women in policing and corrections and the challenges that they face. Could the same be said for women who work in probation and parole? Do they face these same challenges in this male-dominated environment? The answer to this question is yes. Research indicates that women in parole have similar experiences with sexual harassment and marginalization as do women in policing (Ireland & Berg, 2008). Working with highly intense populations also means extensive exposure to acts of violence. Over time, this exposure can desensitize probation officers (Petrillo, 2007).

In addition, women experience high levels of stress as part of their job duties. The presence of stress can be found in four different areas of the job: internal organizational stress, external organizational stress, job and/or task-related stress, and personal stress. Research indicates that male and female probation officers experience different categories of stress. Female probation officers register higher levels of physical stress whereas male probation officers register high levels of internal organization, job-related, and personal stress. However, each of these types of stress was greater for officers in supervisory positions (and men were more likely to serve in these roles). At the same time, it is possible that women have lower registered levels of stress because they are more likely to be aware of the early warning signs of stress and take action (Wells, Colbert & Slate, 2006). Despite this, many women acknowledge that these stressful on-the-job experiences often spill over into their lives. Much of the literature on criminal justice occupations (such as policing and corrections) focuses on the masculine nature of these careers and the challenges that women face within these environments. However, literature on parole officers indicates that female officers utilize gendered strategies as part of their management strategies. Like female police officers, communication skills were invaluable in the daily aspects of their job as a parole officer. As one female parole agent expressed,

> We have to have good communication skills; we have to be able to recognize volatile situations; and you have to be able to know how to handle those situations by using your communication skills. I have been involved in situations that could have easily turned volatile, but my manner, my demeanor, my communication skills, and the manner in which I dealt with these individuals has made a very big difference in the way they have responded to me. (Ireland & Berg, 2008, p. 483)

Developing rapport with their clients was also an important skill that contributed to their on-the-job safety. While male officers were more likely to use force in their cases (a reflection of their identity with policing), female agents aligned themselves with a social worker mentality, which allowed for more of a rehabilitative focus (Ireland & Berg, 2008). Particularly in cases where female officers were involved in supervising male offenders, gender became a way to challenge the offender's perceptions and stereotypes about women. However, male offenders would often challenge these female officers, using tricks from intimidation to flirting to regain some power over the situation. At the same time, their interactions with these offenders gave a unique insight as to how victims experience interactions with these offenders, particularly in cases of intimate partner violence and sexual offenses (Petrillo, 2007). In addition, female officers emphasized the role of respect between themselves and their parolees as a way to manage their caseload. "Parolees, if you treat them well and you do your job, even when you have to lock them up, they will respect you and understand that you are just doing your job. If you treat them like a piece of crap, that's what you're going to get back" (Ireland & Berg, 2008, p. 485).

While parole officers appear to engage in cross sex supervision, probation officers are often assigned caseloads that are specialized, such as around a particular offense (drug crimes, sexual offending), need (mental health treatment), or gender of the offender. Since female probation officers are more likely to be assigned to supervise female offenders, this creates an opportunity to engage in gendered strategies. While these approaches reflect the needs of the offender, it may also be related to how officers do their job. For example, female officers are more likely to engage with their clients on an emotional level and build relationships with their clients. In this way, the probation officer serves as a positive role model for her clients (Wyse, 2013).

Conclusion

At the heart of the research for each of these fields, two major themes emerge—(1) gender can affect the way in which women who work in these fields satisfy the demands of their positions, and (2) gender affects the experiences that they have within their jobs. These factors are multiplied for women of color, whereby race serves as yet another variable through which discrimination and other challenges can persist. For some of the most masculine positions, such as policing and corrections, women must fight against firmly held beliefs that such jobs are inappropriate for women. While equal employment opportunity legislation has opened the doors for access for women in these traditionally male-dominated fields, women still face an uphill battle as they have been denied opportunities for opportunity and promotion throughout history. Despite these struggles, women remain an important presence in these fields with significant contributions that need to be encouraged and acknowledged, particularly for future generations of women in these fields.

Summary

- Traditional male occupations, such as policing and corrections, historically excluded employment options for women on the grounds that the work was too dangerous.
- Early policewomen were involved in crime prevention efforts, primarily with juvenile and female populations.
- While equal opportunity legislation may have opened access for women in policing and corrections, institutional cultures and standards continued to create barriers for women in these occupations for entry and advancement.
- Women in police, corrections, and community supervision use different tools and techniques in their daily experiences in their positions, compared to male officers.
- Few women have successfully navigated to the top levels of their fields in law enforcement and corrections.
- As workers in these fields, women are subjected to issues with job satisfaction, stress, and burnout.
- There are more females employed in probation than any other law enforcement or correctional environment.

KEY TERMS

Baldwin, Lola	Gendered assignments	*Jordan v. Gardner*
Blankenship, Betty	Good ol' boy network	Male inmate preference
Civil Rights Bill	*Griffin v. Michigan Department of Corrections*	Masculine culture
Coffal, Liz		Owens, Marie
Community policing	*Grummett v. Rushen*	Wells, Alice Stebbins

DISCUSSION QUESTIONS

1. Based on the research, how do women do gender within traditional male-dominated criminal justice occupations?

2. What challenges do women who work in criminal justice occupations face that their male counterparts do not?

3. What suggestions can be made to improve the status of women within criminal justice occupations?

WEB RESOURCES

American Correctional Association: http://www.aca.org

Association of Women Executives in Corrections: http://www.awec.us

National Center for Women and Policing: http://www.womenandpolicing.org

Visit **www.sagepub.com/mallicoat2e** to access additional study tools including eFlashcards, web quizzes, web resources, video resources, and SAGE journal articles.

READING 23

As you learned in the section, many women in policing experience sexual harassment on the job. As a minority in this male-dominated occupation, the source of this harassment often comes from within the department. This article by Kimberly Lonsway, Rebecca Paynich, and Jennifer Hall explores the issue of sexual harassment from a mixed methods perspective. Their research begins with a quantitative survey of a large agency and is followed with a qualitative survey with female police officers. This research highlights how sexual harassment can impact female officers both professionally and personally.

Sexual Harassment in Law Enforcement

Incidence, Impact, and Perception

Kimberly A. Lonsway, Rebecca Paynich, and Jennifer N. Hall

A considerable body of research demonstrates that sexual harassment is more common in professions that are nontraditional for women (i.e., where the majority of employees are male and the duties are traditionally defined as masculine)—as compared with fields where women are traditionally employed (Berdahl, 2007; Fitzgerald, Drasgow, Hulin, Gelfand, & Magley, 1997; Glomb, Munson, Hulin, Bergman, & Drasgow, 1999; Gruber, 1998; Mansfield et al., 1991). The present study was designed to examine the incidence, impact, and perception of sexual harassment in law enforcement utilizing a mixed methods approach and two data sources. Using both quantitative and qualitative methods, we offer a detailed picture of the phenomenon and capture some underlying factors that influence the perceptions, responses, and outcomes.

✉ Definitions of Sexual Harassment

Sexual harassment is defined by the U.S. Equal Employment Opportunity Commission (EEOC) as follows:

Unwelcome sexual advances, requests for sexual favors, and other verbal or physical conduct of a sexual nature constitute sexual harassment when this conduct explicitly or implicitly affects an individual's employment, unreasonably interferes with an individual's work performance, or creates an intimidating, hostile, or offensive work environment. (EEOC, 1980, p. 74677)

Yet the legal definition is not the only one available. Sexual harassment has also been defined empirically, based on decades of social-psychological research. For example, Fitzgerald, Swan, and Magley (1997) defined the construct as "unwanted sex-related behavior at work that is appraised by the recipient as offensive, exceeding her resources, or threatening her well-being" (p. 15). This definition was used to develop the Sexual Experiences Questionnaire (SEQ), which is "the most widely-used and validated measure of sexual harassment to date" (Cortina & Berdahl, 2008, p. 471). Items on the SEQ tap three dimensions of sexual harassment. Unwanted sexual attention includes sexually suggestive comments that are made

SOURCE: Lonsway, K. A., Paynich, R., & Hall, J. N. (2013). Sexual harassment in law enforcement: Incidence, impact, and perception. *Police Quarterly,* *16*(2), 177–210.

to or about a person as well as inappropriate touching. Gender harassment includes behaviors such as dirty jokes or stories that are told in the workplace or comments that put women down. Finally, *quid pro quo* literally translates to "this for that." The term is therefore used to describe situations where an employee is forced to submit to unwanted sexual advances as a condition of employment, either with a tangible job reward for complying or punishment for refusing.

Outcomes of Sexual Harassment

Sexual harassment has a range of well-documented negative effects on the psychological and professional well-being of victims (for a comprehensive review, please see Cortina & Berdahl, 2008). These outcomes are seen across a wide variety of workplace contexts, and they remain significant even when controlling for the experience of other stressors (e.g., general job stress, trauma outside of the workplace), other features of the job (occupational level, organizational tenure, workload), personality (negative affectivity, neuroticism, narcissism), and other demographic factors (age, educational level, race; Cortina & Berdahl, 2008, p. 477).

Not surprisingly, this negative impact is typically more severe when the sexually harassing behaviors are experienced with greater frequency (Langhout et al., 2005; Schneider, Swan, & Fitzgerald, 1997). On the other hand, it is apparently not affected by how it is labeled. Rather, the negative impact that victims experience in terms of their physical, psychological, and professional well-being appear to be the same, regardless of whether or not they identify the behavior as sexual harassment (Magley, Hulin, Fitzgerald, & DeNardo, 1999; Munson, Miner, & Hulin, 2001). This is particularly noteworthy, because most victims do not label their experience. Research estimates suggest that fewer than 20% will do so (Magley et al., 1999).

Reporting Behaviors

There is little doubt that most sexually harassing behavior remains unreported. Estimates suggest that fewer than 25% of women file a formal complaint after experiencing sexual harassment, regardless of the specific workplace context (Cochran, Frazier, & Olson, 1997; Cortina, 2004; Culbertson & Rosenfeld, 1994; Schneider et al., 1997). This is true even for women who are sexually *assaulted* by a coworker. One study of women who experienced an attempted or completed workplace rape found that only 21% filed a formal report and 19% quit (Schneider, 1991). The reasons for nonreporting of sexual harassment are numerous, and they include concern that nothing will be done or that reporting may even make the situation worse (Cortina, 2004; Fitzgerald, Swan, & Fischer, 1995; Wasti & Cortina, 2002).

Sexual Harassment in Law Enforcement

Estimates range widely for the incidence and prevalence of sexually harassing behaviors within law enforcement. On one hand, 24% of the police women in one study said that they experience a "constant atmosphere" of offensive remarks (Timmins & Hainsworth, 1989). Yet 100% of the female officers who were interviewed in a second study described experiencing at least one sexually harassing behavior during the course of their career (Haarr, 1997). Most estimates fall somewhere in between, converging on a range from 53% to 77% (Bartol, Bergen, Volckens, & Knoras, 1992; Christopher et al., 1991; Martin, 1994; Nichols, 1995; Robinson, 1993). This suggests that one half to three quarters of the American women who work in law enforcement will be subjected to some form of sexually harassing behavior in their workplace, with sexual and/or sexist remarks being the most common by far. However, most of these studies have utilized only a single item to assess the frequency of such experiences and/or explicitly asked respondents whether they have been "sexually harassed." Both of these practices are problematic. First, any single item will fail to reliably assess the full range of possible experiences with such behavior. Second, questions that explicitly ask about sexual harassment are actually assessing the labeling of these behaviors rather than their objectively defined experiences (Fitzgerald, Magley, Drasgow, & Waldo, 1999).

One exception is the study conducted by Robinson (1993) who surveyed 1,269 female police officers throughout the state of Florida and found that 61% had experienced at least one of the specific behaviors listed on the questionnaire during the last 6 months. Yet very few formally complained, either to someone within their agencies (23%) or outside (15%). One explanation may be that women in law enforcement are less likely than those in other fields to label their experiences as sexual harassment. For example, only 21% of the women in Robinson's study who had experienced one of the behaviors suggested that they had been "sexually harassed." However, little is known about the specific impact of such behavior on police officers and how it might differ by gender. In addition, very little work has sought to explore whether police officers will label such experiences as sexual harassment and, if not, what their process is for appraising such behavior. The present study was conducted to fill this void, using a mixed methods research design. As described in Brent and Kraska (2010), such a design allows for a more comprehensive understanding—in this case, by documenting the wide range of sexually harassing behaviors that women in policing have experienced and offering a rich and nuanced description of their perceptions of those experiences.

Method

Two studies were conducted to explore these issues. *Study 1* involved surveying sworn personnel within a single large law enforcement agency. The survey in *Study 2* was then conducted with a national sample of female police officers.

Study 1

Sampling procedure. The initial sample was created using the roster of 2,602 enlisted personnel within the law enforcement agency. An initial sample of 797 sworn personnel was designed to include all of the women ($n = 82$), all of the minority men ($n = 369$), and a random sample of the White men ($n = 346$). At the time of the survey administration, the agency employed only 2.7% women among their sworn personnel, which was considerably lower than the national average of 12.7% for large agencies and 8.1% for small and rural agencies (Lonsway, 2007).

An effort was also made to oversample respondents with the rank of captain or higher. This increased the initial sample size from 797 to 807. A letter from the agency head was sent to these 807 personnel, informing them of the survey's purpose and procedures. The study was described as a work environment survey, with questions to address "the challenges, rewards, and concerns" associated with their jobs and coworkers. Participants were explicitly informed that the focus was "to determine whether women and minorities experience different issues than their colleagues," and they were told that their responses would be used to guide policy reforms in this area.

Survey administration. Those with the rank of captain or above received their survey questionnaire in the mail. Sworn personnel of the rank of lieutenant or below were directed to report in groups of approximately 50 to the survey administration site at a specified date and time. On reporting to the site, they were welcomed by a member of the research team and provided a brief introduction regarding the purpose and procedure for the survey. Their rights and roles as research participants were then described, and they were reminded that the survey effort was conducted to assist in improving the working conditions at the agency.

Final response rate. Usable surveys were returned from 69 of the 82 women, 293 of the 369 minority men, 301 of the 346 randomly sampled White men, and 16 respondents who did not indicate their gender and/or racial identification. An agency report identified a number of reasons for nonparticipation by the remainder of the sample, which included required court appearances, vacation days, training, emergency responsibilities at the duty station, and extended sick leave. The following survey results are therefore based on the 679 usable surveys returned from the original sample of 807 individuals invited to participate. This represents an excellent response rate of 84.1%.

Sample demographics. Of the 679 officers completing a usable survey questionnaire, 69 (10.2%) were women, 607 (89.4%) were men, and 3 (0.4%) did not indicate their gender. Their breakdown by racial/ethnic identification was 53.8% European American/White, 24.3% African American/Black, 11.5% Hispanic, and 10.5% who indicated another category or provided no response to the question.

Respondents ranged in age from 24 to 54, with an average of 38.8. They reported being with the agency for an average of 14.1 years (with a range from 2 to 32 years) and in their current assignments for an average of 5.7 years (with a range from 1 to 29 years). All but 5 of the 679 survey respondents provided information on their rank. Of these, most were either in line operations (e.g., patrol) or detectives (62.4%), with an additional 30.3% who were sergeants, 5.0% lieutenants, and 2.2% with the rank of captain, major, or above.

Survey instrument. After providing background information, respondents in *Study 1* were asked to complete a number of measures tapping *Work Attitudes and Behaviors, Health and Well-Being,* and *Individual Tolerance of Sexual Harassment.* Measures were selected based on their well-established psychometric properties and prior association with sexual harassment.

Work attitudes and behaviors. Briefly, *Work Withdrawal* and *Job Withdrawal* were assessed with scales developed by Hanisch and Hulin (1990). An abbreviated version of the Job Descriptive Index (originally developed by Smith, Kendall, & Hulin, 1969 and revised by Roznowski, 1989) was used to measure satisfaction with various aspects of the job: *work, coworkers, and supervisors. Job Stress* was then evaluated using a shortened version of the Stress in General Scale (Stanton, Balzer, Smith, Parra, & Ironson, 2001). For both the Job Descriptive Index and Job Stress Scale, several new items were developed for the present study and added to address unique aspects of the law enforcement context. (For more information, see Lonsway, 2007.)

Health and well-being. Next, respondents were asked to complete two measures of their physical and psychological well-being. First was the Satisfaction With Life Scale (Diener, Emmons, Larsen, & Griffin, 1985). Second was the Brief Symptom Inventory (Derogatis, & Spencer, 1983), which taps *depression, anxiety,* and *physical somatization* (i.e., symptoms).

Experiences. Respondents were also asked about the frequency of their experiences (within the past year) of 16 behaviors drawn from the Sexual Experiences Questionnaire (SEQ). This measure was originally developed by Fitzgerald, Drasgow, Hulin, and Gelfand (1993) and revised for use in the present study. Responses were provided on a frequency scale ranging from *never* to *most of the time.* For each respondent, scores were computed for the three SEQ subscales: *unwanted sexual attention, quid pro quo sexual harassment,* and *gender harassment.*

For each individual behavior, respondents were then asked to indicate who perpetrated the behavior: a "coworker," "supervisor," "command staff," or "other." They were also asked whether the behavior was reported to a supervisor or command staff. Options were *not reported, discussed informally,* or *filed a formal complaint.* As a follow-up question, respondents were asked whether they had filed a formal complaint and, if so, whether they experienced retaliation. If they had not filed a formal complaint, they were asked to indicate their reasons.

Labeling. Although SEQ items were written in purely behavioral terms, a question in both studies asked respondents whether they had been "sexually harassed" to determine whether they labeled any situation as such. For a more detailed description of the method and measures used in *Study 1*, please see Lonsway (2007).

Study 2

Sampling procedure. For *Study 2*, a systematic random selection design was employed to identify a national sample of female officers. First, a list of law enforcement agencies was drawn from the *National Directory of Law Enforcement Administrators, Correctional Institutions, and Related Agencies* published by the Public Safety Information Bureau (2002). The number 30 was then randomly chosen from a table, and every 30th agency on the list was selected to receive surveys for their female officers. Agencies were contacted to determine the actual number of female officers they employed and to gain permission from the person in the agency with authority to grant it. Once permission was granted, surveys were sent to a contact person within the agency for distribution to all their female officers.

On nearing the end of the listed agencies, it was discovered that the target sampling frame of 2,000 female officers was not going to be met for the sample. This happened both because some agencies employed few (or no) female officers (often because they were small agencies) and/or because they denied permission to send the surveys. Therefore, a new random number was selected (29) and contacts were made with every 29th agency listed in the directory until the target number of 2,000 female officers was met.

Survey administration and response rate. Surveys were mailed to sampled female officers, and they were returned using a preaddressed, postage paid envelope that was included with the mailed survey. Approximately 2,000 surveys were mailed out, and 531 were returned. This represents a final response rate of approximately 26.6% from the sample of female officers who were identified. For a more detailed description of the method and measures used in *Study 2*, please see Seklecki and Paynich (2007).

Sample demographics. All respondents in *Study 2* were female. Most were White (75.0%), with the remaining 14.3% African American, 6.4% Hispanic, 0.6% Native American, and 1.7% representing other racial/ethnic groups. Only 11 respondents failed to indicate their racial/ethnic identification.

Most women indicated that they were line officers (69.3%), although 16.0% held the rank of sergeant, and approximately 3% had achieved the position of chief or other equivalent rank. Respondents typically worked for a municipal police department (73.6%) or sheriff's office (24.7%). Only two respondents worked for a state police agency and one for a campus agency.

On average, respondents had been employed in law enforcement for 11.25 years, and they had held their current rank for 5.35 years. The average number of sworn officers in their agencies was around 489 (with a median of 120), and the average population served was about 254,057 (with a median of 70,000). The most common assignment for survey respondents was patrol (55.4%) and the next most frequent was investigations (20.7%). The rest of the survey respondents were divided between several other assignments within their agencies.

Survey instrument

Background information. As in *Study 1*, the female officers responding to the survey in *Study 2* were first asked to provide some background information and beliefs and attitudes regarding their employment.

Experiences. Respondents were also asked to indicate how frequently they experienced 15 behaviors during the course of their career in law enforcement. As in *Study 1*, these items were drawn from the SEQ but slightly revised for the present study. Response options included *never*, *once or twice*, and *three or more times*. They were then asked to provide more detailed information about their

experiences with each of the behaviors: "Please describe the situation in more detail (who was involved, did you file a complaint, if so, what was the outcome of the complaint . . .)." Narrative responses were submitted to a process of thematic coding to identify patterns. (For more detailed information about the methods and measures used in *Study 2*, please see Seklecki & Paynich, 2007.)

Thematic coding. To conduct the qualitative research, the research team began by examining the data and identifying themes that appeared to best represent narrative responses. Through collaborative interaction, final coding categories were clarified by adding, removing, or modifying these thematic descriptors. Two independent raters then coded responses for two of the 15 SEQ items, and their initial agreement was calculated (84.6% for one item and 87.4% for the other). Next, they engaged in a process of discussion and debate to clarify the category definitions and recoded the responses that produced initial disagreements. Their level of agreement was recalculated, and it increased to 91.6% and 94.0%.

The raters then coded responses to four additional SEQ items and engaged in the same process of calculating initial level of agreement, clarifying the category definitions, and recoding responses with disagreements. As a result, the final level of agreement for these four items ranged from 91.6% to 100%. The coding definitions were thus finalized, and the raters independently coded the remaining SEQ items. Final agreement levels ranged from 91.6% to 100% for the 15 items, with an average of 96.65%.

Results

Incidence of Behaviors

Overall, 83.5% of the sample in *Study 1* indicated that they had experienced at least one of the behaviors on the SEQ during the past year. This included 82.6% of the men and 92.5% of the women. In *Study 2*, an even higher percentage (93.8%) of the female officers indicated that they experienced at least one of the behaviors during the course of their law enforcement career. Reading Table 23.1 summarizes the percentage of respondents in both studies who experienced each behavior at least once. Please note that for *Study 1*, respondents were only asked about their experiences during the last year. For *Study 2*, it was during the

Reading Table 23.1 Incidence of Behaviors, Most Common Perpetrators, and Percentage of Behaviors Reported

	Percentage Experiencing Behavior at Least Once				Most Common Perpetrators (Study I)	Percentage Filing a Formal Complaint (Study I)
	Study 1: During the Past Year			Study 2: During Law Enforcement Career		
	Overall ($n = 679$)	Men ($n = 607$)	Women ($n = 69$)	Women ($n = 531$)		
Experienced at least one behavior (any SEQ item)	83.5	82.6*	92.5*	93.8		
Unwanted Sexual Attention (SEQ subscale)	21.2	18.2***	48.5***	74.0		
Make sexually suggestive remarks to or about you?[b]	19.0	16.1***	44.9***	71.5	Coworker	0.0
Try to have a romantic or sexual relationship with you even though you tried to let the person know you didn't want to?	2.1	1.2***[a]	10.3***[a]	34.5	Coworker	0.0
Keep on asking you out even after you have said "no?" (*Study 1* only)	1.9	1.5**[a]	5.8**[a]	N/A	Coworker	0.0
Touch you in a way that made you uncomfortable?	1.8	1.2***[a]	7.2***[a]	21.7	Supervisor	8.3
Make forceful attempts to have sex with you?	0.9	1.0[a]	0.0[a]	3.3	Coworker	0.0
Give you any sexual attention that you did not want? (*Study 1* only)	1.3	0.7***[a]	7.2***[a]	N/A	Coworker	0.0
Quid Pro Quo Sexual Harassment (SEQ subscale)	2.5	2.3[a]	4.3[a]	15.2		
Hint that you might get some reward for doing something sexual?	0.9	0.8[a]	1.4[a]	10.2	Coworker	20.0

| | Percentage Experiencing Behavior at Least Once | | | | Most Common Perpetrators (Study I) | Percentage Filing a Formal Complaint (Study I) |
| | Study 1: During the Past Year | | | Study 2: During Law Enforcement Career | | |
	Overall (n – 679)	Men (n – 607)	Women (n – 69)	Women (n – 531)		
Hint at a job benefit of some kind if you were sexual with him or her?	0.3	0.2[a]	1.4[a]	7.1	Coworker	0.0
Make you do something social in order to be better treated on the job? (*Study 1*); Make you do something social (e.g., spend time with him or her) to be treated well on the job (*Study 2*)	1.3	1.3[a]	1.4[a]	5.7	Coworker	0.0
Make you afraid that you would be treated poorly if you didn't do something sexual?	0.4	0.5[a]	0.0[a]	3.4	Supervisor/ coworker	33.3
Treat you badly for refusing to have sex?	0.6	0.5[a]	1.4[a]	3.1	Supervisor	0.0
Gender Harassment (SEQ subscale)	83.2	82.4	91.2	91.3		
Tell dirty stories or jokes? (*Study 1*); Tell inappropriate dirty stories or jokes (*Study 2*)	81.5	80.6	89.7	85.6	Coworker	0.2
Show, use, or hand out dirty pictures or stories (e.g., pornography)?	21.0	22.0	13.0	33.3	Coworker	0.0
Say things to put women down (e.g., saying that women don't make good supervisors)?	30.1	29.1*	40.6*	58.3	Coworker	1.1
Make crude or obscene gestures? (*Study 1 only*)	20.9	21.8	14.5	N/A	Coworker	1.6

(Continued)

Reading Table 23.1 (Continued)

	Percentage Experiencing Behavior at Least Once				Most Common Perpetrators (Study I)	Percentage Filing a Formal Complaint (Study I)
	Study 1: During the Past Year			Study 2: During Law Enforcement Career		
	Overall (n = 679)	Men (n = 607)	Women (n = 69)	Women (n = 531)		
Insult you by calling you a homosexual (e.g., "dyke," "fag," "queer")?[c]	1.9	1.7[a]	4.3[a]	10.7	Coworker	0.0
Sexually harass you?	0.8	0.2***[a]	5.9***[a]	27.2	Coworker	12.5

*Chi-square test of gender difference significant at the level of $p < .05$. **Chi-square test of gender difference significant at the level of $p < .01$. ***Chi-square test of gender difference significant at the level of $p < .001$.

[a]At least one cell had an expected count of less than 5.

[b]In *Study 2* there was one question that asked "to you" and one that asked "about you." They were combined for the purpose of this table.

[c]In *Study 2*, this question specifically asked whether "colleagues" insulted the respondent.

course of their law enforcement career. Thus, it makes sense that the percentage in *Study 2* is higher than in *Study 1*. Reading Table 23.1 also includes the most common perpetrator for each behavior and the percentage of respondents who filed a formal complaint (from *Study 1*).

The Appendix presents descriptive statistics for all quantitative measures, and it therefore offers another view of the frequency of SEQ behaviors. Overall, the mean score of 19.2 on the 16-item SEQ suggests that behaviors were not experienced very often in the past year, with an average item frequency only slightly higher than *never* (1.2). The average item-level score for two of the three subscales was similarly low: 1.1 for unwanted sexual attention, 1.0 for quid pro quo harassment. Only gender harassment was experienced more frequently, with an average item score of 1.5, suggesting a frequency between *once or twice* and *sometimes* in the past year.

Most Frequent Behaviors

As Reading Table 23.1 reveals, a few behaviors were experienced more frequently than others, by respondents in

both samples. Most of these behaviors constituted gender harassment or unwanted sexual attention that was verbal in nature. For example, more than three quarters of the sworn personnel in both studies had heard "dirty stories or jokes" in the workplace during the past year. Other common behaviors in both studies were statements that "put women down," exposure to "dirty pictures or stories (e.g., pornography)," and "sexually suggestive remarks." In *Study 1*, another common behavior was "crude and obscene gestures" (this behavior was not included in *Study 2*). For participants in *Study 1*, these five most common behaviors were all typically committed by a coworker, and they were very rarely reported. The percentage of such behaviors that resulted in a formal complaint ranged from zero to a high of 1.6% (for "crude and obscene gestures").

Unwanted sexual attention that was physical in nature and quid pro quo sexual harassment were experienced less frequently by respondents in both studies. However, they were more likely to be committed by a supervisor and more likely to be reported. As revealed in *Study 1*, the percentage of these behaviors resulting in a formal complaint ranged from zero to 8.3% for unwanted physical touching and

33.3% for quid pro quo behaviors (fear of being treated badly for not engaging in sexual behavior). Almost 1% of the respondents in *Study 1* and more than 3% of the women in *Study 2* indicated that they had experienced forceful attempts to have sex with them. In *Study 1*, all of these respondents were men.

Labeling Sexual Harassment

Only five respondents in *Study 1* (0.7% of the sample) said they had been "sexually harassed" during the past year (four women and one man). In *Study 2*, however, as many as 27.2% of the female officers said they had been "sexually harassed" during their career.

Study 1: Quantitative Analyses

Gender comparisons. Next, gender comparisons were conducted with the three SEQ subscales in *Study 1*, using a Bonferroni correction to control for accumulated error rate ($\alpha = .02$). The only significant effect was found for unwanted sexual attention, $t(74.40) = 3.62$ (equal variances not assumed), $p < .001$.[1] Mean scores suggested that the effect was due to a greater frequency of behaviors being experienced by women as compared to men. Cohen's (1977) d-statistic was computed as .53, suggesting a moderate effect size.[2] No gender differences were seen for the SEQ subscales tapping gender harassment or quid pro quo sexual harassment.

Outcome measures. *Study 1* responses were also examined to explore whether behaviors on the SEQ had an impact on a range of personal and professional outcomes (specifically, the 10 measures described in the Appendix under *Work Attitudes and Behaviors* as well as *Health and Well-Being*). A series of regression equations were run with two predictor variables: the number of years that respondents had worked for their agencies (i.e., tenure) and their current rank.[3] These two variables were first tested alone; then, a total score on the SEQ was added to determine whether it accounted for unique variance in each of the outcomes. A Bonferroni correction was again used for the 10 outcome variables, so alpha was set at .005. Results are presented in Reading Table 23.2, and they reveal that SEQ total scores explained unique variance for every single one of these 10 outcome measures—even when controlling for the

variables of tenure and rank ($p < .005$). Across the 10 outcome measures, R^2 for the original model (with only tenure and rank) ranged from less than .01 to .05. The change in R^2 for this step then ranged from .02 to .06, so the models with SEQ scores predicted a total of 3% to 8% of the variance in the 10 outcome measures.

Reporting and retaliation. Respondents in *Study 1* were next asked to select from a range of options indicating whether they had ever filed a formal complaint in their agency and whether they experienced retaliation as a result. As seen in Reading Table 23.3, most (89.0%) had never filed such a formal complaint. Only 5.3% of the sample indicated that they had "filed at least one formal complaint, but never experienced retaliation as a result." Smaller percentages said they had experienced retaliation as a result of filing a complaint for sexual harassment, sex discrimination other than sexual harassment, race discrimination, or some behavior other than race or sex discrimination. In other words, almost half (47.8%) of those who had filed a formal complaint for any such behavior stated that they had experienced retaliation as a result. Interestingly, only female respondents experienced retaliation after reporting sex discrimination, and only male respondents experienced retaliation after reporting race discrimination.

Reasons for not reporting. As seen in Reading Table 23.1, very few *Study 1* respondents reported any of the behaviors included on the SEQ using a formal complaint process. They were therefore provided with the following prompt: "If you decided NOT to file a formal complaint in any of the situations described above, please indicate your reasons for not doing so."

By far, the most common response to this question was that the "situation was not serious enough to warrant a formal complaint"; this option was endorsed by 49.2% of the sample. Other common responses included "concern about the impact of reporting on my career," concern that "nothing would be done if a complaint were filed," "fear of retaliation by supervisors and/or coworkers," "concern regarding the reaction of supervisors and/or coworkers," and "similar situations have been reported and no action was taken." Reading Table 23.3 shows the gender differences for these responses. For example, women were more likely than men to indicate that they did not report because of "fear of retaliation" or "concern

Reading Table 23.2 Regression Analyses Predicting Personal and Professional Outcomes (*Study 1*)

Variable/Model	Work Withdrawal			Job Withdrawal			Life Satisfaction			Work Satisfaction			Supervisor Satisfaction			Coworker Satisfaction		
	β	R^2	ΔR^2	β	R^2	ΔR^2	β	R^2	ΔR^2	β	R^2	ΔR^2	β	R^2	ΔR^2	β	R^2	ΔR^2
Step 1:		.046***			.025***			.027***			.036***			.018***			.021***	
Tenure	.338*			.242***			−.262***			−.281*			−.214*			−.185***		
Rank	−.275***			−.148*			.194***			.285**			.172*			.232***		
Step 2:		.087***	.041***		.053***	.029***		.049***	.022***		.058***	.022***		.047***	.029***		.071***	.049***
Tenure	.331***			.238***			−.258***			−.277***			−.209***			−.184***		
Rank	−.224***			−.106			.155*			.245***			.128*			.177***		
SEQ	.208***			.173***			−.152***			−.154***			−.174***			−.228***		

Variable/Model	Job Stress			Depression			Anxiety			Physical Somatization		
	β	R^2	ΔR^2	β	R^2	ΔR^2	β	R^2	ΔR^2	β	R^2	ΔR^2
Step 1:		.022***			.011*			.009			.005	
Tenure	.100			.155*			.052			.104		
Rank	.057			−.076			.051			−.101		
Step 2:		.043***	.021***		.027***	.016***		.026***	.016***		.020***	.016***
Tenure	.098			.152*			.049			.101		
Rank	.092			−.044			.083			−.069		
SEQ	.149*			.130***			.131***			.128***		

*$p < .05$. **$p < .01$. ***$p < .005$.

Reading Table 23.3   Reporting and Retaliation (*Study 1*)

	Men (*n* = 607)	Women (*n* = 69)	Total (*n* = 679)
Experienced retaliation as a result of filing a formal complaint			
Never filed a formal complaint	89.3%	85.5%	89.0%
Filed at least one complaint but never experienced retaliation	5.1%	7.2%	5.3%
Experienced retaliation for complaint of sexual harassment	0.2%***	2.9%***	0.4%
Experienced retaliation for complaint of sex discrimination	0.0%***	2.9%***	0.3%
Experienced retaliation for complaint of race discrimination	3.13%	0.0%	2.8%
Experienced retaliation for other complaint	1.5%	0.0%	1.3%
Reasons for not reporting			
Situation was not serious enough	48.9%	50.7%	49.2%
Concern about impact on career	15.7%	23.2%	16.3%
Nothing would be done	15.0%	15.9%	15.2%
Fear of retaliation	13.9%	21.7%	14.6%
Concern about reaction of supervisor/ coworkers	12.7%***	27.5%***	14.1%
No action taken in past	11.0%	15.9%	11.5%
Unfamiliar with reporting procedures	4.5%	5.8%	4.6%
Concern about being fired	1.8%	1.4%	1.8%
Afraid of other person involved	0.8%**	4.3%**	1.2%
Other	9.4%*	18.8%*	10.5%

NOTE: All tests had at least one cell with an expected count of less than 5.

*Chi-square test of gender difference significant at the level of $p < .05$. **Chi-square test of gender difference significant at the level of $p < .01$. ***Chi-square test of gender difference significant at the level of $p < .001$.

regarding the reaction of supervisors and/or coworkers." A smaller percentage of respondents indicated that they were unfamiliar with reporting procedures, they were concerned about being fired because of their probationary employment status, or they were afraid of the person involved in the situation.

Study 1 respondents were also given space in which to write their "other" reasons for not filing a report. By far,

most of these open-ended comments indicated that the situation was either not a problem or something that respondents felt they should handle personally. Many emphasized that the incidents were "just joking," "not hostile," and "all in fun." However, others were concerned that nothing would be done or [that] they wouldn't be able to take the matter further. One respondent stated that the situations were "just part of the job—deal with it," and another suggested that "some things aren't believed." Finally, one man stated that the experience made him a "better officer." Similar themes were echoed in the qualitative data from *Study 2*.

Study 2: Thematic Coding

Study 2 respondents were asked to provide narrative responses describing their experiences with behaviors that were drawn from the SEQ. Responses were categorized based on their SEQ subscale and then assigned codes to capture the response strategies officers used as well as outcomes.

Gender harassment. As previously noted, gender harassment was the type of SEQ behavior that was most commonly experienced by the female officers in *Study 2*. The vast majority (91.3%) indicated they had experienced at least one behavior in this category during the course of their career. Responses in this category were also assigned 1,260 of the 2,544 thematic codes in the *Study 2* analysis (49.6%)—the most codes for any of the SEQ subscales.

In this category, women described incidents where "dirty jokes or stories" were told, pornography was displayed, statements were made to put down women, and respondents were insulted based on their gender or sexual orientation. Respondents also described situations where coworkers questioned their sexual orientation, spread rumors that they were lesbian, or called them derogatory names referring to their (supposed) homosexual orientation. Some noted that this happened after declining romantic offers from coworkers. Others described hearing comments that women do not belong in law enforcement. For example, one woman recalled having a captain who always said, "Why don't you go home and be a normal woman barefoot and pregnant in the kitchen?"

Several women indicated that this type of behavior occurred during *roll call*, the beginning of each shift where officers are oriented and given assignments and information they will need for the day. This is significant, because roll call will almost always be attended by a supervisor (typically the sergeant in charge of the unit/shift).

> Roll call seemed to be the time that this activity took place. Everything from officers exposing their genitalia to bringing sex aid objects to roll call . . .

With respect to gender harassment, some respondents emphasized that women participate in this behavior as well as men and/or stated that they had personally engaged in such behavior.

Unwanted sexual attention. The second most common type of behavior was in the category of unwanted sexual attention. Almost three quarters of the female officers (74.0%) indicated they had experienced at least one behavior in this category during the course of their law enforcement career. Responses in this category were assigned 1,151 of the 2,544 thematic codes (45.2%). Within this category, respondents described situations where someone made sexually suggestive remarks to or about them. Several described this type of behavior as very common.

> I was the undercover officer for a high profile prostitution escort service. An Assistant Chief and Lieutenant said "I'd pay to fuck that." Over 20 years the number of times is too long to list. I have never filed a complaint.

> Co-workers and supervisors alike elude [*sic*] to sexual situations or jokes [on a] nearly daily basis. I would not file a complaint and typically am not offended—if you do complain this would make you an outcast/untouchable.

Several officers also mentioned that they received unwanted sexual attention from citizens, including *drunks and male citizens who get too close as if they are my friend.*

As with gender harassment, some noted that women, as well as men, engage in this behavior.

> Believe it or not most female officers are more sexually suggestive towards men than men are towards females (in the police setting).

This category also included situations where someone tried to establish a romantic or sexual relationship with the respondent or touched them in a way that made them uncomfortable. This often included grabbing women's breast or buttocks, patting them on the buttocks, or rubbing their shoulders to give them an unwanted "massage." Some examples were particularly disturbing, with behaviors that constituted attempted or completed sexual assault.

My Lieutenant slapped me across my ass after he told me that he likes women on their knees in front of him. I was mad. Everybody in the P.D. knew what happened, but no one said a thing.

[I] was drunk at a party and if it wasn't for fellow officers I would have been raped by a supervisor.

On the other hand, some women stated that they liked the sexual attention at work.

Sometimes it is the normal part of male/female relationships. . . . That's how I met my husband (also a police officer) it was welcome then! Now that I'm old (53) no one ever makes remarks like that anymore! How sad.

Quid pro quo sexual harassment. While quid pro quo situations may be the most widely recognized form of sexual harassment, they were the least commonly experienced by female officers participating in *Study 2.* Responses in this category were assigned 102 of the 2,544 thematic codes (4.9%), and 15.2% of *Study 2* respondents indicated that they had experienced this type of behavior during the course of their law enforcement career. Those who did went on to describe situations where someone tried to coerce them into engaging in sexual behavior hinted that they might get a reward for such behavior or made them feel afraid they would be treated badly for not complying.

Once a Captain told me that my life could be real simple or it can be quite difficult and grabbed my breast when he shut the door (closing me in his office) I walked out and my career has been HELL.

In another situation, a female officer indicated that she had applied to teach in the police academy and was told by the person in charge, *If you give me some head, I will give you the position.*

Perhaps not surprisingly, these behaviors appeared to be more likely to involve a supervisor, rather than a peer, subordinate, or someone else (e.g., citizen, suspect).

They also appeared to be more likely to involve a male perpetrator, rather than a woman.

Response Strategies

The women then went on to describe how they responded to such situations. Across all three categories of behavior, the most frequent response was "no complaint filed" (47.6%). While *Study 2* respondents were not required to provide a reason why they did not file a complaint, some indicated that they did not believe it would be productive.

Making a complaint to the Chief or Assistant Chief would do absolutely no good (I know from prior experience).

Others did not report because they were afraid of retaliation (5.9%). For example, one female officer described her concerns about reporting dirty stories and jokes:

I hear this a lot being the only female detective. Some make me feel uncomfortable but I just laugh it off. I am afraid to make a complaint because it would be worse for me. This is still a good old boys department.

Another described similar fears in a more serious situation involving physical assault.

A Captain that was well known for this. He physically assaulted me my first year in law enforcement. I spoke with several people. I decided I wanted to continue working in law enforcement. I would have been labeled if I had complained.

A third officer described fears that kept her from reporting the sexually suggestive comments made at her agency:

Fear of "black sheep" status, fear of retribution, and the possibility of not getting promoted if [it] caused internal conflict.

The second most common theme across the three categories of behavior was that respondents considered it to be "no big deal" (21.3%). Rather, they frequently described sexually suggestive comments, pictures, and stories as "just joking" or "part of the job."

This is the world of law enforcement, it's not for the weak at heart or the prudence of a princess.

Others seemed to characterize this behavior as inevitable in a workplace with mostly men. In fact, many women felt a need to participate in such behavior (especially "dirty jokes or stories"), to be accepted within their law enforcement agencies.

Dark humor, dirty humor, are part of police work. A woman entering police work needs to recognize that and accept it if they wish to be accepted by male peers.

A few even appeared to enjoy the attention that can sometimes accompany this behavior.

A coworker showed me a picture in playboy and said he thought I looked like her. He didn't mean it as derogatory and I didn't take it that way.

However, respondents appeared to be less likely to view a behavior as "no big deal" if it involved statements that put women down or physical touching (rather than jokes or stories).

The third most common strategy was for respondents to handle the situation on their own (15.5%), usually by talking to the person themselves and sometimes enlisting the help of peers.

The officer started to put his hands places he shouldn't. I told him to "knock it off." He did.

Another common theme was the use of humor. For example, in response to a pornographic image shown by a coworker, one woman responded, It looks like a penis—only smaller. Another reportedly told [a] coworker [that if] his own wife didn't want anything to do with him, why should I?

Sometimes, however, women handled the situation using more dramatic and/or physical actions. This appeared to be more likely in response to more severe behaviors.

An officer drove me behind a building and attempted to unbutton my shirt. I threatened to shoot him. No complaint filed.

A road officer who was continuously asking to have sex and grabbing me. I told him to stop several times and finally kneed him in the crotch. It didn't happen again. He is no longer with this department. Also, other officers physically threatened him if he continued.

When I was a rookie officer, a male officer approached me in the parking lot and tried to kiss me. I had to physically restrain him and threaten to file a complaint.

Differences in common response patterns. While these general responses were most common across the three categories of behavior, some variation was also seen. For example, respondents appeared to be less likely to view quid pro quo behavior as "no big deal" or see it as "part of the job." The percentage of codes for "no big deal" was only 8.8% for *quid pro quo sexual harassment* versus 18.8% for *unwanted sexual attention* and 24.5% for *gender harassment*. Similarly, respondents appeared to be more likely to file a formal complaint for *quid pro quo sexual harassment* than *unwanted sexual attention* or *gender harassment*. The percentages were 10.8% versus 5.4% or 3.0%, respectively. They may also have been more likely to handle a situation themselves if it involved *unwanted sexual attention* or *quid pro quo sexual harassment,* rather than *gender harassment* (19.6% and 18.6%, vs. 11.8%).

Less frequent responses. Taken together, 6.6% of codes across all three categories of behavior suggested that an officer either reported the situation informally to a supervisor or filed a formal complaint. In some situations, this did not lead to any satisfactory resolution.

A supervisor consistently made sexually explicit remarks. I filed a complaint and was told by the city administrator that I would never get promoted if I followed through. I dropped the complaint. The supervisor was later fired for sexual harassment of another female employee.

In fact, some women described how a negative response to one complaint deterred them from filing another when similar behavior was experienced again—even if took place in another agency. For example, one officer described two situations where a coworker tried to establish a romantic or sexual relationship that was unwanted:

> Both were Sergeants. First time (he was married) a complaint was filed—nothing done. It was suggested to me that I not file a complaint. Second, I just started with a new agency and there was no way I would.

In other situations, the complaint process appeared to successfully resolve the situation. In fact, at least one officer described how the complaint may have even deterred others from engaging in similar behavior in the future:

> Filed a complaint in my first year in law enforcement. Being the new girl in a district brings on a lot of unwanted attention from other male officers. Since then I have had no problems but the reputation follows me that I will make a complaint so I think people watch what they do and say.

The remaining codes were divided between several response strategies. For example, 5.7% of the responses suggested that the officer simply tried to ignore or tolerate the situation. As one wrote, "I will tolerate it rather than subject myself to the stigma of being a female who filed (cried) sexual harassment." The remaining 2.7% of responses indicated that the officer chose to walk away from the situation, avoid the person or people involved, refuse to participate in the behavior, or talk to someone else about the incident. Less than 1% of the codes suggested that respondents filed a lawsuit or quit their jobs. Some of these individuals moved to another agency, while others left the field of law enforcement entirely.

> A cop (another department) broke into my apartment and went through my things—they categorize this as sexual harassment. Guy was fired, rehired, put on my shift, I sued (hostile work environment). Left department—the guy remained employed.

Outcomes. Finally, participants described the outcome of the situation. Across all three categories of behavior, the most common theme was that the behavior stopped (42.8%). However, the second most common theme was that they experienced retaliation (12.9%).

> A coworker called me a "stupid bitch" [on] several occasions. I eventually had to file a written complaint. The male officer was given a transfer to a "preferred" unit while I was sent back to routine patrol. This was even though the complaint was determined "founded" by our supervisor. In short, I was punished and he was rewarded.

In fact, many officers described situations where the original behavior stopped as a result of their response, but they experienced retaliation nonetheless. As one woman described, the behavior stopped after filing a complaint, but she was *still paying for it*. Retaliation appeared to be particularly common in situations involving *quid pro quo sexual harassment* rather than other types of behavior (38.7% vs. 11.3% for *unwanted sexual attention* and 10.6% for *gender harassment*). To illustrate, one officer recalled that after filing a complaint with the Equal Employment Opportunity Commission (EEOC), *No action [was] taken, [and] they recommended I go somewhere else to work.* Another recounted,

> [A] Sergeant would make comments about how good I looked. He would try and talk to me about the problems he was having with his wife. I would tell him I am not the one he should talk to about this. He would then hold me back in the roll call room after others left to discuss my reports. He would lean over me or sit close, constantly touching my arms, shoulders, etc. I would move away or tell him to stop, I'm uncomfortable. He would retaliate by criticizing my reports or judgment.

The third most common outcome across all three categories of behavior was that the person involved was reprimanded (12.7%). Some officers said that this resolved the situation.

> A supervisor made some remarks that could be taken as off color about another female officer. A complaint was filed and the supervisor was reprimanded. This situation took place more than

once with different supervisors and female officers and the outcome was the same.

However, others noted that they experienced retaliation as a result. To illustrate, one woman described a situation where a fellow officer tried to establish a romantic relationship with her.

> [I] went to a female officer (Sgt) for advice. I was ordered to file another written complaint. He was verbally reprimanded. I got no support, was talked about. Back-up on calls slow. I was transferred to CP [community policing].

The fourth most common outcome was that nothing happened at all (11.6%). As in other situations, the officer may have experienced retaliation despite the lack of disciplinary response to her complaint.

> Scantily clad pictures/posters of females [were] hanging in roll call rooms. [I] complained. I was laughed at. [The] pictures remain. "Other females don't care" was what I was told. I give up.

In a smaller percentage of responses, officers noted that the person involved in the behavior was either fired, demoted, moved, transferred, resigned, or retired (7.1% of codes).

> An instructor at an academy repeatedly asked me "how I like it" while motioning his fingers; in front of a classroom of all male officers. I filed a complaint—(along with other male officers)—and the instructor lost his certification as an instructor.

As in other responses, this does not necessarily mean that the situation was completely resolved. One officer described a situation where an instructor showed pornographic images in class. A complaint was filed and the instructor was dismissed. However, the man in charge of the program told her, *If I had a class full of men, there wouldn't have been a complaint.*

Of the remaining codes, 6.2% involved situations where the person involved in the behavior apologized to the respondent, and 5.8% were handled by someone other than the respondent (e.g., coworker). One officer recounted the following situation:

> A supervisor made a remark about my breasts and I informed if it did not stop a formal complaint would be filed. The supervisor apologized and the remarks stopped.

Less than 1% of the codes involved a lawsuit being settled and/or the person involved in the behavior receiving counseling or being arrested.

Labeling. As previously indicated, about one quarter of the female officers (27.2%) in *Study 2* indicated that they had been "sexually harassed" at some point during their law enforcement career. As one woman said,

> Using the legal definition of sexual harassment the situations I have previously described are sexual harassment. I did not file a complaint in any of the incidents.

Therefore, most did not characterize the SEQ behaviors they had personally experienced as sexual harassment. In fact, many respondents appeared to contrast their experiences with a narrow definition for sexual harassment, for example, by including only quid pro quo situations in their conceptualization or focusing on other forms of discrimination.

> I wouldn't say I was "sexually harassed" because no threats or promises were ever made.

> I define sexual harassment probably in a different sphere, I see it when blatant preference is shown to a male.

> Sexual harassment must be an unwelcome remark, etc. In that regard I have always been able to take a joke and can give it right back. Ask me about discrimination! That's another story.

⊠ Discussion

The present study makes a number of contributions to the existing literature on sexual harassment, particularly with respect to law enforcement. First, *Study 1* and *2* both document a high incidence of behaviors that could potentially be sexually harassing even in comparison with other studies in policing and fields that are nontraditional for women. This difference may be due to the increased methodological rigor with which these behaviors were measured in comparison with past efforts. In both of our studies, we used a modified version of the Sexual Experiences Questionnaire (SEQ), which is the most well-established measure for this purpose.

Higher rates were seen in *Study 1* than *Study 2,* which could be due to differences in the representation of women in the agencies involved in the two studies. As previously noted, the agency involved in *Study 1* had a particularly low representation of women. The divergence could also be related to differences in organizational culture and practices, selectivity bias, or a host of other factors that could have varied between the agencies and officers participating in *Study 1* versus *2*. Perhaps a more likely explanation is found, however, in the different time frames used for describing behaviors in the two studies. *Study 2* asked respondents to describe experiences throughout the course of their entire law enforcement career, whereas *Study 1* asked only about the past year.

Experiences, Reporting, and Retaliation

The results also provide a detailed picture of the types of behaviors that were experienced by survey participants and their strategies for responding. Many of the findings replicate prior research, regarding the relative frequency of various types of behavior, the most common perpetrator of each type, the fact that very few behaviors were reported, the reasons that respondents gave for not reporting them, and the frequency with which respondents experienced retaliation as a result of their response.

For example, both studies document that the most frequent behaviors were found on the gender harassment subscale of the SEQ, including comments and behavior that are sexualized in nature even if they are not targeted toward sexual engagement with a particular individual. This is consistent with recent work demonstrating that women in nontraditional fields are more likely to face gender harassment without the purpose of sexual engagement, rather than targeted sexual behavior such as unwanted sexual attention or quid pro quo sexual harassment

(Leskinen, Cortina, & Kabat, 2011). Analyzing responses from women in the military and federal legal practice, these researchers documented that "nine out of every ten victims had experienced primarily gender harassment, with virtually no unwanted sexual overtures" (p. 25). Such dramatic differences were not seen in our data, but the results of both our studies support their contention that the purpose of such behavior has more to do with gender and power, rather than sexual engagement with a particular individual:

> This conduct is not about misguided attempts to draw women into sexual relationships; quite the contrary, it rejects women and attempts to drive them out of jobs where they are seen to have no place. (Leskinen et al., 2011, pp. 25–26)

On this basis, Leskin and colleagues proposed that the more inclusive term *sex-based harassment* should be used in place of the more conventional—and comparatively narrow—phrase *sexual harassment*. Not only does this alternative terminology more accurately convey the reality of most situations that are experienced by female employees, but it also maps more closely on the language originally used by the EEOC (Leskinen et al., 2011).

Returning to the *Study 1* results, the typical perpetrator of most behaviors on the SEQ was a coworker, rather than a supervisor, subordinate, or other person (e.g., citizen, suspect). This pattern is also seen in prior work demonstrating that coworkers, customers, and clients are a common source of such behavior (Berdahl, 2003; Konik & Cortina, 2008). In fact, this dynamic may be particularly characteristic of gender harassment that does not include a targeted sexual component. In *Study 1,* for example, the *gender harassment* subscale was the only one with coworkers as the most common perpetrators for every single behavior. Whether this pattern holds in other contexts could be a question for future research, as could the potential implications for employees in a range of different workplace settings (including other nontraditional fields for women).

Also consistent with prior research, reporting was more likely for behaviors that involved physical touching or quid pro quo situations. Perhaps not surprisingly, these behaviors were also more likely to be perpetrated by a supervisor, rather than a coworker or subordinate (in *Study 1*). This pattern thus supports previous findings indicating that sexual harassment is more likely to be reported if it is viewed as more severe, and some of the factors that increase the perceived severity include physical touching, quid pro quo situations, and/or behaviors that are perpetrated by a supervisor (Bergman, Langhout, Palmieri, Cortina, & Fitzgerald, 2002; Cochran et al., 1997; Cortina, 2004; Cortina, Fitzgerald, & Drasgow, 2002; DuBois, Faley, Kustis, & Knapp, 1999; Hesson–McInnis & Fitzgerald, 1997; Langhout et al., 2005; Malamut & Offermann, 2001; Wasti & Cortina, 2002).

In this context, it is worth noting that some of the low frequency behaviors (e.g., quid pro quo situations, unwanted physical touching, and forceful attempts to have sex) were experienced by a small but not insignificant number of respondents in both studies. Some of these situations were then described in disturbing detail in the narrative responses of *Study 2* respondents. That such behaviors occur at all should be cause for alarm. Yet this concern is exacerbated by the fact that even such severe behaviors were not typically reported. Prior research suggests that women in nontraditional professions are less likely than those in other fields to file a complaint when they have been sexually harassed (Ilies, Hauserman, Schwochau, & Stibal, 2003).

Our results also document both how frequently officers experience retaliation as a result of their response to these situations and how severe these retaliatory behaviors can be. In *Study 1*, fear of retaliation was one of the most common reasons that officers gave for not reporting SEQ behaviors, and the women in *Study 2* frequently described experiencing retaliation in response to these situations, particularly for those involving quid pro quo sexual harassment. Many women noted that they experience retaliation, regardless of the outcome of the original behavior. For instance, many women described how the retaliation continued even when the original behavior stopped and/or the person involved in the situation was reprimanded or received some other form of discipline. Some women mentioned that this retaliation included a delay or denial of backup, which is particularly troubling.

> The most dangerous form of work retaliation in both law enforcement and firefighting is the failure to provide immediate backup or other assistance in emergency situations. In firefighting, it also includes stealing or tampering with necessary safety equipment. Such acts represent the ultimate form of retaliation unique to the kind of workplace where emergency situations can easily become life-threatening. For many complainants, this is the point at which they begin to fear for their lives and consequently leave the organization. (Harrington & Lonsway, 2007, p. 54)

Our findings thus highlight the work that remains for law enforcement administrators—to ensure that sexually harassing behaviors are not committed or tolerated within their organizations, that they are reported when they occur, and that retaliation does not result.

Gender comparisons. In *Study 1*, quantitative analysis revealed that female officers were more likely than their male colleagues to experience *unwanted sexual attention*. No gender difference was found for the other SEQ subscales (*quid pro quo sexual harassment* or *gender harassment*). This may be partly explained by the fact that the number of women in the *Study 1* sample was considerably smaller than the number of men (69 vs. 594). This difference represents a proportion 1 to 10. Moreover, item-level data in Reading Table 23.1 suggest that almost all of the behaviors were experienced at a higher rate by female as compared to male participants in *Study 1*. With a larger sample size of women, therefore, other subscale differences may have emerged as statistically significant.

The lack of gender differences for two of the three subscales may also be explained by the low frequency of behaviors constituting *quid pro quo sexual harassment* and the high frequency of *gender harassment* (particularly for the item regarding "dirty stories or jokes"). Floor effects for the former and ceiling effects for the latter could have played a significant role. The results from *Study 1* thus fit within the larger context of mixed findings regarding gender. As previously reviewed, most research has historically found that female employees experience sexually harassing behaviors with far greater frequency than their male colleagues. On the other hand, some more recent studies report that men and women have such experiences with comparable frequency, but they are experienced as more upsetting for women than men.

The present results shed light on this issue by suggesting that the gender comparison in law enforcement

Reading 23 Sexual Harassment in Law Enforcement **493**

may depend on the type of behavior being assessed. Many behaviors—particularly those within the category of gender harassment—are common within policing and thus equally likely to be experienced by male and female officers. However, women are still more likely than men to be targeted with unwanted sexual attention. This again highlights the need to tease apart how the dynamics of sex-based harassment might differ for the various types of behavior on the SEQ subscales (i.e., those that do vs. do not include targeted sexual engagement).

These findings also raise the question of whether the specific behaviors experienced by men and women might differ. In their pioneering work, Berdahl, Magley, and Waldo (1996) found that men's experiences with gender harassment can be categorized into three types of behavior: *lewd comments, negative remarks about men, and enforcement of the heterosexual male gender role.* While the present research was not designed to specifically tap these subdimensions of men's experiences with gender harassment, this could prove to be an interesting direction for future research conducted within law enforcement organizations.

Past research also documents that the *impact* of such behavior may vary by gender and that it is determined in large part by whether the experience is appraised as a negative one. The survey instrument used in *Study 1* did not include a measure of how the SEQ behaviors were appraised; therefore, we do not have this information for *Study 1* respondents. However, judging by the narrative responses in *Study 2*, it is reasonable to suggest that many respondents did not view these behaviors very negatively. In the category of responses for *Study 2*, the two most common themes were that "no complaint was filed" and [that] the behavior was seen as "no big deal." Based on the existing research literature, it is also likely that the behaviors were viewed as more bothersome, stressful, or upsetting by the women as compared with the men in *Study 1*.

Nonetheless, experience with the SEQ behaviors exerted a negative impact on a range of personal and professional outcomes for *Study 1* respondents, and this was true for men as well as women. In fact, this finding is consistently reported in the literature, and the message is therefore important for law enforcement administrators who are seeking to eliminate sexual harassment and improve their organization's response. It may be that such behaviors are not typically viewed as a problem by

law enforcement personnel or that their appraisal differs for men versus women. (Unfortunately, the small number of women officers in *Study 1* prevented us from testing the outcome model separately by gender.) Yet such behaviors clearly represent a threat to the well-being of officers, regardless of their personal views or the larger organizational context.

Labeling sexual harassment. As previously noted, most people who experience behaviors on the SEQ do not describe themselves as having been "sexually harassed" (Fitzgerald, Swan, et al., 1997; Magley et al., 1999). Women in nontraditional professions are particularly unlikely to do so (Ilies et al., 2003). Even so, the percentage of *Study 1* respondents who said that they had been sexually harassed is strikingly low (less than 1%), especially given the frequency with which they experienced SEQ behaviors. It is possible that the climate of the particular agency involved in *Study 1* made officers reluctant to label their experiences as sexual harassment. However, this reluctance may also be explained by the more general context of law enforcement and the characteristics of the people who choose to work there:

> Women in law enforcement and firefighting may be especially reluctant to see themselves—or to be seen by others—as "victims"; they typically see themselves as problem-solvers who can manage the situation informally, without filing a formal complaint; they are often unaware of either their right to a workplace environment free of sexual harassment or the policies for reporting and investigating such problems; and they often view sexual harassment as "part of the job" and not a reason to complain. (Harrington & Lonsway, 2007, p. 21)

In contrast, far more respondents in *Study 2* labeled the SEQ behaviors they experienced as sexual harassment, which may be due to some of the same factors that explained their higher incidence rates as compared with *Study 1* (e.g., differences in the agencies and officers involved in the two studies, unknown differences in selectivity bias, and the different time frames for describing behaviors from throughout the course of their career vs. during the past year).

As with reporting behavior, research finds that employees are more likely to label an experience as sexual harassment if it includes physical touching, quid pro quo situations, and/or behaviors that are perpetrated by a supervisor (Fitzgerald, Swan, et al., 1997). This may explain why so few respondents labeled their experiences as sexual harassment; the most common behaviors were from the gender harassment subscale of the SEQ, which does not include the targeted sexual engagement that many people tend to think of as constituting sexual harassment.

While this pattern was not tested in the present study, it is important to keep in mind that labeling does *not* appear to determine the impact of an experience. Rather, negative outcomes result from experiencing SEQ behaviors, regardless of whether or not the target views them as constituting sexual harassment (Magley et al., 1999; Munson et al., 2001). Therefore, our findings highlight the importance of sexual harassment prevention programs for employees, including those in law enforcement organizations. One of the goals can be to properly identify sexual harassment. If the professional context of law enforcement—or the unique context of any particular agency—serves to discourage employees from identifying behaviors as sexual harassment, it is difficult to imagine how it could encourage them to report such behaviors when they are experienced.

Prior research demonstrates that sexual harassment is less common in organizations that have proactive policies and rigorous enforcement (Gruber, 1998; Hesson–McInnis & Fitzgerald, 1997; Pryor, LaVite, & Stoller, 1993). Reporting is also more likely in such an organizational climate, and victims have better outcomes (Fitzgerald, Drasgow, et al., 1997; Hulin, Fitzgerald, & Drasgow, 1996; Zickar, Munson, & Hulin, 1997). Therefore, we hope that the present findings will inform policies and programs to help decrease the frequency of sexual harassment in law enforcement, increase reporting, and reduce the negative impact on all police officers—both male and female.

Limitations

While the current study was conducted with greater methodological rigor than many of its predecessors, some concerns do limit the confidence with which the findings can be generalized. Among these is the small number of women in the *Study 1* sample, particularly for women of color (who are virtually absent). Concern is also warranted by the selectivity of the sampling procedure used for *Study 2*. However, because of the different methodologies used in the two studies, the limitations of one study are counterbalanced to some extent by the strengths of the other. For example, while *Study 1* involved a relatively large sample with an excellent response rate, it was drawn from a single agency. The sampling procedure for *Study 2* involved a greater degree of selectivity, yet respondents came from a large number of agencies. Thus, any cost in terms of the internal validity may have bought gains in external validity.

Taking this point further, male and female respondents in *Study 1* provided a wide range of information, both about their own personal experiences and also about their perceptions of individual and organizational impacts. To that extent, the breadth of information provided in *Study 1* was complemented by the depth of detail offered in the narrative responses from *Study 2*. Similarly, the large number of women in the *Study 2* sample may have helped to offset the relatively small number of women in *Study 1*—yet the lack of male participants in *Study 2* precluded any gender comparisons, which we were able to do in *Study 1*. Finally, no outcome measures were included in *Study 2,* so any conclusions about the impact of such experiences must be made on the basis of *Study 1* data. As in any study combining the use of two methods, we hope that the rich and nuanced descriptions offered in the qualitative data may help to explain some of the complex relationships underlying statistical results in the quantitative analysis.

Future Research

In sum, results of the present study converge with many of the conclusions from past research on sexual harassment in a wide variety of organizational settings. However, some findings diverge, and it is unclear the extent to which these different patterns can be attributed to the general context of the law enforcement profession, the unique context of particular agencies, or other factors. For example, future research could explore whether the rather high incidence of SEQ behaviors seen in this study also applies to other law enforcement agencies as well as organizations in other fields that are nontraditional for women. Finally, future research could also explore whether gender differences are seen in the frequency of unwanted sexual attention versus other forms of sexually harassing behavior—and whether the behaviors are appraised and/or labeled differently by men versus women in law enforcement. Such research could prove invaluable in designing and evaluating workplace programs to eliminate such behavior. As one female officer in *Study 2* concluded,

I have to say we have come a long way in 21 years but [have] a long way to go. I think newer officers will never experience some of the horrible things that went on and that is a good thing.

Appendix

Descriptive Statistics for Measures (*Study 1*)

Scale Name	Response Scale	Coefficient Alpha	Mean (SD)		
			Overall	Men	Women
Work Attitudes and Behaviors					
Work Withdrawal (10 items)	1 = "never" to 5 = "many times"	.77	1.62 (.44)	1.62 (.44)	1.64 (.45)
Job Withdrawal (3 items)	1 = "never" to 5 = "many times"	.76	1.50 (.73)	1.51* (.76)	1.39* (.40)
Work Satisfaction (5 items)	0 = "no," 1 = "?," and 3 = "yes"	.83	2.54 (.72)	2.53* (.73)	2.70* (.59)
Supervisor Satisfaction (7 items)	0 = "no," 1 = "?," and 3 = "yes"	.87	2.33 (.82)	2.33 (.82)	2.33 (.82)
Co-worker Satisfaction (9 items)	0 = "no," 1 = "?," and 3 = "yes"	.81	2.53 (.54)	2.53 (.53)	2.50 (.57)
Job Stress (12 items)	0 = "no," 1.5 = "?," and 3 = "yes"	.87	1.40 (.80)	1.40 (.80)	1.41 (.89)
Health and Well-Being					
Satisfaction With Life Scale (5 items)	1 = "strongly disagree" to 5 = "strongly agree"	.88	3.58 (.82)	3.58 (.83)	3.64 (.72)
Depression (5 items)	1 = "not at all" to 5 = "extremely"	.85	1.25 (.53)	1.26 (.54)	1.23 (.44)
Anxiety (6 items)	1 = "not at all" to 5 = "extremely"	.68	1.17 (.34)	1.16* (.33)	1.27* (.42)
Physical Somatization (7 items)	1 = "not at all" to 5 = "extremely"	.71	1.24 (.29)	1.24 (.30)	1.25 (.25)

(Continued)

(Continued)

Sexual Experiences Questionnaire (SEQ)					
Total score on SEQ (16 items)	1 = "never" to 5 = "most of the time"	.67	19.22 (3.11)	19.16 (3.06)	19.91 (3.52)
Unwanted Sexual Attention (6 items)	1 = "never" to 5 = "most of the time"	.41	6.44 (1.07)	6.37*** (0.99)	7.03*** (1.46)
Quid Pro Quo Harassment (5 items)	1 = "never" to 5 = "most of the time"	.60	5.05 (.37)	5.05 (.38)	5.06 (.29)
Gender Harassment (5 items)	1 = "never" to 5 = "most of the time"	.65	7.74 (2.40)	7.74 (2.40)	7.81 (2.44)

* *T*-test for gender difference significant at the level of $p < .05$.

*** *T*-test for gender difference significant at the level of $p < .001$.

Notes

1. Where noted, *t* tests were conducted with unequal variances, due to a significant difference on Levene's test for the equality of variances. Otherwise, all *t*–test statistics are based on the assumption of equal variances.

2. Linear regression analysis was conducted with *Study 1* data to test whether gender predicts the frequency of *unwanted sexual attention* when the variables of tenure and rank are also included in the equation. This was tested because tenure and rank were both significantly correlated with scores on this SEQ subscale ($p < .05$). Results indicated that the gender difference remained significant ($p < .001$), even when controlling for tenure and rank.

3. Again, the predictive power of tenure and rank were tested because they were significantly correlated with many of the personal and professional outcomes. Analyses were also run controlling for gender, but results suggested that it made virtually no difference in the outcomes.

References

Bartol, C. R., Bergen, G. T., Volckens, J. S., & Knoras, K. M. (1992). Women in small–town policing: Job performance and stress. *Criminal Justice and Behavior, 19,* 240–259.

Berdahl, J. L. (2003, August). The dark side of gender and the lighter side of sex: Exploring unchartered waters in sexual harassment research. Paper presented at the Annual Meeting of the Academy of Management, Seattle, WA.

Berdahl, J. L. (2007). The sexual harassment of uppity women. *Journal of Applied Psychology, 92,* 425–437.

Berdahl, J. L., Magley, V. J., & Waldo, C. R. (1996). The sexual harassment of men? Exploring the concept with theory and data. *Psychology of Women Quarterly, 20,* 527–547.

Bergman, M. E., Langhout, R. D., Palmieri, P. A., Cortina, L. M., & Fitzgerald, L. F. (2002). The (un)reasonableness of reporting: Antecedents and consequences of reporting sexual harassment. *Journal of Applied Psychology, 87,* 230–242.

Brent, J. J., & Kraska, P. B. (2010). Moving beyond our methodological default: A case for mixed methods. *Journal of Criminal Justice Education, 21,* 412–419.

Christopher, W., Arquellas, J., Anderson, R., Barnes, W., Estrada, L., & Kantor, M., Tranquada, R. E. (1991). *Report of the Independent Commission on the Los Angeles Police Department.* Independent Commission on the Los Angeles Police Department. Retrieved from http://www.parc.info/client_files/Special%20Reports/1%20 -%20Chistopher%20Commision.pdf

Cochran, C. C., Frazier, P., & Olson, A. M. (1997). Predictors of responses to unwanted sexual attention. *Psychology of Women Quarterly, 21,* 207–226.

Cohen, J. (1977). *Statistical power for the behavioral sciences.* New York, NY: Academic Press.

Cortina, L. (2004). Hispanic perspectives on sexual harassment and social support. *Personality and Social Psychology Bulletin, 30,* 570–584.

Cortina, L. M., & Berdahl, J. L. (2008). Sexual harassment in organizations: A decade of research in review. In C. Cooper & J. Barling (Eds.), *Handbook of organizational behavior* (pp. 469–497). Thousand Oaks, CA: Sage.

Cortina, L., Fitzgerald, L., & Drasgow, F. (2002). Contextualizing Latina experiences of sexual harassment: Preliminary tests of a structural model. *Basic and Applied Social Psychology, 24,* 295–311.

Culbertson, A., & Rosenfeld, P. (1994). Assessment of sexual harassment in the active-duty Navy. *Military Psychology, 6*(2), 69–93.

Derogatis, L. R., & Spencer, P. M. (1983). *The Brief Symptom Inventory: Administration, scoring, and procedure manual—I.* Baltimore, MD: Clinical Psychometric Research.

Diener, E., Emmons, R. A., Larsen, R. J., & Griffin, S. (1985). The Satisfaction With Life Scale. *Journal of Personality Assessment, 49,* 71–75.

DuBois, C. L. Z., Faley, R. H., Kustis, G. A., & Knapp, D. E. (1999). Perceptions of organizational responses to formal sexual harassment complaints. *Journal of Managerial Issues, 11,* 198–212.

Equal Employment Opportunity Commission (EEOC). (1980). Guidelines on discrimination because of sex (Sect. 1604.11). *Federal Register, 45,* 74676–74677.

Fitzgerald, L. F., Drasgow, F., Hulin, C. L., & Gelfand, M. J. (1993). *The Sexual Experiences Questionnaire: Revised edition* (Unpublished research scale). Chicago: Department of Psychology, University of Illinois.

Fitzgerald, L. F., Drasgow, F., Hulin, C. L., Gelfand, M. J., & Magley, V. J. (1997). Antecedents and consequences of sexual harassment in organizations: A test of an integrated model. *Journal of Applied Psychology, 82,* 578–589.

Fitzgerald, L. F., Magley, V. J., Drasgow, F., & Waldo, C. R. (1999). Measuring sexual harassment in the military: The Sexual Experiences Questionnaire (SEQ–DoD). *Military Psychology, 11,* 243–263.

Fitzgerald, L., Swan, S., & Fischer, K. (1995). Why didn't she just report him? The psychological and legal implications of women's responses to sexual harassment. *Journal of Social Issues, 51*(1), 117–138.

Fitzgerald, L. F., Swan, S., & Magley, V. J. (1997). But was it really sexual harassment? Legal, behavioral, and psychological definitions of the workplace victimization of women. In W. O'Donohue (Ed.), *Sexual harassment: Theory, research, and treatment* (pp. 5–28). Boston, MA: Allyn & Bacon.

Glomb, T. M., Munson, L. J., Hulin, C. L., Bergman, M. E., & Drasgow, F. (1999). Structural equation models of sexual harassment: Longitudinal explorations and cross-sectional generalizations. *Journal of Applied Psychology, 84,* 14–28.

Gruber, J. E. (1998). The impact of male work environments and organizational policies on women's experiences of sexual harassment. *Gender and Society, 12,* 301–320.

Haarr, R. N. (1997). Patterns of interaction in a police patrol bureau: Race and gender barriers to integration. *Justice Quarterly, 14*(1), 54–83.

Hanisch, K. A., & Hulin, C. L. (1990). Job attitudes and organizational withdrawal: An examination of retirement and other voluntary withdrawal behaviors. *Journal of Vocational Behavior, 37,* 60–67.

Harrington, P. E., & Lonsway, K. A. (2007). *Investigating sexual harassment in law enforcement and nontraditional fields for women.* Upper Saddle River, NJ: Prentice-Hall.

Hesson-McInnis, M. S., & Fitzgerald, L. F. (1997). Sexual harassment: A preliminary test of an integrative model. *Journal of Applied Social Psychology, 27,* 877–901.

Hulin, C. L., Fitzgerald, L. F., & Drasgow, F. (1996). Organizational influences on sexual harassment. In M. Stockdale (Ed.), *Sexual Harassment in the Workplace* (Vol. 5, pp. 127–150). Thousand Oaks, CA: Sage.

Ilies, R., Hauserman, N., Schwochau, S., & Stibal, J. (2003). Reported incidence rates of work related sexual harassment in the United States: Using meta-analysis to explain reported rate disparities. *Personnel Psychology, 56,* 607–631.

Konik, J., & Cortina, L. M. (2008). Policing gender at work: Intersections of harassment based on sex and sexuality. *Social Justice Research: Special Issue on Social Behavior and Inequality, 21,* 313–337.

Langhout, R., Bergman, M., Cortina, L., Fitzgerald, L., Drasgow, F., & Williams, J. H. (2005). Sexual harassment severity: Assessing situational and personal determinants and outcomes. *Journal of Applied Social Psychology, 35,* 975–1007.

Leskinen, E. A., Cortina, L. M., & Kabat, D. B. (2011). Gender harassment: Broadening our understanding of sex-based harassment at work. *Law & Human Behavior, 35*(1), 25–39.

Lonsway, K. A. (2007). Are we there yet? The progress of women in one large law enforcement agency. *Women & Criminal Justice, 18*(1/2), 1–48.

Magley, V. J., Hulin, C. L., Fitzgerald, L. F., & DeNardo, M. (1999). Outcomes of self-labeling sexual harassment. *Journal of Applied Psychology, 84,* 390–402.

Malamut, A. B., & Offermann, L. R. (2001). Coping with sexual harassment: Personal, environmental, and cognitive determinants. *Journal of Applied Psychology, 86,* 1152–1166.

Mansfield, P. K., Koch, P. B., Henderson, J., Vicary, J. R., Cohn, M., & Young, E. W. (1991). The job climate for women in traditionally male blue-collar occupations. *Sex Roles, 25,* 63–79.

Martin, S. E. (1994). "Outsider within" the station house: The impact of race and gender and black women police. *Social Problems, 41,* 383–400.

Munson, L., Miner, A., & Hulin, C. (2001). Labeling sexual harassment in the military: An extension and replication. *Journal of Applied Psychology, 86,* 293–303.

Nichols, D. (1995, Summer). The brotherhood: Sexual harassment in police agencies. *Women Police, 29*(2), 10–12.

Pryor, J. B., La Vite, C., & Stoller, L. (1993). A social psychological analysis of sexual harassment: The person/situation interaction. *Journal of Vocational Behavior, 42,* 68–83.

Public Safety Information Bureau. (2002). *National directory of law enforcement administrators, correctional institutions, and related agencies.* Stevens Point, WI: Author.

Robinson, G. V. (1993, December). *Sexual harassment in Florida law enforcement: Panacea or Pandora's box?* Paper presented at the Senior Leadership program with the Florida Criminal Justice Executive Institute. Retrieved from http://www.fdle.state.fl.us/FCJEI/publications .asp

Roznowski, M. (1989). Examination of the measurement properties of the Job Descriptive Index with experimental items. *Journal of Applied Psychology, 74,* 805–814.

Schneider, B. E. (1991). Put up and shut up: Workplace sexual assaults. *Gender & Society, 5,* 533–548.

Schneider, K., Swan, S., & Fitzgerald, L. (1997). Job-related and psychological effects of sexual harassment in the workplace: Empirical evidence from two organizations. *Journal of Applied Psychology, 82,* 401–415.

Seklecki, R., & Paynich, R. (2007). A national survey of female police officers: An overview of findings. *Police Practice and Research, 8*(1), 17–30.

Smith, P. C., Kendall, L., & Hulin, C. L. (1969). *The measurement of satisfaction in work and retirement: A strategy for the study of attitudes.* Chicago, IL: Rand McNally.

Stanton, J. M., Balzer, W. K., Smith, P. C., Parra, L. F., & Ironson, G. (2001). A general measure of work stress: The Stress in General Scale. *Educational and Psychological Measurement, 61,* 866–888.

Timmins, W. M., & Hainsworth, B. E. (1989). Attracting and retaining females in law enforcement: Sex-based problems of women cops in 1988. *International Journal of Offender Therapy and Comparative Criminology, 33,* 197–205.

Wasti, S. A., & Cortina, L. M. (2002). Coping in context: Sociocultural determinants of responses to sexual harassment. *Journal of Personality and Social Psychology, 83,* 394–405.

Zickar, M. J., Munson, L., & Hulin, C. L. (1997). Organizational antecedents of sexual harassment. Unpublished manuscript cited in J. Hunter-Williams, L. F. Fitzgerald, & F. Drasgow, (1999). The effects of organizational practices on sexual harassment and individual outcomes in the Military. *Military Psychology, 11,* 303–328.

DISCUSSION QUESTIONS

1. What types of behaviors were most frequently experienced by female police officers?

2. Discuss the similarities and differences between gender harassment, unwanted sexual attention, and quid pro quo harassment.

3. What are the different outcomes that female officers experienced when they reported sexual harassment by a fellow officer?

READING 24

Like policing, women in corrections have been the minority within an occupation dominated by men. While the number of women in corrections has increased significantly in lower ranks, there continues to be few women in the upper ranks. What factors impact their success in moving up the chain of command? This article uses qualitative research methods to assess the factors that female correctional officers perceive have limited their opportunities to promote to upper level positions.

Promotional Opportunities

How Women in Corrections Perceive Their Chances for Advancement at Work

Cassandra Matthews, Elizabeth Monk-Turner, and Melvina Sumter

Women are in a distinct minority among correctional officers, especially at more advanced ranks; however, Lambert et al. [22] projected that women would soon comprise [*sic*] half of the correctional workforce. In 2005, male correctional officers outnumbered women by a ratio of 2:1 [30].

SOURCE: Matthews, C., Monk-Turner, E., & Sumter, M. (2010). Promotional opportunities: How women in corrections perceive their chances for advancement at work. *Gender Issues, 27,* 53–66.

The greatest gender disparity in correctional officers was at federal facilities where only 13% of correctional officers were women; however, in state facilities, women accounted for 26% of all correctional officers [30]. Much research in criminology and criminal justice has explored the representation of women in corrections; however, less work examines how women themselves perceive their opportunities for advancement in the field of corrections.[1] This work aims to add to this growing body of research.

The first female to head a correctional facility in the United States was Mary Weed [26]. Weed filled her husband's position as warden of Philadelphia's Walnut Street Jail after his death, serving as warden from 1793 to 1796 [26]. Traditionally, females served in administrative and clerical roles within the correctional field in gender segregated facilities. In 1970, California became the first state to employ female correctional officers in male institutions [29]. By 1978, Jurik [18] reported that thirty-three states assigned females to work as correctional officers in males' prisons. By the end of the 1980s, the integration of female officers in male institutions had occurred in almost every system [5, 12, 29].

Prior research has documented that women who work in corrections face negative perceptions by co-workers, problems in being a token "woman" within the correctional hierarchy, harassment, and balancing a home life with a work life [6, 19, 24]. Griffin et al. [15] argued that female correctional workers tend to be perceived negatively by male co-workers and supervisors. Especially in institutional settings, some employees hold the perspective that females cannot perform the job as well or in the same manner as their male counterparts [3, 4]. On the other hand, there is also the perception that females who work in corrections are more of a nurturer or caregiver compared to males [3]. In fact, Crewe [8] maintained that male correctional officers "tend to perceive female officers as a calming, moderating, and a normalizing force, in effect suggesting that certain 'feminine' traits may be advantageous to prison officer work" (397). Further, Crewe [8] argued that male officers oftentimes feel protective of female officers, suggesting "that females are naturally less capable than men at doing the job" (397). In the field of corrections, such perceptions could negatively impact success, suggesting that women

were too soft, pushovers, or in need of protection by others [3].

In addition to negative perceptions, harassment at work is a central concern for women in corrections. Griffin et al. [15] found that male officers viewed females who enter corrections as subject to ridicule, discrimination, and harassment. In fact, Savicki et al. [28] argued that harassment from co-workers was a primary reason people left the field of corrections. Examples of harassment include but are not limited to sexual jokes, sexual innuendos, and/or unwanted physical touching. Savicki et al. [28] found that females in the correctional field were likely to experience sexual harassment in this male-dominant environment [28]. They found that "gender was at least four times as likely to be identified as the primary source of harassment over race, national origin, and religion" (611). Similarly, Kim et al. [20] maintained that female correctional officers encounter sexual harassment from both male prisoners and male co-workers. Likewise, Rader [27] argued that women experience sexual harassment, sexual innuendos, and verbal abuse from male prisoners. Such harassment may affect work performance and self-esteem which impacts promotional opportunities [24, 27, 31].

Female correctional officers face unique problems in balancing work and home life [14]. Cassirer and Reskin [6] argued that employed women continue to feel responsible for domestic work and child care [1, 16, 18]. Lambert et al. [21] concluded that work and family roles remain unbalanced, especially for women in corrections, because these roles are in conflict. Lambert et al. [21] argued that "correctional officers may treat their spouses and children like inmates, barking orders to them and questioning their activities" (148). Further, Lambert et al. [21] maintained that if women correctional officers do not successfully balance home and work roles, then their chance of obtaining a promotion are reduced. Further, given the responsibilities of "home work," some women may not wish to seek promotions since advancement at work would most likely entail less flexible work hours and additional work responsibilities [21].

Promotional Opportunities

Goodman et al. [13] argued that the higher the percentage of lower level management jobs filled by women, the more likely an organization will have women in top management positions. Goodman et al. [13] also found that high turnover in management tended to increase the likelihood that women would be in top management positions. Further, women were more likely to be in top management positions if organizational salaries were lower than average [13]. Notably, if an organization emphasized promotion and development, then the chances of having more females in management increased [13].

Maume [23] found that women managers had fewer promotional opportunities in female than male-dominated job environments. Notably, women who worked with men were more likely to be promoted than those who worked mostly with other women. Maume's [23] work is essentially at odds with Kanter's [19] reasoning that gender promotional gaps should be widest in male-dominated work environments. In sum, Maume [23] argued that promotional opportunities came easier for white men than others. Specifically, Maume [23] said one could think of "a 'glass escalator' for white men, a 'glass ceiling' for others ..." when conceptualizing promotional opportunities by gender and race (483).

The glass ceiling hypothesis proposed than [sic] an invisible barrier blocks women's upward mobility into the higher reaches of occupational hierarchies [17, 25]. England and Farkas [10] explored structured mobility ladders or internal labor markets. Their work expanded the discussion of promotional gaps by recognizing that mobility opportunities in certain jobs are structurally restricted. In other words, regardless of the quality of work one does or individual motivation to advance at work, the chances for upward mobility are poor if the ladders to advance within the organization are not in place [9]. The primary focus of this study is to better understand how women who work in corrections perceive promotional opportunities in the field (both community and institutional).

⊠ Methods

This work utilizes a qualitative method in order to better understand how women perceive promotional opportunities in corrections. After gaining human subject approval, semi-structured phone interviews with women who work or have worked in community and/or institutional corrections in the state of Virginia were conducted between December 2007 and June 2008. Initially, a gatekeeper was identified which allowed us to gain access to additional women who worked in the field. Thus, from this key individual, a snowball sample ensued. Individuals in the sample represent women who work in city, federal, and state correctional facilities. Further, they include women who work at various ranks within corrections including correctional officers, managers and supervisors, and directors.

Each of the women identified agreed to be interviewed. To maintain confidentiality, names, descriptive characteristics of the participants, and the organization they previously or currently worked for were not collected during the interview process. Also, each respondent was given a pseudonym. Each participant was advised at the beginning of the conversation that the information provided would remain confidential. Participants were also advised, and all agreed, that the interview would be taped. Data were collected using a semi-structured interviewing schedule. Respondents were asked a series of questions in order to better understand how women perceived promotional opportunities in the field of corrections. Focus centered on better understanding perceptions regarding promotion in general, how gender differences in the workplace shaped perceptions of promotional opportunities, how women felt about harassment issues at work, and how they perceived problems in balancing home and work life.

Limitations of Methods and Data

Qualitative research techniques allow researchers to better understand problems from the point of view of those offering the information or data. Instead of asking many respondents a multitude of questions, usually with closed-ended response options, qualitative researchers aim to collect more detailed data from a relatively few individuals. The goal in qualitative work is to get to the heart of the matter at hand—to really understand something well as opposed to a superficial gloss of a problem. Thus, qualitative work typically relies on small samples, which poses a thorny issue for methodologists; however, as Creswell [7] writes, one really understands qualitative methods when they know that there is no answer to the question of how large the sample should be. Thus, the primary focus of this work is to better understand, from the perspective of a few female correctional officers, how they understand and feel about opportunities for advancement at work. Clearly, by opting to gather detailed information from a few respondents, this work rests on a convenience sample that was not randomly drawn. Therefore, it is important for the reader to keep in mind that the experiences of these women cannot be generalized to the population of all female correctional officers. Nevertheless, the richness and complexities of experiences these women have related help us all better understand issues related to women's advancement in corrections.

Findings

Of the fourteen women interviewed, the median age was 46 with a range of 34–65 years old. Equal numbers (6 each) of respondents identified their racial background as white and African-American/black. One respondent identified as Asian and another in the other race category. One respondent reported being single, another was single but in a monogamous relationship, seven were married, another was separated, and four were divorced. The vast majority (12) of participants had children. The age of these women's children ranged from seven to thirty-seven, with the average age being 24. All but one participant had received their bachelor's degree; the participant who had not received her bachelor's degree will be graduating later this year.

When asked about their experience with the Department of Corrections, all fourteen work or have worked within the state department. Two women work or have worked in the federal system, and one of the fourteen works or has worked in the local government. Ten women work or have worked in the institutional section of corrections, and another five work or have worked in the community corrections field.

Promotional Experiences

Most (10) of the women in the sample had been promoted at least once while employed in the correctional field. Of the four participants that had not been promoted, each said "yes" when asked if they foresaw promotional opportunities in the future. When asked why they perceived promotions in their future, most said that they had satisfied a requirement necessary for a promotion such as additional training to gain more experience or more education. When the ten participants that had been promoted were asked if they expected additional promotions, one did not give an answer, while four said "yes," three said that they were "unsure" and two said "no" because both were retired.

When asked if there had ever been any person that they felt deserved a promotion but did not receive one while working in the correctional setting, thirteen of the participants said "yes." Most respondents felt that deserving individuals had not been promoted primarily because the process was political and that, for women, the odds of being promoted were simply against them because of their gender. For example, Jennifer said, "It does help to know the right people." Lucy and Marcia said that promotions can be "political;" specifically, Lucy said that "as I changed positions, it seemed to get more political." Likewise, Marcia stated, "It seems whenever a new opportunity comes available, you have to play the game, it's all politics." The participant, Sarah, who said "no," had the following answer, "I feel that everyone that gets a promotion deserves it for one reason or another."

Most (12) respondents felt men had greater promotional opportunities compared to women. Only two women felt promotional opportunities were equal between the genders. None of the respondents felt that women have greater opportunities for promotions in the correctional setting.

Respondents felt men were promoted more than women because they dominated supervisory and managerial positions. For example, Paige stated, "Men [receive more promotions because], they're more dominant in the field." In agreement, Marcia stated, "I would say males because they outnumber the number of women in corrections." Others responded that men knew the right people and that there is a "stigma that women cannot do the job as well as a man." For example, Sarah stated,

> If I had to choose, I would say men. First, because they do dominate the field and secondly, because they usually have that seriousness to them and can be more intimidating to others and a little more forceful in getting a job done.

Jody agreed with the idea that men might be promoted more because they were perceived as capable stating,

From my experience I've seen more men be promoted than women but I don't think that necessarily means that men have more chances than women, I think they might fill the shoes a little better.

When asked if a promotion was important to them, all of the participants said "yes." For example, Kelly explained, "Yes [promotions are important], I want to keep climbing the ladder and try to encourage others to do so." Charlotte echoed similar sentiments when she said, "Yes, [promotions are important], I like the money and responsibility and I'd like more of both."

To better understand how the type of job held shaped a woman's feeling about promotional opportunities, responses were broken down into several broad categories. Of the fourteen respondents, ten were in a higher position of authority (positions ranged from director to assistant director to assistant superintendent to manager to supervisor). All of these women supervised others (management positions). The other four women in our sample were correctional officers (and one intake counselor) with no supervisory responsibilities (general positions).

Within the "general position" group, all saw a promotion in their future. Each said that in order to get this promotion, more training or education was needed. Four women in management positions were unsure about further promotions (three were unsure, one did not answer, and two were retired). Everyone except Natasha, who was classified as being in a general position, reported that they knew someone who desired a promotion but did not get it.

Of the fourteen respondents, the two (Kelly and Britney) who thought that men and women had equal opportunities for advancement were both in a general position. The other twelve felt that men have a greater chance of receiving a promotion. Again, the recurring theme as to why men had greater opportunities for promotion than women was that men simply outnumbered women and that there is and always would be a stigma that women cannot do the job as well as men.

Interactions With Others at Work

Respondents were asked about the amount of interaction while at work with male co-workers. All of these women worked with both men and women on a daily basis; however, the majority of interactions while at work were with men. For example, Jennifer stated that she worked

"pretty much daily [with women], but we're always out numbered by the men." Another participant, Lucy, said, that she worked with women "pretty frequently. But there was always more interaction with men."

Most interactions with men at work were strictly professional; however, some respondents were friendlier with male officers because a friendship was formed outside of work. For instance, Kelly (in a management position) stated,

They're [her interactions with men are] almost always kept professional but there are a few men I work with that I became friends with outside of work and those usually are more friendly.

Another interviewee, Paige (in a general position), said,

There are some officers that intermingle outside of work and become friends but while on duty everyone stays professional for the most part. It could be dangerous if we're not.

When interactions with men were compared to interactions with other women in the correctional setting, respondents reported being more comfortable and friendlier with other women workers. Angelina (in a management position) put it this way,

They're [her interactions with women are] usually more friendly than with men for the most part but we're still all there for a job so we try to keep things professional.

And Paige stated,

I tend to be friendlier or just more comfortable with women sometimes than men but it tends to stay professional also.

Women, in our sample, clearly felt in a minority, or token, position in [the] workplace, consistently reporting a sense that men were dominant in corrections.

Understandings of Sexual Harassment

Respondents were asked to define sexual harassment. While responses differed, most respondents included the terms *sexist jokes, unwanted touching, sexual comments, sexual innuendos,* and *unwanted sexual encounters* in their definitions (see Reading Table 24.1).

Respondents were asked if they had ever experienced sexual harassment. Of the fourteen women in our sample, eight said that they had experienced sexual harassment while employed in the correctional setting. Two of these eight women reported that these encounters of sexual harassment affected their perceptions of promotional opportunities in the correctional setting. Sarah and

Reading Table 24.1 Witness and Definitions of Sexual Harassment and Position

	Witnessed It?	Example/Explanation
Interviewee Managerial Position		
Lucy	No	"But I know it went on. When I was director, sexual harassment was not tolerated. I know it happened but it never happened in front of me and I was a bit slow at realizing it if it did."
Kelly	Yes	"Well, who hasn't in this day and age? The jokes are pretty common, you know, in the locker room or the break room. Um, I wouldn't say I hear them everyday but I would say at least once a week there's always some dirty joke buzzing around. They're not really taken too seriously; I think people know they're not there to hurt anyone's feelings."
Jennifer	No	"I've never personally witnessed anything. I've overheard jokes and heard officers and other colleagues talking amongst themselves—but that was probably me eavesdropping when I shouldn't have."
Marcia	Yes	"Well, who hasn't? Of course in a male dominated field I have heard the raunchy jokes and sexist comments—I have seen the unnecessary flirting and such."
Sarah	Yes	"I've noticed other co-workers deal with it from other co-workers, but I've never seen an offender step out of line. Um, like the touching or I guess grabbing or like a pat on another person's rear." "I've heard the jokes and the sexist comments; I doubt those will ever go away. Well, I had this one time, a long time ago, where a male correctional officer said something like, 'oh I'll do it, since the woman doesn't want to.'"
Stella	No	"I've never witnessed anything like that—I've had my suspicions but I don't know if it does actually happen."
Jody	No	"I've heard the stories or the rumors really but I've never witnessed anything like that."
Nicole	No	"I've never personally witnessed it but I don't doubt that it never happened."
Britney	No	"I have never personally witnessed it. I've heard the stories and been to the trainings at work about it. I've heard the stories that buzz around. Well, one story I've heard is when a counseling session was going on, it was a juvenile offender, his family and two officers, well, they are more like counselors then but it was one male and a female counselor.

(Continued)

Reading Table 24.1 (Continued)

	Witnessed It?	Example/Explanation
		But during this meeting the male counselor said something to the effect of you're just a woman—the boy isn't going to see it your way—he said this to the other female counselor. I think they were talking to the offender and his family on what the juvenile can do to stay out of trouble and excel in school. I'm pretty sure he made his comment in front of the family and the offender. I know the female counselor filed a complaint but I'm not sure if anything ever came of it. But that's what I heard happened and I heard it down the line a bit so I'm not exactly positive what exactly happened."
General Position		
Paige	No	*
Natasha	Yes	"I've heard some sexual jokes at work but that's not uncommon, you know. I haven't heard anything that I have really found too offensive. And I haven't seen or heard of anything dealing with unnecessary touching or anything like that off the top of my head."
Charlotte	Yes	"I've heard jokes around the office every so often."
Candice	Yes	"Of course, I've heard the jokes and I've seen hugging and friendly touching among other workers but I'm not sure if those people were or are in a relationship or not, I think maybe they were but I don't know."

* No answer

Marcia, both in management positions, felt that if they had said something about a sexual harassment encounter that the male co-workers would have looked down on them and [that] they probably would not have been promoted. For instance, Sarah said,

> I think if I would've fought back or just did something that would look like I could out do a male counterpart, I don't think I would've been promoted.

While Marcia agreed,

> I think maybe going back to the question you just asked me, if I would've done something like file a complaint or something, I'm not sure if I would've been promoted. In my experience, it's better to keep a tight lip about some things and just deal with it. I think if I would've done something then I don't know if I would've been trusted to have a higher rank.

Previous literature held that sexual harassment was the most common form of harassment women encounter [28]. This holds for the women in this sample as all have heard about instances of harassment and/or been a victim of sexual harassment. Britney related her concerns about harassment in this way,

> A counseling session [that] was going on; it was a juvenile offender, his family and a two officers . . . one male and a female counselor. During this meeting the male counselor said something to the effect of "you're just a woman"—"the boy isn't going to see it your way"—he said this to the other female counselor. I think they were talking to the offender and his family on what he can do to stay out of trouble and excel in school . . .

Half of the women interviewed had encountered sexist jokes and/or comments on a weekly or sometimes daily basis. For example, in Marcia's interview, she almost sounds sarcastic when she's replying to the question, "Have you ever witnessed another female encountering sexual harassment in the correctional setting"; she stated, "Well, who hasn't?" Her response also suggests that sexual harassment and negative perceptions about women in the correctional field are common. Results support Rader [27] and McMahon [24] who both argued that women were teased, verbally abused, and harassed by male co-workers because of their gender and [that] this by itself can affect the promotional opportunities for women in the correctional field.

☒ Discussion and Policy Implications

Most (12) of the women in the sample felt that men were promoted more than women in the correctional field. For instance, when asked who had greater opportunities for promotions, Lucy stated,

> I would say men because the field is male dominated and there will always be that idea; that stigma that women cannot do the job as well as a man.

None of the women felt that women were in an advantaged position with regard to being promoted at work. Cassirer and Reskin [6] found that women did not place as much importance on promotions as men did. Their research was consistent with Kanter's [19] thesis that men placed a greater emphasis on promotions than women.

Notably, all of the women said that a promotion was important to them. For example, Angelina said, "Yes, without a doubt." Sarah stated, "Yes, of course . . ." And Jennifer affirmed,

> Oh yes . . . when I supervise some officers, I push them—I try to encourage officers . . . [to] work toward being promoted.

Women perceived that men received more promotions and were more likely to be promoted than women. Notably, several women said they felt that if they complained about harassment, their male colleagues would look down on them and [that] they may not be promoted

because of that. Also of concern, women related that the belief continues to hold that men fill the shoes better when in position of higher authority. Nicole put it this way:

> Men do the job that a man can do—there are not a lot of times where a man will admit that a woman can do the same job especially in this field.

This work provides support for Griffin, Armstrong, and Hepburn's [15] argument that harassment at work was problematic for women in corrections. All of [the] women in this sample were either a victim and/or a witness of sexual harassment. Further, for some, there was a sense that if such harassment was reported, then the chance for a promotion in corrections would be diminished. It appears essential for correctional institutions to be sensitive to potential sexual harassment problems at work. Regular workshops focusing on this issue would be worthwhile. Supporting those who bring concerns forward is critical if women are to feel comfortable expressing problems at work. Clearly, women who wish to advance in correctional careers should not be penalized for ever having raised sexual harassment concerns.

Given that women represent a distinct minority among correctional officers, it seems imperative for policy makers to initiate programs to help advance women into these positions. Several initiatives like the following might make a difference. First, women who hold positions of leadership in correctional institutions might officially "mentor" other women and help them think about different promotional opportunities. They could share how they have reached the position they currently hold and what they believed helped in attaining this position. Second, women who express an interest in moving up the career ladder in correctional institutions might receive educational incentives to help attain this goal. Some institutions help those who wish to advance [by offering] the opportunity to attain more education and by providing financial support and attractive work schedules, in return for a time commitment (once the education is complete) to the supporting institution. Finally, if the lack of representation appears entrenched and no improvement in gender diversity is seen across time, it might be appropriate to set guidelines and timetables to reach the goal of gender diversity in corrections. Implementing educational and child care support, such as suggested above, might ensure that women enter these positions which would then lead to other women seeing themselves in such positions and following in their steps. Little research in the correctional field addresses how women feel about their promotional opportunities. This study helps provide some insight and adds to current literature in the field.

Notes

1. In this work, the term *corrections* or the *correctional setting* is conceptualized as being the employment area for the participants, whether it is community, institutional, or administrational. The terms encompass various staff roles that are available, such as counselors, correctional officers, supervisors, superintendents, or directors. Promotional opportunities are defined as job advancements which may or may not include a pay increase and/or supervision of other employees. These promotions can be at a vertical level as well as at a horizontal level.

References

1. Armytage, P., Martyres, K., & Feiner, M. (2000). *Females in corrections: Getting the balance right.* Presented at the Women in Corrections: Staff and Clients Conference convened by the Australian Institute of Criminology in conjunction with the Department for Correctional Services SA, October/ November, Adelaide.

2. Camp, S. D., & Langan, N. P. (2005). Perceptions about minority and female opportunities for job advancements: Are beliefs about equal opportunities fixed? *The Prison Journal, 85,* 399–419.

3. Camp, S. D., Steifer, T. L., & Batchelder, J. A. (1995). *Perceptions of job advancement opportunities: A multilevel investigation of race and gender effects.* Washington, DC: Federal Bureau of Prisons & Indiana State University.

4. Carlson, J. R., Thomas, G., & Anson, R. H. (2004). Cross-gender perceptions of corrections officers in gender-segregated prisons. *Journal of Offender Rehabilitation, 39,* 83–103.

5. Cassirer, N., & Reskin, B. (2000). High hopes: Organizational position, employment experiences, and women's and men's promotion aspirations. *Work and Occupations, 27,* 438.

6. Creswell, J. W. (1994). *Research design: Qualitative and quantitative approaches.* Thousand Oaks, CA: Sage.

7. Crewe, B. (2006). Male prisoners' orientations towards women officers in an England prison. *Punishment & Society, 8,* 395–421.

8. Doeringer, P., & Piore, M. J. (1971). *Internal labor markets and manpower analysis.* Lexington, MA: D.C. Heath.

9. England, P., & Farkas, G. (1986). Households, employment, and gender. NY: Aldine.

10. Fry, L., & Glaser, D. (1987). Gender differences in work adjustment of prison employees. *Journal of Offender Counseling, Services, & Rehabilitation, 12,* 39–52.

11. Goodman, J. S., Fields, D. L., & Blum, T. C. (2003). Cracks in the glass ceiling: In what kind of organizations do women make it to the top? *Group and Organization Management, 28,* 475–501.

12. Griffin, M. (2007). Women as breadwinners. *Women and Criminal Justice, 17,* 1–25.

13. Griffin, M. L., Armstrong, G. S., & Hepburn, J. R. (2005). Correctional officer's perceptions of equitable treatment in the masculinized prison environment. *Criminal Justice Review, 30,* 189–206.

14. Grube-Farrell, B. (2002). Women, work, and occupational segregation in the uniformed services. *AFFILIA, 17,* 332–353.

15. Hulton, M. (2003). Some take the glass escalator, some hit the glass ceiling. *Work and Occupations, 30,* 30–61.

16. Jurik, N. C. (1985). An officer and a lady: Organizational barriers to women working as correctional officers in men's prisons. *Social Problems, 32,* 375–388.

17. Kanter, R. M. (1977). Men and women of the corporation. New York: Basic Books, Inc.

18. Kim, A.-S., Devalve, M., Elizabeth, Q. D., & Johnson, W. W. (2003). Women wardens: Results from a national survey of state correctional executives. *The Prison Journal, 83,* 406–425.

19. Lambert, E. G., Hogan, N. L., & Barton, S. M. (2004). The nature of work-family conflict among correctional staff: An exploratory examination. *Criminal Justice Review, 29,* 145–172.

20. Lambert, E. G., Paoline, E. A., I. I. I., Hogan, N. L., & Baker, D. N. (2007). Gender similarities and differences in correctional staff work attitudes and perceptions of the work environment. *Western Criminology Review, 8,* 16–31.

21. Maume, D. J., Jr. (1999). Glass ceilings and glass escalators: Occupational segregation and race and sex differences in managerial promotions. *Work and Occupations, 26,* 483–509.

22. McMahon, M. (1999). *Women on guard: Discrimination and harassment in corrections.* Toronto, Canada: University of Toronto Press Inc.

23. Morrison, A. (1987). *Breaking the glass ceiling.* NY: Addison-Wesley.

24. Morton, J. (1980). *A study of employment of women correctional officers in state level adult male correctional institutions.* Unpublished doctoral dissertation, University of Georgia, Athens.

25. Rader, N. (2005). Surrendering the solidarity: Considering the relationships among women correctional officers. *Women & Criminal Justice, 16,* 27–42.

26. Savicki, V., Colley, E., & Gjesvold, J. (2003). Harassment as a predictor of job burnout in correctional officers. *Criminal Justice and Behavior, 30,* 602–619.

27. Tewksbury, R., & Collins, S. C. (2006). Aggression levels among correctional officers. *The Prison Journal, 86,* 327–343.

28. U.S. Department of Justice. (2008). *Correctional officers, April 2007*. Washington, DC: Bureau of Statistics.

29. Zimmer, L. E. (1986). *Women guarding men*. Chicago: The University of Chicago Press.

DISCUSSION QUESTIONS

1. Which three reasons do female correctional officers believe have impacted their ability to be promoted?

2. How do female correctional officers perceive their abilities on the job compared to male correctional officers?

3. How do women in corrections experience sexual harassment?

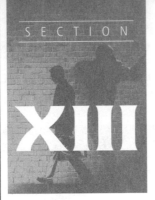

XIII

Women Professionals and the Criminal Justice System

Courts and Victim Services

Women and the Law

Like women in many of the occupations discussed in Section XII, women in the legal field have historically been underrepresented. The 1800s saw several notable examples of women in these occupations. In 1869, Belle Mansfield became the first woman admitted to a state bar (Iowa) in the U.S (Morello, 1986; Robinson, 1890). Charlotte E. Ray became the first African American woman admitted to the bar for the District of Columbia in 1872 (Law Library of Congress, n.d.; Robinson, 1890). By 1879, antidiscrimination laws had changed, and Belva Ann Lockwood became the first woman to practice law before the U.S. Supreme Court (Cook, 1997; Law Library of Congress (n.d.); Smith, 1998). However, it was not until 1918 that the first woman was admitted to the American Bar Association. These appearances by women into the legal profession were rare, and most of these women held positions with low prestige (Drachman, 1998). While times have improved significantly for women in this field, they still endure several challenges based on gender.

Today, women have reached near parity in terms of law school enrollment and faculty positions. Women make up almost half of all students enrolled in law school (47.1% in 2009–2010) with 13.2% of these women identifying as women of color, compared to 10.4% men of color (American Bar Association [ABA], 2012). Women also make up a significant presence among law school faculty. According to the American Bar Association (2010), women make up 54.6% of the tenured, tenure-track, or visiting full-time faculty at law schools across the nation. In addition, more women are finding their way into the top administrative positions within these schools. While women are less likely than men to hold the highest office (26.9% of dean positions are staffed by women), they are more likely than men to hold the office of associate or vice dean (60.6%) and assistant dean or director (69.7%).

▲ Photo 13.1   The number of women in the legal field is increasing. Here, a female lawyer talks with a jury during a trial.

While women have moved up the ranks within the legal academy, the number of male attorneys far exceeds the number of female attorneys in the United States. According to the American Bar Association (2012), only 31% of practicing attorneys in the United States are female. In addition, many positions are inaccessible for women. Women make up only 2% of the managing partners within the 200 largest law firms in the United States. Within Fortune 500 corporations with in-house counsel, women make up only 18% of these positions and only a small proportion (13%) of these are staffed by women of color (National Association for Law Placement, 2010; National Association of Women Lawyers, 2009, 2010). In addition, women are less likely to make partner than men (Noonan, Corcoran, & Courant, 2008). This contributes to significant disparities in pay between men and women as women earn approximately 75% of male salaries (a drop from 80% in 2008; Bureau of Labor Statistics, 2009).

Like many of the fields within the criminal justice system, women in the legal profession also face challenges with balancing the needs of their career with the demands of motherhood and family life. Within the corporate model of the legal system, the emphasis on billable hours requires attorneys to work long hours, both during the week and on weekends. In recent decades, the demand for billable hours by firms on their associates has increased significantly. Even with these high demands, billable hours are only part of the daily work that lawyers might engage in. The demands of this type of position often conflict with family responsibilities. For many women, this conflict results in either delaying the start of a family or choosing their career over motherhood entirely. Others choose to leave their legal positions prior to making partner or leave their positions for ones that are less stressful and afford greater flexibility. In many cases, for women who exercise part-time options in an effort to create **work-family balance,** work and family life are often viewed as less ambitious compared to the male (and other female) counterparts.

While firms may offer opportunities for part-time work, research indicates that few women avail themselves of these opportunities for fear that doing so would damage their potential for career advancement. For those women who chose these career trajectories, research indicates that these positions did not necessarily involve compensatory reductions in workload, forcing many to bring their work home with them, work for which they do not receive compensation. In addition, these women often believed that a reduction in time spent in the office could ultimately affect their chances for promotion and earning potential, and it also fostered negative assumptions regarding their work ethic and level of commitment among their colleagues (Bacik & Drew, 2006). One suggestion to remedy the demands created by the billable hours model is to move toward a value billing (where the costs of the legal work are based on the nature and complexity of the case) or fixed fee (costs are quoted up front for the project) billing system. Both of these models create work efficiency and allow for a greater work-life balance (Durrani & Singh, 2011).

As women in private law practice become discouraged regarding their likelihood of achieving partner status, many make the decision to leave their positions. Indeed, men are two to three times more likely to become partners than women and also earn significantly higher salaries (ABA, 2011). While the decisions to get married, have children, and take time away from their jobs, or reduce their employment status to part-time, do not have a significant effect for men or women in their likelihood to leave private practice, these variables are associated with levels of satisfaction surrounding the balance of work and family needs. Here, satisfaction is the key, not their decisions regarding family status (Noonan & Corcoran, 2008).

The majority of research on women in the legal profession lacks any discussion of how race and ethnicity interact with gender for women of color. What is available indicates that race and ethnicity have significant effects on the gendered nature of legal work. Generally speaking, men were more likely to be assigned high-profile cases, whereas women were assigned cases related to educational and other social issues. In addition, one respondent indicated that although White women and women of other minority groups were more likely to be viewed as "good attorneys," Chicanas were less likely to be viewed as valuable professionals in their field. Here, women of color are put in a position wherein they need to constantly prove themselves to their colleagues. As one female of color commented, "They just didn't appreciate me; (they) didn't think I was capable" (Garcia-Lopez, 2008, p. 598). In addition, Chicana women were more likely than White women to be overburdened with larger, lower profile caseloads. They also felt as though they were the key representatives and spokespersons for their racial-ethnic group. As another observed, "It's like they expect you to answer for the entire Latino population; like you should know everything there is to know about Latinos" (p. 601). Unlike other racial, ethnic, and gender groups, Chicana women attorneys did not define their success by financial achievements. Rather, social justice and helping people in their community play a key function in their concept of success and happiness with their lives and careers (Garcia-Lopez, 2008). In addition, many Latina law associates believe that the **glass ceiling** exists and can limit opportunities for promotion based on their gender and ethnic identity (Foley, Kidder, & Powell, 2002).

Scholars debate whether or not women can achieve equality in the legal profession. Some suggest that as older (and mostly male) partners retire, younger attorneys will be more likely to include a greater representation of women, given the increase in the number of women who attend and graduate from law school (French, 2000). Others argue that this theory neglects the fact that any change in the culture of the law firm will be slow in coming, due to the small numbers of women who choose to work within these types of positions and are successful on the partnership track (Reichman & Sterling, 2001).

Women and the Judiciary

In the judiciary, the representation of women has grown substantially over the last several decades. Although most of the conversations about women in the judiciary focus on the women that have been appointed to the U.S. Supreme Court, we have seen increases in the number of women appointed to the judiciary at all levels in recent times for both the state and federal legal systems. In light of these changes, how is this reflected in the proportion of women who serve in these positions? What is the current status of women in the judiciary?

Most female judges are assigned to courts of general jurisdiction. For example, 92% of women judges in California serve in trial courts (Williams, 2007). Similar trends are noted in the nationwide data, where 84% of women judges serve in courts at the trial level (National Association of Women Lawyers, 2010). While this might seem staggering in terms of the number of women that have been relegated to these lower level positions, we need to think about these data within the context of the number of positions at each level. For example, the majority of all justices (regardless of gender) serve in these general (and other lower level) jurisdiction courts, simply because there are so many opportunities (and high demand) for these positions. In contrast, there are few justices at the appellate and higher levels, which means fewer positions for women in general. However, the proportion of women in these positions is increasing. In particular, the practices set forth by President Bill Clinton in the 1990s were particularly noteworthy, as he appointed more women to judicial positions at the federal appellate level than any other president either before or after him (Goldman, 1995, as cited in Palmer, 2001). Nationwide, women represent 31% of the judges at the state supreme court level. Within the federal level, women

Steve Petteway, photographer for the Supreme Court of the United States

▲ Photo 13.2   The four women of the U.S. Supreme Court. From left to right, Sandra Day O'Connor, Sonia Sotomayor, Ruth Bader Ginsburg, and Elena Kagan.

occupy 48 of the 179 available positions in the Federal Circuit Court of Appeals (26.8%) and 33% in the U.S. Supreme Court (ABA, 2011). So while the physical number of women in these positions is somewhat small, their effect is significant given the few positions that exist at this level.

What factors affect the appointment of women to the judiciary? Williams (2007) suggests that more women receive a judicial appointment as a result of a nonpartisan election, compared to partisan elections. Liberal states are more likely to have women in judicial positions, compared to conservative states. In addition, the presence of female attorneys in the state also increases the representation of women as judges in the trial courts. At the appellate level, three variables affect the representation of women in these positions: (1) As more seats are generally available on the appellate bench, the representation of women at this level increases; (2) as the number of female attorneys in a state increases, so does the number of women judges at the appellate level; (3) states that use the merit selection process to fill seats have an increased number of women on the bench, compared to those states that rely on a partisan election to fill these positions. In addition, research indicates that women in the judiciary have a greater interest in elevating their career trajectory compared to male judges (Jensen & Martinek, 2009).

CASE STUDY

Spotlight on Women and the Supreme Court

The U.S. Supreme Court is an institution unlike any other in the nation. The first Court was established in 1789 with six members: a chief justice and five associate justices. Today, there are a total of nine justices—eight associates plus the chief justice. Over the past 211 years, there have been 112 justices and 17 chief justices.

(Continued)

(Continued)

Turnover on the Court is a slow process as members of the Supreme Court are appointed for life (and many serve until their death; Supreme Court, n.d.). The presence of women on the Supreme Court is a new practice. It wasn't until 1981 that the first female justice was appointed to the Court. To date, there have only been four women to serve on the Supreme Court: Sandra Day O'Connor, Ruth Bader Ginsburg, Sonia Sotomayor, and Elena Kagan.

In 1981, President Ronald Reagan appointed Sandra Day O'Connor as the first woman to grace the Supreme Court's bench. At the time of her appointment, there were few women in high-ranking judicial positions at the state and federal level. O'Connor began her tenure on the Court as a conservative voice, and she voted with her conservative colleagues in the overwhelming majority of her decisions ("Nine Justices," 2004). While she was initially appointed as a conservative voice on the Court, she was not always aligned with the political right and became the swing vote alongside more liberal justices in some high-profile cases before the Court. For example, in *Lawrence v. Texas* (2003), she ruled with her liberal colleagues that laws banning sodomy for homosexuals but not for heterosexuals were unconstitutional. She retired from the Court in January 2006.

O'Connor remained the lone woman on the Court until 1993, when Clinton appointed a second woman to the Court—Ruth Bader Ginsburg. During her tenure as a lawyer, she appeared before the Court on six separate occasions in cases involving women's rights. She was first appointed to the federal bench by President Carter in 1981 to serve on the U.S. Court of Appeals. During her tenure on the Court, Ginsburg has presented a balanced view in her decision making—sometimes voting with her liberal colleagues and other times serving as the swing vote for the conservative voice. One of her noted decisions on gender equality involved the case of *United States v. Virginia* (1996), which involved a challenge against the single sex admission policy of Virginia Military Institute. In writing for the majority opinion, Ginsburg stated that "neither federal nor state government acts compatibly with equal protection when a law or official policy denies to women, simply because they are women, full citizenship stature—equal opportunity to aspire, achieve, participate in and contribute to society based on their individual talents and capacities" (518 U.S. 515, 532).

Recently, Ginsburg has been joined by two additional female justices: Sonia Sotomayor (2009) and Elena Kagan (2010). Their appointments mark a shift in the judiciary of the highest Court in the land. Sotomayor is the first woman of color, a Latina, to serve on the Supreme Court, and the inclusion of Kagan creates a historical first, as this is the first time in history that three women have served simultaneously on the Court.

Sotomayor began her career as a prosecutor and spent time in private practice before she was appointed to the judiciary (federal district court) by President George H. W. Bush in 1991. She was elevated to the Second [U.S. Circuit] Court of Appeals by President Clinton in 1997. Perhaps her most famous decision came in 1995 when she ruled against the administrators of Major League Baseball, and subsequently ended the baseball strike ("Sonia Sotomayor," 2012). As the first appointment of President Obama in 2009, she has been involved in several landmark decisions including health care reform and immigration laws. While a moderate voice early in her career, on the Court she has served as a liberal voice and is often viewed as a champion for the rights of the downtrodden (Savage, 2009).

Few presidents have the opportunity to nominate even one member to the Supreme Court. During his tenure, President Obama has made two appointments. His second appointment came in 2010 with the confirmation of Elena Kagan (Center for American Women and Politics, n.d). Kagan's career included a variety of positions in private practice, tenure at University of Chicago Law and even a stint in the White House as a deputy domestic policy advisor under President Clinton. She became a professor at Harvard Law School and was later named its first woman dean. In 2009, President Obama appointed Kagan to serve as the solicitor general. However, this position was short lived as she was nominated and confirmed to the Supreme Court in 2010. While some viewed her lack of experience in the judiciary as a negative, she has posited herself as one of the more influential leaders on the Court. Indeed, she has participated in two of the recent landmark decisions by the Court involving gay marriage: *Hollingsworth v. Perry* (2013; overturned California's Prop. 8) and *U.S. v. Windsor* (overturned the Defense of Marriage Act). In each of these cases, Kagan sided with the majority opinion in support of gay marriage as a component of fairness and dignity.

With three female justices on the Court, Ginsburg, Sotomayor, and Kagan make history and represent a significant increase of women in the judiciary. While the progress is certainly significant, the long tenure of justices may mean that the addition of more women to the Court will not occur in the near future. However, as new appointees, the voices of Sotomayor and Kagan will certainly shape the decisions of the Court for a significant future.

Does being female affect the way in which judges make decisions? In a study involving hypothetical vignettes, the findings indicated several areas where gender differences existed among judges who participated in the survey. In most of the scenarios, the female judges imposed longer sentences in cases of simple assault and were less likely to award civil damages for these cases. However, when damages were to be awarded, female judges awarded significantly higher monetary levels compared to male judges (Coontz, 2000). When reviewing outcomes in real-life cases, the results are mixed. Research by Steffensmeier and Hebert (1999) finds that women judges tend to be harsher in their sentencing decisions compared to their male counterparts. Controlling for offender characteristics, the presence of a woman on the bench increases both the likelihood of prison time for offenders (10%) and the length of their sentences (+5 months longer). In addition, property offenders and repeat offenders are the ones most likely to bear the brunt of this increased severity when facing a female judge. In contrast, research by McCall (2007) indicates that female judges are generally more liberal in their decision making. Similar research on gender differences in sentencing by Songer, Davis, and Haire (1994) indicates that male and female judges do not differ in judicial decision making in federal cases involving obscenity charges or criminal search and seizure cases, but female judges were significantly more likely to decide in favor of the victim in cases of employment discrimination. At the state supreme court level, research indicates that not only do women tend to vote more liberally in death penalty and obscenity cases but also that the presence of a woman on the court increases the likelihood that the male judges will vote in a liberal fashion (Songer & Crews-Meyer, 2000).

Women and Work in Victim Services

A violation of the criminal law is considered a crime against the state, regardless of the offense or the harm to the victim. Victims have generally played a minor role throughout the criminal justice process and have had limited rights. For example, victims were not entitled to information about the case, nor were they invited to take an active role in the process. The fight for victims' rights began to emerge during the 1970s as a grassroots effort. One of the first victim services programs was the Bay Area Women Against Rape in San Francisco, which was the first rape-crisis center. In 1975, the National Organization for Victim Assistance (NOVA) was created as a resource for victims' rights groups across the United States and provides a voice to the needs of victims of crime (Young & Stein, 2004).

With the increased attention on victims' rights at the national level, the number of agencies began to multiply. While some of these groups were nonprofit community-based organizations, there was also a push for victims' services

© Lynn Johnson/National Geographic Society/Corbis

▲ **Photo 13.3**   Many women are drawn to work in the field of victims' services. Here, a counselor provides support to a young girl at a domestic violence center.

within local and state government bureaus. The funding source varies from organization to organization. While many of these programs receive state and federal funds, these resources alone are not enough to support the needs of the organization. As a result, many programs seek out grants and private subsidies to sustain their efforts (California Emergency Management Agency [Cal EMA], 2011).

While crime and victimizations cut across race, class, and gender lines (as well as other demographic identities), women are disproportionately represented within certain categories of crime, such as rape, sexual assault, and intimate partner abuse. One of the unique factors of many victim service organizations that focus on these particular types of victims is that the workforce tends to be predominately female. In addition, many of these workers identify as survivors of these crimes.

This feminine dynamic within the workplace brings a unique perspective to these agencies, particularly compared to the majority of occupations affiliated with the criminal justice system that are male dominated. Within the victims' services field, feminine traits, such as compassion, care, and support, are a critical part of the daily work environment. Many of the workers in these fields are drawn to this work as a result of their own experiences with crime and victimization, combined with a desire to serve victims with similar backgrounds to their own. At the same time, formal education in fields such as victimology, psychology, criminology, social work, and sociology as well as specialized training on issues such as victim services, law, and the criminal justice system are invaluable for this field (Neff, Patterson, & Johnson, 2012).

However, it is important to consider that victimization is a highly sensitive experience, and the people that work within these fields are often faced with high exposure to emotion within the context of their work. Over time, this can take its toll. The following sections highlight some of the challenges that **victim advocates** face in the workplace with agencies that provide services for victims of intimate partner violence and sexual assault.

Advocates for Intimate Partner Abuse

The decision to seek out assistance in cases of intimate partner abuse can be difficult for many victims. As you learned in Section IV, victims may experience fear and shame as a part of their abuse, believe that nothing can be done to change the situation, or may fail to even identify themselves as a victim. Despite these challenges, the demand for services for victims of these crimes is in high demand. Advocates in these cases may involve a variety of duties, including providing services (or referrals for services), helping victims secure temporary and transitional housing and providing support in legal cases (Camacho & Alarid, 2008; Slattery & Goodman, 2009).

Within the context of their daily work, advocates are exposed to stories filled with episodes of physical, sexual, and psychological abuse. In addition, advocates deal with clients in emergent and pressure filled situations. The intensity of these events can take their toll on advocates and lead to **burnout**. Not only may advocates experience emotional exhaustion due to the high levels of on-the-job stress, these experiences can lead advocates to become less connected to their work and their clients. As a result, many may question whether these costs are worth it and whether it makes a difference (Babin, Palazzolo, & Rivera, 2012). It is when an advocate feels that they are ineffective that the risk for burnout is at its highest. To a certain extent, these feelings of efficacy are perpetuated by the cycle of violence. Victims of intimate partner abuse often leave several times before they are able to completely sever their relationship. When a victim returns to her batterer, the advocate may feel that she has failed. Over time, this can have a significant impact on whether the advocate has sympathy for her client, which in turn can limit delivery of services (Kolb, 2011). In an effort to continue to support their clients, advocates will often excuse or justify their clients' actions so as to not take this decision as a personal rejection. One advocate expressed this experience in the following way:

> It takes the heat off (the client) and it makes it easier, especially with abusers, to say that we made them do it, we made them take out the charges. It's frustrating, but that's what an advocate does. (Kolb, 2011, p. 110)

The emotional nature of work as a domestic violence advocate can have a significant impact on his or her mental health. Advocates may experience their own psychological strain or secondary trauma stress. **Secondary trauma stress** is similar to post-traumatic stress disorder (PTSD) and is defined as "stress resulting from helping or wanting to help a traumatized or suffering person" (Figley, 1995, p. 7). One of the greatest predictors of secondary trauma stress is whether advocates have a history of their own intimate partner abuse (Slattery & Goodman, 2009). Since many advocates in the field have a personal history of victimization by an intimate partner, this is important to consider. However, organizational support structures within the workplace can serve as a protective factor against developing secondary trauma stress (Slattery & Goodman, 2009). Examples of these include fostering an environment of peer-to-peer support among the workers as well as developing formal mentor programs for new employees (Babin et al., 2012).

In addition to protecting themselves from trauma, organizational structures have also served to professionalize the field. Today, many organizations require certificates or specialized training as a prerequisite for employment, with several requiring a college degree. In many ways, this represents a departure from the foundations of domestic violence workers, which were staffed primarily with survivors. The professionalization of these agencies provides not only boundaries between their staffs and their clients but also opens the door to increased resources both for the individual workers (health insurance) as well as for the agency as a whole (Wies, 2008).

Rape-Crisis Workers

As one of the first examples of victims' services in the 1970s, rape-crisis organizations began as community-based grassroots agencies. Initially, these organizations were run primarily by a volunteer and female workforce. Many of these women had survived a rape or sexual assault at some point in their lifetime (Mallicoat, Marquez, & Rosenbaum, 2007). In addition to providing support for victims of sexual assault, many of these early centers worked on legislative actions in pursuit of victims' rights in sexual assault cases (Maier, 2011). During the 1980s and 1990s, rape-crisis organizations began to collaborate with other service providers, such as hospitals, police departments, and other community-based services. While much of the collaboration was driven by the budget cuts and the need to develop new ways to share resources, the effect was a professionalization of these agencies and their missions (Mallicoat et al., 2007). In addition, state governments began to take an interest in making sure that crime victims had access to services (Maier, 2011). As a result, contemporary rape-crisis organizations can provide a variety of services including crisis hotlines (many of which are staffed 24 hours a day), crisis counseling, and legal and medical advocates for victims (Ullman & Townsend, 2007) as well as services for non-English speakers and proactive education on rape and sexual assault (Maier, 2011). While work within these organizations has become a full-time professional occupation, organizations must call on volunteers to help serve the needs of the community (Mallicoat et al., 2007). In addition, today's rape-crisis centers are usually less focused on the political activism that was a core component of the early rape-crisis centers of the 1970s (Maier, 2011).

There is significant variability within the different types of rape-crisis organizations in terms of the types of populations they serve (rural vs. urban and multicultural populations), the types of services that are provided (direct services vs. community outreach), and their connection to other community agencies (Gornick, Burt, & Pitman, 1985). Despite these differences, rape-crisis organizations have a similar philosophy that places victim advocacy as a primary focus (Mallicoat et al., 2007).

Earlier in this section, you learned that the majority of the workforce within a rape-crisis center is female and that many of these women are survivors of sexual victimization. Survivors of these crimes may be drawn to work within this field for a variety of reasons. Many volunteers see working in a rape-crisis organization as a way of giving back to a community that assisted them with their own victimization experience or use it to continue to work through their own victim experience (Mallicoat et al., 2007). Rape-crisis workers also believe that it is their purpose to empower their clients by creating opportunities for the victims to be in control of their lives, which is something that was taken away during their assault (Ullman & Townsend, 2008).

Rape-crisis workers also help to limit or prevent secondary victimization. As you learned in Section II, secondary victimization occurs when victims of sexual assault have a negative experience with the interventions, and these experiences can cause further trauma to the victim as a result. How does this revictimization occur? The process of a police investigation can further traumatize victims, as they are often required to provide the details of their attack multiple times. While the intent of this process is to document the assault in detail, victims can potentially feel that they are blamed for the assault. Other stages of the investigation also carry the risk for potential revictimization, such as the rape exam, which is an extensive process.[1] The rape exam requires specific training of professionals (such as a sexual nurse examiner) in order to ensure that evidence is collected in the correct manner. Errors in this process can not only jeopardize the case but can also cause additional emotional trauma for the victim (Maier, 2008a). As a case moves forward in the criminal justice system, victims may experience additional acts of revictimization. They may receive little information about their case as it moves through the system. They may have to "re-live" the assault when testifying as witness and, in cases where a plea bargain is offered, be denied the opportunity to confront their accuser in court (Kelleher & McGilloway, 2009). However, the presence of an advocate appears to positively impact these difficult events as victims indicate that they encounter less distress as a result of their interactions with the police and medical professionals. Victims also receive an enhanced standard of care by hospital staff when a crisis counselor is present (Campbell, 2006).

While rape-crisis counselors and advocates provide valuable services for victims and the community, these workers can face a number of barriers in their attempts to deliver services. In Section III, you learned about rape myths and how this can lead to misperceptions in society about the reality of these crimes. Research by Ullman and Townsend (2007) acknowledges that this can make it difficult to provide support for the victim. In addition, budget constrictions can limit the ability of a rape-crisis organization to provide services for the victims. Finally, many victims do not know where to turn for help. It is important that rape-crisis organizations not only conduct outreach to let victims know where they can turn for help but also engage in public education to help dismantle these misperceptions about rape and sexual assault (Kelleher & McGilloway, 2009).

Rape and sexual assault exists in every community. However, the availability of services can vary from organization to organization. Those agencies with the largest budgets (and largest staff and number of volunteers) are able to provide the most resources. Most of these agencies are located in larger urban areas. For victims in rural communities, accessible resources may be limited, and workers in these communities face their own set of unique challenges. Consider that in rural communities, anonymity about people and their lives is rare. Everyone knows everybody (and their business) which can limit privacy and jeopardize confidentiality in these cases. Victims may also be less likely to report these assaults, particularly when cases involve a family member or when victims experience backlash and blame for their victimization (Annan, 2011). Victim blaming practices are also heavily influenced by cultural factors, such as the

---

[1]The rape kit involves collecting data from a variety of different places in search of DNA that may have been left from the offender and includes a pelvic exam, scraping under the fingernails, combing for hairs in the pubic region, and oral swabbing.

acceptance of traditional gender roles or conservative religious values, in these rural communities (McGrath, Johnson, & Miller, 2012). Finally, there can be significant challenges in the delivery of services for these victims. Given that rural agencies may draw from a large geographical area, poverty and a lack of available transportation can significantly limit the delivery of support and resources to some communities (McGrath et al., 2012). Despite these challenges, rape-crisis workers in rural communities do see assets to their small stature as they can provide consistent care and attention to their clients as their cases move throughout the system. There is less of a risk that their cases will get handed off to other professionals or get lost within the system. In addition, the tight-knit community allows advocates to develop close relationships with related practitioners, which improves the continuum of care for victims (Annan, 2011).

In Section III, you learned about how women of color have different experiences of sexual assault, which demonstrated in a variety of ways, including prevalence rates, reporting behaviors, disclosure practices, help-seeking behaviors, and responses by the justice system. First, race, ethnicity, and culture have a significant impact on reporting sexual assault. For example, victims in Hindu Indian cultures believe that to be sexually assaulted means that they are no longer "pure," which is a high status symbol within the community. Rather than bring shame to their family, the women have chosen to remain silent and not report these victimizations. Second, the limited availability of resources designed for victims from different races, ethnicities, and cultures can reduce the likelihood that victims will seek out assistance. In addition, many advocates expressed that many victims seemed to accept their victimization, as if this is a normal experience within their community and that it is not necessary to make a big deal about it. Finally, racism can lead to differential treatment of victims of color by the criminal justice system, particularly for cases of interracial victimization. In the words of one advocate,

> If a woman of color is assaulted by a White man there is almost a guarantee of hopelessness—nothing is going to happen. If a White woman is assaulted by a person of color, the whole thing changes. It is going to be on the front page of the news. (Maier, 2008b, p. 311)

Like other occupations within the criminal justice field, rape-crisis workers are faced with issues such as job satisfaction and burnout. While many advocates in this field express high levels of job satisfaction in their work with victims (despite comparatively low salaries), the emotionally taxing nature of the work can lead to high levels of burnout. Earlier in this section, you learned about issues of burnout and secondary trauma for domestic violence advocates and that rape-crisis counselors deal with many of the same issues in the context of their work environments. As a result, it is important that workers balance the demands of work with healthy physical and emotional outlets outside of the workplace (Mallicoat et al., 2007).

◪ Conclusion

Despite the gains of women in traditionally male-dominated criminal justice occupations, they continue to confront a glass ceiling in terms of equal representation, compensation, and opportunity within these fields. In cases such as the legal field, women in these fields become a symbol for all things gender. In other examples such as domestic violence and rape-crisis advocacy work, the organization itself becomes gendered in response to its feminist foundations, and many women are drawn to work within these environments as a result. While equal employment opportunity legislation has opened the doors for access for women in these traditionally male-dominated fields, women still face an uphill battle as they have been denied opportunity and promotion throughout history. In occupations such as attorneys and judges, the proportion of women in these fields has significantly increased in recent decades. While woman are represented at both upper and lower levels of the judiciary, their presence may still be as token females. In the case of victims' services agencies, the majority of these organizations are female centric, creating a unique environment. However, many advocates in these fields suffer from emotional burdens and challenges to gender normative values that can impact their ability to deliver services to victims. Despite these struggles, women remain an important presence in these fields with significant contributions that need to be encouraged and acknowledged, particularly for future generations of women in these fields.

✄ Summary

- Women in the legal field struggle with balancing work demands with family life. These struggles can affect the advancement of women in their field.
- While the number of women in the judiciary has increased, the majority of these positions are at the lower levels.
- Many rape-crisis and intimate partner violence organizations are predominately staffed by women.
- Many women who serve as victims' advocates have their own personal experience with victimization.
- Victim advocates face issues of burnout and secondary trauma that can affect not only their levels of job satisfaction but also their abilities to offer care to victims and survivors of these crimes.
- Advocates working with victims of color need to consider the cultural issues in these communities when providing services and outreach.
- Rural communities face unique considerations in providing services and support for victims of crime.

KEY TERMS

Burnout	Secondary trauma stress	Work-family balance
Glass ceiling	Victim advocates	

DISCUSSION QUESTIONS

1. Based on the research, how do women do gender within the traditional male-dominated legal occupations?

2. What challenges do women who work in law-related occupations face that their male counterparts do not?

3. What suggestions can be made to improve the status of women within law-related occupations?

4. How can organizations help support women in these occupations to improve job satisfaction and limit burnout?

5. How do the challenges for specialized populations (race/ethnicity, culture, and rural environments) impact the delivery of services for victims?

WEB RESOURCES

International Association of Women Judges: http://www.iawj.org

National Association of Women Judges: http://www.nawj.org

National Association of Women Lawyers: http://www.nawl.org

Visit **www.sagepub.com/mallicoat2e** to access additional study tools including eFlashcards, web quizzes, web resources, video resources, and SAGE journal articles.

READING 25

Women's presence on the bench has been steadily increasing. While much of these gains are made at the lower court levels, there have been smaller gains in these upper ranks. This article by Madhavi McCall examines the judicial sentencing practices by state supreme court justices on three areas of criminal justice: search and seizure, domestic violence, and juveniles tried as adults.

Structuring Gender's Impact

Judicial Voting Across Criminal Justice Cases

Madhavi McCall

The nomination of Harriet Miers to replace Sandra Day O'Connor on the U.S. Supreme Court revived public debate on the importance of gender diversity for the judiciary. Scholarly debate during the past quarter century has yet to produce consensus regarding the effects of gender on judicial behavior (e.g., Cook, 1984; E. Martin & Pyle, 2000; Segal, 2000), in part prompting Palmer (2001, p. 237) to assert that neither the question "Once women are on the bench, does it make a difference?" nor the question "What is the impact of increasing numbers of women judges?" has been adequately assessed.

This article systematically addresses these questions of whether gender is a component of a judge's decisional calculus by evaluating the effect of judge gender on judicial voting behavior. Specifically, I examine the voting behavior of male and female state supreme court justices in Fourth Amendment search and seizure cases, cases in which juveniles are tried as adults, and domestic violence cases decided by the state high courts between 1980 and 2000.

Analyses presented here extend the logic of existing arguments regarding the importance of a justice's gender in two ways. First, the range of case types addressed in this study provides the opportunity to assess the scope of influence that a justice's gender may have. That is, this research examines whether behavioral differences between men and women justices are detectable not only in cases commonly viewed as having a gender component (domestic violence) but also in those in which the presumed role of gender may be more subtle (juveniles tried as adults, search and seizure). Second, this study attempts to reconcile certain inconsistent findings of earlier research by asserting that the impact of gender may be contextual. I hypothesize, like several sociologists have for other professions (Dworkin, Chafetz, & Dworkin, 1986; Floge & Merrill, 1986; Kanter, 1977; Yoder, 1991), that women justices may be more willing to express behavioral differences that do exist once the proportion of women extends beyond tokenism. In short, this research taps both of Palmer's (2001) questions by positing that the answer to the first (Does gender matter?) partially depends on understanding the answer to the second (Does increased gender representation matter?).

Using logit analysis and controlling for institutional, legal, and political constraints, I find that women justices

SOURCE: McCall, M. (2008). Structuring gender's impact: Judicial voting across criminal justice cases. *American Politics Research*, *36*(2), 264–296.

NOTE: I would like to thank Alex Bernstein, San Diego State University, and Rowan Rozanski, Colorado State University, for their help in coding the data used in this research.

tend to vote differently than do men. Moreover, such gender effects became more evident after women came to hold an appreciable number of state supreme court seats. In the following sections, I review the existing literature, present research methods, and discuss the findings.

⊠ Review of the Literature on Gender-Based Models of Judicial Decision Making

Many legal scholars argue that judge gender structures judicial behavior and assert that female judges engage in a different decisional calculus than do male judges (Allen & Wall, 1993; Davis, Haire, & Songer, 1993; Gryski, Main, & Dixon, 1986; E. Martin, 1993; E. Martin & Pyle, 2000; M. McCall, 2003a, 2005; Resnik, 1988; Sherry, 1986). However, on many points, research efforts have failed to produce consistent findings (for a review, see Palmer, 2001). For instance, although results tend to indicate that women judges support the women's position in cases that directly affect women's lives (E. Martin & Pyle, 2005; M. McCall, 2003a; Songer, Davis, & Haire, 1994), other studies do not find a different voting pattern between men and women in gender-neutral cases (Allen & Wall, 1993; Gryski, Main, & Dixon, 1986). The perception that gender has a limited impact may not be uncommon among practitioners. For instance, when asked what effect gender has on decisions, Justice Jeanne Coyne of the Minnesota Supreme Court replied that her years on the bench had led her to conclude, "A wise old man and a wise old woman reach the same conclusion" (E. Martin, 1993).

Among scholarly research involving women's rights cases, Davis et al. (1993) find gender differences in sex discrimination cases, and Allen and Wall (1993) find that women are the most liberal court members in women's rights cases. Yet in both studies, the influence of gender is limited to cases dealing with women's issues. More recently, however, E. Martin and Pyle's (2000) study of the Michigan Supreme Court finds gender differences in discrimination and divorce cases but not in sex discrimination or sexual harassment cases, whereas M. McCall (2003a) finds that gender is a significant factor in sexual harassment cases on the state supreme courts. E. Martin and Pyle (2005) expand on their Michigan results by analyzing the impact of judge gender in divorce cases on all 50

state supreme courts and find that judge gender continues to influence case outcomes. The authors find that regardless of political party affiliation, female justices tend to support the female litigant in divorce cases more so than their male brethren. Although a majority of the findings suggest that gender-based voting differences exist among justices in women's rights cases, the results are inconsistent at times (Palmer, 2001).

In cases without an explicit gender component, studies are also inconclusive but often suggest that judge gender is not a relevant factor in case outcome (Palmer, 2001). For instance, Davis (1993) finds that Justice Sandra O'Connor did not consistently vote for the women's rights position, and Davis et al.'s (1993) work concludes that gender is not a significant factor in either obscenity or search and seizure cases decided by U.S. courts of appeals. Earlier work by Walker and Barrow (1985) suggests that women judges are less liberal than are men on economic regulation, criminal justice, personal liberty, and women's policy issues, and Segal (2000) also finds no behavioral differences between men and women justices. However, a recent analysis (M. McCall, 2005) indicates that gender is significant in police brutality cases decided after 1990. Obviously, the results of gender-based judicial studies fail to clarify the relationship between a justice's gender and voting tendencies, and additional analysis is needed.

Although the results of prior research on female justices are inconsistent, the theoretical underpinnings on which these studies are based remain strongly supported (see E. Martin & Pyle, 2005; Sherry, 1986). For instance, most of the literature on gender-based judicial differences suggests that female justices in women's rights cases will support the rights of women (the less dominant group) more strongly than will male justices (Allen & Wall, 1993; Davis et al., 1993; E. Martin & Pyle, 2005; M. M. McCall & M. A. McCall, 2007). I extend this logic and posit that such behavioral differences occur in other case types as well, with women justices manifesting more liberal voting patterns than men, and assert that integrated models of judicial behavior may better reveal such relationships.

Why Liberal?

Given the mixed empirical results of earlier research, the expectation that women judges will exhibit more liberal voting patterns than men, particularly in criminal justice cases, is not intuitively obvious and thus warrants discussion. Beyond the judicial literature (M. McCall, 2005; M. M. McCall & M. A. McCall, 2007), other research suggests that women view crime and crime control differently than do men and that these attitudes are reflected in women's policy preferences. Indeed, for decades, surveys have indicated that women in the general population are much more concerned about crime than are men (Warr, 1990), that women are more likely to be concerned about becoming a victim, even if they live in cities with relatively low crime rates (Marshall, 1991), and that women are more likely to believe that crime rates are increasing (Maguire & Pastore, 1996). Therefore, it may be tempting to conclude that women in general, and perhaps justices specifically, might be more willing to support aggressive crime-control policies and to support greater latitude and discretion for police officers than men.

However, the link between policy preferences and attitudes is much more complex than such a presumed fear–punitiveness connection would suggest (Hurwitz & Smithey, 1998). First, although women may be more fearful of crime, this does not necessarily mean that they will support more stringent law-and-order policies (for a review, see Hurwitz & Smithey, 1998). Indeed, although women are more likely than men to press for longer prison terms and the criminalization of certain acts, women also appear less supportive of the death penalty and are less willing to try juvenile offenders as adults. Furthermore, women are more likely than men to support social and economic programs in an effort to reduce crime rates (Maguire & Pastore, 1996, p. 245; "Which of the Proposals," 1994) and are less likely to support increased funding for prison construction. In addition, women generally are less supportive (Maguire & Pastore, 1996) and women justices are significantly less supportive of police brutality and excessive use of force by police officers (M. McCall, 2005). Such patterns suggest that although women are more concerned about crime generally, they do not necessarily tend to support aggressive measures to stop and control crime.

Second, although most still consider policing to be a male profession (S. Martin & Jurik, 1996), police departments since the 1970s have actively pursued women as officer candidates in part to improve the image of police work that had been tarnished by abuses during the 1960s. Female police officers are seen as more caring and compassionate (see M. A. McCall, 2004). Indeed, surveys have

long indicated that the general population finds women officers more pleasant and respectful than male officers (Sichel, Friedman, Quint, & Smith, 1978). Residents also think that women officers are less corrupt and less likely to abuse police discretion and receive fewer formal citizen complaints (Felkenes, 1991). Women officers themselves view their jobs differently than do men, as they tend to see policing in a social context extending beyond apprehending criminals (Schulz, 1995). Views held by female officers that the role of the police officer should be structured within a larger societal context are consistent with literature on female moral decision making (Gilligan, 1982) and economic voting (Welch & Hibbing, 1992) and may help explain the generally favorable resident assessments of female officers.

Third, Kathlene's (1995) innovative study of Colorado legislators and crime policy preferences suggests that there are differences between men and women legislators. That is, female legislators tend to frame the causes of criminal behavior within a larger societal context, tend to focus on social conditions for the causes of crime, and tend to be more supportive of rehabilitation options for first-time offenders, whereas male legislators tend to focus on the importance of individual choice and appropriate punishment. In addition, Welch (1985) finds that women in the U.S. House of Representatives generally exhibit more liberal voting patterns, and Shevchenko (2002) finds similar patterns of behavior by female legislators in Russia. Some members of the electorate seem to assume the presence of such patterns, as McDermott (1998) finds that voters in low-information elections use candidate gender as a voting cue, stereotyping female as more liberal than male competitors.

Finally, several public law scholars theorize that women justices are more liberal than men justices (Allen & Wall, 1993; Davis et al., 1993; E. Martin & Pyle, 2005; M. McCall, 2005; Songer & Crews-Meyer, 2000). Principally, it is argued by judicial scholars that female judges might reject the zero-sum method of decision making employed by male justices and might instead "suggest innovative resolutions that offer concessions to both sides" (Behuniak-Long, 1992, p. 427), resulting in more contextual decision-making patterns. Indeed, the National Association of Women Judges encourages its members to consider extralegal factors such as social conditions when sentencing juvenile offenders (Dobbin &

Gatowski, 1996) and trains its members to recognize social variables justifying lighter sentences for female offenders (Cicero & DeConstanzo, 2000).

I do not make these points with the intent of suggesting that women are "soft on crime." Rather, although women may consider crime to be as important a social issue as men, women may be less likely to tolerate abuses of individual rights to achieve crime control and less likely, particularly as policymakers, to pursue policy options that fail to address the roots of criminal behavior (Hurwitz & Smithey, 1998). Moreover, although most judicial authors consider liberal voting by female judges in gender-specific cases, part of the logic of these works—that female judges will be more likely to support the nondominant position (M. McCall, 2005)—can be applied to gender-neutral cases as well. Drawing on these different bodies of research, I posit that women justices will be less likely than men to tolerate threats to individual rights to achieve crime control and thus will exhibit more liberal voting tendencies than men in all three issue areas under consideration. Consequently, I posit not only that women judges will exhibit different behavior patterns than men but also hypothesize that these behavioral manifestations will result in women judges casting more liberal votes than men in search and seizure, juveniles tried as adults, and domestic violence cases.

Does the Number of Female Justices Matter?

As Palmer (2001) summarizes, existing research lacks a clear consensus regarding the impact of increasing numbers of women judges. This is a particularly relevant question to tackle given the notable strides by women during the past few decades in obtaining seats on federal (Palmer, 2001) and state (Allen & Wall, 1993; Kay & Sparrow, 2001) benches. While some authors assert that the number of women justices on courts has a substantial effect on decisions (e.g., Allen & Wall, 1993; E. Martin & Pyle, 2000), most research was conducted when there were very few women justices, and these women may have felt greater pressure to conform to the views of other (male) justices (E. Martin & Pyle, 2005). If a woman justice endured such pressure, she likely felt it long before taking the bench, as women constituted a small minority of law students at most schools until fairly recently. For instance, U.S.

Supreme Court Justice Ruth Bader Ginsburg was one of only nine women in her law school class of more than 500 (E. Martin & Pyle, 2005). Thus, it is possible that these women, in part because of their low numbers and in part because of the predominantly male socialization at law school, may have conformed to the conservative (male, crime control) expectations within the legal profession at the time (E. Martin & Pyle, 2005). If these connections were to hold, it would not be surprising that earlier legal studies often found that men and women justices exhibit similar behavioral characteristics.

Although any individual supporting a minority perspective might feel pressured to conform to the majority (Asch, 1951), women might be particularly likely to avoid confrontation in that they tend to exhibit more collegial leadership and relationship styles than do men. Leadership research finds that female officeholders adopt governing styles that are less hierarchical and less conflictual than the decision-making styles used by male officeholders, with women governmental officials leading through an emphasis on mutual respect and noncompetitive power. Flammang (1985) finds this governing style for women county officials, Rinehart (2001) for women mayors, Thomas (1994) for state legislatures, and Barr, Kearns, and Palmer (2002) for women justices.

Such decision-making styles and tendencies may prompt women justices to suppress their preferences in the interest of consensus, unless there is a sufficient number of like-minded cooperative players (a critical mass; McCarthy, 2001). We would expect that pressures to suppress preferred positions and the resulting conformist behavior would diminish as more women enter the profession. Some research on other policymaking bodies supports this logic. For instance, Thomas's (1994) study of state legislatures suggests that women policymakers do not feel comfortable advancing policy preferences unless a critical mass of women legislators is present. Critical mass theory holds that women typically must constitute approximately 15% to 25% of an institution's membership before they will be able to exert much power or influence, although a smaller percentage might suffice in an elite, small-group setting (Barr et al., 2002) such as a court.

In addition, although not directly related to critical mass theories, recent work on partisanship cohort effects also indicates that numbers matter. Sunstein, Schkada, and Ellman (2004) find that the likelihood of liberal votes in sex discrimination cases is significantly higher when all three members of the federal appeals court panel are liberal than when only two of the three are liberal, even though there is a liberal majority in both instances. Justices may find "safety in numbers" when voting against dominant interests.

Indeed, studies in other areas have concluded that having only token representation of women in traditionally male-dominated jobs has a negative impact on the ability of those women to feel comfortable in their jobs and in their interactions with their male colleagues. For instance, Dworkin et al. (1986) find that female public school teachers became more alienated from their work as their numbers declined. Kanter (1977) argues that it is the rarity of high-level saleswomen, not their gender, that appears to impede their chances of advancement and leads to feelings of isolation. Kanter's findings that numerically scarce women in traditionally male-dominated positions tend to feel isolated have been repeatedly studied for dozens of other occupations and have held consistently (see Yoder, 1991). Others report that traditionally dominant majorities engage in heightened discriminatory behavior toward minority groups and that this discriminatory reaction by majorities is most problematic when the minority group is very small (see Yoder, 1991). Together, these works paint a picture of women working in previously male-dominated occupations as isolated, alienated, and discriminated against by their male colleagues. These experiences, and the desire to avoid them, may encourage women in these circumstances to align their behavior with the dominant perspective (see Yoder, 1991).

Extended to the state judiciaries, token women justices may suppress their policy preferences to conform to the predominately male culture. If these women also feel isolated, it is less likely that they will be able to express policy preferences against the dominant interest. Indeed, Sherry (1986) notes that it is important to increase the numbers of women beyond tokenism as this may provide balance to traditionally male judicial perspectives. Others argue that women had to initially become a part of the male-dominant legal culture to obtain high court positions, but as a greater number of women occupied judicial seats, they were more able to act "like women" (McCarthy, 2001; Wefing, 1997). Given that the number of women on state supreme courts has dramatically increased during the past quarter century and that the literature suggests

that beyond the personal characteristics of these women, the numbers of women independently matter, it is appropriate to now reevaluate the influence of gender, taking into consideration the level of female representation. As Smith notes (1994), "Increased gender and racial diversification beyond tokenism may indeed have substantive policy ramifications" (p. 200).

I expect not only that gender matters but also that the effect of gender will be stronger after the number of women on the bench reaches a notable level. Therefore, I examine judicial votes rendered on state supreme courts between 1980 and 2000. In 1980, only 3% of the justices on the high state courts were women, but women held 26% of these judgeships in 2000. This dramatic rise in the number of women allows me to test the importance of the number of women on the bench in two ways. First, Thomas (1994) asserts that minority representation generally is more clearly expressed after a "tipping point" has been reached. Kanter (1977) and Yoder (1991) also address the need for a tipping point in minority representation before the negative effects of tokenism are reduced. Although no one has yet to determine precisely what qualifies as a tipping point, Barr et al. (2002) suggest that tipping under general circumstances might be reached with 15% representation and that a smaller number might suffice in elite, small-group settings. I test a tipping point of 10% female judicial representation on the state supreme courts because state high courts meet the elite, small-group-setting criterion. Second, critical mass and cohort studies suggest that numbers matter on specific courts, and thus, I investigate what impact, if any, women justices on specific benches have on the behavior of their colleagues.

Modeling Judicial Decision Making

As noted, the principal purpose of this article is to add to our understanding of the influence that judge gender has on judicial decision making. To accomplish this, I code the disposition of randomly selected search and seizure, juveniles tried as adults, and domestic violence cases from state supreme courts decided between 1980 and 2000. There were a total of 718 search and seizure votes from 148 cases, 396 juveniles tried as adults votes from 77 cases, and 331 domestic violence votes from 68 cases. The dependent variable is the direction of the justice's vote and is coded 1 if the justice votes for the liberal position, defined as a vote for the defendant in search and seizure cases, for the juvenile in cases where the juvenile was tried as an adult, and for the person raising the issue of domestic violence in domestic violence cases and 0 if the justice votes for the conservative position.

As noted earlier, gender-based studies have found that gender matters more consistently in cases directly dealing with *women's issues*. This connection seems intuitive and is supported not only by judicial research but also by studies of other policymaking bodies both in the United States and abroad (Shevchenko, 2002). However, I posit that judge gender is a factor in a wide variety of cases and therefore examine the voting patterns of judges in criminal justice cases without a necessarily obvious gender component (search and seizure), in cases with a family "care" component (juveniles tried as adults), and in cases with a direct influence on women's lives (domestic violence). These cases provide a continuum of issues on which the influence of gender may vary, allowing for a better understanding of the types of cases in which gender matters. Because the dependent variable is dichotomous, I use logit to conduct the statistical analysis. All variables, unless otherwise noted, are dummy variables coded 1 if the attribute is present and 0 otherwise. Variables used in all three data sets are listed in Reading Table 25.1. Legal variables for each data set are listed in Reading Table 25.2.

Attitudinal Variables

Female. Based on the research summarized above, I expect women justices to be more liberal than male justices, and I include a dummy variable coded 1 if the justice is a woman and 0 if the justice is a man and expect a positive sign on the variable's coefficient. This expectation, however, is dependent on the number of women on the courts, and as such, the gender variable is also used as a component of several interactive "critical mass" variables.

Ideology. Apart from the gender of a justice, some suggest that basic political ideology is central to judicial decisions. Although the attitudinal model (Segal & Spaeth, 1993) is the dominant paradigm used to explain judicial behavior on the federal courts, the notion that a judge's ideology is related to state court judicial decisions is suggested by the literature (Traut & Emmert, 1998); consequently, a consideration of ideology is a necessary component of behavioral analysis. I use Brace, Langer, and Hall's (2000) Party Adjusted Judicial Ideology (PAJID) scores as a measure of judicial ideology. The PAJID matrix runs from 0 (*most conservative*) to 100 (*most liberal*). The score controls for a justice's party identification, and I expect that justices with higher liberal scores will be more inclined to rule for the liberal position, resulting in a positive coefficient value.

Institutional Variables

Behavioral state supreme court research finds that justices are restricted from purely attitudinal voting and has demonstrated that institutional, political, and legal factors constrain voting choices because some justices are elected and do not enjoy life tenure (Hall & Brace, 1989, 1996; M. McCall, 2001, 2003a, 2003b). It follows that the effect of gender cannot be adequately evaluated considering institutional factors (M. McCall, 2005; Smith, 1994).

Method of retention. Although other institutional factors are used as control variables, most state judicial research questions if differences in the method of retention for seats on the state supreme courts influence judicial behavior. Specifically, like others (Hall & Brace, 1989, 1996; M. McCall, 2001, 2003a, 2003b), I posit that elected justices should feel greater pressure to be *tough on crime* than their appointed counterparts, and thus, I expect that justices who must be reelected will be more inclined to vote conservatively on criminal justice issues, controlling for all other factors. The method of retention variable is coded 1 if the justice is elected, excluding merit elections, and 0 if the justice is appointed, and I hold that the method of retention variable will produce a negatively signed coefficient.

Term length. State supreme courts employ a wide range of term lengths, intended to produce variations in levels of judicial accountability. I posit that justices with shorter term lengths are more inclined to render conservative decisions to satisfy the electorate's desire for tough-on-crime politics (Hall & Brace, 1996). This variable is coded in years, and I expect a positive coefficient.

Reading Table 25.1   Description of Institutional, Attitudinal, and Political Independent Variables Used, All Data Sets

Variable	Variable Description
Dependent variable	
Direction of justice's vote	1 if vote for criminally accused; 0 otherwise
Independent variables: Institutional	
Elected	1 if retained through election; 0 otherwise
Job requirements	Composite variable measuring state residency and legal experience requirements
Job training	Composite variable measuring the number of required hours of initial job training and yearly continuing education
Court of appeals	1 if intermediate court of appeals; 0 otherwise
Geographic selection	1 if district-based selection; 0 otherwise
Term length	Number of years of a justice's term
Independent variables: Critical mass	
More than 10% women overall	1 if total number of women on the bench is 10% or higher; 0 otherwise
More than 10% women overall and this vote is cast by a female judge	1 if total number of women on the bench is 10% or higher; 0 otherwise
Vote cast by a male judge sitting with one female judge	1 if vote cast is by a male judge who has one female colleague; 0 otherwise
Vote cast by a male judge sitting with two female judges	1 if vote cast is by a male judge who has two or more female colleagues; 0 otherwise
Vote cast by a female judge sitting with a female colleague	1 if vote cast is by a female judge sitting with one or more female colleagues
Percentage of women in legal profession	Composite variable measuring the overall growth of women in the legal profession
Independent variables: Attitudinal	
Female	1 if female justice; 0 otherwise
Ideology	Brace, Langer, and Hall's (2000) Party Adjusted Judicial Ideology measure
Independent variables: Political	
Retention year	1 if case occurs during a retention year; 0 otherwise

Reading Table 25.2 Description of Legal Independent Variables

Variable	Variable Description
Independent variables: Legal search and seizure	
Warrant or exception to warrant used	1 if search warrant or use a judicially recognized exception to warrant requirement used; 0 otherwise
Probable cause	1 if trial court found probable cause exists; 0 otherwise
Drug crime	1 if drug related case; 0 otherwise
Violent crime	1 if murder, attempted murder, sexual assault, or armed robbery; 0 otherwise
Car search	1 if car search; 0 otherwise
Body search	1 if body search; 0 otherwise
Independent variables: Legal juveniles tried as adults	
Murder case	1 if the juvenile commits murder; 0 otherwise
Sexual assault	1 if the juvenile commits sexual assault; 0 otherwise
Suspect gender	1 if the suspect is female; 0 otherwise
Weapon used	1 if weapon used in crime; 0 otherwise
Drug crime	1 if drug related case; 0 otherwise
Independent variables: Legal domestic violence	
Divorce case	1 if abuse factor in divorce proceedings; 0 otherwise
Sexual assault	1 if victim claims sexual abuse; 0 otherwise
Custody battle	1 if abuse factor in custody battle; 0 otherwise
Female victim	1 if victim is female; 0 otherwise
Justice gender × female victim	1 if vote from a female judge in a case with female victim; 0 otherwise
Battered women defense	1 if battered women's defense used; 0 otherwise
Battered women × female justice	1 if vote from a female judge in case using battered women's defense; 0 otherwise

Intermediate court of appeals. Several state court systems have an intermediate court of appeals that tends to increase the justices' discretion in case selection. Although their research is based on the U.S. Supreme Court, Walker, Epstein, and Dixon (1988) find that voting patterns changed when the Court was given greater discretion in docket selection. The authors find that as judicial discretion in case selection increased, the justices became more likely to choose cases dealing with highly relevant social issues, and these types of cases are more likely to cause ideological splits on the Court. If this analysis can be extended to the state supreme courts, justices might express more liberal policy preferences in states with intermediate courts of appeals because the stakes in any given case are likely to be higher and the cases selected may be more socially relevant.

Initial job training and continuing education. Some states require justices to undergo job training and continuing education exercises. I include a composite job-training variable measuring initial job training and level of continuing education. Although the precise nature of the training exercises differs by state, in part, this education is intended to familiarize and socialize new justices with the norms of the court and to ensure a degree of professionalism (Rottman, Flango, Cantnell, & La Fountain, 1998). Because job training is likely to add to justices' socialization process, and because some authors (Sickels, 1965) suggest the suppression of dissent on state courts is an institutional norm, it follows that female justices dissenting in support of a feminist perspective are more likely to do so on courts with less job training.

Other institutional characteristics. Used as control variables, the legal and residency requirements to be a justice on the high court vary by state. Some states simply require that justices reside in the state and hold a law degree, whereas others demand that justices live in the state for 10 years and possess 10 years of legal experience. I include, again as a composite variable, judicial requirements and contend that states that use a more selective process for filling judicial seats are less likely to encourage liberal votes. In addition, I posit that district-based selection, as opposed to statewide selection, will result in conservative votes. Primarily, if the justice is selected via the district, the potential for evaluation of the justice's voting position is greater because the justice's constituency is smaller. This increase in potential scrutiny should discourage votes that can be perceived as being soft on crime.

Critical Mass Variables

I include six variables to measure how the number of women on the court influences judicial voting behavior. These variables consider not only the overall number of women on the bench and in the legal profession but also the influence that women on a specific bench may have on their male and female colleagues.

More than 10% women overall. To determine if the relative presence of female justices overall has an impact on general voting rates, I calculated the total percentage of female state supreme court justices for each year. As noted, in the elite, small-group setting of state courts of last resort, I test a tipping point of 10% female judicial representation. If the number of female justices overall in the state supreme courts is 10% or greater, this variable is coded 1. If representation is less than 10%, the variable is coded 0. Even with the increased number of women on the bench, the vast majority of the bench is still male, and thus, I expect a negative coefficient on this variable generally.

More than 10% women overall, and vote is cast by a female judge. Although women justices remain in the minority after the presumed tipping point (greater than 10% female inclusion overall), if female justices are influenced by the overall number of women on the state benches, the votes by female justices should reflect the impact of the higher proportion of women. This variable is an interactive term between the female and more than 10% women overall variables and is coded 1 if more than 10% of all state supreme court justices are female and the judge casting the current vote is a female. If the overall percentage female metric is less than 10% and/or if the vote is cast by a male justice, the variable is coded 0. I posit a positive variable coefficient, suggesting that female justices tend to vote in a more liberal manner after the overall proportion of women judges reaches the 10% tipping point.

Vote cast by a male judge serving with one woman judge. Arguably, the presence of a woman on a state supreme court might influence the votes of her colleagues, and the next three variables are intended to model that possibility. In this first variable, the variable is coded 1 if the vote is being cast by a male judge who is sitting with one, and only one, female colleague, and I anticipate a positive variable coefficient, suggesting that the presence of a female justice has a measurable influence on her male colleagues.

Vote cast by a male judge serving with two or more women judges. Assuming the number of women on a court matters and that the presence of one woman might influence her male colleagues, two or more women on a panel should exert greater influence on the male members of the court. This variable is coded 1 if the vote being cast is by a male judge sitting with two or more women judges and 0 otherwise, and I anticipate a positive coefficient on the variable.

Vote cast by a woman judge serving with a woman colleague. If women feel more comfortable advancing policy positions when there are other like-minded individuals on the bench, then it follows that the presence of a female colleague would allow women judges greater opportunity to render liberal decisions. Thus, I posit that this variable, coded 1 if the vote is cast by a female sitting with a female colleague and 0 otherwise, will produce a positive and significant coefficient.

Percentage of women in legal profession. This variable is a composite measuring the number of women in the legal profession during the year in which a case is decided by the state high court. The variable considers the percentage of practicing female attorneys and the percentage of first-year entering female law students. Palmer (2001) suggests that the overall number of women in the legal field "has had a profound impact on the profession and the legal rights of women" (p. 238), and thus, I include a variable representing the growth of females in the legal profession as a whole. Palmer specifically suggests that the influx of female attorneys is important because female lawyers might present different types of legal arguments to judges who might represent a more female-oriented view of the law (see Sherry, 1986), and this might influence the voting behavior of the state high court judges. Thus, especially in women's rights cases, the percentage of women in the legal profession might serve as a proxy variable indicating that changes in judicial voting might partially be related to justices' being exposed to different types of legal, nondominant views of the law that they might not have previously considered. Thus, I expect that as women lawyers increase in number, the judges will cast more liberal votes.

Political Variable

To control for the political context, I include a dummy variable coded 1 if the case occurs during the retention year of a given judge. If a justice were to choose to advocate a policy preference that might be perceived as soft on crime, this vote would influence retention chances less at the beginning of the term. A justice should exhibit a greater tendency to vote conservatively toward a term's end, resulting in a negative coefficient sign. A complete listing of all institutional, attitudinal, and political variables is provided in Reading Table 25.1.

Legal Variables

The legal context of any case likely influences judicial decisions. Because the relevant legal dimensions depend on the type of case, I use different legal variables in the three data sets.

Legal Variables for Search and Seizure Cases

Warrant or exception and probable cause. I expect searches conducted with a warrant or based on an exception to the warrant requirement and/or conducted with probable cause to be more likely to be upheld by the justices than searches conducted without these elements. I use two dummy variables coded 1 if the attribute is present in the case and 0 otherwise and expect negative coefficients on both the warrant and probable cause variables.

Location of search. I posit that the location of the search should be relevant during the decision-making process and use car search and body search variables to test this assertion. In 1968, the U.S. Supreme Court approved safety searches in *Terry v. Ohio* (1968) to ensure officer safety. Most body searches conducted here are labeled as *Terry* stops; therefore, I anticipate that justices will typically uphold the constitutionality of these searches. Car searches present a different scenario. Although the Supreme Court holds that cars merit less protection than do homes or persons (Epstein & Walker, 2001), questions nonetheless persist. The ability of officers to search passengers and closed containers within a car and to search without probable cause but based on reasonable suspicion and other related issues continues to be addressed by courts (Epstein & Walker, 2001). The high court's response to these questions has been increasingly conservative, leaving it to the state courts to protect the criminally accused against unreasonable car searches under state constitutions. As Baum (1995) notes, states' courts tend to adopt more liberal policies when the Supreme Court goes highly conservative, and consequently, I expect a positive coefficient on the car search variable.

Drugs and violent crimes. Apart from the location of a search, I anticipate that searches in connection with drugs and violent crime (classified as sexual assault, murder, attempted murder, and armed robbery) will produce more conservative rulings because justices fear appearing soft on crime. I use a violent crime and a drug variable and expect a negative coefficient on each variable.

Legal Variables for Cases in Which
Juveniles Are Tried as Adults

Murder, sexual assault, drugs, and crimes with weapons. Although juveniles may commit a variety of crimes, I expect that justices are more likely to rule against the defendant juvenile in murder and sexual assault cases (rape–murder cases count as both). I also expect judges to be less lenient if the crime involves a weapon and/or if there are drugs involved in the crime. Thus, I include four dummy variables coded 1 if the charged crime is a murder, is a sexual assault, involves drugs, or involves a weapon and 0 otherwise, and I expect a negative coefficient on all four variables.

Suspect gender. I posit that courts may treat male defendants more harshly than female defendants and include a dummy variable coded 1 for a male suspect. The coefficient is expected to be negatively signed.

Domestic Violence Cases

Divorce, sexual assault, or custody battle. I code the type of case in which the domestic violence claim is made. If the case deals with a divorce, either because the man claims to have received an unfair portion of the marital assets based on a false claim of domestic violence or because the woman is claiming domestic violence and is filing for divorce, I code the divorce variable 1. I code the divorce variable 0 otherwise. I hold that in either circumstance, a divorce case is more likely to result in a vote for the person making the domestic violence claim and that the justices are likely to rule equally in favor of men claiming to be wrongfully accused and women who claim to be abused. I also use a dummy variable to code if the case involves sexual assault. I posit that if the violence occurs in the context of a sexual assault, the justices are more likely to find in favor of the domestic violence claim and thus anticipate a positive coefficient. I finally code if the case is a custody battle and anticipate that the justices will award custody to the spouse claiming to be abused.

Gender of victim. I anticipate that justices will be more supportive of a woman claiming sexual abuse and accordingly code the gender of the victim. This variable is intended to separate actual cases of domestic violence from those in which either (a) the abuser (typically a man) is killed (and is thus the victim in the case at hand) during or after an attack, or (b) the man claims that he has been wrongfully accused of domestic violence, either in a divorce or in a custody case. Because this variable is coded 1 if the victim is a woman, I anticipate a positive coefficient on this variable. I further consider only the behavior of female justices in cases where the victim is a woman and anticipate a positive coefficient on this interaction variable as well.

Battered women's defense. This variable is coded 1 if the woman kills her abuser and uses the battered women's defense and 0 otherwise. I anticipate that the justices will rule against the "victim" and in favor of the battered woman and thus expect a positive coefficient. Moreover, assuming that judge gender differences will be most evident here, I include a variable coded 1 if the vote is rendered by a woman justice and 0 otherwise and anticipate that women justices will rule in favor of the battered women's defense and that the variable will produce a positive coefficient.

Results

In general, the results support the notion that judge gender matters. Collectively, the results suggest that the increased number of women justices has a substantive effect on judicial voting patterns. The influence of gender is more generalized than the current body of literature suggests, and integrated models of judicial decision making produce more complete results.

Search and Seizure Results

I examined 718 votes cast by state supreme court justices from 1980 to 2000 in search and seizure cases in which an explicit privacy violation was asserted by the defendant. I limit search and seizure cases to privacy claims because this eliminates cases arguing faulty warrants, good faith exceptions, unreliable or uncorroborated anonymous tips, scope of searches, searches incident to a valid arrest, and temporal or spatial questions. Regression results are presented in Reading Table 25.3.

Reading Table 25.3 Effects of Independent Variables on Voting for a Liberal Outcome in Search and Seizure Cases, 1980 to 2000

Variable	1980 to 2000 Estimate	SE	Impact
Institutional			
Elected	−2.61***	0.51	−0.43
Job requirements	−0.09	0.07	—
Job training	−0.03**	0.01	−0.01
Court of appeals	0.15	0.45	—
Geographic selection	−0.86	0.73	—
Term length	0.11	0.08	—
Attitudinal			
Female	0.93**	0.46	0.22
Ideology	−0.57	0.44	—
Critical mass variables			
More than 10% women overall	−2.30***	0.51	−0.40
More than 10%, female judge	1.62*	0.94	0.33
Male serving with woman	−0.24	0.37	—
Male serving with two women	4.04***	0.95	0.48
Woman serving with woman	2.48**	1.21	0.42
Percentage of women in legal profession	0.30***	0.08	0.07
Political			
Retention year	−0.36**	0.18	−0.09
Legal			
Car search	1.79***	0.46	0.36
Body search	−1.37***	0.49	−0.30
Violent crime	−3.47***	0.90	−0.47
Drug crime	0.52	0.51	—
Probable cause	−2.08***	0.42	−0.39
Warrant or exception	−3.94***	0.69	−0.48
Constant	−10.19***	3.21	
χ^2	230.54***		
Correctly predicted (%)	85.8		

Variable	1980 to 2000 Estimate	SE	Impact
Nagelkerke R^2	.54		
Reduction of error (%)	44.3		
Degrees of freedom	21		
Number of votes	718		

NOTE: Dependent variable is justice's vote in Fourth Amendment search and seizure cases. Entries are logistic regression coefficients. Significance levels are based on log likelihood χ^2. As per the procedure described in Kmenta (1986, p. 439), I regress each independent variable against all other independent variables to measure the degree of multicollinearity present in this sample. The results of this endeavor indicate multicollinearity is not a major factor in the results. I calculate the impact of each variable using the procedure described in Segal and Spaeth (1993, p. 144). The impact is calculated by measuring the difference in the probability of a vote for the plaintiff when the variable is present as opposed to when it is absent. I use a baseline of a 0.50 prior probability of a vote for the plaintiff.

$*p < .10. **p < .05. ***p < .01.$

Reading Table 25.4 Effects of Independent Variables on Voting for a Liberal Outcome in Juveniles Cases, 1980 to 2000

Variable	1980 to 2000 Estimate	SE	Impact
Institutional			
Elected	−1.73**	0.74	−0.35
Job requirements	0.16*	0.08	0.04
Job training	0.06***	0.02	0.02
Court of appeals	0.95	0.61	—
Geographic selection	−0.38	0.72	—
Term length	−0.09	0.09	—
Attitudinal			
Female	1.68*	1.00	0.34
Ideology	−0.002	0.01	—
Critical mass variables			
More than 10% women overall	0.92	1.85	—
More than 10%, female judge	1.56*	0.86	0.33
Male serving with woman	1.08	1.18	—
Male serving with two women	2.89**	1.43	0.45
Woman serving with woman	0.99**	0.51	0.23
Percentage of women in legal profession	0.27	0.25	—

(Continued)

Reading Table 25.4 (Continued)

Variable	1980 to 2000 Estimate	SE	Impact
Political			
Retention year	0.42	0.49	—
Legal			
Murder	−1.71***	0.68	−0.35
Sexual assault	0.70	1.05	—
Weapon used	−1.79	1.70	—
Suspect is a male	−2.50*	1.45	−0.42
Drugs crime	−0.18***	0.05	−0.04
Constant	3.05	2.25	
χ^2	81.90***		
Correctly predicted (%)	81.7		
Nagelkerke R^2	.50		
Reduction of error (%)	37.5		
Degrees of freedom	20		
Number of votes	396		

NOTE: Dependent variable is justice's vote in cases where juveniles are tried as adults. Entries are logistic regression coefficients. Significance levels are based on log likelihood χ^2. As per the procedure described in Kmenta (1986, p. 439), I regress each independent variable against all other independent variables to measure the degree of multicollinearity present in this sample. The results of this endeavor indicate multicollinearity is a factor in the results, as the murder and sexual assault variables show some correlation. I calculate the impact of each variable using the procedure described in Segal and Spaeth (1993, p. 144). The impact is calculated by measuring the difference in the probability of a vote for the plaintiff when the variable is present as opposed to when it is absent. I use a baseline of a 0.50 prior probability of a vote for the plaintiff.

*$p < .10$. **$p < .05$. ***$p < .01$.

Reading Table 25.5 Effects of Independent Variables on Voting for a Liberal Outcome in Domestic Violence Cases, 1980 to 2000

Variable	1980 to 2000 Estimate	SE	Impact
Institutional			
Elected	5.13***	1.81	0.49
Job requirements	0.65***	0.19	0.16
Job training	0.09**	0.04	0.02
Court of appeals	1.88	2.13	—

Variable	1980 to 2000 Estimate	SE	Impact
Geographic selection	−8.45***	2.26	−0.50
Term length	0.57***	0.19	0.14
Attitudinal			
Female	−4.39***	1.61	−0.49
Ideology	0.02	0.02	—
Critical mass variables			
More than 10% women overall	−0.51	0.98	—
More than 10%, female judge	3.99***	1.38	0.48
Male serving with woman	−0.24	1.30	—
Male serving with two women	2.96**	1.24	−0.45
Woman serving with woman	0.84**	0.40	0.20
Percentage of women in legal profession	0.87	0.78	—
Political			
Retention year	1.57	1.41	—
Legal			
Divorce case	9.24***	2.54	0.50
Sexual assault case	3.27***	1.26	0.46
Custody battle	−3.95***	1.34	−0.48
Female victim	7.01***	2.17	0.50
Female judges and female victim	2.46*	1.53	0.42
Battered women's defense	1.04	1.91	—
Female judges and battered women's defense	5.84***	2.35	0.50
Constant	−62.01***	20.3	
χ^2	85.28***		
Correctly predicted (%)	88.0		
Nagelkerke R^2	.67		
Reduction of error (%)	70		
Degrees of freedom	22		
Number of votes	331		

NOTE: Dependent variable is justice's vote for person making a domestic violence claim. Entries are logistic regression coefficients. Significance levels are based on log likelihood χ^2. As per the procedure described in Kmenta (1986, p. 439), I regress each independent variable against all other independent variables to measure the degree of multicollinearity present in this sample. The results of this endeavor indicate multicollinearity is not a major factor in the results. I calculate the impact of each variable using the procedure described in Segal and Spaeth (1993, p. 144). The impact is calculated by measuring the difference in the probability of a vote for the plaintiff when the variable is present as opposed to when it is absent. I use a baseline of a 0.50 prior probability of a vote for the plaintiff.

*$p < .10$. **$p < .05$. ***$p < .01$.

The findings strongly suggest that the number of women on a court has an impact on judicial voting patterns after controlling for institutional, legal, and attitudinal factors. First, and most relevant to this analysis, the importance of judge gender is evident in this model. The female variable is significant and positive, indicating that female justices exhibit more liberal voting patterns than do their male colleagues. Not only is gender significant, but it is [also] significant in cases that lack an explicit gender component. Perhaps the impact of gender is clearer because the model used here includes institutional and legal factors and is thus more specified than models used in past research.

Moreover, regarding the importance of the number of women on the bench, the critical mass variables show some very interesting results. As the total number of women on the bench increases, the rate of voting for the defendant decreases. Given that men still constitute a majority of the bench, this finding is not surprising. However, the behavior of female judges as the number of women overall increases is also significant, but in this case, the coefficient is positive. Female judges show increases in liberal voting rates as the overall number of women is greater than 10%. The impact of the variable is also substantial. Assuming any litigant has a 50–50 chance of getting a justice's vote, in cases where the overall number of female justices is 10% or higher and the vote is cast by a female justice, the chances of a liberal vote increase by 33 points. Moreover, male judges sitting on a bench with female colleagues show a much stronger tendency to liberal voting, although the results indicate that the presence of one female judge is not sufficient to influence her male colleagues. Rather, male voting patterns do not show any significant behavioral differences until they sit on a bench with two or more female colleagues. When a male justice is sitting with two or more female justices, the probability of a liberal vote increases by 48 points. Interestingly, even in cases without an explicit gender component, the male judges appear to be influenced in behavior by their female colleagues. In addition, female justices sitting with other women are also more likely to hand down liberal rulings. Finally, an overall increase in females in the legal profession leads to an overall increase in liberal voting behavior.

Second, the findings indicate that elected justices are less likely to rule for the criminal defendant than are their appointed counterparts, supporting past institutional research (Hall & Brace, 1989, 1996; M. McCall, 2001, 2003a, 2003b). Moreover, again the impact of the variable is substantial. Assuming there is a 50–50 chance that a justice will vote liberally, the likelihood of a liberal vote decreases by 43 points if the justice is elected. Although the other institutional variables fail to exert consequential effects on voting behavior, the negative and statistically significant coefficient on the retention year variable increases confidence in the idea that justices are aware of and constrained by institutional variables. As justices approach a retention event, they are much less likely to cast liberal votes.

Third, and not surprisingly, legal variables significantly influence vote outcome and produce high impact scores. Justices are less likely to rule for the liberal position if either a warrant or an exception to a warrant exists and if a search is conducted with probable cause. Clearly, both variables indicate that when the search is not considered an abuse of police discretion, the justices are less likely to rule for defendants. In addition, as anticipated, the justices on state supreme courts were less likely to vote liberally in body searches but were more liberal regarding car searches. The type of crime also appears to be related to the rate of liberal voting, with justices far less likely to cast liberal votes when the defendant committed a violent crime, although the drug variable is insignificant.

Not only do several of the variables behave as anticipated, but the model performs well [too]. The predictive value of the model is an impressive 85.8%, produces a Nagelkerke $R2$ of .54, and reduces error by 44.3%. Any attempt to measure the influence of gender in search and seizure cases would seem incomplete without accounting for institutional, legal, political, and attitudinal factors or without considering changes in the general proportion of women on the bench over time.

Juveniles Tried as Adults Results

I also randomly selected cases in which juveniles were tried as adults, examining a total of 396 votes. I present the results in Reading Table 25.4. Findings again support the contention that integrated models of judicial decision making are needed to fully understand the influence of gender on decisions.

First, the female variable produces a significant and positively signed coefficient and indicates that female justices are more likely to render liberal rulings (for the juvenile) than are their male brethren. The significant results on the female variable—a variable that was insignificant in the more neutral search and seizure cases—suggest that female justices show greater behavioral diversification in more family oriented cases. The impact of the female variable is impressive, with the probability of a liberal vote increasing by 34 points if the justice is a female. Indeed, the importance of more women on the bench is again evident in the critical mass variables. In this data set, female judges casting votes when women occupy at least 10% of the court seats are more likely (about two thirds more likely) to render liberal votes than are both male judges and female judges when less than 10% of the court seats are held by women. Also consistent with the Fourth Amendment regression, a male judge sitting with two or more female colleagues appears more likely to rule for the criminal defendant, and a female judge sitting with another female is also more likely to hand down a liberal ruling. Indeed, the chances of a liberal vote in cases where men are serving with two or more women increase by 45 points, and the chances of a liberal vote on courts with two or more women increase by 23 points. Generally, adding women to the state courts appears to matter, with women justices acting in a more liberal manner once the tipping point has been reached, and it seems to matter on specific courts where differential voting patterns of the other judges serving with these women are evident.

Second, even in these more family oriented cases, elections remain a constraint on a judge's ability to render liberal votes, reducing the probability of a liberal vote by 35 points. Perhaps as a result of highly publicized school shootings and violence beginning in the early 1990s and/or because incidents of juvenile violence steadily increased throughout the 1980s, 9 elected justices again appear more conservative in their voting behavior than do appointed justices. The other two statistically significant institutional variables do not exhibit a large substantive impact on the voting decisions, and the remaining three institutional variables fail to garner statistical significance. Last, although statistically significant in the Fourth Amendment data set, the retention year variable does not reach significance, and the variable produces a coefficient that is signed opposite expectations. It may be that public attention to cases before the state supreme court involving juveniles tried as adults is already relatively high, weakening the

importance of the retention year metric. Subsequent research might test this and alternative explanations.

Third, the legal variables are also significant and produce high impact scores, and the results indicate that the type of crime and sex of offender are consequential. Justices are much less likely to rule for juvenile offenders who have committed murder and are less likely to rule for a juvenile in cases in which drugs play a role in the facts, consistent with the notion that justices do not want to appear soft on crime. Although the sexual assault variable fails to garner statistical significance, there is a correlation between the murder and sexual assault variables, and this may account for the insignificant findings. It is possible that with a larger sample size, any differential treatment by judges of murder and sexual assault cases could be more clearly isolated. Although significant at only the .10 level, the sex of the offender also appears to be part of the decisional calculus, with justices far more likely to rule conservatively when the offender is male. Overall, the model performs well, is statistically significant, correctly predicts 81.9% of cases, and produces a Nagelkerke R^2 of .50 and a reduction of error of 37.5%.

Domestic Violence Cases Results

Finally, I conducted statistical analysis on domestic violence cases decided by state supreme courts. There were a total of 331 judicial votes dealing with domestic violence issues. This data set is a bit more complex than the other two sets because both men and women at times are the "victim" of the domestic violence claim. That is, I include not only cases in which men are accused of domestic violence but also cases in which prior abusers (typically men) are the victims of the case at hand (e.g., battered women's defense cases). The data are coded, however, as liberal if the justice votes in support of the domestic violence claim regardless of if the defendant is the abused or a previous abuser. Accordingly, the legal variables used in this data set are particularly important because they help identify the type of case involved. Results of a logit regression on all 331 votes are presented in Reading Table 25.5.

A cursory review of the results indicates that although most of the variables are significant, the institutional and gender variables produce coefficients signed opposite expectations. The legal variables, however, produce anticipated results, and the influence of gender becomes more evident when case type is taken into consideration. Collectively, the results tell an interesting and somewhat complex story of judicial decision-making tendencies.

Starting with the female and legal variables, the data at first glance appear to indicate that female judges are more likely to hand down conservative decisions in domestic violence cases. This potentially counterintuitive finding, however, is perhaps best understood by examining the various contexts of differing case types; the legal variables prove to be critical in this regard. First, if the case involves a female victim—typically cases in which the male is charged with domestic violence—the justices are more likely to render decisions supporting the domestic violence claim. This result is driven in part by the gender of the justice, with women justices more likely than men to rule in favor of the female victim. Moreover, if the woman assaults or kills her abuser and then asserts the battered women's defense, female justices are far more likely than male justices to vote for the woman.

The importance of case type is further demonstrated in the divorce, sexual assault, and custody battle variables. The person claiming to be the victim of domestic violence or sexual assault (typically a woman) is more likely to garner votes. In custody battles, however, the votes typically go against the domestic violence claim. Two factors may explain this finding. First, many of the custody battle votes involved men suing for custody and claiming that they had been wrongfully accused of domestic violence or that they had completed court-mandated therapy and thus were no longer violent. Generally, the justices did not tend to rule for the men in such instances. Second, in some of these cases, women asserted domestic violence for the first time during the custody hearing, without producing adequate documentation that abuse had occurred. The courts seemed leery of these claims and often ruled against the woman's claim of domestic violence.

Regarding the critical mass variables, women judges are significantly more likely than men to hand down liberal rulings once the 10% threshold has been reached, with the probability of a liberal vote increasing by 48 points under this condition. In domestic violence cases—the issue with the strongest gender component of case types presented here—women justices might be inclined to suppress certain (liberal) views until women are present on high courts in significant numbers. Perhaps this inclination reflects an overcompensation by women justices

serving during the early part of the analyzed period in an attempt to avoid the perception of gender bias. Some of this result may be driven by the greater willingness of lawyers to employ and judges to accept the battered women's defense in the later cases in this data set. Although understanding the possible role of such forces must await future research, the results here portray strongly divergent patterns of voting by women judges after the tipping point has been reached. Moreover, voting by male justices trends differently in domestic violence cases than in the search and seizure and juvenile groupings. Unlike in the other two data sets, where men with multiple women colleagues were more likely to hand down liberal rulings, here the male judges sitting with two of more women are more likely to hand down conservative rulings, with the probability of a liberal vote dropping 45 points if a male justice sits with two or more women. It is unclear if this represents a backlash of sorts, with men becoming less likely to espouse a traditionally *feminine position* in an issue area with a strong gender component and as more women join the bench (for related arguments, see Kanter, 1977; Yoder, 1991). Again, these data can only hint at this and encourage additional research on this and other interpretations. Finally, and as in the other data sets, female justices sitting with female colleagues are more likely to render liberal rulings, with the probability of a liberal vote increasing by 20 points under this condition. Overall, the results suggest that the number of female justices matters, but in this data set, the increase in female judges on specific benches may have led some male justices toward more conservative voting patterns.

Second, the results also indicate that elected justices are more likely than appointed ones to render liberal decisions. In this case, however, liberal is defined as a vote for the person making a domestic violence claim, suggesting that elected justices are more likely to render decisions that support victims of domestic violence. Perhaps as an appeal to women voters or as a response to pressure from feminist and other organizations, elected justices appear more responsive to the claims of domestic violence than their appointed brethren. The results suggest that elections have an influence on judicial behavior but that influence is not simply manifest as conservatism in criminal justice cases. Although overall it may be accurate to cast elected justices as being under greater pressure to present a tough stand on law-and-order issues, the justices also appear more sympathetic to cases dealing with nontraditional suspects and abuse victims.

In addition, unlike in the other data sets, the institutional variables are much more relevant here. Throughout all data sets, the geographic selection variable is significant only in the domestic violence model, and the estimates here suggest that district-based selection is more likely to lead to conservative votes. Also, and again only significant in the domestic violence model, the positive coefficient on the "term lengths" variable suggests that as states provide justices with longer tenures on the court between retention events, the justices produce more liberal rulings. Although it is interesting to note that these variables are significant and correctly signed here, without comparable significance in the other data sets, it is difficult to conclude that these factors strongly contribute to judicial decisions in the general case. Again, the model is significant, correctly predicts 88.0% of cases, produces a Nagelkerke R^2 of .67, and reduces error by 70.0%.

Conclusions

This research suggests that men and women state supreme court justices exhibit a different decisional calculus in cases that are gender neutral and in cases that explicitly deal with women's issues. Moreover, it appears that the strength of gender differences is dependent on the number of female justices on the courts. Finally, the results suggest that these differences exist even after controlling for legal, political, and ideological factors. The findings add to our understanding of judicial behavior by placing the role of gender within the institutional context in which it plays out.

Across a range of issue areas, women justices exhibit a different, more liberal voting pattern from their male counterparts. This propensity of women justices to speak with a different voice, however, appears dependent in part on the number of women on the courts. It is not the case in the data sets explored here that gender simply does not matter. Rather, it seems likely that the influence of gender is somewhat suppressed and thus more difficult to detect until women justices achieve a notable presence on state supreme courts. In recent years, when such a threshold has been reached, the gender-based voting differences are significant and align with traditional, theoretical expectations (i.e., Sherry, 1986).

The results are consistent with critical mass theory and the notion that inclusion at the token level tends to suppress the expression of policy preferences. Indeed, the findings of this study on gender, and the partisanship study conducted by Sunstein et al. (2004), suggest that work on cohort effects is worthy of further consideration and that Asch's (1951) original analysis on conforming behavior among college students might be extended to elite group settings as well.

Moreover, institutional factors also appear to be strong determinants of behavior. Specifically, the scholarly research on methods of retention and judicial decisions has produced mixed results, with early efforts failing to substantiate a relationship between elections and decisions and later works (e.g., Hall & Brace, 1989) suggesting that a relationship might exist. Moreover, when a relationship between retention systems and judicial behavior is found, the research often possesses limited application given the narrowness of cases investigated. The findings presented here indicate that the effect of elections is more generalizable than previously suggested; perhaps elections structure judicial behavior in a broader spectrum of cases. As such, the research indicates that studies attempting to delineate the influence of gender should consider institutional constraints on a justice's ability to implement personal policy preferences.

In each of the data sets, the legal factors surrounding any particular case also appear to be strong constraints on judicial behavior. The influence of legal and institutional factors might help explain why the ideology variable was insignificant in all the models. The lack of significance overall of the attitudinal variable is an interesting and important finding because it suggests that although attitudes might be central to judicial decision making on the federal courts, attitudes play a smaller role on courts where the justices are more obligated to follow precedent and must face periodic retention events. Although I do not mean to suggest that judicial ideologies are irrelevant factors in decisions, the results indicate that state justices might be much more constrained by legal and political considerations than is generally recognized.

The results of this research strongly suggest that male and female justices exhibit differential voting patterns in three different criminal justice areas. Although it is premature to assert that "gender matters" in all cases, it would appear that the influence of gender is more generalized than has been previously found and might extend beyond cases explicitly dealing with women's lives. Moreover, the models suggest that past research may have been time bound, not adequately discerning gender-based voting differences because an adequate number of female justices did not occupy judicial positions. In addition, the models indicate that all justices, male and female, are heavily constrained in judicial action by legal and institutional constraints; thus, integrated models that control for these constraints might produce more complete results. However, given the apparently complex nature of judicial decisions that this research suggests, additional research using integrated models conducted on more contemporary supreme courts might determine the extent to which these results can be generalized and the extent to which we can confidently say that gender matters.

◤ References

Allen, D., & Wall, D. (1993). Role orientations and women state supreme court justices. *Judicature, 77,* 156–165.

Asch, S. E. (1951). Effects of group pressure upon the modification and distortion of judgment. In H. Guetzkow (Ed.), *Groups, leadership, and men* (pp. 177–190). Pittsburgh, PA: Carnegie Press.

Barr, M., Kearns, E., & Palmer, B. (2002, April). *Conversational dynamics during oral arguments before the Supreme Court: Does gender play a role?* Paper presented at the annual meeting of the Midwest Political Science Association, Chicago, IL.

Baum, L. (1995). Electing judges. In L. Epstein (Ed.), *Contemplating courts* (pp. 18–43). Washington, DC: Congressional Quarterly Press.

Behuniak-Long, S. (1992). Justice Sandra Day O'Connor and the power of maternal legal thinking. *Review of Politics, 54,* 417–444.

Brace, P., Langer, L., & Hall, M. (2000). Measuring the preferences of state supreme court justices. *Journal of Politics, 62*(2), 387–413.

Cicero, J., & DeConstanzo, E. (2000). *Sentencing women offenders: A training curriculum for judges.* Washington, DC: U.S. Department of Justice.

Cook, B. (1984). Women on the state bench: Correlates of access. In J. Flammang (Ed.), *Political women: Current roles in state and local government* (pp. 191–218). Beverly Hills, CA: Sage.

Davis, S. (1993). The voice of Sandra Day O'Connor. *Judicature, 77,* 134–139.

Davis, S., Haire, S., & Songer, D. (1993). Voting behavior and gender on the U.S. Court of Appeals. *Judicature, 77,* 129–133.

Dobbin, S., & Gatowski, S. (1996). *Juvenile violence: A guide to research.* Reno, NV: National Council of Juvenile and Family Court Judges.

Dworkin, A. G., Chafetz, J. S., & Dworkin, R. J. (1986). The effects of tokenism on work alienation among urban public school teachers. *Work and Occupations, 13,* 399–420.

Epstein, L., & Walker, T. (2001). *Constitutional law for a changing America: Rights, liberties and justice.* Washington, DC: Congressional Quarterly Press.

Felkenes, G. T. (1991). Affirmative action in the Los Angeles Police Department. *Criminal Justice Research Bulletin, 6,* 1–9.

Flammang, J. (1985). Female officials in the feminist capital: The case of Santa Clara County. *Western Political Quarterly, 38,* 94–118.

Floge, L., & Merrill, D. (1986). Tokenism reconsidered: Male nurses and female physicians in a hospital setting. *Social Forces, 64*(4), 925–946.

Gilligan, C. (1982). *In a different voice: Psychological theory and women's development.* Cambridge, MA: Harvard University Press.

Gryski, G., Main, E., & Dixon, W. (1986). Models of state high court decision making in sex discrimination cases. *Journal of Politics, 48,* 143–155.

Hall, M., & Brace, P. (1989). Order in the courts: A neo-institutional approach to judicial consensus. *Western Political Quarterly, 42,* 391–407.

Hall, M., & Brace, P. (1996). Justices' responses to case facts: An interactive model. *American Politics Quarterly, 24*(2), 237–261.

Hurwitz, J., & Smithey, S. (1998). Gender differences on crime and punishment. *Political Research Quarterly, 51,* 89–115.

Kanter, R. M. (1977). Some effects of proportions on group life: Skewed sex ratios and responses to token women. *American Journal of Sociology, 82,* 965–990.

Kathlene, L. (1995). Alternative views of crime: Legislative policy-making in gendered terms. *Journal of Politics, 57,* 696–723.

Kay, H. H., & Sparrow, G. (2001). Symposium and workshop on judging at the University of California, Berkeley School of Law (Boalt Hall), spring semester 2000: Workshop on judging: Does gender make a difference? *Wisconsin Women's Law Journal, 16,* 1–14.

Kmenta, J. (1986). *Elements of econometrics.* New York: Macmillan.

Maguire, K., & Pastore, A. (Eds.). (1996). *Bureau of Justice Statistics sourcebook of criminal justice statistics, 1995.* Washington, DC: Government Printing Office.

Marshall, C. (1991). Fear of crime, community satisfaction and self-protective measures: Perceptions from a Midwestern city. *Journal of Crime and Justice, 14,* 97–121.

Martin, E. (1993). The representative role of women judges. *Judicature, 77,* 166–173.

Martin, E., & Pyle, B. (2000). Gender, race, and partisanship on the Michigan Supreme Court. *Albany Law Review, 63,* 1205–1237.

Martin, E., & Pyle, B. (2005). Women on the courts symposium: State high courts and divorce: The impact of judicial gender. *University of Toledo Law Review, 36,* 923–947.

Martin, S., & Jurik, N. (1996). *Doing justice, doing gender: Women in law and criminal justice occupations.* Thousand Oaks, CA: Sage.

McCall, M. (2001). Campaign contributions and judicial decisions: Can justice be bought? *American Review of Politics, 22*(2), 349–374.

McCall, M. (2003a). Gender, judicial dissent, and issue salience: The voting behavior of state supreme court justices in sexual harassment cases, 1980–1998. *Social Science Journal, 40*(1), 79–97.

McCall, M. (2003b). The politics of judicial elections: The influence of campaign contributions on the voting patterns of Texas Supreme Court justices, 1994–1997. *Politics and Policy, 31*(2), 314–347.

McCall, M. (2005). Court decision making in police brutality cases, 1990–2000. *American Politics Research, 33*(1), 56–80.

McCall, M. A. (2004). *Urban policing levels and the localization of law and order politics.* Unpublished doctoral dissertation, Washington University, St. Louis, MO.

McCall, M. M., & McCall, M. A. (2007). How far does the gender gap extend? Decision making on state supreme courts in Fourth Amendment cases, 1980–2000. *Social Science Journal, 44*, 67–82.

McCarthy, M. (2001). Judicial campaigns: What can they tell us about gender on the bench? *Wisconsin Women's Law Journal, 16*, 87–112.

McDermott, M. (1998). Race and gender cues in low-information elections. *Political Research Quarterly, 51*(4), 895–919.

Palmer, B. (2001). "To do justly": The integration of women into the American judiciary. *PS: Political Science and Politics, 34*(2), 235–239.

Resnik, J. (1988). On the bias: Feminist reconsiderations of the aspirations for our judges. *Southern California Law Review, 61*, 1877–1944.

Rinehart, S. (2001). Do women leaders make a difference? Substance, style and perceptions. In S. Carroll (Ed.), *The impact of women in public office* (pp. 149–165). Bloomington: Indiana University Press.

Rottman, D., Flango, C., Cantrell, M., & La Fountain, N. (1998). *State court organization 1998.* Washington, DC: Bureau of Justice Statistics.

Schulz, D. M. (1995). *From social worker to crimefighter: Women in United States municipal policing.* Westport, CT: Praeger.

Segal, J. (2000). Representative decision making on the federal bench: Clinton's district court appointees. *Political Research Quarterly, 53*(1), 137–150.

Segal, J., & Spaeth, H. (1993). *The Supreme Court and the attitudinal model.* Cambridge, UK: Cambridge University Press.

Sherry, S. (1986). Civic virtue and the feminist voice in constitutional adjudication. *Virginia Law Review, 72*, 543–615.

Shevchenko, I. (2002). Who cares about women's problems? Female legislators in the 1995 and 1999 Russian state dumas. *Europe-Asia Studies, 54*, 1201–1222.

Sichel, J., Friedman, L., Quint, J., & Smith, M. (1978). *Women on patrol: A pilot study of police performance in New York City.* Washington, DC: National Criminal Justice Reference Service.

Sickels, R. (1965). The illusion of judicial consensus: Zoning decisions in the Maryland Court of Appeals. *American Political Science Review, 59*, 100–104.

Smith, S. (1994). Diversifying the judiciary: The influence of gender and race on judging. *Richmond Law Review, 28*, 179–204.

Songer, D., & Crews-Meyer, K. (2000). Does judge gender matter? Decision making in state supreme courts. *Social Science Quarterly, 81*(3), 751–762.

Songer, D., Davis, S., & Haire, S. (1994). A reappraisal of diversification in the federal courts: Gender effects in the courts of appeals. *Journal of Politics, 56*(2), 425–439.

Sunstein, C., Schkade, D., & Ellman, L. (2004). Ideological voting on federal courts of appeals. *Virginia Law Review, 90*, 301–354.

Terry v. Ohio, 392 U.S. 1 (1968).

Thomas, S. (1994). *How women legislate.* New York: Oxford University Press.

Traut, C., & Emmert, C. (1998). Expanding the integrated model of judicial decision making: The California justices and capital punishment. *Journal of Politics, 60*(4), 1166–1180.

Walker, T., & Barrow, D. (1985). The diversification of the federal bench: Policy and process ramifications. *Journal of Politics, 47*(2), 596–616.

Walker, T., Epstein, L., & Dixon, W. (1988). On the mysterious demise of consensual norms in the United States Supreme Court. *Journal of Politics, 50*(2), 361–389.

Warr, M. (1990). Dangerous situations: Social context and fear of victimization. *Social Forces, 68*, 891–907.

Wefing, J. (1997). State supreme court justices: Who are they? *New England Law Review, 32*, 47–88.

Welch, S. 1985. Are women more liberal than men in the U.S. Congress? *Legislative Studies Quarterly, 10*(1), 125–134.

Welch, S., & Hibbing, J. (1992). Financial conditions, gender, and voting in American national elections. *Journal of Politics, 54*, 197–213.

Which of the proposals I'm about to read would be most effective in reducing crime in this country? [Poll, various options, national, 1,682 respondents]. (1994, April 16–19). *Los Angeles Times.*

Yoder, J. (1991). Rethinking tokenism: Looking beyond numbers. *Gender & Society, 5*(2), 178–192.

DISCUSSION QUESTIONS

1. Which factors influence sentencing practices for search and seizure cases? How does gender play a role in these decisions?

2. Which factors influence sentencing practices for domestic violence cases? How does gender play a role in these decisions?

3. Which factors influence sentencing practices for cases of juveniles tried as adults? How does gender play a role in these decisions?

READING 26

In an effort to meet the needs of crime victims, many agencies began as community-based movements to serve the needs of particular crime victims, such as intimate partner violence or rape and sexual assault. This article by Sarah Ullman and Stephanie Townsend looks at the challenges that rape crisis workers face in the delivery of services to victims.

Barriers to Working With Sexual Assault Survivors

A Qualitative Study of Rape Crisis Center Workers

Sarah E. Ullman and Stephanie M. Townsend

Rape crisis centers are uniquely situated to respond to the physical, emotional, and social needs of survivors. Their services focus on three critical areas: 24-hour crisis hotlines, individual and group counseling (often on a short-term basis only), and legal and medical advocacy (Campbell & Martin, 2001). Although there have been few explicit studies on the benefits of receiving rape crisis services, there is evidence that rape crisis center advocates do help victims obtain services from the legal, medical, and mental health systems. In a study of survivors' postassault experiences, Campbell et al. (1999) found that survivors who worked with a rape crisis center advocate experienced significantly less distress than those who did not. In community studies, rape crisis centers are rated as most helpful of a range of support sources by victims seeking help after assault (Filipas & Ullman, 2001; Golding, Siegel, Sorenson, Burnam, & Stein, 1989). A recent study of more than 1,000 sexual assault survivors recruited from the community in a large metropolitan area showed that 16%

sought rape crisis services and 79.3% rated them as helpful—a higher percentage than any of 10 informal and formal support sources assessed (Ullman, Filipas, Townsend, & Starzynski, in press). Despite the potential benefit of crisis services, only 1 in 5 survivors in their sample received these services. Similarly, the numbers of survivors accessing the legal, mental health, and criminal justice systems are also low. Representative community data show that only 11.0% have contact with the legal system, 9.3% seek medical care, and 16.1% obtain mental health services (Golding et al., 1989). Recent convenience samples show higher rates of contact, with 20% to 39% contacting the legal system, 20% to 43% seeking medical care, and 39% to 60% obtaining mental health care (Campbell et al., 1999; Ullman, 1996; Ullman et al., in press). Even the highest of these estimates reflects a relatively low proportion of survivors accessing services that can potentially benefit from them in coping with the physical and psychological effects of sexual violence. This raises questions about whether

SOURCE: Ullman, S. E., & Townsend, S. M. (2007). Barriers to working with sexual assault survivors: A qualitative study of rape crisis center workers. *Violence Against Women, 14*(4), 412–443.

NOTE: This article was partially written while the first author was a faculty scholar at the University of Illinois at Chicago, Great Cities Institute. Earlier portions of this article were presented at the 2003 and 2004 American Society of Criminology meetings. We thank anonymous reviewers of this article for helpful comments.

there are barriers to services that could be mitigated. Specific services for rape victims can be obtained from mental health, medical, and police or legal sources following the crime. Martin (2005) has provided a detailed description of all formal service providers and their roles in relation to serving rape victims. Martin argues that some service providers pose barriers for victims and their advocates because of unique organizational goals that conflict with the goal of enhancing victim recovery. For example, Martin has shown how organizational goals such as police' and prosecutors' need for victims to serve as credible witnesses and hospital personnel's treatment of victims as patients with physical injuries lead them to treat victims in an unresponsive manner. Other work with rape survivors shows that they experience harmful treatment from medical and legal institutions that often revictimize them with negative social reactions (Campbell, 1998; Campbell, Wasco, Ahrens, Sefl, & Barnes, 2001). This evidence suggests that organizational or system barriers lead to harmful responses to victims and likely a lack of therapeutic services. The existence of barriers is further supported by Logan, Evans, Stevenson, and Jordan's (2005) recent focus groups with 30 female clients from rural and urban rape crisis centers that showed barriers of lack of access, availability, and knowledge of services, and unacceptable and/or revictimizing experiences with service providers (e.g., lack of sensitivity by mental health, medical, and criminal justice personnel). These findings regarding secondary victimization are consistent with many other studies of sexual assault victims, showing that survivors report a variety of negative social reactions both from informal and especially from formal support providers. Furthermore, studies show these reactions have harmful effects on psychological symptoms of survivors, including posttraumatic stress disorder (PTSD; Campbell et al., 1999; Davis, Brickman, & Baker, 1991; Ullman, 1996; Ullman et al., in press; Ullman & Filipas, 2001).

Reports from victims are an important source of information regarding barriers to accessing support. An alternative approach is to seek the perspectives of advocates whose role is both to provide direct support and to help victims access resources from other systems. Advocates may be a useful source of information in at least three ways. First, they can help to identify barriers victims face. This approach was used by Campbell (1998), who interviewed rape crisis advocates about their most recent case. Advocates were asked about victims' experiences with the legal, medical, and mental health systems, including what actions were taken by each system, whether those actions fit what the victim wanted, and how readily available the services were. Analyses indicated that there were three patterns in victims' experiences. One group had positive experiences with all three systems, a second group had positive experiences only with the medical system, and a third group had difficult experiences with all three systems. This study revealed differential patterns of responses based on community-level, assault-related, and individual-level variables. It also demonstrated that advocates could be an important source of information about the experiences victims have when seeking support services.

Second, advocates may also be important sources of information about the challenges service providers face when assisting survivors. Burnout and vicarious trauma have been documented as problems in past studies of rape crisis workers (Baird & Jenkins, 2003; Ghahramanlou & Brodbeck, 2000; Schauben & Frazier, 1996) and crime victim support workers generally (see Salston & Figley, 2003, for a review). Yet most research has only studied these psychological symptoms in relation to worker characteristics and client caseloads. It is also important to understand organizational and system-related barriers from the vantage point of those who interface with many survivors during long periods. Social service providers' perspectives in their own words can provide additional insights into the institutional barriers that limit the availability and efficacy of services. Such information may help in understanding the larger context of rape crisis work that contributes to vicarious trauma and burnout in workers.

Third, understanding the perspectives of service providers on service-related barriers can help researchers who are attempting to do collaborative research on sexual violence. Collaborative methods for research and evaluation are especially appropriate when working with violence against women organizations because of the fact that workers in such organizations possess critical knowledge about issues such as client safety and confidentiality (Wasco et al., 2004). It is also beneficial for practitioners who cite benefits of collaboration that include identification of promising practices, validation of local program experiences, obtaining data to support funding requests, and evaluation of client services and programs, whereas researchers cite benefits of gaining new perspectives, generating research ideas, improving project design, and interpreting research findings (National Violence Against Women Prevention Research Center, 2001). However, there are numerous challenges to collaboration between researchers and service providers, including differing priorities, different organizational cultures, and a diversity of professional backgrounds, that give rise to different terminologies (Riger, 1999). Overcoming these challenges and negotiating tensions first requires that researchers understand the context in which service providers work. To foster effective collaborations, it is particularly important that researchers understand the barriers that service providers may face in their work. This can sensitize researchers to the complexities of service provision, thereby allowing for better communication and collaboration.

In summary, although some research has documented barriers faced by survivors to getting help (Campbell, 1998; Campbell et al., 2001; Martin, 2005), further work is needed from service provider perspectives on the barriers they face in advocating for survivors. Therefore, a qualitative interview study was conducted of victim advocates from various rape crisis centers in a large urban area. This was a grounded theory, exploratory study to identify barriers advocates face in their work and how those barriers affect survivors' ability to receive support. Implications for future research and practice with sexual assault survivors are discussed.

Method

Sample

The sample was composed of 25 women who were current or former rape victim advocates working at rape crisis centers in a large Midwestern metropolitan area. This sample is part of a larger study of both clinicians and advocates working at a variety of social service agencies, including rape crisis centers (see Ullman, 2005, for a description of the first author's experience doing these interviews). Participants were recruited using multiple methods. Letters were sent to 60 people working in agencies in the metropolitan area who were listed as participants at the most recent national conference on sexual

violence prevention. All persons who called the researcher or responded to the researcher's phone calls did participate in the study. In response to these letters, 14 interviews were conducted (a 23% response rate). Although the sexual violence conference is a selective source to sample, many eligible participants could be easily identified from that list with contact information for many metropolitan area rape crisis workers who attended the conference. In addition, 10 interviewees were identified by participants referring the interviewer to other people who have worked in the rape crisis field in the area, and one person was located by a chance meeting at a professional function. This resulted in a total sample of 25 advocates, representing 10 distinct agency locations, with an average of 2.80 persons interviewed per location. Nineteen participants were currently working as advocates doing advocacy, referral, and/or crisis counseling at rape crisis centers. Six were former advocates who had worked at rape crisis centers, generally within the past year. Most advocates had done medical advocacy and/or crisis counseling. Two had done primarily legal advocacy, one had done health education, and six had also done administrative work (e.g., volunteer coordinator, director, supervisor) in addition to advocacy. Eight rape crisis centers were freestanding organizations, two programs were contained within a larger social service agency or community mental health center, and one participant worked both on a rape crisis hotline and in a university counseling and advocacy setting. All women had experience working with sexual assault survivors, ranging from 1.5 to 16 years of experience, with an average of 5.14 years of experience (s = 3.83). Eleven workers also had mental health experience doing crisis counseling or other types of therapy with sexual assault survivors, with an average of 3.64 years of experience (s = 6.00). Participants were asked to indicate if they had any or all of four types of training (sexual assault, domestic violence, child abuse, violence against women). Thirteen had all 4 types of training, and 12 had from 1 to 3 types of training. All had training on sexual assault. No further detail was specifically asked about the nature and extent of participants' training. In terms of practice location, 4 worked in suburban locations, 19 worked in the city, and 2 worked in both city and suburban settings. Women were asked to check off all applicable items in a checklist that characterized their treatment orientation. Seventeen endorsed a feminist orientation in their approach to working with survivors, whereas 12 endorsed various other treatment orientations such as client-centered and cognitive behavioral. All participants were women. In terms of education, 1 had a PhD, 7 had master's degrees, 14 had bachelor's degrees, and 3 had some college or an associate's degree. Most women were White ($n = 12$), followed by Hispanic ($n = 6$), Black ($n = 5$), Asian ($n = 1$), and multiracial ($n = 1$). Women's average age was 33.04 years ($s = 9.20$ years). Most women ($n = 12$) were in their 20s, with a range of 25 to 58 years. Two had incomes of $10,000 to $20,000, 11 had incomes from $20,000 to $30,000 per year, 8 earned $30,000 to $40,000 per year, 3 had incomes of $60,000 or more, and 1 refused to provide her income.

Agencies

Services for rape victims in the area from which participants were sampled include a 24-hour hotline for the entire metropolitan area that is run out of the largest rape crisis center in the city. The hotline is coordinated by full-time employees and staffed by trained volunteers 24 hours a day. Other services provided by the area's rape crisis centers include medical and legal advocacy, crisis counseling and referral to other social and mental health services, prevention education, and training to other agencies including police and state's attorneys. Agencies where workers were employed included two large rape crisis centers, one of which had satellite offices in both city and suburban locations. Both of these rape crisis centers had administrative and supervisory staff, advocates, and counselors, with a smaller core of paid, full-time staff and a larger core of volunteer victim advocates who typically went on emergency room calls when rape victims were taken there by police following an assault.

Some workers mainly did crisis counseling and gave referrals to survivors of sexual assault, whereas others did longer-term therapy with survivors or administrative work and supervision of other employees in their agencies. Most advocates did crisis counseling and medical advocacy, with two advocates primarily doing legal advocacy and prevention education to area schools and colleges. Typically, those doing mostly counseling also worked on advocacy needs with clients, some of whom were also receiving therapy from mental health professionals outside of the rape crisis center. Smaller agencies were typically more mental health focused and were often part of community mental health centers, although they still identified as rape crisis centers. They provided the same advocacy and counseling services, but the larger organizations where they were housed also served other populations, such as child victims or clients with general mental health needs. Agencies varied in geographic location and both provider and client demographic characteristics, partially reflecting the agency, its philosophy, and the client population of the specific agency location. For example, agencies in predominantly Black or Hispanic neighborhoods had more staff with similar ethnic backgrounds, whereas agencies located in the downtown central city had a greater proportion of White staff.

Obviously, our study is limited by a small sample from a subset of centers in one metropolitan area, some of whom were former advocates with negative experiences that may have motivated them to participate. No rural advocates were included in this study, which is a limitation because rape crisis center services are much more limited in rural areas (Martin, 2005) and barriers that advocates and victims face may differ in rural arenas (Logan et al., 2005). In addition, only a couple of open ended questions were asked about barriers advocates faced in working with survivors and in their organizations specifically, which were followed up with probes. Detailed questions were not asked about a predetermined list of specific barriers, which may have led to underreporting of certain barriers or more discussion by advocates of the most salient barriers they face. Because only the first author conducted these interviews, age and race matching with advocates was not possible. The first author is a White, middle-aged female, which may have led to fewer or poorer quality data from advocates with different age and ethnic characteristics (see Ullman, 2005, for a discussion of her perceptions of how this may have affected interviews with older, ethnic minority women, in particular).

Procedure

Participants completed in-person interviews at a time and location convenient for them. Most interviews were conducted at their work offices (20) at a convenient time for the women, but 5 preferred to be interviewed at other locations. Interviews were conducted from November 2002 through May 2003 by the first author. Interviews ranged from 45 minutes to 1 hour and 20 minutes in length, with the average interview length of 65.36 minutes (s = 13.36 minutes), and a modal interview length of 1 hour.

Semistructured interviews asked about women's training and work experience with survivors of sexual assault and other relevant work experience, how disclosures of sexual assault tended to occur, how interviewees typically respond to disclosures, difficult and rewarding aspects of working with survivors, barriers to working with survivors and to survivors' obtaining services, and solutions that might improve services to this population. Participants were also asked about their views about the role of mental health professionals in working with sexual assault survivors. Only the data on barriers were analyzed in the current study.

Analysis Strategy

A grounded theory approach was used for data analysis. Four stages of analysis were used. The first stage consisted of open and axial coding (Strauss & Corbin, 1998). Open codes emerged from the text to break the data into discrete parts. Axial coding extended the analysis from the textual level to the conceptual level. The second stage of analysis involved construction of a meta-matrix, which is a master chart that compiles descriptive data from each case into a standard format (Miles & Huberman, 1994). Column headings identified key variables and each row represented a program. This process allowed for the identification of themes that were common to many programs and those that were unique to a small number of programs. The third stage of analysis was the manipulation of the meta-matrix to create submatrices that were conceptually ordered according to key variables (Miles & Huberman, 1994). This process allowed for identification of patterns between variables. The final stage was the creation of analysis forms that summarized the submatrices. In completing these forms, both within-case and cross case analyses were done, in which the content of codes within and then across cases were compared. The goal was to identify and interpret any themes or patterns that could answer the research question of what barriers interfere with survivors receiving help following a sexual assault. The results as described in the following section were based on the final stage of analysis.

Results and Discussion

Advocates identified multiple barriers to their work with survivors at their organizations and in the social systems (e.g., medical, criminal justice) from which survivors seek help. In the sections that follow, each barrier is described by advocates reporting them and how the barrier affected advocates' ability to work with survivors and help them access needed services. To frame the organization of these barriers, Reading Figure 26.1 shows how these themes may be organized hierarchically to show their interrelationships.

Broader societal attitudes discussed first can be viewed as influencing several subgroups of barriers occurring at levels of the (a) organization, (b) staff, and (c) direct services.

Societal Attitudes

Barriers to service provision exist within a larger societal context. At the macro level, it is important to consider how societal attitudes may be reflected in the responses that societal institutions make to rape survivors. Some advocates (36%) spoke about attitudes toward rape manifested in system responses that interfered with advocacy. For example, one advocate discussed the larger barrier of societal denial of the problem of rape:

> We still haven't reached a point in our society where you can even acknowledge this problem for what it is and that's why people can't get over it. I don't care if they're sitting in an office an hour a week and somebody says, yes you have a right to all these feelings, everything else in the world, tells them that they don't. Until we acknowledge that, that's never gonna happen! (Advocate 36)

Race and class biases are also societal barriers reflected in organizations, including rape crisis centers and in institutions that respond to survivors' needs. These types of biases were noted by 56% of participants.

> So it's all based on the story that night what's the story? How credible is the witness? the victim? How credible is the perp? Well, you know racism plays into account, classism plays into account, I mean you name it, it's there. Sexism plays a role, too. (Advocate 3)

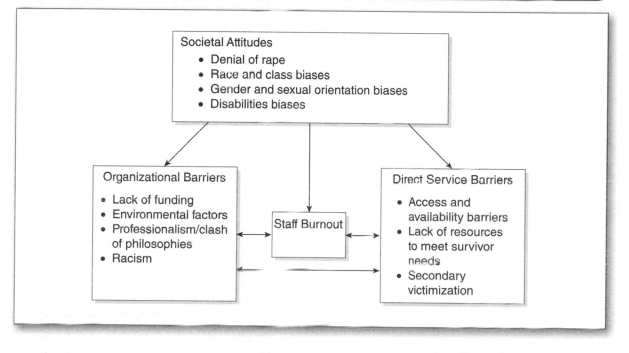

There's always this doubt. I've never heard a person who wasn't of color told: "Well, you can take it back if you want, you know if you tell me that you made it up, then we'll let you go if you try to press charges." They bully young people and particularly young people of color by saying, "I'm giving you a chance to take this back." Police say I'm giving you a chance to tell me the truth, if you're not telling me the truth then you know, you can take it back now, but if we go through with this and we try and prosecute and we find out that you're lying, then you're gonna go to jail, you know? It's like a script. I haven't heard like an older person told that, I've never heard a person who wasn't of color asked those things so, and when I say older, I mean like people in their 40's or 50's unless there was a situation where maybe they were mentally ill or they were a substance abuser. It's always people who are disenfranchised in some form or fashion who are completely silenced and not believed. (Advocate 25)

One participant continued to explain further the ways survivors are treated differently based on gender and sexual orientation:

It's even sexist because male survivors are treated horribly. They don't even take it seriously and act like they deserve it. The impression I've gotten is not as if they're saying that it didn't happen, it was just they deserved it or they must have been doing something to condone it or they must be homosexual so it's because of their lifestyle. I've seen survivors who were not homosexual openly say, well you know, I'm not gay, but all the questioning was geared around that. Did you know the guy, were you in a relationship with him? Why does that matter so? People still have in their minds what the ideal rape victim looks like, behaves like, what type of lifestyle they have. It's amazing to me that we haven't gotten past that. I think it's partly the media and it's partly about just wanting to remain in your comfort zone. (Advocate 25)

Another advocate spoke of problems that survivors with disabilities and immigrants have in getting appropriate responses from service systems:

> I think the hardest work that I've done is with people with any type of disability and with elder people and not because they put up a barrier. It's hard also to work with people with mental illness because it's hard to work with them, and it's hard to make the system to understand them and respect them and their rights. It's also hard with immigrants for the same reason and because law enforcement doesn't cooperate with them and thinks what they're saying or what they think is because of their ethnicity. (Advocate 32)

Clearly, these attitudes make it even more difficult for advocates to help survivors from marginalized groups who suffer from multiple sources of stigmatization and devaluation in the eyes of social institutions that deal with rape victims. It is much more difficult for advocates to combat not only rape stereotypes affecting all rape survivors but also additional stereotypes about "less deserving" rape victims who because of age, race, sexual orientation, occupation, mental illness, or immigration status are viewed as unworthy of the system's attention or response. These attitudes about specific groups of people are ingrained in all members of society to varying degrees and may be more unconscious and well accepted. This may make them even harder for advocates to challenge than rape stereotypes, which probably are less socially acceptable to admit adhering to. These broad societal attitudes undergird specific barriers that are seen at the levels of the organization and staff, and they contribute to barriers that victims face when seeking direct services.

⊠ Organizational Barriers

The high prevalence of rape in combination with widespread denial of this problem contributes to the underresourcing of agencies that serve victims. As a result, rape crisis centers face organizational-level barriers to providing an adequate response to victims' needs. Barriers at this level include a lack of funding and environmental stressors. In the effort to obtain more funding and resources, agencies have come under pressure to adopt organizational practices that are seen as more professional but that in some cases redefine the agencies' focus on advocacy. In addition, organizations are not immune from societal attitudes such as racism that may be manifest in their own practices. Each of these barriers was articulated by participants in this study.

Lack of Funding

The lack of funding was an issue mentioned by 64% of participants. Some described funding as precluding advocates from making a long-term commitment to rape crisis work. This may directly contribute to staff turnover and, therefore, to lower quality services for survivors.

> It's hard to think about making a RCC [rape crisis center] a career for a long time, cause it's impossible, it's very hard to imagine spending the rest of your life working for no more than $35,000 a year and that's after being at an agency for a long time. Especially, I mean I remember that they just made a decision that nobody was going to advance, they were only going to have supervisors that had master's degrees, so everybody that had a BA or BS, that was sort of then the ground level. Some were sort of faced with this dilemma, because there's obviously nowhere else to advance in the agency without having a master's degree but the money and time it would take to get a master's degree and then come back, even the supervisory level is really only going to make $4,000 more. But I went for my master's last year, it would be financially prohibitive even in a supervisory position. So I think that they can also value sort of experience in the field. (Advocate 35)

> I know I'm glad we're getting money, I'm glad to have this done but it's just I think there were some of the people at [Agency X] who left because they had children and the agency doesn't provide child care, you know you can't bring your child, too. I understand that, and so it's cheaper to stay at home with your children than to have day care and work at [Agency X]. The pay is that low for some of the positions, and I don't understand

how in a feminist organization why people have to leave a job. (Advocate 35)

In addition to low salaries, which may contribute to staff turnover, the lack of funding also raises the possibility of competition between agencies for available funds. This was a concern of 16% of participants. One advocate spoke of this in relation to the competition between domestic violence and sexual assault providers for the same dollars:

I think sometimes you run into that sort of change in focus [from rape to domestic violence], I think other times it's really just vying for the same funding. I think the whole DV/ sexual assault thing is that domestic violence has always just been sort of ahead of the ball in terms of getting the funding, the awareness, and getting more people to recognize it as an issue. Plus, I think just in general it's [domestic violence] easier for people to talk about than anything that has to do with sex. That kind of puts you down a couple of notches in terms of who's gonna want to talk to you about it, fund you, and let you into their schools to talk about it. So I think that there has always sort of been that challenge distinguishing sexual assault from domestic violence and getting sexual assault recognized, also a very serious concern that needs attention. (Advocate 10)

The scarcity and competitiveness of funds was also discussed in terms of how it shapes the approaches agencies take to doing their work. One such effect is that agencies may take on new projects because they fear losing the support of grantors, even though the new projects are beyond the scope of what the agency can handle. For example, an advocate complained of a situation when her agency director agreed to provide advocacy to more area hospitals, when advocate resources were already stretched to the limit in covering their existing contracts:

I'm sure it has to do with funding, but I think that there's also a way in which we, as in "we" as a part of this agency get so scared that we're gonna lose funding or not be able to expand services

that we start agreeing to things that are not helpful to the agency. (Advocate 35)

Part of the problem may be that grantors do not recognize the larger context of providing services or the preliminary steps needed to launch an initiative. This can create a mismatch between grantors' expectations and what is actually necessary to carry out community initiatives. One advocate explained this in the context of outreach she did to the [ethnic group name] community:

The [ethnic group name] services program was funded when I started working at the agency and they had staff that was funded by [the state coalition], but the funding was strictly for counseling, and the entire time that I was there, they had a total of 3 or 4 clients, because the outreach had not been done. You can't just open your doors and expect that people are gonna come. What ended up happening with that program was that everyone was aware that we were in danger of losing that funding, and so the manager asked me to come in and make a last minute push to try and drum up some clients. But it was a little late, and actually that was a time when I felt like I was ready to transition into something else anyway, so I said okay, fine, but the more I started working on that, the more I felt like this is just not something that I care to save, because this program was of course conceived in a way that had no consideration or respect for the communities that it was presuming to serve. If the funding was really what it should be, it should be funded to be purely outreach and that's it. We shouldn't even have been funded for counseling at that point in time, which they would have known if they had talked to anybody within those communities. (Advocate 37)

A former advocate with many years in the field explained her broader view of funding in relation to other government priorities. She spoke of federal changes in terms of a shift from funding victim services to funding criminal justice and prosecution-based strategies and a wholesale shift of funds away from violence against women toward issues of gangs and drugs:

There's so many different levels to that because nationally there's nothing available because the funding has been diverted over the last 5 years from victim services into prosecution. And so there's less and less money available to victim services, so a lot of the money comes from things like the Violence Against Women Act and some other kinds of victims' services. But in order to deal with the crime, the current administration strategy is to shift away [from] putting victim services money into prosecution. But the problem is that prosecution money has been transferred into prosecution of gangs and drugs, so the prosecution level of sexual assault, domestic violence, or child sexual abuse has not necessarily increased in correlation with extra money they put into prosecution. (Advocate 38)

She also spoke of the problematic structure of services where duplicate services have been developed in parallel, instead of having centralized services, where common resources can be shared by many different constituencies. Her comments on this matter are especially notable because they contrast with other participants who expressed more concern with maintaining their own agencies' programs and services. This former advocate, however, proposed a centralization of services as a way to make better use of limited funds:

Right now is there are a lot of dollars spent on duplication of services, but what I would like to see is an actual kind of centralization of services that a lot of these violence against women agencies need, so you have a centralization of services that offer legal advocates so that not everybody has these positions. You could have a centralized database where you allow common resources to be funded commonly and collectively and then people can utilize the resources. So if you've got a curriculum development person who's actually being funded from eight different agencies, each of those agencies has to spend less money, but they can all utilize the curricula developed by that kind of a practice system. I think it's what's necessary and I think it's the next part of the maturation process of these agencies. (Advocate 38)

Environmental Factors

Limited funding may also lead to less than ideal settings in which to provide services. Environmental factors within rape crisis centers were cited as barriers to providing services by 8% of advocates. This problem may be greater, however, at smaller agencies and satellite offices. Those mentioning positive environmental characteristics of their work settings (e.g., spacious, peaceful, welcoming) all worked in larger agencies, whereas most of the small number of participants mentioning problems with the work environment (3 out of 4) worked in these smaller settings. Specifically, they talked about problems with lack of privacy and limited space for doing advocacy in their workplace. For example,

In terms of counseling, I've only had about 3 clients coming into the office for legal advocacy where there's no real privacy. I have the cubicle where I sit, but there's no real privacy for a client to come in and talk to me. (Advocate 22)

A related issue regarding the physical work environment was safety concerns, mentioned by one advocate working at a larger agency in the city:

For the first month I was working there, there was no lock on the office door, so I couldn't even lock myself in, and I just remember being terrified at night and being told by the agency that we don't have enough money and there's too many people coming in and out to deal with this problem. (Advocate 35)

Although few advocates in this study mentioned environmental factors, likely because they were not specifically asked about these factors, they seemed important to mention because they may affect advocates in their work with victims. Martin (2005) notes that smaller agencies, particularly rape crisis centers, may be less able to be responsive to victims' needs generally because of their limited resources.

Professionalization of Rape Crisis Centers

Another important organizational characteristic that may affect the ability of advocates to help survivors is the professionalization of rape crisis centers, which was mentioned by 16% of advocates. Research has documented that as many rape crisis centers have become more institutionalized, they have focused more on counseling and advocacy for individual survivors and less on political action and institutional advocacy, as in the past (Campbell, Baker, & Mazurek, 1998). In this study, a major barrier raised by some advocates was professionalization of rape crisis centers. Professionalization and standardization of services has its benefits, such as ensuring that survivors receive quality treatment (e.g., counseling) by well-trained professionals who have specific educational credentials. However, it may also have disadvantages, such as minimizing the traditional feminist or social change perspective, that may be important for challenging systems that fail to meet victims' needs.

Advocates presented two conflicting views on the impact of professionalization of rape crisis centers on survivors receiving their services. Three advocates argued that professionalization (e.g., requiring specific educational credentials) was harmful because it (a) excluded many women who had a vital contribution to make helping rape survivors and (b) led rape crisis centers to hire professionals who were nonfeminist or even antifeminist in their orientation. Another perspective voiced by one advocate in particular was that professionalization (defined as appropriate professional training and demeanor) is important to encourage in rape crisis centers, so that survivors are appropriately treated and the field is taken seriously and supported by external funders. However, this approach may also narrow the range of people whose skills are employed in the field. In this sample, concerns about professionalization were noted more by those workers endorsing a feminist orientation. The advocates quoted below described the manifestation of professionalization of rape crisis work occurring at the organizational level:

> There's a lot of issues like professionalization of the movement that I think is a big problem. Everything is so focused on services. You have people at [Agency X], they had this awesome very powerful woman working there, she'd been doing the work for several years and she was let go, they got rid of her position. We had heard it was because she doesn't have a college degree and that's [Agency X's] formal policy is you have

to have a college degree to do the work. I think that just excludes a lot of very amazing people. (Advocate 29)

> There are ways that agencies could think more about how they are marketing their services, who their staff are, what their priorities are in terms of staffing and where centers and satellites are going to be located, but I think that's not the kind of thing that happens. This is where I start to get really angry because I feel as though I've seen the agencies get more and more professionalized and become more of a system. They all work together more, so they become more and more alike, and it's frustrating because there's this move to say we want all of our counselors to have master's degrees. On the one hand, yeah you would like your sexual assault survivors to get sort of the best kind of counseling that they can, but the master's is not always the best measure of who's best able to provide 10 weeks of crisis counseling. (Advocate 35)

This latter point is likely valid given research showing no correlation of professional training with psychotherapeutic effectiveness (Luborsky et al., 1986; Stein & Lambert, 1984). Professional technical expertise and knowledge do not necessarily predict success. Instead, effective therapists and other support sources have qualities of warmth, empathy, and genuineness (Frank & Frank, 1991), which may not come from professional training or certification.

Limiting staff to those with graduate degrees can also narrow the focus of rape crisis centers. Specifically, the need for activism and social advocacy, not simply counseling, was identified as important for empowering survivors:

> We have to move toward thinking about social advocacy and making change. I see a lot more counselors who are just trained as counselors and don't think about activism. If you're in there empowering your clients, think about how much they can advocate for themselves. Not just with family members or partners, but society. . . . Writing a letter to the editor can be a part of the counseling or therapy, but that gets

lost when they're more traditional, and that's not being stressed in the training. (Advocate 35)

Unfortunately, as agencies professionalize and require more educational credentials, they lose a broader activist focus, which is critical for fighting rape and for empowering survivors, and end up with a narrower, apolitical, individual counseling approach.

Another advocate described the problem of supervisors with clinical credentials who are nonfeminist and yet are hired at rape crisis centers that traditionally espoused and often still espouse a feminist commitment to addressing violence against women:

> They hired a clinical supervisor who was not a feminist, who said that she doesn't understand what feminism's about. But how can you work in a RCC and not be a feminist? I remember one time she came to talk to me about a client she had. She said the woman had gone to make a phone call at like three in the morning, and this woman said, "Well don't you just think that was stupid, I mean that was just asking to get raped." And I said, "I cannot believe you are the clinical supervisor at this agency!" (Advocate 35)

Clearly, such statements are problematic coming from a leader in an organization devoted to eradicating violence against women and sensitive treatment of rape survivors. This may not only affect survivors who have contact with the staff person but also communicate a negative and demoralizing message to advocates about how their organization's leaders view sexual assault survivors.

Although these concerns about professionalization and especially about the hiring of staff based on narrow criteria were shared by many of the advocates, an alternative view was also expressed. An advocate who had left rape crisis work to work on behalf of rape victims in another arena presented a very different view of professionalization. She argued for a "professionalism" that referred to the need for professional behavior in rape crisis centers. This was distinct from the issue of professionalization of rape crisis centers by requiring workers to have advanced degrees:

> A controversial thing that I've said before, and people get mad at me all the time, is I think a lot of victim service agencies adopt a victim mentality of "woe is us, there's nothing we can do, there's too much to be done, we can't do it all, we're stressed out." There is a lack of professionalism in these agencies. . . . I think part of it is, you've gotta professionalize the profession in a way that it hasn't been. I mean we just have not done it and I don't think it has to be that damn stressful as people make it out to be. I think there is a way to do this and I think it has to do with leadership. One of the things I have fought very hard for at [Agency X] is to say, look, if it stresses you out that much, don't do it! (Advocate 38)

I asked how this kind of professionalism differed from the negative side of professionalization of agencies that other advocates expressed to me. She elaborated on the problem:

> Sometimes you hear these young, passionate people are very feminist or who have very strong politics who feel like the model is very apolitical or very service oriented and doesn't have that kind of analysis. But the thing about it is, and maybe this is just me getting older too, is that passion that you find in the college age population. . . . You can't build a workforce on that, cause guess what, those kids grow up and when they hit 25, they quit cause they wanna make more money. I think the problem is people want to build a lot on trying to harness that energy, but that is a fleeting kind of energy, it is not a permanent energy, and so what you have to do is you have to create a channel in which you capture that energy but that can't be the permanent fuel that you run on. The permanent fuel that you run on has to be based on professionals who are in it for the long haul. (Advocate 38)

This quote suggests that both conditions of the work (e.g., low pay) and who it attracts (e.g., young feminists) may lead to staff turnover because of lack of career advancement opportunities in rape crisis centers. She spoke of how she envisioned developing services to address specific functions that agencies sought to fulfill and that such a model would lead to long-term growth instead of functioning in survival mode in the context of limited government resources directed at the problem.

> We need staff people to fulfill these functions. What are the functions that should be fulfilled from a staff perspective, what are the functions from a volunteer perspective and how can we professionalize the whole process so that we're putting appropriate responsibilities on staff, appropriate responsibilities on volunteers, appropriate responsibilities on the boards of directors, appropriate responsibilities on leadership, and we've created some really strong selection tools, retention tools, leadership development tools, so that people in these positions are people who wanna be in these positions for the long haul, and we're actually developing the skills necessary for them to become better as they go along. . . . It's a difference between surviving and thinking about long term growth. I think the way that these organizations are constructed right now is all based on a survival model. I absolutely think this issue [rape] is one of the most underfunded issues in our country, and it's one of the most prevalent issues in our country, and we don't deal with it. But until the rest of the world comes around, we have to do better with what we have. (Advocate 38)

Racism in Rape Crisis Centers

Racism is an issue that has been critically important in the contemporary women's movement generally and in relation to the issue of rape and rape crisis centers specifically (Campbell et al., 2001; Matthews, 1994; Scott, 1998). Racism is not only an issue that must be confronted in the broader society. It must also be confronted within rape crisis centers themselves. If left unaddressed, it undermines an agency's ability to provide quality services to victims of color and replicates within the agency dynamics of oppression that are related to the cultural causes of violence against women. Racism was spontaneously noted to be a problem in rape crisis organizations by 24% of advocates in this study:

> I think the whole rape crisis center thing is still a "White feminist" women's movement thing, and

I think it's still painfully obvious. Especially at a center like X which for the most part is White women. (Advocate 30)

Another advocate voiced her perception that her organization tried to be nonracist by sponsoring events related to women of color, but that action was not tantamount to a thorough organizational critical self-examination and attempt to be truly nonracist in everyday practices:

> We just had this event focused on women of color, which I think is good, but I think in some way it's almost like, well you know, we did that event kind of a thing like, we're not racist, we did that event! (Advocate 29)

Another advocate discussed a systemic issue that she perceived affected workers in her satellite office. The workers all happened to be women of color and were treated with distrust by the manager at the main office of the organization who was White:

> There was, in my mind, a ridiculous conflict with our manager who had a basic lack of trust in people in our office, many of whom had conflicts with her in the past. A lot of us perceived that this was related to the fact that everyone who worked in our office were people of color. (Advocate 37)

Another more structural manifestation of racism was the geographic distribution of services, which resulted in disproportionately poorer access to rape crisis services for women living in predominantly ethnic minority neighborhoods.

> Downtown and the north side is where most services are! There are less on south side, yet huge populations reside there. There are not enough funds to publicize resources or to understand what people want or need. Many White feminists in the field who are college educated need to not "poo-poo" religion. We don't understand different cultural responses. (Advocate 33)

Another former advocate who was an administrator and worked for many years in the [city] rape crisis movement explained the larger context of racism in rape crisis centers. The civil rights movement and the feminist movement really were on parallel but unconnected charts, whether it's the NAACP or the Urban League and the victims' organizations. Different institutions came out of the civil rights movement and civil rights history and then there's sexual assault and domestic violence that really came out of the feminist movement. So now you've got these organizations that are trying to go back and deal with some of these issues. Because they were segregationist in their thinking, which translated into a lot of segregation in their practices. They're trying to heal some of that, but a lot of Black women in their communities don't want to have anything to do with you, because they say: you have not been here for us when we needed you. (Advocate 38)

Although the issue of racism was not mentioned by the majority of advocates in terms of how they were treated by rape crisis centers or as a barrier to their work with survivors, it was mentioned by a few White and ethnic minority women despite the fact that no questions in the interview focused on this topic specifically. This suggests that issues of racism are likely of concern for many advocates working in rape crisis centers. Some women perceive that their organizations have not dealt with this issue fully, which is likely a reflection of the larger context in which racism continues to afflict society and the feminist movement more generally. Insofar as racism alienates ethnic minority women advocates and causes them job stress in working at their organizations, this is a problem that may lead to burnout for these workers and may also indirectly negatively affect their ability to help survivors.

Staff Burnout

Both organizational barriers and the nature of rape crisis centers' work may affect advocates' ability to help survivors by causing stress and burnout. Research has shown vicarious traumatization and burnout are problems for many counselors and advocates working with sexual assault survivors (Baird & Jenkins, 2003; Ghahramanlou & Brodbeck, 2000; Schauben & Frazier, 1995; Wasco & Campbell, 2002), although existing studies have not examined how organizations may specifically contribute to these problems. Not surprisingly, 44% of advocates, particularly ex-advocates (4 out of 6), mentioned factors associated with stress and burnout among workers that were caused by their agency's working conditions.

There's burnout and that can be difficult. But I think that's in any social service setting required to witness everybody else's pain and the impact of that. (Advocate 25)

I think it starts at the top. Funders want you to do as much as you can with as little. And they certainly don't want you to have downtime. They don't see that downtime is actually recovery time so that you can sustain it long term. I think that the way that the jobs are set up is to do this 100% of the time and not to take part time stuff. And I think that's why people get into private practice, because they're so sick of this nonprofit stuff where you just burn your workers out. You exploit either their sense of giving, their naivete or their age. I think young idealistic workers get easily crapped on because they are so passionate. I was so passionate and now I'm like totally cynical and rekindling my passion, but only because I've had a year off already to sort of recover and think about this. (Advocate 31)

Multiple causes of burnout were identified by the advocates. First, a number of them, especially those who had left their agencies because of burnout, cited inadequate supervision as a factor contributing to burnout.

I think it's because there's a lot of supervision problems in rape crisis work and we have supervisors who don't know what our jobs are. Maybe they've done medical [advocacy]. A lot of the executive directors in [city] haven't done any direct service work. My supervisor has done medical, but she has not done legal [advocacy]. There's low accountability in the centers, you have people who are super burnt out and not fired. There are legal advocates who don't do anything, there's a lot of people who don't do anything. Counselors who don't do anything, don't see anyone, you know. (Advocate 29)

I just feel how much can they care about survivors when the frontline people working directly with survivors are treated with blatant disregard for their well-being. I mean that's sort of my cynical perspective at this point. . . . They would say, "Yeah we hear what you're saying and we're working on it," which was the response for 2 years during which they were not working on it. I never felt like I was blamed necessarily, but it certainly was not like, "Oh you're right, we're gonna fix this tomorrow, because this is a problem and you know we see that." It was never like that. Everything was this huge long process, and most things that were addressed were never taken care of or fixed. (Advocate 30)

Other organizational problems that may be related to staff burnout raised mostly by former advocates included lack of adequate pay, lack of support, lack of accountability for work, and even outright abuse of workers that may actually characterize inadequately funded human service agencies in general (Glisson, 2000; Webster & Hackett, 1999).

I don't have to have somebody who's exploiting me, disempowering, abusing me basically, not paying me anything, I mean the money is a part of that too because nobody wants to work for crap. We tell clients we're trained to empower people, but who do we as social workers empower, everybody but ourselves. We're just these little doormats for everybody, and we're encouraged to be that way, because when we speak out, our agencies don't want to hear it. I think there's a problem with social work as a whole that the people who are in the nonprofit and advocacy/victim services are sort of qualitatively poorer than they could be. (Advocate 31)

I mean I don't really know how to frame it, but there are problems of not like getting support, and when people aren't supported, you have a lot of people who don't like their jobs. For instance, someone called and she said, "I tried to work with the legal advocate at this other center on the north side, she had no idea what I was talking about, so can you help me?" I gave her a bunch of information and she asked: "What are you talking

about?" Who is talking to this legal advocate and finding out why she doesn't know what her job is? I mean it's because she's not getting training or support. Why isn't someone addressing it? I think training and support would create better advocacy skills and reduce burnout. (Advocate 29)

When the executive director first came to the agency, she said, I'm gonna do this, this, and this. And we were like, great! And then nothing changed. She didn't do any of what she said she was gonna do. I've said the relationship with the agency, it's like an abusive relationship. The agency's the abuser and the worker is the victim. I felt like there was so many times where I thought, am I crazy? Is it me? It takes a long time to leave and realize that you deserve better! It was so similar, it's really scary looking back at it, it was like a cycle of violence. (Advocate 30)

Organizational factors such as time constraints imposed by rigid work demands and inflexibility in rape crisis centers were also cited as a barrier to advocates' own professional development and their ability to sustain themselves in doing such stressful work. One advocate who had burnt out and left her agency noted,

There's this national women of color against violence conference, and we were told that time volunteering there couldn't be work time which was frustrating because we were networking. It's sort of an inflexibility that became more institutionalized on the grant-making level. You have to count how everyone's time is being spent, but that fails to count how workers sitting around chatting for 2 hours is an important part of self-care and sustaining morale. . . . I just think that there are ways in which the agency doesn't always want to be flexible in terms of hours, yet they expect you to be flexible. They need someone that's gonna stay until 8:00, but they're the same people saying that you can't come in when it's convenient for you. (Advocate 35)

Although past research has suggested that supportive organizations may directly and indirectly promote workers' self-care (Wasco, Campbell, & Clark, 2002), which may reduce stress and burnout, researchers have not directly studied workers' perceptions of how organizations may be unsupportive. This may be partially because of past studies recruiting workers through their organizations (e.g., via executive directors), whereas in this study, workers were recruited directly, not through their organizations, as were former advocates who, not surprisingly, were more negative about their former employers.

It is very important to note that despite these negative aspects of agencies raised by workers, rape crisis centers do extremely positive work with few resources. Comments such as those noted here would likely be reflective of workers' perceptions in any human services organization. These issues may in fact be common yet unlikely to be voiced by workers who are still in the field, as evidenced by the fact that only one current advocate in this study (who was working off site at a hospital doing advocacy) clearly raised these negative criticisms about her organization. This led to interviews with former advocates, all of whom more fully elaborated on this theme. It is not surprising that current workers, most of whom were interviewed at their agencies, would be hesitant to raise these controversial issues.

Barriers to Direct Services

Although societal attitudes, organizational-level variables, and staff burnout affect the availability and quality of services, their effects may not always directly affect individual victims. However, there are barriers to service provision that directly affect individual victims who may be in need of or who may seek services from rape crisis centers and from the legal, medical, and mental health systems. Barriers that occur in the course of providing direct services to victims include limited access to services, the unavailability of specific services, a lack of resources to meet victims' needs, and secondary victimization when services are sought.

Access and Availability of Services to Meet Survivor Needs

The ability to access support services is the starting point for victims to get formal help in coping with sexual assault.

However, barriers to survivors' connecting with existing services were noted by many (44%) of the advocates interviewed. These barriers included stigma of receiving services, geographic location, cost of services, and inadequate availability of services. Some of these barriers appeared to be related to race and geographic location, suggesting that they may differentially affect subgroups of survivors. For example, the stigma of seeking mental health services and geographic location of services were noted as barriers for ethnic minority women. In discussing how ethnic minority women might perceive her agency, one advocate explained,

Why do I want to come downtown to some ritzy, all White counseling center where they're gonna tell me I'm crazy? You know the stereotype. Well, counseling doesn't mean you're the crazy one. Just because we're downtown doesn't mean we're ritzy or we're all Caucasian or all straight or whatever it may be. Many people of communities that are oppressed do not want to come to the services, they want the services to come to them. So we must go out to their communities and meet them on their turf, go into their schools and show that I'm not afraid to come meet you where you're at. I'm not afraid as a White woman to come into your neighborhood. (Advocate 3)

Clearly, if ethnic minority women perceive that going to services means they could be labeled mentally ill or that the service providers will be White, middle-class women who will not identify with them or understand their concerns, this may be enough of a barrier to prevent them from accessing available services. In addition, there may be practical difficulties associated with traveling to organizations that provide services outside survivors' neighborhoods, especially for women who rely on public transportation.

Another frequently cited barrier was the availability of affordable or free services:

One of the most obvious barriers for many survivors is needing resources that are affordable or free. We're really fortunate that all of our services are free because it makes sense that somebody who's the victim of a crime shouldn't have to pay. That's a big worry to survivors that I've worked with—how am I gonna pay for this? Fortunately, in the emergency rooms we can tell them that the law [Sexual Assault Survivors Emergency Treatment Act] pays for your care through the [state] Department of Public Aid. We tell them, if you get a bill, call me, we'll fix it. (Advocate 8)

Unfortunately, advocates also noted that many victims do not realize that rape crisis services are available free of charge, so they may not seek help believing they would have to pay for services they cannot afford. Inadequate availability of services was cited with regard to basic rape crisis services for specific subpopulations and for related needs extending beyond rape crisis including bilingual services and services for disabled women. For example, the lack of bilingual services prevents some women from being able to access formal support, as one advocate described:

The other [barrier] that comes up immediately is living in a city as diverse as [city] is the limited language capabilities that we have and so we serve clients obviously in English. We do have sort of a backup system. And there are several other agencies that do bilingual . . . we have crisis intervention services. So we feel pretty well equipped to handle calls that are monolingual Spanish speakers. But [city] has a large population of Latino people and Polish people and we just can't serve them. (Advocate 6)

The pressing need for bilingual services to serve survivors and their family and friends is clear from the area's demographics. According to the 2000 census, 26% of this urban area's population was Hispanic. In addition, the area has a very large Polish-speaking population. However, rape crisis services in languages other than English are not widely available.

Several advocates also noted the limited services for disabled survivors:

There are limited resources available for people with disabilities. There is the deaf and hard of hearing community that some people describe as disabled. Some people don't see that as a disability, but certainly the resources available for that community are very limited. (Advocate 6)

I am surprised for such a big city there are not rape crisis centers with a focus on disabilities. I just surely thought that there would be all these great programs. I think there was a grant out there a couple of years ago, but the program failed and I don't know why. I think that's sad. (Advocate 1)

The limited availability of services for disabled survivors is particularly notable in light of data showing that disabled persons are at equal or greater risk of sexual victimization than others (Young, Nosek, Howland, Chanpong, & Rintala, 1997).

Resource Barriers That Reduce Direct Services

Resource issues mentioned by 28% of advocates that affect rape crisis centers' capacity to provide direct services included funding constraints, agency inefficiency in using funds, and paperwork required by funders. In addition, the scarcity of resources appears to have resulted in problems with the way organizations are structured and how they treat employees, both of which affect their ability to serve survivors. These organizational issues included poor supervision, unresponsiveness to employees' needs, and inflexibility of organizations.

The most commonly mentioned resource barrier, noted by all of those interviewed, was the sheer lack of funding for rape crisis centers. As one advocate put it,

It really comes down to funding. I mean we can't expand our programs any further. We have waiting lists of hospitals that want us in. We have waiting lists of high schools and colleges that want us doing our prevention programs. We don't have enough people to go out to police stations and be a face that the police officers recognize. We don't have enough people in courthouses that are court watchers to know how judges are ruling, so that we could know who to vote in or vote out. If we had more funding to expand some of our programs, we could make a bigger impact for all victims as a whole. (Advocate 3)

Another frequently cited (52%) problem was that the funding restricts the range of activities in which rape crisis centers can engage. This may mean that survivors in certain areas are unserved or that necessary work is not funded:

> One of the biggest barriers is definitely how funding is set up. For your funding to have a boundary is very frustrating. Even for just basic mental health counseling, you can't see anybody past [a certain street]. But if there's really nothing there for those people, where do they go? There have been times when I've wanted to do a little more community outreach, but my funding only lets me do 1% so it gets a little frustrating, so I think more flexibility would be good. (Advocate 16)

> I think the expectation is higher than what can be provided in the amount of time that the funds allot for it. They don't provide enough up front time for advertising, getting the word out, going into the community before you're supposed to be showing results. Then you're not successful and they take the money away, give it to someone else, and then they run into the same problem. So I think it's sort of a two-fold problem. One coming from the funder's restrictions and then the other just trying to be creative, thinking outside the box of different ways of providing the service. (Advocate 10)

External funding also requires accountability and reporting to the funder. Although only a couple of advocates mentioned burdensome paperwork, they aptly described how it could conflict with efforts to provide crisis advocacy to survivors:

> There was an argument always between the street staff and management (who had to actually answer to funders), and they want to know exactly what this victim's age was, and what that relationship is—if that information is not available. There's a four-page form that you have called an intake form and on there you put the exact time you spent with them, all the medication that

they were given—you know just things that you have to know. I understood the need for it but, my other need was greater [i.e., to be there for her client]. (Advocate 36)

> I know one of their biggest frustrations is time and the sheer amount of paperwork you have to do for a client. I've had a couple of them tell me, if I didn't have to go and do all that paperwork, I could probably see an extra client a day. . . . I think funders are too concerned about numbers. They always want to know how many people? How much money? How many hours? And it doesn't always boil down to that and I think they just don't seem to get that. (Advocate 16)

Secondary Victimization

The final direct services barrier affecting victims noted by advocates was secondary victimization. Because sexual violence has emotional, medical, and legal ramifications, survivors often come into contact with multiple community systems. Navigating these systems can be challenging and, at times, retraumatizing. Often, a main function of advocates is to work on behalf of survivors to ensure that their rights are respected and that they receive all of the assistance to which they are entitled. Consequently, advocates face barriers to working with survivors not only in the context of their own agencies and funders but also in their interactions with other systems. A major barrier mentioned by most (72%) of those interviewed was that survivors experience negative or revictimizing reactions, such as being blamed or disbelieved when telling other people about the assault or seeking formal services. Hospitals were frequently cited as a common first contact for survivors and as a place where they may face unpredictable responses:

> There are certain hospitals in this city that are wonderful. I mean I haven't dealt with very many yet, but I've heard the stories. I mean there are certain ERs that if I had a friend that was raped, I would probably send them to that ER first, even if it was 5 miles out of the way because their staff is compassionate, they're prepared to deal with this issue, they just take a good approach

to it. And then you have other hospitals—it just depends on the luck of the draw. I mean if you've got a physician that's tired or cranky or doesn't want to deal with this or feels like this person has lied or the victim happens to be a prostitute. (Advocate 7)

Certainly one of the barriers is how people treat people who've been sexually assaulted and all the myths that they come to the table with. If the victim's first interaction with whomever they're disclosing to is negative, then that could sort of stop them from seeking other help. If their first contact is the hospital ER and a nurse or a doctor is rude or inappropriate or doesn't believe them, that could just end it right there. They're not gonna want to get help in any other way, they'll forget it, not want to tell anybody else feeling that no one will believe me. If it's the police who respond negatively initially, maybe they won't go on to get medical help. That's a huge barrier. (Advocate 10)

When you do encourage survivors to get help, you're sort of sending them into the lion's den almost. I mean this is a scary thing to go to the hospital and it's kind of a gamble, whether or not the experience is going to go well. It's even worse to have your case taken into the legal system and frankly, I don't know. If I were raped right now, I don't know if I would go to the hospital. I certainly would not prosecute and there's no way I would go to court. So I was beginning to feel while I was there even [at the agency]—how can I be doing this work, telling people what they should do with their case when I wouldn't do it myself? (Advocate 30)

A lot of times they [formal support sources] don't say things in front of the [victims]. But out of the room, nurses and law enforcement would make comments to me that always are out of line, they say too much to me and that's when I get really frustrated. It happens a lot of times where nurses are revictimizing my clients, saying, "Girl, what are you thinking? What were you doing like at 9:00 at night up there?" (Advocate 32)

These reactions to victims by the medical system make it difficult for advocates because they often are unable to protect survivors from further trauma following the rape caused by these negative social reactions from service providers, which research shows are associated with greater PTSD symptoms in survivors (Campbell et al., 1999; Ullman & Filipas, 2001). Because victims need these systems' services and advocates have less power than medical personnel, advocates are put in a bind if they try to confront personnel making negative reactions to victims. Advocates have to work with service providers on an ongoing basis, and although they may try to educate them as best they can, they must walk a fine line in doing so, as they can receive defensive reactions and hostility from these personnel. Even worse, providers' hostility may be taken out on survivors who may subsequently be treated even more poorly. Clearly, this problem adds to advocates' burden because they have to try to support survivors regarding not only the rape and its effects but also the revictimization they are experiencing from system personnel.

Because of problems of secondary victimization within the medical system, advocates also suggested that training of medical personnel was needed. However, pointing this out to those providers often led to anger or denial by personnel who did not appreciate advocates' viewpoints about system responses to survivors.

I mean the hospital situation could also be equally frustrating with people not really knowing how to do exams very well and doctors and nurses that just weren't really trained in how to do these things and didn't really have the bedside manner that we would have liked. We have contracts with various hospitals and we would try to go into hospitals and do trainings with folks in ERs and not only is it hard to do trainings, but when you get there, they're like, "We know how to do our job, we don't need you people having to tell us how to do our jobs." And we would say well actually, we have all these cases where evidence was tampered with or a client is saying that this happened. That shouldn't have happened. So we knew that stuff was happening. And that was often frustrating too. (Advocate 30)

As a consequence of these attitudes, advocates are often unable to effectively ensure that victims' rights are fulfilled and that they get appropriate medical care and proper collection of forensic evidence in the rape kit.

The legal and criminal justice systems were also identified as sources of secondary victimization for survivors.

I think another huge barrier is just the mythology that's out there and is so pervasive. Victim blame is, in my perception, the number one barrier to prosecution that victims face. If they're willing and want to prosecute, what law enforcement looks at primarily is how credible is this person and how credible is their story? Because if they're not credible, this isn't going to stand up in court and we don't want to take it. And there are 101 billion ways to discredit somebody, and I've seen and heard them all. What we know is that people are targeted [for rape] because of their vulnerability and their inability to be credible or tell the story in the way that law enforcement needs it to be told. (Advocate 8)

I get very frustrated with felony review in the state's attorneys office in the sense that unless there is a statement from the offender, we can't charge this individual. The system doesn't like to give options. I've been in with state's attorneys who want the case to go a certain way and they don't give victims all their options and that is one of my jobs—to make sure they're aware of all their options. But sometimes that doesn't sit well with the state's attorneys office. (Advocate 20)

I promised her that she doesn't have to see him [the offender]. She didn't want to press charges, she didn't want him in her life. They had already put him out of the house. He had snuck in. We go to the police station, there's a woman detective who I already knew, I had a history with her, she was awful, awful. She questioned the woman [survivor] in the same room with the suspect handcuffed to a piece of wood on the wall. So we're at the other end of this conference table and he's right there the whole time. It was so unnecessarily abusive. (Advocate 36)

The court system is really awful. If you get a good state's attorney, and there are some out there, that's fine. But most of the time and especially with sexual assault, they don't want to deal with it. We've been training people in the state's attorneys office, but they didn't even want to sit through the training. (Advocate 16)

A former advocate summarized the problems with entering the legal system for rape survivors most clearly:

We still have a system where it's extremely tough for women to come out and allege a rape, let alone go through the process of a trial. . . . I understand the profound expectations people have when they press charges and I know 9 times out of 10 it'll be plea bargained out and you don't get your moment in court. If it does go to trial, you don't ever get to tell your story the way you want to, so I think expectations women have of what it means to go to court are derived from our popular cultural ideal of standing up in court, pointing at somebody and saying he raped me and that of course does not happen. I've said, you know your job as a survivor now is to get stronger and here are all the different options you can use to get stronger. Don't let anybody tell you that the only way to get stronger is through the legal system, cause it will probably not be the result. So, I'm much more brutally honest with them and I think there's a lot of advocates who kind of feed into the mythology of what it means to press charges and that you have to press charges to get rapists off the streets. We're not gettin em off the street! If we do get em off the street, it will be for 5 to 6 months and from what I've seen chances are if a man rapes women, he is either going to participate as a rapist or be victimized by sexual assault in jail. When he gets back on the street, he's a much more dangerous rapist than he was before. I have no faith in the legal system to solve this issue. (Advocate 38).

In summary, secondary victimization from police and legal personnel makes it difficult for advocates to help survivors get any kind of real justice or accountability from the criminal justice system. Advocates can try to support survivors who choose to pursue a criminal case by helping keep them informed about their case and going to court with them, but they have little control over whether a case will be deemed credible and worthy of the prosecutor's time and effort in the first place. Police may also poorly treat survivors, violate their rights, and retraumatize them when they perceive that certain survivors have less value, such as young, ethnic minority women. This makes it extremely difficult for advocates whose goal is to try to empower survivors within an inherently antivictim criminal justice system.

⊠ Conclusions and Study Implications

This study identified a number of barriers that workers in rape crisis centers perceive that survivors face getting services. Consistent with past research on survivors, advocates noted numerous problems with access, availability, affordability, and acceptability of services (Campbell, 1998; Campbell et al., 2001; Logan et al., 2005; Martin, 2005). Our sample of rape crisis center workers mentioned barriers of access and availability to services, funding and resource problems at both organization and system levels, and secondary victimization or insensitivity of service providers, notably medical and criminal justice system personnel. Many interviewees mentioned problems of underfunding of rape crisis centers and difficulty securing help among women in disadvantaged groups such as the homeless, prostitutes, the disabled, and mentally ill. Some barriers also varied by workers' demographic or treatment orientation. Those with higher degrees reported fewer problems with services being insensitive or structural barriers generally. Workers with less formal education cited more structural barriers and services insensitivity and fewer survivor-related barriers. It is unclear if these perceptions were because of the jobs of workers in the organization or differences in individuals with these different degrees. Views about the causes of social problems may also differ for those who elect to gain higher degrees, who may have a greater investment and belief in the system than those who do not.

Most advocates mentioned the problems of secondary victimization by the systems that are supposed to help

women obtain medical treatment and justice. However, workers doing primarily advocacy were more likely than those doing counseling to mention racism and sexism as barriers and service providers' insensitivity toward minorities specifically. Not surprisingly, those endorsing a feminist orientation were more likely to mention barriers related to race, class, and gender bias; professionalization of rape crisis centers; rape myths or societal denial of rape; language barriers; and lack of culturally competent services than were those endorsing nonfeminist treatment orientations. Although both Whites and minorities mentioned issues of racism generally as barriers, ethnic minorities were more likely to mention racist biases of the system specifically, particularly if they were young, compared to Whites. In addition, Latinas mentioned language barriers and familial, cultural, or immigration issues more than others. This finding is consistent with past studies of sexual assault victims who frequently note problems of receiving negative social reactions when seeking help from formal systems (Campbell et al., 1999, 2001; Ullman, 1996; Ullman & Filipas, 2001). In our study, workers also identified barriers associated with language, ethnic minority race, family or culture, immigration, disability, mental illness, prostitution, and young age to be associated with poorer access to services and more secondary victimization by formal service providers, especially medical and criminal justice personnel. Racism was noted in our study as a barrier particularly for younger women in how they were treated as rape victims. Young, ethnic minority women were viewed as being subject to greater police harassment and secondary victimization by medical and criminal justice system personnel.

Although Logan et al.'s (2005) sample mentioned bureaucratic problems and staff incompetence as barriers for women seeking services, these were discussed in relationship to medical and criminal justice systems, not rape crisis centers themselves. Other research by Campbell and Martin (Campbell et al., 2001; Martin, 2005) has also documented problems, particularly with the medical and criminal justice or legal systems' responses to rape victims. Survivors in Logan et al.'s study did not mention any of the numerous problems found in our study, [those] noted by advocates we interviewed in these organizations. This may be because of a number of factors. They may not have had awareness of these problems, given that their contact is more limited than employees of centers studied here. The women were recruited by rape crisis centers, and the focus groups were conducted at the centers, which may have made any problems that arose with those agencies less likely to be mentioned. Women with negative experiences may also have been less likely to have been referred to the study by rape crisis center staff. Finally, their study did not ask women about problems with getting help from rape crisis centers specifically.

However, our study found that various organizational barriers to doing advocacy were professionalization, racism, inflexibility of rape crisis centers, physical space limitations, structure of programs, burnout, and vicarious trauma related to poor supervision; and lack of accountability and caretaking of staff by agencies, corruption, lack of respect for clients in one agency, and paperwork demands. Past research has clearly documented the serious problem of vicarious trauma and burnout in those who work with traumatized populations, including sexual assault survivors (Salston & Figley, 2003; Schauben & Frazier, 1995; Wasco & Campbell, 2002). Racism has also been documented by others studying rape crisis centers (Campbell et al., 2001; Matthews, 1994; Scott, 1998). Professionalization has been noted by other researchers who study rape crisis centers as leading to changes in these organizations (Campbell et al., 1998) such as being less political, which were noted as negative by a number of younger advocates in this study. Clearly, some of the organizational problems noted are related to funding limitations, but others, such as racism, may be associated with professionalization.

These problems did not characterize all agencies, and the worst problems were mentioned by former advocates who likely felt freer to talk about problems in their past work settings but also may have had worse experiences than other employees. Clearly, the small convenience sample of metropolitan area advocates studied presents biases that may not reflect what a random sampling of rape crisis center employees and former employees might report. Further research is needed to determine how widespread these perceptions are and how these issues may be better addressed in rape crisis centers in the future. We caution that these findings should not be taken to mean that rape crisis centers are not doing extremely positive work on behalf of survivors of sexual assault in the community. These problems more likely reflect widely shared, yet often unspoken, experiences of workers in low-paid

human service organizations, all of whom provide critically needed services without adequate funding and societal support (Glisson, 2000; Webster & Hackett, 1999).

Community studies suggest that rape crisis centers are typically rated as one of the most helpful support sources by sexual assault survivors (Filipas & Ullman, 2001; Golding et al., 1989), compared with other formal sources such as mental health, medical, and criminal justice, which are typically rated less favorably. In addition, a recent preliminary descriptive evaluation of rape crisis services in Illinois found that they were an effective use of taxpayer money (Wasco et al., 2004). Despite the findings here of problems in these organizations, some of which were noted to a greater extent by former advocates in the sample, it does not necessarily imply that many survivors are not receiving excellent help from these agencies. Human service agencies, including rape crisis centers, typically receive less funding than needed to serve their client populations and often cannot afford to pay or support workers as much as they ideally would like to. Although efficient use of limited resources is one way to overcome such limitations, clearly sheer amounts of funding and support for providing such services to a population in crisis is a major task that cannot simply be managed by better fiscal management.

More attention is needed for addressing problems related to less-than-optimal resources and support for advocates in particular working in rape crisis centers, and these problems are unlikely to be limited to centers in the metropolitan area studied here. However, it is known that this line of work is related to high burnout, and many current employees mentioned the problems of high turnover in these agencies that offer little chance for promotion or pay increases. Future research on secondary trauma and burnout in rape crisis workers should go beyond studying worker characteristics, training, and work roles and also study organizational characteristics that may also contribute to these negative outcomes.

Martin (2005) has persuasively argued that organizational constraints and goals often result in secondary victimization of rape victims because workers in medical and criminal justice systems follow rules required to do their jobs, which entails practices that often conflict with the needs of rape victims. This implies that organizational change, not only training or education of service system personnel, will be needed to improve rape victims' treatment. Clearly, this exploratory study suggests that more research is needed to understand how rape crisis workers may be better supported in their organizations and in their advocacy efforts generally for survivors in the systems with which they interface. Researchers need to be aware of the stresses faced by rape crisis centers and their workers if they wish to collaborate with them in work that may help to respond to rape in the community. This study's results may also help researchers to better understand the larger context in which survivors attempt to get help from rape crisis centers, the medical system, and the criminal justice system. Without an understanding of the larger context of survivors' help-seeking experiences from both survivors' and service providers' perspectives, researchers may be less able to fully understand how survivors navigate their recovery and their support-seeking experiences following sexual assault. The findings suggest many barriers that rape crisis centers need to address to enhance their advocates' ability to help rape survivors. However, increased resources to these organizations are urgently needed to enable them to make these changes. This is vital given that rape crisis centers are the only support system whose goal is to help victims navigate their recovery and to obtain help from other service systems. Beyond this, the larger societal context of rape and other organizations that deal with rape victims (e.g., hospitals, criminal justice) also need to be adapted or transformed in some way to improve responses to victims following sexual assault.

⊠ References

Baird, S., & Jenkins, S. R. (2003). Vicarious traumatization, secondary traumatic stress, and burnout in sexual assault and domestic violence agency staff. *Violence and Victims, 18,* 71–86.

Campbell, R. (1998). The community response to rape: Victims' experiences with the legal, medical, and mental health systems. *American Journal of Community Psychology, 26,* 355–379.

Campbell, R., Baker, C. K., & Mazurek, T. L. (1998). Remaining radical? Organizational predictors of rape crisis centers' social change initiatives. *American Journal of Community Psychology, 26,* 457–483.

Campbell, R., & Martin, P. Y. (2001). Services for sexual assault survivors: The role of rape crisis centers. In C. M. Renzetti, J. L. Edelson, & R. K. Bergen (Eds.), *Sourcebook on violence against women* (pp. 227–241). Thousand Oaks, CA: Sage.

Campbell, R., Sefl, T., Barnes, H. E., Ahrens, C. E., Wasco, S. M., & Zaragoza-Diesfeld, Y. (1999). Community services for rape survivors: Enhancing psychological well-being or increasing trauma? *Journal of Consulting and Clinical Psychology, 67,* 847–858.

Campbell, R., Wasco, S. M., Ahrens, C. E., Sefl, T., & Barnes, H. E. (2001). Preventing the "second rape": Rape survivors' experiences with community service providers. *Journal of Interpersonal Violence, 16,* 1239–1259.

Davis, R. C., Brickman, E. R., & Baker, T. (1991). Effects of supportive and unsupportive responses of others to rape victims: Effects on concurrent victim adjustment. *American Journal of Community Psychology, 19,* 443–451.

Filipas, H. H., & Ullman, S. E. (2001). Social reactions to sexual assault victims from various support sources. *Violence & Victims, 16,* 673–692.

Frank, J. D., & Frank, J. B. (1991). *Persuasion and healing: A comparative study of psychotherapy* (3rd ed.). Baltimore: Johns Hopkins University Press.

Ghahramanlou, M., & Brodbeck, C. (2000). Predictors of secondary trauma in sexual assault trauma counselors. *International Journal of Emergency Medicine, 2,* 229–240.

Glisson, C. (2000). Organizational climate and culture. In R. Patti (Ed.), *Handbook of social welfare administration* (pp. 195–218). Thousand Oaks, CA: Sage.

Golding, J. M., Siegel, J. M., Sorenson, S. B., Burnam, M. A., & Stein, J. A. (1989). Social support sources following sexual assault. *Journal of Community Psychology, 17,* 92–107.

Logan, T. K., Evans, L., Stevenson, E., & Jordan, C. (2005). Barriers to services for rural and urban rape survivors. *Journal of Interpersonal Violence, 20,* 591–616.

Luborsky, L., Crit, S., Christoph, P., McLellan, A. T., Woody, G., Piper, W., et al. (1986). Do therapists vary much in their success? Findings from four outcome studies. *American Journal of Orthopsychiatry, 56,* 501–512.

Martin, P. Y. (2005). *Rape work: Victims, gender, and emotions in organization and community context.* New York: Routledge.

Matthews, N. (1994). *Confronting rape: The feminist anti-rape movement and the state.* London: Routledge.

Miles, M. B., & Huberman, A. M. (1994). *Qualitative data analysis* (2nd ed.). Thousand Oaks, CA: Sage.

National Violence Against Women Prevention Research Center. (2001, May). *Fostering collaborations to prevent violence against women: Integrating findings from practitioner and researcher focus groups.* Charleston, SC: Author.

Riger, S. (1999). Working together: Challenges in collaborative research on violence against women. *Violence Against Women, 5,* 1099–1117.

Salston, M., & Figley, C. R. (2003). Secondary traumatic stress effects of working with survivors of criminal victimization. *Journal of Traumatic Stress, 16,* 167–174.

Schauben, L. J., & Frazier, P. A. (1995). Vicarious trauma: The effects on female counselors of working with sexual violence survivors. *Psychology of Women Quarterly, 19,* 49–64.

Scott, E. K. (1998). Creating partnerships for change: Alliances and betrayals in the racial politics of two feminist organizations. *Gender & Society, 12,* 400–423.

Stein, D. M., & Lambert, M. J. (1984). On the relationship between therapist experience and psychotherapy outcome. *Clinical Psychology Review, 4,* 127–142.

Strauss, A. L., & Corbin, J. M. (1998). *Basics of qualitative research: Techniques and procedures for developing grounded theory.* Newbury Park, CA: Sage.

Ullman, S. E. (1996). Do social reactions to sexual assault victims vary by support provider? *Violence and Victims, 11,* 143–156.

Ullman, S. E. (2005). Interviewing clinicians and advocates who work with sexual assault survivors: A personal perspective on moving from quantitative to qualitative methods. *Violence Against Women, 11,* 1–27.

Ullman, S. E., & Filipas, H. H. (2001). Predictors of PTSD symptom severity and social reactions in sexual assault victims. *Journal of Traumatic Stress, 14,* 369–389.

Ullman, S. E., Filipas, H. H., Townsend, S. M., & Starzynski, L. L. (in press). Psychosocial correlates of PTSD symptom severity in sexual assault survivors. *Journal of Traumatic Stress.*

Wasco, S. M., & Campbell, R. (2002). Emotional reactions of rape victim advocates: A multiple case study of anger and fear. *Psychology of Women Quarterly, 26,* 120–130.

Wasco, S. M., Campbell, R., & Clark, M. (2002). A multiple case study of rape victim advocates' self-care routines: The influence of organizational context. *American Journal of Community Psychology, 30,* 731–760.

Wasco, S. M., Campbell, R., Howard, A., Mason, G., Staggs, S., Schewe, P., et al. (2004). A statewide evaluation of services provided to rape survivors. *Journal of Interpersonal Violence, 19,* 252–263.

Webster, L., & Hackett, R. K. (1999). Burnout and leadership in community mental health systems. *Administration and Policy in Mental Health, 26,* 387–399.

Young, M. E., Nosek, M. A., Howland, C. A., Chanpong, G., & Rintala, D. H. (1997). Prevalence of abuse of women with disabilities. *Archives of Physical Medicine and Rehabilitation, 78*(Suppl.), S34–S38.

DISCUSSION QUESTIONS

1. Discuss how each of the organizational barriers can limit how rape crisis advocates engage in victim assistance.

2. How has the professionalization of rape crisis centers affected their ability to engage in advocacy work?

3. What barriers exist in providing direct services to victims? How do rape-crisis advocates respond to these challenges?

Glossary

Acquaintance rape: the victim knows the perpetrator; it usually accounts for the majority of rape and sexual assault cases.

Adler, Freda: her works were inspired by the emancipation of women that resulted from the effects of the second wave of feminism. Adler suggested that women's rates of violent crime would increase.

Age-of-consent campaign: designed to protect young women from men who preyed on the innocence of girls by raising the age of sexual consent to 16 or 18 in all states by 1920.

Altruistic: one explanation for infanticide where the mother believes that it is in the best interest of her child to be dead and that the mother is doing a good thing by killing her child.

Attachment: the bond that people have with the values of society as a result of their relationships with family, friends, and social institutions.

Baldwin, Lola: hired in 1908 by the Portland, Oregon, police department to provide supervisory assistance to a group of social workers. Her employment sparked debates as to whether she was a sworn officer or a social worker.

Barefield v. Leach (1974): held that states could not justify disparities in the programs for female inmates based on a smaller female incarcerated population and the costs of program delivery.

Battered women's movement: shelters and counseling programs established throughout the United States to help women in need as a result of the feminist movements in the 1960s and 1970s. It led to systemic changes in how the police and courts handled cases of domestic violence.

Belief: a general acceptance of society's rules.

Blankenship, Betty: one of the first women in the United States to serve as a patrol officer; she worked for the Indianapolis Police Department in 1964, and she helped set the stage for significant changes for the future of policewomen.

Bootstrapping: modern-day practice of institutionalizing girls for status offenses.

Burnout: the feeling of being under high levels of emotional and physical duress. This feeling is often categorized into three stages:

(1) emotional exhaustion due to stress, (2) depersonalization, and (3) reduced personal accomplishment.

Canterino v. Wilson (1982): males and females must be treated equally unless there is a substantial reason that requires a distinction be made.

Chivalry: instances in which women receive preferential treatment by the justice system.

Civil Rights Bill of 1964: focused on eliminating racial discrimination; however, the word *sex* was added to the bill, prohibiting the use of sex as a requirement for hiring.

Coffal, Liz: one of the first women in the United States to serve as a patrol officer for the Indianapolis Police Department in 1964; she helped set the stage for significant changes for the future of policewomen.

Commitment: the investment that an individual has to the normative values of society.

Community policing: a policing strategy that is based on the idea that the community is extremely important in achieving shared goals; it emphasizes community support from its members, which can help reduce crime and fear.

Cooper v. Morin (1980): held that the equal protection clause prevents prison administrators from justifying the disparate treatment of women on the grounds that providing such services for women is inconvenient.

Core rights of victims: vary by jurisdiction; however, the following core rights have been found in many state constitutions: right to attend, right to compensation, right to be heard, right to be informed, right to protection, right to restitution, right to return of property, right to a speedy trial, and right to enforcement.

Custodial institutions: similar to male institutions, women are warehoused and little programming or treatment is offered to the inmates.

Cyberstalking: incidents of stalking that use electronic forms of technology such as e-mail, text, GPS, and the Internet.

Cycle of victimization and offending: explains how young girls often run away from home in an attempt to escape from an abusive situation, usually ending up as offenders themselves.

Cycle of violence: conceptualized by Lenore Walker in 1979 to help explain how perpetrators of intimate partner abuse maintain control over their victims over time. The cycle is made up of three distinct time frames: tension building, the abusive incident, and the honeymoon period.

Dark figure of crime: crimes that are not reported to the police and therefore not represented in official crime statistics, such as the Uniform Crime Reports and the National Incident-Based Reporting System.

Dating violence: intimate partner abuse in relationships where people are unmarried and may or may not be living together; violence that occurs between two people who are unmarried; teenagers are seen as the most at-risk population.

Differential association theory: focuses on the influence that one's social relationships may have in encouraging delinquent behavior. This theory also incorporated various characteristics of the social learning theory, suggesting that criminality is a learned behavior.

Discretionary arrest: police officers have the option to arrest or not arrest the offender based on their free choice within the context of their professional judgment.

Drug-facilitated rape: an unwanted sexual act that occurs after a victim voluntarily or involuntarily consumes drugs or alcohol.

Evil woman hypothesis: women are punished not only for violating the law but also for breaking the socialized norms of gender-role expectations.

Extralegal factors: can include the type of attorney (private or public defender), which can significantly affect the likelihood of pretrial release for women.

Fear of victimization: a gendered experience where women experience higher rates of fear of crime compared to males. This idea is based on the distorted portrayal of the criminal justice system by the media.

Femicide: the killing of women based on gender discrimination. The murders often involve sexual torture and body mutilation.

Feminism: a series of social and political movements (also referred to as the *three waves of feminism*) that advocated for women's rights and gender equality.

Feminist criminology: developed as a reaction against traditional criminology, which failed to address women and girls in research. It reflects several of the themes of gender roles and socialization that resulted from the second wave of feminism.

Feminist pathways perspective: provides some of the best understanding of how women find themselves stuck in a cycle that begins with victimization and leads to offending.

Feminist research methods: process of gathering research that involves placing gender at the center of the conversation, giving women a voice, and changing the relationship between the researcher and the subject to one of care and concern versus objectivity.

Filicide: the homicide of children older than one year of age by their parent.

Formal processing: a petition is filed requesting a court hearing, which can initiate the designation of being labeled as a delinquent.

Fry, Elizabeth: a key figure in the crusade to improve the conditions of incarcerated women in the United Kingdom and an inspiration for the American women's prison reform movement.

Gender gap: refers to the differences in male and female offending for different types of offenses.

Gender-responsive programming: creates parity in offender programming and is designed to meet the unique needs of women. Generally involves consideration of six key principles: gender, environment, relationships, services and supervision, socioeconomic status, and community.

Gender-specific programming: must be able to address the wide variety of needs of the delinquent girl. Efforts by Congress have been made to allocate the resources necessary for analyzing, planning, and implementing these services.

Gendered assignments: job duties that were usually assigned to officers based on their gender; female officers were more inclined to receive social service positions rather than patrol and crime-fighting positions.

Gendered justice: also referred to as *injustice*; it is the discrimination of individuals based on their gender. This idea is often seen in the criminal justice system where females' needs and unique experiences go unmet due to the fact that the theories of offending have come from the male perspective.

Genital mutilation: also known as female circumcision and involves the vandalism or removal of female genitalia for the purposes of protecting girls' virginity and eliminating the potential for sexual pleasure.

Glass ceiling: a term used to describe the invisible barriers that limit the ability of women and minorities from achieving high rank opportunities in the workplace.

Glover v. Johnson (1979): held that the state must provide the same opportunities for education, rehabilitation, and vocational training for female offenders as provided for male offenders.

Good ol' boy network: a social network of people who provide access and grant favors to each other. It is usually made up of elite White males, and they tend to exclude other members of their community.

Griffin v. Michigan Department of Corrections (1982): held that inmates do not possess any rights to be protected against being viewed in stages of undress or naked by a correctional officer, regardless of gender.

Grummett v. Rushen (1985): the pat-down search of a male inmate (including the groin area) does not violate one's Fourth Amendment protection against unreasonable search and seizure.

Hagan, John: developed the power control theory; his research focused on the roles within the family unit, especially that of patriarchy.

Harassment: acts that are indicative of stalking behaviors but do not ignite feelings of fear in the victim.

Hirschi, Travis: proposed the social bonds theory; his research focused primarily on delinquency and the reasons why people may not become involved in criminal activity.

Honor-based violence: murders that are executed by a male family member and are a response to a belief that the woman has offended a family's honor and has brought shame to the family.

Human trafficking: the exploitation and forced labor of individuals for the purposes of prostitution, domestic servitude, and other forms of involuntary servitude in agricultural and factory industries.

Incapacitated rape: an unwanted sexual act that occurs after a victim voluntarily consumes drugs or alcohol.

Incarcerated mothers: have a significant effect on children. The geographical location of the prison and length of sentencing determine whether mothers can have ties with their children; in many cases, the children are either cared for by family members or are placed in foster care.

Infanticide: an act in which a parent kills his or her child within the first year.

Intimate partner abuse: abuse that occurs between individuals who currently have, or have previously had, an intimate relationship.

Involvement: one's level of participation in conventional activities (studying, playing sports, or participating in extracurricular activities).

Jail the offender and protect the victim models: prioritization is given to the prosecution of offenders over the needs of the victims; however, these models are widely criticized due to their limitations and inability to deter individuals from participating in the offenses.

Jordan v. Gardner (1992): the pat-down policy designed to control the introduction of contraband into the facility could be viewed as unconstitutional if conducted by male staff members against female inmates.

Just world hypothesis: society has a need to believe that people deserve whatever comes to them; this paradigm is linked to patterns of victim blaming.

Juvenile delinquency: the repeated committing of crimes by young children and adolescents.

Juvenile Justice and Delinquency Prevention (JJDP) Act of 1974: provides funding for state and local governments to help decrease the number of juvenile delinquents and to help provide community and rehabilitative programs to offenders.

Karo-kari: literally "black man/black woman"; this is a form of premeditated killing of both male and female adulterers and is a part of Pakistan's cultural tradition.

Laub, John: codeveloped the life course theory; his research has primarily focused on the following criminological and sociological topics: deviance, the life course, and juvenile delinquency and justice.

Legal factors: have an impact on the decision-making process for both males and females in different ways. They vary from jurisdiction to jurisdiction and they can range from criminal history to offense severity.

Level of Service Inventory-Revised (LSI-R): a risk assessment tool used for correctional populations.

Life course theory: examines how adverse life events impact criminality over time and can provide insight on both female and male offending patterns.

Lifestyle theory: developed to explore the risks of victimization from personal crimes and seeks to relate the patterns of one's everyday activities to the potential for victimization.

Lombroso, Cesare, and William Ferrero: the first criminologists to investigate the nature of the female offender; they worked together to publish *The Female Offender* in 1985.

Machista: also referred to as *chauvinistic*; in this belief, masculinity is praised and seen as superior.

Male inmate preference: women inmates are perceived as more demanding, defiant, and harder to work with, so male and female officers would much rather work with male inmates.

Mandatory arrest: surfaced during the 1980s and 1990s with the intention to stop domestic violence by deterring offenders. It clarified the roles of police officers when dealing with domestic violence calls and removed the responsibility of arrest from the victim.

Maquiladoras: assembly plants or factories that reside in another country; they are responsible for manufacturing and assembling parts and then shipping the products to the originating country.

Masculine culture: also known as the *male-dominated police culture*; while attempting to gain acceptance into this culture, females are often disrespected and harassed by their male counterparts.

Masked criminality of women: Otto Pollak's theory that suggested that women gain power by deceiving men through sexual playacting, faked sexual responses, and menstruation.

Mendelsohn, Benjamin: distinguished categories of victims based on the responsibility of the victim and the degree to which the victim had the power to make decisions that could alter his or her likelihood of victimization.

Minneapolis Domestic Violence Experiment: helped show the decrease in recidivism rates when an actual arrest was made in misdemeanor domestic violence incidents, in comparison to when a police officer just counseled the aggressor.

National Crime Victimization Survey (NCVS): gathers additional data about crimes to help fill in the gap between reported and unreported crime (also known as the dark figure of crime).

National Incident-Based Reporting System (NIBRS): An incident-based system of crimes reported to the police. The system is administered by the Federal Bureau of Investigation as part of the annual Uniform Crime Reports.

National Intimate Partner and Sexual Violence Survey (NISVS): An annual survey by the Centers for Disease Control designed to measure the prevalence of intimate partner violence, sexual violence, and stalking.

National Violence Against Women Survey (NVAWS): A telephone survey of 8,000 men and 8,000 women in the United States (English and Spanish speaking) that was conducted by the Centers for Policy Research to measure the prevalence of violence against women.

Neonaticide: an act of homicide of an infant during the first 24 hours after the birth of the child.

Net widening: refers to the practice whereby programs such as diversion were developed to inhibit the introduction of youth into the juvenile justice system. However, these programs expanded the reach of the juvenile court and increased the number of youth under the general reach of the system, both informally and formally.

No-drop policies: developed in response to a victim's lack of participation in the prosecution of her batterer; these policies have led to the disempowering of victims.

Owens, Marie: a contender for the title of first female police officer; she worked as a Chicago factory inspector, transferred to the police department in 1891, and allegedly served on the force for 32 years.

Parens patriae: originated in the English Chancery Courts; this practice gives the state custody of children in cases where the child has no parents or the parents are deemed unfit care providers.

Parole: (1) a form of post-incarceration supervision of offenders in the community; (2) a method of releasing offenders from prison prior to the conclusion of their sentence.

Pollak, Otto: wrote *The Criminality of Women* in 1961 to further explain his belief that crime data sources failed to reflect the true extent of female crime.

Post-traumatic stress disorder (PTSD): may develop after a person experiences a traumatic life event. PTSD can include flashbacks, avoidance of emotional contexts, and recurrent nightmares and may inhibit normal daily functioning abilities.

Power control theory: looks at the effects of patriarchy within the family unit as a tool of socialization for gender roles.

Probation: a form of community-based supervision that imposes restrictions and regulations on offenders but allows for them to serve their sentence in the community as compared to jail or prison.

Pseudo-families: the relationship among individuals who are not related; these relationships are common in the prison system and are often created as a means to provide emotional support to one another during their imprisonment.

Pulling a train: also known as *sexed in*; example of the gang initiation process that requires sexual assault by multiple male members.

Rape: sexual intercourse under force, threat of force, or without the legal consent of the individual. In many jurisdictions, the term *rape* specifically applies in cases of penile-vaginal forced intercourse.

Rape myth acceptance: false beliefs that are seen as justifiable causes for sexual aggression against women.

Reauthorization of the Juvenile Justice and Delinquency Prevention (JJDP) Act (1992): acknowledged the need to provide gender-specific services to address the unique needs of female offenders.

Reentry: the transition from an incarcerated setting to the community; it usually involves meetings with parole officers who provide referrals to receive treatment; unsuccessful reentry often leads to recidivism.

Reformatory: a new concept that saw incarceration as an institution designed with the intent to rehabilitate women from their immoral ways.

Resiliency: also known as *protective factors*; these can enable female victims and female offenders to succeed.

Restraining order: available in every jurisdiction; it is designed to provide the victim with the opportunity to separate from the batterer and prohibit the batterer from contacting the victim.

Risk factors for female delinquency: include a poor family relationship, a history of abuse, poor school performance, negative peer relationships, and issues with substance abuse.

Routine activities theory: created to discuss the risk of victimization in property crimes. It suggests that the likelihood of a criminal act or the likelihood of victimization occurs when an offender, a potential victim, and the absence of a guardian that would deter said offender from making contact with the victim are combined.

Same-sex intimate partner abuse: intimate partner abuse that occurs in a same-sex relationship. Research is significantly limited on this issue, and many victims fear reporting these acts or seeking help due to concerns of being "outed" or concerns about homophobia.

Same-sex sexual assault: oftentimes refers to male-on-male assault, due to the limited research on woman-on-woman sexual violence.

Sampson, Robert: codeveloped the *life course theory*; his research has focused on a variety of topics within the fields of criminology and sociology.

Secondary trauma stress (STS): high levels of stress that results from the need and/or desire to help a victim; victim advocates are often affected by this type of stress.

Secondary victimization: the idea that victims become more traumatized after the primary victimization. It can stem from victim blaming or from the process of collecting evidence (physical or testimonial).

Sentencing guidelines: created in conjunction with the Sentencing Reform Act of 1984; the only factors to be considered in imposing a sentence were offense committed, the presence of aggravating or mitigating circumstances, and the criminal history of the offender.

Sexual assault: often used as an umbrella term for all forms of unwanted sexual activity other than rape, sexual assault includes acts, such as penetration other than vaginal-penile penetration, penetration by objects, sodomy, forced oral copulation, sexual touching, and other lewd acts.

Simon, Rita: hypothesized that women would make up a greater proportion of property crimes as a result of their "liberation" from traditional gender roles and restrictions.

Social bond theory: focused on four criteria, or bonds, which prevent people from acting on potential criminological impulses or desires. Travis Hirschi identified these bonds as attachment, commitment, involvement, and belief.

Spousal rape: involves emotional coercion or physical force against a spouse to achieve nonconsensual sexual intercourse; it can often lead to domestic violence.

Stalking: a course of conduct directed at a reasonable person that could cause them to feel fearful. It includes acts such as unwanted phone calls or messages, being followed or spied on, and making unannounced visits.

Status offenses: noncriminal behaviors such as running away, immorality, truancy, and indecent conduct that allowed youth to come under the jurisdiction of the juvenile court.

Statutory rape: sexual activity that is unlawful because it is prohibited by stature or code; it generally involves someone who is not of legal age to give consent.

Stranger rape: the perpetrator is unknown to the victim and is usually associated with a lack of safety, such as walking home at night or not locking the doors.

Street prostitution: an illegal form of prostitution that takes place in public places.

Sutherland, Edwin: proposed the differential association theory; his research focused on one's social relationships and their influence on delinquent behavior.

Symbolic assailant: a perpetrator, often of minority ethnicity, who hides in dark shadows awaiting the abduction, rape, or murder of unknown innocents. He or she attacks at random, is unprovoked, and is difficult to apprehend.

T-visa: visas issued by the United States for victims; the T-visa is issued for human trafficking victims.

Trafficking Victims Protection Act of 2000: designed to punish traffickers, protect victims, and facilitate prevention efforts in the community to fight against human trafficking.

Uniform Crime Reports (UCR): An annual collection of reported crime data from police departments. It is compiled by the Federal Bureau of Investigation.

Victim advocates: trained professionals who support victims of a crime. Victim advocates can provide emotional support, knowledge about the legal process and the rights of crime victims, and provide information and resources for services and assistance.

Victim blaming: shifting the blame of rape from the offender to the victim; by doing so, the confrontation of the realities of victimization is avoided.

Violence Against Women Act (VAWA): passed in 1994; this federal law provides funding for training and research on intimate partner abuse as well as sets forth policies for restitution and civil redress. VAWA established the Office on Violence Against Women within the Department of Justice; it provided funding for battered women's shelters and outreach education, funding for domestic violence training for police and court personnel, and the opportunity for victims to sue for civil damages as a result of violent acts perpetuated against them.

von Hentig, Hans: his theory of victimization highlights 13 categories of victims and focuses on how personal factors such as biological, social, and psychological characteristics influence risk factors for victimization.

Walking the line: gang initiation process for girls in which they are subjected to assault by their fellow gang members.

Welfare Reform Act of 1996: Section 115 of this act bans women with a felony drug conviction from collecting welfare benefits and food stamps.

Wells, Alice Stebbins: the first female police officer hired in the United States by the Los Angeles Police Department in 1920; she advocated for the protection of children and women, especially when it came to sexual education.

Work-family balance: a term used to describe the prioritization of family life (marriage, children, and lifestyle) within the demands of the workplace.

Wraparound services: holistic and culturally sensitive plans for each woman that draw on a coordinated range of services within her community, such as public and mental health systems, addiction recovery, welfare, emergency shelter organizations, and educational and vocational services.

References

Abad-Santos, A. (2013, January 3). Everything you need to know about Steubenville High School football "rape crew." *The Wire.* Retrieved from http://www.thewire.com/national/2013/01/steubenville-high-football-rape-crew/60554/

Abe-Kim, J., Takeuchi, D. T., Hong, S., Zane, N., Sue, S., Spencer, M. S., . . . Alegría, M. (2007). Use of mental health-related services among immigrant and US-born Asian Americans: Results from the National Latino and Asian American Study. *American Journal of Public Health, 97*(1), 91.

Acoca, L., & Dedel, K. (1997). *Identifying the needs of young women in the juvenile justice system.* San Francisco, CA: National Council on Crime and Delinquency.

Acoca, L., & Dedel, K. (1998a). *Identifying the needs of young women in the juvenile justice system.* San Francisco, CA: National Council on Crime and Delinquency.

Acoca, L., & Dedel, K. (1998b). *No place to hide: Understanding and meeting the needs of girls in the California juvenile justice system.* San Francisco, CA: National Council on Crime and Delinquency.

Adler, F. (1975). *Sisters in crime: The rise of the new female criminal.* New York, NY: McGraw-Hill.

After court order, Madonna faces accused in stalker case. (1996, January 4.). *New York Times.* Retrieved from http://www.nytimes.com/1996/01/04/us/after-court-order-madonna-faces-accused-in-stalker-case.html

Agnew, R. (1992). Foundation for a general strain theory of crime and delinquency. *Criminology, 30,* 47–88.

Agosin, M. (2006). *Secrets in the sand: The young women of Juarez.* New York, NY: White Pine Press.

Air Force Times. (2012, December 2). Sex assault victims seeking help sooner. Retrieved from http://www.airforcetimes.com/article/20121202/NEWS/212020308/

Akintunde, D. O. (2010). Female genital mutilation: A socio-cultural gang up against womenhood. *Feminist Theology, 18*(2), 192–205.

Alabama Coalition Against Domestic Violence (ACADV). (n.d.). *Dating violence.* Retrieved from http://www.acadv.org/dating.html

Albonetti, C. A. (1986). Criminality, prosecutorial screening, and uncertainty: Toward a theory of discretionary decision making in felony case processing. *Criminology, 24*(4), 623–645.

Alexy, E. M., Burgess, A. W., Baker, T., & Smoyak, S. A. (2005). Perceptions of cyberstalking among college students. *Brief Treatment and Crisis Intervention, 5*(3), 279–289.

Alpert, E. (2013, February 18). Murder charges filed after woman burned alive in Papua New Guinea. *Los Angeles Times.* Retrieved from http://articles.latimes.com/2013/feb/18/world/la-fg-wn-woman-burned-alive-papua-new-guinea-20130218

Althaus, D. (2010). Ciudad Juarez women still being tortured by killers. *Houston Chronicle.* Retrieved from http://www.chron.com/news/nation-world/article/Ciudad-Juarez-women-still-being-tortured-by-1703010.php

Alvarez, L. (2011, July 5). Casey Anthony not guilty in slaying of daughter. *New York Times.* Retrieved from http://www.nytimes.com/2011/07/06/us/06casey.html?pagewanted=all&_r=0

American Bar Association (ABA). (2010). *Law school staff by gender and ethnicity.* Retrieved from http://www.americanbar.org/content/dam/aba/migrated/legaled/statistics/charts/facultyinformationbygender.authcheckdam.pdf

American Bar Association (ABA). (2011). A current glance at women in the law, 2011. Retrieved from http://www.americanbar.org/content/dam/aba/marketing/women/current_glance_statistics_2011.authcheckdam.pdf

American Bar Association (ABA). (2012). *Goal III Report: An annual report on women's advancement into leadership positions in the American Bar Association.* Retrieved from http://www.americanbar.org/content/dam/aba/administrative/women/2012_goal3_women.authcheckdam.pdf

American Bar Association Commission on Domestic Violence. (2008). *Domestic violence Civil Protection Orders (CPOs) by state.* Retrieved from http://www.americanbar.org/content/dam/aba/migrated/domviol/pdfs/CPO_Protections_for_LGBT_Victims_7_08.authcheckdam.pdf

American Correctional Association. (2007). *Directory of adult and juvenile correctional departments, institutions and agencies and probation and parole authorities.* Alexandria, VA: Author.

American Society of Criminology (ASC). (n.d.). History of the American Society of Criminology. Retrieved from http://www.asc41.com

Americans for the Arts. (2000). Arts facts: Arts programs for at-risk youth. Retrieved from http://www.americansforthearts.org/

sites/default/files/pdf/get_involved/advocacy/research/2008/youth_at_risk08.pdf

Amnesty International. (1999). *Document—Pakistan: Violence against women in the name of honour*. Retrieved from http://amnesty.org/en/library/asset/ASA33/017/1999/en/53f9cc64-e0f2-11dd-be39-2d4003be4450/asa330171999en.html

Amy Elizabeth Fisher. (2014). The Biography.com website. Retrieved from http://www.biography.com/people/amy-fisher-235415.

Anderson, T. L. (2006). Issues facing women prisoners in the early twenty-first century. In C. Renzetti, L. Goodstein, & S. L. Miller (Eds.), *Rethinking gender, crime and justice* (pp. 200–212). Los Angeles: Roxbury.

Annan, S. L. (2011). "It's not just a job. This is where we live. This is our backyard": The experiences of expert legal and advocate providers with sexually assaulted women in rural areas. *Journal of the American Psychiatric Nurses Association, 17*(2), 139–147.

Anuforo, P. O., Oyedele, L., & Pacquiao, D. F. (2004). Comparative study of meanings, beliefs and practices of female circumcision among three Nigerian tribes in the United States and Nigeria. *Journal of Transcultural Nursing, 15*(2), 103–113.

Appier, J. (1998). *Policing women: The sexual politics of law enforcement and the LAPD*. Philadelphia, PA: Temple University Press.

Arin, C. (2001). Femicide in the Name of Honor in Turkey. *Violence against women, 7*(7), 821–825.

Associated Press. (2012, July 21). Air Force instructor sentenced to 20 years in prison after raping female recruit and sexually assaulting several other women. Retrieved from http://www.dailymail.co.uk/news/article-2177097/Lackland-Air-Force-instructor-Luis-Walker-sentenced-20-years-prison-guilty-rape-sexual-assault.html

Australian Bureau of Statistics (ABS) (2014). Recorded crime—Offenders. Retrieved from http://www.abs.gov.au/ausstats/abs@.nsf/Lookup/by%20Subject/4519.0~2012-13~Main%20Features~Offenders,%20Australia~4

Babin, E. A., Palazzolo, K. E., & Rivera, K. D. (2012). Communication skills, social support and burnout among advocates in a domestic violence agency. *Journal of Applied Communication Research, 40*(2), 147–166.

Bachman, R., Zaykowski, H., Lanier, C., Poteyeva, M., & Kallmyer, R. (2010). Estimating the magnitude of rape and sexual assault against American Indian and Alaska Native (AIAN) women. *Australian & New Zealand Journal of Criminology, 43*(2), 199–222.

Bacik, I., & Drew, E. (2006). Struggling with juggling: Gender and work/life balance in the legal professions. *Women's Studies International Forum, 29*, 136–146.

Baillargeon, J., Binswanger, I. A., Penn, J. V., Williams, B. A., & Murray, O. J. (2009). Psychiatric disorders and repeat incarcerations: The revolving prison door. *American Journal of Psychiatry, 166*, 103–109.

Baker, C. K., Holditch Niolon, P., & Oliphant, H. (2009). A descriptive analysis of transitional housing programs for survivors of

intimate partner violence in the United States. *Violence Against Women, 15*(4), 460–481.

Ball, J. D., & Bostaph, L. G. (2009). He versus she: A gender-specific analysis of legal and extralegal effects on pretrial release for felony defendants. *Women and Criminal Justice, 19*(2), 95–119.

Barata, P. C., & Schneider, F. (2004). Battered women add their voices to the debate about the merits of mandatory arrest. *Women's Studies Quarterly, 32*(3/4), 148–163.

Bates, K. A., Bader, C. D., & Mencken, F. C. (2003). Family structure, power-control theory and deviance: Extending power-control theory to include alternate family forms. *Western Criminological Review, 4*(3), 170–190.

Baum, K., Catalano, S., Rand, M., & Rose, K. (2009). *Stalking victimization in the United States*. U.S. Department of Justice, Bureau of Justice Statistics. Retrieved from http://ojp.usdoj.gov/content/pub/pdf/svus.pdf

BBC. (2013, May 7). Profile: Amanda Berry, Georgina De Jesus and Michelle Knight. Retrieved from http://www.bbc.co.uk/news/world-us-canada-22433057

Beck, A. J., Harrison, P. M., & Guerino, P. (2010). Sexual victimization in juvenile facilities reported by youth, 2008–09. U.S. Department of Justice, Bureau of Justice Statistics. Retrieved from http://bjs.ojp.usdoj.gov/content/pub/pdf/svjtry09.pdf

Belenko, S., & Houser, K. A. (2012). Gender differences in prison-based drug treatment participation. *International Journal of Offender Therapy and Comparative Criminology, 56*(5), 790–810.

Belknap, J. (2007). *The invisible woman: Gender, crime and justice*. Belmont, CA: Thomson-Wadsworth.

Belknap, J., Dunn, M., & Holsinger, K. (1997). *Moving toward juvenile justice and youth serving systems that address the distinct experience of the adolescent female* (Report to the Governor). Columbus, OH: Office of Criminal Justice Services.

Belknap, J., & Holsinger, K. (1998). An overview of delinquent girls: How theory and practice failed and the need for innovative change. In R. Zaplin (Ed.), *Female crime and delinquency: Critical perspectives and effective interventions* (pp. 31–64). Gaithersburg, MD: Aspen.

Belknap, J., & Holsinger, K. (2006). The gendered nature of risk factors for delinquency. *Feminist Criminology, 1*(1), 48–71.

Bennett, L., Riger, S., Schewe, P., Howard, A., & Wasco, S. (2004). Effectiveness of hotline, advocacy, counseling, and shelter services for victims of domestic violence: A statewide evaluation. *Journal of Interpersonal Violence, 19*(7), 815–829.

Bennett-Smith, M. (2013, February 7). Accused "witch" Kepari Leniata burned alive by mob in Papua New Guinea. *Huffington Post*. Retrieved from http://www.huffingtonpost.com/2013/02/07/kepari-leniata-young-mother-burned-alive-mob-sorcery-papua-new-guinea_n2638431.html

Bennice, J. A., & Resick, P. A. (2003). Marital rape history, research, and practice. *Trauma, Violence, & Abuse, 4*(3), 228–246.

Bent-Goodley, T. B. (2004). Perceptions of domestic violence: A dialogue with African American women. *Health and Social Work, 29*(4), 307–316.

Berg, A. (2011, September 4). Stop shackling pregnant prisoners. *The Daily Beast.* Retrieved July 10, 2012, from http://www.thedailybeast.com/articles/2011/09/04/stop-shackling-pregnant-prisoners-new-push-to-ban-controversial-practice.html

Bernard, T. J. (1992). *The cycle of juvenile justice.* New York, NY: Oxford University Press.

Bernhard, L. A. (2000). Physical and sexual violence experienced by lesbian and heterosexual women. *Violence Against Women, 6*(1), 68–79.

Beynon, C. M., McVeigh, C., McVeigh, J., Leavey, C., & Bellis, M. A. (2008). The involvement of drugs and alcohol in drug-facilitated sexual assault: A systematic review of the evidence. *Trauma, Violence, & Abuse, 9*(3), 178–188.

Black, M. C., Basile, K. C., Breiding, M. J., Smith, S. G., Walters, M. L., Merrick, M. T., . . . Stevens, M. R. (2011). *The National Intimate Partner and Sexual Violence Survey (NISVS): 2010 summary report.* Atlanta, GA: National Center for Injury Prevention and Control, Centers for Disease Control and Prevention. Retrieved from http://www.cdc.gov/ViolencePrevention/pdf/NISVS_Report2010-a.pdf

Blackwell, B. S., Holleran, D., & Finn, M. A. (2008). The impact of the Pennsylvania sentencing guidelines on sex differences in sentencing. *Journal of Contemporary Criminal Justice, 24*(4), 399–418.

Blackwell, D. B. (2012, June 15). Through my eyes: Surviving sexual assault. Retrieved from http://www.usafa.af.mil/shared/media/document/AFD-120619-023.pdf

Block, C. R. (2003). How can practitioners help an abused woman lower her risk of death. *National Institute of Justice (NIJ) Journal, 250,* 4–7. Retrieved from http://www.ncjrs.gov/pdffiles1/jr000250c.pdf

Block, K. J. (1999). Bringing scouting to prison: Programs and challenges. *The Prison Journal, 79*(2), 269–283.

Block, K. J., & Potthast, M. J. (1998). Girl Scouts Beyond Bars: Facilitating parent-child contact in correctional settings. *Child Welfare, 77*(5), 561–579.

Bloom, B., Owen, B., & Covington, S. (2003). *Gender-responsive strategies: Research, practice, and guiding principles for women offenders.* Washington, DC: National Institute of Corrections. U.S. Department of Justice. Retrieved January 13, 2011, from http://nicic.gov/pubs/2003/018017.pdf

Bloom, B., Owen, B., & Covington, S. (2004). Women offenders and the gendered effects of public policy. *Review of Policy Research, 21*(1), 31–48.

Bloom, B., Owen, B., Deschenes, E. P., & Rosenbaum, J. (2002a). Improving juvenile justice for females: A statewide assessment in California. *Crime and Delinquency, 48*(4), 526–552.

Bloom, B., Owen, B., Deschenes, E. P., & Rosenbaum, J. (2002b). Moving toward justice for female offenders in the new millennium: Modeling gender-specific policies and programs. *Journal of Contemporary Criminal Justice, 18*(1), 37–56.

Blumberg, J. (2007, October 24). A brief history of the Salem witch trials. *The Smithsonian.* Retrieved from http://www.smithsonianmag.com/history/a-brief-history-of-the-salem-witch-trials-175162489/

Bond, C., & Jeffries, S. (2009). Does indigeneity matter? Sentencing indigenous offenders in South Australia's higher courts. *Australian & New Zealand journal of Criminology, 42,* 47–71.

Bond, C. E. W., & Jeffries, S. (2012). Harsher sentences?: Indigeneity and prison sentence length in Western Australia's higher courts. *Journal of Sociology, 48*(3), 266–286.

Bornstein, D. R., Fawcett, J., Sullivan, M., Senturia, K. D., & Shiu-Thornton, S. (2006). Understanding the experiences of lesbian, bisexual and trans survivors of domestic violence. *Journal of Homosexuality, 51*(1), 159–181.

Bourduin, C. M., & Ronis, S. T. (2012). Research note: Individual, family, peer and academic characteristics of female serious juvenile offenders. *Youth Violence and Juvenile Justice, 10*(4), 386–400.

Bowles, M. A., DeHart, D., & Webb, J. R. (2012). Family influences on female offenders' substance use: The role of adverse childhood events among incarcerated women. *Journal of Family Violence, 27,* 681–686.

Boyd, C. (2001). The implications and effects of theories of intergenerational transmission of violence for boys who live with domestic violence. *Australian Domestic & Family Violence Clearinghouse Newsletter, 6,* 6–8.

Boykins, A. D., Alvanzo, A. A., Carson, S., Forte, J., Leisey, M., & Plichta, S. B. (2010). Minority women victims of recent sexual violence: Disparities in incident history. *Journal of Women's Health, 19*(3), 453–461.

Boyle, E. H., McMorris, B. J., & Gomez, M. (2002). Local conformity to international norms: The case of female genital cutting. *International Sociology, 17*(1), 5–33.

Branum, D. (2013, January 8). USAFA reports show increased trust in system, better reporting. *Air Force Print News Today.* Retrieved from http://www.usafa.af.mil/news/story_print.asp?id=123331120

Brennan, P. K. (2006). Sentencing female misdemeanants: An examination of the direct and indirect effects of race/ethnicity. *Justice Quarterly, 23*(1), 60–95.

Brennan, T., Breitenbach, M., Dieterich, W., Salisbury, E. J., & van Voorhis, P. (2012). Women's pathways to serious and habitual crime: A person-centered analysis incorporating gender responsive factors. *Criminal Justice and Behavior, 39*(11), 1481–1508.

Brents, B. G., & Hausbeck, K. (2005). Violence and legalized brothel prostitution in Nevada: Examining safety, risk and prostitution policy. *Journal of Interpersonal Violence, 20*(3), 270–295.

Bright, C. L., Ward, S. K., & Negi, N. J. (2011). "The chain has to be broken": A qualitative investigation of the experiences of young women following juvenile court involvement. *Feminist Criminology, 6*(1), 32–53.

Britton, D. M. (2003). *At work in the iron cage: The prison as a gendered organization.* New York: New York University Press.

Broidy, L., & Agnew, R. (1997). Gender and crime: A general strain theory perspective. *Journal of Research in Crime and Delinquency, 34,* 275–306.

Brown, L. M., Chesney-Lind, M., & Stein, N. (2007). Patriarchy matters: Towards a gendered theory of teen violence and victimization. *Violence Against Women, 13*(12), 1249–1273.

Brown, M., & Bloom, B. (2009). Reentry and renegotiating motherhood: Maternal identity and success on parole. *Crime & Delinquency, 55*(2), 313–336.

Brown, M. J., & Groscup, J. (2009). Perceptions of same-sex domestic violence among crisis center staff. *Journal of Family Violence, 24,* 87–93.

Brumfield, B., & Simpson, D. (2013, October 9). Malala Yousafzai: Accolades, applause and a grim milestone. CNN. Retrieved from http://www.cnn.com/2013/10/09/world/asia/malal-shooting-anniversary/

Brunovskis, A., & Surtees, R. (2012). Coming home: Challenges in family reintegration for trafficked women. *Qualitative Social Work, 12*(4), 454–472.

Brunson, R., & Miller, J. (2006). Gender, race and urban policing: The experience of African American youths. *Gender & Society, 20,* 531–552.

Bryant-Davis, T., Chung, H., & Tillman, S. (2009). From the margins to the center ethnic minority women and the mental health effects of sexual assault. *Trauma, Violence, & Abuse, 10*(4), 330–357.

Bui, H. (2007). The limitations of current approaches to domestic violence. In R. Muraskin (Ed.), *It's a crime* (4th ed., pp. 261–276). Upper Saddle River, NJ: Pearson Prentice Hall.

Bui, H., & Morash, M. (2008). Immigration, masculinity and intimate partner violence from the standpoint of domestic violence service providers and Vietnamese-origin women. *Feminist Criminology, 3*(3), 191–215.

Bunch, J., Clay-Warner, J., & Lei, M. (2012, December 6). Demographic characteristics and victimization risk: Testing the mediating effects of routine activities. *Crime & Delinquency.* Advance online publication. Retrieved from http://cad.sagepub.com/content/early/2012/12/05/0011128712466932.full.pdf+html

Bundeskriminalamt (BKA). (2013). *Police crime statistics yearbook 2012.* Retrieved from http://www.bka.de/nn_195184/EN/Publications/PoliceCrimeStatistics/policeCrimeStatistics__node.html?__nnn=true

Bureau of Justice Statistics (BLS). (2006). *Intimate partner violence.* Office of Justice Programs. Retrieved from http://bjs.ojp.usdoj.gov/content/pub/press/ipvpr.cfm

Bureau of Labor Statistics (BLS). (2009). *Median weekly earnings of full-time wage and salary workers by detailed occupation and sex.* Retrieved from www.bls.gov/cps/cpsaat39.pdf

Bureau of Labor Statistics (BLS). (2014). *Occupational outlook handbook, 2014–15 Edition.* Probation Officers and Correctional Treatment Specialists. Retrieved from http://www.bls.gov/ooh/community-and-social-service/probation-officers-and-correctional-treatment-specialists.htm

Burgess-Jackson, K. (Ed.). (1999). *A most detestable crime: New philosophical essays on rape.* New York, NY: Oxford University Press.

Burgess-Proctor, A. (2006). Intersections of race, class, gender and crime: Future directions for feminist criminology. *Feminist Criminology, 1*(1), 27–47.

Burgess-Proctor, A. (2012). Backfire: Lessons learned when the criminal justice system fails help-seeking battered women. *Journal of Crime and Justice, 35*(1), 68–92.

Burke, J. (2012, November 2). Kashmir parents accused of killing daughter in acid attack. *The Guardian.* Retrieved from http://www.theguardian.com/world/2012/nov/02/paresnts-accused-kashmir-acid-attack

Burton, V. S., Cullen, F. T., Evans, D., Alarid, L. F., & Dunaway, G. (1998). Gender, self-control and crime. *Journal of Research in Crime and Delinquency, 35*(2), 123–147.

Bush-Baskette, S. (1998). The war on drugs as a war on Black women. In S. L. Miller (Ed.), *Crime control and women* (pp. 113–129). Thousand Oaks, CA: Sage.

Bush-Baskette, S. (1999). The war on drugs: A war against women? In S. Cook & S. Davies (Eds.), *Harsh punishment: International experiences of women's imprisonment* (pp. 211–229). Boston, MA: Northeastern University Press.

Bush-Baskette, S. R. (2000, December). The war on drugs and the incarceration of mothers. *Journal of Drug Issues, 30,* 919–928.

Bush-Baskette, S. R. (2010). *Misguided justice: The war on drugs and the incarceration of Black women.* New York, NY: iUniverse.

Bush-Baskette, S. R., & Smith, V. C. (2012). Is meth the new crack for women in the war on drugs? Factors affecting sentencing outcomes for women and parallels between meth and crack. *Feminist Criminology, 7*(1), 48–69.

CableNewsNetwork(CNN). (2001). Patty Hearst profile. Retrieved from http://www.cnn.com/CNN/Programs/people/shows/hearst/profile.html

Calderon Gamboa, J. (2007, Winter). Seeking integral reparations for the murders and disappearances of women in Ciudad Juárez: A gender and cultural perspective. *Human Rights Brief, 14*(2), 31–35. Retrieved from http://www.wcl.american.edu/hrbrief/14/2calderon.pdf

California Emergency Management Agency (Cal EMA). (2011). Victim services programs. Retrieved from http://www.calema.ca.gov/PublicSafetyandVictimServices/Pages/Victim-Services-Programs.aspx

Camacho, C. M., & Alarid, L. F. (2008). The significance of the victim advocate for domestic violence victims in Municipal Court. *Violence and Victims, 23*(3), 288–300.

Campbell, A. (1984). *The girls in the gang.* New Brunswick, NJ: Rutgers University Press.

Campbell, A. (1995). Female participation in gangs. In M.W. Klein, C. L. Maxson, & J. Miller (Eds.), *The modern gang reader* (pp. 70–77). Los Angeles, CA: Roxbury.

Campbell, J., & Carlson. J. R. (2012). Correctional administrators' perceptions of prison nurseries. *Criminal Justice and Behavior, 39*(8), 1063–1074.

Campbell, J. C., Webster, D., Koziol-McLain, J., Block, C. R., Campbell, D., Curry, M. A., . . . Wilt, S. (2003). Assessing risk factors for intimate partner homicide. *National Institute of Justice (NIJ) Journal, 250,* 14–19. Retrieved from http://www.ncjrs.gov/pdffiles1/jr000250e.pdf

Campbell, N. D. (2000). *Using women: Gender, drug policy and social justice.* New York, NY: Routledge.

Campbell, R. (2006). Rape survivors' experiences with the legal and medical systems: Do rape victim advocates make a difference? *Violence Against Women, 12*(1), 30–45.

Canada honor killing trial verdict: Shafia family found guilty. (2012, January 29). *Huffington Post.* Retrieved from http://www.huffingtonpost.com/2012/01/29/canada-honor-killing-shafia-family-guilty_n_1240268.html

Canterino v. Wilson, 546 F. Supp. 174 (W.D. Ky. 1982).

Caputo, G. A., & King, A. (2011). Shoplifting: Work, agency and gender. *Feminist Criminology, 6*(3), 159–177.

Carbone-Lopez, K., Gatewood Owens, J., & Miller, J. (2012). Women's "storylines" of methamphetamine initiation in the Midwest. *Journal of Drug Issues, 42*(3), 226–246.

Carlan, P. E., Nored, L. S., & Downey, R. A. (2011). Officer preferences for male backup: The influence of gender and police partnering. *Journal of Police and Criminal Psychology, 26*(1), 4–10.

Carr, N. T., Hudson, K., Hanks, R. S., & Hunt, A. N. (2008). Gender effects along the juvenile justice system: Evidence of a gendered organization. *Feminist Criminology, 3*(1), 25–43.

Carson, E. A., & Golinelli, D. (2013). Prisoners in 2012—Advance counts. U.S. Department of Justice, Bureau of Justice Statistics. Retrieved from http://www.bjs.gov/content/pub/pdf/p12ac.pdf

Casey Anthony. (2014). The Biography.com website. Retrieved from http://www.biography.com/people/casey-anthony-20660183.

Cass, A., & Mallicoat, S. L. (2014). College student perceptions of victim action: Will targets of stalking report to police? *American Journal of Criminal Justice.* doi: 10.1007/s12103-014-9252-8

Catalano, S. (2007). *Intimate partner violence in the United States.* Bureau of Justice Statistics. U.S. Department of Justice: Washington, DC. Retrieved from http://bjs.ojp.usdoj.gov/content/pub/pdf/IPAus.pdf

Catalano, S. (2012). *Intimate partner violence in the United States.* Bureau of Justice Statistics, Office of Justice Programs. Retrieved from http://bjs.ojp.usdoj.gov/content/intimate/ipv.cfm

Catterall, J. S., Dumais, S. A., & Hampden-Thompson, G. (2012). The Arts and achievement in at-risk youth: Findings from four longitudinal studies. National Endowment for the Arts. Retrieved from http://arts.gov/sites/default/files/Arts-At-Risk-Youth.pdf

CBS News. (2009, February 11). Air Force rape scandal grows. Retrieved August 31, 2012, from http://www.cbsnews.com/2100-201_162-543490.html

Center for American Women and politics. (n.d.). Women on the U.S. Supreme Court. Retrieved from http://www.cawp.rutgers.edu/fast_facts/levels_of_office/USSupremeCourt.php

Centers for Disease Control and Prevention (CDC). (1992–2004). Youth risk behavior surveillance—United States 1991–2004. CDC surveillance summaries. Department of Health and Human Services. Retrieved from http://www.cdc.gov/

Centers for Disease Control and Prevention (CDC). (2003). *Costs of intimate partner violence against women in the United States: 2003.* Atlanta, GA: National Centers for Injury Prevention and Control.

Centers for Disease Control and Prevention (CDC). (n.d.). *Intimate partner violence.* Retrieved from http://www.cdc.gov/Violence Prevention/intimatepartnerviolence/definitions.html

Chamberlain, L. (2007, March 28). 2 cities and 4 bridges where commerce flows. *New York Times, 28.*

Chapman, S. B. (2009). *Inmate-perpetrated harassment: Exploring the gender-specific experience of female correctional officers.* (Doctoral dissertation). City University of New York, New York. Available from ProQuest Dissertations and Theses database, http://media.proquest.com/media/pq/classic/doc/1679173831/fmt/ai/rep/NPDF?_s=uODFIQqrVIzWJxoNj7uj9lddn8I%3D

Chasmar, J. (2013, June 10). Teacher publically tortured, beheaded for witchcraft in Papua New Guinea. *Washington Times.* Retrieved from http://www.washingtontimes.com/news/2013/jun/10/teacher-publicly-tortured-beheaded-witchcraft-papu/

Cheeseman, K. A., & Downey, R. A. (2012). Talking 'bout my generation: The effect on "generation" on correctional employee perceptions of work stress ad job satisfaction. *The Prison Journal, 92*(1), 24–44.

Cheeseman, K. A., & Worley, R. M. (2006). A "captive" audience: Legal responses and remedies to the sexual abuse of female inmates. *Criminal Law Bulletin–Boston, 42*(4), 439.

Chesler, P. (2010). Worldwide trends in honor killings. *Middle East Quarterly, 17*(2), 3–11.

Chesney-Lind, M. (1973). Judicial enforcement of the female sex role. *Issues in Criminology, 8,* 51–70.

Chesney-Lind, M. (1997). *The female offender: Girls, women and crime.* Thousand Oaks, CA: Sage.

Chesney-Lind, M. (2006). Patriarchy, crime and justice: Feminist criminology in an era of backlash. *Feminist Criminology, 1*(1), 6–26.

Chesney-Lind, M., & Shelden, R. G. (2004). *Girls, delinquency and juvenile justice.* Belmont, CA: West/Wadsworth.

Chiricos, T., Padgett, K., & Gertz, M. (2000). Fear, TV news and the reality of crime. *Criminology, 38*(3), 755–786.

Cho, S-Y, Dreher, A., & Neumayer, E. (2011). *The spread of anti-trafficking policies—Evidence from a new index.* Cege Discussion Paper Series No. 119, Georg-August-University of Goettingen, Germany.

Ciong, Z. B., & Huang, J. (2011). Predicting Hmong male and female youth's delinquent behavior: An exploratory study. *Hmong Studies Journal, 12*, 1–34. Retrieved August 15, 2012, from http://www.hmongstudies.org/XiongandHuangHSJ12.pdf

Clear, T., & Frost, N. (2007). Informing public policy. *Criminology & Public Policy, 6*(4), 633–640.

Clements-Nolle, K., Wolden, M., & Bargmann-Losche, J. (2009). Childhood trauma and risk for past and future suicide attempts among women in prison. *Women's Health Issues, 19*, 185–192.

Cloud, J. (2011, June 16). How the Casey Anthony murder case became the social media trial of the century. *Time Magazine.* Retrieved from http://content.time.com/time/nation/article/0,8599,2077969,00.html

Cobbina, J. E., Huebner, B. M., & Berg, M. T. (2012). Men, women and postrelease offending: An examination of the nature of the link between relational ties and recidivism. *Crime & Delinquency, 58*(3), 331–361.

Coffman, K. (2012, April 30). Dougherty gang sentenced in Colorado for police shootout. *Reuters.* Retrieved from http://news.yahoo.com/dougherty-gang-sentenced-colorado-police-shootout-230049502.html

Cohen, A. K. (1955). *Delinquent boys.* Glencoe, IL: Free Press.

Cohen, L. E., & Felson, M. (1979). Social change and crime rate trends: A routine activity approach. *American Sociological Review,* 588–608.

Connor, T. (2013, October 16). Ariel Castro victim reparations bill gets initial approval. NBS News. Retrieved from http://usnews.nbcnews.com/_news/2013/10/16/20988996-ariel-castro-victim-reparations-bill-gets-initial approval?lite

Contreras, R. (2009). "Damn, yo—Who's that girl?" An ethnographic analysis of masculinity in drug robberies. *Journal of Contemporary Ethnography, 38*(4), 465–492.

Cook, C. L., & Fox, K. A. (2012). Testing the relative importance of contemporaneous offenses: The impacts of fear of sexual assault versus fear of physical harm among men and women. *Journal of Criminal Justice 40*(2), 142–151.

Cook, F. A. (1997). Belva Ann Lockwood: For peace, justice, and president. Stanford, CA: Women's Legal History Biography Project, Robert Crown Law Library, Stanford Law School. Retrieved from http://wlh-static.law.stanford.edu/papers/LockwoodB-Cook97.pdf

Cook, J. A., & Fonow, M. M. (1986). Knowledge and women's interests: Issues of epistemology and methodology in feminist sociological research. *Sociological Inquiry, 56*, 2–29.

Coontz, P. (2000). Gender and judicial decisions: Do female judges decide cases differently than male judges? *Gender Issues, 18*(4), 59–73.

Cooper, A., & Smith, E. L. (2011). Homicide trends in the United States. Annual rates for 2009 and 2010. U.S. Department of Justice. Retrieved from http://bjs.ojp.usdoj.gov/content/pub/pdf/htus8008.pdf

Cops, D., & Pleysier, S. (2011). "Doing Gender" in fear of crime: The impact of gender identity on reported levels of fear of crime in adolescents and young adults. *British Journal of Criminology, 51*(1), 58–74.

Corsianos, M. (2009). *Policing and gendered justice: Examining the possibilities.* Toronto, Canada: UTP Higher Education.

Covington, S. (1999). *Helping women recover: A program for treating substance abuse.* San Francisco, CA: Jossey-Bass.

Cox, L., & Speziale, B. (2009). Survivors of stalking: Their voices and lived experiences. *Affilia: Journal of Women and Social Work, 24*(1), 5–18.

Crandall, M., Senturia, K., Sullivan, M., & Shiu-Thornton, S. (2005). No way out: Russian-speaking women's experiences with domestic violence. *Journal of Interpersonal Violence, 20*(8), 941–958.

Crime in the United States 2010 (CIUS). (2010). Forcible rape. Uniform Crime Reports. U.S. Department of Justice, Federal Bureau of Investigation. Retrieved from http://www.fbi.gov/about-us/cjis/ucr/crime-in-the-u.s/2010/crime-in-the-u.s.-2010/violent-crime/rapemain

Crime in the United States 2012 (CIUS). (2012). About crime in the U.S. Uniform Crime Reports. U.S. Department of Justice, Federal Bureau of Investigation. Retrieved from http://www.fbi.gov/about-us/cjis/ucr/crime-in-the-u.s/2012/crime-in-the-u.s.-2012

Crosnoe, R., Erickson, K. G., & Dornbusch, S. M. (2002). Protective functions of family relationships and school factors on the deviant behavior of adolescent boys and girls. *Youth and Society, 33*(4), 515–544.

Curry, G. D., Ball, R. A., & Fox, R. J. (1994). *Gang crime and law enforcement recordkeeping. Research in brief.* Washington, DC: U.S. Department of Justice, Office of Justice Programs, National Institute of Justice. Retrieved September 28, 2010, from http://www.ncjrs.gov/txtfiles/gcrime.txt

Dahl, J. (2012, May 16). Fla. woman Marissa Alexander gets 20 years for "warning shot": Did she stand her ground? CBS News. Retrieved from http://www.cbsnews.com/news/fla-woman-marissa-alexander-gets-20-years-for-warning-shot-did-she-stand-her-ground/

Daigle, L. E., Cullen, F. T., & Wright, J. P. (2007). Gender differences in the predictors of juvenile delinquency: Assessing the generality-specificity debate. *Youth Violence and Juvenile Justice, 5*(3), 254–286.

Dalla, R. L. (2000). Exposing the "pretty woman" myth: A qualitative examination of the lives of female streetwalking prostitutes. *Journal of Sex Research, 37*(4), 344–353.

Dalla, R. L., Xia, Y., & Kennedy, H. (2003). "You just give them what they want and pray they don't kill you": Street-level workers' reports of victimization, personal resources and coping strategies. *Violence Against Women, 9*(11), 1367–1394.

Daly, K. (1994). *Gender, crime, and punishment.* New Haven, CT: Yale University Press.

Daly, K., & Chesney-Lind, M. (1988). Feminism and criminology. *Justice Quarterly, 5*(4), 497–538.

Danner, M. J. E. (2003). Three strikes and it's women who are out: The hidden consequences for women of criminal justice policy reforms. In R. Muraskin (Ed.), *It's a crime: Women and justice* (2nd ed., Chapter 44). Upper Saddle River, NJ: Prentice-Hall.

Davidson, J. T. (2011). Managing risk in the community: How gender matters. In R. Sheehan, G. McIvor, & C. Trotter (Eds.), *Working with women offenders in the community*. New York, NY: Willan.

Davies, K., Block, C. R., & Campbell, J. (2007). Seeking help from the police: Battered women's decisions and experiences. *Criminal Justice Studies, 20*(1), 15–41.

Davis, C. P. (2007). At risk girls and delinquency: Career pathways. *Crime and Delinquency, 53*(3), 408–435.

Davis, K. E., Coker, A. L., & Sanderson, M. (2002). Physical and mental health effects of being stalked for men and women. *Violence and Victims, 17*(4), 429–443.

De Atley, R. (2013, October 28). Sara Kruzan: If sentenced today, hers would be a different story. *The Press-Enterprise*. Retrieved at http://www.pe.com/local-news/local-news-headlines/20131028-kruzan-if-sentenced-today-hers-would-be-a-different-story.ece

De Groof, S. (2008). And my mama said. . . . The (relative) parental influence on fear of crime among adolescent boys and girls. *Youth & Society, 39*(3), 267–293.

De Vaus, D., & Wise, S. (1996, Autumn). Parent's concern for the safety of their children. *Family matters, 43,* 34–38.

DeLisi, M., Beaver, K. M., Vaughn, M. G., Trulson, C. R., Kisloski, A. E., Drury, A. J., & Wright, J. P. (2010). Personality, gender and self-control theory revisited: Results from a sample of institutionalized juvenile delinquents. *Applied Psychology in Criminal Justice, 6*(1), 31–46.

Deluca, M. (2013, August 1). Ariel Castro victim Michelle Knight: "Your hell is just beginning." Retrieved from http://usnews.nbcnews.com/_news/2013/08/01/19813977-ariel-castro-victim-michelle-knight-your-hell-is-just-beginning?lite

Demuth, S., & Steffensmeier, D. (2004). The impact of gender and race-ethnicity in the pretrial release process. *Social Problems, 51*(2), 222–242.

Dennis, M. L., Scott, C. K., Funk, R., & Foss, M. A. (2005). The duration and correlates of addiction and treatment careers. *Journal of Substance Abuse Treatment, 28*(2), S51-S62.

Dershowitz, A. (2011, July 7). Casey Anthony: The system worked. *Wall Street Journal*. Retrieved from http://online.wsj.com/news/articles/SB10001424052702303544604576429783247016492

Diep, F. (2013, June 10). Mississippi will test teen mom babies for statutory rape evidence. *Popular Science*. Retrieved from http://www.popsci.com/science/article/2013-06/new-mississippi-teen-moms-babies-statutory-rape

Dietz, N. A., & Martin, P. Y. (2007). Women who are stalked: Questioning the fear standard. *Violence Against Women, 13*(7), 750–776.

DiMarino, F. (2009). Women as corrections professionals. *Corrections.com.* Retrieved from http://www.corrections.com/articles/21703-women-as-corrections-professionals

Dinan, E. (2005, February 27). Where the Smart boys are 14 years later. *Portsmouth Herald*. Retrieved from http://www.hampton.lib.nh.us/hampton/biog/pamsmart/20050227PH.htm

Dissell, R. (2012, September 2). Rape charges against high school players divide football town of Steubenville, Ohio. Cleveland.com. Retrieved from http://www.cleveland.com/metro/index.ssf/2012/09/rape_charges_divide_football_t.html

Dobash, R., & Dobash, R. E. (1992). *Women, violence and social change*. New York, NY: Routledge.

Dodderidge, J. (1632). *The lawes resolutions of women's rights: Or, the law's provision for women*. London, UK: John More, Rare Book and Special Collections Division, Library of Congress.

Dodge, M. Valcore. L., & Klinger, D. A. (2010). Maintaining separate spheres in policing: Women on SWAT teams. *Women & Criminal Justice, 20*(3), 218–238.

Donovan, P. (1996). Can statutory rape laws be effective in preventing adolescent pregnancy? *Family Planning Perspectives, 29*(1). Retrieved from http://www.guttmacher.org/pubs/journals/2903097.html

Dowler, K. (2003). Media consumption and public attitudes toward crime and justice: The relationship between fear of crime, punitive attitudes, and perceived police effectiveness. *Journal of Criminal Justice and Popular Culture, 10*(2), 109–126.

Downey, M. (2007, October 28). Genarlow Wilson is free . . . But other victims of Georgia's sweeping sex offender laws are not. *Atlanta Journal-Constitution*, p. B1.

Drachman, V. G. (1998). *Sisters in law: Women lawyers in modern American history*. Cambridge, MA: Harvard University Press.

Dugan, L, Nagin, D., & Rosenfeld, R. (2003). Exposure reduction or retaliation: Domestic violence resources on intimate-partner homicide. *Law & Society Review, 37*(1), 169–198.

Durrani, S., & Singh, P. (2011). Women, private practice and billable hours: Time for a total rewards strategy? *Compensation & Benefits Review, 43*(5), 300–305.

Dye, M. H., & Aday, R. H. (2013). "I just wanted to die": Preprison and current suicide ideation among women serving life sentences. *Criminal justice and Behavior, 40*(8), 832–849.

Eghigian, M., & Kirby, K. (2006). Girls in gangs: On the rise in America. *Corrections Today, 68*(2), 48–50.

Einat, T., & Chen. G. (2012). What's love got to do with it? Sex in a female maximum security prison. *The Prison Journal, 92*(4), 484–505.

England, L. (2008, March 17). Rumsfeld knew. *Stern Magazine*. Retrieved August 31, 2012, from http://www.stern.de/politik/ausland/lynndie-england-rumsfeld-knew-614356.html?nv=ct_cb

Esbensen, F. A., & Carson, D. C. (2012). Who are the gangsters? An examination of the age, race/ethnicity, sex and immigration status of self-reported gang members in a seven-city study of American youth. *Journal of Contemporary Criminal Justice, 28*(4), 465–481.

Esbensen, F. A., Deschenes, E. P., & Winfree, L. T., Jr. (1999). Differences between gang girls and gang boys: Results from a multisite survey. *Youth and Society, 31*(1), 27–53.

Esfandiari, G. (2006). Afghanistan: Rights watchdog alarmed at continuing "honor killings." Women's United Nations Report Network. Retrieved from http://www.wunrn.com/news/2006/09_25_06/100106_afghanistan_violence.htm

Estrada, F., & Nilsson A. (2012). Does it cost more to be a female offender? A life-course study of childhood circumstances, crime, drug abuse, and living conditions. *Feminist Criminology, 7*(3), 196–219.

Ewoldt, C. A., Monson, C. M., & Langhinrichsen-Rohling, J. (2000). Attributions about rape in a continuum of dissolving marital relationships. *Journal of Interpersonal Violence, 15*(11), 1175–1183.

Ezell, M., & Levy, M. (2003). An evaluation of an arts program for incarcerated juvenile offenders. *Journal of Correctional Education, 54*(3), 108–114.

Fagel, M. (2013, March 8). Jury questions to Jodi Arias illustrate their frustration with her story. *Huffington Post.* Retrieved from http://www.huffingtonpost.com/mari fagel/jodi-arias-jury questions_b_2825167.html

Farid, M. (2014, January 13). On the shelves: "I am Malala": Her first hand story. *The Jakarta Post.* Retrieved from http://www.thejakartapost.com/news/2014/01/13/on-shelves-i-am-malala-her first-hand-story.html-0

Farley, M. (2004). "Bad for the body, bad for the heart": Prostitution harms women even if legalized or decriminalized. *Violence Against Women, 10*(10), 1087–1125.

Farley, M., & Barkin, H. (1998). Prostitution, violence and post traumatic stress disorder. *Women and Health, 27*(3), 37–49.

Farley, M., & Kelly, V. (2000). Prostitution: A critical review of the medical and social sciences literature. *Women and Criminal Justice, 11*(4), 29–64.

Fattah, E. A., & Sacco, V. F. (1989). *Crime and victimization of the elderly.* New York, NY: Springer-Verlag.

Federal Bureau of Investigation (FBI). (2003). Bank crime statistics 2003. Retrieved from http://www.fbi.gov/stats-services/publications/bank-crime-statistics-2003/bank-crime-statistics-bcs-2003

Federal Bureau of Investigation (FBI). (2011). *Crime in the U.S. 2010: Uniform Crime Reports.* Retrieved from http://www.fbi.gov/about-us/cjis/ucr/crime-in-the-u.s/2010/crime-in-the-u.s.-2010

Federal Bureau of Investigation (FBI). (2012a, January 6). Attorney General Eric Holder announces revisions to the Uniform Crime Report's definition of rape: Date reported on rape will better reflect state criminal codes, victim experiences [Press release]. U.S. Department of Justice, Uniform Crime Reports. Retrieved from http://www.fbi.gov/news/pressrel/press-releases/attorney-general-eric-holder-announces-revisions-to-the-uniform-crime-reports-definition-of-rape

Federal Bureau of Investigation (FBI). (2012b). Crime in the United States, 2012. Retrieved from http://www.fbi.gov/about-us/cjis/ucr/crime-in-the-u.s/2012/crime-in-the-u.s.-2012/cius_home

Federal Bureau of Investigation (FBI). (2012c). UCR program changes definition of rape: Includes all victims and omits requirement of physical force. Criminal Justice Information Service, U. S. Department of Justice. Retrieved from http://www.fbi.gov/about-us/cjis/cjis-link/march-2012/ucr-program-changes-definition-of-rape

Feld, B. C. (2009). Violent girls or relabeled status offenders? An alternative interpretation of the data. *Crime and Delinquency, 55*(2), 241–265.

Felix, Q. (2005). Human rights in Pakistan: Violence and misery for children and women. *Asia News.* Retrieved from http://www.asianews.it/news-en/Human-rights-in-Pakistan: violence-and-misery-for-children-and-women-2554.html

Fellner, J. (2010). Sexually abused: The nightmare of juveniles in confinement. *Huffington Post.* Retrieved August 15, 2012, from http://www.huffingtonpost.com/jamie-fellner/sexually-abused-the-night_b_444240.html

Ferszt, G. G. (2011). Who will speak for me? Advocating for pregnant women in prison. *Policy, Politics & Nursing Practice, 12*(4), 254–256.

Figley, C. R. (1995). Compassion fatigue: Toward a new understanding of the costs of caring. In B. H. Stamm (Ed.), *Secondary traumatic stress: Self-care issues for clinicians, researchers and educators* (2nd ed., pp. 3–28). Lutherville, MD: Sidran.

Fisher, B. S., Cullen, F. T., & Turner, M. G. (2000). The sexual victimization of college women. Series: Research report. *NCJ.* Available from https://www.ncjrs.gov/txtfiles1/nij/182369.txt

Fisher, B. S., Daigle, L. E., & Cullen, F. T. (2010). What distinguishes single from recurrent sexual victims? The role of lifestyle-routine activities and first-incident characteristics. *Justice Quarterly, 27*(1), 102–129.

Fisher, B. S., Daigle, L. E., Cullen, F. T., & Turner, M. G. (2003). Reporting sexual victimization to the police and others: Results from a national-level study of college women. *Criminal Justice and Behavior, 30*(1), 6–38.

Fisher, B. S., & May, D. (2009). College students' crime-related fears on campus: Are far-provoking cues gendered? *Journal of Contemporary Criminal Justice, 25*(3), 300–321.

Fisher, B. S., & Sloan, J. J. (2003). Unraveling the fear of sexual victimization among college women: Is the "shadow of sexual assault" hypothesis supported? *Justice Quarterly, 20,* 633–659.

Fleisher, M. S., & Krienert, J. L. (2004). Life-course events, social networks, and the emergence of violence among female gang members. *Journal of Community Psychology, 32*(5), 607–622.

Fleury-Steiner, R., Bybee, D., Sullivan, C. M., Belknap, J., & Melton, H. C. (2006). Contextual factors impacting battered women's intentions to reuse the criminal legal system. *Journal of Community Psychology, 34*(3), 327–342.

Foley, S., Kidder, D. L., & Powell, G. N. (2002). The perceived glass ceiling and justice perceptions: An investigation of Hispanic law associates. *Journal of Management, 28*(4), 471–496.

Foundation for Women's Health, Research and Development (FORWARD). (2012). *Female genital mutilation.* Retrieved from http://www.forwarduk.org.uk/key-issues/fgm

Fox News. (2014, January 7). One of two teens convicted in Steubenville rape case released. Retrieved from http://www.foxnews.com/us/2014/01/07/one-two-teens-convicted-in-steubenville-rape-case-released/

Franiuk, R., Seefelt, J. L., Cepress, S. L., & Vandello, J. A. (2008). Prevalence and effects of rape myths in the media: The Kobe Bryant case. *Violence Against Women, 14,* 287–309.

Freedman, E. B. (1981). *Their sisters' keepers: Women prison reform in America, 1830–1930.* Ann Arbor: University of Michigan Press.

Freeman, H. (2013, June 18). Nigella Lawson: From domestic goddess to the face of domestic violence. *The Guardian.* Retrieved from http://www.theguardian.com/commentisfree/2013/jun/18/nigella-lawson-domestic-goddess-violence

Freiburger, T. L., & Burke, A. S. (2011). Status offenders in the juvenile court: The effects of gender, race and ethnicity on the adjudication decision. *Youth Violence and Juvenile Justice, 9*(4), 352–365.

Freiburger, T. L., & Hilinski, C. M. (2010). The impact of race, gender and age on the pretrial decision. *Criminal Justice Review, 35*(3), 318–334.

French, S. (2000). Of problems, pitfalls and possibilities: A comprehensive look at female attorneys and law firm partnership. *Women's Rights Law Reporter, 21*(3), 189–216.

Frost, N. A., & Clear, T. R. (2007). Doctoral education in criminology and criminal justice. *Journal of Criminal Justice Education, 18,* 35–52.

Frost, N. A., & Phillips, N. D. (2011): Talking heads: Crime reporting on cable news. *Justice Quarterly, 28*(1), 87–112.

Fus, T. (2006, March). Criminalizing marital rape: A comparison of judicial and legislative approaches. *Vanderbilt Journal of Transnational Law, 39*(2), 481–517.

Gaarder, E., & Belknap, J. (2002). Tenuous borders: Girls transferred to adult court. *Criminology, 40*(3), 481–518.

Garcia, C. A., & Lane, J. (2010). Looking in the rearview mirror: What incarcerated women think girls need from the system. *Feminist Criminology, 5*(3), 227–243.

Garcia, C. A., & Lane, J. (2012). Dealing with the fall-out: Identifying and addressing the role that relationship strain plays in the lives of girls in the juvenile justice system. *Journal of Criminal Justice, 40,* 259–267.

Garcia-Lopez, G. (2008). Nunca te toman en cuenta [They never take you into account]: The challenges of inclusion and strategies for success of Chicana attorneys. *Gender and Society, 22*(5), 590–612.

Gartner, R., & Kruttschnitt, C. (2004). A brief history of doing time: The California Institution for Women in the 1960's and the 1990's. *Law and Society Review, 38*(2), 267–304.

Gast, P. (2011, August 10). Siblings wanted in bank robbery, shootout arrested after chase. CNN. Retrieved from http://www.cnn.com/2011/CRIME/08/11/georgia.three.siblings.manhunt.archives/index.html?iref=allsearch

Gavazzi, S. M., Yarcheck, C. M., & Lim, J.-Y. (2005). Ethnicity, gender, and global risk indicators in the lives of status offenders coming to the attention of the juvenile court. *International Journal of Offender Therapy and Comparative Criminology, 49*(6), 696–710.

Gehring, K., Van Voorhis, P., & Bell, V. (2010). "What Works" for female probationers? An evaluation of the *Moving On* program. *Women, Girls and Criminal Justice, 11*(1), 6–10.

General Accounting Office (GAO). (1999). *Women in prison: Issues and challenges confronting U.S. correctional systems.* Washington, DC: U.S. Department of Justice.

Gerbner, G., & Gross, L. (1980, Summer). The "Mainstreaming" of America: Violence profile no. 11. *Journal of Communication,* 10–29.

Gidycz, C. A., Orchowski, L. M., King, C. R., & Rich, C. L. (2008). Sexual victimization and health-risk behaviors a prospective analysis of college women. *Journal of Interpersonal Violence, 23*(6), 744–763.

Gilbert, E. (2001). Women, race and criminal justice processing. In C. Renzetti & L. Goodstein (Eds.), *Women, crime and criminal justice: Original feminist readings.* Los Angeles, CA: Roxbury.

Gilfus, M. E. (1992). From victims to survivors to offenders: Women's routes of entry and immersion into street crime. *Women and Criminal Justice, 4*(1), 63–89.

Gillum, T. L. (2008). Community response and needs of African American female survivors of domestic violence. *Journal of Interpersonal Violence, 23*(1), 39–57.

Gillum, T. L. (2009). Improving services to African American survivors of IPV: From the voices of recipients of culturally specific services. *Violence Against Women, 15*(1), 57–80.

Girard, A. L., & Senn, C. Y. (2008). The role of the new "date rape drugs" in attributions about date rape. *Journal of Interpersonal Violence, 23*(1), 3–20.

Girl Scouts of America (GSA). (2008). *Third-year evaluation of Girl Scouts Beyond Bars final report.* Retrieved August 22, 2012, from http://www.girlscouts.org/research.pdf/gsbb_report.pdf

Girls Incorporated. (1996). *Prevention and parity: Girls in juvenile justice.* Indianapolis, IN: Girls Incorporated National Resource Center & Office of Juvenile Justice and Delinquency Prevention.

Girshick, L. B. (2002). No sugar, no spice reflections on research on woman-to-woman sexual violence. *Violence Against Women, 8*(12), 1500–1520.

Glaze, L., & Maruschak, L. (2008). *Parents in prison and their minor children.* Washington, DC: U.S. Department of Justice.

Goddard, C., & Bedi, G. (2010). Intimate partner violence and child abuse: A child-centered perspective. *Child Abuse Review, 19,* 5–20.

Gordon, J. A., Proulx, B., & Grant, P. H. (2013). Trepidation among the "keepers": Gendered perceptions of fear and risk of victimization among corrections officers. *American Journal of Criminal Justice, 38,* 245–265.

Gormley, P. (2007). The historical role and views towards victims and the evolution of prosecution policies in domestic violence. In R. Muraskin (Ed.), *It's a crime* (4th ed., Chapt. 13). Upper Saddle River, NJ: Pearson Prentice Hall.

Gornick, J., Burt, M. J., & Pitman, P. J. (1985). Structures and activities of rape crisis centers in the early 1980s. *Crime and Delinquency, 31*, 247–268.

Gottfredson, M., & Hirschi, T. (1990). *A general theory of crime.* Palo Alto, CA: Stanford University Press.

Gover, A. R., Brank, E. M., & MacDonald, J. M. (2007). A specialized domestic violence court in South Carolina: An example of procedural justice for victims and defendants. *Violence Against Women, 13*(6), 603–626.

Gover, A. R., Welton-Mitchell, C., Belknap, J., & Deprince, A. P. (2013). When abuse happens again. Women's reasons for not reporting new incidents of intimate partner abuse to law enforcement. *Women & Criminal Justice, 23*, 99–120.

Greenfeld, L. A. (1997). *Sex offenses and offenders: An analysis of data on rape and sexual assault.* Washington, DC: U.S. Department of Justice, Office of Justice Programs.

Greenfeld, L. A., & Snell, T. L. (2000). *Women offenders.* Washington, DC: Bureau of Justice Statistics. Retrieved October 15, 2010, from http://bjs.ojp.usdoj.gov/content/pub/pdf/wo.pdf

Greer, K. (2008). When women hold the keys: Gender, leadership and correctional policy. Management and Training Institute. Retrieved from http://nicic.gov/Library/023347

Grella, C. E., & Rodriguez, L. (2011). Motivation for treatment among women offenders in prison-based treatment and longitudinal outcomes among those who participate in community aftercare. *Journal of Psychoactive Drugs, 43*(1), 58–67.

Griffin v. Michigan Department of Corrections, 654 F. Supp. 690 (1982).

Griffin, T., & Wooldredge, J. (2006). Sex-based disparities in felony dispositions before versus after sentencing reform in Ohio. *Criminology, 44*(4), 893–923.

Grossman, S. F., & Lundy, M. (2011). Characteristics of women who do and do not receive onsite shelter services from domestic violence programs. *Violence Against Women, 17*(8), 1024–1045.

Grossman, S. F., Lundy, M., George, C. C., & Crabtree-Nelson, S. (2010). Shelter and service receipt for victims of domestic violence in Illinois. *Journal of Interpersonal Violence, 25*(11), 2077–2093.

Grummett v. Rushen, 779 F.2d 491 (1985).

Guerino, P., Harrison, P. M., & Sabol, W. J. (2011). Prisoners in 2010. U.S. Department of Justice, Bureau of Justice Statistics. Retrieved from http://www.bjs.gov/content/pub/pdf/p10.pdf

Guevara, L., Herz, D., & Spohn, C. (2008). Race, gender and legal counsel: Differential outcomes in two juvenile courts. *Youth Violence and Juvenile Justice, 6*(1), 83–104.

Gyimah-Brempong, K., & Price, G. N. (2006). Crime and punishment: And skin hue too? *American Economic Association, 96*(2), 246–250.

Haarr, R. N., & Morash, M. (2013). The effect of rank on police women coping with discrimination and harassment. *Police Quarterly, 16*(4), 395–419.

Hagan, J. (1989). *Structural criminology.* New Brunswick, NJ: Rutgers University Press.

Hall, M., Golder, S., Conley, C. L., & Sawning, S. (2013). Designing programming and interventions for women in the criminal justice system. *American Journal of Criminal Justice, 38*, 27–50.

Hannan, L. (2014, January 10). Marissa Alexander can remain free on bond, but judge clearly upset with home-detention supervisor. *The Florida Times Union.* Retrieved from http://jacksonville.com/breaking-news/2014-01-10/story/marissa-alexander-can-remain-free-bond-judge-clearly-upset-home

Hardesty, J. L., Oswald, R. F., Khaw, L., & Fonseca, C. (2011). Lesbian/bisexual mothers and intimate partner violence: Help seeking in the context of social and legal vulnerability. *Violence Against Women, 17*(1), 28–46.

Harlow, P. (2013, March 17). Guilty verdict in Steubenville rape trial. CNN Transcripts. Retrieved from http://transcripts.cnn.com/TRANSCRIPTS/1303/17/rs.01.html

Harner, H. M., & Riley, S. (2013). The impact of incarceration on women's mental health: Responses from women in a maximum-security prison. *Qualitative Health Research, 23*(1), 26–42.

Harrington, P., & Lonsway, K. A. (2004). Current barriers and future promise for women in policing. In B. R. Price & N. J. Sokoloff (Eds.), *The criminal justice system and women: Offenders, prisoners, victims and workers* (3rd ed., pp. 495–510). Boston, MA: McGraw Hill.

Harris, K. M., & Edlund, M. J. (2005). Self-medication of mental health problems: New evidence from a national survey. *Health Services Research, 40*(1), 117–134.

Harrison, J. (2012). Women in law enforcement: Subverting sexual harassment with social bonds. *Women & Criminal Justice, 22*(3), 226–238. doi: 10.1080/08974454.2012.687964

Harrison, P. M., & Beck, A. J. (2006). Prison and Jail inmates at midyear 2005 [BJS Bulletin]. http://bjs.ojp.usdoj.gov/content/pub/pdf/pjim05.pdf

Hart, T. C., & Rennison, C. M. (2003). *Special report: National Crime Victimization Survey: Reporting crime to the police.* Bureau of Justice Statistics. Retrieved from http://bjs.ojp.usdoj.gov/index.cfm?ty=pbdetail&iid=1142

Hassouneh, D., & Glass, N. (2008). The Influence of gender-role stereotyping on female same sex intimate partner violence. *Violence Against Women, 14*(3), 310–325.

Haynes, D. F. (2004). Used abused arrested and deported: Extending immigration benefits to protect the victims of trafficking and to secure the prosecution of traffickers. *Human rights Quarterly, 26*(2), 221–272.

Heidensohn, F. M. (1985). *Women and crime: The life of the female offender.* New York: New York University Press.

Heimer, K. (1996). Gender, interaction and delinquency: Testing a theory of differential social control. *Social Psychology Quarterly, 59*, 339–361.

Hennessey, M., Ford, J. D., Mahoney, K., Ko, S. J., & Siegfried, C. B. (2004). Trauma among girls in the juvenile justice system. National Child Traumatic Stress Network Juvenile Justice Working Group. Retrieved January 25, 2012, from http://www .nctsn.org/nctsn_assets/pdfs/edu_materials/trauma_among_ girls_in_jjsys.pdf

Hersh, S. M. (2004, May 10). Torture at Abu Ghraib. *The New Yorker*. Retrieved August 31, 2012, from http://www.newyorker .com/archive/2004/05/10/040510fa_fact?currentPage=all

Hessy-Biber, S. N. (2004). *Feminist perspectives on social research*. New York, NY: Oxford University Press.

Higdon, M. (2008). Queer teens and legislative bullies: The cruel and invidious discrimination behind heterosexist statutory rape laws. *UC Davis Law Review, 42*, 195.

Hindelang, M. J., Gottfredson, M. R., & Garofalo, J. (1978). *Victims of personal crime: An empirical foundation for a theory of personal victimization*. Cambridge, MA: Ballinger.

Hines, D. A., Armstrong, J. L., Reed, K. P., & Cameron, A. Y. (2012). Gender differences in sexual assault victimization among college students. *Violence & Victims, 27*(6), 922–940.

Hirsch, A. E. (2001). Bringing back shame: Women, welfare reform and criminal justice. In P. J. Schram & B. Koons-Witt (Eds.), *Gendered (in)justice: Theory and practice in feminist criminology* (pp. 270–286). Long Grove, IL: Waveland Press.

Hirschel, D. (2008). *Domestic violence cases: What research shows about arrest and dual arrest rates*. National Institute of Justice. Retrieved from http://www.nij.gov/nij/publications/dv-dual-arrest-222679/dv-dual-arrest.pdf

Hirschel, D., Buzawa, E., Pattavina, A., Faggiani, D., & Reuland, M. (2007). *Explaining the prevalence, context and consequences of dual arrest in intimate partner cases*. U.S. Department of Justice. Retrieved from https://www.ncjrs.gov/pdffiles1/nij/grants/218355 .pdf

Hirschi, T. (1969). *Causes of delinquency*. Berkeley: University of California Press.

Holsinger, K., & Holsinger, A. M. (2005). Differential pathways to violence and self-injurious behavior: African American and White girls in the juvenile justice system. *Journal of Research in Crime & Delinquency, 42*(2), 211–242.

Hsu, H., & Wu, B. (2011). Female defendants and criminal courts in Taiwan: An observation study. *Asian Criminology, 6*, 1–14.

Huebner, A. J., & Betts, S. C. (2002). Exploring the utility of social control theory for youth development: Issues of attachment, involvement, and gender. *Youth & Society, 34*(2), 123–145.

Huebner, B. M., DeJong, C., & Cobbina, J. (2010). Women coming home: Long-term patterns of recidivism. *Justice Quarterly, 27*(2), 225–254.

Huffington Post. (2013, November 25). Steubenville grand jury investigation: Four more school employees indicted. Retrieved from http://www.huffingtonpost.com/2013/11/25/steubenville-grand-jury-investigation_n_4337646.html?utm_hp_ref= steubenville-rape

Human Rights Watch. (2006). Custody and control: Conditions of confinement in New York's juvenile prisons for girls. Retrieved August 13, 2012, from http://www.hrw.org/sites/default/files/reports/ us0906webwcover.pdf

Hunt, G., & Joe-Laidler, K. (2001). Situations of violence in the lives of girl gang members. *Health Care for Women International, 22*, 363–384.

Hurst, T. E., & Hurst, M. M. (1997). Gender differences in mediation of severe occupational stress among correctional officers. *American Journal of Criminal Justice, 22*(1), 121–137.

Inciardi, J. A., Lockwood, D., & Pottiger, A. E. (1993). *Women and crack-cocaine*. Toronto, Canada: Maxwell Macmillian.

Ingram, E. M. (2007). A comparison of help seeking between Latino and non-Latino victims of intimate partner violence. *Violence Against Women, 13*(2), 159–171.

Inter-American Commission on Human Rights. (2003). The situation of the rights of women in Ciudad Juárez, Mexico: The right to be free from violence and discrimination. Retrieved from http://www.cidh.org/annualrep/2002eng/chap.vi.juarez.htm

International Labour Organization. (2005). *A global alliance against forced labour*. Geneva, Switzerland: United Nations.

Ireland, C., & Berg, B. (2008). Women in parole: Respect and rapport. *International Journal of Offender Therapy and Comparative Criminology, 52*(4), 474–491.

Irwin, J. (2008). (Dis)counted stories: Domestic violence and lesbians. *Qualitative Social Work, 7*(2), 199–215.

Jacobs, A. (2000). *Give 'em a fighting chance: The challenges for women offenders trying to succeed in the community*. Retrieved July 31, 2011, from http://www.wpaonline.org/pdf/ WPA_FightingChance.pdf

James, D. J., & Glaze, L. E. (2006). *Bureau of Justice Statistics Special Report: Mental Health Problems of Prison and Jail Inmates* (NCJ No. 213600). Washington DC: U.S. Department of Justice, Office of Justice Programs.

Jefferies, M. (2013, June 19). Nigella Lawson photos: Charles Saatchi reveals why he accepted police caution but makes no public apology. *The Mirror*. Retrieved from http://www .mirror.co.uk/news/uk-news/nigella-lawson-photos-charles-saatchi-1960358

Jensen, J. M., & Martinek, W. L. (2009). The effects of race and gender on the judicial ambitions of state trial court judges. *Political Research Quarterly, 62*(2), 379–392.

Joe, K., & Chesney-Lind, M. (1995). Just every mother's angel: An analysis of gender and ethnic variation in youth gang membership. *Gender and Society, 9*(4), 408–430.

Johnson, H. (2004). Drugs and crime: A study of incarcerated female offenders. *Australian Institute of Criminology, 63*. Retrieved from http://www.aic.gov.au/documents/E/B/8/%7BEB8A400C-E611–42BF-9B9F-B58E7C5A0694%7DRPP63.pdf

Johnson, I. M. (2007). Victims' perceptions of police response to domestic violence incidents. *Journal of Criminal Justice, 35*, 498–510.

Johnson, J. E., Esposito-Smythers, C., Miranda, R., Rizzo, C. J., Justus, A. N., & Clum, G. (2011). Gender, social support and depression in criminal justice-involved adolescents. *International Journal of Offender Therapy and Comparative Criminology, 55*(7), 1096–1109.

Jones-Brown, D. (2007). Forever the symbolic assailant: The more things change, the more they stay the same. *Criminology & Public Policy, 6*(1), 103–121.

Jordan v. Gardner, 986 F.2d 1137 (1992).

Just Detention International (JDI). (2009). Incarcerated youth at extreme risk of sexual abuse. Retrieved August 15, 2012, from http://www.justdetention.org/en/factsheets/jdifactsheetyouth .pdf

Justice Research and Statistics Association (JRSA). (n.d.). Background and status of incident-based reporting and NIBRS. Retrieved from http://www.jrsa.org/ibrrc/background-status/ nibrs_states.shtml

Karakurt, G., & Silver, K. E. (2013). Emotional abuse in intimate relationships: The role of gender and age. *Violence and Victims, 28*(5), 804–821.

Karandikar, S., Gezinski, L. B., & Meshelemiah, J. C. A. (2013). A qualitative examination of women involved in prostitution in Mumbai, India: The role of family and acquaintances. *International Social Work, 56*(4), 496–515.

Kardam, N. (2005). The dynamics of honor killings in Turkey. Prospects for action. United Nations Development Programme. Retrieved from http://www.unfpa.org/public/publications/ pid/383

Katz, C. M., & Spohn, C. (1995). The effect of race and gender and bail outcomes: A test of an interactive model. *American Journal of Criminal Justice, 19,* 161–184.

Kaukinen, C. (2004). Status compatibility, physical violence, and emotional abuse in intimate relationships. *Journal of Marriage and Family, 66*(2), 452–471.

Kaukinen, C., & DeMaris, A. (2009). Sexual assault and current mental health: The role of help-seeking and police response. *Violence Against Women, 15*(11), 1331–1357.

Kelleher, C., & McGilloway, S. (2009). "Nobody ever chooses this . . .": A qualitative study of service providers working in the sexual violence sector—Key issues and challenges. *Health and Social Care in the Community, 17*(3), 295–303.

Kellermann, A. L., & Mercy, J. A. (1992). Men, women, and murder: Gender specific differences in rates of fatal violence and victimization. *The Journal of Trauma, 33*(1), 1–5.

Kernsmith, P. (2005). Exerting power or striking back: A gendered comparison of motivations for domestic violence perpetration. *Violence and Victims, 20,* 173–185.

Kilpatrick, D. G., Resnick, H. S., Ruggiero, K. J., Conoscenti, L. M., & McCauley, J. (2007). *Drug-facilitated, incapacitated, and forcible rape: A national study.* Charleston, SC: Medical University of South Carolina, National Crime Victims Research & Treatment Center.

Kim, B., Gerber, J., Henderson, C., & Kim, Y. (2012). Applicability of general power-control theory to prosocial and antisocial risk taking behaviors among women in South Korea. *The Prison Journal, 92*(1), 125–150.

Kim, B., & Merlo, A. (2012). In her own voice: Presentations on women, crime and criminal justice at American Society of Criminology meetings from 1999–2008. *Women and Criminal Justice, 22*(1), 66–88.

Kitty, J. M. (2012). "It's like they don't want you to get better": Psy control of women in the carceral context. *Feminism & Psychology, 22*(2), 162–182.

Klein, A. R. (2004). *The criminal justice response to domestic violence.* Belmont, CA: Wadsworth Thomson Learning.

Knoll, C., & Sickmund, M. (2010). *Delinquency cases in juvenile court, 2007.* Office of Justice Programs. Office of Juvenile Justice and Delinquency Prevention. Retrieved December 1, 2010, from http://www.ncjrs.gov/pdffiles1/ojjdp/230168.pdf

Knoll, C., & Sickmund, M. (2012). *Delinquency cases in juvenile court, 2009.* Office of Juvenile Justice and Delinquency Prevention. Retrieved from http://www.ojjdp.gov/pubs/239081.pdf

Koeppel, M. D. H. (2012, November 28). Gender sentencing of rural property offenders in Iowa. *Criminal Justice Policy Review.* Advance online publication. doi:10.1177/0887403412465308

Kolb, K. H. (2011). Sympathy work: Identity and emotion management among victim-advocates and counselors. *Qualitative Sociology, 34,* 101–119.

Koons-Witt, B. (2006). Decision to incarcerate before and after the introduction of sentencing guidelines. *Criminology, 40*(2), 297–328.

Koons-Witt, B. A., Sevigny, E. L., Burrow, J. D., & Hester, R. (2012). Gender and sentencing outcomes in South Carolina: Examining the interactions with race, age, and offense type. *Criminal Justice Police Review, 10,* 1–26.

Kraaij, V., Arensman, E., Garnefski, N., & Kremers, I. (2007). The role of cognitive coping in female victims of stalking. *Journal of Interpersonal Violence, 22*(12), 1603–1612.

Krouse, P. (2013, July 26). Ariel Castro agrees to plea deal: Life in prison, no parole, plus 1,000 years. Retrieved from http://www .cleveland.com/metro/index.ssf/2013/07/ariel_castro_agrees_ to_plea_de.html

Kruttschnitt, C., & Savolianen, J. (2009). Ages of chivalry, places of paternalism: Gender and criminal sentencing in Finland. *European Journal of Criminology, 6*(3), 225–247.

Kuriakose, D. (2013, October 9). Malala Yousafzai: From blogger to Nobel Peace Prize nominee—Timeline. *The Guardian.* Retrieved from http://www.theguardian.com/world/interactive/2013/oct/09/ malala-yousafzai-timeline

Kurshan, N. (2000). *Women and imprisonment in the United States: History and current reality.* Retrieved January 3, 2011, from http://www.prisonactivist.org/archive/women/women-and- imprisonment.html

Kurtz, D. L., Linnemann, T., & Williams, L. S. (2012). Reinventing the matron: The continued importance of gendered images and division of labor in modern policing. *Women & Criminal Justice, 22*(3), 239–263.

Kyckelhahn, T., Beck, A. J., & Cohen, T. H. (2009). Characteristics of suspected human trafficking incidents. Retrieved from http://www.ojp.usdoj.gov/bjs/abstract/cshti08.htm

LaGrange, T. C., & Silverman, R. A. (1999). Low self-control and opportunity: Testing the general theory of crime as an explanation of gender differences in delinquency. *Criminology, 37*(1), 41–72.

Lambert, E. G., Hogan, N. L., Altheimer, I., & Wareham, J. (2010). The effects of different aspects of supervision among female and male correctional staff: A preliminary study. *Criminal Justice Review, 35*, 492–513. doi: 10.1177/0734016810372068

Lambert, E. G., Paoline, E. A. Hogan, N. L., & Baker, D. N. (2007). Gender similarities and differences in correctional staff work attitudes and perceptions of the work environment. *Western Criminology Review, 8*(1), 16–31.

Lambert, E. G., Smith, B., & Geistman, J. (2013). Do men and women differ in the perceptions of stalking: An exploratory study among college students. *Violence and Victims, 28*(2), 195–209.

Lane, J., Gover, A. R., & Dahod, S. (2009). Fear of violent crime among men and women on campus: The impact of perceived risk and fear of sexual assault. *Violence and Victims, 24*(2), 172–192.

Langton, L. (2010). Crime data brief: Women in law enforcement. Bureau of Justice Statistics. Retrieved from http://bjs.ojp.usdoj.gov/content/pub/pdf/wle8708.pdf

Law Library of Congress (n.d.). Women lawyers and state bar admission. The Library of Congress. Retrieved from http://memory.loc.gov/ammem/awhhtml/awlaw3/women_lawyers.html

Lawrence v. Texas, 539 U.S. 558 (2003).

Learner, S. (2012). Scarred for life. *Nursing Standard, 26*(18), 20–21.

Lee, R. K. (1998). Romantic and electronic stalking in a college context. *William and Mary Journal of Women and the Law, 4*, 373–466.

Legal Action Center. (2011). State TANF options drug felon ban. Retrieved August 22, 2012, from http://www.lac.org/doc_library/lac/publications/HIRE_Network_State_TANF_Options_Drug_Felony_Ban.pdf

Leiber, M., Brubaker, S., & Fox, K. (2009). A closer look at the individual and joint effects of gender and race in juvenile justice decision making. *Feminist Criminology, 4*, 333–358.

Leonard, E. B. (1982). *Women, crime, and society.* New York, NY: Longman.

Lerner, M. J. (1980). *The belief in a just world: A fundamental delusion.* New York, NY: Plenum Press.

Lersch, K. M., & Bazley, T. (2012). A paler shade of blue? Women and the police subculture. In R. Muraskin (Ed.), *Women and justice: It's a crime* (5th ed., pp. 514–526). Upper Saddle River, NJ: Prentice-Hall.

Leung, R. (2009, February 11). Abuse of Iraqi POW's by GI's probed. *60 Minutes.* CBS News. Retrieved August 31, 2012, from http://www.cbsnews.com/stories/2004/04/27/60ii/main614063.shtml

Liang, B., Lu, H., & Taylor, M. (2009). Female drug abusers, narcotic offenders and legal punishment in China. *Journal of Criminal Justice, 37*, 133–141.

Like-Haislip, T. Z., & Miofsky, K. (2011). Race, ethnicity, gender and violent victimization. *Race and Justice, 1*(3), 254–276.

Lindgren, J., Stanglin, D., & Alcindor, Y. (2013, August 7). Ariel Castro's house of horror demolished in Cleveland. *USA Today.* Retrieved from http://www.usatoday.com/story/news/nation/2013/08/07/ariel-castro-cleveland-house-abduction/2626855/

Lipari, R. N., Cook, P. J., Rock, L., & Matos, K. (2008). 2006 gender relations survey of active duty members (DMDC Report No. 2007–022). Arlington, VA: Defense Manpower Data Center.

Lipsky, S., Caetano, R., Field, C. A., & Larkin, G. L. (2006). The role of intimate partner violence, race and ethnicity in help-seeking behaviors. *Ethnicity and Health, 11*(1), 81–100.

Littleton, H., Breitkopf, C. R., & Berenson, A. (2008). Beyond the campus unacknowledged rape among low-income women. *Violence Against Women, 14*(3), 269–286.

Logan, T. K., Evans, L., Stevenson, E., & Jordan, C. E. (2005). Barriers to services for rural and urban survivors of rape. *Journal of Interpersonal Violence, 20*(5), 591–616.

Lombroso, C., & Ferrero, W. (1895). *The female offender.* New York, NY: Barnes.

Long, L., & Ullman, S. E. (2013). The impact of multiple traumatic victimization on disclosure and coping mechanisms for Black women. *Feminist Criminology, 8*(4), 295–319.

Lonsway, K. A., & Fitzgerald, L. F. (1994). Rape myths in review. *Psychology of women quarterly, 18*(2), 133–164.

Lonsway, K. A., Paynich, R., & Hall, J. N. (2013). Sexual harassment in law enforcement: Incidence, impact, and perception. *Police Quarterly, 16*(2), 177–210.

Lonsway, K., Carrington, S., Aguirre, P., Wood, M., Moore, M., Harrington, P., . . . Spillar, K. (2002). *Equality denied: The status of women in policing: 2001.* The National Center for Women and Policing. Retrieved from http://www.womenandpolicing.org/PDF/2002_Status_Report.pdf

Lonsway, K., Wood, M., Fickling, M., De Leon, A., Moore, M., Harrington, P., . . . Spillar, K. (2002). *Men, women and police excessive force: A tale of two genders: A content analysis of civil liability cases, sustained allegations and citizen complaints.* The National Center for Women and Policing. Retrieved from http://www.womenandpolicing.org/PDF/2002_Excessive_Force.pdf

Lopez, A. (2012). Scott signs "historic" anti-shackling bill for incarcerated pregnant women. *Florida Independent.* Retrieved July 10, 2012, from http://floridaindependent.com/74661/rick-scott-anti-shackling-bill

Lopez, A. J. (2007). Expert: Victims' path rockier than celebrities'. *Rocky Mountain News.* Retrieved from http://therocky.com/news/2007/mar/15/expert-victims-path-rockier-than-celebrities/

Los Angeles Almanac. (2012). LAPD had the nation's first police woman. Retrieved from http://www.laalmanac.com/crime/cr73b.htm

Lowe, N. C., May, D. C., & Elrod, P. (2008). Theoretical predictors of delinquency among public school students in a mid-southern state: The roles of context and gender. *Youth Violence and Juvenile Justice, 6*(4), 343–362.

Lyons, C. (2006, April 20). "Media circus" atmosphere aggravated case. Retrieved from http://www.hampton.lib.nh.us/hampton/biog/pamsmart/equinox2006_4.htm

MacIntosh, J. (2011, August 9). "Rack" and ruin: Stripper goes on "crime spree" with brothers. *New York Post*. Retrieved from http://www.nypost.com/p/news/national/vixen_faces_rack_ruin_q5hnBQ1AlZJrIImUY4CHCP

Maggard. S. R., Higgins, J. L., & Chappell, A. T. (2013). Pre-dispositional juvenile detention: An analysis of race, gender and intersectionality. *Journal of Crime and Justice, 36*(1), 67–86.

Maguire, B. (1988). Image vs. reality: An analysis of prime-time television crime and police programs. *Journal of Crime and Justice, 11*(1), 165–188.

Maher, L. (1996). Hidden in the light: Occupational norms among crack-using street level sex workers. *Journal of Drug issues, 26*, 143–173.

Maher, L. (2004a). A reserve army: Women and the drug market. In B. Price & N. Sokoloff (Eds.), *The criminal justice system and women: Offenders, prisoners, victims and workers* (3rd ed., pp. 127–146). New York, NY: McGraw-Hill.

Maher L. (2004b). "Hooked on heroin: Drugs and drifters in a glo-balized world." *Addiction, 99*, 929–930.

Mahoney, J. (2013, May 9). Death penalty possible for alleged Cleveland kidnapper, prosecutor says. *The Globe and Mail*. Retrieved from http://web.archive.org/web/20130509221120/http://www.theglobeandmail.com/news/world/kidnap-suspect-ariel-castro-due-in-cleveland-court/article11810618/?cmpid=rss1

Mahoney, J. L., Cairns, B. D., & Farmer, T. W. (2003). Promoting inter-personal competence and educational success through extracur-ricular activity participation. *Journal of Educational Psychology, 95*(2), 109–118.

Maier, S. L. (2008a). "I have heard terrible stories . . ": Rape victim advocates' perceptions of the revictimization of rape victims by the police and medical system. *Violence Against Women, 14*(7), 786–808.

Maier, S. L. (2008b). Rape victim advocates' perception of the influ-ence of race and ethnicity on victims' responses to rape. *Journal of Ethnicity and Criminal Justice, 6*(4), 295–326.

Maier, S. L. (2011). "We belong to them": The costs of funding for rape crisis centers. *Violence Against Women, 17*(11), 1383–1408.

Mallicoat, S. L. (2006, August). *Mary Magdalene project: Kester pro-gram evaluation*. Paper presented at the Program Committee of the Mary Magdalene Project, Van Nuys, CA.

Mallicoat, S. L. (2007). Gendered Justice: Attributional differences between males and females in the juvenile courts. *Feminist Criminology, 2*(1), 4–30.

Mallicoat, S. L. (2011). Lives in transition: A needs assessment of women exiting from prostitution. In R. Muraskin (Ed.), *It's a crime: Women and justice* (4th ed., pp. 241–255). Upper Saddle River, NJ: Prentice-Hall.

Mallicoat, S. L., Marquez, S. A., & Rosenbaum, J. L. (2007). Guiding philosophies for rape crisis centers. In R. Muraskin (Ed.), *It's a crime: Women and criminal justice* (4th ed., pp. 217–225). Upper Saddle River, NJ: Prentice-Hall.

Marks, P. (1993, November 16). Buttafuoco is sentenced to 6 months for rape. *The New York Times*. http://www.nytimes.com/1993/11/16/nyregion/buttafuoco-is-sentenced-to-6-months-for-rape.html

Martin, E. K., Taft, C. T., & Resick, P. A. (2007). A review of marital rape. *Aggression and Violent Behavior, 12*(3), 329–347.

Martin, L. (1991). *A report on the glass ceiling commission*. Washington, DC: U.S. Department of Labor.

Maruschak, L., & Parks, E. R. (2012). Probation and parole in the United States, 2011. U.S. Department of Justice, Bureau of Justice Statistics. Retrieved from http://www.bjs.gov/content/pub/pdf/ppus11.pdf

Mary Katherine Schmitz. (2014). The Biography.com website. Retrieved from http://www.biography.com/people/mary-kay-letourneau-9542379.

Maslin, J. (1987, September 17). Fatal attraction [Review]. Retrieved from http://www.nytimes.com/movie/review?res=9B0DE3DE163CF93BA2575AC0A961948260

Mastony, C. (2010). Was Chicago home to the country's 1st female cop? Researcher uncovers the story of Sgt. Marie Owens. *Chicago Tribune*. Retrieved from http://articles.chicagotribune.com/2010–09–01/news/ct-met-first-police-woman-20100901_1_female-officer-police-officer-female-cop

Mastony, C. (2012, May 23). $4.1 million settlement set for pregnant inmates who said they were shackled before giving birth. *Chicago Tribune*. Retrieved July 10, 2012, from http://articles.chicagotribune.com/2012–05–23/news/ct-met-shackled-pregnant-women 20120523_1_pregnant-women-pregnant-inmates-shackles-and-belly-chains

Matoueda, R. (1992). Reflected appraisals, parental labeling and delinquency: Specifying a symbolic interactionist theory. *American Journal of Sociology, 97*(6), 1577.

Matthews, C., Monk-Turner, E., & Sumter, M. (2010). Promotional opportunities: How women in corrections perceive their chances for advancement at work. *Gender Issues, 27*, 53–66.

Mauer, M. (2013). The changing racial dynamics of women's incar-ceration. The Sentencing Project. Retrieved from http://www.sentencingproject.org/doc/advocacy/Changing%20Racial%20Dynamics%20Webinar%20Slides.pdf

Mayell, H. (2002, February 12). Thousands of women killed for family honor. *National Geographic News, 12*.

McCall, M. (2007). Structuring gender's impact: Judicial voting across criminal justice cases. *American Politics Research, 36*(2), 264–296.

McCartan, L. M., & Gunnison, E. (2010). Individual and relationship factors that differentiate female offenders with and without a sexual abuse history. *Journal of Interpersonal Violence, 25*(8), 1449–1469.

McCoy, L. A., & Miller, H. A. (2013). Comparing gender across risk and recidivism in nonviolent offenders. *Women & Criminal Justice, 23*(2), 143–162.

McGrath, S. A., Johnson, M., & Miller, M. H. (2012). The social ecological challenges of rural victim advocacy: An exploratory study. *Journal of Community Psychology, 40*(5), 588–606.

McKnight, L. R., & Loper, A. B. (2002). The effect of risk and resilience factors on the prediction of delinquency in adolescent girls. *School Psychology International, 23*(2), 186–198.

Mears, D. P., Cochran, J. C., & Bales, W. D. (2012). Gender differences in the effects of prison on recidivism. *Journal of Criminal Justice, 40*, 370–378.

Melton, H. C. (2007). Predicting the occurrence of stalking in relationships characterized by domestic violence. *Journal of Interpersonal Violence, 22*(1), 3–25.

Mendelsohn, B. (1956). A new branch of bio-psychological science: La Victimology. *Revue Internationale de Criminologie et de Police Technique 10*, 782–789.

Merolla, D. (2008). The war on drugs and the gender gap in arrests: A critical perspective. *Critical Sociology, 34*(2), 355–270.

Merton, R. K. (1938). Social structure and anomie. *American Sociological Review, 3*(5), 672–682.

Messina, N., Grella, C. E., Cartier, J., & Torres, S. (2010). A randomized experimental study of gender-responsive substance abuse treatment for women in prison. *Journal of Substance Abuse Treatment, 39*, 97–107.

Meyer, C. L., & Oberman, M. (2001). *Mothers who kill their children: Understanding the acts of moms from Susan Smith to the "Prom mom."* New York, NY: University Press.

Millar, G., Stermac, L., & Addison, M. (2002). Immediate and delayed treatment seeking among adult sexual assault victims. *Women & health, 35*(1), 53–64.

Miller, J. (1994). Race, gender and juvenile justice: An examination of disposition decision-making for delinquent girls. In M. Schwartz & D. Milovanivoc (Eds.), *Race, gender and class in criminology: The intersection* (pp. 219–246). New York, NY: Garland.

Miller, J. (1998a). Gender and victimization risk among young women in gangs. *Journal of Research in Crime and Delinquency, 35*, 429–453.

Miller, J. (1998b). Up it up: Gender and the accomplishment of street robbery. *Criminology, 36*(1), 37–66.

Miller, J. (2000). *One of the guys: Girls, gangs and gender.* Oxford, UK: Oxford University Press.

Miller, L. J. (2003). Denial of pregnancy. In M. G. Spinelli (Ed.), *Infanticide: Psychosocial and legal perspectives on mothers who kill* (pp. 81–104). Washington, DC: American Psychiatric.

Miller, S. (2005). Victims as offenders: The paradox of women's violence in relationships. New Brunswick, NJ: Rutgers University Press.

Miller, S., Loeber, R., & Hipwell, A. (2009). Peer deviance, parenting and disruptive behavior among young girls. *Journal of Abnormal Child Psychology, 37*(2), 139–152.

Miller, S. L., & Meloy, M. L. (2006). Women's use of force: Voices of women arrested for domestic violence. *Violence Against Women, 12*(1), 89–115.

Miller, S. L., & Peterson, E. S. L. (2007). The impact of law enforcement policies on victims of intimate partner violence. In R. Muraskin (Ed.), *It's a crime* (4th ed., Chapt. 14). Upper Saddle River, NJ: Pearson Prentice Hall.

Ministry of Labour in cooperation with the Ministry of Justice and the Ministry of Health and Social Affairs, Government of Sweden. (1998). *Fact sheet*. Stockholm, Sweden: Secretariat for Information and Communication, Ministry of Labour.

Mintz, Z. (2013, June 10). Witch hunts in Papua New Guinea on the rise, killings connected to economic growth and jealousy. *International Business Times*. Retrieved from http://www.ibtimes.com/witch-hunts-papua-new-guinea-rise-killings-connected-economic-growth-jealousy-1298363

Moe, A. M. (2007). Silenced voices and structured survival: Battered women's help seeking. *Violence Against Women, 13*(7), 676–699.

Moe, A. M. (2009). Battered women, children, and the end of abusive relationships. *Afilia: Journal of Women and Social Work, 24*(3), 244–256.

Moffitt, T. E., Caspi, A., Rutter, M., & Silva, P. A. (2001). *Sex differences in antisocial behavior: Conduct disorder, delinquency and violence in the Dunedin Longitudinal Study*. New York, NY: Cambridge University Press.

Molidor, C. E. (1996). Female gang members: A profile of aggression and victimization. *Social Work, 41*(3), 251–257.

Moore, J. W. (1991). *Going down to the barrio: Homeboys and homegirls in change*. Philadelphia, PA: Temple University Press.

Moore, J., & Terrett, C. P. (1998). *Highlights of the 1996 National Youth Gang Survey. Fact sheet*. Washington, DC: U.S. Department of Justice, Office of Justice Programs, Office of Juvenile Justice and Delinquency Prevention.

Morash, M., & Haarr, R. N. (2012). Doing, redoing and undoing gender: Variation in gender identities of women working as police officers. *Feminist Criminology, 7*(1), 3–23.

Morello, K. (1986). *The invisible bar: The woman lawyer in America 1638 to the present*. New York, NY: Random House.

Morgan, K. D. (2013). Issues in female inmate health: Results from a southeastern state. *Women & Criminal Justice, 23*, 121–142.

Moses, M. (1995). Girl Scouts Beyond Bars—A synergistic solution for children of incarcerated parents. *Corrections Today, 57*(7), 124–127.

Mungin, L., & Alsup, D. (2013, September 4). Cleveland kidnapper Ariel Castro dead: Commits suicide in prison. CNN Justice. Retrieved from http://www.cnn.com/2013/09/04/justice/ariel-castro-cleveland-kidnapper-death/

Murtha, T. (2013, March 19). From Big Dan's to Steubenville: A generation later, media coverage of rape still awful. RH Reality Check. Retrieved from http://rhrealitycheck.org/article/2013/03/19/from-big-dans-to-steubenville-a-generation-later-media-coverage-of-rape-still-awful/

Mustaine, E. E., & Tewksbury, R. (2002). Sexual assault of college women: A feminist interpretation of a routine activities analysis. *Criminal Justice Review, 27*(1), 89–123.

Nagel, I., & Hagan, J. (1983). Gender and crime: Offense patterns and criminal court sanctions. In N. Morris and M. Tonry (Eds.), *Crime and justice* (Vol. 4, pp. 91–144). Chicago, IL: University of Chicago Press.

Nagel, I. H., & Johnson, B. L. (2004). The role of gender in a structured sentencing system: Equal treatment, policy choices and the sentencing of female offenders. In P. Schram & B. Koons-Witt (Eds.), *Gendered (in)justice: Theory and practice in feminist criminology.* Long Grove, IL: Waveland Press.

Nash, S. T. (2006). Through Black eyes: African American women's constructions of their experiences with intimate male partner violence. *Violence Against Women, 11*(11), 1420–1440.

National Association for Law Placement. (2010). *Law firm diversity among associates erodes in 2010.* National Association for Law Placement. Retrieved from www.nalp.org/uploads/PressReleases/10NALPWomenMinoritiesPressRel.pdf

National Association of Women Lawyers and The NAWL Foundation. (2009). *Report of the Fourth Annual National Survey on Retention and Promotion of Women in Law Firms.* Retrieved from http://nawl.timberlakepublishing.com/files/2009%20Survey%20Report%20FINAL.pdf

National Association of Women Lawyers and The NAWL Foundation. (2010). *Report of the Fifth Annual National Survey on Retention and Promotion of Women in Law Firms.* Retrieved from http://nawl.timberlakepublishing.com/files/NAWL%202010%20Final(1).pdf

National Coalition Against Domestic Violence. (n.d.). Mission statement and purpose. Retrieved from www.ncadv.org

National Drug Intelligence Center. (n.d.). Drug-facilitated sexual assault fast facts. Retrieved from http://www.justice.gov/archive/ndic/pubs8/8872/index.htm#Top

National Public Radio. (n.d.). Timeline: America's war on drugs. Retrieved July 31, 2011, from http://www.npr.org/templates/story/story.php?storyId=9252490

National Youth Gang Center. (2009). *National Youth Gang Survey analysis.* Retrieved from http://www.nationalgangcenter.gov/Survey-Analysis

Navarro, J. N., & Jasinski, J. L. (2013). Why girls? Using routine activities theory to predict cyberbullying experiences between girls and boys. *Women & Criminal Justice, 23,* 286–303.

Neff, J. L., Patterson, M. M., & Johnson, S. (2012). Meeting the training needs of those who meet the needs of victims: Assessing service providers. *Violence and Victims, 27*(4), 609–632.

Newton, M. (2003). Ciudad Juarez: The serial killers playground. Retrieved from http://www.trutv.com/library/crime/serial_killers/predators/ciudad_juarez/11.html

Ng, C. (2013, March 17). Steubenville, Ohio, football players convicted in rape trial. ABC News. Retrieved from http://abcnews.go.com/US/steubenville-football-players-guilty-ohio-rape-trial/story?id=18748493

Nine justices, ten years: A statistical retrospective. (2004). *Harvard Law Review, 118*(1), 521. Retrieved from http://web.archive.org/web/20060327053526/http://www.harvardlawreview.org/issues/118/Nov04/Nine_Justices_Ten_YearsFTX.pdf

Nixon, K., Tutty, L., Downe, P., Gorkoff, K., & Ursel, J. (2002). The everyday occurrence: Violence in the lives of girls exploited through prostitution. *Violence Against Women, 8*(9), 1016–1043.

Nokomis Foundation. (2002). *We can do better: Helping prostituted women and girls in Grand Rapids make healthy choices: A prostitution round table report to the community.* Retrieved from http://www.nokomisfoundation.org/documents/WeCanDoBetter.pdf

Noonan, M. C., & Corcoran, M. E. (2008). The mommy track and partnership: Temporary delay or dead end? *Annals of the American Academy of Political and Social Science, 596,* 130–150.

Noonan, M. C., Corcoran, M. E., & Courant, P. N. (2008). Is the partnership gap closing for women? Cohort differences in the sex gap in partnership chances. *Social Science Research, 37,* 156–179.

Norton-Hawk, M. (2004). A comparison of pimp and non-pimp controlled women. *Violence Against Women, 10*(2), 189–194.

NY Daily News. (2013, December 20). Congress passed defense bill with provision to crack down on sexual assault in the military. Retrieved from http://www.nydailynews.com/news/politics/sen-gillibrand-military-sexual-assault-bill-passes-article-1.1553722

O'Connor, M. L. (2012). Early policing in the United States: "Help wanted—Women need not apply!" In R. Muraskin (Ed.), *Women and justice: It's a crime* (5th ed., pp. 487–499). Upper Saddle River, NJ: Prentice-Hall.

Odem, M. E. (1995). *Delinquent daughters: Protecting and policing adolescent female sexuality in the United States: 1885–1920.* Chapel Hill. University of North Carolina Press.

Odem, M. E. (1995). Delinquent daughters: Protecting and policing adolescent female sexuality in the United States, 1885–1920. Chapel Hill: University of North Carolina Press.

O'Donnell, P., Richards, M., Pearce, S., & Romero, E. (2012). Gender differences in monitoring and deviant peers as predictors of delinquent behavior among low-income urban African American youth. *Journal of Early Adolescence, 32*(3), 431–459.

Office for National Statistics (2014). *Crime in England and Wales, year ending December 2013.* Retrieved from http://www.ons.gov.uk/ons/dcp171778_360216.pdf

Office on Violence Against Women (OVW). (n.d.). Home. U.S. Department of Justice. Retrieved from http://www.ovw.usdoj.gov

O'Keefe, E. (2013, December 19). Congress approves reforms to address sexual assault, rape in military. *Washington Post.* Retrieved from http://www.washingtonpost.com/politics/congress-poised-to-approve-reforms-to-address-sexual-assault-rape-in-military/2013/12/19/bbd34afa-68c9-11e3-a0b9-249bbb34602c_story.html

Oppel, R. A. (2013, March 17). Ohio teenagers guilty in rape that social media brought to light. *The New York Times.* Retrieved from http://www.nytimes.com/2013/03/18/us/teenagers-found-guilty-in-rape-in-steubenville-ohio.html?pagewanted=all&_r=0

Ortiz, N. R., & Spohn, C. (2014). Mitigating the effect of a criminal record at sentencing: Local life circumstances and substantial assistance departures among recidivists in federal court. *Criminal Justice Policy Review, 25*(1), 3–28.

Owen, B., & Bloom B. (1998). *Modeling gender-specific services in juvenile justice: Final report to the office of criminal justice planning.* Sacramento, CA: OCJP.

OXFAM. (n.d.). Protecting the accused: Sorcery in PNG. Retrieved from http://www.oxfam.org.nz/what-we-do/where-we-work/papua-new-guinea/gender-justice/confronting-sorcery

OXFAM. (2010, October 15). Sorcery beliefs and practices in Gumine: A source of conflict and insecurity. Retrieved from http://www.oxfam.org.nz/sites/default/files/reports/Sorcery_report_FINAL.pdf

Oxman-Martinez, J., & Hanley, J. (2003, February 20). Human smuggling and trafficking: Achieving the goals of the UN protocols? *Cross Border Perspectives: Human Trafficking, 20.*

Ozbay, O., & Ozcan Y. Z. (2008). A test of Hirschi's social bonding theory: A comparison of male and female delinquency. *Internal Journal of Offender Therapy and Comparative Criminology, 52*(2), 134–157.

Pakes, F. (2005). Penalization and retreat: The changing face of Dutch criminal justice. *Criminal Justice, 5*(2), 145–161.

Palmer, B. (2001). Women in the American judiciary: Their influence and impact. *Women and Politics, 23*(3), 91–101.

Panchanadeswaran, S., & Koverola, C. (2005). Voices of battered women in India. *Violence Against Women, 11*(6), 736–758.

Parsons, J., & Bergin, T. (2010). The impact of criminal justice involvement on victims' mental health. *Journal of Traumatic Stress, 23*(2), 182–188. doi:10.1002/jts.20505

Patel, S., & Gadit, A. M. (2008). Karo-kari: A form of honour killing in Pakistan. *Transcultural Psychiatry, 45*(4), 683–694.

Pathe, M., & Mullen, P. E. (1997). The impact of stalkers on their victims. *British Journal of Psychiatry, 170,* 12–17.

Patterson, D., & Campbell, R. (2010). Why rape survivors participate in the criminal justice system. *Journal of Community Psychology, 38*(2), 191–205.

Perona, A. R., Bottoms, B. L., & Sorenson, E. (2006). Research-based guidelines for child forensic interviews. *Journal of Aggression, Maltreatment & Trauma, 12*(3/4), 81–130.

Perry, D. (2010). *The Girls of Murder City: fame, lust, and the beautiful killers that inspired* Chicago. New York, NY: Penguin Group/Viking Press.

Peterselia, J. (2000). Parole and prisoner reentry in the United States. Perspectives. American Probation and Parole Association. Retrieved at http://www.appa-net.org/eweb/resources/pppsw_2013/history.htm

Peterson, F. (2012, July 21). Luis Walker, Lackland boot camp instructor, convicted of rape and sexual assault. *Global Post.* Retrieved September 11, 2012, from http://www.globalpost.com/dispatch/news/regions/americas/united-states/120721/luis-walker-rape-sex-assault-lackland-texas-sexual-air-force-military-boot

Petrillo, M. (2007). Power struggle: Gender issues for female probation officers in the supervision of high risk offenders. *Probation Journal: The Journal of Community and Criminal Justice, 54*(4), 394–406.

Piquero, N. L., Gover, A. R., MacDonald, J. M., & Piquero, A. R. (2005). The influence of delinquent peers on delinquency: Does gender matter? *Youth & Society, 36*(3), 251–275.

Planty, M., Langton, L., Krebs, C., Berzofsky, M., & Smiley-McDonald, H. (2013). Female victims of sexual violence, 1994–2010. U.S. Department of Justice, Bureau of Justice Statistics. Retrieved from http://www.bjs.gov/content/pub/pdf/fvsv9410.pdf

Platt, A. M. (1969). *The child savers.* Chicago, IL: University of Chicago Press.

Pollak, O. (1950). *Criminality of women.* Baltimore, MD: University of Pennsylvania Press.

Pollak, O. (1961). *The criminality of women.* New York, NY: A. S. Barnes.

Pollak, S. (2013, February 7). Woman burned alive for witchcraft in Papua New Guinea. *Time.* Retrieved from http://newsfeed.time.com/2013/02/07/Woman-burned-alive-for-witchcraft-in-Papua-New-Guinea

Pollock, J. M. (1986). *Sex and supervision: Guarding male and female inmates.* New York, NY: Greenwood Press.

Potter, G., & Kappeler, V. (2006). *Constructing crime: Perspectives on making news and social problems* (2nd ed.). Long Grove, IL: Waveland Press.

Potter, H. (2006). An argument for Black feminist criminology. *Feminist Criminology, 1*(2), 106–124.

Potter, H. (2007a). Battered Black women's use of religious services and spirituality for assistance in leaving abusive relationships. *Violence Against Women, 13*(3), 262–284.

Potter, H. (2007b). Battle cries: Understanding and confronting intimate partner abuse against African-American women. New York: New York University Press.

President's Commission on Law Enforcement and the Administration of Justice. (1967). *The challenge of crime in a free society.* Washington DC: U.S. Government Printing Office.

Proano-Raps, T. C., & Meyer, C. L. (2003). Postpartum syndrome and the legal system. In R. Muraskin (Ed.), *It's a crime: Women and justice* (3rd ed., pp. 53–76). Upper Saddle River, NJ: Prentice-Hall.

Pryor, D. W., & Hughes, M. R. (2013). Fear of rape among college women: A social psychological analysis. *Violence and Victims, 28*(3), 443–465.

Quinn, B. (March 19, 2013). Taliban victim Malala Yousafzai starts school in UK. *The Guardian.* Retrieved from http://www.theguardian.com/world/2013/mar/20/taliban-victim-malala-yousafzai-school

Rabe-Hemp, C. (2012). The career trajectories of female police executives. In R. Muraskin (Ed.), *Women and justice: It's a crime* (5th ed., pp. 527–543). Upper Saddle River, NJ: Prentice-Hall.

Rabe-Hemp, C. E. (2008). Survival in an "all boys club": Policewomen and their fight for acceptance. *Policing: An International Journal of Police Strategies and Management, 31*(2), 251–270.

Rabe-Hemp, C. E. (2009). POLICEwomen or PoliceWOMEN? Doing gender and police work. *Feminist Criminology, 4*(2), 114–129.

Raeder, M. S. (1995). The forgotten offender: The effect of the sentencing guidelines and mandatory minimums on women and their children. *Federal Sentencing Reporter, 8,* 157.

Rafferty, Y. (2007). Children for sale: Child trafficking in Southeast Asia. *Child Abuse Review, 16*(6), 401–422.

Rafter, N. H. (1985). *Partial justice: Women in state prisons 1800–1935.* Boston, MA: New England University Press.

Raphael, J. (2000). *Saving Bernice: Battered women, welfare and poverty.* Boston, MA: Northeastern University Press.

Raphael, J. (2004). *Listening to Olivia: Violence, poverty and prostitution.* Boston, MA: Northeastern University Press.

Raphael, J., & Shapiro, D. L. (2004). Violence in indoor and outdoor venues. *Violence Against Women, 10*(2), 126–139.

Raphael, K. G. (2005). Childhood abuse and pain in adulthood: More than a modest relationship? *The Clinical Journal of Pain, 21*(5), 371–373.

Rasche, C. E. (2012). The dislike of female offenders among correctional officers: A need for specialized training. In R. Muraskin (Ed.), *Women and justice: It's a crime* (5th ed., pp. 544–562). Upper Saddle River, NJ: Prentice-Hall.

Rathbone, C. (2005). *A world apart: Women, prison and life behind bars.* New York, NY: Random House.

Raymond, J. G. (2004). Prostitution on demand: Legalizing the buyers as sexual consumers. *Violence Against Women, 10*(10), 1156–1186.

Reichman, N. J., & Sterling, J. S. (2001). Recasting the brass ring: Deconstructing and reconstructing workplace opportunities for women lawyers. *Capital University Law Review, 29,* 923–977.

Reinharz, S. (1992). *Feminist methods in social research.* New York, NY: Oxford University Press.

Rennison, C. M. (2009). A new look at the gender gap in offending. *Women and Criminal Justice, 19,* 171–190.

Renzetti, C. M., Goodstein, L., & Miller, S. E. (2006). *Rethinking gender, crime, and justice: Feminist readings.* New York, NY: Oxford University Press.

Resnick, H., Acierno, R., Holmes, M., Dammeyer, M., & Kilpatrick, D. (2000). Emergency evaluation and intervention with female victims of rape and other violence. *Journal of Clinical Psychology, 56*(10), 1317–1333.

Resnick, P. J. (1970). Murder of the newborn: A psychiatric review of neonaticide. *American Journal of Psychiatry, 126,* 1414–1420.

Revolutionary Worker. (2002). The disappearing women of Juarez. Retrieved from http://revcom.us/a/v24/1161-1170/1166/juarez .htm

Reyns, B. W., & Englebrecht, C. M. (2012). The fear factor: Exploring predictors of fear among stalking victims throughout the stalking encounter. *Crime & Delinquency, 59*(5), 788–808.

Reyns, B. W., Burek, M. W., Henson, B., & Fisher, B. S. (2013). The unintended consequences of digital technology: Exploring the relationship between sexting and cybervictimization. *Journal of Crime and Justice, 36*(1), 1–17.

Rice, S. K., Terry, K. J., Miller, H. V., & Ackerman, A. R. (2007). Research trajectories of female scholars in criminology and criminal justice. *Journal of Criminal Justice Education, 18*(3), 360–384.

Rickert, V. I., Wiemann, C. M., & Vaughan, R. D. (2005). Disclosure of date/acquaintance rape: Who reports and when. *Journal of Pediatric and Adolescent Gynecology, 18*(1), 17–24.

Rideout, M. (2007). May 1, 1990: The shocking death that started a sensation in N.H. Keene Equinox. Retrieved from http://www .hampton.lib.nh.us/hampton/biog/pamsmart/equinox2006_1 .htm

Ritchie, B. E. (2001). Challenges incarcerated women face as they return to their communities: Findings from life history interviews. *Crime and Delinquency, 47*(3), 368–389.

Robinson, L. (1890). Woman lawyers in the United States. *The Green Bag, 2,* 10.

Robison, S. M. (1966). A critical review of the Uniform Crime Reports. *Michigan Law Review, 64*(6), 1031–1054.

Rodriguez, S. F., Curry, T. R., & Lee, G. (2006). Gender differences in criminal sentencing: Do effects vary across violent, property and drug offenses. *Social Science Quarterly, 87*(2), 318–339.

Roe-Sepowitz, D. E. (2012). Juvenile entry into prostitution: The role of emotional abuse. *Violence Against Women, 18*(5), 562–579.

Romero-Daza, N., Weeks, M., & Singer, M. (2003). "Nobody gives a damn if I live or die": Violence, drugs, and street-level prostitution in inner city Hartford, Connecticut. *Medical Anthropology, 22,* 233–259.

Rosenbaum, A. (2009). Batterer intervention programs: A report from the field. *Violence and Victims, 24*(6), 757–770.

Rosenbaum, J. L. (1989). Family dysfunction and female delinquency. *Crime and Delinquency, 35,* 31–44.

Rosenbaum, J. L., & Spivack, S. (2013). *Implementing a gender based arts program for juvenile offenders.* Waltham, MA: Elsevier.

Ross, E. (2013, May 10). Air Force sex scandal heats up. Retrieved from http://www.koaa.com/news/air-force-sex-scandal-heats-up/

Ryder, J. A., & Brisgone, R. E. (2013). Cracked perspectives: Reflections of women and girls in the aftermath of the crack cocaine era. *Feminist Criminology, 8*(1), 40–62.

Ryon, S. B. (2013). Gender as social threat: A study of offender sex, situational factors, gender dynamics and social control. *Journal of Criminal Justice, 41,* 426–437.

Sabina, C., Cuevas, C. A., & Schally, J. L. (2012). Help-seeking in a national sample of victimized Latino women: The influence of victimization types. *Journal of Interpersonal Violence, 27*(1), 40–61.

Salisbury, E. J., Van Voorhis, P., Wright, E., M., & Bauman, A. (2009). Changing probation experiences for female offenders based on women's needs and risk assessment project findings. *Women, Girls and Criminal Justice, 10*(6), 83–84, 92–95.

SAMHSA. (2009). Substance abuse treatment: Addressing the specific needs of women. A treatment improvement protocol TIP 51. Center for Substance Abuse Treatment. Retrieved from http://mentalhealth.samhsa.gov/cmhs/CommunitySupport/women_vio lence/ default.asphttp://bjs.ojp.usdoj.gov/index.cfm?ty=tp&tid=35

Sampson, R. (2003). Acquaintance rape of college students. *Public Health Resources, 92.*

Sampson, R., & Laub, J. (1993). *Crime in the making: Pathways and turning points through life.* Cambridge, MA: Harvard University Press.

Sandifer, J. L. (2008). Evaluating the efficacy of a parenting program for incarcerated mothers. *The Prison Journal, 88*(3), 423–445.

Saulters-Tubbs, C. (1993). Prosecutorial and judicial treatment of female offenders. *Federal Probation, 37–42.*

Savage, D. G. (2009). Sotomayor takes her seat. *American Bar Association Journals, 95*(10), 24–25.

Sawyers, E. T. (1922). History of Santa Clara County, California. Retrieved from http://www.mariposaresearch.net/santaclararesearch/SCBIOS/cfbrattan.html

Schadee, J. (2003). Passport to healthy families. *Corrections Today, 65*(3), 64.

Schalet, A., Hunt, G., & Joe-Laidler, K. (2003). Respectability and autonomy: The articulation and meaning of sexuality among girls in the gang. *Journal of Contemporary Ethnography, 32*(1), 108–143.

Schemo, D. J. (2003, August 29). Rate of rape at academy is put at 12% in survey. Retrieved August 31, 2012, from http://www.nytimes.com/2003/08/29/national/29ACAD.html?th

Schoonmaker, M. H., & Brooks, J.S. (1975). Women in probation and parole, 1974. *Crime & Delinquency, 21*(2), 109–115.

Schoot, E., & Goswami, S. (2001). *Prostitution: A violent reality of homelessness.* Chicago, IL: Chicago Coalition for the Homeless.

Schulz, D. M. (1995). *From social worker to crime fighter: Women in United States municipal policing.* Westport, CT: Praeger.

Schulz, D. M. (2003). Women police chiefs: A statistical profile. *Police Quarterly, 6*(3), 330–345.

Schulze, C. (2012). The policies of United States police departments: Equal access, equal treatment. In R. Muraskin (Ed.), *Women and justice: It's a crime* (5th ed., pp. 500–513). Upper Saddle River, NJ: Prentice-Hall.

Schwartz, M. D., & DeKeseredy, W. S. (2008). Interpersonal violence against women: The role of men. *Journal of Contemporary Criminal Justice, 24*(2), 178–185.

Schwartz, M. D., DeKeseredy, W. S., Tait, D., & Alvi, S. (2001). Male peer support and a feminist routing activities theory: Understanding sexual assault on the college campus. *Justice Quarterly, 18*(3), 623–649.

Scott-Ham, M., & Burton, F. C. (2005). Toxicological findings in cases of alleged drug-facilitated sexual assault in the United Kingdom over a 3-year period. *Journal of clinical forensic medicine, 12*(4), 175.

Sedlak, A. J., McPherson, K. S., & Basena, M. (2013). Nature and risk of victimization: Findings from the survey of youth in residential placement [Bulletin]. Office of Juvenile Justice and Delinquency Prevention. Retrieved from http://www.ojjdp.gov/pubs/240703.pdf

Sellers, C., & Bromley, M. (1996). Violent behavior in college student dating relationships. *Journal of Contemporary Criminal Justice, 12*(1), 1–27.

Sengstock, M. C. (1976). *Culpable victims in Mendelsohn's typology.* Retrieved from https://www.ncjrs.gov/App/publications/Abstract.aspx?id=48998

Sentencing Project. (2006). *Life sentences: Denying welfare benefits to women convicted of drug offenses.* Retrieved December 28, 2010, from http://www.sentencingproject.org/doc/publications/women_smy_lifesentences.pdf

Severance, T. A. (2005). "You know who you can go to": Cooperation and exchange between incarcerated women. *The Prison Journal, 85*(3), 343–367.

Shackling pregnant inmates banned under California law, but many states allow the practice. (2012, October 11). *Huffington Post.* Retrieved from http://www.huffingtonpost.com/2012/10/11/pregnant-women-shackles-giving-birth-two-thirds-33-states_n_1958319.html

Shannon-Lewy, C., & Dull, V. T. (2005). The response of Christian clergy to domestic violence: Help or hindrance? *Aggression and Violent Behavior, 10*(6), 647–659.

Sharma, A. (2013, October 31). Sara Kruzan released from prison 18 years after killing pimp as teen. Retrieved from http://www.kpbs.org/news/2013/oct/31/sara-kruzan-killed-pimp-teen-goes-free/

Sharp, S. F., Peck, B. M., & Hartsfield, J. (2012). Childhood adversity and substance use of women prisoners: A general strain theory approach. *Journal of Criminal Justice, 40*, 202–211.

Sharpe, G. (2009). The trouble with girls today: Professional perspectives on young women's offending. *Youth Justice, 9*(3), 254–269.

Sheeran, T. J. (2013, July 17). Ariel Castro pleads not guilty to 977 counts in Ohio kidnapping indictment. *Huffington Post.* Retrieved from http://www.huffingtonpost.com/2013/07/17/ariel-castro-arraignment-charges_n_3609793.html

Shekarkhar, Z., & Gibson, C. L. (2011). Gender, self-control and offending behaviors among Latino youth. *Journal of Contemporary Criminal Justice, 27*(1), 63–80.

Shelden, R. G. (1981). Sex discrimination in the juvenile justice system: Memphis, Tennessee, 1900–1917. In M. Q. Warren (Ed.), *Comparing male and female offenders* (pp. 52–72). Beverly Hills, CA: Sage.

Shepherd, S. M., Luebbers, S., & Dolan, M. (2013, April–June). Identifying gender differences in an Australian youth offender population. *Sage Open, 3*, 1–12.

Sherman, L. W., & Berk, R. A. (1984). The Minneapolis Domestic Violence Experiment. *Police Foundation Reports.* Retrieved from http://www.policefoundation.org/pdf/minneapolisdve.pdf

Sholchet, C. (2013, May). Jodi Arias guilty of first degree murder: Death penalty possible. CNN. Retrieved from http://www.cnn.com/2013/05/08/justice/arizona-jodi-arias-verdict/

Shufelt, J. L., & Cocozza, J. J. (2006). Youth with mental health disorders in the juvenile justice system: Results from a multi-state prevalence study. National Center for Mental Health and Juvenile Justice. Retrieved January 26, 2012, from http://www.ncmhjj.com/pdfs/publications/PrevalenceRPB.pdf

Silva, S. A., Pires, A. P., Guerreiro, C., & Cardoso, A. (2012). Balancing motherhood and drug addiction: The transition to parenthood of addicted mothers. *Journal of Health Psychology, 18*(3), 359–367.

Silverman, J. G., Raj, A., Mucci, L. A., & Hathaway, J. E. (2001). Dating violence against adolescent girls and associated substance use, unhealthy weight control, sexual risk behavior, pregnancy and suicidality. *Journal of American Medical Association, 285*(5), 572–579.

Silverman, J. R., & Caldwell, R. M. (2008). Peer relationships and violence among female juvenile offenders: An exploration of differences among four racial/ethnic populations. *Criminal Justice and Behavior, 35*(3), 333–343.

Simkhada, P. (2008). Life histories and survival strategies amongst sexually trafficked girls in Nepal. *Children and Society, 22*, 235–248.

Simmons, W. P. (2006, Spring). Remedies for the women of Ciudad Juárez through the Inter-American Court of Human Rights. *Northwestern Journal of International Human Rights, 4*(3). Retrieved from http://www.law.northwestern.edu/journals/jihr/v4/n3/2/Simmons. pdf

Simon, R. (1975). *Women and crime*. Lexington, MA: D. C. Heath.

Skolnick, J. (1966). Justice without trial. New York, NY: Wiley.

Slattery, S. M., & Goodman, L. A. (2009). Secondary traumatic stress among domestic violence advocates: Workplace risk and protective factors. *Violence Against Women, 15*(11), 1358–1379.

Smith, E. L., & Farole, D. J., Jr. (2009). *Profile of intimate partner violence cases in large urban counties*. Bureau of Justice Statistics, U.S. Department of Justice. Retrieved from http://bjs.ojp.usdoj.gov/content/pub/pdf/pipvcluc.pdf

Smith, J. C. (1998). *Rebels in law: Voices in history of Black women lawyers* (KF299.A35 R43 1998). Ann Arbor: University of Michigan.

Smith-Spark, L., & Nyberg, P. (2013, July 31). Nigella Lawson and Charles Saatchi take step toward divorce. CNN. Retrieved at http://www.cnn.com/2013/07/31/world/europe/nigella-lawson-saatchi-divorce/

Smude, L. (2012). Realignment: A new frontier for California criminal justice. In C. Gardiner & S. Mallicoat (Eds.), *California's criminal justice system* (pp. 153–168). Durham, NC: Carolina Academic Press.

Snedker, K. A. (2012). Explaining the gender gap in fear of crime: Assessments of risk and vulnerability among New York City residents. *Feminist Criminology, 7*(2), 75–111.

Snell, C., Sorenson, J., Rodriguez, J. J., & Kuanliang, A. (2009). Gender differences in research productivity among criminal justice and criminology scholars. *Journal of Criminal Justice, 37*(3), 288–295.

Snow, R. L. (2010). *Policewomen who made history: Breaking through the ranks*. Lanham, MD: Rowman and Littlefield.

Snyder, H. N., & Sickmund, M. (2006). *Juvenile offenders and victims: 2006 national report*. National Center for Juvenile Justice. Office of Juvenile Justice and Delinquency Prevention. Retrieved December 1, 2010, from http://www.ojjdp.gov/ojstatbb/nr2006/

Snyder, J. A., Fisher, B. S., Scherer, H. L, & Daigle, L. E. (2012). Unsafe in the camouflage tower: Sexual victimization and perceptions of military academy leadership. *Journal of Interpersonal Violence, 27*(16), 3171–3194.

Snyder, Z. K. (2009). Keeping families together: The importance of maintaining mother-child contact for incarcerated women. *Women & Criminal Justice, 19*, 37–59.

Sokoloff, N. J. (2004). Domestic violence at the crossroads: Violence against poor women and women of color. *Women Studies Quarterly, 32*(3/4), 139–147.

Songer, D. R., & Crews-Meyer, K. A. (2000). Does judge gender matter? Decision making in state supreme courts. *Social Science Quarterly, 8*(3), 750–762.

Songer, D. R., Davis, S., & Haire, S. (1994). A reappraisal of diversification in the federal courts: Gender effects in the court of appeals. *Journal of Politics, 56*(2), 425–439.

Sonia Sotomayor. (2012). *The New York Times*. Retrieved from http://topics.nytimes.com/top/reference/timestopics/people/s/sonia_sotomayor/index.html?8qa

Spencer, G. C. (2004/2005). Her body is a battlefield: The applicability of the Alien Tort Statute to corporate human rights abuses in Juarez, Mexico. *Gonzaga Law Review, 40*, 503.

Spinelli, M. G. (2004). Maternal infanticide associated with mental illness: Prevention and the promise of saved lives. *American Journal of Psychiatry, 161*, 1548–1557.

Spitzberg, B. H., & Cupach, W. R. (2003). What mad pursuit? Obsessive relational intrusion and stalking related phenomena. *Aggression and Violent Behavior, 8*, 345–375.

Spohn, C., & Beichner, D. (2000). Is preferential treatment of female offenders a thing of the past? A multisite study of gender, race, and imprisonment. *Criminal Justice Policy Review, 11*(2), 149–184.

Spohn, C., & Belenko, S. (2013). Do the drugs do the time? The effect of drug abuse on sentences imposed on drug offenders in three U.S. District Courts. *Criminal Justice and Behavior, 40*(6), 646–670.

Spohn, C., & Brennan, P. K. (2011). The joint effects of offender race/ethnicity and gender on substantial assistance departures in federal courts. *Race and Justice 1*(1), 49–78.

Spohn, C., Gruhl, J., & Welch, S. (1987). The impact of the ethnicity and gender of defendants on the decision to reject or dismiss felony charges. *Criminology, 25*(1), 175–192

St. John. P. (2013, October 26). Jerry Brown Oks freedom for woman imprisoned at 16 for killing pimp. *Los Angeles Times*. Retrieved from http://articles.latimes.com/2013/oct/26/local/la-me-ff-kruzan-20131027

Stacy, M. (2012, May 19). Marissa Alexander gets 20 years for firing warning shot. *Huffington Post*. Retrieved from http://www.huffingtonpost.com/2012/05/19/marissa-alexander-gets-20_n_1530035.html

Stalens, L. J., & Finn, M. A. (2000). Gender differences in officers' perceptions and decisions about domestic violence cases. *Women and Criminal Justice, 11*(3), 1–24.

Stangle, H. L. (2008). Murderous Madonna: Femininity, violence, and the myth of postpartum mental disorder in cases of maternal infanticide and filicide. *William and Mary Law Review, 50*, 699–734.

Starzynski, L. L., Ullman, S. E., Townsend, S. M., Long, L. M., & Long, S. M. (2007). What factors predict women's disclosure of sexual assault to mental health professionals? *Journal of Community Psychology, 35*(5), 619–638.

Stattin, H., & Magnusson, D. (1990). *Pubertal maturation in female development* (Vol. 2). Hillsdale, NJ: Erlbaum.

Steer, J. (2013, May 6). Cleveland police: Missing teens Amanda Berry and Gina DeJesus found alive, appear to be OK. Retrieved from http://www.newsnet5.com/news/local-news/cleveland-metro/cleveland-police-dispatch-missing-teens-amanda-berry-and-gina-dejesus-found-alive

Steffensmeier, D., & Allan, E. (1996). Gender and crime: Toward a gendered theory of female offending. *American Review of Sociology, 22*, 459–487.

Steffensmeier, D., & Hebert, C. (1999). Women and men policymakers: Does the judge's gender affect the sentencing of criminal defendants? *Social Forces, 77*(3), 1163–1196.

Steffensmeier, D., Kramer, J., & Streifel, C. (1993). Gender and imprisonment decisions. *Criminology, 31*, 411–446.

Steffensmeier, D., Schwartz, J., Zhong, H., & Ackerman, J. (2005). An assessment of recent trends in girls' violence using diverse longitudinal sources: Is the gender gap closing? *Criminology, 43*, 355–405.

Steffensmeier, D., Zhong, H., Ackerman, J., Schwartz, J. & Agha, S. (2006). Gender gap trends for violent crimes, 1980 to 2003: A UCR-NCVS comparison. *Feminist Criminology, 1*(1), 72–98.

Stevenson, T., & Love, C. (1999). *Her story of domestic violence: A timeline of the battered women's movement.* Safework: California's Domestic Violence Resource. Retrieved from http://www.mincava.umn.edu/documents/herstory/herstory.html

Stewart, C. C., Langan, D., & Hannem, S. (2013). Victim experiences and perspectives on police responses to verbal violence in domestic settings. *Feminist Criminology, 8*(4), 269–294.

Stohr, M. K., Mays, G. L., Lovrich, N. P., & Gallegos, A. M. (1996). *Partial perceptions: Gender, job enrichment and job satisfaction among correctional officers in women's jails.* Paper presented at the Annual Meeting of the Academy of Criminal Justice Sciences, Las Vegas, Nevada.

Strachan, M. (2013, October 29). Target to drop criminal background questions in job applications. *Huffington Post.* Retrieved from http://www.huffingtonpost.com/2013/10/29/target-criminal-history-questions_n_4175407.html

Stringer, E. C., & Barnes, S. L. (2012). Mothering while imprisoned: The effects of family and child dynamics on mothering attitudes. *Family Relations, 61*, 313–326.

Strom, K. J., Warner, T. D., Tichavsky, L., & Zahn, M. A. (2010, September 8). Policing juveniles: Domestic violence arrest policies, gender and police response to child-parent violence. *Crime & Delinquency.* Advance online publication. Retrieved from http://www.sagepub.com/journals/Journal200959

Sullivan, M., Senturia, K., Negash, T., Shiu-Thornton, S., & Giday, B. (2005). For us it's like living in the dark: Ethiopian women's experiences with domestic violence. *Journal of Interpersonal Violence, 20*(8), 922–940.

Supreme Court. (n.d.). The Supreme Court of the United States—History. Retrieved from http://www.judiciary.senate.gov/nominations/SupremeCourt/SupremeCourtHistory.cfm

Surette, R. (2003). The media, the public, and criminal justice policy. *Journal of the Institute of Justice & International Studies, 2*, 39–52.

Sutherland, E., & Cressey, D. (1974). *Criminology* (9th ed.). Philadelphia, PA: H. B. Lippincott.

Sutton, J. R. (1988). Stubborn children: Controlling delinquency in the United States, 1640–1981. Berkeley: University of California Press.

Svensson, R. (2003). Gender differences in adolescent drug use. *Youth and Society, 34*, 300–329.

Svensson, R. (2004). Shame as a consequence of the parent-child relationship: A study of gender differences in juvenile delinquency. *European Journal of Criminology, 1*(4), 477–504.

Tamborra, T. L. (2012). Poor, urban, battered women who are stalked: How can we include their experiences. *Feminist Criminology, 7*(2), 112–129.

Tasca, M., Zatz, M., & Rodriguez, N. (2012). Girls' experiences with violence: An analysis of violence against and by at-risk girls. *Violence Against Women, 18*(6), 672–680.

Taylor, S. C., & Norma, C. (2012). The "symbolic protest" behind women's reporting of sexual assault crime to the police. *Feminist Criminology, 7*(1), 24–47.

Tewksbury, R., & Collins, S. C. (2006). Aggression levels among correctional officers. *The Prison Journal, 86*(3), 327–343.

Tewksbury, R., Connor, D. P., Chesseman, K., & Rivera, B. L. (2012). Female sex offenders' anticipations for reentry: Do they really know what they're in for? *Journal of Crime and Justice, 35*(3), 451–463.

Tewksbury, R., DeMichele, M. T., & Miller, J. M. (2005). Methodological orientations of articles appearing in criminal justice's top journals: Who publishes what and where? *Journal of Criminal Justice Education, 16*(2), 265–382.

The Florida Senate. (2011). Examine Florida's "Romeo and Juliet" law (Issue brief 2012–214). Retrieved from http://www.flsenate.gov/PublishedContent/Session/2012/InterimReports/2012–214cj.pdf

Thompson, M., & Petrovic, M. (2009). Gendered transitions: Within-person changes in employment, family and illicit drug use. *Journal of Research in Crime and Delinquency, 46*(3), 377–408.

Tille, J. E., & Rose, J. C. (2007). Emotional and behavioral problems if 13-to-18 year-old incarcerated female first-time offenders and recidivists. *Youth Violence and Juvenile Justice, 5*(4), 426–435.

Tillman, S., Bryant-Davis, T., Smith, K., & Marks, A. (2010). Shattering silence: Exploring barriers to disclosure for African American sexual assault survivors. *Trauma, violence, & abuse, 11*(2), 59–70.

Tjaden, P. G., & Thoennes, N. (2006). *Extent, nature, and consequences of rape victimization: Findings from the National Violence*

Against Women Survey. Washington, DC: U.S. Department of Justice, Office of Justice Programs, National Institute of Justice.

Topping, A., & Quinn, B. (2013, June 18). Nigella Lawson assault: Charles Saatchi accepts police caution. *The Guardian*. Retrieved from http://www.theguardian.com/uk/2013/jun/18/saatchi-lawson-police-caution-assault?guni=Article:in%20body%201ink

Torre, I. (2013, October 9). Oakistan's educational challenges. CNN. Retrieved from http://www.cnn.com/2013/10/09/world/asia/infographic-pakistan-education/index.html?iid=article_sidebar

Truman, J. L. (2011). *Criminal victimization, 2010*. Washington, DC: Bureau of Justice Statistics.

Truman, J. L., & Planty, M. (2012). Criminal Victimization 2011. Bureau of Justice Statistics, U.S. Department of Justice. Retrieved at http://www.bjs.gov/content/pub/pdf/cv11.pdf

Turrell, S. C., & Cornell-Swanson, L. (2005). Not all alike: Within group differences in seeking help for same-sex relationship abuses. *Journal of Gay & Lesbian Social Services, 18*(1), 77–88.

Turvill, W. (2013, November 1). Saatchi decides not to sue Nigella and reveal the "truth" over their break-up as he "wants to get on with his life." *Daily Mail*. Retrieved from http://www.dailymail.co.uk/news/article-2483393/Charles-Saatchi-wont-sue-Nigella-Lawson-divorce-truth.html

Ullman, S. E., & Townsend, S. M. (2007). Barriers to working with sexual assault providers. *Violence Against Women, 13*(4), 412–443.

Ullman, S. E., & Townsend, S. M. (2008). What is an empowerment approach to working with sexual assault survivors? *Journal of Community Psychology, 36*(3), 299–312.

United Nations. (2000). Protocol to prevent, suppress and punish trafficking in persons, especially women and children. Geneva, Switzerland: Author.

United Nations. (2008). UN-backed container exhibit spotlights plight of sex trafficking victims. UN News Centre. Retrieved from http://www.un.org/apps/news/story.asp?NewsID=25524&Cr=trafficking&Cr1

United Nations. (2010). Impunity for domestic violence, "honor killings" cannot continue. UN News Centre. Retrieved from http://www.un.org/apps/news/story.asp?NewsID=33971&Cr=violence+against+women&Cr1

United Nations Office on Drugs and Crime. (2013). The 2012 United Nations Survey of Crime Trends and Operations of Criminal Justice Systems. Retrieved from https://www.unodc.org/unodc/en/data-and-analysis/statistics/data.html

UN News Centre. (2013, May 31). UN human rights office regrets Papua New Guinea's decision to resume death penalty. Retrieved from http://www.un.org/apps/news/story.asp?NewsID=45049&Cr=death+penalty&Cr1=&Kw1=sorcery&Kw2=&Kw3=#.UtR6byjiOI4

UN: "Sorcery" murders must end. (2013, April 13). *New Zealand Herald*. Retrieved from http://www.nzherald.co.nz/world/news/article.cfm?c_id=2&objectid=10877300

U.S. Bureau of the Census. (2000). Profiles of general demographic characteristics. Retrieved from http://www2.census.gov/census_2000/datasets/demographic_profile/0_United_States/2kh00.pdf

U.S. Census. (2013). Quick facts, Stubenville, OH. Retrieved from http://quickfacts.census.gov/qfd/states/39/3971608.html

U.S. Department of Defense. (2010). *DoD fiscal year (FY) 2009 annual report on sexual assaults in the military services*. Washington, DC: Office of the Secretary of Defense, Sexual Assault Prevention and Response Office. Retrieved from http://www.sapr.mil/media/pdf/reports/fy09_annual_report.pdf

U.S. Department of Health and Human Services. (2011). *National human trafficking resource center fact sheet*. U.S. Department of Health and Human Services. Retrieved from http://www.hhs.gov/

U.S. Department of Justice, Office of Justice Programs. (1998). *New directions from the field: Victims' rights and services for the 21st century*. Washington, DC: U.S. Government Printing Office.

U.S. Department of Justice. (2003). *Criminal victimization, 2003*. Washington, DC: Author.

U.S. Department of State. (2008). *Trafficking in persons report*. U.S. Department of State. Retrieved from http://www.state.gov

U.S. Department of State. (2009). *Trafficking in Persons Report 2009*. U.S. Department of State. Retrieved from http://www.state.gov

U.S. Department of State. (2011). *Trafficking in Persons Report 2011*. U.S. Department of State. Retrieved from http://www.state.gov/j/tip/rls/tiprpt/2010/index.htm

U.S. Department of State. (2012). *Trafficking in Persons Report 2012*. U.S. Department of State. Retrieved from http://www.state.gov

U.S. Department of State. (2013). *Trafficking in Persons Report 2013*. U.S. Department of State. Retrieved from http://www.state.gov/documents/organization/210737.pdf

Valera, R. J., Sawyer, R. G., & Schiraldi, G. R. (2000). Violence and post-traumatic stress disorder in a sample of inner city street prostitutes. *American Journal of Health Studies, 16*(3), 149–155.

Van Voorhis, P., Salisbury, E., Wright, E., & Bauman, A. (2008). *Achieving accurate pictures of risk and identifying gender responsive needs: Two new assessments for women offenders*. Washington, DC: United States Department of Justice, National Institute of Corrections.

Van Wormer, K. S., & Bartollas, C. (2010). *Women and the criminal justice system*. Boston, MA: Allyn and Bacon.

VictimLaw (n.d.). About victims' rights. Retrieved from https://www.victimlaw.org/victimlaw/pages/victimsRight.jsp

Viglione, J., Hannon, L., & DeFina, R. (2011). The impact of light skin on prison time for Black female offenders. *The Social Science Journal, 48*, 250–258.

Visher, C. A. (1983). Gender, police arrest decisions, and notions of chivalry. *Criminology, 21*, 5–28.

von Hentig, H. (1948). The criminal and his victim: Studies in the sociobiology of crime. Cambridge, MA: Yale University Press.

Wagenaar, H. (2006). Democracy and prostitution: Deliberating the legalization of brothels in the Netherlands. *Administration and Society, 38*(2), 198–235.

Walker, L. E. (1979). *The battered woman*. New York, NY: Harper and Row.

Walsh, D. (2012, October 9). Taliban gun down girl who spoke up for rights. *New York Times*. Retrieved from http://www.nytimes.com/2012/10/10/world/asia/teen-school-activist-malala-yousafzai-survives-hit-by-pakistani-taliban.html?pagewanted+all&_r=0

Wang, M. C., Horne, S. G., Levitt, H. M., & Klesges, L. M. (2009). Christian women in IPV relationships: An exploratory study of religious factors. *Journal of Psychology and Christianity, 28*(3), 224–235.

Wang, Y. (2011). Voices from the margin: A case study of a rural lesbian's experience with woman-to-woman sexual violence. *Journal of Lesbian Studies, 15*(2), 166–175.

Warr, M. (1984). Fear of victimization: Why are women and the elderly more afraid. *Social Science Quarterly, 65*(3), 681–702.

Warr, M. (1985). Fear of rape among urban women. *Social problems*, 238–250.

Warshaw, R. (1994). I never called it rape. *Harper Perennial*.

Washington, P. A. (2001). Disclosure patterns of Black female sexual assault survivors. *Violence Against Women, 7*(11), 1254–1283.

Webster v. Reproductive Health Services, 492 U.S. 490 (1989).

Weerman, F. M., & Hoeve, M. (2012). Peers and delinquency: Are sex differences in delinquency explained by peer factors. *European Journal of Criminology, 9*(3), 228–244.

Wells, T., Colbert, S., & Slate, R. N. (2006). Gender matters: Differences in state probation officer stress. *Journal of Contemporary Criminal Justice, 22*(1), 63–79.

Welsh-Huggins, A. (2013a, March 17). Teen in Steubenville rape case: "I could not remember anything." *Huffington Post*. Retrieved from http://www.huffingtonpost.com/2013/03/16/steubenville-rape-case-teen-cant-recall-assault_n_2893398.html?utm_hp_ref=steubenville-rape

Welsh-Huggins, A. (2013b, May 2). Steubenville Rape: Teen girls guilty of threatening rape victim on Twitter. *Huffington Post*. Retrieved from http://www.huffingtonpost.com/2013/05/02/steubenville-rape-teen-girls-guilty-threats-twitter_n_3204301.html

Wesely, J. K. (2006). Considering the context of women's violence: Gender, lived experiences, and cumulative victimization. *Feminist Criminology, 1*(4), 303–328.

West, C. M. (2004). Black women and intimate partner violence: New directions for research. *Journal of Interpersonal Violence, 19*(12), 1487–1493.

West, D. A., & Lichtenstein, B. (2006). Andrea Yates and the criminalization of the filicidal maternal body. *Feminist Criminology, 1*(3), 173–187.

Westervelt, S. D., & Cook, K. J. (2007). Feminist research methods in theory and action: Learning from death row exonerees. In S. Miller (Ed.), *Criminal justice research and practice: Diverse voices from the field* (pp. 21–37). Boston, MA: University Press of New England.

Westmarland, N. (2001). The quantitative/qualitative debate and feminist research: A subjective view of objectivity. *Forum: Qualitative Social Research, 2*(1). Retrieved from http://www.qualitative-research.net/index.php/fqs/article/view/974/2125

Whaley, R. B., Hayes-Smith, J., & Hayes-Smith, R. (2010). Gendered pathways: Gender, mediating factors and the gap in boys' and girls' substance use. *Crime and Delinquency, 59*(5), 651–669.

Whitaker, M. (2014, April 2). Marisa Alexander in court, seeking "stand your ground" immunity. MSNBC. Retrieved from http://www.msnbc.com/politicsnation/florida-mom-seeks-stand-your-ground

Widom, C. S. (1989). The cycle of violence. *Science, 244,* 160–166.

Wies, J. R. (2008). Professionalizing human services: A case of domestic violence shelter advocates. *Human Communication, 67*(2), 221–233.

Williams, M. (2007). Women's representation on state trial and appellate courts. *Social Science Quarterly, 88*(5), 1192–1204.

Wismont, J. M. (2000). The lived pregnancy experience of women in prison. *Journal of Midwifery and Women's Health, 45*(4), 292–300.

Women's Health. (2004). *UMHS Women's Health Program*. Retrieved from http://www.med.umich.edu/whp/newsletters/summer04/p03-dating.html

Women's Prison Association (WPA). (2003). *WPA focus on women and justice: A portrait of women in prison*. Retrieved January 3, 2011, from http://www.wpaonline.org/pdf/Focus_December 2003.pdf

Women's Prison Association (WPA). (2008). *Mentoring women in reentry*. Retrieved January 21, 2011, from http://www.wpaonline.org

Women's Prison Association (WPA). (2009a). *Quick facts: Women and criminal justice 2009*. Retrieved January 5, 2011, from http://www.wpaonline.org

Women's Prison Association (WPA). (2009b). *Mothers, infants and imprisonment: A national look at prison nurseries and community-based alternatives*. Retrieved January 5, 2011, from http://www.wpaonline.com

Women's Prison Association (WPA). (n.d.). Laws banning shackling during childbirth gaining momentum nationwide. Retrieved from http://66.29.139.159/pdf/Shackling%20Brief_final.pdf

Wooditch, A. (2011). The efficacy of the *Trafficking in Persons Report*: A review of the evidence. *Criminal Justice Policy Review, 22*(4), 471–493.

Wooldredge, J., & Griffin, T. (2005). Displaced discretion under Ohio sentencing guidelines. *Journal of Criminal Justice, 33,* 301–316.

World Health Organization. (2012). *Sexual and reproductive health*. Retrieved from http://www.who.int/reproductivehealth/about_us/en/index.html

World Law Direct (2011). Shackling laws. Retrieved from http://www.worldlawdirect.com/forum/law-wiki/43470-shackling-laws.html

Wright, E. M., DeHart, D. D., Koons-Witt, B. A., & Crittenden, C. A. (2013). "Buffers" against crime? Exploring the roles and limitations of positive relationships among women in prison. *Punishment & Society, 15*(1), 71–95.

Wyse, J. J. B. (2013). Rehabilitating criminal selves: Gendered strategies in community corrections. *Gender & Society, 27*(2), 231–255.

Yacoubian, G. S., Urbach, B. J., Larsen, K. L., Johnson, R. J., & Peters, R. J. (2000). A comparison of drug use between prostitutes and other female arrestees. *Journal of Alcohol and Drug Education, 46*(2), 12–26.

Yahne, C. E., Miller, W. R., Irvin-Vitela, L., & Tonigan, J. S. (2002). Magdalena Pilot Project: Motivational outreach to substance abusing women street sex workers. *Journal of Substance Abuse Treatment, 23*(1), 49–53.

Yavuz, N., & Welch, E. W. (2010). Addressing fear of crime in public space: Gender differences in reaction to safety measures in train transit. *Urban Studies, 47*(12), 2491–2515.

Yeum, E. B. B. (2010). Eleventh annual review of gender and sexuality law: Criminal law chapter: Rape, sexual assault and evidentiary matters. *Georgetown Journal of Gender & the Law, 11*, 191–869.

Yirga, W. S., Kassa, N. A., Gebremichael, M. W., & Aro, A. R. (2012). Female genital mutilation: Prevalence, perceptions, and effect on women's health in Kersa district of Ethiopia. *International Journal of Women's Health, 4*(1), 45–54.

Young, M., & Stein, J. (2004). *The history of the crime victims' movement in the United States: A component of the Office for Victims of Crime Oral History Project.* Washington DC: U.S. Department of Justice. Retrieved from https://www.ncjrs.gov/ovc_archives/ncvrw/2005/pdf/historyofcrime.pdf

Zaitzow, B. H., & Thomas, J. (2003). *Women in prison: Gender and social control.* Boulder, CO: Lynne Rienner.

Zaykowski, H., & Gunter, W. D. (2013). Gender differences in victimization risk: Exploring the role of deviant lifestyles. *Violence and Victims, 28*(2), 341–356.

Index

Note: n within a page reference indicates an endnote number.

About the Author

Stacy L. Mallicoat is a Professor of Criminal Justice and Deputy Chair for the Division of Politics, Administration and Justice at California State University, Fullerton. She earned her B.A in Legal Studies and Sociology, with a concentration in Crime and Deviance, from Pacific Lutheran University (Tacoma, WA) in 1997 and received her PhD from the University of Colorado at Boulder in Sociology in 2003. Her primary research interests include feminist criminology and public opinion on the death penalty. She is the author or co-author of four books, including *Women and Crime: The Essentials* (SAGE), *Criminal Justice Policy* (SAGE), and *California's Criminal Justice System* (Carolina Academic Press). Her work also appears in a number of journals such as *Feminist Criminology, Journal of Criminal Justice, American Journal of Criminal Justice, Journal of Ethnicity and Criminal Justice,* and *Southwestern Journal of Criminal Justice,* as well as a number of edited volumes. She is an active member of the American Society of Criminology, the ASC's Division on Women and Crime (where she currently serves as an Executive Counselor), the Western Society of Criminology, and the Academy of Criminal Justice Sciences.